Reclamation of Drastically Disturbed Lands

Reclamation of Drastically Disturbed Lands

Proceedings of a symposium held 9–12 August 1976 at the Ohio Agricultural Research & Experiment Station, Wooster, Ohio. Cosponsors were the American Society of Agronomy, Crop Science Society of America, Soil Science Society of America, American Society of Agricultural Engineers, Society of American Foresters, Society for Range Management, Soil Conservation Society of America, The Institute of Ecology, U.S. Environmental Protection Agency, and the Ohio Agricultural Research & Development Center.

Editorial Committee: FRANK W. SCHALLER, co-editor
PAUL SUTTON, co-editor

Program Planning Committee: PAUL SUTTON, chairman
G. W. BENGTSON
A. E. DUDECK
W. R. GARDNER
C. H. HERBEL
R. J. HUTNIK
J. F. POWERS
L. W. REED
F. W. SCHALLER
R. L. SMITH
N. P. SWANSON
L. W. ZELAZNY

Coordinating Editor: MATTHIAS STELLY

Managing Editor: RICHARD C. DINAUER

Assistant Editor: ELIZABETH L. SHEMA

Published by: American Society of Agronomy
Crop Science Society of America
Soil Science Society of America
Madison, Wisconsin USA

1978

Second Printing 1981

American Society of Agronomy, Inc.
Crop Science Society of America, Inc.
Soil Science Society of America, Inc.
677 South Segoe Road, Madison, Wisconsin 53711 USA

Library of Congress Cataloging in Publication Data

Main entry under title:

Reclamation of drastically disturbed lands

   Includes bibliographies and index.
   1. Reclamation of land—Congresses.
   2. Reclamation of land—United States—Congresses.
   3. Reclamation of land—Canada—Congresses.
   I. Schaller, Frank W., 1914-
  II. Sutton, Paul, 1929-
III. American Society of Agronomy.
S605.R43   333.7'6   78-8745
ISBN 0-89118-052-4

Printed in the United States of America

CONTENTS

4 **Extent of Disturbed Land and Major Reclamation Problems in Canada**

J. V. THIRGOOD

SECTION II—LEGISLATION

SECTION III—CONSIDERATIONS AFFECTING DISTURBANCE TECHNIQUES AND RECLAMATION

11 Environmental and Aesthetic Considerations in Surface Mining Policy

12 Criteria for Selecting Lands That Are Not to be Disturbed

13 Premining Planning to Maximize Effective Land Use and Reclamation

SECTION IV—MATERIALS AND TECHNIQUES FOR HUMID REGIONS

26 Mulch and Chemical Stabilizers for Land Reclamation in Dry Regions

BURGESS L. KAY

27 Improvement of Saline- and Sodium-Affected Disturbed Lands

F. M. SANDOVAL AND W. L. GOULD

28 Use of Irrigation in Reclamation in Dry Regions

R. E. RIES AND A. D. DAY

29   Reclamation Research on Strip-Mined Lands in Dry Regions

J. F. POWER

30   Reclamation of Coal Surface-Mined Land in Western Canada

J. V. THIRGOOD AND P. F. ZIEMKIEWICZ

SECTION VI—RECLAMATION OF LAND DISTURBED FOR OTHER THAN COAL MINING

34 Reclamation of Lands Disturbed by Stone Quarries, Sand and Gravel Pits, and Borrow Pits

BRENT W. BLAUCH

35 Disposition of Dredged Material

RAYMOND J. KRIZEK AND DIMITRIOS K. ATMATZIDIS

36 Vegetating Mine Tailings Ponds

REX F. NIELSON AND H. B. PETERSON

SECTION VII—ANALYTICAL TESTS AND METHODS

40   Applications of Remote Sensing Technology to Disturbed Lands

T. L. COX AND S. G. WITTER

FOREWORD

Some of the drastically disturbed lands resulting from man's activities are surface mining, highway construction, and the dredging of rivers and harbors. In the United States alone over 1.76 million hectares of land have been disturbed by surface mining, about half of this by coal mines. Every year about 40,470 hectares of land are disturbed by coal mining. It is estimated that over 10.8 million additional hectares of land can be stripmined for coal. In the United States over 10.5 million hectares of land have been used for rural transportation right-of-ways. Approximately 27,600 hectares of land are required each year to handle the dredged material from waterways.

Drastically disturbed lands are a hazard to the environment. Water erosion causes sedimentation in stream channels, highway ditches, and water reservoirs. Wind erosion and dust pollution occur in the arid regions. Water movement and chemical changes in mine spoils often lead to serious pollution problems. Proper reclamation, well planned and quickly executed, will minimize such damage and sometimes enable economical, recreational, or aesthetic benefits to accrue on these drastically disturbed lands.

This book provides basic information on the reclamation of drastically disturbed lands. Current and recent reclamation research as related to mining and other land disturbances is presented which will be helpful to students studying reclamation, persons interested in the national problem, or individuals responsible for developing and/or carrying out reclamation plans.

This book is one of a long series of publications provided by the American Society of Agronomy on significant crop, soil, or environmental questions affecting human welfare.

Appreciation is hereby expressed to the co-editors—Dr. Frank W. Schaller and Dr. Paul Sutton—and to the many authors, reviewers, and others who have made this publication possible.

March 1978

JOHNNY W. PENDLETON, *president*
American Society of Agronomy

VIRGIL A. JOHNSON, *president*
Crop Science Society of America

PARKER F. PRATT, *president*
Soil Science Society of America

PREFACE

This book is a compilation of papers presented at a symposium held at Wooster, Ohio, 9–12 August 1976. The major objective of the symposium was to assemble persons involved with the reclamation of drastically disturbed lands for an exchange of information and ideas, and to publish an authoritative, up-to-date treatise which could be used by those interested in land disturbance and its reclamation.

The symposium was jointly sponsored by the American Society of Agronomy, Soil Science Society of America, Crop Science Society of America, Soil Conservation Society of America, American Society of Agricultural Engineers, Society of American Foresters, The Institute of Ecology, Society for Range Management, U.S. Environmental Protection Agency, and the Ohio Agricultural Research and Development Center.

A committee composed of representatives from the sponsoring organizations developed the symposium program. The 42 papers presented represent a cross-section of authors and coauthors from government, universities, and industry in the United States and Canada.

The subject matter in the book covers a wide variety of interests. Much attention is given to research results and field experience involving materials and techniques for reclamation. Chapters are also devoted to the extent and characteristics of disturbed land, chemical, physical, and social factors affecting disturbance and reclamation, and legislative aspects.

The reclamation of lands disturbed by surface mining of coal is given major emphasis. However, chapters are also devoted to lands disturbed by sand, gravel, stone, and phosphate mining, highway construction, dredge and fill operations, and revegetation of mine tailings and ponds which result from mining of copper and uranium. Climatic variations in the U.S. and Canada are handled by chapters specific for regions which are humid, arid, or of an alpine or arctic nature.

In addition to the program committee and authors, recognition is given to other scientists who performed critical reviews of chapters. Special recognition is given to Dr. Matthias Stelly and other members of the American Society of Agronomy headquarters staff for help in conducting the symposium and publishing this book.

March 1978   FRANK W. SCHALLER, *co-editor*
                                          Iowa State University
                                               Ames, Iowa

                                   PAUL SUTTON, *co-editor*
                       Ohio Agricultural Research & Development Center
                                               Wooster, Ohio

CONTRIBUTORS

Donovan Abbott — Head, Minerals and Materials Department, The Research and Productivity Council, Fredericton, New Brunswick, Canada

Earl F. Aldon — Principal Hydrologist, Rocky Mountain Forest and Range Experiment Station, Forest Service, U.S. Department of Agriculture, Albuquerque, New Mexico

Darwin W. Anderson — Research Scientist, Saskatchewan Institute of Pedology, University of Saskatchewan, Saskatoon, Canada

Walter H. Armiger — Research Agronomist, Biological Waste Management and Soil Nitrogen Laboratory, Science and Education Administration, U.S. Department of Agriculture, Beltsville, Maryland

Dimitrios K. Atmatzidis — Visiting Assistant Professor of Civil Engineering, Department of Civil Engineering, The Technological Institute, Northwestern University, Evanston, Illinois

Marshall Augustine — Senior Consultant, Hittman Associates, Inc., Columbia, Maryland

Armand Bauer — Soil Scientist, Northern Great Plains Research Center, Science and Education Administration, U.S. Department of Agriculture, Mandan, North Dakota, formerly, Professor of Soils, North Dakota State University

George W. Bengtson — Research Forester, Soils and Fertilizer Research Branch, Tennessee Valley Authority, Muscle Shoals, Alabama

Orus L. Bennett — Supervisory Soil Scientist, Science and Education Administration, U.S. Department of Agriculture, West Virginia University, Morgantown, West Virginia

William A. Berg — Associate Professor of Agronomy, Agronomy Department, Colorado State University, Fort Collins, Colorado

Roy E. Blaser — University Distinguished Professor of Agronomy, Department of Agronomy, Virginia Polytechnic Institute and State University, Blacksburg, Virginia

Brent W. Blauch — Civil Engineer/Project Manager, Skelly & Loy Engineers and Consultants, Harrisburg, Pennsylvania

William G. Blue — Professor of Soil Science, Soil Science Department, University of Florida, Gainesville, Florida

Kenes C. Bowling — Executive Director, Interstate Mining Compact Commission, Lexington, Kentucky

Thadis W. Box — Dean, College of Natural Resources, Utah State University, Logan, Utah

Ray W. Brown	Plant Physiologist, Intermountain Forest and Range Experiment Station, Forest Service, U.S. Department of Agriculture, Ogden, Utah
John P. Capp	Chemical Engineer, Bureau of Mines, U.S. Department of the Interior, Morgantown, West Virginia
Frank T. Caruccio	Associate Professor, Department of Geology, Environmental Hydrogeology Programs, University of South Carolina, Columbia, South Carolina
Michael L. Clar	Formerly, Engineer (Water Resources), Hittman Associates, Columbia, Maryland; now, Research Assistant, Department of Mineral Engineering, The Pennsylvania State University, University Park, Pennsylvania
Tracy L. Cox	Formerly, Research Scientist, Remote Sensing, The Remote Sensing Institute, South Dakota State University, Brookings, South Dakota; now, Scientific Consultant, Laramie, Wyoming
Willie R. Curtis	Hydrologist, Northeastern Forest Experiment Station, Forest Service, U.S. Department of Agriculture, Berea, Kentucky
Grant Davis	Associate Program Manager and member, Oil Shale Environmental Advisory Panel, Intermountain Forest and Range Experiment Station, Forest Service, U.S. Department of Agriculture, Billings, Montana
A. D. Day	Agronomist and Professor, Department of Plant Sciences, University of Arizona, Tucson, Arizona
Rey S. Decker	Senior Soils Engineer, Hoskins-Western-Sonderegger Consulting Engineers, Lincoln, Nebraska
Eugene E. Farmer	Research Hydrologist, Intermountain Forest and Range Experiment Station, Forest Service, U.S. Department of Agriculture, Ogden, Utah
Sherrill H. Fuchs	Conservation Agronomist, Soil Conservation Service, U.S. Department of Agriculture, Portland, Oregon
Herbert R. Gardner	Soil Scientist, Science and Education Administration, U.S. Department of Agriculture, Fort Collins, Colorado
Glendon W. Gee	Formerly Research Scientist, Soils Department, North Dakota State University, Fargo, North Dakota; now, Senior Research Scientist, Water and Land Resources Department, Batelle-Northwest Laboratories, Richmond, Washington
Gwendelyn Geidel	Research Associate, Environmental Hydrogeology Programs, University of South Carolina, Columbia, South Carolina
Frank W. Glover, Jr.	State Resource Conservationist, Soil Conservation Service, U.S. Department of Agriculture, Morgantown, West Virginia
Walter L. Gould	Associate Professor of Agronomy, Department of Agronomy, New Mexico State University, Las Cruces, New Mexico
Alten F. Grandt	Director of Reclamation-Western Group, Peabody Coal Company, St. Louis, Missouri

Elmore C. Grim

Formerly, Surface Mining Specialist, U.S. Environmental Protection Agency, Cincinnatti, Ohio; now, Director, Division of Forestry, Bureau of Natural Resources, Department for Natural Resources and Environmental Protection, Commonwealth of Kentucky, Frankford, Kentucky

James L. Halderson

Formerly, Agricultural Engineer, Metropolitan Sanitary District of Greater Chicago, Chicago, Illinois; now, Associate Professor of Research, Research and Extension Center, University of Idaho, Aberdeen, Idaho

Ronald D. Hill

Director, Resource Extraction and Handling Division, Industrial Environmental Research Laboratory, U.S. Environmental Protection Agency, Cincinnati, Ohio

George V. Holmberg

Surface Mine Reclamation Specialist, Soil Conservation Service, U.S. Department of Agriculture, Washington, D.C.

William J. Horvath

Regional Representative, National Association of Conservation Districts, Stevens Point, Wisconsin

Sue Johnson

Research Coordinator, Center for Developmental Change, University of Kentucky, Lexington, Kentucky

Wilton Johnson

Mined Land Information Specialist, Division of Environment, U.S. Bureau of Mines, Washington, D.C.

Robert S. Johnston

Research Hydrologist, Intermountain Forest and Range Experiment Station, Forest Service, U.S. Department of Agriculture, Logan, Utah

J. Nick Jones, Jr.

Research Agricultural Engineer, Science and Education Administration, U.S. Department of Agriculture, Virginia Polytechnic Institute and State University, Blacksburg, Virginia

Burgess L. Kay

Specialist in Wildland Seeding, Department of Agronomy and Range Sciences, University of California, Davis, California

Raymond J. Krizek

Professor of Civil Engineering, Department of Civil Engineering, The Technological Institute, Northwestern University, Evanston, Illinois

James R. LaFevers

Environmental Scientist, Energy and Environmental System Division, Argonne National Laboratory, Argonne, Illinois

Erlend L. Mathias

Research Agronomist, Science and Education Administration, U.S. Department of Agriculture, Division of Plant Sciences, West Virginia University, Morgantown, West Virginia

David A. Mays

Agronomist, Soils and Fertilizer Research Branch, Tennessee Valley Authority, Muscle Shoals, Alabama

James D. Mertes

Associate Professor, Department of Park Administration and Landscape Architecture, Texas Tech University, Lubbock, Texas

Rex F. Nielson

Associate Professor of Agronomy, Agriculture Experiment Station, Utah State University, Logan, Utah

Paul E. Packer — Principal Research Forester, Intermountain Forest and Range Experiment Station, Forest Service, U.S. Department of Agriculture, Logan, Utah

Angelos Pagoulatos — Assistant Professor of Agricultural Economics, Department of Agricultural Economics, University of Kentucky, Lexington, Kentucky

James Paone — Chief, Division of Environment, U.S. Bureau of Mines, Washington, D.C.

H. Douglas Perry — Research Associate, Department of Agronomy, Virginia Polytechnic Institute and State University, Blacksburg, Virginia

H. B. Petersen — Professor of Irrigation, Agricultural Engineering Department, Utah State University, Logan, Utah

William T. Plass — Principal Plant Pathologist, Northeastern Forest Experiment Station, Forest Service, U.S. Department of Agriculture, Princeton, West Virginia

J. F. Power — Research Soil Scientist, Northern Great Plains Research Center, U.S. Department of Agriculture, Mandan, North Dakota

R. V. Ramani — Associate Professor of Mining Engineering, Department of Mineral Engineering, The Pennsylvania State University, University Park, Pennsylvania

Alan Randall — Professor of Agricultural Economics, Department of Agricultural Economics, University of Kentucky, Lexington, Kentucky

James M. Riddle — Formerly, Research Assistant, Department of Mineral Mining, The Pennsylvania State University, University Park, Pennsylvania; now, Assistant Professor, Department of Mineral Engineering, Colorado School of Mines, Golden, Colorado

Ronald E. Ries — Range Scientist, Northern Great Plains Research Center, Science and Education Administration, U.S. Department of Agriculture, Mandan, North Dakota

Fred M. Sandoval — Research Soil Scientist, Northern Great Plains Research Center, Science and Education Administration, U.S. Department of Agriculture, Mandan, North Dakota

Lee W. Saperstein — Associate Professor and Section Chairman—Mining Engineering, The Pennsylvania State University, University Park, Pennsylvania

Richard M. Smith — Professor of Agronomy, Division of Plant Sciences, West Virginia University, Morgantown, West Virginia

Andrew A. Sobek — Formerly, Research Assistant III, Plant Sciences Division, West Virginia University, Morgantown, West Virginia; now, Soil Scientist, Energy and Environmental Systems Division, Argonne National Laboratory, Argonne, Illinois

Robert M. Strang

Associate Professor, Faculty of Forestry, University of British Columbia, Vancouver, British Columbia, Canada

Paul H. Struthers

Environmental Specialist, Mined Land, Division of Environment, U.S. Bureau of Mines, Washington, D.C.

J. L. Thames

Professor, Watershed Hydrology, School of Renewable Natural Resources, University of Arizona, Tucson, Arizona

J. V. Thirgood

Professor, Faculty of Forestry, University of British Columbia, Vancouver, British Columbia, Canada

Ashley A. Thornburg

Plant Materials Specialist, Soil Conservation Service, U.S. Department of Agriculture, Lincoln, Nebraska

Robert J. Valleau

Head, Operational Planning Branch, Environmental Coordination Services, Land Conservation and Reclamation Division of Alberta Department of the Environment, Edmonton, Alberta, Canada

Keith Van Cleve

Professor of Forestry (Soils), University of Alaska, Fairbanks, Alaska

T. R. Verma

Assistant Research Professor, Watershed Hydrology, School of Renewal Natural Resources, University of Arizona, Tucson, Arizona

Willis G. Vogel

Range Scientist, Northeastern Forest Experiment Station, Forest Service, U.S. Department of Agriculture, Berea, Kentucky

E. M. Watkin

Department of Crop Science, University of Guelph, Guelph, Ontario, Canada

Scott G. Witter

Formerly, Research Assistant, Remote Sensing Institute, South Dakota State University, Brookings, South Dakota; now, Graduate Research Assistant, Department of Geography, University of Tennessee, Knoxville, Tennessee

David A. Woolhiser

Research Hydraulic Engineer, Science and Education Administration, U.S. Department of Agriculture, Colorado State University Engineering Research Center, Fort Collins, Colorado

D. L. Wright

Formerly, Research Associate, Department of Agronomy, Virginia Polytechnic Institute and State University, Blacksburg, Virginia; now, Extension Agronomist, University of Florida, Agricultural Research and Extension Center, Quincy, Florida

David R. Zenz

Coordinator of Research, Metropolitan Sanitary District of Greater Chicago, Cicero, Illinois

P. F. Ziemkiewicz

Formerly, Graduate Student, Faculty of Forestry, University of British Columbia, Vancouver, British Columbia, Canada; now, Reclamation Research Officer, Alberta Energy and Natural Resources, Edmonton, Alberta, Canada

Chapter 1

The Significance and Responsibility of Rehabilitating Drastically Disturbed Land

THADIS W. BOX

Utah State University
Logan, Utah

I. INTRODUCTION

Man has always disturbed the land. Although the interruption of the pristine state by primitive man was not great, his degree of disturbance was limited only by his low population numbers and his lack of complex tools. Man's early activities did not change the landscape greatly, but his alteration of natural conditions must be considered as land disturbance. Therefore, all lands are disturbed by human activity.

The human animal is responsible for most of the major land disturbances, but there is something in his moral makeup that makes him feel responsible for correcting the results of his actions. This responsibility is deep rooted, not only in Judeo-Christian tradition but also in the religions of many primitive cultures. The Maori of New Zealand say, "The land is a mother that never dies." Many of the African traditional religions tie the concepts of human productivity and afterlife to the ground on which a person was raised (Mbiti, 1969). Disturbance and neglect of the land are thought to alter man's very relationship to God. Both the Old and New Testaments of the Bible teach stewardship of the land resource.

These moral and ethical concerns for the land have best been stated by one of our more recent prophets, Aldo Leopold, in the discussion of his land ethic (Leopold, 1949):

> All ethics so far evolved rest upon a single premise: that the individual is a member of a community of interdependent parts. His instincts prompt him to compete for his place in that community, but his ethics prompt him also to cooperate (perhaps in order that there may be a place to compete for).
>
> The land ethic simply enlarges the boundaries of the community to include soils, water, plants, and animals or collectively: the land.

Thus, Leopold spells out for us the major reasons why we must be concerned with the land and at the same time points out that land is much broader than soil, ground, dirt, or other descriptions of a medium for plant growth. Indeed, land contains all of us. He continues to give us a view of our relationship to the rest of the land (Leopold, 1949):

1

In short, a land ethic changes the role of *Homo sapiens* from conqueror of the land-community to plain member and citizen of it. It implies respect for his fellow members, and also respect for the community as such.

If we accept Leopold's land ethic, then failure to rehabilitate land we disturb is as unthinkable as failure to aid the victims of an automobile crash. To walk away from the strip mine or an eroded wheat field may, in fact, be more damaging to society than the failure to adequately treat the ghastly wounds of a colleague after hitting him in an automobile accident.

Few people indeed would shy from the responsibility of giving aid when one caused direct harm to another human being. Most would agree that society should follow the example of the good Samaritan and aid one who is not a friend. Yet it takes laws to force us to apply the same ethical standards to land we have injured. It has been estimated that only about one person per square mile can be supported on the earth if man exists in a hunter-gatherer economy. The four billion people who now inhabit the earth's surface have systematically altered and disturbed the entire face of the earth (Thomas, 1956). The extent of disturbance may vary with population numbers, stage of economic development, age of the culture, and other factors, but the entire face of the earth—and the moon, as well—has felt the effects of man.

Therefore, what we will concern ourselves with here is the degree of that disturbance. The title of this book indicates that we will be discussing those lands that are drastically disturbed.

II. DRASTIC DISTURBANCE AS A CONCEPT

The concept of drastic disturbance will vary between cultures and between individuals within a culture. For my definition here, I will consider areas to be drastically disturbed if the native vegetation and animal communities have been removed and most of the topsoil is lost, altered, or buried. These drastically disturbed sites will not completely heal themselves within the lifetime of man through normal secondary successional processes. The process of rebuilding the plant community must start from a new growth medium, usually a mixture of subsoil, rocks, and soils. Plants and animals have been completely removed and must reestablish themselves within the area disturbed. The natural process often must be helped by artificially introducing new plant communities or by altering the conditions under which new plant communities may develop.

A. Kinds of Drastically Disturbed Areas

There are a number of kinds of drastically disturbed areas. Perhaps the most common of these are towns and cities, and the roadways between them. Each year thousands of hectares of land are drastically disturbed in the building of transportation systems, shopping centers, housing developments, etc. Biotic communities are destroyed and the soil is covered with concrete and asphalt. However, since the societal objective for these areas is to change land use from natural communities to urban areas, reclamation or rehabilitation is usually not part of the long-term land use plan. Rehabilitation only becomes an issue when a town or roadway is abandoned.

Another major area of drastic disturbance is the road cuts, fills, and shoulders that occur in the normal process of building transportation corridors. These long, narrow scars stretch from coast to coast and meander throughout every state in the nation. In total, they probably represent the largest and most visible areas of drastically disturbed lands. They cut across almost every biotic community and every soil type in the United States. Only a recluse or the blind escape the visual insults of these areas. Some are rehabilitated promptly; others are not. Many times the scars are accepted along with the concrete bridges as inevitable badges of progress.

Mine spoils have received much attention from the public and the Congress since the energy crisis accelerated the development of strip mines for coal, uranium, phosphates, etc. Although the need for energy and minerals dictates a major alteration of the earth's surface, the environmentally conscious society of today also demands that we consider rebuilding or reclaiming the areas disturbed. Some of the newer mines show the results of excellent rehabilitation efforts; the older ones stand as monuments to our insensitivity to the land.

Large areas of eroded farmland and rangeland also contribute high percentages to our total area of drastically disturbed lands. However, in most cases these disturbances occurred slowly and without the fanfare associated with the mining industry. Therefore, they have probably received less attention than those areas recently disturbed.

Regardless of the cause of drastic disturbance, it is apparent today that society will not tolerate land being used and left to heal itself. The thought of leaving it in an unproductive and unaesthetic condition for decades or centuries is no longer an acceptable alternative. The popular press is full of articles demanding restoration, reclamation, or rehabilitation, and almost every state in the Union now has statutes regulating the rebuilding of the landscape following disturbance.

B. Definition of Rebuilding Processes

In this chapter I will follow the standard definitions suggested by the National Academy of Sciences (NAS, 1974) in their estimation of rehabilitation potential of western coal lands. *Restoration* means that the exact conditions of the site before disturbance will be replicated after the disturbance. Thus, complete restoration is seldom, if ever, possible. Some values are always lost or altered. Even in the coal fields of Germany where the landscape is surveyed prior to mining and the location of each tree, rock, and other feature mapped and scheduled for reestablishment in its exact location, it is usually impractical or impossible to exactly restore or duplicate the condition of the original site. In my opinion, restoration should be used only when the surface contains important archaeological and historical artifacts that society wishes to preserve.

Reclamation implies that the site will be habitable to organisms originally present in approximately the same composition and density after the reclamation process has been completed. It is acceptable, however, if the site is made habitable to other organisms that closely approximate the original; that is, they fill the same ecological niche. Most environmentalists support the concept of reclamation and insist that, where possible, the original native species should be used in the reclamation process.

Rehabilitation means that the disturbed site will be returned to a form and productivity in conformity with a prior use plan. It implies that a stable condition will be established that will not deteriorate substantially with the projected land use. It also suggests that the area must be consistent with surrounding aesthetic values. This view of land rebuilding is generally supported by agriculturists. It allows the drastically disturbed landscape to be altered for land uses other than the one that was in effect prior to the disturbance. For example, an area that was originally grazing land may be converted to wheat fields following strip mining operations in the northern Great Plains. It also allows an open pit mine to be converted to a lake and the land use changed from agriculture to a county park. Rehabilitation suggests that several alternative land uses have been examined and the potential for reaching each of them evaluated. It also suggests that the selected land use should be both ecologically stable and of high value to society. If a land use other than that prior to disturbance is selected, the selection implies that someone has determined that the new land use is more beneficial to society than the old.

In all cases, however, it is important that the objective for rebuilding the landscape be established prior to the disturbance. The importance of examining objectives for land after mining applies whether the rebuilding process is to include restoration, reclamation, or rehabilitation.

If restoration is selected as a goal in mining, it is assumed that disturbance will be kept to a minimum, since it is usually not possible to completely restore drastically disturbed land. Techniques for the mining operation will then reflect that goal.

When a goal of reclaiming a landscape is established, it implies that we should disturb only in areas where we can reestablish native communities. This rebuilding process, though not as difficult as that of restoration, is dependent upon much more ecological information and the availability of native plant propagules than is a rehabilitation process. The degree of ecological sophistication is great, and the chance for success may be low.

In rehabilitation we must examine all ecological constraints, determine the needs of society, and plan the site for some new land use prior to developing the rehabilitation plan.

Under ideal conditions, when all alternatives are considered and a proper rehabilitation plan developed prior to disturbance, the benefits for society should be great and any losses associated with disturbance should be only temporary. Unfortunately, this preplanning process has not been part of all mining operations in the past. Lands have simply been disturbed and then rehabilitation imposed on the extraction plan as an afterthought.

III. FUTURE LAND DISTURBANCES

I doubt seriously that we will ever see less drastic disturbance of our landscape than we have today. As the human population continues to grow, it will be increasingly more important to rearrange and distribute goods to meet societal needs. This rearranging and redistributing of the products of the earth can only mean that more disturbance will take place. The changing of the landscape will probably be done to meet society's needs in about four areas.

The first and most obvious need for continued land disturbance is to produce food for a growing world population. The plowing of land to plant a wheatfield or the spading of a flower bed to grow petunias disturbs the natural condition. These disturbances, however, are usually not considered drastic by the public, because it is generally recognized that their products, food or flowers, are good for society. What is not generally recognized is that poor agricultural practices associated with very good intentions and objectives have caused widespread erosion worldwide and are perhaps the single largest contributor to drastically disturbed lands.

In the United States, the erosion-producing land use practices reached their peak in the mid-1930's and resulted in the formation of the Soil Erosion Service (later to become the Soil Conservation Service). The establishment of this government agency marked the first nationwide attempt at rehabilitation of drastically disturbed lands in these United States.

The second major land-disturbing practice is associated with shelter and housing for the human population. The removal of trees has only recently attracted attention as being a major disturbance of land, because forestry, like agriculture, produced useful goods for mankind and was considered a normal part of the development of this county.

As I mentioned earlier, the transportation network in this country is responsible for the most widespread drastic disturbance of landscapes. Highways and railroads cut through mountains, cross plains, and protrude from the marshes of this land. They contribute to the most abundant and most easily seen source of drastic disturbance. However, I maintain that these disturbed areas are not really "seen" because people accept them as a normal part of the road-building process. In other words, they have become accustomed to seeing them and a road cut is very much a part of their normal, everyday experience, whereas a strip mine is not.

Land disturbance necessary to obtain the energy and mineral products for our society probably causes the most drastic disturbance of the landscape of any use. Although it is not widespread, it totally and dramatically changes the landscape. Since it is not accepted as a part of most citizens' everyday life, that is, it is not directly producing food or is not a part of the roadside or the road as they visualize it, this disturbance is somehow viewed as more insulting to the land. Therefore, it is this land use—mining and, more particularly, strip mining—that has caused most of the public outcry and pleas for reclamation.

There are certainly other reasons why lands are drastically disturbed; but regardless of the reasons for the insults to the land, there will likely be more in the future. Society can decide to rebuild the landscape or it can readjust its values to accept the insult. Probably both will occur. There is no doubt that there is a sincere nationwide movement to insure that strip mines are properly rehabilitated. However, one has only to travel our highways to see that the same standard is not applied to all disturbances.

IV. PROBLEMS ASSOCIATED WITH DRASTIC DISTURBANCE

A. On-site Disturbances

A large number of problems are associated with the drastic disturbance of the landscape. In general, those on-site disturbances are relatively small. They may range from a few hundred square kilometers for the total coal mining in the West, or a few thousand hectares for oil shale development, to gravel pits along roadsides, which may be less than a hectare in size.

Problems associated with rehabilitating these areas, regardless of size, primarily deal with the application of technology. In all cases, engineering strategy is involved. Such items as how to best remove the topsoil and store it for future use, the removal of the overburden, and the extraction of the material that is needed for society weigh heavily in the mining plans. The rebuilding of the mass removed so as to have minimal effect on any aquifers involved, placing toxic materials at depths where plants will not readily reach them, and providing for adequate surface hydrology all involve application of modern engineering principles.

Finally, the area must be capped with a medium suitable for plant growth. This may be the topsoil that has been stored previously or it may be materials taken from various strata in the overburden that have the physical characteristics necessary for proper water relationships. In the latter case, it is often necessary to add organic matter and mineral elements to sustain plant growth. In this portion of the rehabilitation process, both engineering principles and those agronomic principles dealing with soil, fertility, and structure have to be utilized.

Once the plant growth medium is in place, the establishment of plants becomes a prime requisite. Here agronomic practices of seed bed preparation, selection of proper species, proper seed placement, and nurturing of the seedlings are of paramount importance. After the seedlings have become established, a management program designed to utilize these plants with animals, either domestic or wild, is incorporated, and a monitoring of the system to assure that minerals are properly cycled and the system is functioning so that it may maintain itself is necessary.

Since, as Leopold (1948) suggests, man is part of the land, the results of rehabilitation must pass public scrutiny and acceptance. Failure to involve the public in the process prior to complete rehabilitation may result in the failure of an otherwise successful effort.

In all cases, problems associated with the rehabilitation of the drastic disturbance of the site itself will involve the application of available technology and the development of new methods and techniques through research (Atwood, 1975).

B. Off-site Disturbances

In most cases the on-site disturbances are receiving attention, but, unfortunately, many times the amount disturbed for the actual mining operation is usually disturbed in roads, transmission lines, dams, etc., necessary for water for the project. These associated projects generally create many more offsite effects than those on the site itself.

The off-site effects directly related to the development of a project can usually be estimated with some degree of accuracy. Most mining companies can calculate the length and width of roads necessary to move the material, the transmission corridors, the development of storage areas, or other factors directly related to their operation. On federal lands the rehabilitation of these off-site areas is usually covered in the leases that permit the extraction of the minerals.

It is far more difficult to estimate the off-site effects of the major land use changes indirectly related to a given land disturbance. For instance, a mining operation of any size will require housing developments, parks, city sewer systems, etc. The boom town effect of a mining development is often difficult to anticipate and even more difficult to regulate. The influx of large numbers of people into an area may create considerable drastic disturbance to the surrounding land area. For instance, the amount of off-road vehicle use has been shown to increase around such mining towns as Rock Springs, Wyo., Vernal, Utah, or other western towns associated with energy development. In these arid environments the drastic disturbance caused by four-wheel drive vehicles climbing the surrounding mountains may cause a greater contribution to sediment load in the surrounding rivers than the mining operations where the drivers of the vehicles work. The loss through vandalism of archaelogical and historical artifacts cannot be estimated. However, these effects were not anticipated in the reclamation reports submitted by mining companies prior to the development of their mines.

One of the major problems associated with rehabilitation of disturbed lands is the lack of adequately trained personnel. The person who reclaims land must be a mixture of engineer, landscape architect, soil scientist, agronomist, ecologist, and social scientist. There is no one ideally trained as a reclamation specialist. Those of us who are now working in the area were usually trained in one field and have gained experience in the others. The National Academy of Sciences' report, *Rehabilitation Potential of Western Coal Lands* (1974), pointed out that one of the major limiting factors in rehabilitating western coal lands was the availability of reclamation specialists trained in the arid environment.

A study at Utah State Univ. was initiated last year to attempt to determine the concepts and skills needed for reclamation specialists. A survey instrument was designed to ask people in private companies and government agencies dealing with mining and rehabilitation to evaluate disciplines, concepts, and skills that would be needed for a person to handle a rehabilitation assignment. Over 550 questionnaires were sent to state, federal, and private organizations known to be involved in mining. The response indicated an overwhelming need for specially trained reclamation specialists. However, many of the respondents indicated they thought it would be almost impossible for a single individual to possess all of the attributes necessary. All indicated that the individual must be trained across disciplines and be conversant with engineers, geologists, soil scientists, agriculturists, and ecologists. In addition, these poeple should have practical experience and be able to apply their training.

I will not attempt to list all of the problems dealing with a given drastic disturbance. I would simply state that the techniques for solving on-site disturbances are usually available or can be developed rapidly through research if enough money is available. On the other hand, it is almost impossible to estimate the total amount of drastic disturbance associated with a given project, whether this be a strip mine in Montana or a new interstate highway across southern California.

C. Rehabilitation, Whose Responsibility?

Rehabilitation, at best, will be costly. The question may be legitimately asked, "Why reclaim the land at all?" Since the area to be disturbed will be relatively small compared with the rest of our land base, why not simply make the disturbed areas into national sacrifice areas? In my opinion this solution is acceptable only if the societal costs of not reclaiming the land are properly evaluated and considered against future uses to which the land may be placed. We have a limited supply of land in the world and it is to society's advantage to keep options for land use open for future generations. Even if it were not to our advantage, I suspect the moral and ethical considerations discussed earlier would dictate that we try to rebuild what we have torn asunder.

If the need for the rehabilitated land is to be in the future, then the question can be legitimately raised as to who should be responsible for that reclamation. Most often it is thought that the one who disturbs the land and derives a profit from that disturbance should also be responsible for reclaiming it. However, many hold that the one who owns the land or, better stated, who holds it in trust has the responsibility for restoration of damages. Here, again, our ethical concern for stewardship shows itself.

It can also be argued that, since the general public is to benefit from reclamation, then the general public should somehow underwrite the costs of reclamation and be responsible to see that areas are restored to former productivity. But how do we make the "public" live up to its responsibilities?

Since answers to the questions of who should reclaim or rehabilitate lands are not clear cut, there must be a need for regulation, and for regulations clearly spelling out by whom and under what conditions will land be reclaimed. In a private, free enterprise economy one cannot expect a corporation or land owner to rehabilitate land unless the costs of rehabilitation are somehow offset by benefit to the company in its quest for a profit. Society can demand that the private sector rehabilitate disturbed sites by passing laws and statutes that insist certain kinds of reclamation practices be undertaken. The meeting of these performance standards then becomes a license to continue operations. In the absence of law, adverse public opinion may affect the profit of the company and therefore force it to operate reclamation or rehabilitation efforts when it is disturbing land.

In practice, both processes are now in operation on the private companies of this country. All the western states except Arizona now have surface mine laws. In addition, many of the states in Appalachia and the Midwest where mining is conducted have laws directing that companies reclaim lands that they disturb, and more laws are being enacted each year. Laws that are already on the books are being revised to make the rehabilitation requirements more stringent and there is still active interest in passing a federal strip mining and rehabilitation law.

In my opinion, most companies go beyond the letter of the law in reclaiming land. No major company now dares leave the land bare. Even if laws were not present, the court of public opinion forces them to take an environmental posture in order to sell their products.

The costs of rehabilitation are normally very high when weighed against the surface use value of the land before mining. However, the cost is usually fairly low when related to the cost of the product removed. For instance, rangelands worth only few hundred dollars per hectare may overlie large coal fields. The cost of reclaiming the land to range productivity may reach several thousands of dollars per hectare; but when the cost is related to the product removed, the cost of reclamation may be only a few cents per ton. In most cases, society will opt for reclamation and force the company to put the landscape back together in a form acceptable to it. Insistence that the coal company reclaim the land at its own expense may appear to be costing the company, but these costs are usually only passed on to the consumer.

V. CONCLUSIONS

Disturbance of land began long before man strated to record his history. The amount of disturbance and the extent of its permanency have been getting larger each year. Actions of *Homo sapiens* are continuing to be more drastic, due to better machines and a greater desire to rearrange the earth's surface to obtain goods and services. As man's population and technology grow, it is likely that the amount of drastically disturbed land will be even larger. However, at the same time, our environmental conscience is developing, and it is likely that we will make an attempt to obtain better land use.

Good land use depends at least in part on three activities. First, the ecological potential of the area must be evaluated. In addition, it is necessary to determine what society wants and needs from the land. And, third, political and social institutions must be developed to allow people to get what they want from the land and stay within its carrying capacity for that particular use.

We know quite a bit about the ecological potential of most of the land that will be disturbed in the future. We may not be as certain about what society will want from the land, but we can assume that they will want the drastically disturbed portions of our landscapes rehabilitated so that other goods and services can be obtained. We can hope that man has learned enough from his mistakes in the past that he will design the institutions necessary to insist that proper rehabilitation be done.

Any rehabilitation effort is site-specific. Preplanning the rehabilitation work is a necessity if the rebuilding program is to be successful. It is essential in the preplanning effort to have a clear idea of what the land use objective will be once the rehabilitation process has been completed.

To a large extent technology is now available for rehabilitation of most of our drastically disturbed lands. In those cases where it is not available it can be developed if research projects are properly designed. If society makes a commitment to rehabilitate the land it drastically disturbs, in my opinion societal loss from land disturbance should be minimal and shortlived. Without a commitment expressed at all levels of government, loss of productivity through disturbance could be tragic.

LITERATURE CITED

Atwood, G. 1975. The strip mining of western coal. Sci. Am. 233:23–29.

Leopold, A. 1949. A sand county almanac and sketches here and there. Oxford University Press, New York, N. Y. 233 p.

Mbiti, J. S. 1969. African religions and philosophy, Heinimann, Nairobi. 289 p.

National Academy of Sciences. 1974. Rehabilitation potential of western coal lands. Ballinger Publ. Co., Cambridge, Mass. 198 p.

Thomas, W. L., Jr. (ed.). 1956. Man's role in changing the face of the earth. Univ. of Chicago Press, Chicago, Ill. 1,193 p.

Copyright © 1978 ASA–CSSA–SSSA
677 South Segoe Road, Madison, WI 53711 USA
Reclamation of Drastically Disturbed Lands

Chapter 2

Extent of Disturbed Lands and Major Reclamation Problems in the United States

JAMES PAONE, PAUL STRUTHERS, AND WILTON JOHNSON

U.S. Bureau of Mines, Washington, D.C.

I. INTRODUCTION

This paper is concerned with the extent of land disturbed by the minerals industry in the United States and the major problems associated with reclaiming those lands. The discussion on the extent of disturbed lands is based on data developed by the U.S. Bureau of Mines from a survey taken to determine how much land was used and reclaimed by the minerals industry from 1930 through 1971. The term *reclaimed* in this report means that reconditioning or restoration work was completed on mined areas and waste disposal areas in compliance with federal, state, or local law.

The principal source of data for the survey was the minerals industry itself. Corroborative data and information were obtained from other federal and state agencies, mining organizations, and trade associations.

The paper includes data obtained on mining operations of all commodities including mines, quarries, pits, mills, and coal preparation plants. Petroleum and natural gas activities are excluded.

II. COMPARISON OF MAJOR LAND USES

The total land area of the United States, excluding Alaska and Hawaii, comprises 917 million ha (2.264 billion acres). Although land supports a variety of uses, its most predominant use is agriculture. According to a report published by the Economic Research Service of the U.S. Department of Agriculture (Frey, 1973), 520 million ha (1.283 billion acres), or 57% of the total land mass, is devoted to agricultural uses. These include land used for cropland, grassland (pasture and range), woodland grazed, and farmsteads and farm roads.

Nonagricultural uses occupy the remaining 397 million ha (981 million acres), or 43% of the total land area. The most significant form of nonagricultural land use is ungrazed forest land. The second most significant form falls within the special use category. This category includes land for development of urban areas, recreation and wildlife, transportation networks, and public installations and facilities.

11

Table 1—Comparison of major land uses in the United States, 1969

Major land use	Land area	
	Million ha	% of total
Agricultural		
Cropland	191.1	20.8
Grassland pasture and range	244.6	26.7
Forest land grazed	80.1	8.7
Farmstead, farm roads	4.6	0.5
Total agricultural land	520.4	56.7
Nonagricultural		
Forest land not grazed	212.6	23.2
Special uses	68.4	7.5
Miscellaneous	114.6	12.4
Mining, 1930–71	1.5	0.2
Total nonagricultural land	397.1	43.3
Total land area	917.5	100.0

Miscellaneous uses also constitute a substantial portion of non-agricultural land. These include uninventoried land and areas of little or no use such as marshes, open swamps, bare rocks, tundra, and desert.

Mining, when compared to other land uses, occupies a very small, almost undiscernible, portion of the nation's land. Despite the attention mining has received over the years, a land utilization survey conducted by the Bureau of Mines (Paone et al., 1974) concluded that mining and its related activities used less than 0.2% of the total land mass during the 41-year period 1930–71, and nearly half of that has been reclaimed. Yet, because of its conspicuous nature and the methods that must be employed to obtain the minerals, mining is looked upon as a major environmental threat. A comparison of various types of land use is shown in Table 1.

III. DESCRIPTION OF MINING METHODS

To state it simply, *mining* can be defined as that process or activity aimed at removing a desired mineral commodity from its natural placement in the earth. There are two methods by which minerals may be removed: surface mining and underground mining. The proximity or depth of the mineral or ore deposit in relation to the earth's surface is a principal factor in determining which method is the most suitable in a given situation.

A. Surface Mining

The surface mining process permits the mineral or ore deposit to be removed through excavations. It is not applicable to all situations. In some instances, the thickness of overburden that must be moved in order to recover a given amount of product places a definite economic limitation upon the operator. In other instances, such as sand and gravel operations, surface mining offers the only practical means of mineral recovery.

The procedure for surface mining generally involves two steps: (i) prospecting or exploration to discover, delineate, and prove the ore body, and (ii) the actual mining or recovery phase. Drill holes and excavations used to intersect or expose the ore body may be numerous and can constitute a serious source of surface disturbance. But excavations made during the recovery process are the primary source of surface disturbance associated with surface mining. Surface mining methods may be classified as (i) open pit mining, (ii) strip mining, (iii) dredging, and (iv) hydraulic mining.

1. OPEN PIT

Open pit mining (open cast mining) includes quarries used to produce limestone, sandstone, marble, and granite; pits used to produce sand and gravel; and large excavations used to produce iron and copper. In open pit mining, the amount of overburden removed is proportionately small compared to the quantity of ore or ore-bearing material produced. Another distinctive feature of open pit mining is the length of time that it is conducted in one place. Because of the thickness of the deposits, some open pit mines operate for years, obtaining large quantities of ore while disturbing a relatively small surface area.

2. STRIP MINING

Strip mining is a term commonly used to describe the surface mining method for recovering coal. There are two general types of strip mining: area stripping and contour stripping.

Area stripping is used in relatively flat terrain, mostly in the midwestern U.S. The process involves removing the overburden atop the coal seam using large shovels, draglines, or bucket wheel excavators capable of handling massive amounts of material. In smaller operations, smaller equipment such as bulldozers may be used. The overburden from the first cut is placed on unmined land adjacent to the cut. The coal is then removed. The process is repeated, placing overburden from subsequent cuts into those previously excavated. Unless the land is reclaimed, this process produces ridges resembling a gigantic washboard.

Contour stripping is practiced in hilly terrain. It is the most widespread method of surface mining coal in some states in the Appalachian Region. The contour stripping process involves removing the overburden over the coal seam, starting at the outcrop and proceeding around the hillside. After the coal is removed, successive cuts are made until the overburden becomes too great to permit the coal to be recovered economically.

3. DREDGING

Dredging is used extensively in placer gold mining. It is also used to recover sand and gravel from streambeds and low-lying lands. The process involves the use of a suction apparatus or various mechanical devices such as ladder or chain buckets, clamshells, and draglines mounted on floating barges.

Dredging is a source of surface disturbance in that it produces tailing piles having a configuration similar to spoil piles left by area strip mining.

4. HYDRAULIC MINING

Hydraulic mining was used quite extensively in the past to produce gold. Today, the process occurs on a limited scale. It involves the use of powerful water jets to break and wash down or erode ore-bearing material. The material is then fed into concentrating devices where the desired product is separated from the waste. Like dredging, hydraulic mining creates a waste disposal problem.

B. Underground Mining

Underground, or deep, mining is used to recover mineral and ore deposits that lie far enough beneath the earth's surface to make surface mining impractical or uneconomical. Underground mines are of several types including shaft mines, drift mines, and slope mines. Shaft mines are used to gain access to mineral deposits that lie far below the earth's surface, while drift and slope mines are used to reach deposits in hilly areas.

Generally, surface disturbance from underground mining occurs when roof support systems are systematically removed or deteriorate, causing total collapse of the rock strata. As a result, minor depressions or massive cave-ins sometimes appear on the surface. In populated areas, subsidence can affect public health and safety and cause extensive property damge.

Depending on whether coal or metal and nonmetallic minerals are being produced, any of several underground mining systems may be employed including room and pillar, longwall, open stope, filled stope, and caved stope.

1. COAL

Room and pillar is the principal method used in underground coal production. However, the longwall method is receiving much attention and application because it has a much higher rate of recovery than is achieved by the room and pillar method.

a. Room and Pillar—In the United States, coal generally occurs in flat-lying deposits and is usually mined by the room and pillar method. This method is characterized, as the name implies, by the excavation of rooms with intervening pillars of coal of adequate size left in place to support the roof. Various types of mechanical mining or continuous mining machines and equipment are used to fragment, load, and transport the coal from the mine. In 1975, about 97% of the U.S. underground coal production of 263 million metric tons was produced by room and pillar methods.

b. Longwall—The longwall mining system employs the use of continuous cutting-conveying machines which are pulled back and forth across the coal face. Roof control with powered self-advancing supports is temporary; such supports, moved forward as the longwall advances, allow the roof to collapse, inducing subsidence which may affect the surface.

2. METAL AND NONMETAL

The remaining three methods (open stope, filled stope, and caved stope) are used almost exclusively in underground mining of metallic and nonmetallic minerals. In actual practice, combinations of two or all three methods may be used.

a. Open Stope—*Open stope* is a term used to describe the room and pillar method of metal mining. An open stope is a cavity from which the ore has been extracted, the only support being pillars of ore, wood, concrete or steel props, or rock. Depending on the size or nature of the deposit, open stopes may be used with or without pillars. The value of the deposit may determine whether pillars are left or whether some form of artificial support is applied.

b. Filled Stope—Filled stope methods are used in medium ground where the ore and surrounding rock are not firm enough to stand alone. Waste filling is added to prevent underground caving and possible surface subsidence. Filling the stope is also a means of disposing of waste material from the mine or processing plant.

c. Caved Stope—Caved stope involves undercutting a deposit, letting it cave in, and pulling the ore out through chutes and other channeling devices installed below the caved areas. Caving methods induce surface subsidence and are generally used in areas where subsidence can be tolerated.

IV. EXTENT OF LAND USED BY MINING

As can be gathered from the foregoing discussion of the various mining processes, the very nature of mining necessitates disturbing the land. Like agriculture, transportation, and urbanization, mining is essential to the nation's well-being.

Disturbed land can be attributed to both surface and underground extractive operations, as well as to areas used for deposition of milling and other processing wastes. Surface areas affected as a result of deteriorating subsurface supports in abandoned underground mines also contribute to the amount of land affected by mining. In 1971, the Bureau of Mines conducted a survey to determine how much land had been used and reclaimed by the mining industry between 1930–71, and for the year 1971 (Paone et al., 1974).

Table 2—Land utilized and reclaimed by the mining industry in the United States, 1930–71

Type of use	Metals		Nonmetals		Fossil fuels†		Total‡	
	Utilized	Reclaimed	Utilized	Reclaimed	Utilized	Reclaimed	Utilized	Reclaimed
Surface mining excavation	58,700	7,040	429,000	102,000	391,000	290,000	879,000	399,000
Overburden and refuse disposal from surface mining	49,800	2,130	118,000	52,200	129,000	108,000	297,000	162,000
Subsidence and disturbance from underground mining	4,940	720	1,850	40	35,600	1,620	42,400	2,400
Disposal of refuse from underground mining	8,860	610	840	70	67,200	8,090	76,900	8,770
Disposal of wastes from milling and processing	89,400	7,000	81,300	9,430	12,900	2,620	184,000	19,100
Total‡	212,000	17,500	631,000	164,000	635,000	410,000	1,480,000	591,000

† Excludes oil and gas operations.
‡ Data may not add to totals shown because of independent rounding.

According to the results of that survey, the domestic minerals industry in that 41-year period utilized 1.48 million ha (3.65 million acres), 0.16% of the total land mass. During the same period, 591,000 ha (1.46 million acres), or 40% of the total area utilized, was reclaimed. In 1971 alone, 83,000 ha (206,000 acres) were utilized and 66,000 ha (163,000 acres) were reclaimed. Thus, the ratio between land used and reclaimed doubled in 1971, compared with the ratio for the 41-year period. Table 2 shows the total amount of land utilized and reclaimed in the United States according to mining function and commodity mined.

A. Land Utilized by Mining Function, 1930–71

Of the total 1.48 million ha (3.65 million acres) used by the minerals industry, about 50% was accounted for by the area of excavation associated with surface mining, 20% by the disposal of overburden and other mine wastes from surface mining, 13% by disposal of mill or processing wastes, and 5% by disposal of underground mine wastes; the remaining 3% was subsided or disturbed as a result of deteriorating underground workings.

Reclamation of 95% of the 591,000 ha reclaimed (1.46 million acres) was performed on land affected by surface mining operations. Included were areas of excavation, 68%, and areas used for disposal of overburden and other mine wastes from surface mining, 27%. The remaining 5% was distributed among mill waste areas, waste from underground mines, and subsided areas.

B. Land Utilized by Mining, by Selected Commodity, 1930-71

On a commodity basis, the production of bituminous coal accounted for the greater portion of land used—40%. The remaining 60% was used to produce all other mineral commodities, including sand and gravel, 18%, stone 14%, clay and copper 5% each, iron ore 3%, phosphate rock 2%, and other minerals 13%.

V. PROJECTED LAND USE—SURFACE COAL MINING

Information on the total amount of land utilized by the mining industry for years beyond 1971 has not been developed by the Bureau of Mines. However, efforts are underway to obtain information to update existing land use data on land utilized in connection with coal mining. The information is being sought from individual coal operators and state mining and reclamation agencies. When the survey is completed, its results will be published in a Bureau of Mines report.

In conjunction with other work, namely "Project Independence," the Bureau of Mines projected the amount of land that will be used by the surface coal mining industry in 1975, 1977, 1980, 1985, and 1990. The data shown in Table 3 are based on surface coal mine yields by state, developed for 1971 and modified to reflect the shift to thicker deposits in the northern Great Plains in the latter part of the projection period. Unlike the data that will be obtained by the previously mentioned study, the areas of reclaimed land, land use for disposal of waste from underground mining, and subsidence are not included in this projection.

VI. MAJOR RECLAMATION PROBLEMS

The principal legislative and technical experience in reclaiming disturbed land has centered on surface mined lands, and most extensively on lands strip mined for coal. The denuded and rough appearance of the

Table 3—Projected regional land use for coal production from surface mining

	Area in ha, by year				
Region	1975	1977	1980	1985	1990
Northern Appalachia	8,000	8,300	9,400	10,800	14,000
Southern Appalachia	5,500	5,700	6,800	8,500	10,300
Midwest	7,200	7,400	8,300	9,900	11,700
Gulf	800	1,400	3,900	5,800	7,200
Northern Great Plains	400	500	600	900	1,100
Rocky Mountain	500	600	600	700	900
Pacific Coast	600	800	1,200	1,900	2,200
Total†	23,000	25,000	31,000	39,000	47,000

† Data may not add to totals because of independent rounding.

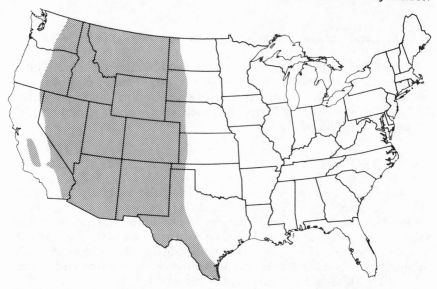

Fig. 1—Regions of gross climate contrast in the contiguous U.S. Shading depicts general area where climate is mostly arid or semiarid except at higher altitudes. (Adapted from Masters & Wolfe, 1974).

strip mined land was the earliest concern, resulting in pioneering efforts in revegetation with trees in regions having natural forest cover. State laws requiring reclamation date back some 30 years or more. Initial requirements for replanting strip mined lands were quickly followed by requirements for regrading. Grading and revegetation remain the basic operations in surface reclamation today, but involve the added directives of water pollution control and concern for land use planning.

The reclamation of areas disturbed by mining is a current, daily operation for industry personnel involved. Practices are used which meet regulatory requirements enforced by inspectors within the bounds of technical and economic constraints and cost effectiveness. The practices are those which experience has proven to give consistent, acceptable results. There is little incentive to change unless a new technique is markedly superior in cost effectiveness. New practices are quickly adopted when required by changes in regulations.

A large part of the western half of the United States has a dry climate as shown in Fig. 1. Land areas classified as tropical, subtropical, and middle latitude deserts and steppes (Masters & Wolfe, 1974) reflect an arid or semiarid climate. Climate is always of concern when reclamation is required in a new region. Past experience elsewhere may not apply and results of reclamation may be different. New conditions encountered always require a period of trial and assessment to establish a basis for realistic requirements and expectations in reclamation. In perspective, prevailing conditions such as topography and geochemistry also vary from place to place and are accommodated to the degree possible by modifications in reclamation practice. It is better to consider climate in a similar vein and proceed with development of appropriate and improved means of reclamation suited to a region. Little purpose is served by making contrasts with other localities.

An opportunity for improvement over natural premining conditions is possible in land reclamation. There has been occasion to create useful flat land where steep land was dominant. Where saline soils occur in dryer climates, the surface conditions causing salinity are disrupted and likely will not be reestablished in reclamation. Other factors in reclamation remain of concern, however, and present the opportunity for better technical definition and improvement in practices.

A. Surface Topography

Premining surface topography influences mine development and the location of facilities including access roads and waste disposal areas, and is of fundamental importance in reclamation since any major change in terrain caused by mining may be viewed as an adverse impact. The surrounding topography serves as the recognized pattern for reclamation grading, even though technical considerations might dictate otherwise. Virtually all land area has some degree of slope caused by natural erosion, and the reestablishment of slopes and drainage channels results in intensified erosion since loose, disturbed materials are less stable than the original consolidated strata. Acceptable modification of slopes by engineering means such as furrows or diversions applied in grading the finished surface, especially in steeper terrain, is urgently needed to control rill and gully erosion during the time required for plant cover establishment. Slopes of concern may approach the limiting angle of repose for spoil materials, generally about 36 to 38 degrees or some 75 to 80% gradient.

B. Land Stability

Lands disturbed in mining and subsequently graded are not only unstable in reference to erosion. They are also subject to settling and possible landslide. Freshly excavated materials occupy a volume in the range of 25% greater than that of the rock prior to excavation. Significant vertical settling occurs unevenly over the surface in time as space between fragments is reduced under force of gravity. Surface features designed for erosion and water control can become ineffective because of settling. The range in effect of settling needs better definition for accommodation in engineering design for water control purpose.

Landslides or mudslides can occur when spoil banks in slopes become saturated. Certain soil materials are more prone to slide than others. A source of water in excess of direct precipitation, either surface or ground water, generally can be found in slide areas. All factors involved and their relative importance need to be identified for guidance in preventing slides. The need is particularly of concern in reference to valley fill placement of spoils.

C. Water Control

The role and control of water are vital considerations in mined land reclamation. Water is essential to success and at times is a cause of difficulties in reclamation. Water management and control, principally at the land surface, is a key element in the results achieved. The most obvious essential requirement for water is moisture supply for plant establishment, survival, and growth. In almost every climate there are periods of moisture stress for plants during the growing season, the probable chief cause of plant mortality in the first year following planting. The stress may be the direct lack of water or caused indirectly by too high concentrations of mineral salts or possibly toxic ions. In any case, measures for moisture conservation can increase plant survival.

Weathering is another essential role of water (Struthers, 1965). Minerals freshly exposed at the land surface are altered by reacting with moisture and atmospheric gases, releasing salts. An increase in moisture in the soil helps to promote weathering, dilute and leach out the mineral salts, and improve the soil condition for plant survival and growth. Runoff also removes salts at the surface but erodes the weathered minerals, causing the cycle to be repeated.

Salts and sediment are considered pollutants in receiving waters. Both may reach surface streams while only the salts reach ground water. Sediment control while freshly disturbed land is still barren of vegetation can be markedly improved by grading the surface to retain or detain water on the land, but appropriate engineering design has yet to be developed for a variety of site conditions and situations encountered. Control methods developed for agricultural lands are helpful, but only rarely applicable because of design limitations.

Surface infiltration of water and percolation through soil materials can alter the composition of dissolved mineral salts, presumably toward equilibrium in the ground water environment. The content of reactive ions is gradually reduced. Some of the salts may resurface in seepage waters on lower slopes. The preferred and essential disposition of mineral salts from disturbed land, either in runoff or by infiltration, has not been determined by pollution control authorities and is in need of investigation, documentation, and recommendation by the scientific community.

D. Soil Conditions

Surface characteristics of lands disturbed in mining have been widely reported. The suitability of some methods used for characterization, however, remains in question, particularly tests developed for agricultural soils. Continued investigation is needed for proper interpretation of spoil and geologic core sample testing, especially in reference to forecasting reclamation results.

One of the characteristics distinguishing soils and spoils is the location of horizons that retard the infiltration and percolation of water, and that direct the development of root growth. Where topsoils are intact, surface infiltration rates are usually higher than the percolation rates of deeper horizons, and the root distribution of plants is mostly in or near the surface. The opposite is generally true of lands disturbed in mining. The contrast has recognized significance in reference to infiltration of moisture for plant use but otherwise has received little attention for applications that may be beneficial in reclamation.

Most past experience in reclamation of disturbed land has been obtained by direct grading and planting of strip mine spoils. A recent innovation and requirement in some states is for removal and reapplication of the original soil on the mined site. Initial results have been reported from investigations of the practice, but longer term observations are urgently needed for guidance of future developments. One area of concern is the desired degree of mixing at the soil-spoil interface, and another is the cost effectiveness of variations of the practice.

E. Revegetation

The revegetation of lands disturbed in mining has received major attention in both application and research effort. The establishment of vegetative cover continues to be the principal means relied upon for erosion control, which has led to a trend toward more use of forage species for close ground cover and less of forest tree species.

The principal areas of investigation both now and in the past have been the search for plants more tolerant to disturbed land conditions and the development of appropriate cultural practices for plant establishment. The testing of different plant species can be an unending task. The evaluation of plants for relative tolerance to site conditions has seldom proven very useful or cost effective beyond the initial period of screening necessary on new soil materials or in new geographic regions. The reason is that site conditions can vary widely, whereas the range in tolerance of different plants to critical conditions is relatively narrow. It is more effective to identify and modify the major site problems. Plant species mixtures suited to the improved site and the climate can then be selected on the basis of maximum surface protection against wind and water erosion, thereby promoting permanent site stability and soil formation. At that point the public interest is served. It would seem justified to allow site use for special purposes during recovery of stable conditions only if compatible with that objective. Extended search for species for the special advantage or purpose of the private land owner is not generally considered to be a public responsibility.

Results of research on cultural methods to improve success in revegetation are seldom reported in reference to cost effectiveness. Where attempts are made at such evaluation the information is helpful, but there appears to be no standard means for the evaluation. The development or evolvement of a standard methodology to denote the cost effectiveness of cultural methods would be of major value.

LITERATURE CITED

Frey, H. T. 1973. Major uses of land in the United States, summary for 1969. USDA-ERS Agric. Econ. Rep. no. 247.

Masters, L. W., and W. C. Wolfe. 1974. The use of weather and climatological data in evaluating the durability of building components and materials. U.S. Natl. Bureau of Standards Tech. Note 838 (Libr. Congr. Card no. 74-600106).

Paone, J., J. L. Morning, and L. Guorgetti. 1974. Land utilization and reclamation in the mining industry, 1930-71. U.S. Bureau of Mines Inf. Circ. 8642.

Struthers, P. H. 1965. Rapid spoil weathering and soil genesis. p. 86-90. *In* Grant Davis, W. W. Ward, and R. E. McDermott (eds.) Proc. Coal Mine Spoil Reclamation Symp., 11-14 Oct. 1965, Pennsylvania State Univ. School of Forest Resour., University Park, Pa.

Chapter 3

Rehabilitation Problems in Alpine and Arctic Regions

RAY W. BROWN, ROBERT S. JOHNSTON, AND KEITH VAN CLEVE

Forest Service, USDA, Ogden, Utah, and
University of Alaska, College, Alaska

I. INTRODUCTION

Mineral exploration, mining, pipeline construction, recreation, and other activities are accelerating on alpine and arctic ecosystems in North America. These ecosystems are threatened with severe disruption; in some areas, esthetic, watershed, and wildlife habitat values have already been seriously damaged. For example, during the past 5 years human disturbance to the Alaskan arctic tundra has increased rapidly as a result of the development of the well-known gas and oil reserves of that region. Also, the largest known deposits of chromium and platinum in the western hemisphere were recently discovered on the alpine tundra of the Beartooth Mountains of Montana, and several mining companies have begun full-scale mining. Although tundra ecosystems constitute a relatively small proportion of the earth's land surface [about 5.4% (Webber, 1974)], their geographical size is in no way proportional to their importance, or to the impacts that disturbances have on them.

Alpine and arctic ecosystems are of vital importance as metropolitan and agricultural watersheds, providing nearly year-round snow accumulation and water storage areas. Also, they are essential wildlife habitats. In arctic tundra regions, strong sociological ties exist between man and his environment. These areas recently were found to contain valuable mineral and fossil fuel resources, which are being rapidly exploited at the expense of this unique ecosystem. In some areas, unregulated recreational activities threaten to destroy the very resource that most appeals to the recreationist. Our lack of knowledge concerning the interactions of various biotic and abiotic components of the tundra ecosystem is the most important limiting factor in the development of effective rehabilitation techniques for disturbed tundra lands. The major challenge in the face of expanding development, however, is not to withdraw all of these areas from reasonable use, but to develop the technology and skills necessary to return these unique ecosystems to a natural, self-sustaining state.

II. CHARACTERISTICS OF ALPINE AND ARCTIC REGIONS

Traditionally, the term *tundra* is used to identify ecosystems in which the vegetation consists of low-growing herbaceous, shrub, or lichen species and where growing season temperatures are too low to permit tree growth (Billings, 1974a, 1974b; Webber, 1974; Love, 1970; Bliss, 1971). More specifically, *tundra* defines treeless regions beyond climatic timberlines in northern latitudes (arctic tundra) and above tree line on high mountains at midlatitudes and southern latitudes (alpine tundra).

Tundra ecosystems in the United States occur in Alaska, the 11 western States, and in a small region in New England. Arctic tundra in the United States is confined to the northern portion of Alaska between the Brooks Range and the Arctic Ocean and along the western coastal regions. However, alpine tundra occurs at higher elevations in mountainous terrain above tree line. The elevation of tree line in the western U. S. decreases from about 3,500 m in the southwest to about 2,000 m in northern Montana, whereas in Alaska tree line occurs at less than 1,000 m in many places. In New England, tree line occurs at about 1,500 m (Hadley & Bliss, 1964).

Although there are some objections to using tree line as the lower or southern boundary of tundra ecosystems (Barry & Ives, 1974; Billings, 1974b), this criterion is widely used because of convenience and generally will be used here. Apparently, however, not all alpine or arctic ecosystems are necessarily *tundra*. Love (1970) pointed out that *subalpine* and *subarctic* ecosystems are subdivisions of the alpine and arctic types, respectively, and should not be construed to mean "below" alpine or arctic. The implication here is that fingers and isolated patches of krummholz and dwarfed trees characteristic of the upper montane zone on mountain slopes and the taiga in arctic regions are full-fledged alpine and arctic ecosystems, respectively. Therefore, the term *tundra* as used here is to be restricted to only those ecosystems in alpine and arctic regions composed of low-growing herbaceous, shrubby, or lichen-dominated communities.

Alpine and arctic environments are generally considered to be severe, at least from man's point of view (Table 1). Generally, both regions are characterized by extremely short growing seasons with low temperatures and snow cover of long duration, but they are climatically similar in few other ways (Barry & Ives, 1974). Alpine areas experience regular diurnal and seasonal regimens of solar radiation relative to their latitude. However, arctic regions may receive virtually no solar radiation for half the year and nearly total daylight during much of the other half. Although both regions may be windy, high windspeeds are more frequent in alpine areas (Bliss, 1956). Mean annual precipitation in the arctic is markedly lower than that received in alpine regions (Barry & Ives, 1974).

Low temperature is a characteristic shared by all tundras and is one of the most important limiting factors in terms of plant productivity in alpine and arctic environments (Billings, 1974b; Tranquillini, 1964; Webber, 1974). Because of these low-growing season temperatures,

Table 1—Comparison of environmental characteristics of an alpine tundra location in
Colorado and an arctic tundra location near Barrow, Alaska
(from Billings & Mooney, 1968)

Component	Alpine tundra	Arctic tundra
Solar radiation		
Highest daily total, ly	780	760
Avg. July intensity, cal cm^{-2} min^{-1}	0.56	0.30
Max. photoperiod	15 hours	84 days
Air temperature $+1$ m, °C		
Annual mean air	-3.3	-12.4
Max. air	18.3	25.6
Jan. mean air	-12.8	-26.7
July mean air	8.3	3.9
Soil temperature -15 cm, °C		
Max. soil	13.3	2.5
Annual mean soil	-1.7	-6.2
Precipitation, annual mean, mm	634	107
Wind, annual mean, km hr^{-1}	29.6	19.3
Growing season, days	60–90	60–90

tundra ecosystems have among the world's lowest biological productivities, ranging between about 10 to 400 dry g m^{-1} year^{-1} (Webber, 1974). The 10°C isotherm during the warmest month of the year has been suggested as the climatic limit for trees in the northern hemisphere (Wardle, 1974). However, Billings (1974b) argued that choice of the isotherm is often arbitrary, its position is not often known, local microclimate affects it, and not all plants obey it. Soils, vegetation, and microclimate are generally more heterogeneous in alpine than in arctic regions due to greater topographical variability. Consequently, air and soil temperatures generally are also more variable in the alpine.

An important characteristic of all arctic tundra regions and some alpine tundra regions is the presence of permanently frozen soils. Permafrost is most often continuous in higher latitudes; in midlatitude tundras, its occurrence is sporadic or relic (Ives, 1974). Also, tundra environments are subject to periodic soil-freezing and frost-heaving cycles during the growing season and severe surface disruption often results.

Although many of the same plant species occur in both alpine and arctic flora, alpine regions are floristically richer and more diverse. Billings (1973) suggested that these differences may be due to the more heterogeneous alpine habitat. Generally, there is an attenuation in floristic richness from low latitude alpine regions through the midlatitude alpine tundras to the arctic tundra and polar deserts of high latitudes (Billings, 1973). Although there are many differences between alpine and arctic regions, floristically and physiognomically they have many similarities. For example, 45% of the species found on the Beartooth Plateau in Montana are also found in the arctic (Billings, 1973). Some species are also circumpolar, being found in virtually all major tundra ecosystems. The floristic similarity between alpine and arctic regions intimately links many common rehabilitation problems. However, it is to be emphasized that differences between these two tundras are significant and that conclusions reached in one are not necessarily applicable to the other.

III. ALPINE AND ARCTIC REHABILITATION PROBLEMS

Disturbances in tundra regions are caused by many factors, but recently man has had by far the greatest impact. His mobility and technological capabilities have, in the span of a few decades, allowed him to roam, prod, explore, excavate, and occasionally enjoy vast expanses of back-country tundra in relative comfort. The resulting impacts in terms of environmental damage have been enormous, but the ecosystem recovery rates by both natural and artificial means to date have been extremely slow or, more commonly, nonexistent.

A. Nature and Extent of the Problem

For the most part, disturbed tundra lands most in need of rehabilitation are those damaged by mining, road construction, pipeline development, and other activities that result in total destruction of the surface ecosystem. A logical beginning in the development of a comprehensive rehabilitation program for disturbed tundra regions is an assessment of the nature and extent of the problem. Since no known data are available, a U.S.-wide survey was undertaken in an effort to document the nature and extent of disturbances on alpine tundra ecosystems. Questionnaires were distributed to all land management agencies known to administer tundra lands requesting their best estimate of the extent of the problem. An analysis of their responses revealed that the following major causes of land disturbance in tundra regions include: (i) grazing by livestock; (ii) recreation, including trail, campsite, and trampling disturbances; (iii) mining, past and present, and mineral exploration sites, construction sites and camps; (iv) roads, permanent and unimproved, and off-road vehicle disturbances; (v) pipelines; (vi) powerlines; (vii) reservoirs; and (viii) other causes, such as fire and landslides (Table 2). The survey also included a category for estimated future disturbance of these lands; however, these estimates were not generally documented in quantitative terms.

Table 2—Summary of the nature and extent of tundra disturbances in the United States

Nature of disturbance	Extent of disturbance			
	Western U.S.	Alaska	New England	Total U.S.
	ha			
Grazing	256,198	unknown	unknown	unknown
Recreation	38,141	unknown	450†	unknown
Mining	34,677	unknown	unknown	unknown
Roads	12,748	unknown	unknown	unknown
Pipelines	683	3,000†	unknown	unknown
Powerlines	289	unknown	unknown	unknown
Reservoirs	274	unknown	unknown	unknown
Other	795	unknown	unknown	unknown
Total disturbance	343,805	18,210†	unknown	unknown
Total area of tundra	2,915,991	74,060,000	4,371	76,980,362
% disturbed	11.8	0.025	unknown	unknown

† Estimated.

The nationwide extent of tundra ecosystems in the United States is about 77 × 10⁶ ha, or about 8.2% of the total U. S. land area. The worldwide extent of tundra ecosystems is about 8 × 10⁸ ha, or about 5% of the earth's total land surface, according to Whittaker (1970). Of the approximately 2.9 × 10⁶ ha of alpine tundra in the western U. S., almost 12% has been disturbed and requires rehabilitation (Table 2). Unfortunately, these kinds of data are not available for the alpine and arctic tundra regions in Alaska. Our estimate of the total extent of tundra in Alaska is about 74 × 10⁶ ha, of which about 52% is arctic tundra and 48% is alpine tundra. About 18 × 10³ ha has been disturbed by various causes, such as mining and roadbuilding. Obviously, the widely publicized Alaska pipeline has contributed a significant proportion of the disturbed land in that state. In New England, the major causes of disturbance to alpine tundra are associated with recreational activities.

The most alarming disclosure of the alpine survey is the apparent lack of regard by land managers for disturbed alpine land. Realistically, some land managers are very aware of the problem, but others appear to be little concerned about these disturbed resources. In a few cases, land managers are totally unaware that tundra ecosystems even exist within their areas of responsibility. The major concern, perhaps understandably, seems to be for resources of high economic return, such as timber and rangelands. It seems absolutely essential that the watershed, wildlife habitat, esthetic, and other values of tundra environments in both alpine and arctic regions be managed with the same degree of concern given other resources.

B. Types of Disturbance

1. GRAZING

Many alpine ranges have been used for summer grazing by livestock, principally sheep, since the mid-1880's (Thilenius, 1975). Heavy grazing pressure and poor management practices caused soil compaction and serious depletion of vegetation, which resulted in severe erosion problems. In addition to increased sediment loads, the bacteriological count in water is affected by concentrated animal use near lakes and watercourses, although the quantitative effects have not been well documented. Grazing has resulted in the greatest extent (> 250,000 ha) of tundra damage, but the degree of disturbance is generally much less severe than that from other uses.

2. RECREATION

Recreational use of alpine areas has rapidly increased in the past decade and is expected to continue to grow. Most of the problems related to this activity are associated with off-road vehicles and concentrated use by pack animals on trails and campsites. These problems are particularly evident on wet sites (Willard & Marr, 1970). Other impacts include trampling of vegetation by foot traffic at campsites, on easily accessible park areas, and on open tundra slopes. Also, water quality problems due to inadequate sanitation facilities at frequently used remote sites is a widespread problem. Recreational activities have disturbed over 38,000 ha (interestingly similar to the figure for mining disturbance). In fact, recreation may now be among the fastest growing causes of disturbance to tundra lands, especially alpine areas (Willard & Marr, 1970, 1971; Marr & Willard, 1970).

3. MINING

Surface disturbances associated with mining, construction sites, work camps, and drill pads are among the most disrupting of man's activities on tundra areas. These disturbances and their associated roads usually result in the complete destruction of the soil, vegetation, and microclimate of an area. The native vegetation, organic matter covering, and the fertile, productive surface soils are removed or buried, thus increasing the erosion potential due to wind and water movement, and further compounding the problems of reestablishing vegetation on the site.

In alpine areas, head cuts and steep faces of mine dumps are particularly susceptible to surface erosion and, in some situations, mass slumping. Local surface water and ground-water flow patterns can also be disrupted by mine operations. In addition to increased sediment loads of streams, water quality can also be seriously degraded. Although reasonably well-controlled, spillage of oil and other petroleum products is a potential source of damage to both the aquatic and the surface environment. McCown et al. (1972) and Deneke et al. (1975) described impacts of crude oil and contaminated soils on plant growth. Mining operations in certain geologic formations can result in the movement of high concentrations of acid and heavy metals into surface and subsurface waters (Johnston et al., 1975). Vegetation, both on site and off site, may be damaged or killed by highly acid water and heavy metal concentrations. Also, the aquatic environment may be destroyed for many miles from the problem source.

Several techniques have been developed to neutralize acid drainage impacts (Skelly & Loy, 1973) but they are expensive and their maintenance requirements make them impractical for use at abandoned mines or poorly accessible sites. These solutions, like many engineering alternatives designed to lessen the impact of erosion and sedimentation problems, are designed to treat the symptoms of problems and not to cure the problems themselves. Over 34,000 ha of alpine tundra have been disturbed by mining in the western U.S. A large percentage of the total area is comprised of abandoned operations.

4. ROADS

Road construction and off-road vehicle use are among the most extensive and severe causes of surface soil disturbance in both alpine and arctic regions. Van Cleve (1975) indicated that vehicular movement to remote sites in the course of oil and gas exploration and in various scientific endeavors is probably the oldest and most widespread cause of substantial disturbance to arctic ground surfaces. Our survey of the extent of alpine soil disturbance in the western U.S. indicates that over 12,000 ha have been drastically disturbed by roads for various uses. This estimate is probably very conservative. Physical disruption and compaction of the surface soil is the most obvious type of disturbance. It may vary in extent from minimal impacts on vegetation and surface soils caused by passage of a single off-road vehicle to the removal and relocation of large quantities of surface material during road construction. Removal or destruction of the protective vegetative and organic cover usually results in serious erosion problems, changes the thermal and water regimens of soils, alters the depth of permafrost, and lowers nutrient status and site productivity. Thermokarsting, the melting of permafrost, results from compaction due to vehicular traffic, and is particularly damaging in areas having a high water table.

Sediment production from roads usually decreases markedly within a few years after construction (Fredricksen, 1965; Dyrness, 1967; Brown & Krygier, 1971). This response appears to be related to rapid revegetation of disturbed lands in more temperate climates; but in tundra areas natural revegetation of such areas is much slower. As a result, once accelerated erosion is initiated, it will continue for a much longer time. Increased sediment production, together with changes in flow regimens caused by disruption of drainage patterns, can also result in stream channel instability, water quality deterioration, and reduced productivity of aquatic environments. These effects have been well documented in other areas, but have not been adequately studied in tundra environments. Better regulation of off-road vehicle use, the development of less damaging transport vehicles, better engineering design standards for roads in these regions, and recent regulations requiring revegetation of disturbances should help alleviate these problems.

5. OTHER DISTURBANCES

Pipelines, powerlines, reservoirs, and other facilities constitute a substantial source of disturbance to tundra regions. The construction of these facilities results in damage similar to that done to tundra ecosystems by roadbuilding and mining. Pipelines, particularly, have had more extensive impacts in arctic regions than in alpine regions. The most obvious example is the well-known Alaska pipeline, which extends through about 150 km of north-slope arctic tundra and about the same amount of alpine tundra.

Fire is an additional factor contributing to tundra disturbances, but it is of far less importance than many other causes. For the most part, fire has been a natural force throughout the evolution of tundra regions, and has had particularly important impacts on the vegetation patterns in the taiga and krummholz types. Wardle (1974) indicated that fire is the most important catastrophic event affecting timberlines. Whether fire is caused by man or lightning, its effects last longer than those of avalanches, windthrow, or insects because fire destroys seedlings, litter, and humus. Tundra vegetation, by virtue of its growth form is somewhat resistant to fire, and the position of most buds and other meristems near the soil surface reduces the threat of mortality.

Depending upon the severity of burns, loss of plant cover and surface-insulating organic matter can change surface albedo and trigger the thaw of frozen ground and soil movement, especially in ice-rich, fine-textured soil (Wein, 1974; Wein & Bliss, 1973; Brown et al., 1969; Viereck, 1973). Fire suppression measures, especially bulldozed firelines in the past, have resulted in substantial soil erosion when constructed in silty, permafrost-dominated soil (Bolstad, 1971). Fire effects have been shown to be minimal with regard to stream chemistry and biology, and erosion arising from the burn contributed only in a minor way to increased stream turbidity (Lotspeich et al., 1970). Intensive fire may result in nutrient depletion by volatilization of nitrogen (Van Cleve, 1975; M. G. Weber, 1975. Nutrient redistribution following fire in tundra and forest tundra. M.S. Thesis. Univ. of New Brunswick, Fredericton. 69 p.). Fire also acts as a rapid decomposer, releasing nutrients contained in relatively unavailable forms in organic matter for reuse by plants (Lutz, 1956).

C. Environmental Factors Affecting Rehabilitation

In terms of the adapted plants and animals that inhabit tundra regions, there is no evidence that the tundra environment is severe. The floristic evolution of these regions reflects an almost total lack of man's influence (Billings, 1973). Yet, in the short span of one century, man's impacts are almost everywhere. In his search for minerals, fossil fuels, forage for livestock, and even for the restitution of his soul, man has left a trail of destruction and debris behind him that may remain for centuries. The often misused terms associated with tundra ecosystems such as *fragile* and *severe* take on a whole new and only too familiar meaning where man and tundra meet.

However, there is little question that tundra environments are among the most rigorous on earth. The unique climatic, geologic, and edaphic features of these regions often provide imposing barriers to traditional rehabilitation efforts.

1. CLIMATIC FACTORS

Among the most important biologically limiting environmental factors in tundra regions are low temperatures (Billings, 1973, 1974a, 1974b). However, other climatic factors are also important, including solar radiation, wind, precipitation, and length of the growing season. In terms of rehabilitation, these climatic factors have been described by Johnston et al. (1975); so they are only briefly summarized here.

a. Temperature—Air temperatures are cool during the growing season, ranging from a mean of about 8°C in midlatitude alpine areas to about 3°C in arctic tundra regions (Billings, 1973). Temperatures may, and often do, fall below 0°C during the growing season, retarding photosynthesis, nutrient and water uptake, and phenological development. They may damage meristematic tissues of all but the most cold-hardy plant species.

b. **Wind**—Windspeeds are usually greater in alpine regions than in arctic regions, and often result in severe desiccation of exposed plant parts during both winter and summer seasons (Johnston et al., 1975). Wind maintains snow-free areas on ridges and slopes, exposing them to severe frost damage and desiccation. Wind blows snow onto lee slopes, shortening the growing season and resulting in abrasive damage to exposed plants. It also erodes fine soil particles from disturbed sites, reducing water- and nutrient-holding capacities.

c. **Solar Radiation**—Solar radiation flux densities are generally higher in alpine regions during the summer than in arctic regions. Of course, the higher alpine intensities should be contrasted with the longer photoperiods in the arctic; however, the arctic receives less biologically active ultraviolet radiation (Caldwell, 1972). Midsummer solar radiation during the day in the alpine may exceed the solar constant, but often averages about 1.6 cal cm^{-2} min^{-1}. High radiation loads in the alpine result in high soil and plant surface temperatures, and promote summer drought and high evaporation.

d. **Frost**—Frost may occur periodically throughout the growing season near the soil surface in tundra environments. Permafrost is continuous in arctic regions, but only occurs sporadically in most alpine areas. Thermokarst results in surface disturbances that can be limiting to plant survival. Needle-ice and other congeliturbation processes cause injury to plants, mainly by lifting young seedlings from the soil and exposing the roots to desiccation. Frost damage is intensified by the removal of vegetation and organic layers. Frost also lowers the soil water potential, limiting water availability to plants.

e. **Growing Season**—The growing season length is similar in both alpine and arctic environments, averaging about 70 to 80 days (Billings, 1973). However, growing season length is highly variable in different years, and may not exceed 45 days in some cases. Also, freezing conditions prevail on many days during the growing season, causing disruption of normal plant phenotypic development. The short growing season precludes the use of most commercially available species, which are not capable of completing their entire life cycles.

f. **Precipitation**—Precipitation in alpine and arctic regions occurs mostly in the form of snow during winter months, but alpine regions receive much greater amounts of total annual precipitation than arctic areas. Billings and Mooney (1968) indicate that the annual precipitation of Niwot Ridge in Colorado (3,476 m elevation) is about 634 mm; at Barrow, Alaska (3 m elevation), it is about 107 mm. On the Beartooth Plateau in Montana, the annual precipitation is about 1,200 mm (Brown & Johnston, 1976). However, as in many alpine areas, these high precipitation levels are really indicative only of lee slopes and depressions and are much higher than those accumulated on windswept ridges and exposed slopes. Then, too, only about 10% of the annual precipitation is received during the growing season on the Beartooth Plateau, as compared with about 50% at Barrow.

2. GEOLOGY AND SOILS

Massive mountain building and erosional processes, profoundly altered by glaciation, are largely responsible for alpine landscapes. Contrasted with the topographical heterogeneity of alpine landforms, the arctic tundra is characterized as a broadly sloping plain, only slightly above sea level and underlain by permanently frozen soils to great depths (Hunt, 1974). As would be expected, a region as large as the North American arctic and alpine tundra contains many varieties of rock types. Predominant rock types in the Rocky Mountains are granites, quartzites, and pegmatites; massive basalts and other volcanic rocks occur in small areas (Retzer, 1974). The great depths of sedimentary materials have largely been eroded, but remnants can still be found in some locations.

Many factors influence the development of soils in the alpine and arctic tundra, including parent material, landform, glaciation and other geomorphic processes, vegetation, biological activity, and climate. More specifically, soil development in these cryopedogenic regions is governed by cold aboveground and subsurface temperatures and by the presence of a permanently frozen substratum at some depth below the surface. The rate of soil development is limited by slow mechanical weathering of the generally hard and resistant rock types of these regions. Cold temperatures and frozen soils inhibit the chemical reactions and biotic activity that contribute to soil genesis. The resulting soils are very young, heterogeneous, and poorly developed. The various soil-forming processes and the classification of arctic and alpine soils were discussed by Retzer (1974) and Rieger (1974).

Permafrost is a phenomenon throughout the arctic and, to a lesser extent, the alpine tundra regions. However, the depth of seasonal thawing varies considerably from site to site. Retzer (1964) described these regions as "possessing a greater variety of unique microlandforms than possibly any other region on the earth's surface due primarily to the freeze-thaw phenomena and the presence of perched watertables over permafrost." This heterogeneity of landforms and soils profoundly complicates rehabilitation efforts, requiring that rehabilitation prescriptions be site specific and frequently for very small restricted areas, rather than having broad and general applicability.

Soils of these regions can generally be classified as either poorly drained or well drained. Poorly drained soils occupy 85 to 90% of the arctic tundra region (Rieger, 1974), but are much less extensive in alpine regions. In arctic tundra regions, percolation of water is controlled by permafrost, and lateral movement of water is slow and confined to upper portions of the soil (Douglas & Tedrow, 1960). Both the depth of the soil and the depth of the organic mat are variable. The nutrient capital of these soils is frequently tied up in the organic layers and, because of the low temperatures and poor drainage, is not released by chemical and biological activity for plant growth. The disruption of organic mats destroys their insulating qualities and causes the depth of thaw to increase. Increasing the depth of thaw may help promote root and vegetative growth on better drained soils but, on poorly drained, fine-textured soils, the removal of the organic mat greatly increases erosion problems. Permafrost areas require special consideration and techniques if they are to be used for construction and other activities.

Well-drained soils are less extensive than poorly drained soils in arctic regions, but they possess unique characteristics important to successful revegetation efforts. These soils are generally thin, coarse-textured, and have low organic matter content. The nutrient capital and exchange capacities of these soils are low and must be considered when fertilizer treatments are prescribed. The low water-holding capacity coupled with periods of low summer rainfall create severe drought conditions. Brown et al. (1976) and Johnston et al. (1975) reported water potentials in an alpine area in the surface 15 cm of soil on disturbed sites that often exceeded −20 bars, which was far lower than the water potentials of adjacent and undisturbed tundra. Although these soil water conditions severely inhibit plant establishment, they are not as severe as those found in tundra desert locations or on windswept ridges and talus slopes. Solifluction, needle-ice formation, and hummocking are common phenomena in alpine and in some arctic regions, but these congeliturbation processes are intensified when surface vegetation and organic matter are removed. The resulting erosion and destruction of young plants greatly compound the rehabilitation problem. Yet another consequence of surface disturbance in alpine areas is the additional loss of fine soil particles due to wind erosion in soils where productivity is already restricted by a lack of fine materials.

Perhaps one of the most severe soil problems in alpine tundra areas results from the exposure of pyrites and other heavy metals. Under these conditions, the pH of the surface soils can become very acid, inhibiting plant growth and retarding absorption of water and nutrients by the roots. The physiological responses by native plants to high heavy-metal concentrations are poorly defined, but they are known to block or to interfere with vital physiological processes.

D. Plant Species Adaptability and Selection

Alpine and arctic plant species are equipped with unique physiological and morphological features that are particularly well adapted to tundra environments. Successful rehabilitation of alpine and arctic disturbances will, in large part, depend upon our ability to recognize these features in the selection of adapted plant species (Brown et al., 1976).

Alpine and arctic vascular plant species are typically low-growing herbaceous or shrub species. Most are perennial (very few are biennial or annual) with large underground root or stem storage systems (Bliss, 1971; Billings & Mooney, 1968; Billings, 1974b). The floras of these regions are generally described as species-poor, consisting of from 200 to 300 species in North American alpine tundra to only slightly more than 100 species in the arctic tundra. These flora generally are composed of graminoids, leafy dicots, cushion dicots, and prostrate shrubs. Most alpine dicots reproduce by seeds, but some vegetative reproduction also occurs. However, arctic dicots typically reproduce vegetatively by means of rhizomes, and only occasionally by seeds (Billings, 1974b; Mooney & Billings, 1961). There is evidence that many graminoids in alpine regions reproduce both by seeds and by rhizomes, particularly on disturbed sites (Brown et al., 1976).

Most alpine and arctic dicots have much greater dry weights of underground parts than of stems and leaves (Mooney & Billings, 1961; Scott & Billings, 1964). For example, Scott and Billings (1964) found that over 79% of the total standing crop of vegetation is below ground in alpine areas; Dennis and Johnson (1970) found up to 90% below ground in the arctic. This below-ground tissue is important for carbohydrate storage during the winter and for the characteristic rapid burst of growth in the spring. Billings (1973) cited evidence that higher root/shoot ratios occur in moist habitats and lower ratios occur in drier areas.

Another unique adaptation of alpine and arctic plants is the preformed shoot and flower buds (Billings, 1974b). These features have particular significance since the short, cold growing season retards normal growth and development characteristic of plants in milder environments. The primordia of these buds often are formed one or two growing seasons before bud break. The adaptive advantages of this characteristic include rapid growth and flowering following spring snowmelt and increasing seasonal temperatures. In these environments, the annual life form is severely pressed to complete its entire life cycle from germination to seed set in one short growing season. Consequently, annual plants are rarely found in tundra flora.

In addition to morphological adaptations, tundra plants have many physiological characteristics that differ from those of plants in milder climates. Billings (1974a, 1974b) summarized the major physiological characteristics of tundra plants, which include:

1) *Life form.* Perennial herbs, prostrate shrubs, or lichens. Except for rosette plants, perennial herbs have the greatest underground biomass.

2) *Seed germination.* Seeds remain dormant at low temperatures; germinate only above freezing; total germination low.

3) *Seedling establishment.* Rare and slow.

4) *Mineral nutrition.* Not well documented. Cold temperatures inhibit nitrogen fixation.

5) *Photosynthesis and respiration.* Occur at high rates when temperature and light are favorable. Optimum rates are at lower temperatures than usual. In the dark, respiration is higher at all temperatures than it is for ordinary plants. Alpine plants have higher light-saturation values than arctic plants.

6) *Drought resistance.* Plants exposed on xeric sites (windswept ridges, frozen soil, or soils deprived of water by growing season drought) attain low water potentials, increase concentrations of

soluble carbohydrates, and close stomates. Some capable of carrying on photosynthesis at very low water potentials.

7) *Breaking of dormancy.* Controlled by temperature and photoperiod.

8) *Growth.* Very rapid at low temperatures, with nitrogen and phosphorus mostly limiting.

9) *Food storage.* Carbohydrates stored underground in perennials, lipids stored in leaves and stems of evergreen shrubs. Stored food is depleted in early summer regrowth.

10) *Winter survival.* Frost resistance of plants closely tied to concentration of soluble carbohydrates.

11) *Flowering.* Buds preformed one or more years before, flowering dependent upon temperature and photoperiod.

12) *Pollination.* Mostly by insects, especially in the alpine tundra. Wind also important in graminoid pollination.

13) *Seed production.* Opportunistic.

14) *Vegetative reproduction.* Most common in the arctic tundra, but also occurs in the alpine tundra; mostly by rhizomes, bulbils, layering.

15) *Dormancy.* Triggered by photoperiod, low temperatures, and drought.

Additional details on the physiological characteristics of tundra plants are available in Billings (1973, 1974a, 1974b), Bliss (1956, 1971), Tranquillini (1964), Johnson and Caldwell (1974, 1975, 1976), Billings et al. (1966), Billings and Mooney (1968), Ehleringer and Miller (1975), Mooney and Billings (1960, 1961), Tieszen (1973), and Johnson (D. A. Johnson. 1975. Gas exchange and water relations of two alpine and two arctic tundra plant species. Ph.D. Dissertation. Utah State Univ., Logan. 114 p.).

One of the major problems associated with rehabilitating tundra disturbances is the selection of adapted plant species (Brown et al., 1976; Johnston et al., 1975; Johnson & Van Cleve, 1975; Van Cleve, 1975). Each plant carries a gene pool of information that defines its ecological and physiological adaptability. Long-term survival in tundra environments is intimately linked to physiological mechanisms similar to those that have evolved in the native species. Many native species provide a vast storehouse of adapted genetic material that until recently has not been widely used in rehabilitation (Sutton, 1975).

Probably more than any other single factor, it is the relative commercial unavailability of native plants that has precluded their widespread use in rehabilitation (Sutton, 1975). This is particularly true of tundra plant species. Very little effort has been focused on the breeding and selection of favorable tundra species for revegetation, except for the work of Mitchell (1972) and Klebesadel (1971, 1974). Breeding and selection programs for tundra species are vitally needed. Using established techniques, these programs could begin to yield valuable information in a relatively short time since the strong selective pressures of tundra environments have narrowed the number of genetic lines that would have to be tested. However, until such a program is begun, rehabilitation work in tundra regions will continue to be restricted largely to the use of commercially available seed sources, most of which are unadapted to the harsh environments of these areas.

Although native plant species offer many advantages for rehabilitation, not all natives are necessarily well adapted for this purpose. Disturbances to the natural environment often result in completely different site conditions to which most natives may not be adapted. Brown et al. (1976) cited evidence that only about 10% of the native vascular species on the Beartooth Plateau in Montana are active natural colonizers on alpine disturbances. Those that are adapted to the altered edaphic conditions are obviously also adapted to the climate and perhaps to the natural cycles of drought, disease, and insect outbreaks. Land disturbances may provide environmental conditions not previously available to some native hybrids (Anderson, 1971). However, adapted native species are commercially unavailable, generally have low seed viability and low seedling vigor, unknown responses to rehabilitation treatments and maintenance requirements, and seed collection from them may be expensive and environmentally damaging.

It is also conceivable that some species introduced from other tundra or similar environments may also be adapted to disturbed tundra conditions. This is still somewhat speculative, however, since research results thus far cast doubt on the longevity of introduced species in tundra regions. Some introduced species may appear to be adapted to disturbed edaphic conditions, but may eventually succumb during long-term exposure to the rigorous tundra climate. For example, Brown et al. (1976) found that stands of commercially available introduced grasses began to deteriorate after only three growing seasons on an alpine mine site, although the native species showed increased vigor and rates of spread. In such cases, however, the introduced species may ameliorate the edaphic conditions sufficiently to allow the eventual establishment of native species.

The use of adapted introduced species will continue to play a vital role in tundra rehabilitation. As Ward (1974) pointed out, it may be unrealistic to expect to ever totally replace the natural plant communities of an area following disturbance. Climatic patterns and other environmental conditions are continuously shifting and may no longer be commensurate with such plant community development.

Not all adapted introduced species are commercially available. Further, many of the unknown autecological characteristics and problems of acquiring seed and other plant parts associated with native species apply to them as well. Unfortunately, very few adapted introduced species that are available commercially are known.

Commercial availability has many advantages. For example, convenience cost per unit of seed is usually lower and, as a result of breeding and selection programs, vigor is higher, growth characteristics are uniform, and responses to rehabilitation treatments are known. However, commercially available species are largely unadapted to tundra conditions and so have many serious disadvantages as well. They tend to be poorly adapted to the tundra climate or to natural periods of drought, disease, or insect infestation cycles. Also, continued maintenance, such as fertilization, may be required to maintain adequate stands. Therefore, availability alone is a weak criterion for species selection.

Although commercially available species will probably continue to play an important role in disturbed tundra rehabilitation, greater use of both adapted native and introduced species is encouraged (Brown et al., 1976; Van Cleve, 1975; Sutton, 1975). In view of the severe nature of disturbed tundra environments (Van Cleve, 1975; Brown et al., 1969; Brown & Johnston, 1976; Brown et al., 1976), a program is needed to develop techniques for producing seed and plants of adapted species. Such large-scale disturbances as the Alaska pipeline (> 1,200 km long) and the projected large-scale development of the Beartooth chromium-platinum reserves in Montana (Stoneberg, 1976) will require vast quantities of adapted plant materials for rehabilitation.

Intensive research on the physiological tolerance limits of plant species is also needed. Although some data are available for a few species, few pertain to plant responses on disturbed tundra soil conditions. At present, selection of plant species for rehabilitation is largely based on qualitative criteria. The techniques and knowledge are presently available to "match" plant physiological requirements with microenvironmental characteristics on specific sites. Although plant colonization and succession studies are very useful (Brown et al., 1976; Johnson & Van Cleve, 1975), they provide only surficial evidence of species adaptability.

Natural selection is a highly efficient mechanism for isolating those individual plants that can compete for soil, water, and nutrients on a severe tundra disturbance. Some of the more important criteria to be considered in selecting adapted plant species for the rehabilitation of disturbed tundra areas include:

1) *Availability.* Collection by hand is very expensive and subject to local environmental conditions. Seed may not be produced every year in tundra environments or may be produced only in small quantities. Collection can be detrimental to the environment.

2) *Growth form.* Low-growing plants with large root systems are better adapted to tundra conditions than larger leafy species. This type of growth form reduces the possibility of mortality due to wind, ice abrasion, and desiccation, results in higher plant temperatures, and provides for abundant carbohydrate storage in the roots. It also benefits plant water relations and nutrient requirements.

3) *Drought resistance.* The severest water stress occurs on windy exposed ridges and snow-free areas. Severe drought is common on disturbed tundra sites during the growing season and has greatest impact on emerging seedlings. High radiation loads, strong winds, and rocky soils with low water-holding capacities are common on alpine tundra disturbances, restricting plant colonization to species that are the most drought resistant.

4) *Mineral nutrition.* Fertility requirements are generally not well known for most species potentially useful for tundra rehabilitation. The cold tundra environment depresses more typical re-

sponses to fertilization. Plants requiring high fertility levels are not recommended.

5) *Reproduction.* Vegetative reproduction capabilities are more desirable since seed production is opportunistic, being limited to the most favorable years. Also, seedlings are rare and slow to develop. Rhizomatous or layering graminoids and dicots are better adapted and provide stable cover most rapidly.

6) *Growth.* The capacity to carry on high rates of photosynthesis and respiration at low temperatures is essential. Plants must be capable of breaking dormancy near 0°C. Root systems should be capable of storing large quantities of carbohydrates. Plants must be capable of completing in about 6 weeks the entire life cycle, including flowering, seed production, and maturation.

7) *Ecotypic variation.* Most tundra species have a broad range of ecological tolerances, reflecting considerable phenotypic or genetic variability, or both. Capacity for ecotypic differentiation is probably more essential in highly variable alpine environments than in arctic regions.

8) *Colonization and succession.* Plant species and ecotypes found growing on old disturbances are evidence of adapted genetic material. However, these individuals may differ genetically from those plants of the same species growing in the immediate vicinity of the disturbance. Succession studies help to isolate adapted plants from which selection criteria should be based.

IV. REHABILITATION OF TUNDRA DISTURBANCES

Vegetation recovery and ultimately ecosystem stability take place very slowly under disturbed tundra conditions. From hundreds to thousands of years may be required for recovery of tundra disturbances where the soil has been lost (Billings, 1973; Willard & Marr, 1970, 1971). Only recently, accelerated research efforts have developed rehabilitation techniques specifically suitable for tundra disturbances (Johnston et al., 1975; Brown & Johnston, 1976; Brown et al., 1976; Van Cleve, 1975, 1973; Johnson & Van Cleve, 1975). The outstanding principle of rehabilitation common to both alpine and arctic regions is that traditional revegetation techniques developed at milder latitudes and elevations do not succeed on tundra disturbances. Highly specific rehabilitation techniques must be developed because of the specialized physiological requirements of adapted plant species and the rigorous atmospheric and edaphic environments of these regions.

The objectives and general considerations of rehabilitation of tundra lands have been discussed in detail by Brown et al. (1976), Johnston et al. (1975), Johnson and Van Cleve (1975), and Van Cleve (1975). Because the rehabilitation of disturbances of tundra lands and of all ecosystems is highly site-specific, the following general recommendations are discussed only in terms of their broadest application and are not to be construed as being equally applicable to all disturbances. Nor is it possible to generalize about the length of time required to achieve successful rehabilitation of disturbed tundras, but almost certainly it will be measured in terms of decades.

a. Species Selection—Plant succession and colonization studies on old disturbances are recommended to aid in identifying adapted native species. Collection of seed or other propagules should be restricted to local populations to reduce the possibility of incorporating unadapted genetic material. The concept of vegetation baseline studies prior to revegetation is recommended (Ward, 1974). The use of adapted introduced species as nurse crops is recommended. They should be included in the seed mixture with the native species. Physiological requirements and growth form must be considered, and species should be selected that are known colonizers on disturbances.

b. Seeding Methods—Alpine land disturbances should be seeded late in the fall just prior to permanent snow accumulation to prevent germination the current year. Alpine areas are generally inaccessible until early summer, at which time conditions may not be favorable for germination and survival (Brown et al., 1976). However, Johnston and Van Cleve (1975) cited evidence that arctic disturbances may be seeded successfully in either the spring or the fall. Fall plantings of both seed and transplant stock will insure that dormancy requirements are met. Techniques must be used to loosen the surface soil and seed must be covered and packed to insure firm contact with the soil particles. Brown et al. (1976) found that firm packing is one of the most important steps in rehabilitation. Merely relying on snowfall, frost action, wind, or other natural processes to cover and pack the seed is not recommended. Species mixtures are specific with site conditions (Brown et al., 1976; Johnson & Van Cleve, 1975; Hernandez, 1973; Troth et al., 1973; Dabbs et al., 1974; Mitchell & McKendrick, 1974; Younkin, 1972; Van Cleve & Manthei, 1973), but generally should include both adapted native and adapted introduced species together. Seeding rates on alpine tundra areas generally range between 28 and 111 kg ha^{-1}, depending upon site conditions and availability of seed (Brown et al., 1976).

c. Fertilizer—Fertilizer applications are absolutely essential for successful and rapid establishment of plants on tundra environments (Brown et al., 1976; Johnson & Van Cleve, 1975; Van Cleve, 1975; Mitchell, 1972; Van Cleve & Manthei, 1971). Application rates of up to about 111 kg ha^{-1} of nitrogen (equivalent) in bulk fertilizer are generally recommended because the cool temperatures of tundra environments lower nutrient availability severely. Also, decomposition rates, microbial activity, and nutrient cycling progress at low rates in tundra environments (Haag, 1972; McCown et al., 1972). Periodic reapplication of fertilizer may be required in many areas. Specific macronutrient and micronutrient requirements should be determined by soil analyses for each disturbance before selecting the rate and kind of fertilizer.

d. Soil Amendments—On acidic soils with a pH below about 5.0, lime should be applied to a depth of about 15 to 30 cm (Brown et al., 1976). Application rates depend upon local soil conditions, but generally about 220 kg ha^{-1} is sufficient, with the possibility that periodic reapplication may be necessary. Topsoil is desirable, but is rarely available in sufficient quantities in tundra environments to be a practical alternative. Organic matter in the form of straw, peat, or manure has resulted in striking increases in plant growth and development on tundra disturbances (Brown et al., 1976). Organic matter improves water and nutrient availability in xeric sterile spoils and should be applied at the rate of about 2,000 to 4,000 kg ha^{-1}.

e. **Transplanting**—Transplanting of native and introduced species has proven to be the most successful rehabilitation technique on alpine disturbances (Brown et al., 1976) and appears to be highly successful in arctic regions as well (Van Cleve, 1975; Johnson & VanCleve, 1975). Pads of tundra plants that have slumped from road cuts and other disturbances can easily be collected and planted. Also, we are currently conducting research on the development of large-scale nursery techniques for growing native tundra species in containers designed for easy transplanting.

V. CONCLUSIONS

The tundra ecosystems of North America are going to become even more important for recreation and as sources of minerals and fossil fuels as demands accelerate. The primary challenge facing us now is to develop rehabilitation methods that are compatible with the rigorous environment characteristic of these regions. Rehabilitation research experience in tundra regions so far provides only tentative optimism. It is obvious that disturbances in these cold environments are going to recover very slowly under the best of conditions. There seems to be little question that additional research is needed to develop rehabilitation techniques for tundra disturbances, but this will not be accomplished by good intentions alone. It seems essential that scientists, land managers, industrialists, recreationists, politicians, and, in fact, society as a whole must assess the commitment to returning disturbed lands to a rehabilitated state. The present extent of that commitment is not at all clear.

The picture is not entirely bleak, however. Rehabilitation results based on the best techniques presently available seem to indicate that some of the more obvious kinds of damage can be partially repaired in a matter of a few years. Some results of the development and selection of adapted plant species are encouraging, and techniques for seeding and planting are being developed in a number of locations. Microenvironmental research on tundra disturbances is quantitatively defining the magnitude of environmental damage in terms of the most important limiting factors for plant growth. Plant succession and colonization research is identifying some of the important native species and ecotypes adapted for survival and growth on disturbed areas and is providing data on site modification and environment amelioration requirements. Plant ecology and physiology research is providing data on the adaptability limits of plant species and ecotypes. These adaptability criteria are being used to select plants for use in rehabilitation programs.

Research is to be encouraged if the site-specific rehabilitation techniques needed are to be developed. Together with those areas subject to severe thermokarsting, the particularly severe disturbances in tundra regions that have resulted in the total loss of soil and have exposed acid-producing pyrites and high concentrations of toxic heavy metals are among the most difficult problems. These areas are beyond our present rehabilitation capabilities; we cannot provide recovery except for the most superficial kinds of "cosmetic" treatments. Rehabilitation problems in such areas are sorely aggravated by rigorous environmental conditions, particularly when wind removes fine soil particles and sweeps away insulating snow. These sites tend to become more xeric with time, retrogressing to polar desertlike conditions.

Our present research efforts need to be intensified and expanded. The need for quick decisions hastily applied on specific sites has diluted much of the basic research progress. Without question, applied research is needed to develop such specialized techniques and methods as transplanting, sodding, and fertilizing; however, the complexity and diversity of the problem extends beyond these matters. Unfortunately, applied research is rapidly outdistancing its needed support from basic research. Rehabilitation is much more than revegetation; the establishment of a grass cover on a disturbance is no guarantee that successional trends will take over and eventually return a site to its natural condition. Research is just beginning to consider such subtle factors as soil microbial activity, wildlife habitat interactions, herbivorous insect impacts, plant physiological processes, and many others. A sense of urgency is needed to launch a comprehensive research effort on the development of rehabilitation programs. Data from both applied and basic research should be used.

In summary, the major rehabilitation problems in alpine and arctic tundra regions that should be considered are:

1) *Climatic factors:*
   a) Low summer temperatures depress growth, development, and nutrient availability,
   b) High winds cause desiccation, soil water evaporation, and erosion of fine soil particles,
   c) High radiation (in alpine tundra) enhances evaporation and high surface temperatures,
   d) Frost action, particularly needle-ice, is common throughout the growing season,
   e) The growing season is short, ranging from 45 to 90 days, and
   f) Low precipitation is common during the growing season in alpine tundra; often it is only 10% of the total mean annual amount.

2) *Soil factors:*
   a) Soils are poorly developed and rocky, resulting in low water-holding capacity (alpine tundra),
   b) Exposed subsoils are infertile,
   c) Oxidation of pyritic subsoils results in low pH,
   d) Permafrost retards water percolation and results in perched water tables following surface disturbance (mainly arctic tundra), and

e) High concentrations of toxic heavy metals and other chemicals are present (mainly alpine tundra).

3) *Biological factors:*

a) Seed and plants of adapted species are not commercially available,

b) Most commercially available species are unadapted,

c) Seed production in tundra regions is sporadic,

d) Seed collection is expensive,

e) Native species have low germination rates and low vigor,

f) The annual life form is unadapted,

g) Shoot growth is slow the first year or two; most initial growth occurs in root system,

h) Most reproduction is by vegetative means,

i) Biological activity in soil is slow to reestablish following disturbance,

j) Physiological requirements of native species are largely unknown, and

k) Roles that primary and secondary successional processes play in shaping ultimate vegetation on tundra disturbances are unknown.

LITERATURE CITED

Anderson, E. 1971. Man as maker of new plants and plant communities. p. 653–666. *In* T. R. Detwyler (ed.) Man's impact on environment. McGraw-Hill, New York.

Barry, R. G., and J. D. Ives. 1974. Introduction. p. 1–13. *In* J. D. Ives and R. G. Barry (eds.) Arctic and alpine environments. Methuen and Co. Ltd., London.

Billings, W. D. 1973. Arctic and alpine vegetation: similarities, differences, and susceptibility to disturbance. BioScience 23:697–704.

Billings, W. D. 1974a. Adaptations and origins of alpine plants. Arc. Alp. Res. 6:129–142.

Billings, W. D. 1974b. Arctic and alpine vegetation: plant adaptations to cold summer climates. p. 403–443. *In* J. D. Ives and R. G. Barry (eds.). Arctic and alpine environments. Methuen and Co. Ltd., London.

Billings, W. D., E. E. C. Clebsch, and H. A. Mooney. 1966. Photosynthesis and respiration rates of Rocky Mountain alpine plants under field conditions. Am. Midl. Nat. 75:34–44.

Billings, W. D., and H. A. Mooney. 1968. The ecology of arctic and alpine plants. Biol. Rev. 43:481–529.

Bliss, L. C. 1956. A comparison of plant development in microenvironments of arctic and alpine tundra. Ecol. Monogr. 26:303–337.

Bliss, L. C. 1971. Arctic and alpine life cycles. Annu. Rev. Ecol. Syst. 2:405–438.

Bolstad, R. 1971. Catline rehabilitation and restoration. p. 107–116. *In* C. W. Slaughter, R. J. Barney, and G. M. Hansen (ed.) Fire in the northern environment. USDA For. Serv., Washington, D. C.

Brown, G. W., and J. T. Krygier. 1971. Clearcut logging and sediment production in the Oregon Coast Range. Water Resour. Res. 7:1189–1199.

Brown, L., W. Rickard, and D. Vietor. 1969. The effect of disturbance on permafrost terrain, Corps of Engineers, U.S. Army Cold Regions Res. and Eng. Lab. Spec. Rep. 138. 14 p.

Brown, R. W., and R. S. Johnston. 1976. Revegetation of an alpine mine disturbance: Beartooth Plateau, Montana. USDA For. Serv. Res. Note INT-206, 8 p. Intermt. For. & Range Exp. Stn., Ogden, Utah.

Brown, R. W., R. S. Johnston, B. Z. Richardson, and E. E. Farmer. 1976. Rehabilitation of alpine disturbances: Beartooth Plateau, Montana. p. 58–73. *In* Proc. Workshop on Revegetation of High Altitude Disturbed Lands. Colorado State Univ. Infor. Serv. 21, Colorado State Univ., Fort Collins.

Caldwell, M. M. 1972. Biologically effective solar ultraviolet irradiation in the arctic. Arct. Alp. Res. 4:39–43.

Dabbs, L., W. Friesen, and S. Mitchell. 1974. Pipeline revegetation. Biol. Rep. Ser. 2, North. Eng. Serv. Co. Ltd., Calgary, Alberta. 67 p.

Deneke, F. J., B. A. McCown, P. I. Coyne, W. Rickard, and J. Brown 1975. Corps of Engineers, U.S. Army Cold Regions Res. and Eng. Lab. oil research in Alaska. USACRREL Res. Rep. 346. Hanover, N.H.

Dennis, J. G., and P. L. Johnson. 1970. Shoot and rhizome root standing crops of tundra vegetation at Barrow, Alaska. Arct. Alp. Res. 2:253–266.

Douglas, L. A., and J. C. F. Tedrow. 1960. Tundra soils of arctic Alaska. Int. Congr. Soil Sci., Trans. 7th (Madison, Wis.) 4:291–304.

Dyrness, C. T. 1967. Mass soil movements in the H. J. Andrews Experimental Forest. USDA For. Serv. Res. Pap. PNW-42. Pac. Northwest For. and Range Exp. Stn., Portland, Oreg. 12 p.

Ehleringer, J. R., and P. C. Miller. 1975. Water relations of selected plant species in the alpine tundra, Colorado. Ecology 56:370–380.

Fredricksen, R. L. 1965. Sedimentation after logging road construction in a small western Oregon watershed. p. 56–59. In Proc. Federal Interagency Sedimentation Conf. Misc. Publ. 970. USDA, Washington, D. C.

Haag, R. W. 1972. Limitation to production in native plant communities in the Mackenzie Delta Region. p. 69–142. In L. C. Bliss and R. W. Wein (eds.) Botanical studies of natural and man modified habitats in eastern Mackenzie Delta Region and the Arctic Islands. ALUR—1971-72. Ottawa, Canada.

Hadley, E. B., and L. C. Bliss. 1964. Energy relationships of alpine plants on Mt. Washington, New Hampshire. Ecol. Monogr. 34:331–357.

Hernandez, H. 1973. Revegetation studies, Norman Wells, Inuvik, and Tuktoyaktuk, N.W.T., and Prudhoe Bay, Alaska. Can. Environ. Prot. Board, Can. Gas Arctic Study Ltd. Interim Rep. 3. 101 p.

Hunt, C. B. 1974. Natural regions of the United States and Canada. W. H. Freeman and Co., San Francisco, Calif. 725 p.

Ives, J. D. 1974. Permafrost. p. 159–194. In J. D. Ives and R. G. Barry (eds.) Arctic and alpine environments. Methuen and Co. Ltd., London.

Johnson, D. A., and M. M. Caldwell. 1974. Field measurements of photosynthesis and leaf growth rates of three alpine plant species. Arct. Alp. Res. 6:245–251.

Johnson, D. A., and M. M. Caldwell. 1975. Gas exchange of four arctic and alpine tundra species in relation to atmospheric and soil moisture stress. Oecologia 21:93–108.

Johnson, D. A., and M. M. Caldwell. 1976. Water potential components, stomatal function, and liquid phase water transport resistances of four arctic and alpine species in relation to moisture stress. Physiol. Plant. 36:271–278.

Johnson, L., and K. Van Cleve. 1975. Revegetation in arctic and subarctic North America—a literature review. Tech. Note 76-15. 72 p. Corps of Engineers, U.S. Army Cold Regions Res. and Eng. Lab., Hanover, N. H.

Johnston, R. S., R. W. Brown, and J. Cravens. 1975. Acid mine rehabilitation problems at high elevations. p. 66–79. In Watershed Manage. Symp., Am. Soc. Civil Eng., Utah State Univ., Logan.

Klebesadel, L. J. 1971. Native Alaskan legumes studied. Agroborealis 3:9–11.

Klebesadel, L. J. 1974. Sweet holygrass, a potentially valuable ally. Agroborealis 6:9–10.

Lotspeich, F. B., E. W. Mueller, and P. J. Frey. 1970. Effects of large scale forest fires on water quality in interior Alaska. Fed. Water Pollut. Control Admin. Rep. 115 p.

Love, D. 1970. Subarctic and subalpine: where and what? Arct. Alp. Res. 2:63–73.

Lutz, H. J. 1956. Ecological effects of forest fires in the interior of Alaska. USDA Tech. Bull. 1133. Washington, D. C.

McCown, R. H., F. J. Deneke, W. Rickard, and L. L. Tieszen. 1972. The response of Alaskan terrestrial plant communities to the presence of petroleum. Symp. Proc. on Impact of Oil Resource Development on Northern Plant Communities. Inst. Arctic Biol., Univ. of Alaska Fairbanks.

Marr, J. W., and B. E. Willard. 1970. Persisting vegetation in an alpine recreation area in the southern Rocky Mountains, Colorado. Biol. Conserv. 2:97–104.

Mitchell, W. W. 1972. Adaptation of species and varieties of grasses for potential use in Alaska. p. 2–6. In Symp. on Impact of Oil Resource Development on Northern Plant Communities. Univ. of Alaska, Fairbanks.

Mitchell, W. W., and J. D. McKendrick. 1974. Tundra rehabilitation research: Prudhoe Bay and Palmer Research Center. Inst. of Agric. Sci., Univ. of Alaska, Fairbanks. 27 p.

Mooney, H. A., and W. D. Billings. 1960. The annual carbohydrate cycle in alpine plants as related to growth. Am. J. Bot. 47:594–598.

Mooney, H. A., and W. D. Billings. 1961. Comparative physiological ecology of arctic and alpine populations of *Oxyria digyna*. Ecol. Monogr. 31:1–29.

Retzer, J. L. 1964. Present soil-forming factors and processes in arctic and alpine regions. Soil Sci. 99:38–44.

Retzer, J. L. 1974. Alpine soils. p. 771–802. In J. D. Ives and R. G. Barry (eds.) Arctic and alpine environments. Methuen and Co. Ltd., London.

Rieger, S. 1974. Arctic soils. p. 747–769. In J. D. Ives and R. G. Barry (eds.) Arctic and alpine environments. Methuen and Co. Ltd., London.

Scott, D., and W. D. Billings. 1964. Effects of environmental factors on standing crop and productivity of an alpine tundra. Ecol. Monogr. 34:243–270.

Skelly and Loy Engineers, Consultants. 1973. Processes, procedures, and methods to control pollution from mining activities. U.S. Environ. Prot. Agency Rep. EPA-430/9-73-011. 390 p.

Stoneberg, R. 1976. The Stillwater Complex—booming again. Montana Outdoors. Jan.–Feb.:19–25.

Sutton, R. K. 1975. Why native plants aren't used more. J. Soil Water Conserv. 30:240–242.

Thilenius, J. F. 1975. Alpine range management in the western United States—principles, practices, and problems. USDA For. Serv. Res. Pap. RM-157. Rocky Mt. For. and Range Exp. Stn., Fort Collins, Colo. 32 p.

Tieszen, L. L. 1973. Photosynthesis and respiration in arctic tundra grasses: field light intensity and temperature responses. Arct. Alp. Res. 5:239–251.

Tranquillini, W. 1964. The physiology of plants at high altitudes. Annu. Rev. Plant Physiol. 15:345–362.

Troth, J. L., W. E. Rickard, F. J. Deneke, and F. R. Koutz. 1973. Artificial revegetation of sites contaminated by refined petroleum spills. Corps of Engineers. U.S. Army Cold Region Res. and Eng. Lab. Tech. Note. Hanover, N.H. 8 p.

Van Cleve, K. 1975. Recovery of disturbed tundra and taiga surfaces in Alaska. Intern. Symp. on Recovery of Damaged Ecosystems. Virginia Polytech. Inst. Blacksburg, Va. 23–25 Mar. 1975.

Van Cleve, K., and J. Manthei. 1971. Revegetation of disturbed tundra taiga surfaces. Alaska Sci. Conf., Univ. of Alaska, Fairbanks. 163 p.

Van Cleve, K., and J. Manthei. 1973. Report on tundra-taiga surface stabilization study. Alyeska Pipeline Serv. Co., Inst. Arctic Biol., Univ. of Alaska, Fairbanks.

Viereck, L. A. 1973. Wildfire in the taiga of Alaska. Quat. Res. 3:465–495.

Ward, R. T. 1974. A concept of natural vegetation baselines. p. 24. In W. A. Berg, J. A. Brown, and R. L. Cuany (eds.) Proc. Workshop on Revegetation of High Altitude Disturbed Lands. Colorado State Univ. Inform. Ser. 10. Colorado State Univ., Fort Collins.

Wardle, P. 1974. Alpine timberlines. p. 371–402. In J. D. Ives and R. G. Barry (eds.) Arctic and alpine environments. Methuen and Co. Ltd., London.

Webber, P. J. 1974. Tundra primary productivity. p. 445–473. In J. D. Ives and R. G. Barry (eds.) Arctic and alpine environments. Methuen and Co. Ltd., London.

Wein, R. W. 1974. Recovery of vegetation in arctic regions after burning. Environ.-Soc. Comm., North. Pipelines, Rep. 74-6, Task Force on Northern Oil Development, Ottawa, Canada. 63 p.

Wein, R. W., and L. C. Bliss. 1973. Changes in arctic *Eriophorum* tussock cummunities following fire. Ecology 54:845–852.

Whittaker, R. H. 1970. Communities and ecosystems. MacMillan Publ. Co., New York. 158 p.

Willard, B. E., and J. W. Marr. 1970. Effects of human activities on alpine tundra ecosystems in Rocky Mountain National Park. Boil. Conserv. 2:257–265.

Willard, B. E., and J. W. Marr. 1971. Recovery of alpine tundra under protection after damage by human activities in the Rocky Mountains of Colorado. Biol. Conserv. 3:181–190.

Younkin, W. E. 1972. Revegetation studies of disturbances in the Mackenzie Delta Region. p. 175–229. In L. C. Bliss and R. W. Wein (eds.) Botanical studies of natural and man-modified habitats in the eastern Mackenzie Delta Region and the Arctic Islands. ALUR 1971-72. Ottawa, Canada.

Chapter 4

Extent of Disturbed Land and Major Reclamation Problems in Canada[1]

J. V. THIRGOOD

University of British Columbia,
Vancouver, British Columbia

I. INTRODUCTION

Canada extends over 9 million square kilometers. East-west this vast area extends 6,919 km from coast to coast and, while the southern boundary is only 96 km to the north of us here in Wooster, Ohio, its northernmost lands extend to within 644 km of the North Pole. There are great physiographic, climatic, biological, socio-economic, and political diversities.

In a previous paper (Thirgood, 1969), the major natural regions and the nature of disturbances within these regions were described. Since 1969, interest in land reclamation has increased and certainly there are more people working in all phases of reclamation. Intercommunication, previously a major weakness, has greatly improved, a notable development in this regard being the establishment of the Canadian Land Reclamation Association in 1975. But overall the situation is relatively little changed, despite greater activity. The effort is still not commensurate with the need, progress has been largely exploratory, and we have still to build a substantial body of well-founded reclamation technology.

Under the Canadian federal structure, natural resources fall within the jurisdiction of the provinces; hence, reclamation requirements are at the discretion of the provincial governments and vary considerably as the provincial need is perceived. The regional descriptions that follow have been contributed by individuals involved in their regional situations and, in general, follow provincial divisions.

II. MINE WASTES IN EASTERN CANADA[2]

A. Nature of Disturbance

Mining of a wide variety of metals, industrial minerals, and coal has taken place in eastern Quebec and the Gaspé Peninsula of Quebec, Labrador, Newfoundland, New Brunswick, and Nova Scotia. The largest

---

[1] Presented by J. V. Thirgood for The Canadian Land Reclamation Association. Sections II through VII are contributed by the individual authors cited in those sections.

amount of environmental disruption has been caused by the mining of coal, iron, base metals (copper, lead, and zinc), and gypsum (Fig. 1).

B. Extent

Coal mine dragline operations have affected 4,600 ha in New Brunswick (Table 1). In Sydney, Nova Scotia, some 100 ha of rock waste has originated from stripping operations (dragline and scraper) and 200 ha are covered by waste dumps from underground mines.

The iron mines and the single titanium mine are open pit operations

[2] Contributed by D. Abbott, Head, Minerals and Materials, Research and Productivity Council, Federicton, New Brunswick, Canada.

Table 1—Land disturbed by mining, eastern Canada

Mining activity	Open pit	Wastes		
		Tailings	Rock/ Overburden	
	——————— ha ———————			
Coal				
N.B. Coal Ltd., N.B.	--	--	4,600	1.800 ha reforestated 1967–74
Cape Breton Dev. Corp., N.S.	--	--	300	20 ha planted ground cover 1975
Other	--	--	50	
			4,950	
Iron, titanium				
Iron Ore Co.,				
Knob Lake, Que.	430		600	
Carol Lake, Lab.	440	100	60	Revegetation trials on tailings
Sept. Iles, Que.	--	160	--	
Wabush Mine, Wabush, Lab.	260	250	40	20 ha tailings revegetated
Que. Cartier Mine,				
Lac Jeannine, Que.	100	280	220	
Mt. Wright, Que.	not yet in production			
Fire Lake, Que.	not yet in production			
Que. Iron & Ti Corp.,				
Lac Allard, Que.	30	--	10	
	1,260	790	930	
Sulphide				
Caspe Copper, Murdockville, Que.	100	780	130	30 ha revegetated tailings dam waste
Anaconda, Caribou, N.B.	5	5	5	
Brunswick M & S, N.B.	15	140	15	
Heath Steele, N.B.	5	75	5	
Other	--	100	20	
	125	1,100	175	
National Gypsum, N.S.	60	--	40	Self-revegetated after 2–3 years
Georgia Pacific, N.S.	--	--	200	
Other	100	--	600	
	160	--	840	

in Quebec and Labrador. At Knob Lake, Quebec, there are 13 major pits, some down to 200 m below surface, and there are over 50 rock dumps which are frequently over 50 m high. Elsewhere, disruption of the land surface is less spectacular. Land affected by iron mining in hectares is as follows: open pits, 1,260; tailings, 790; and rock wastes, 930. In Labrador at Carol Lake and Wabush, tailings disposal is into lakes but elsewhere it is on land.

Wastes from sulphide mining occur in the Gaspé Peninsula, Quebec, New Brunswick, and Newfoundland. At Gaspé Copper Mine Ltd., the

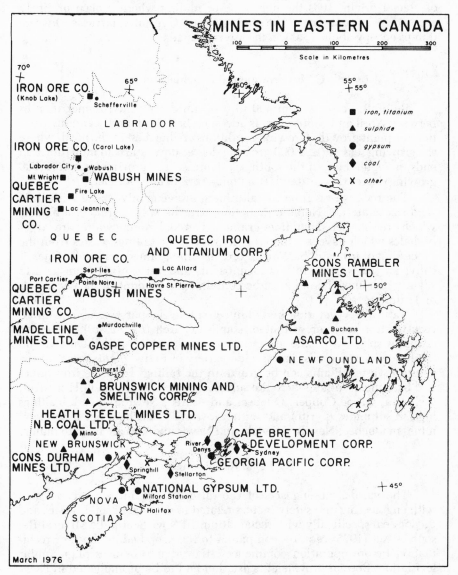

Fig. 1—Mines of Eastern Canada.

area of pits is 100 ha and about 130 ha are occupied by rock wastes. Open
pit operations and rock wastes are not important at the other sulphide
mines. Tailings dams occupy appreciable areas. At Gaspé the three tailings dams cover 780 ha, while the remaining mines have sulphide tailings
over a total of about 320 ha. As the acid mine drainage from certain base
metal mines, particularly in New Brunswick, would contaminate the
drainage system unless controlled, collection systems treat all water
before it leaves the property.

The waste from gypsum operations is the unconsolidated overburden
of glacial origin. It is the only type of mining where broken or finely
crushed rock is not part of the mining waste. Gypsum quarries and waste
dumps occupy about 1,000 ha in eastern Canada.

C. Environmental Considerations

Rainfall, varying from 400 to 600 mm during the summer months
between April and September, is adequate both in quantity and distribution for plant growth. Growing conditions are harshest in the north where
the growing season (± 1,000 growing degree days) starts in mid-June and
ends in September. In the south, by contrast, the growing season (2,600
growing degree days) extends from mid-April to late October.

The rock wastes from metal mining are generally coarse with little
sand-size material. Notable exceptions are the wastes from Knob Lake
which are weathered and finer grained. The coal mining wastes are largely shales which have weathered to a gravel. The tailings wastes from the
processing of iron and base metal ores are fine-grained materials. Chemically, all the wastes are low in nutrients and vary in pH from acid to
slightly aklaline; the more acidic contain toxic amounts of heavy metals
and sulphate.

Natural revegetation by volunteer species is sparse or absent on all
rock wastes; however, volunteer stands of birch (*Betula* sp.) and aspen
(*Populus* sp.), with some ground cover, have established themselves on
the less acid coal spoils, and a wide variety of native plants grow on the
gypsum wastes. Plants can be grown in the tailings from the iron mines
and base metal mines where the sulphide content is low and pH neutral,
such as at Gaspé Copper, Quebec, and Asarco, Newfoundland. Tailings
high in sulphides (pyrite) and with a low pH from the other base metal
mines in Quebec, New Brunswick, and Newfoundland are toxic to plants.

D. Legal Requirements

The various mining acts of the different provinces are concerned
with engineering and safety factors related to disposal of solid wastes and
do not deal specifically with reclamation. In Nova Scotia the Mineral Resources Act (1975) requires companies to file proposed methods of reclamation before operation commences; the other provinces plan similar
legislation. Special provincial legislation had to be promulgated in Newfoundland for the iron mines to dump tailings into lakes.

E. Reclamation Activities

Coal mining wastes were reforested from 1967 to 74 in the Minto area, New Brunswick, where 1,800 ha were planted with 3.8 million trees, viz., jack pine (*Pinus banksiana* Lamb.), red pine (*Pinus resinosa* Ait.), scots pine (*Pinus sylvestris* L.), white pine (*Pinus strobus* L.), blue spruce (*Picea pungens* Engelm.), Norway spruce (*Picea abies* (L.) Karst), white spruce (*Picea glauca* (Moench) Voss), and black locust (*Robinia pseudoacacia* L.). Jack, red, and scots pine have grown most successfully. Some ground cover has been established, with the most successful varieties being white dutch (*Trifolium repens* L.), sweet clover (*Melilotus alba* Desr.), birdsfoot trefoil (*Lotus corniculatus* L.), and red top (*Agrostis alba* L.). In the Sydney area during 1975, ground cover was planted on 18 ha from a coal strip which had been leveled and respread with topsoil. The following seed mix was used: timothy (*Phleum pratense* L.)—60%, alsike clover (*Trifolium hybridum* L.)—15%, red top—15% and perennial rye (*Lolium perenne* L.)—10%. Initial results were encouraging.

Reclamation trials have taken place at Wabush since 1970 where 20 ha have been planted with rye grasses, yellow clover (*Trifolium agrarium* L.), crownvetch (*Coronilla varia* L.), alfalfa (*Medicago sativa* L.), and timothy. Timothy and winter rye (*Secale cereale* L.) were the most successful. Experimental plantings of willow (*Salix* sp.), birch, and red top have taken place on the iron tailings at Carol Lake, Labrador.

At Gaspé Copper Mine, Quebec, 30 ha have been revegetated on the tailings dam walls as a result of revegetation trials which started as far back as 1959. A wide variety of seed mixes have been used in which the most successful species have been red top, cocksfoot (*Dactylis glomerata* L.), barley (*Hordeum vulgare* L.), and perennial rye. Other plants tried have been birdsfoot trefoil and oats (*Avena sativa* L.). Some alders (*Alnus* sp.), birch, and trembling aspen (*Populus tremuloides* Michx.) have been established at the base of the embankments. At the Buchans mine, Newfoundland, revegetation trials were carried out in 1974 with birdsfoot trefoil, Kentucky blue grass (*Poa pratensis* L.), and creeping red fescue (*Festuca rubra* L.). The results were encouraging.

F. Special Problems

Climate is a problem at the mines in northern Quebec and Labrador because of the short growing season. At the other mines the single most important problem, and the most difficult to solve, is that of low pH and factors associated with it.

Coal mine wastes at Minto and Sydney having a pH below 4 are not self-revegetated and attempts at planting have failed. The base metal mine tailings high in sulphides (pyrite) have a pH below 4 and sometimes near 2. In these wastes dissolved heavy metal content and sulphate ion can reach 10,000 ppm. Plants cannot survive in such toxic conditions.

G. Methodologies

At Minto, New Brunswick, most of the coal spoil banks were planted without grading. Only near major highways were the piles leveled for aesthetic reasons. Tree planting was a hand operation at 2.4-m intervals. Costs in 1973 averaged $0.07 per tree, which is equivalent to a reclamation charge of $85 per hectare. Spring planting proved best and survival rates of 90% were obtained. Fertilizer was not used.

At Sydney, Nova Scotia, planting was with a mechanical seeder at a rate of 41 kg seed/ha, followed by harrowing. Liming was at the rate of 6.8 tonne limestone/ha and $12 + 24 + 24$ ($N + P_2O_5 + K_2O$) fertilizer was applied at 0.6 tonne/ha. The cost of backfilling the workings, leveling, and respreading topsoil and seeding was $6,000 to $7,000/ha.

Seeding on the iron tailings at Wabush and Carol Lake, Labrador, were also hand operations. At Wabush the most successful fertilizer was the $8 + 18 + 20$ at 450 kg/ha followed by another 220 kg/ha 6 weeks later. Peat was used on the plots at Carol Lake.

At Gaspé Copper, Quebec, the embankments were seeded by hand at 330 kg/ha and then harrowed by tractor. Humus was sometimes added at a rate of 1,000 m³/ha and $10 + 10 + 10$ fertilizer applied at 330 kg/ha. In the experimental plots at Asarco, Buchans, Newfoundland, up to 1,000 kg $10 + 20 + 20$ fertilizer/ha was added to the experimental plots as well as lime.

III. RECLAMATION IN ONTARIO AND WESTERN QUEBEC[3]

A. Nature and Extent

Several factors are responsible for the amount and varied form of disturbed land that is found in the province of Ontario and the western half of Quebec. Hard rock mining dominates the northern regions of each province. Some of the materials being recovered on a commercial basis are copper, lead, zinc, gold, silver, platinum, nickel, uranium, iron, cobalt, palladium, iridium, rhodium, ruthenium, asbestos, talc, and nepheline syenite. Coal and phosphate mining is also envisaged. By virtue of population concentration in a 1,120-km corridor from Quebec City in the east to Windsor in the west, the demand by industrial, commercial, and residential interests for energy and mineral aggregates is high. This is reflected in well-developed systems for the transmission of oil, gas, and electricity, and for the production of aggregates. The above interests have also been the cause of many disturbed and eroded lakeshores along Lakes Huron, Erie, and Ontario, and along the St. Lawrence River.

Disturbed land has resulted from the disposal of milling wastes, construction of oil, gas, and electric transmission lines, highway construc-

---

[3] Contributed by E. M. Watkin, Department of Crop Science, University of Guelph, Guelph, Ontario, Canada.

tion, residential development, and heavy industrial activity such as steel and fertilizer plants. Equally important, but insidious in nature, is the erosion and resulting stream sedimentation arising from a large and sophisticated agricultural industry. Obviously many of the activities are common to other areas of North America, but their effect on Ontario is often accentuated by the distances involved, as for example an electric power transmission line in northern Ontario approximately 30.5 m wide and 1,400 km long. In such circumstances, reclamation of disturbed land arising from construction represents a major undertaking. Similar problems of distance apply to oil, gas, and highway systems. By comparison to similar activities in the western United States, Africa, and Australasia, hard rock mining activity is small in terms of milling wastes disposed. For example, the average iron property handles between 10,000 and 15,000 tons/day; uranium averages 5,000 tons/day, and gold, 700 tons/day. The largest copper/nickel operation handles only up to 35,000 tons/day compared to Bougainville Copper in the Pacific, where a 200,000 tons/day open pit feeds a 90,000 tons/day concentrator. However, Ontario and western Quebec represent one of the richest mining areas in the world, and what is lacking in individual mine size is compensated for by the fact that the number of significant and active mining operations greatly exceeds 100. In all, some 128 km² of mill wastes are estimated to exist in Ontario today. Unfortunately, no accurate record exists of the amount of disturbed land created by the aforementioned activities.

B. Environmental Conditions

Climatic conditions contrast sharply between the southernmost and more northerly areas of the Ontario/western Quebec region, as shown in Table 2. Although constant reference is made to the harsh winters in the northern regions and the resultant effects on plant establishment and growth, snow cover ameliorates low temperature conditions in the north

Table 2—Comparison of several climatic parameters between southwestern Ontario (Windsor) and northeastern Ontario/northwestern Quebec (Kirkland Lake—Val d'Or)†

Parameters	S.W. Ontario	N.W. Ontario N.E. Quebec
Mean daily temperature (°C)		
Jan.	−3	−17
Apr.	8	1
July	22	17
Oct.	12	5
Mean annual frost free period (days)	165	90
Mean annual length growing season (days)	220	160
Mean May/Sept. precipitation (cm)	36	41
Mean annual snowfall (cm)	80	297

† Composed from several sources, and does not represent exact meteorological station data.

as regards vegetation survival. The most difficult factor affecting reclamation through vegetation establishment is the decrease in the length of the growing season in a southerly to northerly direction. Such decrease increasingly affects the establishment of perennial forage crops, particularly legumes.

C. Legal Requirements

Legal requirements in relation to reclamation of drastically disturbed land are relatively weak in both provinces. The Mining Act of 1970 in Ontario requires rehabilitation of waste disposal areas after the closing down of mining operations. However, in many instances this is not enforceable because by that time many of the smaller mines have either disposed of their assets or run at a loss for several years prior to closing and, consequently, lack available monies for reclamation purposes. Only the larger mining companies having more than one property are in a financial position to undertake rehabilitation when one of their properties is closed out. However, proposed changes in the Mining Act will prevent future nonrehabilitation by initiating a scheme under which specific royalties obtained during the operating life of a mine will have to be used in rehabilitation prior to the surrender of a company's charter as required under the Ontario Business Corporations Act of 1971.

The aggregate extraction industry is governed by a separate act, the Pits and Quarries Control Act of 1971. Under this Act a royalties system is applied per ton of material removed from the pit or quarry operation, the cumulative sum of which is only returned after rehabilitation has been completed to the satisfaction of the Minister of Natural Resources. Much of the environmental and pollution control legislation for which Canada has gained widespread recognition in the past decade applied primarily to air and water pollution control, whether or not such pollution and environmental disturbance has arisen from drastically disturbed land. Reclamation of disturbed land is not subject to legislative control, but the effects of such disturbing activities on the surrounding environment are strongly so.

D. Present Status of Reclamation Activities

Research and field implementation is characterized by the involvement of a few private companies and federal and provincial government ministries in each area in which reclamation is required. These institutions have pioneered new cultural practices, as they apply in Ontario and northwestern Quebec, for the reclamation of pits and quarries, hard rock tailings, highways, and hydroelectric transmission lines. Except in three instances, reclamation research at academic institutions is at a very low level and, in the three instances, funding has been provided by private companies. A considerable volume of information on land reclamation does already exist as a result of the above involvements, but general acceptance and implementation by other private and public institutions remains weak.

E. Special Problems

Two major problems may be easily identified. Those of acid mine drainage from high sulphide-containing mine wastes where iron sulphide content may range to approximately 30%, and shoreline erosion on the Great Lakes. The former is largely a chemical problem due to high acidities which have been formed, while the latter is characterized by severe slope erosion problems created by wave action and varying water levels in the Great Lakes. A problem of high alkalinity and steep slopes is exhibited by asbestos in the Eastern Townships region of Quebec. One problem area to which little attention has been given is that of the reclamation of industrial wastes resulting from such industries as smelting, refining, and manufacturing. Generally, though, many reclamation problems could be fairly easily resolved on a technical basis, requiring only the correct input of current agronomic knowledge of species selection, seeding, and fertilizer methods.

IV. DISTURBED LANDS AND MAJOR RECLAMATION PROBLEMS IN SASKATCHEWAN AND MANITOBA[4]

A. Lignite Coal Strip Mining

Strip mining has resulted in the severe disturbance of approximately 4,300 ha in southern Saskatchewan, with an annual rate of increase of 150 to 200 ha/year (Anderson et al., 1975). The coal in this region is part of the Ravenscrag Formation, equivalent of the Fort Union Group, U.S.A., of Paleocene age. It occurs in as many as eight seams and is mined by stripping to 5- to 35-m depths. Overburden materials include glacial till and related sediments near the surface, and weakly indurated sandstone, siltstone, and shale interbedded with the coal. This region, a former grassland, has a semi-arid, continental climate with average annual precipitation of 400 mm, warm short summers, and long cold winters.

Areas stripped prior to 1973 have a surface configuration of chaotic to parallel ridges or interconnected cones with steep slopes, and open pits. Vegetation has established itself on 16% of this area, mostly on loamy materials with low soluble sodium and salinity levels (Anderson et al., 1975). Native plants such as *Agropyron* and *Poa* grasses, snowberry (*Symphoricarpos* sp.), pasture sage (*Artemisia frigida* Willd.), and others are common, with willow and cottonwood (*Populus* sp.) in moist areas and introduced forage species such as brome grass (*Bromis inermis* Leyss.) and sweet clover doing well. Vegetation is sparse or absent on a large portion of the area, particularly on silty or clayey materials where

[4] Contributed by D. W. Anderson, Research Scientist, Saskatchewan Institute of Pedology, University of Saskatchewan, Saskatoon, Canada.

high Na levels coupled with a dominance of montmorillonite clay have resulted in strong, compact or cemented surface crusts, retarding germination and growth of plants and increasing runoff and erosion on the steep slopes. Salt- or alkali-tolerant plants such as alkali grass [*Distichlis stricta* (Torr.) Rydb.], wild barley (*Hordeum jubatum* L.), and gumweed (*Grindelia perennis* A. Nols) are common on these spoils, as well as numerous weeds from adjacent agricultural lands.

Early reclamation attempts involved a minimum of grading, often just leveling the crests of ridges. Trial plantations of poplar, Scots pine, elm (*Ulmus* sp.), green ash [*Fraxinus pennsylvanicus* var. *lanceolata* (Borkh.) Sarg.], willow and others showed that these trees were not suitable (Flavelle, 1974). Wolf willow (*Elaeagnus commutata* Bernh.), Russian olive (*Elaeagnus angustifolia* L.), and Siberian elm (*Ulmus pumila* L.) were more suited, and recent reclamation projects have included these species. Alfalfa, sweet clover, crested wheat grass [*Agropyron cristatum* (L.) Gaertn.], Russian wild rye grass (*Elymus junceus* Fisch.), and brome grass grew well on nonsodic soils (Halland, 1968).

Present legislation in Saskatchewan requires that mine operators carry out programs for the protection and reclamation of the lands and watercourses affected by mining operations. Statements documenting land characteristics prior to mining and the effects of mining on land, water-courses, wildlife, and local inhabitants, and programs for reclamation as well as for the potential use of the land, are required and must be approved by government authority before mining begins.

Some recently mined lands have been graded to < 12° slope, large boulders removed, and the area seeded to alfalfa—brome forage and trees. These attempts have been relatively successful on loamy, nonsodic materials. Establishment and growth of vegetation on sodic, clayey spoils is a much more difficult problem. Current plans recommend the burial of unsuitable substrates during the mining operation so as to obviate this problem. Stripping and use of topsoil as topgrade material, and the investigation of other forage species are experimental programs. Studies indicate a variety of microclimates related to aspect and slope position within spoil areas (Anderson et al., 1975) and suggest choosing species appropriate to the climates at particular sites, as well as shaping lands so as to create sites suitable for less drought-resistant plants such as trees.

B. Sulfide Mine Tailings

The mining of heavy metals and the resultant sulfide mine tailings occur at three locations in the Canadian Shield region of Saskatchewan and Manitoba. The tailings dump at Flin Flon occupies 300 ha, is bare of vegetation, unsightly, and a source of blowing dust. The very high sulfur content, with an unlimited potential for acid formation, makes vegetative growth difficult or impossible. Small scale agronomic experiments with a variety of species and amendments achieved very limited success, mainly because of the low soil pH which could be alleviated only temporarily with additions of lime (D. A. Ogram, personal communication).

C. Other Disturbed Lands

Ten potash mines in the semiarid to subhumid regions of central Saskatchewan have waste dumps and brine lagoons, of 300 to 400 ha extent at each mine. The extreme salinity of these materials makes revegetation unlikely. Research and monitoring of the possible contamination of adjacent lands by salt dust and of ground water by saline waters is continuing.

Contamination of agricultural lands by spillage of salt water produced in oil extraction is a problem in the oil fields of southern Saskatchewan. The contaminated soils have extremely high Na and salinity levels. Their reclamation is being studied at the Univ. of Saskatchewan.

V. THE EXTENT OF DISTURBED LAND AND MAJOR RECLAMATION PROBLEMS IN ALBERTA[5]

A. Environmental Conditions

Alberta is a province exhibiting wide environmental diversity. Latitude changes from 49 to 60°N, and altitude increases from 152 to > 3,658 m above sea level resulting in at least 10 ecological zones. These zones reflect large geological and physiological differences and extreme variation in floral and faunal characteristics. An ecological zone outline map (Fig. 2) illustrates these regions of environmental diversity.

B. Nature and Extent of Disturbances

Disturbance operation	Presently disturbed hectares	Expected disturbed hectares
Oil and gas	9,614	9,091
Coal (foothills)	3,150	455
Coal (prairie)	2,341	91
Oil sands	2,273	114
Sand and gravel	9,091	4,545

C. Legal Requirements

The Land Surface Conservation and Reclamation Act was instituted in 1972 to deal with specific disturbance operations. The aim of this Act is to provide a framework whereby development proposals can be reviewed in a coordinated manner and the proper site-specific development and reclamation standards can be consistently applied to each successive pro-

[5] Contributed by R. J. Valleau, Operational Planner, Environmental Co-ordination Services, Land Conservation and Reclamation Division, Alberta Department of theEnvironment, Edmonton, Alberta, Canada.

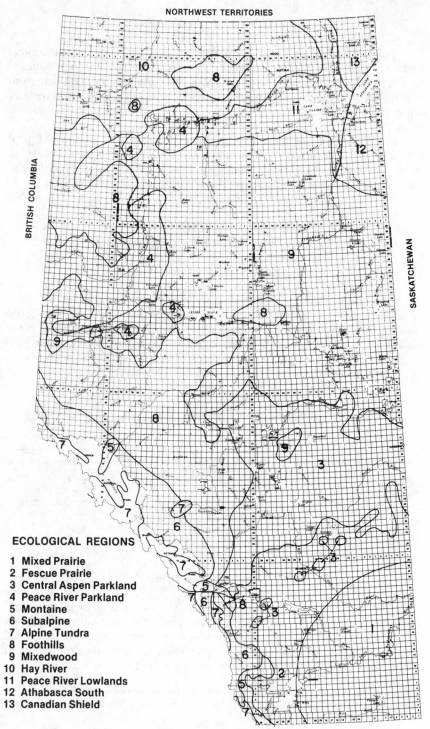

ECOLOGICAL REGIONS

 1 Mixed Prairie
 2 Fescue Prairie
 3 Central Aspen Parkland
 4 Peace River Parkland
 5 Montaine
 6 Subalpine
 7 Alpine Tundra
 8 Foothills
 9 Mixedwood
10 Hay River
11 Peace River Lowlands
12 Athabasca South
13 Canadian Shield

Fig. 2—Alberta: Ecological regions.

posal. This framework makes use of government referral systems for routine applications and environmental impact statements for proposals having more significant impact. The onus remains on the proponent to provide whatever research and technical information is required for the acceptance and approval of a submitted proposal. The Act stresses preventative measures to minimize adverse surface impacts rather than remedial measures.

D. Present Status of Reclamation Activities

For surface disturbances occurring prior to the existence of reclamation legislation, an active government program of reclamation was initiated in 1973. A total of approximately 100 sites including derelict coal mines, gravel pits, abandoned roads and airstrips, oil and gas activities, oil sands activities, sewage lagoons, garbage dumps, and stream crossings have been reclaimed to date. This has involved approximately 909 ha at a cost of $1,300,270. By 1977, it is estimated that 80% of all such sites within the province will have been reclaimed. Reclamation research work is presently being carried out in a rather segmented manner among various private, government, and university groups.

E. Special Problems

The province has three significant problem areas:
1) Ecological zones 1, 2, and 3, in which large reserves of prairie thermal coal lie, is largely an area with saline subsoils and bedrock. Major difficulties in reclaiming these areas back to agricultural production are expected.
2) Vast deposits of oil are located in ecological Zone 7 in the Athabasca Oil Sands deposits. After surface mining, problems are expected in recreating water tables and revegetating sterile and toxic sand.
3) The foothills region of the Rocky Mountains presents special reclamation problems due to geography and altitude. It is included in ecological Zone 5.

F. Significant Advances Made

The general increasing public interest in environmental matters has effected tremendous changes in attitude in government and industry. These changes have resulted in improved reclamation programs, more public participation in assessing potential projects, and more direct government involvement in planning industrial expansion. Two examples of the latter are the recent Coal Policy, in which the government has outlined areas in the province where coal mining is allowed, and the government policy to decentralize further industrial expansion away from the major cities.

VI. NATURE OF DISTURBANCES AND RECLAMATION ACTIVITIES IN BRITISH COLUMBIA[6]

A. Nature and Extent of Disturbances

A rapidly increasing population, accelerating urban and industrial development, smelters and pulp mills, encroachment on estuaries, modification of shore lines, highway development in mountainous country, railway construction, dam-building, province-wide powerlines with 91-m rights-of-way, the logging of 227,000 ha of forest a year, forest fires, forestry and mining access roads, avalanches, and mudslides, all cause drastic environmental disturbance in what is still largely a wilderness province. But none of these activities give rise to the level of public concern that is directed at the more concentrated and spectacular disturbances associated with open pit mining and, therefore, it is to mining, both hard rock and coal, and the related exploration programs, that reclamation requirements are directed.

In fairness, however, the scale of mined-land disturbance is very small in relation to the total area of the province— <0.2% of the total. In consequence, most of the serious land use conflicts have come in the form of externalities to the mining operation, affecting either wildlife, aesthetics, or water quality and the fisheries. Again, these are problems of quite local significance, but nowhere have these problems been more serious than in the Coal Block in the southeastern corner of the province where important coal seams outcrop on the southeast aspect of a series of mountain ridges for a distance of 288 km. These areas, because of the grass/shrub communities they support and favourable snow depths during winter, are critical to the maintenance of large concentrations of deer, elk, and bighorn sheep. Watershed values are also significant because these mountains form the headwaters of the Columbia and associated river systems and support an important sport fishery.

B. Environmental Conditions

There is great diversity of geology, climate, soils, and vegetation. Elevation varies from sea level to over 4,600 m, rainfall from <25 to over 500 mm, and general climate through semidesert, to moist Pacific coast, to alpine and boreal zones. Eleven distinct "biogeoclimatic zones" (Krajina, 1965) are noted. Table 3 shows the general climate and vegetation of these and the distribution of major mining operations within them.

---

[6]Contributed by J. V. Thirgood, Faculty of Forestry, University of British Columbia, Vancouver, B.C., Canada.

C. Legal Requirements

The Mines Regulation Act and Coal Mines Regulation Act of 1969 set out general policy and regulations for mine reclamation. These acts placed the onus on the industry to develop reclamation technology while the government retained an inspection function. Responsibility for administration of the Acts rests with the Department of Mines and Petroleum Resources. With subsequent amendments the provisions now apply to all surface disturbances resulting from surface and underground mineral and coal mines, gravel pits and quarries, and to exploration for coal and minerals. There are requirements for reporting and for bonding up to a maximum of $2,200/hectare and provision for closure for failure to comply. The Provincial Pollution Control Act and Water Act, and the Canada Fisheries Act are other pieces of legislation that can have direct bearing on mining activities.

Dick and Thirgood (1975) and Warden (1976) have reviewed the consequences. Although some progress has been made, the success of these legislative approaches is questionable. The problem lies in the failure to establish satisfactory standards or adequate enforcement and to provide technical expertise. Development has been uncoordinated and "in house". The Reclamation Section of the Provincial Mines Inspectorate has received only nominal staffing. Perhaps our population is still too low and our mines too far from major areas of settlement for continuing expressions of public concern from all but a committed minority.

In view of the extremely varied environmental conditions, it is unlikely that British Columbia shall ever have legislation that details the specific reclamation techniques to be employed. Emphasis will probably remain on standards of reclamation, with guidelines indicating how these can best be achieved. Some progress has been made toward these goals. Site-specific criteria based on specified reclamation land use objectives, surface drainage control, vegetation cover, ecological stability, and plant vigor have been suggested for reclamation standards (Dick, 1974), and the Department of Mines has published reclamation guidelines for exploration operations (McDonald & Dick, 1973).

A new review process gives some hope that, in future, broader social, economic, and environmental implications of major developments will be examined more carefully than they have been in the past. A document *Guidelines for Coal Development* has been drawn up under the authority of the Environment and Land Use Committee (ELUC, 1976). This is a Cabinet committee comprised of the ministers who are responsible for resource use and economic development or who are involved with highways, settlement, and public health services. The Committee is empowered by the Environment and Land Use Act to ". . . ensure that all aspects of preservation and maintenance of the natural environment are fully considered in the administration of land use and resource development commensurate with the maximum beneficial land use and minimize and prevent waste of such resources, and despoilation of the environment

Table 3—Biogeoclimatic zones and the distribution of mining operations in British Columbia

Zone	Major climax species	Land form	Elevation (m)	Climatic classification (Koppen)	Precipitation (mm)	Mean annual temperature (°C)	Number of producing mines	Substances mined
I Coastal Western hemlock	Western hemlock, western red cedar, grand fir, Pacific silver fir	Insular and Pacific Coast mountain areas	0–460 (max. 910)	Cfb Equable mesothermal humid	1,780–6,660	5–10	6	Copper, molybdenum, nickel, iron
II Coastal Douglas-fir	Douglas-fir, grand fir, arbutus, Garry oak	Coastal trough	0–500 (max. 460)	Csb Mediterranean subhumid	690–1,270	9–11	5	Iron, limestone
III Coastal Mountain hemlock	Mountain hemlock, subalpine fir, yellow cedar	Higher elevations Insular & coast mountain areas	300–1,500 (max. 1,800)	Dfc Microthermal Subalpine humid with a heavy snow cover	2,210–4,320	3–7	4	Molybdenum, copper
IV Interior Western hemlock	Western hemlock, western red cedar, western white pine, western larch, grand fir	Canadian Cordillera, interior system (southeast)	360–1,220	Dfb Continental humid	560–1,700	3–8	3	Copper, tungsten lead, zinc
V Interior Douglas-fir	Douglas-fir, ponderosa pine, lodgepole pine, western larch	Canadian Cordillera, interior system (southern)	300–900 (max. 1,340)	Dfb Contenental subhumid	400–560	4–9	15	Coal, copper, barite, lead, zinc
VI Cariboo Aspen, lodgepole pine	Trembling aspen, lodgepole pine, Douglas-fir, white spruce	Canadian Cordillera, interior system (central plateau)	520–910	Dfb Microthermal Continental subhumid	360–510	2–5	4	Molybdenum, copper, diatomaceous earth
VII Ponderosa pine, bunchgrass	Ponderosa pine, blue bunch wheatgrass, big sage	Canadian Cordillera, interior system (southern)	270–760	Bsk Continental cold semiarid to subhumid	180–360	5–10	3	Limestone, silica, copper

(continued on next page)

Table 3—continued.

Zone	Major climax species	Land form	Elevation (m)	Climatic classification (Koppen)	Precipitation (mm)	Mean annual temperature (°C)	Number of producing mines	Substances mined
VIII Engelmann spruce, subalpine fir	Engelmann spruce, subalpine fir, alpine larch, white bark pine	Canadian Cordillera, interior and eastern systems	90-2,290	Dfc Continental Cold humid	410-1,830	0-4	9	Copper, coal,
IX Sub-boreal spruce	White spruce, subalpine fir, trembling aspen, paper birch	Canadian Cordillera, interior system (north-central)	330-850	Dfc Sub-boreal Continental humid	410-640	0-4	4	Mercury, copper
X Boreal spruce	White spruce, black spruce, tamarack paper birch	Interior Plains Region, low elevations, interior system (far north)	170-850	Dfc,Dsb Boreal Continental humid	310-580	-3-3	1	Asbestos
XI Alpine tundra	Western moss heather, pine mountain heather	Mountain tops province-wide	N 900+ SW 1680+ SE 2290+	Dfc,ET Subarctic, Continental Cold tundra	540-2,540	-3--1	3	Asbestos, copper

occasioned thereby . . .." These *Guidelines* are the first real attempt to implement a formalized plan for assessment of major resource developments before they are entered into. The guidelines are designed to identify environmental disruptions and social, economic, and community impacts that may be associated with mine development and production. They outline all the factors that must be investigated in connection with the surface or underground extraction of coal, reclamation, transportation, the provision of power, and the effect on the community and region. Responsibility is placed on the developer to obtain the information required to permit government assessment of the various impacts, and to provide a cost/benefit analysis of the total development. Provision is made for frequent review, particularly with a Coal Steering Committee comprised of representatives of the Department of Mines and Petroleum Resources, the Department of Economic Development, and the ELUC Secretariat. Eventual decision rests first with the ELUC Committee, and finally with the provincial Cabinet. The guidelines and review process seem to promise better integration of coal developments into overall land use and regional planning. Nevertheless, there are many problems in relation to coal mine exploration, reclamation, the operation of existing mines, and the whole hard rock sector that remain to be dealt with.

D. Present Status of Mining and Reclamation Activities: The Mining Industry—Present and Future

Today, large open pit mines account for most of the production of coal and minerals, though many small underground mines still operate. Copper, lead, zinc, tungsten, molybdenum, and asbestos are mined, with similar quantities of iron, nickel, barite, gypsum, mercury, limestone, silica, and diatomaceous earths. Table 4 shows the number of different mining operations presently in production and under permit. The total land area disturbed at present by all mining activities, including exploration, is probably in the neighbourhood of 19,000 ha.

Only 9 out of 49 producing mines are located above the 49th parallel, the center of the province, but recent discoveries indicate that the northwest will likely be the center of future mineral mining activity. In addition, as energy needs sharpen, coal deposits in both the southern Rocky

Table 4—Operating mines in British Columbia

Type of operation	Number of mines	Average area per operation
		——— ha ———
Coal—surface	2	650
Coal—underground	1	20
Metal—surface	16	275
Metal—underground	20	55
Industrial minerals	10	32
Gravel quarries	200 + (estimate)	8
Placer gold	200 + (estimate)	2

Mountains, presently mined largely for export, and the northern Rocky Mountain foothills will probably be developed either by surface or by underground hydraulic methods.

E. Reclamation Progress Since 1969

Most significantly, reclamation has been shown to be biologically possible in most regions of the province, given sympathetic mine development and engineering. Trees, shrubs, grass, and forbs have been established on most waste materials. This is not to say that major problems do not exist, but a significant development is that there is increasing recognition that reclamation is not a matter of a single treatment but of continuing land and vegetation management. The function of artificial revegetation is to provide early stabilization and very largely to prepare the way for and hasten natural invasion and successional processes. Philosophically, reclamation has passed the stage of cosmetic reclamation—concern is for long-term land use compatibility, usually with emphasis on wildlife and watershed values.

Considerable progress has been made in developing techniques for restoring the integrity of watersheds in exploration areas. But of 19,000 ha disturbed by mining and exploration, probably not more than 900 ha have been reclaimed to an acceptable standard and most companies have yet to progress beyond the stage of plot research. Only two companies have reclamation staff and only one is carrying out a sizeable operational program. General shortcomings in present reclamation procedure include: failure to include reclamation needs as a constraint on mining practice, failure to recognize site factors as constraints on vegetation, and lack of emphasis on results and assessment.

F. Special Problems

Most of the reclamation problems arise out of the mountainous conditions. Waste rock is normally disposed of by casting down the mountain side. Surface instability is likely to be the main barrier to reclamation and effects of such factors as degree and length of slope, total rainfall, rainfall intensity, "soil" texture, particle density, aspect, microtopography, and material size range, as they affect stability, are little understood. Much work needs to be done at each mine to determine the maximum angle at which adequate ground cover can be achieved. Much needs to be done to modify mining methods and particularly methods of waste disposal to facilitate reclamation. Slope modification is particularly important. There is a general lack of plant material adapted to site conditions. In general, the emphasis on revegetation has been to use easily obtained coniferous seedlings and broadly based mixtures of commercial grasses and legumes. Attention must be paid to selection of grass and legume species suited to site conditions, to naturally occurring broadleaved trees and shrubs, to native plants in general, and to patterns of local ecological succession. Associated with this is the need for investigating methods for propagation of native plants.

VII. LAND RECLAMATION IN CANADA NORTH OF LATITUDE 60°N. (YUKON AND THE NORTHWEST TERRITORIES)[7]

A. The Setting

In the 3,800,000 km² (1,460,000 mi²) which make up the land mass of northern Canada, one can distinguish at least six major ecoregions (Strang, 1976). They have different characteristics of parent material, climate, and vegetation and so require different land reclamation practices (Fig. 3).

The six ecoregions are:
on the Arctic Islands:
1) Eastern, pre-Cambrian—rugged topography, little or no plant cover;
2) Western, sedimentary—subdued relief, little or no plant cover;
on the Mainland:
3) Tundra—subdued relief, continuous cover of sedges and dwarf shrubs;
4) Boreal—varied relief, none of it extreme;
open spruce or pine forests over lichen and ericaceous shrub ground cover;
5) Alpine—steep terrain, sparse cover;
6) Delta—flat, poorly drained, continuous ground cover, tree cover varies with time since deposition.

The climate increases in severity, that is, aridity and shortness of growing season, from south to north and from west to east.

The most unusual and distinctive feature is the presence of permafrost which is defined (Brown & Kupsch, 1974) as "the thermal condition in soil or rock of having temperatures below 0°C which persist over at least two consecutive winters and the intervening summer". Note that permafrost is a state and not a material and that the definition avoids any mention of soil moisture.

B. Reasons for Reclamation

Reclamation of disturbed sites in Canada's north is required for the same reasons as those which apply in the south—site stabilization and aesthetics. Revegetation alone will not quickly provide a sufficient insulating layer of organic material to restore the thermal equilibrium which existed prior to disturbance and so is incapable of preventing thawing and thermal erosion.

---

[7] Contributed by R. M. Strang, Faculty of Forestry, University of British Columbia, Vancouver, B.C., Canada.

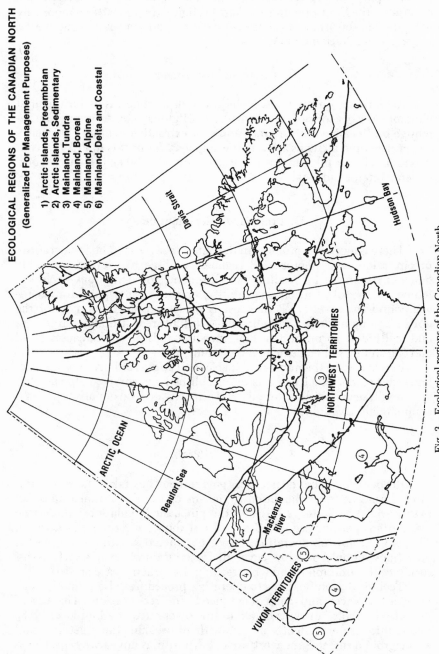

ECOLOGICAL REGIONS OF THE CANADIAN NORTH
(Generalized For Management Purposes)

1) Arctic Islands, Precambrian
2) Arctic Islands, Sedimentary
3) Mainland, Tundra
4) Mainland, Boreal
5) Mainland, Alpine
6) Mainland, Delta and Coastal

Fig. 3—Ecological regions of the Canadian North.

One may ask what the aesthetic requirements are in such a vast and remote area. The answer is simply that the major highway construction program—the Dempster and Mackenzie Highways (the latter temporarily halted)—has tourism as a prime *raison d'etre*, and some mining activity is very close to a National Park.

C. Causes of Disturbance

Exploration for minerals, including hydrocarbons, is by far the most widespread cause of surface disturbance. Highway construction is an intensive but localized disturbance and so is extractive mining. Hydroelectric projects and airstrips are very few and very far between. Pipeline construction will resemble highway construction, if or when it is carried out, in being intense but local.

D. Problems of Reclamation

There is a general problem in the climatic severity. The temperature, precipitation, and photoperiod regimes combine to provide a notably harsh environment for seedling establishment. Soil conditions—cold soil temperatures, low nutrient availability, and frequently poor drainage—compound the severity. Permafrost is present throughout most of the north, adding a further complication—in flat areas it inhibits drainage, and melting of permafrost in high moisture soils on slopes causes rapid and continuing soil movement and erosion.

Furthermore, the number of species and strains of introduced grasses and other plants which can become established and survive in the north is very small, seed is in short supply, and virtually no seed of native species is commercially available.

E. Avoidance of Problems

Recognizing these difficulties, government has taken steps to minimize the needs for reclamation by means of the Territorial Lands Act (Territorial Lands Act, 1971) and the pursuant Regulations. Under the Regulations permits are issued for all but the smallest scale of activity. They set out how an operation is to be conducted, at what season of the year (moving only on snow-covered, frozen grounds avoids surface disturbance, for example), and what reclamation practices are needed.

Technical modifications to operating procedures also minimize surface disturbances and consequent needs for reclamation. The use of "mushroom shoes" or skids bolted to the lower edge of a bulldozer blade allows it to scrape up debris or trash without breaking the vegetation mat at the ground surface; the work area of drill sites is now always protected by a thick layer of gravel, wood chips or comparable insulating material throughout the period of activity to protect the ground surface and maintain thermal stability.

F. Reseeding Mixtures

Despite these precautions, there are occasions when excavation is inescapable and reseeding is necessary, principally for highway or pipeline construction and mining operations. One element in the environmental studies pursued as part of the Mackenzie Valley Pipeline investigation was the testing of agronomic grasses for their suitability in the North. Parallel though smaller scale tests have been carried out by several oil and mining companies and by the Federal Government in its Mackenzie Highway program. Results are far from complete, but there is general agreement on the most suitable seed and fertilizer mix for the Mackenzie and Yukon Valley. Species, strain, and rates of seeding are shown in Table 5.

G. Fertilizer

Requirements are site-specific but a useful general guide is:

1) At seeding: 224 kg phosphate/ha (as 373 kg triple superphosphate/ha)
   112 kg N/ha (as 249 kg urea/ha)
2) After 2 years: 78 ± 11 kg N/ha (as 174 ± 28 kg urea/ha).

Table 5—Species suited for use in the Mackenzie and Yukon Valley

Species and strain	Rate of application
	kg/ha
For tundra sites:	
arctared creeping red fescue (*Festuca rubra* L.)	11.2
nugget Kentucky blue grass (*Poa pratensis* L.)	11.2
engmo timothy (*Phleum pratense* L.)	3.9
frontier reed canary grass (*Phalaris arundinacea* L.)	3.9
meadow foxtail (*Alopecurus pratensis* L.)	3.9
slender wheatgrass (*Agropyron caninum* (L.) Beauv. var *majus*)	3.9
tall Arctic grass (a native species) (*Arctagrostis latifolia* [R.Br.] Griseb.)	9 *
One may also use a quick nurse crop of:	
winter rye (*Lolium perenne* L.)	11.2
For boreal sites:	
boreal creeping red fescue	11.2
common or nugget Kentucky blue grass	11.2
common meadow foxtail (*Alopecurus pratensis* L.) *or* climax timothy	11.2
bluejoint (*Calamagrostis canadensis* (Michx.)	6.7†
(a native species)	
On wet sites:	
frontier reed canary grass	11.2
On dry sites:	
frontier reed canary grass	5.6
revenue slender wheatgrass (*Agropyron trachycaulum* [Link] Malte)	5.6
South of lat. 52°N.:	
alsike clover (inoculated((*Trifolium hybridum* L.)	11.2

† The native species should be applied in two sowings, one-third at the initial seeding, the remaining two-thirds 2 years later with a booster fertilizer dressing.

In the tundra sowing must be early in the season; this is less critical but still desirable in the boreal zone. Requirements for high elevation, mountainous sites, and the eastern mainland have not yet been worked out. Seeding is difficult and of no great benefit in the Arctic archipelago.

LITERATURE CITED

Anderson, D. W., R. E. Redmann, and M. E. Jonescu. 1975. A soil, vegetation and micro-climate inventory of coal strip mine wastes of the Estevan area, Saskatchewan. Energy, Mines and Resources Canada, Ottawa, Canada. 140 p.

Brown, R. J. E., and W. O. Kupsch. 1974. Permafrost terminology. Tech. Mem. III, Nat. Res. Counc., Ottawa, N.R.C. 14274, 62 p. illustr.

Dick, J. H. 1974. Criteria for land reclamation standards in British Columbia. A paper pre-pared for Land Reclamation Short Course EM 6672, 18–20 Mar. 1974. Centre for Con-tinuing Education, Univ. of British Columbia, Vancouver. 7 p.

Dick, J. H., and J. V. Thirgood. 1975. Development of land reclamation in British Colum-bia. In M. K. Wali (ed.) Practices and problems of land reclamation in western North America. Univ. of North Dakota Press, Grand Forks, N. D.

Environment and Land Use Committee. 1976. Guidelines for coal development. Parlia-ment Build., Victoria, British Columbia. 33 p.

Flavelle, Frank. 1974. Experimental tree plantings on Estevan spoil banks—Saskatchewan. p. 189–198. In D. Hocking and W. R. MacDonald (eds.) Proc., Workshop on Disturbed Lands in Alberta. Alberta Environment, Edmonton, Alberta.

Halland, C. 1968. Introducton of tree cover in the Estevan spoil banks. 8th Interm Rep. Saskatchewan Dep. of Nat. Resour., Saskatoon.

Krajina, V. J. 1965. Bioclimatic zones and classification of British Columbia. Ecol. of western North America. 1:1–33.

McDonald, J. D., and J. H. Dick. 1973. Reclamation guidelines for exploration. Inspection and Eng. Div., Dep. of Mines and Pet. Resour., British Columbia. 19 p.

Strang, R. M. 1976. Land use handbook. Environ. Div., Northern Nat. Resour. and Environ. Branch, Dep. of Indian Affairs, Ottawa. Mimeo. illustr.

Territorial Lands Act. 1971. Canada Gazette Part II, 105 (22). SOR/71-580. Queen's Printer, Ottawa.

Thirgood, J. V. 1969. Land reclamation in Canada. A paper presented at the NATO Ad-vanced Study Inst. on the Ecology and Revegetation of Drastically Disturbed Areas held at the Pennsylvania State Univ. Common. For. Res. 49(3)141:227–234. 1970.

Warden, G. 1976. Black pits and vanishing hills. Coal Development in British Columbia. British Columbia Wildlife Fed., Vancouver.

Chapter 5

Citizens' Role in Land Disturbance and Reclamation[1]

GEORGE V. HOLMBERG, WILLIAM J. HORVATH, AND JAMES R. LA FEVERS

USDA, Washington, D.C.; National Association of Conservation Districts, Stevens Point, Wisconsin; and Argonne National Laboratory, Argonne, Illinois, respectively.

I. INTRODUCTION

The citizens' role refers to acts that are intended to influence the behavior of those empowered to make decisions on land disturbance and reclamation. Examples of different participating methods are discussed along with the results of effective participation.

Participation, in most places, will involve governmental decisions, although nongovermental decisions are also considered. Of all the forms of citizen involvement, it appears that the most effective have been in legislation and enforcement. In 38 states, minimum reclamation standards are dictated by law. This indicates that citizens of the state want to have a role in the reclamation of their land and that they are either willing to pay the price for that reclamation or think they will have to pay a higher price (social costs) if there is no reclamation. It is in this context that citizen participation is discussed.

Citizens need to participate in the planning process from the beginning. The most effective results are achieved when industry, citizens, planners, elected officials, and agencies share their experience, knowledge, and goals and jointly create a plan acceptable to all.

Press, radio, and television coverage of reclamation activities and the efforts of community groups make citizens aware of the issues and the importance of the decisionmaking process. Good communication, coordination, and program integration among persons and groups concerned with surface mine reclamation are essential for successful programs. Effective reclamation programs need to include environmental, social, economic, and political issues along with the latest technological advances. Interdisciplinary professionals with divergent backgrounds and viewpoints need to work together.

---

[1] Conclusions and opinions attributed to different organizations are drawn from material either furnished by representatives of the organizations or in the literature cited.

Citizen groups such as national and state mining trade organizations, surface mining reclamation associations, and environmental groups can help provide for effective reclamation programs. They stimulate the public and promote support for reclamation, provide additional information, and exert influence on policy makers. Environmental legislation, through citizen involvement, has resulted in participation by many different agencies at the federal, regional, state, multicounty, county, townships, and municipal levels of government in the reclamation of surface-mined land.

II. LEGISLATION AND ENFORCEMENT

If present legislative and administrative trends continue, according to Imhoff et al. (1976), mined-area programs of states will appear largely as separate responses to individually perceived needs. However, most of the programs now coming on line are directed toward increasing integration of the formerly separate activities of local public planning, private mining, and state-private reclamation. Resource managers and planners, private as well as public, are being called on to join mine operators, engineers, and scientists in addressing the complex technical tasks required in an integration of land planning, mining, and reclamation.

Imhoff et al. (1976) state that the decade of the 1970's has been characterized by new programs that treat mining as an interim land use. This emerging concept, illustrated in Fig. 1, is being expressed increasingly in state legislation.

III. FEDERAL, STATE, AND LOCAL CONTROLS AND PERMITS

Besides the governmental programs specifically termed *mined-area reclamation*, a great many other local and state controls of various kinds pertain to the integrated set of activities that occur over time at the *aver-*

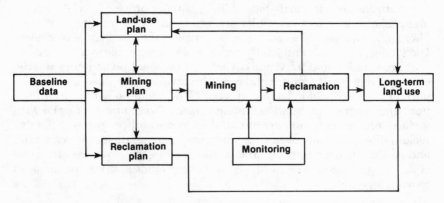

Fig. 1—Sketch of the concept of integrated mining, reclamation, and land use planning. (Modified from Imhoff et al., 1976).

age surface mine site. The number and type of controls vary by locale and by state. Imhoff et al. (1976) have developed a hypothetical example, Table 1, suggesting that the mine operator may have to obtain literally dozens of governmental permits (excluding federal) if the mining, reclamation, and land-use activities that ensue at the site are to be lawful. Table 1 is based on a review of state and local legislation, state and local plans, and environmental impact statements.

It is recognized that there may be some damage from surface mining even with the best planning and land reclamation methods. Somewhere between the extreme concern for the environment and the need for surface mining, there is a common middle ground where both sides can meet. In some places such as the phosphate mining area in Florida, there is competition for land for several uses, including, primarily, agriculture, residential, and the interim mining use. A consideration of human needs and the social, economic, and environmental goals is necessary. Phosphate fertilizer from mining in this area is essential for food production. Most of the country's phosphate is produced in Florida. The many areas of environmental concerns in phosphate mining and related activities are indicated in Table 2, a summary of information prepared by Sarasota County, Florida, for discussion purposes at a meeting on phosphate mining in Washington, D.C., on 12 Mar. 1976.

Imhoff et al. (1976) reviewed all state laws on the reclamation of surface mined areas. They reported that these laws address a progression of private actions or initiatives that vary according to time, place, technology, and economic conditions. These laws function as "constraints" that affect the activities that occur before, during, and after mining. All state mined-area reclamation laws recognize the possible role of local government in such activities as zoning. Several of the mined-area programs require evidence of compliance with local planning controls. A few mined-area programs place local governments in the decisionmaking process with regard to the issuance of mining permits.

The regulating permits that must be obtained to open a new phosphate mine or plant in Florida are listed in the following paragraphs. (Information provided by John Lawson, Holland, and Knight, Tampa, Fla., at a meeting on Florida Phosphate Mining, 15 Mar. 1976).

A. Federal Permits and Approvals

a. **National Pollutant Discharge Elimination System (NPDES)**— This permit is required by the Federal Water Pollution Control Act of 1972 (FWPC Act) for discharge of industrial waste water. If the source being permitted is a "new source" (i.e., constructed after publication of proposed EPA guidelines), EPA must comply with the National Environmental Policy Act of 1969 (NEPA), which may require preparation of an environmental impact statement (EIS). Preparation and approval of the EIS may require 18 to 24 months (or longer if complications arise) and may impose substantial costs on the applicant.

Table 1—Hypothetical example of state and local controls and permits required for a surface
mine (From Imhoff et al., 1976)†

Time period/activity	Zoning and related local land-use controls	State recla-mation controls	Water, air, and noise pollution controls	Other controls, as named
Pre-mining (years 0-4):				
Existing land use	X	--	X	--
Prospecting the area	--	X	--	--
Mineral and economic evaluations	--	X	--	--
Acquisition of rights	--	X	--	State water rights
Surveying & design of mine	--	X	--	--
Natural resources studies	--	X	X	--
Reclamation planning	--	X	--	--
End land-use planning	X	X	--	--
Costs analyses	X	X	X	State and local environmental controls
Obtaining mine permit‡	X	X	--	Waste discharge permits
Constructing roads and buildings‡	X	X	X	State location of development (e.g., as in Maine)
Obtaining utilities	X	--	--	State utilities regulation
Drainage and erosion control‡	--	X	X	State water board
Fencing and screening‡	X	X	--	State fish and game
Environmental monitoring‡	--	X	X	--
Joint Mining and reclamation (years 4 to 30):				
Removal and segregation of soils‡	X	X	--	Local soil & water conservation
Disposal of debris‡	X	X	X	Sanitary land fills
Drilling and blasting‡	X	X	X	State permit
Extracting and hauling minerals‡	X	X	X	State severance taxes
Filling and grading‡	X	X	X	--
Reducing pitwalls or highwalls‡	X	X	X	--
Burying toxic materials‡	X	X	X	--
Revegetation‡	--	X	--	--
Post-mining (4 to 36):				
Vegetation survival studies‡	--	X	--	State agriculture
Pest and weed control‡	X	X	--	State agriculture
Land capability studies	X	X	--	State agriculture
Divesting ownership or rights	X	--	--	Official acceptance of lakes and roads
Water quality performance	X	X	X	State agriculture
Decommissioning mine (dismantling, demolishing, etc.)	X	X	--	State mine abandonment laws
Established end use	X	--	X	--
Recovery of bonds	X	X	--	--

† Does not include controls pertaining to mine safety.
‡ A process that tends to be maintained or repeated, as necessary, throughout much of the life of the mine.

Table 2—Phosphate mining and related activities (A summary of information prepared by Sarasota County, Fla., for discussion purposes at a meeting on phosphate mining in Washington, D.C., on 12 Mar. 1976)

Areas of concern	Unmined ore	Mining	Beneficiation	Phosphorus extract	Manufacturing	Waste products	Land reclamation	Products
Air quality	Radon	Radon; fugitive particulates exhaust emissions	Radon	Radon fluorine particulates SO₂ NH₃	Radon fluorine particulates SO₂ NH₃	Radon from gypsum stacks and manufacturing; particulates; fluorine	Radon particulates exhaust emissions	Radioactive materials in fertilizers and feed supplements
Water quality	Radioactive material fluoride; phosphate	Radioactive materials fluoride; phosphate & turbidity in surface water discharges	Radioactive materials fluoride; flotation process chemicals; slurry transport H₂O quality; leachate from ore storage; PO₄; turbidity in surface water discharges	Radioactive material plant area runoff; spills; discharge of accidentally contaminated process & cooling water	Radioactive material; fluoride; spills; runoff from plant site & storage area; cooling pond recharge quality; discharge of accidentally contaminated process & cooling water	Radioactive materials; fluoride; NH₃; PO₄; turbidity in low pH water from gypsum disposal ponds & in leachate from slime & tailings ponds; disposal of the above into surface waters	Increased recharge potential of mined-out areas may allow movement of leachate from tailings and slimes used in reclamation	Same as air quality; PO₄ in water from products; materials handling, storage, spills, & by-product storage
Water resource (quantity)	Significant in limiting ground water recharge in certain areas	Increased evapotranspiration resulting from formation of lakes in mined-out areas	Large volumes used to transport ore & tailings; wash water; screening & floatation process water		Process water used to manufacture phosphoric acid; cooling water makeup	Transport of wastes to disposal areas uses large volumes of water	Native vegetation; altered to lake-dominated area which will increase evapotranspiration; recharge may be increased	
Land resources		Unreclaimed land has few uses; large areas have been mined or are planned to be mined	Plant site and storage areas	Plant site; storage areas; cooling ponds;	Plant site; storage areas; cooling ponds	Plant site; disposal and storage areas	Large areas needed for disposal; natural topography extensively altered; redistribution of minerals in the strip-mined area from natural sequence.	
Public health	Air quality; water quality; agricultural products contamination; radiation hazards from on-site occupation	Air quality; water quality; aesthetics	Air quality; water quality; aesthetics	Air quality; water quality	Air quality; water quality; aesthetics	Air quality; water quality; contamination of land disposal sites	Air quality; water quality; radiation hazards from on-site occupation	Air quality; water quality; entrance of radioactive materials into the food chain
Energy use		Large user	Large user	Large user	Large user	Waste treatment and disposal is a large user of energy	Land reclamation is a large user of energy	U recovered will supply some energy
Economic impact	Significant agricultural, residential, & recreational potential for unmined areas	Local labor force; supports mining service industries	Local labor force; supports service & process chemicals suppliers	Local labor force; raw materials for local phosphorus based manufacturing	Local labor force; large industrial based local economy	Pollution of air, water and land can lead to a significant economic impact	Significant for long-term continued use of the land	Industry should pay for pollution abatement study programs

b. U.S. Army Corps of Engineers (CORPS) Dredge and Fill—Section 404 of the FWPC Act may require Corps approval for construction or mining activities in certain "wetlands." The Corps may also be required to prepare an EIS, which would involve delays and expenses similar to those involved in the EPA procedure noted in *a*. If an EIS is required by both EPA and the Corps, one statement is prepared jointly by both agencies.

c. Significant Deterioration—Prior to construction of a potential source of air pollution, the applicant must obtain approval from EPA under the Significant Deterioration Rule (40 CFR, Part 52). This rule requires preconstruction review for all new major stationary sources to insure preservation of certain "clean air" areas.

B. State Permits

The Florida Department of Environmental Regulation (DER) requires permits for construction and/or operation of potential sources of pollution, including the facilities described in the following paragraphs.

a. Plant Complexes—In mining operations, a beneficiation facility separates phosphate rock from clay and sand. In chemical fertilizer plants, sulfuric acid is mixed with phosphate rock to produce phosphoric acid, a basic ingredient in the production of phosphatic fertilizers.

In both mining and chemical operations, DER requires a permit application that describes the general size and location of the plant, as well as details of the process flow. Both construction and operation permits are necessary.

b. Industrial Waste Water Facility—This system, as a part of phosphate mining and chemical operations, provides for recirculation of process water. The permit application must include engineering details such as construction specifications and water balance. Both construction and operation permits are required.

c. Dams—Earthen dams are an essential part of the industrial waste water facility and may be constructed only by qualified engineers experienced in this type of work. Detailed criteria, set forth in chapter 17-9, Florida Administrative Code (FAC), must be met in the design of earthen dams used in phosphate mining activities. DER approval must be obtained for construction and operation of earthen dams and related structures.

d. Dredge and Fill—Dredge and fill activities (including phosphate mining and industrial construction) in waters of the state and certain defined wetlands must have a permit from DER. The applicant must affirmatively demonstrate that water quality criteria will be achieved during and after the proposed activity to obtain DER approval.

e. **Air Pollution Sources**—A permit is required for construction and or operation of facilities that may be point sources of air pollutants. Elaborate pollution control devices are required for limiting emissions to defined levels. Computer dispersion modeling may also be required to demonstrate that ambient air standards will be met (and that degradation of ambient standards will not occur).

f. **Significant Degradation**—DER may not allow construction of new point sources if emissions from those sources will cause an increase in concentrations of pollutants over certain defined levels.

g. **Injection Wells**—DER has jurisdiction over ground waters of the state and requires a permit for construction of injection wells. These wells are now being used to recharge aquifers pumped by industrial operations. Injection well permits require that water quality in the aquifers will be maintained.

h. **Sanitary Waste Facilities**—A permit must be obtained for construction and operation of sanitary waste facilities. Design specifications for the facility are submitted by the developer and reviewed by the DER staff.

C. Regional Permits

In Florida, regional water management districts are charged with the responsibility of regulating water use. Much of the phosphate industry lies within the jurisdiction of the Southwest Florida Water Management District (SWFWMD), which administers a set of comprehensive regulations governing use of waters under district jurisdiction.

a. **Works of the District**—SWFWMD rules specify that a permit is required to "connect to, withdraw from, discharge water into, place construction within or across, or otherwise make use of a work of the district. . ." The "works of the district" include various rivers, tributaries, and flood plains within district boundaries.

b. **Storage and Management of Surface Waters**—A SWFWMD permit is required for construction, alteration, abandonment, or removal of any dam, impoundment, reservoir, or appurtenant work that exceeds a minimum size or reroutes, restricts, or alters the rate of flow of a stream or other watercourse draining a watershed that exceeds 5 square miles (12.95 square kilometers). This type of permit is generally required for construction of industrial waste water facilities (impoundments) associated with phosphate mining operations and may also be required for impoundments used by chemical plants.

c. **Consumptive Use and Well Construction**—A permit is required for consumptive use of water above certain limits. Users are limited to an amount based on the "water crop," which is related to the extent of the applicant's landholdings. Permits for construction of wells must also be obtained.

D. Land Use Control and Local Review

a. Development of Regional Impact Statement (DRI)—Chapter 380, Florida Statues, requires a comprehensive assessment of the regional impact expected from major developments. These assessments, commonly referred to as *DRI's*, evaluate the impact on the regional environment, economy, public facilities, public transportation, and housing. DRI's are reviewed by regional planning councils and by the local government (county commissions) and are approved or disapproved only after a public hearing.

b. Zoning Regulations—Additionally, most counties have adopted zoning regulations requiring further approvals before construction of major industrial projects. For example, rezoning and approval of a master mining plan must be obtained before a phosphate mining operation can be started.

c. Reclamation—Reclamation (after mining) is required under most county mining ordinances and under the Florida Severance Tax Law. Topographic, esthetic, and water quality standards are applied by both county and state governments.

IV. ZONING AND LAND USE PLANNING FOR SAND AND GRAVEL MINING

Many citizens are aware of the reclamation needs of sand and gravel pits. These pits are located in every state and generally within or near urban centers where land values are high. Some operations contribute significantly to the sediment load in streams. Unsightly appearance, windblown dust, and noise are also concerns of citizen groups. Wildlife and recreation are common uses associated with the reclamation of these sites, although many sites are also reclaimed for land use such as residential development, forestry, and agriculture. In most places, the land use and reclamation planned for the pits depend on the proximity of the mines to urban communities. Most state surface-mined-area reclamation laws include sand and gravel pits as a mineral or commodity covered under the law. Planned sequential use is also often required by local units of government. An example of some of the requirements for reclamation planning is outlined in the New York State law.

Sand and gravel in New York State is the third most important mined commodity, exceeded only by cement and stone in dollar value. The New York State Mined Land Reclamation Law requires a reclamation plan as well as a mined land-use plan. The reclamation plan is the operator's written proposal for reclamation of the affected areas and includes land use objectives, maps, or other documents as required to describe reclamation as well as, where relevant, grading specifications and the manner and type of revegetation. The two major goals of the Bureau of Mineral Resources, New York State Department of Environmental Conservation, for implementing the program are: (i) assistance in mining development, and (ii) environmental protection assistance.

In areas of rapid urban growth, the construction aggregate industry must meet the urban growth demand for sand and gravel by establishing operations as close to their potential markets as possible due to the low cost, high bulk characteristics of the material and the relatively high transportation cost.

Pickels (1970) reported on the importance of zoning gravel-bearing land for future extraction. This property then would not be totally lost if it were not immediately utilized by the producers. Such land could be a significant contribution to a city's open space program. Sites could be rehabilitated to conform with the particular recreation desires of the local communities or they could be developed in such a manner that they duplicate the character of nonmined open space.

Pickels (1970) pointed out that sand and gravel sites closely resemble urban-suburban recreation areas. Basically, the lengthy period of operations, often 15 to 30 years, and the potential annoyance factors associated with mining are reasons enough for many people to object to any mining. However, it is this stage of mining (excavation) that will generally transform a site into a highly desirable recreation area. Annoyance factors cannot be totally eliminated, but they can be adequately minimized. This can be done in many ways; the more common is to place earth mounds and/or vegetative screens in such a manner that not only are recreation and mining interests physically separated but also noise, unsightly views into the operations area, and dust strategically controlled.

If a producer does desire to rehabilitate his site for recreation use, he should, in most cases, approach development via progressive rehabilitation. This necessitates a predevelopment plan that could allow the site to be utilized for recreation prior to, concurrent with, and subsequent to excavation. Progressive rehabilitation is recommended because:

1) It utilizes already available personnel and equipment. Rehabilitation work could occur during slack periods or during winter slowdowns.

2) It opens the site to recreation use sooner than other methods.

3) It assures the concerned public that recreation development will be the terminal site use.

4) It could be the most economical method of development.

It should be emphasized that nonrehabilitated sites have contributed favorably to outdoor recreation and are considered superior to developed sites by many naturalists, boaters, hunters, and fishermen.

Pickels (1970) states that the final success of any proposed rehabilitation project necessarily depends on the implementation stage or the grading and earthmoving phases of operation. Certain site features must be made to conform to desired recreation use requirements. The major site features to work with are slopes, cut banks, overburden mounds, and depressions. In each situation, size, height, location, stability, and slope gradient are factors to be considered.

It is obvious that such a complex undertaking as transforming a sand and gravel site into a recreation site demands the expertise of various professionals. Although the producer has an adequate understanding of the various mining phases, he could employ the services of a site planner, recreation specialist, and ecologist to assist him in his development of the site. There may also be many others that could be of some service to the operator.

Most sand and gravel sites have high recreation potential. The character of physical terrain features can be altered in numerous ways to conform to the requirements for the desired recreation use. The imagination of the planner and the ability of the producer to recognize recreation potential of a site are probably the foremost considerations for any successful development. The lack of imagination that most present-day rehabilitated sites exhibit probably comes from the assumption that imaginative development costs more than a less imaginative scheme. This does not seem to be a justifiable reason for not considering the best possible solution to any rehabilitation proposal.

It should be realized that rehabilitation for recreation need not be the only re-use potential of any particular site. There may be reasons why a depleted site could be utilized as a sanitary landfill operation and subsequently transformed into a desirable recreation area. Problems originating in the landfill operation would obviously have to be eliminated before any recreation use.

In recent years the rising popularity of recreation-oriented residential developments has been phenomenal. They are generally featured in conjunction with golf courses, lake complexes, and generous open space. There is every reason to believe that depleted sand and gravel sites can be transformed into desirable recreation-oriented living areas. Slopes could easily be stabilized and made to support dwelling units, depressions could be converted into underground parking facilities or indoor recreation areas, and existing water features could serve to tie the total complex together. Pickels (1970) believes that there is a great need for imaginative planning coupled with the realization by the producer and the public that there is unlimited potential waiting to be recognized and channeled in the desired direction.

V. LITIGATION

A number of lawsuits have resulted in enforcing laws involving mining and reclamation of surface-mined lands. An example of this enforcement was recently reported.

According to the Bureau of National Affairs, Inc. (1976), a mining company was fined more than $1 million for its discharges of taconite tailings into Lake Superior. The U.S. District Court for the District of Minnesota fined the company for violating its Minnesota water discharge permit.

The U.S. Department of Interior (1967) special report on *Surface Mining and Our Environment* reported on state control of surface mining on private lands. They state that

experience has shown that to achieve effective results in minimizing or preventing adverse effects from surface mining the following prerequisites are necessary:

1) An informed public that demands action be taken to prevent needless damage to mined lands and adjacent areas.

2) The enactment of legislation which commits the state to a policy of regulating surface mining operations in order to prevent mining practices that are known to cause harmful effects, and requires that mined lands be reclaimed after mining is completed—with stiff penalties for violation of the law.

3) The establishment of an inspection and enforcement staff that is provided with adequate financial resources and the flexibility of authority needed to meet varying local conditions, such as determining that surface mining shall not be permitted where it is known that reclamation is not feasible under present technology.

4) Continuing, timely, and effective control through a system of frequent inspections and consultations with mining operators at all stages of the mining cycle, and equitable imposition of the penalties provided.

VI. ORGANIZED CITIZEN GROUPS

The National Wildlife Federation has published a list of organizations, agencies, and officials concerned with natural resource use and management in the 21st edition of its *Conservation Directory* (Decker, 1976). Many citizen groups listed in this document have concern for surface mine reclamation. Information from statements by these citizen groups on reclamation of surface-mined land is quoted. (The authors of this paper are making no judgment as to the validity of these positions. They are reported here only as information germane to this discussion.)

A. National Wildlife Federation

The National Wildlife Federation has adopted a national policy that includes the following basic principles (Nat. Wildl. Fed., 37th Annual Convention, Washington, D.C., 15–18 Mar. 1973):

1) A total ban should be imposed on strip mining areas of steep slopes or in areas where, because of climatic conditions or other factors, land reclamation cannot be practiced successfully.

2) The extraction of oil shale should be permitted only by underground mining or by in situ methods which prevent water pollution or contamination by radioactivity.

3) Any allowable surface mining can be regulated under strict provisions which assure, through adequate performance bonds, that effective land reclamation efforts are made an integral part of the operations.

This organization expresses the firm belief that strong federal regulations must be authorized, established, and rigidly enforced if surface mining is to be controlled effectively throughout all the states on a uniform basis.

B. Izaak Walton League

The Izaak Walton League of America (Maitland Sharpe, personal communication) has had resolutions on reclaiming surface mined areas for a number of years. At a convention in June 1963, at Cincinnati, Ohio, the league urged "more vigorous enforcement of existing federal and state laws relating to the operation of strip mines and other mineral properties, research in methods of preventing drainage from abandoned mines, and enactment of needed additional statutes to conserve all resource values."

"Additional resolutions that constitute the formal and official policies of the League (Maitland Sharpe, personal communication) have been developed at a number of national meetings since 1963." In 1972, the league recommended (Maitland Sharpe, personal communication):

1) A prohibition on strip mining where even the best reclamation efforts would result in the social, environmental, and economic detriment of an area.
   a. Specifically, they recommend that strip mining be prohibited:
      —On natural slopes greater than 12°;
      —In flood plain on any streams;
      —On land held in trust by the United States for Indians, such as in the Four Corners Area;
      —On all public lands where mining would impair nonexploitive values presently enjoyed by the public under the multiple use system.
2) The inclusion in federal legislation of a provision allowing any citizen to bring suit against the industry on behalf of a public right to a clean environment.
3) The establishment of standardized impact statements prepared on a site-by-site basis describing in clear and simple terms all primary and secondary effects of the operation and circulated for public comment well in advance of the approval of a mining permit.
4) The creation of cooperative agreements among federal, state, and other agencies in the development of land use programs and criteria for past and future surface-mined areas to allow agencies developing river basin plans, air pollution abatement plans, and regional land use plans, greater control and assurance that surface mining will be consistent with an overall management system.
5) That the effects of strip mining and controls to abate its environmental consequences be specifically recognized in existing federal legislation in the areas of air pollution, water pollution, noise pollution, and land use.
6) The creation of a fund to restore orphan lands and to provide research monies to provide better understanding of acid formulation, nutrient deficiency, effects of bacterial action, ground water hydrology, and classification of waste or spoil bank materials in surface-mined areas as well as to improve mining equipment, procedures, slope stabilization, erosion control, and to prevent acid water production.
7) The inclusion of a federal provision requiring that the burden of proof be placed on the strip mine operator to show conclusively that he can restore the land equal to its original use.

The league's reclamation policy has rested (Maitland Sharpe, personal communication) on three fundamental premises:

1) "Full reclamation should be incorporated into and made an integral part of the mining process.

2) Where such reclamation may not be feasible, or cannot be guaranteed, strip mining should be prohibited.

3) Orphan lands damaged by·past mining should be reclaimed with funds collected from current mining operations."

C. National Audubon Society

The National Audubon Society (R. C. Boardman, personal correspondence) states that "not all strip mining has to be bad; the trouble is that often coal is mined in the wrong place and in the wrong way. The society recognizes that America needs coal and states that about two-thirds of the remaining coal seams in potential U.S. strip mining areas *could* be strip mined without permanent damage to the environment. But the society stressed the word 'could' and adds that in 'case after case' this doesn't happen."

In summary, the National Audubon Society asks: "(1) that strip mining be *confined* to areas that can truly be reclaimed; (2) that effecive controls must be established *during* the mining operation; and (3) that full reclamation must be enforced *afterward*."

D. League of Women Voters

The League of Women Voters of the United States' position (Alice Klorons, personal communication) requires "reclamation of lands damaged by such activities as surface mining . . . ."

The League of Women Voters position (Alice Klorans, personal communication) is: "In decisions about land use, public as well as private interests should be respected, with consideration for social, environmental and economic factors. Each level of government must bear appropriate responsibility for planning and managing land resources. It is essential, at a minimum, that an appropriate level of government determine, regulate, and guide critical activities and the use of critical land areas. To guarantee responsive and responsible governmental decisions citizen participation must be built into the planning and management of land resources at every step."

E. Sierra Club

In the *National Wildlife Conservation Directory* (Decker, 1976), the Sierra Club is listed as "a citizens organization with goals to protect and conserve the natural resources of the Sierra Nevada, the United States, and the world; to undertake and publish scientific and educational studies concerning all aspects of man's environment and the natural ecosystems of the world; and to educate the people of the United States and the world to the need to preserve the quality of that environment and the integrity of these ecosystems." In regard to a "Federal Regulatory Program," the Sierra Club (1973) states:

> Given industry and government's shallow commitment to total reclamation, the absence of federal or state land use planning, the absence of federal law and state enforcement of existing laws, and the primitive state of existing technology, it is not unreasonable to conclude that strip mining should be prohibited.
> Perhaps not for all time and in all places, but prohibited until there exist even the most rudimentary mean of making strip miners accountable to a broader public standard of care and caution.
> Short of total prohibition the federal government should:
> —Phase out contour strip mining on steep slopes.
> —Apply a moratorium to new strip mines pending a determination of where reclamation is possible or feasible and capable of being enforced.
> —Establish comprehensive land use and energy policies.
> —Provide for citizen participation in the environmental regulation of coal strip mining.
> —Establish a nationwide program for orphan (abandoned or completed operations) mine reclamation.
> —Develop incentives for research and development of environmentally sound underground mining methods.
> —Reassess coal export policies.
> —Prohibit government purchases of strip-mined coal.

F. Soil Conservation Society of America

The Soil Conservation Society of America (1968) recognizes eight principles that should be considered in arriving at policies and actions governing surface mining, soil and water resource management during and following mining, the productive uses of mined areas:

1) The most important single factor in achieving adequate resource management during and after mining is thorough planning for future productive uses of areas affected by surface mining—preferably prior to mining. Such preplanning would include access roads and refuse disposal as an integral part of the total operation.
   a. The basic capabilities of disturbed lands should guide planning for their future productive use.
   b. Mining operators should use the advice of qualified individuals, institutions, and agencies to aid them with their problems related to planning.
   c. More research is needed to guide planning for protection of adjacent resources during mining and for mined-area use programs.
2) Classification of mined lands is necessary to define their capabilities for productive uses.
   a. More research is required to establish criteria for classifying mined areas according to their physical and chemical characteristics.
   b. Rugged topography presents more problems than gentle topography.
   c. Rock types and mineralogy and chemistry of various types of mineral deposits are important determining factors.

3) The after mining use possibilities of the area affected should be based upon capabilities of the disturbed area, compatibility with adjacent land uses, and the needs and desires of both the landowner and local communities.

a. The factors basic to mined-area use planning are topography, mineral produced, type and techniques of mining operations, disturbed overburden characteristics, environmental geography, socioeconomic needs, and landowner objectives.

b. Overburden analyses are necessary at any particular operation to make possible the proper placement of the maximum amount of overburden materials capable of supporting desirable vegetation so they may be on the surface of the disturbed area.

4) Equipment now available is generally suitable for preparing mined land for productive uses in areas of gentle topography. Better planned use of existing equipment in such areas would solve some of the existing problems. Mining and putting disturbed areas to productive uses is difficult or sometimes economically impractical in rugged topography with present equipment. New types of equipment for mining and making productive uses of mined land would offer distinct advantages, particularly in rough or mountainous country. The mining industry and equipment manufacturers should be encouraged and aided in designing and developing such equipment.

5) In current surface mining operations where opportunities for productive use of mined land do not exist—or where offsite damage can be expected before restoration can be completed—the mined areas, together with the access roads and refuse disposal areas, should be physically isolated from surroundings to prevent damage and adverse impacts to adjacent resources of land and water and to man-made improvements and investments.

6) In planning for future surface mining operations where opportunities for protecting offsite values or making productive uses of the mined land do not exist, operators should be encouraged not to mine such areas.

7) Preparation of surface-mined areas to encourage future productive uses can be greatly enhanced by placing overburden materials, such as massive rocks and acid-producing strata, where they do not become a predominate part of the reformed surface.

a. Materials most suitable for growth of desirable plants should be placed where they may become a part of the reformed surface.

b. Waters capable of supporting fish and other desirable aquatic life should be the goal where impoundments occur or are made.

8) Good housekeeping—maintaining operating areas, including roads and refuse disposal areas in presentable condition—should be an important consideration in the advance planning of operations and should be observed throughout mining and subsequent uses of the disturbed areas. A sense of pride on the part of the operators in doing a good job of mining along with a good job of postmining land use would, within the framework of American business tradition, bring about maximum benefits to all concerned.

G. National Association of Conservation Districts

The National Association of Conservation Districts (NACD) (1975) policy position involves mining, reclamation, and the USDA Forest Service Program, Surface Environment and Mining (SEAM). Their policy is as follows:

We urge the revision of mining laws to make them consistent with protection of the environment and with effective conservation of soil and water resources. We advocate laws requiring that: (1) a permit be obtained from the appropriate agency prior to the start of surface mining operations; (2) a bond be posted for reclamation of land damaged by mining; (3) assurances be obtained that mining will be undertaken with methods deliberately designed to minimize damage to soil and water resources; and (4) a resource conservation plan be adopted for the restoration of surface features following the mining operation.

Approximately two million acres have already been damaged by surface mining in the United States. These surface-mined lands are contributing to the problems of sedimentation and pollution of streams; erosion damage to adjacent timberlands, highways, grazing lands, and farmlands; and they adversely affect the total environment and natural beauty of the landscape.

We recommend that Congress authorize a program whereby the states may utilize the capabilities of the Department of Agriculture and the Department of the Interior to accomplish the reclamation of lands damaged by surface and open pit mining.

We also urge the continuation of research that will contribute to the economic restoration of such areas by landowners.

We favor legislation that would require the conservation and utilizations of topsoil and/or weathered soil materials in all surface mining operations. Productive soil is a natural resource that should not be buried or lost to future generations by surface mining operations.

The Department of Agriculture's SEAM Program, under the leadership of the Forest Service, embodies research, development, and application efforts to harmonize surface mining on public and private lands in the western United States with environmental quality objectives. NACD commends this program which is aimed both at the use of appropriate measures in new mining operations, to protect natural resources and neighboring communities, and the reclamation of previously mined lands.

We urge Congress to provide additional funds to extend this top priority conservation program.

VII. LANDOWNERS GOALS AND DECISIONS

Two contrasting views on surface mining of coal by landowners are reported in the *Rangeman's Journal*. In the June 1975 issue, a Montana rancher (Brewster, 1975) states that many assertions and accusations made against surface mining of coal are not borne out by fact. He contends that the money generated by coal development can accomplish in a short time much-needed range improvements that income from cows has not been able to do. He believes that reclamation to original production is possible and that, with reasonable environmental regulations, surface mining can result in much-needed stimulus to range improvement. In years to come, with the high cost of land, improved and increased range management will be an important factor in feeding the nation. The money from coal development can and will do the job.

The Montana rancher states that the biggest misconception put out by environmentalists is that the whold countryside is going to be torn up. It is his opinion that not more than 10% of any sizable ranch will be disturbed, leaving 90% on which to continue ranching, with coal money from the 10% used to increase the productive capacity of the 90%. This capacity can be increased by several range management practices including water spreading, leveling, seeding, fertilizing, irrigating, and better distribution of range watering facilities, including pipelines. Furthermore, the cow herd could be upgraded by buying better bulls—bulls that ranchers have dreamed about but have not been able to afford.

In an article in the December 1975 issue of the *Rangeman's Journal* another Montana rancher rebuts the compatibility of a livestock and strip mine operation (Bailey, 1975). His concerns with coal mining are summarized as follows:

1) Coal mining is a competitive business and does not lend itself to "good guyism," nor are mining companies concerned with much more than getting the coal out unless forced to do otherwise by legislation.

2) Reclamation techniques in the Northern Plains are still highly experimental, and none has stood the test of drought, time, or the lack of commercial fertilizers.

3) Consideration must be given to the ramifications of a high gasification complex and its supporting facilities within the confines of a ranch along with the strip mine operation.

4) You cannot necessarily mix lots of dollars with spoil material and improve the quantity and quality of forage on the ranch.

VIII. ONSITE EVALUATION OF RECLAMATION

Citizen participation, through evaluations of surface mine reclamation at operating surface mine sites, is very effective. West Virginia Department of Natural Resources, Division of Reclamation, sponsors an annual interagency evaluation field trip. Representatives of conservation districts, private consultants, seeding contractors, environmental groups, newspapers, mine operators, federal and state agencies, West Virginia University, and Virginia Polytechnic Institute, were included in the 122 participants in the interagency evaluation conducted 28 July–1 August 1975. Four days were spent in the field observing reclamation of coal surface-mined areas with a critique on the last day.

The group was divided into 11 working committees on the first day. The chairman of each committee made a report following the field trip. In addition, there were several individual reports. The reports reflected concern for future use of reclaimed areas as well as a need to know what future land use will be needed so that initial disturbance and replacing the material are compatible with intended use. Most observers, especially those who have participated in the evaluation several times, reported that they were impressed by the changes in mining and reclamation techniques over the 5-year period. The consensus was that a plan for mining and reclamation developed before the mining operation starts is the best guide to effective reclamation.

Although many of the evaluations were complimentary about the progress made, there were many suggestions for additional improvement. Many individuals emphasized reclamation measures needed to reduce off-site damages during mining and to aid long-term stability and use. Participants recognized the need for waterways and diversions to safely dispose of surface water from steep slopes. Most of the discussions about conservation measures were on how they could best be constructed to do the job, not on whether they were needed. Proper location and time to construct the measure in relation to other stages in mining were considered.

An added benefit from the evaluation is the education received. It provided a free exchange of ideas in a group with varied responsibilities in reclamation work. It is being used by graduate students from colleges and universities to supplement more detailed course work dealing with or related to industrial disturbance. The evaluation continues to be used by state and federal agencies as a training exercise for their employees.

Plans prepared to meet requirements for a permit continue to improve. The questions about planning seem to be the amount of detail that would be useful and the kind of assistance the mine operator needs to make plan preparation more effective and easier. For example, decision on future land use such as woods and wildlife habitat will satisfy the requirements of West Virginia's law; however, the group observed at least two examples where it was apparent soon after mining started that the areas could be used for many more intensive uses and land use objectives were changed after mining started.

The maintenance needed to insure long-term performance of the reclaimed land continues to be a problem and needs continual study. The problem is most acute where the mine operator does not own the surface and his interest and responsibility end with establishment of satisfactory vegetation. The surface owner is not obligated under the West Virginia Surface Mining and Reclamation Act for maintenance of established structures.

The segregation of spoil material is an accepted practice on all active mine operations. In the past, specifications have been written to save topsoil for spreading on the surface. It has been pointed out many times in the state that the material on the surface may not always be the most favorable for plant growth. On at least two sites visited, the best material from a plant nutrient standpoint was not the surface layer. The benefits from soil testing was discussed in one report.

Disposal of water from steep slopes, especially where a riprapped channel is built in the center of a valley fill, was studied in depth during the evaluation. The need for diversions and the stage in mining at which they should be built was discussed. Rock riprapping a channel, how large the channel should be, and the kind of rock needed was discussed.

The choice of plant species depends on future use of the area. Goals should be to establish vegetation that will stabilize the area and provide desirable harvestable forage. The surface landowner is in the best position to maintain established stands for optimum performance. The report on herbaceous vegetation emphasized the benefits of mulching and the need for topdressing seeded areas 6 months to 1 year after seeding. The need for woody vegetation was discussed.

The stability of large fill areas, such as a valley fill, was discussed. There were special comments about how proper placement, especially at the toe of the slope, affects slope stability.

The committee studying socioeconomic effects recognized that surface mining does make a substantial contribution to total energy needs. The committee also recognized that surface mining cannot be accomplished without disturbing the surface and causing some disruption of the environment.

West Virginia Department of Natural Resources, Division of Reclamation, has demonstrated the utmost in citizen participation through the evaluations made by many different individuals and groups.

IX. CITIZENS' ROLE IN RECLAMATION THROUGH MINING ASSOCIATIONS

A. West Virginia—Coal

West Virginia Surface Mining and Reclamation Association feels that surface mining in the state has outgrown its earlier status as an emotional issue, according to Lusk (1976). This came about through: (i) having a tough state law; (ii) money to enforce the law; (iii) advanced technology in mined-land reclamation; and (iv) an industry that was willing to change.

The *Beckley Post-Herald*, Beckley, West Virginia, 29 July 1975, reported on comments by Ben E. Lusk, President of the West Virginia Surface Mining and Reclamation Association, and Ben Greene, Chief of Reclamation for the Department of Natural Resources, in an article entitled "Land Preserved Through Restripping." They stated that "Highwalls and spoil piles left over from abandoned surface mining operations in the state are being eliminated. Reentering an inactive mine allows the operator full environmental control before, during, and after mining." Due to larger equipment, new methods, and accessibility, restripping is a great benefit to the state's special reclamation program that would normally be responsible for reclaiming such orphaned lands. The operators are totally eliminating the old highwalls which could not be done in most cases through the "Special Reclamation Program." A survey by the Reclamation Division made in 1975 showed, "of the 95 permits issued 35 (36.8%) are recuts and of the 5,900 acres permitted, over 2,000 acres (35%) are previously disturbed by surface mining. However, the most significant factor is that on the restripping permits issued since 20 Mar. 164,802 lineal feet or 29.3 miles of highwall will be totally eliminated."

Restripping enables coal miners to recover coal deposits that were once considered unminable and it eliminates reclaiming old, abandoned surface mines that have scarred the mountains for as long as 30 years or more. A third advantage has to do with the overall amount of land disturbed each year; more coal can be produced but less land will be disturbed.

B. Arizona—Copper

There are many examples of mining companies returning the land to more intensive and more productive use after mining than what it had been used for previously.

An example of this is reclamation work done by City Service Company (Miami Copper Company) on copper mine tailings in Arizona. Some of the mine tailings have been landscaped and used as a trailer court. On another location, the company has topsoiled about 150 acres (60.7 ha) of tailings. The area was seeded and additional native perennial grasses have become established on the area. Most of the area was rated in good to excellent range condition. It is being grazed and yields were estimated to be 10 times the yields of surrounding areas.

The Arizona Mining Association in their publication *This is Copper Country* (Richardson, 1975), discusses Arizona's copper mining industry. The Association recognizes the environmental, economic, and social impacts of the industry.

Over 53% of the nation's newly mined copper in 1974 came from 23 open pit mines and 7 underground mines, which take up less than 102,000 acres (41,279 ha) or about one-seventh of 1% of Arizona's land surface. Arizona also ranks second in the United States in the production of silver and molybdenum, and fourth in production of gold, all largely byproducts of copper mining.

Participation by citizens in reclamation of copper mine tailings is being accomplished in Green Valley, Ariz. Green Valley is a retirement community located about 16 km (10 miles) south of Tuscon, Ariz. Several open pit copper mines are located in the area. Homeowners in Green Valley have formed a committee to work with Cyprus Pima, Amax, and Duval mining companies. The committee is concerned chiefly with scenic beauty, although blowing dust, soil erosion, and restoration of natural wildlife habitat are also concerns. The copper companies have a committee, consisting of company supervisors and a private nurseryman, that works with the citizen group. Several large plantings using containerized plants have been made on the tailing piles. Most of the plants are evergreen desert species that will partially hide the tailing piles throughout the year. The mining companies hire students from the University of Arizona at Tucson as summer help in reclaiming the areas.

Copper pit mines are major tourist attractions in Bisbee, Arizona, "Queen of the Mining Camps." The Lavender Pit Mine, operated by Phelps Dodge Corporation, attracts many visitors. Bus tours of the mine are provided by the City of Bisbee through the Bisbee Chamber of Commerce.

C. Minnesota—Iron

Minnesota's Iron Ranges are also seen as unique and fascinating. Thousands of tourists come to the Iron Ranges each year to watch the mining operations, to marvel at the open pits, and to tour taconite plants.

An Iron Range Trail system is being developed to highlight some of the most interesting attractions on the Iron Ranges. So, in a way, Minnesota's iron mining industry is part of another industry—the tourist industry.

Generally, Minnesota's mining companies have to contend with environmental problems of the use of water, the control of dust, the prevention of erosion, and the stockpiling of overburden and low grade iron-bearing materials that may be of use some time in the future.

Minnesota's iron mining and taconite companies have various programs designed to solve these problems. Tree planting, seeding tailing basin embankments and stockpiles, recirculating water, and dust control systems are some of these programs.

Dickinson (1972), reporting on reclamation work done by Erie Mining Company states that:

> Evidence of progress is the native vegetation seeding into areas that have been stabilized with grasses and legumes. Without treatment, vegetation will not establish itself in a taconite basin for many years. We know this because, for test purposes, we have small tailing areas that are 20 years old which are still devoid of vegetation.

> Probably our greatest satisfaction comes from the knowledge that we are building soil from barren crushed rock. In 1967, we planted tailing with alfalfa and sweet clover and covered it with hay. In 1972, this area was covered with a dense, healthy stand of alfalfa. In this planting is the first indications of soil being formed in the root zone of the test plants.

> At Erie Mining Company, we feel we have demonstrated a sincere stewardship for the environment in which we operate. Our program of multiple resource management provides a balance with taconite mining and processing. In addition to work in tailing stabilization, we are also working in forest management, which includes a wildlife habitat program. These programs were underway well in advance of the enthusiasm of modern environmentalists and present legislation. They show what can be accomplished by the determined cooperation of owners and management to keep mining compatible with the environment.

X. COORDINATED EFFORT OF PRIVATE INDUSTRY, LOCAL, STATE, AND FEDERAL AGENCIES

Citizen involvement was demonstrated in the development of the newly established Environmental Plant Center located at Meeker, Colo. Oil shale and coal development in the Upper Colorado Basin stimulated great interest and tremendous cooperative effort among private industry, and local, state, and federal agencies in establishing the center. There is a severe lack of commercially available native plant materials for suitable reclamation of land disturbed by any type of mining and related developments. The Environmental Plant Center is an offshoot of the plant materials program designed by the Soil Conservation Service more than 30 years ago to provide improved plant materials for specific soil and conservation uses. The immediate need to obtain seeds for revegetation was recognized so the cooperative route of establishing the plant center was chosen. Two Colorado conservation districts, White River and Douglas

Creek, agreed to acquire physical ownership of the land and facility and SCS agreed to provide the technical assistance needed to set up and operate the plant center. SCS provides an advisor for on-site assistance. The Colorado Seed Grower's Association and private oil and coal companies are providing financial support along with cooperating agencies including SCS, Fish and Wildlife Service, Bureau of Land Management, Forest Service, Environmental Protection Agency, and Energy Research and Development Administration.

These supporting groups, plus representatives for Colorado State University, Utah State University, and Wyoming State University, make up an advisory board to establish needs and priorities for work at the plant center.

The plant center is located on 76 ha (189 acres) of irrigated land. Seed collections of native grasses, shrubs, and forbs are underway to begin initial testing in 1976. This is the first step in the systematic program of plant materials centers. Species from plant introduction stations, plant breeders, and research agencies will be compared at this stage of testing. Over 500 accessions of native species have been catalogued at the plant center.

Basic data are recorded and selections are made for advanced evaluations of superior strains. At this stage, the selections will be available for cooperative testing with the other agencies and people working on revegetation problems.

The third step of SCS systematic testing program is to evaluate the selected strains in field plantings under actual use conditions and with conventional equipment by using the best known research methods. Proven strains will be increased and made available to growers for commercial production. Use of soil and site information is a part of the research and testing. Plant communities differ according to soil and climatic conditions. Soil information is available from local SCS field offices and can be a useful tool in correlating and analyzing research results.

XI. COORDINATING ASSISTANCE AT THE LOCAL LEVEL BY CONSERVATION DISTRICTS

Conservation districts, local subdivisions of state government, are in a unique position to coordinate assistance from all available appropriate sources—private and public, local, state, and federal. These districts encourage citizen participation and enlist the assistance of all individuals, agencies, institutions, organizations, and industry in a position to contribute to the solution of soil and water conservation problems associated with surface mine reclamation.

Conservation districts encourage citizens to have a part in creating the kind of environment we all live in and believe that each person has the chance and responsibility to help improve it. More people need to understand the effects of surface mining and other land-disturbing activities on environmental quality and translate their energy into meaningful action.

Surface mining may affect the environment by influencing the quality of the air, land, and water. There are also beneficial environmental effects from surface mining such as creating opportunities to develop recreation areas where none existed before.

SCS and other agencies continue to adapt conservation measures to surface-mined areas and other drastically disturbed areas. New conservation measures have been developed for specific environmental needs and to give the best help possible in "traditional" conservation work that has already made a substantial impact on environmental quality.

Conservation districts and agencies together have some challenges in their mutual efforts on reclamation of land affected by surface mining. They are:

1) To see that all special-interest groups have the opportunity to participate, from the outset, in planning conservation projects;

2) To see that all conservation work is installed with full attention to its overall impact on the environment;

3) To see that all conservation work is properly maintained so that its impact continues to be favorable; and

4) Perhaps the most important of all, to help inform the public accurately about the state of the environment and alternatives for its improvement.

Meaningful individual action and meaningful community planning come from understanding the facts about the condition and the potential of natural resources.

This nation can gain a high standard of living for its citizens without losing those very resources that make this country a good place to live. We have much of the technology; there are growing indications that we have the will and willingness to pay the cost of a high quality environment.

XII. USDA PROGRAM FOR RECLAMATION OF LAND AFFECTED BY MINING

Ward (1976), reporting on the USDA Program for Reclamation of Lands Affected by Mining, discussed the amount of land disturbed by surface mining as related to agricultural production, environmental quality, and rural communities. He reviewed coordination and acceleration of individual efforts of several USDA agencies in reclaiming private and public lands. He stated that

the nation's demand for mineral resources and energy self-sufficiency will result in an increasing amount of land disturbed by mining and mineral processing. An estimated 4.4 million acres of land have already been disturbed by mining. About 1.9 million acres (including 100,000 acres of national forest system lands) remain to be reclaimed. Added to this, nearly 200,000 acres may be disturbed annually during the next decade. By 1990, the rate of disturbance may reach 250,000 acres per year. Some projections indicate that as much as 12–13 million acres may eventually be disturbed. . ..

Surface and subsurface mining of fossil fuels and minerals, and related activities such as coal gasification, oil shale processing, ore reduction and transport of mined commodities create strains on the nation's food and fiber production base, the environment, and rural communitiess. Forest lands of the East, grasslands and croplands of the Midwest, and rangelands of the Northern Great Plains, and elsewhere in the West, are underlain by vast coal resources and other minerals that can be surface mined. The potential for destruction of surface values on these and other rural lands is great.

Without proper planning and reclamation, serious impacts can be expected on agricultural production, environmental quality, and rural communities. These impacts will affect not only mined areas, but will have deleterious effects on surrounding areas and non-mining sectors of the economy.

Since most mineral development takes place in rural America on range, forest, and farm lands, it is the responsibility of the Department of Agriculture to see that the technology and technical assistance is adequate and effective for reclamation of mined lands and that social, environmental, and economic impacts of mining are ameliorated. In recognition of this, there has been established a USDA Program for Reclamation of Lands Affected by Mining. The program is concerned with anticipating and ameliorating the effects of fossil fuel and mineral development on the environment, surface resources, people, and agricultural production. It coordinates and maximizes the impact of USDA agency activities; thus, enabling the Department to exercise federal leadership in reclaiming private and public lands. It also fosters coordination and seeks to avoid duplication with related work of non-USDA agencies.

The Program coordinates and accelerates the individual efforts of several USDA agencies. These agencies are: the Agricultural Stabilization and Conservation Service (ASCS), Agricultural Research Service (ARS), Cooperative State Research Service (CSRS), Economic Research Service (ERS), Extension Service (ES), Forest Service (FS), and the Soil Conservation Service (SCS). They are the ones in USDA that conduct programs directly concerned with the management of soil, water, plants, and animals on rural private and public lands affected by mining.

The Soil Conservation Service implements this policy by working primarily through conservation districts in providing assistance to surface mine operators, individuals, groups, units of government, and others as needed. The SCS maintains needed liaison with other federal, state, and local agencies, units of government, mining companies, and organizations to carry out a coordinated approach in reclamation. The primary goal is to ensure that the disturbing of rural land is done in a reasonable, selective, and orderly manner, without sacrificing our food and fiber production base, quality of living in rural areas, or quality of the environment.

Assistance is provided on soil survey and interpretations for use and management of soils affected by mining. Interdisciplinary assistance is given in four phases of surface mine reclamation work: (i) reclamation planning prior to mining, (ii) applying planned stabilization and conservation treatment during mining operations, (iii) additional reclamation planning and application after mining operations, and (iv) reclamation planning and application assistance on abandoned mined lands. Promising plant materials are tested for mine spoil reclamation.

XIII. BALANCE BETWEEN ECONOMIC DEVELOPMENT AND QUALITY OF THE ENVIRONMENT

There is a continual need for citizen involvement in the planning process to reach a reasonable solution to land use planning. Citizen's role in surface mine reclamation has helped in maintaining a balance between overall energy requirements and the environment. Our rising standards of living and rapidly expanding populations have required large amounts of energy. There is also a necessity for preserving the natural environment essential for quality of living, now and in the future. The conflict between the need for more energy and maintaining or improving the quality of living will depend on the patience, determination, intelligence, and hard work that all concerned are willing to give. Citizen groups can assist in keeping the public well informed so that the environmental considerations, as well as mining and proper reclamation, are well understood.

The real issue is how commodities can be provided without degradation to the environment. Acceptable levels of environmental quality of land, air, and water can be achieved at a price we can afford if all segments of society work together. This involves enacting laws that benefit the public from an environmental and economic standpoint. Multicounty, county, and other local unis of government must help control land use and reclamation through zoning regulations or ordinances. Each citizen needs to accept a fair share of the economic burden and help in changing behavior patterns that contribute to environmental degradation. Mining companies, in many cases, are increasing their efforts in protecting the environment by doing additional research and applying new and better reclamation principles.

Citizens have an important role in land disturbance and reclamation by influencing the behavior of those empowered to make decisions. The most effective results are achieved when industry, citizens, planners, elected officials, and agencies share their experience, knowledge, and goals and create a plan acceptable to all.

LITERATURE CITED

Bailey, D. 1975. Coal—a hard lump to swallow? Rangeman's Journal 2(6):169–170.

Brewster, B. 1975. Can coal befriend the cow? Rangeman's Journal 2(3)72–73.

Bureau of National Affairs, Inc. 1976. Environmental reporter-current developments, section 1, May 7, 7(1):3.

Decker, G. H. 1976. Conservation directory 1976, A list of organizations, agencies, and officials concerned with natural resoure use and management. 21 st ed. Nat. Wildlife Fed., Washington, D.C.

Dickinson, S. 1972. Experiments in propagating plant cover at tailing basins. Min. Congr. J. 58:21–26.

Imhoff, E. A., T. O. Friz, and J. R. LaFevers. 1976. A guide to state programs for the reclamation of surface mined areas. U.S. Geol. Surv. Circ. 731. U.S. Government Printing Office, Washington, D.C.

Lusk, B. E. 1976. The coal industry is being regulated out of business. West Virginia Surface Mining and Reclamation Association's Green Lands Quarterly, Winter, 1976, Charleston, W. Va. p. 4.

National Association of Conservation Districts. 1975. Policy Positions 1975. Nat. Assoc. of Conserv. Dist. Service Dep., League City, Tex.

Pickels, G. 1970. Realizing the recreation potential of sand and gravel sites. Proj. no. 5, Nat. Sand and Gravel Assoc., Univ. of Illinois, Urbana.

Richardson, J. K. 1975. This is copper country (Facts about Arizona's copper mining industry). Arizona Mining Assoc., Phoenix, Ariz.

Sierra Club. 1973. The strip mining of Ameica. Sierra Club, San Francisco, Calif.

Soil Conservation Society of America. 1968. Surface mining problem or opportunity. Soil Conserv. Soc. of Am., Ankeny, Iowa.

U.S. Department of Interior. 1967. A special report to the nation. Surface mining and our environment. U.S. Government Printing Office, Washington, D.C.

Ward, D. J. 1976. USDA Research and Development for Reclamation of Lands Affected by Mining. Report no. 600/7-76.002. p. 182–185. In Proc. of Nat. Conf. on Health, Environmental Effects, and Control Technology of Energy Use. Off. of Energy, Miner. and Ind., Off. of Res. and Dev., USEPA 9–11 Feb. 1976, Sheraton Park Hotel, Washington, D.C.

Copyright © 1978 ASA-CSSA-SSSA
677 South Segoe Road, Madison, WI 53711 USA
Reclamation of Drastically Disturbed Lands

Chapter 6

History of Legislation for Different States

KENES C. BOWLING

*Interstate Mining Compact Comission,
Lexington, Kentucky*

I. INTRODUCTION

Coal was referred to by Greek scholars three centuried before the birth of Christ. It is a matter of record that its use was known in England as early as 852 A.D. Mines were in operation in England 300 years before our continent was discovered. The first operating mine on this continent was opened in 1750 near Richmond, Virginia, and the coal industry has been growing ever since. Initially, much of the mining was by the stripping method. It was on a small scale and involved working in from the surface outcrop of the coal seams by using the pick and shovel and later the horse and scraper. From this humble beginning the surface mining of minerals has emerged into a sophisticated method, employing shovels and drag lines that will move up to 200 cubic yards of overburden in one bite, trucks that may haul up to 180 tons, and single mines that may produce 5 to 7 million tons of coal per year.

Controversy between citizens concerned with the environmental damage that surface mining was doing and the coal industry developed after World War II. Science and technology had introduced larger and more efficient machinery for biting into the mountain slopes of Appalachia in order to meet the increased consumer demand for low cost electricity. Many coal seams neglected for years because of their poor quality or because they were too thin to deep mine were suddenly in demand. In the mountains of Appalachia hundreds of miles of outcrop coal, the seam having been deep-mined many years ago, now become profitable sources for strip-mining operations. The number of acres disturbed by strip mining began to grow. This surface mining was unregulated and left a legacy of thousands of acres of abandoned and useless land and hundreds of miles of streams contaminated by mine drainage and silt. It also brought a cry of anguish from citizens groups who demanded that all forms of strip mining be abolished. This cry was duly noted by governors and legislatures in many states who then began the long road toward enacting laws for controlling the ravages of surface mining and the elimination of abandoned mine land.

The first strip mine legislation was adopted in West Virginia in 1939, then Indiana in 1941, Illinois in 1943, Pennsylvania in 1945, and Ohio in 1947. Let's take four states and trace how their law began and how it has been strengthened through the years as experience was gained through trial and error, not only in reclaiming a mining area but also in new mining techniques. We will use West Virginia not because they were first but because of the tremendous difficulties they have had to overcome due to multi-seam contour stripping on steep slopes; Kentucky because it is unique in that two sets of regulations apply, one for Western Kentucky where area mining is practiced and one for Eastern Kentucky where contour stripping is practiced; Pennsylvania because their law is more or less a model and because of their unique anthracite coal field; and Indiana because theirs is area stripping only.

II. LEGISLATION IN WEST VIRGINIA

In 1939, 37 years ago, the first surface mining control legislation in the United States was enacted in West Virginia. Although limited in scope, it recognized the industry and the disruptive environmental effects associated with its operations. The State Department of Mines was designated as the sole regulatory authority for this act.

The 1939 legislation was amended and notably broadened in 1945, 1947, and 1959. The Department of Mines remained as the only agency concerned with its enforcement. The amendments and additions in 1961, however, mandated the sharing of these regulatory responsibilities. The statutory obligation to insure that surface-mined areas were reclaimed in accordance with the legislative provisions was placed with the Department of Natural Resources and subsequently the Reclamation, Land and Survey Division.

The basic context of surface mining control legislation in West Virginia has changed little over the years since 1939. What has changed considerably, however, is the interpretation of the law and the resultant enforcement program as evidenced by the more complete and technical requirements and regulations. These changes can be traced through the incremental development of the Reclamation Division as follows:

In 1939, the first surface mining control legislation in the nation was adopted, the Department of Mines was the sole regulatory authority, and bonds were set at $150 per acre of coal to be mined—not acreage disturbed.

In 1945, a registration fee of $50 was established, bonding was increased to $500 with a minimum of $1,000, authority was provided for the revocation of permits and forfeiture of bonds, information to be shown in the application was described, and the method of approving the regrading of a mining site was initiated.

In 1947, a special fund was created for deposit of registration fees and forfeited bonds to be used for administration and certain reclamation work.

In 1959, surface mining was defined but excluded augering as a method. The registration fee for surface mining was increased to $100, and was to be deposited in General Revenue not Special Revenue Account. Provisions were made for annual renewal of mining permits at a rate of $50 per year, also to be deposited in General Revenue Account. A bond forfeiture fund was established to be used only for reclaiming affected areas and provisions were made for the release of bonds upon execution of contract with the appropriate Soil Conservation District. Five surface mining divisions were created within the State to be staffed by one inspector each and monitored by a state supervisor. Each inspector was to be appointed and required to serve a probation period of 1 year.

In 1961, reclamation responsibilities were transferred to the newly created Department of Natural Resources, a Division of Reclamation was created, and a bond to be deposited with the Director, Department of Natural Resources was required.

In 1963, the Division of Reclamation was given increased responsibility for reclamation aspects of surface mining. A Special Reclamation Fund and Programs was created and was to be industry-financed at a rate of $30 per proposed disturbed area. A Reclamation Board of Review was created, and the definition of surface mining was expanded to include augering. A requirement was established for proof of bond deposit ($150/acre—minimum of $1,000) to be submitted to the Director, Department of Natural Resources, and that the bond be posted on the entire disturbed area (including access, haulageways, etc.) rather than acres of coal to be removed.

In 1965, the mining of sandstone, sand, and limestone and Federal/State Highway projects were excluded from the provisions of the law.

In 1967, the complete regulatory authority for all surface mining was transferred from the Department of Mines to the Division of Reclamation. A 30-day frequency for inspections of each operation throughout the State was established. A Reclamation Commission was created and the promulgation of Rules and Regulations was required. A prospecting permit was created including application procedure, and a bonding rate ($150/acre). A minimum requirement for insurance coverage of any company making application for mining was established. The bonding rate was increased to a margin of between $100–$500, with the speciic amount determined by the Director (it was set at $300). The mine inspector was given authority to stop any operation in violation and authorization was given for providing triple damages protection to persons whose property might be damaged by surface mining operations.

In 1971, the bonding margin was increased to $600–$1,000. At first the bond was set at $750 per acre but was recently increased to $1,000. The Special Reclamation tax was increased from $30 to $60 per acre. It was required that all drainage be controlled in approved structures and installed prior to commencement of activity. Provisions were made for control of all blasting activity. It was required that all highwalls be eliminated if original slopes were less than 30%. If original slopes were greater than 30% they must be reduced to a maximum of 30 feet. Provisions were made for public notification, adjacent landowner notification, and the filing of protests for any application. Inspection frequency was increased to every 15 days. It was required that grasses must accompany the planting of trees on completed areas. The provision that a bond was to be released if contract was executed with Soil Conservation District was removed. The registration fee was increased to $500 and annual renewal increased to $100. A provision was made for expansion of surface mining to 22 counties of the State, designated as *moratorium counties.*

III. LEGISLATION IN KENTUCKY

Kentucky's first strip mine law was passed in 1954 and, from a reclamation standpoint, little was accomplished. Main requirements of the law were to cover the face of the coal seam and grade spoil banks where practicable. Under this law thousands of acres of orphan lands were created.

When Governor Combs took office in 1960, he found that only a handfull of operators in eastern Kentucky had bothered to obtain a permit from the State as required by law. Administrative hearings and litigation gradually resulted in all operators being placed under the permit and bonding procedures. Amendments to the law in 1962 and 1964 closed certain loopholes in enforcement, required additional material to be placed over the coal seam and auger holes, and added certain grading requirements. So, where the 1954 law required grading spoil banks where practicable, the 1964 amendment now required the overburden to be graded to a rolling topography as defined by regulation. The resulting regulation required grading of the disturbed area so that it could be traversed by farm machinery.

Anyone familiar with strip mining will realize that these regulations on the grading of the stripped area would only be applicable to area-type mining as practiced in western Kentucky. So, in 1965 Governor Edward T. Breathitt instructed the Division of Reclamation to draft new regulations that would control, for the first time, the method of operation on steep mountain slopes. Under the direction of the Director of Reclamation, Elmore Grim, regulations were drafted and public hearings held. In essence, the regulations were designed to limit the cut into the mountainside in relation to the steepness of slope, so that the weight of the resulting overburden placed over and down the slope would not tend to create landslides. The regulations provided that on slopes above 33°, no overburden could be placed downhill below the operation. On slopes between 30 and 33°, the maximum bench width allowed was set at 45 feet. As the slope decreased in steepness, the bench width was allowed to become progressively larger. The 1965 regulations also established for the first time specific vegetative planting requirements designed to achieve quick cover and soil stabilization.

A dramatic change was created by the 1966 law which required grading in relation to area mining. This new legislation called for complete backfilling of the disturbed area to the approximate original contour of the land, with no depressions to accumulate water.

While the new law restricted the amount of spoil that could be pushed down the hill, it was silent on how much spoil could be stacked on the bench. This stacking resulted in added weight on the bench and created the possibility of as many mudslides as did the older method of operations. Therefore, in 1967 the law was amended to provide that on slopes 27° and above, measured downhill from the coal seam where the spoil would be placed, only auger mining could be practiced. The method of strip mining whereby all the overburden was uncovered before picking up the exposed coal was thereby restricted to original slopes of 26° or less. Moreover, on all operations, no spoil could be stacked on the outer one-third portion of the fill bench.

Kentuck's primary concern, when the 1966 law was passed and subsequent regulations adopted, was stabilizing the outslopes resulting from contour stripping. Based on the experience gained from administering the 1966 law, Kentucky in recent years has upgraded their regulations to include water quality control, and the building and reclaiming of haul roads. Regulations, also, have been promulgated to control clay, sand, and gravel operations. Soon their law will cover the surface effects of underground mining. Engineering criteria for head-of-the-hollow fills is being studied.

Kentucky, as do other states, continues to review and upgrade its regulations as the need arises. To assist in this, Governor Julian Carroll has set aside $47,000 each year of the 1976–77 biennium to staff an Environmental Quality Commission. The Commission is made up of seven members, appointed by the Governor to act in an advisory capacity to the Department of Natural Resources and Environmental Protection and to the Governor on matters pertaining to the environment.

IV. LEGISLATION IN PENNSYLVANIA

Pennsylvania is unique in that it has two distinct coal fields, the anthracite or hard coal, and the bituminous, or soft coal. In the first stages of regulation each was under a separate law.

The first Surface Mining Law was enacted in 1941. This law gave the Department of Environmental Resources jurisdiction over coal stripping operations and enabled them to promulgate regulations to protect the health and safety of employees. It was not an environmental protection law.

In 1945, Act 418, which later became the basis for the present law, was adopted. It applied to bituminous coal open pit mines only and required the backfilling of highwalls to cover exposed coal seams from a point 3 feet above the top of the coal seam to the bottom of the pit at an angle not to exceed 45°. The operator was required to level and round the tops of spoil banks to permit planting with trees, shrubs, or grasses. A $200 per acre bond was required and the operator could propose planting of other mined lands in lieu of planting the particular land covered by the bond. Penalties were minimal, but the Act was a beginning toward control of surface coal mines.

In 1947, the first Anthracite Strip Mining law was passed. This law required backfilling of pits within a distance of 75 feet from the centerline of any public road and 200 feed from any dwelling or building. Exposed coal seams had to be covered with 5 feet of earth to provide proper drainage from abandoned pits to prevent breakouts that cause flooding and public safety hazards. The law required leveling and rounding of the tops of spoil banks, and provided for fees to be paid by the operator for planting of the spoil banks. Bonds of $200/acre were required. In 1949 the Act was amended to raise the bonding requirement to $300/acre.

In 1951, the Anthracite Law was amended to require backfilling to distances of 15 feet from the edge of the right of way of any public road. In 1953 language was added to make it clear that the 5-foot cover required over exposed coal seams need not be leveled or planted, indicating that the Department had overstepped its authority and had attempted to get some unauthorized reclamation work accomplished.

In 1956 the Anthracite Law was amended to require the submission of maps each year outlining the areas affected and rehabilitated. It required certification by a professional engineer of completion reports to be filed within 6 months of mine closure. The bituminous law was also amended in 1956 to raise the bonding requirements to $300/acre, to require the submission of certain maps with permit applications, to require monthly reports on each operation, to require annual maps of the lands affected and rehabilitated, and more important, to require backfilling of strip mines for a distance of 75 feet from the right of way of public roads and 200 feet from dwellings and buildings.

In 1959, the penalty section of the bituminous law was amended to require a minimum fine of $500 for failure of any operator to register with the Department.

In 1961, the anthracite bonds were raised to $500/acre, the distance for backfilling was extended to 75 feet from the right of way of public roads and 225 feet from buildings, and backfilling of pits that are not more than 75 feet deep and are within 700 feet of a road or building was required. The backfilling requirement specified that a 45° angle be established from the top of the highwall to the floor of the pit. The 5-foot cover requirement over the top of the exposed coal seam continued in effect for pits located more than 700 feet from roads or building. The penalty section for failure to register as a strip miner was made identical to that contained in the bituminous law.

In 1961, the bituminous bonds were raised to $400 per acre and the cover required over exposed seams was raised to 5 feet. Land that was previously used for growing crops or is located within 750 feet from a group of five homes or public buildings was required to be backfilled from the top of the highwall at an angle not to exceed 45°. Cuts located more than 750 feet from buildings were required to be backfilled at an angle not to exceed 70°.

In 1963, an important enforcement tool was added to the bituminous law. Citizens were given the duty to report violations of the law to the Department and were given the right to bring mandamus actions in the county courts to compel the Department to enforce the law. In the same year the Department was authorized to license bituminous surface operators, to require permits for individual operations, and most important, to require contour or terrace backfilling of all mines. A land reclamation board was established to review individual proposals for alternate types of restoration such as water impoundments. This was the first law with teeth in it.

The Anthracite Law was changed in 1963 to require the annual licensing of operators, to allow the Department to refuse to license an operator if he is in violation of any of the provisions of the act, to require a permit for each individual operation, to require a timetable for backfilling, and to increase bonds of $500 to $1,000/acre. Also, the 1963 law required complete backfilling of all pits less than 100 feet deep, and required backfilling of all pits for a distance of 100 feet from a highway right of way and for 250 feet from any buildings. Pits in excess of 100 feet deep were required to be backfilled as determined by a newly formed land restoration board. Pits were to be backfilled whenever practical as mining progressed. All funds collected as fees, fines, or forfeited bonds were to be used by the Department in reclaiming lands affected by open pit mining.

In 1968, the bituminous law was amended to clarify a problem that had arisen in the mining of clay. Many of t he commercially important clays in Pennsylvania exist in the bituminous coal fields. Some operators attempted to circumvent the law by claiming that they were really mining clay and that the removal of coal was only incidential to the clay mining. The 1968 amendment made it clear that the law applied even if the removal of coal was only incidential to any other purpose. The construction of public highways came under regulation if it was necessary to excavate coal in making highway cuts.

Additional legislation in 1968 required that an operator must complete backfilling on a bituminous strip mine before the necessary backfilling equipment could be removed from the site. A 1970 law allowed the operator to plant a combination of trees, grasses, and shrubs in revegetating backfilled lands. During the years of development of this legislation, amendments were also made to Pennsylvania's Clean Streams Law fixing the responsibility of mine operators for controlling drainage during and after mining.

On 30 November 1971, the Governor signed into law the Surface Mining Conservation and Reclamation Act of 1971. This was the culmination of three and one-half years of public and legislative debate and hearings, and Pennsylvania became one of the first states to regulate all forms of open-pit mining. This Act brought the anthracite and the bituminous coal fields under the same law.

The law defines surface mining to include strip, drift, and auger mining, dredging, quarrying, and leaching from the earth or from waste or stock piles or banks. Underground mining as well as noncommercial extraction of noncoal minerals is exempt from regulation as is the removal of fill from highway burrow pits and the mining of noncoal minerals in amounts that do not exceed 500 tons/acre per year. The latter exemption would amount to the removal of an average of 1.6 inches of limestone per year or 2.5 inches of sand.

The law provides for annual licensing of operators and prohibits the Department from licensing an applicant who has failed to comply with any of the provisions of the Act. An applicant cannot be licensed if any officer, director, or principal owner is or has been associated with another operator who is in violation of any of the provisions of the act.

An operator must obtain a permit for each operation before mining begins. He must submit maps which show the location of the operation, streams, roads, railroads, and utility lines. He must report buildings located within 1000 feet of the affected area along with the names of the owners and the present use of the structures, names of landowners, and the results of test borings. He must also file a reclamation plan which includes the best use to which the land was put prior to mining, the proposed use following reclamation, the manner in which topsoil and subsoil will be conserved and replaced, the manner of compaction of the backfill, a planting program and methods to prevent erosion and siltation, and a detailed timetable for reclamation. Contour or terrace backfilling is required for coal mines. Alternatives to contour or terrace backfill may be proposed for noncoal mines and may include water impoundments, water-oriented real estate developments, recreational areas, industrial sites, or solid waste disposal sites. For noncoal mines, the alternatives to contour or terrace backfilling must not pose a threat to water quality, must be practical and reasonable, must be timely, and must not violate Federal, state, or local laws. The operator must also submit the written consent of the landowners to enter upon the lands within a period of 5 years after the operation is completed for purposes of reclamation, planting, and inspection or construction of treatment facilities to prevent stream pollution.

The operator must also file a certificate of insurance for personal injury and property damage in an amount of at least $100,000. A bond is required in an amount to be determined by the Department. The minimum bond is $5,000 and must be for an amount based on the total estimated cost to the Commonwealth of completing the approved reclamation plan. The period of liability under the bond is for the life of the operation and 5 years thereafter.

If a noncoal operator is removing at least 4 times as much mineral as overburden, and will operate for at least 10 years, he may elect to pay 95% of the bond premium cost to the Commonwealth's reclamation fund in lieu of bonding. This does not excuse the operator from complying with his approved reclamation plan but recognizes the long-term nature of some noncoal operations.

The Act also requires the submission of various operating reports and maps. It authorizes the establishment of rules and regulations to protect the health and safety of persons engaged in surface mining and for the protection of the general public. Conditions that cause a risk of fire, landslide, subsidence, cave-in, or other unsafe, dangerous, or hazardous situations, including unguarded or unfenced open pits, highwalls, spoil banks, water pools, abandoned structures, or equipment or tools, are prohibited.

The Act established a Surface Mining Conservation and Reclamation Fund to receive all monies collected in fees and forfeitures of bonds. The fund is to be used by the Department for the purposes of foresting or re-claiming lands affected by surface mining. The Act also preempts all local ordinances purporting to regulate surface mining, except zoning ordinances.

V. LEGISLATION IN INDIANA

In Indiana, the topography is relatively flat and area mining is used exclusively for the extraction of coal. When the Indiana law was passed the main concern was the reclamation of surface-mined lands to the high-est potential land use.

Surface mine reclamation started in Indiana in 1918 when one mine owner reclaimed the area he surface mined by planting fruit trees. Then in 1926, the members of the newly formed Indiana Coal Association agreed that each mine owner in the association would plant 5 acres for each mining shovel or dragline used in their operation. This type of vol-untary reclamation continued until legislation was passed in 1941. The State of Indiana was second in the nation to pass legislation requiring rec-lamation of these areas. The 1941 Surface Mining Act was concerned pri-marily with revegetation of the areas surface mined and did not require grading.

In 1967, new legislation was enacted that addressed itself to the grading and establishment of vegetation on surface-mined areas. At that time, there were only five other states that had a surface mine reclama-tion law. The 1967 Surface Mine Act required extensive grading of all areas affected by surface mining of coal, clay, and shale. It was the first piece of legislation in the nation that required grading of all areas to a maximum slope of 33.33% or less depending upon land-use capability.

Under the present legislation, operators who propose the surface mining of coal, clay, or shale in the State of Indiana must submit an ap-plication for a permit 60 days before the operation is to start. The applica-tion must be accompanied by fees of $50.00, plus $30.00 for each acre proposed, and bond in the amount of $600/ace or a minimum of $5,000. A reclamation plan is also required with the application. The method of operation, grading work, and procedures to establish vegetation are out-lined within this plan.

The State of Indiana applies various land-use alternatives for re-claiming areas that are surface mined for coal, clay, and shale when considering the application for surface-mining permits. Permits are issued for forests, rangeland, pasture, hay production, row crops, housing devel-opment, building sites, sanitary landfills, recreational areas, wildlife de-velopment, etc.

The land-use selected for reclaiming surface-mined land is de-termined through consideration of many factors to achieve the highest po-tential land-use capability of the area after reclamation. Primary con-sideration is given to the material above the mineral that will be mined and its capability to support vegetation after it has been disturbed. The land use before mining, lease—owner agreements, land use of surround-

Table 1—Use of reclaimed lands as designated by permits issued in Indiana in 1974

	% maximum slope	Acres proposed	% of total
Forest	33⅓	191	4
Range	33⅓	2,475	47
Pasture, hay	25	973	19
Row crop—others	8	1,564	30
Total		5,203	100

ing areas, and operation location are also some of the factors that assist in deciding the reclamation program for each application considered.

The present regulations, effective on 1 January 1968, mandates that no slope shall exceed a maximum of 33.33% for forest and range land uses. The pasture land uses and hay and row crop land uses must not exceed a maximum slope of 25 to 8%, respectively. The laws that were passed in Indiana to reclaim lands affected by surface mining have been successful in obtaining the highest potential land use of the area.

Table 1 illustrates the selection of land use being applied to reclaimed surface-mined land in Indiana. These figures were taken from the permits issued during the calendar year of 1974. If the land uses illustrated in Table 1 were classified as agrarian and nonagrarian, then 96% will be returned to agricultural uses such as beef grazing, hay production, and cereal crops.

Frequently, an area will be surface mined during the early part of any given year. Grading then takes place throughout the summer and early fall. Then winter wheat will be planted for a cover crop of grasses and legumes or left for a mature wheat crop to be harvested. Consequently, the cycle from mining to the harvest of a crop can take place within one growing season or over a 12- to 15-month period.

VI. CONCLUSIONS ON LEGISLATION

What we have attempted to show with these four states is the evolution of surface mining legislation over the past 35 years. You can understand that each state, due to its topography and climatic conditions, had different priorities which were initially emphasized. Pennsylvania, because of the acid conditions created by both underground and surface mining, attacked the acid mine drainage problem. Kentucky placed its emphasis on overburden stabilization and sediment control. Indiana wanted a higher use for the land after mining was completed. As the states gained experience through administering their law, they began to broaden their environmental control.

In 1939, one state (West Virginia) had a surface mine law; today 38 states have environmental controls on the extraction of minerals by surface mining. Table 2, a matrix showing the status and general content of surface-mined area reclamation, graphically shows what the states have been doing. The matrix was compiled by Ed Imhoff, of the U.S. Geological Survey.[1] It represents many hours of work and is the best overall comparison of state standards available.

Are there any problems left that the states must face? Of course there are! How to establish permanent vegetative cover on areas where rainfall may be less than 6 inches per year is a severe problem. Most state surface mine laws require acid-bearing material to be covered with nonacid material; where should this acid material be placed in order to assure there will be no degradation to the ground water? Sound engineering principles have to be developed for "head-of-the-hollow fills" that are economical to build and at the same time would assure permanent stability. New mining techniques that will lessen the temporary environmental damage to the land, air, and water need to be developed. Better engineering criteria for sediment control facilities and haulage roads is needed. And more emphasis has to be placed on the development of specialized reclamation equipment that will assist in revegetating a mined area, and that will help control sediment and water quality. These are just a few things that come to mind, but let's concentrate on the one problem that seems to disturb the general public more than any other, that is, land disturbed by prelaw mining or what is commonly known as *orphan mine land*.

VII. ORPHAN MINE LAND

In 1967, the Department of the Interior conducted a survey which resulted in a published paper entitled "Study of Surface Mining and our Environment."[2] They estimated there were two million acres of land that had no reclamation or were inadequately reclaimed and that it would require an expenditure of $750 million to do just the basic reclamation on these lands. Due to inflation, the cost figure today would far exceed the 1967 cost.

In the face of such a tremendous expenditure of monies, what can the states do to rehabilitate orphaned lands? Well, the states are doing something. Some of them, such as Kentucky and Pennsylvania, have established a revolving fund to reclaim selected areas. This acreage is sold and the money redeposited in the revolving fund to reclaim other areas. Other states including Ohio and Maryland place permit or acreage fees or a minerals tax into a special orphan land reclamation fund. The Tennessee Valley Authority has initiated a 5-year, 22.8 million-dollar plan to do basic reclamation on 87,000 acres of orphan strip mines and coal haul roads in four states, Kentucky, Tennessee, Virginia, and Alabama. Congress approved $2.9 million to get the program started and former President Ford in his budget requested the same amount for fiscal year 1977.

Oklahoma, under the guidance of Ward Padgett, the State Mine Inspector, is embarking on a unique plan for the reclamation of orphan strip

---

[1] E. A. Imhoff, T. O. Friz, and J. R. LaFevers. 1976. A guide to state programs for the reclamation of surface mined areas. U.S. Geol. Surv. Circ. 731. U.S. Government Printing Office, Washington, D.C.

[2] U.S. Department of Interior. 1967. Surface mining and our environment. USDI, Washington, D.C.

Table 2—Matrix of information on state surface mined-area reclamation programs, December 1975

	1	2	3	4	5	6	7	8	9	10	11
						State law					Reclamation—Main act
	Stage of program development								Rules vary by mining method	Control water flow and quality	Reclamation—Main act
	State	Act(s)	Rules and regulations	Technical guidelines	Title of Act(s)	Administering agency(ies)	Mineral or commodity covered	Rules vary by mining method	Control water flow and quality	Conserve and replace topsoil	Backfill and grade
ALABAMA	---------------	X	X	--------	Alabama Surface Mining Act of 1969 and Alabama Surface Mining Reclamation Act of 1975.	Department of Industrial Relations and Surface Mining Reclamation Commission.	All minerals *except* limestone, marble, and dolomite (coal covered by 1975 Act).	-------	X	X	Strike-off top of spoil ridges to width ≧15 ft and cover coal seam with spoil depth ≧10
ALASKA	---------------NOTE: On State lands, reclamation requirements are established by the State of Alaska—on a case-by-case basis—as part of the te a condition of leasing).										
ARIZONA	--------------- NOTE: The State of Arizona applies standard reclamation requirements to State Lands as a condition of mineral leases. Arizona trols (e.g., zoning) and activity permits (e. g., minerals proceeding) to encourage reclamation.										
ARKANSAS	---------------	X	X	X	The Arkansas Open Cut Land Reclamation Act of 1971.	Department of Pollution Control and Ecology.	All minerals __	-------	X	Standards vary according to original natural conditions.	All grades w be ≦33%; blade and grade to ap proximate original su face condi- tions.
CALIFORNIA	---------------	X	--------	--------	Surface Mining and Reclamation Act of 1975.	Department of Conservation (Policy); local governments (Permits and Plans).	All minerals __	-------	X	-----------	-----------
COLORADO	---------------	X	--------	--------	Colorado Open Mining Land Reclamation Act of 1973.	Department of Natural Resources.	Coal, sand, gravel, quarry aggregate, and construction lime- stone.	-------	X	-----------	Strike-off top spoil ridge to width o ≧15 ft. Achieve le or undulat skyline.
CONNECTICUT	----------					NOTE: Local governmental land-use controls and pe					
DELAWARE	-------------					NOTE: Local governmental land-use controls and pe					
FLORIDA	---------------	X	X	--------	Chapter 211, II Florida Statutes.	Department of Natural Resources.	All minerals __	-------	X (Lakes shall support fish or recrea- tion).	X	All grades w be ≦25%. Blend peak ridges, and leys. Deve uninterrup drainage.
GEORGIA	---------------	X	X	X	Georgia Surface Mining Act of 1968, as amended.	Department of Natural Resources.	All minerals __	-------	X	X	Blend peaks, ridges, and valleys int a rolling to graphy sui able for pl growth.
HAWAII	---------------	X	--------	--------	Chap. 181, Sub- title 3, Hawaii Statutes.	Department of Land and Natural Resources.	All minerals, *except* sand, rock, gravel, and construc- tion mate- rials..	-------	X	If necessary for end-use objective.	Strike-off pe and ridges of s and fill de- pressions.
IDAHO	-----------------			--------	The Idaho Sur- face Mining Act.	Department of Lands.	All minerals __	-------	X	Replace overburden to extent reasonably available.	Strike-off rid to width c ≧10 ft an peaks to w of ≧15 ft.
ILLINOIS	---------------	X	X	X	Surface-Mined Land Conser- vation and Reclamation Act.	Department of Mines and Minerals.	All minerals __	-------	X	*Row crops,* 18 in.; *Other uses,* replace as prac- ticable.	Varies by planned u i.e.: origin grade for r crops; ≦3 forest and wildlife; ≦50% hay and pastur

Table 2—Continued.

12	13	14	15	16	17	18	19	20	21	22	23	24
red and standards set				*Requirements for land-use planning*				*Special Provisions*				
reduce chwall pitwall	Bury or neutralize toxic wastes	Revegetate for beneficial use	Other rules or remarks	Resources information required	Alternative uses will be considered	End use will be declared	Role of local public planning	Minerals protected from nonmining development	Exclusion of areas from consideration for mining	Long-range or regional mine planning	Substitute lands allowed	Financial or economic analyses required
ate coal he high- ll, ex- t at al cut.	With 2 ft of earth or permanent water body.	Standards for forests, grasses, and legumes. soil additives may be required.	Construct two access roads per each mile of coal mine highwall. Depth of lakes ≦6 ft.	Hydrology, and land use.	X	X	1975 Act is "... to preempt local ... regulation of coal surface mining ..."	—	—	—	—	—

...ases to mine operators. Most of the mineral deposits of Alaska lie on State or Federal lands (where reclamation requirements are

...ins Federal lands where reclamation requirements are a condition of mineral leases. Some local units of government use land-use con-

12	13	14	15	16	17	18	19	20	21	22	23	24
X	With 3 ft of earth or permanent water body.	X	Construct fire lanes or access in areas of reforestation.	Soils _____	Any "productive use."	X	—	—	—	—	X	—
—	—	—	—	Climate, geology, land use, minerals, population, topography, and water resources.	Operator must declare "potential uses."	X	Act on permits and reclamation plans and establish mining policy in general plans.	State may designate areas reserved for mining.	—	—	—	—
—	—	X (Exceptions for unsuitable areas.)	—	Geology, land use, minerals, topography, and water resources.	—	X	Review for conformity with local land-use controls.	—	—	—	X	—

...ities may be applicable to mining and reclamation.

...ities may be applicable to mining and reclamation.

12	13	14	15	16	17	18	19	20	21	22	23	24
—	—	Plant coverage >80%; bare areas ≦¼ acre.	Established lakes must be at least 3 acres in size and 6 ft in depth.	Land use, minerals, soils, topography (USGS), and water resources.	Consider "landowner's desires."	X	—	Must certify excavations intended for property improvement.	—	—	X	—
X ept in ld ck.)	With 2 ft of soil supporting vegetation.	Attain high quality permanent cover.	—	Land use minerals, population, topography, and water resouces.	—	X	—	—	—	Rules provide for long-range planning updated by annual permits.	X	—
—	—	Quick cover grass crop, followed by reforestation, or conversion to farming.	Carrying capacity of pasture lands will be ≧1 cow per 3 acres.	Soils, topography, and water resources.	Land uses comparable, at least, to premining conditions.	—	—	—	—	—	—	—
—	—	Revegetate to compare to premining conditions.	—	Minerals and water resources.	—	—	—	—	—	—	—	—
rade of 0%.	With 4 ft of water or suitable material.	Replant row crops if soils suitable. Detailed standards for other uses.	Separate permits required for refuse disposal (landfill).	Geology, land use, minerals, soils, topography (USGS), vegetation, water resources, and wildlife.	Agency will "encourage" consideration of multiple land use.	X	County board may recommend land use, and may request hearings.	—	—	Rules "encourage" long-range reclamation planning.	X	Land values, tax base, state & regional economy, employment & effect of plan.

(continued on next page)

Table 2—Continued.

1	2	3	4	5	6	7	8	9	10	11
Stage of program development				State law					Reclamation—Main ac	
State	Act(s)	Rules and regulations	Technical guidelines	Title of Act(s)	Administering agency(ies)	Mineral or commodity covered	Rules vary by mining method	Control water flow and quality	Conserve and replace topsoil	Backfill grade
INDIANA	X	X	X	Chap. 344, Acts of 1967, Indiana Statutes.	Department of Natural Resources.	Coal, clay, and shale.	-------	X	----------	Grades: row crops ≤... pasture a... hay ≤25... forest an... range ≤3... (slope le... limited).
IOWA	X	X	X	An Act Relating to Surface Mining, as amended.	Department of Soil Conservation.	All minerals	--------		X	In coal mine reclamation, strata more suitable than top soil may be used.	Grade spoil ≤25%, except whe... original was steep then, ble... with adja... land.
KANSAS	X	X	X	Mined-Land Conservation and Reclamation Act.	State Corporation Commission.	Coal	--------		X	As necessary to provide plant growth material.	Rolling topography tra... versable planned... Grade ≤2... (slope lengths limited).
KENTUCKY	X	X	X	Chapter 350, Kentucky Revised Statutes.	Department for Natural Resources and Environmental Protection.	All minerals	For contour mining, limits are placed on cut benches and slope.	Detailed standards.	----------	Approximat... original c... tour. Gr... bench tal... to ≤10%
LOUISIANA								NOTE: Local governmental land-use controls and p...		
MAINE	X	X	--------	(1) Mining and Rehabilitation of Land Act, and (2) Site Location of Development Act.	Department of Environmental Protection.	All minerals (sand and gravel are covered only by Site Act).	--------	X	X	X
MARYLAND	X	X	X	Maryland Strip Mining Law.	Energy and Coastal zone Administration.	Coal	Backfilling rules vary by area, terracing, or block-cut methods of mining.	X (pH range 6.8 to 8.5.)	X	Area: approxi mate contour. Terracing: grad... ≤9% and outer slope grade to ≤70%.
MASSACHUSETTS								NOTE: Local governmental land-use controls and p...		
MICHIGAN	X	--------	--------	Mine Reclamation Act of 1970, as amended.	Department of Natural Resources.	All minerals except clay, gravel, marl, peat, or sand.	--------	--------	--------	--------
MINNESOTA	X	--------	--------	Mineland Reclamation Act of 1971, as amended.	Department of Natural Resources.	Metallic minerals.	--------	--------	--------	--------
MISSISSIPPI								NOTE: Local governmental land-use controls and p...		
MISSOURI	X	--------	--------	(1) Reclamation of Mining Lands and (2) The Land Reclamation Act.	Department of Natural Resources.	Act (1) coal and barite; Act (2) clay, limestone, sand, and gravel.	--------	--------	--------	Act (1) tra... versable ar... farming; (2) trave... able for i... tended us... and strike... top of spo... ridges to width of ≥20 ft (forest an... pasture).

Table 2—Continued.

12	13	14	15	16	17	18	19	20	21	22	23	24
ed and standards set								Minerals protected from nonmining development	Exclusion of areas from consideration for mining	Long-range mine planning	Substitute lands allowed	Financial or economic analyses required
				Requirements for land-use planning				Special Provisions				
duce hwall itwall	Bury or neutralize toxic wastes	Revegetate for beneficial use	Other rules or remarks	Resources Information required	Alternative uses will be considered	End use will be declared	Role of local public planning					
ade of %% or ate lake it.	With 2 ft of soil, overburden, or water.	X	Other standards pertain to lakes, soil texture, and waste disposal.	Geology, land use, minerals, soils, topography, and water resources.	X	X	----------	--------	--------	--------	----------Prohibited.	----------
ade ≤33%.	With 2 ft of spoil.	X (Detailed guidelines available.)	----------	Mineral, soils, and water resources.	----------	--------	----------	--------	--------	--------	--------	----------
ade of % unsup ed, as lake.	With 2 ft of spoil or permanent water body.	X	Other standards pertain to removal of boulders and formation of lakes.	Geology, soils, topobraphy (USGS), and water resources.	----------	X	----------	--------	--------	Rules allow 5-yr plans for "contiguous" mined areas.	X	----------
min- face 5"; r min- back- and r coal ft.	With 4 ft of overburden.	X (Detailed guidelines available, e.g., time of planting.)	Other, detailed standards on: access roads, lakes, and sediment control.	Soils, topography (USGS), and water resources.	----------	--------	State permits must comply with local zoning laws.	--------	--------	Rules allow the development of "area plans" for mined areas.	--------	----------
ies may be applicable to mining and reclamation.												
--------	----------	X	----------	Minerals, soils, topography (USGS), vegetation, and water resources.	----------	----------	----------	--------	--------	----------	--------	----------
nate hwall back- and	With 2 ft of overburden.	Quick cover grass crop, followed by vegetation for end uses.	Specific survival standards for the vegetation established through reclamation.	Minerals, soils, topography (USGS), and water resources.	X	X (Attention to land-owner's desires.)	Agency takes cognizance of county planning, zoning, and grading permits.	----------	Land sloping more than 20° (any 200 ft cross-section) is excluded.	"Encouraged." Annual permit renewals provide update.	Pro hibited.	----------
ies may be applicable to mining and reclamation.												
--------	----------	----------	----------	Environmental planning information may be required.	----------	--------	----------	--------	--------	----------	--------	Act mandates studies of economic effects of regulations.
--------	----------	----------	----------	----------	----------	--------	"Rules . . . shall conform with any State and local land-use planning program."	--------	Agency identifies areas. not reclaimable under present technology.	----------	--------	Act mandates consideration of economic effects of regulations.
ities may be applicable to mining and reclamation.												
(1), pe of e will ≤25%.	With 4 ft of earth supportive of vegetation.	Appropriate to type of end use declared.	Exceptions allowed in grading on: Act (1), subdivisions and wildlife; Act (2), flood plains.	----------	X	X	----------	--------	--------	----------	X	----------

(continued on next page)

Table 2—Continued.

	1	2	3	4	5	6	7	8	9	10	11
	Stage of program development				State law					Reclamation—Main act	
	State	Act(s)	Rules and regulations	Technical guidelines	Title of Act(s)	Administering agency(ies)	Mineral or commodity covered	Rules vary by mining method	Control water flow and quality	Conserve and replace topsoil	Backfill and grade
MONTANA		✕	✕	✕ (Partial.)	(1) Montana Strip & Underground Mine Reclamation Act, and (2) Open Cut Mining Act, and (3) Montana Hard-Rock Mining Reclamation Act.	Department of State Lands.	Act (1) Coal and uranium; Act (2) bentonite, clay, phosphate rock, scoria, and sand and gravel; Act (3) other minerals.		Act (1) specific criteria, e.g.—pH range of 6.0 to 9.0.	✕	Act (1) grade to ≦20%.
NEBRASKA								NOTE: Local governmental land-use controls and pe			
NEVADA								NOTE: Local governmental land-use controls and pe			
NEW HAMPSHIRE								NOTE: Local governmental land-use controls and pe			
NEW JERSEY								NOTE: Local governmental land-use controls and pe			
NEW MEXICO		✕	✕		New Mexico Coal Surfacemining Act.	Bureau of Mines and Mineral Resources.	Coal			✕	Topography will be "gently undulating" consistent with proposed end use.
NEW YORK		✕			New York State Mined Land Reclamation Law.	Department of Environmental Conservation.	All minerals and mined topsoil.		✕	✕	✕
NORTH CAROLINA		✕			The Mining Act of 1971.	Department of Natural and Economic Resources.	All minerals			✕	Minimizing earth slides and consistent with future land use.
NORTH DAKOTA		✕	✕		North Dakota Century Code; Reclamation of Strip-Mined Land.	Public Service Commission.	Coal			✕	Replace all available plant growth material, up to 5 ft thickness. Approximate original contour, or serve approved end use.
OHIO		✕	✕		(1) Strip Mine Law, and (2) Surface Mine Law.	Department of Natural Resources.	Act (1) Coal, Act (2) All other minerals.			✕	✕ (or other plant-growth materials.) Approximate original contour, or serve approved end use.
OKLAHOMA		✕			Mining Lands Reclamation Act.	Department of Mines.	All minerals				Topography will be traversable for approved use. Slope box cut over burden will be ≦25°.

Table 2—Continued.

	2(12)	13	14	15	16	17	18	19	20	21	22	23	24
											Special Provisions		
	d and standards set				Requirements for land-use planning				Minerals protected from nonmining development	Exclusion of areas from consideration for mining	Long-range or regional mine planning	Substitute lands allowed	Financial or economic analyses required
		Bury or neutralize toxic wastes	Revegetate for beneficial use	Other rules or remarks	Resources information required	Alternative uses will be considered	End use will be declared	Role of local public planning					
t will ≤20%.	Act (1), backfill with 8 ft of overburden.		Suitable, permanent, diverse and primarily native species.	Effluent standards conform with criteria of State Dept. of Environmental Sciences.	Environmental areas, geology, soils, minerals, topography (USGS), vegetation, water resources (use plan & monitoring system), and wildlife.	----------	X	----------	---------	--------	"Intended mining and reclamation plans" are developed to apply to life of operation.	Prohibited.	Reclamation costs requested of applicant.

...es may be applicable to mining and reclamation.

...es may be applicable to mining and reclamation.

...es may be applicable to mining and reclamation.

...es may be applicable to mining and reclamation.

	2(12)	13	14	15	16	17	18	19	20	21	22	23	24
	------	X	To serve selected end use.	----------	Climate, land use, soils, topography, vegetation, water resources, and wildlife.	X	X		Consultation required with soil and water conservation districts.	----------	--------	--------	----------
safe, le and pati- with ound-ter		X	X	Mining from State-owned submarine lands is covered by another act.	Land use, minerals, topography (USGS), and water resources.	----------	X		Local mining laws and land-use controls, stricter than the Act prevail (but locals must enforce).	----------	--------	--------	----------
		X		X (with appropriate local or State agency approval.)	----------	Land use, minerals, vegetation, and wildlife.	----------	X		----------	--------	--------	--------	----------
of will ≤35%.		----------	X	Remedy any impairment to domestic or livestock water supply.	Geology, land-use preference, minerals, soils, topography, vegetation, and water resources.	X	X		----------	--------	Act conveys authority to delete certain lands from surface mining.	"Extended Mining Plans" cover 10-yr period.	--------	Agency may request estimate of costs of reclamation.
X	X	X	X	----------	Act (1) soils (test borings) and topography, Act (2) soils (test borings or prior operation).	X	X		----------	--------	Act (1) conveys authority to delete certain lands from surface mining.	Act (2) plan covers 10-yr period.	--------	Act (1) applicant provides estimated cost of reclamation.
le to e end- objec-	With 3 ft of overburden.			X (Exemptions: soils with poor texture, toxicity, and nutrient deficiency).	----------	----------	----------	X	----------	--------	---	----------	----------

(continued on next page)

Table 2—Continued.

	1	2	3	4	5	6	7	8	9	10	11
						State law				Reclamation—Main	
	Stage of program development							Rules vary by mining method	Control water flow and quality	Conserve and replace topsoil	Backfill gra
	State	Act(s)	Rules and regulations	Technical guidelines	Title of Act(s)	Administering agency(ies)	Mineral or commodity covered				
OREGON		X	X	_____	Oregon Mined Land Reclamation Act, as amended.	Department of Geology and Mineral Industries.	All minerals __	_____	X	_____	As appro for pla subsequa beneficia use.
PENNSYLVANIA		X	X	_____	Surface Mining Conservation and Reclamation Act, as amended.	Department of Environmental Resources.	All minerals __	_____	X	X (12 in. of soil, conditions permitting, or all available topsoil.	Approxim original tour; te race; o serve a proved use.
RHODE ISLAND									**NOTE: Local governmental land-use controls and**		
SOUTH CAROLINA		X	X	_____	South Carolina Mining Act.	Land Resources Conservation Commission.	All minerals __	_____	X	_____	Minimizir slides a consiste with fu land us
SOUTH DAKOTA		X	X	_____	Surface Mining Land Reclamation Act, as amended.	Department of Agriculture.	All minerals ___	_____	X	X	"Achieve tour m beneficia the pro land us
TENNESSEE		X	X	X	The Tennessee Surface Mining Act.	Department of Conservation.	All minerals *except* dimension stone, limestone, and marble.	*Contour mining* rules apply on slopes >15"; *area mining* on slopes <15"; quarries are a special case.	Detailed standards are in effect.	X	*Contour*: benches hibited slopes > *Area*: Approxi original surface.
TEXAS		X	_____	_____	Texas Surface Mining and Reclamation Act.	Railroad Commission of Texas.	Coal, lignite, and uranium.	_____	X	Use stratum best for plant growth.	Approxima original contour
UTAH		X	X	_____	Mined Land Reclamation Act of 1975.	Department of Natural Resources.	All minerals (including oil-shale and bituminous sands).	_____	X	X	(where "practi
VERMONT		X	_____	_____	Vermont's Land Use and Development Law.	District Environmental Commissions and the Environmental Board.	All minerals ___	_____	_____	_____	_____

Table 2—Continued.

12	13	14	15	16	17	18	19	20	21	22	23	24
								Special Provisions				
				Requirements for land–use planning				Minerals protected from nonmining development	Exclusion of areas from consideration for mining	Long-range or regional mine planning	Substitute lands allowed	Financial or economic analyses required
reduce ghwall pitwall	Bury or neutralize toxic wastes	Revegetate for beneficial use	Other rules or remarks	Resources information required	Alternative uses will be considered	End use will be declared	Role of local public planning					
red and standards set												
ppro-ppriate nned ose-ent ieficial e.	-----------	X	Visual screening. economically practicable; streambank restoration.	-----------	-----------	X	Department may approve local governmental permitting or reviewing in lieu of State.	-----------	-----------	-----------	-----------	-----------
inate hwall.	Varies with existing conditions.	X	Clean Streams Law also directly applicable.	Fisheries, geology, land use, minerals, and water resources.	X	X	-----------	-----------	-----------	-----------	-----------	Applicant provides detailed estimate of reclamation.
ties may be applicable to mining and reclamation.												
-------	X	X (with appropriate local or state agency approval.)	Visual screening may be required.	Land use, topography (USGS), vegetation, and wildlife.	-----------	X	Local soil and water conservation districts review and comment.	-----------	-----------	-----------	X	-----------
will ≤14°.	With 8 ft of topsoil or suitable overburden.	To create self-regenerative growth without irrigation.	Noxious weeds must be controlled.	Land use, soil, minerals, topography, wildlife, vegetation, and water resources.	-----------	X	Incompatibility with local land plans can be basis for rejection of mining request by Agency.	-----------	-----------	-----------	-----------	Applicant provides detailed estimate of reclamation costs.
nate hwall h compacted xe kfill, ed to ch 5°.	With 4 ft of compacted material or permanent water body.	Where approved, permanent growth serving purpose at least as useful as pre-mining.	Standards differ by mineral: coal, phosphate, sand and gravel, clays, shale, and barite.	Land use, minerals, soils, topography (USGS), and water resources.	-----------	X	-----------	-----------	-----------	-----------	-----------	-----------
X	X	Establish diverse self-regenerative cover suitable for approved end use.	Principles stated on lakes, water rights, and ground water; 4-yr responsibility for vegetation.	Hydrologic effects. land capability, land use, minerals, soils, topography, vegetation, water resources, and wildlife.	Determine capacity of land for alternative uses.	X	Notified and comment is recorded.	-----------	Agency can declare "areas unsuitable for mining" (6 criteria).	Applicant must anticipate effects of reclamation over life of mine.	-----------	Agency conducts economic studies relating to item (22).
-------	/X	X (Priority to non-noxious native plants.)	Program is implemented through orders that recognize individual site and mine conditions.	Land use, soils, vegetation, and water resources.	Explore capabilities of land to support a variety of uses.	X	Notified and comments taken under advisement.	-----------	-----------	-----------	-----------	-----------
-------	-----------	-----------	Application for permit is viewed for conformity with State plan or planning principles.	Land capability and land use.	X	X	Action must accord with local plans.	X (Land development permits.)	-----------	-----------	-----------	-----------

(continued on next page)

Table 2—Continued.

1	2	3	4	5	6	7	8	9	10	11
Stage of program development				State law					Reclamation—Main ae	
State	Act(s)	Rules and regulations	Technical guidelines	Title of Act(s)	Administering agency(ies)	Mineral or commodity covered	Rules vary by mining method	Control water flow and quality	Conserve and replace topsoil	Backfill grade
VIRGINIA _____	✗	✗	✗	(1) 45.1–198, and (2) Title 45.1–180, chap. 16.	Department of Conservation and Economic Devolpment.	Act (1) coal. Act (2) All other minerals.	Quarries are a special case—especially in backfilling.	✗	_____	"... retain spoil on bench in far as feasible.
WASHINGTON _____	✗	✗	_____	Surface-Mined Land Reclamation Act.	Department of Natural Resources.	All minerals	Quarries are a special case.	✗	_____	Conform to surround land area
WEST VIRGINIA _____	✗	✗	✗	Article 6, Chap. 20, Code of West Virginia, as amended.	Department of Natural Resources.	All minerals	Grading and backfilling rules vary by *area mining or contour mining.*	Standards set forth in *Drainage Handbook for Surface Mining.*	✗	Fill bench denied o grades >65%; tour min areas wi suitable farm machiner
WISCONSIN _____	✗	_____	_____	Metallic Mining Reclamation Act.	Department of Natural Resources.	Metallic minerals.	_____	✗	✗	✗
WYOMING _____	✗	✗	_____	Wyoming Environmental Quality Act of 1973.	Department of Environmental Quality.	All minerals	Rules vary by *soft rock mining or hard rock mining.*	✗	Use most suitable plant growth materials.	Approxima original tour; te race; or serve ap proved e use.

Table 2—Continued.

12	13	14	15	16	17	18	19	20	21	22	23	24
								Special Provisions				
ed and standards set				Requirements for land-use planning				Minerals protected from nonmining development	Exclusion of areas from consideration for mining	Long-range or regional mine planning	Substitute lands allowed	Financial or economic analyses required
Reduce ghwall pitwall	Bury or neutralize toxic wastes	Revegetate for beneficial use	Other rules or remarks	Resources information required	Alternative uses will be considered	End use will be declared	Role of local public planning					
re-ce... the aximum tent actic-le."	With 4 ft of material suitable for plant growth.	✗	Standards for access roads across highwall; special preparation of soils in erosion-prone areas.	Environmental impact study (implied), land use, minerals, topography (USGS), and water resources.	✗	✗	Local soil and water conservation districts advise.	---------	-------	---------	-------	---------
e of ll in con-lidated, 6%; ll slope rock, 5°.	With 2 ft of clean fill.	✗	Requirements of other agencies relate to water rights, flood plains, and fish and wildlife.	Land use, minerals, topography, and water resources.	---------	✗	Applicant must show legality of action with regard to local zoning.	---------	-------	---------	-------	---------
✗	With 4 ft of material suitable for plant growth.	Detailed standards.	Other detailed requirements exist for back fill and for stream crossings.	Land use, minerals, soils, topography, and water resources.	✗	✗	---------	---------	-------	---------	-------	---------
--------	✗	✗	Screening of site required.	Geology, land use, soils (suitability), topography, and water resources.	---------	-------	Mining, reclamation, and comprehensive plan shall conform to local zoning.	Act mandates a State program discouraging the preclusion of mining.	--------	Agency may require comprehensive long-term plan.	--------	Applicant may be required to show costs data.
lize; pe; nimize ect on dscape.	✗	✗	Protect soil stockpile from winds. Delay mining for archeological or paleontological surveys.	Geology, land use, soils, topography (USGS), vegetation, water resources (use & rights), and wildlife.	---------	Must be ≥ highest previous use of site (as declared by Agency).	County involvement in administration of act.	--------	-------	--------	-------	Socioeconomic analyses may be needed by Agency to set use.

mine lands. On 18 September 1975, the Oklahoma coal operators met and discussed the orphan mine problem. At a second meeting in October further study was made and consideration given to a plan to reclaim those areas where reclamation was feasible. The operators feel that, by adoption of a voluntary program, they can effectively reclaim such areas at less cost than if the state and/or Federal Government enact legislation which would require a special tax for administration and implementation of a law to eliminate spoil areas. A committee, appointed by the operators, met 5 November 1975 to explore the possibilities of practical procedures to accomplish reclamation of orphan mine land. This program, I'm sure, will be followed closely by many states.

Prelaw orphan mine land is just what the name implies, land that was mined prior to reclamation legislation and then abandoned. With surface mine legislation now in effect in the various states, orphan lands should never again occur.

VIII. FUTURE LEGISLATIVE NEEDS

In looking at future needs in legislation you suddenly become aware that this is an area that each state must decide for itself. While the basic model for a surface mine law may apply to all states, encompassing such things as purpose, permitting, licensing, acreage fees, bonding, penalties, etc. there is still the problem of reclamation standards. The states have such diversity in geological, hydrological, and climatic conditions, topography, coal thickness and quality, methods and techniques of mining, marketing the product, and many other variables that it is virtually impossible to have one set of reclamation standards that will suffice for all states. To illustrate this more graphically consider for a moment the Eastern and Western coal fields of West Virginia, where regulations have been promulgated for each distinct coal field because of the difference mentioned above.

It is appropriate to end this chapter by pointing out that the governors and the legislative bodies of the states that have significant surface mining are aware of the environmental problems created by such operations. This is evidenced by the number of states that now have surface mining laws and further evidenced by the continued review and upgrading of present regulations. The 12 states that are members of the Interstate Mining Compact have recognized the need for a forum through which they may exchange useful information concerning the surface mining of solid minerals. The member states of the Compact produce approximately 80 % of the coal produced in these United States. In joining the Compact each party state agrees that within a reasonable time it will formulate and establish an effective program for the conservation and use of mined land by the establishment of standards, enactment of laws, or the continued or improved enforcement of current laws, to accomplish the wise use of their resources.

Copyright © 1978 ASA–CSSA–SSSA
677 South Segoe Road, Madison, WI 53711 USA
Reclamation of Drastically Disturbed Lands

Chapter 7

Industry's Viewpoint of Legislation Affecting Surface-Mined Coal Lands

ALTEN F. GRANDT

Peabody Coal Company,
St. Louis, Missouri

I. INTRODUCTION

The commercial surface mining for coal in this country began near Danville, Ill., in 1866 (Anonymous, 1972). Since surface mining began, lawmakers have been wrangling over what to do about strip-mined land. In Illinois there were 55 separate legislative actions recorded during the period from 1929 to 1962 (Weber, 1962). Similarly, at the federal level, Representative E. Dirksen in 1940 introduced HR 10079, a bill which would have required surface mines to fill the hole or hollow caused by surface mining with the spoil and such additional soil "as may be necessary to make the contour of the land approximately the same as before the mining operation was begun." (Siehl, 1971).

The number of states enacting laws designed specifically for mined area reclamation has increased from one in 1939, with the initial action of West Virginia, to 38 in 1975. In several of the remaining 12 states, draft legislation abounds and all 50 states are likely to have legislation by 1980 (Imhoff et al., 1976).

The stated declaration of policy or purpose of each of these laws also functions as a constraint on activities before, during, and after mining. For example, one of the responsibilities of the particular reclamation legislation is "to ensure the protection of the public interest. . .." This public interest should include not only reclamation, but also the right of interstate commerce to use the fuel.

The coal industry supports realistic legislation that will ensure the achievement of sound reclamation and the protection of the environment.

II. EVALUATION OF EXISTING LEGISLATION

To understand some of Industry's viewpoints regarding legislation (federal, state, or county) it is necessary to understand what is required to make a coal mine. In alphabetic terminology, so familiar today, it can be

117

described as CCC—Coal, Customer, Capital. *Legislation* affects all three.

What is the situation today? Permits of various kinds are required from federal, state, county, and/or municipal agencies. The amount of information required of the operator has multiplied manyfold, which also means that the regulatory agency must spend more man-hours reviewing the application. Many laws include specific time schedules, both for the applicant specifying his lead-time, and for the agency specifying its time for action. For instance, the proposed EPA regulation requiring environmental assessments to be submitted with the application for a National Pollutant Discharge Elimination System (NPDES) water discharge permit states that it must be submitted at least nine months before start of construction of the discharge. The Wyoming Industrial Siting Act specified that the Agency can take 450 days to review a mining permit application before action is required.

There is no uniform standard for permits applicable countrywide. In fact, there is not even uniformity within an individual state, because of the varying conditions that are site-specific to each mine. One of the first steps the operator should perform in developing a new mining venture is to make an assessment of all of the permits anticipated. It is far better to prepare for even the uncertain ones, because it is easy to drop later an unneeded one from the list, but failure to include a needed one at the beginning of development can result in costly time delays. The mine usually cannot commence without having all permits. The omission of just one can prevent opening the mine, thereby exposing the operator to legal action for failure to deliver coal.

What are some of these permits? In this review they will be classified by governmental agency categories.

A. Federal Permits or Approvals

1. MINING/RECLAMATION PLAN APPROVED BY U.S. GEOLOGICAL SURVEY

Under the Federal Mineral Leasing Act of 25 February 1920, approval of the company's mining and reclamation plan had to be obtained from the U.S. Geological Survey (USGS) for federally owned coal.

In the past, the operator first obtained a prospecting permit for a chosen area from the Department of Interior. After proving the reserve, he obtained a preference-right lease and then developed the mining and reclamation plan. This plan was then submitted to the USGS for its approval.

Earlier this year, the Department of Interior proposed a series of regulations dealing with leasing requirements (43 CFR Section 3041), mining and reclamation requirements (30 CFR Section 211), diligence requirements (43 CFR 3500), and commercial quantities (43 CFR 3520). These regulations require the approval of the mining and reclamation plan, which must be in conformance with the specific lease conditions.

Regulation 43 CFR 3041 will govern such aspects as leasing, permitting, licensing, planning procedures, reclamation standards, surface uses, bond requirements, and reports related thereto. Regulation 30 CFR 211 will govern operations for the discovery, testing, development, mining, preparation, and handling of federal coal, and for reclamation. Regulation 43 CFR 3500 requires commencing of coal production from a Logical Mining Unit (LMU) at a rate of 1/40th of unit reserves within 10 years of lease issuance or regulations promulgation, and extraction, processing, and sale of at least 1% of LMU reserves in each calendar year thereafter.

Regulation 43 CFR 3520 defines commercial quantities of coal and requires that preference right lease applicants must show coal contained within a prospecting permit can be developed and marketed at a profit or, in other words, be accompanied by a projected mining plan and a profit-loss statement.

2. NATIONAL POLLUTANT DISCHARGE ELIMINATION SYSTEM

The federal water pollution control act amendments of 1972 established the National Pollutant Discharge Elimination System (NPDES), whereby any facility (a mine) having a water discharge from a point source must apply for a permit, and receive such before commencement of operation of the discharge. The permit can be issued for any period of time, not to exceed five years. Initial application basically requires information relative to the nature and quantity of the discharge, the source from which it comes, the location of the discharge, the receiving stream, and other minimal basic information.

The application is submitted to the regional office of the federal Environmental Protection Agency (EPA), except in those cases where the federal EPA has granted authority to a state agency to issue permits, monitor the discharges, and bring about enforcement actions. Once the agency receives the application, it has no specified time in which to respond. Its usual procedure will be to ask the applicant to supply additional data concerning the sources of water discharge, its expected quantity and quality, and the method of treatment to comply with the effluent limits for the coal industry. It will also request information as to how the discharge will be monitored. The federal EPA is far behind the originally anticipated schedule for issuance of permits for existing facilities.

3. SECTION 404 PERMITS FOR DISCHARGE OF DREDGED OR FILL MATERIAL

The federal Water Pollution Control Act Amendments of 1972, in Section 404, directs the Corps of Engineers to establish regulations controlling the discharge of dredged and fill material in "navigable streams." The full impact of this regulation is not yet fully understood, and the interpretation by various district Corps of Engineer offices is still being defined. As a result of a recent court decision, virtually every stream or tributary thereof will eventually be classified as waters of the United States and come under the jurisdiction of this regulation.

The Corps, on 25 July 1975, promulgated an interim final regulation entitled "Permits for Activities in Navigable Waters or Ocean Waters" concerning the placement of dredged and fill materials in navigable streams and tributaries thereof. The regulations require that anyone who is going to place dredged or fill material into a navigable stream must obtain a permit from the Corps of Engineers. Prior to issuance of a permit, a Section 401 certification from the state Water Pollution Control Agency must be obtained to assure that the coal operation will comply with applicable effluent limitations and water quality standards.

The regulation applied to coastal waters and navigable waters began immediately. Subsequent to 1 July 1976, the placement of such material in a primary tributary of a navigable stream is subject to the permit requirements of the regulations. After 1 July 1977, a permit will be required for this type of activity in any stream which has a normal flow of 5 ft^3/sec or more. These requirements will affect almost every mining operation. The crossing of a stream, diversion of a stream, depositing spoil in a stream bed, and other activities in these waters will fall under this regulation.

4. NATIONAL ENVIRONMENTAL POLICY ACT

In order to comply with the National Environmental Policy Act (NEPA) of 1969, the operator, in most instances, will be required to furnish an environmental report of assessment, after which the USGS will publish a draft environmental impact statement. This must then be the subject of a public hearing, ultimately revised to incorporate comments and concerns, and published as a final envionmental impact statement. After residing with the Council of Environmental Quality for 30 days, the Agency is then free to approve a mining plan.

5. ENERGY MINERALS ACTIVITY RESOURCE SYSTEM

Whenever federally owned coal is involved, the Department of Interior's new leasing policy further extends the time for governmental approvals. The complicated program of the Energy Minerals Activity Resource System (EMARS) is gradually being revealed. To date there have been two impact statements in both draft and final formats. The leasing regulation 43 CFR Part 3041, and mining regulation 30 CFT Part 211 have been issued in draft-proposed and final-proposed format, but not yet promulgated. Regulations have been proposed to define what constitutes "due diligence" of coal development and to describe the discovery of coal in "commercial quantities."

Also a regulation describing EMARS has been proposed and published in the *Federal Register*. The flow chart shown in Fig. 1 describes the four major steps of leasing: Management Framework Plans, Nominations, Environmental Analysis, and Tract Evaluation. Various estimates

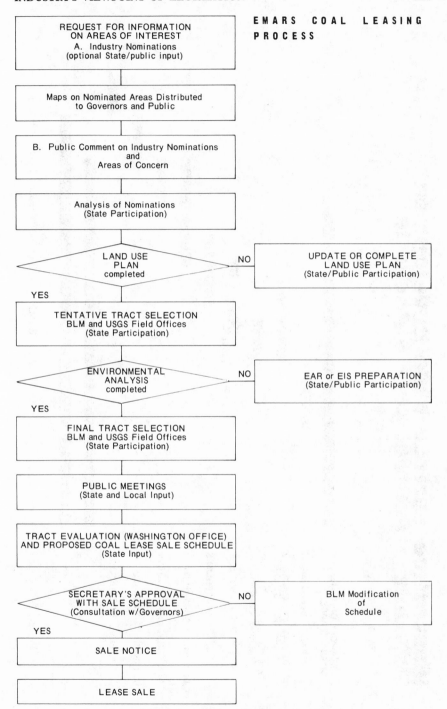

Fig. 1—Flow chart showing the four major steps of leasing under the Energy Minerals Activity Resource System (EMARS). Excerpted from 16 March 1976 *Federal Register.*

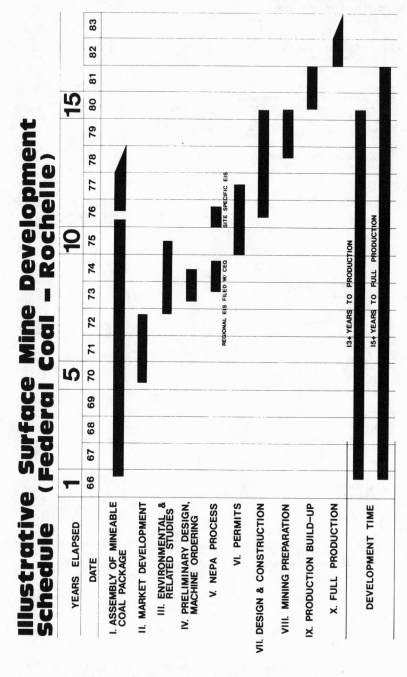

Fig. 2—Surface mine development schedule prior to the adoption of EMARS (Peabody Coal Company, Rochelle, Wyo.).

of time to accomplish this program are being discussed, but our best judgement is approximately 4 years.

It must be realized that this is additional time before issuance of a lease. The impact of this new program on the nation's plans for energy independence has not yet been felt. When added to the 10 to 13 or more years now required from lease issuance to first coal production, it has the potential for another delay. For example, the time required to develop a mine prior to adoption of EMARS is shown in Fig. 2. Peabody began assembly of a mineable coal package in the Rochelle, Wyo., area in 1966. By the time production is realized in early 1980, more than 13 years will have elapsed.

6. FEDERAL COMMUNICATIONS COMMISSION

Most mines require two-way radio service for efficient operation. An application must be made to the Federal Communications Commission (FCC) for a license under Section 1.1305 of the FCC rules. Under this rule the FCC will accept at face value the applicant's statement that "this application is not a major action. . ." Under these conditions, this permit application can proceed without waiting until an Environmental Impact Statement has been completed.

7. OIL SPILL PREVENTION PLAN

Where a mine has oil storage facilities of 650 gallons above ground, or of 20,000 gallons below ground, an oil spill prevention plan must be on file at the mine office, although it need not be filed with the EPA.

8. ENVIRONMENTAL ASSESSMENT FOR EPA NPDES PERMIT

The federal EPA has proposed a regulation requiring the submittal of an environmental assessment with the application for a NPDES permit at least 9 months before start of construction of the discharge. They further indicated at a seminar conducted by the American Bar Association, that it may take as long as 24 months for the EPA to reevaluate and act upon the permit application. A further indication of potential delays and time constraints was the feeling that EPA has the right to deny the permit application if the project was undesirable because of some secondary environmental impact. Thus, even in spite of the fact that the applicant would meet the applicable effluent standards for his industry, he is not assured that he will receive the necessary NPDES permit.

That type of constraint seriously alters the financial commitment (capital) to a new project. Heretofore, the coal operator had reasonable assurance that he would receive the permit, although it may take a longer period of time, and thus was willing to risk the necessary capital. But now faced with a possible denial of the permit application, he must reevaluate how far in advance and how much capital he can risk. This may require some sort of indemnification from the customer in the event the project is delayed or stopped. It must be remembered also that the customer is faced with some of these same constraints because he too must obtain a NPDES permit.

The proposed EPA regulations further state that the applicant may use a third party for development of the necessary environmental assessment. However, if the applicant does use the third party, EPA must approve the selection of the consultant, determine the scope of the work, direct the investigation, and receive the report. The only thing the applicant will receive is the bill. Needless to say, the coal industry has made strong objections to such a procedure.

9. OTHER FEDERAL PERMITS OR ACTIONS

In addition to the major federal permits or approvals discussed above, there may be others required, depending upon the specific mine site. If National Resource Land surface is included in any of the mine areas or under any facilities, a Special Land Use Permit must be obtained from the Bureau of Land Management. Likewise, if Forest Service land is involved, rights-of-way from the Service must be obtained. Finally, if the mine plans include a preparation plant, an Air Pollution Emission Source Permit must be obtained from either the federal EPA or the State depending upon whether or not the state has an approved air quality control implementation plan. None of these permits or approvals will be issued until the NEPA has been satisfied.

There are other approvals required to satisfy the Mine Enforcement Safety Act (MESA). Water, silt, and slurry impoundment design plans must be submitted to MESA for approval. Existing structures must be investigated and certified as safe. The plans for all new structures must be certified and approved prior to construction. Some will be subject to weekly inspection for possible problems. The recent failure of the dam in Idaho, certainly tragic, has further compounded industry's problems.

B. State Permits

The list of state permits also varied, although there is some commonality of certain requirements. Various regulatory agencies, sometimes under a common department and in other cases under different governing bodies, issue permits, monitor performance, and bring enforcement actions on violations.

1. MINING AND RECLAMATION PERMIT

All but 12 states have established regulatory control over surface mining. In those states where coal surface mining is a significant industry, the regulations are more complete and extensive than in states where it is not. The vehicle of regulations is a permit, usually good for 1 to 5 years with renewal provisions.

Some of these are fairly straightforward, even though the requirements may be very stringent. Others, on the other hand, become very complicated, such as in Montana. There, a prospecting permit is required to drill the holes to take samples for analytical data required in the mining-permit application itself. The mining/reclamation permit is an annual requirement with specific designated areas to be mined each year. However, if all of the area designated for mining in a year is not mined, then in no more than 60 and no less than 30 days before the expiration of that permit application must be made for its renewal. Two hundred and forty days before the expiration of a current mining permit, application must be made for a permit to mine the next year's areas. If the Agency decrees that more information is needed, the countdown starts again at 240 days. In addition, another permit must be obtained under the Montana Coal Conservation Act. It, too, is an annual permit. An attempt is being made to have the expiration of the coal mining and reclamation permit, and the coal conservation act permit coincide; however, this desirable goal has not yet been accomplished. It can be readily seen that both the state agencies and applicant can become thoroughly confused on deadlines, permit periods, exact areas under permit, etc.

Some states have all permits expiring on a uniform date, while others have them staggered, depending upon when the original permit was issued. Needless to say, the operator with mines in several states needs a very detailed preplanning and timetable procedure to meet all of the necessary requirements. A reminder system providing a warning well in advance of the expiration of the permit is essential.

2. WATER DISCHARGE PERMIT

Most states require the operator to obtain a water pollution control permit of some sort. These may be in addition to the NPDES permit, even if the state administers that program. Illinois requires a water pollution discharge permit, which limits a greater number of potential contaminants in the effluent than does the federal system. Since the NPDES program, when administered by the federal EPA, requires state certification of the quality of water being discharged, Illinois has been attempting to have total dissolved solids regulated in federal permits. This matter is currently under litigation. The state permit length can vary from a one-time requirement down to as short a time as 1 year.

Many states are now requiring that a sediment control plan and design be included either with the mining/reclamation permit application or submitted prior to mining plan approval. Kentucky, for instance, requires that the engineer-certified plan be approved by the state prior to approval of the mining permit. The construction of the sediment control structure must also be certified. Submittal and approval requires an additional 12 weeks minimum lead time. If the structure is over 6 m (20 feet) in height, it may well take 1 year or longer for approval. Ohio, Montana, and Alabama requirements are similar to those of Kentucky. Wyoming, Utah, and Colorado have as stringent or even more stringent requirements.

3. WATER TREATMENT OPERATOR'S LICENSE

Some states require that the operator of the treatment plant be licensed by the state. Indiana and Colorado have such a requirement, even though the treatment plants may be only settling basins.

4. AIR POLLUTION SOURCE PERMIT

An air pollution permit for fugitive dust, preparation plant heating boilers, and thermal dryers are required by many states. Kentucky, for instance, requires a permit before construction of any facility which will emit the dust. A plan for compliance must be included with the permit application.

5. SOLID WASTE DISPOSAL

If a mine is to dispose of solid waste from any source other than that from the mine, a permit is generally required. This will apply to mines receiving fly ash, bottom ash, breaker reject, pulverizer reject, etc., from a nearby power plant or other source. Some state laws advocate the use of mined lands as sanitary landfills.

6. PERMITS FOR SURFACE EFFECTS OF UNDERGROUND MINES

Kentucky has a new proposed regulation, which has been through the public hearing stage and for which the final regulation is anticipated shortly, that will require annual permits for surface effects of underground mines. The regulation has very detailed, specific engineering design criteria with respect to access roads, haul road, drainageways, etc.

7. NOISE ABATEMENT PLANS

Illinois has a very stringent environmental noise regulation. While it does not have a permit requirement, the operator must gather extensive data to know the amount of noise emanating beyond his property line. If it exceeds certain standards he must take corrective action or stand the risk of enforcement actions being brought against the mine. There is a variance procedure, similar to those for air and water, to cover situations which cannot be corrected, but relief is granted only for limited periods.

8. OTHER STATE PERMITS OR ACTIONS

Some states, Indiana for example, require a construction permit for a mine or any facility having a water discharge. Further, in Wyoming, either an industrial siting permit or a certificate of nonjurisdiction must be obtained. Most states also require either proof that the federal MESA regulations have been satisfied, or state-agency approvals of safety-related aspects of mine operation, such as refuse, mine waste, or gob piles. These may be "life-of-mine" actions or may require periodic renewals.

C. County and Municipal Requirements

In most states, land-use planning legislation has established a mechanism requiring that an area be specifically zoned to allow mining. The general practice is for the county commissioners to designate an area which can be mined within a limited time period. If the commissioners are satisfied with the progress of reclamation they may extend the zone for an additional area. In Wyoming, each municipality controls zoning up to 8 km (5 miles) beyond their corporate limits. In Illinois this distance is 4 km (2½ miles). Some municipalities impose building codes and waste treatment requirements in the extended area.

III. DISCUSSION

The number of permits and regulatory agencies involved clearly shows the need for an elaborate time schedule for filling applications, receiving permits, and coordinating with the development steps of a mine. The complexities involved can probably best be demonstrated by an example of actual Peabody Coal Company experiences.

Peabody was involved in one of the early interpretations and actions under the Corps of Engineering, 404 regulation. In connection with a planned normal extension of its River King Pit no. 6 operation, the Company planned to divert a small creek called Plum Creek and mine the coal under the creekbed. The mining plan submitted called for the diversion of 5.1 km (3.2 miles) of Plum Creek commencing 30.4 km (19 miles) upstream from the point where the Creek enters the Kaskaskia River in Randolph County of southern Illinois.

Initially, the Corps of Engineers indicated in writing that it considered Plum Creek to be within their jurisdiction at the point of diversion, thereby requiring a 404 Permit, and that the diversion would be a major federal action, significantly affecting the quality of the human environment. It thus determined that a full environmental impact statement would be required, activating the complete NEPA process.

Incidentally, the Illinois Environmental Protection Agency would neither certify that the diversion would not have an adverse impact upon Illinois Stream Quality Standards, nor would it waive its right to certify. Without one of these two actions, the Corps of Engineers could not grant approval to the Company even though a complete and final Environmental Impact Statement found that the proposed diversion *would not* adversely affect the quality of the human environment.

Furthermore, the Company did not feel that the Corps had jurisdiction because its study showed that the stream flow was less than the required minimum of 5 ft³/sec. The Corps has recently submitted a letter stating that is does not have jurisdiction in this situation. All these various decisions and changes required a period of 8 months.

The recently adopted Corps of Engineers regulations governing permits under Section 404 of the Federal Water Pollution Control Act Amendments is the most recent addition of lead time, particularly for surface mines. The regulation extends Corps jurisdiction beyond the traditional "navigable waters and tributaries thereof" to virtually all waters of the United States.

According to one Western governor, "it would control, in its final stages, virtually every swimming pool in the State." He realized that the regulation was a reaction to a court decision, but wished that the Corps of Engineers had not reacted with such enthusiasm. At the public hearings on the regulation, most states vigorously opposed what they felt was invasion of states' rights and states' authority by the federal government.

The discussion thus far has concerned itself with the effect of the ever-lengthening permitting process on the development of a coal mine. However, we cannot overlook the fact that without a *Customer* (the second *C*), there would be no coal mine. Coal company sales departments need to recognize this greater lead time for mine development and to impress upon prospective customers that the coal industry can no longer respond in the historic patterns of 2 or 3 years. Not long ago a utility executive remarked that the lead time for a nuclear plant was 10 years, but for a coal plant it would only be 4 or 5 years. That type of thinking needs to be updated.

There is no fixed additional or total time to obtain permits. This affects the *Capital*. Each situation must be analyzed on a site-specific basis. The total number of permits required, as well as the sequence of applying for those permits, must be evaluated early in the planning for a new mine or the expansion or extension of an existing mine. An "educated guess" must be made regarding the anticipated response time from regulatory agencies, possible delays, and potential objectors to the project. Knowledge as to experience of competitors provides some guidance to the maximum permitting time expected.

A delay can materially increase the interest payments on funds already borrowed to finance the project as well as result in possible penalties for failure to deliver coal by the date specified in the contract.

Industry's viewpoint of legislation affecting surface-mined coal lands is aptly summarized by C. E. Smith, Jr., president of Carter Mining, in his statement, "the obstacles to Western Coal development today is regulatory and legislative bottlenecks—a control system which had good intentions, but a poor grasp of the factors which allow development to take place" (Article in *Casper Star Tribune*, Casper, Wyo., 3 February 1976, p. 18).

LITERATURE CITED

Anonymous. 1972. Reclamation of strip mined lands in Illinois. p. 1–16. *In* J. W. Lewis (ed.) 1971–1972 State of Illinois 856. Illinois Blue Book, Sec. of State, Springfield, Ill.

Imhoff, E. A., T. O. Friz, and R. LaFevers, Jr. 1976. A guide to state programs for the reclamation of surface mined areas, USGS Cir. 731. U.S. Government Printing Office, Washington, D.C.

Siehl, G. H. 1971. Legislative proposals concerning surface mining of coal. Senate Comm. on Interior and Insular Affairs, U.S. Government Printing Office 63-958-1971, Washington, D.C.

Weber, L. S. 1962. The administration of the Illinois Strip Mine Reclamation Act. Proc. Ill. Min. Inst. 70:52–59.

Copyright © 1978 ASA–CSSA–SSSA
677 South Segoe Road, Madison, WI 53711 USA
Reclamation of Drastically Disturbed Lands

Chapter 8

Geochemical Factors Affecting Coal Mine Drainage Quality

FRANK T. CARUCCIO AND GWENDELYN GEIDEL
University of South Carolina
Columbia, South Carolina

I. INTRODUCTION

A. Background of the Acid Mine Drainage Problem

To achieve an energy program independent of foreign sources, the United States will undoubtedly exploit the large quantities of coal found within the conterminous United States. Based on projected energy demands and estimated available coal reserves, it has been calculated that an energy supply sufficient to meet our energy needs for the next 200–300 years exists within the coal measures. Large quantities of low sulfur coals of great thickness and at shallow depths are found in the western part of the United States. Some of the problems associated with the extraction of those coals are concerned primarily with the high total dissolved solids (T.D.S.) content of the drainages that will emanate from the mine operations, the preservation of the fertile valleys occupying the proposed mining sites, and the effect that the operations will have on the ground water resources. In contrast, the major problems associated with the strip mines of the bituminous coal fields of Appalachia and the Midwest center about the instability of backfilled areas leading toward mass movement, the reclamation of backfilled mines, and the generation of acidic mine drainages. This chapter addresses itself primarily to the last problem and the possible application of the following geochemical considerations to the reclamation and revegetation of surfaces of backfilled mines.

Acid mine drainage is an extremely acidic iron and sulfate rich drainage that forms under natural conditions when certain coal seams are mined and the associated strata are exposed to a new oxidizing environment. During this process a variety of iron sulfides ($FeS–FeS_2$) are exposed to the atmosphere and oxidize in the presence of oxygen and water to form soluble hydrous iron sulfates. These compounds commonly appear as white and yellow salt crusts on the surface of weathered rock faces. Some of the oxidation products have been identified as melanterite (white crystals of ferrous sulfate), copiapite (yellow crystals of ferric sulfate), halotrichite (white crystals of iron and magnesium sulfate), and alunogenite (white crystals of aluminum sulfate). Natural waters flowing over the weathered surfaces readily dissolve these compounds which hydrolyze in water and form acidic, high sulfate and high iron drainages. Subsequently, the ferrous iron is oxidized to the ferric state, complexing with ferrous and ferric oxyhydroxides that impart the red and yellow color characteristic of acid mine drainage. When the iron hydroxide precipitates on the base of streams, it forms the "yellow boy" that is commonly observed in the streams and drainages of some coal mine areas.

The general chemical reactions explaining the oxidation of FeS_2 and the production of acidity (H^+) are given by the following equations:

$$2FeS_{2(s)} + 7O_2 + 2H_2O = 2Fe^{2+} + 4SO_4^{2-} + 4H^+ \quad [1]$$

$$Fe^{2+} + 1/4 O_2 + H^+ = Fe^{3+} + 1/2 H_2O \quad [2]$$

$$Fe^{3+} + 3H_2O = Fe(OH)_{3(s)} + 3H^+ \quad [3]$$

$$FeS_{2(s)} + 14Fe^{3+} + 8H_2O = 15Fe^{2+} + 2SO_4^{2-} + 16H^+ \quad [4]$$

(Barnes & Romberger, 1968, and Baker, 1975)

The stoichiometry of Eq. [1] shows that 1 mole of FeS_2 will produce 2 moles of H^+ (acidity). In turn, the Fe^{2+} generated by the reaction of Eq. [2] can readily oxidize into Fe^{3+} and produce an additional 2 moles of H^+ (Eq. [3]). In the references cited by Baker (1975), it has been shown that the FeS_2 can also be oxidized in the presence of excess Fe^{3+} in solution with water and further hydrolyze to form additional H^+ (Eq. [4]).

The oxidation of Fe^{2+} to Fe^{3+} usually proceeds slowly under normal conditions, as in Eq. [2] and [3]. Howver, certain iron bacteria act as catalysts and greatly enhance and accelerate the chemical reaction rate. As early as 1919, workers have shown that, "the sulfur oxidation reactions appear to be hastened by the presence of bacteria or some catalytic agent," (Powell & Parr, 1919, in Temple & Koehler, 1954, p. 17). Subsequently, other workers investigating the oxidation rates of sterilized versus innoculated samples showed that certain iron bacteria do indeed catalyze the oxidation reactions involved in acid mine drainage formation and effectively increase the acidity produced.

Three bacteria have been isolated from the acid mine drainage geochemical regimes and identified as being responsible for the catalytic affect. They are *thiobacillus thiooxidans*, a sulfur-oxidizing bacteria; *thiobaccillus ferrooxidans*, a bacterium which oxidizes Fe^{2+} to Fe^{3+}, and *ferrobaccillus ferrooxidans*, another sulfur-oxidizing bacteria (EPA, 1971a). These bacteria are indigenous to aqueous environments with pH values that range from 2.8 to 3.2 and it becomes apparent that the pH of the ground water controls the occurrence and distribution of these bacteria. The geologic conditions leading toward the production of acidity or alkalinity and the implications that these have on the acid mine drainage reactions are discussed further in the following sections.

B. Geochemical Factors Affecting Drainage Quality

1. GENERAL RELATIONSHIPS

From the above discussions it follows that the occurrence of minerals producing acidity and alkalinity, and the various interactions, will ultimately control the quality of coal mine drainage. To some extent, the chemistry of the drainage is further modified by the ion exchange capacity of the material through which the drainage flows. In turn, the natural buffering capacity of the streams and waterways receiving the mine drainages further modifies the chemical composition of the streams in an area. For example, Biesecker and George (1965) showed that the mine drainages from the bituminous coal field of Pennsylvania flow through the reaches of the upper parts of Maryland which are underlain by limestone. In these areas, large concentrations of alkalinity are generated by the surrounding rock which effectively neutralize the acid mine drainages and ameliorate the water quality.

Whether a geologic system will be acidic or alkaline can be ascertained by evaluating the production potentials of the acidity and alkalinity components. If the factors are such that the alkalinity generated exceeds the acidity, then the system remains neutral or basic. The catalyzing bacteria are inhibited and the solubility of Fe^{2+} and Fe^{3+} is greatly reduced, which collectively inhibits the acid production reactions. On the other hand, if the acidity generated within any part of the geochemical system exceeds the alkalinity, the solubility of the FeS_2 is enhanced and the acid production is increased. In addition, the low pH of the system, which controls the distribution of the catalyzing bacteria, will also put additional Fe^{3+} into solution, which increases the acid load in accord with Eq. [4]. It becomes apparent that once the acid reaction begins, it becomes self-propagating, and all acid-producing mechanisms begin to interact in a synergistic manner.

Thus, to evaluate the drainage quality variations that could be expected from particular rock strata, the potential to produce acidity is balancd against the potential to produce alkalinity to determine the net resultant geochemistry. The following sections discuss how various geochemical factors affect the production of acidity or alkalinity and the possible interactions.

2. ACIDITY (SULFUR AS IRON DISULFIDE)

Sulfur in coal and associated strata can occur as organic sulfur, pyritic sulfur, and sulfate sulfur. Organic sulfur is the component that is complexed within the coal plant material and is organically bound within the coal. Generally, the organic sulfur component is not chemically reactive. Recent studies by Caruccio et al. (1977) showed that in eastern Kentucky the organic sulfur content of coal has a consistent average value between 0.35 to 0.5% (weight per weight basis).

Sulfate sulfur commonly represents the weathering products of the disulfides, as outlined in Eq. [1]. In most fresh samples from the areas of study in Kentucky, Pennsylvania, and West Virginia, the oxidation products constitute a small percentage of the total sulfur that is measured and is generally neglected.

Pyritic sulfur (as iron disulfide FeS_2) is the sulfur contained in the sulfide phase. Recent work by Baldwin (1975) has shown that other sulfide phases between zinc, lead, and copper could also form and could account for a minor portion of sulfides within coals. However, the dominant sulfide mineral in coal is marcasite or pyrite.

When samples are analyzed for sulfur content using the LECO combustion method (Caruccio, 1968), all three sulfur components are ignited and measured as total sulfur. Specific analytical tests can be used to determine the mode and occurrence of various types of sulfur. However, in this study all types were collectively ignited and analyzed as total sulfur, expressed as a percentage on a weight per weight basis.

Studies by Mansfield and Spackman (1965), Caruccio (1968), Caruccio et al. (1977), and J. Medlin (Coal Res. Div., USGS, Reston, Va., personal communication) have shown that variations in total sulfur content of coal samples collected from western Pennsylvania and eastern Kentucky usually reflect variations in the pyritic sulfur content. The organic sulfur content within particular coal seams had a narrow range of variance and remained relatively constant as a background value. Consequently, in these areas variations in total sulfur content measure variations in pyritic sulfur contents.

In comparing two strip-mined areas in central Pennsylvania, Caruccio (1968) showed that the occurrence of acid mine drainage could not be related to the sulfur content of the coals and overlying strata. The coals and strata of the two areas, one containing strip mines that produced acidity and the other containing mines with nonacid drainages, had total sulfur contents that were very similar. The microscopic examination of polished samples of coal and rock collected from the nonacid-producing area showed that these samples contained abundant amounts of pyrite, thus supporting the contention that total sulfur measurements reflected pyritic sulfur content. It was reasonably assumed that the pyritic sulfur contents were similar for samples collected from both the acid and nonacid areas.

In a combination of studies, selected samples of coal and rock were placed in leaching chambers and periodically flushed with deionized water. The quality of the leachate collected from each sample was analyzed and the degree of acidity produced by each sample was measured. Representative splits of the samples used in the leaching chambers were analyzed for sulfur contents and cast in molds for polished pellets that were microscopically examined. Caruccio (1968) found that the pyrite morphology was significantly different between the samples that produced acid and those that did not, even though the total sulfur contents were similar. Further, a significant difference in the pyrite morphology was found between the samples collected from the two areas. In samples from the nonacid-producing area, the pyrite commonly had a massive form and appeared to have been deposited after coalification.

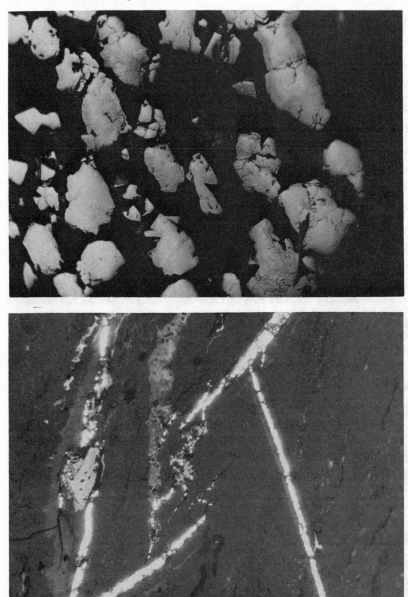

Fig. 1—Photomicrographs of stable pyrite (325×).

Most of the grains were >400 μm and some had a morphology that suggested that the pyrite had replaced plant structures and occupied joints in the coal (Fig. 1). The morphology of other grains not shown but also included in stable pyrite categories are crystals or euhedra of pyrite that commonly have cubical or triangular shapes. These particles, although small in size (between 5–10 μm), are relatively inert. In samples from the

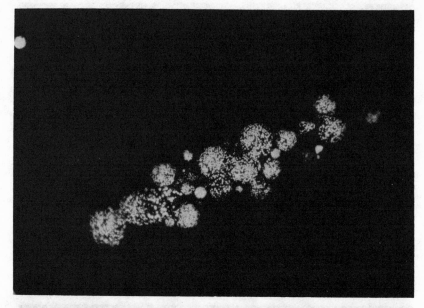

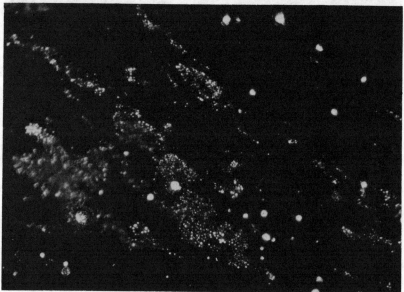

Fig. 2—Photomicrographs of reactive pyrite (325×).

acid-producing area, however, a major portion of the pyrite occurred as clusters of spheres approximately 25 μm in diameter. Each of the spheres was an agglomeration of minute (approximately 0.25 μm) crystals of pyrite that collectively formed the globular morphology (Fig. 2). Gray et al. (1963) called attention to this type of pyrite (often called framboidal pyrite) occurring in the Pittsburgh seam of Pennsylvania.

In a relative sense, the framboidal pyrite is much more reactive than the massive secondary pyrite. Coal and rock samples containing framboidal pyrite exposed to the laboratory atmosphere were noted to readily decompose to produce the salt crusts of oxidation products which commonly appear on the surface of the coal. On the other hand, samples containing coarse-grained particles of pyrite did not show appreciable signs of weathering, and the pyrite remained shiny and brassy for indefinite periods of time. Subsequent studies by Caruccio (1975) showed that the percentages of framboidal pyrite within samples of similar permeabilities multiplied by the total pyrite content of that sample can be used to estimate the acid-producing potential. On this premise, and in view of the limits of alkalinity imposed by the geochemical systems, the occurrence of acid mine drainage can be directly related to the occurrence of framboidal pyrite within a coal seam and associated calcareous deficient strata.

3. ALKALINITY (CALCAREOUS MATERIAL)

The preceeding discussions showed that the amount of acidity produced is dependent upon the amount of iron disulfide that is available for decomposition. Given a fixed amount of O_2 and Fe^{3+}, it follows that coals and strata containing abundant framboidal pyrite will tend to produce acidic mine drainages. However, Caruccio (1968) has shown that the degree of acidity is also a function of the calcium carbonate content of the strata (which has the potential of generating an alkaline, highly buffered, and potentially neutralizing drainage), and the pH of the ground water before mining takes place (which controls the occurrence of the various types of iron bacteria that catalyze the acid-producing chemical reaction and the solubility of iron).

In a strip mine, numerous strata of varying chemical compositions are disturbed by the mining process, and the ultimate quality of the drainage is a blend of all drainage chemistries produced by each rock type. Smith and his associates (1974) have developed a technique that evaluates the acid-base account of various overburden materials which can be used for selected material placement to enhance the revegetation of reclaimed mines. However, their acid estimates are obtained from total pyritic sulfur contents of the rocks without differentiation of pyrite types.

Just as the reactive pyrite content of a stratum generates acidity, the occurrence of calcium carbonate content in the stratigraphic section can generate moderate amounts of alkalinity. At a given partial pressure of CO_2 (pCO_2), infiltrating waters in contact with calcareous materials in the ground water regime generate alkalinity concentrations that are fixed by the pCO_2 and time of contact. The alkalinity can be calculated from the following equation:

$$\log Ca^{2+} \text{ (mg/liter)} = 2.56 + 0.362 \log pCO_2 \qquad [5]$$

and for each mole of calcium produced there are two moles of bicarbonate alkalinity.

In certain areas of the bituminous coal field of Pennsylvania, which are overlain by calcareous glacial drift, alkalinities of infiltrating waters can be as high as 400 mg/liter (as $CaCO_3$). In some nonglaciated areas where the Allegheny and Pottsville formations are exposed, the limited occurrence of calcareous material of the rocks yields ground waters with alkalinities ranging from 120 to 200 mg/liter (as $CaCO_3$, which can effectively neutralize 100 to 200 mg/liter of acidity [as $CaCO_3$]). In consideration of the limited amount of alkalinity generated in the stratigraphic section, the ultimate quality of the mine drainage is largely determined by the amount of acidity that is produced. If the acidity is less than the available alkalinity, the drainage will be neutral; if it is greater, the drainage will be acidic.

Under atmospheric conditions where the partial pressure of carbon dioxide is equal to $10^{-3.5}$ atm, the alkalinity generated by water flowing over calcareous material is about 60 mg/liter (as $CaCO_3$). If a good soil-mulch cover is developed the partial pressure of carbon dioxide in the soil could increase to about 10^{-1} (data taken from Black, 1957) and increase the available alkalinity of infiltrating waters by a factor of eight. This value assumes that the infiltrating waters move slow enough to allow the chemical reaction to go to completion. The development of a good mulch cover requires many years and the resulting high alkalinities may not be realized for some time. However, even assuming the system to be under conditions far from ideal, we could still expect an alkalinity concentration of about 185 mg/liter (as $CaCO_3$) which can effectively neutralize equal amounts of acidity.

The dependency of the generation of alkalinity upon the partial pressure of carbon dioxide, which, in turn, is a function of a soil mulch cover, underscores the necessity of establishing a rapidly growing vegetation cover in order to successfully reclaim an area. To this end, it is urged that there should be an initial planting of carpet grasses and, subsequently, after the grasses have been established, the planting of trees. The grasses will provide a good soil mulch as well as effectively reducing the temperatures of the surface rock fragments, thereby providing for the greater retention of soil moisture. Proper management is required to insure that an effective growth medium is provided at the surface and that tree and grass growth be compatible.

4. pH

In addition to providing a neutralization potential, calcium carbonate also renders the ground water alkaline, which affects the occurrence of the catalyzing iron bacteria and the stability of pyrite. In the absence of calcareous material, the pH of the natural ground water could be < 5.5, which supports the catalyzing iron bacteria and effectively compounds the acid problem. In the presence of calcareous material, the ground waters normally will be alkaline, which effectively inhibits the acid-producing bacteria and reduces the acid potential. Indeed, in some cases, alkaliniity may be favorable to the viability of bacteria that produce basic substances (EPA, 1971a).

The pH of the water is also important in establishing the stability of certain types of pyrite. In a study by Temple and Koehler (1954) on the reactivity and the stability of sulfur balls, the presence of calcium and magnesium was identified in stable pyrite nodules, but noted to be absent in the reactive ones. Significantly, washing the nodules with acid, implying the removal of calcium and magnesium, rendered the inert sample reactive. Assuming that this mechanism applies to the study area, it is apparent that once acidic waters are formed, they will effectively leach the iron disulfides of their protective calcium carbonate and perpetuate the oxidation reaction. The oxidation reaction in turn generates additional mineral acidity which enhances the leaching process, liberating additional acidity for more effective calcareous leaching. In turn, additional Fe^{3+} is placed into solution, which increases the acid-producing reaction of Eq. [4]. Once acidic waters are generated, the mechanism becomes self-propagating.

C. Interactions

Within a hydrogeologic regime, an evaluation of rock–water quality interactions is necessary in order to predict the coal mine drainage quality that is to be expected. In a recent study based in eastern Kentucky, samples of coal were collected and analyzed for the occurrence and distribution of framboidal pyrite within the coal and overlying strata. Previous work has shown that the overlying roof rock can be used to identify the chemical character of the coal. Because of a strong association between the coal and overlying strata, the coal was used to approximate the quality of the overburden which, in turn, was related to the chemical quality of the ground water. Fresh samples of coal were collected from selected locations along the coal seam, and representative portions of each sample were cast in plastic pellets and polished. The polished surface was then examined with a light-reflecting microscope to determine the percentage and distribution of pyrite types, i.e., framboidal percentages vs. secondary.

Within the geologic system, the ground water migrates through the overlying strata and vertically into the coal seam. At the base of the seam the flow encounters the underlying seat earth and, because of the low permeability, moves laterally along the coal (the coal acts as an aquifer) until the water emanates from the coal face. As the water flows through the geologic regime, along joints and fractures, a variety of chemical constituents, including the framboidal pyrite and calcium carbonate are put into solution. Because the water reflects the gross chemical composition of the coal and overlying strata over a larger area, samples of water within the area of study were chemically analyzed and the data were used to complement and substantiate the results obtained from the microscopic examination of the coal samples. In so doing, the interpretations of the microscopic study of the coal samples would have a broader base and could be extended to a regional significance.

II. CASE HISTORY

A. Introduction

The recently completed construction along Interstate I-64 between Grayson and Ashland, Ky., exposed a variety of coal seams which, due to their relatively unweathered state, provided an excellent base for a study relating the occurrence of framboidal pyrite and calcium carbonate to coal mine drainage quality. Extensive detailed mapping of the strata in these roadcuts by Drs. John Horne and John Ferm (Caruccio et al., 1977) enabled them to recognize the environments in which the coals were deposited. These paleoenvironments ranged from alluvial plains through upper delta and lower delta plains grading into tidally influenced back and beach barriers. Accordingly, fresh water coals are associated with alluvial–upper delta plain strata, and marine–brackish water coals are associated with lower delta plain–back barrier strata, with a transitional zone between these two end members.

From the exposures along I-64, numerous samples of coal from all paleoenvironments were collected and analyzed for framboidal pyrite content and for total sulfur analysis. Given the premise that framboidal pyrite is the most reactive of the pyrite types, coupled with the assumption that variations of total sulfur contents reflect variations in pyritic sulfur contents of the samples, the percentage of reactive pyrite of each sample can be calculated.

An empirical relationship between total sulfur and pyritic sulfur had been derived. With many exceptions, the following formula can be used to calculate pyritic sulfur from total sulfur:

$$S_{pyritic} = 0.78\,S_{total} - 0.49.$$

In a field geochemical survey, water samples were collected from springs and water seeps emanating from the coal faces where the coal samples were collected. Because the quality of ground water reflects the overall geochemistry of the strata and represents a larger geologic regime, the analyses of specific chemical quality parameters serve to corroborate the sulfur analyses and the pyrite morphology distribution data.

B. Water Quality Parameters

At each location from which the coals were sampled, the coal face was chiseled away with a hand pick until a water flow was encountered. In most cases, a slow, steady flow could be obtained and, by the proper manipulation of a plastic straw, in juxtaposition with a sample bottle, a sufficient volume of water could be collected for chemical analyses. Of the 48 coal sample locales, 46 had a sufficient water flow that could be collected and subsequently analyzed. Each sample was analyzed for specific chemical parameters that could be readily related to the geochemistry of the strata and which are indicative of a particular chemical reaction. Ultimately, the quality of the drainage could be related to pyrite stability or reactivity. The specific parameters measured and the reason for choosing them are outlined below.

1. pH

The pH reflects the degree of acidity or alkalinity that could be expected from the sample. Within broad limits, the character of the sample could be quickly determined and related to the geochemistry of the strata. To insure that no changes in pH occurred due to changes in temperature, dissolution of gases, etc., all pH measurements were made in the field at the collection site using a portable Photovolt pH meter. Prior to measurement, the meter and electrode were calibrated using the appropriate buffers.

2. CONDUCTIVITY

Within broad estimates, the electrical properties of the solution reflect the ionic strength of a solution. Thus, the conductivity of the water sample can be related to the total dissolved solids content of the water sample and is related to the chemical activity that has taken place within the aquifer or coal seam through which the ground water flowed. Conductivities of samples were measured within a 12-hour period from time of collection using a portable Universal Interloc conductivity meter which was calibrated and standardized against a known conductivity standard solution.

3. ACIDITY

As outlined in the beginning of this paper, the iron disulfide readily oxidizes to produce a ferrous sulfate compound which is readily soluble in water and hydrolyzes to produce acidity and attendant amounts of sulfate. In the absence of neutralization, the measure of the acidity of water flowing from a seam is a good estimate of the amount of reactive pyrite that could be expected to be found in that particular coal seam. In the presence of neutralization, the acidity and alkalinity concentrations are reviewed in conjunction with sulfate concentrations to deduce pyrite reactivity (discussed in following sections). These data coupled with the percentage of framboidal pyrite, as noted to occur in the polished pellets, should approximate the water quality that could be expected from a particular coal seam and the abundance of reactive pyrite present in the seam.

Hot acidities were determined in a laboratory after boiling the sample for 2 minutes. This insured the complete oxidation and hydrolysis of the iron compounds and expelled the carbonic acid acidity. The sample was then titrated with a $0.025N$ sodium hydroxide solution to a pH 7.0 endpoint which was potentiometrically determined (Rainwater & Thatcher, 1960).

4. HARDNESS

In water samples collected for this study, the hardness reflects the presence and relative abundance of either calcium, magnesium, or iron. By examining the hardness data in conjunction with the acidity and pH data, the dominance of a particular cation could be accurately deduced. If, for example, a high hardness content appears, coupled with a high acidity and low pH, one can assume that the primary cation contributing to hardness is soluble iron. If, on the other hand, hardness is present in samples with a low acidity and high pH, it can be correctly assumed that the dominant divalent cation is calcium or magnesium.

Hardness determinations were made in the laboratory by the complexiometric EDTA method as outlined in *Standard Methods* (APHA, 1971).

5. SULFATE

Sulfate concentrations were analyzed by a modified barium chloranilate method outlined in *Method for Chemical Analyses of Water and Wastes* (EPA, 1971b). The chloranilate ion is released in the presence of an acid buffer and develops a wine color that is proportional to the amount of sulfate ion present. The intensity of the color of the filtrate was colorimetrically measured on a B & L Spec-20 meter and related to a standard curve. To preclude cation interferences, the samples were passed through cation exchange columns before adding the reagent.

As noted previously, the decomposition of pyrite produces sulfate, in addition to iron and acidity. On the assumption that the strata do not contain abundant amounts of either gypsum or anhydrite, it could be readily assumed that the primary source of sulfate is the decomposition of reactive pyrite. As such, sulfate contents are an excellent measure of the degree of reactive pyrite present in the section.

6. GENERAL RELATIONSHIPS

The exact nature of the geochemical system of the coal and overlying strata from which the water sample was collected can be quickly ascertained if sulfate data are related to and examined in conjunction with hardness, acidity, and pH. If, for example, a sample has a high sulfate, hardness, and acidity content, coupled with a low pH, it could be readily assumed that that particular stratigraphic section is generating acid mine drainage and contains abundant amounts of reactive pyrite. If, on the other hand, the sample contains low sulfate concentrations, coupled with high hardness, low acidity, and high pH, it could be assumed that the water flowed through strata containing calcareous material and a paucity of reactive pyrite. Finally, if a sample has a high sulfate, high hardness, low acidity, and high pH, it could be assumed that the geochemical system is such that acidity is being generated by reactive pyrite, but is subsequently neutralized by the alkalinity produced by calcareous material present in the section.

Thus, by noting the interrelationships between pH, conductivity, acidity, hardness, and sulfate, the interrelationships and combinations thereof between reactive pyrite (generating acidity) and calcareous material (generating alkalinity) can be effectively determined.

III. DATA AND INTERPRETATIONS

A. Occurrence of Framboidal Pyrite (Acid Production Potential)

The Kentucky field survey which was designed to test the variability of total sulfur content occurring in the channel and column samples of coal seams showed that the percentage of total sulfur varied to a greater degree than had been previously suspected (Caruccio et al., 1977). Marked differences in the sulfur content of samples collected from various geographic areas suggested that similar variations existed within the framboidal pyrite content. In order to make a valid comparison between coals found in different paleoenvironments, an examination of samples common to one geographic location must be made.

Accordingly, the samples collected from Kentucky Interstate 64 between Grayson and Ashland, Kentucky were used for the comparison. The pyritic sulfur and framboidal pyrite percentages for each seam were calculated and plotted as shown in Fig. 3. In this figure, the upper delta plain (fresh water) sequence is represented by the Princess 7 coals, the transitional sequence by the Princess 5 coals, and the lower delta plain (marine–brackish) paleoenvironment is represented by the Tom Cooper and Wolf Creek coals. The results obtained from the I-64 sites were used when comparing coals of differing paleoenvironments, mainly because of the availability of a larger number of samples.

It was originally hypothesized that a preponderance of framboidal pyrite would be associated with the marine–brackish water coal sequences when framboidal pyrite percentages and total sulfur contents of individual samples were plotted within groups of coals from similar paleoenvironments. However, the histograms plotted in Fig. 3 show that framboidal pyrite is found in coals of all paleoenvironments and is not restricted to a marine–transitional environment.

The above hypothesis was tested with a Chi Square test which showed that there was a significant difference in framboidal pyrite content between the upper delta plain coals and the transitional/lower delta plain coals. A one-way analysis of variance showed no measurable difference when the upper delta plain coals and the lower delta plain coals were compared to the transitional ones, but that there was a significant difference (at the 95% level) when the upper delta plain coals were compared to the lower delta plain coals. Inasmuch as the transitional environment is a blend of the extreme environments, it is to be expected that the coals from all three environments would be similar when compared to the "median" environment. However, it is significant that the lower delta

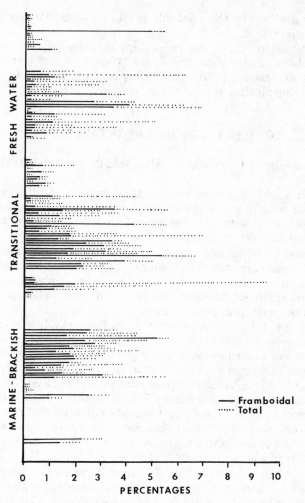

Fig. 3—Total and framboidal pyrite distribution for coals grouped into paleoenvironments.

plain coals contain more framboidal pyrite than the upper delta plain coals.

Because of the variability of total sulfur content within coals, we suspect that a similar variability also exists within the distribution of framboidal pyrite. Although this may reflect the variability of micro-paleoenvironments within one coal seam, it appears that, generally, greater percentages of framboidal pyrite combined with a greater percentage of pyritic sulfur occur in lower delta plain sequences when compared to the upper delta plain-alluvial sequences.

Therefore, within the constraints in interpretations imposed by the variability of total sulfur contents, a positive relationship exists between the occurrence of framboidal pyrite in lower delta plain sequences, and a relative paucity of framboidal pyrite in the upper delta plain sequences.

B. Aqueous Geochemistry

1. OBJECTIVE

The quality of a mine drainage will be the end result of a combination of complex geochemical interactions involving different ions from a variety of sources. It has been shown that the source of acidity, iron, and sulfate in mine drainage can be readily related to the occurrence and decomposition of framboidal pyrite. Calcareous material found within a hydrogeologic environment provides the geochemical system with a natural buffering capacity. Ground water flowing within a geologic section and contacting either or both of these geochemical effects will absorb specific chemical species that reflect either of these reactions or combinations thereof.

This section discusses the effect that ground water chemistry has on the quality of mine drainage produced from a stratigraphic section. Previous results showed that reactive framboidal pyrite is found within all strata of varying paleoenvironments, albeit in greater preponderance within coals associated with strata of marine–brackish water paleoenvironments. As such, acidic drainages would be expected to be produced and emanate throughout the stratigraphic section. However, this anticipation does not consider the profound effect that the natural aqueous geochemistry has on the ultimate quality of mine drainage. The importance of considering the buffering effects of the natural system was best exemplified in the study by Biesecker and George (1966) who showed that streams degraded by acid mine drainage were ameliorated as they flowed through terrains underlain by calcareous strata. In the present study, similar affects by natural buffering systems were also noted to occur.

2. REGIONAL WATER QUALITY CHARACTERISTICS

All locations where coal samples were previously collected were revisitied during the month of June 1975. At most of the locations, water samples were collected and analyzed for field pH, conductivity, acidity, hardness, and sulfate concentrations. In the following discussions, the sulfate, acidity, conductivity, and pH values of water samples collected from the marine–brackish water strata will be contrasted with those collected from the coals of the fresh water strata.

The conductivity data are grouped by various paleoenvironments and plotted in Fig. 4. Acid mine drainages that were sampled during the survey are plotted at the top of the diagram for comparison. Interestingly, higher conductivities are noted for water samples collected from the fresh water sequence than those emanating from the marine–brackish water strata. This water quality trend, high conductivity with high pH, suggests the presence of calcareous material. Obviously, alkalinity measurements would have more directly substantiated this premise but, because of the sampling difficulty and the inability to run alkalinity analyses within 12

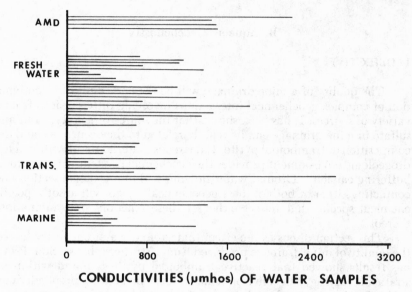

CONDUCTIVITIES (µmhos) OF WATER SAMPLES

Fig. 4—Conductivities of water samples from various paleoenvironments.

hours (thereby precluding valid results), these analyses were not performed.

The sulfate data from the water samples were similarly plotted, grouping samples into various paleoenvironment categories. In Fig. 5, sulfate concentrations are plotted vs. the paleoenvironment of the coal seam. The values for acid drainages collected from the area are included for reference. Again, another interesting trend is observed. Sulfate, whose source is primarily from the decomposition of the sulfide, is abundant in water samples collected from the fresh water strata. Because there are almost three times as many samples collected from this sequence as there are from the marine–brackish water sequence, a sample bias is introduced which may affect the interpretations. Regardless of this potential error, the fact remains that significant amounts of sulfate are found in water samples emanating from the rocks deposited in a fresh water environment. This fact readily substantiates the data presented in Fig. 3, which showed significant percentages of reactive pyrite occurring within coals of fresh water paleoenvironments. The significantly high sulfate concentrations of ground water emanating from the fresh water coals further suggests that framboidal pyrite is present throughout these seams on a regional scale. Equivalent amounts of sulfate are also noted to occur in water samples collected from the transitional and marine–brackish water strata which again substantiate the data derived from the microscopic examination of the pellets.

The significant effect that the natural buffering capacity has on drainage quality becomes further apparent when the sulfate concentrations are plotted against the pH values for the water samples collected from the various paleoenvironments. In Fig. 6, the sulfate vs. pH values

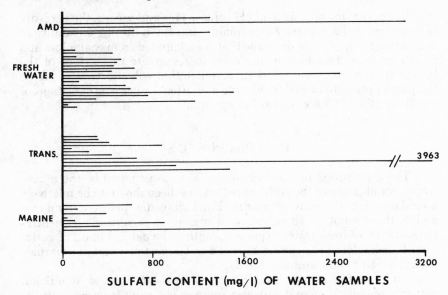

SULFATE CONTENT (mg/l) OF WATER SAMPLES

Fig. 5—Sulfate content of water samples from various paleoenvironments.

of the water samples were plotted according to the paleoenvironment of the source bed.

Interestingly, some water samples collected from strata of a marine-brackish water paleoenvironment have low pH's and high sulfate (exceeding 750 mg/liter), as would be expected if the strata contained reactive acid producing pyrite and no natural buffering capacity. In contrast, water samples from fresh water paleoenvironments containing high sulfate have pH's that approach neutrality. This supports the premise that acid-producing pyrite and no natural buffering capacity. In contrast, tents, but that the acidity is being neutralized by the available alkalinity,

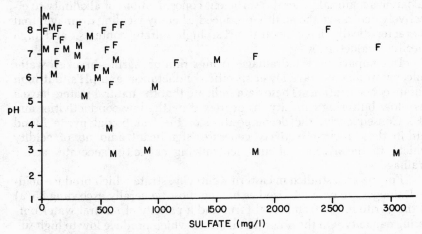

Fig. 6—pH vs. sulfate of water samples from marine *(M)* and fresh water *(F)* strata.

which accounts for near neutral pH values. This underscores the necessity of considering the natural water quality and the buffering capability in evaluating the quality of drainage that is anticipated from coal mines and reclaimed sites. In addition, the need to revegetate the surface of the backfilled mine to provide an organic mulch that will effectively increase the partial pressure of carbon dioxide and affect larger concentrations of alkalinity (Eq. [5]) becomes further apparent.

IV. CONCLUSIONS

The distribution of framboidal pyrite, as ascertained by the microscopic examination of the polished pellets, has been shown to be relatively abundant in coal seams of marine–brackish water paleoenvironments and, although not as abundant, also present in significant concentrations in coals of fresh water sequences. Within the natural limits of variation, framboidal pyrite can be expected to be most prevalent in marine–brackish water and transitional coals.

On a regional basis, water quality analyses showed significant amounts of sulfate present in water samples collected from coals in the fresh water and marine–brackish water strata. The presence of sulfate anion in water samples can be correlated with the occurrence of reactive pyrite in strata. In some cases, large amounts of framboidal pyrite in marine–brackish water coals produced high sulfate-acid drainages.

The presence of sulfate in water samples collected from the fresh water sequence corroborates the results of the microscopic examination of the polished pellets which showed framboidal pyrite to be present in fresh water coal seams. Yet, in the majority of cases, drainages from these strata are neutral and have high specific conductances. These data suggest that the water is flowing through strata that contain reactive pyrite which is decomposing to produce moderate amounts of acidity and sulfate anion. Within other parts of the flow regime, water in contact with calcareous material generates sufficient concentrations of alkalinity to effectively neutralize the acidity produced, thereby yielding drainages that characteristically have neutral pH's, high sulfate contents, and high specific conductances.

In comparison, the drainages from strata of marine–brackish water paleoenvironments have lower specific conductances and pH's, but high sulfate concentrations. These data indicate that the natural waters have a very low buffering capacity, as expressed by the low conductivities and pH. Consequently, the decomposition of the framboidal pyrite found within these rocks effectively generates significant amounts of acidity which, in the absence of any neutralizing capacity, generates acidic drainages.

For the area studied in eastern Kentucky, strata which produce acidic drainages are characterized as having most (generally exceeding 85%) of the pyrite in the framboidal form and a paucity of natural water buffering capacity. On the other hand, strata which produce low to high sulfate-neutral pH drainages usually have 5–30% of the pyrite in the framboidal form and are associated with highly buffered alkaline–water systems. Thus, the prevalence of framboidal pyrite, in combination with the alkalinity of natural waters, determines the quality of drainage from various strata.

During the strip mining operations, rocks capable of generating acidity and alkalinity become disrupted, effectively increasing the surface areas of reactions and magnifying the concentrations of the various water quality components. Studies are now in progress to evaluate the magnitudes of increase in alkalinity and acidity that could be expected when rock layers are fractured. Factors such as jointing patterns, permeability, and physical decomposition characteristics are among the variables being considered.

ACKNOWLEDGMENTS

Drs. John Ferm and John Horne, formerly with the Department of Geology, University of South Carolina, provided the basis for the interpretation and identification of the coal's paleoenvironment. The latter also assisted in the collection of the coal and water samples. Mr. Jeff Baldwin assisted in the field work and collection phases and fabricated most of the pellets used in this study.

The results presented in this paper are part of a larger study that was funded by the Resource Extraction and Handling Division of the Environmental Protection Agency, Grant Number R803895-01-0. Our gratitude is extended to Mr. Elmore Grim for his support and encouragement during the study.

LITERATURE CITED

American Public Health Association. 1971. Standard methods for the examination of water and wastewater. 13th ed. APHA, Washington, D.C.

Baker, M. 1975. Inactive and abandoned underground mines-water pollution prevention and control. EPA-440/9-75-007. USEPA, Washington, D.C.

Baldwin, J. S. 1975. The vertical and lateral distribution of trace elements in the Fire clay coal seam near Hazard, Kentucky. Geol. Soc. of America Abstracts for 1975 National Meeting, G.S.A., Boulder, Colorado.

Barnes, H. L., and S. B. Romberger. 1968. Chemical aspects of acid mine drainage. J. Water Pollut. Control Fed. 40:371–384. Part 1.

Biesecker, J. E., and J. R. George. 1966. Stream quality in Appalachia as related to coal-mine drainage, 1965. Geol. Surv. Cir. 526. U.S. Geological Survey, Washington, D.C.

Black, C. A. 1957. Soil-plant relationships. John Wiley, New York.

Caruccio. F. 1968. An evaluation of factors affecting acid mine drainage production and the ground water interactions in selected areas of western Pennsylvania. p. 107–151. In Preprints of papers presented before the 2nd Symp. on Coal Mine Drainage Res., 14 May 1968, Bituminous Coal Res., Monroeville, Pa.

Caruccio, F. 1975. Estimating the acid potential of coal mine refuse, p. 197–205. In The ecology of resource degradation and renewal. Blackwell Scientific Publ., London, England.

Caruccio., F., J. C. Ferm, J. Horne, G. Geidel, and B. Baganz. 1977. Paleoenvironment of coal and its relation to drainage quality. EPA-600/7-77-067. Natl. Tech. Inf. Serv., Springfield, Va.

Gray, R. J., N. Shapiro, and G. D. Coe. 1963. Distribution and forms of sulfur in a high volatile Pittsburgh coal seam. Trans. Soc. Min Eng. 226:113–121.

Mansfield, S. P., and W. Spackman. 1965. Petrographic composition and sulfur content of selected Pennsylvania bituminous coal seams. SR-50. Coal Res. Sec., Pennsylvania State Univ., University Park, Pa.

Rainwater, F. H., and L. L. Thatcher. 1960. Methods for collection and analysis of water samples. U.S. Geol. Surv. Water Supply Pap. 1454. Supt. of Doc., Washington, D.C.

Smith, R. M., W. Grube, T. Arkle, and A. Sobek. 1974. Mine spoil potentials for soil and water quality. EPA 670/2-74-070. USEPA, Cincinnati, Ohio.

Temple, K. L., and W. A. Koehler. 1954. Drainage from bituminous coal mines. Eng. Exp. Stn. Bull. 25. West Virginia Univ., Morgantown, W. Va.

U.S. Environmental Protection Agency. 1971a. Inorganic sulfur oxidation by iron-oxidizing bacteria. Water Pollut. Control Res. Series. 14010-DAY-06/71. USEPA., Supt. of Doc., Washington, D.C.

U.S. Environmental Protection Agency. 1971b. Methods for chemical analyses of water and wastes. USEPA 16020-07/71. N.E.R.C., Cincinnati, Ohio.

Chapter 9

Physical and Chemical Properties of Overburdens, Spoils, Wastes, and New Soils

RICHARD MERIWETHER SMITH AND ANDREW A. SOBEK

West Virginia University, Morgantown, and
Argonne National Laboratory, Argonne, Illinois, respectively.

I. INTRODUCTION

In this chapter we agree with a modern definition of soil as "the collection of natural bodies of the earth's surface, in places modified or even made by man of earthy materials containing living matter and supporting or capable of supporting plants out-of-doors" (USDA-SCS, 1975). Moreover, we accept the pedologic principle that soils should be defined, classified, and managed in accordance with soil profile properties that can be observed or measured. This viewpoint applies to highly disturbed or manmade soils as well as to soils reflecting all degrees of lesser disturbance. Very few soils have escaped man's influence.

The same principle regarding properties applies to earth or rocks that are to be disturbed and used near the land surface for the creation of new soils and surfaces. The genesis, age, or stratigraphic position of these earthy materials are of interest in this context only insofar as they provide information about properties that will influence the quality of soils being formed. However, sedimentary rock classification by texture, composition, and other properties as discussed by Folk (1954) and Krumbein and Sloss (1963) relates more directly to soil formation by disturbance than genetic or historical classifications. Other obvious variables with functional influences on man-made soils include methods of disturbance, weather or climate, and motivation of operators.

There should be an engineering dictum that advance planning is essential to success in major disturbance activities. It is inconceivable that a responsible engineer would start building a highway, an urban mall, or a surface mine without some appraisal of the rock and soil to be disturbed or used. Recently, we have seen increasing emphasis on planning to avoid pollution as well as planning to achieve economical and technically sound goals in engineering, recreation, or production (USDA Staff, 1968; Anderson, 1971; Glover, 1971; Patterson, 1974). This chapter emphasizes properties of earthy materials (rocks, soils, or wastes) that influence pollution and quality of landscape. Properties considered are oriented toward efficiency of operations and quality of resulting land for anticipated use. This means that practical selectivity determines the choice of properties measured and methods used. Different choices would prevail under a different bias or if absolute scientific objectivity could be achieved. However, properties favored in this chapter are similar to those emphasized previously (Kohnke, 1950; Grandt & Lang, 1958; Chapman, 1967; Knabe, 1964 and 1973).

II. ACTION BEFORE AND DURING MAJOR DISTURBANCES

A. Advance Mapping and Sampling

A modern detailed soil survey at 1:15,000 or 1:20,000 aids planning a major land disturbance such as a surface mine or an urbanization project. Such a survey may lack detail for some needs, but it should provide enough information about the top several feet of land cover to be useful. Profile texture, horizonation, drainage, and general acidic or basic status are indicated by soil units identified. In addition, the topmost horizon would be classed as Mollic (deep, neutral, soft, and dark) or not, providing a clue to usefulness for segregation and replacement after disturbance. Greater detail regarding soils is sometimes needed and is obtained by more intensive study or on-site investigation.

Geologic mapping on a scale of 1:24,000 or larger should be available before major land disturbances. In mining, exploration drilling to determine thickness and quality of coal or mineral can be used to map overlying rock units as well (Smith et al., 1974a and 1976), and to collect appropriate depth samples for field and laboratory analyses. Examples of such sampling are provided by premining planning in Great Britain (Riley & Rinier, 1972; Striffler, 1967); East and West Germany (Knabe, 1964 and 1973); Czechoslovakia (Jonas, 1973 and 1974); Poland (Bauman, 1976); central U.S.., Indiana (Wiram & Deane, 1974), and Illinois, where recent regulations identify properties required for surface, root zone, and nontoxic materials (R. T. Dawe. 1975. Director, Illinois Dep. of Mines and Minerals, informational memorandum); and in West Virginia where selective sampling and analysis is being used by the West Virginia Department of Natural Resources to aid operators in meeting water quality standards (West Virginia DNR, 1976).

Since three-dimensional rock units can change gradually or abruptly, the ideal spacing for analyses must involve judgment. However, one arbitrary suggestion that seems reasonable is that all mining or other disturbance shall be within 1 km of a rock core of column that has been sampled and analyzed by approved methods. More detailed sampling may be judged necessary, depending on complexity indicated by pedologic and geologic mapping. Vertical spacing of samples that has been satisfactory in practice below the A, B, and C horizons of soil profiles is one sample to represent each 30 cm of depth where little detailed attention has been given to rock strata in place. This kind of sampling involves catching the chips expelled by an air drill (West Virginia Univ., 1971; Smith et al., 1974a).

In cases where exploration test cores or fresh high wall exposures have been available, all distinctive horizons thicker than 12 cm are recognized for possible sampling. Thinner layers have been ignored unless properties afforded special interest, in which case they are sampled regardless of thickness. Thick rock members are subdivided and samples taken representing thicknesses of 150 cm or less in thick-bedded or massive sandstone and 90 cm or less in other rock types (shale, mudstone, limestone, intercalate, loess, till, etc.) (Smith et al., 1974a; Sobek et al., 1976. Field and laboratory methods applicable to overburdens and minesoils. US-EPA. In process). Thus, each total section for study and analysis averages approximately one sample per meter.

Decisions regarding sampling should be based on rock types defined in terms of properties. An inexperienced or untrained person should take a sample arbitrarily from near the center of each 30 cm of depth rather than attempting to separate and sample in detail by rock types or soil horizons.

Details of rock type definitions, use of Munsell color books, use of 10% hydrochloric acid to detect carbonates, determining hardness by fingernail, penny, or knife, and certain other field or laboratory clues to important properties have been spelled out for general application (Grube & Smith, 1974; Smith et al., 1974a). Some arbitrariness is essential to consistency in determination of rock and soil properties needed for planning disturbances and future use of land following placement of materials and reclamation.

B. Environmental Objective

It is important to study properties having overriding influence on the primary objectives of the activity. In this paper we are assuming that protection or improvement of the environment is our number one objective. Such an assumption leads to conclusions that environmental objectives either will be achieved or the activity will be prevented. If conditions exist under which the activity is more important to society than the desired environment, then different choices might be required. Economic considerations would provide the logical basis for choices not controlled by immediate environmental concern, but reliable economic calculations must be based on sophisticated assumptions that cannot be accepted casually. For example, the disarmingly simple assumption that surface mining destroys land for posterity leads to the conclusion that such mining should be prevented. But a different assumption about the post-mining valuation results in a different economic conclusion (Grandt & Lang, 1958; Knabe, 1964; Pitsenbarger, 1974 and 1975; Frederick, 1971; Smith, 1971). If surface mining recovers coal or other minerals profitably and improves land at the same time, then we can't afford not to use the surface mining method.

C. Acid-Base Accounting

Acid drainage and toxicity from mining (Temple & Koehler, 1954; Hill, 1970; Berg & Vogel, 1973) and from highway construction (Miller et al., 1976) have received such attention that acid-base accounting, to provide a basis for predicting extreme acidity of disturbed materials and likely associated concentrations of soluble aluminum and iron or other toxic metals, has become a popular method. As described in detail elsewhere (Smith et al., 1976), when paste pH measurements on finely pulverized rock or soil is considered in conjunction with titratable neutralizers as well as immediate and potential maximum acidity expressed as $CaCO_3$ equivalents, satisfactory assurance against excess acidity has been provided. The approach is similar to development of base-acid balances and their successful use in studies near Cottbus, East Germany as described by Knabe (1973). In Germany the balance derives from summation of basic cations vs. actual potential mineral (mostly sulphate) anions.

Complications involved in predicting rates of oxidation and acid formation from pyritic sulphur are such that no generally applicable methods have been recommended. Essential variables influencing rates of acid formation include reactive surface area (Singer & Stumm, 1968), ferric iron (Singer & Stumm, 1968), partial pressure of oxygen (Smith & Shumate, 1970), forms of pyritic sulphur (Caruccio, 1968), catalytic agents (Singer & Stumm, 1968; Caruccio, 1968), pH (Smith & Shumate, 1970), and *Thiobacillas* or *Ferrobacillas* organisms (Wilson, 1965; Wilson & Zuberer, 1976). The possibility of quantifying all of these and possibly other controlling variables in different rock types under diverse field situations is remote. Moreover, precise knowledge regarding oxidation rates is not needed for most real world situations when maximum potential acidity has been determined. Extensive testing by the relatively simple pH and acid-base accounting approach based on maximum immediate acidity plus maximum future sulfate acidity has resolved or indicated reasonable precautions needed in most field situations. Definition of toxic or potentially toxic cases by this means may warn against some materials that will remain satisfactory for many years because of limited pyritic surface area or other control of oxidation rate, but the warning against potential toxicity at some time in the future appears to constitute a wise precaution. Moreover, in practice, most examples have proven to be reasonably clear cut when the pH and acid-base account of particular rock types in stratigraphic sequence are known.

Regardless of intended future land use, we are assuming that acid-toxic or potentially toxic disturbed soils and water are a violation of environmental goals and, hence, are not acceptable. Other properties of disturbed soils may be acceptable for one land use but not for another. Physical stability on steep slopes is a requirement that might be rated essential for all land uses except extensive wildlife and recreation in remote woodland. Favorable, near neutral reaction and favorable plant nutrient levels would be rated desirable, if not essential, wherever production of sensitive agricultural crops was involved.

An example of an acid-base account is given in Fig. 1. Such illustra-

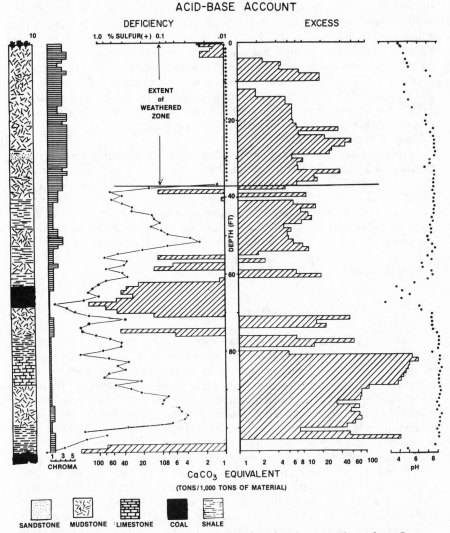

Fig. 1—Overburden properties above the Pittsburgh and Redstone Coals, Barbour County, W. Va. (Grube, 1974).

tions indicate common interrelations found in the Pittsburgh coal basin of Appalachia. Chroma of 2 or lower (Munsell color chips) and increased total sulphur identify the bottom of the zone of pyrite and iron oxidation commonly called the weathering front at a depth of 11.3 m (37 ft). Often this depth approximates 6 m in the eastern U.S. (West Virginia Univ., 1971). However, pH and calcium carbonate equivalent suggest that geologic or pedologic leaching of natural bases has penetrated only to about 6.4 m (21 ft). This difference between depth of pyrite oxidation and depth of carbonate leaching is typical of other cases studied in the Appalachian basins as well as in eastern Interior and western Interior basins (Grube, 1974; Smith et al., 1976). Known cases of pyrite destruction by oxidation deeper than carbonate leaching occur in calcareous mudrocks where water movement is slow and neutralizing capacity exceeds maximum mineral activity. Obviously, low pH, required for *Thiobacillas* activity (Wilson & Zuberer, 1976) is not essential for oxidation of pyritic minerals in the natural environment, although rapid rates of oxidation may be favored by *Thiobacillas* and *Ferrobacillas*. Direct chemical oxidation is the assumed dominant process at near neutral pH. Smith and Shumate (1970) have indicated that the rate of such oxidation increases with increasing pH in the acid range rather than decreasing as expected with the *Thiobacillas* microorganisms.

Application of the suggested definition of *potentially toxic* is well illustrated by Fig. 1. A calcium carbonate deficiency of 5 parts or more per 1,000 parts of material has been used arbitrarily for this definition (Smith et al., 1974c; Smith et al., 1973). In Fig. 1, the soil zone shows a deficiency of 2 to 3 parts per 1,000, corresponding with a pH near 5. This zone would not be considered potentially toxic but some deeper samples, especially between 11.6 m (38 ft) and 23.1 m (76 ft), would be rated potentially acid toxic even though low pH measurements were obtained only in or immediately above the Redstone (upper) coal.

D. Other Appropriate Analyses

Although pH and the acid-base account have been identified as worthy of overriding importance, other properties of overburden should be determined and considered as guides to practices and placement of materials for best results under projected land management. In most cases, operators should be able to increase efficiency of mining and reclamation by carefully considering overburden properties. Successful operators commonly understand the removal and placement of different kinds of materials with proper equipment better than their competitors. However, since emphasis on consistent overburden sampling and analysis is new to many surface miners and other earth movers, some operators have overlooked the opportunities, not only to achieve better reclamation and more valuable land but to increase efficiencies and profits. It is increasingly apparent that successful competition in earth-disturbing activities belongs to those who see opportunities for improved efficiency in the same information required for achieving high quality land by controlled placement and treatment based on properties. After all, the cost of sampling and proper analysis of overburdens is relatively insignificant, since the same cores or borings can be used for mineral exploration and overburden sampling. Then, attention to interpretations rarely fails to indicate significant chemical or physical properties of material that could not possibly be known without these analyses. Such new information should be a key to greater success in many operations.

Development of proof that overburden sampling and analysis is profitable would require a special study of each operation and would depend upon the competence of individuals and machines involved, both with and without the knowledge obtained from analyses. There would be cases where the local people understood the situation so well from experience that information from analyses was not needed. We have encountered such cases in our extensive research. On the other hand, we have experienced cases where the people were frankly confused or uncertain about their overburden problems and were struggling to obtain every possible bit of new information. In additional cases, the people were confident of conditions that didn't exist. Sometimes the misconceptions were obvious or suspected without analyses, but in other cases analyses were required before errors were evident.

Essential features of laboratory analyses that have been applied most successfully to overburdens and man-made soils are as follows:

a. **Paste pH**—A paste pH measurement of powdered rock or soil eliminates the "suspension effect" (Jackson, 1958). The "suspension effect", when a definite soil/water ratio such as 1:1, 1:2, etc., is used, results in a different pH reading when the electrode is placed in the sediment as opposed to the supernatant liquid. The pH of the sediment is usually lower for acid materials. Since materials are toxic to many plants when the pH values are < 4.0 (the range of acidity dominated by mineral acids in soil solution), and solubility of many elements is pH dependent, no other measurement is more useful. Easy preparation is achieved with a 2:1 soil/water ratio which gives a satisfactory paste with most samples. More water can be added to fine-textured material or more sample added to coarse-textured materials if necessary to develop the desired paste for pH measurements.

b. **Total or Pyritic Sulfur**—The total or pyritic sulfur content is measured by a LECO Induction Furnace with Automatic Sulfur Titrator. A sample is heated to approximately 1600°C while a stream of oxygen is passed over the sample. The sulfur dioxide released is collected in a dilute hydrochloric acid solution containing potassium iodide, starch, and a small amount of potassium iodate, and automatically titrated with a standard potassium iodate solution. The total sulfur only accurately quantifies the potential acidity of materials when all sulfur is present as a pyritic mineral; therefore, when gypsum is found in the overburden or when the materials are weathered, the sample is leached with hydrochloric acid and water to remove the sulphates before a total sulfur measurement is taken. Then the stoichiometry of the reaction of the oxidation of FeS_2, the maximum potential acidity can be calculated in terms of $CaCO_3$ equivalents (0.1% sulfur yields sulfuric acid that requires 3.125 parts $CaCO_3$ equivalents to neutralize 1,000 parts of material). When combined with a neutralization potential of the material, a net Acid-Base Account of the material can be made.

c. **Neutralization Potential**—The neutralization potential of overburden materials is the second component of a net Acid-Base Account. The amount of nuetralizers (alkali and alkaline earth cations) present in overburden materials is found by treating the sample with a known amount of standardized hydrochloric acid, heating to insure complete reaction, and titrating with a standardized base. The amount of neutralizers in a given material is now known and a net Acid-Base Account for the material is calculated. If the material has a net deficiency of 5 parts

$CaCO_3$ equivalents per 1,000 parts of material, the material is designated as potentially toxic. Thus, you can find materials in the overburden that will be potentially toxic or that will have an excess of neutralizers.

d. **Fizz Rating of Powdered Samples**—In the laboratory a fizz rating of powdered samples is made by treating a scoop of sample with 10% HCl in a dropwise manner. The relative intensity of fizz is recorded, i.e., no reaction is "0", a visible reaction is "1", a strong effervescence is "3", and a turbulent effervescence which splatters is "5". A visible reaction "1" usually indicates the presence of at least the equivalent of 18.14 metric tons (20 tons) calcium carbonate per thousand tons of material.

e. **Munsell Color of Powered Samples**—The use of Munsell color of powdered samples is restricted mainly to value and chroma, although hue is always recorded. Value is used to distinguish between true high carbonaceous materials and those that contain lesser amounts of carbon or none at all. Materials with a value of 3 or less contain appreciable amounts of carbon and are true Carboliths (high-carbon shales; rider, bone and other impure coals). These materials frequently contain the highest amounts of total sulfur and may be a source of extreme acidity if neutralizers are absent or present in insufficient amounts. Also, these materials contain appreciable amounts of plant nutrients, such as phosphorus.

Chroma, the other important component of color, indicates weathered and nonweathered materials. A chroma of 3 or more indicates that iron oxidation has taken place and there is probably an absence of pyrite. This material may contain small amounts of neutralizers, but will need to be limed and fertilized if it is to be used as "topsoiling" material. However, in materials with a chroma of 2 or less, iron is absent or occurs in reduced form which may include pyrites. This material normally contains higher amounts of neutralizers than similar material with chromas of 3 or more, but lime may still need to be applied to neutralize the acidity that will be produced if pyrites occur.

f. **Electrical Conductivity**—Electrical conductivity of a soil–water extract is accomplished by saturating a sample with distilled water and allowing it to set for 1 hour. The soil water is then extracted using a vacuum and the electrical conductivity of the extract measured. This measurement is commonly used for indicting the concentration of ionized constituents in the extract. If checking for gypsum, allow the soil–water extract to stand for several hours and remeasure the electrical conductivity. If gypsum is present, this electrical conductivity measurement will greatly increase over the first measurement.

g. **Extractable Plant Nutrients**—Dilute hydrochloric and sulfuric acid is regularly used to determine extractable plant nutrients (phosphorus, potassium, calcium, and magnesium). The mixed acids are more effective than hydrochloric acid along as an extracting solution for phosphorus; however, good correlation with crop yield response to phosphorus fertilization occurs only with phosphorus extractable from acid materials. Since neutral and calcareous materials are commonly present in coal overburden, phosphorus should be extracted by sodium bicarbonate, a nondestructive extracting solution. Crop yield response from phosphorus fertilization correlates well with sodium bicarbonate-extractable phosphorus in acid or neutral soils as well as in calcareous soils.

h. **Lime Requirement for Desired pH**—Materials are tested for lime requirement which will raise the pH of these materials to 6.5. There are several methods which can be used and all correlate with Dunn's $CaOH_2$ titration procedure. The rationale of liming to pH 6.5 is as follows: (i) calcium is being added to the soil along with magnesium if dolomitic limestone is used; (ii) mineral acidity is neutralized as well as acidity due to aluminum; (iii) exchangeable aluminum, manganese, and iron are greatly reduced; (iv) microbial populations are changed with the sulfur and iron oxidizers being essentially removed and unavailable to catalyze pyrite oxidation; (v) phosphorus availability is increased (Jackson, 1958; Wilson, 1965).

i. **Rock Hardness**—A rock hardness scale, taken from Moh's scale of hardness, is used primarily to separate rocks into categories as to type of rocks, i.e., sandstone, mudstone, mudrock, etc., and likely persistence as coarse fragments. The scale is most useful and consists of only three hardness categories: (i) < 2.5 or 3.0, rock can be scratched with a fingernail or penny; (ii) from 3.0 to 5.5, rock cannot be scratched with a fingernail but can be scratched with a knife blade; (iii) > 5.5, rock which cannot be scratched with a knife blade. Most potential coarse fragments are harder than 3.0, or with sandstones they ring when hit with a hammer as described by Heald et al. (1974).

j. **Rock Slaking in Water**—Rock slaking in water is a mild weathering procedure that can be used in the field or laboratory. An air-dry fragment is quickly and totally immersed in water trapping air in the pores of the fragment. As the water moves into the pores, the pressure of the trapped air will cause the fragment to explode if the individual particles are not cemented together. This method indicates if the rock or soil will disintegrate easily when exposed to atmospheric conditions. It also gives an idea of the character of the coarse fragments which will be formed.

k. **Physical Weathering Potential**—Another weathering index is the dispersion of rock or soil by shaking in calgon solution. This method is a modification of the dispersion part of the pipette method of doing mechanical analysis of soils. This test can be done in two different ways: (i) materials can be subjected to this vigorous dispersion and then simply separated into two size fractions by passing the dispersed material through a 2-mm sieve; or (ii) the materials can be separated into four size fractions by doing a pipette or hydrometer analysis of the dispersed material which passes a 2-mm sieve. The results obtained by using this method indicate coarse fragment percentages, relative breakdown of overburden materials, and particle sizes of the < 2-mm fraction.

l. **Texture by Observation, Feel, and Mechanical Analysis**—Rock and soil texture by observation are accomplished by studying the material without and with a 10× hand lens, and rating the size of particles. Textures of < 2 mm material is accomplished by feel. A small sample is moistened and kneaded, then rubbed between the thumb and fingers of the hand to detect the sand (gritty), silt (smooth), and/or clay (sticky). This way the dominate textural class can be determined. Finally, soil texture is determined by either the hydrometer or pipette methods in the laboratory, with the pipette method being preferred. Rock textures are measured as described in section k. Textures indicate water and air relations, possibilities of future pan formations, and present zones of excess clay.

m. **Porosity**—Rock and soil porosity can be determined directly or indirectly. Direct determination utilizes a nonpolar liquid to avoid slaking. The indirect method is a calculation of porosity from particle and bulk density measurements. The direct method involves allowing the fragment to saturate after air has been removed from the fragment's pores by vacuum, then weighing the fragment in a saturated state and a dry state to find the amount of solvent held by the fragment. The porosity of the fragment is then calculated. Porosity information of coarse fragments will modify the moisture retention characteristics of highly disturbed soil when coarse fragments are present in large quantities. The stress vs. volume retention of coarse fragments influences the total soil water characteristic (Coile, 1953).

n. **Rock Type**—Rock type is an important parameter for evaluating overburden materials. Sandstones, shales, mudstones, mudrock, limestones, carboliths, etc., must be defined consistently as to properties that dominate and give each rock type certain characteristics unlike any other material. After a long number of samples have been analyzed (Smith et al., 1976), there are certain generalizations that can be made for each rock type, e.g., sandstones without appreciable carbon have a common range of sulfur contents which differ from shales and carboliths, and weathered (high chroma) sandstones differ from unweathered (low chroma) sandstones in amount of sulfur they contain. Therefore, rock type as determined by definition based on properties can indicate a range of properties without analyses (Smith et al., 1974c).

o. **Sodium Adsorbtion Ratio**—The sodium absorbtion ratio (SAR) is used to express an empirical relationship between the relative activity of sodium ions in exchange reactions with a soil. The concentration of sodium, calcium, and magnesium in a saturated soil extract is measured and the SAR is calculated. Since it is well correlated to exchangeable-sodium ratio, values of 12 or higher indicate problems due to salinity (Sandoval et al., 1973). This measurement applies especially in subhumid regions.

E. Choice of Future Land Use

Planning for future use of highly disturbed land is widely recommended and its desirability is seldom disputed. In surface mining, early decisions regarding land use are standard practice in Great Britain (Striffler, 1967; Riley & Rinier, 1972); Germany (Knabe, 1974 and 1973); Poland (Bauman, 1976); Czechoslovakia (Jonas, 1973 and 1974); and the

USSR (Izhevskaya et al., 1974; Nastya et al., 1974). Such decisions have also been emphasized in the United States (Grandt & Lang, 1958; Orton & Galpin, 1945; Tyner et al., 1948; Glover, 1971; Smith, 1971). Emphasis is greater on such decisions where land is used intensively. In cases where relatively low value land is being disturbed, a decision may be made to leave the area in low intensity use and the decision receives little attention. At present in central Illinois, increased attention to planning for high value cultivated cropping naturally follows increasing disturbance of highly valued cropland (R. T. Dawe. 1975. Director, Illinois Dep. of Mines and Minerals, informational memorandum).

In steep terrain or on stony or shallow soils, advance planning is resulting in creation of high value land for intensive use where only low intensity uses were feasible before disturbance (Pitsenbarger, 1974 and 1975). Any idea that highly disturbed soils are automatically low value soils is out of step with modern reality in the United States, as well as in the European countries mentioned. Prices of minesoils per hectare in excess of $2,000 are not uncommon in West Virginia and even land in low intensity uses commands prices in the range of several hundred dollars per hectare. There is economic evidence that under some conditions prevailing land prices reflect locations (Dufresne & Colyer, 1975) more than soil properties. Where properties are being planned carefully and it can be demonstrated that land value will be higher in the long run, if not immediately, the price-dependent factor is soil properties (Greene & Raney, 1974); and (B. C. Greene. 1976. Restoring grossly disturbed land to agricultural and other uses. Invitational papers and abstracts of technical papers. Northeastern Branch Meetings, Am. Soc. of Agron., Morgantown, W. Va. p. 22–25).

Education of land users or prospective purchasers is essential to full appreciation of the importance of overburden and minesoil properties. The negative outlook that highly disturbed soils are automatically inferior must be rejected in order to realize maximum returns from selective placement based on properties. The conclusion of Nobel prize winner Borlaug (1976) that "natures way is not good enough" applies to highly disturbed soils as well as to other aspects of production from the land.

Different kinds of land use known to occur on highly disturbed sites (Grandt & Lang, 1958; USDA Staff, 1968; Pitsenbarger, 1974 and 1975; White & Pitsenbarger, 1973) can be grouped into the following six classes based on observable or measurable properties: (i) multiple uses with few limitations; (ii) rural, urban, recreational, or industrial building sites and grounds; (iii) extensive recreation, including access to remote lands; (iv) production of forest products; (v) pasture, hay, or specialty crops not requiring plowing; and (vi) intensive agriculture, including plowing.

These uses will depend on properties of the replaced, highly disturbed, or man-made soils as well as on shape, slope, and water control. In many cases, the soil and rock materials will satisfy some of the uses indicated but not all uses. It is necessary to find out in advance by mapping, sampling, and analysis whether appropriate earth materials are available to satisfy the preferred use, without amendments or with amendments that can be economically provided. Parameters identified for analysis appear to account for properties of overburden having general, overriding influences in determining successful operations and land suitability for planned use. Other properties of interest represent refinements that may be required by specialists to answer specific questions about soil management or interactions with use. In peculiar situations, proper diagnosis is essential, followed by remedies adapted from science and experience. Many practical field problems cited prove to be a repetition or slight variation of the commonplace. With pH below 4 and accompanying high concentrations of soluble iron and aluminum, there is little reason to start looking for rare toxins when asked to explain why alfalfa or trefoil have failed to grow. With present knowledge, the problem may be how to apply and hold in place enough neutralizing material for a long enough time to adjust and stabilize the pH within a satisfactory range. As soon as research provides cheaper methods, such as more tolerant varieties or effective trace element treatments as discussed by Bennett (1971), these improvements will be adopted. In coal mining situations, either with overburden spoils or with coal wastes, dramatic plant growth failures are usually associated with extreme acidity, which must be moderated by known methods before serious attention is given to details of plant nutrient balances or seeding methods.

Mine wastes may have a variety of uses depending on engineering properties (Moulton et al., 1974). An example is the use of mine refuse and fly ash as road face, as reported by Scott and Wilmoth (1974). It has been indicated (C. Delp. 1976. Soil morphological characteristics, genesis, and classification of West Virginia coal mine refuse. M.S. Thesis. West Virginia Univ., Morgantown) that mine wastes can be studied and classified into several categories of highly disturbed soils. A high percentage of these wastes (carbolithic minesoils) are strongly or extremely acid and require prolonged leaching or neutralizing treatments before they can be fertilized and managed for vigorous plant growth and production. When carbolithic minesoils or mine wastes are used for building sites and grounds (Category 2), crop production is not involved but treatments are required to grow plants for water and wind erosion control, dust prevention, and beautification. The work of Delp (previously cited) and other field observations indicate that vigorous plant growth on mine wastes is not uncommon. Many of these cases involve prolonged natural leaching and natural invasion by plants. In fresh coal wastes, the lime requirement for assured neutralization would be highly variable (Smith et al., 1974a). Neutralization to sufficient depth for vigorous plant root development requires not only adequate rates but protection from erosion until neutralization occurs. Reclamation has been accomplished in Missouri by liming and fertilizing according to soil tests, followed by covering with 22.9 cm (9 inches) or more of favorable minesoil or other soil material (Brundage, 1974); and in southern Illinois a lime rate of 67.2 metric ton/ha (30 U.S. ton/acre per 1% of sulfur), incorporated to 20.3 cm (8 inches), plus annual fertilization has resulted in good, persistent growth of a grass-legume mixture on six different mine waste deposits (J. Sturm. Dir. of Tech. Serv., West Virginia Surface Mining and Reclamation Assoc., Charleston, W. Va., personal communication). In West Virginia, grass seedings on limed and fertilized wastes have been more successful in cool fall weather than in the spring. Legumes can be seeded in the spring following grass establishment (J. White, Vice President of Pioneer Fuel Co., Beckley, W. Va., personal communication). An alternate method that has been successful is treatment with neutral or alkaline fly ash plus fertilization with N and P (Capp & Adams, 1971; Capp & Gillmore, 1974). Success from liming and fertilization alone depends upon deep incorporation of adequate lime, plus mulching to prevent erosion and sufficient rainfall to cause dominance of downward moving water, which is normal in the humid region except during severe drought.

Minesoils with extreme acidity may represent 5% of the total in old workings in Illinois (Grandt & Lang, 1958) and may approach 10% in northern West Virginia (Brown, 1962 and 1971). The impression of this 5 or 10% may be such that a high proportion of questions raised by co-workers or the public involves this relatively small percentage of the total. This is the reason for our conclusion that many problems presented for solution are repetitions of the same problem. The principle of liming to eliminate acidity is well known and generally acceptable, but the mechanics of liming within the restrictions imposed by machinery, time, weather, and erosion may fail to eliminate the extremely acid condition. Unfortunately, there is sometimes a tendency to reject the proven principle rather than to correct the mechanics. Problems of detailed nutrient balances or rare chemical toxins undoubtedly occur, but these represent slight interest compared to elimination of extreme acidity on a small percentage of the total area. There may be little interest in knowing concentrations of soluble elements at pH below 4.0 unless this knowledge can be extrapolated into concentrations at the higher pH being created by liming. One of the most pressing questions in this connection is the behavior of plants with their root systems in soil that ranges from high to low pH and from high to low concentrations of important elements.

III. CLASSIFICATION, MAPPING, AND USE OF NEW SOILS

In order to accommodate highly disturbed or man-made soils within meaningful categories based on properties, a new Suborder of *Soil Taxonomy* (USDA-SCS, 1975) has been suggested (J. C. Sencindiver. 1976. Genesis and classification of minesoils. Ph.D. Dissertation. West Virginia Univ., Morgantown. (in progress); Smith et al., 1974b and 1976). This Suborder (Spolents) has properties 1, 2, and 4 of Orthents plus at least three of nine properties that have been used to provide a unique definition of Spolents. In many cases highly disturbed soils have more than the minimum three of the identifying criteria which follow.

A. Properties of Spolents

a. Disordered Coarse Fragments—If coarse fragments constitute at least 10% of the volume of the control section, they are disordered such that >50% will have their long axis at an angle of at least 10% relative to any plane in the profile. The test for disorder should exclude fragments with longest diameter < 2 or > 25 cm, and should be based on numbers of coarse fragments rather than volume.

b. **Color Mottling Not Associated With Horizonation**—Color mottling occurs without regard to depth or spacing in the profile. The mottling involves color differences of at least two color chips in the standard Munsell soil color charts. This mottling occurs among fines as well as within coarse fragments or between fines and coarse fragments.

c. **Splintery Edges on Fissile Coarse Fragments**—If coarse fragments are fissile, the edges are frayed or splintery rather than smooth.

d. **Bridging Voids**—This refers to coarse fragments bridging across voids as a result of placement of materials leaving discontinuous, irregular pores larger than textural porosity. Such voids are present consistently but vary in frequency, prominence, and size.

e. **Thin Surface Horizon Higher in Fines**—A thin surface horizon or horizon immediately below a surface pavement of coarse fragments, which contains a higher percentage of fines (< 2 mm) than any other horizon in the profile to the bottom of the control section may occur. This horizon ranges from 2.5- to 10-cm thick in most minesoils, but it may be thicker in minesoils that have been "topsoiled".

f. **Local Pockets of Dissimilar Material**—Local pockets of materials, excluding single coarse fragments, that range from 7.6 to 100 cm in horizontal diameter may occur. These pockets have no lateral continuity and are the result of the original placement of materials and not of postdepositional processes. They may differ from the surrounding material in color (two or more Munsell color chips), soil textural, or particle-size class, or dominant rock type constituting the coarse fragments.

g. **Artifacts**—Artifacts may occur within the profile. This includes plastics, glass, paper, metal, tires, logs, etc.

h. **Carbolithic Coarse Fragments**—Disordered carbolithic coarse fragments may occur in noncarbolithic Spolents. These coarse fragments, which are usually associated with the coal, are found in the profile because of moving and mixing of overburden materials.

i. **Irregular Distribution of Oxidizable Organic Carbon**—This irregular distribution of oxidizable carbon with depth in the profile is due to the mixing of overburden materials. Both recent and geologically old carbon compounds are involved.

B. Lower Categories of Spolents

Great groups of Spolents are set apart on the basis of soil temperature and moisture regimes as Udispolents, Ustispolents, etc., in a fashion parallel to the great groups of Orthents and Fluvents. Subgroups are distinguished mainly on lithology of coarse fragments in the control section

(25 to 100 cm), but additional subgroup criteria are essential. Family classes are defined by particle size, mineralogy, soil reaction, and soil temperature.

The emphasis on coarse fragments at the Subgroup level of classification is justified by the fact that minesoils are created from more or less fractured and disintegrated rocks or earth which automatically assume a major role in determining genetic processes as well as use-potentials and management requirements of these soils.

a. Udispolents—Spolents in the udic or humid moisture regime. All Spolents studied to date have been placed in the Udispolents.

b. Subgroups—Seven Classes Defined:

1) Fissile Udispolents—Udispolents where at least 65% of the total coarse fragments within the control section are shales with parallel bedding planes evident at spacings of 5 mm or less, resulting in physical weathering into progressively thinner chips.

2) Plattic Udispolents—Udispolents where at least 65% of the coarse fragments within the control section are sandstones with grain size >0.05 mm.

3) Regolithic Plattic Udispolents—Plattic Udispolents in which 90% or more of the sandstone coarse fragments have interior chroma >2.

4) Carbolithic Udispolents—Udispolents in which >50% of the coarse fragments within the control section have a Munsell soil color value of three or less for the streak or the powder of the coarse fragments. This includes coal, bone coal, and carbon rich shales and muds.

5) Schlickig Udispolents—Udispolents with at least 10% coarse fragments, of which 65% or more consist of mudrocks that do not qualify as fissile and which may or may not fizz in 10% hydrochloric acid (by field test) but fail to qualify for the Kalkig Subgroup.

6) Typic Udispolents—Udispolents that are not dominated by any one rock type with the control section, and do not quality for any other subgroup.

7) Kalkig Udispolents—Udispolents with at least 65% of the coarse fragments in the control section consisting of limestone or calcareous mudrocks that fizz in 10% hydrochloric acid (field test).

8) Matric Udispolents—Udispolents with <10% coarse fragments, by volume, within the control section.

9) Pyrolithic Udispolents—Udispolents with at least 50% of the coarse fragments within the control section consisting of glassy, cindery, or ceramic material that does not qualify for carbolithic but that appears to have formed from the burning of carbolithic material. These coarse fragments are commonly some shade of red, brown, or yellow with observable development of vesicular openings. The coarse fragments are commonly called *red dog* or some other local descriptive name.

10) Other Subgroups—Subgroups that may be required when more Spolents are studied. It is known that Lithic subgroups occur in which the depth to bedrock is <50 cm, but no extensive areas of these soils have been observed. The use of Lithic as a second modifier with any of the Subgroups (one thru nine) would be natural. In the case of mixed rock types

(Typic Udispolents) the appropriate name would by simply Lithic Udispolents.

C. Family Criteria

a. Particle Size—The particle size of West Virginia minesoils is dominantly loamy–skeletal with a few sandy–skeletal and clayey–skeletal. However, nonskeletal minesoils are known to occur. Established particle size definitions in *Soil Taxonomy* (USDA-SCS, 1975) are satisfactory.

b. Mineralogy—The mineralogy of minesoils is assumed to be siliceous for the Plattic and Regolithic Plattic Udispolents and mixed for the other noncarbolithic subgroups until proven otherwise. New mineralogy classes are needed for the Carbolithic Udispolents because of the dominance of coal and other high carbon fragments or glass in classes where burning has occurred. It is proposed to designate the mineralogy as *nigric* if >50% of the appropriate textural fraction consists of black, opaque particles, and *skoric* if >50% is glass. The only other mineralogy class anticipated with the Carbolithic Subgroup is mixed.

c. Reaction—Soil reaction is measured at 25 cm or immediately below any surface layer applied as "topsoil", whichever is deeper. The classification of soil reaction is as follows: (i) *Extremely acid*—pH < 4.0—for all subgroups except carbolithic, which is < 3.0; (ii) *Acid*—pH 4.0 to 5.5, inclusive for all subgroups except carbolithic, which is 3.0 to 5.5, inclusive; (iii) *Neutral*—pH 5.5 to 8.0, inclusive; (iv) *Alkaline*—pH > 8.0.

d. Soil Temperature Class—In West Virginia the soil temperature class is mesic. Other classes occur as defined for Orthents and Fluvents.

D. Phases of Families

It will be desirable to map phases of certain soil families in order to satisfy specific practical needs. For example, steep slope and extremely stony phases would apply to some outslopes in steep terrain. However, the outslopes might be indicated more satisfactorily in mapping by an appropriate elongate symbol rather than an enclosed area. Other useful phases might be: (i) extremely acid surface phase; (ii) weathered topsoil phase; (iii) alkaline geologic topsoil phase; (iv) rough surface phase, where use of farm machinery would not be feasible; (v) loamy surface phase, where plowing for cultivated crops would be practical even on skeletal control sections; and (vi) Mollic surface soil phase, where the top layer meets the criteria for a Mollic epipedon.

Soil testing to determine lime and fertilizer needs for intensive uses would be necessary in addition to the best of classification and mapping. Also, full descriptions of such features as gullies, ponded water, large surface stones, and inclusions of distinctly different minesoils would be a part of the definitions of minesoil mapping units.

Management and land use implications by families are imperfectly tested at present, but several generalizations seem likely to apply. With extremely acid families, for instance, covering with at least 15 cm of favorable material probably would be a standard recommendation, whereas with acid families liming would be feasible for forage seedings; with neutral families no liming would be needed.

From the standpoint of available soil water and fertility, the sandy-skeletal, siliceous families would be generally unfavorable for forage production, but would be favorable for roadways, camping, and certain specialty crops. On the other hand, Schlickig or Kalkig, clayey–skeletal, neutral families would be most productive as meadowlands, but would lack stability for roadways or stability on steep slopes.

E. Spolents Criteria for Suitability Classes

Regarding criteria for new soils, based on overburden study and analysis, we would suggest that the Acid-Base Accounting Method be applied regardless of anticipated land use. In general, the entire profile to 100 cm depth should qualify as *Not Toxic* or *Potentially Toxic* with respect to acidity. In subhumid regions, a comparable approach could assure against excess or toxic alkalinity.

We now have extensive data showing that the Acid-Base Accounting Method does not set unreasonable or unachievable standards for coal overburdens (Smith et al., 1976). On the other hand, in our experience, conforming to the nontoxic standard has prevented near-surface, acid-induced toxicity. Basic or well-buffered neutralizers are so much more abundant than extreme acid-formers in the earth's superficial crust that it is a matter of locating and placing local materials where the acid-formers, if present, will be overwhelmed by the neutralizers. In rare cases, only, would acid-formers predominate throughout the overburden and require extraordinary measures.

Having agreed that avoiding toxicity deserves top priority, we can begin to set standards for minesoil suitability classes: (i) suitable for multiple uses; (ii) suitable for rural, urban, recreational, or industrial building sites and grounds; (iii) suitable for extensive recreation and access: hiking, camping, hunting, etc.; (iv) suitable for production of forest products; (v) suitable for pasture, hay, or other crops not requiring plowing; (vi) suitable for intensive agriculture including plowing.

1. SUITABILITY CLASS 1

The implication here is that few limitations of any kind exist. Weather-resistant rock fragments (tough sandstone, limestone, and ironstone) would anchor the base into old soil or bedrock. The overlying layer would be a broad mix of particle sizes including enough coarse rock fragments to interlock with basal fragments. Subsoil favorable for permeation by plant roots should be medium textured, near neutral in reaction, and high in plant nutrients. The best surface layer would probably be a near-neutral, highly fertile sandy loam with no coarse fragments larger than 75 mm diameter. Significant soil organic matter would be desirable throughout the plant root zone (surface and subsoil to a depth of about 1 m). Weatherable coarse fragments would be desirable throughout the subsoil.

2. SUITABILITY CLASS 2

If primary interest focused on building sites and grounds, the emphasis would be placed on physical strength and stability throughout. A broad mixture of particle sizes (including coarse fragments) would be favorable, with emphasis on packing to high density, and provision for quick, controlled surface drainage. The base should be well anchored with weather-resistant rock fragments.

3. SUITABILITY CLASS 3

Extensive recreation and access would need to emphasize physical stability and drainage, much as for Suitability Class 2, but with more interest in leaving the top layer loose enough for good growth of wildlife food and cover crops of trees, shrubs, and ground cover. Plant nutrient and pH requirements would be satisfied by the nontoxic rule.

4. SUITABILITY CLASS 4

Production land for forest products would be favored most by leaving deep, medium-textured materials relatively unpacked, but shaped for efficient future harvesting (Chapman, 1967). Reaction and plant nutrient would be generally satisfactory for adapted species.

5. SUITABILITY CLASS 5

Suitability for forages and other crops not requiring plowing would emphasize available phosphorus, potash, and other nutrients as well as a deep-rooting zone. Minimum compaction consistent with physical stability would be desirable. High base status would be favorable for most crops. Most coarse fragments in the surface should be smaller than 75 mm diameter and preferably soft enough to be cut with a disk. A relatively high percentage of coarse fragments in subsoils would be tolerable and might be desirable, especially if they were readily weatherable. Specialty crops might require other special properties that could be provided if anticipated.

6. SUITABILITY CLASS 6

Suitability for crops requiring plowing would emphasize relatively few coarse fragments in the plow layer with none coarser than 150 mm diameter. In addition, darkened surface soil or soil organic matter as a source of nitrogen and to favor soil granulation might be important in the plow layer. A sandy loam surface layer might substitute for a finer textured layer with granular structure, especially if the subsoil contained soil organic matter and the profile was fertile.

7. GENERALIZATIONS

In situ production of organic matter and nitrogen by 2 years or more of vigorous legumes and grasses before growing cultivated crops, as practiced in Great Britain (Chadwick, 1973; Riley & Rinier, 1972; Stiffler, 1967), Germany (Heide, 1973; Knabe, 1964 and 1973), Czechoslovakia (Jonas, 1973 and 1974), Poland (Bauman, 1976; J. Libicki, Chief Coordinator, Central Res. Inst. for open-pit mining, personal communication), and the USSR (Izhevskaya et al., 1974; Nastya et al., 1974) should be a satisfactory alternative where darkened surface soil is scarce or unavailable. Where Mollic (deep, soft, dark, neutral) original surface soil is available there is maximum incentive to surface or near-surface replacement of such material, as recommended in central Illinois (Caspall, 1975) and elsewhere (McCormack, 1974) in the region of Mollisols. However, the possibility may be worth considering that even better soils would result from blending the Mollic epipedon into the total root zone (1 to 2 m) rather than placing it arbitrarily on the immediate surface. We endorse the principle stated by Borlaug (1976) that "nature's way isn't good enough". There may be ways to do better, even when considering soils that were naturally productive.

As outlined, all suitability standards assume proper burial, blending, or special treatments to prevent toxic or potentially toxic acidity from occurring. In addition, the standards assume that adequate measures will be taken to control erosion. Quick establishment of effective ground cover on all critical slopes is the basis for erosion control. However, properly designed diversion terraces, stable, loose-rock, or other terrace outlets, mulching, and lime plus fertilization according to chemical tests, are standard aids to ground cover establishments that should not be neglected.

These suggestions for creating Spolents according to plan are feasible only when soil and other overburden properties are studied in advnace and are correlated with pedologic and geologic mapping units. This appears to be the approach favored by many modern operators, regulatory agents, service technicians, research scientists, and legislators. In fact, no feasible alternative appears to have a chance of satisfying the overall demands of modern society for environmental quality as well as for energy, highways, housing, urbanization, and recreation.

F. Profile Properties and Mapping Units

The National Cooperaive Soil Survey in West Virginia has recognized the need for more meaningful mapping units on the 121,500 ha (300,000 acres) of highly disturbed soils in West Virginia and has acted accordingly. To date, 7 descriptive, provisional mapping units based on rock types, coarse fragments, texture, pH at 25 cm in the profile, and dominant mineralogy have been defined and are being used in Monongalia and Marion Counties (Dale Childs, personal communication). These descriptive units correspond with soil families that have been tentatively defined and named under the suggested classification scheme discussed in this paper, which has been offered as an amendment to *Soil Taxonomy* (R. M. Smith, J. C. Sencindiver, C. H. Delp, and K. O. Schmude. 25 Nov. 1976. Memorandum to John Rourke, Chrm., Northeast Soil Taxonomy Comm.). The proposed amendment to *Soil Taxonomy* was endorsed by unanimous vote of participants in the January 1976 Northeastern Work Planning Conference of the National Cooperative Soil Survey.

The point that should be more fully appreciated regarding major disturbance of land surfaces is simply this. We now know enough about soil and rock properties and how to measure or amend them that we can make our new soils as good as we want them to be. The primary question is, how much time and energy are we willing to spend? And if the cost is too high, how can we do it more cheaply?

IV. SUMMARY AND CONCLUSIONS

Major land disturbances should involve advance planning of the entire operation including reclamation designed for some particular land use. The planning should be based on mapping of soil and rock units defined in terms of physical and chemical properties. Units mapped should be sampled and analyzed for properties that influence efficiency and success of the operation. Frequency of sampling should be sufficient to insure that extrapolation of data on pedologic and geologic maps will not be likely to introduce practical contradictions. Measurements must be designed to answer hierarchical questions from the simple to the more complex and from the highly important to the less significant or more easily remedied. This approach has led to emphasis in humid regions on simple measurements of paste pH and acid-base accounting to assure against extreme acid toxicity of soil and water, in accordance with demands of our environmental goals. Under subhumid conditions, electrical conductivity and the sodium adsorption ratio are simple measurements that may demand widespread attention. Other properties deserving high priorities include rock weakness or stability in a near surface environment, soil and rock textures, favorable pH for sensitive plants, adequate phosphorus, potassium, magnesium and calcium, and appropriate density of packing for the intended land use. Concentrations of readily extractable aluminum and other biotoxins is a major environmental concern that correlates closely with pH extremes except when peculiar amendments or wastes cause or intensify conditions.

During major land disturbances, good advance information about soil and rock properties can reduce disturbance costs as well as assure that resulting highly disturbed soils will meet intended standards for projected use.

New soils, on mappable management units, defined by physical and chemical properties, must be nontoxic and may be subdivided conveniently into suitability classes for: (i) all uses with few chemical or physical limitations, (ii) building sites and grounds, (iii) extensive recreation and access, (iv) woodland production products, (v) forage and other crops not requiring plowing, and (vi) crops requiring plowing, with relatively few coarse fragments.

Profile definitions based on properties as well as descriptive mapping units have been adopted provisionally for surface-mined lands in West Virginia and Ohio but have not yet passed through final correlation by the National Cooperative Soil Survey.

Special studies involving similar definitions have been initiated on surface-mined land for correlation with plant performance, both by the U.S. Soil Conservation Service and the U.S. Forest Service. Also, special testing of minesoil classification as a part of Interagency Evaluation of reclamation in West Virginia has been practiced during the past 3 years.

In the Washington, D.C., metropolitan area, man-man urban soil profiles have been studied and provisional mapping units have been used for completion of a survey of these highly disturbed soils, but final correlation has not been completed.

LITERATURE CITED

Anderson, J. C. 1971. Preparation of surface-mined land for revegetation. p. 7–8. In D. M. Bondurant (ed.) Proc. of the Revegetation and Economic Use of Surface-Mined Land and Mine Refuse Symp. School of Mines, College of Agric. and For., Appalachian Center, West Virginia Univ., 2–4 Dec. 1971, Pipestem State Park, W. Va.

Bauman, K. 1976. Reclamation of worked-out terrains in the Polish openpit mining of lignite. In Proc. of 2nd Int. Conf. of West Virginia Surface Mining and Reclamation Assoc. (Wroclaw, Poland), April 1976, WVSMRA, Charleston.

Bennett, O. L. 1971. Grasses and legumes for revegetation of strip-mined areas. p. 23–25. In D. M. Bondurant (ed.) Proc. of the Revegetation and Economic Use of Surface-Mined Land and Mine Refuse Symp., School of Mines, College of Agric. and For., Appalachian Center, West Virginia Univ., 2–4 Dec. 1971, Pipestem State Park, W. Va. West Virginia Univ., Morgantown.

Berg, W. A., and W. G. Vogel. 1973. Toxicity of acid coal mine spoils to plants. I:57–68. In R. J. Hutnik and G. Davis (ed.) Ecology and reclamation of devastated land. Gordon Breach Sci. Publ. Inc., New York.

Borlaug, N. 1976. Nature's way isn't good enough. Am. For. 82:20–21, 58–63.

Brown, J. H. 1962. Success of tree planting on strip-mined areas in West Virginia. West Virginia Univ. Agric. Exp. Stn. Bull. 473. Morgantown, W. Va.

Brown, J. H. 1971. Use of trees for revegetation of surface-mined areas. p. 26–28. In D. M. Bondurant (ed.) Proc. of the Revegetation and Economic Use of Surface-Mined Land and Mine Refuse Symp., School of Mines, College of Agric. and For., Appalachian Center, West Virginia Univ., 2–4 Dec. 1971, Pipestem State Park, W. V. West Virginia Univ., Morgantown.

Brundage, R. S. 1974. Depth of soil covering refuse (gob) vs. quality of vegetation. p. 183–185. In 1st Symp. on Mine and Preparation Plant Refuse Disposal. 22–24 Oct. 1974, Louisville, Ky., Natl. Coal Assoc., Washington, D.C.

Capp, J. P., and L. M. Adams. 1971. Reclamation of coal mine wastes and strip spoil with fly ash. Proc. Am. Chem. Soc., 162nd Natl. Meetings 15(2):1–11.

Capp, J. P., and D. W. Gillmore. 1974. Fly ash from coal burning powerplants: an aid in revegetating coal mine refuse and spoil banks. p. 200–211. In 1st Symp. on Mine and Preparation Plant Refuse Disposal. 22–24 Oct. 1974. Louisville, Ky., Natl. Coal Assoc., Washington, D.C.

Caruccio, F. T. 1968. An evaluation of factors affecting acid mine drainage production and the ground water interactions in selected areas of Western Pennsylvania. p. 107–151. *In* 2nd Symp. on Coal Mine Drainage Research. Coal Industry Advisory Comm. to ORSANCO, 14–15 May 1968, Mellon Inst., Pittsburg, Pa. Bituminous Coal Res., Inc., Monroeville, Pa.

Caspall, F. C. 1975. Soil development on surface mine spoils in Western Illinois. II:221–228. *In* 3rd Symp. on Surface Mining and Reclamation. Natl. Coal Assoc., Washington, D.C.

Chadwick, M. J. 1973. Amendment trials of coal spoil in the north of England. II:175–188. *In* R. J. Hutnik and G. Davis (ed.) Ecology and reclamation of devastated land. Gordon and Breach Sci. Publ. Inc., New York.

Chapman, A. G. 1967. Effects of spoil grading on tree growth. Mining Congr. J. Aug.:93–100.

Coile, T. S. 1953. Moisture content of small stone in soil. Soil Sci. 75:203–207.

Dufresne, A. N., and D. Colyer. 1975. Factors affecting rural land values along corridor E in West Virginia. West Virginia Univ. Agric. Exp. Stn. Bull. 639, Morgantown.

Folk, R. L. 1954. The distinction between grain size and mineral composition in sedimentary rock nomenclature. J. Geol. 62:344–359.

Frederick, G. B. 1971. Industry experience in revegetating with specialty crops. p. 58–59 *In* D. M. Bondurant (ed.) Proc. of the Revegetation and Economic Use of Surface-Mined Land and Mine Refuse Symp. School of Mines, College of Agric. and For., Appalachian Center, West Virginia Univ., 2–4 Dec. 1971, Pipestem State Park, W. Va. West Virginia Univ., Morgantown.

Glover, F. W., Jr. 1971. Surface mine reclamation preplanning. p. 3–4. *In* D. M. Bondurant (ed.) Proc. of the Revegetation and Economic Use of Surface-Mined land and Mine Refuse Symp. School of Mines, College of Agric. and For., Appalachian Center, West Virginia Univ., 2–4 Dec. 1971, Pipestem State Park, W. Va. West Virginia Univ., Morgantown.

Grandt, A. F., and A. L. Lang. 1958. Reclaiming Illinois strip coal land with legumes and grasses. Univ. of Illinois Agric. Exp. Stn. Bull. 628.

Greene, B. C., and W. B. Raney. 1974. West Virginia's controlled placement. p. 5–17. *In* 2nd Research and Applied Technology Symp. on Mined-Land Reclamation. 22–24 Oct. 1974, Louisville, Ky. Natl. Coal Assoc., Washington, D.C.

Grube, W. E., Jr. 1974. Pedologic potential of selected upper Pennsylvania sedimentary rocks using chemical parameters. Ph.D. Dissertation. West Virginia Univ. Univ. Microfilms, Ann Arbor, Mich. (Diss. Abstr. 75-4989).

Grube, W. E., Jr., and R. M. Smith. 1974. Field clues useful for characterization of coal overburden. West Virginia Surface Mining and Reclamation Association Green Lands Quarterly 4(1):24–25, Charleston, W. Va.

Heald, M. T., G. E. Arnold, and R. M. Smith. 1974. Sandstone weathering on surface mine spoil. West Virginia Surface Mining and Reclamation Association Green Lands Quarterly 4(3):19–20, Charleston, W. Va.

Heide, G. 1973. Pedological investigations in the Rhine Brown-Coal Area. II:295–315. *In* R. J. Hutnik and G. Davis (ed.) Ecology and reclamation of devastated land. Gordon and Breach Sci. Publ. Inc., New York.

Hill, R. D. 1970. Elkins mine drainage pollution control demonstration project. p. 284–303. *In* 3rd Symp. on Coal Mine Drainage Research. Bituminous Coal Res., Inc., Monroeville.

Izhevskaya, T. I., A. I. Savich, and V. N. Cheklina. 1974. Sulphide-containing rocks and their significance in recultivation of spoil banks of the brown coal open pits. (In Russian). Intl. Congr. Soil Sci., Trans. 10th (Moscow, USSR). 4:427–432.

Jackson, M. L. 1958. Soil chemical analysis. Prentice Hall, Inc., Englewood Cliffs, N. J.

Jonas, F. 1973. Reclamation of areas damaged by mining activity in Czechoslovakia. II:379–394. *In* R. J. Hutnik and G. Davis (ed.) Ecology and reclamation of devastated land. Gordon and Breach Sci. Publ. Inc., New York.

Jonas, F. 1974. Development of anthropogenous soil on spoil banks originated after lignite mining in Czechoslovakia. Intl. Congr. Soil Sci., Trans. 10th (Moscow, USSR) 4:390–397.

Knabe, W. 1964. Methods and results of strip-mine reclamation in Germany, Ohio J. Sci. 64(2):75–105.

Knabe, W. 1973. Development and application of the "Domsdorf Ameliorative Treatment" on toxic spoil banks of lignite opencast mines in Germany. II:273–295. *In* R. J. Hutnik and G. Davis (ed.) Ecology and reclamation of devastated land. Gordon and Breach Sci. Publ. Inc., New York.

Kohnke, H. 1950. The reclamation of coal mine spoils. Adv. Agron. 2:317–349.

Krumbein, W. C., and L. L. Sloss. 1963. Stratigraphy and sedimentation. 2nd ed. W. H. Freeman and Co., San Francisco.

McCormack, D. E. 1974. Soil reconstruction: for the best soil after mining. p. 150–162. In 2nd Research and Applied Technology Symp. on Mined-Land Reclamation. 22–24 Oct. 1974, Louisville, Ky. Natl. Coal Assoc., Washington, D.C.

Miller, W. L., C. L. Godfrey, W. G. McCully, and G. W. Thomas. 1976. Formation of soil acidity in carbonaceous soil materials exposed by highway excavations in East Texas. Soil Sci. 121:162–169.

Moulton, L. K., D. A. Anderson, S. M. Hussain, and R. K. Seals. 1974. Coal mine refuse: an engineering material. p. 1–25. In 1st Symp. on Mine and Preparation Plant Refuse Disposal. 22–24 Oct. 1974, Louisville, Ky. Natl. Coal Assoc., Washington, D.C.

Nastya, S., K. Rentse, N. Marin, and I. Blazha. 1974. Investigation of agricultural development of lands disturbed by ore mining. (In Russian). Int. Congr. Soil Sci., Trans. 10th (Moscow, USSR) 4:414–419.

Orton, C. R., and S. L. Galpin. 1945. Approved drainage, grading, and plantings for strip-mined lands. West Virginia Univ. Agric. Exp. Stn. Mimeo. Circ. no. 55, Morgantown.

Patterson, J. C. 1974. Planting in urban soils. USDI, Natl. Park Service, Ecological Serv. Bull. no. 1. U.S. Government Printing Office, Washington, D.C.

Pitsenberger, J. E. 1974. Future land use. In F. W. Glover, Jr. (ed.) Annual interagency evaluation of surface mine reclamation in West Virginia report. West Virginia DNR, Div. of Reclamation, Charleston.

Pitsenbarger, J. E. 1975. Future land use. p. 32–33. In F. W. Glover, Jr. (ed.) Annual interagency evaluation of surface mine reclamation in West Virginia report. West Virginia DNR, Div. of Reclamation, Charleston.

Riley, C. V., and J. A. Rinier. 1972. Reclamation and mine tip drainage in Europe. p. 1–14. In 4th Symp. on Coal Mine Drainage Research. Natl. Coal Assoc., 26–27 Apr. 1972, Mellen Inst., Pittsburgh, Pa. Bituminous Coal Res. Inc., Monroeville, Pa.

Sandoval, F. M., J. J. Bond, J. F. Power, and W. O. Willis. 1973. Lignite mine spoils in the Northern Great Plains—characteristics and potential for reclamation. p. 117–133. In Research and Applied Technology Symp. on Mined-Land Reclamation. Natl. Coal Assoc., 7–8 Mar. 1973, William Penn Hotel, Pittsburg, Pa. Bituminous Coal Res., Inc., Monroeville, Pa.

Scott, R. B., and R. C. Wilmoth. 1974. Use of coal mine refuse and fly ash as a road base material. p. 263–275. In 1st Symp. on Mine and Preparation Plant Refuse Disposal. Natl. Coal Assoc., Washington, D.C.

Singer, P. C. and W. Stumm. 1968. Kinetics of the oxidation of ferrous iron. p. 12–34. In 2nd Symp. on Coal Mine Drainage Research. Coal Industry Advisory Comm. to ORSANCO, 14–15 May 1968, Mellon Inst., Pittsburgh, Pa. Bituminous Coal Res., Inc., Monroeville, Pa.

Smith, E. E., and K. S. Shumate. 1970. Sulfide to sulfate reaction mechanism. Water Pollut. Control Res. Series 14010 FPS. USDI, FWQA. Washington, D.C.

Smith, R. M. 1976. Minesoil properties and classification studies. West Virginia Surface Mining and Reclamation Association Green Lands Quarterly 6(1):11, Charleston, W. Va.

Smith, R. M., W. E. Grube, Jr., and J. T. Ammons. 1973. Toxic or potentially toxic materials. West Virginia Surface Mining and Reclamation Association Green Lands Quarterly 3(3):7, Charleston, W. Va.

Smith, R. M. W. E. Grube, Jr., T. Arkle, Jr., and A. A. Sobek. 1974a. Mine spoil potentials for soil and water quality. Environ. Prot. Technol. Series S800745. U.S. Government Printing Office, Washington, D.C.

Smith, R. M., W. E. Grube, Jr., J. C. Sencindiver, R. N. Singh, and A. A. Sobek. 1974b. Properties, processes and energetics of minesoils. Int. Congr. Soil Sci., Trans. 10th (Moscow, USSR) 4:406–413.

Smith, R. M., W. E. Grube, Jr., A. A. Sobek, and R. N. Singh. 1974c. Rock types and laboratory analyses as a basis for managing minesoils. p. 47–52. In 10th Forum on Geology of Industrial Minerals Proc. Ohio State Univ. Dep. of Geol. and Mineral., and Ohio Div. of Geol. Surv., 17–19 Apr. 1974, Columbus, Ohio. Ohio DNR Misc. Rep. no. 1, Columbus.

Smith, R. M., A. A. Sobek, T. Arkle, Jr., J. C. Sencindiver, and J. R. Freeman. 1976. Extensive overburden potentials for soil and water quality. Environ. Prot. Technol. Series. EPA-600/2-76-184. U.S. Government Printing Office, Washington, D.C.

Smith, W. D. 1971. Industry experience in revegetating with trees. p. 55–57. In D. M. Bondurant (ed.) Proc. of the Revegetation and Economic Use of Surface-Mined Land and Mine Refuse Symp., West Virginia Univ., Morgantown.

Striffler, W. D. 1967. Restoration of open-cast coal sites in Great Britain. J. Soil Water Conserv. 22:101–103.

Temple, K. L., and W. A. Koehler. 1954. Drainage from bituminous coal mines. West Virginia Univ. Eng. Stn. Res. Bull. 25, Morgantown.

Tyner, E. H., R. M. Smith, and S. L. Galpin. 1948. Reclamation of strip-mined areas in West Virginia. J. Am. Soc. Agron. 40:313–323.

U.S. Department of Agriculture, SCS, Soil Survey Staff. 1975. Soil taxonomy: a basic system of soil classification for making and interpreting soil surveys. Agric. Handbook no. 436. U.S. Government Printing Office, Washington, D.C.

U.S. Department of Agriculture Staff. 1968. Restoring surface-mined land. USDA Misc. Pub. 1082. U.S. Government Printing Office, Washington, D.C.

West Virginia Department of Natural Resources. 1976. West Virginia surface mining reclamation regulations. State of West Virginia, Charleston. Chap. 30-6. p. 1–25.

West Virginia University. 1971. Mine spoil potentials for water quality and controlled erosion. Water Pollut. Control Res. Series 14010 EJE. U.S. Government Printing Office, Washington, D.C.

White, J. R., and J. E. Pitsenbarger. 1973. Report of special committee on future land use. In F. W. Glover, Jr. (ed.) Annual interagency evaluation of surface mine reclamation in West Virginia report. West Virginia DNR, Div. of Reclamation, Charleston.

Wilson, H. A. 1965. The microbiology of strip mine spoil. West Virginia Univ. Agric. Exp. Stn. Bull. 506T.

Wilson, H. A., and D. A. Zuberer. 1976. Microbiological factors associated with surface mine reclamation. West Virginia Agric. Exp. Stn. Bull. 645T.

Wiram, V. P., and J. A. Deane. 1974. Physical and chemical characteristics of acid-producing sandstone warrant preferential strip and burial mining methods. p. 88–102. In 5th Symp. on Coal Mine Drainage Research. Louisville, Ky., 23–24 Oct. 1974, Natl. Coal Assoc., Washington, D.C.

Chapter 10

Hydrologic and Climatic Factors[1]

H. R. GARDNER AND D. A. WOOLHISER

Agricultural Research Service, USDA,
Fort Collins, Colorado

I. INTRODUCTION

An understanding of water movement over the surface and through the topsoil and spoil is essential in designing techniques to establish vegetation, control erosion, stablize spoils, and control water pollution on drastically disturbed lands. Thus, any general discussion of reclamation of drastically disturbed lands necessarily involves hydrology and climatology.

In this chapter we will consider only those aspects of hydrology and climatology that are important in the reclamation of drastically disturbed lands because detailed discussions would be prohibitively long. We will begin by describing components of the hydrologic cycle to illustrate the physical basis of modifying the hydrologic regime by disturbance and subsequent reclamation activities. We will then describe management approaches to modify the hydrologic cycle to achieve particular goals and, finally, we will consider evaluation of management practices.

II. THE MACROSCALE HYDROLOGIC SYSTEM

In this section we will qualitatively discuss individual components of the hydrologic cycle and examine in more detail those aspects deemed significant in managing drastically disturbed lands.

A. Precipitation

The major uncontrolled inputs to a hydrologic system are precipitation and solar radiation. Because they are not predictable in any deterministic sense they must be considered as dependent stochastic processes with parameters varying in space and time. These two inputs are perhaps the most important determinants of the climate of a region.

A map showing isolines of mean annual precipitation and the loca-

---

[1] Contribution from the Agricultural Research Service, USDA, in cooperation with Colorado State University Experiment Station, Fort Collins, Colorado.

173

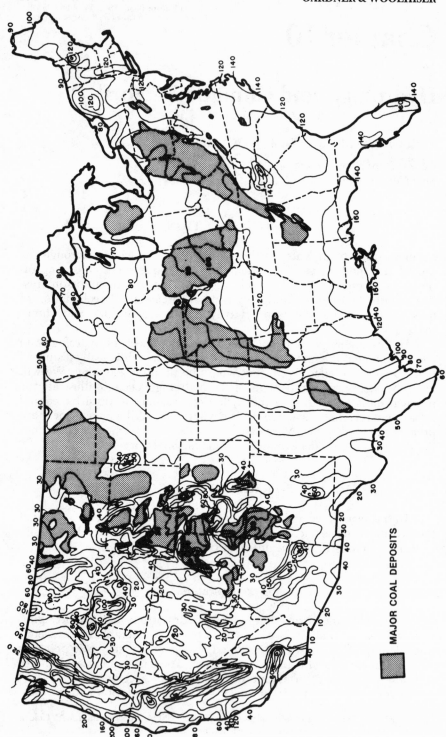

Fig. 1—Mean annual precipitation (cm) and major U.S. coal reserve areas.

MAJOR COAL DEPOSITS

tion of major coal deposits in the conterminous United States is shown in Fig. 1. Average annual precipitation ranges from < 25 cm in parts of the Western coal fields in Arizona, New Mexico, Colorado, and Wyoming to > 125 cm in the Appalachian coal fields. The seasonal distribution of precipitation also varies considerably. The distribution of precipitation is quite uniform throughout the year in western Colorado and the Four Corners area, changing to a pronounced early summer peak in the northern Great Plains, and becoming more nearly uniform in the Appalachian coal fields. The proportion of precipitation that occurs as snow also has a significant effect on the hydrologic water balance. For a detailed description of the climate of the United States see Court (1974).

B. Temperature

Air temperature is dependent on a number of factors included in the heat balance of an air layer near the ground. These factors include incoming and outgoing radiation, soil heat transfer, conduction and mass heat exchange in the air, and latent heat transfer. Those aspects of temperature and radiation balance that are especially important from the hydrologic standpoint are: length of growing season, potential evapotranspiration, precipitation occurring as snow, and frequency of freezing and thawing.

Temperature fluctuations are especially severe in the Western coal fields, with average annual freeze–thaw frequencies ranging from 90 to > 130 in parts of southern Wyoming. This high freeze–thaw frequency accelerates weathering of overburden materials which substantially affects its infiltration characteristics.

The steep slopes characteristic of some surface-mined areas have a significant effect on the microclimate and hydrology. South-facing slopes receive more solar radiation and have higher potential evapotranspiration than north-facing slopes. This difference has a profound effect on vegetation establishment.

Waste coal present in the overburden can lower the albedo and result in high surface temperatures.

C. Evapotranspiration

The hydrologic budget for a soil mass includes terms for precipitation input and losses by evaporation, transpiration, and deep drainage. Deep drainage is of major concern for both humid and arid areas. When the magnitude of total seasonal rainfall is compared to the total potential evapotranspiration (ET) for areas ranging from arid to humid, the total potential ET exceeds the rainfall in an arid region by a considerable margin, while in the humid region the total rainfall can exceed the potential ET by a significant amount. In arid regions it is possible for the plant cover to use almost all of the rainfall in ET and leave essentially none for deep drainage. Occasionally a storm may cause enough infiltration to place some water beyond the influence of plant roots. In areas where winter precipitation accumulates as snow, there may be significant deep percolation even though the ET exceeds precipitation on an annual basis. In more humid regions where the annual rainfall equals or exceeds the potential ET, there may be excess water beyond that required to satisfy plant growth. The excess water will drain below the root zone and eventually appear in the ground water or surface water, carrying with it whatever constituents it might have dissolved on the way.

Potential ET computed by the Thornthwaite method (Thornthwaite, 1948) varied from 60 cm and less in the Western coal field up to approximately 90 cm in Alabama. In the west potential ET is two or three times greater than the precipitation. Consequently, runoff is small and occurs as a result of intense rainfall or infrequent recharge of ground water contributing to streamflow. In the Appalachian fields precipitation is considerably greater than potential ET and mean annual streamflow (surface and subsurface runoff) may be > 50 cm.

The actual rate of ET depends on climatic factors, soil water content, extent of plant cover, and land management techniques. Evapotranspiration can be modified significantly by changing from deep-rooted to shallow-rooted vegetation or vice-versa. If the available water storage capacity in the rooting zone is changed significantly, ET and, consequently, deep drainage will be affected.

D. Infiltration

As snow melts or rain falls on soil, the phenomenon of infiltration governs the amount of water that will enter the soil and thereby exerts a controlling influence on the amount of surface runoff. The major factors involved in determining infiltration are: the slope of the soil surface, the characteristics of the surface, the surface groundcover, and the amount and intensity of the rainfall. Some of the physical, chemical, and biological characteristics of soil that affect infiltration can be manipulated by man through agronomic and engineering practices. The major controlling factor in infiltration will be the characteristics of the top few centimeters of soil. The porosity, pore size distribution, and tortuosity of soil pores have a substantial effect on infiltration rates. Sands have higher infiiltration rates than silts or clays, which have more porosity but have much smaller pore sizes.

In many cases where a topsoil is placed on top of the disturbed material, the topsoil has a saturated hydraulic conductivity which is much less than that of the material below. In this case the infiltration is almost completely determined by the hydraulic conductivity of the surface soil. These topsoil materials are much more affected by rain drop impact than would be the other disturbed materials underlying them. The small particles that result from the breakdown of soil aggregates due to rain drop impact can be carried into larger pores by water and form a thin surface layer with a low hydraulic conductivity. This surface layer then effectively controls the infiltration rate (Edwards & Larson, 1969; Hillel &

Gardner, 1970). Vegetation or mulches protect the soil surface from rain drop impact and reduce crust formation.

Frozen soil usually has a lower infiltration rate than unfrozen soil. If the soil is frozen while at a high water content, a dense, nearly impermeable mass may result. Thus, in the spring a serious runoff hazard may occur on steep slopes where the soils have been frozen while wet.

Repeated cycling of freezing and thawing can have an effect on the infiltration. This effect will depend on the initial soil conditions and whether the soil is a rocky, disturbed, spoil material, or whether it originally was an A or B horizon of a normal soil. Soil tends to increase temporarily in initial infiltration rate, while a spoil material which has not previously been subject to freezing and thawing due to its placement below the surface of the soil tends to break down physically to smaller particles as a result of the freezing and thawing and its hydraulic conductivity decreases.

Slope has a substantial but indirect affect on infiltration. Depression storage is generally greater on flat slopes than on steep slopes and surface water is present longer after rainfall stops, allowing greater infiltration.

Infiltration generally has been described or predicted on the basis of entirely empirical equations, or simplifications of more general equations. Equations presented by Horton (1940) and Holtan (1961) are examples of empirical models. Equations obtained from simplifications of the basic equations or from algebraic approximations of numerical solutions of the basic equations are given by Green and Ampt (1911), Philip (1964), Smith (1972), Mein and Larson (1973), and Brustkern and Morel-Seytoux (1970).

The major stumbling block in estimating infiltration at this time is the necessity of estimating parameters. Holtan and associates have attempted to develop techniques for estimating parameters in the Holtan equation by using information available in soil surveys (England, 1970), or by developing estimates of parameters for various land use or cover factors (Holtan & Creitz, 1967).

E. Surface Runoff

Surface runoff begins when rainfall (or snowmelt) rates exceed the infiltration capacity of the soil and depression storage is filled. Surface runoff is somewhat arbitrarily classified as either overland flow or channel flow. Overland flow is sometimes considered to be thin sheet flow over a relatively smooth surface. However, a more general and realistic definition would be the flow that is occurring outside of the well-defined channel system. The mean velocity of overland flow is directly related to the slope (laminar flow) or the square root of the slope (turbulent flow), and is inversely related to the hydraulic resistance of the surface. The hydraulic resistance varies widely depending on the surface characteristics from a Mannings N of 0.02 for bare soil to 0.4 for a dense turf (Woolhiser, 1975). Differences in hydraulic resistance of this magnitude would result in the depth of water on the rougher surface being approximately six times as great as the depth on the bare soil for the same discharge. The velocity, of course, would be only one-sixth of that on the bare soil. The greater depth on the dense sod would allow much more time for infiltration after the rainfall stopped, resulting in less runoff even if the infiltration characteristics of the soils were the same. The lower velocities on the sod would also result in a much lower erosion potential.

It is anticipated that in many cases surface disturbance will increase surface runoff by decreasing the infiltration rate and lowering hydraulic resistance. These effects will also tend to increase peak flow rates. Increases in surface runoff from rainfall simulations have been observed in the west by Lusby and Toy (1976) and Gilley.[2]

F. Surface Water Storage

Water can be stored on the soil surface in depression storage, within the soil in the unsaturated condition as held against gravity by forces of attraction, or in saturated form in an area where an impermeable barrier serves to balance the force of gravity. All water that is trapped in surface storage either infiltrates or evaporates, with evaporation usually being the smaller quantity. Surface storage may become runoff when surface depressions overflow and rills formed by surface runoff erode barriers, thus allowing a sudden increase in runoff which, in turn, can break down the whole system and cause extensive erosion.

Two beneficial effects of surface storage are to reduce erosion and to increase the water available for plant growth. In areas where excessive amounts of water move through the root zone and contribute to drainage problems, it is desirable to increase the runoff after plant growth has stabilized the surface. Unfortunately, this cannot be done because the slope and surface configuration have already been established. However, the surface storage will decrease as the surface pockets tend to slake down with time. In areas of low rainfall, the same technique can be used on the disturbed areas that are used in agronomic practice to reduce water loss by runoff. Contour furrows in range and pasture have considerable storage immediately after installation. However, the storage capacity is reduced by erosion and trampling by livestock. Neff (1973) found that contour furrows in eastern Montana had only half their original capacity after 6 to 10 years and that the average effective life (storage > 0.13 cm) was about 25 years.

G. Soil Water and Ground Water

Subsurface water storage manifests itself in two ways; storage at less than saturation, and storage at saturation. That which is at less than saturation flows by unsaturated flow from the surface down to the ground water table. The rate of flow depends directly on the amount that gets

---

[2] J. E. Gilley, G. W. Gee, A. Bauer, W. O. Willis, and R. A. Young. 1976. Runoff and erosion characteristics of surface-mined sites in western North Dakota. Am. Soc. Agric. Eng. Pap. no. 76-2027. St. Joseph, Mich.

through the plant root zone without being diverted by evaporation or plant extraction. The amount of water that is below the root zone at a particular time depends on the relationship between the unsaturated hydraulic conductivity and the water content. In areas of extremely low rainfall there may be many years when the net flow downward below the root zone is essentially zero. The plants have extracted all water that was not lost by evaporation. In spoils where the material is rocky with low silt and clay content the unsaturated water-holding capacity is very low, leaving little water that can be temporarily stored in the root zone for plant growth.

In some soils a rather permeable top soil is underlain by a slowly permeable clay layer. If infiltration rates are rapid enough, it is possible for the surface soil to become saturated. The saturated flow will be predominantly in a lateral downslope direction and is known as interflow. This water may reappear on the surface at the foot of the slope or on the side slope whenever the clay layer comes to the surface. There is general agreement among hydrologists that a flow mechanism such as interflow exists; however, there is some argument as to how important it is. Dunne (1970) presented some measurements of subsurface storm flow in Vermont and discussed its relative importance. He concluded that interflow (subsurface storm flow in his terminology) did not contribute significantly to flood hydrographs. This does not mean that this mechanism is unimportant from the standpoint of water quality in some regions. Minshall and Jamison (1965) presented data suggesting that interflow can exist on Midwest Claypan soils. Interflow could be significant on mined areas if permeable top soils are placed on relatively impervious spoil material. This is not likely except in areas with high sodium spoil material.

The effect of surface mining on the amount, direction, and rate of ground water flow depends largely on the geologic and topographic characteristics of the area before mining. In all cases the overburden is shattered and mixed, with a consequent increase in its porosity. Therefore, potential saturated water storage in the overburden will be increased. Whether or not it will serve as a useful aquifer depends on the hydraulic conductivity of the fractured material and the chemical characteristics of the spoil.

Three before-and-after configurations are shown in Fig. 2(a)–(f). In Fig. 2(a) and (b) we see a configuration that occurs in the Yampa Coal Field of western Colorado. When the coal is removed and the shattered overburden is replaced, it appears quite likely that substantial amounts of water will move more deeply than before mining (McWhorter & Rowe, 1976). If rooting depth is decreased due to vegetation type or soil water storage characteristics, it is also likely that water yield will be increased.

In Fig. 2(c) and (d) we see a case that occurs in the Appalachian Plateau region of Ohio. When the coal is removed from a layer that outcrops on both sides of a hill or ridge, a low spot is left in the center. If no drainage way is provided a lake will form in the low spot. Ground water storage may be increased and this area may contribute base flow for a longer period than it did prior to mining.

In Fig. 2(e) and (f) is shown a very thick coal seam with shallow

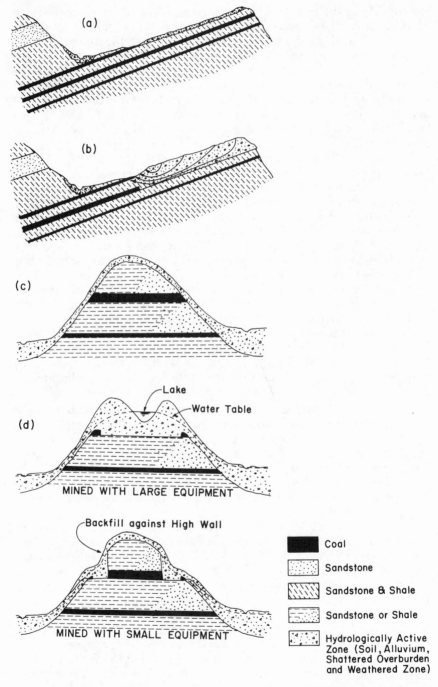

Fig. 2—Before and after configuration of ground water flow in three different types of strata: (a,b) the Yampa Coal Field in western Colorado; (c,d) Appalachian Plateau region of Ohio; (e,f) thick coal seams of northeastern Wyoming.

(e)

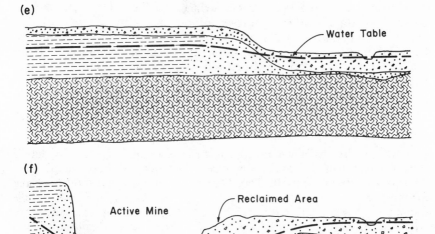

(f)

Coal

Sandstone or Shale

Hydrologically Active
Zone (Soil, Alluvium,
Shattered Overburden
and Weathered Zone)

Fig. 2—Continued.

overburden and subdued topography. This case is similar to some mines in northeastern Wyoming. In this area the coal seams are the major shallow aquifers. During mining the mine will act as a large diameter well and the water level in the aquifer will be drawn down for some distane around the mine. Recharge to the mine from nearby streams may also be induced. After the pit is backfilled, the piezometric surface will eventually approach the original piezometric surface. However, the trnsmissibility characteristics of the area may change and the piezometric surface may be much nearer the ground surface. If the hydraulic conductivity of the spoil is less than the effective conductivity of the coal seam, wells will require a greater draw-down to produce the same amount of water (McWhorter & Rowe, 1976). If the spoil is more permeable the aquifer will be improved insofar as water quantity is concerned. The effects of mining on ground water recharge must also be considered when the disturbed area is large relative to the recharge area.

H. Streamflow

Streamflow includes direct surface runoff (during and shortly after rainfall or snowmelt), interflow, and ground water runoff. Surface mining activities can change the volume of streamflow, its flow duration, and its quality. The proportion of direct surface runoff to total runoff can also be changed significantly. If surface runoff and erosion- were to be increased significantly, the stream channel characteristics would change. For example a large increase in erosion may result in channel aggradation while increases in runoff, base level lowering, or decreases in erosion may result in degradation.

I. Erosion

Erosion begins when raindrops strike the soil surface and detach particles from the soil mass. These soil particles are then available for transport by surface runoff. The shear forces exerted by runoff may also detach particles, resulting in rill erosion. Severe erosion can be especially damaging to reclamation efforts by physically removing seeds and fertilizer, and by removing sufficient topsoil so that the available soil water storage is not adequate for the desired vegetation.

Erosion processes have been studied extensively on agricultural soils (Wischmeier & Smith, 1965) and more recently on severely disturbed areas (Lusby & Toy, 1976)[2]. These studies have shown that the amount of erosion is related to rainfall energy, the steepness and length of slope, and the structural stability of the soil. Vegetal cover absorbs raindrop impact and reduces the velocity of the overland flow, thus reducing erosion. On short slopes splash erosion is significant, but on long slopes and in snowmelt situations rill erosion is predominant.

The amount of erosion from slopes as steep as 20% is directly related to some of the factors already mentioned, such as structural stability of the aggregated particles and the percentage of the total that is rock or gravel. In addition to this, the plant population and character have a great effect on the stability of the surface as the plants reduce raindrop splash and slow the rate of surface runoff. Annual weeds which are undesirable from the standpoint of competing with desirable species have some utility in controlling erosion. As an illustration, Russian thistle (*Salsola kali* L.) grows prolifically in the southern Montana area. In the spring the mine spoils are literally carpeted with thistle. This stabilizes the slopes to a great degree the first year. In subsequent years, seeded species tend to crowd out the thistle and establish a more useful cover. The amount of erosion from the slopes in the first year is probably no greater than that from cultivated lands in many instances.

J. Chemical Transport

Chemicals dissolved in soil water will move at approximately the same rate as the water if the chemicals are not reactive with the soil material. Generally, anions such as chloride and nitrate fall in this category. If there are interactions between the soil solids and the dissolved chemicals, many complex situations can occur. At low water contents, the water moves in unsaturated flow in thin films, and the movement rate will be slow enough that at any given time the solution will be near equilibrium with the solids surrounding it. Cations, such as sodium, calcium and magnesium, are extremely reactive and will readily exchange on and off the soil cation exchange sites. The affinity of the cation to the soil affects its movement rate through the soil in unsaturated flow. The relative affinities of the various cations for most of the soil materials are Ca^{2+} > Mg^{2+} > K^+ = NH_4^+ > Na^+. An examination of this list shows that Na^+ ion moves more rapidly in leaching water and would tend to leach out first. Kurtz and Melsted (1973) discuss this to some degree.

Since the disturbed material generally is quite heterogeneous both on the macro- and on the microscale, the composition of the solution, although in near equilibrium at any one time, could be changing by being passed through the material. This can happen if the material has sufficient exchange capacity to take out of solution some cations and exchange them for others which are in much greater abundance in the layer being passed through. Also, many slightly soluble compounds are available for solution. Equations have been developed that describe or predict leaching of ions, such as nitrate, that have little or no interaction with the medium through which they are moving or else interact purely mechanically, such as in miscible displacement (Burnes, 1975; Gardner, 1965; Nielson & Biggar, 1963). Kurtz and Melsted (1973) have suggested that rain water has been underrated as a weathering agent. They found that water in Illinois streams is often saturated with silicates, showing that active primary silicate weathering may take place with each rain shower that brings good quality water into the soil.

A major concern for water use in disturbed areas is the concentration of salts in the drainage water and its effect on the downstream users of both ground and surface water. In many cases in disturbed materials, available minerals can supply the ground water with soluble salts which can keep the water near saturation with gypsum or reduce the pH in the case of acid formation for an indeterminate time. Thus, the major control mechanism may have to be the bypassing of the drainage part of the hydrologic cycle through the route to ET and runoff. The encouragement of runoff is generally new to our way of thinking but it may have to be studied seriously as an alternative to some of the results of deep drainage and its accompanying transport of chemicals.

III. MANAGEMENT OF FACTORS AFFECTING THE HYDROLOGIC CYCLE

In the preceding section we have discussed components of the hydrologic cycle and changes that might occur when the land is subjected to disturbances such as surface mining. In this section we will consider management factors that can alleviate the effects of land disturbances on the hydrologic cycle.

Within limits, the hydrologic regime of a disturbed area can be modified by reclamation management practices that change the storages or transmission rates within the hydrologic cycle.

A. Topsoil

The two major purposes for the placement of topsoil over spoil are to provide an acceptable growth medium for plants and to provide control of infiltration and runoff of water.

Some spoil materials do not contain materials toxic to plants and, thus, only need addition of required nutrients to provide good ground cover. However, many spoil materials have toxic amounts of some minerals present that prevent good germination and growth of plants. In this case placement of a layer of topsoil over the surface of the spoil may be desirable. McCormack (1974) has suggested that with proper use of soil surveys and soil tests before mining a soil could be reconstituted involving replacement of A and B horizons based on their characteristics. In some cases this could give a soil with a profile as much as 120 cm thick.

In many areas where the original topsoil was only 30–40 cm thick and had no structure, there would be little use in trying to separate the A and B horizons. Simply placing 30 cm of soil back on the surface would be about the best that could be done. Any extremely salty layer would have to be adequately covered by spoil with favorable properties. The depth of topsoil is usually constrained by the amount present before mining. However, the minimum topsoil depth should be based upon requirements of vegetation and the amount expected to be lost by erosion during the vegetation establishment period.

Harbert and Berg (1974) working with spent oil shale used 15 to 30 cm thicknesses of topsoil. A leaching treatment of 100 cm of water was included because the spent oil shale is very salty. Plants grown on 30 cm of topsoil over spoil did well with and without the leaching treatment. Salt moved up to the surface by capillarity in 15-cm topsoil treatments, but not in the 30-cm treatments. The requirement in some states to bury high salt layers under at least 240 cm of better material would alleviate the high salt problem encountered by Harbert and Berg (1974).

Infiltration control by adding topsoil is very important in areas where acid drainage is encountered in conjunction with strip mines. Good et al. (1970) have shown in a study of a deep mine refuse pile that pyrite oxidation was limited to the outer mantle of 10 to 25 cm which had much of the clay removed by leaching. Clay had migrated below the outer layer forming a slowly permeable layer at about 25 cm depth. The rate of pyrite oxidation was essentially constant.

Erosion constantly renews the supply of unreacted material. The placement of a layer of topsoil at least 30 cm thick would reduce the oxidation rate considerably by reducing the amount of water moving through the reactive layer, reducing the oxygen supply available, and reducing the erosion of the reactive layer. The topsoil layer would be much more stable than the uncovered spoil if a good plant cover is established. The current law in Illinois, where this stock pile of spoil was located, required a 120 cm depth of clean earth to be applied to a new refuse pile followed with vegetative cover. Any time that a good growth medium can be placed on top of the spoil in acid-producing areas it will contribute to the reduction of the oxidation of sulfides and production of acid drainage.

B. Surface Configuration

The macro- and microtopography of a disturbed area can be modified to increase depression storage and reduce slope length. Increasing depression storage increases infiltration and decreases direct surface runoff and erosion. Reducing slope length may profoundly reduce on-site erosion and sediment lost from the area with only minor effects on surface runoff. The spoil surface can be modified to retain almost all of the water which will fall in most storms. These techniques have been discussed by Wight (1976). They include gouging and dozer basins used by Hodder et al. (1971) and level bench terracing as used by Haas and Willis (1971).

In arid areas this would be desirable to conserve water and control erosion. In humid areas, particularly on steep-banked mines, configurations that conserve much of the water would cause other problems more serious than that caused by the sedimentation and runoff if the water were only partially contained. When the water is contained on the slopes, the danger of spoil slides can be extreme in humid areas where the normal hillsides may be as steep as 30%. The excess water infiltrated into the soil but not used by plants moves below the root zone and drains through the spoil. This water contributes to the extreme instability of the material and helps to cause the outslope failures. The surface instability caused by the removal of vegetation and replacement of the spoil is responsible for the movement of large amounts of suspended solids by surface erosion, especially during severe storm events. During lesser events there is a much smaller difference in stream discharge (Curtis, 1973).

Outslopes on Eastern strip mines are characteristically quite steep and often are unstable. A special technique to help stabilize the surface for planting of grasses is to form the surface into stair steps of a size ranging from 30 to 90 cm. This has been referred to by Armiger et al. (1976). This technique could be done by a machine as suggested by the above authors or on a larger size scale using a bulldozer.

Contouring is a practice that may be useful in some cases. Tillage and planting operations can be performed on the contour to construct a small amount of surface storage. Contours will reduce runoff and erosion for small rainstorms, but are ineffective on short slopes that are 2 to 8% in slope.

Terrace systems prevent severe rill and gully erosion by reducing the effective slope length. Soil loss is reduced from the strips between terraces and much of the soil lost is redeposited in the terrace channel. The water discharge from the terrace channels must be conveyed to the toe of the slope by means of stabilized outlets or subsurface drains.

Terrace systems prevent severe rill and gully erosion by reducing the effective slope length. Soil loss is reduced from the strips between terraces and much of the soil lost is redeposited in the terrace channel. The water discharge from the terrace channels must be conveyed to the toe of the slope by means of stabilized outlets or subsurface drains.

Graded terraces on cropland have reduced surface runoff in some situations and increased it in others. Level terraces store runoff until it infiltrates and can nearly eliminate surface runoff in areas with low rainfall and permeable soils.

One factor that must be considered is that there may be substantial variations in infiltraton rates on regraded spoils. In Eastern areas, researchers have found that the infiltration rates into spoil piles where the tops were cut off were an order of magnitude less than on the areas filled between piles (Coleman, 1951).

In arid regions, the surface configuration can be used to advantage, not only to discourage runoff, but to concentrate the water into limited areas. If there is a lower limit to the amount of water infiltrated which is necessary to maintain plant growth, then when the rainfall fails to contribute this amount there will be essentially no growth of plants during that period. If the water can be concentrated into smaller areas by controlled runoff and infiltration, then plant growth may be maintained in part of the area that could not have been done without the concentration of the water. This enhances the overall control of wind and water erosion. This technique has been used on farmland successfully where runoff slopes as small as 120 cm wide contribute to a trash-filled slot (Fairbourn & Gardner, 1974). Riley (1969) used this technique effectively in Ohio for toxic salt control with ridges 90 to 120 cm from peak to peak and 60 to 90 cm high. After one winter the ridges were eroded down to about 15 to 45 cm high. The plants growing in the ravines were growing well because of the leaching of salts out of that zone.

In northern areas where rainfall is lacking for good plant production, snow trapping is a useful technique to gain water. Contour furrowing can trap and keep snow and prevent the spring runoff (Wight et al., 1975).

C. Subsoil Layering

During the process of backfilling after strip mining there is an opportunity to place materials back in the pit in a particular sequence of layers if the material was stockpiled properly when removed. If a particular overburden layer is high in salt it can be placed below the plant root zone. This problem occurs in some parts of the Fort Union formation in the northern Great Plains and may occur in other areas.

The necessity of avoiding leaching of sulfates out of zones of high iron sulfides is another problem that can be at least partially controlled by placement of materials. A compact layer which restricts water flow can be placed above the high sulfide materials or the material may be placed below the water table where oxidation of the sulfides will be restricted because of low rates of oxygen diffusion in the water.

When surface layers are rather coarse and have a low water-holding capacity, the water-holding capacity can be increased by the use of a compacted or restricting layer just below the plant root zone. A coarse layer could also achieve the restriction of water flow.

D. Vegetation

Although vegetation on disturbed areas may be used primarily for aesthetic purposes, for wildlife, or for pasture, the first consideration must be its effect on water control. The choice of vegetation to be planted can affect the amount and seasonal variability of ET and thus the hydrologic cycle. Vegetation also affects infiltration and hydraulic resistance of the surface to overland flow. Depth of rooting is also significant in climates where shallow-rooted vegetation is often subjected to water stress. In general, total runoff will be less if a watershed is covered with a deep-rooted evergreen than if covered with a shallow-rooted deciduous species.

The kinds of plants to be grown must also be matched to the rainfall regime and the chemical and physical characteristics of the spoil. Physical characteristics that make plants good soil stabilizers must be considered as secondary to the ability of the plants to grow under the local conditions.

E. Fertility

Adequate fertility is a necessity in every revegetation case to provide for sufficient plant material to stabilize the surface. In many areas sufficient nutrients are not present to support plant life, but with added fertility acceptable revegetation can be achieved (Vogel, 1975).

In some cases surface modification may control levels of salts in such a way as to encourage selective leaching to allow plants to grow. Riley (1969) formed large ridges on the contour which caused runoff from the slopes and increased leaching in the ravines. The salt levels in the material under the ravines was much lower than that in the ridges. Also of major concern is the possible presence of elements in concentrations high enough to create toxicities for the plants or the animals that may consume them.

F. Mulches

Surface mulches interrupt the transfer of energy from the region above the soil surface to the soil. This can involve both the interception of heat energy and kinetic energy. When the soil surface is wet, the rate of transfer of heat energy from the sun and from the air above the soil is a limiting factor in evaporation of soil water. After the soil surface dries the major mechanism of evaporation control lies within the water-transporting properties of the soil. Thus, mulch only effects evaporation during the energy-limiting phase of evaporation. This reduction of evaporation allows a high water content near the surface for a longer time, thus enhancing the opportunity for seed germination and seedling survival.

The interception of raindrops by the mulch decreases the velocity with which the droplets hit the soil surface, thus decreasing the puddling and the splashing of the surface soil. The physical presence of the mulch also reduces the velocity of runoff which has not infiltrated into the soil and thus allows a longer time for infiltration. This action not only reduces the water loss by runoff, but at the same time reduces surface erosion. The reduction of heat energy arriving at the soil surface also reduces the soil surface temperature. This can have extreme importance, particularly in the case of very dark colored materials such as a spoil material intermixed with coal or spent oil shale. Without a mulch the temperature of these materials can reach levels that are lethal to small seedlings.

Seedlings can be established without a mulch even in arid areas, but the success is much greater with some type of protecting mulch. In Wyoming (May et al., 1971) various mulches tried gave from 6 to 8 times as many seedlings the first year as the check.

Hydroseeding with a range of amounts and types of mulch material has achieved good success in Eastern areas.

On a sandy clay loam with a slope of 2.5:1, Barnett et al. (1967) found an increase in stand of 1.5 to 2 times as many plants with a reduction of sediment loss to about one-tenth when using a variety of mulches compared to a bare slope. The runoff from a very wet slope was not reduced with mulch when compared to the bare slope, but the surface was quite well stabilized.

The addition of a mulch often increases the total infiltration which can increase the leaching of salts out of the surface material. This can prepare the surface for better plant growth at an earlier time than without a mulch (Vogel, 1975).

G. Supplemental Water

The major purposes of supplemental water are to help with germination and establishment of plants and to reduce salts and toxic ion concentrations in the surface layers of the disturbed areas. The best time to get good establishment without irrigation is immediately after a large rain when there is already a good supply of soil water. This combination of conditions may occur infrequently in the Southwest. Even when these conditions do occur the probability of sufficient water over a sustained period of time is small. The use of supplemental water is an obvious alternative.

In the San Juan Basin of New Mexico where the annual precipitation averages 15 to 20 cm, Aldon (1975) has successfully used supplemental sprinkler and drip irrigation to establish shrubs. During the irrigated period, the number of plants that can be supported by the land is greater than the number that could be supported under the natural rainfall regime. As a result the plant population will be reduced after termination of the irrigation. Because of the time necessary for the plant community to equilibrate with the rainfall regime, it is necessary to wait for at least two growing seasons before evaluating the success of the planting.

The use of supplemental water to reduce salt content of surface materials can be effective, but probably will not be used often since most state regulations that apply to strip mining require a certain amount of acceptable topsoil to be replaced on top of spoil material.

Leaching trials on spent soil shale (Harbert & Berg, 1974) have shown that 100 cm of leach water applied by sprinklers to the shale material before placement of topsoil effectively reduced the soluble salt concentration to acceptable levels. However, with 15 cm topsoil placed on top of the shale after leaching, the water rose to the surface by capillarity and caused a collecting of salts within the topsoil. Apparently the topsoil thickness was not adequate to keep the salts from rising to the surface.

Water harvesting can also be considered as a technique for applying supplemental water. In arid areas this technique for applying supplemental water has been used to obtain water for shrubs in range reseeding (Aldon, 1975) and as a farming technique (Wight, 1976). It has been quite effective. The use of the harvested water has also been effective in selective leaching of salts from surface materials (Riley, 1969).

One of the problems that cannot be solved with supplemental water is the removal of salts by leaching when the dissolved salts are coming from rock in the spoil. The leaching water can remove salts for years with no decrease in concentration of the salts in the water because of the almost unlimited supply in the rocks.

IV. EVALUATION OF CONSEQUENCES OF MANAGEMENT

Evaluating the hydrologic consequences of a management practice implies that a procedure is available to quantitatively predict a flow or storage component of the hydrologic cycle for that practice and also for some alternative. In many cases a weaker evaluation involving only a ranking of practices with respect to a hydrologic variable is sufficient. The Universal Soil Loss Equation (USLE) as applied to agricultural areas is an example of the former in that one could estimate that the average annual erosion from a field would be X_1 tons per year for a contoured row crop and X_2 tons per year for a terraced contoured row crop. Evaluation capabilities for disturbed lands are presently in the second category. We may be able to say that there will be more erosion with practice A than with practice B, but we cannot say how much. A ranking is adequate if the cost C_B of practice B is equal to or less than the cost C_A of practice A. However, if $C_B > C_A$ we need to know if the reduction in erosion is worth the difference in cost.

Quantitative evaluations require the development of models of water, chemical, and sediment transport on disturbed areas. Models represent our descriptions of how water, sediment, and chemicals move on disturbed areas under alternative management practices. The models should not violate the basic physical principles of hydrology and should also incorporate the principles of chemistry, biology, and plant science needed to describe a biological system. Such models also include a number of empirical laws and, therefore, require extensive field data.

Little research has been done on the hydrologic effects of drastic disturbance and reclamation, and the research that has been done has developed ranking criteria for limited aspects of hydrology. One of the difficult problems in hydrologic research in disturbed areas is that the system is in a transient state during the research period. This invalidates many traditional research procedures which assume the system is in a quasi-equilibrium condition.

Many studies of hydrology on disturbed lands are currently in progress. Hopefully the results from these studies can be integrated into quantitative prediction models that can be used by mine managers and regulatory agencies to design management procedures to achieve specific goals.

ACKNOWLEDGMENT

This paper is a contribution from the Agricultural Research Service, U.S. Department of Agriculture, in cooperation with the Colorado State University Experiment Station. This research was supported in part by funds from the U.S. Environmental Protection Agency thru EPA-IAG-D6-E763.

LITERATURE CITED

Aldon, E. F. 1975. Techniques for establishing native plants on coal mine spoil in New Mexico. p. 21–27. In 3rd Symp. on Surface Mining and Reclamation. Vol. 1. 21–23 Oct. 1975, Louisville, Ky. Natl. Coal Assoc., Washington, D.C.

Armiger, W. H., J. N. Jones, and O. L. Bennett. 1976. Revegetation of land disturbed by strip mining of coal in Appalachia. USDA-ARS, ARS-NE-71, Beltsville, Md. 38 p.

Barnett, A. P., E. G. Diselsen, and E. C. Richardson. 1967. Evaluation of mulching methods for erosion control on newly prepared and seeded highway back slopes. Agron. J. 59: 83–85.

Brustkern, R. L., and H. J. Morel-Seytoux. 1970. Analytical treatment of two-phase infiltration. J. Hydrology Div. Proc. Am. Soc. of Civil Eng. 96 (HY12):2535–2548.

Burnes, I. G. 1975. An equation to predict the leaching of surface applied nitrate. J. Agric. Sci. Camb. 85:443–454.

Coleman, G. B. 1951. A study of water infiltration in the spoil banks in central Pennsylvania. J. For. 49:574–579.

Court, A. 1974. The climate of the conterminous United States. p. 193–344. In R. A. Bryson and F. K. Hare (eds.) World survey of climatology, Vol. II. Climate of North America. Am. Elsevier Sci. Publ. Co., New York.

Curtis, W. R. 1973. Effects of strip mining on the hydrology of small mountain watersheds in Appalachia. p. 145–157. In Russell J. Hutnik and Grant Davis (eds.) Ecology and reclamation of devastated land. Gordon and Breach Sci. Publ., Inc., New York.

Dunne, T. 1970. Runoff production in a humid area. USDA-ARS, ARS 41-160, Washington, D.C. 107 p.

Edwards, W. M., and W. E. Larson. 1969. Infiltration of water into soils as influenced by surface seal development. Trans. Am. Soc. Agric. Eng. 12(4):463, 465, 470.

England, C. B. 1970. Land capability: A hydrologic response unit in agricultural watersheds. USDA-ARS, ARS 41-172, Washington, D.C. 12 p.

Fairbourn, M., and H. R. Gardner. 1974. Field use of micro-watersheds with verical mulch. Agron. J. 66:740–744.

Gardner, W. R. 1965. Movement of nitrogen in soil. In W. V. Bartholomew and F. E. Clark (eds.) Soil nitrogen. Agronomy 10:550–572. Am. Soc. of Agron., Madison, Wis.

Good, D. M., V. T. Ricca, and K. S. Shumate. 1970. The relation of refuse pile hydrology to acid production. p. 145–151. In 3rd Symp. on Coal Mine Drainage Research, 19–20 May 1970, Coal Advisory Comm. to Ohio River Valley Water Sanit. Comm., Pittsburg, Pa. Bituminous Coal Res., Inc., Monroeville, Pa.

Green, W. H., and G. A. Ampt. 1911. Studies on soil physics: I. Flow of air and water through soils. J. Agric. Sci. 4:1–24.

Haas, H. J., and W. O. Willis. 1971. Water storage and alfalfa production on level benches in the northern Plains. J. Soil Water Conserv. 26:151–154.

Harbert, H. P., and W. A. Berg. 1974. Vegetation stabilization of spent oil shales. Colorado State Univ., Environ. Res. Center, Tech. Rep. no. 4, Fort Collins.

Hillel, D., and W. R. Gardner. 1970. Transient infiltration into crust-topped profiles. Soil Sci. 109:69–76.

Hodder, R. L., B. W. Sindelar, J. Buchalz, and D. F. Ryerson. 1971. Coal mine land reclamation research. Res. Rep. 20, Montana Agric. Exp. Stn., Mont. State Univ., Bozeman.

Holtan, H. N. 1961. A concept for infiltration estimates in watershed engineering. USDA-ARS, ARS 41-51, Washington, D.C. 25 p.

Holtan, H. N., and N. R. Creitz. 1967. Floods and their computation. Intl. Assoc. of Sci. Hydrol. Pub. no. 85, Gentbrugge, Belgium. p. 756–767.

Horton, R. E. 1940. An approach toward physical interpretation of infiltration capacity. Soil Sci. Soc. Am. Proc. 5:399–417.

Kurtz, L. T., and S. W. Melsted. 1973. Movement of chemicals in soils by water. Soil Sci. 115:231–239.

Lusby, G. C., and T. J. Toy. 1976. An evaluation of surface-mine spoils area restoration in Wyoming using rainfall simulation. p. 375–386. In Earth surface processes. John Wiley & Sons, Ltd., New York.

May, M., R. Lang, L. Lujan, P. Jacoby, and W. Thompson. 1971. Reclamation of strip mine spoil banks in Wyoming. Res. J. 51, Univ. of Wyoming Agric. Exp. Stn., Laramie.

McCormack, D. E. 1974. Soil reconstruction: For the best soil after mining. p. 150–161. In 2nd Res. and Applied Technology Symp. on Mined-Land Reclamation. Louisville, Ky.

McWhorter, D. B., and J. W. Rowe. 1976. Inorganic water quality in a surface mined watershed. Am. Geophys. Union Symp. on Methodologies for Environ. Assessments in Energy Dev. Regions. 8 Dec. 1976, San Francisco, Calif. Am. Geophy. Union, Washington, D.C.

Mein, R. G., and C. L. Larson. 1973. Modeling infiltration during a steady rain. Water Resour. Res. 9(2):384–394.

Minshall, N. E., and V. C. Jamison. 1965. Interflow in claypan soils. Water Resour. Res. 1(3):381–390.

Neff, E. L. 1973. Water storage capacity of contour furrows in Montana. J. Range Manage. 26(4):298–301.

Nielson, D. R., and J. W. Biggar. 1963. Miscible displacement: Mixing in glass beads. Soil Sci. Soc. Am. Proc. 27:10–13.

Philip, J. R. 1964. An infiltration equation with physical significance. Soil Sci. 77:153–157.

Riley, C. V. 1969. Chemical alternations of strip mine spoil by furrow grading—revegetation success. p. 315–330. In R. J. Hutnik and Grant Davis (eds.) Ecology and reclamation of devastated land. Gordon & Breach, New York.

Smith, R. E. 1972. The infiltration envelope: Results from a theoretical infiltrometer. J. Hydrol. 17(1/2):1–21.

Thornthwaite, C. E. 1948. An approach towards a rational classification of climate. Geogr. Rev. 38:55–94.

Vogel, W. G. 1975. Requirements and use of fertilizer, lime, and mulch for vegetating acid mine spoils. p. 152–169. In R. J. Hutnik and Grant Davis (eds.) Ecology and reclamation of devastated land. Gordon & Breach, New York.

Wight, J. R. 1976. Land surface modifications and their effects on range and forest watersheds. Proc. of the 5th Workshop of the United States/Australia Rangelands Panel, Boise, Idaho, 15–22 June 1975. In Harold F. Heady, Donna H. Falkenborg, and J. Paul Riley (eds.) Watershed management on range and forest lands. Utah Water Res. Lab., Utah State Univ., Logan, Utah.

Wight, J. R., E. L. Neff, and F. H. Siddoway. 1975. Snow management on eastern Montana rangelands. In Proc. of the Snow Manage. on the Great Plains Symp. 29 July Bismarck, N. Dak. Res. Comm. of Great Plains Agric. Counc. Publ. 73, Agric. Exp. Stn., Univ. of Nebraska, Lincoln.

Wischmeier, W. H., and D. D. Smith. 1965. Predicting rainfall erosion losses from cropland east of the Rocky Mountains. USDA-ARS Agric. Hbk. 282, Washington, D.C.

Woolhiser, D. A. 1975. Simulation of unsteady overland flow. p. 485–508. In K. Mahmood and V. Yevjevich (eds.) Unsteady flow in open channels, Vol. II. Water Resour. Publ., Fort Collins, Colo.

Copyright © 1978 ASA–CSSA–SSSA
677 South Segoe Road, Madison, WI 53711 USA
Reclamation of Drastically Disturbed Lands

Chapter 11

Environmental and Aesthetic Considerations in Surface Mining Policy

ALAN RANDALL, SUE JOHNSON, AND ANGELOS PAGOULATOS
University of Kentucky
Lexington, Kentucky

I. INTRODUCTION

Surface mining activities have a major impact on the quality of environmental resources and, thus, on the value that people can derive from environmental resources and amenities. In the absence of adequate provision for prevention of off-site damages and subsequent land reclamation, potential later uses of the affected environmental resources are diminished in value. Damage prevention and reclamation procedures are costly, but offer the potential of reducing the environmental losses and, in some cases, actually increasing the value of certain resources in particular uses above the level prior to mining.

Given an adequate array of data about the damages from surface mining in various environments, the cost and effectiveness of the alternative damage prevention and reclamation techniques, and the value of environmental resources of various qualities in alternative uses, it would be possible to answer some important policy questions. In what, if any, environments should surface mining be prohibited? What degree of damage prevention and reclamation is appropriate in each environment mined?

In this chapter, we present an economic framework for analysis of environmental quality issues. The environmental impacts of surface mining for coal are discussed and the small, emerging body of research on the economic and social value of environmental improvements is selectively reviewed. Finally, we present some preliminary results of ongoing research to quantify environmental perceptions and preferences and the economic value of environmental improvements in a region of surface mining activity in eastern Kentucky.

II. RESOURCE USE AND ENVIRONMENTAL QUALITY: AN ECONOMIC PERSPECTIVE

Environment refers to the totality of natural resources, including the intricate interrelationships among living and nonliving things which constitute ecosystems and biomes. Environmental damage occurs when waste constituents from one resource use affect the quantity and quality of a re-

193

source supply in such a manner as to (i) preclude, (ii) increase the costs, or (iii) reduce the benefits of a later use of the resource. Not all changes in resource quality are damaging; some changes may be beneficial to later uses.

Environmental quality changes are economically relevant when they affect (adversely, in the case of damages) later uses of resources to meet the needs of people. In ascribing dollar values to the costs of environmental damages, later uses of affected resources must be traced and dollar values determined for the preclusion of later uses, losses in productivity of later uses, and increased costs of treatments to improve or restore the quality of resources for later uses.

Efficient investment in environmental improvements may be pursued using the benefit/cost framework of analysis. The benefits of environmental improvements may be conceptualized in terms of cost avoidance: the benefits are equal to the costs of potential damage which is avoided. The costs of environmental improvements may be calculated directly, except in the case where mining of an area is prohibited for environmental reasons. In that case, the costs are equal to the potential profits which are lost as a result of the decision not to mine. Given the necessary economic information, the efficient level of investment in environmental improvements may be calculated: damage should be reduced to that point where the benefits from an additional step are just equal to the costs of that step, given that total benefits exceed total costs.[1]

This simple and straightforward framework finds its most acceptable use in analyzing environmental quality changes of a short-term nature. When the cause of disturbance is eliminated, the environment returns to its prior condition. However, many environmental quality changes (for example, the drastic land disturbance associated with surface mining) may be reversed only at great expense, if at all. Irreversible changes, even if they may not seem damaging at the time they occur, may preclude options for resource use which may become feasible in the future due to technological developments and changes in demand. Foreclosure of future options must be evaluated as a cost of achieving present goals. While it is often difficult to place dollar values on these types of foreclosed options, it is appropriate to view irreversible environmental change with a good deal of apprehension. In particular, it is dangerous, even if we are unable to say how dangerous, to allow irreversible change to an environmental resource which has no close substitutes.

III. ENVIRONMENTAL IMPACTS OF SURFACE MINING

In the period from 1930 to 1971, more than 3.6 million acres of land in the United States were used for surface mining, and barely 40% was reclaimed (Table 1). Mining for fossil fuels (for the most part, coal) ac-

---

[1] This economic framework is, of necessity, highly simplified. It focuses on the trade-off between environmental benefits and disposable income. These, however, are not the only important concerns. Other goals such as full employment, price stability, and income distribution are important. Environmental improvements must necessarily be pursued in conjunction with these other goals.

Table 1—Land utilized and reclaimed by the mining industry in the United States in 1930–71, by area of mining activity

Type of use	Metals		Nonmetals		Fossil fuels‡		Total§	
	Utilized	Reclaimed	Utilized	Reclaimed	Utilized	Reclaimed	Utilized	Reclaimed
				acres				
Surface area mined (area of excavation only	145,000	17,400	1,060,000	253,000	966,000	716,000	2,170,000	987,000
Area used for disposal of overburden and other mine waste from surface mining	123,000	5,270	291,000	129,000	320,000	268,000	733,000	402,000
Surface area subsided or disturbed as a result of underground workings	12,200	1,780	4,570	100	87,900	4,000	105,000	5,870
Surface area used for disposal of underground mine waste	21,900	1,500	2,080	180	166,000	20,000	190,000	21,600
Surface area used for disposal of mill or processing waste	221,000	17,300	210,000	23,300	31,900	6,480	454,000	47,100
Total	524,000	43,300	1,560,000	406,000	1,570,000	1,010,000	3,650,000	1,460,000

† Source: Paone et al., 1974.
‡ Excludes oil and gas operations.
§ Data may not add to totals shown because of independent rounding.

counted for 43% of the total land used in surface mining. The reclamation performance of the coal industry has been better than that of the other surface mining industries: two-thirds of the land used has been reclaimed to some degree. Every state has been impacted by surface mining, but West Virginia, Pennsylvania, Ohio, and Kentucky have been affected more than the others (Paone et al., 1974).

Data for years more recent than 1971 are unavailable. However, such data, were it available, would show continued and accelerated surface mining, gradual improvement in the reclamation performance of the coal surface mining industry, and some shifts in the geographic distribution of the industry, the most notable being an expansion in the states of the upper great plains.

Surface mining of coal generates environmental damages in several ways. The disturbance of land and its vegetative cover, and the removal and deposition of overburden may increase the amount of runoff following rain and the concentration of soil particles suspended in the runoff. The frequency and severity of floods may be increased and the problem of siltation exacerbated. Water quality may be adversely affected by increased sediment and concentration of harmful chemicals in the runoff which enters the system of streams and aquifers. Surface mining may result in increased incidence of erosion and slides, reducing the productivity of land in agricultural and forest uses, and perhaps destroying productive land and/or buildings and structures. Explosions due to blasting in surface mining operations may destroy productive property and create noise which disturbs natural ecosystems and is aesthetically unpleasant. The process of disturbing the land surface and the removal and deposition of overburden destroys natural ecosystems and the aesthetic quality of the landscape, diminishing its value for recreational and other purposes for which aesthetic characteristics are important. In summary, the adverse effects of surface mining on resource quality seem most severe and long lasting in the case of land and water resources. Noise pollution and air pollution from dust are relatively confined in space and time, being localized in the vicinity of the mine and ceasing to be problems when the mining operation stops.

Later uses of land which are affected include agriculture, forestry, extraction of minerals, transportation, residential, commercial, and industrial uses, and the maintenance of scenery and land-based ecosystems. These last mentioned uses are crucial for recreational, scenic, and other aesthetic uses of land. The water resource is used for most of these same purposes, as well as for navigation and the maintenance of fresh-water ecosystems.

The severity of the environmental impacts of surface mining vary widely from situation to situation. Severity of impact depends on the extent of surface mining in the affected region, the technique of surface mining and the methods of handling overburden and disposal of wastes, the depth of overburden, the slope of the land, and the topographical, climatic, geological, hydrological, and ecological features of the environment mined. Thus, the economic value of the damage associated with surface mining will vary among mining sites, as well as among the different mining regions of the country.

The aesthetic and environmental benefits of off-site damage prevention and reclamation, in conceptual terms, are equal to the value of potential damages to later resource uses which are avoided. Techniques for estimating the value of damage avoided vary widely depending on the particular resource and type of resource use considered and the degree to which the value of the resoure in that use is reflected in observable market prices.

Many of the benefits from reclamation and off-site prevention are directly reflected in the market. For convenience, we call them *market benefits*. Several examples may be helpful. Water for residential, commercial, and industrial uses may be treated to improve its quality. Provided that the water after treatment is adequate for these uses, the increment in observable water treatment costs attributable to mining in the absence of damage prevention practices may be used to estimate the benefits to those water uses of implementing damage prevention practices. Similarly, if surface mining reduces the output of the agricultural and forestry industries in the vicinity, and reclamation practices would restore that output, the foregone net economic returns to those industries may be used. If surface mining activities cause slides, erosion, land subsidence, or increased flooding, the value of real property destroyed is an indicator of the potential benefits of damage prevention.

Other kinds of benefits from environmental improvements, although they may be of substantial value to resource users, are not directly reflected in the observed movement of market variables. These *nonmarket benefits* must be measured or imputed indirectly.[2] These kinds of benefits include the restoration and maintenance of aesthetic, scenic, and recreational resources.

While nonmarket environmental costs of surface mining are difficult to measure, they are of particular importance. Mining creates an irreversible change in landscape and stream aesthetics and to ecosystems exposed to mining and its off-site impacts. Successful reclamation, especially in mountain and arid environments, is unable to return the environment to its original aesthetic condition. The reclaimed environment may be useful and aesthetically pleasing, perhaps more so to some people than the original, but it is not the same as the original. Research (discussed below) has indicated that alternative aesthetic environments are perceived differently. Unique environments have no exact substitutes, and it cannot be assumed that two equally pleasing environments are direct substitutes,

---

[2] The terms, *nonmarket benefits* and *nonmarket costs*, sacrifice precision for the sake of brevity. Many of these benefits and costs are at least partially and indirectly reflected in the market. Aesthetic damages, for example, may show up in the market indirectly through declining revenues in businesses which serve tourists and recreationists, and in decreasing relative values of residential land. Several researchers have claimed success in measuring at least part of the social costs of air pollution by observing the price of residential land in a geographic cross-section of neighborhoods exposed to differing concentrations of pollutants (Freeman, 1974).

one for the other. Irreversible change to an environment which has few close substitutes is a serious matter.

These considerations suggest that substantial attention should be directed to quantifying the environmental perceptions and preferences of people and, to the extent feasible, the economic value of various aesthetic environments.

IV. MEASURING THE COSTS AND BENEFITS OF PREVENTING ENVIRONMENTAL DAMAGE

In this section, we discuss the economic costs and benefits of damage prevention and surface mine reclamation in central and southern Appalachia, using the results of the most reliable studies yet completed.

A. Costs of Damage Prevention and Land Reclamation

The costs of reclamation in the Appalachian coalfields have been estimated (Carlsmith et al., 1974). At the risk of oversimplification, we will attempt to summarize the preliminary results of that study.[3] Average operating costs (at 1972 prices) for basic reclamation (defined as spoil stabilization sufficient to prevent off-site damages from groundslides, erosion, and water runoff) were in the range of $0.25 to $0.60 per ton of coal produced. Full reclamation (defined as basic reclamation plus the return of the land to a state of useful productivity and restoration and enhancement of landscape aesthetics) would cost in the range of $0.65 to $0.90 per ton (in 1972 dollars).

B. Market Benefits

Very little research has been completed on estimation of the benefits of reclamation. As we have indicated above, the theoretical concepts for estimating the market benefits of reclamation are well defined. For the most part, however, the empirical relationships, even in the physical and biological areas, are not well known and work to estimate the economic relationships has just begun.

In Appalachian Tennessee, the benefits from reclamation in five case study watersheds were estimated to fall in the range of $0.60 to $1.40 (in 1973 dollars) per ton of coal mined (Bohm et al., 1975). Since aesthetic and social considerations were not fully incorporated into those estimates, they may be considered estimates of the market benefits. This evidence, fragmentary as it is, suggests that in Appalachia the costs of basic reclamation and full reclamation in some cases are exceeded by the market benefits.

---

[3] In Carlsmith et al. (1974), reclamation costs were related to mining method, subregion in which mining occurred, total annual subregional output, highwall height, and slope of the terrain.

C. Nonmarket Benefits: Aesthetic, Scenic, and Recreational

Nonmarket benefits of reclamation consist mostly of benefits from uses for which the aesthetic quality and ecological diversity of the environment are important. Sightseeing and aesthetic enjoyment, nature study, outdoor recreation, hunting, and fishing are some of these uses. In order to estimate the nonmarket benefits of reclamation, it is necessary to have information on the way in which humans perceive environments and their environmental preferences. Economic estimation of nonmarket benefits requires evidence of the trade-offs which people find acceptable between disposable income and environmental aesthetics. In this section, we examine the existing literature. In the following section, some preliminary results of on-going research being conducted by the authors is presented.

Research to measure *environmental perceptions and preferences* has been underway for several years. Techniques have been developed and are subject to continued efforts at refinement, and some initial empirical results are available.

Leopold and Marchand (1968) and Leopold (1969) have measured the uniqueness of small streams, using uniqueness ratios based on subjective estimates of biologic uniqueness and human interest uniqueness. These kinds of studies have potential applicability to decision making about surface mining since our economic framework warns that the environmental losses from irreversible change in highly unique environments (i.e., those with few substitutes) may be very high. Dearinger et al. (1973) have developed a method of using color slides and a semantic differential rating method to determine people's preferences among natural landscapes. Milbrath (1975) has developed a comprehensive instrument for measuring people's responses to various environmental elements, in terms of valence (an indicator of pleasure or displeasure) and importance to the individual.

While these kinds of techniques have yet to be applied in studying the environmental impacts of surface mining, some results have been obtained in other settings. These results are at least suggestive for our purposes. Stark landscapes (e.g., deserts, winter pastures, and lava flows) are not perceived as beautiful by most people, although the presence of flowing water in the scene helps mitigate the perceived ugliness (Dearinger, 1968; Dearinger et al., 1973; Calvin et al., 1972). These same studies indicate that people usually agree on very beautiful and very ugly aspects of scenes and disagree considerably on the less extreme or more commonplace aspects. Where people have widely different preferences, the formation of aesthetic preference is influenced more by occupation and lifestyle than by such variables as age and sex. These studies and another by David (1971) suggest that perception of negative aspects of outdoor enbironment is largely visual, although the sense of smell may be another source of negative stimuli.

There is some evidence that people prefer natural to man-made environments (Zube, 1974). This finding suggests that the unmined environment may be aesthetically preferred to the reclaimed environment. An associated finding is that people prefer more complex visual patterns in the environment to simple ones (Pyron, 1972). This suggests that people may not respond positively where surface mines on relatively flat land are reclaimed, leaving a fairly monotonous landscape. On the other hand, it is not impossible that reclaimed mines on steep, wooded slopes may heighten landscape diversity. Whether the net aesthetic impact is positive (in response to increased diversity) or negative (in response to the manmade nature of the reclaimed sections) is a question awaiting research.

It is known that recreational and aesthetic uses of the environment are closely related. At one extreme, wilderness-seeking recreationists consider the aesthetic experience to be the most important aspect of recreation (Shafer & Mietz, 1969). If a drastically disturbed environment is to be restored for recreational use, its value in that use will be heavily dependent on its aesthetic quality.

Economists have, during the last 20 years, paid attention to the economic *value of nonmarket goods.* Using and improving the techniques suggested and applied by Davis (1963) and Clawson and Knetch (1966), economists have succeeding in valuing the recreation experience to the point where recreation values are routinely included in economic analyses of the benefits and costs of water resources development projects. The benefits of preserving natural environments, as an alternative to developing them in ways which cause irreversible change, have been estimated (Fisher et al., 1972). For valuation of the benefits of air pollution abatement, two quite different techniques have been applied, with some success. There is a body of literature (reviewed in Freeman, 1974) which relates differentials in the value of residential land to different ambient concentrations of air pollutants, in order to estimate the economic value of air pollution controls. An alternative approach based on questionnaire techniques has been used (Randall et al., 1974; and Brookshire et al., 1976) for the same purpose. Respondents in personal interviews are confronted with hypothetical situations which require them to examine trade-offs between economic goods and environmental amenities, and forced to make rational choices. The techniques used in the studies led by Randall and Brookshire, called bidding games, generate results which can be aggregated to provide dollar estimates of the total value of aesthetic environmental improvements.[4] Randall et al. (1974) estimated that the annual benefits of eliminating emissions from a single huge coal burning electric power plant amounted to $24 million annually. Brookshire et al. (1976) closely replicated those results.

The findings of these studies tell us nothing specific about the nonmarket benefits from surface mine reclamation. However, they do establish the fact that economists have succeeded in valuing some nonmarket environmental goods and, at least in some circumstances, the economic benefits from aesthetic environmental improvements are measurable and substantial.

---

[4] A number of other formats have been used for playing trade-off games. For example, the priority evaluator, used successfully by Pendse and Wyckoff (1974), indicates rational trade-offs but does not generate aggregate dollars values for environmental amenities.

V. EMPIRICAL FINDINGS FROM A CASE STUDY OF THE BENEFITS OF RECLAMATION

The authors are currently involved in a case study, as yet unfinished, to estimate the economic value of the benefits of reclamation of surface-mined land in eastern Kentucky. The study area is the area in the watershed of the North Fork of the Kentucky River, an area of about 1,600 square miles (4,144 km²). The terrain is mountainous, with narrow valleys, and is typical of the central and southern Appalachian coalfields. The area has experienced both deep and surface mining for coal, and surface mining has expanded in recent years. In 1974, there were 157 active surface mines, which produced 11.2 million tons of coal (U.S. Bureau of Mines, 1975). Permits for surface mining of 21,500 acres were active as of 31 March 1976.

The population is in the neighborhood of 80,000, living in small towns, villages, and the countryside. Hazard, the largest city, has a population of around 9,000. Coal mining is the major basic industry, far surpassing agriculture and forestry in the value of output.

As this paper goes to press, some preliminary results on the subjects of environmental perceptions and the economic value of aesthetic environmental improvements are available.

A. Environmental Perceptions

Four environmental quality packages, each consisting of four representative color photographs, were presented to respondents. The four packages represented the regional environment (i) surface mined with no reclamation, (ii) surface mined with a moderate level of reclamation, (iii) surface mined with full reclamation, and (iv) never mined. Within each package, the photographs represented the broad landscape, intermediate distance landscapes, and flowing streams.

Respondents ranked all four packages on two scales: one measuring the pleasure or displeasure engendered by the environment and the other measuring how much impact the environment had on the respondent's sense of well-being. A composite scale, where the minimum score can be interpreted as "offends me greatly" and the maximum score as "pleases me greatly," was calculated for each respondent. Results (Table 2) indicate that the unreclaimed environment was perceived very negatively, while the never-mined environment was perceived very positively. Partial reclamation reduced the perceived negative impacts of surface mining, while state-of-the-art reclamation resulted in positive perceptions of the environments. However, the never-mined environment was preferred to the fully reclaimed environment. Respondents perceived that surface mining, even with the best available reclamation practices, creates irreversible change in environmental quality. These findings were highly significant, in the statistical sense (Table 2).

Table 2—Environment perceptions and preferences (North Fork of the
Kentucky River Region, 1976) †

Environment	Mean score**	SE (mean)
Mined, no reclamation	-9.65	0.32
Mined, partial reclamation	-2.38	0.46
Mined, state-of-the-art reclamation	7.88	0.29
Never mined	11.50	0.13

** All mean scores were significantly different from each other at the 0.01 level of confidence.
† Scale: Offends me greatly − 12, ... , 12 pleases me greatly.

B. Economic Values

A series of bidding games was played with respondents, using the same four packages of photographs to represent alternative levels of regional environmental quality. The bidding games determined the willingness of respondents to pay for improvement of the environment, starting with the mining but no reclamation level of quality. Each game challenged the respondent with a particular trade-off problem; environmental improvement could be obtained only at some economic cost. In one game, the cost was an increase in the price of coal and, eventually, in the cost of living; in another, it was an increase in the price of electricity produced from coal; in the third, it was a direct payment into an "environmental improvement fund."

The results of the bidding games (Table 3) indicated that respondents placed a high value on aesthetic environmental improvements. An increase in the price of coal of $6.77 was considered acceptable, in order to

Table 3—Bidding game results (North Fork of the Kentucky River region, 1976)**

Game 1. An acceptable increase in the price of coal

Level of reclamation	Mean ($/ton)	SE (mean)
Back to original	9.30	1.31
State-of-the-art	6.77	1.02
Partial	4.01	0.80

Game 2. An acceptable increase in the household electricity bill

Level of reclamation	Mean (% increase)	SE (mean)
Back to original	15.20	1.32
State-of-the-art	11.31	0.99
Partial	7.25	0.72

Game 3. An acceptable monthly payment per household

Level of reclamation	Mean ($/mo)	SE (mean)
Back to original	5.95	0.44
State-of-the-art	4.87	0.40
Partial	3.43	0.39

** All mean bids were significantly different from 0, at the 0.01 level of confidence.

obtain the state-of-the-art level of reclamation. Alternatively, an increase of 11% in electricity bills, or a direct monthly payment of $4.87 per household was considered acceptable. Partial reclamation was valued positively but less than full reclamation. If reclamation was capable of restoring the environment to its original condition, that would be worth even more than state-of-the-art reclamation.

These basic data will eventually permit more complete analyses of the costs and benefits of surface mine reclamation. However, one conclusion can be drawn immediately: The residents of the North Fork region believe that the aesthetic benefits of full reclamation are sufficiently high to justify an increase of about $6.75 in the price of coal. The results of Carlsmith et al. (1974), if updated to 1976 prices, suggest that full reclamation would cost about $1.50 per ton of coal mined.

VI. CONCLUDING COMMENTS

The environmental and aesthetic impacts of drastic land disturbance in general, and surface mining in particular, are substantial. Adverse environmental impacts lower the quality of life for people and are therefore just as consequential as any other adverse economic impact. Economic efficiency in surface mining requires that reclamation proceed until the benefits of an additional step are just equal to its costs, provided that total benefits exceed total cost. Where the net returns from mining are less than the value of the environmental losses after all economically feasible reclamation has been completed, mining should not be undertaken.

We have somewhat arbitrarily divided the benefits from reclamation into *market* and *nonmarket* categories. The empirical evidence currently available, which is fragmentary at best, suggests that the market benefits from basic reclamation and, in some cases, full reclamation in Appalachia exceed the cost. If, in addition, the nonmarket benefits are positive, the economic case for reclamation would be sound.

Studies of environmental perceptions and preferences, in situations other than surface mining, have shown that there are good reasons to expect (i) that nonmarket benefits from reclamation may be positive and (ii) that the reclaimed environment may be perceived as inferior to similar but unmined environments. A case study in a surface mining region of eastern Kentucky has confirmed these expectations. Preliminary results indicate that unreclaimed environments are perceived very negatively; partially reclaimed environments, slightly negatively; fully reclaimed environments, quite positively; and never-mined environments even more positively. Nonmarket benefits of reclamation appear to be positive and substantial.

With the completion of the research currently being undertaken by the authors, it may be possible to compare the aggregate benefits and costs of various levels of surface mine reclamation, and to provide highly valuable input for the policy decision process.

LITERATURE CITED

Bohm, R., J. Moore, and F. Schmidt-Bleek. 1975. Benefits and costs of surface mine reclamation in Appalachia. p. 441–447. *In* M. G. Morgan (ed.) Energy and man: technological and social aspects of energy. Inst. of Electrical and Electronic Engineers Press, New York.

Brookshire, D., B. Ives, and W. Schultze. 1976. The valuation of aesthetic preferences. Working Pap. Ser. Resour. Econ. Prog., Univ. of New Mexico, Albuquerque.

Calvin, J., J. Dearinger, and M. Cartin. 1972. An attempt at assessing preferences for natural landscapes. Environ. Behav. 4:447–470.

Carlsmith, R., R. Spore, and E. Nephew. 1974. Systems studies of coal production. Progress Rep. Oak Ridge Nat. Lab., Oak Ridge, Tenn.

Clawson, M., and J. Knetch. 1966. Economics of outdoor recreation. Johns Hopkins University Press, Baltimore.

David, E. 1971. Public perception of water quality. Water Resour. Res. 7:453–457.

Davis, R. 1963. Recreation planning as an economic problem. Nat. Resour. J. 3:239–249.

Dearinger, J. 1968. Esthetic and recreational potential of small naturalistic streams near urban areas. Res. Rep. 13. Water Resour. Res. Inst., Lexington, Ky.

Dearinger, J., G. Woolwine, C. Scroggin, D. Dolan, and J. Calvin. 1973. Measuring intangible values of natural streams—Part II. Res. Rep. 66. Water Resour. Res. Inst., Lexington, Ky.

Fisher, A., J. Krutilla, and C. Ciccehetti. 1972. The economics of environmental preservation: a theoretical and empirical analysis. Am. Econ. Rev. 62:605–619.

Freeman, A. 1974. On estimating air pollution control benefits from land value studies. J. Environ. Econ. Manage. 1:74–83.

Leopold, L. 1969. Landscape esthetics. Nat. Hist. 78:36–45.

Leopold, L., and M. Marchard. 1968. On the quantitative inventory of the riverscape. Water Resour. Res. 4:709–711.

Milbrath, L. W. 1975. Environmental beliefs: a tale of two counties. Social Sci. Res. Center, State Univ. of New York, Buffalo. 114 p.

Paone, J., J. Morning, and L. Giorgetti. 1974. Land utilization in the mining industry, 1930–71. Bur. of Mines Inf. Circ. 8042. U.S. Dep. of Interior, Washington, D.C.

Pendse, D., and J. Wyckoff. 1974. A systematic evaluation of environmental perceptions, preferences and trade-off values in water resource analysis. Res. Rep. 25. Water Resourc. Res. Inst., Corvallis, Oreg.

Pyron, B. 1972. Form and diversity in human habitats. Environ. Behav. 4:87–120.

Randall, A., B. Ives, and C. Eastman. 1974. Bidding games for valuation of aesthetic environmental improvements. J. Environ. Econ. Mgt. 1:132–149.

Shafer, E., and J. Mietz. 1969. Aesthetic and emotional experiences rate high with northwest wilderness hikers. Envion. Behav. 1:87–197.

U.S. Bureau of Mines. 1975. Coal—bituminous and lignite in 1974. Miner. Ind. Surv., Washington, D.C.

Zube, E. 1974. Cross-disciplinary and intermode agreement on the description and evaluation of landscape resources. Environ. Behav. 6:69–89.

Chapter 12

Criteria for Selecting Lands That Are Not to be Disturbed

JAMES D. MERTES

Texas Tech University
Lubbock, Texas

I. DEFINITION

Lands that are not to be disturbed are generally defined as those land and/or water areas which, because of some biophysical, historical, or cultural characteristics, are determined to be unique, highly productive, rare, fragile, perishable, or, as they function in their natural state, hazardous to human health, safety, and welfare. Such areas oftentimes are unrecognized by a community as having significant economic and societal benefit if left undisturbed. In the past many such areas were disturbed, the results of which often led to environmental backlashes of catastrophic proportions. Flood damage, property destroyed by mudslides and avalanches, and aquifer recharge areas sealed off by concrete are only a few examples of the costly social lessons communities too often learn the hard way. Many lands which are drastically disturbed in the process of extracting minerals such as gravel and coal are considered ecologically sensitive. This classification most often reflects the kinds of problems associated with the land during mining. In many instances it is virtually impossible to reclaim land following the extent of disturbance required for open surface mining. These lands should be considered extremely sensitive and prime candidates for exclusion from mining. *Why?* Because through some set of decisions lands which should not have been converted were utilized for purposes which are not in keeping with the natural character of the land.

To be more specific, sensitive lands, or lands which should not be disturbed, are land areas whose destruction or disturbance will immediately affect the life of community by either (i) creating hazards such as flooding or landslides, (ii) destroying important public resources such as water supplies and water quality of lakes and rivers, or (iii) wasting important productive lands and renewable resources (Thurow et al., 1975).

Lands not to be disturbed are unique in the sense that they cannot be disturbed without some resultant cost. This does not mean, however, that when valuable resources are found beneath the land surface of sensitive lands they cannot be developed. Resource development, guided by proper performance standards, can, in many instances, hold site disturbance to a minimum. Appropriate measures for mitigation, internalization of negative externalities, and restitution can be planned into the resource development program.

II. ECOLOGICAL FUNCTIONS

One reason for not disturbing lands in many of the categories previously identified is the important ecological function they perform. Oftentimes these functions or processes are important, not only in terms of a local or regional ecosystem, but also because of resource or amenity value they may provide. The marsh or wetland, for example, provides a unique and diversified natural area, while also serving to collect runoff and filter water into an aquifer from which a local community may draw all or some of its water. Forested hillsides which provide amenity values and outdoor recreation opportunities also form the watershed for a stream which may flow into a coastal estuary.

Other areas simply serve as places where natural occurrences take place. Flooding is a natural occurrence, and it takes place in that area within the stream profile known as the *floodplain*. Floodplains should not be drastically disturbed. Seismic activity is a known occurrence in many areas. These areas should not be disturbed. In any instance where the land disturbance would result in people, property, or a natural system being placed in jeopardy, development of the land resource in question should be given serious consideration.

It is fundamental in the environmental planning process that, in order to determine what lands should not be disturbed, a scientific, systematic objective, and acceptable procedure for discovering, evaluating, describing, and prioritizing our sensitive lands is needed. The identification process is the most critical. Many approaches to this process have been developed over the past decade. Names like McHarg, Lewis, and Hills come to mind immediately.

A brief review of the procedural aspects of the process will be helpful. Stover (1975) suggests that developing a system for identifying lands deserving protection calls for a three-pronged approach to analyzing land and water resources. First, outstanding natural areas of great ecological significance must be identified. Those are areas which should be considered as first-priority sites. Second, it must be determined which of the remaining resources can and should be developed and which should be retained as open space recreational–natural areas to help preserve ecological diversity. Finally, for the land determined to be best suited for development, land capability analysis should be conducted to ascertain how much development the area can support (Stover, 1975). The resource inventory can be accomplished by systematically surveying an entire region in terms of a detailed set of variables and then, through analysis of multiple and interacting factors, screening the region for land and water areas which meet a set of criteria adopted for critical area designation (U.S. Army Corps of Engineers, 1974).

Any natural area classification system should accomplish the following objectives (Sargent & Brande, 1976):

1) The system should be readily understandable by those who will use it;
2) It should be based on the judgment of natural scientists and local citizens; and
3) It should be reasonable and objective in order to withstand legal challenges.

Several approaches employing various criteria for use in identifying sensitive lands are examined. These objectives should be kept clearly in mind.

The early work of Angus Hills in the area of biophysical land classification systems laid the foundation for the ecological determinism of McHarg and the environmental quality parameters analysis of Lewis (Belknap & Furtado, 1967). All three processes have been utilized in several land use analysis studies (McHarg, 1971; Wells et al., 1975).

Attention to the critical or sensitive nature of certain lands and their limited capability to withstand drastic disturbance has been the focal point of several recent studies in a variety of resource settings. McHarg and associates studied the complex ecosystem of the southern coastal region to determine appropriate development guidelines for the Woodlands New Community in Harris County, Texas. Major elements of the study included a complex soil survey, vegetation analysis, hydrologic assessment, and microclimatic study (McHarg et al., 1973). The Tahoe Regional Planning Commission undertook a wide array of environmental studies to determine the suitability of lands around the lake for disturbance to accommodate various intensities of development. Major concerns were the steep topography, shallow, easily erodable soils, vegetation, subsurface geology, and surface drainage. The Tahoe studies ultimately led to the development of a land suitability map which identified those areas suited for low, moderate, and high intensity development using certain land development performance standards. The map also identified those land areas which by virtue of their natural features are areas which should not be disturbed under any conditions (Bailey, 1975).

Many special studies have been conducted to develop, test, validate, and refine procedures for inventorying and assessing critical areas. MacConnell has prepared a manual for classifying land-use and vegetative cover using remote sensing data. The procedure is intended to refine the state land use inventory for Massachusetts. Critical lands are identified through the process (MacConnell, 1975). New York State has a similar state-wide land use and resource analysis system which identified critical and sensitive lands (Hardy & Shelton, 1970). The Vermont Land Capability Study grouped land on a state-wide scale into several capability and suitability classes. Lands above 2,500 feet elevation, for example, which are the higher altitude forest, watershed, and shallow soils areas, are not suited for development (Vermont State Planning Off., 1974). The Bureau of Economic Geology in Texas has prepared an environmental atlas for portions of the coastal zone. Sensitive lands and hazard areas are mapped and the development constraints are clearly described (Fisher et al., 1972).

Colorado is one of many western states with a state-wide program for identifying special lands which should not be disturbed or, if so, only with special care. The most critical areas, from the standpoint of human safety and public interest, are the high mountain avalanche areas, meadows, and wildlife areas (Colorado Land Use Commission, 1974). An excellent source of state resource management programs dealing with critical areas is found in a January, 1976, summary prepared by the U.S. Geological Survey (Off. of Land and Water Plan., 1976).

Several special studies dealing with the delineation of lands designated as critical, sensitive, or capable of minimal disturbance have been conducted recently. Many of these have been designed to be used as a framework for identifying sites which should be reserved and managed as open space, nature preserves, natural areas, research natural areas, or limited recreation areas. These lands include historic cultural and scenic areas which have social, economic, environmental, and recreational values.

Recently, the Office of Land Use and Water Planning of the Interior Department prepared a set of methods and techniques for developing a critical area program (USGS, 1976). A similar set of guidelines was prepared by the U.S. Army Corps of Engineers for use in planning for the management of critical areas (U.S. Army Corps of Engineers, 1974).

III. GUIDANCE SYSTEMS FOR SENSITIVE LANDS

Discussion of the topic of critical lands, sensitive areas, or preserving natural diversity oftentimes suggests that use of such areas be restricted to passive, extensive types of activities which are primarily nonconsumptive in nature. In many instances, based on the character of the lands in question, these kinds of uses may indeed be the most appropriate. In other situations, certain uses may be compatible if effective measures are taken to minimize the resultant damages. In short, this simply means to hold the on-site disturbances to a minimum and internalize to the greatest extent possible all negative externalities (impacts or implications) associated with the activity. If this can be accomplished in an economically feasible and socially acceptable manner, there should be no hesitancy to deny society the use of certain and often vital natural resources.

When we speak of uses of land, we mean those actions of man which usually result in some form of conversion or modification of the land from its natural state. Uses in this context refer to activities such as timber harvesting, dredging, filling, excavating, channelizing, plowing, urbanization, grading, burning, drilling, blasting, and the like. Each activity generates certain side effects which occur at the time of or shortly after the disturbance. Many of these side effects remain active for a considerable period after the initial disturbance flow off-site, becoming cumulative in terms of the chain of effects they generate far beyond the site. Examples of these situations include dust, noise, smoke, falling rock, vibration, glare, and water pollution.

The logical question at this point is *can we make any use or uses of these sensitive lands?* The answer in many cases is *yes*. This *yes*, however, should be conditioned by the application of a rigid set of environmental performance standards. Use of sensitive lands, or any land for that matter, should as a rule conform to the following criteria:

1) Uses which respect the ecological integrity of the land;
2) Uses which provide a reasonable economic return to both the owner and society;
3) Uses which minimize potential public harm; and
4) Uses which minimize future external social costs.

In disputes involving the management of sensitive lands, or land in general, where individual goals and community goals conflict, the courts have generally ruled that in seeking a balance the landowner must be allowed a reasonable economic use of the land. Also, in the case where urgently needed public resources are needed, provisions have been made to allow what could be defined as a reasonable economic return to society.

The term which has troubled and frustrated all who have wrestled with the question is what is meant by the term *reasonable economic return*. Certainly, most rational individuals would not define *reasonable* as extracting every unit of profit regardless of the negative environmental impact of the activity. On the other hand, it seems difficult to justify the total restriction of people from land, particularly private land, unless, of course, the public is willing and able to pay the full cost of removing the land and its resources from the market. Reasonableness as applied here suggests intelligence and prudence, balanced with uses of the land which are consistent with sound principles of environmental planning and management.

Land uses which minimize potential public harm are acceptable on fragile sites, given the appropriate performance standards. These kinds of uses do not invite people to place themselves, their homes, and communities in unnecessary hazard situations. This also suggests that a considerable savings may result from avoiding the public cost of expensive and not always fail-safe protective devices. Dams, levees, costly foundations, extra-strength construction; these are fine if one espouses this long-time love affair with the concrete truck! Many would argue that, given enough engineering talent, any land area can be developed regardless of the natural character of the land, so long as an abundance of low cost energy and resources is readily available. This does not include the cost of subsidized insurance for development in flood plains and coastal zones. While not developing many lands which should not be disturbed may result in an increase in value of residual developable lands, the cost can be at least partially offset by lowering the social cost of those activities which are necessary to make the land developable.

It has been shown that many incompatible uses of sensitive lands often require the development of expensive protective structures which are paid for with public funds. If an environmental function—often termed an evil of nature—occurs, lives and property can be lost. These are the kinds of external social costs which, if not completely eliminated, can be substantially mitigated through appropriate land use management practices. There is no sound rationale to justify the redistribution of public wealth to subsidize land development in areas where environmental planning would dictate otherwise. If a rare, unique, or irreplaceable natural, historical, or cultural resource is lost or irreparably damaged as a result of unwise land conversion or development, society suffers a loss. While the magnitude of such loss may be difficult to measure, certainly no one can deny nor ignore the magnitude of public outcry which has arisen in recent years when such areas are being threatened. The amount of money spent on acquisition, protection, and litigation on behalf of wise use of sensitive lands or to prevent the disturbance of lands which are not to be disturbed bears testimony to the opportunity costs and social value of these resources.

A. Public Policy for Lands That Are Not to be Disturbed

Public interest in the proper management of sensitive lands is not of recent origin. From George Perkins Marsh to the modern day environmental crusaders, the development of land conservation programs has been based on two philosophical concepts. First, lands of unique character which include scenery, wildlife habitat, and other resources with no market value should be owned and managed by the government as parks, wildlife refuges, and conservancies. Second, through a vast program of economic incentives, land owners could be enticed to adopt those conservation practices which would yield short run returns on the investment. In some instances, these programs have been contradictory, to wit, federal funds to acquire wetlands for wildlife habitat and federal funds to help farmers drain wetlands to increase the supply of tillable land.

State and local governments have used their taxing, regulatory, fiscal, and eminent domain authorities to effect land conservation and management through what has come to be known as the *land use guidance system* (Kaiser & Reichert, 1975).

Aside from taxation, public spending, and fee or less than fee acquisition of certain property or development rights, the remaining land management tools involve the imposition of some constraints on the owner's use of his property. In each instance, the application of these constraints must be for the express purpose of protecting the general health, safety, and welfare of the community. The principal test which is applied in questions of excess application of these contraints is whether the public gain far exceeds the private loss to the extent that the landowner's residual opportunities do not afford reasonable economic use of the property. In other words, when the public tries to get something for nothing, some serious questions as to the constitutionality of the action can be raised.

B. Major Issues

The subject of public values and private property rights is the focal issue in any discussion of how to deal with the question of protecting lands which should not be disturbed. This topic has been the subject of massive volumes of legal and economic literature in the past several years (Bosselman et al., 1975). The issues can be grouped into several doctrinal categories:

1) The public interest-public pay doctrine;
2) The prevention of public harm or provision of public safety doctrine; and
3) The elastic public welfare doctrine.

Each of these involves some element of suspension of private property rights. If the public believes it is in the public interest to restrict all economically beneficial uses of certain lands, thereby depriving the owner of any reasonable use and enjoyment of the property, outright fee simple public ownership is the appropriate course of action. Short of public abrogation of the public trust responsibility, the public can be assured that the land resource in question will not be disturbed. The loss of the resources and tax revenue represents the exercised opportunity cost.

Less than public stewardship via fee interest in sensitive lands involves entry into the often murky gray area of imposed restrictions which promote the public interest yet do not constitute a taking of the property or right to use the property. This has become a very emotional and doctrinally varied area of concern to all involved in the planning and management of sensitive lands. Application of the police power and its justification vary considerably among states and geographic–political regions of the country. Several examples will illustrate these have been selected.

1. PUBLIC INTEREST-PUBLIC PAY DOCTRINE

The first example falls into the public interest–public pay doctrine category. The case is a 1963 New Jersey case (Morris County Land Improvement Co. v. Parsippany-Troy Hills TP., 1963). Here we have Parsippany-Troy Hills, which is a large, sprawling township in Morris County. The county at this time, 1962, had a great deal of vacant land which was being rapidly converted to urban development. A population explosion had hit the county which generated a host of planning and zoning problems.

The area in question is a large swamp of some 1,500 acres known as Troy Meadows. The area was formed during the last glacial period. In addition to being a complex ecological area, the swampland serves as a lowland drainage basin for surrounding higher lands.

Environmental research and analysis had established that the area was unsuitable for fill unless the top two layers of decomposed material were removed. Its appropriate uses in the natural state included the raising of fish and growing of aquatic plants.

At the time of the litigation, there were no active land uses in the Parsippany-Troy Hills portion of Troy Meadows. At that time, about 75% of the area was owned by Wildlife Preservation, Inc., a private noncommercial tax-paying corporation interested in conservation and preservation of the natural state of the area as a *public or quasi-public* wildlife sanctuary and nature study refuge. This organization has been active in urging local officials to restrict use of *all* the land accordingly. It opposed any activity which would be biologically adverse to the swamp or wildlife therein.

At the time the plaintiff acquired his sixty-six acres, the land was zoned to the most restrictive residential classification of the Township ordinance. A subsequent amendment to the ordinance for the area of Troy Meadows forbade any new use of land or change in existing use (except for agricultural purposes of the growing of fish, water fowl, and water plants), the dumping or other disposal of material, or any change in the natural or existing grade of the land without obtaining a special permit from the Township Committee.

The plaintiff made no attempt to use his land until 1959 when he began filling along the edge of a road without a permit. Wildlife Preservation, Inc., complained and in 1960 the plaintiff was granted limited permission to place fill adjacent to the road to a depth of 300 feet at his own risk.

In 1960, the Township, after extensive ecological studies of the meadowland, established the Meadowland Development Zone. The purpose of the zone was to establish those permitted uses which were deemed to be compatible with the site, as well as provisions for special exceptions. Permitted uses included agriculture, raising of woody plants, commercial greenhouses, and outdoor recreation.

The plaintiff argued that the Meadowland permitted uses amounted, for the most part, to strict regulation of land reclamation in aid of uses allowed as of right. He continued to fill his land after the adoption of the Meadowland Development Zone. He then applied for and was denied an exception to continue the land-filling operation, along with excavation of an 18-acre reservoir. The plaintiff argued that denial of the exception constituted a taking of the plaintiff's property without compensation and that, among other things, such a denial was unreasonable and arbitrary.

The township argued on the basis that the swamp served as a natural flood water reservoir and that to fill or change the character of the swamp was not in the public interest. A great deal of ecological evidence to support this contention was presented. During the trial, the judge visited the area and inspected the swamp.

After dealing with the other legal issues, the New Jersey Supreme Court proceeded to take head on the critical issues of whether the restrictions placed on the plaintiff's land constituted a taking. The court recognized the prime objective of the regulation was to retain the land substantially in its natural state. What disturbed the court was that many of the permitted uses provided the landowner no means of realizing a reasonable economic return from his property, i.e., outdoor recreational uses to be operated only by some governmental unit and conservation uses and activities. The court concluded that the main purpose of the regulations was to achieve a public benefit. While the purposes of the regulations were viewed as laudable public purposes, the court viewed the restrictions as far too restrictive and, as such, constitutionally unreasonable and confiscatory. The court recognized that draining and filling the marsh would be necessary to make the land usable; however, it felt that some reclamation was possible without destroying the function of the entire meadowland. In concluding, the court suggested that if the public desired the area for public use it should be acquired from the owner at fair market value.

2. PREVENTION OF PUBLIC HARM DOCTRINE

A similar case with a diffeent ending illustrates the prevention of public harm or provision of public safety doctrine (Just v. Marinette County, 1972).

In this instance, the State of Wisconsin had passed legislation requiring counties to adopt a shoreland zoning ordinance which, among other things, requires a special permit to change the natural character of land within 1,000 feet of a navigable lake and 300 feet of a navigable river. The county is required to enforce the regulations promulgated by the Department of Natural Resources to protect navigable waters and public rights therein from degradation and deterioration which results from uncontrolled use and development of shorelands (Wis. Stat. Annot. 59.971 [1,6], 144.26).

The statute defines wetlands, establishes the state's role of trustee of its navigable waters through use of the police power to promote public health, safety, convenience, and general welfare, and establishes the permitted and conditional uses. Permitted uses include such activities as harvesting wild crops, sustained yield forestry, hunting, fishing, hiking, agriculture, and certain kinds of filling and draining under permit.

The case in question involves Mr. Ron Just who, in 1961, several years prior to the passage of the ordinance, purchased some 36 acres on the south shore of Lake Noquebay, a navigable lake in Marinette County. The land had 1,266.7 feet of lake frontage. Just purchased the land partially for personal use and partially for resale. From 1964 Just sold parcels having lake frontage.

In February 1968 6 months after the effective date of the ordinance, Ron Just, without securing a conditional use permit, hauled 1,040 yd^2 of sand onto his property and filled an area approximately 20 ft wide along the shoreline. More than 500 ft^2 of the fill was upon wetlands located contiguous to the water and which had surface drainage towards the lake.

The county sought a mandatory injunction to restrain Just from placing fill on their property without first obtaining a conditional use permit as required by ordinance. Just sought a declaratory judgment stating that: (i) the shoreland ordinance of Marinette County was unconstitutional, (ii) their property was not "wetland as defined in the ordinance," and (iii) the prohibition against the filling of wetlands was unconstitutional.

The court began by identifying the real issue as to whether the conservancy district provisions and the wetlands filling restrictions are unconstitutional because they amount to a constructive taking of the plaintiff's property without just compensation.

The court examined the concept of public benefit in contrast to public harm and the scope of an owner's use of his property. It reasoned that if the land is used in its natural form and if its character is not changed in contradiction to what nature intended, there is no public harm and still an opportunity of private benefit. In this case, the court looked at the wetland as closely interrelated with other wetlands and to the purity of water, navigation, fishing, and scenic beauty. Because people now understand this relationship more fully, the court reasoned, they view these lands as an essential part of the balance of nature.

The court then raised the question: *is the ownership of a parcel of land so absolute that man can change its nature to suit any of his purposes?* The court felt that if the change resulted in a public harm, then it was not beyond the reasonable application of the police power to restrict uses to those which were in harmony with the natural state of the land. In this instance, the court felt the permitted uses were consistent with nature and reasonable. The Wisconsin court dismissed the conclusion in Morris County Land Improvement by reasoning that filling a swamp not otherwise commercially usable is not in and of itself an existing use which is prevented but rather is the preparation for some future use which is not indigenous to a swamp. The creation of commercial value was not considered as important as the protection of natural values. Thus, there could be no diminution of value as the owners contend, particularly when changing the character of the land is at the expense of harm to public rights. The court did not view this as a taking and dismissed the case.

3. PUBLIC WELFARE DOCTRINE

A third case serves to illustrate an emerging view of the public welfare doctrine. The case involves a denial by the Adirondack Park Agency of a petition by property owners to construct boat houses on their property on a peninsula on Oseetah Lake (McCormick v. Lawrence, 1975).

The Adirondack Park Agency was created by the New York Legislature to control land use within the park, thereby protecting and preserving the park values. The petitioners desired to build a boat dock into Oseetah Lake. The agency felt this dock would impair the visual values and aesthetic qualities of that region of the park. The legislature mandated that the agency "shall not approve any project. . .or grant a permit therefore, unless it first determines that such project meets the following criteria. . .(3) The project would not have an undue adverse impact upon the natural, scenic, aesthetic, ecological, wildlife, historic, recreational, or open space resources of the park. . . ." (N. Y. Exec. Law 805 84-10, 1976).

The court, after viewing the exhibits, determined that denial of the permit was not an abuse of the police power nor a taking. The court concluded that aesthetic considerations alone generate a sufficient impact on the public welfare to warrant an exercise of the police power where such considerations relate to unique features of the locality. Thus, the denial was neither arbitrary nor unreasonable; the owners could still use and enjoy their property.

4. COMPOSITE OF DOCTRINES

The fourth example involves all four doctrinal issues illustrated in two flood plain zoning cases. In both instances, the question of excessive use of the police power to restrict use of the flood plain land to non economically feasible uses was the issue. The public interest, prevention of public harm, and public safety and welfare all came to bear on each case. If these lands should not be disturbed, then what is the appropriate and equitable course of public action?

In a Pennsylvania case, the Commonwealth Court of Pennsylvania affirmed a lower court ruling which held that after the owner's land, which was previously zoned commercial, was rezoned flood plain, thereby limiting use of the land to such activities as cultivating and harvesting crops and grazing animals, the owner could not avail himself of compensation under provisions of eminent domain (Gabel v. Thornbury Township, Delaware County, 1973). The court did not feel that the restrictions so limited the use of Gabel's property that the public interest could be served without acquiring the property by the payment of compensation.

In a California case, the landowners sought inverse condemnation action against the county, alleging that the zoning of their property under the county flood plain ordinance amounted to a taking without compensation (Turner v. County of Del Norte, 1972). The Superior Court held that the county ordinance prohibiting specified types of buildings in areas subject to flooding and limiting the use of land in such areas to parks, recreation, and agriculture did not constitute unlawful taking of property within such areas. Proof of the area being subject to flooding, and therefore a potential risk to life and property located in the flood plain, was established in part from Corps of Engineers flood plain studies of the lower Klamath River. The Corps accepted the flood plain zoning provisions as adequate flood plain management. The court found sufficient evidence to suggest the reasonableness of the ordinance in relation to the promotion of the health, safety, general welfare, and prosperity of the community. There was evidence of a frequency of flooding which would eventually destroy any permanent residences built on this land and endanger the health of the occupants and, further, that buildings in the flood plain property would increase flood heights which could conceivably increase the hazard to other buildings away from the zoned area.

When contrasting Morris and Just, we see two similar situations, yet two opposing views on how to deal with lands which someone believes should not be disturbed. In McCormick, the court took a giant step in ruling that aesthetics are a legitimate concept within the general police powers. Thus, we recognize that aesthetic, scenic, and visual aspects of land are such to suggest that on the basis of possibly impairing these intrinsic qualities certain lands should not be disturbed. In this instance, the social values of the undisturbed shoreline of Oseetah Lake were of a higher value than that of the boathouses to the owners of the property. Here again we find a situation where the legislature had determined that the state was to ". . .insure optimum overall conservation, protection, preservation, development and use of the unique scenic, aesthetic, wildlife, recreational open space, historic, ecological, and natural resources of the Adirondack park" (N. Y. Exec. Law 805 84-10. 1974).

Many believe the Just decision was very unfair as far as Mr. Ron Just was concerned. If, indeed, the public was to benefit from not having Just's land disturbed, and Just's residual value, based on the permitted uses, is diminished considerably, then does not this imposition and diminution constitute a taking rather than a mere regulation?

One common feature of all the cases reviewed was the existence of an ordinance which prescribed certain permitted uses for the sensitive land. These uses, which may not have the highest economic value, were activities which did not require disturbing the land and disrupting its ecological function. In some instances, certain uses, such as nature study, hiking trails, wildlife preserves, and harvesting of wild crops, have little or no market value. On the other hand, the record does not show the economic magnitude of the potential public harm, the public savings from preventing the harm, and the economic value of the water purified through the natural purifying plant.

5. SECURING DEVELOPMENT RIGHTS

Another approach to the protection of lands which should not be disturbed is to simply purchase the land in fee, or the appropriate development rights. Many states are using one or a combination of these techniques to preserve valuable farm, forest, wetland, and other valuable open space lands.

6. SOCIAL AND ECONOMIC IMPLICATIONS

Certainly there are other economic and social benefits associated with the decision not to disturb sensitive lands. The problem, of course, eventually reduces down to a basic issue. Someone other than the public owns the land and may not agree with what the land capability assessment says about the land. Take, for example, the owner of land on the shore of Lake Tahoe. When the land was purchased several years ago, the buyer probably didn't know he was investing in a land resource that should not be disturbed. He may have paid $10,000 an acre for the real estate which today may be worth $80,000 an acre. What happens when he awakens one fine morning to discover he owns not valuable real estate but a valuable ecological resource which a public body says should not be developed in order to protect the public interest? At this point, perhaps the land is worth $2,000 an acre. As these acres are taken out of the active development market, land which is determined to be suitable for development jumps in value. What we have here is a classical Donald Hagman "Windfall for Wipeout" situation (Hagman, 1974). Whoever benefits from the protection of Lake Tahoe and the lucky individual who owns the developable land are the winners.

A solution to this problem is needed. This solution must occur within the framework of our political-economic system. We must, as Professor Hagman strongly urges, find a way to capture the exact increments of gain from the reapers of windfalls and as equitably as possible compensate the owners of those lands which should not be disturbed (Hagman, 1976). Several approaches to resolving this issue have been suggested. Concepts such as transfer payments, compensable regulations, real estate transfer tax, and graduated capital gains tax are being suggested as ways of helping public bodies balance windfalls against wipeouts.

In an example involving wetlands management, the State of New Jersey designated approximately 140 acres of the owner's property as coastal wetland pursuant to the authority granted under its wetlands act. The effect of the order was to prohibit any "regulated activity" without a permit. The court rejected the argument that this action constituted a taking requiring compensation. The court concluded that since the legislature determined that preservation of wetlands was in the public interest and that reasonable uses were provided, the restriction was not a taking of the owner's property. The court indicated that such an owner must exhaust all statutory procedures for determining appropriate uses for the land (Sand Point Harbor, Inc. v. Sullivan, 1975).

Restriction of the use of land to open space compatible uses in contemplation of future public acquisition has always been held an unreasonable use of the police power. In a recent California case, the court struck down a downzoning of open land from high density development to open space and conservation land with residential development limited to the construction of one dwelling per 10-acre lot. In this case the regulation was both unreasonable and confiscatory (Eldridge v. City of Palo Alto, 1975).

In the first two cases, the application of performance standards allowed for reasonable uses of the property consistent with sound environmental management. In Eldridge, the city should have either acquired the land in fee or developed a land development program allowing for appropriate uses and a reasonable economic return on the property.

C. Development of Performance Standards

A second major area of current interest is the public policy shift from conventional police power restrictions to the broader use of performance standards and unified permit systems. Performance standards combine certain features of zoning and the permit system to form a less arbitrary and more reasonable land use guidance system.

Conventional zoning places compatible land uses in districts. Other uses may be allowed if they meet certain conditions which are often imposed in an arbitrary fashion. Performance standards require the planner and decision-maker to look at the effect or impact of the proposed use rather than the use per se. This requires a great deal of indepth information about the environmental characteristics—size, physical appearance, land, water, energy and transporation requirements, waste generation, and including measurable units of noise, emissions, etc.

For any given site or development, performance standards set the absolutes which must be met in order to accommodate the limitations of the site with the needs of the development. In short, a development which ordinarily may not be desirable in a sensitive area could become compatible if it were economically feasible to meet the established performance standards. In this manner the greatest number of negative externalities are internalized, thereby protecting the ecological values of the site while permitting a higher level of economic utility.

The information needed to prepare performance standards is complex and extensive. Most of the ecological data is usually prepared by a public agency. The unified permit system requires the developer to provide a considerable amount of information about his site and the scope and character of his development. This information can be reviewed by the appropriate persons with knowledge of a particular aspect of the site or development.

1. DEVELOPMENT PERMIT PROCESS

A very good example of this type of permit system is that used in Vermont. The Vermont State Land Use and Development Plan Law requires prospective land developers and subdividers to prepare a development permit (Vt. Statutes Annot., 1976). A permit must be obtained for certain kinds of land use activities including construction above an elevation of 2,500 feet, commercial or industrial construction on more than 1 acre of land, construction of 10 or more housing or dwelling units, construction of a site involving 10 acres or more, or facilities requiring separate sewage disposal facilities.

The permit is a comprehensive document covering all aspects of the project including information about the site and performance aspects of the development, such as air pollution, sanitary waste discharge, runoff, and physical appearance. The permit is reviewed by a local board as well as a state land use board. The burden of proof falls on the applicant to show the proposed development fits the suitability determination of the site and will have no adverse environmental implications. The state may call upon technical experts to visit the site and offer independent evaluations of the information contained in the applicant's permit.

In approving a development permit, the board must be satisfied that the proposed project will have no adverse impacts on air or water quality, soil erosion, municipal utilities, traffic congestion, educational facilities, parks, aesthetics, historic sites, and unique natural areas.

The Vermont system is basically an effective system of guiding development in sensitive areas (Heeter, 1976). Most litigation to date has involved procedural rather than substantive matters. In many instances the boards' findings are difficult to refute, leaving the developer the choice of either modifying his proposal or seeking an alternative site. This system is potentially the most comprehensive in the nation as a vehicle for applying performance standards to guide the development of sensitive lands (Healy, 1976). Observation suggests that the quality of land development in Vermont has greatly improved in the past 4 years.

2. THE PROCESS IN OPERATION

A recent case illustrates the effectiveness of the Vermont permit system which incorporates certain performance standards (In re Wildlife Wonderland, Inc., 1975). A developer who had received a permit for a commercial game farm from the regional environmental commission was subsequently denied by the State Environmental Board. The farm would utilize 65 acres of a 600-acre tract. Attendance was projected at 100,000 visitors from late spring through early fall.

The Board found that the farm would present water and air pollution problems, create an adverse impact on aesthetics, cause unreasonable soil erosion, endanger public investments in public lands, interfere with public uses of those lands, and be detrimental to the public health, safety, and general welfare. These findings were backed up by indepth studies which established that the performance of the development was not such that it could meet the environmental quality standards for areas in which it was proposed (Am. Soc. of Plan. Off., 1976). This case clearly illustrates how the system can respond when an attempt is made to develop lands which should not be disturbed.

Combining these features, the permissible level of disturbance is that which is consistent with the planning and management objectives that have been promulgated. Thus, the performance zone is defined by both the environmental quality standards for the site and the list of acceptable impacts. The community, in establishing the performance standards for an area such as Troy Meadowlands, sets the minimum level of contamination and insures that this level will not be exceeded.

Environmentally sensitive areas can accommodate uses that do not require extensive construction. Simply permitting certain uses may not insure that the use is compatible with the natural processes at the site. Environmental performance criteria specify those uses which are compatible with the land as it functions naturally.

The use of environmental performance criteria requires the identification and description of the natural processes that are closely associated with public health, safety, and welfare and that provide the community important benefits ignored by the market. A level at which a community desires the natural processes to operate is then established. Any development of land must be done in such a way that the natural processes continue to function at this level.

Environmental performance criteria encourage compatible uses as well as innovative land use planning and design. This encourages the landowner to find the best use for his site. The burden of proof shifts from planner to landowner, who must show his proposed development can measure up to the standards. Uses which are not compatible with the natural systems are easily separated and suggested for transferral to more desirable sites. In short, the system does nothing more than attempt to preserve or maintain the performance of the natural system already there.

The current national focus on the problems associated with the reclamation of drastically disturbed lands suggests an urgent need to develop workable performance standards for various kinds of mining operations. This is being accomplished to some extent by means of state statutes which prescribe certain premining, operation, and post-mining procedures intended to facilitate in an environmentally acceptable manner the most feasible restoration of the mine site. Much of the technology discussed by scientists and engineers in this book represents the kind of information which forms the basis for promulgating performance requirements. In many of the chapters the procedures recommended, if followed, would so reshape the land as to significantly enhance its potential for a wide spectrum of economically sound uses. Also, application of these procedures would significantly reduce the number of undesirable aspects of the mining which have triggered strong community opposition.

The performance standard focuses on how the land functions. The community sets a specific measurable limit at which the key functions of a sensitive area must operate; the developer must then show that his development will meet those standards. The community sets forth its policy objectives and frames its guidance system to meet those objectives. If at any time the development fails to meet the standards, it can be corrected or severe penalties imposed.

The criteria for selecting lands that are not to be disturbed and some of the techniques for managing these lands have been discussed in this chapter. The process is complex, highly technical, and requires a high level of scientific input. Public understanding and support for wise and prudent management of these lands appears to be increasing. Future prospects to avoid many of the past problems resulting from improper use of these kinds of lands appear bright.

LITERATURE CITED

American Society of Planning Officials. 1976. Land Use Law and Zoning Digest, Vol. 28, No. 3, 143. p. 13–14.

Bailey, R. G. 1975. Land capability classification of the Lake Tahoe Basin, California-Nevada: A guide for planning. USDA-FS, in cooperation with the Tahoe Regional Planning Agency, South Lake Tahoe, Calif.

Belknap, R. K., and J. G. Furtado. 1967. Three approaches to environmental resource analysis. Conserv. Found., Washington, D.C.

Bosselman, F., D. Collies, and J. Banta. 1975. The taking issue: An analysis of the constitutional limits of land use control. Council on Environ. Qual. U.S. Government Printing Office, Washington, D.C.

Colorado Land Use Commission. 1974. Priority areas of environmental concern in Colorado. Colorado Land Use Comm., Denver.

Eldridge v. City of Palo Alto. 124 Cal. Rptr. S47. 26 Sept. 1975.

Fisher, W. L., J. H. McGowen, L. F. Brown, Jr., and C. G. Groat. 1972. Environmental geologic atlas of the Texas Coastal Zone—Galveston-Houston Area. Bur. of Econ. Geol. Univ. of Texas at Auston.

Gaebel v. Thornbury Township, Delaware County, 303 A.2d 57. 24 June 1973.

Hagman, D. G. 1974. New deal: Trading windfalls for wipeouts. Planning, The American Society of Planning Officials Magazine. 40:9–9.

Hagman, D. G. 1976. The taking issue: The HFH: et al. Round. Land Use Law and Zoning Digest 28(2):5–9.

Hardy, E. E., and R. L. Shelton. 1970. Inventorying New York's land use and natural resources. N.Y. Food Life Sci. Bull. 3:4.

Healy, R. G. 1976. Land use and the states. Johns Hopkins Press, Baltimore.

Heeter, D. G. 1976. Act 250: Alive and basically well. Land Use Law and Zoning Digest 28:3–5.

Just v. Marinette County. 201 N.W. 2d 761. 31 Oct. 1972.

Kaiser, E. J., and P. A. Reichert. 1975. Land use guidance system planning for environmental quality. Nat. Resour. J. 15:3–529.

MacConnell, W. P. 1975. Classification manual, land use and vegetative cover mapping. Massachusetts Agric. Exp. Stn. Res. Bull. no. 631. Amherst, Mass.

McCormick, v. Lawrence. 372 N.Y.S. 2d 156. 11 Aug. 1975.

McHarg, I. L. 1971. Amelia Island, Florida: A report on the master planning process for a new recreational community. Wallace, McHarg, Roberts & Todd, Philadelphia.

McHarg, I. L., J. Sutton, and A. W. Spirn. 1973. Woodlands new community guidelines for site planning. Wallace, McHarg, Roberts & Todd, Philadelphia.

Morris County Land Improvement Company vs. Parsippany-Troy Hills Township. 193 A.2d 232. 23 July 1963.

New York Executive Law E 805, 806. (McKinney, 1976).

Office of Land and Water Planning. 1975. Critical areas: A guidebook for development of state programs. U.S. Dep. of Interior, Washington, D.C.

Office of Land and Water Planning. 1976. State resource management programs primer: Critical areas and information/data handling. U.S. Dep. of Interior, Washington, D.C.

Sands Point Harbor, Inc. v. Sullivan. 346 A.2d 612. 12 Oct. 1975.

Sargent, F. O., and J. H. Brande. 1976. Classifying and evaluating unique natural areas for planning purposes. J. Soil Water Conserv. 31:3–113.

Stover, E. J. (ed.) 1975. Protecting nature's estate: Techniques for saving land. U.S. Government Printing Office, Washington, D.C.

Thurow, C., W. Toner, and D. Erley. 1975. Performance controls for sensitive lands: A practical guide for local administrators. Am. Soc. of Planning Off., Chicago.

Turner v. County of Del Norte. 101 Col. Rptr. 93. 7 March 1972.

U.S. Army Corps of Engineers. 1974. Planning considerations for statewide inventories of critical environmental areas: A reference guide. Smithsonian Instit., Washington, D.C.

U.S. Geological Survey. 1976. Methods and techniques for critical area development. Tech. Support Rep. A, U.S. Dep. of Interior, Washington, D.C.

Vermont State Planning Office. 1974. Vermont land capability. Vermont State Plan. Off., Montpelier.

Vermont Statutes Annotated. 1976. T 10.0 6001 Pt. 5. Ch. 151. State Land Use and Development Plans.

Wildlife Wonderland, Inc. v. State of Vermont. 346 Atlantic, 2d 645, 133 VT. 507 (1975).

Wells, D. M., J. D. Mertes, B. L. Allen, and A. N. Glick. 1975. Procedure for selecting a minimal environmental impact routing for a water conveyance canal. Water Resour. Bull. 11:4–714.

Wisconsin Statues Annotated 59.971 (West, 1957).

Copyright © 1978 ASA–CSSA–SSSA
677 South Segoe Road, Madison, WI 53711 USA
Reclamation of Drastically Disturbed Lands

Chapter 13

Premining Planning to Maximize Effective Land Use and Reclamation

JAMES M. RIDDLE AND LEE W. SAPERSTEIN

Colorado School of Mines, Golden, Colorado, and The Pennsylvania State University, University Park, Pennsylvania, respectively

I. INTRODUCTION

In all industries, but particularly in mining, planning is recognized as the key to success. Extremely large capital investments and commitments of manpower and resources are common. Mining companies expect their investments to be repaid over short periods of time; therefore, the opening of a new mine should follow a preconceived plan in which optimum return is foremost.

However, attention in recent years to land disturbance and its subsequent restoration has increased the scope and depth of the mining engineer's field of concern. The traditional direction of engineering activity has two components, as shown in Fig. 1. One component relates to the actual mining activity: removal of material from the earth's crust and a conversion of that material to a marketable commodity. The second component has involved the pure-market economy, public system of supply and demand for minerals.

Today the mining engineer's field is more complex. It has been altered by the additional and related concerns of environmental quality. The mining plan must consider public demands for environmental quality as well as demands for minerals. The public voice these demands because they desire more subjective and aesthetic "goods" as well as the real-money value of mined products. Such public demands for extra-production environmental quality are expressed by considerable government activity. The mine plan is frequently scrutinized by a score or more of governmental agencies. A view of this more involved system of mine-planning analysis is presented as Fig. 2.

The major part of any planning process is to combine (i) formulation and definition of the problem with (ii) identification of the data necessary to solve the problem and the techniques by which such data can and will be analyzed. The vogue term for such an analysis is *preplanning*, which is best viewed as either a redundant misnomer or an ellipsis. That is, since planning should obviously occur "pre" anything, perhaps the term *pre-mining planning* is best used to define *the formulation of the problem and identification of the future steps to be taken in dealing with it.*

223

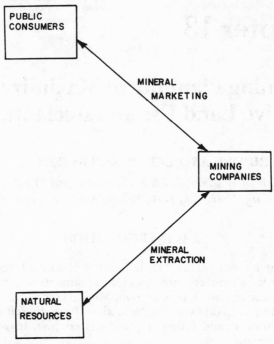

Fig. 1—The traditional mine-planning system.

II. THE MINE PLANNING PROBLEM—ITS SCOPE AND DEPTH

A. The General Problem

A total systems approach to problem solution is a flow process of six parts: formulation (of the problem), identification (of data and techniques), collection (of data), assessment (of the data by such techniques), preliminary solution, interplay, and final solution. After any phase it may be necessary to repeat an earlier phase if analysis has been insufficient to continue further. When interplay and discussion lead to the conclusion that all aspects have been examined, the planning process has been completed.

The decision to mine or not to mine is complex in its own right. Based on the assumption that mining is to take place, the specific planning problem may be formulated as (i) the maximization of production and (ii) the maintenance of certain environmental quality resources, specifically land use. These objectives are further constrained by (i) the objective of the company to operate at a profit and (ii) limitations arising from the scarce nature of a variety of resources with which mining is involved. Recalling Fig. 2, it may be seen that mining is a series of actions taken to extract resources from nature and to provide them as commodities to the public while returning and restoring some resources to the environment. These actions influence the well-being derived by the public. The planner should recognize that in relating the characteristics of the environment,

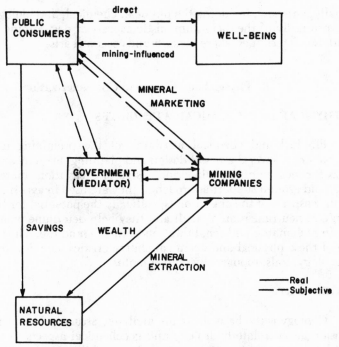

Fig. 2—The contemporary mine-planning system.

the activities of mining, and the impacts to the public, it is only mining's activities with which he deals. He cannot alter what is present or how the public reacts, except by modifying the function of the mining activity, which is merely one link in an interconnected process.

The first planning problem, then, is to learn as much as possible about this intricate system of real and emotional value flows. A first step is to inventory or list the many resources present prior to mining. Then the activities of mining can be listed and, for each activity, the planner can determine which resources are to be consumed or altered. As a final step to determining the scope, depth, and interconnections of the mining proposal, the planner can then consider where the outputs of his activities will occur. Knowing the what, where, when, and how of both resource consumption and output of value and resources can help the planner determine the actual benefits and costs which would arise from an alternative plan. Mine planning is essentially formulating several alternative approaches, determining the benefits and costs expected in each alternative, and selecting the best of these as the *ultimate optimum mining plan*. Such a plan is generally the one most positive in total value and is still consistent, in total, with the constraints and desires of public, government, and company.

In the specific case of optimizing land use and reclamation, there are several types of basic information, including physical, chemical, biological, and socio-humanistic characteristics. The various phases and unit operations of mining represent the activities which are to be planned.

Finally, a review, including the physical, chemical, and biological nature but primarily of the socio-humanistic aspects of post-mining alternative land use, determines where benefits and costs will arise.

B. Physical and Chemical Characterization

1. PHYSICAL AND CHEMICAL ATTRIBUTES

Physical and chemical attributes of the premining environment are factors in several areas of design and planning. Such measures are the basis for most mining engineering design of excavation, materials handling, and ground support approaches; they are used in assessing the water quality aspects of the operation (specifically the potential for both formation and neutralization of acid) and they help determine what the needs are in reclamaton and rehabilitation to future land use. The specific listing of these physical and chemical characteristics includes consideration of geology, soils, topography, and climate.

2. GEOLOGY

Geology is the basis for many analyses. Structural and stratigraphic considerations relate hydrology and geochemical aspects to mining and rehabilitation, aid investigations of slope stability, and relate to the occurrence of sulfur in the coal, rock, and overburden of the mine. Three forms of sulfur occur commonly in association with coal: organic, pyritic, and sulfate sulfur. Organic sulfur is distributed uniformly throughout the coal in a stable form which does not contribute to mine drainage. Likewise, sulfate sulfur in fresh coal comprises a low (< 0.05) percentage, and is not an important contribution to mine drainage (R. R. Parizek. 1975. Occurrence of sulfur in coal. *In* Unpublished In-house Quarterly Rep. no. 2, 20 Dec. 1975, EPA Grant no. R803882-01-0, from Dep. of Mineral Eng., Pennsylvania State Univ., to Extraction Technol. Branch, USEPA).

Pyritic or sulfide sulfur, the most environmentally important occurrence, can appear as either pyrite or marcasite. Both minerals have the same chemical formula, FeS_2, but differ in physical structure. They occur either in macroscopic or microscopic scale, or both. Pyrite in shales and wasted coal remains in the spoil at the mine site, representing a new, more detrimental, depositional form for the further action of water and the formation of acid mine drainage. The occurrence of sulfur in and with coal is well documented in the literature (U.S. Bur. of Mines, 1975).

The deposition of organic material and its transformation to coal is recognized as a characteristic sequence. A repeating sequence, or cyclothem, of strata is found in many basins, particularly in the Appalachian Interior Basin. Changes in cyclothem geology can be traced on a regional basis. The cyclical pattern of coal geology is important for characterization of the general physical and chemical nature of the mining environment. Well-developed and traceable cyclothems occur throughout Ohio, Pennsylvania, and West Virginia. A typical sequence (Branson, 1962) would include: marine shale or limestone; coal; underclay; fresh-water limestone; and sandstone and shale. By identifying the particular cyclothemic nature of a given coal deposit, delineating the status of deposition (alluvial, upper delta, lower delta, or shoreline conditions), the mineralogy, petrology, and mechanical properties relative to mine engineering and water quality implications may be inferred.

3. SOILS

Soils are an important consideration of premining evaluation, although not so much in terms of which soils are present before mining except to assure restoration to an equal condition. Of primary concern are the characteristics of the material to be restored and rehabilitated to serve as soil, particularly topsoil, after mining. It is seen in many older mining districts that spoil banks are only sparsely revegetated, in part due to the lack of nutrients in the form of a topsoil, and in part due to the water flow characteristics of the restored strata. In cases where bedrock material, shale, sandstone, siltstone, and fire-clay have been generously mixed with, or have totally replaced, the original topsoil covering, a minimum of fine-grained matrix material and organic matter is available to serve either as a source of nutrients or for moisture-holding purposes. High infiltration capacity, high porosity, and high permeability are all too commonly encountered in situations where no attempt is made at top-layer restoration.

Regrading of spoils can be insufficient to provide a growth medium; therefore, characterization of the future soil strata should include either provision for replacement of existing soil strata or complete rebuilding of a topsoil strata. Techniques for rebuilding soil will be covered later in the section on methods. A few of these can be mentioned here, however, and include reconditioning with lime or limestone, fertilizing, pH adjustment, and other nonspecific amendments such as the addition of mulch, fly ash, or sewage sludge.

4. TOPOGRAPHY AND CLIMATE

Topography and climate should be considered for several reasons, including identification of the type of mining to be practiced, determination of operating problems associated with extremes of terrain and weather, assuming suitability of methods for revegetation, and delimiting alternatives for future use, either urban or agrarian.

General features of terrain influence the selection of area mining vs. contour mining. In contour mining, the terrain may indicate a preference among the several alternatives. Extremes in climate and terrain influence the selection of equipment to be used in these methods and determines desirable planting periods. For example, high rain or snowfall is not conducive to operating small trucks on steep grades, and may cause topsoil washout and erosion.

General aspects of the terrain and climate or, specifically, characterization of the climax biome of the area, influences selection of revegeta-

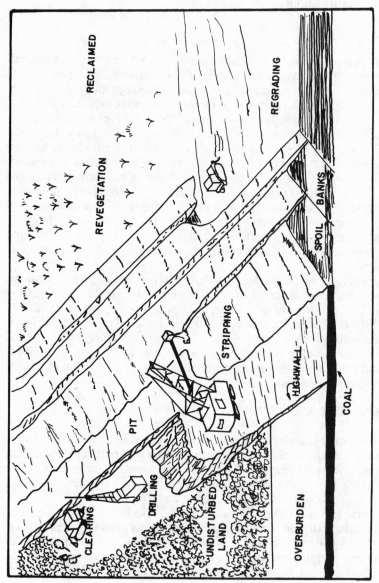

Fig. 3— Area mining with concurrent reclamation (after Grim & Hill, 1974).

tion approaches. The moderate and "normal" conditions of the Eastern United States pose fewer problems. In the Western United States, the arid to semiarid deserts and grasslands consist of vegetative systems that are more difficult to restore. In either case, the revegetation should be matched and meshed with natural biological progression.

5. HYDROLOGY

Hydrology, both surface and underground, is a crucial element. Understanding the surface-mine planning problem requires a knowledge of the flows of water in and near the mine. Erosion and sediment production are the immediate concerns in the critical postmining, prerevegetation time period. Controlling sediment and erosion in storms and the mine drainage phenomenon are two major long-term problems.

Solutions to these problems cannot be achieved by considering only surface or subsurface flow; a complex, composite hydrogeological system is present. Variations in topography, soils, geology, and hydrology account for many and widely scattered types of mine drainage observed in a region or even in a smaller area.

In conducting hydrology studies, it should be recognized that (i) intermediate, deep, and shallow ground water systems are present, (ii) quality and quantity of water do relate directly to past and present mining activity, and (iii) no natural deposit can be considered as isolated from water flows (impermeable). If surface and underground water flows are understood, adverse water quality effects can be avoided or controlled by several techniques. These techniques include controlling and altering drainage by diversion, regrading, compacting, and layering fill or, more extensively, control of ground water by a system of collector and disposal wells. Contact between spoil and water can be reduced through revegetation which, at the same time, increases water interception and evapotranspiration. Other effects of mine drainage can be reduced through limestone or lime application and burial of toxic (acid-forming) material.

C. Mining Design Bounds

1. SURFACE MINE DEVELOPMENT

Surface mine development may follow one of several alternative approaches. Considerations of terrain and overburden depth generally combine to indicate an overall approach. Specific details of unit operations are based on more specific characteristics of the overburden and the coal as well as the reclamation plan.

2. TERRAIN

Terrain influences the selection of the general approach. For relatively flat terrain, typical of the Midwest to Far West, area mining is common (Fig. 3). Contour mining (Fig. 4) is practiced in more rolling to steep

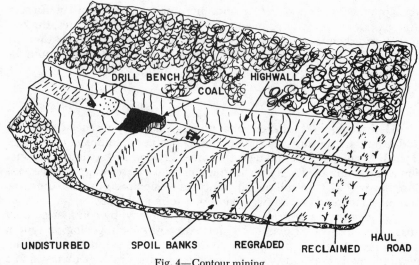

UNDISTURBED   SPOIL BANKS   REGRADED   RECLAIMED   HAUL
                                                                    ROAD
Fig. 4—Contour mining.

terrain. Accepted practice calls mining on slopes steeper than 12° *contour mining*. In other contour-mining areas, under special conditions of overburden thickness and extent of coal, contour mining may take the form of mountain top-removal mining (Fig. 5), which resembles area mining in many ways.

3. OVERBURDEN PROPERTIES

Overburden properties, depth of overburden, and general mining approach are elements in the design of the unit operations of overburden removal, or stripping. A variety of systems can be used to expose the coal seam for extraction. These depend on the physical and chemical characteristics of the overburden, and the production or stripping rate desired. Of primary concern is the overburden thickness. This variable often determines the dimensions of the pit. Of addditional importance is the strength and composition of the overburden. These factors affect the choice of excavating machinery and determine whether blasting is required.

4. SEAM PROPERTIES

Seam properties, on the same order as overburden properties, are elements to the design of the unit operation of coal handling. In both overburden removal and coal handling, thick and easily dug material may be directly loaded by large-scale equipment such as stripping shovels or draglines. Thin or hard material must be drilled and blasted, and handled by smaller systems such as loader-truck or small shovel-truck applications. Easily dug material, or even material which must be blasted but will break uniformly and predictably in size, is handled by the earth-moving giants, shovels, draglines, and bucket-wheel excavators.

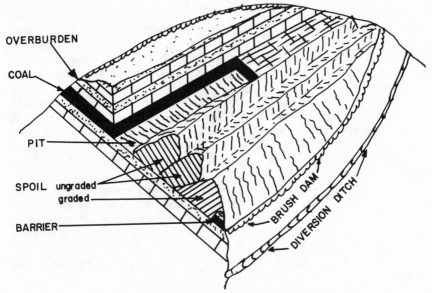

OVERBURDEN

COAL

PIT

SPOIL ungraded
      graded

BARRIER

BRUSH DAM

DIVERSION DITCH

Fig. 5—Mountain-top removal.

D. Biological Characterization

1. PLANTS AND ANIMALS

Plants and animals common to the mining area should be studied from several perspectives. The number of species present and the population of each species help in gauging the absolute stability of a life system and its degree of development, and may be useful in predicting the ability of a system to respond to lowered environmental quality. Air and land animals may be in the classes of economic, unique, or endangered species and require specific consideration. The mine planner is more concerned, however, with the plant community on the land and with the lant and animal life of streams and lakes he may be affecting. The existing plant community may be used as a guideline for revegetation, and efforts in reclamation may be directed to establishing a climax floral biome. Aquatic studies reveal the self-purification capabilities of waters which may receive discharge and, hence, the level of discharge contamination which could be accepted.

2. SOCIO-HUMANISTIC FACTORS

Socio-humanistic factors are hard to define. They are emotional and qualitative, not the logical numbers with which engineers prefer to work. Nonetheless, a good planner must consider the population profile and attitudes of the public, current uses of the land, and any plans for future land use which have been made.

Public attitudes and other characteristics of the population determine whether mining is desired or how well it may be accepted compared to other present and future land uses. Work ethics and current employment influence the availability of a work force. Aesthetic or historic value of the land may be so great that the public will exert every political pressure available to control mining with laws, regulations, prohibitions, or zoning restrictions.

Current land-use forms are usually the objectives of reclamation. However, the planner may find it desirable to follow the pattern of use rather than absolute, original restoration. Forested hillside land adjoining a pasture may be more desirable as a pasture after mining, or orphaned mined land in a wilderness area may be more worthwhile if reclaimed as a forest.

Future land-use plans contrary to premining use are not generally provided for in laws and regulations. These may call for completely changing the existing environment and require a variance from the laws. An example is that of mountain top-removal mining, which leaves flat areas suitable for urbanization. In many cases, subdivision development or recreational uses may be greatly enhanced and assisted by the mining activity.

III. IDENTIFICATION OF POSTMINING
ALTERNATIVE LAND USES

A. General Approaches

Identifying current and future land uses can be expanded to include specific postmining uses. Details of short- and long-term alternatives must be assessed to assure that the necessary planning steps are taken.

B. Short-Term Uses

The immediate and short-term uses for virtually any mined land are agricultural, as most states require reclamation by planting prior to release of bond. With rare exception, a mining company must reclaim and rehabilitate to a specified, near-natural, though not specifically agricultural, state before proceeding to any long-term use. The best approach to defining short-term postmining use, then, is to key the use to long-term development plans.

C. Long-Term Uses

Long-term postmining land use is generally expected to be on at least as high a level as that use prior to mining. Obviously, the definition of level of land use is subjective. It is perhaps more appropriate to consider levels of postmining and long-term uses to be those that are as acceptable to those parties involved as the premining uses.

Predominant land uses in current mining areas are agriculture, wildlife habitat, and/or recreation. These may be simple to re-form in the postmining state. From a mining engineer's perspective there are five general levels of involvement to which the land could be committed in the future. These are, in ascending order of level of involvement,

1) "Wilderness," or unimproved use;
2) Limited agriculture or recreation, with little development, such as grazing, hunting or fishing; timber land;
3) Developed agriculture or recreation, such as crop land, water sports, and vacation resorts;
4) Suburban dwelling or light commercial and light industry; and
5) Urban dwelling or heavy commercial and heavy industry.

It is interesting to note that more intense involvement, such as suburban and urban development, with which higher land value is typically associated, usually requires drastic land disturbance. The reclamation steps to such end use are generally less expensive and involved. Most of the cost and effort is in the installation of new use. In contrast, to return a previously wilderness area to a near-wilderness state may require extensive restoration and rehabilitation efforts at high cost to the mining company.

It may then be of definite economic advantage to plan an alternative future use at high-intensity level. The cost of reclamation as a mining process can be minimized. High intensity use ensures relief of the mining company from long-term responsibility. In many cases, such a goal is a part of preplanning, and is accepted as the ultimate definition of preplanning. However, the social value of a shopping center or residential area in the middle of nowhere is questionable.

Delineation of alternative long-term uses, then, requires compliance with socio-economic and public constraints as well as with goals of the mining company. In recognition of public welfare, governments are developed to exercise collective-action mechanisms: laws, regulations, and planning and zoning, in general. A complication exists, however, in that no comprehensive federal base exists for such actions, and few state acts have been adopted. Such laws are primarily at the county or municipal levels, where logistics, finances, and technological capabilities may be limited.

Planning goals in determining acceptable long-range alternatives will vary according to the incentives of government. In the most rigorous of cases, the alternatives may be extremely limited by zoning restrictions or predetermined long-range land use plans for the region. In the least restrictive cases, virtually any alternative may be acceptable on a legal basis. In either case, the alternatives will usually have varying degrees of acceptability to the public.

From a practical viewpoint, the process defies specific detailing. The long-term use must be linked to the mining plan in space, time, and concept. Such linking is perhaps achieved by minimizing disturbance unnecessary for the determined future use, and minimizing those reclamation activities that are not a part of the normal mining process.

IV. ANALYSIS OF METHODS NEEDED TO ACHIEVE IDENTIFIED SHORT- AND LONG-TERM USES

A. Types of Feasibility

The acceptability of a given use plan is limited by two considerations. The proposal must be technologically feasible, that is, the engineering design must be consistent with the capabilities of men and equipment. In addition, the project must be economically feasible, that is, there is a limit to the capital investment and operating expenses which can be met by the company. The analysis of such considerations may be divided into two aspects: technical feasbility studies and economic feasibility studies.

B. Technical Feasibility Studies

1. TECHNICAL FEASIBILITY

Technical feasibility requires achieving future land use plans which can be developed concurrently and integrally with mining. In any pollution-control development, add-on methods are insufficient in the long run; meaningful control is achieved through systematic design. If mining, as an activity, leaves disorganized chaos, then reclamation efforts are generally limited to short-term and cosmetic screening of that chaos. If mining leaves a firm foundation, or restoration of integrity, then a positive reclamation can develop from such an orderly base. The technical aspects of rehabilitation and restoration develop the foundation, frame the future land use, and combine with a long-term program to finish and maintain the structure.

2. MINING-RECLAMATION REQUIREMENTS

Mining-reclamation requirements for possible land-use alternatives will vary with the desired type and degree of restoration. In most cases, toxic material must be segregated and sealed so that it will be innoccuous in the future. Other less desirable material such as boulders or impermeable clays may be hidden in a like manner. A definitive restoration or adaptation of surface contour will be required. Some material must be replaced to serve as a topsoil or surface-covering layer. It is usually necessary to amend the topsoil with fertilizer, mulch, and other conditioning agents to enhance growth. The goal of premining planning and scheduling is to develop such steps as an integral part of the mining method.

In the standard surface mining approaches of today, selective replacement of material is relatively simple. Contour mining approaches such as block-cut, box-cut, haul-back, mountain-top removal and modified area mining are generally flexible enough to allow segregation and selective replacement. (Characteristics of these methods are reviewed in

Chapter 14 of this book, "Surface Mining—A Review of Practices and Progress in Land Disturbance Control," by R. V. Ramani and E. C. Grim). Larger scale methods such as area mining are less flexible; however, careful control of overburden handling should allow selectivity in backfilling.

The question of restoration vs. adaption of contour is one which is decided by the general mining approach. In strict contour mining, in which the seam is followed around a hill, the restoration to approximate original contour with excess spoil disposal in valley fills is generally most appropriate. In mountain top-removal mining, the result is a flat land area. If large areas of flat land are not particularly desired, the indicated approach may be to restore some degree of relief by practicing modified area mining. Small hills, terraces, and shallow hollows may enhance future use potential for grazing or wildlife purposes. Area mining restoration is almost exclusively to original contour in areas of Ohio and west where premining use is for crops. In areas such as western Pennsylvania, the agricultural value of lands, however, may be greatly increased by changing steeply rolling mining lands to a more tillable topography.

The concerns of backfilling address two major areas of long-term concern: (i) slopes and stability (by both mass failure and surface erosion) and (ii) water quality maintenance. In reality, these two aspects become inseparable. The primary source of slope failure is the prolonged action of water, through erosion, and mass wasting. The primary result of water's actions on slopes is erosion and sediment production. One of the primary concerns of water quality control is sediment.

The interconnection of stability and erosion control is enhanced by apparently conflicting approaches to these problems. Gross stability is enhanced by establishing grade and cover to minimize infiltration and permeation. Conversely, erosion and sediment control are achieved by encouraging infiltration and permeation to minimize runoff. A third complicating factor is that prevention of acid drainage may require either basic approach, depending on the particulars of the situation.

The proper approach would entail, first, the establishment of as heavy a cover crop after backfilling as possible, to encourage vegetative interception and evapotranspiration as opposed to surface or subsurface runoff. However, not all of the water can be handled in this manner. Provision must be made for storms by designing clean-running interceptions and diversions for excessive rainfall. Stability and subsurface quality are inherent in the design of fills and backfills. If a suitable, large-rock drainage base and contact zone is established at the base contact of the fill, slippage can be minimized while rapid drainage of ground water is enhanced. Figure 6 presents a typical design for a backfill section with toxic material present. Notice that there are two possible piezometric surfaces for ground water flow, both of which are isolated from the toxic material.

Such approaches to water quality and the control of stability are exemplified by the head-of-hollow or valley-fill concept (Fig. 7). Since the valley fill is, presumptively, the most stably designed of any surface-mining backfill operations, the considerations of its design present the concepts to be employed in any backfilling operation. While these plans

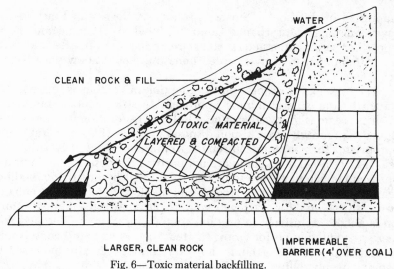

LARGER, CLEAN ROCK

IMPERMEABLE
BARRIER (4' OVER COAL)

Fig. 6—Toxic material backfilling.

are included in Chapter 14 of this book (Ramani and Grim), they are reviewed here also.

The first step in construction of a valley fill is to scalp the area to be filled of vegetation and to remove topsoil. By clearing to a predominantly mineral soil or rock base, the greatest cohesive contact can be achieved to minimize slope failure. Next, rock-filled or French drains are constructed in all natural drainages to assure that water travelling along its natural path will minimally contact fine and toxic material. Then, the fill is brought up, not by dumping from the top but by layering in 4-foot lifts from the toe of the fill and working back to the valley wall, as in Fig. 7. As the fill is raised, the French drains are raised with the fill to provide a relatively clean drainway for stormwater runoff. The bringing up in layers, which are compacted, provides for a heterogeneous fill with greater stability as compared to the physically and hydrologically less stable mixing of fines on solids which occurs if dumping is from the top, as in Fig. 8. Final finishing with minimal (2 to 1) outslopes, terraces, and a crowned top bench should assure that normal water will innoccuously infiltrate while storm water runoff can be cleanly diverted. As a final precaution, of course, a sediment catchment basin is usually constructed at the toe of the hill. Such construction is the ultimate for any backfill method, but may be excessive for simple area mining.

Replacement of topsoil is practiced in mining where required by regulations. It may be either directly specified or required to develop postmining vegetation. An interesting question to be raised is *what is topsoil?* Despite all of the answers that could be given, is there a definition of topsoil, for mining-regulation purposes, which would be upheld in a court of law? In southern Illinois, the question may be quite easy to answer. In eastern Kentucky and southern West Virginia, however, a distinct topsoil is often lacking, and growth may be as good or better in the 'B' and lower horizons; therefore, in a mining engineering sense, the dictum of topsoil replacement could best be viewed as a requirement to re-

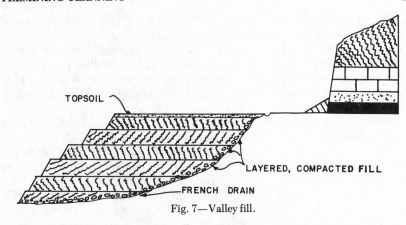

TOPSOIL

LAYERED, COMPACTED FILL

FRENCH DRAIN

Fig. 7—Valley fill.

place or establish a layer of material of specific thickness, having certain physical and chemical characteristics and, primarily, capable of supporting some specific vegetation. In premining planning, attention is to be directed at identifying all strata potentially adaptable as such a surface covering. If topsoil replacement is required by law, and a topsoil is limited or not available, such synthetic topsoil should be placed on top of the spoil immediately under such top-covering as is available.

Extensive or exotic soil amendments are avoided by the mining industry because of the cost involved. Common approaches involve the addition of lime, mulch, and fertilizer only as needed. In some cases, it may be necessary to add "exotic" materials to the soil to enhance revegetation, but such requirements are generally determined through extensive services or consultants.

Many mulches have been used to assist in establishing vegetative cover. Straw or hay can be manually applied but they, as well as wood chips, are often spread mechanically or hydropneumatically. Rapid-

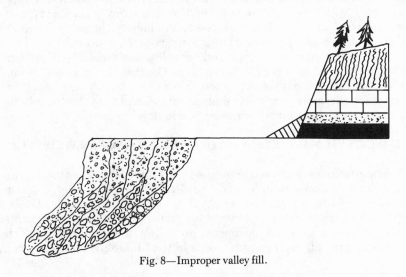

Fig. 8—Improper valley fill.

growing annual plants and small grains can be used to establish ground cover, to leave organic matter in the soil, and to serve as a mulch for perennial establishment. While the past practices of mine operators neglected such steps, often the practice today is to establish quick-cover/mulch crops prior to topsoiling, thus assuring vegetative stabilization and enhancing the organic content and water-holding capability of the surface layer.

Fly ash, the residue of coal-fired boilers, can be applied to increase nutrients, moisture, and alkalinity and to ameliorate toxic materials present. The trace elements contained in fly ash are often important micronutrients; fly ash is also rich in the common macronutrients except for nitrogen. Nitrogen deficiency can be handled by planting legumes such as inoculated clover (*Trifolium* L.), alfalfa (*Medicago sativa* L.), and vetch (*Vicia* L.). The use of fly ash may be particularly attractive when a power plant is located at or near the mine, since the ash must be disposed of in some manner anyway (Adams, 1971).

Stabilized sewage sludge is another recyclable amendment to reclaimed mined land. Sludge is rich in nutrients and may reduce acidity as well as provide stable organic matter to form a humus. A related type of amendment is composting with municipal waste, which has been practiced in other countries but has seen limited application in the United States. Care must be taken, however, to avoid poisoning the soil with too high a level of heavy metals and salt from the sludge (Grim & Hill, 1974).

Natural or volunteer revegetation is slow to develop, as the spoils are likely to be low in nutrients, perhaps toxic, and the surrounding vegetation is usually mature, established, and a poor source of seeds. The extent of amendments should be based on rapid establishment of a cover crop and the continuation of cover, once established, to assure control of water quality.

All plans for reclamation should be approved, of course, by the responsible permitting agency. Proper attention to segregation, backfilling and grading, topsoil restoration, and amendments to establish a rapid cover crop which will ultimately yield to dominant species maximizes these efforts. Currently, however, the technology is limited so far as the reclamation of arid or semi-arid lands in the west are concerned.

Assuming proper restoration and rehabilitation are achieved, rededication of the land may require more time. Grazing, for example, should not be allowed immediately on a new cover crop. In any case, establishment of long-term use is not definitely accomplished at the end of mining, but may require long-term maintenance and development.

3. LONG-TERM MAINTENANCE TO SUPPORT LONGER LIVED USES

Long-term maintenance to support longer lived uses consists of monitoring slopes to assure stability and of controlling water quality. Slope instability is one long-term problem that is difficult to reconcile. Once a slope has failed it is virtually impossible to return the fill to a permanently stable form. As mentioned previously, proper attention to drainage of the fill area and the physical considerations of the fill are the key elements in stability. If these factors are not closely and carefully planned, long-term stability will be questionable.

Even in the best efforts of surface restoration there is a likelihood of local, minor, and shallow failure. Of course, the common-sense approach is to keep all surfaces as minimally sloped as possible and certainly under the angle of repose. Parallel slumping or minor ravine formation is corrected by refilling, compacting, and rapid establishment of cover. Another mitigating action may be to place interceptor and diversion channels to reduce downslope flow while local instabilities are being corrected.

Where the coal mine drainage phenomenon cannot be prevented, a long-term program to neutralize the discharge will be necessary. In most surface-mining situations much of the necessary layout will be present in sediment-control ponds. What is required is a mechanism for the addition of limestone, lime, anhydrous ammonia (where no discharge to surface drainage is encountered), soda ash, sodium hydroxide, or other suitable neutralizing reagent. Good planning to minimize acid formation through isolation of toxic material and concurrent backfilling is still the best approach to the control of acid coal-mine drainage.

One other aspect of long-term commitments is the maintenance of sediment and erosion control installations. With appropriate planning and no unusual storms, such problems may be minimal. However, control structures may become clogged or filled. Provisions for postmining cleaning and clearing should be included in the premining plan. Various laws require that ponds over certain maximum depths must be inspected regularly, and this factor may limit their planned size. Sediment ponds should be sized with downstream communities in mind.

C. Economic Feasibility Studies

Mining is performed by companies. Their intention is to maximize the wealth of the company, typically by achieving a maximum return on investment. In the system of analysis as explained in the introduction to this chapter, it is apparent that the goal of the planning engineer is to

Table 1—Sample reclamation costs in the Monongahela River Basin (Doyle et al., 1974)

Item	Cost†
Backfilling and grading	$ 3,100/ha
Refuse bank contouring and grading	$ 2,470/ha
Soil cover for graded refuse bank	$ 6,175/ha
Refuse bank removal and burial	$ 1.30/m^3
Soil cover at burial site	$ 0.61/m^2
Clearing and grubbing	$ 740/ha
Revegetation	$ 750–775/ha
Mine drainage treatment plant:	
Capital cost, where Q = m^3 per second flow	$153,345 × $Q^{0.72}$
Operation cost	$ 0.0534/m^3 treated

† 1 ha = 2.48 acres; 1 m^3 = 1.31 yd^3; 1 m^2 = 1.19 yd^2; 1 m^{3}s^{-1} = 2.28 million gallons per day.

maximize economic return to the company consistent with the constraints and incentives of the public and the government. At the mine level, the planner must consider the direct cash costs (Table 1) of reclamation, the internal costs, as well as the real-money returns he expects. On a company level, the planner must consider the constraining aspects of the public welfare, the external and sometimes noncash costs and benefits of his operation.

The consideration by benefit-cost analysis of internal, direct costs and income from mineral sales is the traditional approach to engineering planning. If, however, premining planning is truly to maximize effective land use and reclamation, it is necessary for the planner to alter the scope of investigation to include the socio-humanistic benefits and costs as are currently bargained through mining-reclamation regulations. This goal cannot be reached by the traditional and all too quantitative engineering approach; qualitative analysis and subjectivity are required. The premining planner certainly must carefully assess all of the hard-data aspects of his operation, but must consider present use, desired future use, and the intensity and locality of preference of alternative uses. By linking a mining plan with concurrent restoration and rehabilitation to provide a maximum of social welfare through present use as mining, reclamation, and commitment to best alternative future use, the planner can truly realize such maximization.

LITERATURE CITED

Adams, L. M., J. P. Capp, and E. Eisentrout. 1971. Reclamation of acidic coal mine spoil with fly ash. Rep. of Investig. no. 7504, U.S. Bur. of Mines. U.S. Government Printing Office, Washington, D.C.

Branson, C. C. 1962. Pennsylvania system of central Appalachians. p. 97–117. In Pennsylvania System in the United States—a Symposium. Am. Assoc. of Petroleum Geologists.

Doyle, F. J., H. G. Bhatt, and J. R. Rapp. 1974. Analysis of pollution control costs. Environ. Prot. Technol. Ser. no. EPA-670/2-74-009. USEPA, U.S. Government Printing Office, Washington, D.C.

Grim, E. C., and R. D. Hill. 1974. Environmental protection in surface mining of coal. Environ. Prot. Technol. Ser. no. EPA-670/2-74-093. USEPA, U.S. Government Printing Office, Washington, D.C.

U.S. Bureau of Mines. 1975. The reserve base of U.S. coals by sulfur content (1. The eastern states). U.S. Bur. of Mines Circ. 8680. U.S. Government Printing Office, Washington, D.C.

SUGGESTED ADDITIONAL REFERENCES

Goldberg, E. F., and Garrett Power. 1972. Legal problems of coal mine reclamation. Water Pollut. Control Res. Ser. 14010 FZU 03/72, USEPA, U.S. Government Printing Office, Washington, D.C.

Skelly and Loy, Engineers–Consultants. 1975. Economic engineering analysis of U.S. surface coal mines and effective land reclamation. U.S. Bur. of Mines Contract Rep. no. S0241049. Skelly and Loy, Harrisburg, Pa.

Copyright © 1978 ASA–CSSA–SSSA
677 South Segoe Road, Madison, WI 53711 USA
Reclamation of Drastically Disturbed Lands

Chapter 14

Surface Mining—A Review of Practices and Progress in Land Disturbance Control

R. V. RAMANI AND ELMORE C. GRIM

The Pennsylvania State University, University Park, Pennsylvania, and Division of Forestry, Frankfort, Kentucky, respectively

I. INTRODUCTION

Mining, perhaps with the exception of agriculture, is the most basic of all industries. Even in agriculture, much of the fertilizer consists of minerals initially mined and processed and finally enriched to the chemical form. In fact, it is doubtful that there is any aspect of human life as it exists today which does not require the products of mining. Exploitation of mineral resources is a must if better standards of living are to be attained, since mining affects practically every other phase of industrialization, and provides the basics for sustained growth. There are some fundamental differences between mineral resources and other resources. These are that the mineral riches are highly localized, limited, and nonrenewable, and that as long as they are in the ground they serve a very limited purpose.

In the most elementary form, mining is materials handling. It is a process of extracting in situ material (solid, liquid, or gas) from the crust or bowels of the earth. In this sense, removal of gas and oil from underground chambers and the recovery of subterranean water can be considered as mining. In this chapter, however, the discussion will be limited to mining of the solid resources, not so much because the other two forms are in any way less important, but because most minerals—both metallic and nonmetallic—are found and mined in the solid state.

Decisions on whether an ore body will be mined or not, and the mining method to be practiced on a given ore body, depend on many technological, economic, and social factors. The various mining methods can be classified as surface or underground depending on whether the ore body is recovered from operations on the surface of the earth, or from operations in underground openings, approached from suitably located surface openings. More often, technological factors constrain the mining engineer to a single mining method and the economic and social factors determine whether the deposit can be mined at all. While there are many environmental considerations similar to both types of mining, this chapter will address itself only to surface mining. The importance of surface

241

mining can hardly be overemphasized. It is known that over 90% of the mined products are obtained through this method. In fact, more than 75% of the land affected by surface-mining is the result of surface mining of coal, crushed stone, and sand and gravel. In subsequent sections of this chapter, land considerations and surface mining equipment and methods are briefly covered. The section on mining methods includes an extended discussion on some recent innovative methods for improved land utilization in surface coal mining.

II. LAND CONSIDERATIONS

Competition for land for soil and water, living space, recreation, and industry is becoming more intense. Mineral exploration, development, extraction, and processing all have different impacts and conflict with these essential uses. More importantly, because of the very nature of the nonrenewability of a mineral deposit, mining is necessarily a temporary activity, to be abandoned sooner or later. Therefore, it is necessary to be concerned with the concurrent and sequential land use for optimum land utilization. The allocation of land for agriculture, forest, wildlife, urban growth, recreation, transportation, and so forth is compounded by political, economic, sociological, and ecological considerations, and when some of these lands hold mineral riches, the big question is: *How can one mine these riches without impairing the utility values for satisfying land demands during and after mining?* While this is too frequently interpreted as a problem, it should also be recognized as an opportunity to remold the surface for a desirable end-use.

Land disturbances from surface mining can be substantial unless adequate preventive measures are taken. The problem has grown to enormous proportions in recent years, for the following technological reasons: as easily mineable and richer deposits are fast being extracted and, in some cases, completely exhausted, attention has been directed towards mining larger tracts of lower-grade, higher-cost deposits. In strip-mining, the ratio of overburden thickness to that of coal has been increasing. In either case, current operations are involved with handling more material, and often from greater depths, than theretofore. The need to exploit vast reserves with thick cover and heavy relief has resulted in the development of larger and more powerful equipment which can displace and remove enormous amounts of materials at a much faster rate.

Land damages that are cited against surface mining are mainly due to the destruction of surface topographies and soil conditions that existed before mining commenced. Oftentimes, the potential productivity of the soil for plant growth as compared to that of the soil prior to mining is greatly reduced. Soils that are are churned up by these operations are often chemically active, and toxic, thereby becoming a source for water pollution. In fact, the cast overburden (spoil) resulting from surface mining does not resemble any type of soil that has been classified by the Agricultural Experiment Stations (Sawyer & Crowe, 1968). Also, if the overburden is a massive rock formation, huge blocks of rock occur in the graded spoil which make it difficult for the smooth passage of farm machinery. Much larger areas are also affected by the unconsolidated spoil heaps and voids. These conditions affect drainage patterns. Here the natural processes of erosion and sedimentation are accelerated, often moving huge volumes of soil into receiving streams. When not properly guarded and maintained against dumping waste and refuse, these sites become potential health hazards. Finally, the steep walls created as a result of thick burdens and heavy relief, coupled with the possibility of ground movement with lapse of time, present a safety hazard in inhabited neighborhoods. A much larger area may also be affected by the associated haulroads, and by preparation and processing plants.

Since an extensive coverage of this subject is presented elsewhere (Grim & Hill, 1974; Ramani, 1974), an abstract of the major environmental effects due to the various surface mining unit operations is presented in Table 1. Surface mining without control results in serious blights and hazards to public health, contaminates air and water resources, adversely affects land values, creates public nuisances, and generally interferes with community development. In fact, the controversy with regard to surface mining of coal is so intense that some concerned persons are seeking a complete ban on strip-mining of coal and recommend substitution of coal stripping with a greater amount of underground mining. However, there are certain factors in favor of surface mining as opposed to underground mining, viz:

1) Workmen's health and safety aspects are better in surface mining than in underground mining;
2) Surface mining is economically more attractive because of less equipment, capital, and manpower needed, and generally lower lead times to start;
3) Technologically, in shallow covers, underground mining may not be feasible;
4) Environmentally, the effects of surface mining are known and can be controlled, but the long-term effects of underground mining on subsidence and water problems are difficult to assess and predict (Stefanko et al., 1973).

Rehabilitation of surface-mined lands is, however, a tangible program. In fact, strip-mined land, abandoned open-pits, and spoil and waste piles are being shaped and graded, and stabilized and seeded, and reverted back to productive use with proper care and management. Mined area spoil banks that can be revegetated present minor problems, and have great potential for development. Various reclamation programs that are being actively pursued include returning the ground for agricultural and livestock farming, for reforestation, for recreation, and for housing and industrial sites. The possibilities for development under these conditions are limited only by one's imagination. On the other hand, marginal and problem spoils require greater attention. In many areas, local, state, and federal governments have several environmental standards which the mining industry has to meet. In addition to the Federal Strip Mining Legislation, new or amended surface-mine regulations are in force in more than 35 states. Whether there is a law or not, the importance of good mining practices that will make provisions to minimize, if not eliminate, the environmental damages, can hardly be overemphasized.

III. SURFACE MINING EQUIPMENT

The history of surface mining equipment, particularly the excavation machinery, is not very clearly defined. When strip-mining began in Danville, Illinois, in 1866, the overburden was removed by horsedrawn plows and scrapers, and hauled away in wheelbarrows and carts—a far cry from the excavation equipment in use today which is capable of handling several thousand cubic meters of material per hour. At the present time, production rates at many surface mining operations are dwarfing those of the Panama Canal and other well-known earth moving projects which are frequently identified as massive undertakings.

Several pieces of equipment are used in a surface mining operation. The power shovel is a widely used piece of equipment. There are two types of shovels currently used as mining tools: the stripping shovel (Fig. 1) and the quarry-mine (or loading) shovel (Fig. 2). The common method of shovel application in stripping overburden for coal overcasting is shown in Fig. 3. The shovel usually sits in the pit, digs the bank, and de-

Fig. 1—A 95-m³ stripping shovel.

Table 1—Potential major effects of surface mining unit operations on land, water and air resources

Surface mining unit operations:

1. Exploration
2. Area dewatering diversion, etc.
3. Drilling
4. Blasting
5. Stripping (overburden removal)
6. Haulage
7. Top soil or other soil storage
8. Maintenance
9. Beneficiation

Resource	Effect	1	2	3	4	5	6	7	8	9
Land and soil	Soil erosion	*	*				*	*		
	Overburden swelling				*					
	Toxic strata	*	*				*			
	Soil inversion				*					
	Soil stability				*					
	Landslides			*						
	Spoil piles					*	*			
	Oil spills		*	*					*	
	Coal spills					*				
Water	Aquifer effects	*		*	*					
	Runoff alteration			*	*	*				
	Sediments	*				*	*			
	Toxic substances	*							*	
	Groundwater contamination	*					*		*	
	Industrial effluents								*	
	Sludge								*	
Air	Exhaust emissions	*			*	*		*		
	Dust	*	*	*	*	*	*	*	*	
	Noise	*	*	*	*	*	*	*	*	*
	Other (welding, etc.)						*		*	
	Blasting fumes				*					
Wildlife	Habitat altered	*			*	*		*		
	Species diversity					*				
	Aquatic life					*				
	Animal essentials					*				
	Accident/Deaths					*	*			
	Soil organisms					*	*	*		
	Vegetation potential							*		
	Wildlife disturbed	*			*	*	*		*	*
Other	Aesthetic				*		*		*	*
	Dangerous material				*				*	

Fig. 2—A loading shovel fills a truck.

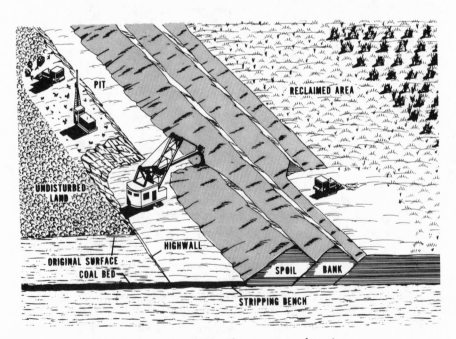

Fig. 3—Area strip mining with concurrent reclamation.

posits the overburden in the adjacent mined-out area. The ability of the shovel to spoil the material is the limiting factor in a given deposit. The quarry-mine shovel is carefully sized according to the capacity of the haul units into which it will be dumping its load. The haul units usually are large off-highway trucks.

Draglines are the most common stripping equipment used in surface mining of coal. As opposed to the shovel, it operates on the surface and has a greater range of spoiling (Fig. 4). The largest shovels and draglines in operation today have bucket capacities of 140 and 170 m³, respectively. Today draglines are becoming more popular than shovels. Draglines provide greater flexibility, work on higher bench heights, and move more cover per hour.

While shovels and draglines are cyclic equipment, bucket wheel excavators are continuous excavation machines capable of removing up to 12,000 m³/hour. Wheel excavators hold considerable promise where conditions are favorable. Ideally, this machine has the capability for continuous overburden removal, and selective placement of the soil and strata (Fig. 5). In the United States, wheel excavators usually operate in tandem with another major stripping machine (Fig. 6).

Fig. 4—A 90-m³ dragline with a 90-m boom. Note the coal-loading shovel and truck in the pit.

Fig. 5—Bucket wheel excavator, dragline, coal-loading shovel, trucks, and a dozer ripper are employed in this operation.

Fig. 6—An operation in Illinois using bucket wheel excavator, stripping shovel, loading shovel, and trucks.

Drilling for fragmentation is commonly done with rotary type units capable of hole diameters from 14 to 40 cm with vertical drilling more common (Fig. 7). However, horizontal side wall drilling has been introduced in several coal stripping operations.

There are several methods of material transportation from the pit. Off-highway trucks are the most commonly used haulage vehicle. These vehicles are obtainable with bottom dump, rear dump, or side dump capability. In surface coal mines, where the overburden is hauled away, the rear-dump trucks are commonly employed, whereas it is common to employ bottom-dump trucks for coal transportation. Trucks are available in sizes varying from 35 tons to 350 tons. The various possible combinations of the different equipment available for the extraction of a deposit are shown in Fig. 8.

Fig. 7—A rotary drill for overburden drilling.

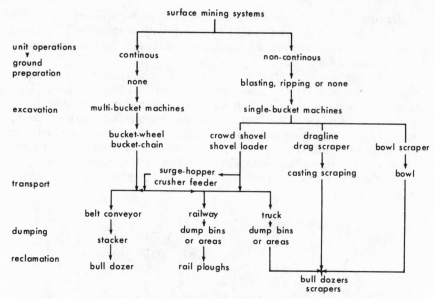

Fig. 8—Equipment application for surface mining systems (Atkinson, 1971).

IV. METHODS OF SURFACE MINING

Surface mining is a very broad term and refers to the removal of the soil and strata over a mineral or a fuel deposit to remove the deposit itself. It is conducted in a relatively simple sequence of operations which includes the unit operations of: (i) scalping the surface, (ii) drilling, (iii) blasting, (iv) stripping or overburden removal, including waste haulage, (v) ore (or coal) loading, (vi) ore (or coal) haulage, and (vii) reclamation. Other operations include building drainage systems, waste handling, and top soil storage. Associated with the mining operations are plants for beneficiation, such as mineral processing or coal preparation plants.

The mining techniques for a particular region are largely dictated by the geologic and topographic conditions, and may not include all the unit operations mentioned above. Even where the techniques are comparable generally, equipment choices and the mode of operation may not be the same. Surface-mining techniques can be broadly classified into contour mining, area strip mining, and open-pit mining. Other methods include auger mining, quarrying, pit mining, hydraulic mining, and dredging. A brief discussion of each of the methods, generally following the description given by Imhoff et al. (1976), is provided in this section.

A. Open-Pit Mining

Open-pit mines are used primarily to extract metallic minerals from near-surface ore bodies. Generally there are two basic types of open-pit operation. One involves the reduction of a hill or a large mound

Fig. 9—Open-pit copper mine in Arizona, near Tucson (Photo: U.S. Geological Survey).

containing ore. The other involves the digging out of a hole containing the ore below ground. The mines in the latter category (Fig. 9) tend to be deep—some in excess of 300 m. As one works down, the pit floor becomes narrower. Mining usually continues uninterrupted for many years and produces large amounts of waste rock and *tailing*, the term for the finely ground waste rock and chemically leached material from which valuable minerals have been extracted. With mines in the former case, the operating floor of the pit widens as one works down the hill from the top.

Reclamation of open-pit mines is difficult because of the constraints represented by: (i) large volumes of wastes (up to 90% of material mined in copper mines is waste); (ii) sharp differences in physical and chemical characteristics of wastes from the same pit; and (iii) the deep excavation left when mining is concluded. Large acreages of land—sometimes hundreds of acres per mine—are used for waste disposal. Reclamation of tailing ponds is difficult because of the fine-grained nature of the waste, which tends to become windblown when dry and physically unstable when wet. Because of textural and chemical problems, tailings are difficult to revegetate, though revegetation has been accomplished on some of the wastes from open-pit mines. Coarse rock wastes are sometimes used as aggregate, and overburden has been used for agriculture. Active open pits, as compared to area coal mines, provide fewer opportunities for simultaneous mining and reclamation because of inherent conflicts in land use that prevail as long as mining is underway. When mining ceases, the problem of sequential use of the pit is tied primarily to economic feasibility.

Where a thick coal seam is overlain by a shallow cover, it is usually extracted by open-pit mining methods. Some of the reserves in the Western United States are recovered by open-pit coal mining. Shown in Fig. 10 is the method of operation in an open-pit coal mine in Wyoming where pan scrapers remove overburden with the assistance of bulldozers. The dozer pushes the scrapers downgrade during the loading operations at point A and another dozer pushes the scraper dumped material into the mined-out area of the pit at point B, thereby ensuring concurrent reclamation.

B. Quarrying

Quarries are used to extract stone for ornamental and building purposes or as a source of crushed stone for construction materials or chemicals. Quarries vary considerably in size and depth, depending upon the

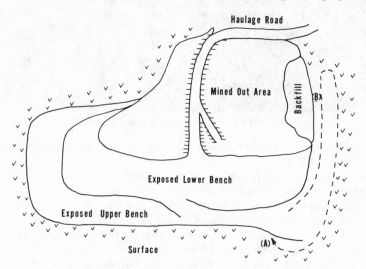

Fig. 10—Plan view of a Wyoming open-pit coal mine.

Fig. 11—Limestone quarry in Wisconsin (Photo: U.S. Geological Survey).

quality, use, and physical characteristics of the rock mined (Fig. 11). Quarries generally are not as deep as open-pit mines, although depths in excess of 60 m are not uncommon. Normally, quarries are active for extended periods of time, some operations continuing for more than 100 years. Waste rock production from quarries is small, and therefore surface disposal of waste is usually not a serious problem. Reclamation of a quarry site commonly is difficult because of steep sides, great depths, and lack of drainage. Reclamation of quarry sites for recreational purposes has the most potential. One state, Pennsylvania, now requires a reclamation plan for all quarries. Most such plans involve turning the quarry into a water impoundment.

C. Pit Mining

Pits are the most common type of excavation for sand, gravel, or clay. They tend to be shallow—rarely exceeding 30 m in depth—and generally have limited surface extent (Fig. 12). The large number of pits is

Fig. 12—Sand and gravel operation near Raleigh, N.C.

the result of the high demand for sand and gravel and the relatively small volume of these materials normally in any one deposit. Most communities are served by one or more sand and gravel pits. Clay pits are dug less frequently than sand and gravel pits but are nonetheless numerous. Relatively little waste is produced by pit mining. Unmarketable overburden or other materials may be bypassed during mining or returned to the pit after processing. The extent of reclamation of pits varies rather directly according to the nearness of urban communities. Urban lands are generally valuable, and reclamation of pits for planned sequential use is often required by local units of government. In the Midwestern United States many pits have been reclaimed for water-oriented residential development.

Fig. 13—Area coal mine in Indiana, showing soil removal underway on left, overburden removal by dragline in the background, coal removal from floor of cut in the center, and ungraded spoil ridges in the right foreground (Photo: U.S. Geological Survey).

D. Area Mining

Area mining is used to extract near-surface bedded deposits in flat-lying terrain. Coal, coastal-plain phosphate, kaolin, and bauxite are most commonly extracted using area mining methods. The overburden is removed from the first cut, followed by removal of the mineral material. A second parallel cut is then made, and the overburden removed is placed into the pit resulting from the first cut. The series of parallel cuts progresses across the property until the depth of overburden and coal or ore characteristics make the mine uneconomic, or until property boundaries are reached (Fig. 3). Some area mines now reach depths of 100 m. Disposal and burial of preparation-plant wastes, power-plant fly ash, and like materials are achieved in some active mining areas. Large tracts of land tend to be disturbed by area mining, but only a narrow tract of land is unreclaimed at any given time (Fig. 13). Area mines have been reclaimed for agricultural, residential, and recreational purposes.

E. Contour Mining

Contour mining is used principally to extract coal that crops out along the sides of steep hills, the mine following the coal seam around the hillside. The overburden above the coal is removed, followed by the coal. Handling of overburden creates problems in contour mining because of the little working space available. Historically, overburden removal involved casting the overburden down hill slopes (Fig. 14). This practice has

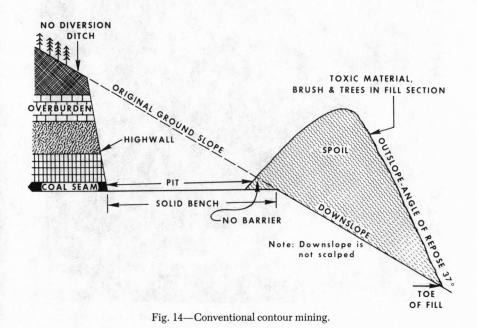

Fig. 14—Conventional contour mining.

come under severe criticism and is no longer practiced. Modern practice emphasizes replacing overburden in the contour mine immediately after coal removal.

F. Auger Mining

Auger mining utilizes cutting heads as large as two meters in diameter that can penetrate several meters in a horizontal direction into a coal seam and extract the coal. Auger mining is used commonly with contour mining to recover reserves of coal from the existing highwall (Fig. 15). When the overburden becomes too thick to allow economical contour stripping to continue, and underground mining would be uneconomical or hazardous, an auger is used to remove additional coal. Auger mining has come under severe criticism from the environmental control point of view, particularly with regard to water pollution. Recent advancements in contour mining (e.g., mountain top-removal method) may be substituted if the reserves are large enough.

Auger mining requires that the last strip cut be left open for access of equipment and removal of the coal. Thus, the final reclamation of the

Fig. 15—Auger used to drill laterally into a coal bed exposed in contour mining.

contour mine must be delayed until extraction of coal by the auger is complete.

G. Dredge Mining

Dredge mining involves the continuous removal and processing of unconsolidated mineral deposits. The dredge is basically a floating platform (Fig. 16) containing continuous digging or suction equipment to extract the mineral, and processing equipment to segregate and remove the valuable mineral fraction. Dredges are used in the United States to mine sand and gravel deposits and placer gold deposits where water is available to float a dredge. Dredging of sand and gravel results commonly in creation of a lake, as most of the excavated material is removed for sale. Dredging for gold, however, results in removal of but a minute portion of the material handled by the dredge. Waste disposal and subsequent reclamation of gold-dredged land is a considerable problem because waste material from gold dredging is stacked behind the dredge, creating spoil piles not unlike those of area mining. Reclamation of this waste is difficult be-

Fig. 16—Dredge mining for gold near Yuba City, Calif. (Photo: Sacramento Bee, Sacramento, Calif.).

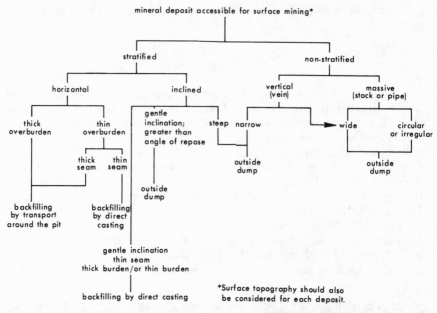

Fig. 17—Influence of geological factors in surface-mine design (Thomas, 1973).

cause of the gravelly nature of the waste, lack of topsoil to reestablish plant growth after mining, and potential for flooding due to the location of most dredging operations in stream beds and valley floors.

H. Summary

The influence of geological factors, particularly the dip, the thickness of the deposit, and the thickness of the cover, are determining factors in the selection of a method. This is clearly brought out in Fig. 17.

While broad generalizations are not always correct, some seem to hold with regard to coal stripping. Contour mining is widely practiced in the steep hills and rolling terrains of the eastern U.S. In the interior region, area mining is more predominant. In the West, mostly shallow overburden and thick coal seams in a semiarid climate are mined by area and open-pit methods.

V. MODERN MINING METHODS FOR LAND-USE ENHANCEMENT

One of the findings of the Department of Interior's study, *Surface Mining and Our Environment* (1967), is that "some damage from surface mining is inevitable even with the best mining and land restoration methods. But much can be done to prevent damage and to reclaim mined lands. . . Basic reclamation comprises remedial measures necessary to alleviate or eliminate conditions . . . such as: erosion, flooding, water pollution, damage to aquatic and wildlife habitat, barriers to access, and hazards to public safety."

While the initial concern from the environmental standpoint was the ability to reclaim the land in a satisfactory manner, today the environmental studies prior to launching a strip mine are much more detailed. For example, Evans and Tate (1975) report that more than $500,000 was spent over a 2-year period to develop base line data on several factors for the Black Thunder surface mine in Wyoming. Such studies point to the recognition of the fact that any attempt to extract nature's wealth involves a change in the physical, biological, social, physiosocial, biosocial, and psychosocial factors. From the initial construction of access facilities to prospect and explore, to the final closing down of mining and beneficiation operations, the ecosystem balance is continually altered. Therefore, to preserve the potential of the land for more permanent utilization, mining systems must be designed such that during and after mining, if the land value cannot be improved, at least adverse environmental impacts can be minimized (Battelle Columbus Lab., 1975).

The future of surface mining, particularly coal stripping, hinges partially upon the ability to reclaim land in a satisfactory manner. Where the environmental impacts cannot be clearly ascertained, it may be that the natural resource should not be mined at all. However, in a majority of instances, knowledge and technology are available to do a better job than heretofore. Fortunately, coal companies, in addition to advancing their inputs to state and federal legislation, are experimenting with several extraction and reclamation techniques. Since conventional contour mining has come under great criticism, several new methods have been proposed and are being practiced on the steep slopes of the eastern United States. Haul-back methods as opposed to conventional overcasting methods have become popular. Haul-back methods provide the flexibility to separate topsoil, segregate toxic materials, and generally facilitate the placement of spoil in a desired sequence. Two important methods in this category are the *Block-cut Method*, and the *Head-of-Hollow Fill Method*. The latter is often associated with yet another method known as the *Mountain Top-Removal Method*.

In the western United States, though direct overcasting with a dragline is more common, other methods have been successfully employed: (i) dozer-scraper combinations, as is commonly employed in major earthmoving and road-construction projects (Fig. 18), and (ii) open-pit type shovel and truck operations. With these two systems, the basic advantage of flexibility and selectivity with regard to overburden placement cannot be overemphasized.

A. Head-of-Hollow Fill and Mountain Top-Removal Methods

The Head-of-Hollow Fill method basically consists of storing the overburden material in narrow, steep-sided valleys according to a well-engineered plan. The Mountain Top-Removal method is an adaptation of

Fig. 18—A pusher-scraper combination for top soil and overburden removal.

the area mining method to contour mining. In this method, the entire mountain tops are removed down to the coal seam in a series of parallel cuts. Excess overburden that cannot be retained on the mined area is transported to Head-of-Hollow Fills, stored on ridges, or placed in natural depressions. In either case, the methods produce plateaus of level, rolling land that may have great value in mountainous terrains. A careful analysis of the cut-and-fill problem associated with both the methods must be done. The overburden generated through the mining operation must completely fill the hollow selected for the purpose. Several cross sections of the hollow fills, sequences of mining and filling, material placement, and haulage road construction deserve critical evaluation.

Several important procedures are followed in adapting the Head-of-Hollow Fill and Mountain Top-Removal methods to a particular area. The head-of-hollow selected for filling is scalped of vegetative cover. Topsoil is removed and stored for later use. Check dams or silt control structures are built downstream from the hollow fill (Fig. 19). The natural drainway in the hollow is deepened. The minimum width recommended for the drain is 4.56 m. A French drain is built in this drainway with rocks not less than 0.36 m in size in any one dimension (Fig. 20 and 21). The fill is built in layers, 1.2 m thick, beginning at the toe of the valley (Fig. 22). The overburden material is deposited in uniform horizontal layers and then compacted with haulage equipment. Each layer of fill is so built that the face of the fill has an outer slope no steeper than two horizontal to one vertical, and usually has crowned terraces (Fig. 23). Some operators have graded the face to approximately 22° from the horizontal, eliminating crowned terraces. However, long slopes without interruptions, such as diversion ditches, are more prone to excessive erosion from surface run-

Fig. 19—A check dam, downstream from a hollow fill.

off; therefore, where the face of the fill is not stepped, diversion ditches at a minimum of every 15 m vertical height of the fill is recommended. Revegetation of the hollow fill face, usually with hydroseeding, is done as soon as the fill height increases.

In the Mountain Top-Removal method, a large portion of the fill is stored on the mountain top, graded, and then seeded. When mining is completed, the mountain top is completely covered with a 6- to 12-m layer of spoil, and is graded nearly flat. The excess overburden material is deposited in a head-of-hollow fill following all the above procedures (Fig. 24 and 25). Several head-of-hollow fills have lasted through seven winters with no slides, and with little or no erosion.

Fig. 20—A distant view of the French drain.

Fig. 21—The boulders that form the core of the French drain must be large in size.

Fig. 22—The valley fill is built from bottom up in layers.

Fig. 23—A completed head-of-hollow fill.

Fig. 24—Mountain top-removal method. Note the head-of-hollow in the front being prepared for valley fill.

Fig. 25—Large area of level ground created as a result of contour mining in West Virginia.

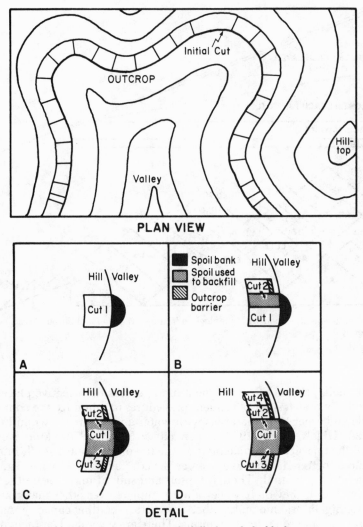

PLAN VIEW

DETAIL

Fig. 26—Contour mining around a hillside with the block system.

B. Block-Cut Method

The Block-cut method is a simple innovation of conventional contour strip mining for steep terrain. It is basically an adaptation of the area mining method, where an initial box-cut is made into the hillside. This cut is two or three times as wide as subsequent cuts, and goes into the hillside to a depth at which the surface mining of the coal is economical. Since mobile equipment (scrapers, front-end loaders, bull-dozers, etc.) are more commonly used, from cut 1, subsequent cuts are taken in either direction (Fig. 26) (Maneval, 1972; Saperstein & Secor, 1973). The spoil from cut 1 is pushed down the hill to be hauled back later into the cut. However, the spoil from subsequent cuts is stored in the previous cut.

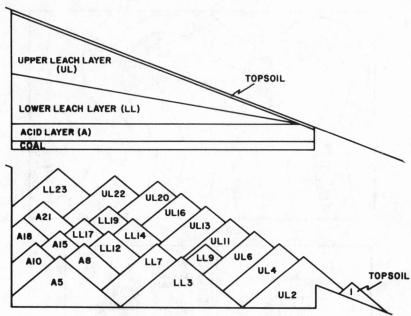

Fig. 27—Movement of spoil within a block to insure segregation and burial of acid-bearing material.

Additionally, the mobile equipment used permits the selective placement of spoil. Two such spoil-placement procedures to minimize the contact of pyritic and other toxic materials with water and air are shown in Fig. 27 and 28 (Hill & Grim, 1975; Saperstein & Secor, 1973). Moreover, by saving the topsoil and replacing it on the top of the graded spoil, in many instances, better results have been achieved, particularly with regard to revegetation potential. Though topsoil and subsoil may not be the most ideal material, they do have certain advantages over other materials, including higher organic matter, better moisture-holding capacity, natural seed source, and soil microorganisms. There are several advantages of this method over conventional contour stripping, the major ones among these being as follows:

1) Spoil is not deposited on the down slopes and, therefore, the dangerous landslide problem associated with conventional contour stripping is eliminated.

2) Since the spoil is stored in the pit itself, it allows for effective burial of the exposed highwall. In addition to the cosmetic desirability of this action, it results in a better control of water seepage and run-off problems, as well as of sedimentation and erosion problems.

3) More importantly, the amount of area disturbed by this method is approximately 60% less than that by conventional contour mining.

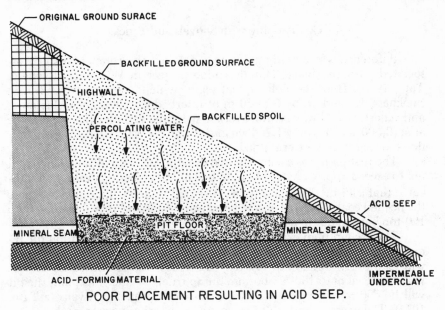

POOR PLACEMENT RESULTING IN ACID SEEP.

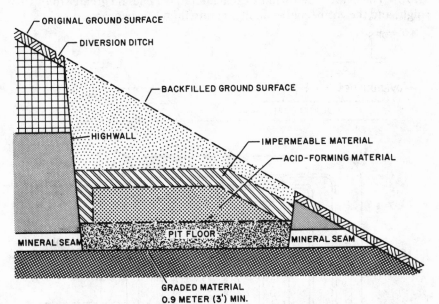

PROPER PLACEMENT FOR ACID FORMING MATERIAL BURIAL

Fig. 28—Spoil placement for better environmental impact.

4) While no new safety hazards are introduced, the use of mobile equipment leads to easy removal and storage of topsoil, and selective mining and placement of toxic materials; it also generally facilitates concurrent reclamation.

C. Stripping with Shovels and Trucks

Reference was already made to a detailed environmental study associated with the Black Thunder mine project in Wyoming (Evans & Tate, 1975). Here the Roland coal seam, which averages over 18 m in thickness, is overlain by 6 to 60 m of interbedded claystones, siltstones, and sandstones. However, the average stripping ratio for the entire lease area (6,500 acres) is only 1.7. Two basic mine plans for producing 7.5 million tons per year were examined.

The first plan was a conventional dragline pit with ultimate highwall not to exceed approximately 40 m in height. Engineering evaluation indicated that a 45-m³ dragline with a 100-m, 30° boom will be able to expose the needed coal. The coal was to be mined by a 24-m³ shovel loading onto 120-ton bottom dump trucks.

The second plan examined was a truck and shovel operation for removing overburden as well as for loading out coal. Here, 24-m³ shovels will load overburden onto 170-ton end dump trucks, and 34-m³ shovels will load coal onto 180-ton bottom dump trucks. Under this plan, the pit will be 600 m in length, and 300 m in width (Fig. 29) (Evans & Tate, 1975). The overburden will be excavated in benches no greater than 16 m high, and the entire coal seam in no more than two benches.

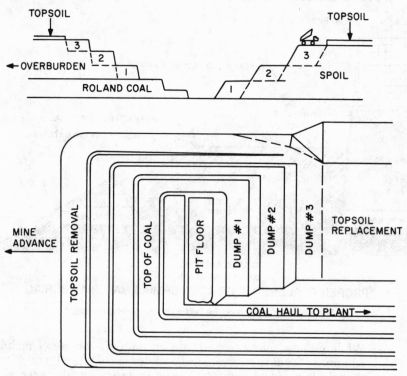

Fig. 29—Truck-and-shovel mining method for Atlantic Richfield's Black Thunder Mine in Wyoming.

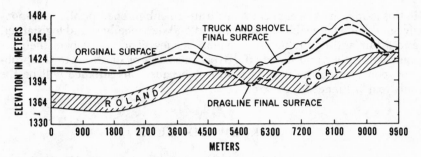

Fig. 30—Truck-and-shovel final surface compared with dragline final surface.

The economics of the two plans indicated that overburden removal costs would be about 12¢ per cubic meter with draglines, whereas it would be about 30¢ per cubic meter with shovels and trucks; i.e., a cost advantage of 18¢ per cubic meter for the dragline. The company has decided to go along with the shovel-truck method.

While the flexibility of the shovel-truck method to increase production can clearly be recognized as opposed to that of the dragline system, the great advantages of the shovel-truck system are in the ability to selectively place the spoils. In fact, the overburden conditions can be closely monitored, and the placement of the overburden so achieved to insure: (i) burial of toxic materials; (ii) topsoil replacement; (iii) desired stratigraphic sequence in the spoil; (iv) desired quality of coal by blending in the pit; and (v) greater recovery of coal.

Shown in Fig. 30 are the cross-sections that will be achieved under the two mining systems (Evans & Tate, 1975). The problem with the dragline is that the material can be carried to only about 100 m, and then only in a direction perpendicular to the line of travel. With shovel and truck systems such limitations as to the length or direction of travel do not exist, thereby leading to a flatter valley configuration. The advantages of this configuration are that: (i) it is amenable to reestablishment of grasses and grazing, (ii) it minimizes the overall erosion potential, and (iii) it permits the reconstruction of meadows and lakes. In fact, the improved reclamation potential was a key factor in the selection of the shovel-truck method.

VI. CONCLUSION

The problem of environmental control is of serious proportions and rightly deserves the present attention given to it. As a basic industry, mining today is charged with the responsibility of supplying raw materials to meet the ever-increasing demand from a growing population. This chapter has briefly reviewed the practices and progress in surface mining with regard to land disturbance control.

Environmental problems do not demand an "either-or" answer, but rather a search for a realistic solution. There are several things needed to make a success of the environmental campaign. Since there are no losers in this game, the key elements constitute an enlightened public, a responsive and knowledgeable operator, good and technically sound legislation, and a fair and equitable enforcement agency. They must pool their resources together and move effectively in search of solutions to the problems confronting the mining industry, because this alliance will be the only real "Alliance for Progress."

ACKNOWLEDGMENT

The authors would like to express their thanks to the National Coal Association for providing us with photographs. Thanks are also due to Mr. Imhoff of the U.S. Geological Survey for permission to use photographs and descriptions from the Geological Survey Circular no. 731.

LITERATURE CITED

Atkinson, T. 1971. Selection of open-pit excavating and loading equipment. Inst. Min. Metall., Trans., Sect. A 80(776):101–129.

Battelle Columbus Laboratories. 1975. Energy from coal: guidelines for the preparation of environmental impact statement. NTIS Pub. PB 242-960, U.S. Dep. of Commerce, Springfield, Va.

Evans, H. W., and J. Tate. 1975. Black Thunder mining planning and environment. Preprint 75-F-128, Soc. of Mining Engineers, Am. Inst. of Mining Engineers, New York.

Grim, E. C., and R. D. Hill. 1974. Environmental protection in surface mining of coal. EPA Pub. no. 670/2-74-093, Cincinnati, Ohio.

Hill, R. D., and E. C. Grim. 1975. Environmental Factors in Surface Mine Recovery. Symp. on Restoration and Recovery of Damaged Ecosystems. Virginia Polytechnic Inst. and State Univ., Blacksburg, Va. Available from EPA, Cincinnati, Ohio.

Imhoff, E. A., T. O. Fritz, and J. R. LaFevers. 1976. A guide to state programs for the reclamation of surface mined area. Geol. Surv. Civ. 731. U.S. Dep. of the Interior, Washington, D.C.

Maneval, D. R. 1972. Coal mining vs. environment: a reconciliation in Pennsylvania. Appalachia (J. of the Appalachian Regional Comm.) 5(4):10–40.

Ramani, R. V. 1974. Environmental concerns and decisions for the mining industry. J. Inst. Eng. (India), Part MM 54(2):45–49.

Saperstein, L. W., and E. S. Secor. 1973. The Block Method of stripping. Preprint 73-F-51, Soc. of Mining Engineers, Am. Inst. of Mining Engineers, New York.

Sawyer, L. E., and J. M. Crowl. 1968. Land reclamation. p. 247–266. In E. P. Pfleider (ed.) Surface mining. Am. Inst. of Mining Engineers, N. Y.

Stefanko, R., R. V. Ramani, and M. R. Ferko. 1973. Analysis of strip mining methods and equipment selection. Res. and Dev. Rep. no. 61. Interim Rep. no. 7. Off. of Coal Res. U.S. Dep. of the Interior, Washington, D.C.

Thomas, L. J. 1973. An introduction to mining. Hicks, Smith & Sons, Sydney.

U.S. Department of the Interior. 1967. Surface mining and our environment. USDI, Washington, D.C.

Copyright © 1978 ASA–CSSA–SSSA
677 South Segoe Road, Madison, WI 53711 USA
Reclamation of Drastically Disturbed Lands

Chapter 15

Grading and Shaping for Erosion Control and Rapid Vegetative Establishment in Humid Regions

FRANK GLOVER, MARSHALL AUGUSTINE, AND
MICHAEL CLAR

*Soil Conservation Service, USDA, Morgantown, West Virginia and
Hittman Associates, Inc., Columbia, Maryland, respectively.*

I. INTRODUCTION

Erosion control of lands in humid areas drastically disturbed by coal surface mining is strongly influenced by four principal factors: climate, soils, vegetation, and topography. The climate for any given region is fixed; man's control is very limited. He can, however, schedule sensitive field operations around the local weather patterns. Vegetation is the most flexible of these factors. Plant materials are available for almost any situation in the humid regions of the United States, provided their establishment is supported by known conservation measures, and the soils and topography are suitable. Because of the nature of surface mining operations, the soils and topography must be reconstructed by grading and shaping, which provide the greatest possibility for control. Grading and shaping consist of selecting and placing the best soil material on the surface and manipulating the soils and topography to control the effective length of slopes, safely dispose of storm runoff, and improve vegetative establishment.

II. OBJECTIVES

The basic objective of an erosion control program for a surface-mined area is to stabilize the disturbed area. When the area is stabilized, the volume of sediment generated will be minimized and off-site damage reduced. Therefore, the principal objective of grading and shaping operations should be to manipulate the soil and topography to assist in the control of surface runoff, thus reducing erosion and improving effective vegetative establishment.

In addition, there are several secondary objectives. The grading and shaping features of an erosion control program must also be compatible with the land use planned for the area after mining and reclamation are

271

completed. The soil and topography required should be identified before making the grading plan.

Plans for grading and shaping should include making full use of the materials or land resources at the site. Large rocks and boulders can be buried or they can be placed on toeslopes to make use of their properties of resistance to weathering. If durable, they can be used as rip-rap for stabilizing waterways or as special features on recreation sites. Brush and other woody materials can be windrowed at the toe of fills and used as a partial filter. They can be fed through a woodchipper and used as a mulch for soil stabilization. The potential use of all materials at the site should be considered in preparing the mining plan and in determining the use of the land after mining.

As a minimum, the grading and sloping operations must conform to state laws. Most states have grading specifications included in their reclamation requirements. These specifications usually require that the peaks and ridges be reduced by grading to a rolling, sloping, or terraced topography. Areas reclaimed for uses such as forest plantation and wildlife may require less grading than for other uses. In addition, some states require that acid-forming material be covered with a minimum depth (0.6 to 1.2 m; 2 to 4 feet) of material suitable to support plant growth. Most states have set a time limit on the completion of the reclamation operations; a 2- to 3-year limit is most common.

III. SOIL CHARACTERISTICS

Soil materials resulting from mining have physical and chemical characteristics unique to each site. The physical-chemical characteristics of the soil materials at a particular site must be known and considered in planning the shaping and grading operations. The characteristics that most influence the stated objectives include the toxicity or potential toxicity of the material and the capacity to hold water.

Potentially toxic acid-forming material can be handled in two ways. It can be buried in the surface mine pit or it can be neutralized by adding lime. If the toxic material is identified, segregated, and stockpiled, it can easily be placed in the bottom of the pit. There are fewer problems in establishing and maintaining vegetation where potentially high acid-forming materials are covered with soil material favorable to plant growth.

The water-holding capacity of the material is the key to erosion control on most sites. Other characteristics that have a strong influence on the erosion potential of a soil are texture, organic-matter content, percent slope, and effective length of slope.

Soil texture refers to the size and proportion of particles making up a particular soil. Soil texture classes are determined by the relative amounts of sand, silt, and clay. If sand is dominant, the soil is coarse-textured or "light" and allows water to infiltrate more rapidly. Too much sand, however, may make the soil too droughty for plant establishment. Clay particles are dominant in fine-textured or "heavy" soils, which are often quite cohesive and slow to erode. Soils high in silt and very fine sand and low in clay and organic matter are generally the most erodible.

Organic matter is plant and animal residue in various stages of decomposition. The organic matter content of a soil has an inverse relationship to erodibility. As the amount of organic matter in a soil increases, the capacity of the soil to absorb surface water increases. As a result, runoff is reduced. Soil materials that result from mining operations are generally lacking in near-surface concentrations of soil organic matter. Deficiencies in near-surface organic matter can be remedied through establishment of vegetative cover and proper maintenance. Superior long-range benefits may be obtained by controlled deep incorporation of organic matter recovered from the original surface soil.

The ability of a soil to hold water depends on texture, depth, organic-matter content, and pore size distribution. Soils that are able to hold large quantities of water are desirable from a plant growth standpoint, although some clays with excessive water holding capacity cause problems.

IV. GRADING CONSIDERATIONS

A. Scheduling and Seasonal Limitations

Seasonal climatic variations play an important role in the scheduling of grading operations. The amount of rainfall and runoff during different periods of the year influences erosion. Because the soil is so vulnerable to erosion during the grading activities, those activities should be scheduled to coincide with the periods of low precipitation. The spring and early summer months often have the highest precipitation rates. Therefore, the bulk of grading operations, especially in critical areas, should be scheduled for midsummer and fall.

Soil stability is another consideration. Proper compaction cannot usually be obtained during the winter months when the ground is frozen. In early spring the ground is often too wet to be handled properly, and mud can impede the operation of grading equipment.

If there is a choice, it is better to grade during the most favorable time for seeding. From a moisture and temperature point of view, April, May, and June in the spring, and late August, September, and October in the fall, are the best times to seed for uniform emergence and seedling growth in West Virginia, Maryland, and Virginia.

B. Topographic Manipulations

The rate of runoff and, correspondingly, the rate of soil erosion can be controlled by manipulating the slope gradient and effective length of slope. Such control is particularly significant in area mining and mountaintop mining.

Slope design should be based on the erodibility of the surface soils, as well as the need to stabilize against mass earth movement. Return to approximate original contour, as required by most state laws, may not be desirable in all cases. A reduction in relief and an overall flattening of the topography is not only desirable from an erosion control standpoint, but may be necessary to convert the site to another type of land use. It must be remembered that shorter and flatter slopes are less erodible.

Where there is little flexibility as to the overall configuration of the slope, as is often the case with contour mining in steep terrain, diversion structures, such as reverse benches or terraces, ditches, and dikes, can be constructed above and along the spoil slopes to decreae the overall length of the slope.

C. Soil Surface Manipulations

The soil surface can be manipulated to reduce and detain runoff. Manipulation includes roughening and loosening the soil, mulching and revegetation, topsoiling, and adding soil amendments.

A roughened and loosened soil surface improves water infiltration, slows the movement of surface runoff, and benefits plant growth. Common methods of loosening and/or roughening a soil surface include scarification, tracking, and contour benching or furrowing. Scarification is usually accomplished by disking or harrowing on the ground contour, but it can also be done by a crawler tractor equipped with ripper bars or by dragging the teeth on the bucket of a front-end loader over the ground.

Tracking is done on steep slopes where equipment cannot be moved safely along the ground contour. It is accomplished by running a cleated crawler tractor up and down the slope. When this method is used, it is important that the cleat marks overlap. The cleats leave shallow grooves that run parallel to the contour. If the slope is not too steep, furrows can be made on contours by angling the dozer blade. Some overtopping of these furrows occurs, but they help control erosion.

The prompt establishment of a cover of vegetation or the placement of a fibrous, organic mulch on a denuded soil surface also reduces and detains surface flow. Additionally, it stabilizes the soil. Vegetation or mulch protects the surface and prevents the soil from being compacted and sealed during a rainfall. Live vegetation and mulching materials make the soil more porous and will increase water infiltration.

The permeability of the surface soil also has a major bearing on the rate of surface runoff. If the soil remaining after grading is highly impermeable, it may be desirable to top-dress the graded area with a more suitable soil if it is available. This process should enhance revegetation efforts. Decreased surface runoff is a secondary benefit.

D. Types of Equipment

Commonly used equipment for grading and shaping are dozers, pull scrapers, motor scrapers, trucks, and high lifts. Power shovels, gradalls, and draglines are sometimes used in the backfilling operation.

The types of equipment used influence the quality of the final grading and shaping. Some compaction is needed to improve slope stability. However, the surface or root zone should be loose to permit water movement and good plant growth. The type of equipment used will have an effect on these conditions.

V. GUIDELINES FOR GRADING AND SHAPING

On the basis of the foregoing discussion, a number of guidelines have been developed to optimize the benefits from the grading and shaping. These guidelines fall into six major categories: scheduling of operations, soil placement, utilization of existing materials, control of runoff water, land use considerations, and selection of equipment.

1. SCHEDULING OF OPERATIONS

Grading and shaping operations should be scheduled with two objectives in mind. The first objective is to minimize the total surface area disturbed at any one time. The second objective is to schedule earth-moving operations which consider seasonal climatic variations. The schedule should require the shaping and grading operations, including seedbed preparation and mulching, to be conducted as a continuous operation during the best seasons of the year.

2. SOIL PLACEMENT

Two major objectives in placing soil materials resulting from mining operations are (i) to provide a stable soil mass and (ii) to provide a suitable growth medium. These objectives are extremely difficult, if not impossible, to attain without a thorough analysis of the overburden materials during preplanning. This analysis will identify potentially toxic materials that must be buried or neutralized. It will also identify the layer of the soil that would be most desirable for plant growth. The occurrence of ground water, particularly aquifers or springs that might saturate and threaten the stability of the soil mass, can also be identified and provided for in the soil reconstruction process. Reconstruction should replace acid soils with nonacid soil material; replace infertile soils with more fertile soil material; replace hardpans and relatively shallow root zones with deeper soils; and provide boulder-free surface soils.

3. UTILIZATION OF EXISTING MATERIALS

Grading and shaping plans should take advantage of materials present at the site. If clayey materials are present in the overburden material, they can be used to segregate toxic soil materials, create an artificial ground water table, and line the walls and bottoms of water-holding impoundments. Large rocks and boulders, which are usually buried, can also be used to anchor the toes of outslopes and stabilize sloping soils.

They can also be broken down and used as rip-rap to stabilize slopes, water courses, and outfalls. Nonmarketable woody plant materials, which are usually buried, can be processed through a wood chipper and used as a mulch. Before a decision is made to discard any material, it should be thoroughly evaluated for possible use.

4. CONTROL OF RUNOFF

Grading and shaping are major considerations in the control of runoff. Runoff can be controlled through a combination of surface soil manipulations, topographic shaping, and erosion control structures. Selected measures are listed in Table 1.

Soil surface manipulations include roughening and loosening the soil, mulching and revegetation, topsoiling, and adding soil amendments. Mulching and revegetation are not strictly shaping and grading operations, but they are generally inseparable from these operations. The shaping and grading operations by themselves cannot do much to prevent rainfall erosion. The impact of falling raindrops can be controlled quickly with mulches and the rapid establishment of grasses and legumes. The preparation of the soil surface through soil surface manipulations will help to keep the mulch in place and establish vegetation.

Topographic shaping is used to control the rate of runoff and to reduce the rate of soil erosion. This objective is accomplished by manipulating the gradient, length, and shape of the slope. In addition, topographic shaping has a major influence on the stability of the slopes. Slope design, therefore, should be based on the erodibility of the surface soils and the stability against landslides.

5. LAND USE CONSIDERATIONS

The grading and shaping operations must recognize the needs of the postmining land use. These requirements and characteristics vary considerably among the many possible land uses, which include reforestation, recreation, agriculture, and urban development. The elements with the greatest possible variance affecting land use include slope length and steepness, water supply, storm runoff handling, and selection of plant materials.

6. SELECTION OF EQUIPMENT

The selection of the proper size and kind of equipment for grading and shaping is important. A large piece of equipment (D-9 or greater) provides the greatest capacity to move earth. However, it may not be the most economical for grading and finishing the job to the required standards.

Most successful operators have found that a large dozer (D-9 or equal) can be used for backfilling and rough grading. After this stage, use of a smaller dozer (D-7 or equal) has proved to be the most economical, mainly because of its greater maneuverability. This smaller size equip-

CONSERVATION MEASURE	DESCRIPTION	APPLICABILITY	EQUIPMENT REQUIRED	LIMITATIONS	DESIGN REQUIREMENTS	MAINTENANCE REQUIREMENTS
GRASSED WATERWAY	A grassed waterway is a natural or man-made drainageway of parabolic or trapezoidal cross-section that is stabilized by suitable vegetation. The flow is normally wide and shallow and conveys runoff down the slope. The purpose of the structure is to convey runoff without causing damage by erosion.	Grassed waterways are used where added channel capacity and/or stabilization is required to control erosion resulting from concentrated runoff and where such control can be achieved by this practice alone or in combination with others. Not suitable where seepage flow occurs.	Dozer (D-7 or equal) Motor grader	Limited to mild gradients (less than 10%) and low velocities (less than 10 fps)	Formal design is required. The following factors must be considered: • capacity • velocity and grade • cross-section • outlets • stabilization	Periodic inspection is required. Key inspection items include: • erosion of sides • grade changes • outlet structure Repair or replace vegetation killed or washed out
PAVED CHUTE OR FLUME	A paved chute or flume is a channel lined with bituminous concrete, portland cement concrete, or comparable non-erodible material, such as grouted rip-rap, placed to extend from the top of a slope to the bottom of a slope. The purpose of the structure is to convey surface runoff safely down slopes without causing erosion.	A paved chute or flume is to be used where concentrated flow of surface runoff must be conveyed down a slope and velocities or soil condition are too severe for vegetation.	Dozer (D-7 or equal) Backhoe	The maximum allowable drainage area should be 36 acres for temporary structures based on SCS design criteria.	Formal design criteria are not required for temporary structures. SCS criteria are available. Permanent structures require formal design including: • flow computations • structure capacity • inlet and outlet • stabilization • structural stability	Periodic inspection is required. Key inspection items are: • piping at inlet • scour at outlet • settlement of structure • structural deterioration
PIPE SLOPE DRAIN	A pipe slope drain is a flexible tubing and/or rigid pipe with prefabricated entrance section, temporarily placed to extend from the top of a slope to the bottom of a slope. The purpose of the structure is to convey surface runoff safely down slopes without causing erosion.	Pipe slope drains are to be used where concentrated flow of surface runoff must be conveyed down a slope in a nonerosive manner.	Dozer (D-7 or equal) Backhoe	The maximum allowable drainage area shall be five acres.	Formal design not required. Tables relating pipe diameter size to drainage area are included in SCS standards and specifications. No potential freezing of inflow and plugging should be permitted.	Periodic inspection is required. Key inspection items are: • piping at inlet • scour at outlet • anchoring of pipe

(continued on next page)

Table 1—continued

CONSERVATION MEASURE	DESCRIPTION	APPLICABILITY	EQUIPMENT REQUIRED	LIMITATIONS	DESIGN REQUIREMENTS	MAINTENANCE REQUIREMENTS
BENCHES	Benching is a method of erosion control accomplished by converting a long continuous slope to a series of stairs and steps. The bench reduces runoff velocities by reducing effective slope length, collects sediment, and provides access to slopes for seeding, mulching, and maintenance.	Benches are used primarily to break up long smooth slopes.	Dozer (D-7 or equal)	Can be used on slopes up to 25 to 30 percent. Are difficult to construct.	Design considerations include: · location · selection of outlets · terrace spacing · terrace length	Should be inspected periodically and sediment buildup should be removed. Must check for breaches in the terrace where rilling and gullying will occur.
LEVEL SPREADER	A level spreader is an outlet constructed at zero percent grade across the slope whereby concentrated runoff may be discharged at nonerosive velocities onto disturbed areas stabilized by existing vegetation. The purpose of the structure is to convert concentrated runoff to sheet flow and to outlet it onto stabilized areas.	The level spreader is used only in those situations where the spreader can be constructed on undisturbed soil, where the area directly below the level lip is stabilized by existing vegetation, and where the water will not be reconcentrated immediately below the point of discharge.	Dozer (D-7 or equal) Motor grader	The level spreader is difficult to construct. the lip must be perfectly level. The spreader is limited to 1 cfs per foot of length based on the peak rate of runoff. The minimum length shall be five feet and the maximum length shall be 20 feet.	Formal design is not required. A Standard Specification is available from SCS.	Periodic inspection is required. Lip should be kept free of sediment and checked to see that gullies do not form.
SEDIMENT TRAP	A sediment trap is a small temporary basin formed by an excavation and/or embankment to intercept sedimen-laden runoff and retain the sediment. The purpose of a sediment trap is to intercept sediment-laden runoff and, thereby, trap sediment. In so doing, drainageways, properties, and rights-of-way below the trap are protected from sedimentation.	Sediment traps are installed in roadway ditches and in small drainageways within and at the periphery of the disturbed area.	Dozer (D-7 or equal) Backhoe	Sediment traps are limited to very small drainage areas.	A formal design is required. Design considerations should include: · drainage area · location · trap size · trap clean out · embankment · excavation · outlet	Frequent inspection and clean out are required.

	Description	Application	Equipment	Design	Inspection
SEDIMENT BASIN	A sediment basin is a basin constructed on a waterway to impound runoff coming from the mine site. The pond is formed by placing an earthen dam across the waterway, by excavating a depression, or by a combination of the two means. The purpose of a sediment basin is to remove sediment from runoff and thus protect streams, properties, and rights-of-way below the sediment basin.	A sediment basin applies where physical site conditions or land ownership restrictions preclude the installation of erosion control measures to adequately control runoff, erosion, and sedimentation. Basins are installed below the mining operation on the major walkways and act as a last line of defense against off-site sediment damage.	Dozer (D-7 or equal) Backhow	Use of temporary detention basins is limited to sites where: (1) failure of the structure would not result in loss of life, damage to homes or buildings, or interruption of use or service of public roads or utilities; (2) the basin is to be removed within a specified time after the beginning of construction of the basin.	A formal design is required. Design criteria vary from state to state. Design considerations include: • location • size of basin • spillways—principal —emergency • sediment handling and disposal • quality embankment materials	Regular inspection is required. Should be checked after major storms for damages. Sediment must be removed from the basin when the storage capacity falls below half the total volume. The sediment removed must be disposed of properly.
CHECK DAM	A check dam is a structure to stabilize the grade or to control head cutting in natural or artificial channels. Check dams are used to reduce or prevent excessive erosion by reduction of velocities in watercourses or by providing partially lined channel sections or structures that can withstand high flow velocities.	Check dams are used where the capability of earth and/or vegetative measures is exceeded in the safe handling of water at permissible velocities, where excessive grade or overall conditions occur, or where water is to be lowered from one elevation to another.	Dozer (D-7 or equal) Backhoe	Limited to upper stream reaches of watershed.	A formal design is required. Design considerations include: • size of dam • type of material • control section • toe stabilization • upstream effects of impoundment	Periodic inspection is required. Should be checked after major storms for damages. Key inspection items include: • sediment accumulation • erosion at toe • breaches in dam
ROUGHENED SURFACE	Mechanical roughening of regraded areas is a technique which is practiced to enhance water infiltration, slow the movement of surface runoff and thereby collect sediment, and benefit plant growth.	This technique is often used to reduce soil erosion on large flat areas and on long and steep slopes.	Highlift with bucket teeth Motor grader with scarifer Subsoiler	Applicable only to newly graded areas.	Not applicable.	Not applicable.

(continued on next page)

Table 1—continued

CONSERVATION MEASURE	DESCRIPTION	APPLICABILITY	EQUIPMENT REQUIRED	LIMITATIONS	DESIGN REQUIREMENTS	MAINTENANCE REQUIREMENTS
RIPRAP, RUBBLE, GABIONS	Riprap, rubble or gabions are layer of loose rock or aggregate placed over erodible soil surfaces. The purpose of riprap is to protect the soil surface from the erosive forces of water.	These practices are used where the soil conditions, water turbulence and velocity, expected vegetative cover, and groundwater conditions are such that the soil may erode under the design flow conditions. The materials may be used, as appropriate, at such places as culvert outlets, channel banks and/or bottoms, roadside ditches, and steep slopes.	Backhoe Highlift	These materials should only be used where vegetation or mulch prove insufficient to stabilize the area.	A formal design may be required. Design considerations include: · size of stone · filter blanket or bedding · method of placement	Occasional inspection will be required. Key inspection items are: · breaches in bedding · stability of sub-base
AGGREGATE COVER	A layer of gravel or crushed rock ranging in thickness from four to eight inches.	A layer of crushed aggregate can be used to stabilize a soil surface, thus minimizing erosion. This method is almost exclusively used to stabilize haul roads. It allows construction traffic in adverse weather and may be used as part of a permanent base construction of paved areas.	Backhoe Highlift	Generally only used on areas subject to heavy traffic such as haul roads, shop areas, etc.	A formal design is required.	Occasional inspection will be required.

	Description	Function	Equipment	Use/Limitations	Design	Maintenance
DIVERSION DITCH	A diversion ditch is a ridge of compacted soil placed above, below, or around a disturbed area to intercept runoff and divert it to a stable disposal area	Generally used above a newly constructed fill and cut slope to prevent excessive erosion of the slope until more permanent drainage features are installed, or the slope is stabilized with vegetation	Dozer (D-7 or equal) Motor grader	Is the least durable diversion structure, and should be used to provide protection for short periods of time, and when relatively small amounts of runoff are to be handled. Limited to drainage area less than 5 acres	A formal design is not required. Construction Specifications are available from SCS	Should be inspected after every storm. Damage repair should be immediate
DIVERSION SWALE (DITCH)	A diversion swale is an excavated, temporary drainageway used above and below disturbed areas to intercept runoff and divert it to a safe disposal area	It can be constructed at the downstream perimeter of a disturbed area to collect and transport sediment-laden water to a sediment trapping device. Or it can be used at the upstream perimeter to prevent storm runoff from entering the disturbed area	Dozer (D-7 or equal) Motor grader	Should not be constructed outside the property lines without obtaining legal easements from affected, adjacent property owners. Limited to drainage areas less than 5 acres	A formal design is not required. However the following factors should be checked. · runoff volume and velocity · Slope length and steepness · Soil type · Outlet location Construction specifications are available from SCS	Should be inspected periodically to check for sediment buildup. Cleanout is needed when capacity reduced
DIVERSION	A diversion is a permanent or temporary drainageway constructed by excavating a shallow ditch along the hillside and a soil dike along the downhill edge of the ditch with the excavated soil	Diversions can be used in place of the dike or swale but they are primarily used to provide long-term runoff control on long slopes subject to heavy flow concentrations. A diversion or water bar can be used on abandoned haul roads to intercept runoff flowing along the roadway and divert it to a safe outslope disposal point	Dozer (D-7 or equal) Motor grader	Should be used on slopes of 15 percent or less	When used as a temporary structure, a formal design is not required. When permanent structures are installed the following factors must be examined: · capacity · velocity and grade · cross-section · outlet · stabilization	Periodic inspection. Structure must be accessible to maintenance equipment. Damage from breaching or silting should be repaired immediately

ment has the capability to final-grade closer to requirements and to construct water disposal measures. Long blades and the overall physical size of large dozers limit their use in constructing these water disposal measures.

Equipment selection is also governed by the distance earth has to be moved. General guides are as follows:

Up to 300 feet (91.4 m)—Dozer
300 feet to 1,000 feet (304.8 m)—Pull scraper
1,000 feet or greater—Motor scraper

VI. APPLICABLE CONSERVATION MEASURES

Numerous conservation measures have been developed to supplement the grading and shaping operations in controlling erosion and establishing effective vegetation. The applicable measures fall into two major categories: measures for runoff control and measures for soil stabilization.

A. Measures for Runoff Control

Measures used in controlling runoff can be grouped into three types according to their function. The three basic functions are:

1) reduction and detention of runoff,
2) interception and diversion of runoff, and
3) conveyance of safe disposal of concentrated flow.

Measures to reduce and detain runoff include those practices discussed under surface soil manipulation and topographic manipulation. Included in these practices are:

1) roughening and loosening the soil,
2) mulching and revegetation,
3) topsoiling and soil amendments,
4) reduction of slope length and gradient, and
5) use of concave slopes.

Interception and diversion practices are used to intercept runoff before it reaches a critical area and to divert it to a safe disposal area. These practices perform two important functions at surface coal mines. They isolate onsite critical areas (i.e., raw spoils, partially stabilized spoils, highwalls, access roads, and other areas) from offsite runoff. In addition, they control runoff velocities on steep or long spoil slopes and abandoned access roads. Interception and diversion is accomplished through the use of various conservation structures, including reverse benches or terraces, cross-slope ditches, earth dikes, and combined ditch and dike (diversion). Table 1 summarizes the characteristics of many of these practices.

The diversion and the interception of runoff necessitate the conveyance and disposal of concentrated flows. Safe conveyance of concentrated flow requires practices that reduce the velocity of runoff or maintain low velocity and, as a result, control its ability to detach and transport soil particles. In handling concentrated flow, the objective is to safely convey the water without erosion. This is accomplished by designing the measures to withstand the expected velocities. For most vegetated waterways there must be only intermittent flow, and velocity cannot exceed 5.0 feet/sec (1.5 m/sec). If greater velocities are expected or base flow or seepage occurs, structural protection is needed such as rip-rap or concrete linings. Other structures such as culverts and chutes can also be used to convey concentrated flows to safe outlets. Temporary storage of runoff in impoundments and energy dissipators (level spreaders, concrete or road blocks, etc.) are other methods that may be used.

B. Measures for Soil Stabilization

The second category of erosion control measures is soil stabilization. Soil stabilization practices are designed to protect the soil from the erosive action of rainfall, ensuing runoff, and wind. Stabilization measures can be either vegetative or nonvegetative, and either short- or long-term.

Vegetative stabilization refers to the use of different types of vegetation to protect the soil from erosion. Nonvegetative stabilization, on the other hand, refers to a multitude of practices that use materials other than vegetation, such as mulch, gravel, etc., in preventing soil erosion. A combination of both vegetative and nonvegetative measures is usually required.

Chapter 16

Plant Materials and Their Requirements for Growth in Humid Regions[1]

O. L. BENNETT, E. L. MATHIAS, W. H. ARMIGER, AND
J. N. JONES, JR.

Agricultural Research Service, USDA
Morgantown, West Virginia, and Beltsville, Maryland

I. INTRODUCTION

Disturbed land surfaces usually should be revegetated as quickly as possible to avoid serious erosion (Bennett, 1973; Bennett et al., 1972; Hill, 1975). Grasses, legumes, trees, and shrubs can be planted on most sites but their growth may be hindered by low pH, lack of available plant nutrients, toxicities, improper selection of adapted varieties, and climatic factors (Bassett, 1964; Berg & Vogel, 1968; Davis et al., 1965; Dickson, 1971; Fleming et al., 1974; Grube et al., 1973; Katz, 1939; Palazzo & Duell, 1974; Russel, 1950; Stone, 1953; Tresher, 1970; Wilson, 1953). A wide variety of plant species can be used on disturbed land areas if their specific growth requirements are met. This chapter will deal with the more desirable species and their specific growth requirements on disturbed lands.

Many experiments have been conducted to determine adaptation of various plant species for revegetation and stabilization of disturbed areas in the eastern U.S. (Bennett, 1971; Bennett, 1973; Blazer et al., 1962; Brown, 1962 and 1971; Costin, 1967; Curtis, 1971; Davidson & Sowa, 1974; Derr & Mann, 1971; Everett et al., 1973; Green et al., 1973; Mellinger et al., 1966; Ruffner, 1955–65; Ruffner & Hall, 1963; Ruffner & Steiner, 1969; Shears, 1971; Struthers, 1960; Sutton, 1970; Sutton, 1973; Troll & Zak, 1972; Vogel & Berg, 1968; Webb, 1975). Some of the species are economically important, while others have only erosion control, soil stabilization, or aesthetic values (Hottenstein, 1970; Korns, 1971). Many of the disturbed soil areas in the eastern U.S. are characterized by poor chemical and physical properties and may constitute serious revegetation problems (Jones et al., 1973; Jones et al., 1975b; Mezapow-

[1] Cooperative studies between the Northeastern Region, Agricultural Research Service, USDA, Morgantown, West Virginia and Beltsville, Maryland; West Virginia University Agric. Exp. Stn., Morgantown, West Virginia and Virginia Polytechnic Institute Agric. Exp. Stn., Blacksburg, Virginia. Research supported in part by Environ. Prot. Agency, Grant no. EPA-IAG D5-E763.

skyj & Brider, 1970; Miller & Budy, 1974; Struthers, 1960; and Sutton, 1970). Much of the research has been conducted to find species that will grow under adverse soil and climatic conditions either with or without soil amendments.

II. FORAGE GRASSES

Several grass species are important in stabilizing the soil against erosion (Heath et al., 1973). Both the annual and the perennial species have a place in planning future land use, whether it be for soil stabilization per se, aesthetic value (Partain, 1974), or for economic production potential. Grasses that have shown promise for use in low pH soil in the eastern U.S. include weeping lovegrass (*Eragrostis curvula* Schrad), bermudagrass varieties (*Cynodon dactylis* L.), tall fescue (*Festuca arundinacea* L.), chewings fescue (*Festuca rubra* L.), switchgrass (*Panicum virgatum* L.), red top (*Agrostis alba* L.), colonial bentgrass (*Agrostis tennuis* Sibth), creeping bentgrass (*Agrostis palustris* Huds), velvet bentgrass (*Agrostis canina* L.), deer tongue (*Panicum clandestinum* L.), big bluestem (*Andropogon gerardi* Vitman), little bluestem (*Andropogon scoparius* Michx), and broomsedge bluestem (*Andropogon virginicus* L.). Of the species listed, weeping lovegrass and bermudagrass seem to be the most tolerant of extremely low pH soil.

Weeping lovegrass was introduced from East Africa and has been used extensively for erosion control and forage production on low fertility soils. It is a perennial bunch grass with an extensive but shallow fibrous root system, grows 1.5 m high, and forms a fairly large bunch. It will grow on soils with a pH of less than 4.0 if adequate fertilizer and lime are applied to inactivate toxic concentrations of Al and Mn. It is one of the fastest germinating and easiest grass species to establish on disturbed land areas. Weeping lovegrass is very tolerant of high aluminum soils (Fleming et al., 1974). Growth was excellent on low pH (3.8) spoils in West Virginia, and almost 6,000 kg/ha of oven-dry forage was produced (Table 1).

Bermudagrass is one of the most promising grasses for use on low pH disturbed soils in the southeastern U.S. (Bennett, 1973; Bennett et al., 1972). The area of adaptation extends from Indiana and Pennsylvania southward to the southern tip of Florida. Most bermudagrass strains will tolerate low pH and high concentrations of Fe, Al, and Mn. Bermudagrass is deep rooted, fast growing, and produces a good quality forage. It spreads by underground rhizomes and above-ground stolons and can be propagated either vegetatively or by direct seeding. The productive forage varieties—Coastal, Midland, and Tufcote—are sterile hybrids and must be propagated vegetatively by using stolons and rhizomes. The Tufcote variety is more tolerant of low pH than are Coastal or Midland; however, all three have been grown successfully in soils with pH's as low as 3.5, with low levels of lime, and moderate fertilizer applications. An available source of N, P, K, Ca, and Mg *must* be available for normal growth. Bermudagrass will respond to very high N applications. Many strains of common bermudagrass can be found throughout the eastern U.S. from

Table 1—Response of weeping lovegrass to lime and fertilizer at White Oak Mountain, W. Va. (Data adapted from Armiger et al., 1976)

Treatments†	Yield			
	1970	1971	1972	1971 pH
	——— kg/ha ———			
No lime, no phosphorus	1,557	3,196	3,304	3.52
4,200 kg/ha phosphate rock	4,907	5,776	4,702	3.80
8,400 kg/ha phosphate rock	4,661	5,051	4,191	4.15
840 kg/ha superphosphate	4,144	5,051	4,702	3.45
1,680 kg/ha superphosphate	4,066	5,186	3,949	3.08
17.9 metric tons dolomite	921	--	3,788	5.65
17.9 metric tons dolomite + 8,400 kg/ha phosphate rock	1,072	--	2,391	5.86
17.9 metric tons dolomite + 840 kg/ha superphosphate	4,552	4,190	4,164	5.67
17.9 metric tons dolomite + 1,680 kg/ha superphosphate	3,761	2,714	6,878	5.90

† 140 kg/ha of N and 110 kg/ha of K were applied to the experimental area as uniform amendments.
‡ Weeping lovegrass survival diminishing with crownvetch becoming the dominant plant species.

Pennsylvania southward. However, they are less productive than the three varieties mentioned.

Tall fescue has been used extensively alone and in combination with other grasses and legumes on disturbed land areas throughout the Eastern U.S. It is a deep-rooted, long-lived perennial which tends to form bunches and is propagated by seeding. Tall fescue grows well if the pH is 4.5 or above and it is one of the more drought-resistant grasses suited for the eastern U.S.; however, it grows best in well-fertilized, moist, medium- to heavy-textured soils. A good fertilization program with N, P, K, Ca, and Mg should be followed for long-term maintenance and survival. Tall fescue is used extensively on strip mine spoils (Bennett, 1973; Jones et al., 1975b; Plass, 1968), roadbanks (Blazer et al., 1962; Green et al., 1973; Johnson et al., 1971; Johnson, 1957; Perry et al., 1975; Roadside Development, 1960; Rovine, 1975), construction sites, and waterways.

Chewings fescue (sub. sp. *commutata*) and red fescue are two of the finer stemmed fescues utilized on disturbed land areas in the eastern U.S. They are tolerant of low pHs (4.5), drought, and shade. Fertilization and climatic requirements are similar to those of tall fescue. Besides tall fescue and red fescues, about 100 species of *Festuca* are adapted to the U.S. The fescues are ideally suited for conservation, since they produce a deep fibrous root system for holding soil particles in place.

Red top grows well throughout the eastern U.S., except in the drier regions of the deep south. Red top grows on very acid soils, on clayey soils of low fertility, and on poorly drained soils. It is a perennial grass with both upright and creeping stems. Although red top will produce fairly well on unproductive soils, it will respond to lime and fertilizer, especially N, P, and K. Other *Agrostis* species include colonial bentgrass, creeping bentgrass, and velvet bentgrass. Most bentgrasses will grow on low-pH disturbed soil areas and produce an effective cover. In general, they are shade-tolerant and will do well under heavy traffic.

Several blue stem species will grow on disturbed land areas in the eastern U.S. The most important species are big bluestem and little bluestem. These warm season grasses have a strong, deep root system with short underground stems, thereby producing a sod highly resistant to erosion. Big bluestem will be about 1½ m tall when mature and grows best on moist, well-drained soils with a pH range from 6.0 to 7.5. It will grow on low fertility soils but is better adapted to the higher fertility soils. Little bluestem grows about 1 m and is more drought-resistant than big bluestem. It can be found on gravelly soils, on ridges, and in other exposed locations in the Appalachian region. Little bluestem has been invading some of the acid mine soils (pH 4.5 and higher) of that region. The unavailability of seed and problems with establishment have been major factors limiting the use of bluestem varieties on strip mine spoils in the eastern U.S. Broomsedge bluestem will invade abandoned low pH strip mine areas in the eastern U.S. and grow on soils of extremely low fertility. Broomsedge is shallow-rooted with low quality forage and is considered an undesirable weed in most areas. However, it does provide some soil protection on extremely low pH (3.5 to 5.5) spoil areas.

Yellow indiangrass (*Sorghastrum nutans* [L.] Nash) is a perennial grass similar to big bluestem that will grow under rather infertile soil conditions. It has not been widely used on disturbed land areas in the eastern U.S., but its use may become more prominent with further evaluation.

Switchgrass, a perennial sod-forming grass adapted to most areas in the eastern U.S., has shown considerable promise for use as a pasture and hay crop on the better strip-mined areas. It is a broad-leaved, coarse-stemmed plant which grows about 1.25 m high and spreads slowly by short rhizomes. It is adapted to fertile, moist soils. However, it will produce better growth and cover on droughty, infertile, eroded soils than will most introduced grasses. Switchgrass is used extensively for wind and water erosion control, mainly because of its large seedling growth and high forage yielding ability. Cultivars of switchgrass will grow throughout the eastern U.S. However, blackwell switchgrass is better adapted to the middle and northern part of the eastern states. Blackwell switchgrass is a rust-resistant cultivar adapted to strip mine spoils with a pH of 4.0 and higher. It will respond to both lime and fertilizer and should be fertilized with a complete fertilizer to obtain good ground cover and hay yields (Table 2).

Some of the more agriculturally important grass species adapted to better soil conditions include: bromegrass (*Bromus inermis* Leyss), timothy (*Phleum pratense* L.), orchardgrass (*Dactylis glomerata* L.), perennial rye grass (*Lolium perenne* L.), Italian ryegrass (*Lolium multiflorum* Lam.), Kentucky bluegrass (*Poa pratensis* L.), Canadian bluegrass (*Poa compressa* L.), Reed canarygrass (*Phalaris arundinacea* L.), Dallisgrass (*Paspalum dilatatum* Poir), Bahiagrass (*Paspalum notatum* Flugge), and, in special situations, lawn grasses including *Zoysia japonica* Steud and *Zoysia matrella*. In addition to the common grasses, several of the cereal grains such as rye (*Secale cereale* L.), oats (*Avena sativa* L.),

Table 2—Blackwell switchgrass yields as affected by lime and phosphate treatments at Bolt Mountain, W. Va. (Data adapted from Armiger et al., 1976)

Spoil amendments/ha†	Yield			
	1972†	1973	1974	Total
	metric tons/ha			
4.5 metric tons phosphate rock + 9 metric tons dolomite	8.7	11.9	13.9	34.5
9 metric tons phosphate rock + 6.7 metric tons dolomite	6.5	12.1	9.9	28.5
13.5 metric tons phosphate rock + 4.5 metric tons dolomite	8.5	15.5	11.4	35.4
24 metric tons phosphate rock	10.1	12.1	12.3	34.5
155 kg/ha P (superphosphate) + 6.7 metric tons dolomite	3.6	9.18	11.0	23.7

† All plots amended with uniform application of 112 kg/ha of N and K.

wheat (*Triticum aestivum* L.), and barley (*Hordeum vulgare* L.) are used mainly as companion crops.

Bromegrasses are cool-season pasture and forage grasses that are deep-rooted, rhizomatous, and form a heavy sod. In general, the bromegrasses are highly palatable and have excellent drought resistance. Smooth bromegrass is one of the most widely used of the cultivated bromegrasses. It will withstand soil pHs in a medium range (5 to 6) and will provide excellent erosion control on farm field waterways, roadbanks, and strip mine spoils, especially when used with a legume. The forage quality of smooth bromegrass compares favorably with that of other cool-season grasses; however, its yield is restricted in the humid region by diseases (rust). Forage yield on acid (pH 5.0) strip mine spoils has ranged from 3.5 to 8 metric tons/ha (Table 3).

Timothy is a cool-season species, adapted to the cooler climates of the northeastern U.S. but not to the southern region. It will grow on acid soils (pH 5.0 to 6.5) where lime and fertilizer have been applied. Timothy is primarily grown for hay, but it produces a good sod for erosion control on disturbed areas, especially when used in combination with legume species. Forage yields on acid strip mine spoils in the Northeastern U.S. have been in the range of 4 to 8 metric tons/ha.

Orchardgrass can be grown successfully on acid disturbed soils in the eastern U.S. where lime and fertilizer have been applied and soil pH ranges from 4.5 to 7.0. Orchardgrass can be grown from southeastern Canada to the northern part of the Gulf states and from the Atlantic Ocean to the eastern Great Plains. It is probably the most common forage species other than bluegrass in the northern Appalachian mountain region. Orchardgrass reportedly is more heat tolerant than either timothy or Kentucky bluegrass but less so than smooth brome or tall fescue. Orchardgrass is shade-tolerant and will persist and be moderately productive on shallow, infertile soils. However, it responds to fertilization, especially N, P, and K, and becomes very competitive when nutrients are available. It can be grown alone, but does very well with legume species like alfalfa and clover. Orchardgrass has been extensively seeded on the

Table 3—Yields of four grass species over a 4-year period as affected by fertility treatments on White Oak Mountain, W. Va.

| | Dry forage yields | | | | | | | | | | | | | | | |
| | Bromegrass | | | | Orchardgrass | | | | Ky 31 tall fescue | | | | Timothy | | | |
Treatments†	1971	1972	1973	1974	1971	1972	1973	1974	1971	1972	1973	1974	1971	1972	1973	1974
								metric tons/ha								
70 P (super)	7.6	4.25	6.3	7.2	6.0	2.9	6.3	7.4	8.1	6.0	7.4	7.6	--	6.3	8.5	9.4
70 P (super) + 125 K	4.0	3.6	5.6	7.2	5.6	3.4	7.4	6.3	6.5	5.6	7.2	7.4	--	4.9	8.5	8.5
70 P (super) + 4 metric tons lime	6.7	4.0	6.3	7.6	6.7	3.4	5.2	6.7	8.3	5.8	7.2	8.3	--	4.9	7.4	9.2
12 metric tons phosphate rock + 125 K	6.0	4.5	6.9	8.7	6.9	3.9	7.2	8.3	8.7	6.0	9.0	8.7	--	5.8	9.4	10.5
12 metric tons phosphate rock	6.0	3.9	6.3	10.1	6.5	3.6	8.3	8.3	8.5	6.3	9.0	10.3	--	5.8	10.5	11.0

† 55 kg/ha of N applied before seeding. Thereafter, 225 kg/ha of N was topdressed in the springs of 1972, 1973, and 1974.

better quality strip mine spoils in the eastern U.S. for soil stabilization, forage production, and grazing. It is usually one of the invader species on the newly graded mine spoils.

The ryegrasses, both perennial and annual, have been used in seeding mixtures on disturbed land areas throughout middle and southern Appalachia. Ryegrasses are considered bunch grasses with no creeping habit of growth. They are generally used as a component for pasture mixtures and are commonly used for pasture, hay, silage, soil conservation, and turf. They can be seeded alone or with other species of grasses and legumes. In many places in the southeastern U.S., annual rye grasses are used to establish a cover for soil protection during the winter. During recent years, strains of perennial ryegrass have been developed for use in the northeastern U.S. However, in general, ryegrasses are less winter-hardy than certain other forage species such as timothy and orchardgrass. The ryegrasses can be grown on a wide range of soil types but will not withstand extremely low temperatures, drought, or poor fertility. Soil pH should be in the range of 5.5 to 7.0.

Kentucky bluegrass is used extensively throughout the northeastern U.S. to obtain a fast cover on disturbed land areas. It is persistent in most of the states, including Alaska, and has a wide soil adaptation. It does best on highly productive soils of limestone origin. Evidently, Kentucky bluegrass was introduced along the Atlantic coast by the early settlers around the 16th century and was carried west and south into the Great Lakes region and the Mississippi Valley. Even though Kentucky bluegrass has a wide soil adaptation, it has rather exacting nutrient and climatic requirements. Soil fertility must be in the high range, with a pH of at least 5.5. Optimum air temperature for Kentucky bluegrass ranges between 15.5 and 32.2C (Heath et al., 1973). Growth is best on northern exposures, or at higher elevations. Although Kentucky bluegrass will grow better in open sunlight, it will grow in slightly shaded situations if moisture and nutrients are favorable. Cool, moist conditions are generally required for optimum growth. It will generally go dormant during dry weather, but will survive severe drought. Kentucky bluegrass is a perennial and produces a dense rhizomatous sod under favorable conditions. It will respond favorably to both irrigation and high nitrogen fertilization.

Canadian bluegrass grows in about the same climatic conditions as Kentucky bluegrass; however, it is dominant only on soils that are acid, droughty, or deficient in N, P, or other nutrients. The optimum temperature for Canadian bluegrass is between 27 and 32°C, but roots and rhizomes develop best at approximately 10°C. Canadian bluegrass produces a blue-green forage, flattened stems, and short, compact panicles. It does not produce as many base leaves as Kentucky bluegrass and matures later in the season. The cultural management of Canadian bluegrass is similar to that of Kentucky bluegrass.

Reed canarygrass is believed to be a native of the Canary Islands, from which it gets its name. Reed canarygrass is a tall, coarse, sod-forming, cool-season perennial which tends to form clumps. It spreads by short, underground, scaley rhizomes and usually forms a dense root system. Reed canarygrass is used on the wet areas on disturbed lands. However, it is more drought-tolerant than many of the cool-season grasses grown in the humid regions. It will withstand flooding for as long as 50 days and will tolerate pHs in the range 4.9 to 8.2. Reed canarygrass is adapted throughout most of the Appalachian region and in the northern half of the United States. It responds readily to fertilization, especially to nitrogen, and will produce high yields under ideal conditions. Reed canarygrass is generally used for pasture, hay, and silage, but has become a vital part of many soil conservation programs. It is one of the main grass species used for vegetating areas where liquid sewage and fluids from municipal and industrial wastes are spray-irrigated on the soil. Reed canarygrass is excellent for gully control because its vigorous spreading growth prevents soil erosion. Small pieces of sod can be planted with a manure spreader in waterways and disced into the soil with good success or it can be seeded directly onto areas where a plant cover is needed.

Dallisgrass is native to South America but was introduced in the United States about 1842. This species is adapted to climates from New Jersey southward to Florida and westward to Texas. Moisture requirements are generally high—requiring as much as 76 cm a year. It will grow on a wide variety of soils but grows best on moist, fertile, clayey, and clay loam bottom lands. With proper fertilization, it will grow on sandy soils but is not well-suited to these conditions. In the southeastern U.S., it is used extensively in grass-legume seeding mixtures on disturbed land areas, especially along highway rights-of-way, construction projects, and better quality strip-mined areas.

Bahiagrass was introduced from South America in 1913. It is widely grown in the southeastern U.S., mainly along the Gulf Coast and Florida. It is adapted to a wide range of coastal plains soils and does well on sandy soils with a pH of 5.5 to 6.5. Once established, it grows well on the drier soils with relatively low fertility. Bahiagrass is a deep-rooted, warm-season perennial that produces short, stout rhizomes and forms a thick sod. It is an excellent species for use on disturbed land areas in the region where adapted. In its region of adaptation, Bahiagrass is tolerant to a wide range of soil conditions, is resistant to weed encroachment, establishes by seed, is relatively free from insects and diseases, produces good growth on soils of low fertility, and withstands close grazing or clipping. The main cultivars of Bahiagrass are Argentine, Pensacola, Paraquay, and Tifhi I and Tifhi II. The last two cultivars were developed by Dr. Glen Burton at the ARS Georgia Coastal Plains Station. The Pensacola variety is used extensively for preventing erosion and for stabilizing the shoulders along road rights-of-way in the southeastern U.S.

Japanese and Korean lawn grass (*Zoysia japonica* Steud) are used on disturbed land areas mainly in the southeastern U.S. They form a low-growing dense sod and spread by rhizomes. They are generally used for lawns and disturbed areas where a low-growing, dense sod is required. They will respond to fertilization, but excessive fertilization is not desirable. Once established, a good, dense sod can be maintained at low cost for several years.

Small grains have been used for revegetation of disturbed land areas throughout the eastern U.S. These are cool-season annuals and are suited to a wide range of soil and climatic conditions, but vary in their soil suitability and preference. Small grain species are usually used to get a quick cover and then used as mulch or nurse crops for more permanent grasses and legume species (Jones et al., 1975a). Rye is more productive than the other small grain species on acid, low-fertility sandy soils or on poorly drained soils. In general, rye can survive lower temperatures than the other small-grained species. Barley (*Hordeum* spp.) is more winter-hardy than oats, but less hardy than rye. In addition, barley is sensitive to wet soil conditions. However, barley and wheat varieties vary considerably in their tolerance to low pH.

Oats grow best in cool, moist climates and are more tolerant than barley to wet soil. They also tolerate a wider soil pH range and soil conditions than does wheat or barley. Spring oats are usually used in the northeastern U.S., whereas winter oats are used more in the southeastern U.S.

III. FORAGE LEGUMES

Several legume species have been used successfully on disturbed lands in the eastern U.S. Some legumes are best used alone; others do better in combinations with grasses and other legumes. The species selected should be adapted to the local environmental conditions. The leguminosae family is the second largest family of agriculturally important plants and comprises several hundred species. Use of legumes on disturbed land areas is extremely important, since they supply a readily available source of nitrogen for non-legume plants, increase the nitrogen content of the soil, aid in protecting soil surface from erosion, and have a beneficial influence on the number, kinds, and activity of various desirable soil organisms. Agriculturally important legume species tested on disturbed land areas in the eastern U.S. include alfalfa (*Medicago sativa* L.), white clovers (*Trifolium repens* L.), crimson clover (*Trifolium incarnatum* L.), birdsfoot trefoil (*Lotus corniculatus* L.), lespedezas (*Lespedeza cuneata, L. stipulacea*), red clover (*Trifolium pratense* L.), crownvetch (*Coronilla varia* L.), hairy vetch (*Vicia villosa* Roth). Other species that have been successfully tested include flatpea (*Lathyrus sylvestris* L.), kura clover (*Trifolium ambiguum* Bieb), zigzag clover (*Trifolium medium* L.), sweet clover (*Melilotus alba* Desr), and yellow sweet clover (*Melilotus officinalis* L.).

Alfalfa is probably the best known forage legume in the United States and throughout the world. It is adapted to a wide range of soil and climatic conditions, but good drainage and fertilization are essential. Its use on disturbed land areas is limited to the better soils where pH has been corrected to the 6 to 7 range. Its deep-penetrating taproot system makes it relatively drought-tolerant and highly desirable in grass-legume mixtures. In studies in West Virginia, an application of dolomitic limestone and raw rock phosphate enabled alfalfa growth on acid strip mine spoils. It is better adapted to the strip mine spoil derived from limestone or calcareous shale overburden than to acid sandstone areas.

White clover has been used extensively in seeding mixtures for use on disturbed lands in the eastern U.S. Ladino white clover was used in the

Table 4—Forage yield and ground cover from selected legumes and legume-grass mixture on a surface mine spoil†

Forage	Ground cover				Yield‡			
	1972		1973					
	Legume fraction	Total	Legume fraction	Total	1971	1972	1973	Average
	%				metric tons/ha			
Chesapeake red clover alone	76**	86 a-c	70 a-c	83 a-c	2.9 b-d	1.6 ef	2.8 b-d	2.4
—with Ky 31 fescue	37 b-e	98 a	40 c-f	100 a	3.9 a-d	4.9 ab	5.3 a-c	4.7
Kenland red clover alone	72 a	81 a-c	75 a-c	86 a-c	4.6 a-d	2.7 b-f	4.2 a-d	3.8
—with Ky 31 fescue	26 c-e	99 a	31 d-f	98 ab	3.7 a-d	4.9 ab	5.6 ab	4.7
Pennscott red clover alone	79 a	91 a	85 ab	92 a-c	4.2 a-d	2.1 d-f	3.7 a-d	3.3
—with Ky 31 fescue	52 a-d	99 a	46 c-e	100 a	5.7 ab	4.0 b-e	5.8 ab	5.2
Mammoth red clover alone	59 a-c	71 bc	45 c-e	55 d	3.0 b-d	2.2 d-f	2.5 cd	2.6
—with Ky 31 fescue	20 de	99 a	39 c-f	100 a	6.1 ab	4.5 a-d	4.1 a-d	4.9
Alsike clover alone	84 a	87 a-c	40 c-f	55 d	2.5 cd	2.8 b-f	3.5 a-d	2.9
—with Ky 31 fescue	20 de	100 a	47 c-e	98 ab	3.2 a-d	4.8 ab	4.0 a-d	4.0
White dutch clover alone	79 a	88 ab	67 a-d	82 a-c	2.3 cd	0.8 f	2.0 d	1.7
—with Merion bluegrass plus creeping red fescue	36 b-e	100 a	52 b-e	100 a	3.1 a-d	1.9 ef	3.5 a-d	2.8
Ladino clover alone	67 ab	86 a-c	53 b-e	71 cd	2.1 cd	1.3 f	3.1 a-d	2.2
—with Merion bluegrass plus creeping red fescue	34 b-e	96 a	53 b-e	100 a	4.9 a-d	0.8 f	5.1 a-c	3.6
Wild white clover alone	76 a	86 a-c	60 a-d	76 b-d	2.7 cd	0.8 f	1.8 d	1.8
—with Merion bluegrass plus creeping red fescue	17 e	99 a	41 c-f	97 ab	3.6 a-d	1.6 ef	2.9 b-d	2.7
Crownvetch alone	80 a	94 a	90 a	96 ab	1.4 d	2.0 ef	6.0 a	3.1
—with Ky 31 fescue	21 de	99 a	65 a-d	99 ab	2.9 cd	4.0 b-e	4.7 a-d	3.9
Sweet clover (yellow) alone	19 e	67 c	11 ef	58 d	3.3 a-d	2.4 c-f	1.8 d	2.5
—with Ky 31 fescue	15 e	97 a	7 f	97 ab	6.4 a	6.7 a	3.3 a-d	5.5

** Any two values in the same column having a letter in common are not significantly different at the 5% level.
† Jones et al., 1975.   ‡ Average of three replicates.

northeastern U.S. during the early 1930's and was later utilized extensively in North Central and southeastern U.S. White clover strains are adapted throughout the eastern U.S. from Maine to Florida and have been used extensively as pasture plants in grass-legume mixtures and in seeding mixtures with grasses for a permanent stabilization of drastically disturbed soil areas. White clover is best adapted to well-drained soils with a pH of 6 to 7 (McConkey, 1935). However, strains of white clover have been grown at pH's of 4 to 5. In eastern Canada, natural selections of white clover have developed a primary taproot, which may grow to more than a meter depth but dies during the second year of growth. White clover is probably the most important pasture legume in the temperate zone and is almost always associated with a companion grass. It is used extensively in grass legume mixtures on strip mine areas, roadbanks, and construction sites throughout the eastern U.S. On strip mine spoil, a mixture of tall fescue and ladino clover gave much better soil protection and total yield than did ladino clover used alone (Jones et al., 1975a) (Table 4).

Crimson clover can be used on disturbed land areas throughout the southeastern U.S. It is used on highway rights-of-way and roadbanks, strip-mined areas, and construction sites in mixtures with grasses and other legumes. Crimson clover is widely grown as a winter annual from the Gulf Coast northward to Maryland, Ohio, and Illinois. It is tolerant of medium soil acidity (pH 5.0 to 8.0) but not to calcareous soil. It is a valuable crop for winter grazing and has become increasingly popular since the development of reseeding or volunteering varieties. It is an excellent plant for stabilizing a soil since it makes rapid fall seedling growth, forms a dense cover, and prevents erosion during the winter months. The central taproot is supported by many fibrous roots. Crimson clover grows better at a lower temperature than most other clover species in the area of adaptation. Good fertilization (P, K, Ca, Mg) is required for maximum growth.

Birdsfoot trefoil is a perennial forage legume used for pasture, hay and silage in the northwest and north central U.S. In these areas birdsfoot trefoil is used extensively in grass-legume mixtures on disturbed land areas, particularly acid strip mine spoils. It will grow on poorly drained, droughty, infertile, acid, or even alkaline soils. Birdsfoot trefoil has a well-developed taproot system with numerous lateral branches and will root to a depth of more than 1 m under good soil conditions. Isolated plants have been found growing on acid strip mine spoils with a 3.5 pH. Apparently, genetic variation is sufficient to allow for selection of acid-tolerant strains. The two main varieties of birdsfoot trefoil grown in the northeastern U.S. are Empire and Viking.

The lespedezas, both annual and perennial, are important legume species used mainly in the southeastern U.S. for hay, pasture, and soil improvement. Most lespedeza species are adapted to low pH (4.5–6.5), infertile soils. However, most varieties respond favorably to lime and to mixed fertilizers on deficient soils. Lespedezas are adapted to a wide range of soil types and soil fertility levels. Many of the lespedezas will grow without soil treatment on eroded, acid soils low in P and other plant nutrients. However, they grow best on the more productive, well-drained soils. The two annual species, *Lespedeza striata* (Thunb) H&A and *Lespedeza stipulacea* maxim, introduced from the Orient are agriculturally important throughout the area of adaptation. They may be used alone or in combination with grass species. The most common species of lespedeza used on disturbed land areas is sericea (*Lespedeza cuneatea* L.). Sericea lespedeza is a long-lived perennial with coarse stems covered with many trifoliate leaflets. If uncut it will grow 1.5 to 2 m tall and develop an extensively branched, deep, taproot system. Sericea lespedeza is used widely for pasture, hay, and soil conservation. It is used extensively for erosion control on disturbed land areas, like strip mines and roadbanks, throughout the southeastern U.S. *Lespedeza bicolor* Turcz. is a shrubby species used for erosion control and for food and cover for wildlife. The Natob cultivar is adapted as far north as Illinois and Indiana, but grows best under more southern conditions. *Bicolor* will grow under adverse soil conditions with low fertility and pH. This plant may grow 6 to 8 m tall under ideal conditions, and is often used as an ornamental because of its profuse colorful flowers.

Red clover is a forage legume which can be grown alone or in combination with grasses. It is probably the most important legume in the northeastern U.S. and is used for hay, pasture, and soil improvement. It develops a deep taproot system with many branching fibrous roots. Because of insect and disease damage, it may act as a biannual rather than a perennial in many sections of the northeastern U.S. Several cultivars and strains of red clover have been used successfully on disturbed land areas, and some are adapted to the southernmost regions of eastern U.S. Red clover will grow on acid soils (pH 4.5) but maximum yields are obtained on fertile, well-drained soils of high moisture-holding capacity. Both calcium and phosphorus are necessary for best growth. Red clover is often sown in combination with companion nurse crops such as oats, flax, barley, or winter wheat. The main cultivars of red clover grown in the eastern U.S. are Chesapeake, Kenland, Pennscott, and Mammoth.

Crownvetch has become one of the most widely used perennial legume species on disturbed lands in the eastern U.S. (Ruffner & Hall, 1963). It is commonly used on roadbanks, difficult industrial sites, and strip-mined areas. Although growth is best on fertile, well-drained soils with a pH of 6 or above, some strains of crownvetch have been grown successfully on strip-mined areas in Pennsylvania, West Virginia, and Maryland with pH's as low as 3.5 where calcium and phosphorus were applied. Crownvetch has a deep penetrating taproot and numerous lateral roots. Adventitious buds can produce new shoots from any of the roots or rhizomes. Its use as a forage plant is not well understood; however, it is being used for grazing by ruminant animals. The three most widely used cultivars of crownvetch are Penngift, Emerald, and Chemung. In general, crownvetch germinates slowly and seedlings grow poorly compared with other legumes. However, once plants are firmly established, growth is vigorous and aggressive. It is an excellent soil conservation plant, a long-lived perennial, spreads rapidly after initial establishment and grows well on eroded soils. In West Virginia, crownvetch has done well when protected by weeping lovegrass, which produces a quick ground cover and protection for the slow-growing crownvetch seedlings.

The true vetches, *Vicia*, contain several species, including about 15 native to the United States. Several may be grown on disturbed soils and acid strip mine spoils with pH range of 4.5 to 8.2. Vetches are often seeded with small grains for hay, silage, or pasture. Probably the best known species is hairy vetch, which is adapted to a wide variety of soil conditions with pH range of 4.8 to 8.2. Lime and P are needed for good growth on acid mine spoils. It is winter-hardy and will withstand below zero temperatures. It may be grown in practically all U.S. areas. It is well-adapted for soil improvement and its matting type of growth helps protect the soil from erosion. *Vicia* species are common invaders along roadways in the southern U.S. The addition of organic matter from vetch improves the physical condition and adds plant food to the soil. Vetches are palatable to livestock and their feeding value is comparable to that of clovers (Brown, 1962). Other species of *Vicia* used on disturbed soils are common (*saliva* L.), Hungarian (*V. panmonica*, Crantz), and purple (*V. benghalensia* L.), but these are adapted only to southern U.S.

Flatpea is a long-lived rhizomatous legume. It is a viny plant with tendril-bearing stems which usually form a dense mat, making it valuable as a conservation plant (Ruffner, 1955–65). It will grow in low pH (4.0) soil and is very drought-resistant. Its primary use is to establish cover on critical outer slope areas, but it also has value as wildlife food and cover. To date, its value as a livestock feed is not fully known.

The extensive deep taproot system of the flat pea seemed to make it drought-resistant and an ideal plant species for low-pH strip mine spoil stabilization. Observation plots were established with flat pea along the edge of the bench area and the outer slope of a site in West Virginia that was characterized by a spoil pH of 2.8. The area was amended with phosphate rock, dolomitic limestone, and N. The flatpea made excellent growth with these nutrients and survival was excellent through four growing seasons. Flatpea seems to be a very promising leguminous plant species for revegetation purposes on acid mine spoils, but seed sources are limited (Armiger et al., 1976).

Kura clover and zigzag clover are two legumes about which very little is known. Kura clover has highly desirable agronomic qualities and spreads extensively by rhizomes (Keim, 1954). It is winter-hardy and resistant to some diseases. Kura is attractive to bees because of its nectar content. The extensive root system and low pH tolerance (4.5) makes it extremely valuable as a soil-conserving plant for revegetating acid strip mine spoils and disturbed land areas. Kura clover is drought-resistant, but it can grow under conditions that are too wet for successful alfalfa production. Only recently have effective cultures of rhizobium been available in the U.S. that would produce active bacteria in nodules on the roots.

The establishment of kura clover depends upon a balanced fertility program. It is potentially a heavy seed-producing crop, but mature pods shatter readily, a characteristic that would make it valuable when it is left to grow continuously without harvest. Kura was slow-growing in the first year on acid strip mine spoil of West Virginia but, thereafter, it formed a dense sod by spreading vegetatively by underground rhizomes (Armiger et al., 1976).

Zigzag clover is a long-lived perennial with a rhizomatous root system (Kawnacka, 1961). It was reported growing on a dry hillside in Massachusetts and in other parts of the country before 1860. Zigzag has shown an adaptation to the unglaciated-sandstone shale soils of Indiana. These soils were waterlogged in winter and very droughty in summer. The clover grew exceptionally well in the soils and was not affected by winter heaving. Zigzag clover is compatible when grown in grass mixtures and is highly disease and insect resistant. It is a low seed producer and, consequently, it is not a well-known legume.

Kura and zigzag clovers have been grown successfully on strip mine spoil at two locations in West Virginia with pH range from 2.8 to 4.0. Both clovers responded to spoil amendments of dolomitic limestone and phosphate rock. The kura clover was inoculated with a rhizobium culture that had been isolated at the Beltsville Agricultural Research Center and found to produce effective nodules. Good stands of both species have persisted through 1975 (Armiger et al., 1976).

Kudzu (*Pueraria lobata* [Willd]) is a fast-growing, coarse, stoloniferous vine used for hay and erosion control mainly in the southern U.S. Under adverse conditions, establishment and complete ground cover may be slow. However, once established, it provides excellent plant cover for erosion control. Kudzu has been used on strip-mined areas mainly to cover the highwall and steep outer slopes. The crowns or seedlings should be planted in good soil at the top of the highwall or near the top of the outer slope. A complete fertilizer plus lime should be applied for establishment. Plants will do well at pH 5.0 and above. Plants will invade surrounding soils with pH of 3.0 to 3.5. Rooting is at the nodes; however, plants can be propagated by seed. Stems can grow to 20- to 25-m lengths in one growing season. Kudzu is nutritionally equivalent to alfalfa and both the foliage and vines are highly palatable. In accessible areas, it can be conrolled by overgrazing with cattle.

IV. TREES AND SHRUBS

Early attempts to discuss soils in connection with silvicultural practices were made by Cotta (1809), Hundeshagen (1938), Sprengle (1832), and Schubler (1938) as reported by Wilde (1958). Since then, many have conducted research relating tree survival and growth to its environment (Russell, 1971). Widely different, and often conflicting results have been obtained in tree fertilization studies, depending on soils, pH, available moisture, location, and climate. This is shown in fertilization studies with nitrogen (Beilmann, 1934; Heiberg & White, 1951; Hobbs, 1944; Walker et al., 1955), phosphorus (Barnes & Ralston, 1953; Fletcher & Ochrymowych, 1955; Heiberg & White, 1951; Hobbs, 1944; Walker et al., 1955), potassium (Heiberg & White, 1951; Hobbs, 1944; Walker et al., 1955), calcium (Baker, 1950; Fletcher & Ochrymowych, 1955; Walker et al., 1955), magnesium (Stone, 1953; Walker et al., 1955), iron (Chadwich, 1936; Walker et al., 1955), manganese (Brauchen & Southwich, 1941), zinc (Wilson, 1953), sulfur (Walker et al., 1955), and boron (Walker et al., 1955). Some species require a relatively good soil with plenty of nutrients whereas other species grow well on acid spoil banks of strip-mined waste areas. Location may greatly alter growth requirements within species. Black walnut (*Juglans nigra* L.) is confined to rich soils of near neutral reaction near the northern boundary of its distribution but grows well on acid, leached soils in the southern U.S. Heavy fertilization of trees for rapid growth is not as feasible as would be true for agronomic crops. Seedlings of maximum weight produced by heavy applications of fertilizer usually have succulent tissue, unbalanced top-root ratio, and other unsatisfactory properties which lower their ability to survive on cutover land.

Nitrogen is the element most often shown to be beneficial in fertilization studies (McDermid, 1960). Under conditions of well-aerated soils adequately supplied with organic matter, microorganisms supply sufficient available N by converting protein-like compounds into nitrate and ammonia (Russel, 1950). Disturbed land areas such as surface mine spoils void of organic matter are apt to show N deficiency.

The optimum pH ranges given for trees are at best crude estimates. The effect of soil reaction is often considerably modified by climate, nutrients, and other factors. For example, white oak (*Quercus alba* L.), tulip poplar (*Liriodendron tulipitera* L.), sycamore (*Platanus occidentalis* L.), and other exacting hardwoods of North America have at times shown fast growth on fine-textured soils with a pH as low as 4.6 (Wilde, 1950). Calcium is removed from the soil in relatively large quantities by both hardwoods and pines. On an average site, hardwoods utilize about three times as much Ca as pines, which helps explain the greater tolerance of pines for acidity (Baker, 1950). Indications are that the pH range for most conifers is wide (Crowther & Benzian, 1952).

Water is perhaps the most important raw material used in tree growth, at least with regard to quantity for survival and growth. It is the principal constituent of protoplasm, a solvent for materials in translocation, and is essential for maintenance of cell turgidity (Kramer, 1962). Baker (1950) defined a no-growth day as one when moisture tension in the surface 30 cm reached or exceeded 4 atm, and assumed diameter growth to be negligible on such days. A single saw-log pine can remove up to 375 liters of water from a moist soil on a hot day (Burns, 1959). In Arkansas, stands of pure pine removed water at about the same rate as stands of pure hardwood (Zahner, 1955). However, in one study the rate of photosynthesis declined more rapidly in pine than in the associated hardwood with decreasing soil moisture (Bormann, 1953). In addition to need for water, trees differ widely in their ability to withstand excess water. Trees such as willows (*Salix* sp.), cottonwood (*Populus* sp.), sycamore (*Platanus* sp.), gum (*Liquidambar* sp.), and spruce (*Picea* sp.) can tolerate prolonged inflow of ground water (Wilde, 1958).

Sunlight is important in the survival and composition in forest succession. After vegetation is removed from an area, the first trees to establish are shade-intolerant species such as pines (*Pinus* sp.) and aspens (*Populus* sp.). Shade-tolerant species such as spruce (*Picea* sp.), hemlock (*Tsuga* sp.), and hard maple (*Acer* sp.) began to establish themselves in 20- to 30-year-old stands (Wilde, 1958). As a rule hardwoods make as much, or more, growth under partial light intensities as under full sunlight. Pine trees have rounded needles in dense clusters which result in the scattering of light and mutual shading. This is one reason why pines can maintain a high photosynthetic rate at light intensities sufficiently high as to retard photosynthesis of a more shade-tolerant species (Kramer & Decker, 1944; Spurr & Barnes, 1973). Photosynthesis begins at a very low light intensity, and most tolerant broadleaf species attain maximum photosynthesis at 20 to 30% of full sunlight (Kramer, 1958).

In mountainous areas, the amount of sunlight that reaches the plant depends on slope orientation. In the Northern Hemisphere, south-facing slopes receive more radiation per unit area than north-facing slopes. In mixed upland oak forests of the Appalachian Mountains, northeast-facing slopes are about 15% more productive than south- and west-facing slopes.

Air pollution should be given some consideration to species selection for planting in an industralized area. Highly sensitive conifers include western larch (*Larix occidentalis* Nutt.), Douglas fir (*Pseudotsuga menziesii* [mirb] *Franco* var. *Menziesii*), and Ponderosa pine (*Pinus ponderosa* Laws.) (Katz, 1939). Fluorides have been responsible for widespread mortality of coniferous trees near smelters, refineries, and power plants (Tresher, 1970). Red maple (*Acer rubrum* L.) and sugar maple (*Acer saccharum* marsh.) were found to be tolerant of air pollutants (Gordon & Gorham, 1963).

Several tree species can be utilized on disturbed land areas in the eastern U.S. However, in general, trees should follow after the spoil has been stabilized with herbaceous species, like grasses and legumes, or be planted with them. On many drastically disturbed areas trees may offer the only logical choice of vegetation where a future monetary return is expected. They do provide long-term cover with little or no additional care and maintenance. The same precautions should be exercised in selecting tree species for use on disturbed land areas as in selecting grasses and legumes. The soil acidity, availability of plant nutrients, chemical and physical properties of spoil material, topography influences, and the overall environmental factors must be considered.

Several tree species have been used on disturbed land areas in the eastern U.S., but only a few have been grown successfully on the more acid strip mine spoils (Ruffner & Steiner, 1969). The more common species used include black locust (*Robinia pseudoacacia* L.), European black alder (*Alnus glutinosa*), autumn olive (*Elaeagnus umbellata*), white pine (*Pinus strobus*), scotch pine (*Pinus sylvestris*), Virginia pine (*Pinus virginiano*), short leaf pine (*Pinus echinata*), red pine (*Pinus resinosa*), Norway spruce (*Picea abies*), European and Japanese larch (*Larix decidua, Larix leptolepis*), and bristly locust (*Robinia hispida*). Other hardwoods not as commonly used include yellow poplar, hybrid poplars, red oak, sycamore, river birch, maples, cottonwoods, and aspens.

Black locust is used extensively on spoil banks throughout eastern U.S. because of survival, growth, and adaptablity (Brown, 1962; Everett et al., 1970). Black locust occurs naturally in the Appalachian Mountains at elevations below 1,075 m. It will grow on a variety of soils but does not do well on excessively dry or compact soils. Limestone soils are especially favorable. Optimum pH is in the range of 6.0 to 7.5, but black locust will grow at pH 4.0–4.5. Growth is retarded if the soil is poorly drained, and black locust does best in open areas without competition from other trees. It will establish on the more difficult sites and produces seed at an early age. It is a legume and adds both N and organic matter to the soil. However, its multiple stem growth habit and susceptibility to damage by the locust borer limit its use as a marketable product. A dominant stem variety has been developed and is used to a limited extent. However, damage from the locust borer has been extensive in most locations.

Bristly locust (*Robinia hispida*) can be used on extremely low pH (3.5 areas and on critical areas where there is little possibility of using the area immediately for economic benefit. It spreads very rapidly from both seed and from adventitious buds formed from the roots. It provides good cover for wildlife.

European black alder is a possible alternative to black locust on disturbed land areas (Ruffner & Steiner, 1969). It grows rapidly, adds N to the soil, and can be used for pulp wood. It survives under about the same soil and climatic conditions as black locust. European alder or black alder grows on soils ranging from loamy to clayey, but will grow under extremely rocky conditions, and will tolerate a very low (4.0) soil pH (U.S. SCS, 1971). It grows under low moisture, and under conditions ranging from poorly drained to dry (Ruffner & Steiner, 1969).

Virginia pine or scrub pine is adapted to southeastern U.S. and grows well on a wide variety of soils. It is best adapted to moderately well-drained, clay, loam, or sandy loam soils. Virginia pine seedlings are more tolerant of low moisture than most pines and will grow under quite dry conditions. Optimum pH range is from 5.0 to 6.0, but this species will grow on disturbed areas with pH as low as 4.6 (Spurway, 1941). Growth is best at elevations of from 30 to 770 m. Virginia pine is shade-intolerant and seedlings require direct sunlight for good growth. Nutrient supply and balance are important for good growth. Virginia pine is more aggressive on the poorer sites than other associated pines (Den Vye, 1948).

Pitch pine (*Pinus rigida* Mill.) grows over a wide geographic range and environmental conditions. It is usually restricted to the shallow sandy or gravelly textured, less fertile soils. Optimum pH range is from 4.5 to 5.0 but it is found on soils with a pH as low as 3.5. Pitch pine is adapted to a wide range of soil moisture conditions from excessively drained to very poorly drained. In Pennsylvania, it usually is not found above an elevation of 615 m (Illich & Aughanbaugh, 1930), but in the Smokey Mountains it is found as high as 1,386 m (Whittaker, 1956). Pitch pine is shade-intolerant.

Shortleaf pine occupies the widest range of any of the southeastern pines, and is least exacting with regard to temperature and moisture. It will grow on a wide variety of acid soils and is used extensively on disturbed land areas in the southeastern U.S. Optimum pH range is 4.5 to 6.0 and it will not tolerate a high pH. Shortleaf pine is shade-intolerant.

Eastern white pine offers an excellent possibility for use on disturbed sites in northern Appalachia (Ruffner & Steiner, 1969). The climatic range is cool and humid. It has grown on practically all the soils within its range (Frothingham, 1914). It is most closely associated with well-drained, sandy soils but also grows on loams and silty soils, whether drainage is good or poor. Optimum pH for growth is 4.5 to 6.0 but it will grow at a higher pH than most pines. It is classed as intermediate in shade tolerance (Baker, 1949). In the seedling stage white pine is susceptible to competition because its growth is slow compared to associated species.

Yellow poplar (*Liriodendron tulipifera* L.) or tulip poplar grows under a variety of climatic conditions throughout eastern U.S. It grows best on moderately moist, well-drained soils, and does not do well on very wet or very dry sites. At the northern part of its range where low temperatures are limiting, it usually is found in valleys and stream bottoms below 300 m. In the southern Appalachians it is found at elevations as high as 1,385 m. Yellow poplar is shade intolerant but can overcome some competition because it grows rapidly. It has been shown to make poor radial growth on N-deficient soils (Mitchell & Chandler, 1939). It usually does not do well on disturbed sites such as surface-mined areas, but good growth has been reported on better sites where moisture and other conditions were favorable (Brown, 1962).

Red spruce (*Picea rubens* Sarg.) grows best in the higher parts of the southern Appalachian mountains where atmospheric humidity and rainfall are greater during the growing season (Korstain, 1937). Optimum pH for growth is in the range of 4.5 to 5.0 but good growth is common on soils with a pH of 4.0. Red spruce often grows on sites unfavorable for other species such as steep rocky slopes, thin soils, and wet bottom-lands. In West Virginia, it is limited to elevations above 1,075 m, and in Tennessee and North Carolina to above 1,385 m. The rate of growth of red spruce is strongly affected by light. It will live in dense shade for years, but requires near full sunlight for best development. The degree of shade tolerance is influenced by fertility and climate.

American sycamore (*Platanus occidentalis* L.) grows best along streams and in bottomlands where there is a good supply of water, and can usually tolerate fluctuations in the ground water level. It seldom makes good growth on eroded, old fields. However, it is recommended for planting on all types of coal-stripped lands (Polter et al., 1951). Optimum pH for good growth is in the range of from 6.0 to 7.5. In the Appalachian Mountains it grows at elevations to 300 m in the northern part and to 770 m in the southern part. It is generally classed as intermediate in shade tolerance.

White oak (*Quercus alba* L.) grows under a wide range of climatic conditions and over a wide range of soils and site conditions. It does best on deep, well-drained loamy soils, but growth is good on all but the driest, shallow soils. Nutrients are usually not a limiting factor except on very sandy soils. Optimum pH range is from 5.5 to 8.0. It does not do well on wet bottomlands. White oak is classed as intermediate in shade tolerance.

Northern red oak (*Quercus rubra* L.) will grow on soils ranging from clay to loamy sands and from deep to shallow rocky soils. Available soil moisture is a critical factor in early survival and growth of red oak seedlings, especially on disturbed sites. Optimum pH range for red oak is from 5.0 to 7.0. It is intermediate in shade tolerance and, among the oaks, it is less tolerant than white oak.

Autumn olive is a woody shrub used extensively for wildlife, food, and cover on surface-mined areas throughout the Appalachian region. It will survive at low spoil pH conditions (4.0) and is adapted to a wide range in soil and climatic conditions.

The European (*Larix decidua*) and Japanese larch (*Larix leptolepis*) have been used to a limited extent on mine spoils in northern Appalachia with some success. Under ideal conditions, growth can be very rapid; however, the European larch is usually susceptible to late spring frost injury.

Birch (*Betula populifolia* Marsh) will grow on soils of low fertility from West Virginia through southern Ontario, Canada. Growth is good on a wide range of soils within this area. In the Pennsylvanian mountain areas, it is one of the common species invading the acid strip mine spoils. The soil pH range is between 4.5 and 6.5. River Birch (*B. nigra*) can be found along bottom lands and on the disturbed areas with higher moisture content.

LITERATURE CITED

Armiger, W. H., J. N. Jones, Jr., and O. L. Bennett. 1976. Revegetation of land disturbed by strip mining of coal in Appalachia. USDA Pub. ARS-NE-71 (August). 38 p.

Baker, F. S. 1949. A revised tolerance table. J. For. 47:179–181.

Baker, F. S. 1950. Principles of silviculture. 1st ed. McGraw-Hill Book Co., Inc., New York. p. 151–207.

Barnes, R. L., and C. W. Ralston. 1953. The effect of colloidal phosphate on height growth of slash pine plantations. Res. Notes Univ. of Florida For. School, University Press, Blacksburg, Va. 2 p.

Bassett, J. R. 1964. Tree growth as affected by soil moisture. Soil Sci. Soc. Am. Proc. 28: 436–438.

Beilmann, A. P. 1934. Experiment on the fertilization of shade trees. Proc. Nat. Shade Trees Conf. 10:114–126.

Bennett, O. L. 1971. Grasses and legumes for revegetation of strip-mined areas. p. 23–45. *In* Proc. Revegetation and Economic Use of Surface-Mined Land and Mine Refuse Symp., West Virginia Univ., Morgantown, WV, 2–4 Dec. 1971. University Press, Morgantown.

Bennett, O. L. 1973. Vegetation to heal scares. p. 249–253. Proc. 28th Annl. Meeting Soil Conserv. Soc. of Am. SCSA Hot Springs, Ark., Sept. 30–Oct. 3.

Bennett, O. L., J. N. Jones, Jr., W. H. Armiger, and P. E. Lundberg. 1972. New techniques for revegetation of strip-mined areas. p. 50–55. Proc. 27th Annl. Meeting of Soil Conserv. Soc. of Am., Portland, Ore., October.

Berg, W. A., and W. G. Vogel. 1968. Manganese toxicity of legumes. U.S. For. Serv. Res. Pap.-NE119, USDA, p. 12.

Blaser, R. E., G. W. Thomas, C. R. Brooks, G. J. Shoop, and J. B. Martin, Jr. 1962. Turf establishment and maintenance along highway cuts. Sch. of Eng. Appl. Sci., Univ. of Va., Reprint No. 6, University Press, Blacksburg.

Bormann, F. H. 1953. Factors determining the role of loblolly pine and sweet gum in the early old-field succession in the Piedmont of North Carolina. Ecol. Monogr. 23:339–358.

Brauchen, O. L., and R. W. Southwich. 1941. Correction of manganese deficiency symptoms of walnut tree. Proc. Am. Soc. Hortic. Sci. 39:133–136.

Brown, J. H. 1962. Success of tree planting of strip-mined areas in West Virginia. West Virginia Univ. Agr. Exp. St. Bull. 473, University Press, Morgantown. 34 p.

Brown, J. H. 1971. Use of trees for revegetation and economic use of surface-mined areas. p. 26–29. Proc. Revegetation and Economic Use of Surface-Mined Land and Mine Refuse Symp., Dec. 2–4, 1971. West Virginia Univ., Morgantown, WV, Univesity Press.

Burns, P. Y. (ed.). 1959. Southern forest soils. La. State Univ. Press, Baton Rouge, La.

Chadwich, L. C. 1936. Chlorosis of pin-oaks. Proc. Am. Soc. Hortic. Sci. 33:669–673.

Costin, A. B. 1967. Grasses and grasslands in relation to soil conservation. p. 236–258. In C. Barnard (ed.) Grasses and grasslands. MacMillan & Co. Ltd., London.

Crowther, E. M., and B. Benzian. 1952. Subcommittee on nutrition problems in forest nurseries. Summary report on 1950 experiments, Rep. For. Res. (London) 1950–1951:113–122.

Curtis, W. R. 1971. Vegetating strip-mine spoils for runoff and erosion control. p. 40–41. Proc. Revegetation and Economic Use of Surface-Mined Land and Mine Refuse Symp., West Virginia University, Morgantown, WV.

Davidson, W. H., and E. A. Sowa. 1974. Early attempts to vegetate coal mine spoils with container grown seedlings. In R. W. Tinus, W. I. Stein, and W. E. Balmer (ed.) Proc. N. Amer. Containerized Forest Tree Seedling Symp., Denver Co. Great Plains Agr. Council, Pub. no. 68, 458 p. U.S. Government Printing Office, Washington, D.C.

Davis, G., R. W. Ruble, J. F. Ibberson, W. H. Wheeler, E. G. Musser, R. D. Shipman, and W. G. Jones. 1965. A guide for revegetating bituminous strip mine spoils. By Pa. Res. Comm. on Coal Mine Spoil Revegetation in Pa., Harrisburg, Pa.

Den Vye, D. 1948. Virginia pine in southern Indiana. Acad. Sci. Proc. 57:77–80.

Derr, H. J., and W. F. Mann, Jr. 1971. Direct-seeding pines in the South. USDA For. Serv. Agric. Handbook 391. U.S. Government Printing Office, Washington, D.C.

Dickson, R. E. 1971. The effects of soil moisture, texture, and nutrient levels on the growth of black walnut. N. Cent. Forest Exp. Stn., St. Paul, Minn. 6 p-illus. USDA Res. Pap. NC-66.

Everett, H. W., F. B. Gaffney, and G. V. Schultz. 1970. Evolution of woody plants and development of establishment procedures for direct seeding and for vegetative reproduction. (Interim Rep. for period 1966–1969) Maryland Project HPR-Project, AW 67-75-46, University Press, Blackburg, Va.

Everett, H. W., C. R. Anderson, G. V. Schultz, and R. F. Dudley. 1973. Direct establishment of shrubs and other woody vegetation. Publ. State Highway Admin. Bur. of Res., Brooklandville, Md. Sec. 3, p. 21–28.

Fleming, A. L., J. W. Schwartz, and C. D. Foy. 1974. Chemical factors controlling the adaptation of weeping lovegrass and tall fescue to acid. Agron. J. 66:715–719.

Fletcher, D. W., and J. Ochrymowych. 1955. Mineral nutrition and growth of eastern red cedar in Missouri. Res. Bull. 577, Mo. Agric. Exp. Stn., 15 p.

Frothingham, E. H. 1914. White pine under forest management. USDA Bull. 13, U.S. Government Printing Office, Washington, D.C. 70 p.

Gordon, A. G., and E. Gorham. 1963. Ecological aspects of air pollution from an iron-sintering plant at Wawa, Ontario. Can. J. Bot. 41:1063–1078.

Green, J. T., R. E. Blaser, and H. D. Perry. 1973. Establishing presistent vegetation on cuts and fills along West Virginia Highways. W. Va. Dept. of Highway Res. Proj. 26—Phase II, Charleston, W. Va.

Grube, W. E., Jr., R. M. Smith, R. N. Singh, and A. A. Sobek. 1973. Characterization of coal overburden materials and mine soils in advance of surface mining. p. 134–152. Proc. Research and Applied Technology Symp. on Mined Land Reclamation. 7–8 Mar. 1973, Pittsburgh, Pa. Bituminous Coal Res., Inc., Monroeville, Pa.

Heath, M. E., D. S. Metcalfe, and R. E. Barnes. 1973. Forages—the science of grassland agriculture. 3rd ed. Iowa State Univ. Press, Ames.

Heiberg, W. O., and D. P. White. 1951. Potassium deficiency of reforested pine and spruce stands in northern New York. Soil Sci. Soc. Am. Proc. 15:369–376.

Hill, R. D. 1975. Non-point pollution from mining and mineral extraction. p. 67–81. Proc. Southeastern Reg. Conf. Non-Point Sources of Water Pollution, Blacksburg, VA (VA Water Resources Research Center). May.

Hobbs, C. H. 1944. Studies on mineral deficiency in pine. Plant Physiol. 19:590–602.

Hottenstein, W. L. 1970. Erosion control, safety, and esthetics on the roadsides—summary of current practices. Public Roads 36(2).

Illich, J. S., and J. E. Aughanbaugh. 1930. Pitch pine in Pennsylvania. Pa. Dept. For. and Water Res. Bull. 2. 108 p.

Johnson, A. G., D. B. White, M. H. Smithberg, and L. C. Snyder. 1971. Development of ground covers for highway slopes. Final Rep. Investigation 615, Univ. of Minn. Dept. of Hortic. Sci., St. Paul.

Johnson, A. W. 1961. Highway erosion control. Am. Soc. Agric. Eng. Trans. 4(1):144–152.

Jones, J. N., Jr., W. H. Armiger, and G. C. Hungate. 1973. Soil ledges improve stabilization of outer slopes in mined spoil. p. 250–259. In Proc. 1st Res. and Applied Tech. Symp. on Mined Land Recl. 7–8 Mar. 1973, Pittsburgh, Pa. National Coal Assoc., Monroeville, Pa.

Jones, J. N., Jr., W. H. Armiger, and O. L. Bennett. 1975a. A two-step system for revegetation of strip mine spoils. J. Environ. Qual. 4:233–235.

Jones, J. N., Jr., W. H. Armiger, and O. L. Bennett. 1975b. Forage grasses aid the transition from spoil to soil. p. 185–194. Proc. 3rd Symp. on Surface Mining and Recl. Vol. 2 NCA/BCR, Louisville, Kentucky. October 21–23.

Katz, M. (ed.). 1939. Effect of sulfur dioxide on vegetation. Nat. Res. Counc. Canada Publ. 815, Ottawa. 447 p.

Kawnacka, M. 1961. Preliminary observations on zigzag clover. Natl. Sci. Found. and Dept. of Agric. Centralny Instytut Informacji Naukowo-Techniczneh Ekononiczne, Warszawa, Poland.

Keim, W. F. 1954. Status of trifolium ambiguum as a forage legume. Dept. of Botany and Plant Pathology, Iowa State College, Ames, Iowa.

Kohnke, H. 1950. The reclamation of coal mine spoils. Adv. Agron. 2:318–349. Academic Press, Inc., New York.

Korns, C. H. 1971. Roadside horticulture vegetation (a terminal report). Mississippi State Highway Dept., Vol. 2. Jackson, Miss.

Korstain, C. F. 1937. Perpetuation of spruce on cutover and burned lands in the higher southern Appalachia Mountains. Ecol. Mono. 7:125–167.

Kramer, P. J. 1958. Photosynthesis of trees as affected by their environment. p. 157–186. In K. V. Thiaman (ed.) Physiology of forest trees. Ronald Press Co., New York.

Kramer, P. J. 1962. The role of water in tree growth. p. 171–182. In T. T. Kozlowski (ed.) Tree growth. Ronald Press Co., New York.

Kramer, P. J., and J. P. Decker. 1944. Relation between light intensity and rate of photosynthesis of loblolly pine and certain hardwoods. Plant Physiol. 19:350–358.

McConkey, D. 1935. The origin and ecological adaptation of the agricultural grasses, clovers, and alfalfa of eastern Canada. Herb. Rev. 3:185–192.

McDermid, R. W. (ed.). 1960. The use of chemicals in southern forests. La. State Univ. Press, Baton Rouge, La.

Mellinger, R. H., W. Glover, and J. G. Hall. 1966. Results of revegetation of strip mine spoil by soil conservation districts in West Virginia. West Virginia Univ. Agr. Exp. Sta. Bull. 540.

Mezapowskyj, M., and R. Brider. 1970. Hydroseeding on anthracite coal-mine spoils. USDA For. Ser. Res. Note NE-124. U.S. Government Printing Office, Washington, D.C.

Miller, E. L., and J. D. Budy. 1974. Field survival of container-grown Jeffrey pine seedlings outplanted on adverse sites. Proc. North Am. Containerized Forest Tree Seedling Symp., Denver, Co. Ed. by R. W. Tinus, W. I. Stein, and W. E. Balmer, Wash., D.C. Great Plains Agr. Council, Pb. no. 68. U.S. Government Printing Office, Washington, D.C.

Mitchell, H. J., and R. F. Chandler. 1939. The nitrogen nutrition and growth of certain deciduous trees of Northeastern U.S. Black Roch. For. Bull. 11. 94 p. U.S. Government Printing Office, Washington, D.C.

National Research Council. 1960. Roadside development. A selected bibliography. Bibliogr. 26. Natl. Res. Counc., Highw. Res. Board, Comm. on Roadside Dev., Washington, D.C. p. 11–17.

Palazzo, A. A., and R. W. Duell. 1974. Responses of grasses and legumes to soil pH. Agron. J. 66:678–682.

Partain, L. E. 1974. Grass for protection, safety, beauty, recreation. p. 204–215. In Grasslands. Iowa State Univ. Press, Ames. Iowa.

Perry, H. D., D. L. Wright, and R. F. Blaser. 1975. Producing vegetation on highway slopes concurrently with and subsequent to highway construction. Final Rep. Proj. 40 for West Virginia Dept. of Highways, FH WA-WV, Charleston, W. Va.

Plass, W. T. 1968. Tree survival and growth of fescue covered spoil bank. U.S. Forest Ser. Res. Note NE-90. U.S. Government Printing Office, Washington, D.C.

Polter, H. S., S. Weitzman, and G. R. Trimble, Jr. 1951. Reforestation of strip-mined lands in West Virginia. U.S. For. Serv. NE For. Exp. Stn. Pap. 43. 20 p.

Rovine, Russel. 1975. The future of roadside management general views and specific moves. Rural and Urban Roads. Feb., p. 11–12.

Ruffner, J. D. 1955–65. An evaluation of species planted on coal strip mine spoil in West Virginia for stabilization purposes. Soil Conserv. Serv. Pub., Morgantown, WV.

Ruffner, J. E., and J. C. Hall. 1963. Crownvetch in West Virginia. West Virginia Univ. Agric. Exp. Stn. Bull. 487, Morgantown, WV.

Ruffner, J. D., and W. W. Steiner. 1969. Evaluation of plants for use on critical sites. Int. Symp. on Ecology and Revegetation of Drastically Disturbed Areas, Penn. State Univ., University Park, Pa. Aug. 3–6.

Russel, E. J. 1950. Soil condition and plant growth. 8th ed. Longman, London.

Russell, T. E. 1971. Planting and direct seeding hardwoods in the southern Appalachians. p. 60–65. In Proc. of Symp. on Southern Appalachian Hardwoods, USDA-FS. U.S. Government Printing Office, Washington, D.C.

Shears, G. A. 1971. Experience in revegetation of highway cuts and fills. p. 33–36. Proc. Revegetation and Economic Use of Surface-Mined Land and Mine Refuse Symp., West Virginia Univ., University Press, Morgantown, WV, Dec. 2–4.

Spurr, S. H., and B. V. Barnes. 1973. 2nd ed. Forest ecology. Ronald Press Co., New York. 571 p.

Spurway, C. H. 1941. Soil reaction (pH) preferences of plants. Michigan State College Agric. Exp. Stn. Bull. 306. 36 p.

Stone, E. L. 1953. Magnesium deficiency in some northeastern pines. Soil Sci. Soc. Am. Proc. 17:297–300.

Struthers, P. H. 1960. Forage seedings help reclaim areas on spoil banks. Ohio Farm and Home Res. 45(1). Ohio Agr. Res. & Devel. Center, Wooster, Ohio.

Sutton, P. 1970. Restoring productivity of coal mine spoils. Ohio Farm and Home Res. 62. Ohio Agr. Res. & Devel. Center, Wooster, Ohio.

Sutton, P. 1973. Reclamation of toxic strip mine spoil banks. Ohio Farm and Home Res. p. 18–20. Ohio Agr. Res. & Devel. Center, Wooster, Ohio.

Tresher, M. 1970. Environment and plant response. McGraw-Hill Book Co., Inc., New York. 422 p.

Troll, J., and J. M. Zak. 1972. The use of grasses, mulches, and woody perennials for rapid stabilization of roadsides. In The use of adaptable plant species for roadside cover in Mass., Tech. Rep. 23-R5-Roadside Development. 160 p.

U.S. Department of Agriculture. Silvics of forest trees of the United States. 1965. Agr. Handbook 271, USDA-FS. 762 p.

U.S. Soil Conservation Service. 1971. Kentucky guide for classification used and vegetative treatment of surface mine spoil. Lexington, Ky. 20 p.

Vogel, W. G., and W. A. Berg. 1968. Grasses and legumes for cover on acid strip mine spoils. J. Soil Water Conserv. 23:88–90.

Walker, R. B., S. P. Gessel, and P. G. Haddock. 1955. Greenhouse studies in mineral requirements of conifers. Western red cedar. For. Sci. 1:51–60.

Webb, D. M. 1975. Revegetation possible for abandoned strip mined lands. Maryland Conservationist, 7–9 p.

Whittaker, R. H. 1956. Vegetation of the Great Smokey Mountains. Ecol. Monogr. 26:1–80.

Wilde, S. A. 1950. A simple soil air permeameter. Agron. J. 42:522.

Wilde, S. A. 1958. Forest soils. Ronald Press Co., New York. 537 p.

Copyright © 1978 ASA–CSSA–SSSA
677 South Segoe Road, Madison, WI 53711 USA
Reclamation of Drastically Disturbed Lands

Chapter 17

Lime and Fertilizer Use in Land Reclamation in Humid Regions

D. A. MAYS AND G. W. BENGTSON

Tennessee Valley Authority
Muscle Shoals, Alabama

I. INTRODUCTION

Denuded, apparently sterile, spoils resulting from surface mining may be bare only because no seed source was naturally present or because none was supplied by man to initiate revegetation; or severe and frequent erosion may have inhibited seedling establishment. However, in most instances, some serious acidity, infertility, or salinity problem is the cause of poor plant growth.

Extreme acidity in the pH range of 2.5 to 4.0 does not in itself inhibit plant growth. A more serious aspect of the problem is that aluminum and manganese concentrations in the soil solution are at high levels when the pH is below 4.0. Both elements are toxic to plant roots at appreciable concentrations in the soil solution. Potentially detrimental soluble iron may also be present at low pH level.

While acidity has often received the blame for barren spoils, severe deficiencies of plant nutrients, particularly nitrogen (N) and phosphorus (P), are actually more widespread than growth-limiting soil acidity. The purpose of this chapter is to discuss the occurrence and correction of these acidity and infertility problems.

II. LIME NEEDS

A. Source and Extent of pH Problems

1. NATURALLY ACID STRATA

Growth-limiting acidity in strip mine spoils has two basic origins. Some overburden may consist primarily of sandstones or shales which are acid because of the low base content of the parent material. When these materials are deposited at the surface during mining or regrading their low pH and infertility precludes successful revegetation without amendment.

When acid layers are thin relative to the total depth of overburden, it is possible to bury the acid material under spoil with more favorable pH during the mining operation. However, situations exist where the overburden may be 25 m or more in depth, with all but the top 1 or 2 m being too acid. Where these unfavorable ratios of good to acid spoil exist, burial of the entire acid layer by conventional mining techniques is almost impossible; heavy liming, topsoiling, or prohibition of mining may then be necessary.

2. OXIDATION OF SULFUR COMPOUNDS

The most common cause of surface spoil acidity is careless placement of sulfur-bearing overburden layers and waste coal on the spoil surface during mining. Iron pyrite (FeS_2) is a prevalent sulfur-bearing mineral in coal seams and adjacent layers. Freshly uncovered coal or pyritic spoil is not strongly acid but upon prolonged exposure to the air the sulfur (S) is oxidized to sulfuric acid (H_2SO_4). This causes the extremely low pH spoil that occurs in such situations. Weathered pyritic spoils commonly have pH values ranging from 2.2 to 3.5.

While strongly acid nonpyritic overburdens can be successfully and permanently improved by applying sufficient lime to neutralize the existing acidity, pyritic spoils have very high residual acidity potentials which must be satisfied. Oxidation of S may continue to produce H_2SO_4 in excess of the amount removed by leaching for many years after mining. If sufficient lime is not added to neutralize this acid as it is formed, a spoil will again become too acid to support plant growth within a year or two after liming.

3. GEOGRAPHICAL OCCURRENCE

It is impossible to characterize adequately the extent and geographical distribution of acid mine spoils on the basis of the data which currently exist; no regional or nationwide compilations have been made. Almost all of the strongly acid spoils in the United States occur in the humid areas from Iowa eastward and southward where the coal deposits tend to be high in S. Acid spoils are rare in the Northern Great Plains lignite and subbituminous fields and in the four-corners area of the southwest where coal deposits generally contain little S. However, spoils in those areas are usually somewhat alkaline and often have salt or sodium problems which are as difficult to remedy as low pH.

The extent of acid spoils has been estimated in a few states. For example, Einspahr et al. (1955) estimated that 38% of some 2,300 ha of spoils in Iowa at that time had a pH of 4.0 or less.

Plass and Vogel (1973) reported that, of 39 different spoils representing 10 different coal seams in southern West Virginia, only 5% of all samples had a pH of 4.0 or less, while 27% had a pH between 4.1 and 5.0. All of the more acid samples were collected from only 3 of the 10 seams represented in the study. A recent Forest Service study in Kentucky identified nine problem seams in southeastern Kentucky, three in eastern Kentucky, but none in northeastern Kentucky. Some acid spoils also occur in western Kentucky. Several of the acid seams in eastern Kentucky also occur in Tennessee.

The limited information available indicates that spoils with growth-limiting pH levels probably represent only a small fraction of all the disturbed land which requires revegetation. If the best techniques of premining overburden analysis such as those suggested by Despard (1974), Grube et al. (1973), and others were combined with careful spoil segregation during mining, it seems likely that few spoils would have surface pH levels so low as to inhibit revegetation.

B. Determining the Lime Requirement of Spoils

Numerous methods for determination of pH or lime requirement have been developed. While there are significant differences in accuracy among methods, none are useful unless combined with an adequate spoil sampling procedure. Because of the great diversity that exists in many spoils, the planning of a logical sampling procedure for each tract is of extreme importance.

Mine spoils may vary greatly in pH or fertility characteristics within a single hectare because of the great amount of soil horizon mixing that occurs during overburden removal. Each area of more than one-fourth to one-half hectare in size which appears to be different in color, texture, or other physical condition should be treated as a separate sampling unit. After a tract has been separated into sampling units, one should obtain from 10 to 20 subsamples from each unit for compositing to form a representative sample for chemical analysis. Subsamples should be taken with a soil sampling tube to a depth of 10 to 15 cm. It is seldom useful to analyze spoil samples from lower horizons.

The glass electrode pH meter is the standard instrument used for pH determination. A pH of 7 indicates neutrality, those below 7 are acid, and those above 7 are alkaline. Since pH is a logarithmic scale, a soil at pH 4 is 10 times more acid than at pH 5 and 100 times more acid than at pH 6.

A water solution is usually used for pH determination with agricultural soils. However, the soluble salts often found in spoils may reduce the pH values by 0.5 to 1.0 units. After the salts are leached out by rainfall the pH may increase by this amount. Thus, the use of a solution of $0.002M$ $CaCl_2$ may give truer pH values with spoil than water solutions.

Several colorimetric methods of pH determination are cheaper or more convenient than the pH meter for only a few samples, but accuracy of these methods is poor and the results should be interpreted with great care. Berg (1969) compared pH by 6 colorimetric methods and a pH meter on 100 Kentucky spoils. His results (Table 1) show the lack of precision which is often obtained with colorimetric methods.

The standard water or buffer pH test indicates the active acidity of the sample with no indication of the amount of residual acid-forming potential. If adequate lime recommendations are to be made for pyritic spoils both the amount of total sulfides and pH must be determined. Barn-

Table 1—Percentage of readings from six pH determination methods falling within a given
deviation of pH meter readings (Berg, 1969)

Method and pH range†	Deviation, in pH units of				
	0.2	0.5	1.0	2.0	3.0
LaMotte-Morgan:					
2.7–4.5	58	92	100	--	--
4.6–6.0	49	87	100	--	--
6.1–8.3	44	80	100	--	--
LaMotte-Morgan modification:					
2.7–4.5	44	100	--	--	--
4.6–6.0	51	80	100	--	--
6.1–8.3	52	88	100	--	--
Soiltex:					
2.7–4.5	44	83	97	100	--
4.6–6.0	33	59	92	100	--
6.1–8.3	16	44	84	100	--
Hellige-Truog:					
2.7–4.5	42	75	97	100	--
4.6–6.0	23	62	97	100	--
6.1–8.3	12	44	72	100	--
Hydrion Papers:					
2.7–4.5	56	97	100	--	--
4.6–6.0	8	31	77	100	--
6.1–8.3	0	0	0	48	100
Kelway pH Tester:					
2.7–4.5	6	33	50	92	100
4.6–6.0	0	3	10	87	100
6.1–8.3	44	68	80	100	--

† Number of spoil samples within the ranges, as determined by pH meter: 2.7 to 4.5—36;
4.6 to 6.0—39; 6.1 to 8.3—25.

hisel and his associates in Kentucky (R. I. Barnhisel, personal communication, 1976) use a sulfide test which employs hydrogen peroxide (H_2O_2) to oxidize the sulfides to H_2SO_4, which is then titrated with sodium hydroxide (NaOH) to pH 7.0. The amount and normality of NaOH required is used to calculate the meq (H^+)/100 g of spoil. This information can then be used to estimate the amount of agricultural lime needed to neutralize the potential acidity related to the pyrite content of the spoil (Barnhisel, 1975).

For a given pH the lime requirement increases with decreasing soil particle size. Since there is limited knowledge of the relationship of pH to lime requirement for many spoils, additional correlations are needed, particularly for spoils that occur in large acreages. The current liming recommendations for spoils in Kentucky are shown in Table 2 (Barnhisel, 1975).

C. pH Requirements of Plants

Most crop plants, as well as many shrubs and deciduous trees, grow best in the pH range from 5.5 to 7.5, while pines grow best at somewhat lower pH. However, there are numerous exceptions and plants can be

Table 2—Recommended ground limestone rates for Kentucky spoils (Barnhisel, 1975)

Buffer pH	Agricultural lime required to adjust spoil to pH	
	5.5	6.4
	metric tons/ha	
6.7–6.3	2– 4	5– 9
6.3–5.9	5– 9	9–13
5.9–5.3	9–13	13–18
5.3–5.0	13–18	18–25
5.0–4.5	18–25	25–34
4.5–4.0	25–34	34–56
below 4.0	34–56	>56

found which will tolerate pH levels as low as 3.5. Prior to the widespread regrading of spoils, liming was usually not technically or economically feasible. Then many workers searched for plants which could grow at low pH and species were often chosen primarily for tolerance to low pH with little regard for their economic usefulness. With the present level of technology it seems more desirable to adjust the spoil pH so that plants offering the best economic or aesthetic advantages can be grown.

Adams and Pearson (1967) and Woodruff (1967) reported the minimum pH levels at which a number of crop plants achieve near-maximum production (Table 3). These species would likely survive at somewhat lower pH levels but with lower productivity levels.

Plass (1974) compared 7 species of direct-seeded pines on 12 spoils with pH ranging from 2.5 to 8.4. He found good survival except at pH's below 3.8 or above 7.8. He concluded that loblolly (*Pinus taeda* L.) and longleaf (*Pinus palustris* Mill.) pine appeared to be best adapted to spoils and that pines grew best between pH 4.1 and 5.0.

Vogel and Berg (1968) found that weeping lovegrass (*Eragrostis curvula* [Schrad.] Nees) and switchgrass (*Panicum virgatum* L.) made satisfactory growth in the greenhouse on pH 4.1 spoil material. In field studies they found that birdsfoot trefoil (*Lotus corniculatus* L.) and sericea lespedeza [*Lespedeza cuneata* (Dumont) G. Don] grew on spoils as

Table 3—Crop plant pH requirements (Adams & Pearson, 1967; and Woodruff, 1967)

Crop	Minimum pH for good productivity
Barley	4.8
Bermudagrass	4.5
Blueberries	4.0
Buckwheat	5.0
Clover	5.5
Corn	4.8
Fescue	5.2
Lespedeza	5.5
Oats	<5.0
Rye	5.0
Sorghum	4.8
Soybeans	<5.0
Sweet clover	6.5
Wheat	5.5

acid as pH 4.5. Black locust (*Robinia pseudoacacia* L.) is reported to grow well at pH 4.0 while the shrub, bristly locust (*Robinia hispida* L.), will survive a pH of 3.5 (Bennett, 1973).

D. Importance of Lime Quality

Barber (1967) discussed liming materials in great detail. Lime quality and, thus, value are affected by both chemical and physical factors. Almost all liming of extensive acreages is done with ground limestone. Calcitic or high calcium limestone is primarily calcium carbonate ($CaCO_3$), while dolomitic limestone also contains magnesium carbonate ($MgCO_3$).

The chemical effectiveness of limestone is measured by its $CaCO_3$ equivalence. Pure dolomitic limestone has a higher equivalence than pure calcitic limestone but is more slowly soluble. In most states agricultural lime which is offered for sale must be tested for its $CaCO_3$ equivalence and particle size. High quality lime should have a $CaCO_3$ equivalency of at least 90%; limestone of low purity may not be worth the hauling and spreading cost.

The effectiveness of limestone in correcting soil acidity depends on rapid dissolution, which increases with fineness of grinding. All particles should pass a 60-mesh or finer screen to be effective within a few weeks. Particles larger than about 10-mesh (granular fertilizer size) are of very limited usefulness. Because of the need for rapid pH adjustment, acid spoils would seem to need the best lime, but one often sees coarse, poor quality lime being applied on such sites.

In addition to agricultural lime, marl, blast furnace slag, cement plant flue dust, and byproduct lime from various industrial processes can also be used as liming agents. These materials are effective, but the supply is limited and localized, and they are of little real importance.

E. Application and Incorporation

Most lime is now distributed with spinner-type spreaders mounted on trucks. This is an economical method but, unless truck operators are well trained, very uneven distribution can result. Freshly limed fields have been observed on which the rate was at least twice as high in the center of the swath as at the edges. Uniform spreading is highly desirable. Acceptable distribution patterns of both lime and fertilizer require adequate training and supervision of spreader truck operators.

Lime should be incorporated whenever possible. Mays (unpublished TVA data) compared lime surface-applied, disked-in, and plowed under on a sod. Soil pH changes were greater and more rapid with incorporation than with surface application. No pH change could be noted after 20 months below a depth of 15 cm even with 50% of the lime plowed down. Four and one-half years after liming the effects of surface applications could be detected at depths of 7.5 to 15 cm, and incorporated lime had affected pH to a depth of 45 cm. Rapid pH adjustment is necessary in revegetation work; thus, incorporation seems to be required.

Surface application followed by disking is the usual practice if lime applications are no greater than 10 to 20 metric tons/ha. However, for extremely high lime rates split application, with part being plowed under, is often recommended. The opportunity for this is somewhat limited on spoils that are rocky or otherwise difficult to plow.

F. Special Techniques

Lime coating of legume seeds has received little attention in the United States. However, in New Zealand and Australia the practice is common because liming is often uneconomical. It is said to allow the successful establishment of legumes on soils which are at least 0.5 pH units too acid for conventional seeding techniques. A sticking agent such as methyl cellulose or gum arabic is used to coat legume seeds with a mixture of innoculum, finely ground lime, sometimes phosphate rock, and molybdenum if deficient for rhizobia (Hastings et al., 1966). This technique should be investigated because of the need to supply N to strip mine sites as fertilizer or by use of legumes.

III. FERTILIZER NEEDS

A. Nutrient Status of Disturbed Areas

1. NITROGEN

Lack of N in spoil materials of the eastern coal fields has been reported by many workers including Plass (1972), Czapowskyj (1973), Bengtson et al. (1973b), Mays and Bengtson (1974), and Vogel (1975). Almost all of the N available to plants in undisturbed soil is found in the top 30 to 60 cm of the profile. Most of the N is held in various soil organic matter fractions but small amounts of NO_3 and NH_4 may be in the soil solution or adsorbed on clay minerals. During mining operations the surface layers are usually buried so deeply that the nutrients they contain are not available to plants. Mine-spoil N deficiency is usually much more severe than N deficiency of infertile undisturbed soil.

Power et al. (1974a) reported that Paleocene shales in North Dakota and Montana contain exchangeable ammonium below a depth of 10 m. When this material is left on the surface and exposed to oxygen after mining it has the potential of nitrifying and supplying significant amounts of N to plants.

2. PHOSPHORUS

Phosphorus supplies are often moderately to severely deficient on strip-mined sites. Plass and Vogel (1973) analyzed 10 samples from each of 39 spoils from southern West Virginia. They found the P concentration to be very low in 52%, low in 35%, and medium in 13% of the samples tested.

Adequate P for survival of transplanted tree seedlings may be insufficient for direct-seeded trees or herbaceous plants. Zarger et al (1973) found that direct-seeded loblolly pines emerged but failed to grow sufficiently large to survive the winter without applied P. Similar results were reported for red (*Trifolium pratense* L.) and ladino (*Trifolium repens* L. var. Ladino) clover and orchardgrass (*Dactylis glomerata* L.) (Mays & Bengtson, 1974). Severe P deficiency in exposed subsoils has also been reported by Moldenhauer et al. (1962) in the loess soils of the several states in the Missouri River valley and by Power et al. (1974b) in the Northern Great Plains area.

3. POTASSIUM

Einsphar et al. (1955), Berg (1973), Bengtson et al. (1973b), Power et al. (1974b), Mays and Bengtson (1974), Vogel (1975), and others have concluded that the majority of mine spoils contain adequate amounts of potassium (K) for revegetation. Potassium is usually contained in the subsoil minerals in sufficient amounts that natural spoil weathering releases enough K for plant growth, particularly where only modest growth rates for erosion control and cover are desired. Where spoils are reclaimed with the objective of growing high-producing agricultural crops such as corn (*Zea mays* L.), alfalfa (*Medicago sativa* L.), or hybrid bermudagrass (*Cynodon dactylon* [L.] Pers.), supplemental fertilization may be needed.

4. OTHER NUTRIENTS

The literature contains little evidence that deficiencies of secondary and micronutrients limit plant growth on mine spoils. As with K, though, it is quite possible that a move toward high levels of productivity on spoils will result in the appearance of deficiency symptoms. Changes in effective secondary and micronutrient supplies are also side effects of pH adjustment. Liming increases the supply of soil Ca, often by several fold, and may also add Mg. All of the micronutrients except boron (B) are less available to plants above a pH of 5.0 to 5.5, while B availability increases with pH. Micronutrient deficiencies seldom cause problems in the soil pH range between 5.0 and 6.5 except for a few crops.

B. Fertilizer Needs for Establishing Vegetation

1. GRASSES AND LEGUMES

The amount and kind of fertilizer needed to establish vegetation on a disturbed area depend both on the native fertility of the spoil and the type of plants to be established. Transplanted seedling trees will survive on sites which are too infertile for successful direct seeding of trees or herbaceous species. Since legumes can be expected to supply most of their own N through symbiotic fixation, they can be successfully seeded with less fertilizer N than grasses. However, legumes have a somewhat higher requirement for P than grasses.

Few experiments have been conducted to compare several rates of the various plant nutrients on which to base refined fertilizer rate recommendations. However, fertilizer cost (usually from $40 to $80/ha) is a very minor part of reclamation expense, while lime may cost several hundred dollars and regrading may cost from $2,000 to $6,000/ha. Thus, if application of at least adequate amounts of the needed nutrients is assured, a precise fertilizer recommendation may not be critical.

Most experiments on disturbed lands have included fertilizer rates similar to those recommended for seedling establishment on infertile agricultural lands. Rates usually range from 50 to 100 kg of N/ha and 40 to 80 kg of P/ha. However, it is likely that these P rates are inadequate for maximum plant growth in many instances. Potassium is often not applied unless a complete fertilizer is used as the N and P source. May et al. (1973) used similar N and P rates in revegetating kaolin mine spoils. Mays and Bengtson (1974) compared P application rates of 28, 56, and 112 kg/ha for fall seeding of several forage species on a sandy, very infertile spoil. The 56-kg rate resulted in winter survival of only about 60% of tall fescue (*Festuca arundinacea* Schreb.) and orchardgrass seedlings and about 30% of red and ladino clover; 28 kg was totally inadequate, while 112 kg resulted in good survival of all species. Application of additional P the spring following seeding was no better than low rates at seeding with no spring application.

2. TREES

Because of their ability to survive and often prosper in acid, infertile, and otherwise harsh soil environments, forest tree seedlings (most often pines) are widely used in land revegetation programs. Part of this hardiness is associated with the inherent low nutrient requirements of these species. But more important, and less commonly recognized, (i) these seedlings come to the field *generally* in a state of "luxury consumption" of nutrients taken up from the heavily fertilized nurserybeds; they can, through internal recycling, grow rather well for several months or more with minimal external nutrient supplies; (ii) they also generally come infected by or invested with mycorrhizae, the unique fungus-roots which enable them to exploit the soil volume thoroughly in their vicinity, making the most of available nutrients and moisture. Thus, if pines alone were to be established, liming would be unnecessary on many sites (pines will grow well at pH levels as low as 4.5); fertilizer requirements might well be rather different from regimes prescribed for herbaceous plants.

However, most drastically disturbed spoil is subject to erosion and it is economically unfeasible to plant sufficient tree seedlings or to establish a dense stand by direct seeding to control erosion. It is generally better to establish a quick cover of herbaceous plants following grading and to plant trees into this cover, usually several months to a year later.

Since nutrient requirements for survival and modest growth of forest tree seedlings are rather low, and because they are effective users of even rather strongly fixed phosphates due to their mycorrhizal habit, any lime-fertilizer program that will produce even a temporarily vigorous cover of grasses or legumes will be adequate for the followup planting of trees. Research in several locales in the Appalachian coalfields indicates that, even on the most infertile spoils, approximately 50 kg each of N and P/ha applied to herbaceous cover prior to tree planting or to plantings of the trees alone is sufficient to ensure good survival and early growth of tree seedlings. Overfertilization, particularly with N, is more of a threat to newly transplanted tree seedlings than is nutrient deficiency because overtopping of the tree seedlings by luxuriant herbaceous cover usually results in heavy tree mortality.

The physical difficulties in transplanting forest tree seedlings onto regraded spoils have encouraged research on establishment of forest trees on such sites by direct seeding. This research has shown that success is dependent upon some of the same factors important for seeding herbaceous plants (a favorable seedbed, protection of seed from predators, and sufficient nutrients). Zarger et al. (1973) found that on spoil deficient in N and P, application of at least 50 kg/ha of each element at seeding or early in the growing season was essential to permit sufficient seedling growth to protect against frost heaving in the first winter. Near complete mortality due to frost heaving was observed in excellent seedling stands whose growth was stunted by N and P deficiency.

Although several researchers have found it possible to establish acceptable stands of trees on disturbed land by direct seeding, the problem of soil erosion is even worse than in tree stands established by planting nursery stock. Attempts to establish mixed stands of herbaceous plants and forest trees by simultaneous seeding have not been very encouraging (Bengtson et al., 1973b) because newly germinated tree seedlings are poor competitors against most herbaceous plants, especially those fertilized adequately. Even seedling transplants have problems competing with certain types of herbaceous cover when the transplanting is done simultaneously with establishment of the cover (Vogel, 1973). Thus, it appears that the delayed planting of forest tree seedlings into temporary or permanent herbaceous cover will continue to be favored for sites where forest cover is desired.

Of great significance in the performance of tree transplants on spoil is the work of Marx (1976) who has found that selective inoculation of roots of pines with *Pisolithus tinctorius* fungi greatly enhances the growth of seedlings transplanted to adverse sites over that obtained with transplants bearing mycorrhizae formed with fungi of other species commonly found in nursery soils. This selective inoculation appears to reduce the trees' needs for supplemental fertilization. Parallel work with hardwood species and other fungi shows similarly encouraging results.

C. Long-Range Fertility Requirements

1. NEEDS FOR MAINTENANCE OF COVER

Most spoils do not receive maintenance applications of fertilizer after they have been revegetated and the mining company is released from a performance bond. If adequate P has been applied before seeding, legumes are present to fix N, and minerals continue to release K, no maintenance fertilizer applications are needed. However, an inspection of revegetated strip mines reveals that this favorable combination of circumstances seldom exists.

Probably N is the nutrient most needed for maintenance. Where grasses and nonleguminous trees are grown, very little nonfertilizer N enters the ecosystem except for the small amount in rainfall or that fixed by algae on the soil surface. At the same time, N is lost through leaching of mineralized NO_3 from the spoil, through volatilization of NH_3 from decaying plant material at the soil surface, or is permanently immobilized in woody vegetation.

The best way of supplying maintenance amounts of N to revegetated spoils is through the use of well-inoculated legumes planted in association with grasses or as understory vegetation with trees. Bengtson (unpublished TVA data) found that sericea lespedeza seeded in newly transplanted loblolly pines supplied sufficient N for excellent tree growth for 7 years on a site on which at least biennial N fertilizer applications of about 100 kg/ha were necessary to maintain growth and color of pines growing without a legume companion crop.

If a spoil is well fertilized with P at seeding, maintenance fertilization is less critical than with N because little or no P leaves the ecosystem. While soluble P is often "fixed" in less soluble mineral forms in the soil, the fixed P is often at least partly available to plants.

2. NEEDS FOR PROFITABLE PRODUCTION LEVELS

a. **Forage and Row Crops**—When profitable crop production is the primary objective of strip mine revegetation, sufficient fertilizer must be added to compensate for that lost to leaching and volatilization, fixed in the soil, and removed in the crop. Cropping may also create a need for K fertilization because harvested crops may remove K more rapidly than minerals release new K to the soil solution.

Fertilizer requirements are considerably higher for harvested than for grazed crops. A forage grass yielding 6,000 kg/ha may remove 150 kg of N, 20 kg of P, and 120 kg of K/ha in a hay crop. If the same crop is grazed, nutrient removal from the ecosystem will be less than 50 kg of N, about 10 kg of P, and 20 kg of K/ha because of nutrient recycling in the dung and urine. Also only 50 to 60% of the forage will be grazed.

Most if not all the production-oriented fertilizer trials with mine spoil forages have been evaluated by clipping to simulate hay management. Mays and Bengtson (1974) found that red clover-tall fescue mixture yielded 0.2, 1.2, and 5.1 metric tons/ha with 0, 28, and 56 kg of P/ha annually and only slightly more when K was added. In the same area tall fescue alone yielded 1.2, 4.2, and 6.5 metric tons/ha of forage when fertilized with 56, 112, and 224 kg of N/ha plus adequate P. They found that common and midland bermudagrass responded to both N and P (Table 4) and produced as much as 18 to 19 metric tons/ha with 448 kg of N and 112 kg of P/ha.

Bennett (1971) reported that midland and Tufcote bermudagrass

Table 4—Bermudagrass yields as affected by applied N and P (Mays & Bengtson, 1974)

Fertilizer rate		Bermudagrass yield	
N	P	Common	Midland
kg/ha		metric tons/ha	
112	0	6.0	2.9
224	0	6.2	4.0
336	0	6.9	4.0
448	0	8.7	3.1
112	112	7.4	5.6
224	112	11.4	9.4
336	112	18.1	13.2
448	112	19.0	18.1

yielded more than 11 metric tons of hay/ha in West Virginia when fertilized with phosphate rock or lime plus 112 kg of K and 224 kg of N/ha. May et al. (1973) found that coastal bermudagrass and bahiagrass (*Paspalum notatum* Flugge) yielded 10.9 and 8.8 metric tons/ha, respectively, on kaolin spoils fertilized with 448 kg of N, 90 kg of P, and 186 kg of K/ha.

There is little information available on the fertility needs for row or fruit crops grown on strip-mined areas. Mays (unpublished TVA data) found that newly planted grapes (*Vitus labrusca* L.) growing on spoil material responded to somewhat higher rates of N and P than are generally recommended for undisturbed land. It seems likely that fertilizer rates somewhat higher than those recommended for low fertility, undisturbed land should be appropriate for crop production on strip-mined sites where specific information is not available.

b. Forestry Crops—Nutrient requirements differ widely among tree species. The pines, particularly "pioneer" species such as Virginia pine (*Pinus virginiana* mill.) and loblolly pine, are among the least demanding of all. Provided the spoil is not more acid than pH 4.0 and contains native "extractable" P in excess of 2 ppm (by the Bray no. 1 procedure; Berg, 1973), these trees can survive and make sufficient growth to provide protective cover with no applied fertilizer on all but the most exceptional sites. However, if the land use plan calls for timber harvest, many infertile sites will require application of at least 50 kg P/ha, preferably broadcast at the time of planting. If legumes are not a part of the understory, application of N fertilizer is also likely to be required at least once before harvest. On highly infertile sites, applications of 100 kg N/ha beginning at stand age 3 and at 3- to 5-year intervals thereafter might be necessary to maintain the rates of growth common on good forest soils. Such fertilization programs are far too costly to be borne by income from timber harvest alone. Such sites would better be put to nontimber uses or be upgraded through the use of herbaceous legumes or N-fixing tree species. Of the latter, European black alder (*Alnus glutinosa* [L.] Gaertn.) appears to have wide adaptability and better potential for forest products than the more commonly planted black locust.

Many disturbed soils are adequately supplied with N for good growth of forest trees; this is particularly so for certain shale-containing spoils, which contain substantial quantities of fossil N which is released upon weathering (Cornwell & Stone, 1973). These sites are more suitable for planting of hardwoods, such as native and hybrid poplars which have distinctly higher N requirements.

Deficiencies in nutrients other than N and P are rare for forest tree species; however, the peculiarities associated with disturbed soils may induce deficiencies and/or toxicities even among the micronutrients (Stone, 1968). Timber harvesting, particularly if it involves whole-tree harvesting, may remove sufficient nutrients to induce second-generation deficiencies in macronutrients such as Ca, Mg, and K, which had been sufficient for the trees planted on the rapidly-weathering original spoil.

D. Methods of Determining Fertility Needs

1. SOIL TESTING

The procedures for obtaining representative soil samples were discussed in the section on pH testing. Generally, soils are tested only to determine pH, P, and K levels. Soil N tests are not precise enough to be useful in making fertilizer recommendations.

All of the state agricultural experiment stations maintain soil testing laboratories which test soil or spoil samples for a modest fee, usually about $2 or $3 per sample. In addition, there are numerous commercial soil testing laboratories where similar services are performed. Unfortunately, all laboratories are not equally careful and all do not provide similar fertilizer recommendations based on a similar soil test result. Thus, care in selecting a testing facility is necessary.

Berg (1973) compared several extractants for P and K tests on 63 spoils which represented 21 coal seams in eastern Kentucky and adjoining states. For P he found that $0.03N$ HCl + $0.025N$ NH_4F (Bray no. 1) gave significantly higher correlation with plant growth than $0.05N$ HCl + $0.025N$ H_2SO_4 (double-acid method), or $0.15N$ H_2SO_4. The relationship between grass growth and P supply measured by the Bray no. 1 test is shown in Fig. 1.

In testing spoils for K supply, $1.0N$ amonium acetate, $0.05N$ HCl + $0.025N$ H_2SO_4, and $0.15N$ H_2SO_4 gave similar results. Plant response to applied K was not noted on any of the spoils tested; thus, soil tests were not correlated with plant response. As part of the same study Berg evaluated the effect of spoil particle size on the Bray no. 1 P test. He found that test results for particles < 2 mm were similar to those for coarse fragments. He concluded that routine sample preparation procedures need not be modified for testing spoils with coarse fragments, at least when the spoils are derived from Pennsylvanian shales.

2. PLANT RESPONSE

Biological responses have been used for assessing the nutrient supply of soils for many years. A small pot technique using rye (*Secale cereale* L.) seedlings (Neubauer test) was used at one time to evaluate the relative

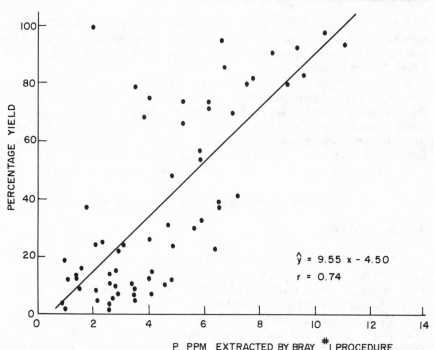

Fig. 1—Percentage yield of grass on 63 N-fertilized spoils as related to Bray no. 1 extractable P (Berg, 1973).

productivity of different soils. With the advent of quick and relatively cheap chemical analysis methods for soils, biological assays are no longer used for routine soil testing. However, this does not preclude the use of visual indications of nutrient deficiency in assessing the fertility level of some spoils.

Nitrogen deficiency is probably the easiest nutritional problem to identify visually. Growth vigor is reduced below that noted on fertile soil and the plant has a light green color. Very obvious visual symptoms can exist before the deficiency becomes so severe as to cause a loss of stand. The visual symptoms of N deficiency can be corrected in a very few days by application of N fertilizer.

Phosphorus deficiency symptoms are less noticeable than those of N deficiency, so that P can seriously limit growth before visual symptoms are obvious. The authors have witnessed severe P deficiency symptoms on tall fescue but only at a fertility level where growth was extremely limited. Phosphorus deficiency in tall fescue is characterized by stunted dark green plants with some purplish tinge. In severe cases the leaf tips are rolled and necrotic.

Stunted growth associated with development of purplish leaf pigmentation of pine seedlings is often associated with P deficiency. On older trees, P deficiency is characterized by short needles and thin crowns resulting from premature shedding of needles.

Table 5—Nutrient deficiency concentrations of several forage crops
(Martin & Matocha, 1973)

Crop	Age	Deficiency concentration			
		N	P	K	S
			%		
Alfalfa	Early bloom	--	<0.20	<0.80	<0.20
Red clover	--	--	<0.20	<1.25	<0.20
Ladino clover	--	--	<0.20	<1.25	<0.20
Common and midland bermudagrass	4 to 5 weeks	<1.70	<0.22	<1.50	<0.12
Orchardgrass	3 to 4 weeks	<2.4	<0.18	<2.0	<0.12
Tall Fescue	5 to 6 weeks	<2.5	<0.24	<2.2	--
Kentucky bluegrass	4 to 6 weeks	<2.1	<0.18	<1.5	--

3. FOLIAR ANALYSIS

The book, *Soil Testing and Plant Analysis* (Walsh & Beaton, eds., 1973) contains an extensive review of plant tissue analysis. Plant analysis is often useful, but there are many problems which limit its application.

Concentrations of most nutrients are highly dependent on the plant portion sampled and age of tissue. Use of tissue analysis to compare effects of several treatments within an experiment makes possible the sampling of comparable plant tissue and reliable comparisons. However, if tissue analysis is used to compare the nutritional status of a crop in the field with published standards it is difficult to insure comparable samples. Tissue analysis does not seem at all suitable for evaluating the nutrient status of an unharvested maintenance-type crop cover.

Martin and Matocha (1973) compiled estimates of deficient, critical, and adequate nutrient concentration levels for several forage crops from a great many U.S. research workers. There was lack of agreement on the plant parts to sample and adequate concentrations of the various nutrients. Table 5 summarizes probable nutrient deficiency levels for several forage crops.

Sampling of plant tissue and interpretation of results are far less precise arts than is the use of common analytical procedures. Since disturbed area revegetation is also a rather imprecise science, great care should be exercised in the use of foliar analysis to diagnose nutritional deficiencies of plants growing on these areas. A minimum requirement should be a knowledge of the standard techniques used for each plant species.

E. Fertilizer Application Techniques

The trend toward extensive regrading of disturbed areas makes possible similar fertilizer application techniques as used for the usual agricultural soils. Fertilizer which is applied for establishment should be broadcast and incorporated into the seed bed with a disk or other implement prior to planting. The high rates usually needed in revegetation cannot be applied in the row with the seed or in tree planting holes as seedling injury or destruction will occur. If a hydroseeder is to be used for planting and mulching an area, the fertilizer is usually added to the tank mix and applied along with the seed and mulch. Once permanent vegetation is established, only surface applications are possible. Nitrogen and K are sufficiently soluble to move into the soil with the first rain. While P is considered to be relatively immobile, the literature contains ample evidence that sod crops are able to obtain adequate P from surface applications.

Fertilizer can be readily applied with truck or trailer-mounted spinner-type spreaders if the terrain is not too rough. More difficult sites can often be treated with smaller tractor-mounted equipment. As with lime spreading, care should be given to training operators so that adequate swath overlap is maintained to assure uniform spreading. Conventional hopper-type spreaders can be used, but the swath width is usually limited to 2.5 to 3.5 m, as compared to 15 to 18 m for spinner-type spreaders. Low clearance makes hopper spreaders vulnerable to damage from rocks and other obstructions that may result from less than perfect grading. If fluid fertilizers are available and economically attractive they can also be applied with various types of broadcast spreaders which give a coverage of 15 m or more wide. However, applying fluid fertilizers to established vegetation may cause some foliage burning.

F. Characteristics of Available Fertilizers

Although the number of commercial fertilizer grades is almost endless, the job of amending disturbed soils can be done with a few basic fertilizer materials.

1. NITROGEN SOURCES

Although many N fertilizers are available, ammonium nitrate (AN 33.5–0–0) and urea (45–0–0) claim most of the commercial market. Both are completely water soluble and are mainly used in granular or prilled form; urea-AN fertilizer solutions are also available.

Both solid AN and urea are widely used as topdressings for forages and for forest tree crops. Ammonium nitrate is preferred at planting because urea releases ammonia upon hydrolysis which can kill germinating seed and where topdressing is followed by dry, warm windy weather, which could result in volatile loss of N as ammonia from hydrolyzing urea. Urea is favored in some situations to reduce transportation costs.

2. PHOSPHORUS SOURCES

Where the need is for correction of simple P deficiency, granular triple superphosphate (TSP, 0–46–0) is excellent because of its high water solubility, high P content, ease of handling and application,

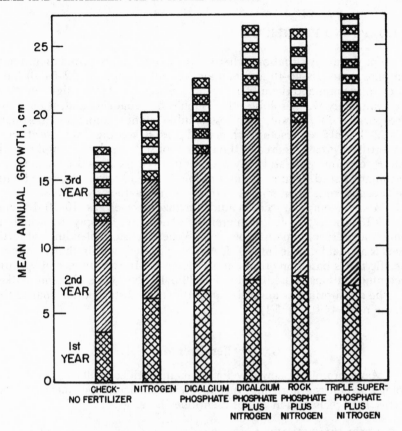

Fig. 2—Black locust growth as affected by fertilizer treatment (Plass, 1972).

ready availability, and relatively low cost. It is also widely used in blending of compound ("mixed") fertilizers. Ordinary superphosphate (OSP, 0–20–0) was once the most common source, but now is not widely used in the United States because of its low P content. The only other "straight P" source of any importance today is finely ground phosphate rock (PR, 0–32–0). This water-insoluble material was shown by Plass (1972) to be useful as an alternative to TSP on some highly acid soils and spoils (Fig. 2). For maximum effectiveness PR must be broadcast and incorporated into the soil. It undergoes gradual dissolution for its P available to plants. This slow release of P by PR is a disadvantage for young plants, which require soluble P for early growth, but this can be an advantage for supplying long-term P needs on certain acid soils subject to strong P fixation. The PR may provide a better sustained supply of P to meet the long-term needs of the crop. Primary limitations to wider use of PR are its low analysis relative to TSP, and the difficulty of broadcasting the fine material uniformly. (See Section G, "New Fertilizer Materials," for some promising means of overcoming this problem.)

3. COMPOUND FERTILIZERS

For the many situations where both N and P are required diammonium phosphate (18–46–0) and ammonium polyphosphate (12–54–0) have much to recommend them. Their plant nutrient content is high and they are completely water soluble; they should be broadcast and, if possible, incorporated in the soil. The less soluble monoammonium phosphate (11–52–0) is also satisfactory when used prior to seeding. Incorporation of the fertilizer greatly increases the volume of soil which can supply available P to plant roots and may also reduce the likelihood of damage to germinating seed. Diammonium phosphate should never be banded with seed because, like urea, it releases toxic ammonia upon hydrolysis.

Many "complete" compound fertilizers, such as 10–10–10 and 13–13–13 are available commercially. These also supply K, which is sometimes deficient on disturbed soils. Where "custom blending" of fertilizers is available, ratios of N/P/K can be specified, within limits, to meet specific needs based on crops and soil analysis. In the absence of specific recommendations, a 3:4:0.8 of N/P/K (3:9:1 of $N/P_2O_5/K_2O$) is more likely to be appropriate as an initial amendment of disturbed soil than is the common 1:0.44:0.8 (1:1:1).

G. New Fertilizer Materials

Many promising new developments in fertilizer materials and technology are on the horizon. Only a few of particular pertinence to disturbed land reclamation will be mentioned here.

1. SULFUR-COATED UREA

Disturbed soils may be highly porous, low in cation exchange capacity, capable of supporting few soil microorganisms, devoid of plant roots, and often lacking much of the N retention capacity of normal soils. Conventional soluble N sources, such as AN and urea, may leach rapidly through them. Disturbed lands are also often remote and difficult to traverse; hence, repeated application of N to maintain a continuous supply for normal plant development is difficult. A slow-release N source offers a potential solution to this dual problem on disturbed lands. Of the several commercial and experimental slow-release N sources on the current scene, including urea-formaldehyde, isobutylidene diurea, and magnesium ammonium phosphate, sulfur-coated urea (SCU) appears to have the most promise in terms of performance and cost. Urea granules are coated with molten S and other minor coating components to produce SCU. It has a N content of 35–40%, depending upon coating weight. Greenhouse and field tests show that SCU can be made to release N over a period of from several months to two years or more. It is particularly useful on long-lived crop plants, such as sugarcane (*Saccharum officinarum* L.), pineapple (*Ananas comosus*), and forage grasses. It also appears to have potential for a wide variety of uses on disturbed lands.

2. GROUND PHOSPHATE ROCK

Because of the merits of PR previously mentioned, and of the difficulties in applying the powdered material, attempts are being made to develop improved methods for broadcasting PR.

Granulation of PR has been achieved by two methods: (i) cogranulation of PR with urea, yielding a product of 26-13-0 analysis and (ii) granulation after partial acidulation of PR. The latter partially acidulated, granulated, ground PR provides both water-soluble and slowly soluble P; a possible disadvantage is the slow disintegration of the granules.

A technique to apply PR as a stable slurry has recently been developed. This makes possible the use of conventional equipment. A logical next step is the blending of NP liquid fertilizer, such as 10-34-0 into the PR slurry; this would provide a higher P analysis and would create a material having both N and P, the latter in both water-soluble and water-insoluble forms. Such a product should have great utility for plow-down application before seeding reclaimed land.

H. Foliar Feeding and "Miracle" Fertilizers

Foliar feeding with small amounts of fertilizer at low concentration is distinguished from fluid fertilizer application in which large amounts of concentrated fertilizers are applied. Foliar application has been successfully used to correct micronutrient deficiencies for 20 years or more. This technique has worked well with materials which need be applied at rates of only a few hundred grams to a few kilograms per hectare. Several micronutrients are readily absorbed through leaves and deficiency symptoms are corrected in a very few days. Iron deficiency of azaleas (*Rhododendron* spp.), zoysiagrass (*Zoysia matrella* (L.) Merr.), and sorghum (*Sorghum vulgare* Pers.), and boron deficiency in cotton (*Gossypium hirstum* L.) and grapes are examples of problems which can be corrected by this method.

Numerous landscaping contractors and specialty fertilizer dealers have promoted foliar application of N, P, and K for all sorts of ornamental and crop plants. Fertilizer solutions must be very dilute, 3 to 4 % N for instance, with very low concentrations of K to completely avoid burning of foliage. Thus, amounts of plant nutrients which can be applied are low and relatively large volumes of water must be transported to the site. In addition, soluble K sources cost about twice as much as KCl. These factors make foliar feeding expensive and the results are often mainly cosmetic with little actual increase in productivity. Thus, foliar feeding can be justified in only a few specialty situations and certainly not on mine-spoil plantings.

Periodically, various "miracle" fertilizers are introduced to agriculture or the specialty trade. These materials are variously advertised as containing a broad spectrum of essential micronutrients or certain magical organic compounds, or as having some unique characteristics as liming agents. A common characteristic of all such materials is a grossly inflated price relative to the actual plant nutrient content.

Special micronutrient mixes are of absolutely no value in situations where none of the added elements are deficient. Even where a micronutrient is deficient, it can be obtained in a standard carrier of that nutrient much cheaper than in a shotgun mixture containing many micronutrients.

Most of the miracle products, particularly liquid ones, carry only nominal amounts of N, P, K, and secondary nutrients, and a little attention to the nutrient concentration versus price relationship should convince most people that such products are of very marginal value.

IV. LIME AND FERTILIZER RESEARCH TECHNIQUES

The primary objective of lime and fertilizer trials on disturbed land should be to find out how much of what soil amendments are needed for satisfactory revegetation for erosion control and cover or profitable crop production. Plant nutrient and lime requirements for any type of soil or spoil cannot be determined unless each nutrient is evaluated in the presence of adequate amounts of all other nutrients. Experiments in which spoils are treated with heavy rates of lime and complete fertilizer are little more than demonstrations that full soil treatment results in improved vegetative cover and tell nothing about the kind or amount of nutrients needed.

In order to properly evaluate nutrient needs, each nutrient should be applied at two and preferably three rates with all other nutrients and lime being applied at rates needed for near maximum growth. Such experiments require many treatments and fairly large areas if done in the field. For instance, an experiment with 3 N, 3 P, and 3 lime rates requires 27 treatments which should be replicated 3 or 4 times, making a total experiment size of 81 or 108 plots.

The rates which are chosen should represent a broad range, with rate one being too low, rate 3 being too high, and the middle rate being near what the researcher judges to be optimum. The results can then be plotted as nutrient response curves. If the application rates have been properly chosen the response curves will give a good indication of the optimum amounts needed.

The appropriate plot size will vary tremendously depending on the class of plants to be grown. For forage crops, plots 2 m wide and 6 to 8 m long are adequate. Row crops should be grown in four- to six-row plots at least 10 m in length. Plots for tree experiments may be as much as 20 m square to allow for enough individual trees for a good sample.

When nothing at all is known about the fertility needs of a spoil, preliminary screening trials can be conducted in pot culture either outdoors or in a greenhouse. This allows the use of a great many treatments and is sufficiently precise to assess the relative availability of the various nutrients. Fertilizer requirements for maximum growth are much higher in the restricted rooting environment of the greenhouse pot than in the same soil in the field. Thus, field trials are necessary to refine the information obtained in the greenhouse.

Response research should not be limited by concerns about what treatments are economically feasible. A great many researchers working on both undisturbed and disturbed lands have failed to achieve optimum production levels or the best vegetative cover because they were overly concerned that the cost of necessary treatment was not economically feasible. To base research solely on what seems feasible today is to ignore the fact that economic, social, and legal considerations are constantly changing.

V. RESEARCH NEEDS

Most lime and fertilizer research conducted thus far has been oriented toward using these amendments to obtain some kind of cover on disturbed land. However, for 25 years or more a few scientists have recognized that strip-mined lands should be used for their highest economic potential and have based their research on that objective. It seems that the time has come when lime and fertilizer research as well as other research on disturbed areas should be oriented toward the optimum production of economically or socially useful products. If wildlife cover or recreational areas are needed, sufficient soil amendments should be added to develop useful and desirable facilities. Where agricultural or forestry production is the goal, research should be oriented toward production of maximum yields. Very little additional research should be devoted to development of cover for erosion control only. Land of all kinds is too valuable to allow disturbed areas to be stabilized with no further use or benefit in mind.

LITERATURE CITED

Adams, F., and R. W. Pearson. 1967. Crop response to lime in the Southern United States and Puerto Rico. In R. W. Pearson and Fred Adams (eds.) Soil acidity and liming. Agronomy 12:161–206.

Barber, S. A. 1967. Liming materials and practices. In R. W. Pearson and Fred Adams (eds.) Soil acidity and liming. Agronomy 12:125–160. Am. Soc. of Agron., Madison, Wis.

Barnhisel, R. I. 1975. Lime and fertilizer recommendations for reclamation of surface-mined spoils. Agric. 40. Dep. of Agron., Univ. of Kentucky, Lexington. 4 p.

Bengtson, G. W., S. E. Allen, D. A. Mays, and T. G. Zarger. 1973a. Use of fertilizers to speed pine establishment on reclaimed coal-mine spoil in northeastern Alabama: I. Greenhouse experiments. p. 199–225. In R. J. Hutnik and G. Davis (eds.) Ecology and reclamation of devastated land. Gordon and Breach, London.

Bengtson, G. W., D. A. Mays, and J. C. Allen. 1973b. Revegetation of coal spoil in northeastern Alabama: effects of timing of seeding and fertilization on establishment of pine-grass mixtures. p. 208–214. In Proc. 1st Res. and Applied Technol. Symp. on Mined Land Reclamation. Bituminous Coal Res. Inst., Monroeville, Pa.

Bennett, O. L. 1971. Grasses and legumes for revegetation of strip-mined areas. p. 23–25. In Proc. Revegetation and Economic Use of Surface-Mined Land and Mine Refuse Symp., West Virginia Univ., Morgantown.

Bennett, O. L. 1973. Vegetation to heal scars. Proc. Annual Meeting of Soil Conserv. Soc. of Am. Vol. 28. p. 249.

Berg, W. A. 1969. Determining pH of strip-mine spoils. USDA For. Serv. Res. Note NE-98. 7 p.

Berg, W. A. 1973. Evaluation of P and K soil fertility tests on coal-mine spoils. p. 93–103. In P. J. Hutnik and G. Davis (eds.) Ecology and reclamation of devastated land. Gordon and Breach, London. Vol. 1.

Cornwell, S. M., and E. L. Stone. 1973. Spoil type lithology and foliar composition of *Betula populifolia*. p. 105–120. *In* Russell J. Hutnik and Grant Davis (eds.) Ecology of devastated lands. Gordon and Breach, New York.

Czapowskj, M. M. 1973. Establishing forest on surface-mined land as related to fertility and fertilization. *In* Forest Fertilization Symp. Proc. USDA For. Serv. Gen. Tech. Rep. NE 3.

Despard, T. L. 1974. Avoid problem spoils through overburden analysis. USDA For. Serv. Gen. Tech. Rep. NE 10. 4 p.

Einspahr, D. W., A. L. McComb, F. F. Riecken, and W. D. Schrader. 1955. Coal spoil-bank materials as a medium for plant growth. Proc. Iowa Academy of Sci. 62:329–344.

Grube, W. E., Jr., R. M. Smith, R. N. Singh, and A. A. Sobek. 1973. Characterization of coal overburden materials and minesoils in advance of surface mining. p. 134–152. *In* Proc. 1st Research and Applied Technology Symp. on Mined Land Reclamation. Bituminous Coal Res., Inc., Monroeville, Pa.

Hastings, A., R. M. Greenwood, and M. H. Procter. 1966. Legume inoculation in New Zealand. New Zealand Div. of Sci. and Ind. Res. Inf. Series no. 58 37 p.

Martin, W. E., and J. E. Matocha. 1973. Plant analysis as an aid in fertilization of forage crops. p. 393–426. *In* L. M. Walsh and J. D. Beaton (eds.) Soil testing and plant analysis. Soil Sci. Soc. of Am., Madison, Wis.

Marx, D. H. 1976. The use of specific mycorrhizal fungi on tree roots in forestation of disturbed lands. p. 47–65. *In* Proc. Conf. on Forestation of Disturbed Surface Areas, Birmingham, Ala., 14–15 Apr. 1976. USDA-For. Serv., Southeast Area, Div. of State and Private Forestry. Atlanta, Ga.

May, J. T., C. L. Parks, and H. F. Perkins. 1973. Establishment of grasses and tree vegetation on spoil from kaolin clay strip mining. p. 137–147. *In* R. J. Hutnik and G. Davis (eds.) Ecology and reclamation of devastated land. Gordon and Breach, London.

Mays, D. A., and G. W. Bengtson. 1974. Fertilizer effects on forage crops on strip-mined land in northeast Alabama. TVA, Natl. Fertilizer Dev. Center, Bull. Y-74. p. 23.

Moldenhauer, W. C., G. Holmberg, and W. D. Shrader. 1962. Establishing vegetation on exposed subsoil in the Monona-Ida-Hamburg soil association area of Kansas, Iowa, Missouri, and Nebraska. Agric. Information Bull. no. 251, ARS-USDA, SCS. 14 p.

Plass, W. T. 1972. Fertilization treatments increase black locust growth on extremely acid surface-mine spoils. Tree Planters Notes 23(4):10–12. USDA-FS, Washington, D.C.

Plass, W. T. 1974. Factors affecting the establishment of direct seeded pine on surface-mine spoils. U.S. For. Serv. Res. Pap. NE-290. 5 p.

Plass, W. T., and Vogel, W. G. 1973. Chemical properties and particle size distribution of 39 surface-mine spoils in southern West Virginia. USDA For. Serv. Res. Pap. NE-276. 8 p.

Power, J. F., J. J. Bond, F. M. Sandoval, and W. O. Willis. 1974a. Nitrification in Paleocene shales. Science 183:1077–1079.

Power, J. F., W. O. Willis, F. M. Sandoval, and J. J. Bond. 1974b. Can productivity of mined land be restored in North Dakota. North Dakota Agric. Exp. Stn. Farm Res. 31(6):30–32.

Stone, E. L. 1968. Microelement nutrition of forest trees: a review. p. 132–179. *In* Forest Fertilization: Theory and Practice. Proc. of a Symp. TVA, Muscle Shoals, Alabama.

Vogel, W. G. 1973. The effect of herbaceous vegetation on survival and growth of trees planted on coal-mine spoils. p. 197–205. *In* Proc. 1st Res. and Applied Technol. Symp. on Mined Land Reclamation. Bituminous Coal Res. Inst., Monroeville, Pa.

Vogel, W. G. 1975. Requirements and use of fertilizer, lime, and mulch for vegetating acid-mine spoils. Proc. 3rd Res. and Applied Technol. Symp. on Mined Land Reclamation. Bituminous Coal Res. Inst., Monroeville, Pa. 3:152–170.

Vogel, W. G., and W. B. Berg. 1968. Grasses and legumes for cover on acid strip-mine spoils. J. Soil Water Conserv. 23:89–91.

Walsh, L. M., and J. D. Beaton (eds.). 1973. Soil testing and plant analysis. Soil Sci. Soc. of Am., Madison, Wis. 491 p.

Woodruff, C. M. 1967. Crop response to liming in the Midwestern United States. *In* R. W. Pearson and Fred Adams (eds.) Soil acidity and liming. Agronomy 12:207–231. Am. Soc. of Agron., Madison, Wis.

Zarger, T. G., G. W. Bengtson, J. C. Allen, and D. A. Mays. 1973. Use of fertilizers to speed pine establishment on reclaimed coal-mine spoil in northeastern Alabama: II. Field experiments. p. 227–236. *In* R. J. Hutnik and G. Davis (eds.) Ecology and reclamation of devastated land. Gordon and Breach, London.

Copyright © 1978 ASA–CSSA–SSSA
677 South Segoe Road, Madison, WI 53711 USA
Reclamation of Drastically Disturbed Lands

Chapter 18

Use of Mulches and Soil Stabilizers for Land Reclamation in the Eastern United States

WILLIAM T. PLASS

Forest Service, USDA
Northeastern Forest Experiment Station, Princeton, West Virginia

I. INTRODUCTION

The use of a mulch or soil stabilizer is one of several treatment options in any plan for reclaiming drastically disturbed areas. Mulches or soil stabilizers should be used as an aid in reclamation and not as a substitute for proper fertilization, grading, and shaping for vegetating and stabilizing the area.

In the humid eastern U.S., many disturbed areas such as highway road banks, surface-mined areas, and construction sites in steep terrain have slopes that are very conducive to soil erosion prior to the establishment of a good vegetative cover. Mulches or soil stabilizers can help control erosion caused by surface runoff prior to the establishment of vegetation. The value of these treatments is more evident on sites that have chemical or physical characteristics that delay the establishment of plants and limit their growth.

For this discussion, mulches are defined as organic or inorganic materials applied to the soil surface. They protect the seed, reduce erosion, modify extremes in surface soil temperatures, and reduce evaporation. The organic materials may supply a limited amount of plant nutrients.

Soil stabilizers are organic or inorganic chemical products applied to the soil surface in water solutions. They form a protective film on the soil surface or infiltrate the soil and physically bind the soil particles together. A soil stabilizer temporarily stabilizes soil against wind and water erosion and prevents evaporation of water from the soil surface.

Treatments can be used that combine a mulch and a soil stabilizer. A number of products and materials are available, many of which have specific attributes and limitations. In order to select the best material to use, the basic characteristics of all available materials should be evaluated. Selection of treatment should be based on requirements for erosion control, and on site and climate variables that may affect the establishment of vegetation and the cost of achieving the site-protection objectives.

329

II. MULCHES

Mulches may be processed or unprocessed materials, including raw residues from agriculture or industry, processed residues, and manufactured products. These materials differ mainly in the physical characteristics of the individual pieces or fibers. The durability of a mulch relates to its physical chracteristics. Durability is defined as the length of time the mulch provides effective site protection.

A. Agricultural Residues

Raw residues from agriculture are often used as mulches, the most common being straw and hay. These are applied at rates of 2,240 to 4,480 kg/ha after the disturbed area has been fertilized and seeded. Resistance to wind or water movement may be increased by the use of asphalt or chemical tacks or by crimping into the ground with a disc. The use of mulches may need to be restricted if the danger of transmitting a plant disease is high. If undesirable seeds have been harvested with the straw or hay, undesirable plants may energe and conflict with establishment of the desired plant species.

A straw or hay mulch effectively dissipates the energy of falling raindrops, thus minimizing the detachment of soil that is caused by the impact of rainfall. Erosion by surface runoff will be reduced if the straw and hay mulches make extensive contact with the soil surface; if the mulch is perched above the surface, sheet and rill erosion may occur beneath the mulch. Also, mulches will increase the rate of infiltration and decrease the rate of evaporation. Both are important in increasing the water available for plant growth under drouth conditions.

Other agricultural residues that may be used as mulches are peanut hulls, corn cobs, and bagasse, a residue from sugar cane mills. Many of these materials need to be reprocessed before they can be used as mulch. In some cases, the pieces are reduced in size by grinding, shredding, or milling (hammer mill). Others need to be dried before being transported and applied. Packaging is an expensive measure that may not be justified unless there exists a well-developed market for the mulch. Most agricultural residues are delivered to the application site in bulk.

B. Wood Residues

Residues such as bark, sawdust, and wood chips from sawmills and other wood-processing plants have been used with good results. Raw or processed hardwood bark is gaining recognition as an excellent material for erosion control (Yocum et al., 1971). The weight of the material and its interlocking rough fibers contribute to its effectiveness. Concern that toxic components of hardwood bark will affect the establishment and growth of plants has been overemphasized. Laboratory or field research has identified only a few minor hardwood species that have documented toxicities. Wood chips, sawdust, and pine bark are less desirable than hardwood bark, since they are light in weight and have a tendency to float in runoff water.

Equipment has been developed to apply these materials efficiently at costs competitive with other products (Emanuel, 1970; Sarles, 1973). Experience has shown that application rates of 56 to 94 m³/ha for bark, wood chips, and sawdust have provided acceptable site protection for a variety of sites. The range of effective rates reflects variability in site conditions and seasonal weather patterns.

Reprocessed waste paper, often referred to as *wood cellulose*, makes a desirable mulch that can be applied with a hydroseeder. The fibers in this material are usually short, so the durability of the mulch may be less than that of long-fibered materials. Some reprocessed waste paper has a higher moisture content than processed wood fiber mulches. Moisture content should be considered in determining application rates from a predetermined air-dried weight per hectare.

Processed wood fiber mulches, prepared from selected woods, are widely used. They are applied with hydroseeders. The product is sold in bales that are easily handled and conveniently stored. The degree of compaction during baling may influence the rate at which the wood fiber mulch can be added to the mixing tank of the hydroseeder. Rates of application that provide a mulching effect range from 1,120 to 1,680 kg/ha. Lower application rates may be used, but effectiveness of this material as a mulch is proportional to the rate of application. Low rates of application of wood fiber may increase the dispersion of seed in the slurry. Colored mulch will mark treated areas. The durability of this short-fibered mulch is short, even when the rates of application are high.

The value of other mulches in establishing vegetation may be compromised if, for the sake of convenience, a slurry containing a mixture of seed, fertilizer, and wood fiber is applied. Application of such a mixture provides an opportunity for some of the seed to be perched above the ground in a web of mulch. A tender, germinating seedling perched in this porous medium is vulnerable to extremes of temperature and to desiccation. The probability of seed damage or seedling mortality is related to the species being seeded, the amount of mulch applied, and the season of seeding. A more effective practice is to apply the seed and fertilizer first, and the wood fiber mulch subsequently. This procedure may be particularly useful in areas of low rainfall or when prolonged dry periods may occur.

III. SOIL STABILIZERS

The use of soil stabilizers for controlling erosion of drastically disturbed sites is a relatively recent development. At present these materials are limited to use on problem areas where their relatively high cost is justified. The use of soil stabilizers may also be restricted by lack of information about rates of application for specific sites.

Stabilizers are applied to the soil surface in water solutions. Most of them infiltrate no more than the upper 2.5 cm of soil and bind the soil particles together to form an erosion-resisting crust. Others form a thin film on the surface that provides temporary protection against soil movement.

Soil stabilizers are often classified by their basic formulas, e.g., polyvinyl acetates, acrylic copolymers, elastometric emulsions, and natural vegetable gums. Similar products may differ from each other because of additives mixed with basic formula. These additives may affect curing time, crust durability, and moisture infiltration rates.

There are many products available for use as soil stabilizers. Due to the large number of products on the market and the variations among products that have a similar basic formula, a discussion of soil stabilizers may become quite complex. Variables which may influence the effectiveness of stabilizers are (i) dilution rate with water, (ii) soil properties and climatic conditions, and (iii) amendments added to the solution to aid in establishing vegetation.

Selection of a product should be based on intended use, cost, availability, and field test results, if available. Reviews of laboratory tests that document the physical stability of soils treated with specific soil stabilizers will aid in the selection of a soil stabilizer or a group of soil stabilizers for a specific site (Gabriels & DeBoodt, 1973). Standardized test procedures have been developed to determine resistence to water erosion, resistence to penetration, and compressive strength (Morrison, 1971).

Weathering tests may also be used to compare products and treatments. Shallow flats filled with soil of known physical characteristics are treated with soil stabilizers and exposed to natural or artificial weathering (Kay & Mearns, 1973; Kay, 1976). The flats may be inclined at various angles or arranged to provide different exposures to the sun. Seed and fertilizer may be applied to the flats so that plant response to the treatments can be determined.

Recently, laboratory tests have been developed to evaluate those characteristics of product or treatment that may affect the establishment or growth of vegetation. The permeability of the soil crust to water or water vapor is important. Most soil-stabilizer treatments will not fill all soil pores, and moisture and air will move through the soil crust. The physical characteristics of both the soil and the treatment materials will determine the percentage of the total pore space that is filled during treatment. Measurements of loss of soil moisture and rates of infiltration reflect changes in porosity of the soil after treatment. The permeability of a crust to water vapor may affect the extent of evaporation losses which, in turn, affects the amount of soil moisture available for seed germination and plant growth.

An ideal soil stabilizer treatment would not restrict infiltration. How a treatment affects infiltration depends on both the product and the dilution ratio. Some treatments may actually increase infiltration during intense rainfall by preventing the detachment of fine soil particles that would ordinarily fill the pores of surface soil and temporarily restrict infiltration (Hendrickson, 1938).

Tough crusts can physically restrict the emergence of some plant species. Small-seeded grasses and legumes may have difficulty in penetrating tough crusts; large-seeded species of grasses would probably be less affected. Selection of species for seeding may be important when some soil stabilizers are used.

After selecting a soil stabilizer for a site the rate of application is determined after consideration of the configuration of the area, the soil type, and the expected interval between application and the development of an effective vegetative cover. The soil stabilizer should be applied on a weight basis (kilograms of dry solids per unit area) and at a standardized dilution rate to produce the type of crust that will reduce erosion and not prevent seed germination. Compatible amendments and seed are added to the solution which is applied when the condition of both soil and atmosphere will complement the treatment. Strict procedural control should be observed on critical sites.

In the humid eastern states, all stabilizer treatments may be expected to become less effective with time because of a complex interaction among edaphic, climatic, and atmospheric variables. Generally, treatment with a soil stabilizer is expected to achieve effective control of erosion until the vegetative cover develops to a size and density that will protect the site. On many sites, such protection can be achieved within a 6- to 8-week period during the growing season.

Soil stabilizers usually require more precise preparation before application than do mulches. One advantage of soil stabilizers is that all the materials required to establish a vegetative cover can be applied in one operation, whereas, for many mulches, application of seed and fertilizer must precede application of the mulch.

A secondary benefit from the use of soil stabilizers is a reduction in seed loss because of surface runoff; the soil stabilizer holds the seeds in place until they germinate. This fact is particularly important on extremely steep slopes. It has also been observed that soil stabilizers reduce friction in the hydromulcher's pipelines, pumps, and application hoses, thus reducing wear on these vital parts and making application of the slurry more efficient.

IV. COMBINING MULCHES AND STABILIZERS

An attractive alternative to separate treatment with a mulch or a soil stabilizer utilizes a combination of a wood fiber or wood cellulose mulch and a soil stabilizer. In this combination, the desirable characteristics of the materials complement each other. Low rates of application of the combination should provide site protection comparable to that achieved by a high rate of either product used alone. There is evidence that the effective life of a wood fiber or wood cellulose mulch is extended when it is used in combination with a soil stabilizer.

Many stabilizers may also be used as chemical tacks to hold straw, hay, or other lightweight mulches in place. The chemical stabilizer binds the individual pieces of mulch together and increases the resistance of the material to the movement of wind or water. The strength of the bond and the effective life of the treatment depend on the amount of soil stabilizer applied.

V. VEGETATIVE MULCHES

Use of vegetative mulches in situ should also be considered in the humid eastern U.S. Quick-developing annual grasses such as rye (*Secale cereale* L.), wheat (*Triticum aestivum* L.), Japanese millet (*Echinochloa crusgalli* var. *frumentacea*), Foxtail millet (*Setaria italica* L.) are sown after adequate fertilizer and other soil amendments have been applied to maximize growth. Species of grasses are selected that are compatible with the season during which they will be grown. Also, the permanent grass and legume species that will be the permanent vegetation is often seeded when the mulch grass is seeded. Care must be taken not to seed the fast-growing mulch grasses at so high a rate that it will be too competitive for the establishment of the permanent species.

The mulch grass provides a ground cover while it is growing and continues to protect the site after it has matured and died. The root system of the mulches in situ anchor the dead stems and leaves of the plants in place so that they provide a protective mulch that may be effective for 1 year or more. Another possibility would be to seed the permanent grass and legume species in this mulch. Under this condition a seed soil contact must be made so good seed germination will be obtained.

VI. APPLICATION METHODS

Important considerations in selecting a mulch or soil stabilizer are the cost at the point of application and the commercial availability of the equipment needed for application of the material. In selecting equipment consideration must be given to the terrain that must be covered. Wheel-type equipment cannot be used on very steep slopes, therefore, the equipment must have a range that will cover these areas.

Materials such as hay, straw, or bagasse are delivered to the site in compact bales, and commercially available blowers apply the baled material. These blowers may be equipped with an attachment that sprays a chemical tack on the mulch as it is being discharged.

Many commercially available mulches, such as wood fiber and wood cellulose products, are designed for application by hydroseeders. The amount of wood fiber or wood cellulose that can be added to a hydro-seeder is limited by the capacity of the pumps and circulation system. An 11.4-kl hydroseeder has the capacity to pump a slurry containing 1,120 to 1,680 kg of wood fiber or wood cellulose. Two or more hydroseeder loads may be required to achieve the desired rate of application.

The costs of soil stabilizers may be readily obtained from dealers and conventional pumps or hydroseeders can be used to apply the material.

Agricultural or organic industrial wastes have a potential value as a mulch, and their cost at the production site may be low. Some of these wastes must be reprocessed and packaged to make them suitable for application by conventional equipment. Others can be used without reprocessing or packaging, and can be transported to the site in bulk. Any rehandling of the material at the site prior to application may significantly increase costs. Physical characteristics of the mulch may be such that specialized application equipment must be used if it is to be spread efficiently and economically.

The cost of labor and support equipment to service and operate conventional application equipment efficiently may be an important consideration in selecting an erosion-control material. A three-man crew can efficiently service and operate a hydroseeder. In addition to the hydroseeder, a supply truck is required to haul the mulch or soil stabilizer, seed, fertilizer, and other soil amendments. Blowers that apply straw, hay, or other baled mulches require a five-man crew and one or two supply trucks. Additional equipment, such as a hydroseeder, is required to spread seed, fertilizer, and other soil amendments. This equipment may be operated by the five-man mulching crew.

VII. EROSION CONTROL AND PLANT ESTABLISHMENT

Research data and experience provide a basis for making generalized comparisons of a few of the materials more commonly used in the eastern United States. Straw and hay are the most commonly used erosion-control materials. Considerable evidence exists for their effectiveness in erosion control when they are applied at rates of 2,240 to 4,480 kg/ha. Movement of the mulches by wind can be minimized by applying an asphalt or chemical tack. The establishment of vegetation is often enhanced by the use of a hay or straw mulch. The use of these materials has sometimes been restricted by contamination of the mulch with noxious weed seeds or with organisms that cause diseases in agricultural crops.

Field studies indicate that hay, straw, or bark is essential to the establishment of grasses and legumes on extremely acid surface mine spoils (Vogel, 1975). The density of grasses and legumes on plots treated with lime and fertilizer was less than that on plots treated with lime, fertilizer, and mulch. It is believed that the mulch aids leaching of toxic ions by reducing the frequency of wetting and drying cycles of the surface. Greater surface moisture under a thick mulch reduces the loss of soil moisture and accelerates leaching.

Wood fiber and wood cellulose mulches are used extensively in the eastern U.S., being applied at rates of 1,120 to 1,680 kg/ha. Their popularity is related to the ease of application and to the fact that all materials needed for revegetation can be applied in one operation. These materials are not as effective as straw or hay for controlling erosion. There is evidence that these mulches may reduce the percentage of seeds germinating and slow plant growth. The percentage of seeds germinating may be reduced when seed is suspended above the soil surface in a loose web of fibers and subjected to moisture stress during wetting and drying cycles.

Higher seeding rates may be used to compensate for these losses or the seed can be applied in one application and the mulch in a second application. Slower plant growth has been demonstrated on areas mulched with wood fiber, but no specific cause of this delay has been identified (Plass, 1973).

The limited use of chemical stabilizers or of wood fiber with a stabilizer has produced inconsistent results. The number of materials used, variations in the rate of application, and the variability in soils and climate make it difficult to generalize results for any of the stabilizers. There is evidence that a few materials have been more widely used than others, and that agencies regulating the use of erosion control products have approved the use of several materials. This finding indicates that soil stabilizers are recognized as effective materials for controlling erosion. It is assumed that their use will expand as specific recommendations for effective methods of application are developed. Reductions in the loss of seed from surface runoff may enhance the establishment of vegetation. Materials that reduce evaporation or increase infiltration rates would also benefit plant growth. There is no evidence of chemical inhibition of germination or growth.

Residues from the wood-conversion industries are important mulching materials in some localities. Those that are supplied in bulk usually have a limited market area because of transportation costs. The lack of efficient application equipment has restricted the use of these products. Recently, new equipment has been developed that will apply these mulches, as well as other agricultural or organic industrial wastes. Rates of application are often expressed in cubic meters, since wastes from wood-processing plants show extreme variation in moisture content. Application rates relating to weight must be based on air-dry weights to assure uniformity. Residues from wood-processing plants may be effective materials for controlling erosion. The hardwood bark products are less subject to movement by wind and water than are wood chips. Wood chips are light in weight when dry, and may be moved by strong winds and runoff water. There is evidence that plant establishment and growth are improved when these mulches are used. Denitrification is not a serious problem, since the individual particles are large and decompose slowly. However, if the bark is m ixed with the soil during seed bed preparation, approximately 30 kg/ha of additional nitrogen is required.

Other types of mulches such as peanut hulls, corn cobs, and bagasse are used locally and may be very effective, but they are less important on a regional basis. Intensified marketing efforts could expand the use of such materials if they were packaged and priced competitively.

LITERATURE CITED

Emanuel, D. M. 1970. Power mulchers can apply hardwood bark mulch. USDA For. Serv. Res. Note NE-135. 6 p.

Gabriels, D., and M. De Boodt. 1975. Erosion reduction factors for chemically treated soils: a laboratory experiment. p. 95–102. In W. R. Gardner and W. C. Moldenhauer (ed.) Soil conditioners. SSSA Spec. Publ. no. 7, Soil Sci. Soc. Am., Madison, Wis.

Hendrickson, B. H. 1938. The choking of pore space in the soil and its relation to runoff and erosion. Trans. Am. Geophys. Union 15:500–505.

Kay, B. L. 1976. Hydroseeding, straw, and chemicals for erosion control. p. 16. *In* Proc. 1976 Soil Erosion Sediment. Short Course at Washington State Univ., Olympia. Publ. by Washington State Univ., Pullman.

Kay, B. L., and Ray Mearns. 1973. Erosion-control treatments on fine sand. Agron. Prog. Rep. 58, Univ. of California Agric. Exp. Stn., Davis, Calif.

Morrison, W. R. 1971. Chemical stabilization of soils. Laboratory and field evaluation of several petrochemical liquids for soil stabilization. Bur. of Reclam. REC-ERC-71-30, U.S. Dep. of Interior, Denver, Colo.

Plass, W. T. 1973. Chemical soil stabilizers for surface-mine reclamation. p. 118–122. *In* Soil erosion: causes and mechanisms; prevention and control. Spec. Rep. 135, Highway Res. Board, Washington, D.C.

Sarles, R. L. 1973. New equipment for bark application. p. 7–24. *In* Technological options in bark utilization. Proc. Bark Residue Sess., Annual Meet. For. Proc. Res. Soc. June 1973. Anaheim, Calif.

Vogel, W. G. 1975. Requirements and use of fertilizer, lime, and mulch for vegetating acid mine spoils. Proc. NCA/BCR Conf. Expo II, Louisville, Ky. Bituminous Coal Res., Inc., Monroeville, Pa.

Yocum, T. R., D. C. Saupe, and S. K. Sipp. 1971. Shredded hardwood bark mulch—an effective material for erosion control and roadside slope stabilization. University of Ill. Exp. Stn. For. Res. Rep. 71-4, Urbana, Ill. 51 p.

Copyright © 1978 ASA–CSSA–SSSA
677 South Segoe Road, Madison, WI 53711 USA
Reclamation of Drastically Disturbed Lands

Chapter 19

Power Plant Fly Ash Utilization for Land Reclamation in the Eastern United States

JOHN P. CAPP

U.S. Department of the Interior
Bureau of Mines, Morgantown, West Virginia

I. INTRODUCTION

The extractive industries that produce minerals by surface mining methods have been increasingly criticized and censured by conservation groups, government agencies, and citizens for not adhering to standards and regulations pertaining to good reclamation practices. In the northern Appalachian basin, where large areas are disturbed to produce coal, this criticism has reached sizeable proportions and threatens the continued use of surface mining methods in some areas. However, it is improbable that surface mining will be abolished; what is more likely to occur is the enactment of regulations by the various mining states to control this type of industry. Thus, spoil banks will still require reclamation and revegetation, but in accordance with higher standards. In addition, greater attention will be directed toward the thousands of acres of abandoned or so-called "orphaned" areas and the problems associated with their reclamation.

To mention reclamation standards and proper reclamation procedures in this context presumes the existence of knowledge accumulated over many years which can be used to set up guidelines. Serious gaps exist however, and the search for new methods, new techniques, better equipment, and materials is widening by the industry, universities, and government agencies.

This paper describes a study in which the U.S. Bureau of Mines engineers at Morgantown, W. Va., developed a procedure for utilizing the special soil-making characteristics of power plant fly ash to aid in the restoration of disturbed lands. Besides returning waste areas to productive use, successful reclamation of spoil areas with fly ash helps solve fly ash disposal problems (Adams et al., 1972; Capp & Adams, 1971).

Development of the pulverized fuel burner, the cyclone burner, and the electrostatic precipitator resulted in the production and collection of large quantities of fly ash, cinders, and bottom ash. In the three decades since the end of World War II, an estimated 416 million metric tons of ash have been produced in the United States, but only about 10%, or 42 million metric tons, has been utilized. If present ash production trends continue, another 272 million metric tons will have accumulated by 1980. Since the current annual utilization rate of this waste material amounts to only 16% of the total produced, it is apparent that continued effort is desirable to develop new outlets and expand existing ones.

It is truly amazing when one considers that, if all the land disturbed or utilized by the mining industry (1930–1976) had been reclaimed by the fly ash technique, approximately 421 million metric tons[1] of ash would have been utilized. Since 421 million metric tons represents an amount that is only slightly larger than the amount of fly ash and bottom ash produced during the same period, the disposal problem would thus have been eliminated.

II. BACKGROUND AND PERSPECTIVE

The properties of spoils and coal refuse that restrict and limit plant growth are acidity, compacted surface, coarse texture, and dark color. On steep outslopes, the effects are compounded by erosion, runoff, and difficulty in operating machinery. Although spoil and refuse may vary widely in composition and character, they all represent potential soil-making material. As the original material weathers, breaks down, oxidizes, and is leached, conditions for plant growth and survival improve, but it may take many years before this happens. On the other hand, fly ash has the capability of speeding up the timetable and making it possible to reestablish life on these barren wastes. The soil formation process is the result of many factors, and fly ash aids this process by eliminating or reducing those spoil and refuse properties that restrict plant growth.

The physical and chemical effects derived from the use of fly ash for reclamation or in agriculture can be attributed to its source and how it is produced. Coal, the source of the ash, was formed from plant substances preserved from complete decay in a favorable environment and then altered by various chemical and physical agents that included heat, pressure, and deposition of sedimentary materials. After the coal is pulverized and burned in the boilers of large power-generating plants, the fly ash is collected as a powdery residue.

The ash is comprised of compounds of silicon, aluminum, iron, and calcium; smaller amounts of compounds containing magnesium, titanium, sodium, and potassium; and traces of compounds having boron, copper, manganese, molybdenum, zinc and other elements. The range of these elements in representative ashes from the eastern United States is given in Table 1. These compounds occur in the ash primarily as complex silicates, oxides, and sulfates, along with lesser amounts of carbonates and phosphates.

Physically, fly ash consists mostly of finely divided spheroids of siliceous glass ranging from 1 to 50 μm in diameter. A minor fraction consists of

---

[1] Based on application of 224 metric tons of ash/ha and 1.88 million ha disturbed. (Latter value estimated from U.S. Bureau of Mines Inf. Circ. 8642).

Table 1—Range of elemental composition of seven fly ashes used in surface mine reclamation demonstrations

Element	Range, %
Calcium	0.2 – 4.1
Magnesium	0.1 – 0.8
Potassium	1.7 – 3.2
Phosphorus	0.1 – 0.2
Carbon	1.0 –38.1
Sodium	0.1 – 0.6
Sulfur	0.15 – 0.40
Boron	0.005– 0.045
Copper	0.004– 0.020
Manganese	0.000– 0.030
Molybdenum	0.002– 0.310
Zinc	0.008– 0.020
Iron	5.1 –16.0
Aluminum	10.3 –19.7
Silicon	21.6 –28.4

larger irregularly shaped particles, some opaque and some transparent or translucent. Carbon is also present, chiefly in the form of irregularly shaped particles of coke.

With the exception of nitrogen, fly ash contains many of the elements essential for plant growth; hence, this power plant waste has potential as a soil amendment to correct deficiencies in some soils.

The principal chemical effect of adding large quantities of fly ash to soil is the neutralization of soil acids. While it is known that some fly ashes are neutral or acid, it appears that most are sufficiently alkaline to increase the pH of soil, strip spoil, and coal mine refuse. Table 2 lists the sites that have been treated with fly ash during the period 1965–1975. All of the areas were initially very acid, but after fly ash was applied the pH was increased to levels suitable for plants. Current pH levels range from 5 to 7.5, depending to some extent on the age of the site. Since the areas received only one fly ash application and the oldest is more than 10 years old, it must be concluded that this treatment is relatively permanent. However, it should be pointed out that the treatment is a surface effect and the lower layers remain extremely acid. For example, samples taken at various depth intervals down to 56 cm show a decrease in pH values with depth (Table 3).

Size fraction data in Table 3 show that the addition of fly ash also modifies the particle size distribution of the spoil. This is because fly ash is made up mostly of the fine sand-silt size particles. In the cases of coarse- and fine-textured soils, the modification results in the formation of a medium-textured soil. These soils generally have the most plant-available moisture.

From a practical point of view, an increase in the moisture-holding capacity as well as the other benefits of fly ash-treated spoils was noted in all the field experiments (Capp et al., 1967, 1975). Additional laboratory test data on recently treated plots show an increase in available water of 4% for the spoil and about 6% for the refuse (Table 4). These increases

Table 2—Characteristics of coal waste areas treated with fly ash

Site	Year initiated	Type†	Hectares	Original pH	Application		Ash pH	Average current pH of site	Condition of vegetative cover
					Rate	Source of ash			
					metric tons				
Albright no. 1	1966	SM	0.4	2.6-2.3	448-1,792	Albright	11.4	5.6	Excellent
Ft. Martin	1968	SM	2.0	3.1-4.7	336	Ft. Martin	11.9	6.9	Excellent
Shannopin	1971	RD	4.0	Variable	Variable	Ft. Martin	11.9	7.4	Good
Stewartstown	1970	SM	26.0	2.5-3.3	336	Ft. Martin	11.9	7.4	Excellent
Cassville	1971	RD	8.0	3.0-3.8	336	Ft. Martin	11.9	6.0	Good
Bunker	1970	RD	0.4	2.7-3.0	336	Ft. Martin	11.9	7.1	Excellent
Century	1973	RD	8.0	2.7	448	Harrison	11.5	6.8	Poor
Powhatan Point	1972	RD	2.5	2.8	448	Berger	9.1	7.4	Good
Rex Coal Co.	1973	SM	4.0	4.5	448	Harrison	11.5	7.2	Fair
Ashley	1973	RD	2.0	3.1	672	Hunlock Ck	3.8	6.8	Fair
Westover	1965	SM	0.2	2.3-3.8	Up to 672	Albright	11.4	5.1	Good
Albright no. 2	1974	SM	13.0	3.1	1,120	Albright	7.7	5.2	Good

† SM = Surface mine spoil; RD = Refuse dump (gob pile).

Table 3—Change in character of spoil material at Albright site (1,792 metric tons/ha)

Fly ash application		Fraction			
Depth interval	Minus 2-mm fraction	Sand	Clay	Silt	pH
cm	%		%		
8–30	83	38.8	8.2	53.0	5.5
38–46	47	54.8	23.2	22.0	3.5
51–56	37	72.8	9.2	18.0	2.9

Table 4—Available water in surface mine spoil, coal mine refuse and fly ash
mixtures of these materials†

	Moisture content 1/3 bar (field capacity)	Moisture content 15 bar (wilt point)	Available moisture
		%	
Stewartstown spoil, untreated control area	13.90	4.76	9.14
Stewartstown spoil, fly ash-treated, 337 metric tons/ha	16.94	3.49	13.45
Cassville refuse, control	21.85	9.17	12.68
Cassville refuse, fly ash-treated, 336 metric tons/ha	23.89	5.43	18.46

† Data on <2 mm fraction.

are significant and could be beneficial to plants during periods of drought stress.

III. CONDUCTIVITY STUDIES

The electrical conductivity of fly ashes tested thus far range from 1.5 to 2.3 mmho/cm. Coal mine refuse generally ranges from about 0.5 to >3.0 mmho/cm, while surface mine spoils range from 0.2 to about 2.0 mmho/cm. Where a fly ash was blended with a low conductivity spoil (e.g., 0.21 mmho/cm), the conductivity of the mixture increased to 0.66 mmho/cm. When fly ash was blended with a high conductivity coal mine refuse (e.g., 3.23 mmho/cm), conductivity of the mixture decreased to 2.51 mmho/cm. Where conductivities of both materials are similar, very little change in the mixture is noted.

It appears that the older fly ash-treated areas have had more of the soluble salts leached out, but a high concentration of salts remains in the plow layer of the newer sites.

This phenomena may help to explain why, in areas of high salt concentration, there are early germination and seedling growth problems with more rapid germination and healthier growth after the area has been leached for several seasons.

The source of fly ash, the condition of the spoil, and the degree of mixing, along with the amount of precipitation, can be determining factors in how much elapsed time is required before vegetation on the problem areas shows a minimum of visible salt damage.

IV. FLY ASH STUDIES BY OTHERS

The basic chemical and physical benefits from utilization of fly ash on agricultural soils have been studied extensively in the United States at the Virginia Polytechnic Institute and State University. These investigations indicate that the boron, molybdenum, zinc, phosphorus, and potassium in fly ash are available to plants and that the waste product can be used to correct deficiencies of these elements when properly applied (Martens & Plank, 1973; Martens & Beahm, 1976). Significant changes in particle size distribution and bulk density were also noted that led to an increase in pore space and available moisture when fly ash was applied to certain soils at the rate of 430 metric tons/ha (Jones & Amos, 1976).

An investigation has been initiated at the University of Alabama to provide a quantitative analysis of growth for various species of plants growing on raw and fly ash-amended strip mine spoils (Wochock et al., 1976). This study has demonstrated a direct relationship between the fly ash treatment rate and such parameters as dry weight, root-shoot ratios, nodulation, and nitrogen fixation.

A full-scale demonstration project is being evaluated at this time as a joint effort of the Department of Environmental Resources, the State of Pennsylvania, and the U.S. Environmental Protection Agency under contract to Ackenheil and Associates-Geo. Systems, Inc., of Pittsburgh, Pa. Fly ash was applied to approximately 73 ha at rates up to 448 metric tons/ha. The location of the demonstration is the Hillman State Park in Washington County, Pa., where a former strip-mined area totaling 1,479 ha is being reclaimed for recreational purposes (Daugherty & Holzen, 1976).

A new and interesting approach to develop better methods of fly ash disposal came to light at the 4th International Ash Utilization Symposium. The concept concerns burial of the waste product in impermeable clay-lined pits or cells. The cells are then covered with the earth originally removed and shaped into mounds that blend into the surrounding landscape (Shively, 1976).

In a similar operation, ash disposal contractors have been transporting ash from power plants at Mt. Storm, W. Va., and Masontown, Pa., to strip mines near the plants and subsequently reclaiming the areas to blend into the landscape.

At the Belle Valley Area Center near Caldwell, Ohio, the Bureau of Mines and the Ohio Agricultural Research and Development Center are evaluating the combinations of fly ash, sewage sludge, and waste cement dust for use in reclaiming acid strip-mine spoils. The objective is to establish the treatment rates for these materials and utilize the special benefits supplied by each one for optimum effect. Results are not yet available on this work.

V. FLY ASH RECLAMATION TECHNIQUE

The basic treatment procedure developed from this experimental program begins with sampling and analysis of both waste material and the available fly ash. From these analyses application rates are determined. Fly ash is delivered to the site and unloaded at specified points to ease spreading requirements. The fly ash is then blended into the surface material by plowing, scarifing, ripping, or similar actions. A seed bed is prepared, seeded, fertilized, and mulched where necessary.

Before a site is treated with fly ash, the area must be leveled and/or contoured, toxic materials buried, land surveyed, and soil samples taken. Soil samples are analyzed to determine acidity, pH, moisture-holding capacity, nutrient deficiencies or fertilizer requirements, soil salinity, and textural classification and/or screen analysis. Samples of soil should be representative of the area from which they were obtained. This information will help evaluate the area for potential reclamation with fly ash.

Fly ash samples from area power plants are analyzed for alkalinity, pH, conductivity, texture, and chemical make-up. Selection of the fly ash for use in the particular site treatment is then based upon evaluation of these properties and upon the distance of the power plant from the reclamation site. Location becomes crucial because hauling costs will greatly affect the overall fly ash reclamation costs.

The amount of fly ash that is applied to the surface of an area depends upon the relative acidity of the spoil and upon the neutralizing power of the fly ash. The acidity of the spoil and alkalinity of the fly ash can be established by titration or by measurement of pH. For most cases, the latter method is easier and is the one used by the Bureau in working with these materials. The amount of fly ash to be added to a spoil by this method is determined empirically by measuring the pH of several fly ash-spoil mixtures (e.g., 0, 20, and 50% by weight). Since the amount of fly ash required will depend upon the characteristics of both the spoil and the fly ash, and because these are quite variable, the amount of fly ash to be used in the treatment may have to be raised or lowered accordingly to obtain the desired pH level of 7.0.

After the fly ash has been delivered to the site, it is spread in as even a layer as possible to give the desired application rate. The thickness of the layer will depend upon the bulk density of the fly ash as received on the site.[2] Spreading can be done by grader, dozer, front-end loader, or other equipment that may be available for such purposes.

Mixing of fly ash and spoil is accomplished by plow and disk or rototiller. Time and care should be taken during this part of the operation to achieve adequate mixing of the two materials. To accomplish this, it may be necessary to plow and cross-plow the area several times, depending on the fly ash application rate and the nature of the spoil. During the disking operation, the disk should be followed by a cultipacker or drag to prepare a good seed bed suitable for grass seed.

---

[2] A layer of typical fly ash will weigh approximately 100 metric tons/ha per cm of thickness.

Table 5—Typical seed mixture sown on fly ash-treated spoil or refuse

Seed	Weight
	%
Kentucky 31 fescue (*Festuca arundinacea*)	35
Red top grass (*Argostis alba*)	14
Orchard grass (*Dactylis glomerrta*)	18
Rye grass (*Lolium perenne*)	28
Birdsfoot trefoil (*Lotus corniculatus*)	5

The nature of the waste materials, the fly ash, and the surface conditions of the site dictate the choice of machinery to be employed. Farm machines, such as tractors, plows, chisels, harrows, disks, spreaders, and packers, have been effectively used where spoil or refuse was not too rocky or compacted and the terrain was suitable. At other sites, heavy construction-type equipment, including bulldozers, front-end loaders, rototillers, rippers and heavy-duty disks, has been required to work the soil because of exessive compaction of surface material, large rocks, and uneven terrain. Large dump trucks of the type commonly used to haul coal have been utilized to deliver the required quantities of fly ash to the site.

The seed application rate generally utilized was 52 kg/ha. Both dry seeding and hydroseeding methods are acceptable and a mulch is recommended on all slopes. Although seeding may be done almost any time, the chances of success are best if it is done in the early spring or autumn. If seeding is done in midsummer, a mulch is highly recommended, even on flat areas.

The amount of fertilizer required on a treated site should be determined by laboratory analysis. In general, a minimum of 1,120 kg/ha of 10–10–10 analysis fertilizer is recommended, or any equivalent substitute is acceptable at the time of treatment. The appearance of the vegetation during the first two seasons should be evaluated for color, vigor, and growth. If the condition is poor, additional fertilizer application is recommended as determined by laboratory test.

The grasses most successfully used on the fly ash-treated plots are given in Table 5. Birdsfoot trefoil (Empire variety), a legume, also gave good results. The symbiotic nitrogen-fixation activity between legumes and root nodule bacteria is well known, and the use of these plants is encouraged to build up and maintain nitrogen fertility of the reclaimed land, especially where application of chemical fertilizers is impractical.

1. DRY MATTER YIELDS

Dry matter yields are indicative of the beneficial effects of fly ash treatment. At the first fly ash-treated site, an average yield of 2.44 metric tons/ha was obtained from the fly ash-treated areas, while the limestone-treated control plot at the same site produced only 1.21 metric tons/ha. Similar yields were obtained from the other fly ash-treated areas.

During the third year after treatment at the Albright site, fertilizer (N, P, and K) rates were increased to determine how a more intensive management program would affect yields.

Since nitrogen is most easily lost by leaching, it was applied in equal portions of 78 kg/ha as urea in the spring and after the first two cuttings. Spring applications of P and K were 101 kg/ha of each from 0–15–30 analysis granulated fertilizer. This treatment increased yields and permitted three cuttings instead of the usual one or two per year. Average dry matter yields from all the plots for the first, second, and third cuttings were 3.6, 5.15, and 8.51 metric tons/ha, respectively, which compares favorably with those obtained at the West Virginia University Agronomy Farm, Reedsville, W. Va., in high fertilization-rate experiments with these same perennial tall grasses. The grass-legume mixture on this plot has continued to yield quantities of hay and forage comparable to surrounding undisturbed fields and pastures up to the present time.

2. PLANT MATERIAL COMPOSITION

The data in Table 6 compares the elemental make-up of plant material grown on fly ash-treated coal wastes with that of plants from the farm soils. These data show that plant materials grown on fly ash-treated refuse and spoils contain generally less potassium, phosphorus, calcium, magnesium, and nitrogen, but higher amounts of iron, copper, boron, manganese, aluminum, and strontium as compared to that from farm soils. Although the fly ash may contain higher than average amounts of trace elements found in soils, the uptake of these elements from ash-

Table 6—Range of composition of dry forage† from Agronomy Farm and spoil coal mine refuse for 1970 and 1972 (Albright, Ft. Martin, Stewartstown, and Bunker sites)

Element	Fly ash-treated spoil, refuse		Farm soil	
	%			
P	0.14–	0.28	0.20–	0.55
K	0.64–	1.70	2.86–	4.03
Ca	0.29–	0.82	0.49–	1.01
Mg	0.03–	0.17	0.39–	0.29
N	0.09–	3.0		3.9
	ppm			
Fe	53	–216	44	–103
Mo	1.7 –	3.5	1.8 –	3.5
Cu	7	– 19	8	– 9
Zn	12	– 28	19	– 29
B	20	–300	14	– 23
Mn	135	–254	71	–160
Al	53	–218	30	– 53
Sr	13	– 99	17	– 32
Ba	0	– 34	16	– 19

† Includes grass and legumes.

treated spoils was not above the limits likely to cause problems with either plants or animals. The exceptions to this are boron and aluminum. Soils normally contain 4 to 88 ppm total boron, of which generally about 50% of the total amount present is soluble. One fly ash used extensively in the Bureau experiments (Fort Martin) had 450 ppm of boron and, although it is unlikely that this is all available boron, this may account for some of the toxicity symptoms sometimes found during the first year after seeding on the fly ash-spoil mixtures. This condition, however, seems to disappear and not recur after continued growth. Analysis of dry plant tissue shows a range of 20 to 300 ppm boron, with the higher concentration in plants grown on the more recently treated acres. Leaching probably accounts for the decreased boron uptake by plants in later years.

Higher aluminum values are probably associated with low pH. It is reemphasized that the fly ash treatment is a surface effect and that low pH spoils material may contact roots of plants growing in the surface layer, providing the opportunity for the plant to absorb soluble aluminum.

VI. PLANT SELECTIVITY TRIALS

In the spring of 1972, several species of plant seeds were obtained from the Plant Materials Centers of the U.S. Department of Agriculture, Soil Conservation Service, for testing germination, growth, and survival. Selection of species for the trial was limited to those plants known to have

Table 7—Plant selectivity trials

Scientific name	Condition and survival rate	
	Summer 1972	Summer 1973
Agropyron intermedium 'Dahe' (Intermediate wheatgrass)	Good	Good
Ammophila breviliqulata (American beachgrass)	Poor	Poor
Andropogon caucasica (Caucasian bluestem)	Poor	Failure
Andropogon gerardi (Big bluestem)	Poor	Few plants
Elymus sabulosus (Wild rye)	Failure	Failure
Eragrostis curvula (Weeping lovegrass)	Excellent	Plants appear dead
Galega officinalis (Common goatsrue)	Fair	Good
Lathyrus sylvestris 'Lathco' (Peavine flatpea)	Poor	Fair
Lotus corniculatus (Birdsfoot trefoil)	Failure	Failure
Lotus tenuis (birdsfoot trefoil, narrow leaf)	Failure	Failure
Panicum amarulum (Coastal panic grass)	Fair	Poor
Panicum clandestinum (Deertongue)	Poor	Fair
Panicum vergatum 'Blackwell' (Switch grass)	Good	Good
Panicum vergatum (Carthage switchgrass)	Fair	Good
Polygonum cuspidatum Ky. 600 (Knotweed)	Fair	Good
Polygonum cuspidatum Ky. 795 (Knotweed)	Failure	Failure
Polygonum cuspidatum Ky. 1416 (Knotweed)	Failure	Failure
Sorgastrum nutans (Indian grass)	Failure	Failure
Coronilla varia L. (Crown vetch)	Very poor	Failure
Lotus corniculatus (Empire birdsfoot trefoil)	Good	Excellent
Melilotus officinalis (Yellow sweet clover)	Excellent	Excellent

tolerance for saline soils and/or alkali soils because some of the fly ash spoil/refuse mixtures fall into those categories. Ten-by-ten-foot-square (3.05-m-square) plots were prepared with a garden rotary tiller after treatment at the rate of 336 metric tons/ha of fly ash and then hand-seeded with the selected seeds. The selected species are listed in Table 7 and rated in general overall performance from the viewpoint of covering ability, vigor, quantity of surviving plants, and appearance. Those that have ratings of good or excellent have potential as useful plant materials for fly ash-reclaimed spoils.

VII. TREE RESPONSE ON SURFACE MINE SPOILS TREATED WITH FLY ASH

The question of tree survival and growth on spoils treated with fly ash has been brought up many times. To find out how trees would respond to these materials, the Bureau and the U.S. Forest Service[3] jointly planted tree seedlings at several of the sites spanning a period of several years through 1971.

The initial attempts to establish tree and shrub seedlings met with little success. When planted soon after the fly ash was applied, many of the species died during the first growing season, and those that survived usually died during the second year.

Although the spoil on all sites was extremely acid before treatment, the fly ash neutralized some of the acidity, and the soil pH after treatment indicated some species of trees and shrubs could survive if acidity-related factors were the principal contributing cause of death. Apparently other factors, such as the soluble components of the fly ash, or a chemical interaction between the fly ash and the acid spoil material, contributed to the poor survival rate. However, at one site (Albright site) that had been treated with fly ash 4 years before the trees were planted, some species survived very well. At the time of planting, the grass and legume cover was growing vigorously, and completely occupied the site. It was speculated that weathering and leaching may have contributed to the success of the surviving trees.

Nine coniferous species, six hardwood tree species, and four deciduous shrub species were planted in groups of four at the Albright site. The study was replicated on three adjacent blocks. After three growing seasons, the species with the highest survival were crabapple, 100% survival; and red oak, 67% survival (Table 8). Both species made very slow growth. Survival for European alder, Scotch pine, and Norway spruce was 58%. The alder grew very well and averaged 4.5 feet in height after three growing seasons. Black walnut, white pine, pitch pine, silky dogwood, and red pine survival ranged from 33 to 50%. All of these species grew very slowly. Japanese larch, European larch, autumn olive, shortleaf pine, tartarian honeysuckle, yellow poplar, sycamore, black locust, and Virginia pine were considered failures.

---

[3] Northeastern For. Exp. Stn., Wood Products Marketing Lab., Princeton, W. Va.

Table 8—Tree survival and growth on the Albright site three years after planting

Species	Average height of all living trees			Survival on all plots		
	Growing season†			Growing season†		
	1	2	3	1	2	3
	——— feet ———			——— % ———		
Crabapple (*Malus* sp.)	1.2	1.4	1.4	100	100	100
Red oak (*Quercus borealis*)	0.8	0.9	1.1	100	100	67
European alder (*Alnus glutinosa*)	1.3	2.5	4.5	83	58	58
Scotch pine (*Pinus sylvestris*)	0.6	0.8	1.0	58	58	58
Norway spruce (*Picea abies*)	0.8	1.1	1.2	67	67	58
Black walnut (*Juglans nigra*)	1.2	1.0	1.4	100	75	50
White pine (*Pinus strobus*)	0.7	1.2	1.7	67	50	42
Pitch pine (*Pinus rigida*)	1.0	1.3	1.7	92	58	33
Silky dogwood (*Cornus amomum*)	1.2	1.0	2.1	58	42	33
Red pine (*Pinus resinosa*)	0.4	0.8	1.0	100	75	33
Japanese larch (*Larix leppolepis*)	1.2	1.0	2.3	42	8	8
Autumn olive (*Elaeagnus umbellata*)	1.2	2.6	4.3	17	8	8
Tartarian honeysuckle (*Lonicera tartarica*)	0.6	1.0	2.4	25	8	8
Shortleaf pine (*Pinus echinata*)	1.0	1.5	--	83	50	--
Yellow poplar (*Liriodendron tulipifera*)	0.4	0.5	--	33	17	--
Sycamore (*Plantanus occidentalis*)	0.6	--	--	42	--	--
Black locust (*Robinia pseudoacacia*)	0.9	0.8	--	17	8	--
Virginia pine (*Pinus virginiana*)	0.2	--	--	17	--	--
European larch (*Larix decidua*)	1.4	--	--	17	--	--

† Total height and survival were determined at the end of each growing season.

Although it is difficult to evaluate the effect of the dense grass and legume cover on survival, this factor may have contributed to mortality in some species, but it probably was not responsible for all mortality. Therefore, the cause of death was probably a combination of the fly ash treatment and the ground cover density. The species that failed were the most intolerant to the site conditions. The species with the highest survival should be considered for future tests on fly ash-treated areas.

In 1973, the Bureau and the West Virginia University Department of Forestry jointly planted tree seedlings at two of the sites where almost complete failures were previously experienced at these locations. Austrian pine from several seed sources, autumn olive, European alder, and black locust were the species planted. The 1974 overall survival rate for two replications at the Stewartston site (treated 1 and 2 years prior to planting) was 17 and 57%. At the Fort Martin site (treated 4 years prior to planting) the survival rate was 68%. Foliage analyses showed significant differences in the quantity of elements absorbed by the trees at different locations and by trees from different seed sources planted on the same site. Trees planted on the 1- and 2-year-old fly ash treatments exhibited boron toxicity, but those planted on the 4-year-old fly ash treatment site rarely showed such symptoms. Although survival was good for seedlings from all but one source, the survival data cannot be extrapolated because rainfall frequency and amount were above average for this area. Another series of plantings would better correlate these factors.

These plantings indicate several variables may determine the survival of trees planted on fly ash-treated surface mine spoil. These include the following:

1) The pH of the spoil before treatment;
2) The fly ash sources and the rate of application;
3) The establishment of an herbaceous ground cover before planting;
4) The fertilization treatment and the composition of the herbaceous ground cover seeded before planting;
5) The time interval between fly ash treatment and planting; and
6) The species of trees or shrubs planted.

The emphasis in past studies has been on the selection of species that can be successfully established on fly ash-treated areas. Since a few promising species have been identified, it seems appropriate to use these to evaluate other factors that may contribute to tree survival.

VIII. FLY ASH RECLAMATION COSTS

Reclamation costs depend on many variables, including the terrain, mine spoil type and age, acreage, equipment used, and degree of reclamation. Based on experience to date, the cost of vegetating fly ash-treated areas is estimated at about $1,232/ha, as given in Table 9. According to the Department of Natural Resources of the State of West Virginia, the 25-ha Stewartstown site which serves as a basis for this table is one of the worst in northern West Virginia. It had been previously "leveled" for a flat fee, and some additional machine time had to be subsequently expended to provide access roads. The latter work is included in spreading and ripping costs. Fly ash costs depend on the quantity needed to neutralize a particular spoil with a given fly ash and the distance from the power plant to the reclamation area. Fly ash for this project was obtained without charge; cost reflects transportation charges only. Spreading and ripping (mixing) charges are actual and would vary with the type of equipment used.

Table 9—Reclamation cost of surface-mined spoil †

Item	Cost/hectare
Fly ash‡	$ 463.68
Spreading and ripping§	440.00
Fertilizer¶	185.33
Seed#	65.56
Fertilizing and seeding	40.77
Soil testing	37.07
Total	$1,232.41

† Land acquisition, leveling and supervision are not included.
‡ 336 metric tons fly ash/ha at delivered cost (16 km from power station) at $1.10/ton (Fly ash provided at no cost). $0.28/metric ton loading fee.
§ 20 machine hours/ha at $22/hour.
¶ 1,120 kg of 10–10–10/ha.
# 52 kg of seed mixture/ha.

Table 10—Equivalent cost of materials found in fly ash

Material	%	Amount of 336-metric ton application	Market value
CaO	6.8	23	$ 136.70†
K₂O + P₂O₅	3.3	8.4	1.142.40‡
Fine sand & silt	89.9	302	755.00§
		Total	$2,034.10

† Lime at $5.90/metric ton.
‡ Fertilizer at $136/metric ton.
§ Fine sand and silt at $2.50/metric ton.

Four states, Ohio, Pennsylvania, West Virginia, and Kentucky, produce nearly 7¼ million metric tons of fly ash per year, in close proximity to the leading counties for strip coal production in each of the states. There is great potential for utilizing fly ash in reclamation in this region by employing the back haul concept wherein trucks that haul coal to the powerplant deliver fly ash to the surface mine area on the return trip. A mutually beneficial arrangement between the coal operator and the power company provides the operator, on the one hand, with a material that aids in reclamation and, on the other hand, gives the power company the opportunity to usefully dispose of a troublesome waste product.

In many cases the fly ash can be obtained for a nominal loading charge and the cost of transportation from the plant to the site. If the backhaul concept is applied, the hauling cost can be considerably reduced compared with the straight haul charge.

Seeding, fertilizing, and testing costs obviously are negligible compared with the three major cost items—fly ash delivery, fly ash spreading, and cultivation. Since the cost of reclamation by fly ash treatment is related only indirectly to the leveling method, as any other reclamation procedure would be, leveling costs are not included in the overall estimate.

Estimates in the surface mining industry range from $1,730 to $2,470/ha for earth moving, seeding, fertilizer, and soil conditioning. However, a closer examination of the $464/ha costs ascribed to fly ash indicates that the actual market value of materials found in the ash and added in the reclamation totaled $2,041, as assessed in Table 10. Although these ingredients would not be purchased in this form, and indeed, not all of these materials would be in a plant-available form in fly ash, the exercise emphasizes values for fly ash not ordinarily considered.

Costs in restoring refuse dumps are also attractive. The standard practice is to cover the refuse with 15 to 60 cm of earth at a cost of up to $1,600/ha. Since leveling, fertilizer, and seed costs would be similar in either case, the same results can be accomplished with 448 tons/ha of fly ash. The savings are obvious, and additional land does not have to be disturbed to obtain borrow material.

Although these costs should be confirmed on a much larger scale, it appears that the fly ash technique can successfully compete with other spoil reclamation methods and is much cheaper than soil cover for most coal refuse piles.

Increased interest and participation of coal-mining and power-generating companies in promoting fly ash for reclamation of waste areas will lead to more information on reclamation practices and costs.

Fly ash is available in large quantities throughout the United States and many of the source locations are presently within economical hauling radius of surface mining operations, especially if a haul-back type of delivery is negotiated between the power company and the coal operator. As power plants in the future add on flue gas lime scrubbers, and easy disposal sites near the plant become unavailable, the use of fly ash for reclamation will become increasingly attractive.

LITERATURE CITED

Adams, L. M., J. P. Capp, and D. W. Gillmore. 1972. Coal mine spoil and refuse bank reclamation with powerplant fly ash. Compost Sci. 13(6):20–26.

Capp, J. P., and L. M. Adams. 1971. Reclamation of coal mine wastes and strip spoil with fly ash. Preprint, 162nd Nat. Meet., Am. Chem. Soc., Washington, D.C., 13–17 Sept. 1971, Vol. 15, no. 2. 12 p.

Capp, J. P., and C. F. Engle. 1967. Fly ash in agriculture. p. 269–279. In Fly Ash Utilization Symp., Pittsburgh, Pa., Aug. 1967. U.S. Bur. of Mines Inf. Circ. 8640. U.S. Gov. Printing Office, Washington, D.C.

Capp, J. P., D. W. Gillmore, and D. G. Simpson. 1975. Coal waste stabilization by enhanced vegetation. Min. Congr. J. 61(5):44–49.

Daugherty, M. T., and H. H. Holzen. 1976. The Hillman fly ash demonstration project—a case study of mass utilization. p. 632–641. In 4th Int. Ash Utilization Symp., St. Louis, Mo., 24–25 Mar. 1976. ERDA, Morgantown Energy Res. Center, Morgantown, W. Va. MERC/SP-76/4.

Jones, C. C., and D. F. Amos. 1976. Physical changes in Virginia soils resulting from the addition of high rates of fly ash. p. 624–631. In 4th Int. Fly Ash Utilization Symp., St. Louis, Mo., 24–25 Mar. 1976. ERDA, Morgantown Energy Res. Center, Morgantown, W. Va., MERC/SP-76/4.

Martens, D. C., and B. R. Beahm. 1976. Growth of plants in fly ash-amended soils. p. 657–664. In 4th Int. Ash Utilization Symp., St. Louis, Mo., 24–25 Mar. 1976. ERDA, Morgantown Energy Res. Center, Morgantown, W. Va., MERC/SP-76/4.

Martens, D. C., and C. O. Plank. 1973. Basic soil benefits from ash utilization. p. 269–279. In 3rd Int. Ash Utilization Symp., Pittsburgh, Pa., 13–14 Mar. 1973. U.S. Bur. of Mines Inf. Circ. 8640. U.S. Gov. Printing Office, Washington, D.C.

Shivley, W. W. 1976. Landforms from fly ash. p. 293–299. In 4th Int. Ash Utilization Symp., St. Louis, Mo., 24–25 Mar. 1976. ERDA, Morgantown Energy Res. Center, Morgantown, W. Va., MERC/SP-76/4.

Wochock, Z. S., J. L. Fail, and M. Hosmer. 1976. Analysis of plant growth in fly ash amended soils. p. 642–656. In 4th Int. Ash Utilization Symp., St. Louis, Mo., 24–25 Mar. 1976. ERDA, Morgantown Energy Res. Center, Morgantown, W. Va., MERC/SP-76/4.

Copyright © 1978 ASA–CSSA–SSSA
677 South Segoe Road, Madison, WI 53711 USA
Reclamation of Drastically Disturbed Lands

Chapter 20

Use of Municipal Sewage Sludge in Reclamation of Soils

JAMES L. HALDERSON AND DAVID R. ZENZ

The Metropolitan Sanitary District of Greater Chicago
Chicago, Illinois

I. INTRODUCTION

The use of municipal sewage sludge for rebuilding topsoil offers a capability which is not available with other methods. As a stabilized material, sludge does not cause burning of plants, can be applied in sufficient quantities to rebuild topsoil at one time, and is available in quantity from large municipalities. Sludge can be transported and applied as a liquid or a solid, although the liquid forms result in handling of great weight.

A number of sludge utilization sites have been ongoing for a sufficient period of time to establish the feasibility of using organic matter from sludge to rebuild topsoil. Operational experience is available for handling systems, application systems, quantities required per acre, and the response of various types of vegetation. Predictions can be made, to a reasonable degree of accuracy, regarding the performance at a new site. The single most important cost factor for most utilization sites will be the transportation costs for moving the sludge from the source of production to the site for utilization.

This chapter will be oriented toward the practical aspects of operating a sludge utilization site for reclaiming land. A complete but brief discussion of all phases of operation will be presented.

II. BENEFITS OF LAND RECLAMATION

A. To Reduce Restricted Site Usage

The basic reasons for site reclamation are: (i) provide for surface topography to permit good drainage but not cause uncontrollable erosion, (ii) improve soil tilth to promote good plant growth, (iii) modify the chemical conditions of the soil to prevent acidic leaching or toxic salt conditions, and (iv) remove debris to provide for agricultural usage. For soils throughout the world, soil fertility plays the most important role in soil productivity, although climate has a large influence. However, the cost of reclamation must be weighed against the benefits of the reclaimed land. Reduced environmental contamination and increased agricultural productivity are the primary benefits of reclamation.

B. Environmental Problem Correction

Contamination from a site can be caused by a number of factors. Particulate matter might leave the site due to wind or water erosion. This situation is most normally correctable by changing site conditions such as soil tilth or slope to reduce the basic conditions which produced the problem.

The chemical composition of water leaving the site, either as overland flow or as ground water, could be such that undesirable responses are triggered elsewhere. Excessive plant nutrients such as nitrogen, phosphorus, and potassium can cause undesirable plant growth in streams and lakes and degrade drinking water quality. Acidic water leaving the site might contain very high concentrations of solubilized heavy metals or might seriously decrease normal aquatic life in the receiving streams or lakes.

Site deficiencies are correctable to varying degrees of effectiveness and cost. Many times it is economically unfeasible to upgrade a particular site to permit the most intensive usage, that is, agriculture. However, many environmental site difficulties can be minimized or removed by providing site conditions which promote a dense vegetative growth.

III. PROPERTIES OF MUNICIPAL SEWAGE SLUDGE

A. Chemical Characteristics

Sewage sludge is derived from the organic and inorganic matter removed from waste water at sewage treatment plants. The nature of the sludge, its chemical, physical, and biological properties, are determined by the type of treatment employed at the sewage treatment plant and, more importantly, the influent sewage.

The influent sewage varies tremendously depending on the nature of the inputs to the sewage treatment plant. It is safe to say that the more industrialized a community becomes the higher are the levels of many constituents present in the influent sewage. However, it is inaccurate to assign responsibility to industrial sources for all the constituents present. A recent study in New York City by Klein et al. (1974) showed that the residential fraction of Cu, Cr, Ni, Zn, and Cd was 47, 28, 25, 42, and 49%, respectively, of the total metal load in the sewage plant influent. Obviously, the residential community is responsible for many of the constituents present in influent sewage and, ultimately, the sludge produced from the treatment of such waste water. In addition to the type of influent sewage, the type of treatment employed at a waste water treatment plant greatly influences the constituents present in sewage sludge. The first treatment process normally employed at most plants is primary treatment. In this process, those solids which will settle out of sewage are removed when it is passed through quiescent holding tanks. At the normal detention times used in these tanks (0.75 to 1.5 hours), approximately 30 to 60% of the suspended solids are removed. After primary treatment sewage can be additionally treated by a secondary process which is usually biological. Biological treatment takes many forms but involves using the sewage as a nutrient source for a mixed culture of microorganisms. The excess organisms of the process are the sludge produced (secondary sludge).

The waste water solids produced by both primary and secondary treatment are liquid in nature. Such sludges can be dried and sold as organic fertilizer or subjected to other stabilization procedures. There are a variety of stabilization procedures available but most involve a biological process where reduction in organic and pathogen content occurs. After stabilization, the resulting sludge can be handled as a liquid or further concentrated by a variety of methods to a drier, solid-like product.

Some typical fertilizer values of sewage sludge can be seen in Table 1, which gives the concentrations of the major plant nutrients from various sources in the midwest and eastern U.S. The N, P, and K are the major elements which aid plant growth.

The metal content of sludges from the Metropolitan Sanitary District of Greater Chicago, seven states in the United States, and 42 locations in England and Wales (Berrow & Weber, 1972) is presented in Table 2. The range of metal levels is great but this is not uncommon in sludges and indicates the highly variable nature of the product. A comparison of the metal data from the Chicago District, which has strict regulations on metal contents of sewage released to the sewers from industrial sources, with the seven states of the United States and Great Britain shows the effects of industrial waste regulations. The Chicago District sludge had less

Table 1—Major plant nutrients present in various sewage sludge sources

Constituent	Chicago WSW†		Illinois—24 Cities		Seven states in U.S.‡	
	Range	Median	Range	Mean	Range	Mean
			% dry weight basis			
Total N	4.2 –9.6	6.8	2.6–9.8	5.4	0.03 –17.6	3.2
NH₃-N	1.5 –5.0	3.1	0.1–6.1	1.8	0.0005– 6.7	0.7
P	1.1 –8.1	2.8	0.7–4.9	2.4	0.04 – 6.1	1.8
S	0.35–1.3	0.98	--	--	--	--
K	0.2 –0.8	0.4	--	--	0.008 – 1.9	0.3
Ca	0.3 –4.8	2.1	--	--	0.1 –25	5.1
Mg	0.6 –1.7	1.1	--	--	0.03 – 2.0	0.5
Na	0.2 –0.7	0.25	--	--	0.009 – 2.7	0.4

† West-Southwest sewage treatment plant.
‡ These data are from Agric. Exp. Stn. Committee on Utilization and Disposal of Municipal, Industrial, and Agricultural Processing Wastes on Land and represent select cities in seven states.

Table 2—Metal content of various sewage sludge sources

Metal	Chicago WSW† Range	Median	Seven states in U.S. ‡ Range	Mean	Great Britain§ Range	Median
			μg/g, dry weight basis			
Ag					5– 150	20
As			6– 230	53		
B			4– 757	114	15– 1,000	50
Ba			21– 8,980	618	150– 4,000	1,500
Bo					1– 30	3
Bi					12– 100	25
Cd	120– 312	197			60– 1,500	--
Co			1– 18	5.3	2– 260	12
Cr	11– 4,120	2,400	17–99,000	3,290	40– 8,800	250
Cu	680– 2,270	1,380	84–10,400	1,260	200– 8,000	800
Fe	15,400–49,000	36,300	400–90,000	12,900	6,000–62,000	21,000
Ga					1– 20	8
Hg	0.8–7.5	3.2			--	--
La					30– 150	60
Li					10– 150	40
Mn	120– 550	370	18– 7,100	400	150– 2,500	400
Mo			5– 39	27	2– 30	5
Ni	186– 840	355	10– 3,515	426	20– 5,300	80
Pb	304– 1,160	680	13–19,700	1,670	120– 3,000	700
Sc					2– 15	5
Sn					40– 700	120
Sr					80– 2,000	300
Ti					1,000– 4,500	2,000
V					20– 400	60
Y					15– 100	40
Zn	1,670– 4,850	2,770	13–27,800	2,900	700–49,000	3,000
Zr					30– 3,000	150

† West-Southwest sewage treatment plant.
‡ Unpublished data from Agric. Exp. Stn. Committee on Utilization and Disposal of Municipal, Industrial, and Agricultural Processing Wastes on Land.
§ Berrow and Weber (1972).

Cr, Ni, and Pb than the other seven states reported; however, in relation to Great Britain, the Chicago District sludge had a higher metal content. The residual pesticide content is generally very low. Chawla et al. (1974) reported the total organofloride insecticide content of four cities in Ontario, Canada, to range from 20 to 103 mg/liter, and the polychlorinated biphenyls (PCB) content of these sludges to range from 74 to 112 mg/liter. Analysis of five waste water treatment plant sludge sources from the District showed the PCB content to be less than 50 mg/liter.

B. Physical Characteristics

The physical properties of sewage sludge depend on the untreated waste water, the type and extent of the waste water treatment, and the method of sludge stabilization. A dense, granular sludge may be produced from primary sludge, while waste-activated sludge from secondary treatment results in a sludge containing mostly bacterial cells which are viscous and difficult to dewater. The distribution of water in sewage solids was estimated by Bjorkman (1969) to be 70% between cells, 22% adhesion and capillar water, and 8% absorption and intracellular fluids. Peterson et al. (1973) reported that the particle size of waste-activated sludge was as follows: 99% <9 μm and 60% <3 μm. The density of the sewage sludge was determined by McCalla et al. (1977) to be 0.58 g/cm^3 for heat-dried waste-activated sludge, 1.01 g/cm^3 for liquid digested sludge, 1.08 g/cm^3 for lagoon digested sludge, and 1.2 gm/cm^3 for aged Imhoff sludge with a solids content of 25 through 60%.

Most sewage sludges behave as a thixotropic psuedoplastic (non-neutonian) fluid when pumped. That is, they become less viscous when mixed. This makes accurate calculations of friction losses quite difficult. Rimkus and Heil (1975) found that the plastic viscosity and yield stress varied as an exponential function of sludge solids content. For a lagoon sludge having a 13% solids content, with a density of 1.08 g/cm^3, they reported a plastic viscosity of 0.79 poise and yield stress of 232 dyn/cm^2.

C. Biological Properties

The possibility of sewage sludge emitting odor is greatly reduced if the sludge has been well stabilized by anaerobic digestion. Well-stabilized sludge can be safely left on the soil surface without worry of odor or vermin infestation. Hinesly et al. (1974) reported a 99% decrease of fecal coliform in 30 days of dessication on the soil surface. Burd (1968) reported a 99.8% bacterial reduction after 30 days of mesophilic anaerobic diges-tion and, further, that pathogenic organisms die during 7 to 10 days of digestion.

Research by Meyer et al. (1971) with the porcine enterovirus (ECPO-1) using germfree 10-day piglets to test virus viability indicated that no porcine enterovirus survived in the sewage sludge digester after 5 days. Reed et al. (J. M. Reed, J. D. Fenters, and C. Lue-Hing. 1975. The effect of ammonia on Poliovirus Type 1. Abstr. of the Annual Meeting, Am. Soc. of Microbiol.) reported on an incubation study using digested sludge supernatant in which all innoculated Ecko virus were inactivated in 2 days, Coxsackie B4 in 3 days, and polio virus type 1 in 5 days. In studies by Bertucci et al. (1977), 250-ml laboratory anaerobic digesters, contain-ing 200 ml of digesting sludge, were innoculated with poliovirus type 1, coxsackievirus type A-9, coxsackievirus type B-4, and echovirus type 11. After 24 hours there was an inactivation of 93.8, 97.5, 89.5, and 58%, respectively. At the end of 48 hours of digestion, the respective inactiva-tions were 98.5, 99.7, 98.6, and 92.5% for the previously listed viruses.

In most programs which use sewage sludge as a nutrient source and soil amendment, there will be many times when the sludge must be held until the weather or other farming operations allow for its application to the fields. During this storage, further reduction in virus and bacterial counts can be expected. Berg (1966) determined the time in days required for 99.9% reduction in the number of virus and bacteria by storage of untreated sludge at different temperatures. His data clearly showed that time and increased temperature decreased virus survival.

IV. SITE PREPARATION

A. Topographic Modification

The amount of modification required at the reclamation site depends primarily upon the initial site conditions and upon the type of final utilization that the site will receive. To a smaller degree, the type of application system which will be used to apply sludge at the site could influence the topography changes.

Agricultural utilization of the site, following reclamation, generally requires the most restrictive slope conditions. Short slopes of 5–10% can be readily cropped on most types of soil, but slopes of 5% or less are more desirable. The land should not be graded flat in most cases, except for soils with a high infiltration rate, or surface ponding of water can be a problem. Agricultural machinery can generally operate on slopes that are too steep to permit good erosion control practices. Therefore, one needs to primarily design a site for suitable erosion control. Information on proper slopes, lengths of slopes, and suitable types of vegetation can be obtained from the USDA Soil Conservation Service (SCS) for any basic type of soil at the reclamation site.

Perhaps the primary purpose of reclaiming the site might be to establish sufficient vegetation to reduce soil erosion to an acceptable level. If this is to be the end utilization, then slopes can be 20% or more, which can considerably reduce the amount of soil to move during site preparation.

B. Debris Removal

The degree to which the soil must be free of rocks, trees, steel cable, and other foreign material depends upon how the site is to be utilized after reclamation. If agricultural activities are to follow, the top 60 cm of soil should be completely free of foreign material of any significant size. Small diameter rocks and wood do not generally cause great difficulty with agricultural machinery. Many types of rock pickers are commercially available for doing a good job on rock removal. Rock rakes can windrow surface rocks in some situations to permit greater efficiency of the rock picker.

If the site is to be vegetated primarily for erosion control, then debris removal must be considered in view of the manner in which the sludge is to be applied. If dry sludge is to be applied, then debris of greater than 30 cm in diameter should be removed from the top 30 cm of soil. To obtain significant benefits of sludge, it should be incorporated into the soil. Con-

ventional agricultural tillage equipment can be used to do the incorporation. If liquid sludge is to be applied by equipment which trails an irrigation hose, then rock removal must generally be very extensive or accelerated wear of the hose can result. Since many combinations of sludge application systems and final site utilization are possible, debris removal
should be considered with the entire operation in mind.

C. Hydrology Control

One of the major environmental tasks at the application site is to prevent contamination of surface and subsurface water with soluble components of the sludge. Nitrogen is usually the component which is most
mobile. If nitrogen can be controlled, other potential runoff contaminants are also usually controlled.

Two basic approaches can be taken to control the problem. Sludge
can be applied by incorporation or injection to minimize the amount of
sludge which is subject to contact by rain water. In most instances such
control is sufficient for the problem. However, the sludge application
rate, climatic conditions, soil type, and topographic conditions at the site
all influence the potential for a problem.

To provide for more complete control, the application area can be
bermed and runoff collection basins installed as schematically shown in
Fig. 1. Runoff water can then be tested to insure freedom from contamination prior to release to the natural watercourse. Contaminated
water can be purified by applying to adjacent land for infiltration or, in
some instances, additional storage time will correct the problem. Field
berms serve the dual purpose of directing application field runoff water to
the retention basin and excluding overland flow from surrounding areas
to minimize the size of the retention basin.

The federal guidelines (USEPA, 1976b) which currently apply to
livestock feed lots under the NPDES systems can be used as a general indicator of regulatory requirements for a sludge application area. The associated problems and their solutions are quite similar. Several states currently have adopted standards for sludge utilization projects but the
federal standards are, as yet, not adopted. However, the appropriate
regulatory agency should be contacted for specific site requirements.

To protect the ground water from contamination, several relatively
straightforward steps can be taken. Initially, the potential reclamation
site should be surveyed to determine the type of soil, depth of soil, depth
to the water table, and any short circuits between the soil surface and the
ground water. Once the site has been determined suitable for application,
the application volume should be controlled to be in correspondence to
the crop and soil system's capability of utilizing or retaining the applied
components. As for surface waters, nitrogen will most likely be the first
component to leach through to ground waters. Wells can be used to
monitor the ground water by taking samples at several depths to determine the progression of the area of component saturation. The need for

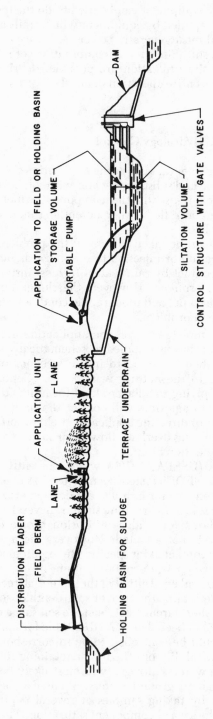

FARM FIELD SCHEMATIC OPERATION

Fig. 1—The runoff control system recycles water which does not meet standards.

ground water monitoring should be in relationship to application quantities and the ability of the site to handle the applied components.

V. HANDLING AND APPLICATION SYSTEMS

A. Dry Solids

If sludge is sufficiently dry—usually meaning a solids content of 30% or greater—it can be handled with conventional end loading equipment and applied with agricultural manure spreaders. Very dry material such as heat-dried sludge can have a substantial dust problem when it is being handled and applied, as it is normally less than 5% in moisture content.

Transportation to the site for stockpiling, or for direct application, can normally be done by truck if distances are relatively short. For longer distance, railroad cars can be used or, in special instances, barges can be efficiently used if multiple loading and unloading can be minimized.

Heat-dried sludge will flow quite readily but most other dry sludge forms are quite difficult to flow by gravity. Hopper bottom trucks or rail cars will not usually allow sludge to flow out the bottom when the doors are opened if the sludge has the characteristics of compost or solids from a sand-drying bed. Such sludge is of a semifiberous nature which tends to compact during transportation. It will bridge across quite large openings. The handling properties of the sludge should be considered before a specific handling system is selected. On-site storage of dry sludge should only be considered for materials which have been well stabilized. If such is done, site storage considerations should primarily center on the stock pile location. Overland flow of surface water should not come into contact with the sludge and any drainage from the pile should be collected in a storage basin. Drainage water can be quite high in soluble plant nutrients, suspended solids, and coliform. Collected water can be disposed of by applying to adjacent land.

It should be pointed out that considerable care should be used in evaluating costs for alternate transportation and application systems because >50% of the total sludge utilization costs are often spent in this part of the system.

B. For Liquids and Slurries

Solids content of sludges which have been applied to land as a liquid have ranged from essentially 0 to 12%. The basic components of a liquid handling system involve the transportation unit to haul sludge to the utilization site, on-site storage facilities, pumping equipment for removing stored sludge, distribution equipment for conveying sludge to the specific application location, and some type of application equipment. These various components will be discussed below in the order that they appear above.

1. TRANSPORTATION

The transportation unit for hauling sludge to the general vicinity of the application site is generally determined by volume and by hauling distances. For small quantities and short distances—perhaps 80 km or less by round trip—tank trucks can be effectively utilized. Tank trucks are often equipped with distribution equipment for direct application to the land without the need for on-site storage and reloading. Larger quantities and greater distances require railroad cars or barges. Pipelines are usually excluded because of the need for flexibility of location at the application site due to limitations on the volume which can be applied with environmental safety on any specific area. Regulatory agencies usually impose some maximum loading limit.

If barging is employed, there is the likelihood that one addition transfer system will be needed to take the sludge from the barge and transport it to storage. Rail cars have the potential of unloading directly into storage.

2. STORAGE

On-site storage basins are usually of earthen construction with some type of a liner to eliminate seepage. Compacted clay of several feet in depth has often served as the liner. Basins should be of sufficient size to provide for flexibility in the stored volume without creating a crisis for incoming or outgoing material. The basins should be so located as to avoid potential environmental problems. Building on flood plains or gravel banks, locating immediately upwind of residential areas, or storing insufficiently stabilized sludges should be avoided and can be avoided by advance planning.

3. REMOVAL FROM STORAGE

The fact that sludge solids will settle during liquid storage can be an advantage or a disadvantage. If removal equipment such as a dredge is available, or if the cover water (supernatant) is removed, sludge which has a higher solids content than that which was transported to the holding basin can be removed for application. However, to remove the solids without removing the supernatant beforehand generally requires more expensive equipment. Raft or shore-mounted pumps encounter problems because settled sludge solids do not flow well in a lateral direction without encouragement from mechanical or hydraulic means. The class of pumps which have been often used are of the open impeller, high head, centrifugal design.

4. DISTRIBUTION

Surface-laid pipelines are most often used to convey sludge from on-site storage to the area of application. Buried piping has been used in some instances because of the freedom from freezing damage and a less obstructed soil surface. The burial of pipe increases the initial cost, however. Tank trucks can also be used for infrequent applications but are seldom found in combination with storage basins because of the larger volume of material normally being handled with this system.

Although not conclusively established at this time, it appears that booster pumps along the distribution line are superior to a single set of pumps at the source whenever the pumped sludge solids content exceeds approximately 5 to 6%. Many installations with lines of 3 to 6 km in length use only source-located pumps if the 5 to 6% solids content is not exceeded.

5. APPLICATION

Several methods are available for applying liquid sludge to the soil. To a considerable degree there is a cost tradeoff between capital expenditures and operational expenditures, although not for all systems. Other factors can influence the choice of application systems. For example, sufficiently strong odors of the sludge being applied could dictate that soil incorporation or injection must be used. The following discussion will be concerned with generalities of the available systems with some comments included on associated strong and weak points of each system.

Gated pipe can be used for application onto areas which have been very carefully graded to maintain constant slopes. The sludge is applied, through the variable-sized gates, at the top of the slopes, and distributes by gravity. Difficulty is generally encountered in maintaining proportionate flow to the area being covered by a particular gate because of varia-

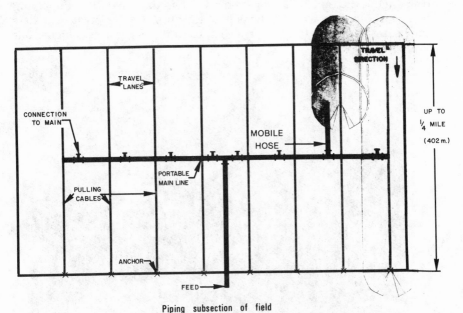

Piping subsection of field

Fig. 2—Schematic layout for a traveling sprinkler.

Fig. 3—A traveling sprinkler working corn.

tions in solids concentration, variations in dynamic pressure at the gate, and nonuniform soil surface conditions. Another surface application system which overcomes some of the above-noted limitations is the large-sized sprinkler, most notably travelers and center pivots. Figure 2 shows a schematic layout for a traveling sprinkler. A rectangular area of approximately 4 ha maximum can be applied to in a single pass. Nozzle sizes range from approximately 2.5–5.0 cm. Nozzle plugging from sludge solids limits the small nozzle sizes, while pump capacity limits the upper size. Major factors in using traveling sprinklers (Fig. 3) are spray drift, runoff from high instantaneous application rates, and the capability of applying to an existing crop without damage to the crop. Center pivot sprinklers can be used similarly to travelers. Their capital cost per acre is higher but

Fig. 4—A tank-type injector (courtesy Starline).

Fig. 5—An injector connected to a mobile hose (courtesy Briscoe-Maphis).

operational costs are lower. Center pivots are not well suited for small or irregularly shaped fields.

Units which can till the sludge into the soil at the time of application are shown in Fig. 4, 5, and 6. Figure 4 shows a tank type injector, while Fig. 5 shows an injector connected to a mobile irrigation hose, as for a traveling sprinkler. Figure 6 shows an incorporation disk. The major difference between an injector and an incorporator is that an injector covers a greater portion of the applied sludge with soil. Lesser differences are: (i) an injector generally requires more power, (ii) an injector can apply to a grass cover crop without totally destroying it, (iii) greater application per unit area can be obtained from an incorporator, and (iv) an incorporator better handles soil obstructions such as rock. The schematic of Fig. 2 applies also to the mobile hose-supplied injector and incorporator. These units can apply to approximately 4 ha in one setting. The solids content

Fig. 6—An incorporation disk.

can generally be higher (12%) for tillage units than for sprinkler application (6%).

Flow rates to either sprinkler or tillage units primarily depend upon pumps and distribution line parameters. The major advantage of tillage application units over sprinklers and gated pipe is that a greater portion of the sludge remains where it is applied. In the event that odors are a major problem, tillage can effectively reduce the problem. Capital costs for tillage units are substantial (approximately $50,000 per applicator and tractor with 1976 values), as are operational costs. Rubber-tired tractors can lack traction under wet surface conditions in the field, even though subsurface soil is dry.

VI. APPLICATION QUANTITIES

A. Organic Matter

Organic matter in the soil is necessary to maintain good soil structure, increase the cation exchange capacity to reduce elemental leaching, improve water relations, and provide for a continuous supply, though limited, of plant nutrients through mineralization. A high level of soil organic matter should not be the end objective, however: a combination of sound management practices, fertilizers, lime, and cultural practices is needed to accomplish the end objective, be it agricultural production for a profit or erosion control to stabilize the soil.

When using sewage sludges to increase the organic matter content, it is necessary that some measurements be made of the portion of the total dry sludge solids which are organic. Depending upon the type and stability of sludge, this figure can vary considerably. Unstabilized sludges can have upwards of 75–80% of the dry matter as organic, whereas anaerobically digested sludge might typically have 40–50% of the dry solid being organic matter. Most soils range from 1 to 6% in organic matter depending upon soil texture, soil temperature, type of vegetation, cultural practices, and extent of soil drainage.

B. Nutrient Application Rates

This section will be directed toward the efficient utilization of the plant nutrients in sludge. In effect, such utilization will tend to maximize the value of sludge when used as a fertilizer. However, the overall cost of application might not be minimized in this procedure because of cost factors other than fertilizer value being involved in the total application costs.

A typical plant nutrient analysis of 5:2.5:0.4 (N, P, and K, respectively, on a % of dry matter basis) is representative for municipal sludges. It is not important that these figures be used with great precision because commercial fertilizers used in agriculture can be as high as 82% N, 26% P, and 50% K. Since most sludges do not have the proper proportions of plant nutrients, commercial fertilizers can and should be used to provide a nutrient balance. Sludges can be used to supply the majority of the annual nutrient needs of agricultural crops.

To determine the sludge application rate for supplying plant nutrients, the following example is given. Consider a corn (*Zea mays* L.) crop that is harvested for grain. This crop removes from the field approximately 168 kg of N, 28 to 34 kg of P, and 39 kg of K. Sludge with a plant nutrient analysis of 5:2.5:0.4 will be used to replace the elements removed. Each 100 kg of dry sludge supplies 5 kg N, 2.5 kg P, and 0.4 kg K. Therefore, 3,360 kg/ha of dry sludge would provide the 168 kg N, 1,120 kg/ha of dry sludge would supply the 28 kg of P, and 9,800 kg/ha is required to supply the 38 kg of K. One can readily observe that one solution to the problem is to meet the entire P needs by applying sludge and then provide the remainder of the N and K with commercial fertilizers. Since P concentrations in soils are not harmful if kept within certain limitations (Hinesly et al., 1974), one could apply 3,360 kg/ha of dry sludge. This meets the N needs, supplies excess P, and supplies 13 kg of K. The remaining 26 kg of K can be supplied by applying 52 kg/ha of a 0:0:50 commercial fertilizer.

One further problem associated with utilizing sludge for nutrient requirements exists. Depending upon the type of sludge, much of the N can be in the organic matter. To make such N available for use of plants requires that soil microorganisms decompose the organic matter. Such decomposition is usually referred to as *mineralization* and it is the annual mineralization rate which is important. There is popular belief that 20% of organic nitrogen in anaerobically stabilized sludges will decompose the first year following application and, therefore, be available for plant use (Hinesly et al., 1974; Harrison & Goodson, 1974). However, there is considerable disagreement on such a number. Some full scale field responses suggest a figure of 5 to 10% as being more appropriate.

There is not general agreement on appropriate mineralization rates for the second and subsequent years or for other types of sludges such as heat-dried. Ranges of 3 to 20% have been noted for second year rates and as high as 50% for first year rates of some sludges and livestock manures. It is important that reliable mineralization rates be established as agricultural production through the use of sludge must produce competitive yields. Fortunately, mineralization rate problems do not apply so critically to phosphorus or potassium.

One needs to know the total nitrogen analysis figure for the sludge as well as how the nitrogen is proportioned between the liquid and the solids. All nitrogen in the liquid is considered to be readily available for plant use. However, depending upon the application method, some of this nitrogen may be lost through volatilization or leaching.

For systems which immediately incorporate sludge into the soil, more nitrogen will be available for first year plant use than for systems which apply without early incorporation. Some documents (Keeney et al., 1975) suggest that essentially all ammonium nitrogen is retained in the soil and available for plants if sludge is promptly incorporated. The volatilization figure appears to be quite site-dependent as some field responses would suggest a volatilization figure of approximately 50% even for incorporated sludges (Metrop. Sanit. Dist. of Greater Chicago, unpublished data).

In the previous example, by using a 20% mineralization rate for the first year, and also by considering a liquid sludge of 5% solids with half of the total nitrogen to be in the organic state and an availability of 80% of nitrogen in the liquid, only 1.25 kg of nitrogen per liquid metric ton is available to the corn crop the first year. That is,

1) 1,000 kg/metric ton × 5% solids × 2.5% organic N × 20% availability = 0.25 kg/metric ton organic N

2) 1,000 kg/metric ton × 5% solids × 2.5% NH_3-N × 80% availability = 1.0 kg metric ton NH_3-N

1.25 kg/metric ton total available N

Thus, to supply the total N requirement of the corn crop, 135 metric tons of liquid sludge/ha (about 1.3 cm deep over the entire ha) would have to be applied in the first year. Local persons can be readily found to aid in proper calculations along the above-noted lines. County agricultural extension agents, high school vocational agricultural instructors, and dealers in commercial fertilizers are several sources of such aid.

C. Heavy Metal Limitations

There is concern among many scientists that the levels of metallic elements present in sewage sludge could be phytotoxic to plants and/or be taken up by plants and be carried into the food chain. After many years of successful use of sludge in England, Paris, Berlin, and other places, the question of phytotoxicity has been chiefly addressed. Unless the soil itself has abnormal metal levels or low pH, phytotoxicity is not a significant cause for concern. In general, the chief question concerning metal constituents in sewage sludge applied to land has in the past few years centered around possible public health problems with dietary increases in metal intake.

The USEPA has released various drafts of a policy statement which proposes quidelines for the utilization and disposal of sludges for publically owned treatment works. The drafts released before the most recent (3 June 1976) version, which appeared in the Federal Register, contained limitations on levels of heavy metals in sludge applied to land and also presented an equation which limited the total application of sludge based upon its zinc, copper, and nickel content. Although this version of the guidelines does not contain either numerical limitations on specific heavy metals or the above-mentioned equation (the draft now assigns USDA and FDA this responsibility), the earlier drafts which did contain such limitations had a pronounced impact on state agencies formulating their own guidelines.

The Wisconsin Department of Natural Resources in Technical Bulletin No. 88 has published guidelines on sludge application to land. The "guidelines can be used for screening the land application alternative, evaluation of environmental effects . . . and for developing a land application program . . ." (Keeney et al., 1975). The guideline restricts total applications of sludge by limiting total "metal equivalent" applications on a pounds per acre basis to not more than 65 times the soil cation exchange capacity (CEC) in meq/100 g of soil. Metal equivalents of a specific sludge are calculated using the following formula:

$$\frac{(\text{ppm Zn}) + 2\,(\text{ppm Cu}) + 4\,(\text{ppm Ni})}{500}$$

In addition, yearly applications are limited to a maximum of 2.24 kg/ha of cadmium with a total site lifetime maximum of 22.4 kg/ha. The lifetime limitation which calculates to be smaller by either of the above equivalent methods or the maximum application of 22.4 kg/ha of Cd takes precedence.

A task force appointed by Roy M. Kottman, Director of the Ohio Agricultural Research and Development center, published, in July of 1975, an *Ohio Guide for Land Application of Sludge*. The guideline was designed "to assist landowners in making decisions as they consider the application of sludge to their land."

The Ohio guide quotes drafts of USEPA guidelines (prior to 3 June 1976) and suggests that the following equation "should be used for situations of slightly acid to neutral soils where pH can be maintained at 6.5 or higher at all times."

$$\text{Total amount of sludge (dry tons/acre)} =$$

$$\frac{\text{CEC} \times 32,700}{(\text{ppm Zn}) + 2\,(\text{ppm Cu}) + 4\,(\text{ppm Ni})} - 200,$$

where
   CEC = cation exchange capacity of soil before sludge application (meq/100 g) and
   ppm = parts per million or mg metal/kg dry weight of sludge.

For soils with a pH below 6.5, the 32,700 figure is changed to 16,350 to calculate maximum total loading, while for forest soils with a pH below 6.5, this figure is reduced to 8,175.

Basically, the Wisconsin, Ohio, and USEPA guidelines have adopted the recommendation of Chaney (1973) who has presented what appears to be a rather straightforward empirical model. He assumed that the soil has a limited capacity to fix or chelate the metals present in sludge applied to land. Also, he assumed that the more sludge one applies the greater will be the metal level in the resulting grain. The concept of limiting the amount of sludge applied to the soil and, therefore, the metal levels in the crop grown is an easily understood concept. However, this concept must be examined in the light of scientific inquiry. The metals present in sewage sludge are not all in ionic form and many are tied up as metal salts or organic complexes. Upon application to soil, the conditions for metal uptake are complex and depend upon soil type, soil pH, type of crop, etc.

An extensive study of the metal uptake of crops grown with sludge has been conducted by Hinesly et al. (1974). A field study was set up on several soils occupying part of the cultivated area on the University of Illinois Northwest Agronomy Research Center near Joliet, Ill. A main objective of the study was to determine how the chemical changes occuring in sludge-fertilized plots would effect soybean and corn nutrition and the extent of changes in metal levels in these crops.

Digested sludge from the West-Southwest and Calumet treatment plants of the Metropolitan Sanitary District of Greater Chicago was applied by furrow irrigation as often as weather conditions permitted, including application following crop harvesting. Corn and soybeans were grown with total applications of sludge to the corn reaching 450 metric tons/ha by 1975 and total application to soybeans reaching 314 metric tons/ha by 1974, as reported by Lue-Hing et al. in 1976.

Table 3 shows the cadmium concentration in the tissues of soybeans and corn grain grown on the University of Illinois plots. The values reported are for plots which received commercial fertilizer only, 1/4, 1/2, and the maximum yearly sludge application. It should be noted that all soybean plots received 224 kg/ha of elemental K.

The greatest increases in the content of cadmium in soybean grain occurred in plants grown on maximum sludge-treated plots in 1972. In this year, the soybean yields were low due to what was reported to be P toxicity.

It can be seen, if one examines the table carefully, that grain metal levels are directly influenced by increasing sludge applications in any given year. However, it appears that metal levels are not related to accumulated sludge application; in other words, grain metal levels do not increase with greater accumulations of applied sludge.

Table 3 presents also the levels of metals in the grain of native corn plants at the University of Illinois Northwest Agronomy Research Center

Table 3—Cd concentration in grain following various application rates of digested sludge (Lue-Hing et al., 1976)

| | Sludge application rate | | | | | | | |
| | Soybeans | | | | Corn grain | | | |
Year	0	1/4 Max	1/2 Max	Max	0	1/4 Max	1/2 Max	Max
	ppm dry weight							
1970	0.06	0.32	0.54	1.02	0.30	0.60	0.79	1.00
1971	0.27	0.41	0.90	1.55	0.14	0.70	0.65	0.92
1972	0.29	0.49	0.94	3.00	0.14	0.45	0.83	1.10
1973	0.18	0.31	0.55	0.75	0.08	0.15	0.35	0.61
1974†	0.31	0.31	0.57	0.92	0.08	0.18	0.40	0.81
1974‡	0.13	0.23	0.35	0.35	--	--	--	--
1975†	0.07	0.34	0.72	1.69	0.06	0.17	0.28	0.51
1975‡	0.12	0.18	0.34	0.46	--	--	--	--

† For soybeans, sludge applications were resumed after harvest in 1973.
‡ For soybeans, sludge applications were discontinued following one application in 1972.

Table 4—Total maximum annual and accumulative applications of digested sludge for corn and soybean grain production (Lue-Hing et al., 1976)

Year	Corn grain				Soybeans			
	Annual sludge solids		Accumulative sludge solids		Annual sludge solids		Accumulative sludge solids	
	metric tons/ha	tons (U.S.)/ acre	metric tons/ha	tons (U.S.)/ acre	metric tons/ha	tons (U.S.)/ acre	metric tons/ha	tons (U.S.)/ acre
1968	51.5	(23.0)	51.5	(23.0)	--	--	--	--
1969	48.3	(21.6)	99.8	(44.6)	42.8	(19.1)	42.8	(19.1)
1970	52.7	(23.5)	152.5	(68.1)	59.3	(26.4)	102.0	(45.5)
1971	128.4	(57.3)	280.9	(125.4)	134.9	(60.2)	236.9	(105.7)
1972	25.6	(11.4)	306.5	(136.8)	4.8‡	(2.1)	241.7	(107.8)
1973	62.2	(27.7)	368.6	(164.5)	13.7	(6.1)	255.4	(113.9)
1974	48.8	(21.8)	417.4	(186.2)	58.6	(26.1)	314	(140.0)
1975	32.6†	(14.6)	450†	(200.7)	--	--	--	--

† Estimated.
‡ Application was discontinued on some soybean plots after the 1972 year.

which were fertilized with sludge at the rate described above and shown in Table 4. In these experiments, a field with only commercial fertilizer application was used as a control (check) plot. Again, rates of sludge application equal to 1/4 and 1/2 of the maximum yearly sludge application were used. A total of 450 metric tons/ha were applied to the maximum treated plot through 1975.

The cadmium content in corn grain was increased by greater applications of sludge. However, Cd concentration in corn grain was not increased by increasing years of sludge application. Concentration levels of Cd reached a fairly constant value and these levels were not changed by increasing accumulative amounts of sludge applied in subsequent years.

Kirkham (1975) studied the chemical characteristics of corn plants which had been grown on sludge-fertilized soils at Dayton, Ohio. She reported that the concentration of the metals Cd, Cu, Ni, and Zn in corn grain were within those concentration ranges normally observed in commercially grown crops. The significance of Kirkham's data lies in the fact that these corn fields had been used for sludge application continuously for over 35 years, with applications of 28 metric tons/ha per year. Of equal significance also is the fact that the Cd content of the sludges applied ranged between 800 and 830 mg/kg and the Zn/Cd ratio ranged between 10.1 and 13.1. USDA draft criteria currently calls for a Zn/Cd ratio of 66 or greater and would not have permitted more than 16 metric tons/ha, ultimately, of the Dayton sludge because of Cd concentration.

The data of Hinesly and Kirkham indicate that, contrary to what has been stated by some regulatory agencies, there is no direct relationship between accumulative sludge application and plant tissue or grain metal levels. In addition, the evidence indicates that continuous fertilization with sewage sludge does not result in abnormally high plant metal levels.

These data indicate that metal level accumulation is not a significant hazard when application amounts do not generally exceed plant nitrogen requirements. Following initial sludge application to reclaim a disturbed land, sludge applications to maintain a cover crop or row crop can be used in order to satisfy nitrogen requirements with no significant plant tissue or grain metal hazard.

VII. RECLAMATION SITE RESPONSES

The following discussion will center around responses which have been obtained from reclamation and agricultural utilization sites where municipal sludge has been used to achieve the response. Numerous sites where sludge has been used are known to exist but record keeping at many sites is such that little, if any, correlation is possible between the sludge application and a particular response.

A. Organic Matter Addition

Section VI-A of this chapter discusses the detailed aspects involved in predetermining the amount of sludge required to achieve a certain increase in soil organic matter content. Table 5 (Halderson & Peterson, 1976) shows two fields which have received sludge with an accumulative amount of 91.3 dry metric tons/ha for field 3 and 73.8 dry metric tons/ha for field 20. It should be noted that field 3 is a strip-mined field which was in pasture prior to sludge utilization, while field 20 is place land which has been in row crops continuously for many years. Field 20 shows an actual organic matter increase of 0.56% above the baseline year of 1972, whereas the calculated percent of increase is 0.82% based upon 73.8 dry metric tons application at 45% organic matter. The calculated change for field 3 is 0.75% but the change in tillage practices on the field—from pasture to row crop—has masked the response from the baseline year.

B. Soil pH

One of the major difficulties with strip-mined soils and oftentimes with other soils that remain after a particular operation, is that the soil pH is so low or high that most vegetation cannot become established. Soil pH often is less than 4.0 or greater than 10.0 at these sites.

At a reclamation project in the Shawnee National Forest in southern Illinois, the Forest Service (Cunningham et al., 1975) has been reclaiming strip-mined land for several years. The land is being reclaimed to provide sufficient permanent vegetation to improve local water quality and aesthetics. Preliminary testing, prior to initiation of the full scale operation in 1974, showed that an application of 336 to 560 dry metric tons/ha was required to increase soil pH from approximately 2.5 to greater than 6.0. This change was sufficient to accomplish the desired objectives. Comparisons were made to agricultural limestone and commercial ferti-

Table 5—Response of soil to sludge application (Halderson & Peterson, 1976)

Sludge applied dry metric tons/ha per year	Year	Soil organic carbon†
Field 3—Strip-mined soil		
10.3	1972	1.24
3.4	1973	0.86
54.7	1974	0.96
22.9	1975	1.23
Field 20—Undisturbed soil		
0	1972	1.89
0.9	1973	2.25
52.5	1974	2.46
20.4	1975	2.03

† Samples taken in spring of year following the year noted.

lizers with municipal sludge being judged the most effective in accomplishing the objective.

C. Crop Yields

There are numerous sources of information for determining the crop response to municipal sludge fertilization. In general, the information indicates that yields for typical agricultural crops are fully as great as would be obtained from the use of commercial fertilizers. However, it should be pointed out, as is done in detail in section VI-B of this chapter, that most sludges are not sufficiently balanced in major plant nutrients. Commercial fertilizers can be readily used to accomplish a balance.

A test conducted by the University of Illinois (M. D. Thorne, Agronomy Dep. personal communications) in 1974 with two rates of commercial fertilizer, livestock manure, and municipal sludge resulted in respective yields of 103.2, 151.3, 137.2, and 172.3 kg/ha of corn, corrected for moisture. Since no supplemental potash was added to the sludge, it is clear that the soil was able to provide sufficient potash to produce a good yield. Continuing such a practice would deplete the soil's supply of potash and result in a lower yield. For the above-noted results, sludge was applied as a liquid. Solids content was unspecified but was probably less than 5%.

The only detrimental aspect that has been noted with use of municipal sludge has been in temporary inhibition of seed germination in some instance if freshly digested sludge is applied close to the time of planting. This problem can be readily avoided by sludge application several weeks before planting or by waiting until the plants are well out of the ground before applying. For stabilized sludges, burning of plants is not generally a problem because salt concentrations are generally lower in comparison to unstabilized sludges or livestock manures. In arid areas accumulation of salt in the topsoil can be a problem with sludge utilization where insufficent water is available to leach the excess salts down below the root zone.

D. Heavy Metals in Crops

There are at least several crops—corn, wheat, soybeans—that can be grown on a site to avoid associated heavy metal problems. Other crops can likely be grown with equal assurance. However, documented evidence is not available in some instances.

The most noteable example of a study (Kirkham, 1975) of heavy metal uptake by crops was done on a site in Ohio where municipal sludge had been applied for some 35 years. Corn was grown on the site in 1973 and was analyzed for various heavy metals. Soils were also analyzed to determine the concentration of heavy metals.

Site results indicate that heavy metal concentrations in corn grain are in the upper range of concentrations that are to be found in grain normally grown. Reconstructed heavy metal applications at the site were noted as being 40–100 times higher than rates recommended by USEPA (1976a), yet the increase in concentration in the grain was small. From such information one can conclude that there should be little likelihood of encountering heavy metal problems if good site management is practiced. Soil pH should be maintained at 6.5 or above, crops should be selected which are known to not concentrate excessive amounts of heavy metals, and application quantities per season should be limited to approximately 45–56 dry metric tons/ha if crops are to be grown that year. If greater application quantities are practiced, a 1-year fallow period seems advisable before growing a marketable crop after discontinuance of high annual application rates, or heavy metal analysis should be conducted on the part of the crop which will be marketed.

LITERATURE CITED

Berg, G. 1966. I. Virus transmission by the water vehicle. II. Virus removal by sewage treatment procedures. Health Library Sci. 3(2):90.

Berrow, N. L., and J. Webber. 1972. Trace elements in sewage sludge. J. Sci. Food Agric. 23:93–100.

Bertucci, J., C. Lue-Hing, D. R. Zenz, and S. J. Sedita. 1977. Inactivation of viruses during anaerobic digestion. J. Water Pollut. Control Fed. 49:1642–1651.

Bjorkman, A. 1969. Heat processing of sewage sludge. p. 670–686. In 4th Congr. of the Int. Res. Group on Refuse Disposal, 2–5 June 1969, Bosle, Switzerland.

Burd, R. S. 1968. A study of sludge handling and disposal. Water Pollut. Control Fed. Res. Ser. Pub. no. WP-20-4.

Chaney, R. L. 1973. Crop and food chain effects of toxic elements in sludges and effluents. p. 129–141. In Proc. of the Joint Conf. on Recycling Municipal Sludges and Effluents on Land, USEPA and USDA, 8–13 July 1973, Univ. of Illinois, Champaign-Urbana. Natl. Assoc. of State Univ. and Land Grant Colleges, Washington, D.C.

Chawla, V. K., J. P. Stephenson, and D. Liu. 1974. Biological characteristics of digested chemical sewage sludges. p. 63–64. In Proc. Sludge Handling and Disposal Seminar, 18–19 Sept. 1974, Environ. Canada, Toronto, Ontario.

Cunningham, R. S., C. K. Losche, and R. K. Holtje. 1975. Water quality implications of strip-mined reclamation by wastewater sludge. p. 643–647. In Proc. 2nd Natl. Conf. on Complete Water Reuse, 4–8 May 1975, Am. Inst. of Chem. Eng. and USEPA, Chicago, Ill.

Grooms, G. C. (ed.). 1975. Ohio guide for land application of sewage sludge. Bull. 598. Coop. Ext. Serv., Ohio State Univ., Columbus, Ohio.

Halderson, J. L., and J. R. Peterson. 1976. Environmental monitoring at agricultural sites for sludge utilization. ASAE Pap. no. 76-2064. Metrop. Sanit. Dist. of Greater Chicago, Chicago, Ill.

Harrison, J. R., and J. B. Goodson. 1974. Process design manual for sludge treatment and disposal, USEPA Technol. Transfer, Washington, D.C.

Hinesly, T. D., O. D. Braids, R. I. Dick, R. L. Jones, and J. E. Molina. 1974. Agricultural benefits and environmental changes resulting from the use of digested sewage on field crops. USEPA Rep. SW-30d. Univ. of Illinois, Urbana.

Keeney, D. R., K. W. Lee, and L. M. Walsh. 1975. Wisconsin guidelines for the application of wastewater sludge to agricultural land in Wisconsin. Tech. Bull. no. 88, Dep. of Nat. Resour., Madison, Wis.

Klein, L. A., M. Lang, N. Nash, and S. L. Kirschner. 1974. Sources of metals in New York City wastewater. Water Pollut. Control Fed. 46:2653-2662.

Kirkham, M. B. 1975. Trace elements in corn grown on long-term sludge disposal site. Environ. Sci. Technol. 9(8):765-768.

Lue-Hing, C., T. D. Hinesly, J. R. Peterson, and D. R. Zenz. 1976. Heavy metals uptake and control strategies associated with sewage sludge fertilized crops. In Proc. of the 1976 Natl. Conf. on Municipal Sludge Manage. and Disposal, Sept. 1976, USEPA and Environ. Qual. Systems, Inc., St. Louis, Mo. Inf. Transfer, Inc., Rockville, Md.

McCalla, T. M., J. R. Peterson, and C. Lue-Hing. 1977. Properties of agricultural and municipal wastes. p. 2-43. In L. F. Elliott and F. J. Stevenson (eds.) Soils for management of organic wastes and waste water. Soil Sci. Soc. of Am., Madison, Wis.

Meyer, R. C., F. C. Hines, H. R. Isaacson, and T. D. Hinesly. 1971. Porcine enterovirus survival and anaerobic sludge digestion. p. 183. In Proc. Int. Symp. on Livestock Wastes, Ohio State Univ., Columbus, Ohio. Am. Soc. of Agric. Eng., St. Joseph, Mich.

Peterson, J. R., C. Lue-Hing, and D. R. Zenz. 1973. Chemical and biological quality of municipal sludge. p. 26-37. In W. E. Sopper and L. T. Kardos (eds.) Recycling treated municipal wastewater and sludge through forest and cropland. Pennsylvania State Univ. Press, University Park.

Rimkus, R. R., and R. W. Heil. 1975. The rheology of plastic sewage sludge. p. 722-740. In Proc. 2nd Natl. Conf. on Complete Water Reuse, 4-8 May 1975, Am. Inst. of Chem. Eng. and USEPA, Chicago, Ill.

U.S. Environmental Protection Agency. 1976a. Municipal sludge management, environmental factors. Fed. Regist. 41(100):22531-22544.

U.S. Environmental Protection Agency. 1976b. State program elements necessary for participation in the National Pollutant Discharge Elimination System. Fed. Regist. 41(54):11458-11461.

Copyright © 1978 ASA–CSSA–SSSA
677 South Segoe Road, Madison, WI 53711 USA
Reclamation of Drastically Disturbed Lands

Chapter 21

Reclamation Research on Coal Surface-Mined Lands in the Humid East

WILLIS G. VOGEL AND WILLIE R. CURTIS

Forest Service, USDA
Northeastern Forest Experiment Station, Berea, Kentucky

I. INTRODUCTION

Research in the reclamation of lands surface mined for coal is not a new activity in the eastern United States. Revegetation research was begun on abandoned coal mine spoils in southeastern Ohio as early as the mid-1930's (Lane, 1968). Most of the research in the 1940's and 1950's was in revegetation and soil science. Research in other disciplines and fields of science such as hydrology, geology, and engineering is more recent. The involvement of all these sciences in reclamation research is one result of an increasing concern for preventing environmental problems as well as correcting them.

Most of the past and present reclamation research involves the physical, chemical, and biological sciences. Researchers in these fields have solved or can solve most of the reclamation problems related to their fields. However, many problems arise in the application of their results because of the economic, social, philosophical, and political ramifications of surface mining. Research in these disciplines, too, will help solve some of the reclamation and environmental problems. But the results of all research must be applicable to the situation and they must be used by the mining industry, legislative and enforcement agencies, and consumers for the benefit of society as a whole.

II. RESULTS AND APPLICATION OF RECLAMATION RESEARCH

A. Revegetation Research

1. REFORESTATION

Most of the early research was concerned with the forestation of spoils in the relatively gentle terrain of the Midwest. The establishment of herbaceous cover usually was not attempted unless someone wanted pasture. Formal or designed reforestation research was conducted primarily by the Central States and Northeastern Forest Experiment Stations of the U.S. Forest Service. Tree planting experiments were also conducted by several of the state agricultural experiment stations, including those of Ohio, Indiana, Iowa, Pennsylvania, and West Virginia, and by a few individuals at other colleges. Some of the early reforestation experiments were not formal research. Nevertheless, they provided a great deal of valuable information. Plantings of a nonresearch nature were made primarily by industry-related groups such as reclamation associations and coal producer associations and by individual mining companies. Some of the first research plantings were made in the 1930's. A large number of research plots were established in the 1940's and 1950's.

These reforestation studies identified species of planted trees that survived and grew best on a variety of surface mine spoils. One group of old Forest Service research plots in Kansas was remeasured 22 years after planting and a black walnut (*Juglans nigra* L.) plantation was remeasured about 34 years after planting (Geyer, 1971; Geyer & Naughton, 1970; Geyer & Rogers, 1972). However, most of the research publications presented results of measurements taken from several months after planting to as long as 10 years after planting. Thus, much of the published data is for plantations 10 years old or less. The results of much of this earlier reforestation research were compiled and published by Limstrom (1960). Numerous other reports that were written at about the same time are listed in the various bibliographies on surface mining and reclamation (Funk, 1962; Frawley, 1971; Munn, 1973; Bituminous Coal Research, Inc., 1975; Czapowskyj, 1976).

This early research resulted in the publication of lists of recommended species and tree planting guides in several of the coal mining states. These guides have been used in the planting of thousands of acres of mine spoil. Many of the recently published planting and revegetation guides still are based largely upon those earlier research publications. Unfortunately, most of the older tree planting experiments have not been reevaluated in recent years. Possibly, changes in species survival, growth, and forest composition during the past 10 to 20 years would provide some new insights into strip mine forestation and alter some of the earlier recommendations.

The Northeastern Forest Experiment Station through its Berea strip mine research project is directing a reevaluation of some of the older strip mine research plantings in Indiana, Ohio, Illinois, Missouri, Kansas, and Oklahoma. Although the results of this evaluation are not yet ready for publication, they show that high-value tree species can be successfully planted and grown on surface-mined land.

Numerous plantings of trees have been made on extremely acid spoils where only a few of the trees survived. Some researchers believe that the surviving trees differ genetically from the dead ones in that they can withstand the extremely acid conditions. Unfortunately, follow-up genetic studies usually have not been performed on these trees to determine whether genetics or growth medium was responsible for their success. A comparison of 57 open-pollinated Virginia pine progeny (*Pinus virginiana*

Mill.) planted on acid spoils showed that survival and growth were significantly better for some progeny than for others (Thor et al., 1974). Indications were that more intensive genetic selection and breeding could probably produce trees of even greater tolerance to acidity or other spoil factors. Similar results with herbaceous materials may also be possible.

The amount of reforestation research on strip mines has been reduced in recent years. Part of this reduction is due to the illusion that most of the answers on species selection are already known. A more important factor is the emphasis on establishing herbaceous vegetation because of the need for erosion control (most state laws require it). Herbaceous vegetation is easier to plant and provides a protective ground cover faster than woody vegetation, and it is usually cheaper to establish it alone than combined with trees. This can be an economic advantage to mine operators in those states that release revegetation bonds as soon as 70 to 80% cover of perennial vegetation is established. Furthermore, when successfully established, the herbage can be used for grazing livestock—a rather quick economic return from the reclaimed land compared to reforestation. In some coal mining areas of the Midwest and East, the immediate establishment of grain and row crops is being encouraged. Apparently, more people are becoming aware of the various uses that can be made of reclaimed surface-mined land.

2. HERBACEOUS COVER

Research on the use of herbaceous species was conducted and reported as early as the mid-1940's (Tyner & Smith, 1945). Subsequently, species trials and other research on the establishment of herbaceous cover have been conducted by the Soil Conservation Service, the Forest Service, the Agricultural Research Service, and various state experiment stations (Grandt & Lang, 1958; Vogel & Berg, 1968; Bennett, 1971; Ruffner & Steiner, 1973). The results of their experiments have been incorporated into revegetation guides and manuals published by federal, state, and private agencies and into revegetation regulations by the surface mine regulatory agencies in several states. In most of these guides the best species for quick temporary cover and for long-term cover are recommended for several types of spoil. We will not discuss the various species because the use of plant materials is being discussed in several other chapters of this book.

A major reason for quick establishment of herbaceous cover is erosion control. Results of one of our studies in eastern Kentucky showed that, most of the time, herbaceous vegetative cover could be established by summer seeding as well as by spring and fall seeding. Summer annuals were used to provide the quick temporary cover for seedings made in May to August. With the application of this information, erosion can be reduced by seeding immediately after grading in the summer months instead of waiting until fall or the following spring. In addition, by seeding immediately after grading one can take advantage of the freshly prepared seedbed (Vogel, 1974).

Many of the researchers that become involved in surface mine revegetation experiments will, first of all, evaluate the adaptability of plant species and varieties of species to grow on mine spoils. But the results of species evaluations on spoils in one area are not always applicable on spoils in other areas, even within the humid East. For example, spoil with a pH of about 4.5 in Kentucky can be just as toxic to plants as spoil with a pH of about 4.0 in Pennsylvania. This happens because chemical and physical characteristics differ in different spoils, even in those with the same pH. Unfortunately, some researchers do not adequately analyze or adequately report their analyses of the spoils they are using, but report only pH. Then, on the basis of their species evaluations, they define pH ranges or limits for various plant species and imply that these pH limits apply to all mine spoils.

3. MYCORRHIZAL FUNGI AND OTHER MICROORGANISMS

One of the most exciting and productive efforts in plant research is with the mycorrhizal fungi. Some of the first observations and studies of ectomycorrhizae on surface mine spoils were reported by Schramm (1966). He concluded that early ectomycorrhizal development was essential for seedling establishment of several tree species on anthracite wastes in Pennsylvania. More recently, Marx (1975) has shown that pine seedlings planted on acid mine spoils survived and grew better when inoculated with *Pisolithus tinctorius*, an ectomycorrhizal fungus. On an acid spoil in Kentucky, where pine had been planted several times without success, Marx planted Virginia pine—some grown in the nursery with *Pisolithus* and some with *Thelephora terrestris* ectomycorrhizae (the latter is the most common associate in nursery beds). Survival of seedlings with *Thelephora* ectomycorrhizae was only 1.5%; but of those with *Pisolithus* it was 45.5%. The latter seedlings made significant growth in one growing season; the *Pisolithus* fungus had completely colonized the roots and adjacent soil.

Application of this research will result in greater success in reforestation; specific mycorrhizae can be chosen for specific sites and species. Secondly, these results show promise that survival and growth of plants with endomycorrhizae also can be improved by research into varieties of fungi that will persist on mine spoils.

The most comprehensive research on microbiology of surface mine spoil was reported by Wilson (1965). One important application of this work is that it shows that mine spoils are not necessarily sterile. Indeed, even unvegetated mine spoils contain populations of microorganisms, although the populations are smaller than in forest or agricultural land. Wilson's work also helps to explain why, as a result of microbial buildups, vegetation of low vigor may suddenly become quite vigorous.

Some research has been done in selecting strains of *Rhizobium* that will more effectively nodulate legumes (Rothwell, 1973; James Menzies, ARS, Beltsville, Md., unpublished data). Results have shown that some strains of *Rhizobium* bacteria are more efficient than others in nodulating legumes under adverse spoil conditions. Development of a commercial supply of these strains for inoculating legume seed would greatly enhance the establishment and growth of legumes on problem mine spoils.

The role of soil fungi (*Aspergillus* spp.) in modifying acid spoil to permit growth of selected vegetation has also been studied. Results indicate that survival and growth of vegetation were increased by inoculating the acid spoil with culture filtrates of *Aspergillus* (Fred M. Rothwell, mimeo report to TVA, July 1968).

Studies show that various forms of soil fauna will bury, consume, and alter the leaf litter and humus on revegetated mine spoils (Vimmerstedt & Finney, 1973). It is obvious that the establishment and normal succession of soil fauna are important in the reestablishment of a forest ecosystem on reclaimed land. However, it has not yet been shown to be practical to hasten the development of the forest ecosystem by artificially applying soil fauna over large areas of reclaimed spoils. The best approach seems to be the manipulation of revegetation procedures to provide the most suitable habitat for natural succession of soil fauna.

4. TREES AND HERBACEOUS COVER COMBINED

Planting both trees and herbaceous species is often desired and required in reclaiming surface mine spoils in the humid East. The herbaceous species provide rapid cover for erosion control; the trees provide a long-term cover and contribute to the reestablishment of a forest ecosystem. Trees also provide a potential merchantable product. Herbaceous cover usually is competitive with planted tree seedlings, especially when the herbaceous cover is established first.

In a field study on coal mine spoils in Kentucky, we measured the effect of herbaceous cover on tree survival and growth (Vogel, 1973). In some plots grass alone or grass with legumes were sown concurrently with the planting of four tree species. In other plots trees were planted without grasses or legumes. After three growing seasons, the herbaceous vegetation (95% ground cover) had not seriously reduced survival of trees, but had greatly suppressed their growth. In the first two growing seasons, grass was the main component of the vegetative cover in all of the seeded plots; but, in the third growing season, the legumes became the dominant component in the plots that had been sown to the grass-legume mixture. In the fourth and fifth growing seasons, the growth of trees in the plots sown to the grass-legume mixture exceeded that in plots with grass only and in plots with no herbaceous cover (Table 1). These trees have not been recently remeasured, but the trees with a legume understory appear more vigorous than trees without legumes. Apparently tree growth is being enhanced by the nitrogen fixed by the legumes, whereas grass alone suppresses tree growth. Neumann (1973) suggests that, in mine spoil reforestation programs, legumes are important in the early development of a favorable environment for soil fauna but grass is not. Thus, in addition to fixing nitrogen, legumes may provide other benefits to trees.

We were successful with another method for establishing trees and herbaceous cover together. A grass-legume seed mixture and fertilizer were applied on the spoil in strips about 1.6 m wide. The seeded strips

Table 1—Average height growth of trees planted with and without herbaceous ground covers

Tree species	Cover treatment†	Cumulative growth	
		1968 to 1970	1971 and 1972
		cm	
Cottonwood			
(*Populus deltoides* Bartr.)	1	183	135
	2	202	150
	3	74	91
	4	95	191
Sycamore			
(*Platanus occidentalis* L.)	1	127	101
	2	139	104
	3	28	44
	4	34	146
Virginia pine			
(*Pinus virginiana* Mill.)	1	93	124
	2	93	114
	3	63	113
	4	74	137
Loblolly pine			
(*Pinus taeda* L.)	1	67	114
	2	80	124
	3	45	104
	4	60	134

† 1 = no treatment; 2 = fertilizer applied (67 kg/ha N and 49 kg/ha P); 3 = fertilizer plus grass (Ky-31 fescue and weeping lovegrass [*Eragrostis curvula* (Schrad.) Nees]); and 4 = fertilizer plus grass plus legumes (sericea lespedeza and Korean lespedeza [*Lespedeza stipulacea* Maxim.]).

were alternated with strips about 0.9 m wide on which hybrid poplar cuttings (*Populus* L. spp.) were planted but no seed or fertilizer was applied. In the first growing season the herbaceous species provided nearly total cover in the 1.6 m-strips (about 60 to 70% of the total disturbed area), but in the unseeded belts the trees were free of herbaceous competition. In the third and fourth growing seasons the herbaceous vegetation filled in the unseeded strips, but by that time the trees had grown taller than the herbaceous cover and were not suppressed by it. This method will work best on areas where the strips of seed and fertilizer can be applied by farm implements. On sloping areas the strips should run on the contour.

In practice, many of the combination plantings of herbaceous and woody species are made with direct-seeded black locust (*Robinia pseudoacacia* L.) and a grass-legume mixture. The concept of planting seedlings of other tree species with the herbaceous cover has not been fully accepted. In the past, most reforestation studies have been short term. The short-term conclusion was that trees could not be grown with herbaceous competition. Today, fewer trees are being planted, partly because of higher labor costs and other problems associated with planting crews. Besides, the revegetation regulations in some states unwittingly discourage tree planting by providing bond release as soon as the requirements for herbaceous vegetation cover are met. Then, too, some surface owners do not want trees—they want pastures.

5. ALLELOPATHY

Another area of research that promises interesting and exciting results is allelopathy. Research in plant physiology shows that substances present in plants or parts of plants of some species can inhibit seed germination and root or shoot growth of other species (Rice, 1974). Little, if any, research in this field has been done in relation to revegetating surface mines. Possibly, some of the relationships that we now call competition among plant types and species are in reality allelopathic inhibitions. For example, studies at the Ohio Agricultural Research and Development Center in Wooster showed that the growth of germinated red oak seeds (*Quercus rubra* L.) was inhibited when they were watered daily with extracts from crownvetch foliage (*Coronilla varia* L.) (Merlyn Larson, unpublished data).

Research on allelopathy should have much application to revegetating surface mines. For example, it should provide more knowledge about compatible or nonallelopathic combinations of woody and herbaceous species.

B. Mine Soil Research

1. CHEMICAL PROPERTIES

Research on surface mine soils (spoils) is inseparable from revegetation research. Much research has been done on the chemical properties of spoils and their relation to the establishment and growth of vegetation. Studies of the nutrient status of spoils and vegetation response to fertilization have been especially valuable to successful reclamation (Tyner & Smith, 1945; Grandt & Lang, 1958; Berg, 1973; Zarger et al., 1973; Mays & Bengtson, 1974). These and other researchers have shown that spoils most often are deficient in plant-available phosphorus and nitrogen, but on some spoils native phosphorus is adequate for plant growth. Potassium may be low in spoils in a few areas, but on most spoils potassium fertilization is not required for establishing a vegetative cover. Use of the appropriate kinds and amounts of fertilizer has increased revegetation success manyfold, especially with herbaceous vegetation.

Refertilization may be necessary for long-term maintenance of a productive herbaceous cover on some spoils. But on many spoils, refertilization is not required, especially where perennial legumes such as sericea lespedeza (*Lespedeza cuneata* [Dumont], G. Don) crownvetch, or flat pea (*Lathyrus sylvestris* L.) are established and the herbage is not repeatedly removed. Phosphorus fertilizer usually is needed for rapid initial establishment of legumes, but after the legume plants are well established they seem to be adequately supplied with phosphorus from either the spoil material or the recycled plant material or both.

Extreme acidity prevents successful revegetation on some surface mine spoils in the humid East. At low pH values (extreme acidity) certain elements such as aluminum and manganese are toxic to plants (Berg & Vogel, 1973; Fleming et al., 1974). Several years ago, the standard treatment before attempting to vegetate extremely acid spoils (pH < 3.5) was simply to let the spoils weather, allowing the oxidation of acid-producing pyritic materials and leaching of the acid (Kohnke, 1950). On some spoils this required many years before vegetation could be established.

More recently, researchers have shown that the acidity and toxicity can be reduced or alleviated with various amendments. Adding lime to acid spoils reduces the solubility of the toxic elements and usually helps to provide a suitable balance of calcium and magnesium for optimum plant growth.

Some of the acid spoils in some parts of Appalachia are reported to be low in magnesium and can be amended with dolomite (Arminger et al., 1976). But, in other areas of Appalachia, the application of dolomite to some acid spoils may inhibit vegetation establishment. In a greenhouse experiment at Berea, we found that liming with finely ground dolomite inhibited the establishment of both Ky-31 fescue (*Festuca arundinacea* Schreb.) and birdsfoot trefoil (*Lotus corniculatus* L.) in some spoils. In other spoils, it inhibited establishment of trefoil but not fescue, and in yet other spoils the dolomite did not inhibit trefoil or fescue. Examples of the three situations are presented in Table 2. The spoils that were used in the greenhouse pots were composed of about one-half soil-size (< 2 mm) material and one-half material to 13 mm size. The amount of lime applied was based on the neutralizing value of each type of liming material. To raise pH to the intended 5.5, agricultural limestone was applied at 19.6, 11.1, and 4.2 g/1,000 g of spoil to the Huckleberry, River Gem, and Jellico spoils.

Some types of waste products also are useful for amending extremely acid spoils. For example, addition of large quantities of organic materials such as barnyard manure, composted municipal wastes, and sewage sludge will reduce acidity and provide nutrients for plant growth (Sopper & Kardos, 1972; Scanlon et al., 1973). However, sewage sludge from some sources is not recommended for this use because the sludge contains toxic levels of heavy metals.

Covering acid spoil with topsoil is recommended by some people. We are now doing research in Pennsylvania to learn more about the effects of topsoiling on soil microbiology, soil and spoil chemical and physical properties, and vegetation establishment. More research is needed to identify the problems and benefits of topsoiling before it is required by law as a standard reclamation practice in the eastern United States.

Mulches usually help in establishing stands of seeded vegetation, especially in summer seedings and on droughty, dark-colored, and south-facing spoils. Mulch also aids vegetation establishment on extremely acid spoils that have been limed (Vogel, 1975). In one of our studies a mulch of shredded bark hastened the establishment of vegetative cover on extremely acid spoils (pH 2.4) that had been limed, fertilized, and sown to a grass-legume mixture. In addition, the first year's herbage yield on mulched spoils was double the yield on unmulched spoil. The legume component of herbage was about 10 times greater on the mulched spoil. In a related ex-

Table 2—Herbage yields and pH in spoils limed with hydrated lime, limestone, and dolomite†

| | Spoil pH (limed) | | | Herbage yields | | | | | |
| | Actual§ | | | Hydrated lime | | Agricultural lime | | Dolomite | |
Intended‡	Hydrated	Agricultural	Dolomite	Fescue	Trefoil	Fescue	Trefoil	Fescue	Trefoil
						g per pot			
			Huckleberry spoil (pH 2.2, before liming)						
4.5	4.3	4.1	6.7	2.0	3.2	0.0	0.0	0.0	0.0
5.5(x)	5.1	4.4	7.0	2.1	4.9	0.1	0.0	0.1	0.0
6.5	6.7	4.7	7.3	3.4	4.3	0.6	0.0	0.1	0.0
2× ¶	--	6.5	7.5	--	--	2.7	2.9	0.1	0.0
			River Gem spoil (pH 2.9)						
4.5	4.2	4.5	5.4	4.8	3.6	4.2	0.6	5.3	0.1
5.5(x)	4.9	5.0	6.1	4.6	2.9	4.1	0.9	5.2	0.0
6.5	5.5	5.5	5.9	4.0	4.5	3.9	1.3	5.1	0.1
2× ¶	--	6.4	7.3	--	--	3.6	1.3	4.9	0.0
			Jellico spoil (pH 4.0)						
4.5	4.1	4.0	4.4	4.5	2.8	3.9	0.9	4.1	2.0
5.5(x)	4.4	4.6	5.4	3.8	5.0	3.7	2.3	4.0	2.1
6.5	5.5	5.1	6.7	3.7	4.8	3.6	2.8	4.5	1.4
2×¶	--	6.4	6.9	--	--	3.7	2.1	4.6	1.2

† Hydrated lime: neutralizing value 135%; agricultural limestone: 1.5% Mg, neutralizing value 94%, 49% passed 50-mesh sieve; dolomite: 12.5% Mg, neutralizing value 95%, 100% passed 60-mesh sieve.
‡ The $CaCO_3$ equivalent needed to attain intended pH was derived from neutralization curves determined by liming the spoils with known increments of $Ca(OH)_2$. Wetting and drying cycles were continued until pH remained stable.
§ pH of spoils after herbage was harvested (approximately 90 days growth).
¶ Rate of lime was twice the amount applied to the pH 5.5 pots. Not applied with hydrated lime.

periment, tree leaves collected from residential lawns were mixed into acid spoil that had been limed. The leaves provided benefits to vegetation establishment and growth similar to those provided by bark mulch.

Soil tests are useful for evaluating factors that limit or prevent revegetation of mine spoils. But limitations of the tests should be recognized. Berg (1969) compared several field kits with the pH meter for testing pH of spoils. He reported that kits that use several indicator dyes agreed more closely with the pH meter than did kits with one indicator dye. Some of the methods were grossly inaccurate. In other studies Berg (1973) found that the Bray no. 1 test for phosphorus correlated significantly with plant growth response to added phosphorus in nitrogen-fertilized spoils derived from rocks of the Pennsylvanian age. Subsequent work has shown that this test does not always correlate well on high pH or alkaline spoils, or on acid spoils limed to neutrality.

Some of the standard agronomic tests for determining lime requirements of soils may provide inaccurate results for liming acid spoils. For example, tests on fresh or unweathered acid spoils may not reflect the total potential of a spoil to produce acid because the acid-producing sulfides may continue to oxidize for a long period of time.

Results of research on soil tests provide guidelines to soil testing labs and field technicians who are responsible for providing mine operators and reclamation people with liming and fertilizing recommendations. This research also makes us aware that some common soil tests may not provide valid results when used for analyzing mine spoils.

2. PHYSICAL PROPERTIES

Some research has been done on the physical properties of spoil, but it has been less useful to reclamation than research on chemical properties. Usually, the land reclaimer "lives with" physical problems of spoil instead of trying to correct them. A premining analysis of the overburden could be used to determine how to separate or mix different rock materials during mining and grading so that the material left on and near the surface has acceptable properties (Despard, 1974). This approach can be applied to both physical and chemical properties of overburden (Grube et al., 1973).

Mine spoils in the eastern United States can vary greatly in physical characteristics from one region to another and even within regions depending on mining procedures. Most mine spoils contain a large proportion of coarse fragments (> 2 mm in diameter), some as much as 80% by volume. This results in low water-holding capacity and causes problems in seedbed preparation. Textures of the soil-size fraction of spoils range from sand to clay, but in most spoils textures are loamy. Spoils with < 50% coarse fragments and a loamy texture of the soil-size fraction seem best as plant growth media. Bulk densities of spoils have been reported from < 1.2 g/cm^3 to > 2 g/cm^3. These densities usually were higher than those of adjacent undisturbed soils. Weathering, growth of deep-rooted plants, accumulation of organic matter, and other soil-forming processes tend to decrease the density of spoils as well as alter other physical and chemical properties.

Mine spoils are a mixture of rock overburden and soil, but they do have certain properties that can be used for classification. Studies of spoil properties have led to a proposed classification system (Smith et al., 1976). The purpose of spoil or minesoil classification is to help identify significant characteristics of the soil, assemble knowledge about them, see their relationship to one another and to their environment, and develop principles of behavior and response to management practices and uses. Long-range minesoil classification and mapping will provide a basis for proper subsequent treatment and management for specialized uses.

C. Hydrologic Research

Surface mining can greatly affect streamflow, sediment load, and water quality of streams. Problems with stormflow, erosion, and sedimentation usually are more serious with contour stripping than with area-type surface mining. Much of the hydrologic research has been concerned with monitoring water quality and with controlling erosion and sedimentation in mined watersheds in the Appalachian region.

Excessive runoff and erosion are major adverse effects of surface mining. Studies in eastern Kentucky show that peak flows of streams are directly related to the percentage of area disturbed during mining. In the watersheds studied, peak flow rates increased threefold to fivefold after mining. Lag time was reduced, thus increasing the rate at which storm runoff peaked (Curtis, 1972).

In the Beaver Creek study area in south central Kentucky, the annual sediment yield from a contour-mined watershed averaged over 665 metric tons/km^2 during the 4 years after mining, compared to 8.75 metric tons for the unmined watersheds. Ninety-six percent of the erosion in the mined watershed was attributed to the disturbed area, which covered only 10.4% of the watershed (Collier et al., 1970). In one of the watersheds that we studied in eastern Kentucky, suspended sediment concentrations were as high as 46,400 mg/liter in streams during active mining periods. A corresponding value for a nearby unmined watershed was 150 mg/liter.

Erosion and subsequent sedimentation destroy aquatic life in the streams below mined watersheds. Following surface mining in an eastern Kentucky watershed, fish were eliminated from the headwaters and progressively on downstream. Benthic food organisms were reduced in number and variety by at least 90%. Reproduction in darters and minnows was curtailed, either by the prevention of mating or by killing of fry and eggs (Branson & Batch, 1972). Continued siltation from the surface-mining operations has prevented the recovery of fish populations and caused the loss of populations of several more species. Results of such studies clearly show the severity of damage caused by erosion and the need for preventing and controlling it.

As one approach to trapping sediment, several settling basins were constructed in streams close to mined areas in eastern Kentucky. The pools in the basins were then surveyed at 6-month intervals to determine the amount of accumulated sediment. The measurements of accumulated sediment were used to develop design criteria for the capacity of debris basins required by regulation (Davis & Hines, 1973). Recent measurements in these watersheds showed that, in a period of 4.5 to 7 years, the accumulated sediment yields ranged from 91 to 396 m^3/ha of disturbed land (Table 3). In addition this study has shown that methods of mining

Table 3—Summary of sediment yield from five watersheds in eastern Kentucky

Watershed	Watershed area	Area disturbed	Years measured	Sediment yield
	ha	ha		m^3/ha
South Fork of Quicksand Creek	166	100	4.5	91.4
Miller Branch	77	43	7	274.3
Mullins Right Fork	132	28	7	152.4
Mullins Left Fork	54	33	7	365.8
Leatherwood	251	198	5.5	396.3

and handling overburden are major factors affecting sediment yield. The smallest yield of sediment was measured in a watershed that was mined by the mountaintop removal method. Reclamation measures, especially a quickly established vegetative ground cover, were also shown to be important because the highest sediment yields were measured during the first 6-month period after mining. Thereafter, sediment yield for any 6-month period was about one-half of the yield for the previous 6-month period (Curtis, 1974).

The results of erosion and sedimentation studies show that sediment control measures must be planned for all phases of the mining operation—from selective movement and placement of overburden during mining to the establishment of a vegetative cover as soon as possible after mining is completed. For example, results from one of our Forest Service studies showed that contour terraces constructed on gently sloping spoils cut storm peak runoff rates and sediment yields in half. Also, the vegetative cover was established more quickly on the terraced plots, partly because of better seedbed preparation and partly because of improved moisture conditions (Curtis, 1971).

Chemical pollution of streams follows disturbance caused by surface mining. We have sampled several small streams in mined watersheds in eastern Kentucky and southern West Virginia, some for as long as 8 years (Dyer & Curtis, 1977). In most cases the sampling was done on a weekly basis. Tests included chemical analyses for Ca, Mg, Al, Na, Mn, K, Zn, Fe, HCO_3^-, Cl, SO_4^{2-}, and SiO_2, as well as for pH and specific conductance. Statistical analyses indicate that the specific conductance of the water in these streams can be used to predict the quantity of constituents such as SO_4^{2-}, HCO_3^-, Ca, and Mg that are in solution. Monthly sampling was found to be adequate to establish trends in stream water quality (Curtis, 1976). Application of these research results may be forthcoming when environmental control regulations require sampling and monitoring of all nonpoint water pollution sources.

D. Geologic Research

Even though geologic research is basic to much of the mining and reclamation activities, it has not received as much attention as other fields of reclamation research. Much of the published research on overburden and soil characteristics has been done by Smith and his associates at West Virginia University (Grube et al., 1973; Smith et al., 1976). A strong effort in reclamation-related geologic research is now being made at the Berea research unit of the U.S. Forest Service.

A major goal of geologic research is to obtain knowledge of the chemical and physical properties of overburden prior to site disturbance and use this knowledge to predict conditions that will prevail after mining is undertaken. This will allow a reclamation plan to be developed before mining begins, rather than after environmental damage has been incurred. For example, engineering research is concerned with designing stable spoil banks and with the physical, chemical, and geometrical parameters of overburden and spoil that determine this stability. Geologic data are essential for describing the physical and chemical parameters.

In relation to hydrologic research, geologic studies can identify the clay minerals and other clay-size particles that erode easily and cause increased turbidity and sediment load in streams. It is important to identify these sediment constituents because the character of suspended and bedload materials in a stream has significant influence on the chemical quality of water.

Use of the results of overburden analysis has already proved helpful in achieving successful revegetation and improving quality of runoff water. Berg and May (1969) sampled and analyzed overburden strata above six coal seams in eastern Kentucky. On several of the seams, the acid strata were relatively thin, located close to the coal, and could be easily identified by sight. Thus, the mine operator was able to separate and bury the toxic strata. In fact, he was required to do so by law. This simple requirement to bury toxic materials caused a reduction in the number of acid spoil banks and revegetation success was increased.

On other coal seams the overburden analyses showed that the acid rock was in a thick stratum located some distance above the coal, or in several strata. Some of the acid strata could not easily be recognized by sight because they were similar in appearance to nonacid strata. Thus, it would be difficult for the mine operator to identify and separate acid strata during the mining operation. The alternative measures would then be to stop mining or, if mining continued, intensify the effort to prevent acid spoils by analyzing all strata and identifying and segregating the acid strata at each mine, or ameliorate the acid spoils with lime and other amendments.

Overburden sampling and analyses were later made on other eastern Kentucky coal seams by Despard (1974). Again, it was shown that color of strata could not be relied on to identify acid strata, but it was useful in identifying nonacid or "safe" strata.

Visible presence of pyrite is another indicator that can be used in the field to help locate strata that may produce acid spoil. Oxidation of pyrite in overburden that has been exposed to weathering is the predominant source of acid in spoil. Sometimes pyrite can be seen in the overburden strata; it should be considered potentially acid-producing. But failure to see pyrite does not mean that it is not present. In many rocks, especially black shales, pyrite may be present in a highly dispersed, fine-grained form that is visible only under a microscope. If present in sufficient amounts, this form of pyrite is actually more harmful than the visible type. In fact some of the pyrite that is easily recognizable by eye possesses a crystal structure that is relatively inert to oxidation, but the fine-grained type is usually more susceptible to oxidation and also has a very large surface area on which oxidation occurs. In analyzing overburden, all fine-grained strata such as shales and claystones should be carefully checked for pyrite.

In testing for pH, fresh rock should be allowed to weather so that oxidizable pyrite will have a chance to produce acid before the pH determination is made. The pH readings even on freshly mined and graded spoil can sometimes be misleading: initially, the pH may indicate that a spoil is nontoxic, but the spoil may become acid after several months of weathering.

E. Wildlife Management Research

Surface mining destroys or disrupts wildlife habitat, but usually the disruption is temporary. The establishment of biotic communities on mined land is nearly always an asset to some form of wildlife. In some mined areas, fish and game bird and mammal populations have increased even to the point of having a significant impact on local fishing and hunting activities. The older area-stripped lands of Indiana, Illinois, Missouri, and eastern Kansas with their interspersion of ponds, marshes, and rolling woodlands, and the grouse-rich outslope perimeters of West Virginia, are examples.

Most of the published information on wildlife and its habitat is of the descriptive type, mainly documentation of surveys made several years after cessation of mining activity (Riley, 1954; Klimstra, 1959; Holland, 1973; and many others). The reports often lacked detail on premining conditions, mining history, and land use patterns after mining. The largest proportion of the publications relate to terrestrial habitat—many to the suitability and propagation of wildlife forage and cover plants.

There is a lack of research information concerned specifically with establishing, increasing, and managing game and nongame populations on reclaimed surface mines. There is comparatively little information published on the impact of surface mining activity on changes in populations, food habits, and vigor of the resident birds, mammals, and aquatic fauna. Changes in land use patterns and their effect on wildlife composition and human use also have received little study.

Some reports combine postmining surveys with management assumptions for particular species or species groups, for example fur-bearers (Yeager, 1942), bobwhite quail (Vohs & Birkenholz, 1962), cottontail rabbit (Burton, 1964) and song birds (Karr, 1968). However, most of these management-oriented papers are general or nonspecific in nature and contain assumptions drawn from basic habitat management principles instead of actual surface mine research experiences. Few, if any, studies have been made of wildlife populations and habitat before, during, and after surface mining of a specific area.

Some of the publications on forage and cover species and planting patterns provided the basis for planting guides and reclamation handbooks published by various government agencies and reclamation associations (Riley, 1957; Ruffner, 1965; Rawson, 1971; and others). No doubt these guides have been very beneficial in establishing and improving wildlife habitat on many surface mines. But, unfortunately, some people still believe that reclamation for wildlife habitat requires only that a few plants of recommended species be planted along with the usual revegetation strategy. Also, wildlife habitat is often considered an added benefit or by-product of standard reclamation procedures. It may be true that any type of vegetative community has some degree of benefit for wildlife, but the maximum benefit for wildlife will probably be achieved by designing the shape of spoils, providing adequate water facilities, and planting suited vegetation species in desired patterns or inducing the development of diverse native plant communities during the revegetation effort.

F. Engineering Research

Engineering research is discussed here last, but it is not any less important than other types of reclamation research. In fact, after premining geologic research, engineering is chronologically the next most important step in the process of good reclamation. Many of the reclamation goals can be more easily achieved and many reclamation problems avoided by planned and properly engineered mining. Unfortunately, engineering research is very expensive and has not received as much attention as revegetation and mine-soil research. Said another way, emphasis has too often been placed on trying to cure or cover up environmental problems that might have been prevented by application of proper engineering techniques during mining and spoil placement.

For some phases of the mining operation, research on engineering problems is not needed nearly as much as simple adherence to already established basic engineering principles. For example, design and construction of haul roads require mainly the application of existing road-construction criteria. Likewise, criteria and recommendations for the proper abandonment of haul roads are also available (Weigle, 1965). Yet basic engineering principles that will help reduce erosion and other environmental damage are not followed on the majority of mining operations.

Surface mining in the mountainous Appalachian coal field causes serious erosion and stability problems. Active research on mining procedures that prevent or reduce these problems is lagging. Much of the engineering research is still in the theoretical stage—hypothesizing and modeling. New mining methods that have the potential for improving reclamation have been developed, mostly by the mining industry through trial and error and on-the-job improvisation. Examples of these developments are the block method (Saperstein & Secor, 1973) and the modified block-cut method (Heine & Guckert, 1973). These methods eliminate double handling of spoil, reduce the amount of land disruption, and increase chances of successful vegetation. Thus, these methods are attractive both aesthetically and financially, especially in contour-type stripping. A method of multiple seam mining and reclamation is being studied on steep slopes in Tennessee by the Tennessee Valley Authority (Allen, 1973). The method is designed to mine coal without leaving highwalls and unstable spoil piles.

A survey was made of about 90 surface mines in eastern Kentucky with special attention given to a total of 178 spoil slides that had occurred on these mines (Williams, 1973). Neither the frequency nor severity of spoil slides was directly related to the steepness of the natural terrain. In-

Table 4—Summary of spoil slide survey

Terrain slope angle	Number of slides	Length of mined outcrop	Amount of mined outcrop in slides
%		km	%
<25	14	12.72	3.0
25–42	31	74.51	3.9
43–50	74	58.38	9.2
51–58	20	75.19	3.5
59–65	21	13.86	14.1
>65	18	20.35	9.7
All sites	178	255.01	6.0

stead, spoil slides occurred with high frequencies where arbitrary guidelines had permitted spoil to be placed upon the outslope in volumes greater than would be allowed by accepted engineering criteria (Table 4). Nearly 50% of the slides occurred either in or close to natural drainages. Only one slide occurred on the point of a ridge; all others occurred on sites with nearly straight or gently curving contours.

The results of this survey also provide evidence that simply prescribing bench width limits for the different site slope angles will not prevent spoil slides. Site slope angle is only one criterion to be considered. Other factors, such as spoil shear strength, spoil dump shape, and moisture content of the spoil will often override the influence of site slope. Thus, engineering research must include studies of mechanical and physical properties of the various overburden materials.

III. CONCLUSIONS

In this paper we have discussed some of the reclamation research that has been done and is presently being done on surface-mined lands in the eastern United States. This paper is by no means an exhaustive review of all past and present research. The discussion of some subjects, such as revegetation with herbaceous species, was limited because these subjects should be discussed in detail in other chapters in this book. Details of much of the research can be learned from publications, most of which are listed in the several bibliographies cited in our text.

Results of some of the past research have been used in everyday surface mine reclamation. Examples are the planting of adapted woody and herbaceous species and the use of fertilizer. However, results of some research have not been applied. For example, early reforestation studies showed that on some spoils in some areas, grading of spoil banks was detrimental to survival and growth of planted tree seedlings. Yet, this knowledge has been largely ignored because grading is now a common, and usually required, practice whether or not tree planting is required.

Some reclamation regulations are written and passed without the supportive evidence of research. In some cases, research findings may indicate that, instead of reducing environmental damage, certain regulations are actually contributing to it. Thus, there should be more recognition of reclamation research by the various segments of society that are concerned with surface mining.

ACKNOWLEDGMENT

The authors wish to thank the other scientists at the Northeastern Forest Experiment Station's Strip-Mine Reclamation Research Project in Berea, Ky., for their contributions to this paper.

LITERATURE CITED

Allen, N., Jr. 1973. Experimental multiple seam mining and reclamation on steep mountain slopes. p. 98–104. In Research and Applied Technology Symp. on Mined-Land Reclamation. 7–8 Mar. 1973, Pittsburgh, Pa. Bituminous Coal Res., Inc., Monroeville, Pa.

Arminger, W. H., J. N. Jones, and O. L. Bennett. 1976. Revegetation of land disturbed by strip mining of coal in Appalachia. USDA-ARS-NE-71. ARS, Beltsville, Md.

Bennett, O. L. 1971. Grasses and legumes for revegetation of strip-mined areas. p. 23–25. In Proc. Revegetation and Economic Use of Surface-Mined Land and Mine Refuse Symp. 2–4 Dec. 1971, Pipestem State Park, W. Va. West Virginia Univ., Morgantown.

Berg, W. A. 1969. Determining pH of strip mine spoils. USDA For. Serv. Res. Note NE-98. Northeast. For. Exp. Stn., Upper Darby, Pa.

Berg, W. A. 1973. Evaluation of P and K soil fertility tests on coal-mine spoils. p. 93–104. In R. J. Hutnik and G. Davis (ed.) Ecology and reclamation of devastated land, Vol. I. Gordon and Breach, New York.

Berg, W. A., and R. F. May. 1969. Acidity and plant-available phosphorus in strata overlying coal seams. Min. Congr. J. 55:31–34.

Berg, W. A., and W. G. Vogel. 1973. Toxicity of acid coal-mine spoils to plants. p. 57–68. In R. J. Hutnik and G. Davis (ed.) Ecology and reclamation of devastated land, Vol. I. Gordon and Breach, New York.

Bituminous Coal Research, Inc. 1975. Reclamation of coal mined-land, a bibliography with abstracts. Bituminous Coal Research, Inc., Monroeville, Pa.

Branson, B. A., and D. L. Batch. 1972. Effects of strip mining on small-stream fishes in east-central Kentucky. Proc. Biol. Soc. Wash. 84:507–517.

Burton, J. P. 1964. Cover type utilization by the cottontail rabbit in a southern Indiana coal-stripped land. Final Rep., Dep. For. and Conserv. Purdue Univ., W. Lafayette, Ind.

Collier, C. R., R. J. Pickering, and J. J. Musser. 1970. Influences of strip mining on the hydrologic environment of parts of Beaver Creek basin, Kentucky, 1955–66. USGS Prof. Pap. 427-C. U.S. Government Printing Office, Washington, D.C.

Curtis, W. R. 1971. Terraces reduce runoff and erosion on surface-mine benches. J. Soil Water Conserv. 26:198–199.

Curtis, W. R. 1972. Strip-mining increases flood potential of mountain watersheds. p. 357–360. In Proc. Natl. Symp. on Watersheds in Transition. 19–22 June 1972, Fort Collins, Colo. Am. Water Resour. Assoc. and Colorado State Univ., Fort Collins.

Curtis, W. R. 1974. Sediment yield from strip-mined watersheds in eastern Kentucky. p. 88–100. In Proc. 2nd Research and Applied Technology Symp. on Mined-Land Reclamation. 22–24 Oct. 1974, Louisville, Ky. Natl. Coal Assoc., Washington, D.C.

Curtis, W. R. 1976. Sampling for water quality. In Proc. 8th Materials Research Symp. Methods and Standards for Environmental Measurement. 20–24 Sept. 1976. Gaithersburg, Md. U.S. Dep. Commer., Natl. Bur. Stand., Washington, D.C.

Czapowskyj, M. M. 1976. Annotated bibliography on the ecology and reclamation of drastically disturbed areas. USDA For. Serv. Gen. Tech. Rep. NE-21. Northeastern For. Exp. Stn., Upper Darby, Pa.

Davis, J. R., and B. J. Hines. 1973. Debris basin capacity needs based on measured sediment accumulation from strip-mined areas in eastern Kentucky. p. 260–276. *In* Proc. Research and Applied Technology Symp. on Mined-Land Reclamation. 7–8 Mar. 1973, Pittsburgh, Pa. Bituminous Coal Res., Inc., Monroeville, Pa.

Despard, T. L. 1974. Avoid problem spoils through overburden analysis. USDA For. Serv. Gen. Tech. Rep. NE-10. Northeast. For. Exp. Stn., Upper Darby, Pa.

Dyer, K. L., and W. R. Curtis. 1977. Effect of strip mining on water quality in small streams in eastern Kentucky, 1967–1975. USDA For. Serv. Res. Pap. NE-372. Northeast. For. Exp. Stn., Upper Darby, Pa.

Fleming, A. L., J. W. Schwartz, and C. D. Foy. 1974. Chemical factors controlling the adaptation of weeping lovegrass and tall fescue to acid mine spoils. Agron. J. 66:715–719.

Frawley, M. L. 1971. Surface mined areas: control and reclamation of environmental damage, a bibliography. Bibliogr. Ser. 27, U.S. Dep. of Interior Off. Lib. Serv., Washington, D.C.

Funk, D. T. 1962. A revised bibliography of strip-mine reclamation. USDA For. Serv. Central States For. Exp. Stn. Misc. Release 35, Columbus, Ohio.

Geyer, W. A. 1971. Timber growth on graded and ungraded strip-mine spoil banks in southeast Kansas. Trans. Kansas Acad. Sci. 74:318–324.

Geyer, W. A., and G. G. Naughton. 1970. Growth and management of black walnut (*Juglans nigra* L.) on strip-mined lands in southeastern Kansas. Trans. Kansas Acad. Sci. 73:491–501.

Geyer, W. A., and N. F. Rogers. 1972. Spoils change and tree growth on coal-mined spoils in Kansas. J. Soil Water Conserv. 27:114–116.

Grandt, A. F., and A. L. Lang. 1958. Reclaiming Illinois strip coal land with legumes and grasses. Ill. Agric. Exp. Stn. Bull. 628. Urbana, Ill.

Grube, W. E., Jr., R. M. Smith, R. N. Singh, A. A. Sobek. 1973. Characterization of coal overburden materials and minesoils in advance of surface mining. p. 134–151. *In* Proc. Research and Applied Technology Symp. on Mined-Land Reclamation. 7–8 Mar. 1973, Pittsburgh, Pa. Bituminous Coal Res., Inc., Monroeville, Pa.

Heine, W. N., and W. E. Guckert. 1973. A new method of surface coal mining in steep terrain. p. 105–116. *In* Proc. Research and Applied Technology Symp. on Mined-Land Reclamation. 7–8 Mar. 1973, Pittsburgh, Pa. Bituminous Coal Res., Inc., Monroeville, Pa.

Holland, F. R. 1973. Wildlife benefits from strip-mine reclamation. p. 377–388. *In* R. J. Hutnik and G. Davis (ed.) Ecology and reclamation of devastated land, Vol. I. Gordon and Breach, New York.

Karr, J. R. 1968. Habitat and avian diversity on strip-mined land in eastern-central Illinois. Condor 70:348–357.

Klimstra, W. D. 1959. The potential of wildlife management on strip-mined areas. Ill. Wildl. 14:5–9.

Kohnke, H. 1950. The reclamation of coal mine spoils. p. 317–349. *In* A. G. Norman (ed.) Advances in agronomy, Vol. II. Academic Press, Inc., New York.

Lane, R. D. 1968. Forest Service reclamation research. Min. Congr. J. 54:38–42.

Limstrom, G. A. 1960. Forestation of strip-mined land in the central states. USDA Agric. Handb. 166. U.S. Government Printing Office, Washington, D.C.

Marx, D. H. 1975. Mycorrhizae and establishment of trees on strip-mined land. Ohio J. Sci. 75:288–297.

Mays, D. A., and G. W. Bengtson. 1974. Fertilizer effects on forage crops on strip-mined land in northeast Alabama. TVA, Natl. Fert. Dev. Cent. Bull. Y-74, Muscle Shoals, Ala.

Munn, R. F. 1973. Strip mining: an annotated bibliography. West Virginia Univ. Library, Morgantown.

Neumann, U. 1973. Succession of soil fauna in afforested spoil banks of the brown-coal mining district of Cologne. p. 335–348. *In* R. J. Hutnik and G. Davis (ed.) Ecology and reclamation of devastated land, Vol. I. Gordon and Breach, New York.

Rawson, J. W. 1971. Surface mining and wildlife. p. 37–39. *In* Proc. Revegetation and Economic Use of Surface-Mined Land and Mine Refuse Symp. 2–4 Dec. 1971, Pipestem State Park, W. Va. West Virginia Univ., Morgantown.

Rice, E. L. 1974. Allelopathy. Academic Press, New York.

Riley, C. V. 1954. The utilization of reclaimed coal striplands for the production of wildlife. Trans. 19th N. Am. Wildl. Nat. Resour. Congr. p. 324–337.

Riley, C. V. 1957. Reclamation of coal strip-mined lands with reference to wildlife plantings. J. Wildl. Manage. 21:402–413.

Rothwell, F. M. 1973. Nodulation by various strains of Rhizobium with Robinia pseudoacacia seedlings planted in strip-mine spoil. p. 349–355. In R. J. Hutnik and G. Davis (ed.) Ecology and reclamation of devastated land, Vol. I. Gordon and Breach, New York.

Ruffner, J. D. 1965. Adaptation and performance of shrubs in mine spoil reclamation. p. 117–123. In Proc. Coal Mine Spoil Reclamation Symp., 11–14 Oct. 1965, Pennsylvania State Univ., University Park, Pa.

Ruffner, J. D., and W. W. Steiner. 1973. Evaluation of plants for use on critical sites. p. 3–12. In R. J. Hutnik and G. Davis (ed.) Ecology and reclamation of devastated land, Vol. II. Gordon and Breach, New York.

Saperstein, L. W., and E. S. Secor. 1973. Improved reclamation potential with the block method of contour stripping. p. 1–14. In Proc. Research and Applied Technology Symp. on Mined-Land Reclamation. 7–8 Mar. 1973, Pittsburgh, Pa. Bituminous Coal Res., Inc., Monroeville, Pa.

Scanlon, D. H., C. Duggan, and S. D. Bean. 1973. Evaluation of municipal compost for strip mine reclamation. Compost Sci. 14:4–8.

Schramm, J. E. 1966. Plant colonization studies on black wastes from anthracite mining in Pennsylvania. Am. Philos. Soc. Trans. N.S. 56 (Part 1):1–194.

Smith, R. M., A. A. Sobek, T. Arkle, Jr., J. C. Sencindiver, and J. R. Freeman. 1976. Extensive overburden potentials for soil and water quality. Environ. Protec. Tech. Series EPA-600/2-76-184. USEPA, Cincinnati, Ohio.

Sopper, W. E., and L. T. Kardos. 1972. Municipal waste water aids revegetation of strip-mined spoil banks. J. For. 70:612–615.

Thor, E., W. T. Plass, and G. Rink. 1974. Breeding Virginia pine for better growth on acid spoil. p. 168–174. In Proc. 2nd Research and Applied Technology Symp. on Mined-Land Reclamation. 22–24 Oct. 1974, Louisville, Ky. Natl. Coal Assoc., Washington, D.C.

Tyner, E. H., and R. M. Smith. 1945. The reclamation of the strip-mined coal lands of West Virginia with forage species. Soil Sci. Soc. Am. Proc. 10:429–436.

Vimmerstedt, J. P., and J. H. Finney. 1973. Importance of earthworm introduction on litter burial and nutrient distribution in Ohio strip-mine spoil banks. Soil Sci. Soc. Am. Proc. 37:388–391.

Vogel, W. G. 1973. The effect of herbaceous vegetation on survival and growth of trees planted on coal-mine spoils. p. 197–207. In Proc. Research and Applied Technology Symp. on Mined-Land Reclamation. 7–8 Mar. 1973, Pittsburgh, Pa. Bituminous Coal Res., Inc., Monroeville, Pa.

Vogel, W. G. 1974. All season seeding of herbaceous vegetation for cover on Appalachian strip-mine spoils. p. 175–186. In Proc. 2nd Research and Applied Technology Symp. on Mined-Land Reclamation. 22–24 Oct. 1974, Louisville, Ky. Natl. Coal Assoc., Washington, D.C.

Vogel, W. G. 1975. Requirements and use of fertilizer, lime, and mulch for vegetating acid mine spoil. p. 152–170. In Proc. 3rd Symp. on Surface Mining and Reclamation. 21–23 Oct. 1975, Louisville, Ky. Natl. Coal Assoc., Washington, D.C.

Vogel, W. G., and W. A. Berg. 1968. Grasses and legumes for cover on acid strip mine spoils. J. Soil Water Conserv. 23:89–91.

Vohs, P. A., Jr., and D. E. Birkenholz. 1962. Response of bobwhite quail to management on some Illinois strip-mine lands. Trans. Ill. Acad. Sci. 55:13–19.

Weigle, W. K. 1965. Designing coal-haul roads for good drainage. USDA Central States For. Exp. Stn. Handb. Northeast. For. Exp. Stn., Upper Darby, Pa.

Williams, G. P. 1973. Changed spoil dump shape increases stability on contour strip mines. p. 243–249. In Proc. Research and Applied Technology Symp. on Mined-Land Reclamation. 7–8 Mar. 1973, Pittsburgh, Pa. Bituminous Coal Res., Inc., Monroeville, Pa.

Wilson, H. A. 1965. The microbiology of strip-mine spoil. W. Va. Agric. Exp. Stn. Bull. 506T, Morgantown, W. Va.

Yeager, L. E. 1942. Coal-stripped land as a mammal habitat, with special reference to fur animals. Am. Midl. Nat. 27:613–635.

Zarger, T. G., G. W. Benstson, J. C. Allen, and D. A. Mays. 1973. Use of fertilizers to speed pine establishment on reclaimed coal-mine spoil in northeastern Alabama: II. Field experiments. p. 227–236. In R. J. Hutnik and G. Davis (ed.) Ecology and reclamation of devastated land, Vol. II. Gordon and Breach, New York.

Copyright © 1978 ASA–CSSA–SSSA
677 South Segoe Road, Madison, WI 53711 USA
Reclamation of Drastically Disturbed Lands

Chapter 22

Grading and Shaping for Erosion Control and Vegetative Establishment in Dry Regions

T. R. VERMA AND J. L. THAMES

University of Arizona
Tucson, Arizona

I. INTRODUCTION

The dry regions of the western United States are well known for their rich mineral deposits and harsh climatic conditions. These areas contain more than 60% of the strippable coal reserves in the United States. Furthermore, the size of these coal fields and the sulphur content of the coal should result in intensive development of energy in the western U.S. Extensive deposits of copper, silver, uranium, oil shale, and other minerals of this semiarid and arid region are crucial for the healthy economic growth of the United States.

The withdrawal and processing of these natural resources disturb land. Impact on the natural environment and ecological parameters is obvious. Soil erosion and sediment processes are accelerated mainly due to lack of protective vegetative cover. Apart from an increased vulnerability of the exposed material to erosion processes, the premining hydrological conditions are irreversibly changed by the operations of stripping and regrading. The problem of environmental degradation and impact can be alleviated by reclamation. Grading and revegetating practices are proving to be the most effective and successful means of erosion and sediment control for a long-lasting and ecologically balanced reclamation of these drastically disturbed lands. Most of the drastically disturbed land in the arid and semiarid regions is a result of mining activities of various sorts. Disturbances and topography resulting from mining activities usually vary from a series of ungraded spoil banks with steep and unstable slopes, the deep pits, to gently rolling or nearly level plateaus. Recontouring of these disturbed areas varies from one state to another depending upon requirements of the mined-area restoration laws. Some voluntary regulatory landscaping programs aimed at some specific post-mining land use are also quite common in the states which do not have reclamation laws.

Most strip mining in the arid and semiarid regions of the western U.S. is done by the contour-furrow method, where successive contour furrows are cut to expose the coal, then filled with spoil from the next furrow after the coal is removed. Recontouring of the spoil material follows two to three rows behind the active cut. Usually, the objective is a landscape which blends in well with the natural topography of the area. Open pit and underground mining are often used for minerals such as copper, sand and gravel, and for oil shale.

Reclamation and revegetation of these disturbed areas in the semiarid and arid western U.S. are slow processes, primarily due to dry and harsh climatic conditions. Erosion and sedimentation are high. Spoil material toxicity is not a problem (Thames & Verma, 1975). Aldon and Springfield (1975) point out that native plant species seem to offer the best possibility for establishment and survival. On-site conservation of precipitation is crucial for vegetative establishment since strip mining of the coal is most extensive in the semiarid and arid regions of the western U.S. Most of the disturbed land is directly or indirectly related to the coal mining industry. This paper deals with grading and shaping for erosion control and vegetative establishment in reclaiming these disturbed lands.

Site stabilization should be the prime goal in grading the mine spoils. Erosion control and vegetative establishment on unstable slopes would be extremely difficult and uneconomical. Gradients of the spoil slopes should be reduced to a degree that will provide mechanical stability and will be conducive to erosion control and vegetative establishment.

II. NEED FOR ON-SITE MOISTURE CONSERVATION

In the semiarid and arid regions, water is the key factor that determines success or failure of revegetating efforts. Runoff rates are high because regraded spoil material has steep slopes which are devoid of vegetative cover. The spoil material is low in organic-matter content and has no well-defined structure. Infiltration rates and plant-available water capacity are quite low. Post-reclamation land uses are mostly grazing in the semiarid and arid regions. Irrigation is often recommended as the means of establishing vegetative cover. However, surface water resources are not dependable and, therefore, irrigation practices to rehabilitate these drastically disturbed areas are uneconomical and impractical. On-site moisture conservation should be the prime consideration in revegetating the areas which receive more than 25 cm of precipitation annually. Effective vegetative cover can be established by on-site moisture conservation practices in most of the semiarid regions of the western U.S. that are considered suitable for dryland farming.

In reality, the amount of precipitation received annually is not the most important factor in the Western states dryland areas. Annual distribution, i.e., winter precipitation vs. summer precipitation, largely affects the success of the revegetation efforts at a given precipitation range. The mean annual temperature and the wind velocity are other climatic factors that can have a controlling influence on on-site moisture conservation for revegetation of the regraded disturbed lands.

Evaporation from land surfaces amounts to a considerable loss of moisture in arid and semiarid regions. Viets (1966) estimated that from one-fourth to one-half of the water lost from a crop is evaporated from the soil surface. On the recontoured disturbed lands these losses are even higher. These losses should be reduced to make moisture conservation effective for vegetative establishment.

III. RETENTION OF RAINFALL AND SNOWMELT RUNOFF

Grading of the spoil material is an expensive but most important phase of reclamation. In the dry regions, moisture conservation should be the main consideration in landscaping and recontouring of the spoil material. Landscape planning should allow maximum retention of the runoff from rainfall and snowmelt. Grading plans should be based on variables such as the amount, intensity, and distribution of annual precipitation, planned end-use of the reclaimed area, type of spoil material, and feasibility of supplemental irrigation. Runoff retention will aid in vegetative establishment and erosion control.

A. Techniques

Grading and shaping techniques for maximum retention of rainfall and snowmelt on drastically disturbed lands will vary according to their post reclamation land use, landscape, precipitation, and the cost of reclamation. In general, contour terracing, contour furrowing, contour trenching, constructing small basins, pitting, surface manipulating, mulching, topsoiling, and tillage are the most commonly used techniques for maximum retention and conservation of runoff. Most of these mechanical and cultural techniques have a dual role for erosion control and moisture conservation. These techniques are specifically designed to modify slopes; to control the velocity and direction of runoff; to trap and retain water on the site in terraces, furrows, small basins, ponds, pits; and to deliberately retard the flow of water as it moves off the disturbed areas.

1. CONTOUR TERRACING, FURROWING, AND TRENCHING

Contour terracing, contour furrowing, and contour trenching, when properly designed and laid out on the regraded disturbed areas, have two functions: (i) to break up the watershed slopes, and (ii) to provide for retention and slow release of runoff.

Contour terraces are quite effective in spreading and retaining the runoff for moisture conservation. There are two categories of terraces—one based on slope characteristics and the other, on shape. On the basis of slope, the terraces are referred to as level terraces or graded terraces. Level terraces are built on contour intervals which are determined from intensity, duration, and distribution of precipitation; from the infiltration and water-holding capacity of the soil; and from the slope characteristics for the disturbed areas. These are designed to retain all the on-site precipitation. Graded terraces are generally used for erosion control and carry runoff water to planned outlets.

Based on shape, there are three categories of terraces: broad base terraces, conservation bench terraces, and simple bench terraces. Conservation bench terraces have been found quite effective in runoff retention and conservation on steep and lengthy slopes of disturbed areas. Contour furrows are also quite effective for runoff retention and conservation (Wight & Siddoway, 1972; Hubbard & Smoliek, 1953; Branso et al., 1966). These furrows are usually 10 to 30 cm deep and spaced up to 1.5 m apart. These furrows form miniature terraces and retain water for conservation.

On relatively level sites small basins can be constructed by placing small dikes at intervals of 2 to 12 m. Stringham (1975) indicated that the effectiveness of contour furrows for runoff retention is greatly enhanced if they are used with small basins.

Pits can also be used for runoff retention and moisture conservation on recontoured disturbed lands in the arid and semiarid regions. Effectiveness of the pitting technique has been studied by Anderson and Swanson (1949), Barnes (1950), Moldenhauer and Amemiya (1969), and Wight and Siddoway (1972). Shallow pits are dug in the surface of the recontoured spoil material (Thames & Verma, 1975).

2. TILLAGE PRACTICES

Tillage practices are necessary for compaction relief. Heavy machineries that are used for recontouring the spoil material cause compaction. Infiltration rates into the compacted material are greatly reduced. Tillage practices are necessary for the preparation of suitable seed bed for vegetative establishment. Tillage loosens the compacted surface and thus facilitates runoff intake and retention. Tillage practices should be adapted to best suit the post reclamation land use. In the arid and semiarid regions grazing is the most common post-reclamation land use. Tillage practices for these regraded disturbed lands, therefore, should be planned for maximum moisture conservation for establishing a vegetative cover and to help control runoff and erosion. Contour tillage practices will add to the effectiveness of the other soil and water conservation measures. Tillage practices also reduce evaporation and, thus, help in moisture conservation and vegetative establishment.

Hodder (1975) has tested some surface manipulation techniques to study the water retention capabilities of several configurations. These configurations included deep chiseling, offset-listering, gouging, and dozer basins.

Deep chiseling is a surface treatment that loosens compacted surfaces on the regraded disturbed sites. Deep chiseling a series of parallel furrows on the contours effectively impedes and retains runoff. The technique is effective on relatively flat slopes during the first spring to help establish a vegetative cover. The effects of this technique in increasing moisture conservation are temporary and it should be used in conjunction with other soil and water conservation measures.

Off-set listering, a surface configuration of alternately arranged elongated pits (about 15 cm deep and 1.2 m long), is effective for runoff retention and moisture conservation. Another surface manipulation technique, gouging, is a series of depressions (about 25 cm deep, 45 cm wide, and 65 cm long). This surface configuration is most suited to gentle slopes and relatively flat areas. It causes differential melting of snow in winter and early spring and, thus, is quite effective in snow-melt runoff retention and moisture conservation.

Dozer basins are quite similar to small basins which are described earlier. A bulldozer is used to place these basins at a desired contour interval. Dozer basins are about 60 cm deep with their length variable according to the size of the dozer blade. These basins are largely designed to accomplish goals similar to those of terracing but without the precision, hazards, and expense of the latter technique (Hodder, 1975).

3. TOPSOIL DRESSING

Topsoil dressing on recontoured spoil materials and disturbed lands of the semiarid and arid regions is used to insure an effective and fast vegetative establishment. It provides a suitable growth medium for plants, and has a high infiltration rate due to its friable and porous nature. Topsoil dressing should be done on stable and compacted slopes. The expenses involved in topsoil dressing are exorbitant and, therefore, if the reclamation plans call for this measure, the quality of the topsoil to be used should be evaluated. Topsoil dressing should only be recommended if soil of good quality existed before land disturbances took place. Good quality topsoil is scarce or nonexistent in many areas of the arid and semiarid regions, where soils are quite poor in plant nutrients and organic matter content (Verma & Thames, 1975). The nature and the size of the disturbed area, and its post-reclamation use, are also important in deciding for or against topsoil dressing. For example, topsoil dressing is effective for vegetative establishment on regraded copper tailing ponds in southern Arizona where topsoil is locally available (Rodiek et al., 1976). But there is no use of topsoil dressing on the recontoured coal mine spoils on the Black Mesa, Arizona, where there is no difference in the physical and chemical characteristics of the overburden material and the undisturbed soils (Verma & Thames, 1975).

4. MULCHING

Mulching practices are well known for their effective but temporary role in soil and water conservation on disturbed areas. They provide protection for the soil surface against erosion, retard evaporation, and increase infiltration of rainwater. Different types of materials are used for mulch. Wood fiber is the most common and effective mulch for erosion control and moisture conservation on disturbed lands of the arid and semiarid regions. Mulching, like topsoil dressing, is quite expensive and its application should only be considered on steep slopes.

5. WATER HARVESTING

Water harvesting is a technique in which runoff efficiency is induced on certain upland portions of a watershed and this water is then used on the remainder of the watershed to provide additional soil moisture for establishing effective vegetative cover. Recontoured disturbed areas in the arid and semiarid region have a potential for water harvesting.[1] Several artificial methods can be used to make a catchment more impervious. Water from surface runoff is stored in reservoirs and can be used for supplemental irrigation.

6. WATER SPREADING

Water spreading can also be used for establishing vegetative cover on the recontoured disturbed lands. In arid and semiarid regions, the limited rainfall usually falls during short, intense storms. Runoff rates are high. Runoff from intense storms and from snowmelt can be diverted on to relatively flat portions of the lower watersheds to provide additional soil moisture.

7. SUPPLEMENTAL IRRIGATION

Supplemental irrigation is an expensive but effective way of establishing vegetative cover on disturbed areas of the arid and semiarid regions. In most of the arid and semiarid regions ground water resources are deep and costly to tap. Surface water resources are not usually dependable. Availability of good quality water for irrigation should be evaluated before planning an irrigation system. Several irrigation systems, such as drip, sprinkler, and trickle, can be used to supplement the soil moisture availability for facilitating vegetative establishment. Planning for an irrigation system should be based on water supply, slope conditions, economics, and post-reclamation uses of the disturbed land.

B. Design and Field Layout

Mechanical structures should be specifically designed to modify slopes, to control the velocity and direction of runoff, and to check the runoff as it moves off the recontoured spoil material. The field layout should also provide for sufficient runoff and sediment catchment area. Thames and Verma (1975) indicated that if mechanical treatments were applied to contain a 25-year storm where it fell on-site, assuming 40% runoff efficiency, considerable effort and expense would be involved in the field design and layout. For example, it would be necessary to construct 14,000 pits, or 60 contour furrows, or 495 basins per ha. Under

---

[1] T. R. Verma and J. L. Thames. 1976. Water harvesting potential on surface-mined lands on Black Mesa, Arizona. Soil Conserv. Soc. Annual Meet., Southern Sec., Mobile, Ala. 2–4 Feb. 1976.

favorable conditions the life expectancy of these treatments is in the order of 3 or 4 years.

The design and field layout of runoff retention measures should be based on hydrologic conditions, proper land management, post-reclamation land use, and other reclamation requirements of the area. Depending upon the slope conditions and post reclamation land use, grading and shaping of the disturbed areas may call for the field design and layout of more than one soil and water conservation measure. For example, contour furrows and pitting could be used to substantiate the effectiveness of contour terraces in controlling soil erosion and runoff on steep and long slopes. Mechanical surface manipulations such as listering and gouging could be used to increase runoff retention and to reduce erosion on relatively level landscapes.

Intensive data on hydrologic parameters of the disturbed area should be used to estimate quantity of runoff retention. Factors such as the intensity, duration, distribution of precipitation, and the infiltration rates of the spoil material should be considered for the design and field layout of the soil and water conservation measures.

Major soil and water conservation measures used to reduce gradients and slope lengths to a degree that will provide mechanical stability can be made more effective when used with conservation tillage, mulching, and cultural practices.

Water spreading, water harvesting, and supplemental irrigation systems add to the available soil moisture for vegetative establishment. The design and field layout of these systems require careful planning. Their failure may cause serious erosion and flood problems.

C. Maintenance

Proper maintenance of the soil and water conservation measures should be a crucial phase of the reclamation plan. Most of the runoff retention measures are temporary and should be maintained long enough to facilitate effective vegetative establishment on the disturbed areas. Failure of the runoff water retention measures in one part of the watershed may cause serious damage to the measures in the other downslope parts. Design and field layout defects that may appear after the first rainfall event should be corrected immediately. Negligence in proper maintenance of runoff water retention systems may result in much heavier costs later. Maintenance costs are usually high in the beginning but decline to a fairly low figure after an effective vegetative establishment. Grazing is the most common post-reclamation land use in the arid and semiarid regions. Restricted or controlled grazing practices would result in low maintenance costs.

IV. FINAL CONTOUR

Final contour or final cut could be left open for water storage on the site. In some states legislation forbids the use of final cut for water storage. Water quality of the surface runoff from the recontoured catchment area should be evaluated before regrading the final cut for water storage. Site planning for the final cut should be based upon post-reclamation land use of the disturbed area; for example, if the post-reclamation land use is grazing then the final cut could be used for water storage for livestock.

Final cut should be graded and shaped to stable slope conditions. The grading and shaping of the final cut should provide such depth that, after evaporation losses occur, sufficient water will remain to supply the demand. Minimum depth should be 4 m in the arid and semiarid conditions. The minimum depth of water should extend over an area equal to at least one-sixteenth, and if possible, up to one-fourth of the surface area. In the arid and semiarid regions, there should be enough catchment area to supply surface runoff for the pond created by grading the final cut. It should be properly compacted and sealed to reduce high seepage losses.

Final cut can also be used as a fresh water body for recreational, fisheries, or irrigational uses.

V. EROSION CONTROL

A. Water Erosion

Soil erosion by water is a complex natural process that is affected by numerous interrelated factors. Drastic land disturbances result in a landscape that is devoid of vegetation and much more vulnerable to the action of erosive agents, rainfall, and runoff.

Splash, sheet, rill, and gully are the most common types of soil erosion by water on recontoured spoil materials and other drastically disturbed areas. Land slides and mass movements are also found on some steep and unstable slopes. Deposition and sedimentation are the end results of these erosion processes. A number of treatments are applicable for erosion control on disturbed lands of the arid and semiarid regions. Minor grading and shaping modification of the recontoured spoil materials or of the regraded disturbed areas, when used in combination with erosion control treatments, are effective in controlling soil erosion and sedimentation processes and help in the establishment and maintenance of vegetation. The following treatments are used for the prevention and control of water erosion on the disturbed lands of semiarid and arid regions.

1. MECHANICAL TREATMENTS

Mechanical structures can provide both temporary and permanent measures for erosion control by reducing and modifying the energy involved in the erosion process. Their main emphasis should be on prevention of erosion rather than on cosmetic treatment. Structural measures include diversions, waterways, buried outlets, terraces, berms, numerous types of grade control structures, chutes, retarding structures, and debris basins. In the arid and semiarid regions, erosion control measures should be aimed at slope stability and soil moisture conservation to facilitate effective vegetative establishment for erosion control. Design and field lay-out of the mechanical structures for erosion control should be a part of a reclamation plan.

In the arid and semiarid regions, diversions should usually be de-signed for runoff spreading and retention. Their purpose is to intercept surface runoff and divert it in a planned direction at a nonerosive veloci-ty. Diversion structures can be in the form of a swale, terrace, or dike.

Mechanical structures should be properly maintained for their effec-tiveness in erosion control measures.

2. CHEMICAL TREATMENTS

Different types of mulches and soil binders have been used to stabilize the soil surface against erosion. Soil stabilization through the use of these chemicals is mostly temporary and provides effective erosion con-trol until the vegetative establishment. Soil binders can be mixed with mulches for their application on the disturbed areas.

Organic or inorganic mulches applied to the disturbed areas protect the soil against the impact of raindrops, intercept surface runoff, protect the seed, reduce temperature ranges (uniform soil temperatures), and re-duce evaporation. Their application is well known for temporary erosion control measures on agricultural lands.

Soil binders can also be organic or inorganic materials usually in the form of emulsions or aqueous solutions. They penetrate the soil surface.

Plass (1973) reported the effectiveness of mulches and soil stabilizers for erosion control. Rodiek et al. (1976) used a mixture of Silva-fiber and Petroset-SB on regraded abandoned mine spoils and found it effective for erosion control and vegetative establishment.

A mixture of mulches such as wood fiber and soil binders is becoming a common practice for temporary erosion control measures on disturbed areas. The mixture is applied with a hydroseeder. Seeds and fertilizers can also be mixed with the soil binder and mulch for application.

Straw, hay, and different types of fibrous materials are also classified as mulches. Their application varies according to the type of material and the nature of the disturbed areas. Jute, cotton, and paper netting, as well as fiber-glass matting, can be used for temporary erosion control measures on disturbed lands.

3. CULTURAL TREATMENT

Proper land management practices are important for the mainten-ance and effectiveness of mechanical and chemical erosion control meas-ures and for vegetative establishment and successful reclamation of the disturbed lands. These practices include conservation cropping systems, contour tillage, contour cultivation, and proper use of pastures and ranges through controlled or deferred grazing practices. These practices are mostly used in conjunction with the mechanical and chemical erosion control measures.

4. BIOLOGICAL TREATMENTS

Effective vegetation is the key to erosion control and successful reclamation of the disturbed lands. Proper vegetative cover should be achieved through crop and soil management practices. The techniques of revegetation on the disturbed land have been discussed elsewhere in this chapter.

B. Wind Erosion

Wind erosion, also referred to as *soil blowing*, is a serious problem in the arid and semiarid regions. Lack of vegetative cover on disturbed land increases the vulnerability of the land to the erosive action of wind. Low soil moisture, high wind velocities, and exposed soil material on the surface of the recontoured disturbed land, all add to the wind erosion hazard. Wind erosion control measures are necessary to facilitate effective vegetative establishment and maintenance.

Two major types of the wind erosion control measures are used. The first type retards surface wind velocities and the second type affects the soil characteristics.

Wind breaks, shelterbelts, and contour strips are effective in controlling wind erosion by reducing wind velocities at the surface. Shrubs and trees for wind breaks and shelterbelts should be planted as early as possible. Supplemental irrigation systems can be used for getting these vegetative barriers established.

Soil management practices such as mulching, use of soil binders, controlled grazing, tillage, and conservation farming should be used for soil moisture conservation and for the improvement of soil structure. These practices, discussed in the earlier part of this chapter, control wind erosion and facilitate vegetative establishment.

VI. CONCLUSIONS

Grading and shaping of the recontoured disturbed land for vegetative establishment and erosion control should be an important part of reclamation plans in the arid and semiarid regions. Soil erosion control measures should be aimed at the on-site conservation of precipitation to facilitate vegetative establishment. Post-reclamation land use should be conducive to soil moisture conservation and erosion control through effective vegetative cover. In the arid and semiarid regions, water is the key factor that determines the success or failure of revegetation efforts. It is alternately a blessing and a threat; the problem is to maximize the one and minimize the other. Grading and shaping of the disturbed land should be aimed at reducing erosive forces of water and retaining it on site for use by vegetation.

LITERATURE CITED

Aldon, E. F., and H. W. Springfield. 1975. Problems and techniques in revegetating coal mine spoil in New Mexico. p. 122–132. In M. K. Wali (ed.). Practices and problems of land reclamation in Western North America. Univ. of North Dakota Press, Grand Forks, N. Dak.

Anderson, D., and A. R. Swanson. 1949. Machinery for seedbed preparation and seeding on Southwestern ranges. J. Watershed Manage. 2:64–66.

Barnes, O. K. 1950. Mechanical treatment on Wyoming range land. J. Range Manage. 3: 198–203.

Branso, F. A., R. F. Miller, and I. S. McQueen. 1966. Contour furrowing, pitting, and ripping on rangelands of the Western United States. J. Range Manag. 19:182–190.

Hodder, R. L. 1975. Montana reclamation problems and remedial techniques. p. 90–106. In M. K. Wali (ed.) Practices and problems of land reclamation in Western North America. Univ. of North Dakota Press, Grand Forks, N. Dak.

Hubbard, W. A., and S. Smoliak. 1953. Effect of contour dykes and furrows on short grass prairie. J. Range Manag. 6:55–62.

Moldenhauer, W. C., and M. Amemiya. 1969. Tillage practices for controlling cropland erosion. J. Soil Water Conserv. 24:19–21.

Plass, W. T. 1973. Chemical soil stabilizers for surface mine reclamation. In Soil erosion: causes and mechanisms, prevention and control. Highway Res. Bd., Spec. Rep. 135: 118–122.

Rodiek, J., T. R. Verma, and J. L. Thames. 1976. Disturbed land rehabilitation in Lynx Creek Watershed. J. Landsc. Plan. 2:265–282.

Stringham, G. E. 1975. Watershed rehabilitation: cultural and mechanical considerations. p. 91–104. In J. L. Thames and J. N. Fischer (ed.) Watershed management in arid zones. School of Renewable Nat. Resour., Univ. of Arizona, Tucson, Ariz.

Thames, J. L., and T. R. Verma. 1975. Coal mine reclamation on the Black Mesa and Four Corners areas of Northeastern Arizona. p. 48–64. In M. K. Wali (ed.) Practices and problems of land reclamation in Western North America. Univ. of North Dakota Press, Grand Forks, N. Dak.

Verma, T. R., and J. L. Thames. 1975. Rehabilitation of land disturbed by mining coal in Arizona. J. Soil Water Conserv. 30:129–131.

Viets, F. G., Jr. 1966. Increasing water use efficiency by soil management. p. 259–274. In W. H. Pierre, D. Kirkham, J. Pesek, and R. H. Shaw (eds.) Plant environment and efficient water use. Am. Soc. of Agron., Madison, Wis.

Wight, J. R., and F. H. Siddoway. 1972. Improving precipitation-use efficiency on rangeland by surface modifications. J. Soil Water Conserv. 27:170–174.

Copyright © 1978 ASA–CSSA–SSSA
677 South Segoe Road, Madison, WI 53711 USA
Reclamation of Drastically Disturbed Lands

Chapter 23

Plant Materials and Requirements for Growth in Dry Regions

A. A. THORNBURG AND S. H. FUCHS

Soil Conservation Service, USDA
Lincoln, Nebraska and Portland, Oregon

I. INTRODUCTION

The rate of land disturbance for many purposes has increased rapidly during the past few years. The public demands that disturbed areas be returned to beneficial uses, that environmental quality be maintained or improved, and that reclaimed areas be aesthetically pleasing. The criteria for selection of species for the dry regions of the United States are discussed. Also treated are some of the principles concerned with selection and use of introduced species compared with native plants and the composition of mixtures.

II. DESCRIPTION OF THE AREA

The dry regions, for the purpose of this chapter, are considered to approximate the subhumid, semiarid, and arid climatic provinces of the United States as described by Thornthwaite (1931). These include most of the western U.S. bordered on the east from central Wisconsin through eastern Texas. Within this area annual precipitation ranges from less than 15 to more than 115 cm. The frost-free period may be less than 90 days to yearlong, and the temperature regimen may be cool, warm, or tropical. Moisture varies from adequate at all seasons, to deficient at all seasons, to seasonal deficiencies. In addition to these wide ranges of climatic factors, the fluctuations in some areas over a period of years may be great. Thornthwaite (1941) made an analysis of 35 years of data for Jamestown, N.D., which is classified as a dry subhumid climate. He found the climatic distribution to be humid 1 year, moist subhumid 15 years, dry subhumid 13 years, semiarid 5 years, and arid 1 year.

411

The dry regions have been divided into nine general plant growth regions for the purpose of discussing species adaptation. These are described in Section VII.

III. CRITERIA FOR SELECTION OF SPECIES

The selection of the proper species for any planting should be based on the climate and soils, and on the use and management planned. Good (1953) points out that plant distribution is controlled primarily by climate and secondarily by edaphic factors, and that plant functions are limited by definite ranges of tolerances for particular factors. The limiting factors are increased, or at least accentuated, in dry climates, with moisture and its seasonal availability being most critical. The water-holding capacity of the soil affects the composition of the natural vegetation. This is more pronounced in the subhumid and semiarid areas than in humid areas or in extremely dry climates. In arid regions many soil and site characteristics and their interactions, such as slope, exposure, toxic conditons, and biotic relationships, become critical limiting factors.

There are fewer alternatives for land use in dry areas as compared with humid areas; however, within the dry regions opportunities for most land uses occur. On any one site the alternatives may be limited. The availability of plant materials may dictate the land use on some sites, rather than the usual situation where species are chosen for a selected land use.

Many tools are available as guidelines for selection of species. Descriptions of natural vegetation have been prepared for most regions. Kuchler (1964) mapped the potential natural vegetation of the conterminous United States. Additional guidance on species is provded by Dice (1943) in his descriptions of the biotic provinces of North America. The plant growth regions of F. L. Mulford, as published in Van Dersal (1939), provided the principal criteria for the selection of regions treated in this paper.

Cold tolerance of plants is a primary consideration. The *Plant Hardiness Zone Map* published by the U.S. Department of Agriculture-Agricultural Research Service (1960), delineates hardiness zones based primarily on minimum temperatures. The cold hardiness ratings for many species of woody plants are listed.

The major land resource areas described by Austin (1965) provide an excellent basis for delineating areas of adaptation of plants. Though vegetation is not described, land resource regions are separated into 156 major land resource areas. These areas are characterized by particular patterns of soil, climate, water resources, and land use.

Rehabilitation-response units for reclamation of surface-mined areas in Montana and Wyoming were described by Packer (1974). These units were based on the characteristics of the soils, suitability and availability of native species, and the amount and distribution of precipitation. The soil associations of the Great Plains as described by Aandahl (1972) provided the basic units.

The major soil limitations for vegetative purposes are: droughtiness, fine textures, claypan soils, wetness, salinity, alkalinity, acidity, shallow depth, and toxicity or severe nutrient imbalance. Slope, stoniness, degree of erosion, and the amount of surface materials available for reclamation, are also important within the climatic range of adaptation of each species.

The objective in many reclamation plantings in the drier regions appears to be to return the area to climax vegetation. In almost every instance the soils are not the same as before the disturbance occurred, and it would seem in many cases that species lower in the successional stage may be better adapted and more easily established. A discussion of some of the species adapted to different regions is included in Section VII.

IV. ADAPTED ECOTYPES AND CULTIVARS

The concept of ecotypes as developed by Tureson (1922) is well established. The common definition is that an *ecotype* is a population of plants that has become genetically differentiated in response to the conditions of a particular habitat. Each ecotype reflects the conditions of elevation, precipitation, temperature, growing season, and soil and site conditions of its origin.

Some species have restricted ranges of adaptation, others may be found over large areas. A widely distributed species may occupy many sites or be restricted to specific types of soils or moisture conditions within its range. The species as a whole is almost invariably made up of numerous ecotypes, often with narrow ranges of adaptation. Though some ecotypes or developed cultivars may grow over a wide range, satisfactory performance may be restricted and the establishment of a self-perpetuating stand may be limited to a small area or to specific sites.

Where improved adapted materials are not available, the experience of the Soil Conservation Service, as reported by Copper (1957), has been that an ecotype can be moved about 400 to 500 km north or 150 to 250 km south of the point of origin to areas of comparable soils and climate and give satisfactory performance. Movement east or west may be greater or less, depending on changes in elevation and precipitation. Some species have wider ecological amplitude and appear to perform satisfactorily over wider ranges of conditions. Materials moved farther from the point of origin do not maintain themselves in competition with either the local ecotypes of the same species or with other species. The most noticeable responses are that plants moved northward grow a larger proportion of the available growing season than local ecotypes and are generally leafier. They perform well until moved too far north to produce a seed or fruit crop, or when they suffer winter injury. As plants are moved south they do not utilize the growing season available, are usually less vigorous, and are more susceptible to disease.

The selection of the proper ecotype or cultivar is as important as the species selection. The cultivars of native plants are mostly selected ecotypes that exhibit superior performance for defined areas. The areas of adaptation follow the principles for those of native ecotypes, though the range of adaptation is often greater.

V. SINGLE SPECIES VERSUS MIXTURES

Whether a single species or a mixture is selected depends on several factors, including the planned use, the desire to have the planting blend with the surrounding vegetation, and whether more than one species is available for the planned use on the site. Public demand, or legislation in some states, may be addressed to diversity. Compatibility of species becomes important. The limiting factors for obtaining success on disturbed areas will probably be different on the site to be reclaimed than on the adjacent undisturbed area, where a number of species may be growing together in what appears to be a stable community. The adjacent area is often made up of several plant communities and, even where the same species are represented, they may occur in different proportions. The reclaimed area will not, under the most careful procedures, be the same as before the disturbance. Species interactions are complex, and species that may be compatible on one site may not be, at least to the same degree, on a different site.

The composition of a plant community, though appearing to be stable, may change over a short period of time. Weaver and Albertson (1944) found that in Kansas the character of the plant community was severely modified by drought. In one study the importance of little bluestem (see a complete list of plant species in Table 1) declined from approximately 80% of the ground cover in 1932 to 4% in 1937. Sideoats grama and blue grama increased from insignificant amounts to make up, respectively, 60 and 30% of the cover in 1939. Coupland (1958) reviewed many studies of the Great Plains and concluded that a complete description of a vegetation type should include an indication of the extent to which it may progress in favoring the mid-grasses during moist periods, and the short grasses during droughty ones. Otherwise the same community may be variously characterized by different workers at different times. It was concluded by Savage and Costello (1948) that the survival of native species in disturbed areas does not always follow the same trends as in undisturbed areas. They found that naturally regrassed, abandoned farm lands withstood the effects of the 1933 to 1936 drought much better than did the vegetation on adjacent rangeland that had never been plowed.

The selection of aesthetically pleasing materials may also be of a single species or a mixture. Selection for appearance is important, since public approval will be based largely on appearance rather than the effectiveness for the planned use. The concept of what is attractive will vary with the experience of the viewer. Some persons prefer a site that is planted to a single species that is maintained in a manicured condition, or is of uniform height, color, and texture. Others abhor anything except a diverse cover that does not contrast with the surrounding area, which may or may not be natural. Though some prefer diversity, it is suspected that a majority of lay people more readily accept a uniform cover.

Table 1—Plant species available for reclamation†

Common name	Scientific name
Catclaw	*Acacia greggii* A. Gray
Thickspike wheatgrass	*Agropyron dasystachyum* (Hook.) Scribn.
Crested wheatgrass	*Agropyron desertorum* (Fisch.) Schult.
Tall wheatgrass	*Agropyron elongatum* (Host) Beauv.
Beardless wheatgrass	*Agropyron inerme* (Scribn. & Smith) Rydb.
Intermediate wheatgrass	*Agropyron intermedium* (Host) Beauv.
Streambank wheatgrass	*Agropyron riparium* Scribn.
Siberian wheatgrass	*Agropyron sibiricum* (Willd.) Beauv.
Western wheatgrass	*Agropyron smithii* Rydb.
Bluebunch wheatgrass	*Agropyron spicatum* (Pursh) Scribn. & Smith
Slender wheatgrass	*Agropyron trachycaulum* (Link) Malte
Pubescent wheatgrass	*Agropyron trichophorum* (Link) Richt.
European black alder	*Alnus glutinosa* (L.) Gaertn.
Creeping foxtail	*Alopecurus arundinaceus* Poir.
Caucasian bluestem	*Andropogon caucasicus* Trin.
Big bluestem	*Andropogon gerardi* Vitman
Yellow bluestem	*Andropogon ischaemum* L.
Seacoast bluestem	*Andropogon littoralis* Nash
Silver bluestem	*Andropogon saccharoides* Swartz
Little bluestem	*Andropogon scoparius* Michx.
Threeawns	*Aristida* spp. L.
Sagebrush	*Artemisia* spp. L.
Big sagebrush	*Artemisia tridentata* Nutt.
Saltbush	*Atriplex* spp. L.
Fourwing saltbush	*Atriplex canescens* (Pursh) Nutt.
Nuttall saltbush	*Atriplex nuttallii* Wats.
Goldfields	*Baeria chrysostoma* Fisch. & Mey.
Gramagrass	*Bouteloua* spp. Lag.
Sideoats grama	*Bouteloua curtipendula* (Michx.) Torr.
Black grama	*Bouteloua eriopoda* (Torr.) Torr.
Blue grama	*Bouteloua gracilis* (H.B.K.) Lag.
Smooth brome	*Bromus inermis* Leyss.
Soft chess	*Bromus mollis* L.
Buffalograss	*Buchloe dactyloides* (Nutt.) Engelm.
Prairie sandreed	*Calamovilfa longifolia* (Hook.) Scribn.
Siberian peashrub	*Caragana arborescens* Lam.
Hackberry	*Celtis* spp. L.
Common hackberry	*Celtis occidentalis* L.
Big sandbur	*Cenchrus myosuroides* H.B.K.
Rubber rabbitbrush	*Chrysothamnus nauseosus* (Pall.) Britt.
Silky dogwood	*Cornus amomum* Mill.
Red-osier dogwood	*Cornus stolonifera* Michx.
Crownvetch	*Coronilla varia* L.
Orchardgrass	*Dactylis glomerata* L.
Desert saltgrass	*Distichlis stricta* (Torr.) Rydb.
Russian-olive	*Elaeagnus angustifolia* L.
Autumnolive	*Elaeagnus umbellata* Thunb.
Sand lovegrass	*Eragrostis trichodes* (Nutt.) Wood
California poppy	*Eschscholtzia californica* Cham.
Winterfat	*Eurotia lanata* (Pursh) Moq.
Tall fescue	*Festuca arundinacea* Schreb.
Idaho fescue	*Festuca idahoensis* Elmer
Hard fescue	*Festuca ovina duriuscula* (L.) Koch
Tarbush	*Flourensia cernua* DC
Ocotillo	*Fouquieria splendens* Engelm.
Triangle bur-sage	*Franseria deltoidea* Torr.

(continued on next page)

Table 1—continued

Common name	Scientific name
White bur-sage	*Franseria dumosa* A. Gray
Green ash	*Fraxinus pennsylvanica* Marsh.
Spiny hopsage	*Grayia spinosa* (Hook.) Moq.
Tanglehead	*Heteropogon contortus* (L.) Beauv.
Curlymesquite	*Hilaria belangeri* (Steud.) Nash
Big galleta	*Hilaria rigida* (Thurb.) Benth.
Black walnut	*Juglans nigra* L.
Juniper	*Juniperus* spp.
Rocky Mountain juniper	*Juniperus scopulorum* Sarg.
Eastern red cedar	*Juniperus virginiana* L.
Creosotebush	*Larrea divaricata* Cav.
Green sprangletop	*Leptochloa dubia* (H.B.K.) Nees.
Wimmera ryegrass	*Lolium rigidum* Gaud.
Amur honeysuckle	*Lonicera maackii* Maxim.
Tatarian honeysuckle	*Lonicera tatarica* L.
Birdsfoot trefoil	*Lotus corniculatus* L.
Osage-orange	*Maclura pomifera* (Raf.) Schneid.
Siberian crabapple	*Malus baccata* (L.) Borkh.
Manchurian crabapple	*Malus baccata mandschurica* (Maxim.) Schneid.
Alfalfa	*Medicago sativa* L.
White sweetclover	*Melilotus alba* Desr.
Bush muhly	*Muhlenbergia porteri* Scribn.
Indian ricegrass	*Oryzopsis hymenoides* (Roem. & Schult.) Ricker
Blue panicgrass	*Panicum antidotale* Retz.
Kleingrass	*Panicum coloratum* L.
Vine-mesquite	*Panicum obtusum* H.B.K.
Switchgrass	*Panicum virgatum* L.
Buffelgrass	*Pennisetum ciliare* (L.) Link.
Reed canarygrass	*Phalaris arundinacea* L.
Timothy	*Phleum pratense* L.
Pines	*Pinus* sp. L.
Pinyon pine	*Pinus edulis* Engelm.
Ponderosa pine	*Pinus ponderosa* Laws.
Indianwheat	*Plantago* sp. L.
Big bluegrass	*Poa ampla* Merr.
Kentucky bluegrass	*Poa pratensis* L.
Poplars	*Populus* sp. L.
Black cherry	*Prunus serotina* Ehrh.
Chokecherry	*Prunus virginiana* L.
Oaks	*Quercus* sp. L.
Skunkbush sumac	*Rhus trilobata* Nutt.
Natalgrass	*Rhynchelytrum roseum* (Nees) Stapf. & Hubb.
Black locust	*Robinia pseudoacacia* L.
Willows	*Salix* sp. L.
Plains bristlegrass	*Setaria macrostachya* H.B.K.
Silver buffaloberry	*Shepherdia argentea* (Pursh) Nutt.
Indiangrass	*Sorghastrum nutans* (L.) Nash
Alkali sacaton	*Sporobolus airoides* (Torr.) Torr.
Green needlegrass	*Stipa viridula* Trin.
Crinkleawn	*Trachypogon montufari* (H.B.K.) Nees
Arizona cottontop	*Trichachne californica* (Benth) Chase
Two-flower trichloris	*Trichloris crinita* (Lag.) Parodi
Rose clover	*Trifolium hirtum* All.
Crimson clover	*Trifolium incarnatum* L.
Black haw	*Viburnum prunifolium* L.
Woolypod vetch	*Vicia dasycarpa* Tenore
Yucca	*Yucca* spp. L.

† The authorities are from Soil Conservation Service, USDA. 1971. National list of scientific plant names. 282 p.

Even after the species have been selected, the proportionate amounts are not easily determined. The successful experiences of the past 30 to 40 years of seeding range mixtures and planting critical areas appears to be the best guide to the opportunities for success of either a single species or mixtures. As more species, especially of forbs and shrubs, become available, their evaluation in mixtures will need to be made, especially of the proportionate amounts of each.

VI. INTRODUCED VERSUS NATIVE SPECIES

The debate continues over the merits of introduced and native species of plants. The use of introduced species for reclamation of disturbed areas is a controversial subject in many parts of the western U.S.; however, introduced species are readily accepted in humid areas. Legislation may specify that disturbed areas be returned to a diverse cover of native plants. Some groups are so fervent in their demands for native vegetation that to suggest an introduced species borders on the subversive. This has on occasion resulted in unadapted ecotypes of native species being used instead of adapted introduced species. Such a philosophy imposes limitations on the uses that can be made of an area to be reclaimed.

There is some justification for the opposition to introduced species, because some are relatively short-lived in the arid and semiarid climates. Reestablishment may be hazardous, especially on fragile sites, and it is important that long-lived or self-perpetuating stands be obtained. The condemnation of all introduced species is not justified. Some introduced species, such as crested wheatgrass and pubescent wheatgrass, have performed well for decades. Tall wheatgrass has been superior to any native species on many saline sites.

Cover to reduce erosion and sedimentation has been the primary consideration in reclamation activities, as it should be; however, agricultural production needs to receive more attention. Introduced species generally exhibit greater agronomic potential, such as response to fertility and management. Where irrigation is to be a continued practice on reclaimed areas, introduced species have greater production potential. There are also opportunities in semi-arid and subhumid areas, where sufficient moisture is available, to develop good, producing dry-land pastures of introduced species.

Introduced species generally exhibit a greater range of adaptation to soils and climate; however, they also require a higher level of management to provide long-term protection. Species selection may be more dependent on availability than desirability for some sites and areas. Seed and planting stock of introduced plants are more readily available. This situation is improving as the U.S. Department of Agriculture Soil Conservation Service plant materials centers, and other agencies and universities have accelerated selection and development of native grasses, forbs, and woody plants.

In conclusion there is a place for both adapted introduced and adapted native plants for reclaiming disturbed lands. Species selection should be based on the use planned and on the specific site conditions, not on whether a plant is introduced or native.

VII. ADAPTED SPECIES FOR SELECTED REGIONS

The drier portions of the United States are divided into nine plant growth regions for the purposes of this paper. The primary guides for these delineations were Thornthwaite's climatic provinces and Mulford's plant growth regions. A complete list of plants available for reclamation of disturbed lands in this area would number into the hundreds. Adaptation of species to precipitation zones and soil textures is the most common method for recommending species and cultivars; however, this is not practical for large geographic areas, because precipitation distribution and effectiveness differ, and adaptation to temperature and other climatic factors becomes limiting.

Examples of species that have exhibited satisfactory performance in each plant growth region are noted. Little attempt has been made to name cultivars or their ranges of adaptation. The species were selected from performance in field plantings conducted by the U.S. Department of Agriculture, Soil Conservation Service, results of research by other agencies and universities, and from descriptions of native vegetation. Hafenrichter (1958) presented considerable information on adaptation of species and cultivars for major regions of the United States. The species, including cultivars, that have been most useful in the Pacific Northwest and the intermountain areas of the western U.S. were treated by Hafenrichter et al. (1968).

A. Western Great Lakes

This region includes Wisconsin, eastern Minnesota, and the western upper peninsula of Michigan. The climate is classified as humid and cool with moisture adequate at all seasons. The annual precipitation is mostly 60 to 75 cm and ranges from 50 to 90 cm. The frost-free period is 100 to 140 days and the average annual temperature 2 to 7°C. the natural vegetation was forest over most of the area.

A large number of species are adapted to the soils and climate of this area. Availability of materials for use on disturbed lands is not a problem. The common grasses, generally used in mixtures with a legume, are tall fescue, smooth brome, and timothy. Kentucky bluegrass and orchardgrass are also well adapted. 'Garrison' creeping foxtail and reed canarygrass perform well on wet sites. The most commonly used legumes are birdsfoot trefoil and crownvetch. Numerous species of woody plants can be used depending on specific site conditons. Siberian crabapple, several species of poplars, tatarian and Amur honeysuckles, silky dogwood, red-osier dogwood, European black alder, black cherry, and green ash perform well. Autumnolive is adapted to the southern portion of this area.

B. Northern and Central Prairies

This is the region known as the *Corn Belt* and *true prairie*. The vegetation was formerly hardwood forest interspersed with tall grass prairie. The climate is subhumid, cool in the northern portion to warm in the remainder of the area, with moisture generally adequate at all seasons. The annual precipitation is mostly 60 to 75 cm, but ranges from 50 to 115 cm. The frost-free period is between 140 and 180 days. The average annual temperature ranges from 7 to 13°C.

A number of introduced and native plants are available for this area and can be selected according to the planned use. Introduced grasses adapted to the area are Kentucky bluegrass, tall fescue, smooth brome, timothy, and orchardgrass. Reed canarygrass is adapted to wet areas. Switchgrass, big bluestem, and Indiangrass are well adapted warm season natives. Birdsfoot trefoil, crownvetch, and alfalfa are commonly used legumes.

Woody species that have been successful include autumnolive, European black alder, poplar species, tatarian honeysuckle, Amur honeysuckle, black cherry, eastern red cedar, pines, oaks, black walnut, green ash, black locust, black haw, and osage-orange.

C. Northern Great Plains

This plant growth region includes most of the Dakotas and Nebraska west to the foothills of the Rocky Mountains and includes northeastern Colorado. The climate is mostly semiarid and cool with a moisture deficiency at all seasons. The elevation ranges from about 450 to 1,800 m. The annual precipitation is between 25 and 60 cm and the frost-free period is 100 to 160 days. The average annual temperature is about 7°C. The natural vegetation is mostly cool season grasses.

The native wheatgrass—western, thickspike, bluebunch, streambank, and slender—are used extensively in mixtures. Western wheatgrass should be included in most mixtures, although for special purposes thickspike or streambank wheatgrass are more appropriate. Named cultivars are available of several native species and adapted ecotypes from harvests of native stands are available for others. Blue grama performs well for cover but is generally not available. Green needlegrass is an important component of mixtures except in the drier portions. On favorable sites big bluestem, little bluestem, and switchgrass provide opportunities for color or for a different season of use. Prairie sandreed is adapted to sandy soils throughout the region. 'Garrison' creeping foxtail and reed canarygrass are adapted to wet sites.

Crested wheatgrass has been used extensively and is long-lived in this climate. Intermediate and pubescent wheatgrasses are useful as introduced pastures. The use of smooth brome and tall fescue is limited to the eastern portions of the Northern Great Plains where the annual precipitation exceeds 50 cm. Alfalfa and white sweetclover are the only legumes used in most of the area for reclamation plantings.

Many native and introduced woody plants are adapted for conservation plantings. Fallowing to provide additional moisture is required for establishment of most woody plants and cultivation must be continued for satisfactory performance of all but a few native shrubs. These practices are not compatible with most reclamation objectives, limiting the use of woody species to favorable moisture situations. Some woody plants useful in this area, if moisture and management are provided, are Russian-olive, green ash, skunkbush sumac, Siberian crabapple, Manchurian crabapple, silver buffaloberry, tatarian honeysuckle, chokecherry, Siberian peashrub, Rocky Mountain juniper, and willow species.

D. Southern Great Plains

The Southern Great Plains, for the purposes of this chapter, are considered to be the area from southcentral Nebraska and southeastern Colorado to central Texas. The climate is mostly semi-arid and warm, with moisture deficient at all seasons. The annual precipitation is mostly 50 to 75 cm. The frost-free period is mostly 160 to 180 days but ranges from 150 to 240 days. The average annual temperature is 10 to 18°C. The native vegetation is mostly warm season grasses.

The most common native grasses of value in reclaiming drastically disturbed lands include big bluestem, little bluestem, Indiangrass, switchgrass, buffalograss, blue grama, sideoats grama, and sand lovegrass. Introduced Old World bluestems such as yellow bluestem, Caucasian bluestem, and introduced Kleingrass, blue panicgrass, and buffelgrass are important in the southern and central portions of this plant growth region. Alfalfa and white sweetclover are the most commonly used legumes. Russian-olive is a satisfactory woody species in the northern portions and along the foothills of the Rocky Mountains. Junipers, hackberry, and shunkbush sumac are important native species. Osage-orange is well adapted to the eastern part of this area. Desirable woody plants require special management for use on most drastically disturbed lands.

E. Southern Plains

This area is the Rio Grande Plains of south and southwest Texas. The climate is semi-arid to arid and warm with a deficiency of moisture at all seasons. The elevation is from sea level to about 700 m. The annual precipitation is 35 to 65 cm. The frost-free period is 220 to 240 days. The average annual temperature is between 16 and 21°C. The native vegetation was originally grassland and savannah, but the area now has a severe brush problem.

The characteristic grasses on sandy soils are seacoast bluestem, two-flower trichloris, silver bluestem, big sandbur, and tanglehead. The dominants on clay and clay loams are silver bluestem, Arizona cottontop, buffalograss, curlymesquite, and grama grasses. Indiangrass, switchgrass, seacoast bluestem, and crinkleawn are common in the oak savannahs.

Old World bluestems, such as yellow and Caucasian bluestems, are satisfactory only where additional moisture is made available. Natalgrass and two-flower trichloris have shown promise in reclamation plantings.

F. Southern Plateaus

This semi-arid to arid, cool to warm climatic area has a deficiency of moisture at all seasons. The area is made up of the 750- to 2,400-m plateaus of western Texas, New Mexico, and Arizona. The frost-free period ranges from 120 to 240 days and the average annual temperature is between 10 and 18°C. The annual precipitation averages from 25 to 50 cm. The area includes a large variety of ecological conditions resulting in many plant associations. Creosote-tarbush desert shrub, grama grassland, yucca and juniper savannahs, pinyon pine, oak, and some ponderosa pine associations occur. Little bluestem, sideoats grama, green sprangletop, Arizona cottontop, bush muhly, plains bristlegrass, vine-mesquite, blue grama, black grama and many other species are common and are useful in reclamation plantings, depending on the site and elevation.

G. Intermountain Desertic Basins

This plant growth region occupies the extensive intermountain basins from southern Nevada and Utah north through Washington, and includes the basin areas of Wyoming. It is a semiarid and cool climate with moisture deficient at all seasons. The precipitation over most of the area is greater in the winter. The elevation ranges from about 600 to 2,400 meters. The average annual precipitation is from 12 to 50 cm and the frost-free period 100 to 160 days. The average annual temperature is 7 to 13°C. The natural vegetation ranges from almost pure stands of short grasses to desert shrub. There are extensive areas dominated by big sagebrush or other sagebrush species.

A wide variety of species of grasses is available for this area, though for some sites the alternatives are few. Among the most commonly used species are the introduced Siberian wheatgrass, crested wheatgrass, intermediate wheatgrass, pubescent wheatgrass, tall wheatgrass, and hard fescue. Native grasses used include bluebunch wheatgrass, beardless wheatgrass, big bluegrass, Idaho fescue, and Indian ricegrass. Four-wing and Nuttall saltbush have performed well in trials. Woody species are limited, though junipers, Russian-olive, shunkbush sumac, and other native and introduced woody plants are adapted to the climate where moisture is adequate.

H. Desert Southwest

This is the desert of southwestern Arizona, southern Nevada, and southern California. The climate is arid, warm to tropical, and moisture is deficient at all seasons. The average annual precipitation ranges from less than 12 to 25 cm and the average annual temperatures from 16 to 24°C. The frost-free period averages 240 days and may exceed 340 days. The elevation is from below sea level to about 1,200 m.

Creosotebush may occur in almost pure stands or with tarbush. Triangle bur-sage, white bur-sage, rubber rabbitbrush, and ocotillo are prominent on some sites. Large numbers of annual and perennial forbs are present. Saltbushes, winterfat, and spiny hopsage are common. The few grasses present in the understory are largely big galleta, desert saltgrass, grama grasses, and species of threeawns.

Only minor success has been obtained in establishing vegetation on disturbed lands in the desert Southwest. Irrigation for establishment may be essential in some areas, and the longevity of stands when irrigation is discontinued is not known. Big galleta and bush muhly show promise. Native shrubs such as creosotebush, fourwing saltbush, and catclaw have also been established. Reseeding annuals such as goldfields, California poppy, and Indianwheat have also shown promise.

I. California Valleys

The climate of the central California Valleys is classified as semiarid to arid and warm and the moisture is deficient at all seasons. The average annual precipitation is 12 to 25 cm over much of the area and as much as 60 cm in the surrounding higher elevations. The precipitation distribution is characterized by a long dry summer. The average annual temperature is mostly 16 to 24°C but may be 13°C in the north. The frost-free period is 230 to 350 days.

The largest area of grassland lies around the edge of the central valley and is dominated by annual species. The only areas remaining in grass in the valley are usually too alkaline for crop production. The grasses remaining in these sites are desert saltgrass and alkali sacaton.

Recommended for seeding in the area of more than 40 cm annual precipitation is a mixture of 'Luna' pubescent wheatgrass, 'Palestine' orchardgrass, and rose clover. Crimson clover, California poppy, and 'Blando' brome can be added.

Inland in the 30-cm precipitation areas a mixture of 'Blando' brome, Wimmera ryegrass, and 'Lana' woolypod vetch is recommended. In the 15- to 30-cm precipitation zone 'Blando' brome (soft chess) and rose clover are used.

VIII. CONCLUSIONS

Many species have value for the reclamation of drastically disturbed areas in the drier areas of the United States. The selection of adapted ecotypes and adapted cultivars is as important as species selection. Alternative land uses are feasible in much of this area, but the land use for some site conditions may be limited by the availability of planting materials. Each drastically disturbed site should be considered to be unique. Local authorities should be consulted for sources of adapted materials and be relied on for establishment techniques and dates before reclamation is attempted.

LITERATURE CITED

Aandahl, A. R. 1972. Soils of the Great Plains—a detailed map of the soil associations of the Great Plains. P. O. Box 81242, Lincoln, Nebr.

Austin, M. E. 1965. Land resource regions and major land resource areas of the United States. USDA Agric. Handb. no. 296. U.S. Government Printing Office, Washington, D.C.

Cooper, H. W. 1957. Some plant materials and improved techniques used in soil and water conservation in the Great Plains. J. Soil Water Conserv. 12:163–168.

Coupland, R. T. 1958. The effects of fluctuations in weather upon the grasslands of the Great Plains. Bot. Rev. 24:273–317.

Dice, L. R. 1943. The biotic provinces of North America. Univ. Mich. Press, Ann Arbor.

Good, R. D. 1953. The geography of flowering plants. 2nd ed. Longmans, Green and Co., New York.

Hafenrichter, A. L. 1958. New grasses and legumes for soil and water conservation. Adv. Agron. 10:349–406.

Hafenrichter, A. L., J. L. Schwendiman, H. L. Harris, R. S. MacLauchlan, and H. W. Miller. 1968. Grasses and legumes for soil conservation in the Pacific Northwest and Great Basin states. USDA Agric. Handb. no. 339, U.S. Government Printing Office, Washington, D.C.

Kuchler, A. W. 1964. Potential natural vegetation of the conterminous United States. Am. Geog. Soc., New York.

Packer, P. E. 1974. Rehabilitation potentials and limitations of surface-mined land in the northern Great Plains. USDA For. Serv. Gen. Tech. Rep. INT 14., Ogden, Utah.

Savage, D. A., and D. F. Costello. 1948. The southern Great Plains—the region and its needs. p. 503–506. Yrbk Agric., USDA, Washington, D.C.

Thornthwaite, C. W. 1931. The climates of North America according to a new classification. Geog. Rev. 21:633–655.

Thornthwaite, C. W. 1941. Climate and settlement in the Great Plains. Agric. Yrbk., USDA. Washington, D.C. p. 177–187.

Tureson, G. 1922. The genotypical responses of the plant species to habitat. Hereditas 3: 211–350.

U.S. Department of Agriculture-Agricultural Research Service. 1960. Plant hardiness zone map. USDA, Misc. Publ. no. 814, Washington, D.C.

Van Dersal, W. R. 1939. Native woody plants of the United States, their erosion-control and wildlife values. USDA Misc. Publ. 303. Washington, D.C.

Weaver, J. E., and F. W. Albertson. 1944. Nature and degree of recovery of grassland from the great drought of 1933–1940. Ecol. Monogr. 14:393–479.

Copyright © 1978 ASA–CSSA–SSSA
677 South Segoe Road, Madison, WI 53711 USA
Reclamation of Drastically Disturbed Lands

Chapter 24

Revegetation Techniques for Dry Regions

PAUL E. PACKER AND EARL F. ALDON

Forest Service, USDA
Intermountain Forest & Range Experiment Station
Logan, Utah, and
Rocky Mountain Forest & Range Experiment Station
Albuquerque, New Mexico

I. INTRODUCTION

Ever-increasing demands for coal, coupled with technological advancement in extraction techniques, have increased surface mining of coal. Effects on the environment have varied, mainly in degree rather than in kind. Surface coal mining has not been a major contributor to air pollution. Consequences of surface mining have been most noticeable on the land. Vegetation has been destroyed, soils have been turned upside down, and large areas have been left as bare, unsightly spoil banks. Natural beauty and topography have been greatly altered. Some areas have lost their productivity; only a small percentage of strip-mined lands has been restored. Surface mining for coal has polluted surface and ground water resources in those parts of the country where the coal has a high sulfur content. Fortunately, surface mining for coal in the dry regions of the western U.S. is expected to have less serious effect on water resources than that encountered in the eastern coalfields.

Revegetating surface-mined lands involves shaping spoil piles to desirable configurations, application of available surface soil, and planting of suitable vegetation. Major factors influencing success of surface-mine revegetation programs are (i) the chemical, hydrologic, and physical characteristics of reshaped spoil materials as they influence productivity; (ii) the climatic characteristics of the site reflected by amounts and distribution of precipitation and the potential for evapotranspiration; and (iii) the availability of seeds and propagated plant parts of both native and suitable introduced plant species. Current revegetation concepts entail returning sites as nearly as possible to their original condition. Hills and valleys are created to simulate natural variety in the landscape. On drier sites, temporary irrigation can facilitate better or more rapid response of seeded or planted vegetation. Land disturbance involved in re-vegetation treatments often creates conditions conducive to wind and water erosion (for example, soil may be compacted by some of the operations and sediment levels in streams may be temporarily increased). However, environmental damage resulting from revegetation treatments is generally ephemeral and necessary if sites are to be brought to their former or higher productive capacities, to their original or improved vegetation covers, and to their former or more suitable uses.

A. The Semiarid Region—Northern Great Plains

The largest deposit of coal in the semiarid West is the Northern Great Plains Coal Province, which occupies approximately 36.6 million ha and contains about 1.4 trillion metric tons of coal, or about one-half of the nation's total coal resource. Approximately 1 million ha, or 2.8% of the area, are underlain by about 72.8 billion metric tons at depths considered to be mineable from the surface. These 72.8 billion tons constitute about 60% of this country's coal reserves that can be mined from the surface. During the next two decades surface mines may bare an average of more than 4,000 ha/year, which then would require revegetation (Northern Great Plains Resour. Progr. Rep., 1975).

B. The Arid Region—Southwestern Deserts

The principal coalfields in the southwest U.S. are found in southwestern Colorado, in northeastern Arizona at Black Mesa, and in northern New Mexico in the Raton and San Juan Basins. This discussion will be limited to the Black Mesa and San Juan coalfields, both of which are in the Four Corners area where the states of Arizona, Utah, Colorado, and New Mexico meet.

II. ENVIRONMENTAL FACTORS AFFECTING REVEGETATION IN DRY REGIONS

A. The Semiarid Region—Northern Great Plains

1. PRECIPITATION AMOUNT AND DISTRIBUTION

The climate of the Northern Great Plains is semiarid (Thornthwaite, 1931). In the semiarid western U.S., the most important climatic factors determining relative agricultural success are the amount of seasonal precipitation and its distribution. In some years, the amount of precipitation

Table 1—Areas of the Northern Great Plains that can be mined from the surface for coal occur in various precipitation zones

Area	Precipitation zones						
	mm						
	<300	300 to 325	325 to 350	350 to 375	375 to 400	400 to 425	>425
Ha	14,321	224,875	91,451	112,555	334,649	250,333	24,119
%	1.4	21.4	8.7	10.7	31.7	23.8	2.3

and its seasonal distribution are adequate for successful agriculture; in others, precipitation is so reduced that successful crop production is unlikely. In 37 years at several Northern Great Plains stations, observations based upon the precipitation-evaporation index (Thornthwaite, 1941) show no superhumid years: 1 humid year; 1 moist, subhumid year; 5 dry, subhumid years; 25 semiarid years; and 5 arid years. Thornthwaite (1941) wrote: "In the desert, you know what to expect of the climate and plan accordingly. The same is true of the humid regions. Man has been badly fooled by the semiarid regions because they are sometimes humid, sometimes desert, and sometimes a cross between the two. Yet, it is possible to make allowances for this too, once the climate is understood."

Average annual precipitation ranges from about 200 to 600 mm in the western semiarid surface coal mine areas. More than 90% of the area receives between 300 and 425 mm. In the Northern Great Plains, precipitation is heaviest from April to September, providing up to 75% of the annual amount. Summer rains are mostly thunderstorms, usually from the Gulf of Mexico. Prevailing wind is from the west—and the Western Great Plains are noted for their winds, which quickly dry soils in summer and blow snow into drifts in winter. During the growing season, distribution of precipitation is usually favorable, being light in the spring, heavy during the summer, and reduced during the fall. A difference of only 25 mm of rainfall during the growing season can affect significantly the potential for revegetation. Coal areas of the Northern Great Plains that are mineable from the surface occur in various precipitation zones as shown in Table 1 (Packer, 1974).

2. PHYSIOGRAPHY AND GEOLOGY

The Northern Great Plains Coal Province lies entirely within Fenneman's Great Plains Physiographic Province (Fenneman, 1931). The topography is predominantly plains, rolling hills, and some badland areas characterized by breaks or sharply eroded hills. Elevations range from about 1,500 m above sea level on the west to about 600 m along the eastern boundary. Average slope is approximately 2 m/km. Streams drain generally easterly and southeasterly.

Geologic formations containing Northern Great Plains coal consist of 500 to 1,000 m of sandstone, shale, limestone, and conglomerate. Most beds are nearly horizontal. In general, the shallowest overburden and the thickest coal beds are in Wyoming. Overburden becomes progressively thicker and more sodic and coal beds become thinner as one travels from Wyoming northward into eastern Montana and then eastward into North Dakota. Accordingly, surface mining of any given tonnage of coal in eastern Wyoming will disturb a smaller area of land and so will require revegetation of fewer hectares than will the mining of an equivalent tonnage of coal in eastern Montana or western North Dakota.

3. SOIL AND SPOIL CHARACTERISTICS

There are 42 major identifiable soil associations in the Northern Great Plains (Aandahl, 1972). Only 18 of these 42 associations occupy coal areas of the Northern Great Plains that can be mined from the surface. Each of these 18 soil associations has been characterized with respect to its physiography, vegetative productivity, and soil stability (Aandahl, 1972). Table 2 shows that the coal land that can be mined from the surface in the Northern Great Plains occupies soil associations having various physiographic, productivity, and stability characteristics.

Inspection of Table 2 reveals that the soil associations characterized by the gentlest topography and the shallowest slopes generally have the highest vegetative productivity and the best soil stability. These differ-

Table 2—Areas of the Northern Great Plains that can be mined from the surface for coal occupy soil associations having varying physiographic, productivity, and stability characteristics

Soil association characteristics	Soil association numbers (Aandahl, 1972)								
	19	21	23	24	25	26	27	30	31
Topography	Undu-lating	Undu-lating	Undu-lating	Rolling	Rolling	Rolling	Rolling	Rolling	Hilly
Slope steepness (%)	<8	<8	<8	<16	<16	<16	<16	<16	<30
Productivity	Good	Good	Good	Good	Very good	Good	Fairly good	Fairly good	Fair
Stability	Very good	Good	Good	Good	Good	Good	Fair	Fairly good	Poor
Area (thousands of ha)	38.2	7.0	15.1	47.2	101.5	45.2	24.1	35.2	149.7
Area (%) 3.6	3.6	0.7	1.4	4.5	9.7	4.3	2.3	3.3	14.2

	Soil association numbers (Aandahl, 1972)								
	33	35	44	109	111	117	121	123	184
Topography	Hilly	Steep	Hilly	Rolling	Hilly	Rolling	Steep	Hilly	Steep
Slope steepness (%)	<30	>30	<30	<16	<30	<30	>30	<30	>30
Productivity	Fair	Fair	Fairly poor	Very poor	Poor	Poor	Very poor	Poor	Very poor
Stability	Poor	Very poor	Fairly poor	Fair	Fairly poor	Fair	Very poor	Poor	Very poor
Area (thousands of ha)	25.1	58.3	144.7	31.2	6.0	146.7	6.0	131.4	39.2
Area (%)	2.4	5.5	13.8	3.0	0.6	13.9	0.6	12.5	3.7

Table 3—Areas occupied by different vegetation types on Northern Great Plains coal
lands that can be mined from the surface

					Vegetation types				
Area	Flood plain	Bad- lands	Shortgrass prairie	Mid- shortgrass prairie	Midgrass prairie	Sagebrush grassland	Sagebrush steppe	Mid- tallgrass prairie	Ponderosa pine forest
Ha (thousands)	13.1	24.1	60.3	151.7	412.0	246.2	47.2	13.1	84.4
%	1.2	2.3	5.7	14.4	39.2	23.4	4.5	1.2	8.0

ences in soil quality can greatly influence the success of spoil revegetation
following surface mining.

4. VEGETATION TYPES

Grasses dominate the vegetation of the Northern Great Plains Coal
Province. Chief among these are wheatgrasses (*Agropyron* spp.), needle
grasses (*Stipa* spp.), grama grasses (*Bouteloua* spp.), bluestems (*Andropogon* spp.), and fescues (*Festuca* spp.). The cold-desert biome, dominated by sagebrush (*Artemisia* spp.), and the montane-coniferous forest
biome, dominated by ponderosa pine (*Pinus ponderosa* var. *Scopulorum*
Engelm), also occur, especially in the western part of the province. The
deciduous forest biome is represented by cottonwood (*Populus* spp.),
willow (*Salix* spp.), and ash (*Fraxinus* spp.), which dominate the bottom
lands along rivers and their tributaries.

Sixteen broad vegetation types have been recognized in the Northern
Great Plains Coal Province (Kuchler, 1964). Nine of these types occur on
areas where coal is obtainable from the surface (Table 3).

These vegetation types represent the potential for reestablishment of
native plant cover on surface mines where surface soil has been replaced.
In the more moist and fertile portions of the Northern Great Plains,
mostly in North Dakota, agriculture rather than native cover may be used
to revegetate the depleted lands of surface mines. Except for agricultural
uses and for such occasional specialized reclamation opportunities as development of a park, a lake, or a marsh, the greatest potential for rehabilitating surface mines lies in using the native plant species that characterize a given area.

B. The Arid Region—Southwestern Deserts

1. CLIMATE AND WEATHER

The southwestern coalfields under discussion can be characterized
as having an arid continental climate, relatively cloud-free skies, high diurnal temperatures, and infrequent precipitation.

Annual precipitation varies considerably from year to year and ranges from 150 to 200 mm at lower elevations to 300 to 500 mm at higher elevations. About 50% of the total precipitation falls during the summer months—July through October. Spring and fall are drier. April, May, and June are the driest and windiest months. Summer storms are convective, of short duration and high intensity, and occur in the late afternoon. The average monthly precipitation during the winter is about 13 mm, is associated with Pacific frontal activity, and is uniformly distributed.

Winter temperatures vary from a mean maximum of 6 to 7°C to a mean minimum of −1 to −7°C. Summer daily temperatures range from highs of 22 to 30°C, rarely exceeding 38°C, to lows around 14°C.

High and gusty winds occur throughout the year and are generally from the southwest during the windiest season.

2. PHYSIOGRAPHY AND GEOLOGY

The Black Mesa is within the Navajo Indian Reservation in northeastern Arizona. It is a massive and moderately dissected highland covering about 849,870 ha that arises abruptly to a maximum elevation of about 2,469 m along its northern boundary, then descends gently to a plain of rolling hills near the Little Colorado River to the south. It is characterized by high sandstone cliffs overlying Cretaceous rocks. The southern part of the mesa is dissected into box canyons and gently dipping rock platforms (Thames & Verma, 1975).

The mining areas in the San Juan Basin are characterized by broad, gently sloping-to-rolling plains and valleys with locally prominent outcrops of sandstone and shale, mesas, buttes, and ridges. Elevation ranges from 1,524 to 2,134 m. The largest coal deposits are in the Fruitland Formation of Late Cretaceous age. This formation is a sequence of irregular gray, brown, and black shales; tan, yellowish-brown, and white sandstones; and coal. The major coals occur near the base of the formation.

Spoils are leveled to a rolling topography after mining, but before planting. All interior slopes are graded to less than 5%. Spoils from the Fruitland Formation show physical and chemical characteristics as follows (Aldon et al., 1976):

Sand, %	22.7
Silt, %	24.4
Clay, %	52.9
Texture class	Clay
Sodium absorption ratio	40.1
Electrical conductivity of saturation extract (mmhos/cm)	8.0
Determined from saturation extract:	
pH	8.0
Na (ppm in soil)	1,850
Ca (ppm in soil)	141
Mg (ppm in soil)	45
NO_3 (ppm in soil)	68
P (ppm in soil)	8.5

The Navajo Fruitland coalfield, at present the largest and best known coalfield in New Mexico, is defined as the area underlain by coal that can be stripped from the Fruitland Formation within the Navajo Indian Reservation. The coal is of subbituminous rank. Sulfur content averages somewhat less than 0.80%.

Another large area, the Bisti Fruitland area, contains an estimated 1,696 million metric tons of subbituminous high-ash, low-sulfur coal in the Fruitland Formation. This area adjoins the east edge of the Navajo Reservation and lies from 48 to 80 km south of Farmington. It represents the greatest undeveloped reserve in the San Juan Basin (Aldon & Springfield, 1975b).

3. SOIL AND SPOIL CHARACTERISTICS

Most soils on Black Mesa are poorly developed and badly eroded. Organic matter content and plant nutrients are low. Rock outcrops are common. Most soils exhibit pH values in excess of 7.0 and so are on the basic side of neutral (Thames & Verma, 1975).

There are three major kinds of soils in the San Juan Basin: Entisols, Aridisols, and miscellaneous land types. The Entisols and Aridisols occur in close association. Entisols are present on eolian sands, deep alluvium, and on old pediment surfaces. Generally, two great groups of Aridisols recognized in the area (Camborthids and Haplargids) are moderately permeable, deep, and developed over eolian and alluvial sediments. Miscellaneous land types are eroded areas (badlands) that include shale and sandstone outcrops (Gould et al., 1975).

4. VEGETATION TYPES AND ANIMAL LIFE

The sandy soils support an open grassland with a scattering of shrubs. The shaley, saline soils and the thin breaks and badlands support mainly low-growing shrubs. Principal grasses of the area include galleta (*Hilaria jamesii* Benth.), alkali sacaton (*Sporobolus airoides* Torr.), and Indian ricegrass (*Oryzopsis hymenoides* Ricker). Shadscale (*Atriplex confertifolia* [Terr. and Frem.] Wats.) and Nuttall saltbush (*Atriplex nuttallii* Wats.) are the most important shrub species. At higher elevations, pinyons (*Pinus edulis* Engelm) and junipers (*Juniperus* spp.) are found scattered on mesa tops (Aldon & Springfield, 1975b). Where rainfall is from 200 to 300 mm, the area is dominated by big sagebrush (*Artemisia tridentata* Nutt.).

Other common shrubs in both the sagebrush association and the pinyon-juniper association are fourwing saltbush (*Atriplex canescens* [Pursh] Nutt.), Greene rabbitbrush (*Chrysothamnus greenei* [A. Gray] Greene), pale wolfberry (*Lycium pallidum* Miers), and the subshrubs snakeweed (*Gutierrezia sarothrae* [Pursh] Britton and Rusby), and winterfat (*Eurotia lanata* [Pursh] Moq). Greasewood (*Sarcobatus vermiculatus* [Hook.] Torr.) and big rabbitbrush (*Chrysothamnus nauseosus* [Pall.] Britt.) occur on the lowest sites, generally along the many arroyos dissecting the valleys (Earl F. Aldon, unpublished data).

Domestic livestock dominate the animal life on the area. This is the habitat of such small mammals as woodrats, ground squirrels, mice, gophers, and rabbits. Lizards and rattlesnakes also occur. Ravens, sparrows, wrens, quail, jays, doves, and hawks have been seen (Thames & Verma, 1975; Westinghouse Electric Corp., 1975). Deer and antelope are at higher elevations.

5. NATIVE CULTURAL CHARACTERISTICS

Most of the coal-producing lands in Arizona and New Mexico are Indian lands. Mining companies lease from Indian tribes; however, Indian culture creates special problems in the management of reclaimed mine land.

The Taylor Grazing Act, when passed in 1934, provided for 18 grazing districts to be set up within the Navajo Indian Reservation. Chapters were later established within the grazing districts. Chapters are usually tied to such public entities as communities and schools. Houses were built to provide a social setting for the people. The grazing capacity of each district was established by the Taylor Grazing Act. This grazing capacity was divided among and grazing permits were issued to the owners of livestock living there at the time.

Families have increased since the early 1930's, and permits have been divided by probate—when an original permit owner died, the permit was distributed among his surviving heirs. Each heir would then begin with his own established permit. At present, each grazing district elects a grazing committee that manages the grazing affairs of that district. The committee resolves the distribution of grazing rights to members of a particular family within the district. The districts also elect members to the Navajo Tribal Council.

Sheep grazing provides the major source of food and income for these people. When mining begins, grazing stops on the portion of land being mined. Those with grazing rights have no place else to go. They cannot just move their animals down the road because they do not have grazing rights on other families' lands. Occasionally, a family will allow members of their clan to graze part of their unmined lands, but this puts additional pressures on those lands.

Sheepherding, a traditional way of life, is upset when mining begins on leased lands. Of course, people are compensated for improvements on their land that are lost, but they cannot be compensated for loss of their way of life while the land is being mined and for the time it takes to complete reclamation. As a result of wanting to get back on their land as quickly as possible to continue sheepherding, they exert tremendous pressure on the mining companies. Thus, reclamation efforts must be intensified in the southwestern U.S. to return the land to sheep production as quickly as possible.

Occasionally, mining damages significant landmarks or ceremonial sites. In such cases, local residents must decide whether or not to allow mining to proceed.

III. REVEGETATION TECHNIQUES FOR DRY REGIONS

A. The Semiarid Region—Northern Great Plains

1. AMENDMENTS FOR REVEGETATION

Properties of spoils created by mining coal from the surface in semi-arid areas of the western U.S. vary widely. The overburden materials of coal beds and the spoil materials created by removing the overburden are characteristically alkaline, the pH ranging from about 7.2 to 8.5. Coal spoils commonly contain soluble salts, chief among which are sodium, calcium, and magnesium sulfates. Most spoils also contain appreciable quantities of calcium carbonate, but small amounts of readily soluble chlorides, carbonates, or bicarbonates (Sandoval et al., 1973).

These spoils provide a poor environment for growth of desirable vegetation. The poorest environments potentially are where sodic soft shale contains montmorillonitic clays and small amounts of organic matter and is close to the surface. The best environments potentially are those associated with a thick mantle of glacial till, loess, or alluvium overlying coal-bearing shale formations.

Physical and chemical properties of spoils that discourage good plant growth can usually be circumvented or improved. Two basic approaches have been used to treat mine spoils for better plant growth—cover undesirable spoils with suitable soil materials or apply amendments designed to alter the chemical properties of the spoils.

a. **Topsoiling**—The spreading of natural surface soil on spoils has a number of beneficial effects upon revegetation of mined land. It provides fertility not usually encountered in raw spoils. It furnishes a source for renewed microbiological activity to improve soil-building processes. It has better infiltration and soil-stability characteristics. Of concern is the upward migration of sodium from spoils into overlying soil materials. Current research indicates that sodium does migrate, but may not extend past the bottom few centimeters of topsoil. Within the next few years, soil depths required for various amounts of plant production on spoils and topsoil materials possessing different chemical and physical properties should be specified.

b. **Chemical Amendments**—Where suitable topsoil materials are not available to cover spoils, chemical reclamation of raw spoils may be achieved by: (i) replacing sodium adsorbed on clay particles with polyvalent cations (preferably calcium) through base exchange reactions, and (ii) percolating water through the spoils to leach displaced sodium below the root zone. Generally, if gypsum and sulfur are applied to moderately sodic spoils with sodium adsorption ratios of less than 15, revegetation after mining will be successful. For highly sodic spoils, those with sodium adsorption ratios in excess of 15, gypsum and sulfur treatments may reduce the sodium hazard over a period of 3 or 4 years. Research results (Doering & Willis, 1975; Richardson et al., 1975) indicate that effective chemical reclamation of highly sodic spoils by leaching with calcium chloride solution can be achieved in a matter of days.

c. **Organic Amendments**—Sewage sludge, manure, straw, and wood fiber are effective in improving alkaline spoils for plant growth. The organic matter comprising these amendments can tie up sodium, thereby reducing its availability and toxicity to plants. Organic amendments also improve spoil structure and water-holding capacity, and provide plant nutrients (Dean & Haven, 1971; Sutton, 1973). Organic amendments should be tilled into spoils. Growth of roots may be limited initially to the depth of mixing. Several years may be required before the untreated spoils below the zone of mixing improve enough to support plant roots. Mixing of the sewage sludge, manure, and other amendments high in organic matter appears to be almost as suitable for plant growth as replacement of topsoil (Richardson et al., 1975).

2. MULCHES FOR REVEGETATION

Surface mulches of various kinds effectively modify environmental factors to benefit plant growth. Organic surface mulches conserve moisture, reduce temperatures, prevent erosion, and supply organic acids and essential plant nutrients.

Straw, hay, sawdust, wood chips, wood fiber, manure, and sewage sludge are all available in quantities needed for use as mulches on coal strip mines. Effective mulching requires efficient distribution of mulch over the area to be treated and a means for keeping the mulch in place. Several methods can be employed to spread and tack down mulches on mine spoils, even those too steep to accommodate farm machinery. Straw, hay, and sawdust can be blown onto the site with a straw mulcher. Concurrent with spreading, straw and hay can be tacked down by using an asphalt emulsion applicator. Where spoils have slopes of less than 3 to 1, straw and hay can be tacked down by cutting them into the soil with a crimper, thereby simulating a stubble stand. Wood fiber, manure, and sewage sludge can all be applied with a hydromulcher. Numerous chemical stabilizers are available for use in tacking down these mulches as well as improving the surface stability of spoils.

Too much mulch can cause excessive water loss to spoils by interception of precipitation followed by evaporation (Weaver & Rowen, 1952). Deep mulch can also retard the initiation of growth because the soil warms slowly (Hopkins, 1954).

Recent evaluations of the effectiveness of various soil erosion controls (Packer et al., 1976) indicate that straw probably is the most effective and widely used of the mulches commonly employed on highway cuts and fills. Straw is also an effective mulch on coal strip mines in the semiarid coal regions of the West. A straw mulch consisting of about 1,700 to 2,200 kg/ha tacked down with about 2,800 liters/ha of asphalt emulsion is an effective, economical mulching system (Hodder et al., 1970).

3. FERTILIZERS FOR REVEGETATION

Analyses of spoil materials from surface coal mines in the Northern Great Plains have consistently shown nutrient deficiencies, particularly in nitrogen (N) and phosphorus (P) (Sandoval et al., 1973). Spoils in Wyoming and Montana that characterize the drier portions of the Northern Great Plains Coal Province are predominantly deficient in P (Sindelar et al., 1973). On the other hand, spoils in North Dakota that characterize the more moist portion of the Northern Great Plains Coal Province are chiefly deficient in N.

Currently recommended rates for fertilizing topsoiled mine spoils are 84 kg/ha of available N and 112 kg/ha of available P (Hodder & Sindelar, 1972). These rates are capable of producing average herbage yields on 2- and 3-year-old perennial grass stands of from 2,500 to 4,500 kg/ha. These rates of fertilizer application are moderate in relation to rates currently applied to increase forage production on farm and range lands (Heide & Larsen, 1969).

Information on N availability in spoils of western coal mines indicates that production of plants economically on spoils requires continual N fertilization (Power et al., 1974). In eastern Montana, the average yield of fertilized 2-year-old stands of introduced and native grasses on topsoiled spoils was nearly five times greater than the 990 kg/ha produced by undisturbed, unfertilized native range (Richardson et al., 1975). Similar grass stands on fertilized, irrigated, raw spoils produced more than four times the amount on native range. Even fertilized, unirrigated, raw spoils produced two and one-half times the herbage yielded by native range. Other studies have shown that fertilized spoils can produce as much forage as fertilized native range under identical climatic conditions (Hodder & Atkinson, 1974). What is not known is the degree of dependence that vegetation established on mine spoils has on continued fertilization. Long-range nutrient requirements of plant communities on mine spoils still must be determined.

4. SEEDING METHODS FOR REVEGETATION

a. Time of Seeding—Spoils should be seeded immediately ahead of the longest period of favorable growing conditions. Where winter temperatures are low and mine spoils remain bare of snow for long periods, seedlings must either be well established before the winter period or else seeded so late that germination does not occur until spring. Late fall seedings reduce the loss of seed to rodents because many of these animals hibernate (Plummer et al., 1968). Cool-season grasses seeded in late fall are protected by the snowpack. They germinate under snow when temperatures rise above freezing and establish as spring conditions become favorable for growth (Hull, 1960). Spring seeding must frequently be postponed—short periods of good conditions often are interspersed with periods that are either too wet or too dry. Wet spoils, unsuited to heavy equipment, may delay seeding until late spring. Such delays can be detrimental to seedling survival where the summer is hot and dry.

Range seedings are usually restricted to late fall or early spring because late summer and early fall moisture conditions are usually unfavorable for seedling establishment. Late fall seedings are best where mixtures of grass, forbs, and shrubs are used because the winter period provides stratification of the seed. Late fall seedings can be destroyed if the soil is not stabilized by mulching for protection against wind erosion. Early spring seedings in March and, to a lesser degree, in April have produced moderately good stands of vegetation. However, May and September seedings have usually been failures.

b. Seedbed Preparation—Another important element of successful seeding on mine spoils is proper preparation of seedbeds. Most coal mine spoils become compacted and must be ripped or disked and harrowed before seeding. If farm equipment is to be used for these purposes, the steepness of graded spoil dump slopes should not exceed approximately 3 to 1.

c. Seeding Methods—Wherever possible, grass and legume seeds should be drilled. The recommended planting depth is 10 to 20 mm and is best accomplished by using a drill equipped with depth bands and culti-packer wheels.

Broadcast seeding is satisfactory for small or inaccessible areas. The surface should be rough enough for the seed to be covered. Roughening is best accomplished by harrowing or disking. Broadcast seeding is also satisfactory when mine spoils are seeded immediately after they are graded and before the surface has become crusted.

Hydroseeding alone has not usually produced good stands of vegetation on strip mine spoils in semiarid areas. However, where drilling or broadcast seeding are followed by hydrofertilizing and mulching, good stands of vegetation can be obtained.

In general, aerial seedings have not been satisfactory on mine spoils in the semiarid West. If spoil surfaces are rough enough for wind or rain action to cover the seed, satisfactory stands might be obtained, but the uncertainties are great.

d. Seeding Rates—Research and experience have shown that drastically disturbed sites characterized by adverse conditions for plant growth generally require much heavier seeding rates for development of satisfactory stands of vegetation than do sites that have retained their topsoil and some plant cover intact (Cook et al., 1974). The quantity of seed to be planted varies with seeding conditons, species to be planted, and method of seeding. Where gentle north-facing slopes are drilled with grass species charcterized by small seeds, seeding rates of 5 to 6 kg/ha are appropriate. As much as 10 to 12 kg/ha may be necessary where species having larger seeds are used. If seeding conditions are severe, such as are frequently encountered on steep slopes or south-facing aspects, seeding rates should be increased to as much as 18 to 22 kg/ha. Drill rows should ordinarily be spaced 20 to 40 cm apart and the seed drilled into mine spoils to a depth of from 6 to 13 mm. Where broadcast seeding is used, seeding rates should be approximately double those employed for drilling.

5. PLANTING METHODS FOR REVEGETATION

Shrubs and, to a lesser degree, trees are obvious and important components of several native forest and range habitat types underlain by surface-mineable coal in the semiarid western U.S. Shrubs are dominant species in a number of plant communities and often become dominant on heavily grazed rangeland. Although some shrub species produce valuable livestock forage (Dietz, 1969), shrubs are particularly important in providing food and cover for birds and wild animals (Julander et al., 1961; Martinka, 1967). In the western part of the Northern Great Plains Coal Province, both sage grouse and pronghorn antelope are dependent on shrubs, particularly sagebrush, for food and cover.

A number of shrub species are particularly adapted to droughty and saline sites due to structural and physiological adaptation of roots and foliage (Kozlowski, 1972; Orshan, 1972). Both aridity and adverse sodic soil conditions are major environmental factors that can limit revegetation of surface mine sites. A few species of shrubs and trees can be established from seed quite successfully during growing seasons of average to above-average precipitation. For the most part, however, reliance on establishment of shrubs and trees from seed is risky. A much higher degree of success can be obtained by transplanting nursery-grown seedling stock.

Shrubs and trees from 1 to 2 years old have been used for planting semiarid western coal spoils. Comparisons of plantings of bare-root stock and stock in degradable containers indicate that survival of the containerized plants greatly exceeds that of the bare-root plants in most instances. The degree of success and speed of response in forcing deep root development of containerized shrubs and trees are not only functions of the plant species but also depend upon the potting soil texture and the composition of the containing tube. Arrangement of soils in sequence from coarse sand at the top to fine silt loam at the bottom has been found essential in order to obtain percolation of water and yet provide an adequate reservoir to catch moisture and retain it in the bottom of the tube in order to stimulate root growth downward.

A hardening period of several weeks in a lath house preceding planting is important in order to prevent sunburn and to acclimate tender greenhouse-grown plants to drying winds and cold temperatures. The factor most limiting to revegetation of semiarid strip coal mines is too little moisture. Risk of failure in any given year is sufficiently high to warrant additional effort and expense in order to avoid replanting shrubs and trees. Current research approaches involve cross-wind furrowing and mulching to conserve moisture and trickle irrigation systems to provide supplemental moisture for one or two growing seasons at most.

6. PLANT MATERIALS FOR REVEGETATION

Plant species available for revegetating coal mine spoils in the Northern Great Plains include a number of native and introduced grasses and legumes. Additionally, several shrubs and trees are adapted for use here.

In the shortgrass prairie type, where the elevation is approximately

1,500 m and the annual precipitation varies from 250 to 400 m, the most suitable grasses for revegetating are mainly cold-season grasses. The best native species include western wheatgrass (*Agropyron smithii* Rydb.), blue grama (*Bouteloua gracilis* [HBK.] Lag.), sideoats grama (*Bouteloua curtipendula* [Michx.] Torr.), and buffalograss (*Buchloe dactyloides* [Nutt.] Engelm.). Adapted introduced grasses include smooth brome (*Bromus inermis* Leyss.), crested wheatgrass (*Agropyron cristatum* [L.] Gaertn.), and Russian wildrye (*Elymus junceus* Fisch.). Native shrubs that characterize this type are big sagebrush, big rabbitbrush, and little rabbitbrush (*Chrysothamnus viscidiflorus* [Hook.] Nutt.).

In the midgrass prairie type of central and eastern North and South Dakota, where the elevation is about 450 m and the annual precipitation ranges from 400 to 500 mm, native grasses that are highly successful for revegetation are mostly cold-season grasses and include western wheatgrass, thickspike wheatgrass (*Agropyron dasystachym* [Hook.] Scribn.), green needlegrass (*Stipa viridula* Trin.), hard fescue (*Festuca ovina* var. *duriuscula* [L.] Koch.), blue grama, side oats grama, and big bluestem (*Andropogon gerardi* Vitman). Adapted introduced grasses include smooth brome, intermediate wheatgrass (*Agropyron intermedium* [Host.] Beauv.), pubescent wheatgrass (*Agropyron trichophorum* [Link] Richt.), crested wheatgrass, and Russian wildrye. An important legume suitable for use here is yellow sweet clover (*Melilotus officinalis* [L.] Lam).

In the Sand Hills region, at an elevation of approximately 600 m where the annual precipitation ranges from 400 to 560 mm, the most appropriate grass species for revegetation appear to be such warm-season grasses as switchgrass (*Panicum virgatum* L.), big bluestem, sand bluestem (*Andropogon hallii* Hack.), sand lovegrass (*Eragrostis trichodes* [Nutt.] Wood), sand reed grass (*Calamovilfa longifolia* [Hook.] Scribn.), and sand drop seed (*Sporobolus cryptandrus* [Torr.] A. Gray). Yellow sweet clover is also an important legume here.

In the forested areas of southwestern South Dakota, northeastern Wyoming, and southeastern Montana, at elevations of about 1,800 m where annual precipitation ranges from 300 to 460 mm, the most suitable grasses are cool-season species. Here the most important native grasses are slender wheatgrass (*Agropyron trachycaulum* [Link] Malte.), mountain bromegrass (*Bromus marginatus* Nees), Idaho fescue (*Festuca idahoensis* Elmer), tall fescue (*Festuca arundinacea* Schreb.), hard fescue, orchardgrass (*Dactylis glomerata* L.), tall oatgrass (*Arrhenatherum elatius* [L.] Presl.), and pinegrass (*Calamagrostis rubescens* Buckl.). Important introduced species include crested and intermediate wheatgrasses. Native shrubs suitable for planting mine spoils in this area include buffaloberry (*Shepherdia argentea* [Pursh] Nutt.), sumac (*Rhus glabra* L.), and snowberry (*Symphoricarpos* spp.).

Saline-alkali swales are common in valley basins of the western part of the Northern Great Plains, at elevations of from 1,000 to 1,500 m where annual precipitation is generally not more than 250 mm. Suitable grasses for revegetation of these sites include native alkali sacaton, tall wheatgrass (*Agropyron elongatum* Host.), and the introduced Russian wildrye. Native shrubs best adapted for revegetation on these saline sites include fourwing saltbush, greasewood, and winterfat.

The use to be made of revegetated strip mine areas should be considered when selecting species and methods for planting. If grazing by domestic livestock is a primary concern, then appropriate species palatable to livestock should be chosen. Where wildlife is a major concern, revegetation projects that use a large component of browse species and some trees would be desirable.

Plant materials that exhibit high tolerance for highly saline conditions are needed for revegetation purposes. New plants adapted to highly alkaline and saline soils are being developed through at least three avenues of investigation: (i) selection of better adapted natural ecotypes, (ii) breeding of more suitable fertile hybrids, and (iii) genetic engineering, involving alteration of plant germ plasm to better meet stresses of the surface environment.

7. EQUIPMENT FOR REVEGETATION

Seeds of most native species desirable for revegetation are not produced commercially. Consequently, they are in extremely short supply and can generally be obtained only by making special efforts to collect them from wild stands. An effective backpack seed collector is needed to collect such seed, especially on rough topography. Several of these seed collectors have been in the research and development stage but none is actually available for widespread use.

One of the most useful pieces of equipment for revegetating mine spoils is a small crawler tractor with a wider than normal beam between the tracks. Such tractors are available with a track beam approximately 1 m wider than that of conventional tractors. This piece of equipment permits safe, cross-slope operation on slopes with a steepness as great as 2.5 to 1. This tractor should be equipped with a hydraulic ripper and a hydraulic three-point lift at the rear. The ripper provides a means for loosening compacted spoils and the three-point lift permits the use of a variety of seeding, planting, mulching, fertilizing, and cultivating equipment that can be used across the slope on the contour without sliding downhill.

Several types of drills are well suited for seeding different types of soil textures and conditions. One of these, the Nesbet[1] single- or double-disk drill with depth bands, is very useful in sandy or sandy loam soils. Another is the rangeland single-disk, deep-furrow drill or the single-disk semideep furrow drill for clay loam soils that have been previously tilled, such as mine spoils. Still another is the Nobel drill, a drill adapted to compacted rocky or gravelly soils.

One of the most useful pieces of equipment for seeding mine spoils is the seeder-cultipacker. This equipment, which looks somewhat like a small disk, has wheels alined to cut furrows, a drill behind the wheels to put seed in these furrows, and another set of wheels behind and offset

---

[1] Use of trade or firm names is for reader information only, and does not constitute endorsement by the U.S. Department of Agriculture of any commercial product or service.

from the drill furrows. This arrangement results in seeding and in covering and compacting the seed in one operation. The cultipacker is also useful for covering seed that has been broadcast.

Two types of equipment are commonly used to scatter seed directly on the soil surface (broadcast seeding). One type is known as the fan or airblast seeder. Small portable hand-held versions of the fan seeder are known as cyclone seeders. The other type is the hydroseeder, which applies seed mixed with water as a spray. However seed is spread, it must be covered with soil in some way if it is to germinate and become established. Seed can be covered by using harrows and disks or a small sheepsfoot roller.

Where straw and hay are used as mulches, they can be blown onto the spoils with a straw blower and then tacked down in one of two ways: by asphalt emulsions blown on with the mulch or by cutting the mulch into the spoils with a mulch crimper to produce a stubble effect.

We wish to emphasize that good revegetation jobs are not obtained by attempting to economize with makeshift equipment. Good revegetation requires use of the right types of equipment. The increased success obtained will more than offset equipment costs.

B. The Arid-Region—Southwestern Deserts

1. AMENDMENTS FOR REVEGETATION

A laboratory study showed that manure, sawdust, bark, and straw did not affect the emergence and early growth of mountain rye and fourwing saltbush on 3-year-old mine spoils (Aldon & Springfield, 1973). Fourwing saltbush showed a trend toward better emergence and taller seedlings where organic matter was incorporated in the spoil material. In other greenhouse tests using mountain rye and adding bark to topsoil and spoil, the effect of the added bark was negligible on emergence but leaf length and ovendry weights were depressed (Aldon et al., 1975).

Field tests are underway using sulfuric acid, bottom ash, gypsum, and sawdust as amendments to spoils. Preliminary data indicate some beneficial effects of bottom ash and gypsum after the first growing season. A longer time is needed to determine whether or not the effect can be sustained.

In 1974, six areas of about 0.2 ha each were topsoiled on the Western Coal Company spoils near Farmington, New Mexico. When soil treatments were compared, the best establishment and growth of plants were on the areas that had 10 cm of surface soil incorporated into the spoil plus an additional 20 cm of soil applied over the top. The treatments of 0, 30, and 46 cm of surface soil over the spoil were consistently ranked as least favorable. On one of the three locations where surface soil was not added, no plants were established (Gould et al., 1975). Wind erosion occurred on the nonmulched areas and deposition on the mulched areas. Much of the surface soil in the Fruitland coalfield area is eolian sand and, if used extensively as a surface material, will constitute a severe erosion hazard unless a mulch is used to stabilize the soil (Gould et al., 1975).

At present, topsoil is being tested at various mines. Different depths and mixing combinations are under investigation.

2. MULCHES FOR REVEGETATION

Investigations in New Mexico have shown the advantages of using mulch for establishing perennial species. For summer seeding near Santa Fe, the most effective mulch material was straw or a white petroleum resin. These materials reduced moisture losses and lowered midafternoon temperatures in the top 2.5 cm of soil during the time seeds were germinating and seedlings emerging (Springfield, 1972).

Straw spread at a rate of 2,240 kg/ha and rototilled into the top 8 cm of spoil was effective in the establishment of fourwing saltbush transplants and seeded alkali sacaton on mine spoils in New Mexico (Aldon, 1975c).

Gould et al. (1975) used 0, 2,240, and 4,480 kg/ha of a straw mulch in seeding spoils under irrigation. He felt that mulching may have been detrimental to establishment of native range plants because of the competition from the grain and weeds. Clean straw or hay would have eliminated this problem.

In general, hay mulch of 3,360 kg/ha crimped in twice provides a stable long-lasting mulch on mine spoils in the southwestern U.S. On light soils, a sheepsfoot roller crimps straw well.

3. FERTILIZERS FOR REVEGETATION

Emergence of fourwing saltbush and alkali sacaton seedlings was not affected by combinations of three different levels of N and P on 2-year-old mine spoils from the Fourcorners area of New Mexico (Aldon et al., 1976). Plant height and yield were affected by N and P applied at 90 and 180 kg/ha in all combinations. Neither species yielded more if either element was applied alone. Combinations of N and P increased yields of both species two to three times. Alkali sacaton yielded the most when N and P were applied at the higher level 1 month after seeding. Doubling the fertilizer level to obtain this additional yield, however, would probably be uneconomical. The higher levels of fertilizer did not increase the yield of fourwing saltbush over what was obtained at the lower level. Applying fertilizer at the time of seeding appeared best for saltbush, whereas delaying fertilizer application (especially P) until a month after seeding gave alkali sacaton some benefits (Aldon et al., 1976). In studies of mountain rye grown on mine spoils, a 10–5–5 fertilizer applied at a rate of 896 and 1,792 kg/ha increased leaf length and plant weights in both spoil and topsoil in nearly all treatments (Aldon et al., 1975). The same rates of fertilizer application did not affect the emergence and height growth of fourwing saltbush and only slightly affected the yield of western wheatgrass after 90 days (Aldon et al., 1975).

There is some advantage in using a combination of fast-release and slow-release forms of fertilizer for both immediate and longer lasting effects. Application of N during the second growing season also increases the total foliage cover in a shorter time. The addition of fertilizer after seedling emergence is recommended in dry areas (Natl. Acad. of Sci. 1974).

4. NEWLY DEVELOPED MATERIALS.

Endomycorrhizal associations are found on members of many plant families. These symbiotic fungal associations with plant roots benefit plant growth by increasing nutrient absorption (including that of normally unavailable P), reducing internal plant resistance to water flow, and improving water uptake. The advantages of endomycorrhizal associations in arid environments are obvious.

Studies of mycorrhizae in the southwestern U.S. grew out of finding that transplants of fourwing saltbush grew better if some soil from beneath a growing shrub was added to the potting mix. Followup studies indicated inoculated plants grew better and accumulated more P than plants grown on sterile soil (Williams et al., 1974). This laboratory finding was then tested in the field on mine spoils near Gallup, New Mexico. Transplants growing on inoculated and uninoculated (sterile) soil were planted on a steep outslope of 3-year-old spoil in 1972. Survival after 1 year was 37% for inoculated plants and 22% for uninoculated plants. Since many plants were buried with sediment or uprooted by frost heave, the test was repeated in 1973. By 1975, after two growing seasons, survival was better among inoculated plants (95%) than among uninoculated plants (84%). In addition, plant height and diameter were significantly greater (41.7 vs. 27.4 cm height and 35.8 vs. 21.3 cm diameter) on plants that were inoculated with endomycorrhizal spores (Aldon, 1975a). Seventeen important field shrubs have been examined for endomycorrhizae. Plants with endomycorrhizae include fourwing saltbush, winterfat, mountain serviceberry (*Amelanchier oreophilus* A. Nels.), Utah serviceberry (*Amelanchier utahensis* Koehne), true mountain mahogany (*Cercocarpus montanus* Raf.), Apache plume (*Fallugia paradoxa* [D. Don] Endl.), rock spirea (*Holodiscus dumosus* [Nutt.] Heller), bitterbrush (*Purshia tridentata* [Pursh] DC.), fendlerbush (*Fendlera rupicola* Gray), mock orange (*Philadelphus microphyllus* Gray), Gambel oak (*Quercus gambelii* Nutt.), snowberry, big sagebrush, and skunkbush sumac (*Rhus trilobata* Nutt.) (Williams & Aldon, 1976).

5. SEEDING METHODS FOR REVEGETATION

Direct-seeding trials of fourwing saltbush have been conducted on spoils at the Navajo Mine in New Mexico. In one seeding on terraces in 1973, a wet winter and early spring provided good residual soil moisture. At the end of the first growing season 83% of the straw-mulched seedlings and 71% of the untreated plants were alive. A white mulch that reflected radiation produced 80% survival (Aldon & Springfield, 1975b).

Unfortunately, sheep and goats destroyed these plants the next spring and prevented followup evaluations.

At another Navajo Mine site, a direct seeding was made on a small low-lying area in March of 1973. By May, about 400 plants had germinated. By September, over half of the plants had survived. One year later, survival was still 58% and plants averaged 55.9 cm in height and 43.2 cm in diameter (Aldon & Springfield, 1975b).

Drilling of seed is by far the most common method of planting on reclaimed areas. The seed is covered to a proper depth, distribution of seed is uniform, and the rate of seeding is controlled. The rangeland drill has worked best on mined areas of the southwestern U.S. (Currier, 1973). The rangeland drill is a rugged seeder with high clearance designed to work on rough sites. It can be converted to a deep-furrow implement by removing the depth bands. The disks are cupped enough to make good furrows. The depth of the furrow is controlled by taking off or adding disk arm weights. Weights up to 32 kg have been used under some conditions. The feed on this drill will not handle trashy seed (Currier, 1973).

6. PLANTING METHODS FOR REVEGETATION

Techniques for planting alkali sacaton seed have been worked out on unmined areas (Aldon, 1975b). Because this species has exacting establishment requirements, the following agronomic steps are necessary for its establishment: (i) plant when soil water is at least 14% or higher (1 atm tension or less); (ii) plant when probabilities for weekly precipitation are greatest and soil temperatures will be near 30°C; (iii) use large seeds at least 1 year old; (iv) saturate the planting site just prior to planting; (v) cover seeds with about 13 mm of mulch to keep them moist and dark; and (vi) if storms at planting site do not deposit at least 6 mm of rain within the first 5 days, rewater to bring the soil to saturation.

Field planting of fourwing saltbush seedlings on unmined areas has also been described (Aldon, 1973). Plant in areas that will be flooded periodically, but not inundated more than 30 hours. In the southwestern U.S., it is important to wait until the probability for sizable (10 mm plus) summer thunderstorms exceeds 50%, generally in late July or early August. Soil water stress should be < 2 atm of tension.

Seedlings should be planted before 1000 hours to minimize stress on plants. Plants should be shaded or covered and watered well while being transported to the planting site.

Make a 10-cm-deep hole, insert plant band, and tamp soil around it. Plant bands at ground level, not below. Roots apparently need not be laid straight down; they can be bent, but not broken.

Plant at 1.5-m spacing. It is unreasonable to expect greater plant densities through revegetation than would be found on undisturbed sites. In favorable years, plants can grow 0.6 m tall the first year.

Cover transplanted seedlings with straw to minimize stresses. Spray straw mulch and fourwing saltbush plants with a 1:1 mixture of water and animal repellent (Aldon, 1973).

7. PLANT MATERIALS FOR REVEGETATION

a. **Seeding vs. Transplants**—Survival of 3-month-old fourwing salt-bush transplants under drip irrigation on coal mine spoils after two growing seasons was twice that of seeded plants (393 vs. 194).

In one other test on mine spoils, transplant plugs of western wheatgrass (grown for 6 weeks in styrofoam blocks) were field planted by four planting methods. Nearby seeded plots 1.4 m^2 in size were seeded at the rate of 26.8 kg/ha or 646 seeds/m^2. Only 24% of the seed produced plants that survived in contrast to 100% survival of the plugs. The transplants survived all combinations of treatments. The use of plugs is more expensive, but ways of reducing these costs are being sought since survival is so good.

b. **Grasses, Forbs, Shrubs, Trees**—At present, the most promising species to plant on mine spoils are alkali sacaton, western wheatgrass, fourwing saltbush, and Indian ricegrass. Depending on elevation and precipitation other species have been tried with sporadic success. They include crested wheatgrass, slender wheatgrass, Siberian wheatgrass (*Agropyron sibiricum* [Willd.] Beauv.), sand dropseed, and yellow sweetclover. Rates of seeding range from 300 to 650 seeds/m^2 or the equivalent of 14 to 27 kg/ha of seeded mixtures.

Good stands of alkali sacaton have resulted when pure live seed was applied at a rate of 3 kg/ha.

Russian-olive (*Elaeagnus angustifolia* L.), Siberian peashrub (*Caragana arborescens* Lam.), rubber rabbitbrush, koshia (*Kochia prostrata* Wats.), and New Mexico olive (*Forestiera neomexicana* A. Gray) transplants have grown on mine spoil with varying success depending on seasonal moisture conditions.

Pinyon pines were planted on some mine spoils in New Mexico in 1974. In a study of two planting dates, April and July, a fertilizer tablet was placed in each planting hole, some trees were inoculated with an ectomycorrhiza and an antitranspirant was applied to the leaves of others. These three treatments were tested alone and in all combinations. Survival after the first growing season was high, but at least two growing seasons will be needed to determine whether or not survival can be sustained. Plantings appear to receive some benefit from inoculation and antitranspirant treatments.

IV. SOME NEW TECHNIQUES AND THEIR USES

A. The Semiarid Region—Northern Great Plains

Erratic climatic conditions, especially in the amounts and distribution of precipitation, remain the dominant factor in success or failure of revegetation efforts on strip mine sites carved from semiarid rangeland ecosystems. Accordingly, addition of irrigation water is sometimes desirable and even necessary to the establishment and survival of seedlings. Without some irrigation water during years of below-average precipitation, revegetation efforts may fail.

Many subsurface and some surface water supplies have high sodium contents. Accordingly, newly planted mine spoils must be carefully irrigated. Frequently, irrigation water is used in association with appropriate soil amendments to prevent development of unfavorable saline conditions. Ordinarily, one growing season of supplemental irrigation is enough to establish a new stand.

a. **Overhead Sprinkler Irrigation Systems**—Automatic overhead sprinkler systems, with nozzles that emit very fine drops, have proven extremely satisfactory for supplemental irrigation of new grass stands. The small drops, approaching a mist, greatly reduce the simulated raindrop impact on the soil surface and so facilitate infiltration and reduce overland flow and soil erosion.

b. **Trickle Irrigation**—Similarly, automatic trickle irrigation systems have proved to be very successful for supplemental irrigation of young shrubs and trees.

c. **Subsurface Irrigation**—Subsurface irrigation systems, designed to emit water into spoils just below the surface, thereby reducing surface evaporational losses, have not been used in the semiarid portions of the western U.S. to any appreciable degree. Greater use has been made of them in the arid desert regions.

B. The Arid Region—Southwestern Deserts

1. SUPPLEMENTAL IRRIGATION

a. **Overhead**—The biggest problem in vegetation establishment on mine spoils may not be the toxicity or the infertility of the spoil materials, but the difficulty of getting moisture into them. This problem can be partially solved by irrigation. In areas receiving < 200 mm of precipitation, irrigation is necessary if reclamation is to keep abreast of mining. For this reason, several irrigation methods were tested at the Navajo Mine. But, when irrigation is used to establish vegetation the question arises as to what happens when the water is turned off. How will plants be maintained on low amounts of natural precipitation (at the Navajo Mine average annual precipitation is 155 mm) and erratic frequency patterns? To help answer these questions, two types (steep slope and gentle slope) of artificial floodways were installed in 1973 to study plant establishment using irrigation. Sprinkler irrigation pipes were arranged in each floodway and fitted with sprinkler heads. Water was applied at a rate of 13 mm twice a week—about 254 mm was applied during the first growing season. No water was applied the second growing season (Aldon, 1975c).

Five randomized blocks were marked off in each floodway. Each block consisted of two plots, one for alkali sacaton and the other for fourwing saltbush. Alkali sacaton was seeded in rows, in collars, and by being broadcast into a straw mulch. In addition, 3-month-old transplants of fourwing saltbush were planted in the floodways in three ways: (i) with straw around the base of each plant; (ii) with paraffin surrounding each plant to collect and conserve moisture; and (iii) with the entire plot mulched with straw.

An average of 86 alkali sacaton seedlings per m² were alive throughout all treatments after the first growing season. Eighty-six seedlings per m² under irrigation for the first season is good initial establishment under field conditions. Twenty-eight percent of these survived after 2 years, even though precipitation averaged only half of normal during the second growing season. The average stand at the end of the second year had 25 plants per m². The most practical way to plant is in furrows; 24 plants per m² survived where this method was employed (Aldon, 1975b). Spoil piles with long, high slopes greater than 10% were detrimental to plant survival. Gentle, undulating topography where 33 seedlings per m² developed proved to be best for establishment.

After 2 years, over 70% of the fourwing saltbushes were alive on the undulating floodway. This stocking is at a rate of one plant per m².

b. Drip or Trickle—Drip irrigation is a method that allows water to drip slowly from small emitters along a pipe. Two 30-m lengths of 13-mm plastic pipe were laid about 6.1 m apart on graded spoil material. Emitters were located at 30-cm intervals along 18 m of each line. Each line was connected to a water source. Three-month-old transplants of fourwing saltbush and western wheatgrass were planted alternately at each emitter. Ten transplants of each species (controls) were planted between the lines, but were not watered.

Seedlings were transplanted in mid-September 1973 and were watered twice a week (eight waterings) until the first hard frost. Discharge rates under gravity feed were 5 liters per emitter per hour. Each emitter delivered about 15 liters per watering. Plants were not irrigated in 1974.

Plant survival and growth were measured 13 and 22 months after planting. Results after the second growing season showed 73% of the fourwing saltbush and 68% of the western wheatgrass transplants were alive. Survival of unirrigated plants was significantly less, and survivors were half as large as irrigated plants (Aldon, 1975c).

2. WATER HARVESTING TECHNIQUES

The first week of a transplant's life is probably the most critical, especially under harsh conditions. To enhance survival during these critical days, several steps should be followed. The most important is to plant when soil moisture levels are optimum and probabilities for weekly precipitation are the greatest.

Low-cost methods for increasing runoff and concentrating it on shrubs to enhance growth and survival were tested beginning in 1972. In a small field test, ground paraffin and black polyethylene were used around fourwing saltbush transplants to catch rainfall. The effective water-collecting area was 0.4 m². Paraffin was applied at the rate of 3.7

kg/m². The paraffin melts into the soil at 54°C and forms a surface coating that repels rain. Runoff from summer storms added an average of 19 mm more moisture to the plants than the untreated plots received with 51 mm of summer precipitation (Aldon & Springfield, 1975a). Greater growth of the transplants reflected the increase in available moisture. The plants, only 5 cm tall at the start of the experiment, were the following heights 75 days later: untreated, 15 cm; paraffin, 23 cm; polyethylene, 36 cm.

In a simultaneous study, 50 plants of Siberian peashrub (*Caragana arborescens*) were planted on mine spoils near Gallup, New Mexico. Seedlings were planted in shallow basins, and paraffin and polyethylene were applied as in the previously described studies. No precipitation fell for the first 2 weeks after planting—after that time it was low. All plants survived, but those treated with ground paraffin showed better vigor. One year later, plants that received extra water were larger, as the following averages show:

	Height, cm	Diameter, cm	Size index (height × diameter)
No treatment	23	8	178
Ground paraffin	25	11	280
Polyethylene	41	16	637

In addition to paraffin, a silicone spray emulsion was tested on spoil material to evaluate its potential for repelling water, thus concentrating runoff. Both the strength and the water repellency of the silicone crusts were reduced by rates of application and runoff concentrations high enough to fracture the crusts.

Both the ground paraffin and the polyethylene treatments appear suitable for harvesting water to aid plant establishment on coal mine spoils. They are now undergoing large-scale pilot tests at two mine sites where growth and survival of western wheatgrass and fourwing saltbush are being followed. Areas shaped at ratios of 6:1 and 12:1 (water yield to planted area) have been treated with paraffin and silicone. Survival after the first growing season shows a slight benefit from both shapes and repellents. More time will be needed to properly assess the value and longevity of the treatments under field conditions (Aldon & Springfield, 1975b).

V. OTHER NEEDS FOR REVEGETATION—PROPER MANAGEMENT OF REVEGETATED STANDS

A. The Semiarid Region—Northern Great Plains

Revegetation of such drastically disturbed sites as surface mine spoils is somewhat similar to planting and landscaping the yard of one's newly built home. It would be unthinkable to carefully plant a lawn, shrubs, trees, and flowerbeds and then leave the plantings without further attention. It should be equally unthinkable to do everything necessary to ensure successful rehabilitation of mine spoils and then to forfeit the entire effort for lack of necessary subsequent care. The land must be managed during and after revegetation. When necessary, management involves measures to control destruction of new vegetation by insects, rodents, livestock, and big game. Such measures may include fencing or the use of repellents to prevent or discourage such damage (Packer, 1974).

Some spoils in the Northern Great Plains are quite resistant to erosion by water and wind; others are not. The most highly erodible spoils, which usually contain more sodium than most, come from deep overburden layers in the North Dakota portion of the Northern Great Plains. This area also receives the most rainfall. In general, these conditions combine to produce high overland flow and soil erosion hazards from mine spoils. Under these conditions, it is desirable, probably even necessary, to prevent or control surface instability if vegetation is to be established. Prevention or reduction of surface runoff and soil erosion from mine spoils can be achieved by a combination of measures, including grading to gentle slopes, terracing, pitting, and mulching. Failure to stabilize spoil surfaces against raindrop and runoff impacts during or immediately after seeding and planting usually results in revegetation failure.

B. The Arid Region—Southwestern Deserts

Proper management of reclaimed areas is absolutely necessary. A few head of domestic livestock can and have eliminated reclamation efforts in a short time. In addition, rodents must be managed and wildlife must be carefully watched to keep them from destroying stands before plants are able to support themselves (Aldon & Springfield, 1975b).

Thames and Verma (1975) recognized this problem and stated: "At present the regraded mine spoil is not vegetated on Black Mesa despite several repeated seedings. The primary reason reseeding has met with poor success is unrestricted grazing. Revegetation will continue to be unsuccessful as long as grazing remains uncontrolled."

Thus far, managers have had little experience with insects or diseases that may attack stands in the southwestern deserts, but these may cause problems. An advantage of using native vegetation is that it may be better able to withstand these pathogens.

LITERATURE CITED

Aandahl, A. R. 1972. Soils of the Great Plains—A detailed map of the soil associations of the Great Plains. Soil Conserv. Serv., Lincoln, Nebr.

Aldon, E. F. 1973. Revegetating disturbed areas in the semiarid Southwest. J. Soil Water Conserv. 28:223–225.

Aldon, E. F. 1975a. Endomycorrhizae enhance survival and growth of fourwing saltbush on coal mine spoils. USDA For. Serv. Res. Note RM-294. Rocky Mt. For. and Range Exp. Stn., Fort Collins, Colo.

Aldon, E. F. 1975b. Establishing alkali sacaton on harsh sites in the Southwest. J. Range Manag. 28:129–132.

Aldon, E. F. 1975c. Techniques for establishing native plants on coal mine spoils in New Mexico. p. 21–28. In 3rd Symp. on Surface Mining and Reclamation, Vol. 1, NCA/BCR Coal Conf. and Expo II, Louisville, Ky., Oct. 1975. Natl. Coal Assoc., Washington, D.C. 243 p.

Aldon, E. F., and H. W. Springfield. 1973. Revegetating coal mine spoils in New Mexico: a laboratory study. USDA For. Serv. Res. Note RM-245. Rocky Mt. For. and Range Exp. Stn., Fort Collins, Colo.

Aldon, E. F., and H. W. Springfield. 1975a. Using paraffin and polyethylene to harvest water for growing shrubs. p. 251–257. In Proc. Water Harvesting Symp., Phoenix, Ariz., 26–28 Mar. 1974. ARS W-22, USDA-ARS, Tucson, Ariz.

Aldon, E. F., and H. W. Springfield. 1975b. Problems and techniques in revegetating coal mine spoils in New Mexico. p. 122. In Mohan Wali (ed.) Practices and problems of land reclamation in western North America. Univ. North Dakota Press, Grand Forks.

Aldon, E. F., H. W. Springfield, and G. Garcia. 1975. Can soil amendments aid revegetation of New Mexico coal mine spoils? USDA For. Serv. Res. Note RM-292. Rocky Mt. For. and Range Exp. Stn., Fort Collins, Colo.

Aldon, E. F., H. W. Springfield, and D. G. Scholl. 1976. Fertilizer response of alkali sacaton and fourwing saltbush grown on coal mine spoil. USDA For. Serv. Res. Note RM-306. Rocky Mt. For. and Range Exp. Stn., Fort Collins, Colo.

Cook, C. W., R. M. Hyde, and P. L. Sims. 1974. Revegetation guide lines for surface mined areas. Sci. Ser. 16. Range Sci. Dep., Colo. State Univ., Fort Collins.

Currier, W. F. 1973. Basic principles of seed planting. p. 225–232. In Proc. 1st Research and Applied Technology Symp. on Mined-land Reclamation, NCA/BCR Coal Conf., Pittsburgh, Pa., Mar. 1973. Bituminous Coal Res. Inc., Monroeville, Pa.

Dean, K. C., and R. Haven. 1971. Vegetative stabilization of mill tailings using municipal and mineral wastes. Environ. Qual. Conf. for the Extractive Industries. July 1970. Salt Lake City, Utah, Am. Inst. Metall. Eng. USDI Bur. Mines, Salt Lake City Metall. Res. Cent.

Dietz, D. R. 1969. Nutritive value of shrubs. In Proc. Int. Symp. on wildland shrubs—their biology and utilization. USDA For. Serv. Gen. Tech. Rep. INT-1. Intermt. For. and Range Exp. Stn., Ogden, Utah.

Doering, E. J., and W. O. Willis. 1975. Chemical reclamation of sodic strip-mine spoils. USDA-ARS-NC-20, Bismarck, N. Dak.

Fenneman, N. M. 1931. Physiography of the Western United States. 1st ed. McGraw-Hill Book Co., New York.

Gould, W. L., D. Rai, and P. J. Wierenga. 1975. Problems in reclamation of coal mine spoils in New Mexico. p. 107–121. In Mohan Wali (ed.) Practices and problems of land reclamation in western North America. Univ. North Dakota Press, Grand Forks.

Heide, W. G., and D. K. Larsen. 1969. Fertilizer use in Montana with comparison 1954–1967. Mont. Agric. Exp. Stn. Bull. 628.

Hodder, R. L., and R. G. Atkinson. 1974. Peabody Coal Co., Big Sky, Mine reclamation research. Mont. Agric. Exp. Stn. Res. Rep. 48.

Hodder, R. L., D. E. Reirson, R. Mogan, and J. Buckhold. 1970. Coal mine spoils reclamation research project. Western Energy Co., Colstrip, Mont. Mont. Agric. Exp. Stn. Res. Rep. 8.

Hodder, R. L., and B. W. Sindelar. 1972. Progress in reclamation research in Montana. Mont. Agric. Exp. Stn. Misc. Publ. 11.

Hopkins, H. H. 1954. Effects of mulch upon certain factors of the grassland environment. J. Range Manag. 7:255–258.

Hull, A. C., Jr. 1960. Winter germination of intermediate wheatgrass on mountain lands. J. Range Manag. 13:257–260.

Julander, O., W. L. Robinette, and D. A. Jones. 1961. Relation of summer range conditions to mule deer herd productivity. J. Wildl. Manag. 25:54–60.

Kozlowski, T. T. 1972. Physiology of water stress. In Proc. Intl. Symp. on Wildland Shrubs— Their Biology and Utilization. July 1971, Logan, Utah. USDA For. Serv. Gen. Tech. Rep. INT-1. Intermt. For. and Range Exp. Stn., Ogden, Utah.

Kuchler, A. W. 1964. The potential natural vegetation of the conterminous United States. Am. Geogr. Soc. Spec. Publ. 36, New York.

Martinka, C. J. 1967. Mortality of northern Montana pronghorn in a severe winter. J. Wildl. Manag. 31:159–164.

National Academy of Sciences. 1974. Rehabilitation potential of western coal lands. Ballinger Publ. Co., Cambridge, Mass.

Orshan, G. 1972. Morphological and physical plasticity in relation to drought. *In* Proc. Int. Symp. on Wildland Shrubs—Their Biology and Utilization, July 1971, Logan, Utah. USDA For. Serv. Gen. Tech. Rep. INT-1. Intermt. For. and Range Exp. Stn., Ogden, Utah.

Packer, P. E. 1974. Rehabilitation potentials and limitations of surface-mined land in the Northern Great Plains. USDA For. Serv. Gen. Tech. Rep. INT-14. Intermt. For. and Range Exp. Stn., Ogden, Utah.

Packer, P. E., C. C. Clyde, E. Israelson, E. Farmer, and J. Fletcher. 1976. Erosion control during highway construction—a manual of principles and practices for erosion control. Rep. of Transp. Res. Bd., Natl. Acad. of Sci., Washington, D.C.

Power, J. F., J. J. Bond, F. M. Sandoval, and W. O. Willis. 1974. Nitrification in paleocene shale. Science 183:1077–1079.

Plummer, A. P., P. R. Christensen, and S. B. Monsen. 1968. Restoring big game range in Utah. Publ. 68–73, Utah Div. Fish and Game, Salt Lake City.

Richardson, B. Z., E. E. Farmer, R. W. Brown, and P. E. Packer. 1975. Rehabilitation research and its application on a surface-mined area of eastern Montana. *In* Proc. Fort Union Coal Field Symp., Montana Acad. of Sci. 3:247–265. Billings, Mont.

Sandoval, R. M., J. J. Bond, J. F. Power, and W. O. Willis. 1973. Lignite mine spoils in the Northern Great Plains—characteristics and potential for reclamation. p. 117–133. *In* Proc. 1st Research and Applied Tech. Symp. on Mined Land Reclamation. Bituminous Coal Res., Inc., Monroeville, Pa. 7–8 Mar. 1973, Pittsburgh, Pa.

Sindelar, V. W., R. L. Hodder, and M. E. Majerus. 1973. Surface mined land reclamation research in Montana. Prog. Rep. 1972–73. Mont. Agric. Exp. Stn. Res. Rep. 40.

Springfield, H. W. 1972. Using mulches to establish woody chenopods. p. 382–391. *In* Intl. Symp. on wildland shrubs, their biology and utilization. USDA For. Serv. Gen. Tech. Rep. INT-1. Intermt. For. and Range Exp. Stn., Ogden, Utah.

Sutton, P. 1973. Establishment of vegetation on toxic coal mine spoils. p. 153–158. *In* Proc. 1st Research and Applied Tech. Symp. on Mined Land Reclamation, 7–8 Mar. 1973, Pittsburgh, Pa. Bituminous Coal Res., Inc., Monroeville, Pa.

Thames, J. L., and T. R. Verma. 1975. Coal mine reclamation on the Black Mesa and the Four Corners areas of Northeastern Arizona. p. 48–64. *In* Mohan Wali (ed.) Practices and problems of land reclamation in western North America. Univ. North Dakota Press, Grand Forks.

Thornthwaite, C. W. 1931. The climates of North America according to a new classification. Geogr. Rev. 21:633–655.

Thornthwaite, C. W. 1941. Climate and settlement in the Great Plains. p. 177–188. *In* USDA Yearbook of Agriculture. U.S. Government Printing Office, Washington, D.C.

U.S. Department of Interior. 1975. Effects of coal development in the Northern Great Plains: A review of major issues and consequences at different rates of development. Northern Great Plains Resour. Program Rep. USDI, Denver, Colo.

Weaver, J. E., and N. W. Rowen. 1952. Effects of excessive natural mulch on development, yields, and structure of native grassland. Bot. Gaz. 114:1–19.

Westinghouse Electric Corporation. 1975. Terrestrial survey of Navajo mine lease associated with the Four Corners Power Plant 1974. Report to Utah Intl. Inc., Fruitland, N. Mex. Westinghouse Electric Corp., Pittsburgh, Pa.

Williams, S. E., and E. F. Aldon. 1976. Endomycorrhizal (vesicular arbuscular) associations of some arid zone shrubs. Southwest. Nat. 20:437–444.

Williams, S. E., A. G. Wollum, II, and E. F. Aldon. 1974. Growth of *Atriplex canescens* (Pursh) Nutt. improved by formation of vesicular-arbuscular mycorrhizae. Soil Sci. Soc. Am. Proc. 38:962–965.

Chapter 25

Correction of Nutrient Deficiencies and Toxicities in Strip-Mined Lands in Semiarid and Arid Regions

ARMAND BAUER, WILLIAM A. BERG, AND WALTER L. GOULD

Agricultural Research Service, USDA, Mandan, North Dakota
Colorado State University, Fort Collins, Colorado, and
New Mexico State University, Las Cruces, New Mexico

I. INTRODUCTION

Nutrient deficiencies in soils are common and widespread in semiarid and arid regions. However, responses to fertilizers applied to correct these deficiencies are not always forthcoming because of the overriding influence of water supply and its distribution on plant growth and reproduction; frequently water is more limiting than nutrients. Areal extent of soils affected by toxic concentrations of nutrients is very small in comparison to areal extent of deficiencies, but toxicity correction is often more difficult to achieve than correction of deficiencies.

Available soil-derived elements essential for plant growth originate primarily from the zone of maximum organic matter accumulation. Thus, the concentration of these available forms usually decreases with depth (notable exceptions can be Ca, Mg, and K). Accumulations of essential nutrients at toxic levels, on the other hand, may occur at any depth within the rooting zone.

The overburden disturbed by strip mining is variable in chemical properties, varying within mine sites as well as among sites (ARS and N. Dak. Agric. Exp. Stn. Res. Staff, 1975; Sandoval et al., 1973). Through the stripping process, stratified materials are mixed and, in general, inverted. With additional "disturbance" occurring as a result of leveling, a given characteristic within the normal root zone can vary widely within a short distance, horizontally and vertically. One characteristic common to all spoils is the lack of organic matter and, hence, a major source of essential available nutrients for plant growth.

The present reclamation laws of some of the western states require stockpiling of suitable plant rooting medium and its placement on leveled spoils. Some state laws further require that the suitable plant rooting medium be applied in stages so that a mixture of the A horizon and much of the B horizon is at the immediate surface. The occurrence of nutrient deficiencies and toxicities of strip-mined lands can be expected to vary with the suitability of the material placed at the surface as a plant rooting medium, and with the thickness of these suitable materials. Correction procedures, especially fertilization, can be expected to vary because indigenous nutrient levels and crop yield potentials will vary with suitability and thickness of the plant growth medium.

II. THE PROBLEM

A. Deficiencies and Toxicities

Deficiencies of the majority of soil-derived essential nutrients have been reported in soils of the semiarid and arid regions; the exceptions are the micronutrients Mo and Cl. However, the degree of deficiency and the areal extent over which deficiency occurs vary greatly depending upon such factors as soil properties and characteristics, prevailing climatic conditions, species, crop yield, and past and present soil management practices.

In areal extent, the most widespread soil deficiencies occur with the macroelements N and P, which are deficient in soils varying widely in texture and organic matter content. Potassium deficiency occurs primarily in coarse- and moderately coarse-textured soils of low cation exchange capacity. However, yield increases to fertilizer K application have been obtained even on soils of high exchangeable K levels (Skogley, 1976).

Soil deficiencies of S and of micronutrients occur to a very limited extent in comparison to the areal extent of N and P deficiencies. Sulfur deficiency in Western and Great Plains coal-mining states usually is manifested on coarse-textured, well-drained, low organic matter soils (Beaton et al., 1971) or areas where erosion has removed the solum. Micronutrient deficiencies invariably occur on only a limited portion of a given field. Deficiencies of B, Cu, Fe, Mn, and Zn were reported in soils of these coal-mining states (Berger, 1962). While Mo deficiencies in crops have been reported in nearly every agricultural area of the world (Johnson, 1966), deficiency apparently has not been detected in soils in these states.

Confirmed nutrient deficiencies in spoils of the Fort Union and Wasatch group (the geological formations containing most of the coal in the Northern Great Plains) have been limited to N and P (ARS and N. Dak. Agric. Exp. Stn. Res. Staff, 1975). However, soil fertility studies have been conducted for only a relatively brief time period and have seldom included other nutrients as variables. Nitrogen may not be deficient in freshly exposed shales because of the relatively high concentration of exchangeable NH_4^+ (Power et al., 1974), but N deficiency is prevalent in spoils of low cation exchange capacity. The shales of high exchangeable NH_4^+, nevertheless, may become deficient in N due to utilization by plants of adsorbed NH_4^+ and of the NO_3^- transformed from NH_4^+ by oxidation. While P levels are very low in core samples of overburden materials in the Fruitland formation in New Mexico, low soil water content in this arid area may be a greater limiting factor to plant growth (W. L. Gould, 1976, unpublished data). Nitrogen and P deficiencies pose major revegetation problems on spoils exposed by surface mining of uranium and limestone, as well as coal, in Colorado (Berg, 1975). Deficiency of K is suspected in isolated areas of Wyoming (personal communication from Paul Singleton).

Toxic concentrations of nutrient elements in spoils are essentially limited to micronutrients. Copper, zinc, and manganese are potential toxic problems on some mine tailings in Utah (personal communication from Rex Nielsen). In these cases, toxicities are very limited in areal extent or, as in the case of the Se in Montana, associated with a specific stratum (personal communication from Hayden Ferguson). Boron toxicity may pose a problem in revegetation of carbonaceous shales exposed by coal mining in northwestern New Mexico (Miyamoto et al., 1975; W. L. Gould, 1976, unpublished data), on spent oil shales (Agronomy Dep., Colorado State Univ.), and leonardite or coal slack. Toxicity of B appears to be associated with materials containing biologically inert C. The potential accumulation of Mo in forages to levels toxic to ruminants has been characterized by Vlek in soils irrigated with water from Mo mining areas (P. L. G. Vlek, 1976. Molybdenum in Colorado soils. Ph.D. dissertation. Colorado State Univ., Fort Collins. 192. p.). Harbert and Berg (1974) reported high levels of Mo in forage grown on spent oil shales.

While not specifically deficient or toxic because of concentration levels, Ca and Mg, both usually present in relatively large quantities in some strata of the overburden or even in soil profiles (ARS and N. Dak. Agric. Exp. Stn. Res. Staff, 1975; Sandoval et al., 1973), may present nutritional problems because of the ratio of one to the other. Crop production is not considered to be affected so long as Mg does not exceed Ca on an equivalent basis (Doll & Lucas, 1973). Hunter (1949) reported no yield influence on alfalfa when Ca/Mg ratio variations ranged from 1:4 to 32:1. However, Ca/Mg ratio in some overburden strata exceeds 1:10.

B. Soil Tests for Evaluation of Nutrient Needs

Soil testing to detect nutrient deficiencies and predict fertilizer treatments as corrective measures is utilized in all of the coal-mining states. There is variation among states in extraction solutions and analytical detection methods used (NCR 13 Soil Testing Comm., 1975), and differences in interpretations of the analytical data in terms of concentration levels which constitute specific degrees of toxicity, sufficiency, or deficiency. Also, the number of nutrients for which tests are conducted vary, because deficiencies are not universally present. The soil tests offered and testing procedures are listed in Table 1 for several western states. In addition to the listed tests for nutrients, tests for pH, soluble salt concentration, and texture are provided.

Adaptability of tests, now used for undisturbed soils, for use on reclaimed land is expected to be dependent upon the thickness of "topsoil" or suitable plant growth medium covering the smoothed spoils. Where the thickness is equal to or thicker than the sampling depth utilized for the particular nutrient at undisturbed sites, applicability as to detection of

Table 1—Testing methods utilized in several western states to detect soil nutrient status

State	N	P	K	Micronutrients
		Nutrients		
Colorado	NO_3[†], NH_4[‡], O.M.[§]	————————	NH_4HCO_3-DTPA	————————
Montana	NO_3	$NaHCO_3$	††	--
New Mexico	NO_3	$NaHCO_3$, H_2O	$NH_4C_2H_3O_2$	DTPA (Zn,Fe)
North Dakota	NO_3	$NaHCO_3$	$NH_4C_2H_3O_2$	DTPA (Zn,Fe)
Wyoming	O.M.[‡‡]	$NaHCO_3$	$NH_4C_2H_3O_2$	--

† NO_3-N test (NCR-13, 1975). Samples are taken to at least 30 cm, and as much as the 60-cm depth.
‡ NH_4-N test.
§ Organic matter, modified Walkley-Black (Graham, 1959).
¶ Olsen et al. (1954).
# Pratt (1965).
†† Correlation and calibration studies are underway (Skogley, 1976).
‡‡ Organic matter, easily oxidizable by $KMnO_4$ (Richard et al., 1960).

deficiency is likely; but adjustments in treatment rate may be necessary depending upon characteristics of underlying materials. Where the thickness of suitable plant rooting medium present on spoils is less than the depth sampled at undisturbed sites, applicability is uncertain and needs to be investigated. However, on spoils without suitable plant rooting medium on the surface, factors other than fertility may be most limiting, obviating the need for testing and fertilizer additions.

The range in chemical characteristics occurring in profiles of undisturbed soils is wide enough to encompass the characteristics associated with spoil materials (Omodt et al., 1975). Hence, procedures for extraction and analysis, which have been developed to evaluate specific nutrient ions in soils covering wide ranges of characteristics, could be expected to encompass the characteristics found in spoils and be suitable for those purposes. This is illustrated with examples.

Example (a)—Appreciable error can be introduced in the evaluation of exchangeable K in saline soils using $1.0N$ $NH_4C_2H_3O_2$, because of the quantity of water-soluble K included in the extract. This potential error is circumvented by use of duplicate samples, one in which water-soluble K is determined and then subtracted from the quantity in the sample subjected to the $NH_4C_2H_3O_2$ extraction (Pratt, 1965).

Example (b)—The $NaHCO_3$ extracts of soils at times contain soluble organic constituents that need to be removed by adsorption on carbon black or reduced to avoid interference in colorimetric P analysis. The use of ascorbic acid to reduce the molybdiphosphate complex, and analysis with a spectrophotometer with a wave length set at 882 nm is a method of overcoming the problem (Watanabe & Olsen, 1965). However, organic constituents in $NaHCO_3$ extracts of mine spoils containing appreciable quantities of coal fragments are insufficiently reduced by ascorbic acid to avoid interference, and require treatment with carbon black (personal communication with J. F. Power).

C. Plant Species Response to Fertilizers on Unmined Sites

Land use of areas presently mined and areas of strippable reserves is, essentially, agricultural. Grazing of native and introduced species constitutes the dominant agricultural use (Packer, 1974), except in North Dakota where about 42% of the area underlain by strippable coal is cultivated and devoted to production of dryland small grain crops. Alfalfa also is grown on relatively limited areas (Sandoval et al., 1973).

Native range plants of the Northern Great Plains area include species such as wheatgrasses (*Agropyron*), needlegrasses (*Stipa*), grama grasses (*Bouteloua*), bluestems (*Andropogan*), fescues (*Festuca*), and dryland sedges (*Carex*) (Packer, 1974), with sagebrush (*Artemisia*) and rabbit brush (*Chrysothammus*) in overgrazed areas of the short-grass prairie. Overall development and growth patterns of individual species in the grassland are variously affected by N fertilization rate (Goetz, 1970; Power & Alessi, 1971; Wight & Black, 1972). Nutrient needs among species can be expected to vary widely because of differences in the capacity to remove nutrients from soil or even the capacity to utilize different ionic species. Supplemental needs of fertilizer nutrients may vary too, especially N, because some native species are N fixers.

Only limited data exist of the uptake of nutrients at various phenological stages of grasses. Woodmansee (communication from Robert Woodmansee) determined that the total N uptake (above and below soil surface) by grass species of a representative short grass prairie to maintain population stability is about 30 kg/ha, and that maximum uptake occurs during the exponential growth phase. Most efficient utilization would require that N application be made prior to the start of this growth phase. Beeson (1941) tabulated data of mineral composition of numerous plant species, including some introduced grasses.

Nutrient needs of small grain crops (wheat [*Triticum* L.], oats [*Avena* L.], and barley [*Hordeum* L.]) are documented (Tisdale & Nelson, 1966), including proportionate amounts of the total uptake at phenological stages (Boatwright & Haas, 1961). Such data are useful from the standpoint of determining total needs and also from the standpoint of timing of fertilizer application. Timing can have an effect on the efficient utilization of applied fertilizers because of potential chemical and biological immobilization, or losses by physical means such a runoff and erosion. In general, the closer the time of application to onset of plant need in relation to occurrence of deficiency, the more efficient the utilization (this assumes placement so that plant roots can intercept the nutrients).

Information is sparse on nutrient needs of adapted woody species, planted on disturbed lands in the western states. An increase resulting from inoculation with mycorrhizae in the growth rate of fourwing saltbush (*Atriplex canscens*) planted on coal-mine spoils has been reported by Aldon (1975). Mycorrhizae are known to increase the availability of certain nutrients, particularly P, to woody species.

Bare-root shrubs have been planted each year for 4 years on shaley

Table 2—Shrub vigor ratings, made visually, as influenced by spot P fertilization
of limestone spoils in Colorado

Species	Nonfertilized			P-fertilized[†]		
	Good	Fair	Poor	Good	Fair	Poor
			%			
Rhus trilobata	51	31	18	71	21	8
Rosa sp.	66	26	8	72	15	13
Caragana arborescens	18	26	54	39	42	9

† 20 g per shrub.

(60% shale fragments) silty clay spoils generated by limestone mining in northeastern Colorado (Agronomy Dep., Colorado State Univ.). The calcareous spoils are deficient in P (2 ppm by $NaHCO_3$ test) and N. Concentrated superphosphate at the rate of 20 g of P per shrub was applied to the spoil in two slits 15 cm deep spaced 10 cm on either side of one half of the shrubs. Overall survival was 66% for P-fertilized shrubs and 70% for nonfertilized shrubs; the difference is not statistically different. Results of vigor ratings after five growing seasons on shrubs planted in 1970 are given in Table 2. The positive effect of P fertilization is highly significant. The data suggest that the response to fertilizer P is greater for *Caragana* than *Rhus* or *Rosa*, although the fertilizer—species interaction was not significant at the 5% level.

D. Fertilizer Application Techniques

Fertilizer application techniques for most efficient utilization of the applied nutrient will vary with factors affecting its mobility in soil, and with plant and microbial immobilization rate. Efficiency of utilization can be considered to be greatest when time of nutrient application together with proper positioning for uptake corresponds precisely to the time of greatest plant need. However, a myriad of factors, predictable and unpredictable, as well as logistics, essentially preclude the utmost in precision.

More alternatives to fertilizer application appear to exist for nutrients mobile in soil than those nonmobile, because positioning is less critical. But, failures are legion where reliance is placed on precipitation in semiarid regions to move mobile nutrients into position for uptake.

Immobile nutrients, such as P, are essentially limited to preplant soil incorporation, or application during planting with suitable drill attachment equipment. Immobile nutrients placed above the seed are "positionally" unavailable because the emerging radicle grows downward. Actively growing plants with roots near the surface can absorb immobile nutrients applied to the surface when the surface is moist. But the average frequency of adequate water at the surface in these regions is low because of rainfall frequency. Nevertheless, responses to surface-applied P of native grassland have been reported (Wight & Black, 1972).

Mobile nutrients, such as NO_3-N, can be applied either before, during, or at planting. Because mobile nutrients are highly soluble in water, placement of such materials in contact with seed at planting can cause germination problems because of a "salt-effect," that is, a reduction in available water surrounding the seed. The quantity of fertilizer material that can be placed in contact with the seed without posing germination problems varies with plant species and available soil water content surrounding the seed.

Application of nutrients in quantities to meet crop needs for more than a season, or in quantities which for several years thereafter require only so-called "maintenance" application rates, usually results in less efficient utilization of the nutrient than do annual applications at rates needed to meet crop requirements. This applies to both mobile and immobile nutrients. Reduction in efficiency is attributed to time-related chemical fixation and biological immobilization processes or, in the case of mobile nutrients, to displacement by percolating soil water. However, timing of fertilizer N at rates up to 540 kg/ha did not affect cumulative grass yields when applied all in one year, or one-third applied in each of 3 years, or one-sixth in each of 6 years, even though yields were increased by fertilizer N rate (Power & Alessi, 1971). Thus, where leaching is not a potential hazard, fertilizer application rates to meet needs for several years may be feasible. However, N applied at 1,120 kg/ha by Smith et al. (1968) was destructive to the vegetation. Application by band or row placement to improve efficiency of utilization of immobile nutrients can lead to development of plant nutritional problems if the quantity applied is too high. The most obvious, and perhaps best documented of these phenomena, is the effect of excess row-applied P upon inducement of Zn deficiency in corn and grain sorghum grown on calcareous soils (Langin et al., 1962).

E. Role of Water in Fertilizer Response

Water has an over-riding effect on plant growth and yield and, hence, on the amount of a nutrient needed to correct an existing deficiency of a given degree (Bauer et al., 1966).

The supply of stored available soil water at seeding within the plant rooting zone is correlated with yield response of spring-seeded annual crops to fertilizer and, hence, is useful as a criterion in determining yield potential, as well as providing a basis for predicting the fertilizer rate required to correct a deficiency of a given degree (Bauer et al., 1967). However, final yields are affected also by growing season precipitation supply and distribution, and by other climatic factors, all of which cannot be predicted. One approach to the problem of the unpredictable climatic factor in making fertilizer recommendations is to assume normal precipitation and climatic conditions, with the realization that rates applied may not be optimum. Growth response of perennial grasses to fertilizer N as affected by the available water supply has been documented by Smika et al. (1965). Response to N increased as either stored soil water or growing season precipitation increased.

The pollution potential as a consequence of mobile nutrients moving through the soil profile is essentially negligible in semiarid areas supporting vegetation perennially. Approximately 75% of the normal precipitation in the Great Plains region falls during the growing season. The amount and distribution is normally such that the available water reservoir in soils supporting vegetation is sufficiently depleted between precipitation events so that water received from the next precipitation rarely moves beyond the rooting zone, and invariably is depleted to the rooting depth by the time the crop is harvested. Power (1972) reported, for example, that water movement into the 180-cm depth of a silt loam soil supporting grasses occurred only during two periods from 1917 to 1958. In both cases, above average annual precipitation occurred for 2 or more successive years. Where summerfallow is included in annual cropping sequences, however, mobile nutrients can be leached below the root zone.

III. STATE OF THE RESEARCH ON CORRECTION OF NUTRIENT DEFICIENCIES

Nitrogen and phosphorus are recognized as being deficient in greatest areal extent and to the greatest degree in surface-mined lands. It is for this reason that these nutrients are tested first in mined-land fertility research. The authors know of no data from field studies which evaluate other nutrient deficiencies.

Most field studies to date directed to fertility research on mined land have involved two rates of fertilizer nutrient—none and some (Sandoval et al., 1973; Farmer et al., 1974). The "some" has been an application of a quantity assuming adequacy, based on previous experiences on undisturbed sites. Such an approach is useful in confirming deficiency, or sufficiency when yield levels are "high," and provides information on the degree to which soil test correlations developed for unmined land apply to mined land. If such correlations apply to mined lands, soil test interpretations applicable to the undisturbed dryland situation may be applicable also to the disturbed area where the spoils are covered with suitable plant rooting medium. Principal research efforts needed would appear to be to confirm the efficacy of soil test methods and standards in current use on undisturbed soils to assess fertility needs on disturbed sites.

Soil fertility studies in the greenhouse and climate-controlled chambers serve useful purposes (i) in evaluating relative differences in fertility among soils, plant rooting media, or plant species; (ii) in diagnosis of nutrient uptake by plants at specific growth stage, or the cause of foliar aberrations; and (iii) to a limited extent, in evaluation of nutrient placement, especially of nonmobile ions. But these studies serve little, if any, purpose in evaluating fertilizer application rates needed in the field. Growth responses to different rates of fertilizer may be observed in greenhouse or climate-controlled chambers (Aldon & Springfield, 1973). However, because of restricted rooting volumes and the control of climatic variables, especially water application, the field situation is not simulated. Calibration studies, that is, fitting the fertility nutrient application rate to the degree of deficiency, needs to be done with crop response evaluations under field conditions.

Soil fertility investigations were established on spoils in North Dakota in 1975 with wheat, corn, and grasses in which either N or P was applied at more than two rates. Wheat and corn trials were established at the Consolidation Coal Company on an area leveled to 9% slope in 1973 and covered with 60 cm of suitable plant rooting medium, primarily a mixture of the solum, during the summer of 1974. All combinations were evaluated of (i) P broadcast applications at 0 and 45 kg/ha followed by incorporation with a disk, (ii) P applied by drill or planter attachment at rates of 0 and 12 kg/ha on wheat and 0 and 18 kg/ha on corn, and (iii) N applications broadcast after planting at rates of 0, 22, 44, and 67 kg/ha on wheat and 0, 34, 67, and 101 kg/ha on corn. Data of site chemical characteristics are provided in Table 3.

A second set of trials with wheat and corn was conducted at Knife River Coal Company in which all combinations of the following were studied: (i) four "topsoil" thicknesses—5, 15, 30, and 60 cm; (ii) three fertilizer P rates—0, 34 and 101 kg/ha P placed at the spoil/topsoil interface; and (iii) three fertilizer P rates—0, 11 and 34 kg/ha applied by drill or planter attachment. A uniform rate of fertilizer N was applied—67 kg/ha on wheat and 90 kg/ha on corn. Data of site chemical characteristics are provided in Table 3.

A grass-legume mixture, seeded by Baukol-Noonan Coal Company in 1973 on leveled spoil material without topsoil, was fertilized with all combinations of five fertilizer P rates 0, 6, 17, 50, and 151 kg/ha broadcast in

Table 3—Chemical characteristics of soil and spoil materials at research sites in North Dakota, 1975

		Mine sites		
Parameter	Depth	Consolidation	Knife River	Baukol-Noonan
	cm			
Soil				
N, as NO$_3$,† kg	0–60	69	9	12¶
P,‡ kg	0–15	6	7	8¶
K,§ kg	0–15	122	208	166¶
pH	0–15	7.5	7.8	7.4
EC mmhos/cm	0–15	1.0	0.3	--
Spoil				
EC, mmhos/cm#	0–30	5.3	4.0	4.0
SAR††	0–30	8	7	1

† 50 kg to 60-cm depth is rated "high" and 9 kg to 60-cm depth is "very low" by NDSU Soil Test Standards; water extraction (NCR-13 Soil Testing Comm., 1975).

‡ 6 to 8 kg is rated "low"; NaHCO$_3$ soluble (Olsen et al., 1954).

§ >95 kg is rated "high" and >136 "very high"; $1N$ NH$_4$C$_2$H$_3$O$_2$ (NCR-13 Soil Testing Comm., 1975).

¶ Sampled autumn 1975.

Saturation extract.

†† Sodium adsorption ratio.

Table 4—Spring wheat grain and straw yield at Consolidation Coal Co. as affected by
fertilizer P rate and placement and fertilizer N rate, 1975†‡

P broadcast, kg/ha	P drill, kg/ha	N rate, kg/ha				
		0	22	45	67	Mean
		kg/ha				
		Grain				
0	0	548	718	813	843	732a*
0	12	880	913	1,156	981	981b
45	0	1,108	934	1,599	880	1,129c
45	12	1,095	941	1,747	867	1,162c
	Mean	1,042b	994b	1,055b	914a	
		Straw				
0	0	1,213	1,706	1,236	1,245	1,351a
0	12	1,819	1,823	1,995	1,888	1,882b
45	0	2,518	2,466	2,499	2,369	2,463c
45	12	2,748	2,681	2,499	2,276	2,551c
	Mean	2,074ab	2,171b	2,057ab	1,944a	

* Mean values followed by different letters, for appropriate comparisons, differ at the 5%
level, according to Duncan's multiple range test.
† Research from which these and data in subsequent tables were derived was supported by
Old West Regional Comm. Grant no. 10470016.
‡ The P broadcast × P drill interaction was significant at the 7% level for grain and straw.

October 1974, and 34, 67, and 134 kg N/ha in the spring 1975. Site-char-
acteristic data are provided in Table 3.

Data to show the effect of fertilizer treatments on crop yields at the
three sites are presented in Tables 4 through 8. The data illustrate the efficacy of the soil test procedures and interpretive standards developed to
predict fertilizer needs on undisturbed soils under dryland farming, in
predicting nutrient deficiency and fertilizer requirements on leveled
spoils covered with "topsoil," or suitable plant rooting medium.

Spring wheat and corn yields were increased by fertilizer P, as was
"predicted" by soil test. Wheat grain yields at the Consolidation
site, on 9% slope, were approximately equal to yields on farms in the
vicinity of the mine on fields cropped in 1974 to wheat, but about 50%

Table 5—Corn silage yield at Consolidation Coal Co. as affected by fertilizer P rate
and placement and fertilizer N rate, 1975†

P broadcast kg/ha	P drill, kg/ha	N rate, kg/ha				
		0	34	67	101	Mean
		kg/ha, 70% H$_2$O				
0	0	8,482	10,201	7,351	7,587	8,470a‡
0	18	10,437	11,250	9,931	8,246	9,966b
45	0	9,777	10,531	9,872	11,321	10,378b
45	18	9,931	11,050	10,119	10,590	10,425b
	Mean	9,660a	10,755b	9,318a	9,506a	

† The P broadcast × P drill interaction was significant at the 7.7% level.
‡ See Table 4 for explanation.

Table 6—Spring wheat grain and straw yield at Knife River Coal Co. as affected by fertilizer P rate and placement and by topsoil thickness, 1975**

P drill, kg/ha	P broadcast, kg/ha	Topsoil, cm				Mean
		5	15	30	60	
				kg/ha		
			Grain			
0	0	65	63	136	179	
	34	112	75	172	204	
	101	129	148	149	236	139a†
11	0	207	234	239	287	
	34	120	177	211	227	
	101	81	128	213	262	198b
34	0	120	168	197	283	
	34	96	119	297	230	
	101	95	148	264	256	189b
	Mean	114a	140ab	208bc	241c	
			Straw			
0	0	375	332	726	970	
	34	568	436	729	965	
	101	544	670	827	1,157	691a
11	0	674	1,098	997	990	
	34	594	660	1,253	1,222	
	101	449	567	1,280	1,346	927c
34	0	576	510	633	1,075	
	34	551	596	927	1,290	
	101	601	646	977	1,236	802b
	Mean	548a	612a	927b	1,139b	

** P broadcast variance for straw was significant at the 1% level.
† See Table 4 for explanation.

lower than on fields fallowed in 1974. Wheat grain yields were much lower at the Knife River site. The low yields at the Knife River site occurred because dry "topsoil" was placed on the spoil shortly before planting. Because of low rainfall after planting, the "topsoil" was not recharged with water, and water severely limited growth. (This illustrates the difficulty of calibrating soil tests under these conditions).

Table 7—Corn silage yield at Knife River Coal Co. as affected by drilled fertilizer P rates and topsoil thickness†

P drill, kg/ha	Topsoil, cm				Mean
	5	15	30	60	
		kg/ha, 70% H_2O			
0	1,583	2,359	3,647	5,290	3,220a‡
11	2,486	3,244	3,726	6,376	3,960b
34	2,516	3,218	4,677	6,719	4,284b
Mean	2,195a	2,940ab	4,019b	6,131c	

† Broadcast fertilizer P at the soil/spoil interface did not affect yield.
‡ See Table 4 for explanation.

Table 8—Grass-legume mixture yield at Baukol-Noonan Coal Co. as affected by
fertilizer N and P rate, 1975[†]

N rate, kg/ha	P rate, kg/ha					
	0	6	17	50	151	Mean
	kg/ha					
34	1,244	1,236	1,335	1,208	1,530	1,310a[‡]
67	1,250	1,552	1,448	1,343	1,304	1,379a
134	1,683	2,045	1,985	1,808	1,635	1,831b

† Fertilizer P did not increase yield.
‡ See Table 4 for explanation.

Application of 12 kg/ha P by drill attachment was not sufficient for maximum attainable wheat grain yields at Consolidation, but 11 kg/ha applied by the same method at Knife River was adequate where yields were lower because of less stored water. The "predicted" P rate for correction of "low" testing undisturbed soils is about 11 to 12 kg/ha P by soil testing standards. These results on spoils suggest that recommended rates of P fertilization based on P soil test interpretations for correction of a given deficiency test level may need upward revision for spoils.

Corn silage yields at both sites were increased by fertilizer P banded 5 cm below and 5 cm to the side of the seed (Tables 5 and 7). In these two cases, the interpretation of P soil test data applicable to undisturbed sites was applicable on the leveled spoil covered with topsoil, at the yield levels attained.

Fertilizer N decreased wheat grain yield when applied at 67 kg/ha N, but lower rates had no effect on yield at the Consolidation site (Table 4). Straw yields, too, were lowest at the 67 kg/ha N rate. Soil test methods diagnosed a "high" available N level; no fertilizer N would be recommended. Thus, the "prediction" of sufficiency level and rate was correct.

The grass-legume yields (Table 8) were increased by fertilizer N but not P. The former was "predicted" by soil test but not the latter. While no data are presented for a nonfertilizer N treatment, visual observations of the grass-legume plant growth surrounding the site left no doubt that yields were increased by fertilizer N applied at the two lowest N rates. Fertilizer P did not effect increases when the rating was "low" by standards developed for small grain crops.

Soil test analyses of stockpiled soil materials, principally all or most of the solum, indicate that the NO_3-N levels ranged from deficiency to sufficiency between different stockpiles and at different depths within a stockpile (Table 9). These data indicate, too, that the range in NO_3^- concentration was greater than the range of either P or K. This suggests that the number of samples needed to representatively assess the available N status of stockpiled materials may be greater than that needed for P or K. After placement on leveled spoils, the available N status can be expected to change more rapidly and extensively under conditions favoring microbial activity than either P or K, but not necessarily at a uniform rate. This change in NO_3^- level compounds the sampling problems of stockpiled soil materials.

Table 9—Soil test analyses of "topsoil" from six stockpiles in North Dakota, 1976

Stockpile	Nutrient	Sampling depth, cm									
		0–30	30–61	61–76	76–102	102–127	127–152	152–178	178–202	202–229	229–254
		kg/15 cm									
1	N, as NO₃†	16	2	2	2	3	2	2	4	--	--
2		8	9	9	6	6	4	5	6	15	11
3		13	10	11	21	11	9	7	5	4	3
4		3	5	4	4	4	3	--	--	--	--
5		5	17	20	20	13	5	2	3	3	5
6		5	3	7	5	17	6	4	3	2	3
1	P‡	6	5	5	5	6	5	6	6	--	--
2		5	6	3	3	4	4	4	3	2	3
3		5	5	4	7	5	5	4	4	5	5
4		5	4	5	8	5	7	--	--	--	--
5		2	3	4	8	8	6	4	3	4	5
6		3	3	6	4	5	4	5	3	1	4
1	K§	200	159	118	91	100	166	207	127	--	--
2		143	153	137	151	158	150	150	152	144	138
3		147	144	143	161	150	152	127	125	132	138
4		136	129	132	179	129	154	--	--	--	--
5		114	143	202	193	207	177	138	148	191	120
6		107	111	114	111	125	102	98	93	57	73

† Water-soluble NO₃.
‡ NaHCO₃ soluble P.
§ 1N NH₄C₂H₃O₂ extractable K.

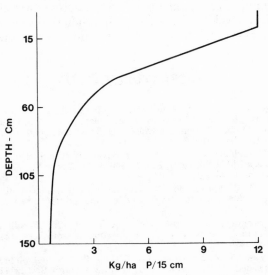

Fig. 1—Sodium bicarbonate-soluble P in Morton silt loam to 152 cm.

The P level of the stockpiled materials was relatively uniform and consistently deficient. This outcome is not unexpected since the amount of NaHCO₃ soluble P decreases sharply with soil profile depth (Zubriski, 1971) (Fig. 1), and the stockpiled materials represent, essentially, the solum. Further, P deficiency is widespread in North Dakota soils (Bauer et al., 1966).

Potassium, extractable with $NH_4C_2H_3O_2$, is present in large enough quantities to be rated as "high" to "very high" in virtually every sample. These ratings are consistent with those of the great majority of soils tested in the state.

IV. SUMMARY

Nutrient deficiencies, especially of N and P, are widespread in soils of the semiarid and arid regions and are expected to be the major nutritional problem in spoilbank reclamation from the standpoint of areal extent and distribution. Known deficiencies of other nutrients exist in soils of the region, but the areal distribution is low in comparison to N and P. Nutrients concentrations present at levels toxic to plants are virtually unknown in soils of the region, but Se accumulations in plants in parts of the region can be toxic to animals. Instances of B toxicity have been documented in spoil materials containing biologically inert C.

Soil test procedures presently utilized provide a means of deficiency detection. Soil test interpretations relative to rate of fertilizer application needed to correct the deficiency, however, may depend on the kind of plant rooting medium present at the spoil surface and its thickness. Where plant rooting medium consists of soil materials from essentially all of the solum, corrective rates may be expected to be equal to those required on undisturbed soils of equal deficiency. But as the thickness of organic matter-containing plant rooting medium decreases, corrective rates for a given deficiency level are expected to be higher, provided some other factor does not alter the potential yield level of the crop grown.

LITERATURE CITED

Agricultural Research Service and North Dakota Agricultural Experiment Station Research Staffs. 1975. Progress report on research on reclamation of strip-mined lands in the Northern Great Plains. Northern Great Plains Res. Center and North Dakota Agric. Exp. Stn. Progress Rep. 20 p.

Aldon, E. F. 1975. Endomycorrhizae enhance survival and growth of fourwing saltbush on coal mine spoils. USDA For. Serv. Res. Note RM-294, Rocky Mt. For. and Range Exp. Stn., Fort Collins, Colo. 2 p.

Aldon, E. F., and H. W. Springfield. 1973. Revegetating coal mine spoils in New Mexico. USDA For. Serv. Res. Note RM-245. Rocky Mt. For. and Range Exp. Stn., Fort Collins, Colo. 4 p.

Bauer, A., E. B. Norum, J. C. Zubriski, and R. A. Young. 1966. Fertilizer for small grain production on summerfallow in North Dakota. North Dakota Agric. Exp. Stn. Bull. 461, Fargo, N. Dak. 54 p.

Bauer, A., E. H. Vasey, R. A. Young, and J. L. Ozbun. 1967. Stored soil moisture best guide to nitrogen needed. North Dakota Agric. Exp. Stn. Farm Res. 24(11):15–24, Fargo, N. Dak.

Beaton, J. D., S. L. Tisdale, and J. Platou. 1971. Crop responses to sulfur in North America. The Sulfur Inst. Tech. Bull. no. 18, Washington, D.C. 39 p.

Beeson, K. C. 1941. The mineral composition of crops with particular reference to the soils in which they were grown. USDA Misc. Pub. No. 369, Washington, D.C. 164 p.

Berg, W. A. 1975. Revegetation of land disturbed by surface mining in Colorado. p. 79–89. In M. K. Wali (ed.) Practices and problems of land reclamation in Western North America. Univ. of North Dakota Press, Grand Forks.

Berger, K. C. 1962. Micronutrient deficiencies in the United States. J. Agric. Food Chem. 10: 178–181.

Boatwright, G. O., and H. J. Haas. 1961. Development and composition of spring wheat as influenced by nitrogen and phosphorus fertilization. Agron. J. 53:33–35.

Doll, E. C., and R. E. Lucas. 1973. Testing soils for potassium, calcium and magnesium. p. 133–151. In Leo M. Walsh and James D. Beaton (ed.) Soil testing and plant analysis. Soil Sci. Soc. Am., Madison, Wis.

Farmer, E. E., R. W. Brown, B. Z. Richardson, and P. E. Packer. 1974. Revegetation research on the Decker Coal Mine in southeastern Montana. USDA For. Serv. Res. Pap. INT-162, Intermt. For. and Range Exp. Stn., Ogden, Utah. 12 p.

Goetz, H. 1970. Growth and development of Northern Great Plains species in relation to nitrogen fertilization. J. Range Mange. 23:112–117.

Graham, E. R. 1959. An explanation of the theory and methods of soil testing. Missouri Agric. Exp. Stn. Bull. 734.

Harbert, H. P., and W. A. Berg. 1974. Vegetative stablization of spent oil shales. Colorado State Univ. Environ. Resour. Center Tech. Rep. 4, Fort Collins, Colo. 40 p.

Hunter, A. S. 1949. Yield and composition of alfalfa as affected by variations in the calcium-magnesium ratio in the soil. Soil Sci. 67:53–62.

Johnson, C. M. 1966. Molybdenum. p. 286–301. In H. D. Chapman (ed.) Diagnostic criteria for plants and soils. Univ. of California Div. of Agric. Sci., Berkeley, Calif.

Langin, E. J., R. C. Ward, R. A. Olson, and H. F. Rhoades. 1962. Factors responsible for poor response of corn and grain sorghum to phosphorus fertilization: II. Lime and P placement effects on P-Zn relations. Soil Sci. Soc. Am. Proc. 26:574–578.

Miyamoto, S., W. L. Gould, and D. Rai. 1975. Characterizing overburden materials before surface mining in the Fruitland Formation of northwestern New Mexico. p. 80–92. In Proc. 3rd Symp. on Surface Mining and Reclamation, 21–24 Oct. 1975, Louisville, Ky. Vol. 1. Natl. Coal Assoc., Washington, D.C.

NCR-13 Soil Testing Committee. 1975. Recommended chemical soil test procedures for the North Central Region. North Dakota Agric. Exp. Stn. Bull. no. 499. Fargo, N. Dak. 23 p.

Olsen, S. R., C. V. Cole, F. S. Watanabe, and L. A. Dean. 1954. Estimation of available phosphorus in soils by extraction with sodium bicarbonate. USDA Cir. 939:1–9, Washington, D.C.

Omodt, H. W., F. W. Schroer, and D. D. Patterson. 1975. The properties of important agricultural soils as criteria for mined land reclamation. North Dakota Agric. Exp. Stn. Bull. 492, Fargo, N. Dak. 52 p.

Packer, P. E. 1974. Rehabilitation potentials and limitations of surface-mined land in the Northern Great Plains. USDA For. Serv. Gen. Tech. Rep. INT-14. Intermt. For. and Range Exp. Stn., Ogden, Utah.

Power, J. F. 1972. Nitrate enrichment of soils and water under dryland in the Great Plains. p. 119–136. In Control of agriculture-related pollution in the Great Plains. Great Plains Agric. Counc. Publ. no. 60, Nebraska Agric. Exp. Stn., Lincoln, Nebr.

Power, J. F., and J. Alessi. 1971. Nitrogen fertilization of semi-arid grasslands: Plant growth and soil mineral N levels. Agron. J. 63:277–280.

Power, J. F., J. J. Bond, F. M. Sandoval, and W. O. Willis. 1974. Nitrification in Paleocene shales. Science 183:1077–1079.

Pratt, P. F. 1965. Potassium. In C. A. Black et al. (ed.) Methods of soil analysis, Part 2. Chemical and biological properties. Agronomy 9:1022–1030. Am. Soc. of Agron., Madison, Wis.

Richard, T. A., O. J. Attoe, S. Moskal, and E. Truog. 1960. A chemical method for determining available soil nitrogen. Int. Congr. Soil Sci., Trans. 7th (Madison, Wis.) Vol. II: 28–35.

Sandoval, F. M., J. J. Bond, J. F. Power, and W. O. Willis. 1973. Lignite mine spoils in the Northern Great Plains—Characteristics and potential for reclamation. p. 117–133. In Proc. 1st Res. and Applied Tech. Symp. on Mined-land Reclamation, Pittsburgh, Pa., 7–8 Mar. 1973, Natl. Coal Assoc. Bituminous Coal Res., Inc., Monroeville, Pa.

Skogley, E. O. 1976. Potassium in Montana soils. Montana Agric. Exp. Stn. Res. Rep. 88, Bozeman, Mont. 62 p.

Smika, D. E., H. J. Haas, and J. F. Power. 1965. Effects of moisture and nitrogen fertilizer on growth and water use by native grasses. Agron. J. 57:483–486.

Smith, A. D., A. Johnston, L. E. Lutwich, and S. Smoliak. 1968. Fertilizer response of fescue grassland vegetation. Can. J. Soil Sci. 48:125–132.

Soltanpour, P. N., and A. P. Schwab. 1977. A new test for simultaneous extraction of macro- and micro-nutrients in alkaline soils. Commun. Soil Sci. Plant Anal. 8:195–207.

Tisdale, S. L., and W. L. Nelson. 1966. Soil fertility and fertilizers. 2nd ed. The MacMillan Co., New York.

Watanabe, F. S., and S. R. Olsen. 1965. Test of an ascorbic acid method for determining phosphorus in water and $NaHCO_3$ extracts from soil. Soil Sci. Soc. Am. Proc. 29:677–678.

Wight, J. R., and A. L. Black. 1972. Energy fixation and precipitation-use efficiency in a fertilized rangeland ecosystem of the Northern Great Plains. J. Range Manage. 25:376–380.

Zubriski, J. C. 1971. Relationships between forms of soil phosphorus, some indexes of phosphorus availability, and growth of sudangrass in greenhouse trials. Agron. J. 63:421–425.

Chapter 26

Mulch and Chemical Stabilizers for Land Reclamation in Dry Regions

BURGESS L. KAY

University of California
Davis, California

I. INTRODUCTION

Land reclamation may take longer in dry regions than where moisture is adequate and well distributed, and revegetation efforts may need to be more intensive. Mulching nearly always shortens the time needed to establish a suitable plant cover. The conventional mulches of agricultural or industrial residues have recently encountered competition from many chemical stabilizers or mulches introduced largely as supplements to the increasingly popular hydraulic methods (hydroseeding-application of a water slurry of seed, fertilizer, mulch, etc.).

Seed coverage with soil to the proper depth is essential in dry regions. Mulch, particularly hydromulching, is sometimes substituted for seed coverage when moisture is adequate. Showing the most promise in excessively dry areas are mulches applied after seed has been covered to the proper depth with soil, as with a grain drill (Springfield, 1971).

Mulches can both protect soil and enhance plant establishment. The soil is protected by shielding it from raindrop impact, retarding water flow and soil movement by trapping silt on the sites, increasing water penetration, and sometimes shedding water. Properly anchored, mulches may reduce wind velocity. They enhance plant establishment by holding seed and fertilizer in place, retaining moisture, preventing crusting, and modifying temperatures.

Mulches on dry sites may also encourage plant suicide! Properly mulched seeds may often be fooled into germinating with the first rainfall and soon die from lack of sufficient moisture for continued growth. The use of soil mulch (seed coverage) is probably the best insurance against such a calamity. Soil which is sufficiently wet for a long enough period to effect germination is more likely to sustain plant growth than is a surface organic mulch. Also planting as near as practical to a date when adequate moisture is expected may avoid this problem.

467

II. ORGANIC MULCHES

Organic mulches are often an agricultural crop residue or industrial by-product. The price usually reflects transport and handling cost more than any intrinsic value of the product.

Most organic mulches require additional nitrogen to compensate for the tie-up of nitrogen in the decomposition process.

Effectiveness is roughly related to the size and shape of the mulch particles. Long, narrow particles are superior to finely ground products. A discussion of the organic mulches commonly used follows.

A. Straw and Hay

Straw and hay are the mulches used most often in the western U.S. Cereals are a major crop in dry regions of the United States, and straw left on the site of production is often considered a liability because its decomposition ties up nitrogen needed for the next crop. Straw availability should be increased by current restrictions on removing this crop residue by burning in place. Clean grain straw, free of noxious weeds, is preferred. The straw can be expected to contain 0.5 to 5.0% cereal seed by weight, which may result in considerable plant cover in the first year. This provides additional erosion protection but may also be prohibitively competitive with the planted erosion-control or beautification mixture. Rice straw (*Oryza sativa* L.) is sometimes used because neither the rice nor associated weeds could be expected to grow on most nonirrigated disturbed lands. In areas where cereal crops are not common, hay is sometimes used but is normally more expensive than straw. Wild-grass hay may be a valuable source of native plant material if cut when the seeds are ripe but not shattered.

The mulch effect of straw can be expected to increase plant establishment. Meyer et al. (1971) obtained fescue-bluegrass establishment of 3, 28, and 42% with respective surface straw mulch treatments of 0, 2.25, and 4.5 metric tons/ha.

Straw can be applied with specially designed straw blowers or spread by hand. Commercial mulch spreaders or straw blowers advertise a capability of up to 13.6 metric tons/hour and distances to 26 m. The length of the applied straw may be important and can be controlled in most blowers by adjusting or removing the flail chains. Baled straw may also be relatively long or short, depending on agricultural practices. Straw to be crimped or punched should be relatively long to be incorporated into the soil effectively and still leave tufts or whisker dams. Rice straw is wiry, does not shatter readily, and consequently does not blow as well as straw of wheat (*Triticum aestivum* L.), barley (*Hordeum vulgare* L.), or oats (*Avena sativa* L.). It may come out of the blower in "bird nests." Blown straw (other than rice) lies down in closer contact with the soil than hand-spread straw and is anchored more successfully with a tackifier (substance sprayed on straw to hold it in place). Wind is a serious limiting factor in applying straw, though it can be an asset in making applications downwind. Dust, a problem in urban areas, can be overcome by injecting water into the airstream used to blow the straw.

The amount of straw to be used will depend on the erodability of the site (soil type, rainfall, and length and steepness of slope), kind of straw (Grib, 1967), and whether plant growth is to be encouraged. Increasing rates of straw give increasing protection. Meyer et al. (1970) show that as little as 1.1 metric tons reduced soil losses by two-thirds, while 9 metric tons/ha reduced losses by 95%. Straw to be crimped is commonly used at 4.5 metric tons/ha, while straw punched into fill slopes in California is at 9 metric tons/ha in a split application and rolling operation (4.5 metric tons each). Straw to be held down with a net should be limited to 3.4 to 4.5 metric tons/ha, and straw held with a tackifier at 2.5 to 3.4 metric tons/ha if plant growth is important. Too much straw will smother seedlings by intercepting all light or forming a physical barrier. Also, some grass straw (notably annual ryegrass [Lolium multiflorum Lam.]) may contain inhibitors that have a toxic effect if used in excess. A good rule of thumb is that some soil should be visible if plant growth is wanted. Higher rates of straw may, of course, still satisfy these requirements if the straws are vertically oriented (like tufts) by crimping or punching. Excessive straw on the surface may be a fire hazard.

Straw or hay usually needs to be held in place until plant growth starts. The problem is wind, not water. Water puddles the soil around the straw and helps hold it in place. Also, wet straw "mats down" and is not easily moved. Common methods of holding straw in place are crimping, disking, or rolling into the soil; covering with a net or wire; or spraying with a chemical tackifier. Swanson et al. (1967) found similar protection from prairie hay applied as a loose mulch or anchored with a disk packer.

Crimping is accomplished with commercial machines which utilize blunt, notched disks which are forced into the soil by a weighted tractor-drawn carriage. They will not penetrate hard soils and cannot be pulled on steep slopes.

Rolling or "punching" is done with a specially designed roller. A sheepsfoot roller, commonly used in soil compaction, is not satisfactory for incorporating straw. Specifications of the California Department of Transportation (1975) contain the following provisions: "Roller shall be equipped with straight studs, made of approximately 2.2 cm steel plate, placed approximately 20 cm apart, and staggered. The studs shall not be less than 15 cm long nor more than 15 cm wide and shall be rounded to prevent withdrawing the straw from the soil. The roller shall be of such weight as to incorporate the straw sufficiently into the soil so that the straw will not support combustion, and will have a uniform surface."

The roller may be tractor-drawn on flat areas or gentle slopes, whereas on steeper slopes with top-of-slope access the roller may be lowered by gravity and raised by a winch in "yo-yo" fashion, commonly from a flat-bed truck. Requirements are soil soft enough for the roller teeth to penetrate, and access to the top of the slope. This is a common treatment on highway fill slopes in California. It can be used on much steeper slopes than a crimper can. Punched straw may not be as effective as contour crimped straw, because of the staggered arrangement of punched straw as opposed to the "whisker dams" made by crimping (Barnett et al., 1967).

A variety of nets have been used to hold straw in place: twisted-woven kraft paper, plastic fabric, poultry netting, concrete reinforcing wire, and even jute. Price and the length of service required should determine the product used. These should be anchored at enough points to prevent the net from whipping in the wind, which rearranges the straw.

Perhaps the most common method of holding straw is use of a tackifier. This method may be used on relatively steep slopes which have limited access and soil too hard for crimping or punching. Asphalt emulsion, the tackifier used most commonly, is applied at 19 to 47 hl/ha—either over the top of the straw or applied simultaneously with the straw-blowing operation. Recent tests have shown that 56 hl is superior to 37 hl, and that 19 hl/ha is not satisfactory.[1] Wood fiber, or new products used in combination with wood fiber, have been demonstrated to be equally effective, similar in cost, and environmentally more acceptable (Table 1). Terratack I is a gum derived from guar (*Cyamopsis tetragonoloba* D.C.), Terratack II is semirefined seaweed extracts, and Ecology Controls M Binder is a gum from plantain (*Plantago insularis* Eastw.). The remaining products are emulsions used in making adhesives, paints, and other products. Though wood fiber alone is effective as a short-term tackifier, glue must be added to give protection beyond a few weeks. Increasing the rate/ha of any of the materials will increase their effectiveness.

---

[1] B. L. Kay. 1976. Hydroseeding, straw, and chemicals for erosion control. Agron. Prog. Rep. no. 77. UC Agronomy-Davis. 14 p. Mimeo.

Table 1—Effect of tackifier products on wind stability of barley straw broadcast at 2,240 kg/ha

Product	Rate/ha			Wind speed (km/hour) at which 50% of straw was blown away
	Chemical	Fiber	Water	
		kg	hl	
None				14
SS-1 asphalt	1,869 liters			64
SS-1 asphalt	3,738 liters			129
SS-1 asphalt	5,607 liters			135
Fiber only		542		75
Fiber only		824		135
Fiber only		1,104		135
Terratack I	45 kg	280	150	111
Terratack II	50 kg	168	70	132
Ecology Control M-Binder	100 kg	168	70	135
Styrene butadiene copolymer emulsion	561 liters	84	37	135
Polyvinyl acetate	935 liters	280	93	87
Copolymer of methacrylates and acrylates	935 liters	280	93	122

B. Hydromulching

Hydromulching is a mulch applied in a water slurry. This same slurry may also contain seed, fertilizer, erosion-control compounds, growth regulators, soil amendments, etc., and is increasingly popular because of low labor requirements. Mulches must have a particle size small enough for ready pumping through 1-cm nozzles, and must not be too buoyant to remain in suspension with moderate agitation. Used most commonly are specially manufactured fibers of alder (*Alnus* sp. L.) and aspen (*Populus tremuloides* Michx.). Western hemlock (*Tsuga heterophylla* [Rafn.] Sarg.), also used, is more difficult to pump. Many recycled paper and agricultural products have been marketed or tested. Among those marketed are office waste, corrugated boxes (PFM), chopped newspaper, and seed screenings. Also tested by the author were whole and ground rice hulls, ground cereal straw, ryegrass straw (both defiberized and NaOH-treated), and washed dairy waste.

The most important quality of a hydromulching material is that it must adhere to the soil even on steep slopes and hold the seed in place during heavy rainfall impact and wind. If it fails in those functions, other characteristics (water-holding capacity, appearance, cost, etc.) are not important.

Hydromulching materials have been tested (by the author) by applying them to the surface of greenhouse flats of 28 by 48 cm filled with decomposed granite. The flats were inclined at 45° (1:1 slope) and subjected to artificial rainfall of 3-mm drops falling 4.5 m from a 2.54-cm grid at 15 cm of water/hour. Virgin wood fibers of aspen and alder offered considerable soil protection (Fig. 1) and were consistently superior to all other products. The only recycled products to approach their effectiveness were the PFM products made from corrugated boxes. One lot of these fibers had been separated on the basis of length, with the shorter fibers being recycled into other paper products. These longest fibers were at least equal to the virgin wood fibers. Tests of commercial PFM products, however, do not always produce such satisfactory results, apparently because they contain a high proportion of short fibers. Commercial materials made of office waste and seed screenings are vastly inferior. These and other recycled materials wash from the slope with the first raindrops. A satisfactory material could probably be made from recycled material if more attention were paid to fiber length.

Another important property of mulch is its moisture-holding characteristics. A standard procedure for measuring this characteristic has been developed by the California Department of Transportation (Hoover, 1976). In general, products with the longest fibers and best slope-adhering characteristics also have the highest moisture-holding capacity.

Commercial fibers are usually dyed with a fugitive green dye which lasts only a few hours or days. This visual aid assists in obtaining an even distribution on the slope.

Rates of hydromulch vary from 0.6 to 3.4 metric tons/ha. The rate of 0.6 metric tons/ha is suggested as necessary to protect seed in passing

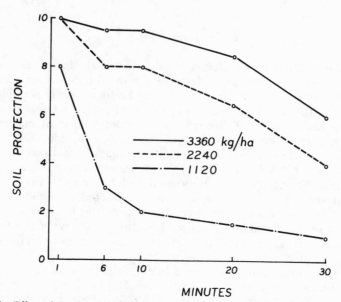

Fig. 1—Effect of simulated rainfall of 3-mm drops at 15 cm/hour on soil protection rating (10 = excellent, 1 = none) on three rates of wood fiber mulch.

through the centrifugal pumps commonly used in hydroseeding.[1] A minimum of 1.1 metric tons/ha is necessary to hold the seed on a slope. No consistent "mulch effect" has been observed with less than 1.7 metric tons/ha. Currier (1970) expressed some concern that "60–70% of the seed hangs up in the mulch and has little or no chance to get its primary roots into mineral soil." Studies with wood fiber showed that, under conditions of adequate moisture, small grass seeds such as Durar hard fescue (*Festuca ovina* var. *duriscula* [L.] Koch.) could emerge through as much as 10 metric tons/ha and readily emerge from between two 1-metric ton layers.[2] Placing the seed on top of 2.3 metric tons speeded emergence and total germination of orchardgrass (*Dactylis glomerata* L.) and did not reduce emergence of any of the other five species tested.

Under limited moisture created by applying the mulch over seed broadcast on greenhouse flats filled with various problem soils, inclining the flats at slopes of 1:1, 1.5:1, or 2:1 (horizontal to vertical measurement) and exposing them to natural rainfall yielded the data in Table 2. On the steepest slopes (1:1 and 1.5:1), 1.1 to 2.3 metric tons of fiber was necessary to hold the seed in place. Without that amount, no seedlings were established. On the flatter 2:1 slopes, the 1.1-metric ton rate did not improve the stand, whereas 2.3 metric tons did. Increasing the rate to 3.4 metric tons increased the number of seedlings on the most severe test with either decomposed granite or fine sand. Recent tests by the author near Lake Tahoe, California, show 5 metric tons/ha to result in good grass

[2]B. L. Kay. 1973. Wood fiber mulch studies. Agronomy Progress Report no. 52, UC Agronomy-Davis. 6 p. Mimeo.

Table 2—Effect of hydromulch fiber rate on emergence of blando bromegrass (*Bromus mollis* L.) on different soils and slope gradients

Treatment	Approximate kg/ha	Number of seedlings/0.1 m²					
		Decomposed granite				Clay loam	Fine sand
		2:1	1.5:1	1:1	1:1	1:1	1:1
None		8	1	0	0	0	0
Wood fiber	1,120	6	14	11	0	93	0
Wood fiber	2,240	28	31	29	15	282	3
Wood fiber	3,360	38	38	22	62	323	17
L.S.D.$_{0.05}$		12	9	9	12	73	11

stands, while 3.4 metric tons/ha produced only few seedlings because of excessive frost heaving.

Wood fiber is an essential addition to most hydraulically applied chemicals, including straw tackifiers. Many soil-binding chemicals will not hold seed, fertilizer, or straw to a slope unless wood fiber is included.

C. Wood Residues

Wood residues (woodchips and bark) can be used effectively if locally available as a waste from the forest-product industry or chipped on the site during land clearance. Smaller wood-residue particles, such as shavings or sawdust, would be subject to wind loss. Woodchips and bark can be applied with a conventional straw-blower to a distance of 18 m (Emanuel, 1971). The rate must be twice that of straw to obtain the same soil protection (Meyer et al., 1972) or even as much as six times the straw rate (Swanson et al., 1965). Observations in California indicate that uneven distribution often results in poor or no plant establishment in the heavier (100% ground cover) applications.

D. Fabric or Mats

Fabric or mats, including jute, excelsior, and woven paper or plastic fibers, are provided in rolls to be fastened to the soil with wire staples. Fiberglass roving (which is blown on with compressed air and tacked with asphalt emulsion) is also available as a nonbiodegradable substitute. Use of these products is limited by their cost and effectiveness. They require high labor inputs for installation, cost at least four times as much as tacked straw, and are not adapted to fitting to rough surfaces or rocky areas. Erosion from beneath these products is common because they do not have intimate contact with the soil. They must be heavy enough or anchored in enough spots to prevent wind whipping. Several reports indicate they are not as effective as straw (Springfield, 1971). They have the advantage of being weed-free but may be unsightly, a fire hazard, or (in some cases) nonbiodegradable or too rapidly biodegradable to be effective. Dudeck et al. (1970) found excelsior mat or jute to yield the best seedling grass of eleven mulch treatments tested. Swanson et al. (1967) found jute, excelsior, and prairie hay or fiberglass anchored with asphalt emulsion to be the best of 11 treatments.

Mats would be used only on small areas, such as to repair failures of other treatments, where time and cost factors are of secondary importance. They should be maintained to repair tears, etc., before wind or water can cause extensive damage.

III. CHEMICALS

Chemicals to be used as a mulch, humectant (a substance that absorbs or helps another substance retain moisture), or soil binder are usually applied in a water carrier or as part of a hydroseeding slurry. They are expensive and very specialized, and must be used correctly for maximum effectiveness. They are not substitutes for sound agricultural or engineering practices, regardless of glowing advertisements. Products are discussed here as either natural organic substances to be used as part of a seeding, or plastic emulsions which may be used with a seeding or alone as a soil binder.

A. Natural Organic Substances

Natural organic substances are generally advertised to hold fiber in place, promote germination, hold moisture, and retard erosion. Most sales literature acknowledges that fiber should be used with the product. Within this group we have tested Bio Binder, Ecology Control M-Binder, Kelgum, Petroset SB, Terratack I, Terratack III, and Verdyol Super.

Virgin wood fiber generally holds very well by itself. Under extreme wind conditions, increasing the rates of fiber application proved to be as good as adding a chemical. The high application cost, however, may make it cheaper to add the chemical than to double the fiber rate. This may or may not give the same plant-mulch effect as adding more fiber. Many of the products did not provide additional erosion protection, and one of them gave poorer results than using the fiber alone. One product (Ecology Control M-Binder) at 112 kg/ha has held fiber in place, improved grass stands, and reduced erosion better than fiber alone in some of the more severe tests (sandy soil, steepest slopes, most wind and rain). Terratack III (a seaweed derivative) shows promise at 45 kg/ha. Most of these products are not compatible with commercial fertilizers, and require a separate application. Most of them allow easier pumping of the hydromulch slurry.

B. Synthetic Emulsions

Plastic emulsions have been used for about a decade to bind surface soil particles for protection from wind and water erosion (Armbrust & Lyles, 1975; Gabriels & De Boodt, 1975). Their use has been limited, however, by relatively high cost and by numerous reports of ineffectiveness and negative effects on plant establishment (Sheldon & Bradshaw, 1977). Among the emulsions used are polyvinyl acetate homopolymers or vinyl acrylic copolymers, generally called PVA. Commercial versions are Aerospray 70, Crust 500, Curasol AE, Enviro, MGS, Stickum, Terra Krete, and Soil Bond. Soil Seal, similar in effectiveness, is a copolymer of methacrylates and acrylates. A new chemical group under current test is styrene butadiene (SBR). All are an intimate mixture of high-molecular-weight polymeric particles dispersed in a continuous aqueous phase. They are basic ingredients in paint, glue, and other products.

1. EFFECTIVENESS AND RATE

Plastic emulsions give better initial protection than do other commonly used erosion-control practices. The optimum rate determined by the California Department of Transportation is 1,120 kg/ha of dry solids (about 1,870 liters/ha) for the polyvinyl acetates (840–1,232 kg/ha on various soils). Most emulsions are about 1.09 kg/liter, and 55% solids. Recent tests compared PVA with an experimental SBR from Amsco Division, Union Oil Company, at rates of 560 and 1,120 kg/ha solids and at low fiber (0.3 metric tons/ha) and high fiber (1.7 metric tons/ha). Applying the emulsion (560 kg/ha) over the top of 1.7 metric tons/ha of wood fiber (split application) greatly increased the effectiveness of SBR, but not PVA. With low fiber, SBR at 560 kg was similar in effectiveness to PVA at 1,120 kg (Fig. 2).

2. DILUTION RATE

All products tested to date are sold as a liquid concentrate to mix with water. The amount of water used is critical. Figures 3 and 4 illustrate the relative effectiveness of dilution rates of 5:1 (water to PVA concentrate) to 40:1 at 1,120 kg and 560 kg of PVA solids per hectare.

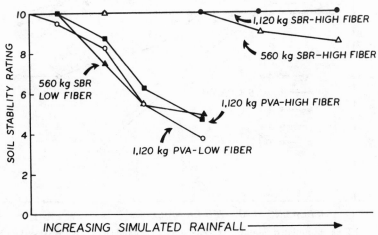

Fig. 2—Effect of simulated rainfall on surface stability of sand treated with PVA or SBR with low (0.3 metric tons/ha) fiber or high (1.7 metric tons/ha) fiber.

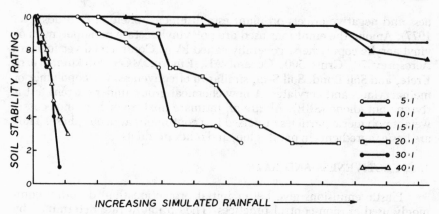

Fig. 3—Effect of simulated rainfall on the surface stability of sand treated with 1,120 kg/ha PVA solids at dilution rates of 5:1 through 40:1.

Dilutions of 5:1 to 10:1 PVA are obviously far more effective than higher dilutions (Fig. 3). Comparison of dilution rates of 1:1 with 10:1, show 4:1 to be too little water, with 5:1–7:1 optimum, 8:1 and 9:1 satisfactory, and 10:1 less effective (Fig. 4). All of the above tests were conducted on dry sand. Emulsions were applied to a horizontal surface of 28 by 48 cm and allowed to cure at about 18°C for at least 2 days. The surface was then inclined at 1:1 (steeper than the natural angle of repose of sand). The surface was then exposed to artificial rainfall with 15-cm/hour, 3-mm drops (Fig. 1), or 15 cm/hour composed of 5 cm/hour, 2-mm drops, plus 10 cm/hour as a mist (Fig. 2, 3, 4). Some treatments survived over 3 m of the latter type of rainfall.

The optimum dilution rate could be expected to be different with other products, on other soil materials, and with other soil-temperature

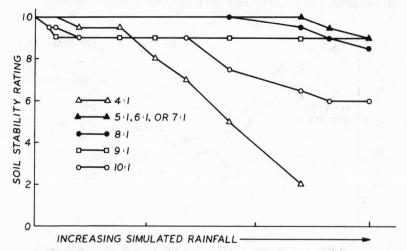

Fig. 4—Effect of simulated rainfall on surface stability of sand treated with 560 kg/ha PVA at dilution rates of 4:1 through 10:1.

and moisture conditions. Since moisture present in the soil contributes to the dilution rate, a lower dilution rate should be used when moisture is already present. Avoid any dilution which produces runoff. Application to dry soils may be preferable because the moisture already present on a site will vary within the site. In applications to warm surfaces, avoid minimum dilution rates; instead, use extra water to compensate for the faster drying. Optimum dilution is far less critical for SBR. Tested were 6:1, 12:1, 24:1, and 36:1 at 560 kg/ha solids. The lower three dilution rates, all equally effective, were superior to the 36:1 dilution.

The poor performances of commercial applications can often be traced to the use of too much water. When the emulsion is applied as a component of hydroseeding, a frequent practice, the water required to carry the wood fiber and other components is often greater than the desired PVA dilution. Hydroseeding machines will normally pump 3–5% fiber by weight. If the contract called for 1,680 kg fiber and 18.7 hl PVA the dilution rate would be 30:1 at 3% and 18:1 at 5%. (Both the liquid and solid effect of the PVA as well as the possibility of an easier pumping effect of PVA are ignored in these calculations as a safety factor to avoid a plugged hydroseeder full of expensive components). This means that the PVA must be applied separately—after the first application (containing the fiber, seed, and fertilizer). A material which is less restrictive as to dilution rates would then be advantageous by allowing a single rather than split application.

3. CURING OF EMULSION FILM

A primary limitation of emulsions is the restriction placed on curing. The minimum curing temperatures generally recommended are 13°C for PVA and 4°C for SBR. Also required are proper drying conditions. Fog will prolong by many days the curing time of either emulsion, and rain before the emulsion is properly cured may prove the crust to be ineffective. A logical use of the materials would be when the construction project is halted for the winter. Unfortunately, however, weather conditions which halt construction are the same as those which slow the curing of emulsions.

4. EFFECT ON PLANTS

Plastic emulsions are not generally toxic to plants even if sprayed directly on them. They commonly reduce establishment, however, and delay emergence of grass seedlings (Fig. 5). Grass seedlings may have a tip burn. These problems are apparently the effect of fertilizer used with the emulsion and seed, rather than the emulsion itself. The emulsion prevents the fertilizer salts from leaching away from the germinating seed.

The most practical way so far of offsetting reduced seedling numbers has been to increase the seeding rate. Doubling the rate of blando bromegrass (*Bromus mollis* L.) from 56 to 112 kg/ha has generally compensated for plant losses due to fertilizer, and sometimes resulted in an increase in numbers, ground cover, and pounds of grass growth. Wood fiber

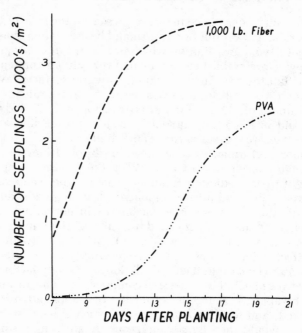

Fig. 5—Effect of soil treatments on emergence of fertilized grass seedlings.

is an essential part of an emulsion treatment, particularly if seeds are used. PVA emulsions will not stick seed or fertilizer to a soil slope. Unless a fiber is added the seed and fertilizer will wash off readily. Do not apply fiber and seed after the emulsion, for they will wash off.

5. OTHER CONSIDERATIONS

Freezing temperatures destroy all uncured emulsions. Do not store concentrates at freezing temperatures. Biological activity also may limit the storage life of emulsions. Do not store for extended periods without consulting the manufacturer. Crusts formed by emulsions may shed most of the rainfall. Therefore, they may limit plant establishment and growth in low-rainfall areas and with soils of low water-holding capacity. Crusts are not self-healing. The treated area must be protected from vehicles and animals, and breaks should be repaired. Crusts will not survive frost heaving. The emulsion could be used very effectively with transplanted shrubs. A soil-active herbicide could be used with them to provide a weed-free erosion-control program.

IV. SOIL AND ROCK MULCHES

Soil and rock mulches are often overlooked as the most practical solution to plant establishment and soil protection problems. The microsites created by rough seedbeds or rock provide seed coverage, separation of seed and fertilizer, and a mulch effect.

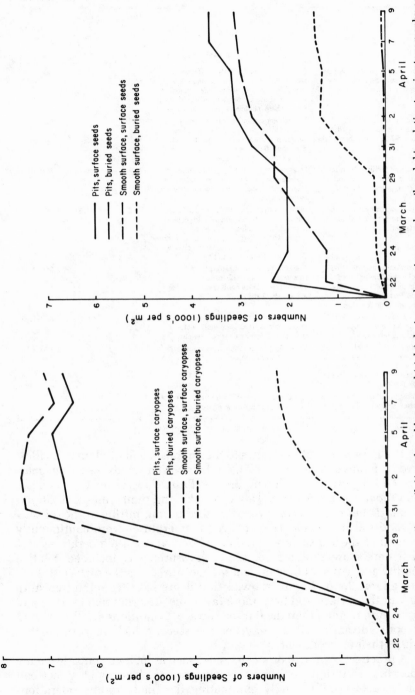

Fig. 6—Seedling emergence of downy brome (*left*) and tumble mustard (*right*) during early spring on a clay soil seeded in relation to microtopography and seed burial (This illustration was originally published in *Weed Science*. Vol. 20, p. 351 and 352. Reproduction is by permission of the editor of *Weed Science* and the authors).

Table 3—Summary of methods and costs of common erosion-control practices in California†

Treatment	Comments	Preger-mination erosion effective-ness‡	Effective-ness on plant establish-ment‡	Approxi-mate cost per ha, $§
1) Seed and fertilizer broadcast on the surface, no soil coverage or mulch.	Inexpensive and fast. Most effective on rough seedbeds with minimum slope and erodability where seed will cover naturally with soil. Suitable for remote or critical areas where machinery cannot be taken.	1	1–4	600
2) Hydroseeding or hydromulching (seed + fertilizer) with 187 kg wood fiber, 4.7 hl water/ha.	Effectiveness similar to broadcasting seed and fertilizer. Not enough fiber to hold seed in place or produce a mulch effect. Seed distribution would be improved by increased volume of water.	1	1–4	600
3) Seed and fertilizer broadcast and covered with soil (raking or dragging a chain, etc.).	Does not require special equipment. Generally a very effective treatment. Labor cost is high on areas not accessible to equipment.	1	3–4	800
4) Hydromulching with 1,680 wood fiber (plus seed and fertilizer).	Most common hydromulch mix in California. Advantages include holding seed and fertilizer in place on steep and smooth slopes where there may not be an alternative method. Only a minimal mulch effect. Cost is much higher than two.	2	3–5	1,050–1,300
5) Hydromulching with 1,680 kg/ha woodfiber plus an organic glue: Ecology Control, Terratack III, etc., plus seed and fertilizer.	The addition of an organic glue will sometimes improve fiber holding and germination. Does not increase labor or machinery cost.	2+	3–6	1,350–1,600
6) Hydromulching with 2,340–3,360 kg/ha wood fiber plus seed and fertilizer.	Produces a true mulch effect and some erosion protection. Commonly better results than 1,180 kg fiber or fiber plus glue.	2–3	4–7	1,300–1,850
7) Seed and fertilizer broadcast and covered with soil as in three above, but followed with hydromulch of wood fiber at 2,240–3,360 kg/ha.	Very effective; combines advantages of coverage and mulching.	2–3	6–8	1,700–2,100

All of the above treatments offer only minimal protection from the impact of raindrops and water flowing over the surface, but are all weed-free.

(continued on next page)

The importance of microsites to the establishment of plants was illustrated by Evans and Young (1972). In their Nevada study, seedling emergence and the growth of downy brome (*Bromus tectorum* L.), medusahead (*Taeniatherum asperum* [Sim.] Nevski) and tumblemustard (*Sisymbrium altissimum* L.) were favored by seed burial, pitting of the soil surface, and soil movement (Fig. 6). Air temperatures were continuously measured at the soil surface and 3 cm above, and soil temperatures at 1 and 3 cm below the surface. Other measurements included relative humidity at a height of 0.3 cm, and soil moisture from the surface to 1 cm deep, and at 3 cm. Results showed that depressed sites retain moisture longer at the surface and have more favorable atmospheric moisture and temperature regimes than the flat soil surface. Conditions are also created for more adequate soil coverage of the seeds, which in turn further modifies their environment.

A practical approach on steep slopes, such as highway cuts, is the use of benches, serrations, or simply rough grading. The rough effect can often be achieved by simply eliminating the final grading operation. Special pitting equipment is available for nearly-level sites.

Table 3—continued

Treatment	Comments	Preger-mination erosion effective-ness‡	Effective-ness on plant establish-ment‡	Approxi-mate cost per ha, $§
8) Straw or hay broadcast with straw blower on the surface at 3,360 kg/ha and tacked down (asphalt emulsion, Terratack II, etc.). Seed and fertilizer broadcast with hydroseeder or by hand.	Common elsewhere in U.S. Very effective as energy absorber and mulch. Straw forms small dams to hold some soil. May be weedy, depending on straw source. Not for slopes steeper than 2:1. Cost would increase significantly if slopes over 15 m from access, or application is uphill.	5–7	8–10	1,600
9) Straw broadcast at 4,480 kg/ha, rolled to incorporate (punched), another 4,480 kg straw broadcast and rolled, and fertilized. Seed and ferti-lizer broadcast with hydro-seeder or by hand.	Common on difficult fill slopes in Cali-fornia. Very effective. Not possible on most cut slopes. Very weedy. Cost would increase significantly if slopes over 15 m from access.	6–8	8–10	2,200–2,600
10) Roll-out mats (jute, excelsior, etc.). Held in place with wire staples. Seed and fertilize as in one or two.	Some are a good mulch, weed-free, adapted to small areas. Can be installed any season, cuts or fills. Unsightly. Difficult to install on rocky soils.	5–7	5–10	6,000–14,000
11) Polyethylene sheets (4-mil). Seed and fertilize as in one or two, use clear plastic; black if no seed is used.	Useful for temporary control. Can be installed any season. Unsightly, wind is a problem in installation and maintenance. May be difficult to establish plants.	10	?	5,900–6,700
12) Seed and fertilizer broadcast, or hydromulched in fiber (treatment two or four), fol-lowed by erosion-control chemical such as polyvinyl acetate at 6:1 silution (6 parts water), at 1,120 kg solid/ha (approx. 757 liters PVA).	Very expensive but will hold soil and seed in some very difficult conditions. May restrict penetration of water into soil. Will not cure below 13°C. Not effective on soils which crack or frost-heave. Will not support animal or vehicle traffic.	10 +	?	2,600–3,400

† Adapted from B. L. Kay, 1976. Hydroseeding, straw, and chemicals for erosion control. Agronomy Prog. Rep. no. 77, UC Agronomy-Davis. 14 p. Mimeo.

‡ 1 = minimal, 10 = excellent.

§ Assumes seed plus fertilizer = $150.00, fiber $136/metric ton, Ecology Control $2.75/kg, PVA $0.79/liter, 5,678 liter hydroseeder with 2-man crew $55.00/hour, labor $13/hour, straw $45/metric ton, straw mulcher with 4-man crew $64/hour (applies 1.8 metric tons/hour), and markup of 30% for overhead (including equipment depreciation) and profit. Cost figures were derived from conversations with contractors, and by review of recent California Dep. of Transportation contracts.

Mulches of crushed stone or gravel 2.5 cm deep provided more effec-tive erosion control than 4,480 kg/ha of straw, and heavier rates of stone were even more effective (Meyer et al., 1972). Field observations in Nevada and California also show a ground-cover of gravel to be effective for reducing wind and water erosion and encouraging invasion by in-digenous plant species.

V. WASTES, FLY ASH, SEWAGE

Wastes, fly ash, and sewage are of very limited use in dry regions because the areas of potential use are usually remote from the source of the waste. Current investigations run more toward use of these materials in commercial fertilizers or in agriculture.

In the short term, sewage sludge can be used on pastures or range. It is transported as a 10% slurry, which limits the distance it can be trans-ported even though it should be a good fertilizer. More extensive use in agriculture is limited by health department considerations, such as micro-organisms, trace elements (cadmium, etc.), and perhaps, in the long term, heavy metals.

VI. RELATIVE EFFECTIVENESS AND ECONOMICS

Mulching practices vary considerably in cost and effectiveness. Some-times the characteristics of the site to be stabilized determine the only practical treatment. Usually, however, there are alternative methods which should be considered.

Seed coverage and mulch should be the first consideration. Seed germination and plant establishment will be improved more by seed coverage than by any other treatment. Mulch treatments increase in effectiveness with both the amount of mulch per hectare and the length of the fiber. While it is possible to apply excessive amounts of mulch, economic considerations usually prevent this. The importance of fiber length, however, should not be overlooked. Increasing the fiber length (as from wood cellulose fiber to straw) may greatly increase the effectiveness of erosion control and germination (Kill & Foote, 1971). This relatively large increase in effectiveness can be achieved at little or no increase in cost. Even increasing the length of wood-cellulose fiber from a recycled paper product to virgin wood fiber improves results with little effect on cost. Table 3 compares relative effectiveness and costs as observed on roadside erosion-control projects in California. Ranges of cost figures are based on conversations with contractors and review of California Department of Transportation contract bids (all bids, not just low bids) for the 1973–1975 period. Labor costs are at a union scale.

The most expensive practice is not necessarily the most effective. For example, straw plus a tackifier is more effective for both erosion control and plant establishment than many of the more expensive treatments. A rough seedbed or covering the seed may be the cheapest and most effective treatment for establishing vegetation.

ACKNOWLEDGMENT

Appreciation for assistance in obtaining cost data is expressed to Bob Crowell, Cagwin and Dorward Co.; Roger Hallin, California Department of Transportation; Jack Hatton, Sta-Soil Corp.; and Dave Westergard, Grass Growers Co.

LITERATURE CITED

Armbrust, D. V., and L. Lyles. 1975. Soil stabilizers to control wind erosion. p. 77–82. *In* Soil conditioners. SSSA Spec. Pub. no. 7, Soil Sci. Soc. of Am., Madison, Wis.

Barnett, A. P., E. G. Diseker, and E. C. Richardson. 1967. Evaluation of mulching methods for erosion control on newly prepared and seeded highway backslopes. Agron. J. 59:83–85.

Currier, W. F. 1971. Methods of seeding. p. 106–111. *In* Proc. Critical Area Stabilization Workshop, 27–29 Apr. 1971, N. Mex. Interagency Range Comm., USDA-ARS, Las Cruces, N. Mex. 197 p.

Dudeck, A. E., N. P. Swanson, L. N. Mielke, and A. R. Dedrick. 1970. Mulches for grass establishment on fill slopes. Agron. J. 62:810–812.

Emanuel, D. M. 1971. Power mulcher can apply hardwood bark mulch. USDA For. Serv. Res. Note NE-135.

Evans, R. A., and J. A. Young. 1972. Microsite requirements for establishment of annual rangeland weeds. Weed Sci. 20:350–356.

Gabriels, D., and M. De Boodt. 1975. Erosion reduction factors for chemically treated soils: a laboratory experiment. p. 95–102. *In* Soil conditioners. SSSA Spec. Pub. no. 7, Soil Sci. Soc. of Am., Madison, Wis.

Grib, B. W. 1967. Percent soil cover by six vegetative mulches. Agron. J. 59:610–611.

Hoover, T. 1976. Water-holding capacity for hydromulch. California Dep. of Transp. Tech. Rep. CA-DOT-TL-2167-1-76-36. 21 p.

Kill, K. D., and L. E. Foote. 1971. Comparisons of long and short-fibered mulches. Trans. Am. Soc. Agric. Eng. 14:942–944.

Meyer, L. D., W. H. Wischmeier, and G. R. Foster. 1970. Mulch rates required for erosion control on steep slopes. Soil Sci. Soc. Am. Proc. 34:928–931.

Meyer, L. D., W. H. Wischmeier, and W. H. Daniel. 1971. Erosion, runoff, and revegetation of denuded construction sites. Trans. Am. Soc. Agric. Eng. 14:138–141.

Meyer, L. D., C. B. Johnson, and G. R. Foster. 1972. Stone and woodchip mulches for erosion control on construction sites. J. Soil Water Conserv. 27:264–269.

Sheldon, J. C., and A. D. Bradshaw. 1977. The development of a hydraulic seeding technique for unstable sand slopes. I. Effects of fertilizers, mulches, and stabilizers. J. Appl. Ecol. 14:905–918.

Springfield, H. W. 1971. Selection and limitations of mulching materials for stabilizing critical areas. p. 128–161. *In* Proc. Critical Area Stabilization Workshop, 27–29 April 1971, Albuquerque, N. Mex. USDA-ARS, Box 698, Las Cruces, N. Mex. 197 p.

State of California, Business and Transportation Agency, Department of Transportation. 1975. Standard specifications. 625 p.

Swanson, N. P., A. R. Dedrick, H. E. Weakly, and H. R. Haise. 1965. Evaluation of mulches for water-erosion control. Trans. Am. Soc. Agric. Eng. 8:438–440.

Swanson, N. P., A. R. Dedrick, and A. E. Dudeck. 1967. Protecting steep construction slopes against water erosion. Natl. Res. Counc., Natl. Acad. of Sci., Highw. Res. Rec. 206. p. 46–52.

Chapter 27

Improvement of Saline- and Sodium-Affected Disturbed Lands[1]

F. M. SANDOVAL AND W. L. GOULD

Agricultural Research Service, USDA,
Northern Great Plains Research Center, Mandan, North Dakota, and
New Mexico State University, Las Cruces, New Mexico

I. INTRODUCTION

The need for reclamation on mined areas of the western U.S. has become acute with the recent acceleration in surface mining of coal. Coal seams at depths suitable for surface mining occur over extensive areas used for agricultural production. Since agricultural land is a limited resource, mined lands must be reclaimed to maintain the resource and for environmental reasons.

Reclamation involves the grading and revegetating of areas that are disturbed. Potential for revegetation is closely related to the chemical and physical characteristics of disturbed soils. The quantity and kinds of soluble salts in the plant growth medium are especially important in reclamation in the western U.S.

Most of the information we review herein comes from research on agricultural soils. Research to date shows that we can transfer much of this technology to mined land spoils; therefore, we will use the words *soil* and *spoil* more or less interchangeably and recognize the difference where warranted.

Salt-affected soils contain sufficient soluble salts or exchangeable Na, or both, to restrict plant growth. Excessive soil salts can make land less productive or cause complete crop failures. The accumulation of soluble salts in soils is one of the most serious problems associated with irrigation agriculture in arid regions. However, the salt hazard is not peculiar to irrigated areas, where problems have received major emphasis.

Salt-affected soils are characterized and classified on their content of soluble salts and the exchangeable Na percentage. Based on these determinations the soil is classified as saline (excess soluble salts), sodic (excess exchangeable Na), and saline-sodic or sodic-saline (excess of salts and exchangeable Na).

The main salinity effect is the increase in osmotic pressure of the soil

[1] Contribution from North Central Region, Agricultural Research Service, U.S. Department of Agriculture, and Department of Agronomy, New Mexico State University.

485

solution, with subsequent impedance of water uptake by plants. Specific ion toxicity is recognized and should not be ignored. Sodic soils are distinguished from saline soils because they require special treatment for improvement and management. When exchangeable Na is excessive, there is lack of soil structural stability among soil particles and water infiltration is restricted.

Research on sodic soils in recent years has helped to clarify the reversible equilibrium relation between soluble and exchangeable or adsorbed Na in the presence of other cations. Present knowledge indicates that the salinization and cation-exchange processes in salty soils are reversible and frequently controllable. The basic principles for reclaiming and managing these soils have been generally understood and applied for many years. Newer technology increases the efficiency for application of this knowledge.

II. FORMATION AND ORIGIN OF SALTS

The basic source of soil salts is the primary minerals in the exposed layer of the earth's crust. During the process of chemical weathering, which involves hydrolysis, hydration, solution, oxidation, carbonation, and other processes, salt constituents are gradually released and made soluble. The salts are then transported by surface water and ground water to lower-elevation areas. Saline soils usually occur in areas that receive salts from other locations, and water is the primary carrier. In a few cases, saline soils have formed from weathering alone.

Saline soils occur primarily in regions of arid or semiarid climate. In humid regions the soluble salts are leached and are transported by streams to the oceans. In arid regions, leaching and transport of soluble salts is less complete because of the more limited rainfall and higher evaporation rates. A build-up of soluble salts commonly occurs in soils with low permeability, in depressional areas that collect drainage water, or in areas subject to seepage or occasional flooding.

The soluble salts that accumulate in soil consist principally of Ca^{2+}, Mg^{2+}, and Na^+ cations and SO_4^{2-} and Cl^- anions. Other ions found in smaller quantities are: K^+, HCO_3^-, CO_3^{2+}, and NO_3^-. The above cations, plus Cl^- and S, are constituents of rocks and minerals. Bicarbonate ions are formed as a result of solution of CO_2 in water. Carbonate and HCO_3^- are interrelated depending upon the pH of the solution, with appreciable amounts of soluble CO_3^{2+} present only at pH of 8.5 or higher.

Some geologic materials are higher in salts than others, and their elemental composition is highly variable. The composition of four types of rock which commonly overlie coal beds and serve as parent materials for soil, and as such during weathering release elements which form salts, are shown in Table 1 as discussed by Jackson (1964). The Ca of salty soils is primarily from the mineral calcite. Magnesium, from minerals like augite, hornblend, and montmorillonite, is very commonly found as dolomite and Mg-substituted calcite. Sodium occurs as NaCl, Na_2SO_4, and sometimes as Na_2CO_3 and other salts (Jackson, 1964).

Table 1—Elemental composition of rocks of the earth's crust

Compound or element	% Composition†			
	Igneous 95%	Shale 4%	Sandstone 0.75%	Limestone 0.25%
SiO_2	59.12	58.11	78.31	5.19
Al_2O_3	15.34	15.40	4.76	0.81
Fe_2O_3	3.08	4.02	1.08 }	0.54
FeO	3.80	2.45	0.30 }	
TiO_2	1.05	0.65	0.25	0.06
CaO	5.08	3.10	5.50	42.57
MgO	3.49	2.44	1.16	7.89
MnO	0.12	tr	tr	0.05
K_2O	3.13	3.24	1.32	0.33
Na_2O	3.84	1.30	0.45	0.05
CO_2	0.10	2.63	5.04	41.54
P_2O_5	0.30	0.17	0.08	0.04
SO_3	--	0.65	0.07	0.05
S	0.05	--	--	0.09
H_2O	1.15	4.99	1.63	0.77

† % indicates percent of rocks in earth's crust.

Shales, especially of marine origin, supply large quantities of soluble salts. Since shales and similar materials weather and erode and the alluvium is leached or traversed by waters, large quantities of salts are removed and redeposited. Thus, the kind of geological formation from which drainage water has come, or through which it passes, largely determines the salt composition of the soil.

III. GENERAL CHARACTERISTICS

A. Saline Soils

Saline soils contain soluble salts in concentrations that interfere with the growth of most crop plants. By definition, the electrical conductance (EC) of a saturation extract must be > 4 mmho/cm at 25°C (U.S. Salinity Lab. Staff, 1954). The nature of the salts does not affect the definition since the principal basis of the classification is the relationship between the EC and the ability of plants to use soil water. When adequate drainage is established, the excessive soluble salts can be removed from the root zone by leaching and the soil returned to normal productivity.

The salts present in saline soils consist mostly of neutral salts, like chlorides and sulfates of Ca, Mg, and Na. Sodium seldom comprises more than half of the soluble cations. Small amounts of bicarbonate may occur, but soluble carbonates are usually absent. Salts of low solubility, such as $CaSO_4$ (gypsum) and Ca and Mg carbonates (lime), may be present.

Saline soils are generally flocculated, so their permeability to water often equals or exceeds that of similar nonsaline soils. These soils can often be recognized by the white crusts of salt on the surface, or by an oily appearing surface. Stunted plants or dark green leaves with occasional tip-burn or marginal burn often indicates salinity.

B. Sodic Soils

Soils with an exchangeable Na percentage (ESP) >15 and with or without appreciable salinity are termed *sodic*. These soils contain sufficient exchangeable Na to interfere with the growth of most crop plants, and pH is usually alkaline (U.S. Salinity Lab. Staff, 1954).

The soil solution of sodic soils may be low in soluble salts but the dominant cation is Na^+. The main anions present are SO_4^{2-}, Cl^-, and HCO_3^-. The CO_3^{2-} anion is appreciably present in the soil solution only when the pH is above 8.5. At high pH and in the presence of CO_3^{2-} ions Ca and Mg are precipitated, so highly alkaline soil solutions usually contain only small amounts of these cations. As the ESP increases the soil becomes dispersed, is less permeable to water, and exhibits poor structural stability. The deterioration of soil structure at high levels of exchangeable Na has been well known for many years. Poor soil physical condition of mined land in the western U.S. has been related to increasing levels of exchangeable Na (Rai et al., 1974; Sandoval et al., 1973a and 1973b).

The hydraulic conductivity is determined to a considerable extent by the ESP and the solute content of the infiltrating fluid. Reeve (1958) expressed hydraulic conductivity in terms of ESP as a function of time. Gardner et al. (1959) studied unsaturated flow in sodic soil and observed that when the ESP was above 25%, the diffusivity was reduced as much as 1,000-fold if the electrolyte concentration was decreased from 300 to 3 meq/liter.

C. Saline-Sodic Soils

Soils with an EC >4 mmhos/cm and an ESP >15 are termed *saline-sodic* (U.S. Salinity Lab. Staff, 1954). These soils have high content of both soluble salts and high levels of adsorbed Na. Drainage and leaching of saline-sodic soils in the absence of Ca, may lead to the formation of a sodic condition. If gypsum is present, or added, the soil may be reclaimed with adequate drainage to a productive level.

IV. PLANT GROWTH RELATIONSHIPS

The sensitivity of plants to salted-soil conditions may be due to (i) the low availability of water because of osmotic potential limitations or poor infiltration restrictions, (ii) toxic effects by specific ions, or (iii) to adverse nutritional conditions often associated with sodic soils. The principal effect on plants by soluble salts is to reduce water availability (Bernstein, 1961; Wiklander, 1964). Gauch and Wadleigh (1944) demonstrated progressive reduction of growth of beans in solution culture with increasing salinity. Except for Na_2CO_3, salts of different ionic composition have about the same influence on water availability at comparable osmotic concentrations. Thorup (1969) reported that plants growing in Na_2CO_3 solutions wilted rapidly, while those growing in NaCl solutions of equal Na^+ ion concentration and equal or greater osmotic pressure made good growth. The higher pH of Na_2CO_3 seemed to be a factor in water uptake. At pH 9.3, roots were discolored and root tips and laterals blackened, and water uptake reduced from 300 to 20 ml/day. He concluded roots were damaged and plants wilted as a direct effect of pH.

At times a plant may be intolerant of a single ion species in the accumulating salts and its growth rate decreases because of toxicity rather than because of a reduction in water uptake. Each of the elements common to soil salts may be toxic to some plants, but Cl and Na were toxic most often. Boron salts often accumulate in saline soils, resulting in toxic B levels for plants.

Sodium effects on plants which are distinct from the effects of excessive concentrations of soluble salts seem due to highly caustic effects of the CO_3^{2-} ion, and direct and indirect effects of exchangeable Na. High alkalinity (high pH) damage seems due to the dissolving effect on organic matter with the formation of soluble Na-humates. A statistical study of pH relationships with adsorbed Na was made by Fireman and Wadleigh (1951).

One cause of poor plant growth on sodic soils is the inability of the plant to obtain an adequate supply of Ca. Thorne (1944b) observed that yield and Ca content of tomatoes decreased markedly with an ESP > 40 in the absence of $CaCO_3$. Bower and Turk (1945) reported that Ca and Mg deficiencies may occur in sodic calcareous soils of high pH. Chang and Dregne (1955a, 1955b) studied both the effect of adsorbed Na on soil physical properties, and mineral uptake in cotton (*Gossypium hirsutum* L.) and alfalfa (*Medicago sativa* L.), and noted that decreased yield was associated with an increase in Na content and a corresponding decrease in Ca of plant tissue. They proposed the term *sodium-induced calcium deficiency* for plant nutrition. A solution culture study indicated that Na did not affect the content of K, Ca, or Mg in cotton leaves at pH 5 or 6, but poor root aeration decreased accumulation of K, Ca, and Mg, and increased Na (Sowell & Rouse, 1958).

Ries et al. (1976) observed that red clover (*Trifolium pratense* L.) grown in a Mg-saline calcareous mine spoil showed Ca deficiency and that Canby bluegrass (*Poa canbyi* [Scribn.] Piper) and green needlegrass (*Stipa viridula* Trin.) showed specific ion toxicity or nutritional disorders above the osmotic effect.

Sodium dominates soil most frequently in the alkaline range. Under this situation, P solubility increases rapidly because of the formation of soluble Na-phosphate compounds. In calcareous soils with appreciable exchangeable Na, P-solubility is usually high because Ca solubility is depressed and Na-phosphates are formed. However, soluble P is assimilated somewhat less readily under alkaline conditions than under neutral or slightly acid conditions (Thorne & Peterson, 1954).

There is some evidence that NO_3-N formation is reduced in sodic soils. Studies in Arizona (Breazeale & McGeorge, 1931) indicated that a root contact-solution with pH higher than 7.6 may impede NO_3-N absorption by plants even though the pH is not sufficiently high to be directly toxic to plants.

Nitrogen mineralization was found limiting in a sodic soil; this was attributed to the lack of readily decomposable organic N-compounds (Cairns, 1963). While appreciable quantities of exchangeable NH_4 are frequently present below 10 m in the sodic overburden of coal lands within the Fort Union geologic group, mineralizable organic N forms were lacking (Sandoval et al., 1973a).

Greenway (1963) has reported that NaCl reduced K uptake in barley shoots and roots during salt stress. On the other hand, Hutcheson and co-workers (1959) observed that Na seemed to have little effect upon plant growth when supplied in nutrient solutions with or without K. However, they concluded that Na may partially substitute for K at low K levels. Sodium adsorption seemed to be strongly inhibited by excess K, but only part of the K-adsorption was inhibited by excess Na when maize seedlings were used as the indicator crop (Bange, 1959). Greenhouse studies by Bains and Fireman (1964) indicated that high levels of exchangeable Na generally caused an increase in the absorption of Na, N, and Mo and a decrease in the absorption of Ca, K, S, Mn, Cu, Zn, B, and Cl. They used five crops in their study and further concluded that sorghum (*Sorghum vulgare* Pers.) is a good crop for studying exchangeable Na-fertility interrelationships.

V. ION EXCHANGE PHENOMENA AND AFFECTING FACTORS

A. Theoretical Aspects

Ion exchange is the reversible process by which cations and anions are exchanged between solid and liquid phases, and between solid phases if in close contact. Adsorption implies the increase or accumulation of an ion species on a solid caused by ion exchange, while desorption refers to the replacement or release of adsorbed ions.

The soil is a heterogeneous system of solid, liquid, and gaseous components in various proportions. The solid component of the soil is made up of minerals and organic matter in more or less discrete particles. The soil solution acts as the medium by which chemical reactions are made possible. Because of the property of the soil material to bind and exchange cations and anions, many of these reactions are made possible.

The ion-exchange property of a soil is due almost entirely to the clay and silt fractions (< 20 μm) and the organic matter, the colloidal material of the soil being most important. Soil particles have an amphoteric character, i.e., they have both positive and negative charges, as evidenced by their power to bind both cations and anions. The negative charge increases and the positive charge decreases with rising pH of the soil solution. At pH levels normally encountered the net charge is negative and, in the vast majority of sodic soils, the positive charge is comparatively very small. Negative charges will adsorb and are neutralized by an equivalent amount of oppositely charged cations—the exchangeable or counter-ions which are held to the surface mainly by Coulomb forces and Van der Waals-London forces.

The exchangeable ions are distributed within a certain space around the soil particles forming a diffuse layer or swarm of ions. The structure of this layer for a given particle is determined by (i) the surface charge density, (ii) kind of counter-ion, (iii) the temperature, and (iv) the concentration of electrolytes in the soil solution. The exchangeable ions are surrounded by water molecules—this is called the *inner* or *micellar* solution as opposed to the *outer* or *intermicellar* solution of free electrolytes. Due to thermal motion, electrolytes migrate into the diffuse layer and distribute themselves so that (i) the concentration of counter-ions decreases from the surface outward, and (ii) the concentration of negative ions increases in the same direction. The electric attraction on exchangeable ions and osmotic pressure are counteracting forces, which balance each other at equilibrium. Wiklander (1964) has given an excellent description and review of the exchange theory.

Adsorbed cations are combined chemically with the soil particles, but they may be replaced by other cations occurring in the soil solution. The fact that the adsorbed cations can interchange freely with adjacent cations in the soil solution makes reasonable the assumption that the proportion of the various cations on the exchange complex will be related to their concentration in the soil solution. Normally in soils of dry regions Ca^{2+} and Mg^{2+} are the principal cations in the soil solution and on the exchange complex. Upon the accumulation of soluble salts, Na^+ often becomes the dominant cation in solution. It may become dominant due to precipitation of Ca and Mg compounds or because of Na^+ increase. The solubility limits of Ca- and Mg-sulfates and carbonates are often exceeded as the soil solution becomes concentrated through evaporation or plant use and a subsequent precipitation of Ca and Mg compounds is followed with a corresponding increase in the relative proportion of Na^+.

The dilution of a soil-water system containing monovalent and divalent cations displaces the equilibrium in such a direction that the adsorption of divalent ions increases and the adsorption of monovalent ions decreases. Bower and Goertzen (1958) reported that, when water is added to soil containing both adsorbed Na and $CaCO_3$, hydrolysis of the $CaCO_3$ takes place and the resulting Ca brought into solution replaces some of the adsorbed Na, as indicated in the following equation:

$$2\,Na^+_{(adsorbed)} + CaCO_3 + H_2O \rightleftharpoons Ca^{2+}_{(adsorbed)} + 2\,Na^+ + HCO_3^- + OH^-.$$

Under equilibrium conditions the extent to which the reaction proceeded to the right increased as the water content in the soil increased.

The solubility of $CaCO_3$ is markedly affected by pH (U.S. Salinity Lab., 1954), as shown in Table 2. The soil solution of calcareous soils in which neutral Na salts have accumulated should contain Ca^{2+}, CO_3^{2-}, and HCO_3^- ions, in addition to Na^+ ions and the anions associated with the neutral salts. A reaction which causes the pH to increase will decrease the

Table 2—Calcium carbonate solubility as affected by pH of the salt-saturated solution

Solution pH	Solubility, meq/liter
6.21	19.3
6.50	14.4
7.12	7.1
7.85	2.7
8.60	1.1
9.20	0.82
10.12	0.36

solubility of $CaCO_3$ and cause it to be precipitated, e.g., when Na_2CO_3 is introduced. Conversely, a reaction in the acid direction will increase Ca^{2+} ions in solution.

B. Practical Applications

Either the ESP or the sodium adsorption ratio (SAR) is used widely for characterizing the Na^+ status of soils and they are the basis of the definition for sodic soils. Bower and Hatcher (1962) have stated that exchangeable Na tends to be underestimated in highly saline-sodic soils due to negative adsorption effects. They felt that ESP might best be estimated from the SAR and that the SAR of an equilibrium extract is perhaps the best value for relating Na- status to plant growth.

The SAR is an empirical mathematical expression developed by the U.S. Salinity Laboratory Staff (1964) that is accepted widely by researchers. It is defined as:

$$SAR = Na/[(Ca + Mg)/2]^{1/2},$$

where concentrations are expressed in meq/liter in saturation extracts.

The SAR takes into consideration changes in both concentration and composition of the salts present in the soil solution that are in equilibrium with the soil. A high correlation coefficient was found by the U.S. Salinity Laboratory Staff (1954) between the SAR and ESP on soils from nine western states. Sandoval and coworkers (1971, 1973) found the SAR highly correlated with ESP in saline soils and mine spoils of the Northern Great Plains.

The most distinguishing characteristic of sodic soils is their lack of stability. Conditions that favor dispersion are colloids at a high state of hydration, a low electrolyte content, a pH reading far from the isoelectric point, and absence of oppositely charged colloids in the same system. High montmorillonitic clay content, in combination with low organic matter levels, enhance the dispersion effect. Conversely, conditions that favor flocculation are dehydration, a high electrolyte content, a pH reading at the isoelectric point, and the presence of an oppositely charged colloid. Barshad (1964) discusses dispersion and flocculation in more detail.

The behavior of soil colloids is influenced by many factors. The colloidal particle consists of: (i) a crystalline core (the clay minerals—principally montmorillonite in sodic soils), which forms the main mass of the clay particle; (ii) gel-like silicates of indefinite composition; and (iii) humus matter. The last two phases are attached to the surface of the silicate core by both physical and chemical means. It is the combination of all three phases which can be designated as a "surface complex" that is responsible for the dynamic nature of the clay particle. Depending upon changes in the soil environment, the composition of the surface complex can be modified to fit prevailing conditions, and these modifications will alter the colloidal properties.

Cation adsorption, being a surface phenomenon, is identified primarily with the clay and organic matter fractions of soils. Adsorbed cations may be replaced by other cations that occur in the soil solution. Sodium, calcium, and magnesium cations are exchangeable. Wiklander (1964) concluded that there is no single universal order of the replacing power of cations. The replacing power is found to increase in the same order as the lyotropic series which would place $Na^+ < K^+$ and for the alkaline earth ions $Mg^{2+} < Ca^{2+}$. However, when monovalent and divalent ions are combined, the replacing power appears to vary considerably with the nature of the exchanger and the concentration of the solution. Wiklander (1964) cites evidence that the kind of clay mineral is important for the relative replacing power and that the adsorption of monovalent ions in relation to divalent ions increases with concentration. The replacing power in soils follows the order: trivalent > divalent > monovalent. Other ion characteristics that influence replacing power are size in hydrated and nonhydrated conditions, and polarizability and polarizing power. The less hydrated the ion, the more tightly it is held.

The position and behavior of the H^+ ion may be of particular interest in some solonized soil areas which overlie coal fields in the Northern Great Plains, where the coal is frequently acidic. Wiklander (1964) felt that the replacing power of H is intimately connected with the acid strength of the exchanger, and H is acid potential-determining. The weaker the acid properties, the smaller the active fraction of the potential acidity and the stronger the replacing power of H^+. On a study he conducted with NH_4-saturated sulfonic acid resin. Wiklander found the following order of replacing power:

$$Li^+ < H^+ < Na^+ < K^+ < Mg^{2+} < Ca^{2+} < Sr^{2+} < Ba^{2+}.$$

The relative replacing power of the common basic cations is, generally, accepted as $Na^+ < K^+ < Mg^{2+} < Ca^{2+}$. Fortunately, Ca^{2+} and Mg^{2+} cations are more strongly adsorbed than Na^+; in fact, at equivalent solution concentrations, the amounts of Ca^{2+} and Mg^{2+} adsorbed are several times that for Na^+. Sodium must comprise about half or more of the soluble cation concentration before appreciable amounts are adsorbed by the exchange complex (U.S. Salinity Lab. Staff, 1954).

The roles of K^+ and Mg^{2+} are not definitely established. While most researchers feel that neither K^+ nor Mg^{2+} contributes to the destruction of soil structure, a few investigators have not agreed. Reeve and coworkers

(1954) compared effects of exchangeable Na⁺ and K⁺ by means of permeability ratios of air to water and modulus of rupture determinations. The permeability ratio is a measure of stability upon wetting and modulus of rupture measures crusting degree. They concluded that both properties increased markedly with Na⁺ increase, whereas K⁺ increases had little effect.

Martin and Richards (1959) concluded that increasing exchangeable K⁺ or NH_4^+ only slightly reduced aggregation of the < 5 μm particles of three soils but greatly reduced water conductivity; increasing exchangeable H⁺ increased the dispersing action of the monovalent cations Na⁺, K⁺, and NH_4^+. In a later study they noted (Martin et al., 1964) that the same quantities of exchangeable Na⁺ reduced hydraulic conductivity more in acid than neutral soil—H⁺ caused Na⁺ to be more effective as a dispersant.

Lagerwerff (1958) concluded that under conditions of equilibrium the composition of the solution phase fully characterized the environment of the plant root—the adsorbed cations per se had no direct effect.

VI. MANAGEMENT AND IMPROVEMENT

A. Principles

The improvement of saline, sodic, and saline-sodic soils has been given attention by many. Most of the principles accepted today came about largely as a result of work done by Gedroiz, de Sigmond, and Kelley. These principles are well known and have been applied many times. They include: (i) establishment of drainage to lower water tables, (ii) leaching of excess soluble salts, (iii) the replacement of exchangeable Na directly or indirectly, and (iv) the rearrangement and aggregation of soil particles to improve soil structure. The last principle has been stressed by fewer researchers and seems to merit further study in sodic soil amelioration work.

The addition of organic matter to sodic soil with subsequent improvement of structure has been recognized for many years. Myers (1937) concluded that organic matter improves soil structure by interacting with the inorganic cation exchangeable material in a manner which tends to prevent swelling and dispersion. Organic matter also serves as energy material for the microbial populations, which can promote stable aggregation of soil particles. Kinds and numbers of soil microorganisms are affected more by organic matter additions than by cation composition of the soil and microbially induced aggregation can be secured at high levels of Na⁺ saturation (Aldrich & Martin, 1954; Hubbell & Staten, 1951). Aldrich and Martin (1954) observed that microbial populations were not reduced by soil cation composition, and that increases in adsorbed Na⁺ markedly increased bacteria and actinomycetes in incubated treatments. Fungi are more responsive to changes in soil pH, preferring an acid to alkaline pH.

The transmission rate of water through sodic soil depends considerably upon the salt concentration of the water (Kelley, 1951). Permeability

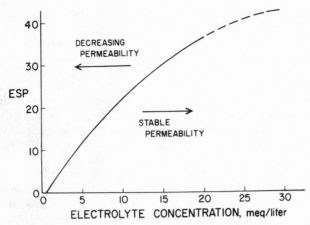

Fig. 1—Relationship of soil exchangeable sodium percentage (ESP) and electrolyte concentration in a mixed ion system of soil solution to permeability.

of sodic soils may decrease when leached with nonsaline water and will increase by leaching with saline water (Christiansen, 1947; Fireman & Bodman, 1940). Reeve and Bower (1960) obtained a thirtyfold increase in hydraulic conductivity with saline water containing divalent cations and reduced the ESP from 39 to 5. Quirk and Schoefield (1955) obtained quantitative data on the effect of electrolyte concentration on soil permeability (Fig. 1) and pointed out the advantages of using high-salt waters for reclamation purposes. The amount of Ca^{2+}, which must be supplied to saturate the soil with divalent cations, defined as the *Ca-deficit*, can be estimated from samples before treatment with saline leaching waters (Schofield & Taylor, 1961). The amount of gypsum needed to prevent deterioration of soil structure, while it is being leached into a salt-free condition, can then be calculated.

Boawn and coworkers (1952) obtained increased productivity with gypsum treatments on a saline-sodic soil in the Yakima Valley of Washington. They observed that leaching without the amendment effected some removal of adsorbed Na^+ but the rate was impractically slow due to reduced permeability. More than 1 year was needed for reclamation, and they observed that, as the exchangeable Na near the surface was lowered, adsorbed Na increased in the subsoil.

Gypsum applied in a saline-sodic soil in combination with leaching did not result in reducing adsorbed Na^+ in a poorly drained Colorado area that was gypsiferous below 23 cm (Amemiya et al., 1956), although soluble salts and adsorbed Na^+ were materially decreased by leaching only.

In Oregon studies (Bower et al., 1951) involved a "slick-spot" type of sodic soil that was noncalcareous near the surface, shallow plowed or disked amendment effect was as follows: Adsorbed Na^+ was replaced most with S, followed by manure plus S, gypsum, and manure plus gypsum. Sulfur, however, depressed crop yields because of acidity.

Chang and Dregne (1955a) showed that several amendments could be effective for reclaiming calcareous saline-sodic soils of southern New

Mexico. Gypsum or sulfur were effective but gypsum was more effective than sulfur. Calcium chloride and hydrochloric acid were also effective, but chloride toxicity to barley was evident in a greenhouse test. They emphasized the need of ample water supplies for effective reclamation.

In laboratory tests Arbol et al. (1975) found that surface application of gypsum was more effective than gypsum mixed throughout a saline-sodic soil in increasing the exchangeable Ca^{2+} and hydraulic conductivity. The soluble carbonates were precipitated when gypsum was mixed with the soil but only a small portion precipitated from surface application.

Reitmeier et al. (1948) reported on studies in California where infiltration was increased with gypsum and organic matter. When the soil was allowed to dry to the wilting percentage, subsequent infiltration rates exceeded those obtained initially by gypsum and organic treatment.

In the southwestern United States, concentrated H_2SO_4 has shown promise for reclaiming calcareous sodic soils. In Arizona, surface applications of concentrated H_2SO_4 at rates of 3 to 10 metric tons/ha followed by leaching increased water infiltration rates and successfully reclaimed sodic and saline soil for growing sorghum (Miyamoto & Stroehlein, 1975; Thorne, 1944a). Concentrated H_2SO_4 sprinkled at a rate of 12 metric tons/ha was far superior to equivalent amounts of gypsum or elemental S when evaluated in terms of yield of mixed pastures over a 2-year period on a Na-saturated soil (Overstreet et al., 1951). Greenhouse tests demonstrated that sodic soil, treated with H_2SO_4, produced equal or greater yields of sorghum and alfalfa (*Medicago sativa* L.) than soil treated with equivalent rates of gypsum, and the uptake of Fe and P was greater (Miyamoto et al., 1975b). Sulfuric acid treatment of P-deficient calcareous soils increased the water and CO_2-saturated, water-soluble P by several fold. In another greenhouse test, concentrated H_2SO_4 increased the growth of five species of range grass and also increased the CO_2-extractable P and EDTA-extractable Fe in the soil (Ryan et al., 1975). Preliminary laboratory tests (unpublished work by W. L. Gould) on the water penetration of sodic overburden material of the Fruitland Formation in New Mexico showed no penetration after the initial wetting of the surface 1 cm with distilled water, while the rate of water movement was 1 cm/hour after applications of H_2SO_4 to the surface of a soil column at the rate of 10 metric tons/ha.

Solonetzic-type sodic soils frequently have native gypsum in their subsoils (Sandoval et al., 1959; Sandoval & Reichman, 1971). By deep plowing Ca is provided to replace the adsorbed Na and these soils' physical condition is improved with subsequent increase in productivity with irrigation in arid areas (Rasmussen et al., 1964), and with natural precipitation in the northern Plains and in Canada (Cairns, 1962; Sandoval et al., 1972).

B. Chemical Reactions from Amendments

The chemical reactions which take place upon the application of amendments depend on the nature of the soil, the amendment, and the environmental conditions. The choice of the amendments will be dependent on character of the soil, the case, and availability of the amendment. Gypsum, sulfur, or lime are more commonly used; therefore, these reaction equations are given and discussed. Important reactions involving other useful amendments have likewise been given and are discussed by Kelley (1951) and the U.S. Salinity Laboratory Staff (1954).

1) *For calcareous soils* (X = the soil colloid)

    a. Gypsum: $2\,NaX + CaSO_4 \rightleftharpoons Ca\,X_2 + Na_2SO_4$

    b. Sulfur: [1] $2S + 3O_2 \rightleftharpoons 2\,SO_3$ (microbial oxidation)

        [2] $2\,SO_3 + 2\,H_2O \rightleftharpoons 2\,H_2SO_4$

        [3] $2\,H_2SO_4 + 2\,CaCO_3 \rightleftharpoons 2\,CaSO_4 + 2\,CO_2 + 2\,H_2O$

        [4] $4\,NaX + 2\,CaSO_4 \rightleftharpoons 2\,Ca\,X_2 + 2\,Na_2SO_4$

        [3'] $2\,H_2SO_4 + 4\,CaCO_3 \rightleftharpoons 2\,CaSO_4 + 2\,Ca(HCO_3)_2$

        [4'] $2\,CaSO_4 + 4\,NaX \rightleftharpoons 2\,Ca\,X_2 + 2\,Na_2SO_4$

        $2\,Ca(HCO_3)_2 + 4\,NaX \rightleftharpoons 2\,Ca\,X_2 + 4\,NaHCO_3$

    c. Sulfuric acid: Same as Eq. [3] and [4], or [3'] and [4'] for S.

Under the last two equations the $Ca(HCO_3)_2$, as well as the $CaSO_4$, would be available for reaction with the exchangeable Na, and one atom of S when oxidized to H_2SO_4 could, theoretically, result in the replacement of four Na ions by Ca. A high moisture level, low soil temperatures, and the release of CO_2 by plant roots would favor the formation of $Ca(HCO_3)_2$ as a product of the reaction.

2) *For noncalcareous soils* (X = the soil colloid)
    a. Gypsum: Same as for calcareous soils.
    b. Sulfur: Eq. [1] and [2] are the same as for calcareous soils.

    [3] $2\,H_2SO_4 + 4\,NaX \rightleftharpoons 4\,HX + 2\,Na_2SO_4$

This reaction might result in extremely acid soil conditions, which occurred in Oregon (Bower et al., 1951).

    c. Limestone: [1] $2\,NaX + CaCO_3 \rightleftharpoons Ca\,X_2 + Na_2CO_3$

Another possibility—where adsorbed H is present:

    [1] $NaX + H_2O \rightleftharpoons NaOH + HX$

    [2] $2\,HX + CaCO_3 \rightleftharpoons CaX + CO_2 + H_2O$

The Na_2SO_4 formed in the reactions using gypsum, S, or H_2SO_4 must be removed by leaching or else the reactions will be prevented from completion. Excessive concentration of Na_2SO_4 will lower the solubility of gypsum and reduce the replacement of exchangeable Na with Ca. The value of S or H_2SO_4 depends chiefly on the presence of $CaCO_3$. In noncalcareous soils, S cannot be expected to be effective and the resulting acidification may further reduce crop production. Likewise, in all except acid soils, the solubility of limestone is too low to bring appreciable Ca into solution. Consequently, the limestone reaction proceeds extremely slowly, if at all.

Chemical amendments, like gypsum, S, and limestone, normally are applied broadcast and then incorporated with the soil by disking or plowing. Thorough incorporation is especially important when S is used to insure a satisfactory rate of reaction.

The initial biological oxidation of S takes place gradually and several months may elapse before the effect is apparent. The oxidation process is generally more rapid in warmer soils. The soil should be kept moist since water is essential for the oxidation of S.

Concentrated H_2SO_4 is hazardous to handle, and special equipment is used to spray it on the soil surface. Air pollution control regulations have created a surplus of H_2SO_4 and S in some areas, so their use for reclamation of sodic mine spoils is a possible disposal method.

C. Leaching

The reclamation of salt-affected soils consists of the removal by leaching of excess soluble salts and exchangeable sodium from the plant root zone. Most efficient leaching in the western U.S. can usually be accomplished with irrigation water. The role of irrigation for mined land reclamation is discussed elsewhere in this book.

The effectiveness of leaching under nonirrigated conditions is dependent upon the amount and intensity of precipitation, the evapotranspiration, and the soil water-holding capacity. Soluble salts are carried with the water to the maximum depth of penetration. Effective leaching means removal of salts from the plant root zone and redeposition deep enough to prevent damage from upward return. Water movement to these depths can occur only when there is a net excess of precipitation over evapotranspiration. The frequency of these occurrences is usually related to the precipitation received. Deeper and more effective leaching will occur more often in areas of moderate to high precipitation than in areas of low rainfall. Runoff and less leaching will occur if precipitation intensity is greater than the infiltration rate into the soil. Land slopes and relief are also factors which influence water entry. Runoff is greater on sparsely vegetated areas than on grassed prairie-type landscapes.

A soil water deficit occurs whenever evapotranspiration exceeds the precipitation. In the arid southwestern U.S., where the season of maximum rainfall is during the warmest summer months, there is little likelihood of accumulating soil water during the growing season, except where the runoff waters concentrate. In contrast, the period of maximum precipitation in semiarid areas north of New Mexico is generally during the spring and early summer, and it is not uncommon to get percolation of soil water below the root-zone of indigenous grasses. Highest salinity in native grassland near Colstrip, Montana, was in the sandy colluvial material below the root zone at depths from 1.5 to 8 m (Power et al., 1975). This distribution suggests that soluble salts were leached from the root zone and were concentrated in the underlying material, resulting in a zone of maximum salinity at the maximum depth to which precipitation sometimes penetrates. Occasionally in the arid southwestern U.S., winter precipitation will provide soil moisture that penetrates below the root zone. In the semiarid and dryer climates, the wetter years are relatively much more important than the dry years in their effect upon soil moisture movement (Arkley, 1963).

The soil water-holding capacity influences the depth of water penetration, i.e., more water is needed for deep percolation in fine-textured than in coarse-textured soils because of the difference in water retention. Arkley (1963) obtained a high correlation between observed depth of $CaCO_3$ accumulation and calculated depth of water movement, using from climatic data the average seasonal excess of precipitation over evapotranspiration and taking into account the water-holding capacity of the soil.

Surface mine spoils in the western U.S. are frequently very fine textured and are sodic (Miyamoto et al., 1975a; Rai et al., 1974; Sandoval et al., 1973a and 1973b). Spoil material with these characteristics will have slow water infiltration rates and high water-holding capacity. Consequently, the moisture that enters the spoil material will usually be retained in the upper few cm and will be lost by evaporation. Leaching and soil development will progress at a very slow rate, especially in arid areas, as is illustrated by the very shallow, saline soils developing from shales in the Fruitland Formation in New Mexico. Chemical amendments are of little value under natural conditions because the precipitation is too scanty to leach the salts out of the root zone. In areas of higher precipitation, sodic spoils might eventually be reclaimed, as evidenced in North Dakota where, after 3 years, the SAR of the surface 15 cm was reduced 35% with gypsum (Power et al., 1975); Sandoval et al., 1973 and 1973b).

D. Burying and Covering Severely Affected Materials

The preferred method for reclaiming saline-sodic mine spoils is to cover the graded spoils with suitable soil materials, or bury undesirable material with overburden of better quality. In the stripping operation strata of poor quality, because of salinity, sodicity, or other reasons, can be deposited so that they can be buried or covered with overburden of better quality during the mining operation. In typical surface mining operations using a dragline, the lowest strata are usually deposited last. Premining knowledge of the characteristics of undesirable overburden will permit planning of the mining operation so that poor quality material can be covered and the better quality soil and overburden put on top.

Stockpiling topsoil and replacing it on the graded sodic spoils is an effective method for reducing sodic damage. Sandoval et al. (1973a and 1973b) in North Dakota found that as little as 5 cm of good quality topsoil over sodic spoils (SAR 25 to 30) enhanced plant growth and production, increased water infiltration, reduced surface crusting, and reduced runoff. The average production of perennial grasses over a 3-year period on these sodic spoils was 1,740 kg/ha in plots topdressed with 5 cm of topsoil, as compared with 310 kg/ha without topsoil (Power et al., 1976; USDA-ARS, 1975). On moderately sodic spoils (SAR 15) the yield on plots with topsoil was 30% greater than on spoils without topsoil.

Infiltration tests conducted on the fourth year after treatments, where the SAR was 25, showed that greater infiltration was obtained on plots receiving 5 cm of topsoil, with and without straw or gypsum, than in plots where no topsoil was added (Fig. 2). The effect of topsoil was largely lost by mixing it into the top 15 cm of spoil. The 5-cm topsoil treatment seemed to act as a permanent mulch, preventing the spoil surface from sealing, thereby increasing infiltration and plant growth. Runoff from nonvegetated plots on a 2% slope was greatest from untreated spoil and lowest from plots with 5 cm of topsoil (USDA-ARS, 1975).

In recent studies (unpublished work by the senior author) on North Dakota silty clay loam sodic spoils (ESP = 25, EC = 3) covered with up to 30 cm of good quality loam topsoil and fertilized with N and P, high yields (4,020 kg/ha) of crested wheatgrass (*Agropyron desertorum* [Fisch.] Schult.) were obtained initially. However, after 4 years, there was a severe and progressive decline in yields (1,890 kg/ha) which was largely attributed to a deterioration of topsoil quality. Upward migration of soluble Na caused an increase in adsorbed Na in the respread topsoil immediately over the spoil. These observations suggest that the sustained level of productivity on treated land may be lower than the initial produc-

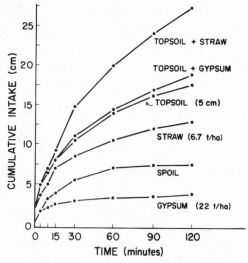

Fig. 2—Effect of surface treatment on North Dakota sodic mine spoil on water infiltration, 4 years after treatment.

tivity. Therefore, quantity of good quality soil materials applied to cover sodic spoils should allow for some topsoil deterioration.

Where gypsum was used in combination with the respread topsoil, it seemed to serve as a deterent to sodic level increases in the topsoil (unpublished work by the senior author).

In northwestern New Mexico, better stands of native range species were established with irrigation in plots receiving 20 to 45 cm of topsoil than on saline-sodic spoil material (unpublished work of W. L. Gould). Plants in plots receiving topsoil grew more vigorously than plants in spoil plots at the end of the second growing season. Richardson et al. (1975) reported that the average production of perennial grasses in the year after seeding on unfertilized plots receiving topsoil was five- to sixfold greater than on irrigated or nonirrigated Montana spoil. The productivity of fertilized plots receiving topsoil was slightly better than spoil plots under irrigation, and nearly twice as great as on fertilized, nonirrigated spoil.

The effect of thickness and quality of applied topsoil is being studied in North Dakota by Powers et al. (1976). Wedge-shaped experiments were constructed in which subsoil from the BC horizons was spread over impermeable sodic spoils (SAR = 26) to depths increasing from 0 to 2 m. Either 0, 20, or 60 cm of AB horizon soil was spread over the subsoil wedge. A fourth treatment involved mixing topsoil and subsoil in the wedge in a 1:3 ratio as the wedge was constructed. Yields of spring wheat (*Triticum sativum* var. vulgare Vilm. Blumengartn.) from the first crop harvested are given in Table 3. Plant growth and yield increased as depth of soil material increased to about the 70 cm thickness. For each type of soil material used, the yield leveled off differently depending on material quality. Data for crested wheatgrass and alfalfa followed the same trend as those shown in Table 3. Under the conditions found in western North Dakota, it seems that about 70 cm of soil material is needed for maximum yield, with the level of productivity determined by quality of the material over spoil. However, time will be required to determine the extent of upward Na migration and extent of deterioration for the applied soil.

Table 3—Yields of first harvest of spring wheat grain as affected by thickness of applied topsoil and applied subsoil materials over North Dakota sodic mine spoil

Subsoil thickness	Topsoil thickness, cm			
	0	20	60	Mixed†
cm			kg/ha	
10	800	1,606	1,962	1,055
30	1,062	1,915	2,016	1,344
50	1,196	1,956	2,050	1,472
70	1,290	1,942	2,050	1,505
90	1,263	1,982	1,935	1,559
110	1,250	1,949	2,009	1,478
130	1,317	2,029	2,076	1,512
150	1,250	1,922	2,130	1,452

† Topsoil (AB horizons) and subsoil (BC horizons) mixed 1:3 ratio.

LITERATURE CITED

Aldrich, D. G., and J. P. Martin. 1954. A chemical-microbiological study of effects of exchangeable cations in soil aggregates. Soil Sci. Soc. Am. Proc. 18:276–283.

Amemiya, M., C. W. Robinson, and E. W. Cowley. 1956. Reclamation of a saline-alkaline soil in the Upper Colorado River Basin. Soil Sci. Soc. Am. Proc. 20:423–425.

Arbol, I. P., I. S. Dahiya, and D. R. Rhumbla. 1975. On the method of determining gypsum requirement of soils. Soil Sci. 120:30–36.

Arkley, R. J. 1963. Calculation of carbonate and water movement in soil from climatic data. Soil Sci. 96:239–248.

Bains, S. S., and M. Fireman. 1964. Effect of exchangeable sodium percentage on the growth and absorption of essential nutrients and sodium by five crop plants. Agron. J. 56:432–453.

Bange, G. G. J. 1959. Interactions in the potassium and sodium absorption by intact maize seedlings. Plant Soil 11:17–29.

Barshad, I. 1964. Chemistry of soil development. p. 1–70. In F. E. Bear (ed.) Chemistry of the soil. Am. Chem. Soc. Monogr., Reinholt Publ. Corp., New York.

Bernstein, L. 1961. Osmotic adjustment of plants to saline media. I. Steady state. Am. J. Bot. 48:909–918.

Boawn, C., F. Turner, Jr., C. D. Moodie, and C. A. Bower. 1952. Reclamation of a saline-alkali soil by leaching and gypsum treatments using sugar beets as an indicator crop. Proc. Am. Soc. Sugar Beet Tech. p. 138–145.

Bower, C. A., and J. O. Goertzen. 1958. Replacement of adsorbed sodium in soils by hydrolysis of calcium carbonate. Soil Sci. Soc. Am. Proc. 22:33–35.

Bower, C. A., and J. T. Hatcher. 1962. Characterization of salt-affected soils with respect to sodium. Soil Sci. 93:275–280.

Bower, C. A., L. R. Swarner, A. W. Marsh, and F. M. Tilston. 1951. The improvement of an alkali soil by treatment with manure and chemical amendments. Oregon Agric. Exp. Stn. Tech. Bull. 22. p. 5–37.

Bower, C. A., and L. M. Turk. 1945. Calcium and magnesium deficiencies in alkali soils. J. Am. Soc. Agron. 38:723–727.

Breazeale, J. F., and W. T. McGeorge. 1931. Nutritional disorders in alkaline soils as caused by deficiency of CO_2. Univ. of Ariz. Agric. Exp. Stn. Tech. Bull. 41.

Cairns, R. R. 1962. Some effects of deep working on solonetz soil. Can. J. Soil Sci. 42:273–275.

Cairns, R. R. 1963. Nitrogen mineralization in solonetizic soil samples and some influencing factors. Can. J. Soil Sci. 43:387–392.

Chang, C. W., and H. E. Dregne. 1955a. Reclamation of salt- and sodium-affected soils in the Mesilla Valley. New Mexico Agric. Exp. Stn. Bull. 401.

Chang, C. W., and H. E. Dregne. 1955b. Effect of exchangeable sodium on soil properties and on growth and cation content of alfalfa and cotton. Soil Sci. Soc. Am. Proc. 19:29–35.

Christiansen, J. E. 1947. Some permeability characteristics of saline and alkaline soils. Agric. Eng. 28:147–150, 153.

Fireman, M., and G. B. Bodman. 1940. Effect of saline irrigation water upon permeability. Soil Sci. Soc. Am. Proc. 4:71–77.

Fireman, M., and C. H. Wadleigh. 1951. A statistical study of the relation between pH and the exchangeable sodium percentage of western soils. Soil Sci. 71:273–285.

Gardner, W. R., M. S. Mayhugh, J. O. Goertzen, and C. A. Bower. 1959. Effect of electrolyte concentration and exchangeable sodium percentage on diffusivity of water in soils. Soil Sci. 88:270–274.

Gauch, H. G., and C. H. Wadleigh. 1944. Effects of high salt concentrations on growth of bean plants. Bot. Gaz. 105:379–387.

Greenway, H. 1963. Plant responses to saline substrates. III. Effect of nutrient concentration on the growth and ion uptake of Hordeum vulgare during a sodium chloride stress. Aust. J. Biol. Sci. 16:616–628.

Hubbell, D. S., and G. Staten. 1951. Studies on soil structure. New Mexico Agric. Exp. Stn. Tech. Bull. 363.

Hutcheson, T. B., Jr., W. G. Woltz, and S. B. McCaleb. 1959. Potassium-sodium interrelationships. Soil Sci. 87:28–35.

Jackson, M. L. 1964. Chemical composition of soils. p. 71–142. In F. E. Bear (ed.) Chemistry of the soil. Am. Chem. Soc. Monogr., Reinholt Publ. Corp., New York.

Kelley, W. P. 1951. Alkali soils: their formation, properties and reclamation. Am. Chem. Soc. Monogr. Reinhold Publ. Corp., New York.

Lagerwerff, J. V. 1958. Comparable effects of absorbed and dissolved cations on plant growth. Soil Sci. 86:63–69.

Martin, J. P., and S. J. Richards. 1959. Influence of exchangeable hydrogen and calcium, and of sodium, potassium and ammonium at different hydrogen levels on certain physical properties of soils. Soil Sci. Soc. Am. Proc. 23:335–338.

Martin, J. P., S. J. Richards, and P. F. Pratt. 1964. Relationship of exchangeable Na percentage at different soil pH levels to hydraulic conductivity. Soil Sci. Soc. Am. Proc. 28: 620–627.

Miyamoto, S., W. L. Gould, and D. Rai. 1975a. Characterizing overburden materials before surface mining in the Fruitland Formation of Northwestern New Mexico. p. 80–94. In Proc. NCA/BCR 3rd Symp. on Surface Mining and Reclamation, 21–23 Oct. 1975. Louisville, Ky. Natl. Coal Assoc., Washington, D.C.

Miyamoto, S., and J. L. Stroehlein. 1975. Sulfuric acid for increasing water penetration into some Arizona soils. Prog. Agric. Ariz. 29:13–16.

Miyamoto, S., and J. L. Stroehlein. 1975. Sulfuric acid for increasing water penetration into some Arizona soils. Prog. Agric. Agriz. 29:13–16.

Myers, H. E. 1937. Physio-chemical reactions between organic and inorganic soil colloids as related to aggregate formation. Soil Sci. 44:331–359.

Overstreet, R., J. C. Martin, and H. M. King. 1951. Gypsum, sulfur and sulfuric acid for reclaiming an alkali soil of the Fresno series. Hilgardia 21:113–127.

Power, J. F., R. E. Ries, F. M. Sandoval, and W. O. Willis. 1975. Factors restricting revegetation of strip mine spoils. p. 336–346. In Proc. Fort Union Coal Field Symp., 25 Apr. 1975, Montana Acad. of Sci., Billings, Mont.

Power, J. F., R. W. Ries, and F. M. Sandoval. 1976. Use of soil materials on spoils—Effect of thickness and quality. N. D. Farm Res. 34(1):23–24.

Quirk, J. P., and R. H. Schofield. 1955. The effect of electrolyte concentration in soil permeability. J. Soil Sci. 6:163–178.

Rai, D., P. J. Wierenga, and W. L. Gould. 1974. Chemical and Physical properties of core samples from a coal-bearing formation in San Juan County, New Mexico. New Mexico Agric. Exp. Stn. Res. Rep. 287.

Rasmussen, W. W., G. C. Lewis, and M. A. Fosberg. 1964. Improvement of Chilcott-Sebree (Solodized-solonetz) slick spot soils in Southwestern Idaho. USDA-ARS 41-91, Beltsville, Md.

Reeve, R. C. 1958. The transmission of water by soils as influenced by chemical and physical properties. 5th Int. Congr. Agric. Eng. Trans., Brussels, Belgium. 1:21–32.

Reeve, R. C., and C. A. Bower. 1960. Use of high-salt waters as a flocculant and source of divalent cations for reclaiming sodic soils. Soil Sci. 90:139–144.

Reeve, R. C., C. A. Bower, R. H. Brooks, and F. B. Gschwend. 1954. A comparison of the effects of exchangeable sodium and potassium upon the physical condition of soils. Soil Sci. Soc. Am. Proc. 18:130–132.

Reitmeier, R. F., J. E. Christiansen, R. E. Moore, and W. W. Aldrich. 1948. Effect of gypsum, organic matter and drying on infiltration of sodium water into a fine sandy loam. USDA Tech. Bull. 937, Washington, D.C.

Richardson, B. Z., E. E. Farmer, R. W. Brown, and P. E. Packer. 1975. Rehabilitation research and its application on a surface mined area of eastern Montana. p. 247–265. In Proc. Fort Union Coal Field Symp. 25 Apr. 1975, Montana Acad. of Sci., Billings, Mont.

Ries, R. E., F. M. Sandoval, J. F. Power, and W. O. Willis. 1976. Perennial forage species response to sodium and magnesium sulfate in mine spoil. p. 173–183. In Proc. 4th Symp. Surface Mining and Reclamation., NCA/BCR Coal Conf., 19–21 Oct. 1976. Louisville, Ky. Natl. Coal Assoc., Washington, D.C.

Ryan, J., J. L. Stroehlein, and S. Miyamoto. 1975. Effect of surface-applied sulfuric acid on growth and nutrient availability of five range grasses in calcareous soils. J. Range Manag. 28:411–414.

Sandoval, F. M., J. J. Bond, and G. A. Reichman. 1972. Deep plowing and chemical amendment effect on a sodic claypan soil. Trans. Am. Soc. Agric. Eng. 15(4):681.

Sandoval, F. M., J. J. Bond, J. F. Power, and W. O. Willis. 1973a. Lignite mine spoils in the Northern Great Plains—Characteristics and potential for reclamation. p. 117–133. *In* Proc. Res. and Applied Tech. Symp. on Mined-Land Reclamation, 22–24 Oct. 1973, Natl. Coal Assoc., Pittsburgh, Pa.

Sandoval, F. M., J. J. Bond, J. F. Power, and W. O. Willis. 1973b. Lignite mine spoils in the Northern Great Plains—Characteristics and potential for reclamation. p. 1–24. *In* M. K. Wali (ed.) Some environmental aspects of strip mining in North Dakota. Educ. Ser. 5, N. Dak. Geol. Surv., Grand Forks, N. Dak.

Sandoval, F. M., M. A. Fosberg, and G. C. Lewis. 1959. A characterization of the Sebree-Chilcott soil series association (slick spots) in Idaho. Soil Sci. Soc. Am. Proc. 23:317–332.

Sandoval, F. M., and G. A. Reichman. 1971. Some properties of solonetzic (sodic) soils in western North Dakota. Can. J. Soil Sci. 51:143–155.

Schofield, R. K., and A. W. Taylor. 1961. A method for the measurement of the calcium deficit in saline soils. J. Soil Sci. 12:269–275.

Sowell, W. F., and R. D. Rouse. 1958. Effect of Na on cation content of leaves and boll production of cotton plants grown in solution cultures in growth chambers. Soil Sci. 86: 70–74.

Thorne, D. W. 1944a. The use of acidifying materials on calcareous soils. J. Am. Soc. Agron. 37:815–828.

Thorne, D. W. 1944b. Growth and nutrition of tomato plants as influenced by exchangeable sodium, calcium, and potassium. Soil Sci. Soc. Am. Proc. 9:185–189.

Thorne, D. W., and H. B. Peterson. 1954. Irrigated soils. Their fertility and management. 2nd ed. The Blakiston Co., Inc., New York.

Thorup, J. T. 1969. pH effect on root growth and water uptake by plants. Agron. J. 61:225–227.

U.S. Salinity Laboratory Staff. 1954. Diagnosis and improvement of saline and alkali soils. USDA Hbk. no. 60, U.S. Government Printing Office, Washington, D.C.

U.S. Department of Agriculture-Agricultural Research Service. 1975. Progress report on research on reclamation of strip-mined land in the Northern Great Plains. USDA-ARS, Mandan, N. Dak. 20 p.

Wiklander, L. 1964. Cation and anion exchange phenomena. p. 163–203. *In* F. E. Bear (ed.) Chemistry of the soil. Am. Chem. Soc. Monogr., Reinholt Publ. Corp., New York.

Chapter 28

Use of Irrigation in Reclamation in Dry Regions[1]

R. E. RIES AND A. D. DAY

Agricultural Research Service, USDA
Northern Great Plains Research Center, Mandan, North Dakota, and
University of Arizona, Tucson, Arizona

I. INTRODUCTION

Advances in agricultural technology have allowed man to support a larger population than permitted by the natural ecological restraints for a non-agricultural culture. Irrigation is one of the important technological advances which enhances crop production even in drought years and contributes substantially to food production for an increasing world population.

Irrigation is not new anywhere in the world. Gulhati and Smith (1967), in a short review of irrigation history, noted that irrigation was used in the southwestern U.S. by early Indian cultures to grow crops on a limited but effective scale. Later, new irrigation techniques and crops were introduced by the Spanish Americans. By the nineteenth century, Mormans and other Anglo-Americans used irrigation to grow crops needed for their livelihood. With legislation, like the Desert Land Act of 1877 and the Carey Act of 1894, Congress attempted to stimulate state and private participation in the development of irrigated agriculture in the West. The Reclamation Act of 1902 and its amendments involved the Federal Government directly in the development of irrigation projects.

The U.S. Department of Agriculture (1948) documented the needs and importance of irrigated agriculture in the western U.S. as of the middle of the twentieth century. Considerable information is available on the practice of irrigated agriculture as summarized by Hagen et al. (1967). Today, we may be at the beginning of a new chapter of irrigation history in the United States. With the extensive development of surface mining in the semiarid and arid West and the commitment to restore these lands to a reasonable level of productivity, a new type of irrigation is developing. The Study Committee on the Potential for Rehabilitating Lands Surface Mined for Coal in the Western United States (1974), after comparing successful and unsuccessful revegetation efforts on many

---

[1] Contribution from the North Central Region, Agricultural Research Service, U.S. Department of Agriculture, and College of Agriculture, University of Arizona.

acres, concluded that the best techniques for revegetating disturbed land-scapes must include "the sparing addition of irrigation water, if needed, during the period of seedling establishment." Irrigating to establish perennial plant communities, followed by termination of irrigation, in-volves purposes and techniques different from the historic objective of supplying plants with sufficient water to produce optimum yield and quality of desired crops.

II. ROLE OF IRRIGATION FOR RECLAMATION

A. Problems in Plant Establishment Without Irrigation

Lack of water to support vegetative communities is a major concern for all workers involved in disturbed-land revegetation in the semiarid and arid western U.S. May (1975) pointed out that nearly half of the sur-face area of the continental U.S. west of the Mississippi River receives less than 38 cm/year (15 inches/year). He emphasized that much of the water received as precipitation is not available for germination, establishment, and growth of vegetation because of losses to sublimation, surface runoff, and evaporation. He estimates that of 23 cm (9 inches) received by an area annually, only 10 to 13 cm (4 to 5 inches) are used by plants.

Yearly and monthly irregularity of occurrence of limited precipita-tion is a second problem. In Fig. 1, the yearly total and average precipita-tion is given for the last 25 years at the Northern Great Plains Research Center, Mandan, North Dakota. Of particular interest is the year-to-year fluctuation in annual precipitation as well as the series of dry years from 1957 through 1962. Figure 2 presents the 60-year maximum, minimum,

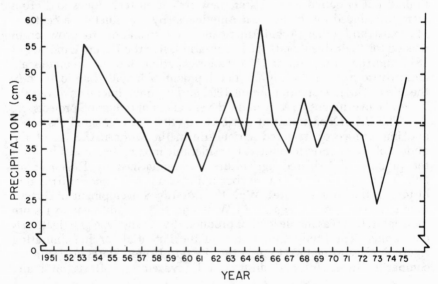

Fig. 1—Variation in annual precipitation as compared to the average over a 25-year period at Mandan, N. Dak.

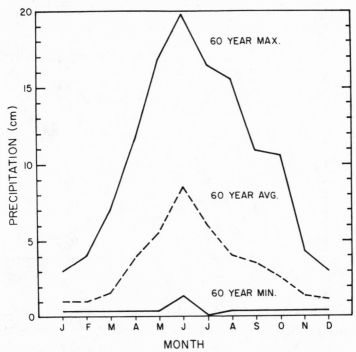

Fig. 2—The 60-year maximum, minimum, and average monthly precipitation at Mandan, N. Dak.

and average monthly precipitation for the same location as above. The range in the precipitation received for the critical month of June over the 60-year period varied from 1.1 to 19.6 cm, with an average of 8.7 cm. In Fig. 3, average monthly precipitation at Mandan for a 60-year period is compared with 1975 monthly precipitation to show the high deviation from the mean possible during any month of the same year. From Jan. to June 1975, precipitation was normal to greatly above normal; but, from July through Nov., precipitation was below the 60-year average. Such variable patterns of precipitation can cause a newly seeded plant community severe water stress and can influence the successful establishment of certain species, or possibly the entire seeding.

Perennial plant communities reproduce naturally by seed when environmental conditions are favorable. Conditions for the reproduction of a certain species may occur only 1 or 2 years out of 10. Perhaps another species within the same community can successfully reproduce from seeds 5 years out of 10. Thus, under natural conditions plant species do not reproduce from seed each year. A perennial community is more closed and protected from excessive erosion than is land in preparation for revegetation after mining. Established communities can wait for that year when conditions are favorable for reproduction of certain species by seed. Mined land needs vegetation established on it as soon as possible to protect it from excessive erosion. Often weedy species play an important role in

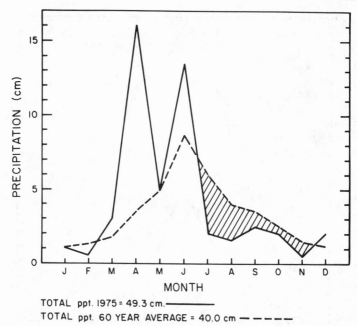

TOTAL ppt. 1975 = 49.3 cm.————
TOTAL ppt. 60 YEAR AVERAGE = 40.0 cm — — — — —

Fig. 3—Monthly precipitation for 1975 as compared with monthly 60-year average, Mandan, N. Dak.

partial protection of these lands, but if revegetation fails in a given year the land is exposed to greater erosion hazards and, because mining continues, twice as many hectares must be revegetated the following year.

It is understandable that when we plan to revegetate a certain number of hectares of mined land every year, and depend on natural precipitation, we can expect failure to establish certain or all species, occasionally, due to lack of water. The risk of failure and associated problems related to the lack of adequate soil water is proportional to the aridity of the area being revegetated. Supplementing natural precipitation with limited amounts of water can help overcome the problems caused by irregular and limited precipitation and can often insure successful revegetation where failure due to lack of water is imminent.

Other characteristics of land to be revegetated, like soil or spoil salinity, can greatly reduce the effectiveness of limited or untimely precipitation. High concentrations of soluble salts (> 4 mmhos/cm) increase the osmotic tension of the soil solution and decrease the water available for plant use. If the salt is composed primarily of Na ions, the soils become dispersed, lack aggregation, and contain few large or continuous pores through which water and air can pass. Water movement into and through such soils or spoils is greatly reduced, surface runoff is increased, and water storage is decreased.

Particle-size distribution, expressed as percentages of sand, silt, and clay, also influences water movement, storage, and availability. Materials with high sand contents permit water to infiltrate and percolate readily, but store very little water for later use by plants. When spoil or soil contains 80% or more sand, droughty conditions may exist. Materials with high clay contents have low rates of infiltration and percolation, but can store considerable quantities of water for later plant use. Infiltration and percolation into spoil or soil material with 40% or more clay is generally slow enough to cause problems. Fine-textured materials which contain Na ions are extremely impermeable. Characteristics of soil or spoils which reduce water intake, permeability, and storage must be considered if irrigation is used. Some of these considerations will be discussed later in this paper.

Characteristics such as the organic matter content of a soil-spoil complex and the amount of plant residue present at the surface can enhance the effectiveness of limited precipitation. Organic matter stimulates aggregation which makes for better water and air movement in a soil or spoil system. Plant residue can serve as a mulch and can substantially reduce soil water loss.

B. Irrigation for Plant Establishment

Irrigation as a tool in the reclamation of surface disturbed lands can be divided into two primary uses: first, to supply supplemental water to the new plant community during its establishment period, and, second, to supply excess water to leach undesirable water soluble constituents to greater depth in the soil-spoil complex. The work of several investigators who have used irrigation for the establishment of vegetation on mine spoils is reported in the following section. (For additional information see Chapter 24, "Revegetation Techniques for Dry Regions," by Packer and Aldon).

Very limited success has been reported in plot work with seeded and planted species on coal mine spoils near Nucla, Colorado, where precipitation is about 28 cm/year (Berg, 1975). These authors believe that there are three management alternatives for revegetation for low precipitation areas. First, seed without irrigation at the proper time, using good cultural practices, but be prepared for failures. Second, use mulches which retain water and improve the chances of establishment of vegetation in any given year. Third, use sprinkler irrigation to provide supplemental water for establishment. Berg and his colleagues have established satisfactory stands using 46 cm of supplemental water over a 2-mo period in a 28-cm/year precipitation zone.

May et al. (1971) reported using irrigation as one of several treatments in establishing vegetation on coal strip-mine spoils near Kemmerer, Wyoming [23.9 cm/year (9.42 in/year) precipitation]. They initiated irrigated plots to study the establishment of *Agropyron intermedium* (intermediate wheatgrass), *Agropyron cristatum* (crested wheatgrass), *Elymus junceus* (Russian wildrye), *Bromus inermis* (smooth bromegrass), and *Trifolium hybridum* (Alsike clover) on 9-year-old spoils in June 1966. Water from a nearby pit, suitable for livestock and agricultural purposes, was sprinkler-applied at a rate of 5 cm/hour (2 in/hour) with applications every 4 to 6 hours during a 2-day period in June and July. Irrigation resulted in some erosion because of the slow intake rate of the clay spoil. They concluded that sufficient water at planting and establishment was critical to stand success of seeded grasses and that irrigation, like snow collection, was one technique for adding supplemental water.

Berg (1972), in reviewing the stabilization of mine wastes, cited several instances where sprinkler irrigation was used to supply added water for revegetation, control blowing sand, and, in some cases, to maintain stands. Harbert and Berg (1974) used irrigation for leaching and establishment as one of several treatments to revegetate spent oil shale at two Colorado sites. After leaching to move soluble salts deeper into the profile at Anvil Points [precipitation 30 cm/year (12 in/year)], a mixture of native grasses and shrubs was seeded 11 June 1973. Sprinkler irrigation was used to add 47 cm (18.5 in) of supplemental water during June and July. Following leaching at Piceance Basin [precipitation 43 cm/year (17 in/year)], another mixture of grasses, forbs, and shrubs was seeded 26 June 1974 and a total of 28 cm (11.0 in) of supplemental water was added for establishment until 19 July. Seedling establishment was good at Anvil Points, but stands were thin and plots were reseeded at Piceance Basin.

Farmer et al. (1974) used irrigation as one treatment for establishing native and introduced species at Decker Coal Mine in southeastern Montana (precipitation about 39 cm/year). Soil textures of the study area varied from a sandy loam to a clay. Plots were sprinkler-irrigated from 18 May through 4 Oct. 1973 at a rate of 3.81 cm/week (1.5 in/week) in five daily applications of 0.8 cm (0.3 in). Ground water from a nearby pit was used for irrigation even though it was of low quality, primarily because of high Na content. First-season yields were highest on irrigated plots with no indications that using low-quality irrigation water adversely affected yield, although it greatly increased the exchangeable soil Na and required correction by applying $CaCl_2$.

Balzer et al. (1975) reported reclamation efforts by Utah International, Inc., at its Navajo Mine near Farmington, New Mexico, located in high desert country with sparse vegetation (21 cm/year of precipitation). Early work with supplemental irrigation has convinced them that this practice is crucial to successful early revegetation. The authors point out the difference between irrigating test plots and irrigating over 200 ha/year (500 acres/year) which they plan for the future. To prepare for this change, two 8-ha (20-acre) test plots were established in 1974 to evaluate drip and sprinkler irrigation systems (Aldon et al., 1976). Under both drip and sprinkler irrigation, the authors found species emergence and survival improved by the application of more frequent and higher levels of water.

In revegetation studies near Farmington, New Mexico (precipitation about 13 to 30 cm/year), Gould et al. (1975) considered the probability of successful revegetation without supplemental irrigation very low. Probability of successful regeneration without supplemental irrigation was better in the Gallup, New Mexico, area (precipitation from 30 to 36 cm/year). The authors found that using supplemental irrigation for establishment in 1974 on the Western Coal Company spoils near Farmington resulted in suitable stands of all species as compared with no emergence on nonirrigated plots. In this study, seeding took place in late July and irrigation began on 20 Aug. and was continued until 12 Oct. Total water applied was 13 to 19 cm. Low application rates were used with 76 mm applied in an initial 3-day period and the rest applied in 7- to 15-mm amounts at 3- to 7-day intervals. At these low application rates by sprinklers, no erosion occurred.

Aldon (1975) reported using sprinkler and drip irrigation for plant establishment along with other cultural treatments on reshaped spoils near Farmington, New Mexico. Water was applied by sprinkler at a rate of 1.3 cm (0.5 inches) twice weekly. A total of 25.4 cm (10 inches) was applied during the first growing season with no supplemental water added the second season. At the end of the first growing season, eight alkali sacaton (*Sporobolis airoides*) seedling/0.1 m^2 (seedling/feet^2) were alive, providing a good initial stand using irrigation. At the end of the second season, even though precipitation was only half of normal, 28% of the seedlings survived. In the second part of this study, water was applied using two 30.5-m (100-feet) lengths of 1.3-cm (0.5-inch) diameter drip-irrigation lines. Emitters were placed every 30.5 cm (every foot) along 18 m (60 feet) of each line and 3-mo old transplants of fourwind saltbush (*Atriplex canescens*) or western wheatgrass (*Agropyron smithii*) were planted at each emitter in mid-Sept. The transplants were irrigated twice weekly until the first hard frost. Under this gravity-feed drip system, the discharge rate of water was 5.3 liter (1.4 U.S. gallons)/emitter per hour. At each watering 15 liters (4 U.S. gallons) of water/emitter were delivered. Water was not used the second season. Survival for both species was significantly better than for control (nonirrigated) plants.

Drip irrigation has been used successfully for establishment of desert vegetation on the "berm" of Cu tailing deposits south of Tucson, Arizona (Aljibury, n.d.). Bengson (1975) reported optimistic results from drip irrigation on disturbed areas near Casa Grande, Arizona [precipitation 15 to 20 cm/year (6 to 8 inches/year)]. Desert shrub species were planted in 1974 and were scheduled to receive one to two 8-hour/week irrigations. Each emitter supplied 3.8 liter/hour (1 U.S. gallon/hour) or a total 30.4 liters (8 U.S. gallons) per irrigation or a volume flow of 144 lpm (38 gpm) at 1.05 kg/cm^2 (15 psi) pressure. Tensiometers were used to adjust the initial irrigation schedule to weather conditions and plant size. After establishment, the plants were subjected to a hardening-off period by gradually reducing the supplemental water supplied by drip irrigation.

The need to supply supplemental water during revegetation of disturbed lands in the semiarid and arid western U.S. generally increases as one moves from the Northern Great Plains (precipitation 40 cm/year to the deserts of the Southwest (precipitation 15 to 20 cm/year). Many localized areas receive precipitation amounts approaching those of the deserts (Kemmerer, Wyo., with 24 cm/year of precipitation). The entire area is characterized by irregular precipitation patterns and several months of drought can occur at any time. Normally, successful revegetation without irrigation is better in zones which receive over 30 cm/year of precipitation, but unsuccessful attempts can occur. Use of irrigation for plant establishment in areas where supplemental water is not an absolute necessity depends on benefits to be gained. Examples include continual seeding as land is prepared, weed control, better species composition, higher production, and more utility of the perennial communities established on disturbed lands. If the revegetative failures which can occur are intolerable from a standpoint of cost, surface soil loss, delays, or for other reasons, the use of irrigation to insure the success of a seeding may be warranted.

C. Irrigation for Leaching

Frequently, spoil material left after mining or tailings left after mineral extraction are high in soluble constituents which will restrict vegetation establishment and growth. Sufficient water can be applied to surpass the water storage capacity of a material so that the excess water can move these soluble constituents below the potential root zone, or at least below a large portion of the root zone, as long as sufficient drainage is available. At Anvil Points in Colorado, Harbert and Berg (1974) reduced high soluble salt concentration in spent oil shale by leaching with sprinkler irrigation [applying 102 cm (40 inches) of water at a rate of 0.4 cm/hour (0.16 inches/hour) for two 5-day periods]. Soluble salts in the soil-solution extract were decreased from 15 to less than 2 mmhos/cm in the first 1.2-m (4-foot) depth. At Piceance Basin, spent oil shale was leached with 51 cm (20 inches) of water in the fall and an additional 102 cm (40 inches) of water the next spring, at 0.4 cm/hour (0.16 inches/hour) for 6 hours/day. This process resulted in variable movement of the soluble salts. They attributed the differences between the two leaching responses to better quality water, lower bulk densities, more continuous leaching, and less wind with lower air temperatures during leaching at Anvil Points than at Piceance Basin.

Leaching can move soluble constituents, if hydraulic conductivity and drainage of the materials permits sufficient water intake and permeability to accomplish leaching and deep percolation. The high-salt leaching technique to improve hydraulic conductivity of sodic spoils has been reported by Doering and Willis (1975). Spoils with about 26% exchangeable-Na and very low permeability were leached with several concentrations of $CaCl_2$. Calcium supplied by the $CaCl_2$ replaced Na^+ on exchange sites, causing flocculation, and permanently increased permeability, which then made it possible to leach soluble salts below the root zone. Although such treatment is expensive, it demonstrates another use of leaching in reclamation.

Leaching as a reclamation tool is not used extensively in the West because most reclamation laws require that suitable soil be saved and replaced after mining, and water in the quantities needed for leaching is often absent. If sufficient surface soil or other suitable growth medium is available for replacement over sodic or saline soils, leaching is not necessary. If, however, suitable soil material is lacking and sufficient water is available, irrigation for leaching provides a tool to extend the root zone in saline or even in sodic spoils (after $CaCl_2$ treatment).

III. WATER FOR RECLAMATION

Irrigation to supplement natural precipitation during the establishment of vegetation requires considerably less water than that needed to produce high yields and high quality crops. Figure 2 shows that 27 cm of supplemental water are needed to increase the minimum amount of precipitation received at Mandan during the past 60 years for the months of May, June, July, Aug., and Sept., to the average received for those months during the same period. This is equal to 2,700 m³/ha, or 108,000 m³ to revegetate 40 ha. In comparison, Cassel and Bauer (1976) concluded that a minimum of 56 cm or 224,000 m³ of water distributed throughout the growing season would be needed to irrigate 40 ha of sugarbeets (*Beta vulgaris*) in southeastern North Dakota during a year of normal temperatures. Another factor reducing the total water needed each season for establishment irrigation at any one mine is the limited area to be revegetated yearly if seedings in all years are successful. Irrigation for leaching requires large quantities of water because the total water storage capacity of soil, spoil, or tailing materials must be met before leaching will take place. The amount of water needed will vary with the texture of the system to be leached.

If supplemental irrigation is to be used in reclamation of surface disturbed lands, a water source of suitable quality is essential. Two sources for this water are surface water and ground water.

A. Surface Water

Water is valuable and in great demand over much of the semiarid and arid West. Some water needed for reclamation may be supplied by large rivers, like the Yellowstone, Missouri, Colorado, and Green. Smaller rivers, like the Little Missouri, Tongue, Powder, Belle Fourche, Delores, and San Juan, may provide varying amounts of irrigation water if properly managed. With short-duration, high-intensity storms, characteristic over much of the West, even smaller, intermittent streams and watersheds may be harvested to supply supplemental surface water. Harvesting and storage of water for later use from rain or melting snow should not be discounted as a source of surface water for supplemental irrigation. Generally, the right to use surface water is controlled by water right laws, which vary from state to state, and effect the availability of this water for reclamation purposes.

B. Ground Water

Ground water is a second source of water for supplemental irrigation. At some locations, water from the mining pit is continually pumped out. Frequently aquifers are severed in the mining process and provide a potential source of water for supplemental irrigation. Sometimes nearby stock water wells or water table monitoring wells are available. These wells could possibly be used to provide needed irrigation water. Water collected and stored from even low-yielding wells can, over time, provide a substantial amount of water for limited irrigation. Like surface water, the right to use ground water is generally controlled by state statutes.

C. Water Quality

Any discussion of sources of supplemental irrigation water for re-vegetation of disturbed areas must consider the water quality. The U.S. Salinity Laboratory Staff (1954) outlined the following characteristics as important for irrigation water quality: (i) total concentration of soluble salts, (ii) relative proportion of Na to other cations, (iii) concentration of B or other toxic elements, and (iv) under some conditions, the bicarbonate concentration as related to the concentration of Ca plus Mg. Wilcox and Durum (1967) also provide a discussion of irrigation water quality. These references, listing criteria for water used for sustained crop production, can provide a basis for initial decisions on quality of supplemental irriga-tion water. Actual standards of quality for water to supplement natural precipitation for one or two seasons during the establishment of perennial communities have not been established.

IV. IRRIGATION METHODS FOR RECLAMATION

The extensive body of knowledge concerning production irrigation can be used to develop initial irrigation techniques for establishing vege-tation on disturbed lands. Certain differences exist between irrigated agriculture and irrigation for vegetation establishment. First, the purpose of irrigated agriculture is to provide enough water to stimulate yield and quality of crops year after year. Irrigating for establishment, however, is to supply enough water in addition to precipitation to ensure establish-ment [the naturalization of a plant in a new habitat or range typically in-volving successful growth, survival, and reproduction (Gove, 1968)] both initially and after irrigation is terminated. A second difference is that irri-gating for establishment may require a certain amount of water stress on the plants being established, whereas irrigation for production and quality strives to eliminate water stress. Another major difference be-tween the two types of irrigation is in the amounts of water required—the quantities needed for supplemental irrigation for establishment are ap-preciably less. Finally, the effect of irrigation on root growth and distri-bution is more important when irrigating for establishment than for irri-gated agriculture.

These differences in purpose and principle must be considered when existing agricultural irrigation concepts and techniques are modified to develop irrigation practices for the establishment of vegetation on dis-turbed lands.

A. Irrigation Management and Problems

Neither type of irrigation eliminates the need for good sound cultural and management practices, and sometimes may increase the need for better management.

Plant species to be used for revegetating an area must be well-adapted to the environmental conditions of the area. Plants native to the area are, of course, adapted, but this does not preclude the use of well-adapted introduced species. The seed source used should also be compatible with the area at which the seeding is to take place.

The same management concerns that have been documented as important in irrigated agriculture must be considered when using irrigation on disturbed land to supplement natural precipitation during revegetation. These factors are application rates, irrigation scheduling, nutrient requirement, infiltration, drainage, soil erosion, salt problems, water quality, chemical and physical characteristics of the soil or spoil, and economics.

1. APPLICATION RATES FOR RECLAMATION IRRIGATION

Special consideration will need to be given to water infiltration and subsurface movement when irrigating disturbed lands. The rates of application of irrigation water for each area will need to be considered individually. Initial rates can be determined using infiltration tests (Haise et al., 1956). Use of their technique on sodic mine spoil in North Dakota showed an average intake rate over a 2-hour period of 4 cm/hour. The rate was 7.4 cm/hour during the first hour and 0.5 cm/hour for the second hour. This decrease in intake rate is important in calculating initial rates and durations of irrigation.

Since many state laws require the stockpiling and replacing of surface soil, many areas of disturbed land will have an abrupt textural interface between replaced surface soil and spoil materials. If water movement into the underlying spoil is restricted, water may move laterally along the interface, potentially giving rise to the development of seeps. On steep slopes, slippage may occur. Using heavy equipment in reshaping spoil and replacing surface soil may, under some conditions, result in compaction, reducing water intake and movement. In some locations and with certain spoils, water repellency has been reported (personal correspondence, Dr. Walter L. Gould, New Mexico State Univ., Las Cruces, N. Mex.). The occurrence of such materials drastically limits water movement. Further information on this subject can be obtained from Debano and Letey (1969).

Water application rates for disturbed lands will need to be carefully controlled and monitored. Very low rates may be required under some conditions and information and technical developments for turfgrass irrigation may be worth considering (Lunt & Seeley, 1967). Other possibilities may involve increasing water intake rates where possible (Henderson & Haise, 1967). If application rates exceed intake of the soil-spoil comex, surface water flow and erosion will occur. If slopes are involved, erosion may be increased.

2. AMOUNT, FREQUENCY, AND DURATION OF IRRIGATION FOR ESTABLISHMENT

Data are limited on the amount and frequency of water needed as precipitation or supplemental irrigation for many grass and forb species used in revegetation work. Even less is known about water requirements for plant establishment, as compared with production and quality. Few data are available on the length of time vegetation should be irrigated for establishment.

Willard (1966) discussed the reasons for failure of forage seedings and outlined the basic cultural considerations involved in establishing new seedlings. Hamilton et al. (1945) discussed the contemporary cultural practices, many of which are still pertinent, including establishment of irrigated pastures. These agronomists recommended that the surface soil should not be permitted to crust or dry within the first 18 to 20 days after seeding. When precipitation did not supply the moisture needed to accomplish this, irrigation was used. Keller and Carlson (1967) discussed the establishment of irrigated perennial forage crops. The differences between irrigating for establishment followed by the termination of irrigation and irrigating for establishment followed by continued production irrigation need to be investigated. Questions involved include the amounts of irrigation water to apply, frequency of application required, and duration of supplementing natural precipitation needed to establish a stand that can sustain itself and provide forage after irrigation is terminated.

Perhaps the initial amount of water and frequency of irrigation for establishing vegetation should be related to natural precipitation amounts and patterns. Each mining area has received precipitation that has allowed adapted species to establish, survive, reproduce, and provide forage. When these species are reestablished, the amounts and frequencies of supplemental water plus precipitation may need to follow the precipitation amounts and patterns of a specific year (perhaps the average year for that location). If the species to be established are known to require more favorable water conditions, a watering schedule that simulates a year with above average precipitation could be followed. Such a system would maintain watering levels comparable to the total precipitation of the area and will not keep the plants totally free from water stress. Scheduling irrigation by methods like the above would be less artificial and arbitrary and can perhaps result in better survival after irrigation is terminated than would irrigation based on the apparent need of the vegetation.

Frequent irrigation of turf grass has been associated with significantly fewer and shallower roots (Madison & Hagan, 1962). The depth, lateral distribution, and volume of root systems are important to plant survival after irrigation is terminated and during drought periods. For this reason, frequency of irrigation for establishing new stands must be clearly understood. Danielson (1967) provided an excellent review of the relationship of root systems to irrigation. Management to encourage deep-rooting and lateral extension of roots into the subsoil may be one of the most important factors in insuring survival of vegetation after irrigation is terminated.

Data are limited on the length of time natural precipitation will have to be supplemented with irrigation to achieve the desired establishment. Weaver and Clements (1938) reported that even a short drought period after germination is detrimental to the establishment of plants. Also, competition for water is known to be critical for most herbs. Grasses have a critical need for water when tillering and during new root development. Water stress at this time results in greater mortality. This stage is reached at about 44 days of age for blue grama (*Bouteloua gracilis*) (Clements & Weaver, 1924). Woody species are susceptible to drought in midsummer and later. Older plants, of all classes of vegetation, were better able to resist adverse conditions. Sampson (1914), working in the Wallowa Mountains in northeastern Oregon with about 43 cm/year (17 inches/year) precipitation, found that after the first season seedling loss due to climatic conditions was minor.

Some very recent work with blue grama has found that, for successful establishment, adventitious roots must be developed. For this to happen, blue grama seedlings require two properly spaced periods of damp, cloudy weather, one for emergence and one for development of adventitious roots (Personal communication, Dr. A. M. Wilson, plant physiologist, USDA-ARS, Crop Res. Lab., Colorado State Univ., Fort Collins, Colo.). Under natural conditions, these two wet periods often fail to occur. This information does show that a very limited amount of supplemental water at the right time could make a big difference in the success of blue grama seedings.

Based on current information, one season of irrigation should be planned as a minimum. This allows supplementing natural precipitation for a complete cycle of vegetational development, until a period of natural dormancy. If other than early season planting is used, at least 6 to 10 weeks of growing weather with favorable water supply should be allowed for plant development. Possibly more than one season of supplementing precipitation will be needed for establishment in more arid areas or for certain species, but, in most cases, supplemental irrigation to insure favorable soil water during the first season of plant development should help the success of revegetation tremendously. Research data are needed to better define this requirement.

Plant density may decrease somewhat after termination of irrigation as the stand adjusts to the new available water supply. Such density reductions are not detrimental, as long as the stabilized density is near that expected for the climatic conditions in the area. As competition becomes greater after irrigation is terminated, the best-adapted individuals should survive. Berg (1975) lowered the seeding rates, when sprinkler irrigation was used for establishment, so that resultant stands would have densities similar to natural stands in the area. However, thin stands resulted, so they recommended seeding at normal rates and letting the stand thin naturally.

B. Irrigation Systems

Two methods of irrigation (drip and sprinkler) seem most suitable for use in reclamation. Present technology and systems can provide a basis for future development of irrigation units specifically designed for use on disturbed lands. Irrigation units should be designed with the characteristics of the disturbed area to be irrigated in mind. The Soil Conservation Service and State Extension Services can be contacted for technical assistance.

1. DRIP IRRIGATION

Drip or trickle irrigation, defined as the frequent or daily application of water to localized areas through emitters at a rate that will balance water used by evapotranspiration, is gaining in popularity and is being used experimentally for establishing vegetation on disturbed areas. The system is composed of a plastic pipeline on the surface with emitters placed at some distance apart. Plants are placed at each emitter and the amount of water for their growth is controlled by adjusting the emitters or the pressure in the water line. The advantages of this technique are water conservation, restricted area for weeds, dual water and nutrient application, use on steep slopes, use of more saline water, and improved water penetration (Aljibury, n.d.). Drip irrigation is popular in areas with high aridity, where water supplies are extremely limited, and where high value crops are grown (Fangmeier, 1972). Use of this system is being studied for revegetation in the arid areas of Arizona and New Mexico.

2. SPRINKLER IRRIGATION

Sprinkler irrigation, a fast-growing, popular method of irrigation, is most often used in irrigating disturbed lands, with both solid set and moving types having application. Advantages of this method are adaptability to irregular topography, relatively uniform water distribution, application rates that minimize soil loss, dual water and fertilizer application, and more effective water use (thus allowing more acres to be irrigated per unit flow of water) (Schwalen & Frost, 1963). The low rates of application by sprinkler are especially desirable when the goal of irrigation is leaching. New sprinkler irrigation developments are continually being made (Pair et al., 1975; Halderman & Frost, 1968). Further adaptation of sprinkler irrigation for use in the revegetation of disturbed land seems very promising.

V. THE FUTURE OF IRRIGATION FOR RECLAMATION

The need for the addition of supplemental water through irrigation has generally been realized and accepted as necessary in areas where precipitation is minimal. Further use of irrigation as a tool in reclamation will depend upon the benefits to be gained. Irrigation is not new and much is known about its use and techniques. This knowledge provides a basis for further development of techniques and principles which apply more specifically to irrigation for plant establishment. Many facets about such irrigation need to be better understood and applied. Supplemental irrigation is a promising tool in establishing perennial plant communities of high productivity and utility on areas disturbed by energy and other mineral development, but it also has potential in improving deteriorated rangeland communities by establishing new communities with more desirable species.

LITERATURE CITED

Aldon, E. F. 1975. Techniques for establishing native plants on coal mine spoils in New Mexico. p. 21–28. *In* Proc. 3rd Symp. on Surface Mining and Reclamation. NCA/BCR Coal Conf. and Expo. II, Louisville, Ky., Oct. 1975. Natl. Coal Assoc., Washington, D.C. 243 p.

Aldon, E. F., H. W. Springfield, and W. E. Sowards. 1976. Demonstration test of two irrigation systems for plant establishment on coal mine spoils. *In* Proc. 4th Symp. of Surface Mining and Reclamation, 1:201–214. NCA/BCR Coal Conf. and Expo. III, Louisville, Ky., Oct. 1976. Natl. Coal Assoc., Washington, D.C. 276 p.

Aljibury, F. n.d. Drip irrigation practices and application. Drip Irrig. News 1(3):1–4.

Balzer, J. L., D. B. Crouch, R. W. Poyser, and W. Sowards. 1975. A venture into reclamation. Min. Congr. J. 61(1):24–29.

Bengson, S. A. 1975. Drip irrigation for revegetating steep slopes in acid environments. Prog. Agric. Ariz. 15(1):3–5, 12.

Berg, W. A. 1972. Vegetative stabilization of mine wastes. p. 24–26. *In* Mining Yearbook. Colorado Mining Assoc., Denver, Colo.

Berg, W. A. 1975. Revegetation of land disturbed by surface mining in Colorado. p. 79–89. *In* M. K. Wali (ed.) Practice and problems of land reclamation in western North America. Univ. of North Dakota Press, Grand Forks, N. Dak.

Cassel, D. K., and A. Bauer. 1976. Irrigation schedules for sugarbeets on medium and coarse textured soil in the northern Great Plains. Agron. J. 68:45–48.

Clements, F. E., and J. E. Weaver. 1924. Experimental vegetation. Publ. 355. Carnegie Inst., Washington, D.C.

Danielson, R. E. 1967. Root systems in relation to irrigation. *In* R. M. Hagan, H. R. Haise, and T. W. Edminster (ed.) Irrigation of agricultural lands. Agronomy 11:390–424. Am. Soc. of Agron., Madison, Wis.

Debano, L. F., and J. Letey. 1969. Water-repellent soils. Proc. Symp. on Water Repellent Soils, 6–10 May 1968, Dry Land Res. Inst. of Calif. and Natl. Sci. Found., Univ. of Calif., Riverside. Univ. of Calif. Press, Berkley. 351 p.

Doering, E. J., and W. O. Willis. 1975. Chemical reclamation of sodic strip-mine spoils. USDA-ARS-NC 20, Peoria, Ill.

Fangmeier, D. D. 1972. Is drip irrigation for Arizona? Prog. Agric. Ariz. 24(3):6, 7, and 15.

Farmer, E. E., R. W. Brown, B. Z. Richardson, and P. E. Packer. 1974. Revegetation research on the Decker Coal Mine in southeastern Montana. USDA For. Serv. Res. Pap. INT-162, Ogden, Utah. 12 p.

Gould, W. L., D. Rai, and P. J. Wierenga. 1975. Problems in reclamation of coal mine spoils. p. 107–121. *In* M. K. Wali (ed.) Practice and problems of land reclamation in western North America. Univ. of North Dakota Press, Grand Forks, N. Dak.

Gove, P. B. 1968. Webster's third new international dictionary. G & C Merriam Co., Springfield, Mass.

Gulhati, N. D., and W. C. Smith. 1967. Irrigated agriculture: An historical review. *In* R. M. Hagan, H. R. Haise, and T. W. Edminster (ed.) Irrigation of agricultural lands. Agronomy 11:3–11. Am. Soc. of Agron., Madison, Wis.

Hagan, R. M., H. R. Haise, and T. W. Edminster (eds.). 1967. Irrigation of agricultural lands. Agronomy 11. Am. Soc. of Agron., Madison, Wis. 1180 p.

Haise, H. R., W. W. Donnan, J. T. Phelan, L. F. Lawhon, and D. G. Shockley. 1956. The use of cylinder infiltrometers to determine the intake characteristics of irrigated soils. USDA-ARS 41-7, Washington, D.C.

Halderman, A. D., and K. R. Frost. 1968. Sprinkler irrigation in Arizona. Ariz. Cooper. Ext. Serv. and Agric. Exp. Stn. Bull. A-56, Tucson, Ariz. 30 p.

Hamilton, J. G., G. F. Brown, H. E. Tower, and W. Collins, Jr. 1945. Irrigated pastures for forage production and soil conservation. USDA Farmers' Bull. no. 1973, Washington, D.C. 30 p.

Harbert, H. P., and W. A. Berg. 1974. Vegetation stabilization of spent oil shales. Colorado State Univ. Tech. Rep. no. 4, Fort Collins, Colo. 40 p.

Henderson, D. W., and H. R. Haise. 1967. Control of water intake rates. In R. M. Hagan, H. R. Haise, and T. W. Edminster (eds.) Irrigation of agricultural lands. Agronomy 11: 925–940. Am. Soc. of Agron., Madison, Wis.

Keller, W., and C. W. Carlson. 1967. Forage crops. In R. M. Hagen, H. R. Haise, and T. W. Edminster (eds.) Irrigation of agricultural lands. Agronomy 11:607–621. Am. Soc. of Agron., Madison, Wis.

Lunt, O. R., and J. G. Seeley. 1967. Turfgrass, flowers and other ornamentals. In R. M. Hagan, H. R. Haise, and T. W. Edminster (eds.) Irrigation of agricultural lands. Agronomy 11:753–768. Am. Soc. of Agron., Madison, Wis.

Madison, J. H., and R. M. Hagan. 1962. Extraction of soil moisture by Merion bluegrass (Poa pratensis L. 'Merion') turf, as affected by irrigation frequency, mowing height, and other cultural operations. Agron. J. 54:157–160.

May, M. 1975. Moisture relationships and treatments in revegetating strip mines in the arid West. J. Range Manag. 28(4):334–335.

May, M., R. Lang, L. Lujan, P. Jacoby, and W. Thompson. 1971. Reclamation of strip mine spoil banks in Wyoming. Univ. of Wyoming, Agric. Exp. Stn. Res. J. 51, Laramie, Wyo. 32 p.

Pair, C. H., W. W. Hinz, C. Reid, and K. R. Frost. 1975. Sprinkler irrigation. Sprinkler Irrigation Assoc., Silver Springs, Md. 601 p.

Sampson, A. W. 1914. Natural revegetation of range land based upon growth requirements and life history of the vegetation. USDA, J. Agric. Res. (Washington, D.C.) III(2): 93–171.

Schwalen, H. C., and K. R. Frost. 1963. Sprinkler irrigation. Ariz. Agric. Exp. Stn. and Coop. Ext. Serv. Bull. A-24, Tucson, Ariz. 39 p.

Study Committee on the Potential for Rehabilitating Lands Surface Mined for Coal in the Western United States. 1974. Rehabilitation potential of western coal lands. Ballinger Publ. Co., Cambridge, Mass. 198 p.

U.S. Department of Agriculture. 1948. Irrigation agriculture in the West. USDA Misc. Publ. 670, Washington, D.C. 39 p.

U.S. Salinity Laboratory Staff. 1954. Diagnosis and improvement of saline and alkali soils. USDA Agric. Hbk. no. 60, Washington, D.C. 160 p.

Weaver, J. E., and F. E. Clements. 1938. Plant ecology. McGraw-Hill Book Co., Inc., New York. 601 p.

Wilcox, L. V., and W. H. Durum. 1967. Quality of irrigation water. In R. M. Hagan, H. R. Haise, and T. W. Edminster (eds.) Irrigation of agricultural lands. Agronomy 11:104–122. Am. Soc. of Agron., Madison, Wis.

Willard, C. J. 1966. Establishment of new seedings. p. 368–381. In H. D. Hughes, M. E. Heath, and D. S. Metcalfe (eds.) Forages. Iowa State Univ. Press, Ames, Iowa.

Copyright © 1978 ASA–CSSA–SSSA
677 South Segoe Road, Madison, WI 53711 USA
Reclamation of Drastically Disturbed Lands

Chapter 29

Reclamation Research on Strip-Mined Lands in Dry Regions

J. F. POWER

Agricultural Research Service, USDA
Northern Great Plains Research Center, Mandan, North Dakota
(now located at the Agronomy Dep., Univ. of Nebraska, Lincoln, Nebr.)

I. INTRODUCTION

Research on the reclamation of land disturbed by strip mining for coal in dry regions is currently being conducted by many scientists employed by several different organizations in each state and province of the western United States and Canada where mining is significant. The purpose of this chapter is to outline the history of reclamation research; to describe the natural resources used in reclamation; to review the kind of research information available and the kind needed to properly utilize each of the natural resources; and to show how this information is used in developing reclaimed land. This chapter is an overview of the state of the art and indicates the direction needed in the future. No attempt is made in this chapter to catalog the various research activities currently in progress. Frequently, the reader will be referred to other chapters in this publication for detailed information on several aspects of reclamation.

II. HISTORY OF SURFACE MINING IN THE WESTERN U.S.

Attempts to restore productivity to land disturbed by strip mining is a relatively new concept in North America, particularly in dry regions. Historically, thousands of hectares in several states were disturbed during the nineteenth century by surface mining, especially by dredging for gold and other materials. Much of this area today remains in the same condition as when it was abandoned decades ago. Likewise, extensive areas of gravel, rock, and clay pits have been abandoned and remain drastically disturbed. Generally, however, mining of this nature was relatively localized and shallow, frequently permitting some degree of natural revegetation of disturbed areas.

In the early 1900's, railroads crossed the dry regions of North America, and coal was a prime fuel to power the locomotives. Thus, extensive coal mining operations were developed. Because many western coal deposits are found at relatively shallow depths, open-pit mining operations were frequently established, utilizing steam shovels for the stripping. Thus, modern day strip-mining was initiated on a commercial scale.

Spoils resulting from these early strip mine operations were usually abandoned after the coal was extracted. Little was known about the ability of such areas to revegetate naturally and, generally, the question had little relevance since there was then little incentive or apparent need to reclaim mined lands. As a result, reclamation research in the western U.S. was practically nonexistent.

By the 1950's, diesel locomotives generally replaced steam locomotives, eliminating much of the need to mine coal in the West. This resulted in most of the strip mines opened some 20 to 40 years earlier being partially or completely closed. However, by the late 1960's and especially in the early 1970's, it became apparent that a dramatic and rapid expansion of coal mining in the West was imminent. First, federal air-pollution standards adopted during this period made it imperative for many industries to seek low sulfur coal, a type of coal prevalent in the West. Second, continued growth in electrical power requirements of the nation dictated the need for new coal sources and electrical generating plants, preferably away from centers of population to lessen potential environmental and social impacts. Third, the dependence of the United States on foreign oil imports and accompanying increases in oil prices in the early 1970's encouraged the development of Western coal as an alternate energy source because of its relatively low mining cost. Consequently, coal production in many of the major Western coal-producing States is doubling each year or two, and projections are for greater expansions in production to continue for the next several decades.

III. ATTITUDES TOWARD RECLAMATION

Before 1970, a relatively small area in the western U.S. had been disturbed by strip-mining, providing very little impetus for research to develop reclamation technology. However, as a result of present and projected future development, tens of thousands of hectares may be disturbed annually, with a potential total area of disturbance of several million hectares. Thus, the need for sound reclamation technology in the West is now apparent.

The demands of today's society, as expressed in recent reclamation laws of many Western states, are not just to stabilize soil and vegetation on disturbed areas, but rather to restore disturbed areas to full agricultural productivity. Almost all of the land underlain by coal is presently used as grazing or cropland, and most is expected to be returned to similar use after mining. The prevailing phiosophy in these laws is to develop mined land to a condition that will allow the highest potential agricultural use, as dictated by the properties of the soil and overburden and by the local climate. Reclamation of this nature is expected to provide ours and future generations with the flexibility of using the area for any purpose for which it is suited.

IV. USE OF NATURAL RESOURCES IN RECLAMATION

The natural resources available at a mine site are the materials used in restoration of productivity: namely, (i) climate, (ii) soils, (iii) overburden, (iv) water, and (v) vegetation. Information on the extent, characteristics, nature, availability, and other parameters of each of these resources must be available to properly reclaim an area.

A. Climate

Of the various parameters of climate, air temperature and precipitation are usually most important. Information is needed on daily and seasonal maximum and minimum temperatures, and on length of frost-free growing season. Monthly precipitation means, some indication of variability of these means, and amounts of precipitation received as snow are of prime importance. Other information usually of lesser importance is monthly and seasonal data on wind velocity and direction, radiation, relative humidity, and open-pan evaporation. Mining of an area would not be expected to appreciably change the climatic resources within that area.

Frequently, the needed information on climate is not available at a proposed mining site, so weather stations are established. Data collected in the few years between the date when a weather station is established and when reclamation plans are developed are usually too limited to permit any estimation of long-term means or variability. Such variability is illustrated in Table 1 which shows the monthly precipitation obtained at Mandan, North Dakota, for 1973, 1974, and 1975, compared to the 61-year means. High variability is a characteritic of climatic data in most dry regions.

When short-term on-site data are inadequate, long-term U.S. Weather Bureau records from the nearest recording station in a similar climatic zone are frequently used. In the Western states and provinces, such records are often available only at distances of 50 to 100 km and often at appreciably different elevations. Therefore, sometimes reclamation plans have to be developed with inadequate climatic information.

Information about climate is a necessary requirement before reclamation plans can be developed. Adequate data on seasonal and

Table 1—Monthly precipitation for 3- and 61-year mean at Mandan, N. Dak.

Year	Jan.	Feb.	Mar.	Apr.	May	June	July	Aug.	Sept.	Oct.	Nov.	Dec.	Total
						mm							
1973	1	1	3	22	63	18	19	5	56	37	4	12	241
1974	1	5	3	73	84	51	57	38	5	30	4	11	358
1975	9	3	36	162	55	136	17	16	21	18	3	18	494
61-year Avg.	10	10	18	40	55	87	59	42	35	23	13	10	402

annual precipitation and temperature provide a basis for making a first approximation regarding the adaptability of various plant species and the potential production of these species. In most coal fields in western North America, precipitation is usually deficient for the maximum growth of most plant species. As a consequence, most reclamation practices are, in essence, the application of technology that effectively stores precipitation within the plant root zone and enhances efficient utilization of this stored water by the growing plant. In general then, reclamation ideally minimizes or eliminates runoff and leaching while maximizing plant growth.

B. Soils

Ideally, information on soil characteristics and extent can be obtained from a detailed soil survey of the region. If conducted in accord with procedures used in the National Cooperative Soil Survey, information will be provided on the location and extent of each soil type present in the proposed mine area. From this information, estimates can be made of the quality of each soil horizon as a potential media for plant growth. Also, the volume of soil from each soil horizon present within the proposed area can be calculated, which will permit calculation of the average amount of soil material available to save and its thickness when spread on the surface of spoils after regrading.

C. Overburden

Physical and chemical properties of overburden materials can be determined before mining by systematically collecting samples by drilling and analyzing them. Analyses of primary concern include texture, pH and water content (saturation percentage) of the saturated paste, electrical conductivity, and soluble Ca, Mg, and Na in the saturation extract. Other characteristics which are sometimes of concern are soluble boron content, cation exchange capacity, exchangeable cations, gypsum and calcium carbonate equivalents, and carbonate, bicarbonate, sulfate, chloride, and nitrate content of the saturation extract. By using research information from this symposium and other sources, plant growth potential of overburden materials can be predicted from the data derived from the above analyses.

In collecting and analyzing samples to characterize overburden materials, several precautions must be observed to permit valid interpretation of the resulting data. Power and Sandoval (1976) found that in sandy overburden materials, drilling fluids that contained appreciable quantities of soluble salts, either with or without additives, could seriously contaminate samples. They found that data for analysis of samples collected directly from the fresh highwall agreed best with data for analysis of shavings collected from pneumatic (dry) drilling (Table 2). Also, in laboratory analysis of samples, it is important to follow in detail standardized procedures, like those outlined by the U.S. Salinity Laboratory Staff

Table 2—Soluble Na content in saturation extract of overburden samples collected by several methods

Drilling method	Depth, m								
	0–1.5	1.5–3	3–4.5	4.5–6	6–7.5	7.5–9	9–10.5	10.5–12	0–12
	meq/liter								
Air	1.22	0.77	0.95	0.68	1.31	0.92	1.03	1.06	0.99
Low salt water	1.09	2.39	1.30	2.22	2.39	2.61	1.61	2.09	1.96
Drilling mud	1.61	7.83	7.83	8.70	5.00	9.30	5.87	4.58	6.34
High salt water	2.24	7.39	8.17	4.45	3.94	3.33	2.50	3.17	4.40
Polymer	2.76	1.34	1.24	1.30	1.24	1.20	1.39	1.30	1.47
Highwall	1.56	1.03	0.78	0.70	0.61	0.81	0.61	0.74	0.76

(1954) or by Black (1965). Consequences of deviating from these procedures are discussed more fully in other chapters of this publication.

D. Water

The availability of water in the dry regions of North America generally overshadows all other factors in regulating plant growth. The primary source of water is natural precipitation, although in some areas precipitation may be augmented by irrigation or by ground water. Also, the properties of soils and overburden determine to a large extent the movement and storage of water within the root zone. Again, details of various aspects of water supply and management are being discussed in other chapters. In the final analysis, however, successful reclamation in dry regions depends upon the availability of technology to collect and conserve water in the potential root zone, and to utilize this water efficiently for plant growth. Almost every activity associated with reclamation in the western U.S. is aimed at one or another aspect of this goal—to efficiently conserve and utilize water.

E. Vegetation

The fifth natural resource used in reclamation is the biotic resource, especially vegetative materials. A wide spectrum of plant species is available for use in reclamation, and the actual species or combination of species used depends mainly upon the expected average water availability in the root zone and on the anticipated use of the area after reclamation. On most areas suitable for mining in the West, present vegetation is comprised of perennial species, especially grasses and forbs. However, in relatively localized regions over 50% of the area may be in annual crops, especially wheat and other small grains. Land use after mining will probably resemble that existing before mining.

Of special concern in many parts of the western U.S. is revegetation by perennial species designated as being "native"—species present before settlement by the white man. Frequently, we do not possess the technology with which we can reestablish these species, both on land disturbed and not disturbed by man. Included in this category are many shrubs and forbs found on the rangeland, and many of the various warm-season grasses (especially in the mixed and short-grass prairie regions). For many species a seed source is also lacking. However, other more recently introduced species are frequently available to fulfill many of the functions of these difficult-to-establish "native" species. Consequently, questions need to be answered regarding the acceptability of such substitutions. Many of the problems relating to species are discussed in detail elsewhere in this symposium.

V. RESEARCH ON RECLAMATION

Basically, reclamation, as used here, is the process of utilizing natural resources in a manner that is economically feasible, and that will allow development of the plant growth potentials permitted by these resources themselves. Therefore, considerable research is needed, first, to determine these plant-growth potentials and, second, to develop guidelines for the proper management of the natural resources to provide the desired product. In dry regions, because of the overwhelming influence of water, these two steps essentially amount to conducting research to develop capacity to store the precipitation received within the normal rooting depth, and to develop "soil" and vegetative management practices that will enhance the utilization of this water by useful vegetation. Included are problems related to both vegetative establishment and to vegetative growth and production.

Various aspects of reclamation research are currently being conducted by many agencies throughout western United States and Canada. No attempt is made in this paper to identify all these projects since several agencies are keeping current inventories of research activities (Old West Regional Commission & U.S. Forest Service SEAM Program, 1975; Bituminous Coal Research, 1975). Some of these agencies with a major involvement in the United States are State Agricultural Experiment Stations, universities, U.S. Department of Agriculture (ARS, SCS, ERS, FS), U.S. Department of Interior (BLM, USBM, USBR, USGS, USFWS), EPA, ERDA, Old West Regional Commission, and others. Mining companies are also extensively involved in most of these research activities.

A. Climate

Research related to climate consists mainly of inventorying precipitation and temperature data. Since great variability of both precipitation and temperature is characteristic of dry regions, information is needed about the magnitude by which these climatic parameters vary, in both time and space. Climatologists or other scientists at most of the State Agricultural Experiment Stations have summarized climatological data for their state and many have calculated variability for at least some of the key locations. Frequently, variability is expressed on a probability basis, as calculated from an incomplete gamma function or other appropriate statistical treatment. Several examples of precipitation probability information are available (Heerman et al., 1971; Ramirez, 1974; and Shaw et al., 1960). With this type of information, it is possible to determine the probability of receiving any predetermined amount of precipitation for any period of time during the year. Information of this nature is valuable in scheduling many operations. For example, it is desirable to receive frequent rain and moderate temperatures when cool season grasses are germinating. The probability of experiencing these conditions can be determined by reference to proper probability tables for the particular locale.

B. Soils

The basic inventory for the soil resource is the National Cooperative Soil Survey conducted by the Soil Conservation Service (USDA), State Agricultural Experiment Stations, and sometimes other agencies. From such a survey, the areal extent and nature of soil present in a given area can be determined. Unfortunately, however, in many areas where mining is active, this survey is less than 50% completed. For some purposes, general soil association maps, which are available on a much larger scale, serve the need as well as the detailed survey. However, the detailed survey information is necessary to develop on-site reclamation plans. Most state enforcement agencies require a detailed soil survey before mining can begin.

Although the soil survey information will provide data on quantity and quality of soil material present, considerable research is needed to relate soil quantity and quality to plant-growth potentials. Some research of this type is in progress at various locations throughout the western U.S. In many states reclamation laws require that suitable soil material be saved and returned to reshaped spoils. Some rather arbitrary definitions of the word *suitable* have been adopted in these states until more detailed research information provides a better scientific basis for this definition.

To illustrate the influence of quality and thickness of soil material on plant growth, data are presented in Fig. 1 on 1975 hard red spring wheat (*Triticum aestivum*) yields at the Glenharold Mine, Stanton, North Dakota. In this experiment spoils containing over 50% clay and with over 25% exchangeable Na were used. Subsoil and topsoil was either mixed or applied in separate layers. Topsoil consisted of the A horizons of Temvik silt loam (Typic haplorboroll), while subsoil was primarily B, C, and sometimes upper D horizon materials derived from loess and glacial till. Adequate N and P fertilizers were added.

In all instances grain yields in Fig. 1 increased as thickness of soil increased to about 60 to 75 cm—beyond 75 cm no significant increases in yield were recorded. Yields were lowest for plots receiving only subsoil,

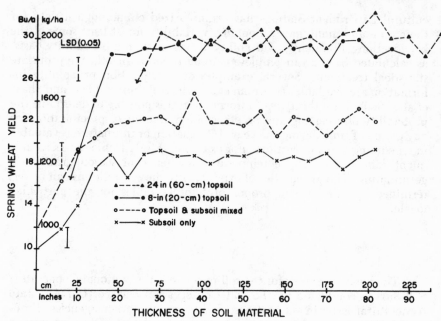

Fig. 1—1975 spring wheat yields as affected by thickness of topsoil and subsoil over spoils, Stanton, N. Dak.

followed by plots with subsoil and topsoil mixed, and greatest yields were obtained from plots with either 20 or 60 cm topsoil spread over the subsoil. The yield level at which response curves levelled off, therefore, increased as quality of soil material increased. Mixing subsoil and topsoil merely diluted the topsoil effect. Similar results have also been obtained using alfalfa (*Medicago sativa*) and several perennial grasses as test crops.

These results suggest that, under the conditions of this experiment, 75 cm of soil material over spoils is sufficient for maximum yields, regardless of the quality of the soil material used. However, because of the adverse characteristics of the spoils beneath, there is potential for salinization or for water-logging of the soil immediately above the spoils. Thus, available data are insufficient to fully solve the problem. Also, if other crops or topsoil, subsoil, or spoils of different characteristics had been used, results may have differed. Therefore, much more research is needed to answer questions related to thickness and quality of soil material spread on spoils.

C. Overburden

Identification and quantification of those overburden characteristics of most importance in regulating plant establishment, growth, and quality is a research problem of highest priority. When this information is available, relatively accurate predictions can be made regarding water relationships that will be encountered in spoils after mining. Since in dry regions water-related properties of spoils regulate vegetative response, the ability of a material to absorb and hold water determines to a large extent the reclamation activities that need to be used to successfully restore productivity. In addition, laboratory analyses of overburden samples can also be used to detect other factors that may limit potential productivity—especially potential deficiencies or toxicities of many elements.

Much research has already been conducted on unmined land throughout the dry regions of North America relating growth of various plant species to physical and chemical properties of the growth media. Thus, much information obtained from unmined land can be applied to interpreting results of laboratory analyses of spoils and overburden. Often correlations between plant growth and levels or intensities of the different soil properties used for unmined land have yet to be verified for use on mined land. Before this can be accomplished, however, acceptance of uniform methods of analysis of overburden and spoils must be accepted and adhered to—otherwise correlations and subsequent interpretations in terms of plant growth potential are meaningless.

Research is in progress at several locations to develop methodology for altering adverse properties of spoils and overburden, once these properties have been identified. However, present efforts associated with this research appear to be inadequate to meet the problems. On a relatively narrow subject, like Na content of spoils, for example, research is in progress at only a few locations to determine the amount of Na replacement that can be expected from various amendments, and how replacement can best be achieved in the field. Very little research is being conducted on the interactions between the effects of gypsum and topsoil thickness when spread on sodic spoils. Additional studies need to be conducted on the basic chemistry of spoils—for example, why does it seem that the solubility of both gypsum and calcium carbonate in some spoils is sometimes lower than one would predict. Likewise, the correlations of plant growth with content of available N and P in spoils or in reclaimed land have not been developed. At only a few locations is research in progress to understand changes that occur with time in overburden properties, or how we can manage these changes to enhance reclamation.

D. Water Supplies

Research on hydrological properties of overburden and spoils is in progress at several locations in the dry regions. In most states with major mining activities, at least one comprehensive study in hydrology is in progress. Collectively, the results of this research will define the water cycle in mined land and will provide some information on how we can manage the water cycle to enhance plant growth. However, in connection with the needed research on altering properties of spoils through amendments, the effects on hydrological characteristics need to be determined. Rather than only determine what happens to water on mined land, more research is needed to determine how we can manage water to maximum benefit. This will require continued active cooperation between hydrologists, soil scientists, agronomists, range scientists, and other disciplines.

A very real opportunity seems to exist to utilize supplemental irrigation for the establishment of perennial species on mined land. This subject is discussed in more detail in another chapter of this symposium. Basically, however, if species adapted to the local climate are used, it appears that the use of supplemental irrigation during critical water-deficient periods during stand establishment may enhance stands of a number of difficult-to-establish species. For example, this technique seems to offer a means of successfully establishing warm season species in the Northern Great Plains, and of increasing establishment of adapted grass and forb species in the arid Southwest. If well-adapted species are used, there is no evidence that they will not survive when irrigation is discontinued after establishment. Also, with judicious selection of timing and amount of irrigation water applied, the quantity of irrigation water required for establishment in a typical mining operation would usually be about 5 to 20 cm/ha annually. Probably, water quality could be somewhat lower than that of water normally used for irrigated crops. In most Western mining areas it would be possible to find this quantity of water of some quality annually. Further research is needed to determine the effect of water quality on stand establishment, however.

E. Plant Materials

In essentially every state, research is in progress to evaluate plant materials for use in reclamation of mined land. In general, most of this work involves the screening of available genetic stock for survival and growth under various combinations of spoils and topsoil with widely differing properties and in different climatic zones of western North America. Major emphasis is being placed on perennial grass species, but at several locations forbs and woody species are also being evaluated. In a few instances, supplemental irrigation (including trickle irrigation) is included as a variable. Annual crop species are being evaluated for use on spoils in only a few states. This research should be expanded since several coal fields are located in areas where over 50% of the land is now cultivated.

To date in most field tests with perennials, the procedure followed is simply to plant a nursery and then evaluate survival and production visually. Sometimes, annual growth is also measured. In very few instances are actual counts of plant density made periodically. Thus, information collected is frequently more subjective than objective. There is a need for expansion of nurseries of perennial species that are evaluated by scientifically and statistically sound methodology.

Another problem of major concern is to properly define the environment under which a given species is best adapted. This is especially important in establishing woody species for wildlife habitats—if planted at the wrong locations in the landscape, such plantings usually fail or are ineffective as wildlife habitat.

Response of various genetic pools of grass species are being evaluated for use on mined land in North Dakota to identify materials useful in a breeding program. In addition, certain selections are being evaluated on spoils covered with varying thicknesses of soil materials to determine the effect of this variable upon plant densities and dry matter production.

Success of seedling establishment on mine spoils is usually greatest for the cool season grasses, especially in the Northern Great Plains. Crested wheatgrass (*Agropyron desertorum*) is probably the species most easily established and most widely adapted. Western wheatgrass (*Agropyron smithii*, Rydb.) is also widely adapted and used in reseeding mine spoils. Other species frequently encountered are slender wheatgrass (*Agropyron trachycaulum*), green needlegrass (*Stipa viridula*), Russian wildrye (*Elymus junceus*), and smooth bromegrass (*Bromus inermis*). Warm season grasses sometimes found include blue grama (*Bouteloua gracilis*), side-oats grama (*Bouteloua curtipendula*), switchgrass (*Panicum virgatum*), and alkali sacaton (*Sporobolus airoides*). Most common legumes are alfalfa (*Medicago sativa*) and yellow sweetclover (*Melitotus officinalis*).

Most of the evaluation of plant materials for use on mined land is being done in monocultures. In only a few instances are species mixtures being evaluated, yet the rangeland being destroyed often contains over 40 individual plant species. Experiments are in progress at very few locations to develop technology by which native climax species can be restored. Prairie hay is sometimes used as a seed source for many perennial species in a few such studies. Likewise, research is only now beginning on management of grasslands established on reclaimed land.

A large void in information exists with regard to mutual compatability or competition of various species when seeded on reclaimed mined land. The basic question of how to successfully establish a mixture of species which will provide season-long grazing of nutritious forage and provide soil erosion protection is largely unsolved. Many scientists believe that through using various combinations of adapted species (both so-called "native" and "introduced"), a grassland ecosystem can be created on mined land that will serve the same major functions as the native climax ecosystem, but will also be considerably more productive. At a few locations this concept is presently being studied.

VI. DECISIONS REGARDING APPLICATION OF RESEARCH RESULTS

A. Potential Land Use

Information and data are required to enable mining organizations, enforcing agencies, land users, and others to arrive at sound decisions on using reclaimed areas. Potential uses have to be evaluated and some priorities set. Potential uses are determined first by various parameters of the five natural resources listed previously and, second, by how these natural resources have been blended together in the mining and reclamation processes. Ideally, blending of resources in the reclamation process results in a landscape where all potential uses, as limited by the nature and properties of the natural resources, are possible. This allows land users and planning organizations maximum flexibility in deciding which of these potential land uses best fits the needs of society and the landowner at that particular time. If this procedure is followed, it will then be possible to use each hectare within its capabilities.

Considerable research is needed to reach the above ideal goal in arriving at land-use decisions for reclaimed land. Many of the specific research needs have been identified in earlier parts of this chapter. Basically, however, at one time or another, most of the information and data, and their interpretations, are derived from research. Fortunately, the backlog of information gained from decades of dryland research on soils and plants grown on unmined land in dry regions can often be applied to reclaimed mined lands. Additional information relating to the unique properties of mine spoils and subsequent man-made soils is derived from much of the reclamation research currently in progress. Questions for which specific research information is incomplete or lacking have been identified to some extent in this paper.

Types of land-use most frequently encountered in mined areas in dry regions are grazing, crop production, wildlife, recreation, and forestry—in more or less decreasing order of area involved. With a few exceptions, similar areas of these same types of land-use will probably be developed on mined land.

B. Grazing

Semiarid and arid grass lands, in climax vegetation, are usually relatively low in carrying capacity when used for grazing. On unmined land productivity is increased by improved livestock and grazing management, fertilization, reseeding, or interseeding—especially with improved species—and by other such practices. In principle, most of these practices can also be used to improve carrying capacity of reclaimed land use for grazing. However, almost no research has been conducted on improved practices for grazing of land reclaimed after mining. Recently, two grazing trials have been established on mined land, one in Montana and one in North Dakota. At this stage of development, questions of prime concern in these studies include: will reclaimed mined land withstand intensive or even abusive grazing; how do we adequately measure and quantify changes in vegetation and soil properties resulting from grazing; and similar questions. Research on the more detailed aspects of grazing management remains to be initiated.

C. Crop Production

At only a few locations in the western U.S. is research being conducted on agronomic aspects of crop production on mined land, although this type of land use could constitute up to 20% of the land area disturbed by mining. The primary crop involved is hard red wheat (spring and winter), but barley, oats, alfalfa, and other harvested crops are also of concern. The assumption is generally made that information acquired on crop production practices for unmined land also applies to mined land. However, the validity of this assumption is largely undetermined. One of the major research needs is to determine if fertilizer and tillage practices for crop production on mined land differ appreciably from those on unmined land. Also, the effects of mining and reclamation upon the nutritional quality of crops needs to be studied, with special attention to potential toxicity problems in animals or humans consuming these products.

D. Wildlife

Use of reclaimed land for wildlife production and habitat can be of great significance. Like unmined land, much of the wildlife use will involve multiple use with other activities, especially grazing. In addition, it will frequently be desirable to set aside selected tracts specifically for wildlife habitat, such as wooded draws, potholes, and marshes. Such combination of land use integrated into the landscape will provide the food and protection required for several wildlife species important in western North America.

The concept exists that unreclaimed or poorly reclaimed mined land is a desirable wildlife habitat. However, this idea is largely false; rather, the statement that such land has little value, except as wildlife habitat, would be more correct. Wildlife is another crop that can be harvested from an area, and wildlife depends primarily upon vegetative growth for food and protection. The more productive a site, generally, the greater potential it has as a habitat for wildlife. Thus, low-quality land is usually a much poorer habitat for wildlife than is productive land—land that produces ample vegetation for food and protection. The main advantage of reserving poorly reclaimed land for wildlife is the fact that wildlife disturbance is minimized on such land because very few other types of land use are possible.

The habitats of most wildlife species are known, so research required is again a matter of developing technology to produce vegetation on mined land. In the case of wildlife, however, the species of vegetation being produced may be somewhat different than those used for livestock grazing or cropland. Generally, forbs, shrubs, and woody perennials are important for many wildlife species. Proper integration of these specialized species of plants into their proper niches in the landscape is another research problem that has hardly been approached. Generally, however, the research approach required is similar to that for other land uses—to identify the growth requirements of the plant species of concern, and to develop technology to meet these requirements at the time and locations required.

E. Recreation and Forestry

Much of the discussion regarding wildlife also applies to land developed for recreational uses. Again, vegetation, along with water and its development, are the resources of prime concern for this land use. And again, the research required is to learn the requirements of the vegetative species desired, and to develop technology whereby these requirements can be met.

Generally, land devoted to forestry after mining in dry regions will probably be of minor importance. Only a very small fraction of the land disturbed by mining produces commercial forestry products before mining. Except for the mountainous areas, tree propogation is a very hazardous activity in most arid and semiarid regions of western North America. Such areas are a poor habitat for commercial forestry operation. Cottonwood, various hardwoods, and a few coniferous species are presently found along stream valleys and in wetter parts of the landscape in these regions. However, these trees serve more as a wildlife habitat than as a source of forest products. Consequently, with localized exceptions, research needs on tree propogation on mined land in the West are largely those associated with development on wildlife habitat, and the need for forestry research as such is relatively minor. The use of single-row field windbreaks on reclaimed land has not been investigated.

VII. CONCLUSIONS

Research on reclamation of strip-mined land in dry regions has accelerated greatly in the last 5 years. Before the 1960's, essentially no effort to reclaim mined land was involved, and practically no specific research was conducted. Research was initiated in the 1960's at a few scattered locations, usually utilizing almost strictly a field approach comparing species adaptability, surface configuration, and other such practices. Until early in the 1970's, very little of this research was supported by laboratory analysis of the soils and overburden, vegetation, and water. The inclusion of analytical data added a new dimension to reclamation research, providing definition of the nature and properties of the resources being utilized in reclamation. This made it possible to define the major problems in reclamation and to provide a scientific basis for interpretation of results. Previously, most reclamation research was by trial-and-error without adequate definition of problems or interpretation of results. Also in the early 1970's, extensive hydrological and geological research was initiated, utilizing the best in scientific techniques. Presently these various aspects of reclamation research are rapidly proceeding at many locations. Funding for this activity has also increased several orders of magnitude within the past decade—from no more than a few tens of thousands to tens of millions of dollars annually.

In this chapter current research needs, as visualized by this author, have been identified. At present, most of these research needs do have some limited activity in progress. The need in most cases is to expand the activity to provide better in-depth and site-specific information. Many of these needs relate to long-term aspects of reclamation—stability of vegetative communities, creation of manmade soils, landscape stability, etc. Research to date has identified the major reclamation problems in most locations, and has devised methodology to correct many of these problems. Through the research conducted to date, steps necessary for the successful restoration of productivity to mined areas have become apparent. These may be summarized as:

1) Determine the nature, properties, and extent of the natural resources available (climate, soil, overburden, water, and vegetation);
2) Relate these factors to potential growth of the plant species of major concern; and
3) Develop economically feasible mining methods which will enable maximum development of plant growth potentials after mining.

The last of these three steps requires the assistance of professional mining research scientists. This expertise is generally beyond the scope of most agricultural scientists. Proper integration of plant growth requirements into mine-plan development is presently being initiated in some instances. However, sometimes changes in mining method may be required, thereby tying the need for reclamation research and mining research together.

LITERATURE CITED

Bituminous Coal Research, Inc. 1975. Reclamation of coal mined-land—A bibliography with abstracts. Bituminous Coal Res., Monroeville, Pa. 188 p.

Black, C. E. (ed.). 1965. Methods of soil analysis, Parts 1 and 2. Am. Soc. of Agron., Madison, Wis.

Heermann, D. F., M. D. Finkner, and E. A. Hiler. 1971. Probability of sequences of wet and dry days for 11 western states and Texas. Colorado State Univ. Exp. Stn. Tech. Bull. 117, Fort Collins, Colo.

Old West Regional Commission and USDA Forest Service SEAM. 1975. Energy Res. Inf. System, Vol. 1, no. 1, Billings, Mont.

Power, J. F., and F. M. Sandoval. 1976. Effect of sampling method on results of chemical analysis of overburden samples. Mining Congr. J. 62(4):37–41.

Ramirez, J. M. 1974. The agro-climatology of North Dakota. North Dakota Coop. Ext. Ser. Bull. 15 and 16, Fargo, N. Dak.

Shaw, R. H., G. L. Barger, and R. F. Dale. 1960. Precipitation probabilities in the North Central States. Univ. of Missouri Agric. Exp. Stn. Bull. 753, Columbia, Mo.

U.S. Salinity Laboratory Staff. 1954. Diagnosis and improvement of saline and alkali-soils. USDA Hbk. 60, U.S. Sup. of Public Documents, Washington, D.C.

Chapter 30

Reclamation of Coal Surface-Mined Land in Western Canada

J. V. THIRGOOD AND P. F. ZIEMKIEWICZ

University of British Columbia
Vancouver, British Columbia

I. SURFACE MINING OF COAL IN ALBERTA

Coal mining in Alberta began in 1835. The industry is now expanding at an unprecedented rate following a severe 20-year slump. This expansion has resulted in rapid growth of surface mining in the agricultural lands of the plains and the expansion of surface mining activity in the mountains and foothills. Prospects for provincial energy needs suggest increasing activity in Alberta's coal sector. A major portion of this increase is likely to result from surface mining techniques.

A. Biophysiography

Alberta's major coal deposits are found in three of its physiographic regions: mountains, foothills, and plains. The following discussion briefly characterizes these regions.

a. **Mountains**—These are areas of subalpine forest of subalpine fir (*Abies lasiocarpa* [Hook] Nutt.) and Englemann spruce (*Picea englemannii*, Parry) as well as alpine tundra. Steep slopes, thin, easily disturbed soils, and severe climate combine to make this region particularly susceptible to long-term degradation. This region is high in aesthetic, watershed, wildlife, and recreational values.

b. **Foothills**—This is a transitional region between mountains and plains. It is transversed by many major watercourses serving Alberta's agricultural industry. Vegetation consists of various grassland-parkland-forest combinations. Grazing, fisheries, wildlife, forestry, and recreational values are all significant in this region with susceptibility to damage high, although perhaps lower than in the mountains.

c. **Plains**—This is a region of flat to gently rolling topography encompassing several ecological types. These include prairie grassland, aspen parkland, and aspen (*Populus tremuloides*, Michx.), white spruce (*Picea glauca* [Moench] Voss) mixed forest. Farming, grazing, forestry, and wildlife values are predominant. Although the potential for damage through surface mining certainly exists here, it is perhaps lower than in either the mountains or the foothills.

B. Extent and Distribution

At present about 25 to 50 billion tons of coal can be recovered by conventional underground or surface mining techniques in Alberta. Potential coal-bearing formations underlie much of the southwestern Alberta plains and extend over a wide range of climatic and vegetative zones. About 34,317 km^2 of this plains area is classed as moderate to high in coal development potential; however, the area suitable for surface mining is probably closer to 2,590 km^2 (Mellon, 1972).

Whereas the plains coal formations are roughly horizontal, those of the foothills are completely folded and faulted with attendant difficulties in exploration and exploitation. Generally, the coal of the western foothills is of a medium to low volatile bituminous type (coking coal), while that of the plains is of a high volatile bituminous type more suitable for thermal power production.

Available estimates indicate that at least 130 km^2 of the foothills region could be strip mined for coal in the next 20 years. This estimate does not account for surface disturbances resulting from access roads, plant sites, town sites, and other support facilities (Mellon, 1972). Difficulties of mining in steep terrain on the foothills and mountains, plus folding and faulting of the seams, make it unlikely that many more surface mines will be developed in these areas in the future. On the other hand, most of the deposits underlying the plains are potentially mineable by surface techniques.

Although the total area disturbance by surface mining in Alberta is small in relation to the total areas of the province, effects caused by siltation, pollution, and transportation may be much larger than the area actually disturbed by extraction. Exploration for coal has and may continue to disturb much more surface area than the actual mining operations.

C. Impacts of Mining

In 1972, consultants to Alberta's Environment Conservation Authority indicated that physical and chemical impacts may occur from surface mining activity. Sheet or gully erosion are more likely to occur and have more widespread effects in the foothills and mountain regions than in the plains. Erosion and consequent siltation effects may result from: exploration activities, actual mining operations, or access and haul roads. Slides may result from slippage of disturbed slopes or from movement of spoil dumps.

Chemical impacts are not expected to be of major concern as Alberta's coal deposits are low in sulphur. However, increased alkalinity and precipitation of iron compounds may constitute hazards to mountain streams. Processing plants may also pose hazards resulting from waste disposal.

D. Reclamation Practices

Most reclamation programs in the mountains of Alberta employ the same basic methods. Generally, the area is resloped to some extent and the headwall somewhat backfilled. Since the mountain soils are very thin and most of the mining operations 5 to 10 years old, the original soils are either buried or scattered by the time reclamation begins. Therefore, the "soil" is usually marine shales and oxidized coal in varying states of decomposition. Since this substrata is often low in nutrients, particularly nitrogen, fertilization is nearly always included at the time of seeding. The seed mixes virtually always consist of some combination of the following agronomic hay crops:

Crested wheatgrass (*Agropyron cristatum* [L.] Gaertn.)
Intermediate wheatgrass (*A. intermedium* [Host] Beauv.)
Redtop (*Agrostis alba* L.)
Smooth brome (*Bromus inermis* Leys.)
Orchard grass (*Dactylis glomerata* L.)
Canada bluegrass (*Poa compressa* L.)
Kentucky bluegrass (*P. pratensis* L.)
Red fescue (*Festuca rubra* L.)
Perennial ryegrass (*Lolium perenne* L.)
Timothy (*Phleum pratense* L.)
Alfalfa (*Medicago sativa* L.)
Red clover (*Trifolium pratense* L.)
White clover (*T. repens* L.)
Sweet clover (*Melilotus alba* Desr.)
(*M. officinalis* [L.] Lam.)

These are usually spread with hand-held cyclone seeders or a hydroseeder, Mulches are sometimes used. Some reclamation programs involve the use of conifer seedlings or hardwood cuttings.

E. Reclamation Problems and Research

Certainly, the climate of the Canadian Rockies will continue to pose special problems in reestablishing vegetative cover on disturbed areas. The following environmental descriptions (Lesko et al., 1975) of the Luscar Mining areas illustrate the conditions under which many of Alberta's reclamation programs must operate.

Luscar is located in west central Alberta, about 40 km south of Hinton at 53°N and 117°E. The region includes both the Rocky Mountain foothills and Mountain Region (Dumanski et al., 1972), adjacent to the Nikanassin Range. Elevations vary from 1,600 m in the valley bottoms to 2,550 m on Luscar Mountain. The climate is subhumid continental with large diurnal and annual temperature ranges. Frequent warm, dry winds (chinooks) during the winter result in rapid changes from extreme cold to thaw conditions in a few hours.

Meteorological observations near Luscar at 1,600 m elevation between 13 May and 17 Aug. 1972 indicated that maximum daily temperatures and potential evapotranspirations occurred in late May and early August. This pattern is the result of a precipitation peak in midsummer.

The soil in the Luscar area was frozen in some places in early May but average soil temperatures were within the range 3.3 to 7.6°C, depending on the soil depth. By 7 June the average soil temperatures had risen to over 12°C at depths of 0, 15, and 30 cm. Average soil moistures between depths of 0 and 15 cm were measured at 31.0, 16.5, 30.4, and 32.8% on 2 May, 7 June, 3 July and 4 Aug., respectively. The lowest soil moistures coincide with high evapotranspirative demand and drought in late May and early June. Storage of winter precipitation is minimal and most of the recharge occurred in June and July.

The Luscar mining area lies within the east slope Rockies section of the subalpine forest region (Rowe, 1972). It contains four forest communities. Two of the communities are dominated by Engleman spruce and alpine fir. Ground vegetation is dominated by stiff club moss (*Lycopodiom annotinum* L.) or by bunchberry (*Cornus canadensis* L.). Lodgepole pine (*Pinus contorta* Loudon var. *latifolia* [Hook] Nutt.) and quaking aspen (*Populus tremuloides* Michx.) are the dominant trees in the other two communities. Pinegrass (*Calamagrostis rubescens* Buckl.) dominates the ground vegetation on the moderately well-drained soil, while bearberry (*Arctostaphylos uva-ursi* [L.] Spreng) on the drier slopes distinguishes the other community.

Soils of the area are orthic gray luvisols and degraded eutric brunisols. Some regosolic soils also occur in actively eroding river banks (Dumanski et al., 1972).

From the preceding discussion the following limiting factors to mountain reclamation emerge: i) long, potentially unstable slopes; ii) a short, cool growing season; and iii) periods of summer drought.

Current knowledge of techniques for reclamation of surface land disturbance in Alberta largely results from the efforts of individual mining companies, rather than from a province-wide, systematic research program. The Alberta Department of Lands and Forests and the Canadian Forest Service have carried out reclamation experimentation and some mining companies have been apparently successful in reclaiming disturbed lands. These efforts, however, do not justify the conclusion that the state of research knowledge is adequate or even extensive. In fact, no extensive body of reclamation literature is available as yet for Alberta or elsewhere in Canada (Smith, 1974).

Smith (1974) cites the following critical areas in which our knowledge is deficient:

1) Genetics of native high-elevation plant species;
2) Transport of divalent metallic ions resulting from land surface upheavel and resulting impacts on water quality;
3) Impacts of surface disturbance on soil microorganisms and resulting influences on biological productivity; and
4) Effects of destruction of perched water tables.

Two additional areas may be included:

5) Long-term nutrient and population dynamics; and
6) Ecological amplitude of reclamation species.
This list is by no means complete. Assuredly, it will grow as reclamation programs develop.

Most reclamation research programs on coal-mined areas in Alberta are centred on the immediate effects of various fertilizer, mulch, and physiographic and soil treatments on the success of various agronomic seed mixes. Virtually all of these programs are only a few years old, so long-term effects are impossible to assess. Also, inconsistent and often subjective quantification of experimental results combine with a frequent lack of statistical rigor and standard nomenclature to make evaluation difficult.

The Canadian Forest Service has established a reclamation research program on coal mining disturbances at Luscar, Alberta (Lesko et al., 1975). This program breaks with precedent by employing controlled experimental procedures, by using statistical treatment of data, and, above all, by publishing the results.

The Alberta Forest Service's reclamation research efforts have concentrated on afforestation of coal disturbances (Selner, 1973). Early results of this work over the work of several decades in Appalachia that show that reclamation programs involving tree planting on bare, steep slopes are highly prone to failure. It seems obvious that an immediate cover of herbaceous species is necessary to check erosion while the trees become established. The statement ". . .afforestation is a valuable, economically sound method of reclamation, even in localities where grass cannot be established" (Selner, 1973), ignores the circumstance that currently used commercial agronomic varieties may be physiologically less fitted to alpine environments than other naturally occurring grasses. Certainly, the failure of low-elevation agronomic species in subalpine conditions does not justify the conclusion that herbaceous vegetation per se is unfit for high elevation reclamation efforts. The Alberta Forest Service has established high elevation test plots along the Continental Divide which in 10 years' time should yield valuable information as to which species will and will not persist at high elevations. However, the use of agronomic species will continue to leave the "native vs. introduced" question unanswered.

F. Regulatory Legislation

Regulation of surface disturbances in Alberta falls under the Land Surface Conservation and Reclamation Act of 1972. The Act applies to all Alberta lands except those disturbed for agricultural or residential purposes. A surface disturbance is defined as any exposure, cover, erosion, or any other degradation of the land surface. The following discussion outlines the salient features of the Act (from Harrington, 1974).

The Minister of the Environment may enter into an agreement with property owners with the purpose of restricting uses which would damage watersheds, shorelines, and valley breaks. (Compensation for the loss of use to the owner must be provided by the government.)

The Minister may also order submission of an environmental impact statement.

Any person violating any provision of the Act is subject to a stop order issued by the Minister which may be appealed before the Environment Conservation Authority.

The Minister may issue a Restricted Geophysical Operations Order restricting such operations within any specified area of Alberta or during a particular time of year.

In the event of environmental degradation resulting from mining operations, the Minister may recommend to the Lieutenant Governor that the Minister of Mines and Minerals be authorized to acquire by exchange, purchase, or expropriation any interest in mines and minerals.

Prior to commencement of a surface-disturbing operation, the operator must submit for approval plans and specifications detailing the development and reclamation programs.

The type and amount of security deposits will be determined by authorized review committees. These committees will be the Crown Minerals Disposition Committee, the Exploration Review Committee, and the Reclamation and Development Review Committee. These will assess conflict areas and recommend solutions, review exploration proposals, and review mining and subsequent reclamation plans, respectively. These committees will have the power to accept or reject proposals brought before them.

Finally, Alberta has developed a set of Land Conservation Guidelines. These are meant to provide protection against erosion on steep or long, gradual slopes by requiring maintenance of vegetation in critical locations and in specified patterns. Distances are specified to ensure that surface-disturbing activities do not impinge on shorelands and watercourses.

The Alberta Environment Conservation Authority (1976) has recently published a report in which the performance of the Coal Exploration Review Committee was discussed. The Report concluded that the Coal Exploration Review Committee had generally been consistent in its application of guidelines in making recommendations to the Deputy Minister of Lands and Forests. The following cases are meant to be illustrative of the nature of problems and solutions consequent to applications for exploration permits:

1) A company, after several warnings to complete its program of reclamation, was found to have undertaken unauthorized exploration. The company's letter of authority was revoked; the company was penalized $2,000 for violation of conditions of the letter of authority, and was forced to carry out reclamation of all of its work. Following completion of reclamation, the company was again given a letter of authority for further exploration.

2) A company made application for exploration which was objected to by the Fish and Wildlife representative on the Coal Exploration Review Committee. The objections were overruled by the Deputy Minister of Lands and Forests and an exploration letter of authority was granted.

3) A company made application for further exploration in an area to which the Fish and Wildlife Division raised objections as did the Alberta Fish and Game Association. The exploration was revised sufficiently to overcome the objections of the Fish and Wildlife Division, but the Alberta Fish and Game Association continued its objections. The letter of authority was granted.

4) A company was given approval with 23 conditions attached for an exploration program. The company asked for and received consent to delay reclamation. The Coal Exploration Review Committee then noted mistakes in the file and the Committee then recommended that no further exploration be allowed. The company had, in addition, not progressively kept up with reclamation. Further exploration was refused.

5) An application for further exploration was turned down because reclamation of previous work was unsatisfactory. Upon satisfactory completion of reclamation, a new exploration letter of authority was granted, but special conditions were attached. Because of interference with wildlife, a drill program was approved on condition that it was to be carried out by helicopter while trenching was to be done by hand. No ground access was to be constructed. The company was warned about harassment of sheep and elk. The program was carried out successfully and final inspection only required that 45 gallon fuel drums be picked up.

6) An application was made for coal exploration in an alpine restricted development area. Approval was withheld. The company availed itself of assistance from government departments and from members of the legislative assembly. The company outlined its great expenditures to date and felt that it had been misled. The Minister of Lands and Forests, despite considerable pressure, maintained his position and exploration permission was withheld in view of the Environment Conservation Authority's pending Report and Recommendations on the Land Use and Resource Development in the Eastern Slopes. The Minister also invited debate in the legislature on the matter. The final communication to the company was that no exploration would be allowed.

Alberta's policies regarding mining disturbances are still evolving. When this chapter was written the Alberta Government had issued a statement "A Coal Development Policy for Alberta." Severe restrictions have been placed on coal exploration and development. Table 1 summarizes the situation. None or very little activity will be allowed in the foothills and Rocky Mountain areas nor in areas where reconciliation of mining with other land uses is not possible or where there is environmental sensitivity.

Where existing leases are effected the government will buy the leases "for sums commensurate with expenditures which have been made." If new leases are issued they will be for periods of 15 years and will be issued only if there is a reasonable chance that commercial mining operations will be allowed.

The scale of mining will be determined on the basis that Alberta's

Table 1—Summary of classification of Alberta lands for purposes of coal exploration and development (Alberta Dep. of Energy and Nat. Resour., 1976)

	Category			
	1 Mountains and other	2 Mountains and foothills	3 Plains and northern	4
	Includes areas for which:	*Includes areas in the foothills and mountains for which:*	*Includes areas outside of the foothills and mountains for which:*	*Includes all areas not placed in Categories 1 and 2*
Criteria	1. Alternative land uses have been established not reconcilable with coal operations	1. The preferred land or resource use remains to be determined	1. Potential land use conflicts remain to be resolved, especially with respect to agricultural lands	
	2. Environmental sensitivity is high	2. Environmental sensitivity is moderate, except for specific situations of high sensitivity	2. Environmental sensitivity is not critical, except for specific situations	
		3. Infrastructure facilities are generally absent	3. Infrastructure facilities are generally absent or only partly developed	
Exploration	None	Limited exploration permitted under strict control	Exploration permitted under normal approval procedures	Exploration permitted under normal approval procedures
Development	None	Restricted development underground or in-situ only	Restricted development	Development permitted under normal approval procedures
Existing leases	1. Sell back to government *or* 2. Continue to expiration of term†	1. Sell back to government *or* 2. Continue with option to renew	1. Sell back to government *or* 2. Continue with option to renew	Continue with option to renew
New dispositions	None	1. Applications for leases accepted where exploration approved 2. Leases issued where development approved	1. Applications for leases accepted where exploration approved 2. Leases issued where development approved	Leases issued

† But without option to renew except in certain leases originally granted by Canada.

"present and all foreseeable future needs" must be assured. These include present and future power plants, metallurgical operations, others including petrochemical industries, surface and in situ gasification, and coal liquifaction. Permits for mining developments to serve markets outside Alberta "will be granted where it is found in the public interest." This applies both to export markets and also to markets in other Canadian provinces.

Emphasis is clearly on prevention rather than cure. No development will be permitted in major recreational areas, wilderness areas, or other ecologically fragile areas. Most significantly, the new policy rules out further surface mining in the Rocky Mountain and foothills regions which will be open only to tightly-regulated exploration. The rate of expansion of surface mining will clearly be influenced if export outside the province —the primary force behind the rapid development of Western Canadian coals of recent years—is not to be a valid reason for the granting of leases.

II. SURFACE MINING OF COAL IN BRITISH COLUMBIA

Nearly 3,642 km² of British Columbia's land were under license for coal exploration in 1975. Two-thirds of this area was on public lands. While British Columbia's coal deposits are widely distributed, present surface coal mining activities are confined to the Fernie coal block in the East Kootenay Region of southeastern British Columbia. British Columbia's coal production has increased tenfold since 1969, from nearly 900,000 to 10,000,000 metric tons in 1973—the vast majority of this going to Japan. The value of this production has risen even more dramatically from $6,817,155 in 1969, to $154,393,643 in 1974. This expansion of British Columbia's coal industry will soon cause it to succeed copper and molybdenum as the mainstay of British Columbia's number two industry—mining.

A. Biophysiography

Under the system of Rowe (1972) Canada was divided into 11 forest regions, 6 of these are found in British Columbia. Later, Krajina (1965) distinguished 11 "biogeoclimatic zones" within the province. These zones are characterized by similar macroclimatic and pedogenic processes combining to support distinct plant communities.

Virtually all of British Columbia's surface coal mining occurs in the interior Douglas fir and Englemann spruce subalpine-fir biogeoclimatic zones. The interior Douglas fir zone occurs between 300 and 1,200 m elevation, receiving 40 to 56 cm precipitation per year. The climate is described by Koppen (1957) as continental subhumid and the characteristic tree species are: Douglas fir (*Pseudotsuga menziesii* [Mirbel] Franco.), lodgepole pine, ponderosa pine (*Pinus ponderosa* Dougl.), and western larch (*Larix occidentalis* Nutt.). This zone represents the lower elevations of coal mining in southeastern British Columbia. Due to an extensive history of fire, much of this zone is dominated by lodgepole pine interspersed with shrub-grassland communities on most of the southerly exposures. The higher elevations of mining activity are within the Englemann spruce—subalpine fire biogeoclimatic zone. This zone is found between 900 and 2,300 m elevation and receives an average of 40 to 180 cm of precipitation per year. The climate is continental cold humid. The major tree species in this zone are Englemann spruce, subalpine fir, alpine larch (*Larix lyalii* Parl.), and white bark pine (*Pinus albicaulis* Englem.). This zone is characterized by long, cold winters, areas of deep snow accumulation, and other areas blown free of snow. Summers are short, cool, and frequently dry. Exposure, high winds, steep slopes, and frosts throughout the growing season make this zone problemistic for reclamation purposes.

B. Extent and Distribution

The total of British Columbia's coal reserves were estimated by the B.C. Department of Mines and Petroleum Resources to be 59.2 billion metric tons as of 31 Dec. 1973. Medium and low-volatile bituminous coal, used to make coke, comprised 95% of this total. British Columbia's reserves of coal constitute 69% of Canada's total reserves of coking coal. Thermal coal reserves were estimated at 3.0 billion metric tons. However, the Department of Mines indicated that this figure will rise as thermal coal exploration increases from previously low levels. For example, exploration of the Hat Creek field in south central British Columbia recently revealed a previously unknown coal deposit 5 km long, 1 km wide, and 600 m thick, totaling a half billion metric tons of thermal coal.

The Department of Mines indicated that only 19%, or 1.3 billion metric tons, of the coking coal reserves are mineable under present technological and economic restraints. Nonetheless, $14 million was spent in 1973 for prospecting, exploration, and further development of operating mines.

At the current rate of extraction (7.6 million metric tons per year) coking coal reserves are estimated by the Department of Mines to be able to produce for another 100 years. However, it is unlikely that this rate of extraction will remain static or that the known reserves will remain unchanged.

Although the major coal deposits of British Columbia occur in the intermountain basins of the East Kootenay and the Sukanka region of northeastern B.C., the province has other widely scattered deposits of thermal coal which will increase in importance as energy demand increases. British Columbia Hydro is currently studying the Hat Creek deposit for power generation. Other deposits on Vancouver Island and the Queen Charlotte Islands may also be developed in the near future along with other smaller fields in the interior. The Groundhog deposits of northwest B.C., currently abandoned, may also become a future source of energy.

C. Impacts of Mining

About 90% of British Columbia's coal production results from mines utilizing surface mining techniques. These mines are all in the East Kootenay region of British Columbia where overburden up to 213 m thick is encountered; overburden depths of 68.5 m are common (Warden, 1976). Two mines comprise the bulk of British Columbia's coal production—Fording Coal Ltd. and Kaiser Resources Ltd. Each of these mines produce roughly 4 to 5 million metric tons of coal annually. Fording and Kaiser operations are centered on the Elk River and Crowsnest coal fields, respectively.

The overburden in both coal fields is composed mainly of sandstone, carbonaceous and calcareous shales, and some conglomerate. Spoil materials range in pH from 4.0 to 8.6. The coal mined is of coking quality and low sulphur content (0.3–0.4%). Due to this low sulphur content stream acidification has not yet become a problem.

Considerable debate has occurred over the impact of surface mining in the East Kootenays on the region's wildlife populations. The B.C. Wildlife Federation indicated in 1968 that 90% of the important big game range in the upper Elk River watershed was covered by coal licenses. The Federation cites destruction of this winter range, critical to the survival of the region's considerable wildlife resource, impaired water quality, and increased hunter access through exploration roads as major causes of concern.

Naturally, the visual impact of surface mining is dramatic. So is the air pollution arising from coal preparation, storage, and disposal areas.

D. Reclamation Practices

Reclamation methods in British Columbia, where practised, usually involve some degree of resloping, benching, planting of trees, or seeding with agronomic herbaceous species and fertilization. The initial seed and fertilizer treatments are usually broadcast and harrowed. Subsequent treatments are simply broadcast. Conservation of topsoil and its reapplication is a foreign concept to most B.C. mine engineers. Consequently, revegetation efforts must begin on decomposing shale and oxidized coal waste. The sterility and lack of cation exchange capacity of these spoils necessitate repeated expensive fertilizer applications in the hope of developing something resembling a conservative soil-plant nutrient cycle.

Low success rates have been reported for coniferous plantings. Deciduous trees and shrubs have proven more successful despite heavy browsing pressure and *Populus trichocarpa* cuttings have been successfully employed up to 1,675 m elevation by Kaiser Resources (Milligan et al., 1975).

E. Reclamation Problems and Research

The major problem of surface mining in the East Kootenays results from the amount of overburden encountered in reaching the numerous 1.5- to 15-m-thick seams which range in elevation from 1,060 to 2,130 m elevations. Since these seams lie within steep-sided mountains, overburden disposal becomes a major problem.

Gardiner (1974), commenting on the Fording Mine, indicated that waste rock will eventually extend over 600 ha in the Fording River valley and adjacent slopes. Continuation of present mining and disposal methods will result in rock dumps ranging up to 300 m in height with a considerable portion of the surface covered by coarse rock and containing insufficient soil to support (vascular) plant life. Although early experimental work suggests that under favorable conditions plants may survive on this coarse material at Fording, severe physical limitations resulting from current disposal methods will make revegetation efforts unsuccessful over much of the waste rock disposal area.

Major earth slides in overburden dumps at both Kaiser Resources and Fording Coal operations indicate severe engineering failures in dump design. However, even where slope macrostability has been achieved, surface instability and erosion often hinder plant establishment. In response, the reclamation staff at Kaiser Resources have proposed a complete redesign of the present long, steep dumps lying at the angle of repose to what appears to be a revegetation angle of repose—26° (Milligan et al., 1975). This plan is now being implemented.

Kaiser Resources is the only large surface coal mine in British Columbia with a history of field-scale reclamation efforts. Its sites of reclamation activity range from 1,176 to 2,190 m elevation. Since 1969 there has been an evolution from predominant emphasis on tree planting, through trees with a ground cover of agronomic species, to the present practices of establishment of a grass cover with later planting of trees and shrubs. The concept is one of continuing vegetation management and successional development rather than of a single treatment. Emphasis is placed on the conservation of islands of natural vegetation and individual plants, where these remain, to provide nuclei for the reinvasion of natural vegetation. Concern is for watershed values and wildlife habitat. To date, apparently vigorous agronomic plant communities have been established up to 1,868 m elevation. Only one 10-ha site has been treated in the subalpine zone at 2,190 m elevation. In August 1975, aerial standing crop at this site was 136 kg ha^{-1}, while at the 1,868-m site it was 1,400 kg ha^{-1} (Ziemkiewicz, 1975).

High elevation reclamation research from the United States is replete with examples of agronomic species which gave initially impressive results but declined dramatically within about 5 years. Thus, reclamationists are often misled by early results. Present reliance on currently available agronomic species can at best be described as a stop gap measure at high elevations until physiologically adapted species become commercially available. It is imperative that future subalpine–alpine plot research include native as well as adapted agronomic species, although seed procurement is often a major problem.

Reclamation research on coal-mined disturbed lands has been carried out by the individual mining companies. Consequently, much of the resulting information becomes "in house" knowledge. Since most reclamation research is not published in refereed journals it is not subject to criticism, does not necessarily involve valid experimental design, and, most importantly, is not available to other reclamationists. The resulting isolation results in the argument heard in Alberta as well as in British Columbia: "Our conditions at this mine are unique, we have nothing to learn from anyone else." Or, more sophisticatedly, "Our reclamation must be site specific." This parochialism only leads to much duplicated effort and the relearning of expensive lessons. In fact, conditions in western Canada are not entirely unique. The difficulty of establishing stable vegetation on extremely steep slopes was recorded from Europe, North America, and elsewhere by Brierly (1956), Hall (1957), and Ashley,[1] and earlier writers of the inter-war period, the turn of the century, and before. This was done long before the dumps of western Canada were "designed."

Current research into the reclamation of coal-mined disturbed lands in British Columbia centers on formulation of workable agronomic seed mixes. While Fording Coal Ltd.'s program emphasizes plot research (Gardiner, 1975), Kaiser Resource's program has employed multivariate regression techniques to examine correlations between both site physiographic and soil factors and aerial standing crops of the 13 agronomic species used in its revegetation work over the past several years. Programs

[1] R. H. Ashley. 1950. The invasion and development of natural vegetation on spoil banks in central Pennsylvania. M.F. Thesis. Pennsylvania State Univ., University Park.

of this nature will eliminate much of the guesswork currently involved in formulating seed mixes.

However, such questions as stability and winter range value of the revegetation plant communities remain unanswered. Kaiser Resources has just begun a long-term nutrient-cycling study in which the vegetation-soil nutrient cycles on apparently stable reclaimed areas and apparently unstable high-elevation reclaimed areas will be compared to those of native, undisturbed grassland communities of similar physiography.

F. Regulatory Legislation

Reclamation of surface-mined disturbed lands is required under Section 8 of the Coal Mines Regulation Act, and Section 11 of the Mines Regulation Act. Amendments to these Acts have brought exploration and all other surface disturbances resulting from mining under legislation. Both Acts begin: "It is the duty of every owner, agent or manager of a mine to institute and carry out a program for the protection and reclamation of the surface of the land and watercourses affected thereby, and, on the discontinuance or abandonment of a mine, to undertake and complete the program to leave the land and watercourses in a condition satisfactory to the Minister. . . ." Briefly, both Acts require:

1) A report to be submitted to the Minister of Mines and Petroleum Resources prior to the commencement of operations containing:
   a) A map showing the location and extent of the mine, and the location of lakes, streams, and inhabited places in the vicinity;
   b) Particulars of the nature of the mining operation including the anticipated area to be occupied during the lifetime of the mine;
   c) Particulars of the nature and present uses of the land to be used; and
   d) A program for land reclamation and conservation with particular reference to:
      i) the location of the land,
      ii) the effect of the program on livestock, wildlife, watercourses, farms, and inhabited places in the vicinity of the mine, and the appearance of the minesite, and
      iii) the potential use of the land, having regard to its best and fullest use, and its importance for existing and future timber, grazing, water, recreation, wildlife and mining;
2) Review of the report by a standing committee composed of other resource agencies in the case of producing mines and coal exploration;
3) A bond not to exceed $500 (later raised to $1,000) per acre of disturbance;
4) Issue of a surface work permit with such special terms and conditions as the Minister sees fit to prescribe;
5) Continual and progressive reclamation over the life of the mine, and annual submission of a report on the progress of reclamation research and operations; and

6) Closure of the mine and forfeiture of the bond in the case of non-compliance with any sections of the Act or permit.

British Columbia's reclamation legislation was enacted in 1969. After 7 years it is possible to evaluate its effectiveness. Dick and Thirgood (1975) indicated that there has been considerable reluctance on the part of the Inspection and Engineering Division of the Department of Mines and Petroleum Resources to reject reports that are clearly below standard. Also, staff levels adequate to the task have not been provided.

The intent of this legislation was to avoid setting firm regulations until research and experience provided some indication of reclamation potentials and requirements. Industry was left with the task of developing reclamation technology while the Department of Mines and Petroleum Resources served only in an inspection capacity.

Dick and Thirgood (1975) reported that this approach has failed. While some reports of activities and proposals have been very comprehensive, others have been quite the opposite. While the mining method, waste disposal systems, macroslope stability, and facilities design may have been discussed in great detail, the actual process of revegetation has too often been treated much more lightly. In the absence of a strong coordinated program of research and development commensurate with the need, the body of accumulated knowledge remains quite inadequate for a reclamation task that is perhaps unequalled in its severity.

A new review process gives some hope that, in the future, broader social, economic, and environmental implications of major developments will be examined more carefully than they have been in the past. A document, *Guidelines for Coal Development*, has been drawn up under the authority of the Environment and Land Use Committee. This is a Cabinet committee comprised of the ministers responsible for resource use and economic development or who are involved with highways, settlement, and public health services. The Committee is empowered by the Environment and Land Use Act to ". . .ensure that all aspects of preservation and maintenance of the natural environment are fully considered in the administration of land use and resource development commensurate with the maximum beneficial land use and minimize and prevent waste of such resources, and despoilation of the environment occasioned thereby. . .."

These *Guidelines* are the first real attempt to implement a formalized plan for assessment of major resource developments before they are entered into. The guidelines are designed to identify environmental disruptions and social, economic, and community impacts that may be associated with mine development and production. They outline all the factors that must be investigated in connection with the surface or underground extraction of coal, reclamation, transportation, the provision of power, and the effect on the community and region. Responsibility is placed on the developer to obtain the information required to permit government assessment of the various impacts, and to provide a cost/benefit analysis of the total development. Provision is made for frequent review, particularly with a Coal Steering Committee comprised of representatives of the Department of Mines and Petroleum Resources, the Department of Economic Development, and the Environment and Land Use

Committee's Secretariat. Eventual decision rests first with the Environment and Land Use Committee, and finally with the provincial Cabinet. The guidelines and review process seem to promise better integration of coal developments into overall land use and regional planning. nevertheless, there are many problems in relation to coal mine exploraton, reclamation, and the operation of existing mines that remain to be dealt with.

III. CONCLUSIONS

Both Alberta and British Columbia are huge, diverse areas with surface coal mining activities occurring in a variety of biophysiographic regions. Surface mining systems range from extensive area stripping on the plains to the intensive pit-type mines of the mountains.

While all the problems attendant to mining on the plains are not yet understood, the reclamation of mountainous country, particularly subalpine and alpine regions, should prove most difficult due to steep slopes, lack of proper seedbed, and harsh macro- and microclimates. Large-scale dump failures, stream siltation, and dust pollution can be serious problems in mountainous country.

Western Canada is still far from developing a body of reclamation knowledge commensurate with the need. Most research is carried on by individual mining companies. Only in Alberta has an attempt been made to coordinate research efforts through government agencies.

Both Alberta and British Columbia have legislation and guidelines regulating reclamation. British Columbia's regulatory agencies are understaffed and the laws under-enforced. Reports from Alberta suggest that its legislation is dramatically more effective in its application.

LITERATURE CITED

Alberta Department of Energy and Natural Resources. 1976. A coal development policy for Alberta. Alberta Dep. of Energy and Nat. Resour., Edmonton. 37 p. plus append.

Alberta Environment and Conservation Authority. 1976. Review of coal exploration policies and programs in the eastern slopes of Alberta. Alberta Environ. Conserv. Auth., Edmonton.

Brierly, J. K. 1976. Some preliminary observations on the ecology of pit heaps. J. Ecol. 44(2): 383–390.

Dick, J. H., and J. V. Thirgood. 1975. Development of land reclamation in British Columbia. In M. K. Wali (ed.) Practices and problems of land reclamation in Western North America. Univ. of North Dakota Press, Grand Forks, N. Dak.

Dumanski, J., T. M. Macyk, C. F. Veauvy, and J. D. Lindsay. 1972. Soil survey and land cultivation of the Hinton-Edson area, Alberta. Alberta Inst. Pedol., Rep. no. S-71-31, Edmonton.

Gardiner, R. T. 1974. Mined-land reclamation research at Cominco Ltd. operations in British Columbia. A paper prepared for "Land Reclamation Short Course", Cent. for Continuing Educ., U.B.C., Vancouver, March 1974.

Hall, I. G. 1957. The ecology of disused pit heaps in England. J. Ecol. 45(3):689–720.

Harrington, D. G. 1974. Application of the Land Surface Conservation and Reclamation Act. In D. Hoaking and W. R. MacDonald (eds.) Proc. of a Workshop on Reclamation of Disturbed Lands in Alberta. Northern For. Res. Centre Inf. Rep. NOR-X-116, Edmonton.

Koppen, W. 1957. Atlas of Canada. Dep. of Mines and Tech. Surv., Ottawa, Canada.

Krajina, V. J. 1965. Ecology of Western North America. Vol. 1. Univ. of British Columbia, Vancouver. p. 112.

Lesko, G. L., H. M. Etter, and T. M. Dillon. 1975. Species selection, seedling establishment and early growth on coal mine spoils at Luscar, Alberta. Northern For. Res. Center Inf. Rep. NOR-X-117, Edmonton.

Mellon, G. B. 1972. Representing the Research Council of Alberta (Geology Division). *In* The impact on the environment of surface mining in Alberta. Summary of the public hearings. Environ. Conserv. Author., Edmonton, Alta.

Milligan, A., R. Berdusco, and J. Wiebe. 1975. Five years of reclamation, Kaiser Resources Ltd. Prepared by the Environ. Serv. Dep., Kaiser Resour., Ltd., Sparwood, B.C.

Rowe, J. S. 1972. Forest regions of Canada. Dep. of Environ., Canadian For. Serv. Publ. 1300. 172 p.

Selner, J. 1973. Surface mine reclamation research in Alberta. Progr. Rep. for 1973. Alberta For. Serv., Edmonton, Alta.

Smith, S. B. 1974. Disturbed environments. *In* D. Hocking and W. R. MacDonald (eds.) Proc. of a Workshop on Reclamation of Disturbed Lands in Alberta. Northern For. Res. Center Inf. Rep. NOR-X-116, Edmonton.

Warden, G. 1976. Black pits and vanishing hills, coal development in British Columbia. B.C. Wildl. Fed., Vancouver, B.C.

Ziemkiewicz, P. F. 1975. Reclamation research methods on coal mine wastes with particular reference to species evaluation and selection. *In* Proc. of the Canadian Land Reclamation Assoc. Univ. of Guelph, Guelph, Ontario.

Copyright © 1978 ASA–CSSA–SSSA
677 South Segoe Road, Madison, WI 53711 USA
Reclamation of Drastically Disturbed Lands

Chapter 31

Persistent Low Maintenance Vegetation for Erosion Control and Aesthetics in Highway Corridors[1]

D. L. WRIGHT, H. D. PERRY, AND R. E. BLASER

*Virginia Polytechnic Institute and State University,
Blacksburg, Virginia*

I. INTRODUCTION

Environments in old or newly constructed highway corridors in the United States vary in climax vegetation from semitropical with forest-grass, humid-temperate with forest, prairie with tall to short grasses, and semiarid, arid, and desert regions with sparse vegetative cover.

From the viewpoint of erosion, pollution, and aesthetics, two major problems are encountered in highway corridors: (i) erosion by wind and water during the construction phase before stabilization with vegetation, and (ii) concurrently controlling erosion and plant succession to a persistent vegetative cover requiring little or no maintenance. Due to the recent fuel crisis and high costs of labor, materials, equipment, and repairs, cultural practices must be implemented to obtain vegetative covers that require little or no fertilizer or mowing maintenance subsequent to establishment. New construction disturbs natural contours, drainage areas, and climax vegetation to cause potential wind and water erosion and pollution. Erosion control practices to minimize off-site pollution from construction sites in highway corridors depend on grading methods, slope preparation, soil surface conditions, soil amendments, mulches, species and varieties in mixtures, and obtaining a desirable, persistent vegetation through plant succession.

Principles on preparing cut, fill, and median slopes; mulching and tackifying processes; soil amendments; and seed mixtures; water control in drainage ways; and special siltation control measures during and sub-

---

[1] Much of the information provided herein was obtained by the Virginia Polytechnic Institute and State University Research Division through research grants from the individual highway departments of Virginia and West Virginia in cooperation with the U.S. Department of Transportation, Federal Highway Administration.

The contents of this paper reflect the views of the authors who are responsible for the facts and the accuracy of the data presented herein. The contents do not necessarily reflect the official views, policy, or specifications of the Federal Highway Administration, Virginia Department of Highways, or the West Virginia Department of Highways.

sequent to construction will be described as used in the Appalachian and Piedmont regions. The principles will generally apply to all highway corridors of the United States. The procedures for obtaining a persistent vegetative cover by plant succession that requires little or no soil amendments subsequent to establishment or the necessity for mowing will especially apply to regions with sufficient precipitation to promote adequate vegetative growth to prevent and/or minimize erosion.

II. ARRESTING EROSION DURING NEW CONSTRUCTION

The grading operations for new highways or other construction activities cause uncontrolled water flows initially from small bare soil areas. Subsequently, the combined and uncontrolled flows from many small areas carry soil particles with the amount enlarging at momentous proportions with increasing distance from the initial erosion sites. Thus, the many small localized disturbed areas with seemingly insignificant movements of water and soil within the initial grading operations often assemble massive and rapid flows of water with coarse and fine sediments, causing severe damage in highway corridors as well as flooding and contaminating downstream drainage systems. Even the initial slow flows of clear water from many small sites, when grading is initiated in a highway contract, cause progressively larger erosive flows of water. Thus, it is imperative to minimize water flow at the very first minisites of initial grading operations.

Although macroclimatic environments cannot be changed, the microclimatic environment may be altered by grading and construction procedures (Goss et al., 1970; Green et al., 1973a; Wischmeier, 1973; Wright et al., 1975). Increased water infiltration to reduce erosion and pollution by runoff water during construction can be controlled or minimized in four primary ways: (i) grade slopes as shallow as practical; (ii) employ grading and soil management to encourage water infiltration and reduce runoff; (iii) establish vegetative covers as the slopes are being constructed to hold soil materials in place and encourage water infiltration; and (iv) use rock or concrete drains for containing and removing concentrated flows of water. It is estimated that it costs about twice as much to maintain 45° (1:1) slopes as 27° (2:1) slopes because of seeding, fertilization, refertilizing, removing sloughed material from ditches, and drainage receptacles. Therefore, initial construction planning, especially the design and grading of slopes, should consider both the short- and long-range maintenance programs and pollution problems that could potentially be encountered and or eliminated for the duration of the highway.

Cut, fill, and median slopes should be as shallow as practical, as the amount and speed of runoff water and potential erosion during and after torrential rains is directly allied with the steepness and length of slopes. The shallowness of slopes depends on many factors (right-of-way, soil material, and cost of construction operations). Micaceous and sandy soils are usually more erodable than heavy-textured soils due to the weakness of the shear plane and lack of cohesiveness; hence, such slopes should be shallow. During winter even light precipitation can cause severe rilling and erosion on shallow bare slopes.

A. Grading Cut Slopes

For long, sloping cuts, the grading operation should begin with establishing diversion ditches at the apex of cuts to impede and disburse water from slopes above the area to be graded (Fig. 1). Slopes should generally be no steeper than 33° (1.5:1), because the shallower slopes are less erosive and vegetation can more easily be established on them. The steepness of cut slopes should be determined by the length of grade, soil and rock materials, topography, width of highway corridor, and ease of establishing vegetation. For example, it is more difficult to establish vegetation on "hot" sunny slopes than on "cool" shaded slopes; hence, shallow slopes on sunny exposures would facilitate the establishment of vegetation (Wright et al., 1975). Conversely, undecomposed rocky materials on cuts may be nearly vertical.

Slopes steeper than 18° (3:1) should be stair-step graded, left rough, or grooved. Stair-step grading may be used on any materials soft enough to be ripped with a dozer. Slopes steeper than 27° (2:1) should be stair-step graded (Fig. 2). The ratio of the vertical cut distance to the horizontal distance should be less than 1:1, and sloping toward the vertical

Fig. 1—Long, hard and smooth cut slopes cause vegetative covers to develop slowly. The low infiltration causes high rates of uncontrolled water flows and severe rilling and erosion.

Fig. 2—*Top:* Stair-step grading of cut slopes encourages infiltration and impedes water flow to minimize erosion and sedimentation in ditch lines. *Bottom:* This grading method creates a favorable environment for establishing vegetation while construction proceeds.

Fig. 3—*Top:* Bench grading with broad benches to catch falling materials creates very steep back slopes, making it difficult to obtain protective vegetation. *Bottom:* Erosion and sedimentation into ditches are serious problems. Sediment dams were made with rocks to reduce clogging of drains and culverts.

wall to catch sloughing soil, increase infiltration, and reduce runoff. The individual vertical cuts should generally not be more than 60 to 90 cm on soft soil materials and not over 100 cm in rocky materials (Blaser & Perry, 1975; Green et al., 1974; Perry et al., 1975; Wright et al., 1975). The heights and widths of the steps may vary within a cut.

Soft rock with subsoil material is ideal for stair-step grading and establishing vegetation during grading operations. Areas in the mountainous region of the western U.S. use topsoil on such stair-steps where vegetation is desired, because the infertile granite material weathers slowly and allows little water infiltration (Foote et al., 1970).

The numerous steps improve water infiltration and generally nullify sheet erosion, rilling, and pollution of runoff waters (Blaser et al., 1975b). Sloughing and falling materials and precipitation intercepted by horizontal steps cover much of the lime, fertilizer, and seeds to promote germination and seedling growth, and to enhance the establishment of a vegetative cover. Stair-step grading also augments encroachment of persistent leguminous vegetative cover, such as crownvetch (*Coronilla varia* L.) (Wright et al., 1975). Note on Fig. 2 that stair-step grading prevented an accumulation of mud and water at slope bases that usually occurs in drainage ways with conventional smooth, hard surfaces on cut slopes and also with bench grading (Fig. 3).

The surface of cut slopes less than 27° (2:1) should be "rough" and undulating with stones left in place (Fig. 4). High and low places giving

Fig. 4—Slopes 27° (2:1) or flatter should be roughened and loosened leaving ridges and furrows perpendicular to the slope to increase water infiltration and to promote vegetative growth.

Fig. 5—Conventional smooth grading and hard surfaces of steep slopes make it difficult to establish seedlings and vegetation due to little water infiltration and severe erosion. Such slopes should have special mulch treatment such as straw tacked with woodfiber.

variable microenvironments speed up the establishment of vegetative cover because of some coverage of seed and fertilizer and improved moisture.

The detrimental practice of constructing slopes with smooth, hard surfaces gives a false impression of "finished grading" and a job well done, but vegetation often fails (Fig. 1 and 5). Rough slope surfaces with rocks left in place give an "ugly" appearance to the novice, but encourages water infiltration, speeds up establishment of vegetation, and decreases the rate of water flow into drainage ways. The increased water infiltration and populations of both cereal rye (*Secale cereale* L.) and Kentucky 31 fescue (*Festuca arundinacea* Schreb.) plants from rough as compared to smooth slope surfaces is given in Tables 1 and 2. Roughened surfaces with topsoil or subsoil increased soil moisture and decreased soil surface temperature, which increased germination, plant density, height, and protective cover (Woodruff & Blaser, 1970a). When comparing rough graded subsoil with topsoil placed over the smooth subsoil, there was a fourfold improvement in vegetative cover for the rough-graded subsoil 3 months after seeding (Table 2).

Slopes along highways with smooth hard surfaces should be grooved or roughened to aid in establishing vegetation before the application of seed, soil amendments, and mulch. The grooves should be 8 to 15 cm deep, parallel to the highway, and spaced 38 to 60 cm apart (Fig. 6). Such

Table 1—The influence of surface conditions of a subsoil with and without topsoil on temperature and moisture of soils (Data taken on 30 May 1975)

Sampling depth	15 cm topsoil, over subsoil				Subsoil alone			
	Rough surface[†]		Smooth surface[‡]		Rough surface[†]		Smooth surface[‡]	
	Moisture	Temp.	Moisture	Temp.	Moisture	Temp.	Moisture	Temp.
cm	%	°C	%	°C	%	°C	%	°C
0–5	13.9	25	11.6	30	15.3	22	11.2	28
5–20	16.1		12.8		18.9		12.4	

† Traversed perpendicular to slopes with a road grader with tiller feet. Lime, fertilizer, seed, and mulch were uniformly applied on the surface. The experiment was established on 25 Apr. 1974.
‡ Conventional hard and smooth surface finish grading.

grooves collect sloughing soil, seed, and soil amendments, and enhance the rate of obtaining a protective vegetative cover (Perry et al., 1975).

Of the four types of slope surfaces discussed, rough slope surfaces, or stair-step grading, is more desirable than smooth slope surfaces with or without lateral grooves for obtaining a vegetative cover quickly.

B. Grading Fill Slopes

It is generally easier to obtain vegetative covers for erosion control on fill slopes than on cut slopes because less compacted rock and soil materials encourage water infiltration and root growth (Fig. 7). However, the common practice of blading and/or tracking fill slopes with a dozer is usually objectionable because compaction inhibits water infiltration and aeration, causing poor growth. Also, seeds and fertilizer on such hard surfaces are apt to wash away. Tracking clayey and silty soil materials,

Table 2—The influence of surface conditions of a subsoil with and without topsoil on plant density, vegetative cover, and height of cool season grasses*

Graded surface	15 cm topsoil over subsoil				Subsoil alone			
	30 May 1975			20 July 1975	30 May 1975			20 July 1975
	Plants/ m²	Vegetative cover, %	Height, cm	Vegetative cover, %	Plants/ m²	Vegetative cover, %	Height, cm	Vegetative cover, %
Rough and furrowed†	1,140a	39a	8.3a	100	1,520a	38a	8.8a	100
Smooth finish grading	260b	10b	4.8b	25	400b	7b	3.8b	21

* Means in a vertical column followed by different letters are significantly different at the 5% level of probability.
† Traversed perpendicular to slopes with a road grader with tiller feet. Lime, fertilizer, seed, and mulch were uniformly applied on the surface. The experiment was established on 24 Apr. 1974.

Fig. 6—Grooving of hard, smooth cuts improves seedling establishment and growth of grasses and legumes. The entire area had a uniform surface application of lime, fertilizer, and seed. The hard and smooth areas between the grooves allowed little water infiltration and seedling growth.

Fig. 7—Rocks and uneven surfaces on fill slopes impede water flow-off and enhance vegetative establishment by creating favorable microenvironments. Straw applied to rough slopes need not be tacked. A vegetative cover is established quickly to control erosion.

Fig. 8—Tracked, compacted fill slopes on clay and silt material restrict water infiltration resulting in rilling and erosion from hard rains. Such slopes need to be reseeded, but it is difficult to establish seedlings in rills.

especially when wet, causes severe surface compaction which augments water runoff and erosion. The weight and downslope slippage of dozers cause soil materials to form hard clods between the cleats that are severed from soil contact. These conditions cause water to flow around and under the "cleated clods;" hence, during heavy rains surface water accumulates and the massive downflows on slopes cause severe sheet and gully erosion (Fig. 8). The xeric environments associated with the severed "clods" make it difficult to establish vegetative cover. Tracking sandy materials may be desirable if the tracks leave indentations perpendicular to the slope. Tracking parallel to the slope is especially objectionable as the vertical rills, inadvertently occurring with such operations, leave channels for accelerated water movement down slopes.

When constructing fill slopes, berms and down troughs (rock, plastic, or other material) should be constructed on each side of the fill lift to direct water movement off the slope. As lifts of the fill slope are constructed, the soil and rock materials falling naturally onto the slope surface should not be removed. Variable steepness, looseness, and undulations within a fill slope create desirable minienvironments for establishing and maintaining vegetation. Also, by allowing materials to fall naturally, the variable contours inhibit water runoff. Colluvial materials "flow" when supersaturated and should not be used in highway fills (Fig. 9). During fill slope construction, the slope area should be properly designed and constructed from the onset to make regrading of slopes unnecessary

Fig. 9—Sloughing often occurs where soils were tracked and compacted. Undulations and rocks left in place usually prevent sloughing.

after seeding. Seedings should be made every week or whenever the lift is elevated 3 to 4.5 m. The vegetation established at the base will settle suspended soil by slowing water movement from above as construction proceeds. Excellent vegetative cover to nullify erosion usually occurs from one seeding on rough, loose fill slopes; however, tracked compacted fill slopes usually have sparse vegetation due to rilling and erosion and require several seedings and refertilizations to establish satisfactory vegetative covers.

Smoothing of fill slopes may be justified where mowing is necessary. However, fill slopes steeper than 2:1 should never be mowed. Leaving fill slopes very rough with rocks falling naturally is desirable as it will often prevent movement or flow of soil material.

C. Grading Medians

Highway medians constructed in mountainous topography often become severely eroded because of the accelerated flows of water concentrated in "V"-bottom drainage ways, making it virtually impossible to establish a vegetative cover to reduce or prevent erosion. This accelerated flow of water causes severe gullying in drainage ways and often plugs culverts and causes downstream pollution.

The slopes of medians with little or slow water movement in drainage ways should generally be shallow ($< 15°$ [4:1]) to reduce hazards to motorists. The compacted surfaces of graded medians are poor environments for water control and seedling establishment (Allmaras et al., 1973; Blaser, 1962a; Carson & Blaser, 1963; Dickens & Orr, 1969; Green et al., 1973a and 1973b; Hottenstein, 1969; Willis & Amemiya, 1973; Woodruff & Blaser, 1970a and 1970b). Thus, the slopes should be loosened and roughened with a spiked dozer blade or strong cultivation tool to leave furrows 5 to 10 cm deep and 15 to 25 cm apart, paralleling the drainage way. This will encourage water infiltration and establishment of vegetation (Fig. 10).

Results from many experiments show vastly improved vegetation and erosion control with rough vs. smooth surfaces. The drainage ways in medians should be constructed with flat bottoms 90 cm wide, rather than the conventional "V"-shaped ditches. The latter concentrate and accelerate the flow of water, encourage erosion, and make it difficult to establish vegetation.

Medians and drainage ways in level topography may be seeded, fertilized, and mulched without special erosion control measures. Lime and fertilizer should be incorporated into the soil to a depth of 10 to 15 cm; seed and mulch should then be surface-applied.

In medians where considerable water flow is expected (generally not to exceed a depth of 5 cm), the ditch may be straw mulched using 4,480 to 6,720 kg/ha of straw tacked with 1,270 to 1,695 liters of asphalt.

For slopes in drainage ways where rather fast water flow is expected, special precautions must be used for stabilization. Where massive and fast flows of water are expected, the only solution is the construction of concrete or asphalt ditches or the equivalent.

The best and surest way of establishing vegetation in drainage ditches where high velocities of water are expected is by direct sodding. It is recommended that the sod be high quality bluegrass-Kentucky 31 fescue mixture, being at least 25% bluegrass (Poa pratensis L.) or creeping red fescue (Festuca rubra L.) in the northeastern U.S. Fertilization, watering, and cultural practices for laying sod should be used.

Jute matting or excelsior materials are superior to asphalted straw but inferior to direct sodding for establishing vegetation in water ways in medians (Fig. 11). The best way to use jute matting is: (i) incorporate soil amendments and leave rough surfaces; (ii) apply seed to surface; (iii) apply straw at 4,480 kg/ha; and (iv) install jute or other appropriate netting over the straw. Instructions for installing jute or other matting should be rigidly followed.

D. Topsoiling

Topsoiling is necessary for establishing vegetation in the following situations:

1) To cover xeric rocky environments;
2) To cover and restrict root contact as with soil materials containing high amounts of pyrites;

Fig. 10—*Top:* Foreground shows conventional smooth, hard grading with little vegetation; background shows rough, loose tillage with vigorous seedlings. *Bottom:* A closeup of the roughened, cloddy subsoil shows excellent stands and growth of seedlings 21 days after seeding. All slopes were mulched with woodfiber.

Fig. 11—Excelsior matting in a ditch along a new highway facilitates growth of seedlings, while controlling erosion. Similar results may be obtained with properly installed jute matting.

3) Where special ornamentals that demand especially good soil fertility and aeration are to be planted;
4) Where a quality turfgrass lawn is wanted, as at rest areas, and highway corridors adjacent to urban areas; and
5) In medians and shoulders, when good topsoil would otherwise be discarded.

Excluding number 5, when applying topsoil to the previously described areas, it should be applied from 25 to 50 cm in depth.

The slopes should be as shallow as possible; topsoil will not usually adhere in place on slopes steeper than 2:1 (Blaser & Woodruff, 1968; Jacobs et al., 1967; Smith, 1973). The slopes should be rough-graded, stair-stepped, or grooved with undulations perpendicular to the slope. This encourages some mixing of the topsoil with the subsoil material to form a bond between the two. The stair-steps or grooves also reduce soil and water runoff. Topsoil should be applied to a depth of about 10 cm, leaving the final surface roughened. Another alternative is to apply the topsoil and then till it with grooves perpendicular to the slope and to a depth of 15 to 20 cm to insure bonding with the subsoil (Wright et al., 1975).

The economics and the potential problems commonly associated with topsoiled areas must be considered. Topsoiling is expensive, costing $5,000 to $10,000/ha, and its use usually delays seeding operations, which

Fig. 12—Topsoil placed over smooth, hard subsoil material on cuts is subject to flow-off as shown above. The subsoil should be roughened before applying topsoil or mixed with the subsoil.

increases the possibility of erosion and pollution. Also, most topsoil contains weed seeds which cause dense weed canopies that shade out desirable species unless the area is reseeded or herbicides are applied. Also, topsoils in humid regions are usually of poor quality (low in pH, fertility, and organic matter).

Potentially beneficial effects from topsoils on sloping cuts, fills, and medians in highway corridors are often nullified and are usually associated with less than desirable slope surface preparation and topsoil application practices. On slopes with hard smooth surfaces and those with vertical rills from prolonged exposure, topsoiling is often useless because of severe sloughing and erosion. Supersaturation at the soil-subsoil interface causes massive sloughing of the loose topsoil (Fig. 12).

The need for topsoiling should be limited to the five areas mentioned previously, as good vegetative covers can be established quickly on properly amended slopes with surfaces composed of subsoil-rock materials.

Grading and preparing subsoil materials as discussed earlier often give more desirable seedbeds than topsoils. As compared with topsoil, the clay content of subsoils provides high moisture availability and deters leaching because of cation retention; the lower silt content of subsoils often reduces sealing of surface pores, thereby reducing runoff due to increased water infiltration.

Experiments show that rough-graded subsoil slopes can be superior to topsoil for grass and legume establishment (Table 3). The better soil

Table 3—Plant populations and vegetative cover as influenced by subsoil conditions,
topsoiling, and fertilizer incorporation. Established 22 May 1972†

Treatments	Plants		Data on 22 July 1972			Crownvetch cover after 2 years
	Crown-vetch	Grass	Vegetative cover	Bulk density‡	Total porosity‡	
	——— m² ———		%	g/cm	——— % ———	
a) Subsoil smooth and hard with lime, fertilizer, mulch, and seed surface applied (conventional method)	80c	160c	22c	1.76	42.1	100
b) Subsoil roughened and loosened with tiller feet of a road grader, then lightly rototilled leaving a cloddy surface (other treatments as in (a))	440a	800a	72a	1.38	51.4	100
c) Same as (b) except lime and fertilizer applied first	480a	930a	74a	1.44	59.9	100
d) Same as (a) but with 10 cm of topsoil and all treatments surface-applied	180b	680b	66b	1.42	53.0	100

† The subsoil pH was 5.3 at the date of seeding. The treatments were: seed mixture—Kentucky 31 fescue at 84, redtop at 2.24, annual ryegrass at 5.6, and crownvetch at 22.4 kg/ha; a 10–20–10 fertilizer at 1,120 kg/ha, lime at 4,480 kg/ha, and woodfiber mulch at 480 kg/ha.

‡ Bulk density (wt/vol) and total porosity (pore space in %) were made on the 0–3 cm soil layer.

moisture on the subsoil rather than the topsoil material (Table 2) was a primary factor responsible for the improvement in plant density. Clayey clods from a roughened subsoil resisted breakdown and crusting to slow down surface water movement allowing better infiltration than the topsoiled slope. Rough-grading of subsoil materials created a loose soil environment as noted by a decrease in bulk density and an increase in porosity when compared to the compacted subsoils for "finished" grading (Table 3).

Establishing excellent leguminous-grass canopies avoids degeneration of grassy vegetation due to the low organic matter-N fertility in subsoil materials. In the humid southern region, winter annuals such as crimson clover (*Trifolium incarnatum* L.) and white clover (*Trifolium repens* L.) and summer legumes such as lespedeza (*Lespedeza striata* Hook. & Arn.) are widely adapted and serve as N-suppliers to perpetuate grass-legume covers (Woodruff & Blaser, 1971).

Legumes such as crownvetch, alfalfa (*Medicago sativa* L.), red clover (*Trifolium pratense* L.), and white clover are broadly adapted to a wide range of central and northern latitudes and altitudes on subsoil materials that are properly graded and amended in the more humid regions

(Blaser & Ward, 1958; Brooks & Blaser, 1964; Carson & Blaser, 1963; Donald, 1963; Shoop et al., 1961; Wright et al., 1975; Zak et al., 1972). In the Appalachian and Piedmont regions, crownvetch or sericea lespedeza (*Lespedeza cuneata* [*sericea*] Don.) have persisted for two decades on various subsoil materials without any maintenance treatments. The longevity is attributed to supplying needed lime and nutrients before seeding and the recycling of the various essential nutrients.

E. Soil Amendments

Controlling erosion from bare soil areas during highway construction is achieved quickly and economically by establishing a protective vegetative cover, which cannot be obtained without adequate and balanced fertility and a favorable pH. The lime and nutrient requirements vary with soils and for species; hence, soil materials should be sampled and analyzed by competent laboratories in making lime and fertilizer recommendations for soils and species adapted to various regions.

The native species and natural woody vegetation in humid regions are generally tolerant of soil acidity and low fertility; however, they establish slowly and require long periods to develop dense protective vegetation (Blaser & McKee, 1967; Zak et al., 1972). The introduced and improved grasses and legumes that develop protective vegetative covers quickly in highway construction projects generally require relatively high fertility and soil pH conditions.

Soil N is the primary limiting nutrient and most costly for grass growth; thus, soil amendments should be planned to grow legumes where adaped. Legume-grass associations eliminate the need for costly N fertilization to maintain dense vegetative canopies for erosion control (Woodruff & Blaser, 1970a).

Where adapted, successful growth of legumes requires a favorable soil pH and mineral balance. Semitropical legumes such as lespedeza species are tolerant of the high acidity, low Ca, low P, and high Al complex common in soils in the humid southeastern U.S. region (McKee et al., 1965a; Wright et al., 1975). Conversely, legumes of temperate origin require medium to high soil pH values with low Al availability and medium to high values for P, Ca, Mg, and K. Except for a few environments, other nutrients such as S and micronutrients are usually adequate. Although applying certain elements may stimulate growth, the objective is to obtain a persistent protective cover of desirable botanical components rather than high yield. Excessive growth is objectionable because of diseases, rodents, and increased mowing and other management problems.

However, liberal applications of lime and P, when needed, are essential for maintaining a protective cover of persistent leguminous species requiring little or no maintenance. Liberal applications of lime have long-lasting residual effects for supplying Ca and Mg and counteracting soil acidity. Phosphorus is generally very low in soils in humid regions and low in availability under high soil pH conditions in the arid regions. Liberal applications are desirable and necessary because the release of P for plant growth is often slow because of chemical fixation with Fe, Al, or Ca, depending on pH. Leaching of P is nil and very low for Ca and Mg; with the recycling (canopies and roots to soil to canopies) of these nutrients, high rates of applications last for decades and are relatively inexpensive. Thus, applications of 2 to 10 metric tons/ha of lime, pending soil properties, and 200 to 350 kg/ha of P as P_2O_5, have maintained persistent and invading legumes such as crownvetch in the Piedmont and Appalachian regions for decades (Blaser et al., 1975a).

F. Mulches, Nets, and Binders

Mulch materials are used for temporary erosion control of bare soils and to simultaneously improve the soil environment for establishing vegetation quickly by augmenting germination and seedling growth. Organic mulches, straw-like materials, and wood products of fiber, chips, and bark moderate soil temperatures and improve moisture relationships; plastic-type materials are generally ineffective (Barkley et al., 1965; Blaser, 1962b; McCreery et al., 1975; McKee et al., 1964). The many experiments with various organic and inorganic nets on steep cut slopes in the Appalachian and Piedmont areas have usually resulted in seeding failures. It is practically impossible to establish a continuous soil-net contact; therefore, water flows under nets cause serious erosion (Fig. 13).

Of the approximately 15 chemical binders and soil stabilizers used in highway corridors on many soil and subsoil materials, all have proven unsatisfactory when used alone for erosion control and seedling establishment (Perry et al., 1975; Wright et al., 1975). With the exception of asphalt, the materials now on the market for binding organic mulches have been ineffective or of such short duration as to make them impractical and economically unfeasible. Laboratory tests show desirable results from some binders, but experiments on slopes along highways have nullified such favorable laboratory results. Binding straw on slopes with 840 kg/ha of woodfiber has given exceptionally good and prolonged straw stabilization, being superior to any binder and avoiding pollution possibilities (Fig. 14) (Wright et al., 1975). Tacking straw with woodfiber gives excellent results in a two-step operation: (i) apply straw, and (ii) apply the seed-woodfiber-soil amendment slurry. This procedure gives results similar to the three-step operation: (i) applying the seed-soil amendment slurry, (ii) applying straw, and (iii) tacking with woodfiber.

It is imperative to apply mulches liberally in harsh environments, as on smooth, hard slopes and "hot" slope exposures, and to provide prolonged mulch stabilizations, as with straw tacked with woodfiber for midsummer or winter seedings (Blaser et al., 1961; McCreery et al., 1975; McKee et al., 1964 and 1965b). High rates of mulch materials are less important for rough, loose graded slopes since the roughness per se creates favorable microenvironments by coverage of seed and fertilizer, aiding germination and growth (Fig. 15).

Mulch materials and rates of application vary with season. For example, straw, woodbark, and wood chips are superior to woodfiber during stress periods when germination and seedling development are slow.

Fig. 13—Nets for slope stabilization are undesirable because of labor involved in installation. Poor net-soil contact causes erosion under the nets, resulting in seeding failures.

Fig. 14—Straw tacked with 840 kg/ha of woodfiber stabilizes straw for prolonged periods, aids in vegetative establishment, and avoids pollution and contamination that could occur with chemical tacking agents.

Fig. 15—Sloughing soil material from the vertical walls of a 25-cm stair-step grading facilitates coverage of seed and soil amendments creating favorable microenvironments for
germination and growth. Excellent seedling stands occurred on horizontal steps. Area with
poor vegetation and sloughing in foreground was left smooth.

1) *Mulches for Favorable Spring or Late Summer Seeding Season*—
Mulch with 3,360 kg/ha of straw, 1,350 kg/ha of woodfiber, or 30
m³ of woodbark or woodchips. If slopes are stair-step graded or in
a rough, loose condition, the mulch rates may be reduced or even
omitted on cool (shaded) slopes. Chemical binders need not be
used during these favorable seasons, although straw may be
tacked with 840 kg/ha of woodfiber on steep slopes.

2) *Mulches for the Late Spring-Summer Season*—Moisture stress and
high air and soil temperatures make straw, woodbark, or woodchips superior to woodfiber for conserving moisture and moder-
ating temperatures to enhance germination and the establishment
of seedlings. Straw on smooth, hard slopes and flat areas should
generally be tacked with asphalt at 210 liter/ha or, preferably,
woodfiber at 840 kg/ha. When applied to rough, loose soil sur-
faced, straw need not be tacked unless the areas have high winds,
traffic air currents, or steep slopes. Woodbark or woodchips
should not generally be used on slopes steeper than 2:1 and do not
need binders. Woodfiber at 2,240 kg/ha should be used on slopes
steeper than 1.5:1 and may be substituted for straw and woodbark when they are unavailable. Rates of applying mulches for
summer seedings are:

a) Straw or grass hay free of weed seeds at 3,360 to 4,480 kg/ha.
b) Woodbark or woodchips at 90 to 140 m³/ha.
c) Woodfiber at 1,680 to 2,240 kg/ha.
3) *Mulches for Winter*—Prolonged soil stabilization during winter (Nov. to Mar.) is imperative since protection from vegetative cover is not likely to be attained until spring. Persistent mulches to be used during hard freezing and thawing conditions are:
a) Straw at 4.5 metric tons/ha tacked with 840 kg/ha of woodfiber.
b) Straw at 4.5 metric tons/ha tacked with asphalt at 2,800 liters/ha, or other suitable chemical binders yet to be ascertained.
c) Woodbark or woodchips at 140 m³/ha without binders. It is best to reserve woodbark or woodchips for the most difficult environments, as for winter stabilization.

G. Hydro- vs. Other Seeding and Fertilizer Techniques

The hydro-method is the most practical method for applying mulch, seed, and soil amendments on steep slopes. However, surface applications of seed, lime, and P, especially on smooth, hard slope surfaces, are inferior to incorporating these materials. It is especially desirable to incorporate lime and P, as these materials are positionally fixed, with movement into soil and subsoil materials being slow. Thus, on traversable slopes it is economical and desirable to apply soil amendments in dry form, and incorporate them into the surface 10 to 20 cm. Seeding with a grain drill or other machines for seed coverage improves moisture status in the soil-seed zone. Also, passing over straw mulch to partially imbed it into soils with cut-away disk is an excellent means of stabilization.

H. Designing Seed Mixtures

Erosion is minimized during grading and denuding operations in highway corridors by establishing a fast-developing vegetative cover. Dense plant canopies reduce raindrop impact onto the soil surface and avoid soil deflocculation and clogging of pores, thereby encouraging water infiltration and reducing runoff waters that cause erosion. The roots of rapidly developing plant covers bind soil materials and increase soil granulation and porosity.

When designing seed mixtures within regions in the United States, it is necessary to alter species components and ratios of species in mixtures to obtain vegetative cover rapidly at various seasons to minimize erosion as construction proceeds (Blaser, 1963; Blaser et al., 1968; Duell & Schmidt, 1974; Powell et al., 1967a; Schmidt et al., 1967; Schmidt & Blaser, 1969; Woodruff et al., 1972). The changing environments, differential adaptations of species, and seedling vigor for different seasonal seedings must be concurrently considered in designing mixtures. Furthermore, the species and seeding rates in mixtures should be planned to give a series of changing species, for example, plant succession shifting from fast-developing temporary species such as cereal grains, ryegrasses, and German millet (*Setaria italica* [L.] Beauv.), to secondary species such as the fescues, bluegrass, and lovegrass (*Eragrostis curvula* [Schrad.] Nees.), to persistent species that develop slowly such as crownvetch, sericea lespedeza, and woody species.

For example, the seed mixtures in the Appalachian and Piedmont regions are designed to obtain a protective cover by mulching and a succession of specis as follows:

1) *Primary Stage*—Bare soil protected with mulch → temporary vegetation from companion annual grasses that germinate quickly and produce vigorous seedlings during specific seasons, such as annual ryegrass (*Lolium multiflorum* Lam.) and cereal rye during the cool seasons or German millet during summer (Fig. 16).

2) *Secondary Stage*—Temporary vegetation → perennial grasses, such as tall fescue, creeping red fescue, and bluegrass. These perennial grasses are often short-lived unless they are mowed and fertilized, especially with N.

3) *Final Stage, Alternative I*—Perennial grasses → perennial persistent legumes requiring little or no maintenance, such as sericea lespedeza and crownvetch. These occur with restricted or preferably no mowing.

Fig. 16—Excellent crownvetch was established into an undisturbed cereal rye canopy. Winter or summer annuals provide excellent in situ mulch for overseeding persistent legumes. Dense, competitive, temporary canopies may be killed by applying herbicides concurrently with seed to eliminate competition.

4) *Final Stage, Alternative II*—Perennial grasses → woody perennials, if left unmowed and unfertilized to reduce canopy competition from grasses. The succession period to woody species may require many years, pending species and natural or artificial seeding. Legume species are excluded to reduce canopy competition.

5) *Final Stage, Alternative III*—Perennial grasses → conditioned stage by mowing managements and N fertilization.

Competition from dense canopies of fast-growing annual species are lethal to desirable persistent species; hence, after annuals die, erosion occurs. All desirable species giving persistent covers have rather poor seedling vigor; thus, the density of the quick developing canopies should be controlled by using low seeding rates to minimize competition. The major species, seeding rates, and seasons of seeding for various states are given in Table 4.

Table 4—Rates and seasons of seeding and species in states in various regions

	Rate of seeding, kg/ha	Seeding season			
		Spring	Summer	Fall	Winter
A. Ohio, Indiana, Illinois, Michigan, Wisconsin, Iowa, Missouri, and Minnesota.					
Ky 31 fescue	50	X	X	X	X
Perennial ryegrass (*Lolium perenne* L.)	28	X	X	X	X
Kentucky bluegrass	34	X		X	
Annual ryegrass	7	X		X	X
Redtop	11	X		X	
Ladino clover	7	X			
Creeping red fescue	45	X	X	X	X
Winter vetch (*Vicia villosa* Roth)	45			X	X
Crownvetch	22	X	X	X	
Birdsfoot trefoil	22	X			
Cereal rye	100			X	X
German millet	28		X		
Alsike clover	14	X		X	
B. Virginia West Virginia, Tennessee, North Carolina, Kentucky, Askansas, Missouri, Maryland, southern Ohio, Indiana, and Illinois.					
Ky 31 fescue	56	X	X	X	X
Redtop	5	X			
White clover	7	X			
Annual lespedeza	22		X		
Weeping lovegrass	7		X		
Bermudagrass (common)	8		X		
Annual ryegrass	7	X		X	X
Crimson clover	22				X
Crownvetch	22	X	X	X	
Sericea lespedeza	40	X	X	X	
Bluegrass	55	X		X	
Red fescue	45	X		X	X
Perennial ryegrass	28	X		X	X
Cereal rye	100				X
German millet	28		X		

(continued on next page)

Table 4—continued

	Rate of seeding, kg/ha	Seeding season			
		Spring	Summer	Fall	Winter

C. Maine, New Hampshire, Vermont, Massachusetts, Rhode Island, New York, Pennsylvania, Connecticut, and New Jersey.

Ky 31 fescue	50	X	X	X	X
Perennial ryegrass	11	X	X	X	X
Creeping red fescue	45	X	X	X	X
Red clover	11	X			
Birdsfoot trefoil	17	X		X	
Crownvetch	22	X	X	X	
Annual ryegrass	7	X		X	X
Cereal rye	100				X
White clover	6	X			
Bentgrass	6	X			
Redtop	10	X		X	
Weeping lovegrass	11		X		
German millet	28		X		
Kentucky bluegrass	33	X		X	

D. Central and southern Louisiana, Mississippi, Alabama, Arkansas, Georgia, South Carolina, Florida, West Tennessee, East Texas, and Coastal Plains of North Carolina and Virginia.

Annual lespedeza (Kobe or Korean)	22	X	X		
Bahiagrass (Pensacola or Wilmington)	45	X	X	X	
Bermudagrass (common)	11		X		
Brunswickgrass	45		X		
Crimson clover	28	X		X	X
Rye	78			X	X
Sericea lespedeza	40		X		
Crownvetch	22	X		X	
Tall fescue (Ky 31)	45	X		X	X
Weeping lovegrass	7	X	X		
German millet	28		X		
White clover	7	X			
Sudangrass	28		X		
Redtop	8	X		X	

E. Arizona, New Mexico, Nevada, Southern California, and West Texas.

Yellow bluestem (*Andropogon Virginicus* L.)	3.0	X		X	
Weeping lovegrass	6.7	X	X		
Lehman lovegrass (*Eragrostis lehmanniana* Nees)	2.2	X	X		
Sand dropseed	1.1	X	X		
Sacaton (*Sporobolus wrightii* munro)	22	X	X		
Black gramagrass (*Bouteloua eriopoda* Lag)	2.2		X		
Sibergian wheatgrass (*Agropyron sibiricum* Beauv)	2.2	X		X	
Blue grama	3.3	X			
Indian ricegrass (*Oryzopsis hymenoides* Richer)	2.2			X	
Yellow sweet clover	3.3	X		X	
Crested wheatgrass	5.6	X		X	
Smooth bromegrass (*Bromus inermis* Leyss)	5.6	X	X		X

(continued on next page)

Table 4—continued

	Rate of seeding, kg/ha	Seeding season			
		Spring	Summer	Fall	Winter

F. Eastern Washington and Oregon, Idaho, Northern Nevada, and Utah.

Crested wheatgrass	5.6	X		X	
Smooth bromegrass	11	X		X	
Slender wheatgrass	5.6	X		X	
Streambank wheatgrass	8.9	X		X	
Hard fescue	13.4	X		X	
Big bluegrass (*Poa ampla* Merr.)	11.2	X			
Western wheatgrass (*Agropyron smithii* Rydb)	8.9	X		X	
Pubescent wheatgrass (*Agropyron trichophorum* (Link) Richt)	4.4	X		X	

G. Western Washington, Oregon, Alaska, and Northwest California.

White clover	4.4	X		X	
Colonial bentgrass (*Agrostis tenuis* L.)	3.3	X	X	X	
Red fescue	22	X	X	X	
Perennial ryegrass	8.9	X	X	X	
Chewings fescue (*Festuca rubra* var. *commutata* Gaud.)	16.8	X		X	
Kentucky bluegrass	5.6	X		X	
Annual ryegrass	112		X	X	X
Barley (*Hordeum vulgare* L.)	112				X
Crownvetch	28	X			

H. North Dakota, South Dakota, Montana, Nebraska, Kansas, Wyoming, Colorado, Oklahoma, Central Texas, and Western Minnesota.

Bromegrass	14	X		X	
Intermediate wheatgrass	7.8	X		X	
Crested wheatgrass	14	X		X	
Kentucky bluegrass	30	X		X	
Perennial ryegrass	3.3	X		X	
White clover	5	X		X	
Reed canarygrass	2.2	X		X	
Switchgrass	2.2		X		
Indiangrass	2.2		X		
Sideoats grama	2.2		X		
Little bluestem	1.1		X		
Alfalfa	7.8	X		X	
Red clover	5.6	X		X	
Hairy vetch	14	X		X	
Buffalograss	4.5		X		
Blue grama	1.1		X		
Slender wheatgrass	7.8	X		X	
Green needlegrass	2.2	X		X	
Western wheatgrass	5.6	X		X	
Green sprangletop	4.5		X		
Weeping lovegrass	4.5		X		
Sericea lespedeza	28	X		X	
Cereals (wheat, rye, oats, barley)	90	X		X	
Ky 31 fescue	28	X		X	
Bermudagrass	7		X		

I. Multistep Seeding and Fertilization

Seeding contracts should specify a 75 to 95% vegetative cover with 50% of the botanical components being persistent legumes or 80% persistent grasses where legumes are not adapted or desired. This assumes that a persistent vegetative cover requiring no additional seed and fertilizer will develop through plant invasion and succession. Presently, a large percentage of the initial contract seedings have a rapidly degenerating grassy vegetation that must be reseeded because of short-lived species and inadequate soil amendments.

It is usually impossible to obtain a satisfactory vegetation from one initial seeding because of the rigorous environments in highway corridors; the soil-biotic-climatic complex cannot be sufficiently manipulated. The principle of multistep seeding is to apply specified seed and soil amendments in two to three applications at dates ranging from 2 to 12 months apart to take advantage of favorable conditions for establishing or stimulating desirable species when initial seedings fail to provide a protective vegetation of desirable persistent species. The second or third step operations, pending vegetation from initial seeding, may include fertilizer, when suitable species degenerate, rhizobia inoculants when nodulation of legumes fail, seed if soil amendments are suitable, or a seed-soil amendment-woodfiber slurry for areas with poor vegetative cover.

The multi-step principle used in the Appalachian and Piedmont regions has been very successful for obtaining desirable persistent vegetative covers requiring little or no maintenance. Exhibits for multi-step applications are:

1) For seeding in all seasons during construction operations:
   a) Step 1. Establish a temporary canopy during summer with a German millet-fertilizer-woodfiber slurry.
      Step 2. Apply cool season species with additional fertilizer during late summer-early fall. Frost or maturity kills millet, providing an in situ noncompetitive mulch canopy.
   b) Step 1. Establish a temporary canopy during winter with a cereal rye-cool season species-fertilizer-wood-fiber slurry over a straw mulch.
      Step 2. Apply a light application of fertilizer with either crownvetch or serica lespedeza and perennial grasses if needed in March. Alternative Step 2. Add paraquat to slurry if cereal rye canopy is dense and tall (aggressive).
2) Favorable spring season, one or two-step operations:
   a) One-step procedure. Use recommended rates as 110 kg seed, 1,700 kg of a 10-20-10 fertilizer, and 1,700 kg/ha of woodfiber.
   b) Two-step procedure. Step 1. Apply woodfiber at 100% of the rate and other materials at 75% of the rate in Alternative (a) above. Step 2. Apply the rest of the materials during late summer, pending stands, applying materials at higher rates where vegetation is sparse.

Table 5—Recommendations for several-step fertilization in different seasons for erosion and siltation control†

Season‡	Fertilization
A. Favorable spring, cool-moist environments	Apply 1,100 kg/ha 10–20–10 at seeding and 550 kg/ha 10–20–10/acre the next fall
B. Late spring-mid summer	(a) With weeping lovegrass-perennial species, use 1,100 kg/ha 10–20–10/acre at seeding, 550 kg/ha the following spring.§ (b) With German millet use 850 kg/ha 10–20–10 at seeding and 850 kg/ha in the fall.§
C. Favorable cool moist periods, summer-early fall	1,100 kg/ha 10–20–10 at seeding and 550 kg/ha next spring
D. Mid-late fall	Apply 1,100 kg/ha 10–20–10 at seeding and 550 kg/ha the following spring
E. Winter seedings	Apply 1,100 kg/ha 10–20–10 at seeding and 550 kg/ha the next spring

† Lime should be applied according to soil test recommendations.
‡ The actual dates within each seeding period vary with physiographic regions.
§ Perennial grasses and legumes should be used during all seasons as discussed in section H of this chapter and used as recommended for various management practices and slope conditions.

An alternative for Step 2 is to apply around 200 kg/ha of P as P_2O_5 and 20 kg/ha of crownvetch when grass cover is sufficiently protective. It is assumed that lime is not needed due to a favorable pH. Fertilizer recommendations used with multi-step seeding in the Virginias are given in Table 5.

When using the multi-step seeding procedure with a given amount of seed or fertilizer, the chances of arresting erosion and obtaining a persistent cover are better than for a single application because:

1) Environmental risk for generating cover is minimal with seeding dates for the multi-step applications.

2) The risk of stand failure from unexpected catastrophies such as torrential rains, drought, and freezing are reduced. There is invariably some soil, seed, and fertilizer movement down slopes, even on shallow ones due to torrential rains or channeling of accumulated water from rainfall. Thus, with one-step methods some soil areas will be left without seed and fertilizer and, hence, no vegetative cover. Such bare areas become enlarged in subsequent years and soil and water movement may become serious. This can be avoided with multi-step principles.

3) The mortality of seedlings from surface concentrations of N and K salts is reduced by the lighter applications (Verghese et al., 1970).

4) There is a chance of saving materials as the initial application may produce a satisfactory vegetative cover, making the second application unnecessary.

5) The multi-step procedures almost assure excellent productive covers as a responsibility by contractors.

6) Degeneration of young stands often starts 6 months after seeding

in subsoil materials before legumes become established; hence, a 2- or 3-step method would improve growth, persistance, and longevity of vegetation.

7) The competition from grasses that suppresses legumes can be controlled by applying no N in Step 2.

8) When desirable species seeded in Step 1 are depressed by weed competition, Step 2 can be made later when weed competition is not serious, as in the fall season.

9) The multi-step method is desirable when grassy covers are to be mowed and maintained. Step 2 could be composed of primarily a slowly available source of N to prolong its longevity.

J. Improving Sparse Vegetation

Sparse vegetation in highway corridors is common in all regions of the United States because of inadequate lime and fertility, use of unadapted and short-lived species, the low soil N status, absence of legumes, competition from aggressive weeds or companion species, catastrophies such as flooding, and poor, unacceptable stands from initial one-step seeding operations.

The soils should be tested to apply nutrients to obtain persistent species, especially legumes. Renovation of sparse canopies with legumes should be initiated while grass cover is adequate to control erosion without applying N. Nitrogen stimulates grasses causing moisture and light competition. This depresses legumes, causing them to fail. Lime, P, and K applications, if needed, stimulate legume seedings and their invasion (Blaser & Woodruff, 1968; Blaser et al., 1975a). For example, slopes with a 50% grass cover or greater have given excellent crownvetch stands when seeded at about 40 kg/ha along with 170 kg/ha of P as P_2O_5 and 850 kg/ha of woodfiber.

For sparse grass stands of 30 to 50% cover, it is usually necessary to apply 50% of the recommended grasses, around 300 kg of P as P_2O_5 and 60 kg/ha of N, along with woodfiber at 1,680 kg/ha and full legume seeding rates.

When maintaining grassy vegetation, fertilizers, especially N, should be applied before degeneration and erosion occur. Rates of N should be as low as possible to avoid overstimulation of growth and problems with mowing management and maintaining vegetation. Autumn season N applications thicken shoot density, decrease weeds, and avoid overstimulation of growth in spring (Blaser & Perry, 1975; Powell et al., 1967b).

III. FUTURE RESEARCH NEEDS

Major areas needing additional research are:

1) The primary need for highway corridor stabilization is the adaptation of persistent, low-growing legumes requiring little mowing

or fertilizer maintenance. Legumes should eliminate costly refertilization and reseeding since soils are invariably low in N. Several species, such as flat pea (*Lathyrus sylvestris* L.) and sweet pea (*L. latifolius*) are promising in the southeastern U.S. region.

2) A primary need in the humid region for cool and warm season grasses is to develop minimum mowing practices for controlling weeds while maintaining an aesthetically pleasing turf. The many millions of dollars spent yearly on hand and tractor mowing operations may be reduced by timely mowing of grasses and weeds to minimize spraying.

3) Another need is the broad problem of developing both temporary and perennial species that may be established during critical erosion periods, especially during winter seasons.

4) Uniform low-growing species of grasses and legumes need to be developed that persist under stress conditions and low fertility, needing no mowing.

5) Various states and regions should investigate the concepts of rough and stair-step grading with different soil and subsoil materials, in various environments and with different plant species, to control erosion and establish vegetative covers quickly.

6) Direct seeding and other methods of encouraging rapid invasion of woody species and low growing shrubs in different regions should be investigated. Many linear miles in highway systems, by plant succession, should develop into a persistent woody vegetation requiring no fertility or mowing maintenance. Direct seeding of woody species has given inconclusive or negative results.

7) The introduction of new legumes and woody species necessitates studies of their effects on wildlife.

8) Highways in the future should be planned to use less area to minimize the exploitation of productive soils needed for food production to avoid hunger for future generations. The advice of agronomists, geologists, and economists should be sought when planning highways.

9) Recent findings in erosion control and establishment of vegetative covers should be disseminated to educate administrators and those directly in charge of construction operations in the form of handbooks or other media to implement the advanced practices of erosion control and vegetative establishment.

ACKNOWLEDGMENT

Research findings and principles reported herein were achieved by personnel of the Agronomy Department of Virginia Polytechnic Institute and State University in cooperation with the West Virginia and Virginia Department of Highways, Federal Highway Administration, and the Virginia Highway Research Council.

LITERATURE CITED

Allmaras, R. R., A. L. Black, and R. W. Rickman. 1973. Tillage, soil environment, and root growth. p. 62–87. *In* Conservation tillage. Natl. Conf. Soil Conserv. Soc. of Am., 28–30 Mar. 1973, Ankeny, Iowa.

Barkley, D. G., R. E. Blaser, and R. E. Schmidt. 1965. Effect of mulches on microclimate and turf establishment. Agron. J. 57:189–192.

Blaser, R. E. 1962a. Methods of maintaining and reseeding deteriorated highway slopes. Dep. of Landsc. Archit., Ohio State Univ., and the Ohio Dep. of Highw. p. 87–93.

Blaser, R. E. 1962b. Soil mulches for grassing. Natl. Acad. of Sci. Highw. Res. Bd., Roadside Dev. Washington, D.C. 1030:15–20.

Blaser, R. E. 1963. Principles for making up seed mixtures for roadside seedings. Natl. Acad. of Sci. Highw. Res. Bd., Roadside Dev. Washington, D.C. 1120:79–84.

Blaser, R. E., and C. Y. Ward. 1958. Seeding highway slopes as influenced by lime and fertilizer and adaptation of species. Natl. Acad. of Sci. Highw. Res. Bd., Roadside Dev. Washington, D.C. 613:21–39.

Blaser, R. E., G. W. Thomas, C. R. Brooks, G. J. Shoop, and J. B. Martin. 1961. Turf establishment and maintenance along highways. Natl. Acad. of Sci. Highw. Res. Bd., Roadside Dev. Washington, D.C. 928:5–17.

Blaser, R. E., and W. H. McKee, Jr. 1967. Regeneration of woody vegetation along roadsides. Natl. Acad. of Sci. Highw. Res. Bd., Roadside Dev. Washington, D.C. 161:104–116.

Blaser, R. E., and J. M. Woodruff. 1968. The need for specifying two- or three-step seeding and fertilization practices for establishing sod on highways. Natl. Acad. of Sci. Highw. Res. Bd., Highw. Res. Rec. Washington, D.C. 246:44–49.

Blaser, R. E., J. T. Green, Jr., and D. L. Wright. 1975a. Establishing vegetation for erosion control in the Piedmont region. p. 235–259. *In* Methods of quickly vegetating soils of low productivity. EPA-440/9-75-006. USEPA, Washington, D.C.

Blaser, R. E., and H. D. Perry. 1975. Establishing vegetation for erosion control along highways in the Appalachian region. Chap. 8. EPA-440/9-75-006. USEPA, Washington, D.C.

Blaser, R. E., D. L. Wright, and H. D. Perry. 1975b. Erosion control during highway construction. Rural and Urban Roads. 13(4):38–40.

Brooks, C. R., and R. E. Blaser. 1964. Effect of fertilizer slurries used with hydro-seeding on seed viability. Highw. Res. Rec. 53:30–34.

Carson, E. W., Jr., and R. E. Blaser. 1963. Establishing sericea lespedeza on highway slopes. Natl. Acad. of Sci. Highw. Res. Bd., Roadside Dev. Washington, D.C. 1030:3–14.

Dickens, R., and H. P. Orr. 1969. Roadside vegetation and erosion control. HPR Rep. no. 44. Auburn Univ., School of Agric. in cooperation with Alabama Highw. Dep. and Fed. Highw. Admin. Dep. of Agron. and Soils, Auburn Univ., Auburn, Ala.

Donald, C. M. 1963. Competition among crop and pasture plants. Adv. Agron. 15:1–118.

Duell, R. W., and R. M. Schmit. 1974. Grass varieties for roadsides. p. 541–551. *In* E. C. Roberts (ed.) Proc. 2nd Int. Turgrass Res. Conf., 19–24 June 1974, Blacksburg, Va., Int. Turfgrass Soc. in cooperation with the Am. Soc. of Agron. and the Crop Sci. Soc. of Am.

Foote, L. E., D. L. Kill, and H. Bolland. 1970. Erosion prevention and turf establishment manual. Off. of Mater. Constr. Div., Minnesota Dep. of Highw.

Goss, R. L., R. M. Blanchard, and W. R. Melton. 1970. The establishment of vegetation on non-topsoiled slopes in Washington. Final Rep. Y-1009. Prepared jointly by Washington State Highw. Comm. and Washington State Univ. Agric. Res. Center in cooperation with Fed. Highw. Admin. Dep. of Agron. and Soils, Washington State Univ., Pullman.

Green, J. T., Jr., R. E. Blaser, and H. D. Perry. 1973a. Establishing persistent vegetation on cuts and fills along West Virginia highways. Final Rep. for the West Virginia Dep. of Highw. and the U.S. Dep. of Transp., Fed. Highw. Admin., Bur. of Public Roads. Proj. 26, Phase II. Agron. Dep., Virginia Polytechnic and State Univ., Blacksburg.

Green, J. T., Jr., J. M. Woodruff, and R. E. Blaser. 1973b. Stabilizing disturbed areas during highway construction for pollution control. Final Rep. for the Virginia Dep. of Highw., Virginia Highw. Res. Counc., U.S. Dep. of Transp., and Fed. Highw. Admin.

Green, J. T., Jr., H. D. Perry, J. M. Woodruff, and R. E. Blaser. 1974. Suitability of cool and warm season species for dormant winter seedings. p. 551–568. *In* E. C. Roberts (ed.) Proc. 2nd Int. Turfgrass Res. Conf., 19–24 June 1974, Blacksburg, Va., Int. Turfgrass Soc. in cooperation with the Am. Soc. of Agron. and the Crop Sci. Soc. of Am.

Hottenstein, W. L. 1969. Highway roadsides. *In* A. A. Hanson and F. V. Juska (eds.) Turf-grass Science Agronomy 14:603–637. Am. Soc. of Agron., Madison, Wis.

Jacobs, J. A., O. N. Andrews, Jr., C. L. Murdock, and L. E. Foote. 1967. Turf establishment on highway right-of-way slopes—a review. Highw. Res. Rec. 161:71–103.

McCreery, R. A., E. G. Diseker, and R. M. Lawrence, Jr. 1975. Mulch treatments. GDOT Res. Proj. no. 6907, Dep. of Agron., Univ. of Georgia, Athens.

McKee, W. H., R. E. Blaser, and D. W. Barkley. 1964. Mulches for steep cut slopes. Natl. Acad. of Sci. Highw. Res. Bd., Highw. Res. 54:35–42.

McKee, W. H., R. E. Blaser, A. J. Powell, R. B. Cooper, U. Yadar, and P. Bosshart. 1965a. The establishing and maintenance of vegetation on various environments along interstate highways. Annual Rep. Virginia Agric. Exp. Stn. in cooperation with the Virginia Counc. of Highw. Invest. and Res. and U.S. Bur. of Public Roads. p. 60.

McKee, W. H., A. J. Powell, Jr., R. B. Cooper, and R. E. Blaser. 1965b. Microclimate conditions found on highway slope facings as related to adaptation of species. Natl. Acad. of Sci. Highw. Res. Bd., Highw. Res. Rec. 93:38–43.

Perry, H. D., D. L. Wright, and R. E. Blaser. 1975. Project 40: Producing vegetation on highway slopes concurrently with and subsequent to highway construction. Final Rep. Agron. Dep., Virginia Polytechnic Inst. and State Univ., Blacksburg.

Powell, A. J., R. E. Blaser, and R. E. Schmidt. 1967a. Physiology and color aspects of turf-grass with fall and winter nitrogen. Agron. J. 59:303–307.

Powell, A. J., R. E. Blaser, and R. E. Schmidt. 1967b. Effect of nitrogen on winter root growth of bentgrass. Agron. J. 59:529–530.

Schmidt, R. E., R. E. Blaser, and M. T. Carter. 1967. Evaluation of turfgrass for Virginia. Res. Div., V.P.I. Bull. 12. Agron. Dep., Virginia Polytechnic and State Univ., Blacksburg.

Schmidt, R. E., and R. E. Blaser. 1969. Ecology and turf management. *In* A. A. Hanson and F. V. Juska (eds.) Turfgrass Science Agronomy 8:217–239. Am. Soc. of Agron., Madison, Wis.

Shoop, G. J., C. R. Brooks, R. E. Blaser, and G. W. Thomas. 1961. Differential responses of grasses and legumes to liming and phosphorus fertilization. Agron. J. 53:111–115.

Smith, N. 1973. On preserving topsoil. p. 217–219. *In* Conservation tillage. Natl. Conf. Soil Conserv. Soc. of Am. 28–30 Mar. 1973, Ankeny, Iowa.

Verghese, G. K., R. E. Hanes, L. W. Zelazny, and R. E. Blaser. 1970. Sodium chloride up-take distribution in grasses as influenced by fertility and complimentary ion competition. Highw. Res. Rec. 335:13–19.

Willis, W. O., and M. Amemiya. 1973. Tillage management principles: soil temperature effects. p. 22–42. *In* Conservation tillage. Natl. Conf. Soil Conserv. Soc. of Am. 28–30 Mar. 1973, Ankeny, Iowa.

Wischmeier, W. H. 1973. Conservation tillage to control water erosion. p. 133–141. *In* Conservation tillage. Natl. Conf. Soil Conserv. Soc. of Am., 28–30 Mar. 1973, Ankeny, Iowa.

Woodruff, J. M., and R. E. Blaser. 1970a. Establishing and maintaining turf on steep slopes along Virginia highways. Annual Rep. for the Virginia Dep. of Highw. and U.S. Bur. of Public Roads, Agron. Dep., Virginia Polytechnic and State Univ., Blacksburg.

Woodruff, J. M., and R. E. Blaser. 1970b. Establishing crownvetch on steep slopes in Virginia. Natl. Acad. of Sci. Highw. Res. Bd., Highw. Res. Rec. Washington, D.C. 335: 19–28.

Woodruff, J. M., and R. E. Blaser. 1971. Stabilizing disturbed areas during highway construction for pollution control. Interim Rep. HPR Code 0754, Dep. of Agron., Virginia Polytechnic Inst. and State Univ., Res. Div., Blacksburg.

Woodruff, J. M., J. T. Green, Jr., and R. E. Blaser. 1972. Weeping lovegrass for highway slopes in the Virginias. Natl. Acad. of Sci. Highw. Res. Bd., Highway Res. Rec. Washington, D.C. 411:7–14.

Wright, D. L., H. D. Perry, J. T. Green, Jr., and R. E. Blaser. 1975. Manual for establishing a vegetative cover in highway corridors of Virginia. Virginia Polytechnic Inst. and State Univ., Blacksburg.

Zak, J. M., J. Troll, J. R. Havis, H. M. Yegian, P. A. Kaskeski, W. W. Hamilton, and L. C. Hyde. 1972. The use of adaptable plant species for roadside cover in Massachusetts. Final Rep. 23-R5-Roadside Dev. Univ. of Massachusetts, Amherst.

Chapter 32

Reclamation of Lands Mined for Phosphate

EUGENE E. FARMER AND WILLIAM G. BLUE

*Forest Service, USDA,
Intermountain Forest and Range Experiment Station, Logan, Utah, and
University of Florida, Gainesville, Florida*

I. INTRODUCTION

In 1973, the United States production of phosphate rock was about 3.8×10^7 metric tons. This was about 39% of the world total. The United States has four major phosphate rock-producing areas: (i) Florida, (ii) North Carolina, (iii) Tennessee, and (iv) the western States of Idaho, Montana, Utah, and Wyoming. The production in the western area primarily comes from the State of Idaho. Phosphate rock statistics for the Florida and North Carolina areas are usually lumped together. Of the United States production in 1973, the combined Florida and North Carolina areas produced 81.7%, Tennessee produced 6.0%, and the western area 12.3%.

Phosphate rock production in the United States is not a static figure but is affected by market conditions and world production, primarily by the phosphate production in Morocco. However, trends in United States production have been forecast by the Bureau of Mines, U.S. Department of Interior (Stowasser, 1975) (Fig. 1). This forecast is based on present production rates, future production plans, demand projections, and estimated phosphate reserves based on current economics. Phosphate reserves are often based on market price and mining costs. By definition, a phosphate reserve is a deposit that can be economically mined today, but a phosphate resource is a deposit that could be mined only if the product price was higher or mining costs were lower (J. L. Weaver in a presentation to the Am. Chem. Soc., New York, N.Y., 6 Apr. 1976).

The projections shown in Fig. 1 indicate that phosphate production in the western area and North Carolina is trending upward all the way to the year 2015. Tennessee production will terminate in about 1990. Only short-term Florida phosphate production will trend upward; phosphate production is expected to start a steep downward slide about 1995. Phosphate demand in the United States is expected to exceed production for

585

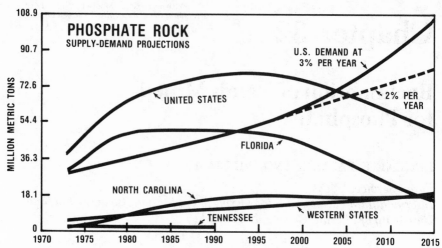

Fig. 1—Projected United States phosphate demand and supply from the major producing areas.

the first time between the years of 2000 and 2005. Of particular interest to this paper is the more than 50 % increase in phosphate rock production in the United States between the years 1976 and 1997. This is indicative of the large job of reclaiming land mined for phosphate. Reclamation technology should be supplying solutions to problems right now. In many cases, technology is supplying answers, in others, technology is being developed. But some problems are not being approached nor even worked on.

Reclamation problems in each of the four major producing areas are, in some respects, unique to each area. However, there are other problems that are, or will be, common among the geographic areas. These are covered in the following pages.

Fortunately, a good deal of reclamation know-how already exists. We were impressed on several occasions with imaginative approaches to reclamation problems by mining companies or land management agencies. Unfortunately, much of this information is poorly documented. Too much reclamation information either is not disseminated or is passed along by word of mouth. Consequently, simple, but important, mistakes are made over and over. Nearly all revegetation failures are preventable. That is, the reasons for failure can be identified and corrected.

Lastly, *revegetation* is often used synonymously with *reclamation*. The words are not synonyms. Land reclamation means more than simple revegetation; it also implies an intended land use. In most cases, Tennessee excepted, the intended use of reclaimed mined-out lands is so vaguely stated and poorly defined that full reclamation is the exception rather than the rule. However, until the uses of reclaimed lands are better defined, vegetative stabilization serves a vital function. It preserves the alternatives of future land uses so that such uses can be selected by future generations. We owe future generations that much.

II. WESTERN PHOSPHATE AREA (IDAHO, WYOMING, UTAH, MONTANA)

Phosphorite deposits occur in the marine phosphoria formation of Permian age (225 million years ago) in Idaho, Wyoming, Utah, and Montana. These deposits crop out over an area of approximately 350,000 km² in the four states and represent one of the largest available reserves of phosphate rock in the world (Coffman & Service, 1967; Popoff & Service, 1965; Service, 1966; Service & Petersen, 1967; Service & Popoff, 1964).

A significant part of the phosphate rock in the western phosphate area occurs in southeastern Idaho (Day, 1973). Idaho contains about 80% of the reserves of the western field and about 35% of the United States reserves. Idaho reserves are estimated at slightly over 1 billion metric tons using the current economics and mining technology. Most of the present mining and proposals for new mining operations are located near the town of Soda Springs, Idaho.

A. Physiography and Vegetation

The western phosphate field is in the Middle Rocky Mountains physiographic province. The Idaho portion of the western field is characterized by a series of north- and northwest-trending mountain ranges and valleys. In the area around Soda Springs, Idaho, the local relief may be as great as 600 m and the elevation of the entire area is over 1,370 m. The highest point in the western phosphate field is nearly 3,950 m in elevation.

The sagebrush-grass vegetative type predominates in the valleys, although marshland sometimes occurs along bottomlands. With increasing elevation, the sagebrush-grass type grades into the mountain-brush cover type. This gradation occurs at elevations between 1,500 and 2,130 m. The conifer-aspen type occupies the highest elevations.

B. Climate

Climate of the western field is strongly affected by the north- and south-trending mountain ranges and valleys. These mountain ranges are almost perpendicular to the prevailing west and northwest winds. Variability of climate between valley and mountain locations is pronounced. Mean annual precipitation ranges from about 25 cm in some of the drier valley bottoms to about 127 cm in some mountain locations. Precipitation tends to increase with increasing elevation, but the relationship is variable depending upon aspect, height of the ridgetops, slope steepness, and direction of prevailing winds, among other things. Increased precipitation at higher elevations is more pronounced in winter than in summer. Usually less than half of the annual precipitation falls during the warm season (May–Oct.). Most of the cold season (Nov.–Apr.) precipitation falls as snow—the proportion increasing with altitude.

The growing season (nonfreezing period) averages 142 days at Pocatello, Idaho, one of the warmest points in the western field. At many mountain locations, the growing season is less than 60 days. Temperatures of less than 0°C have been recorded during every month of the year at Conda, Idaho, and Afton, Wyoming, both valley locations. Frost hazard persists all summer at all elevations over 2,130 m. Maximum summer temperatures are generally warm at all elevations, but large (19°C) diurnal temperature ranges, caused by cloudless days and radiation cooling at night, are common. Minimum winter temperatures are influenced by arctic air masses moving down the west side of the Rocky Mountains. These arctic air masses may bring several consecutive days of subzero temperatures. At Afton, Wyoming (1,864 m elevation), the record cold temperature is −48°C.

C. Soils

For the most part, soils of the western phosphate field have not been mapped in detail. There are at least 16, and probably more great soil groups, that range from desertic Sierozen soils (Aridisols) to the cold, subhumid gray-wooded soils (Alfisols). In the major phosphate areas of southeastern Idaho, the principal great soil groups are the subhumid chernozem and chestnut prairie soils (Mollisols) and the gray-wooded soils (Alfisols). On these soils, organic matter accumulates rapidly and the soil surface horizons are thick and dark. On the steepest slopes, the soils are immature lithosols (Entisols) and regosols (Inceptisols).

Most of the soils underlying forest and brush vegetative types are residual and have developed from sedimentary parent materials—limestone, cherts, and sandstone. Soil pH is nearly neutral, ranging from slightly basic to slightly acid.

Since surface mining for phosphate violently disrupts the surface soils, the properties of the subsoils and parent materials become even more important than the properties of the surface soils. Unfortunately, information on subsoils is even more sketchy than information on surface soils. However, it is important to note that subsoil phytotoxicity is rare to nonexistent. Very dark waste shale materials can create revegetation problems because of high summertime surface temperatures when they are placed on the surface of waste dumps. However, the current practice is to bury these dark materials.

D. Mining Methods and Technology

In the western phosphate area, the sedimentary beds have been severely faulted and folded by crustal deformation. Local sections may dip at any angle from nearly horizontal to vertical. Erosion has occasionally exposed the phosphate-bearing formations in narrow bands along the flanks of the simpler folds or in the irregular fringes of the more complexly folded and faulted areas. Except for an underground mine in Montana, all of the phosphate ore is stripmined. Most of the mines use scrapers and bulldozers to remove the overburden and to mine the phosphate ore. In southeastern Idaho, the main bed ores, suitable for use in wet-process phosphoric acid plants, and furnace shale, used in electric furnaces for the recovery of elemental phosphorus, are selectively mined.

The phosphate ore is classified as main bed ore if the grade is from 31 to 32% P_2O_5, and as furnace shale if the grade is 24 to 26% P_2O_5. The furnace shale is usually nodulized preparatory to charging the elemental phosphorus-producing electric furnaces. Furnace shale may also be beneficiated to produce a 31 to 32% P_2O_5 grade product for wet-process phosphoric acid manufacture. Main bed ores may also be mixed with low grade furnace shales to produce a product suitable for producing elemental phosphorus in the electric furnaces. Ore mined in the western field is usually hauled by truck or moved by rail to the processing plants.

Adverse environmental impacts of phosphate mining are associated with the construction of overburden waste dumps, often in mountainous terrain, and with the construction of transportation systems and plant and safety facilities. Of these, the waste dumps pose the greatest problems of reclamation and the greatest chance for greatly accelerated soil erosion with consequent deterioration of water quality and impacts on stream fisheries. Reduced soil productivity and adverse effects on mountain esthetics are thought to be additional reclamation problems, but their extent and severity are still unresolved.

E. Plant Species Adapted to Waste Dump Revegetation

Reclamation of overburden waste dumps resulting from stripmining is a relatively new undertaking in the western field. Prior to 1970, if revegetation of waste dumps was undertaken, it was often as an afterthought conducted on a trial and error basis. More recently, this situation has changed and the operating companies include reclamation planning in their overall mining plans. Beginning in about 1970, the Forest Service in cooperation with several companies initiated a systematic search for answers to the reclamation problems of waste dumps (USDA For. Serv., 1971). Part of this search centers on plant species adapted to the newly created waste dumps. Although the list is not exhaustive, the plant species in Table 1 appear to offer considerable promise of sustaining a permanent, self-repairing, surface-stabilizing plant cover, especially when seeded onto dumps that have been topdressed with 20 to 30 cm of topsoil or loamy middle waste shale materials.

Particularly in southeastern Idaho, but throughout the western phosphate field, there are many differing viewpoints on the desirability of using native instead of introduced species and of using alfalfa. Opinions also vary as to which species and mixtures of species to use when revegetating waste dumps. These questions have not been resolved. However, it seems clear that mining companies will have to use seed mixtures or plant-

Table 1—Plant species adapted to waste dump vegetation

Native species	Introduced species
Grasses	
Basin wildrye (*Elymus cinereus* Scribn. and Merr.)	Timothy (*Phleum pratense* L.)
Mountain brome (*Bromus marginatus* Nees; Steud.)	Orchardgrass (*Dactylis glomerata* L., Europe)
Western wheatgrass (*Agropyron smithii* Jones)	Smooth brome, Manchar (*Bromus inermis* Leyss., Europe)
Rough fescue (*Festuca scrabrella* Torr.; Hook.)	Intermediate wheatgrass (*Agropyron intermedium* [Host] Beauv., ESS)
Squirreltail (*Sitanion hystrix* J. G. Smith)	Pubescent wheatgrass (*Agropyron intermedium*, var. Luna)
Slender wheatgrass (*Agropyron trachycaulum* Steud.)	Crested wheatgrass (*Agropyron cristatum* [L.] Gaertn.)
Forbs	
None recommended at this time	Alfalfa (*Medicago sativa* L.)
	Yellow sweetclover (*Melilotus officinalis* [L.] Lam.)
Trees and shrubs	
Chokecherry (*Prunus melanocarpa* A. Nels.)	Russian olive (*Elaeagnus angustifolia* L.)
Snowberry (*Symphoricarpos occidentalis* Hook.)	Black locust (*Robina pseudo-acacia* L.)
Bitterbrush (*Purshia tridentata* [Pursh] DC.)	
Aspen (*Populus tremuloides* Michx.)	

ing stock that can be obtained through commercial sources. Unfortunately, most native grass seeds are not available commercially and native tree and shrub planting stock is only occasionally available through commercial sources. Therefore, at least for the next several years, most revegetation will be accomplished with introduced species.

F. Waste Dump Considerations

1. SORTING WASTE MATERIALS

In the western phosphate area, phosphoria formations often outcrop on mountainsides or on mountain ridges, far above the adjacent valleys. The economics of the mining operation dictate that waste overburden materials either be backfilled into the open pit or be disposed of as mountainside waste dumps. At this time, backfilling all open pits is not commonly practiced. In some cases, both the mine operator and the regulatory agencies are reluctant to backfill because, at some future date, the pit may be economically mined to greater depths. Although opinions on this practice vary, it seems both sensible and in the interests of conservation to mine the pit to the fullest possible extent even if that means keeping it open for a long time.

Construction of waste dumps is the usual method of disposing of overburden. Overburden materials are sorted for sequencing into the waste dump for two reasons: (i) to promote the mass stability of the dump and (ii) to ease dump revegetation. Mountainside waste dumps have an inherent mass stability problem due to the effects of gravity and slippage along the natural interface of ground-waste material. If a waste dump becomes saturated with water, mass stability is also reduced due to high soil-pore pressures and increased lubrication of cleavage planes within the dump or within the natural ground (Jeppson et al., 1974). The natural instabilities usually are successfully overcome by using waste chert and limestone rock for constructing the core of the dump and, where possible, by utilizing natural terrain features to stabilize the toe of the dump. After the dump has reached its final size or volume, the waste materials are topdressed with 15 to 45 cm of natural topsoils, shallow subsoil materials, or both. Or they may be topdressed with deeper lying materials (usually derived from shale parent materials) that have many soil-like features, a loamy or silty-loam texture, medium brown color, and no phytotoxic properties. In most cases, these soil-like waste shale materials are as easily revegetated as are the natural topsoils and shallow subsoils.

Sorting of waste materials for dump construction usually requires areas for the temporary storage of these wastes. However, when several dumps are under construction simultaneously, te ~~orary storage areas may not be required. In either case, building of storage areas and re-handling of wastes or increased hauling distances create additional, but unavoidable, costs.

2. SHAPING AND GRADING

Shaping and grading the slopes of waste dumps in the western field is a relatively new operation only coming into common practice in the last 5 to 6 years. Shaping and grading is done for three reasons: (i) to promote increased surface soil stability, (ii) to allow revegetation with farm-type equipment, and (iii) to increase the esthetic appeal by blending the shapes of waste dumps more neatly into the surrounding terrain. One of us (Farmer) believes that high surface-soil erodibility is one of the major causes of past reclamation failures and offers a high potential for adverse stream and fisheries impacts due to sedimentation. Shaping and grading followed by prompt and serious revegetation efforts offer the best chance of preventing these adverse impacts (Cooke et al., 1974).

3. HYDROLOGY, SOIL EROSION, AND WATER QUALITY

Research studies with hard data describing hydrologic properties and soil erosion characteristics of phosphate waste dumps are lacking. The effects of mining on surface runoff volumes, areal infiltration and percolation of water, and ground water supplies are confined to educated guesses and uninformed speculation.

Several state and federal agencies, as well as the mining companies, routinely sample springs, seepage flows, and streamflow for both chemical and physical water quality parameters. Except for one case of mass failure caused by improper waste dump construction, the authors are not aware of any serious loss of surface water quality due to mining disturbances.

G. Successful Revegetation Methods

Beginning in 1966, the Intermountain Forest and Range Experiment Station in cooperation with the Monsanto Company started a small research effort to stabilize and revegetate phosphate mining wastes in southern Idaho (USDA For. Serv., 1971). In 1972, the effort was expanded and today the research is on a continuing basis in cooperation with three companies: (i) The Monsanto Company, (ii) Beker Industries Corporation, and (iii) the Stauffer Chemical Company. The objectives of the research are:

1) To determine the minimum combination of treatments necessary to achieve an acceptable stand of grasses, forbs, and shrubs;
2) To assess the short- and long-term merits of grass mixtures consisting of (i) all introduced grasses, (ii) all native grasses, and (iii) a mixture of native and introduced grasses; and
3) To evaluate the influence of various soil cultural practices, such as seedbed preparation, upon stand establishment.

The following is a summary of the most important conclusions through 1975.

1. FERTILIZER

Fertilizer is required to promote rapid growth of newly seeded grass stands. Heavy initial grass stands are desirable both from the viewpoint of providing ground cover for erosion protection of surface soils and for providing both above- and below-ground organic matter to the waste materials. Since surface soils of mining waste dumps are practically devoid of organic matter, heavy additions in the form of surface litter and dead root systems increase the exchange capacity of the soils. This increased exchange capacity is vital to the nutrient cycling ability of these waste materials and, therefore, affects their capability for supplying needed plant nutrients on a continuing basis.

Recommended fertilizer rates are normally based on soil analyses of the waste materials. The nitrogen level of fresh overburden material is negligible; phosphorus levels are usually adequate; potassium is usually low. During the spring and early summer of the first two growing seasons, plant macronutrient levels for vigorous grass growth are adjusted to: nitrate-N—50 ppm, P—30 ppm, and K—150 ppm. This is an unrefined fertilizer prescription, but it does produce excellent grass yields.

Levels of plant micronutrients in overburden materials have not been investigated.

2. TOPSOIL

Topsoil, in the context used here, includes both natural topsoils and shallow subsoils. It also includes selected overburden materials of medium brown color, with loam or silty-loam textures. Topsoil spread to a depth of at least 20 cm over mining wastes is a desirable revegetation treatment. The highest yielding, fastest growing grass stands have invariably been on fertilized, topsoiled plots.

3. IRRIGATION

Irrigation is probably not a prerequisite for establishing acceptable grass stands during years of average precipitation. However, even in years of above average precipitation, irrigation during the late spring and early summer months will increase the yield of both new seedings and established grass stands. During dry spring periods (an unusual occurrence), irrigation could save a new seeding that would otherwise be lost. The effects of removing irrigation from grass stands established with irrigation are now being investigated. Compared with nonirrigated stands, effects during the first 2 years without irrigation do not appear to be adverse.

4. MULCH

Surface mulching of newly seeded areas with either wood fiber (hydromulching) or blown straw crimped into the soil promotes the germination and emergence of grass seedlings. These mulches also help to protect the soil surface against wind and water erosion. During the second and third years of growth, surface mulch may have a negative effect on grass yield unless sufficient nitrogen is applied to maintain an acceptable carbon/nitrogen ratio in the soil during the period of mulch decomposition. Mulch application rates between 2,500 and 3,400 kg/ha are satisfactory.

5. SEED MIXTURE

Grass seed mixtures consisting of all native species, all introduced species, or a mixture of the two, are being investigated. During the first three growing seasons, the introduced grasses produced more vegetation than the native mixture with the difference depending on other treatments, such as fertilizer and mulch. On fertilized, topsoiled plots differences in the production of native and introduced grasses are small, about 4%. Also, there are several items other than grass production that deserve consideration. These include the long-term ability to survive adverse conditions of soil chemistry, climate, insects, and disease. Definitive evaluation of grass mixtures will take longer than 3 years. Perhaps the most important question to be answered is to what degree the initial seed mixture affects the ability of the resulting stands to perpetuate a self-repairing ground cover that will protect the surface against erosion. The resulting stands should also provide other values, such as forage, and wildlife cover, with the least maintenance inputs. As yet, the initial seed mixture cannot be evaluated in these terms.

6. SEEDING RATE

Seeding rates varying from 28 to 100 kg/ha are being evaluated. To date the results are inconclusive. However, optimum seeding rates are influenced by many variables, such as planting method, season of planting, fertilizer rate, and whether or not a surface mulch is used. Seeding rate also appears to have an influence on weed density—high rates of grass seed discourage weeds. During one growing season, no adverse effects have been detected from the 100 kg/ha seeding rate. Pending a more refined recommendation, we are currently advising seeding rates of 45 to 55 kg/ha for fall plantings on fertilized, unmulched sites.

7. SEASON OF PLANTING

Spring plantings have not been investigated very thoroughly. However, the recommended planting season is from late September until snowfall. A few of the mining companies do employ spring seeding with apparent success. However, in the authors' experience fall-planted grasses are more productive and vigorous than spring-planted grasses, especially in the first two growing seasons.

8. SITE PREPARATION

The degree of success of a revegetation effort is strongly influenced by site preparation. Mine waste dumps present an undesirable environment for plant growth that can best be overcome with a "farming" approach. Very steep slopes (steeper than 2.5:1) are incompatible with a farming approach for several reasons: (i) slopes steeper than about 2.5:1 cannot be safely worked on the contour (rollover hazard); (ii) seed and fertilizer are moved through erosional processes resulting in poor seedling distribution (bare spots); and (iii) seeder-packers or seed drills do not operate properly on very steep slopes when operated on the contour (poor seed planting). Therefore, we recommend that waste dumps be constructed so that the faces are not steeper than 2.5:1.

It is often necessary to rip the surface materials to allow water, air, and root penetration into the mining wastes. The depth of ripping is conditioned by the measured soil bulk densities. At bulk densities over 1.65 g/cm^3, we recommend ripping to about 50 cm. At bulk densities of about 1.4 g/cm^3, ripping to 30 cm is usually sufficient. Lower bulk densities do not require ripping. However, the surface bulk density of most waste dumps is greater than 1.4 g/cm^3.

After ripping, the site should be thoroughly harrowed, first to a depth of about 10 to 15 cm and then again to about 5 cm. This operation loosens up the surface and granulates the soil for a fine seedbed. We have had good success with the vibrating-shank type of harrow, such as the Swedish Triple-K. Standard springtooth harrows are less suited for seedbed preparation at mine dumps.

Seeding and then firming the seed into the seedbed can be accomplished in one operation with either a seeder-packer or a seed drill. We have had good success with the seeder-packer and recommend its use over the seed drill whenever the seed mixture is composed of a wide range of seed sizes. Since the seeder-packer plants at multiple depths at least some seeds in every size class are planted at the proper depth.

H. Land Use on Reclaimed Mining Disturbances

Mining disturbances in the western phosphate area are predominantly situated on wild lands, both forest and range lands. A small amount of mining is located adjacent to agricultural lands, mostly hay land. Therefore, the major use of reclaimed areas is grazing by both domestic and wild animals. These areas also offer a limited amount of wildlife cover. Urbanization with the subsequent demand for more intensive uses of reclaimed mining disturbances is not expected in the foreseeable future.

III. TENNESSEE

Of the three major phosphate-producing areas of the United States, Tennessee produces the least. In 1975, Tennessee produced 5% of the total phosphate rock mined in the United States. The commercial phosphate deposits in Tennessee are expected to be depleted by the year 2000 if the present levels of production are maintained.

The Tennessee phosphate deposits are Ordovician, some 400 million years old (Smith & Whitlatch, 1940). The deposits were originally of marine origin but have been altered, probably several times. That is, the phosphate deposits were eroded, dissolved, and reprecipitated. In the Ordovician period, the area of what is now central Tennessee, from Alabama to Kentucky, was dominated by a huge geologic arch, the Cincinnati Arch (Wilson, 1973). This arch ran through the areas that are now Columbia, Franklin, and Nashville, Tennessee. Through geologic time, the Cincinnati Arch was uplifted above the ancient ocean level. The uplifting and faulting cracked the arch and weathering and erosional processes were begun. The Cincinnati Arch contained multiple limestone deposits, two of which contained phosphoria. These phosphoria deposits, weathered through geologic time, were moved and redeposited or reprecipitated. Most of the original deposits were undoubtedly lost, washed into the Gulf of Mexico. The modern-day phosphoria deposits are scattered and relatively small in areal coverage. Commercial deposits run from less than 1 ha up to as large as 40 ha, probably averaging about 8 ha.

Phosphate overburden depths range from zero to 6 m, averaging 2.5 m in thickness. Ore deposits run to 7.5 m thick, but average about 1.8 m.

The ore is not mined if the ratio of overburden to ore exceeds 3 to 1. The overburden materials are stripped off by a dragline with a capacity of about 2 m³, and the ore is dug with the same equipment. Blasting is not necessary. Ore is trucked directly to the beneficiating plants or trucked to a railhead. At the beneficiating plant, the ore is slurried, washed, and classified at 325 mesh to increase the grade before it is processed. All of the phosphate rock produced in Tennessee goes into electric furnaces for the production of elemental phosphorus. After being washed and classified, the ore is dried and nodulized before charging the electric furnaces.

A. Physiography and Climate

The central basin of Tennessee, from the Tennessee River Valley on the west to the Cumberland Plateau on the east is a rolling plain averaging about 183 m in elevation. Elevations range from about 90 to 300 m.

In middle Tennessee, the average annual precipitation varies from 115 to 127 cm. The precipitation is almost evenly distributed over the year. The cold season (Oct.–Mar.) receives about 55% of the total while the warm season (Apr.–Sept.) receives about 45%. October is the driest month (5.6 cm) and January is the wettest (14.7 cm). At Franklin, Tennessee, the average growing season (above-freezing period) is 192 days, from mid-April well into October. The average January maximum and minimum temperatures are 10 and −1°C, respectively. For July, the average maximum and minimum temperatures are 32 and 19°C, respectively. This climate is very favorable for the revegetation of mining disturbances.

B. Revegetation

Frequently, phosphate mining in middle Tennessee is done in close association with agriculture. Reclaimed mining lands probably are most frequently used for pasture or grain production.

It can be fairly stated that the major problems of reclaiming land mined for phosphate in middle Tennessee have been resolved.

The majority of phosphate lands in middle Tennessee are privately owned and any single deposit constitutes a relatively small acreage. The original land owner usually retains title to the land, selling only the phosphoria. The owner also frequently specifies the vegetation to be used in the postmining reclamation. However, reclamation must also comply with regulations of the State of Tennessee, Division of Surface Mining.

Grading overburden piles and shaping them back to the approximate original land configuration follow closely behind the mining operation. State regulations allow no more than 90 days between mining and reclamation grading on any given area. Since fall (Sept. and Oct.) is the preferred season for reseeding, graded lands usually sit fallow until that time. Spring seeding is also used, usually at the request of the land owner. Agricultural limestone at the rate of 2200 kg/ha may be applied, followed by fertilizer. Ammonium nitrate and potash are commonly used, each at the rate of 112 kg/ha. The lime and fertilizer are disked into the soil and the site is harrowed.

Reseeding is done with a seed drill. The vegetation species most frequently used is fescue (*Festuca* spp.) orchardgrass, and sericea lespedeza (*Lespedeza cuneata* [Dum.-Cours.] G. Don). Spring seedings may employ weeping lovegrass (*Eragrotis* Beauv. *curvula* [Schrad.] Nees.) and sorghum (*Sorghum* spp. L. Moench). Seeding rates vary from 56 to 112 kg/ha depending upon the rockiness of the site; stoney soils receive the heavier seeding rates. Occasionally reclaimed lands can be sowed directly to a small grain crop, usually barley (*Hordeum vulgare* L.) or oats (*Avena sativa* L.). More often the site is held in grass cover for several years before growing grain crops.

Prior to 1967, there were no state regulations controlling surface mining. As a result, there are some unreclaimed, nonagricultural lands mined for phosphate in Tennessee. This acreage is not known to the authors, but it is probably relatively small. Even on abandoned mining areas, there is a heavy cover of volunteer vegetation.

Perhaps the largest unresolved reclamation problem of phosphate mining in middle Tennessee concerns the slime ponds that result from ore beneficiation. The phosphate slimes are clays and silts held behind earthfill dams at depths of from 9 to 60 m. Each pond may be several hundred hectares in size. These phosphatic clays are extremely slow drying, their revegetation potential is low, and their sole value is to provide wildlife habitat for birds and small mammals. Cattails and willows rapidly invade these ponds. With the present reclamation technology these ponds cannot be returned to a more productive use for a very long time—perhaps 20 to 30 years—after their construction. Slime pond reclamation presents the largest challenge and the greatest opportunity in the whole field of phosphate mining reclamation.

IV. NORTH CAROLINA

The phosphate deposits of North Carolina were deposited as chemical precipitates in a restricted marine basin with water depths from about 46 to 183 m. The deposits date from the middle Miocene age (15 million years ago). They are located largely in Beaufort County on both sides of the Pamlico River. The phosphorite lies within the Atlantic Coastal Plain sequence, which, in Beaufort County, is approximately monoclinal with a slight eastward dip.

The phosphorite formation, called the Pungo River Formation, covers approximately 181,000 ha. The formation ranges in thickness from a few centimeters on the west side to over 36 m near the south shore of the Pamlico River. The overburden varies from 12 to 70 m in thickness, but 18 to 30 m is typical in the deposits now being mined. The Pungo River Formation is composed of interbedded phosphatic sands, silts, and clays, diatomaceous clays, and phosphatic limestone.

A stratigraphic and paleoenvironmental study of the Pungo River

Formation (Gibson, 1967) correlates the foraminifera and mollusca of the formation with those of other stratigraphic units. These studies have led to the conclusion that the phosphate beds were laid down in cool waters ranging in depth to 183 m. The deposition took place within a marine basin.

Examinations by Rooney and Kerr (1967) also suggest chemical precipitation in a large shallow lagoon or estuary. The phosphate mineral francolite formed colloidal agglomerates with small ocean organisms and settled to the sea floor as pellets less than 4 mm in diameter. Other evidence suggests that the phosphorite deposits were later altered, possibly by intermittent breaching of the ancient lagoon barrier. The presence of volcanic glass implies a relationship between the phosphorite and ancient marine volcanoes. Perhaps a widespread ashfall of long duration killed great numbers of marine organisms. Their subsequent decay contributed additional phosphate. Except for minor variations, the phosphorite is an uncemented mixture of sand-sized phosphate pellets, sand- and silt-sized quartz grains, and clay minerals.

Phosphate reserves of the Pungo River Formation are variously estimated as ranging between 1.8 and 4.5 billion metric tons. The phosphate resources of the area, that is, those deposits that cannot now be economically mined, may reach 9 billion metric tons. Regardless of the accuracy of these estimates, it seems clear that phosphate mining in the Pungo River Formation will be carried on for a long time.

A. Climate

The climate of the North Carolina phosphate area is strongly moderated by its proximity to the Atlantic Ocean. The elevation ranges from sea level to about 15 m. The average annual precipitation at New Bern, North Carolina, is about 140 cm. The warm season (Apr.–Sept.) is slightly wetter than the cold season (Oct.–Mar.). On the average, 60% of the annual precipitation occurs during the warm season and 40% during the cold season. October is the driest month (8 cm) and July is the wettest (21 cm). At New Bern, North Carolina, the length of the freeze-free period is 241 days, from late March to mid-November. The average January maximum and minimum temperatures are 15 and 2°C, respectively. For July the average maximum and minimum temperatures are 32 and 22°C.

B. Mining Methods and Technology

North Carolina phosphate is mined by removing the surface 12 m of overburden using an electric-powered dredge with a 76-cm cutter head. The dredged material is pumped as a slurry into previously mined areas and is used as landfill. After the dredging operation, the area is drained in preparation for mining with draglines. Draglines remove the remaining 12 to 18 m of overburden material and cast it into an adjacent just-mined cut. The phosphoritic material is also dug with a dragline and the ore is piled on the bank of the dragline cut. A second dragline is used to feed the ore from the storage pile into a sump, where high-pressure water jets are used to slurry the ore. The ore is then pumped in a pipeline to the wash plant. The ore is screened to remove oversize particles and is washed (200 mesh) to remove the clay and silt. After washing, the phosphate ore goes through a flotation process where the quartz sand is separated from the phosphate. The phosphate concentrate is either calcined to remove carbonaceous material or dried.

At this point, the ore is either ready for shipment to customers in bulk or as feedstock for the fertilizer plant. The beneficiating operation has also produced two waste products, sand tailings and phosphate slimes.

Essentially all phosphate rock produced for domestic consumption is used to produce wet-process phosphoric acid. Sulphuric acid digests phosphate rock. The products are phosphoric acid and a waste impure gypsum. The phosphoric acid can be processed to produce other fertilizers, such as triple superphosphate or diammonium phosphate.

C. Revegetation and Stabilization

Reclamation of the North Carolina lands mined for phosphate has proceeded by fits and starts. On the one hand, there are few good examples of reclamation of mined land, although more than 49 ha are said to have been reclaimed. On the other hand, the development of a new industry on a new and atypical phosphate deposit is fraught with difficulties. This is a large operation and certainly will become the largest single producer of phosphate rock in the United States. Mining and reclamation plans have evolved since the mine was opened in 1966. Mined lands are comprised of revegetated areas of varying success, areas undergoing reclamation, dredged lakes, and gypsum storage piles.

The mining operation produces four waste products: (i) normal overburden, (ii) sand tailings, (iii) phosphatic clay slimes, and (iv) waste gypsum. Each waste has its own revegetation and reclamation problems.

Overburden wastes can probably be revegetated and stabilized without great difficulty. These materials are coarse textured and will tend to be somewhat droughty and possess a low soil cation exchange capacity. These are certainly not new problems to the field of mined land reclamation. Lime is necessary on native topsoils that are used for reclamation purposes. However, lime is not used on overburden materials and sand tailings. Seed mixtures of tall fescue (Festuca spp. [Torr.] Hook.), ladino clover [Trifolium repens L. forma lodigense (Hort. ex Gams.)], and annual rye (Lolium spp. L.) drilled on well-fertilized overburden should do well. Coastal bermudagrass (Cynodon sp. Rich) has been sprigged during the spring and has provided forage for cattle during the summer. Both initial and maintenance fertilization programs will probably be necessary. Long-term land productivity as compared to levels before mining is an unresolved question. However, a revegetation program aimed toward building levels of soil organic matter should yield soils of acceptable quality for agriculture or forestry. A new scheme, mixing phosphatic clays with the overburden materials, is expected to achieve marked increases in soil productivity.

Sand tailings will be used primarily as landfill. However, it is highly probable that sand tailings will also be left on the surface, requiring revegetation and stabilization. If the phosphatic slimes can successfully be mixed with sand tailings on an operational scale, the reclamation problems will be greatly diminished. Slimes have already been mixed with sand tailings on a pilot scale. Slime mixing is a difficult operation. Slimes are slurried at 5 to 8% solids. If they are run in on sand tailings, they simply float on the surface of the sand. As the fines settle out, they seal the surface pores. After the water evaporates, the residue is a hard, much-cracked, thin crust. If sand tailings are run in on slime slurries, the slimes float to the surface around the edge of the sand tailings. The final result is the same as that just mentioned.

One mixing method under test consists of running a slime slurry onto dredged overburden or sand tailings. After the surface water has drained, the slurry is worked with crawler tractors pulling large agricultural disks. The mixing operation takes considerable time, effort, and money. As the surface layers dry out, the operation is repeated. Slime mixing has two desirable effects: (i) the mixture of slime and sand has a significantly greater cation exchange capacity and nutrient cycling ability than sand tailings alone, and (ii) it will reduce the magnitude of the slime disposal problem. However, with all candor, the influence of mixing slime with sand tailings will have small influence on the total slime disposal problem.

The problems of reclaiming slime ponds will be covered under the "Florida" section (V.) of this paper. At this point, let it suffice to state that slime ponds represent a very difficult problem. Reclamation answers are being pursued by both the phosphate industry and by governmental agencies. The problems remain unresolved. In North Carolina, one 300-ha slime pond is expected to be filled in 1976. A new, larger pond is under construction.

One of the basic goals of reclamation is to create a soil that will have the potential to grow most crops adapted to the area. Reclamation programs are aimed at building higher levels of soil cation exchange capacity and water-holding capacity. Such soils will probably be of acceptable quality for agriculture and forestry.

Whenever phosphate rock is reacted with sulphuric acid to produce phosphoric acid, an impure gypsum waste also results. This gypsum is a byproduct of every wet-process phosphoric acid fertilizer plant. Gypsum piles may be unobtrusive around small fertilizer plants. However, near Aurora, North Carolina, the gypsum pile is imposing, and it grows by some 2 million metric tons per year. Currently, it is probably the largest single object along the Coastal Plain of North Carolina. The osmotic potential, pH, and mineral impurities probably make revegetation impossible. A small amount of the gypsum is used as a peanut fertilizer. The material is only marginally suitable for wallboard. The use of the waste gypsum as a landfill is being investigated, but that use seems unlikely. How, or whether, these gypsum piles can ever be put to some productive use is unknown. American ingenuity is challenged to either put this waste material to use as a raw material or to perform the cosmetic and stabilizing effect of vegetating the waste.

The last reclamation consideration to be mentioned for North Carolina involves the amount of sand or overburden materials physically available for reclamation. The general premining level of the area presently being mined is only a few meters (perhaps 3) above sea level. The bottom of the phosphorite bed is as deep as 50 m. Obviously, the mining operation is being accomplished largely below sea level. Approximately 40% of the phosphate ore is usable production and is removed from the site as a marketable product. An additional 20% of the ore is phosphatic slimes and is stored on the surface. Therefore, only the overburden materials and approximately 40% of the original phosphate ore are available for the creation of new lands. In order to maintain above sea level elevations for the newly created lands, a substantial fraction of the mined area will have to be reclaimed as freshwater lakes; the water will be supplied by surface runoff and the underlying aquifer. If mining continues, there appears to be no alternative, unless the gypsum byproduct can be used as landfill.

Short-term land use on reclaimed lands will probably involve farm (pasture) or forest lands situated in a land-and-lakes setting. The reclaimed lands are also suitable for either residential or commercial use.

V. FLORIDA

A. Physiography

Florida's phosphate deposits were apparently derived from the Alum Bluff Formation of the middle Miocene Epoch. This formation has been described as being composed of micaceous sand, sandy clay, Fuller's earth, and phosphate limestone (Cooke, 1945). The Alum Bluff Formation is subdivided into three formations including the Hawthorn Formation in Peninsular Florida. The Hawthorn Formation varies in thickness from approximately 65 to 130 m. It was deposited on Tampa limestone and sometimes on Ocala limestone. The Hawthorn Formation is the parent material from which hard rock phosphate of north Peninsular Florida (Sellards, 1913a, 1913b) and the central Peninsular Florida pebble phosphate deposits (Sellards, 1914) were derived. It also forms the bedrock on which the pebble phosphate lies. The pebble phosphate beds are residual from erosion of the Hawthorn Formation and are referred to as the *Bone Valley Formation* of the Pliocene Epoch. The hard rock phosphate was apparently formed by dissolution of phosphate from the Hawthorn Formation and reprecipitation in solution holes in the underlying limestone. At the end of the Miocene Epoch, the entire Florida peninsula was dry land, but its extension was only to the vicinity of Tampa. The typical part of the Bone Valley Formation apparently was deposited as a result of solution and erosion in a broad delta of a stream that opened southward into the ocean. A large part of the phosphate was laid down outside the estuary in the open sea and has not been well defined or exploited. The Bone Valley Formation, which averages 3 to 4 m in thickness (Matson, 1915), is overlain by sandy materials from marine terraces of the Pleistocene Epoch. According to Cooke (1945), five marine terraces ranging in elevation from 8 to 55 m are involved. The central Florida Peninsular pebble phosphate area is located primarily in Polk, Hillsborough, and Hardee Counties and is approximately 80 km in the north-south direction and 64 km in the east-west direction. More recently, pebble phosphate has been discovered in Hamilton County in north Florida.

B. Climate

The climate in the central Florida Peninsular phosphate mining area is subtropical. Temperatures are moderated by lakes, the Gulf of Mexico, and the Atlantic Ocean. Mean annual temperature is about 22°C with a minimum of 16°C in January and a maximum of 27°C in July and August. The average date of the first killing frost is 9 Dec. and the last is 14 Feb. Rainfall averages about 133 cm/year with extremes ranging from approximately 100 to 180 cm/year. Rainfall is seasonal with about 60% occurring from June through September.

C. Soils

Soils in this area have developed from unconsolidated marine sand terraces of the Pleistocene Epoch that cover the Bone Valley Formation (Leighty et al., 1950; Patrick & Mikkelson, 1971; Fowler et al., 1927). The terraces are the Coharie, 55.8 to 70.5 m elevation; Sunderland, 32.8 to 55.8 m; Wicomico, 23.0 to 32.8 m; Penholaway, 13.8 to 23.0 m; Talbot, 8.2 to 13.8 m; and Pamlico, 8.2 m. The higher terraces, which extend down the center of the Peninsula, indicate thick layers of sand over the colloidal material in the Hawthorn Formation; thus, water passes through the sands and into small lakes and streams creating deep, well-drained soils. The Lakeland soil series is characteristic of this area. Most of the pebble phosphate mining is currently carried out at elevations of 32.8 to 49.2 m. The soils over the actual mining area have developed on the Sunderland and Wicomico Terraces. The land on these lower terraces is relatively flat and, because of the proximity of layers with finely divided material, poorly drained. These areas are generally termed *flatwoods* and soils are primarily Spodosols. Myakka, Immokalee, and Ona are soil series characteristic of the Spodosols. There are slightly raised knolls and ridges interspersed within the flatwoods that give rise to soils of somewhat better drainage typified by the Blanton Series. Shallow ponds caused by solution of the underlying limestone are also interspersed in the flatwoods. With the exception of some soils that are influenced by shallow marl or phosphate deposits, soil series are not confined to a particular marine terrace.

Native vegetation (Henderson, 1939) on the Spodosols consists of longleaf pine (*Pinus australis* Michx. f.), wiregrass (*Aristida* spp.), *Sporo-*

bolus spp., saw palmetto (*Serenoa repens* Bartr. Small), gallberry (*Ilex glabra* L.), and runner oak (*Quercus minima* Sarg.). The higher knolls within the flatwoods characteristically are covered with longleaf pine, turkey oak (*Quercus cinera* Michx.), runner oak, and wiregrass. The ponded areas are dominated by cypress (*Taxodium asendens* Brough.) and transitional areas are covered with longleaf pine, cypress, and wax myrtle (*Myrica cerifera* L.) intermixed.

D. Mining Methods and Residue Reclamation

Pebble phosphate in Florida is mined by removing the overburden with large draglines that have 30- to 36-m^3 capacities. The overburden is usually placed in mined-out areas (land from which the phosphate matrix has been removed). The matrix, which consists of approximately one-third each of usable phosphate, quartz sand, and colloidal phosphate and clay (Hortenstine & Rothwell, 1972), is then excavated and dumped into a depression where it is dispersed by high-pressure water jets. The entire matrix (phosphate pebbles, clay, and quartz sand) is then moved hydraulically from the mine to the beneficiation plant where the phosphate particles are separated by a series of processes, including washing, screening, and flotation. The remaining material includes quartz sand and the clay-colloidal size phosphate mixture, which constitutes the slimes or colloidal phosphate (U.S. Dep. of Interior, 1975). These materials are disposed of separately since they will not remain physically mixed. The slime is moved hydraulically at 2 to 5% solids from the beneficiation plant to large retaining ponds, generally constructed on land already mined. This fine material settles rather rapidly and the supernatant water is reused in phosphate processing. Approximately 40,000 liters of water are used per metric ton of phosphate product; approximately 80% of the water is recycled and 20% is new water needed because of water retention by the colloidal material. The slime, which may be 10 to 15 m deep in the retaining ponds, dewaters very slowly. After several years, it may reach a concentration of only 20 to 30% solids. The dikes for the retaining ponds are constructed with water control structures extending above the slime surface in the pond and under the dike; these may be opened to remove surface water and drainage may be adjusted as the surface is lowered by loss of internal water.

Vegetation develops rapidly on the pond surface. Islands of cattails (*Typha latifolia*) may become established in ponds still in the filling stage. As the slime surface dries, woody species including a willow (*Salix* spp.) and wax myrtle become abundant. Reclamation of the slime ponds presents a difficult problem.

The quartz sand is also moved hydraulically from the beneficiation plant to the disposal area at 30 to 40% solids. Much of it is returned to mined-out areas. Water drains readily from the sand; individual piles of loose, unconsolidated sand, which are frequently in excess of 20 m above the original soil surface, cover large areas. These sands, if ideally processed, are essentially devoid of plant nutrients and become extremely dry during the dry season. Observed vegetation has consisted mostly of poorly developed bunches of natal grass (*Rhynchedytrum repens* [Willd.]) and a few sparsely growing unidentified weeds.

Mining of the pebble phosphate began about 1890. Wang et al. (1974) indicated that over 36,500 ha of land had been mined by 1974 in central and north Florida and that 1,900 ha were being mined annually. The rate of mining has been accelerated somewhat to meet demands for phosphate so that the total area mined at present is likely on the order of 40,000 ha. Approximately 1,200 ha of the 1,900 ha mined annually is used for phosphate slime disposal. Wang et al. (1974) quoted the Florida Phosphate Council as claiming that 4,000 ha of land had been reclaimed by 1965 (Sweeney, 1971), but, with continued effort toward reclamation, 26,300 ha remained unreclaimed by 1974. From these values, one can calculate that unreclaimed land is on the order of 12,000 ha. According to Wang et al. (1974), slime ponds occupy 60 to 70 % of the mined-out land. The area of unreclaimed slime ponds at present probably approaches 16,000 to 20,000 ha. Wang et al. (1974) indicated that the colloidal content of the phosphate matrix becomes less in the south-southwest direction of the central Florida deposits. New mining operations must expand in that direction so that reclamation will be somewhat less difficult in the future.

Research studies are in progress to develop techniques that will permit mixing of the colloidal material and sand tailings for disposal or to layer the slime and sand tailings. If these studies are successful, reclamation of these materials will be simplified (Custred, 1975; Lamont et al., 1975). Meanwhile, the mining companies are continuing to construct retaining dikes for disposal of the colloidal material and sand tailings separately.

Reclamation of the mined-out areas is a relatively minor problem where nothing has been done or sand tailings have been added. The major problem is an economic consideration of movement of earth. Reclamation consists of leveling or shaping the land. The quality of the resulting "soil" is variable depending on the depth of quartz sand and its mixture with more finely divided material. Organic matter could be enhanced by scraping and stock piling the surface soil (0 to 15 cm) prior to mining for subsequent spreading on the surface of reclaimed lands, but this is not generally done. The value, relative cost, and inconvenience of saving the surface soil have not been determined.

Where exposed, the sand tailing deposits represent a difficult problem from the standpoint of establishing a highly productive agricultural soil. This material is essentially quartz sand with no organic matter, very low nutrient content, and low cation exchange capacity. Hortenstine and Rothwell (1972) attempted reclamation of this material by addition of 35 and 70 metric tons/ha of municipal compost, which contained 80 % moisture and a fertilizer with N-P-K composition of 10-4.4-8.3 at 1 metric ton/ha. Yields of sorghum (*Sorghum bicolor* L. Moench) and oats were increased tremendously by these treatments, but highest yields were low compared with those expected from well-fertilized soil. Organic carbon and cation exchange capacity increase markedly by addition of municipal compost, but still remain relatively low. Since these treatments did not result in a highly productive soil, a study in progress includes dry phosphate slime incorporated at 336 metric tons/ha alone and together with organic material from a stock-piled surface soil (1.22% carbon) at 1,450 metric tons/ha and from ovendry sewage sludge (12.37% carbon) at 45 metric tons/ha, all with complete fertilization including micronutrients. Cation exchange capacity of the phosphate slime was 24 meq/100 g. Sand tailings without treatment and amended sand tailings constitute the main plots. Hopefully, some of these treatments will increase the cation exchange capacity and moisture-holding capacity sufficiently to provide an area that will be productive with normal fertilizer inputs. Warm season perennial grasses commonly used for pastures in this area, including Pensacola bahiagrass (*Paspalum notatum* Flugge), Transvala digitgrass (*Digitaria decumbens* Stent.), and selections of McCaleb stargrass (*Cynodon aethiopicus* Clayton and Harlan), UF-4 stargrass (*Cynodon nlemfluensis* Clayton and Harlan), and Callie bermudagrass (*Cynodon* spp.) have been planted as subplots. In addition, corn (*Zea mays* L.) and a sorghum-sudan grass hybrid have been used. Forage legumes are Florida 66 alfalfa (*Medicago sativa* L.), *Stylosanthes hamata* (L.) Taub., Siratro (*Macroptilium atropurpureum* DC. [Urb.]), *Vigna* spp., and *Glycine* spp.

Removal of water from the phosphate slime material is the most difficult problem associated with reclamation of phosphate mining residues. Factors customarily involved in dewatering the phosphate slimes are time, evaporation of water from the slime surface, and evapotranspiration from plants growing in the slime ponds. Plants growing on the slime surface are usually mowed as circumstances permit to increase light penetration to the surface and evaporation. This may increase drying at the surface, but does little for dewatering below the surface crust, which must be accomplished to permit operation of agricultural machinery. To maximize drying, surface water can and must be drained through the water control structures. We believe growth of these plants is limited, especially by inadequate N. We are now attempting to increase the rate of drying by use of high rates of N fertilizer superimposed on native vegetation and some introduced grass species including *Echinochloa polystachya* [(H.B.K.) Hitche] and *Hemarthria altissima* (Poir.) Stapf and Hubb.

Particle size distribution and P concentration of typical phosphate slime material are shown in the following tabulation:

Particle size, μm	Distribution, %	P content, %
> 20	6	7.0
10–20	7	7.4
6–10	7	7.4
4–6	5	7.4
2–4	5	7.9
1–2	5	7.4
< 1	65	5.2

As the phosphate slime is dewatered in a pond, shrinkage is greatest at the side furthest from the filling pipe because the smallest, most hydrated particles settle last. Thus, an elevation gradient is established that provides surface drainage. Hydraulic conductivity of the slime is extremely low as evidenced by laboratory studies. The slime is a distinct blue at depths of 30 to 40 cm, indicating an anaerobic condition. The status of flooded soils with respect to oxygen and nutrients was discussed by Patrick and Mikkelson (1971).

The objective of a current experiment with a slime pond sufficiently dry to permit reclamation is to develop a surface soil with better aeration than the slime by addition of sand and of sewage sludge. These materials will be incorporated to a depth of 22 cm. Complete fertilization including micronutrients will be used. Unamended and amended slime treatments constitute the main plots. Subplots have been planted to warm season grass species, Pensacola bahaigrass, Transvala digitgrass, McCaleb stargrass, UF-4 stargrass, and *Hemarthria altissima,* and to legumes, hairy indigo (*Indigofera hirsuta* L.), *Aeschynomene americana* L., *A. falcata* (Poir.) DC., *Stylosanthes hamata* L. Taub., and alfalfa (*Medicago sativa* L.).

None of these experiments has progressed enough for us to arrive at conclusions, but growth differences from amendments on the sand tailings were immediately apparent.

VI. OUTLOOK FOR THE FUTURE

We are optimistic about the future of reclaiming land mined for phosphate in the United States for three reasons: (i) extensive and serious efforts toward reclaiming land mined for phosphate is a relatively new activity that has only taken place in the last 10 years; (ii) large advances in revegetation and stabilization of mined land have already been made and technology transfer to potential users is proceeding; and (iii) we perceive a new sense of determination from a growing number of mining companies to turn mining wastes into productive lands for agriculture or commercial uses.

The technology for reclaiming and stabilizing overburden wastes is well developed, and has proven successful on thousands of hectares. On the other hand, it is also true that large areas of mined-out lands have been abandoned. These abandoned areas were largely mined prior to 1968. Unless the present land owners are stimulated to reclaim these areas they will probably not be reclaimed. Land reclamation is an expensive proposition and where the costs cannot be borne immediately after mining, it is not likely to be accomplished without governmental intervention.

The best examples of reclaimed lands are on overburden materials. The mining companies have developed techniques for burying the wastes that are the most difficult to revegetate and stabilize—chert rock and black shales in the western area and sand tailings in the southeastern area. Even so, some of these difficult materials are most certainly going to be left on the surface. They will require additional research and development.

Mixing of phosphatic slimes (clay and silt) with sand tailings is a promising effort now being investigated by private companies and governmental agencies. Development of a successful, operational-scale mixing method would not only improve the productivity of the resulting sand-slime mix, but would also reduce the areas required for surface storage of phosphatic slimes.

Storage ponds for phosphate slimes are a problem wherever phosphate ores are beneficiated in wet-wash plants. Currently, this is a small, practically negligible problem in the western phosphate field, but is well known in Tennessee, Florida, and North Carolina. As the western area increases production, the areas used as storage will grow. Since the western phosphate field is in mountainous terrain, storage areas will probably be confined to the more productive valley sites rather than in mountain draws.

If slime ponds represent a largely unresolved problem in the southeastern phosphate areas it should be recognized that they also represent an opportunity. The opportunity is to put thousands of hectares of land back into productive agricultural uses. Dewatering of slime ponds and reclamation for agricultural purposes are being investigated by state and federal agencies, private research organizations, and mining companies.

As a conservative estimate, more than 2.5×10^8 metric tons of by-product gypsum was in storage in the United States in 1977. Not only are these gypsum piles esthetically unappealing and occupying large storage areas, but they represent a tremendous untapped resource of P_2O_5 (1.6×10^6 metric tons), CaF_2 (3.5×10^6 metric tons), metal oxides (1.3×10^6 metric tons), and $CaCO_3$ (1.8×10^8 metric tons) (Sweeney & Timmons, 1973). It seems inconceivable to us that these materials will not be put to use at some future date. In the meantime, revegetation possibilities for both stabilization and beautification should be investigated. We are not aware of any work being done in this area.

In summary, there are good reasons for being optimistic about the future of lands mined for phosphate. No major technological problems exist, although there is room for improvement in plant macronutrient and micronutrient prescriptions, plant successional trends, long-term maintenance needs, and vegetative species selection. A further reason for optimism for lands mined in the future is the current industry practice of incorporating reclamation plans into mining plans. The importance of this hand-in-hand approach to mining and reclamation is difficult to overstate.

LITERATURE CITED

Coffman, J. S., and A. L. Service. 1967. An evaluation of the western phosphate industry and its resources (in five parts), Part 4. Wyoming and Utah. USDI, Bur. of Mines, Rep. Invest. 6934, Washington, D.C.

Cooke, C. W. 1945. Geology of Florida. Fla. Geol. Surv. Bull. 29, Tallahassee, Fla. p. 339. p. 339.

Cooke, C. W., R. M. Hyde, and P. L. Sims. 1974. Revegetation guidelines for surface mined areas. Colo. State Univ., Range Sci. Dep., Sci. Ser. 16, Fort Collins, Colo.

Custred, U. K. 1975. Land building with phosphate wastes. In C. L. Mantell (ed.) Solid wastes, Chap. VIII. 3. John Wiley and Sons, Inc., New York.

Day, R. L. 1973. Trends in the phosphate industry of Idaho and the western phosphate field. Idaho Bur. of Mines and Geol. Pamph. 55, Moscow, Idaho. 63 p.

Fowler, E. D., A. E. Taylor, E. W. Knobel, and others. 1927. Soil survey of Hillsborough County, Florida. Bur. Chem. and Soils in cooperation with the Fla. State Geol. Surv., Tallahassee, Fla.

Gibson, T. G. 1967. Stratigraphy and paleoenvironment of the phosphatic Miocene strata of North Carolina. Geol. Soc. Am. Bull. 78:631–650.

Henderson, J. R. 1939. The soils of Florida. Fla. Agric. Exp. Stn. Bull. 334, Gainesville, Fla. p. 67.

Hortenstine, C. C., and D. F. Rothwell. 1972. Use of municipal compost in reclamation of phosphate-mining sand tailings. J. Environ. Qual. 1:415–418.

Jeppson, R. W., R. W. Hill, and C. E. Israelsen. 1974. Slope stability of overburden spoil dumps from surface phosphate mines in southeastern Idaho. Utah Water Res. Lab., PRWG 140-1, Utah State Univ., Logan.

Lamont, W. E., J. T. McLendon, L. W. Clements, Jr., and I. L. Field. 1975. Characterization studies of Florida phosphate slimes. USDI, Bur. of Mines, Rep. Invest. 8089. Washington, D.C.

Leighty, L. G., V. W. Carlisle, O. E. Cruz, and others. 1950. Soil survey of Hillsborough County, Florida. USDA in cooperation with Fla. Agric. Exp. Stn., U.S. Government Printing Office, Washington, D.C.

Matson, G. C. 1915. The phosphate deposits of Florida. U.S. Geol. Surv. Bull. 604, Washington, D.C. p. 101.

Patrick, W. H., Jr., and D. S. Mikkelson. 1971. Plant nutrient behavior in flooded soil. p. 187–215. In R. A. Olson (ed. comm. chm.) Fertilizer technology and use. 2nd ed. Soil Sci. Soc. of Am., Madison, Wis.

Popoff, C. C., and A. L. Service. 1965. An evaluation of the western phosphate industry and its resources (in 5 parts), Part 2. Montana. USDI, Bur. of Mines, Rep. Invest. 6611, Washington, D.C.

Rooney, T. P., and P. F. Kerr. 1967. Mineralogic nature and origin of phospharite, Beaufort County, North Carolina. Geol. Soc. Am. Bull. 78:731–748.

Sellards, E. H. 1913a. Elevations in Florida. p. 81–101. In 5th Annual Rep., Fla. Geol. Surv. Tallahassee, Fla.

Sellards, E. H. 1913b. Origin of the hard rock phosphates of Florida. p. 27–80. In 5th Annual Rep., Fla. Geol. Surv., Tallahassee, Fla.

Sellards, E. H. 1914. The pebble phosphates of Florida. p. 29–116. In 7th Annual Rep., Fla. Geol. Surv., Tallahassee, Fla.

Service, A. L. 1966. An evaluation of the western phosphate industry and its resources (in 5 parts), Part 3. Idaho. USDI, Bur. of Mines, Rep. Invest. 6801, Washington, D.C.

Service, A. L., and N. S. Petersen. 1967. An evaluation of the western phosphate industry and its resources (in 5 parts), Part 5. Trends and outlook. USDI, Bur. of Mines, Rep. Invest. 6935, Washington, D.C.

Service, A. L., and C. C. Popoff. 1964. An evaluation of the western phosphate industry and its resources (in 5 parts): 1. Introductory review. USDI, Bur. of Mines, Rep. Invest. 6485, Washington, D.C.

Smith, R. W., and G. I. Whitlatch. 1940. The phosphate resources of Tennessee. State of Tenn. Dep. of Conserv., Div. of Geol., Bull. 48, Nashville, Tenn.

Stowasser, W. F. 1975. Phosphate rock. In Mineral facts and problems, 1975 ed. Preprint Bull. 667. USDI, Bur. of Mines, Washington, D.C.

Sweeney, J. W. 1971. Land use conflicts and phosphate mining in Florida. State of Florida, Div. of Interior Resour., Bur. of Geol., Inf. Circ. 72, Tallahassee, Fla.

Sweeney, J. W., and B. J. Timmons. 1973. Availability and potential utilization of byproduct gypsum in Florida phosphate operations. State of Fla., Div. of Interior Resour., Bur. of Geol., Spec. Publ. 18, Tallahassee, Fla.

Wang, K. L., B. W. Klein, and A. F. Powell. 1974. Economic significance of the Florida phosphate industry, p. 51. USDI Bur. of Mines, Inf. Circ. 8653, Washington, D.C.

Wilson, C. W., Jr. 1973. Annotated bibliography of the geology of Tennessee January 1961 through December 1970. Tenn. Div. of Geol., Bull. 71, Nashville, Tenn.

U.S. Department of Interior. 1975. The Florida phosphate slimes problem, a review and bibliography. Bur. of Mines Inf. Circ. 8668, Washington, D.C.

U.S. Department of Agriculture, Forest Service. 1971. Surface mine rehabilitation, report of cooperative administrative study to rehabilitate phosphate strip-mined sites, Caribou National Forest. Monsanto Co., J. R. Simplot Co., F. M. C. Corp., El Paso Products Co. Publ. USDA For. Serv., Intermt. Reg., Ogden, Utah.

Copyright © 1978 ASA–CSSA–SSSA
677 South Segoe Road, Madison, WI 53711 USA
Reclamation of Drastically Disturbed Lands

Chapter 33

Oil Shale

GRANT DAVIS

USDA, Forest Service, Billings, Montana

I. DEFINITION: WHAT IS OIL SHALE?

Oil shale is a fine-grained, sedimentary rock containing an organic material called *kerogen*, a rubbery solid that yields oil upon heating. Kerogen originates from the remains of plants and animals that accumulated in the bottoms of large stagnant bodies of water. The partially decayed remains mixed with clay and sand formed a muddy, calcareous deposit. As additional sediments accumulated above, the weight of the overlying materials compressed the organic-rich mixture into marlestone, although *oil shale* is the term most commonly used. Kerogen is actually an incompletely developed oil; geologic conditions never provided the heat or pressure necessary to convert it to oil.

Upon heating the shale to the pryolysis temperature, the kerogen gives up oil. Both gas and carbonaceous residue also are formed. Shale oils have a high pour point and high viscosity, contain less than 10% naptha, and less than 1% sulfur. Shale oil is unlike petroleum in that it contains relatively large quantities of nitrogen and oxygen compounds, as well as unsaturates. Generally, shale oil can be considered similar to crude oil and refined into the same products (Schramm, 1975).

II. WHERE OIL SHALE IS FOUND

A. Major Deposits and Resource Estimates

Oil shale is not as rare as one may think. It is found in many places in the United States and throughout the world. In-place oil resources from shale are measured in liters/metric ton. Although most resource estimates are based on 42 or 63 liters/metric ton (10 or 15 gallons/ton) or richer, 104 liters/metric ton (25 gallons/ton) shale is considered the minimum content for commercial operations with current technology and demand-supply-price situation.

The world's largest known hydrocarbon deposit is located in the United States in the oil shales of the Green River Formation of Colorado, Utah, and Wyoming. Recent estimates put the total resource at 318 trillion liters (2 trillion barrels) in shale 42 liters/metric ton (10 gallons/ton) or richer, including 95 trillion liters (600 billion barrels) in shales richer than 104 liters/metric ton (25 gallons/ton). Oil shale is found in at least 30 states, including Alaska. Although not as rich or thick as the Green River oil shales, the Devonian "black" shales of the central U.S. constitute a large energy source. These marine sediments occur from Texas to New York and from Alabama to Michigan and may contain almost 159 trillion liters (1 trillion barrels) of plus-42-liter/metric ton (10-gallon/ton) shale.

Outside the United States oil shale is known to exist in at least seven provinces in Canada. South America has the Irati shale, second only to the U.S. deposits. Other deposits are found in Africa, Asia, Australia, and Europe. Many of the deposits are undiscovered or unappraised because interest in commercial production is relatively new, but there may be over 47 quadtrillion liters (300 trillion barrels) in plus-42-liter/metric ton (10-gallon/ton) shale in the world (Schramm, 1975).

B. The Green River Formation

Because commercial production of shale oil in the United States will involve the Green River Formation, further description is necessary in order to explain reclamation and other problems related to development. Oil shale deposits of commercial interest underlie an area of approximately 65,000 km^2 in northwestern Colorado, eastern Utah, and southern Wyoming. About 80% of these deposits occur beneath public lands administered by the Department of Interior. Approximately 80% or 76 trillion liters (480 billion barrels of oil) of the richest oil shale deposits are located in the Piceance Creek Basin in northwestern Colorado (Schramm, 1975).

The land area above the Green River Formation is part of the Uintah Province. The plateau is gently rolling, but there are steep, picturesque cliffs where the Colorado River cuts through. The climate can be classed as arid to semiarid, ranging from 15 to 51 cm precipitation in Utah shale country and from 25 to 62.5 cm in the Piceance Basin. The amount of precipitation depends on altitude which rises from less than 1,800 m to more than 2,700 m. Precipitation is rather evenly distributed throughout the year, and over half occurs as snowfall. Soils are generally saline and shallow except in the valley bottoms. Natural vegetation is sparse, but quite variable because of the differences in soils and altitude. Riparian woodland occurs along the rivers, most of the lower areas support sagebrush-greasewood (*Artemisia-Sarcobatus* spp.) types, uplands are covered with mixed mountain shrubs and Pinyon-Juniper (*Pinus-Juniperus* spp.) woodlands, and the high elevations support Douglas-fir (*Pseudotsuga menziesii* [Mirb.] Franco) and Aspen forests (*Populus* spp.) (Cook, 1974).

The harsh climate and lack of available water have a great influence on land use and population distribution. The area is sparsely populated, and towns as well as transportation systems are found along the river bottoms. Most of the land is used for grazing livestock, about 5% is irrigated cropland, and the rest is wilderness and timberland; less than 1% is urban. The Piceance Basin is the wintering range for one of the largest migratory mule deer herds in the western U.S. Elk and wild horses as well as other wildlife also use the area. Consequently, tourism as well as agriculture are the leading components of the regional economy, but mining and oil and gas are also important factors (Thorne Ecol. Inst., 1975; USDI, 1974).

III. HOW OIL SHALE IS MINED

Present technology will allow only conventional methods of mining—underground and surface. In situ and modified in situ methods are in the experimental stage of development. Although the in situ processes also involve underground retorting, they will be discussed in the mining section.

Underground mining will follow conventional room and pillar techniques with some modification. Since the oil shales are several hundred feet thick, the rooms can be quite large and can be conducted on several levels. The operations are closer to limestone mining than coal mining. This method allows operators to select the richer zones of shale, of which about 75% can be extracted at each level. However, multilevel operations must leave undisturbed shale between levels, and this results in about 15% recovery of total in-place resources. There may also be some attempts at block caving.

Surface mining operations would be similar to the large copper mine excavations and are more suitable to Colorado than Utah or Wyoming. About 16 trillion liters (100 billion barrels) of oil could be recovered from the Piceance Basin by open pit methods assuming a 1:1 vertical ratio of overburden to ore of plus-63-liters/metric ton (15-gallons/ton) shale. This would amount to 7% of the area of the Basin. Because the pits must have a 1:1 side slope, only 65% of the ore could be recovered in early stages of operation, but the recovery would increase as the pits became larger and mined as a continuous "moving pit." Even with a 1:1 overburden-ore ratio, the open pits could be over 300 m deep and several kilometers wide at the surface.

In situ methods involve fracturing and heating the shale in place. Holes would be bored into the shale, heat would be by gas, steam, or establishing a fire in the fractured shale, and production wells would pump out the shale oil. There are several advantages to this approach: it takes fewer people to operate, uses less water, and generates less waste in both overburden and spent shale. Because in situ methods could be applied to low-grade oil shales, there is an advantage in recovering oil from deposits that would not be mined using conventional techniques. In spite of the obvious advantages, attempts at in situ recovery of oil have not been very successful, but research is continuing.

Modified in situ processes generally involve a combination of underground mining with underground retorting. Cavities are made in the shale similar to conventional room and pillar mining, and this shale is removed and retorted above ground. Shale overlying the cavity is drilled and blasted, so the base of a cylinder or cone of rubble falls into the cavity. The rubble is fired, and oil is recovered from the base. There are still some technical problems associated with this technique, but it appears to be more feasible than pure in situ processes.

Conventional oil shale mining has enormous waste disposal problems associated with the operations. Open pit mines require surface disposal of overburden, which may be several hundred feet thick, until the pit becomes large enough to fill in the back slopes of the pit as operations move forward. Disposal of waste rock from underground operations is also a problem, but less so than for open pit mines. Storage of low-grade shale which is removed in the mining process but not profitable to retort under present conditions may also have to be stored on the surface and revegetated until it can be recovered at a later date.

The most difficult waste disposal problem by far is the spent shale from surface retorting operations. A good rule of thumb is 0.9 metric tons/day (1 ton/day) waste for 159 liters/day (1 barrel/day) oil. For example, a 16 million liters (100,000 barrels) of shale oil a day operation will produce enough spent shale to fill a canyon 600 m wide, 60 m deep, and 16 km long. For underground mining, all of this material would have to be placed on the surface because underground disposal is considered impractical at the present time. A large portion of the spent shale produced by open pit mining could be placed back in the pit, but some would have to be disposed of on the surface until the hole becomes large enough to backfill (Schram, 1974; USDI, 1974).

IV. HOW OIL SHALE IS RETORTED

Shale oil is produced by crushing the rock, heating it to 482°C or higher to decompose the kerogen, and condensing the oily vapors. This process is called *retorting*. There are several processes based on these general principles that are in various stages of development.

The U.S. Bureau of Mines tested one of the earliest gas-combustion retorts at its Anvil Points, Colorado, project. This was a vertical vessel through which crushed shale moved down by gravity and hot-recycled gases moved up from the bottom. The combustion of these gases along with some residual carbon in the spent shale heated the raw shale to retorting temperature. The oil vapors went off through the top. The Paraho retort works on the same general principle and was tested during the mid 1970's at the Anvil Points facility. The Union Oil retort reverses the flow of gas and shale, with hot gases moving downwards in the vessel, shale being fed through the bottom, and spent shale coming off the top. The Petrosix process is a variation of the vertical retort which uses an external furnace to heat the recycled gas.

The Oil Shale Corporation (TOSCO) has developed the TOSCO II process which uses hot ceramic balls to heat the shale in a horizontal, rotary-type retort. Superior Oil uses a circular grate retort that resembles a large doughnut. This process can also utilize the nahcolite and dawsonite minerals found in oil shale. The Lurgi-Ruhrgas process, developed in West Germany during the 1950's, uses solid heat carriers, such as hot shale residue in a horizontal cylinder with a screw conveyer.

It is important to understand the various processes because each results in a different type of spent shale that will have to be stabilized and revegetated during the reclamation process. The TOSCO II process produces a finely ground spent shale, and the Union Oil process results in large clinkers. The other processes result in spent shale of various sizes falling in between these extremes. Each process will require its own reclamation technique which will be discussed in a later section (Schramm, 1974; USDI, 1974).

V. PROBLEMS OF OIL SHALE DEVELOPMENT

As you would expect in any new industry, the development of oil shale is beset with numerous problems. Difficulties cover a broad spectrum: economic, political, social, technical, and environmental.

The economic problems have a long history. False starts in the past have been halted by discoveries of new sources of oil which made production of shale oil uneconomical. Development is capital intensive. It costs about 1 billion dollars per plant, and oil shale development must compete for capital with other enterprises which may give quicker and higher returns. A discounted cash flow rate of 10% would mean oil would have to sell for $14.20 for 159 liters (1 barrel), and a 15% rate would require a price of $21.70. Since the world price for foreign crude is around $14.00 per 159 liters (1 barrel) delivered to the United States, the lower rate is more realistic. Private capital is not available at this rate (Katell & Wellman, 1974).

A major political problem is the lack of a clear federal energy policy and the role shale oil will play in energy development. However, most of the serious political problems are also tied to economics. A congressional bill to help provide capital for oil shale went down to defeat in December 1975. Although shale oil could possibly compete with $14 per 159 liters (1 barrel) foreign oil, an energy bill (HR 3474) signed into law last December pegs domestic oil at $7.66 per 159 liters (1 barrel), a price too low to compete unless shale oil is subsidized. Also, there has been much talk in Congress about breaking up the big oil companies, and this is not conducive to long-term, billion dollar investments of capital. The other political problems are similar to most energy developments involving mining and conversion plants: permits and legal disputes involving land, water, right-of-way, etc. Although there appears to be enough water available for projected industry demands, the politics of water use and rights can be a tremendous problem in itself (Weeks et al., 1974).

Social problems are hard to separate from the political. There is an undercurrent of antidevelopment feeling throughout the western U.S. Much of this sentiment is directed to the influx of more people which accompanies development, as much as to new industry per se. You will find a difference in general attitude towards oil shale development among the state governments of Colorado, Utah, and Wyoming. Even within Colorado there is a regional difference in that the town of Rangely and the western slope generally favor oil shale development, while the town of Meeker and the eastern slope do not. The impact of newcomers is more of a local problem. Although the projected increase of 20,000 additional people over the first 10 years does not sound overwhelming in more populated areas of the country, this will double and triple the size of many communities in shale country. Local people are very leary of the "boom-bust" image of previous mining developments. Even with planned community expansion, the "front-end load" of providing housing and facilities before the increased tax base provides the capital is a problem that has to be addressed. Oil shale developed in Utah poses another unique social problem. It will affect the 1,600 members of the Uintah and Ouray Indian tribes and their 400,000-ha reservations. These Northern Ute Indian lands may contain 159 billion liters (1 billion barrels) of shale oil. They are faced with the dilemma of how to participate in a new industry and, at the same time, preserve the culture of their small tribes.

Many technical problems have to be solved in the mining and retorting processes as the oil shale industry moves toward commercial production. There is always a time-consuming and costly "shakedown" period as a new industry starts up. Because large amounts of material have to be mined, retorted, and disposed of, present technology results in a relatively low net energy return compared to other energy sources. Even if unlimited capital were available, the logistics of obtaining special equipment and materials and finding enough skilled labor to construct and run the plants would have to be overcome.

Environmental problems are associated with both the retorting and mining processes but, because no commercial plants are in operation, most problems are speculative at this time. The air pollution potential is especially uncertain. Most of the oil shale lies within or near what the U.S. Environmental Protection Agency (EPA) considers Class I areas. Because any change in air quality of these "pristine" areas would be considered "significant," the effect of the new regulations could restrict the number of plants and require the best available control technology at greatly increased costs of development. Although there is some concern about carcenogenic potency of shale oil, animal tests show it is similar to many conventional petroleum products and less carcenogenic than some industrial fuel oils and coal products.

For the most part, oil shale mining operations will result in environmental impact similar to that from mining other minerals. One major exception is the disposal of spent shale. As mentioned previously, large volumes must be placed on the surface, stabilized, and rehabilitated. Although most of the remainder of this chapter will deal with technology for reclaiming areas disturbed by mining oil shale, it should be obvious from the above that this difficult task is just one of the many problems confronting future development of oil shale.

VI. THE OIL SHALE PROTOTYPE PROGRAM

Since the United States owns most of the oil shale, the U.S. Department of Interior started a prototype program in November 1973. The purpose was to generate the essential information concerning the commercial feasibility and environmental impacts of an oil shale industry prior to full-scale development. Six tracts were set up, but bids were received only on the two in Colorado and on two adjacent tracts in Utah. Each tract was about 2,000 ha in size and was to be operated for at least 20 years. It was proposed that each of the Colorado tracts would support an 8-million liter (50,000 barrel) per day operation and the two Utah tracts would support a 16-million liter (100,000 barrel) per day operation. The companies were required to obtain 2 years of environmental baseline data and present a detailed development plan of their proposed operations.

To help monitor the environmental concerns, the U.S. Department of Interior formed an Oil Shale Environmental Advisory Panel early in 1974. The Panel was composed of representatives from several agencies within the U.S. Department of Interior, other Federal departments, state representatives, and environmentalists. The Panel acted as an advisory body to the U.S. Geological Survey Oil Shale Supervisor on environmental matters.

The oil shale prototype program is significant because it is a unique experiment to evaluate an industry and to use a panel of experts to monitor environmental impacts before major development of a natural resource takes place. It is also important because millions of dollars were spent on each lease area to obtain environmental baseline data (Rocky Mountain Oil and Gas Assoc., 1975). These areas thus became some of the most intensely studied areas in the world. By evaluating the methods used to obtain and put the data to use, guides can be developed to help set up similar baseline studies in a cost-effective manner for other activities and for environmental impact statements.

VII. RECLAMATION OF DISTURBED AREAS

Because mining for oil shale will result in several kinds of waste materials, different techniques for reclaiming each type must be used. Spent shale disposal piles will cover large surface areas. Waste rock which is discarded to reach oil shale will also be deposited on the surface. Low-grade shale which cannot be retorted profitably under current conditions may be stockpiled for later recovery. Because spent shale may be covered with soil, it will be necessary to scrape up topsoil and store it in piles until ready for use. So, each of these materials must be stabilized and revegetated either temporarily or permanently according to future use. Other disturbances such as roads, drilling pads, plant sites, and impoundments are also associated with oil shale mining.

Because spent shale is unique to oil shale operations, and also the biggest problem, we will concentrate on it. The other materials are similar to those produced from other types of mining, and some technology is available and transferrable in part to oil shale operations. As mentioned previously, it is important to remember that spent shale may differ depending on shale characteristics and retorting process. Regardless of the type of spent shale produced, reclamation techniques must be developed to solve the major problems of stability, hydrology, and revegetation.

A. Stability

Spent shale may cover large areas at great depths. Although the material is relatively stable, not much experience with such large masses is available for application on spent shale. The finer spent shales when moistened become quite hard when compacted and allowed to "set". Some heat of reaction may occur. The surface of the piles will probably be wetted and compacted to prevent infiltration of water which could lead to failure within the interior or base of the piles. The pressure produced by the weight of disposal piles may cause some problem of failure on materials below the piles. The U.S. Bureau of Mines is studying some of the problems of spent shale disposal.

B. Hydrology

It would be undesirable to have water enter the piles of spent shale because salts could infiltrate into the surface or ground water systems. Infiltration rates are naturally rather low in the finer materials due partly to their resistance to wetting. Melting of snow which builds up on the piles may be controlled by surface compaction, diversion ditches, sediment basins below the piles, and revegetating the surface (Colorado State Univ., 1971).

C. Revegetation

Vegetation can be established directly on spent shale, or the piles can be covered with soil and then revegetated. Revegetating raw shale is the most difficult task. If the piles have been compacted, the surface must be loosened to the depth of the root zone. Spent shale is high in salts, but it can be leached. However, it may take well over 100 cm of water to do an effective job. Then there is a problem of disposing of the leach water. There is also a tendency for salts to work toward the surface, causing resalinization of the leached zone. Unless soil amendments can effectively tie up the salts, revegetated shale may have to be leached periodically.

Spent shale is deficient in N and P, but commercial fertilizers have been used with good success. The dark color of spent shale results in high surface temperatures, but mulching has been effective in plant establishment.

Plant adaptability trials in the greenhouse and the field indicate that several salt-tolerant native and introduced species will grow on raw shale. Successful revegetation has been accomplished experimentally by using containerized seedlings and clumps of native vegetation transplanted from surrounding areas. The Soil Conservation Service has established a plant materials center at Meeker, Colorado, to provide seeds and plants for revegetating areas disturbed in oil shale development.

Supplementary irrigation will probably be necessary until plants are established on spent shale piles. If the spent shale is leached, the same irrigation system can be used for supplementary irrigation.

Topsoiling the piles of spent shale may enable vegetation to be established more easily. There is still some concern that salts may move up from the spent shale into the soil layer (Cook, 1974; Herbert & Berg, 1974). Three different methods of using topsoil on spent shale piles have been proposed by the leasees of the prototype oil shale areas (Detailed Developmental Plans for Ca, Cb, Ua, Ub Oil Shale Tracts. Office Copies USGS Area Office, Grand Junction, Colo.). One proposes to spread soil directly on shale piles. Another proposes to place a layer of overburden rubble over the shale with a layer of soil on top. It is speculated that the rubble will prevent movement of salts from the spent shale up into the soil. The third proposal is to terrace the slopes of spent shale piles to collect water in trenches which will be filled with topsoil (McKell, 1976).

All these alternatives will have to be tried on a large scale to determine which are most cost effective. Additional research is under way to develop new ways to revegetate these difficult sites.

Once vegetation is established on the piles of spent shale, research on proper management practices will have to follow. Studies will have to be installed to determine rates and frequency of refertilization and supplementary irrigation, proper species mixtures for various uses, plant succession, and the best livestock and wildlife management practices.

Much of the work in rehabilitation of spent shale and related disturbed areas is just getting started. It will take several years before even the basic information is developed. However, it is encouraging that reclamation research has started so early in the development of oil shale. One must remember that there are no ongoing commercial operations, and scientists have to get their reservations in early just to obtain spent shale from the experimental retorts.

In summary, it is the opinion of this author that technology for successfully reclaiming disturbances from oil shale operations will be available long before other problems associated with oil shale development are solved.

LITERATURE CITED

Colorado State University, 1971. Water pollution potential of spent oil shale residues. USEPA Grant no. 14030. 116 p.

Cook, C. W. (Coordinator). 1974. Surface rehabilitation of land disturbances resulting from oil shale development. Environ. Resour. Center, Colorado State Univ. Inf. Ser. no. 11. 56 p.

Herbert, H. P., and W. A. Berg. 1971. Vegetative stabilization of spent oil shales. Environ. Resour. Center, Colorado State Univ. Tech. Rep. 4. 40 p.

Katell, S., and P. Wellman. 1974. An economic analysis of oil shale operations featuring gas combustion retorting. U.S. Dep. of Interior, Bur. of Mines. Tech. Prog. Rep. 81. 18 p.

McKell, C. M. 1976. Achieving effective revegetation of disposed processed oil shale: A program emphasizing natural methods in an arid environment. Agric. Exp. Stn., Utah State Univ. Land Rehab. Ser. no. 1. 17 p.

Rocky Mountain Oil and Gas Association. 1975. Summary of industry oil shale environmental studies and selected bibliography of oil shale environmental references. Rocky Mountain Oil and Gas Assoc., Denver, Colo. 31 p.

Schramm, L. W. 1975. Mineral facts and problems—shale oil. U.S. Dep. of Interior, Bur. of Mines Bull. 667. 26 p.

Thorne Ecological Institute. 1975. Wildlife and oil shale—a problem analysis and research program. U.S. Dep. of Interior, Fish and Wildlife Serv., Off. of Biol. Serv. 112 p.

U.S. Department of Interior, Federal Energy Administration. 1974. Project Independence—potential future role of oil shale: Prospects and constraints. U.S. Government Printing Office Stock no. 4118-0016. 495 p.

Weeks, J. B., G. H. Leavesley, F. A. Welder, and G. J. Saulnier, Jr. 1974. Simulated effects of oil-shale development on the hydrology of Piceance Basin, Colorado. U.S. Dep. of Interior Geol. Surv. Prof. Pap. 908. 84 p.

Copyright © 1978 ASA–CSSA–SSSA
677 South Segoe Road, Madison, WI 53711 USA
Reclamation of Drastically Disturbed Lands

Chapter 34

Reclamation of Lands Disturbed by Stone Quarries, Sand and Gravel Pits, and Borrow Pits

BRENT W. BLAUCH

Skelly & Loy
Harrisburg, Pennsylvania

I. INTRODUCTION

Stone quarries, sand and gravel pits, and borrow pits are familiar to all who have been in communities where construction is, or has been, a major industry. With emphasis placed on community growth and expansion, we sometimes take for granted the ready availability of aggregate used in concrete, bituminous paving, cinder blocks, and the like. However, we may not fully realize that the quarry or gravel pit supplying our construction industry is becoming depleted or is being encroached upon by rapid suburban growth. An old quarry, which at one time was in the midst of a farmer's field, may now be found surrounded by industrial, commercial, or residential developments. Who would have thought 50 years ago this quarry would *ever* cause a problem to neighbors?

We cannot make the same mistake today that we made in the past—that is, fail to consider what will become of new quarries, gravel pits, or fill borrow areas 50 or 100 years from now or whenever they are depleted and abandoned. Will we have planned a feasible, safe, future land use, or will we have simply created another hole in the ground of no use, or possibly even a nuisance? With over one-third of the total surface-mined land attributed to stone, sand, and gravel operations, we must continue to consider methods which make these areas suitable for beneficial post-mine use.

II. GENERAL CHARACTERISTICS

Stone quarries and sand and gravel pits are known for their longevity. Although dependent upon size of deposit, production, and market, these surface mine areas have operating lives generally upwards from 30 years and oftentimes continue productive operation through several generations of owners. Long-range planning for such an operation is obviously not an easy task; how can we effectively plan a compatible land-reuse for our children's grandchildren?

With these areas having long operating lives, one might assume land area disturbance to be extensive over the life of the mine. However, this is not always the case. For example, one limestone quarry in Lancaster County, Pennsylvania, has been operating since the late 1800's and has only disturbed a total of about 14 ha. Another pit opened 20 years ago currently extends over a 40-ha tract. Although geologic characteristics have significant influence on the size of an operating area (i.e., thin, flat-lying veins vs. massive, thick deposits), other factors such as ground water elevations, zoning, land ownership, production, and surrounding land use patterns also have direct effects on pit expanse.

With wide variations in size of stone quarries, sand and gravel pits, and borrow areas, it follows that pit configurations and site characteristics are equally as varied. For ease of discussion, let us define those areas where consolidated materials are extracted to be *quarries*, and areas where unconsolidated materials are removed to be *pits*.

A. Quarries

Quarries can generally be classified as one of three types (Bauer, 1968 and 1970):

1) Side hill—where mining begins near the base of a hill or moun-and proceeds into the slope, thus establishing highwall faces on three sides with one end of the quarry open.

2) Open pit—where excavation begins in relatively flat-lying ter-rain, and proceeds downward creating a large, multisided, open hole.

3) Combination—where operations combine side hill excavation with open pit developments.

One of the most distinguishing characteristics of a quarry is the rock highwall which encompasses the mining area. Although many approaches have been incorporated to reclaim these faces, they still remain the number one problem in effective quarry area reclamation. Other characteristics of quarries include:

1) Overburden storage and/or disposal areas—after removal, over-burden is generally stored as a mound along the limit of mining, on piles for future reclamation use, or as backfill material in mined-out areas.

2) Waste disposal areas—usually, quarries produce only small quantities of waste or nonusable byproducts, commonly consisting of dense settling pond sludges, particulates from dust collecting systems, and soft, friable rock not suitable for aggregate. Non-toxic in nature, these materials are often disposed in overburden storage areas.

3) Support areas—an integral part of nearly every quarry is the processing plant, settling ponds, and stockpile areas. These areas do

not cause major problems for rehabilitation, and generally can be integrated with the mine reclamation scheme.

B. Sand and Gravel Pits

Unlike quarries, sand and gravel pits are not easily categorized. Ultimate pit configurations are predominately dictated by the type and shape of the deposit, while mining methods, size of operation, and surrounding topographic features also contribute to final mine area characteristics. Although nearly as varied in configuration as the number of sites themselves, sand and gravel pits do have some common features which can be isolated for discussion.

As stated earlier, mine characteristics are generally dependent upon site geology and the form of the mineral deposit. The following define several common types of sand and gravel operations as related to depositional environment (Schellie & Bauer, 1968; Schellie & Rogier, 1963).

1) Hilltop deposit—in areas where the deposit lies near the hill top or actually forms a hill, mining begins near the base and continues through the hill. As overburden is removed in advance of mining, it is replaced in the mined-out pit. Eventually the entire hill is removed, resulting in a gentle, rolling topography.

2) Dune deposit—sand dunes are ideal for easy extraction but far less than ideal for easy reclamation. With steep slopes commonly surrounding depleted deposits and general lack of overburden materials, effective after-use planning becomes extremely difficult.

3) Wet and dry pocket deposits—a majority of sand and gravel operators extract from pocket type deposits, usually very irregular in areal extent and depth. To accommodate the nonuniformity of the deposit, mining does not follow a symmetrical pattern of excavation, thus creating random depressions in the mined-out floor. If operations intersect the local ground water table, then any portion of the pit mined below that elevation can be expected to fill with water upon site abandonment.

An unavoidable characteristic of nearly every sand and gravel pit is settling ponds. By nature, sand and gravel deposits contain fine-grained silt, sand, and clay particles which must be washed from the desired product. A significant percentage of all materials extracted from the pit is wasted from processing facilities as silt-laden water. To accommodate these waste loadings, large settling ponds must be constructed, which sometimes encompass more area than the pit. As sediments accumulate in these ponds, cleaning, enlargement, or basin relocation become imperative. It is not uncommon to convert mined-out areas into basins, thus providing positive land-forming reclamation through sediment deposition. In fact, some well-planned operations give special consideration to pond locations and waste discharge pipe placement to maximize the land-forming potential of discarded materials.

Similar in some respects to quarries, aggregate pits also require stockpile and plant areas, maintenance areas, and overburden disposal areas for effective mine operation. As with quarries, these areas can easily be incorporated into nearly any reclamation scheme, although preplanning the location of such areas can greatly enhance post-mining land utilization.

C. Borrow Pits

Though not usually considered as a mining operation, borrow areas do generate land configuration schemes similar in nature to unconsolidated aggregate excavations. Many construction projects, particularly highway and site development ventures, require extensive earthwork maneuvers to establish design grades. At times there are insufficient materials available on site to achieve these grades, and it becomes necessary to "borrow" fill from another location to meet project design requirements.

Generally, borrow pits are side hill-type excavations, resulting in a level floor partially surrounded by steep slopes. Though usually considerably smaller than quarries or sand and gravel pits, borrow pits still can pose problems to effective land utilization if not properly reclaimed. Few regulations exist concerning borrow excavations, and rehabilitating these areas is normally left up to the desires of the landowner and commitments of the contractor. However, in some states, erosion and sedimentation control plans and permits are required for construction activities, usually resulting with the contractor's commitment to revegetate a borrow area to ensure minimal erosion losses. Borrow pits need not remain as unattractive, nonusable excavations. With sufficient preplanning and possibly some overall community research, borrow operations could be implemented as part of site development work on a future project area.

III. PROBLEMS OF RECLAMATION

A. Physical Restraints

One of the most significant problems inherent in most mines is that of steep slope or highwall reclamation. Final reclamation schemes must consider how to "treat" these areas with relation to the height and extent of exposed faces. In unconsolidated pits, regrading steep slopes to acceptable, usable grades is relatively easy to achieve. Unfortunately, this is not the case with consolidated rock highwalls, common to quarrying operations.

Reclaiming rock faces can be approached in several ways. If reclamation is taken to mean merely "public protection", then a chainlink fence or an earthen mound planted with thorny vegetation established along the crest of the face will suffice. This type approach is often implemented where a quarry or open pit will be utilized as a water supply reservoir or other nonpublic use. If a reclamation scheme involves establishing recreation facilities in or around the quarry, then not only will highwall crest protection be needed, but the face should be benched to impede rock falls and protect areas near the toe of the wall. To enhance the appearance of these benches, they are sometimes covered with over-burden and planted with grasses and seedlings.

In some instances, a rock highwall will not be compatible with a pro-posed post-mine plan. It then becomes necessary to consider methods of face reduction or elimination, which usually involves some degree of blasting or backfilling. When highwall heights exceed 30 m, questions begin to arise as to the benefits of face elimination, due to increased drill-ing and blasting costs, backfilling costs, availability of materials, and pos-sible loss of reserves. Perhaps it would be more beneficial to regrade or eliminate only portions of the highwall, and allow some faces to remain in strategic locations.

Another problem associated with reclaiming quarries and sand and gravel pits is storage and replacement of overburden and topsoil. If little or no overburden or topsoil exists prior to mining, reclamation activities, especially revegetation, will be seriously inhibited. On the other hand, large amounts of overburden or topsoil can seriously inhibit mining ac-tivities, through insufficient space to store or dispose of those materials. Before mining begins, it is important to know exactly how much over-burden and topsoil will be encountered, and what the reclamation scheme will be. How much overburden and topsoil will need to be con-served for reclamation implementation, or how the reclamation plan can be revised to accommodate the lack of such materials is dependent upon this information.

It is necessary to consider the configuration and extent of the reserve while planning future mined-land uses. Of course, the rehabilitative ap-proach and the mine site parameters must be compatible. With wide vari-ations in the types of mineral deposit, not every reclamation scheme can be applied to any site. In fact, some sites may only be receptive to one or two ideas.

One particular characteristic of the deposit which has considerable impact on reclamation planning is location of the water table. Will water be encountered during extraction of the reserve? If so, at what depth and how far below that level will the mine progress? If water is encountered, chances are post-mine land use will favor some sort of water impound-ment. To maximize use of water areas or adjoining land areas, it becomes important to assess the expected level of water after mining, in relation to potential outlet zones, the expected range of fluctuation in water level, and the expected areal extent of the impoundment. With any impound-ment reclamation plan, care must be taken to protect youthful explorers (and their older counterparts) against possible drownings. Highwall bar-riers (as discussed earlier) and underwater safety benches around the shoreline assist in supplying this protection.

Ground water infiltration into mined-out areas is not the only source of water-oriented reclamation. Settling ponds, particularly the larger ponds associated with sand and gravel operations, can contribute as much or more water area than the pit. However, it is not always practical or de-sirable to allow settling basins to remain as part of post-mine land use, in which case ponds must be dewatered, dried, backfilled, and regraded. Unfortunately, "reclaimed" pond and basin areas are not very suitable for most building construction, due to soft unconsolidated sediment accumulations. Instead, these areas are generally graded to acceptable agricultural type contours, suitable for parks, recreation, farming, or parking lots.

Reclamation problems are not totally site confined. Proximity of highways, streams, and public utilities, and adjacent or nearby land uses can also affect reclamation. For example, if an open pit has been developed and there is not sufficient water infiltration to achieve an acceptable impoundment elevation, consideration could be given to relocating a nearby stream through the pit. This will not only provide a more usable reclamation plan, but may also improve stream water quality through settling of suspended sediments. On the other hand, locations of public utility lines (water, electric, sewer) may prohibit desired regrading configurations, thus precluding implementation of an otherwise acceptable scheme. Prior to any decisions on post-mine land use, it is extremely important to consider all aspects of the site and surrounding areas to ensure that the selected approach will be both achievable and usable.

B. Regulatory Restraints

Although reclamation schemes are most influenced by the physical setting, legal restraints and regulations can also have a significant impact on reclamation alternatives. Some states have adopted "All Surface Mining" legislation, which requires all surface mine operators to submit a mining-reclamation plan for approval. A permit, issued for each operating site, delineates reclamation procedures to be followed. Any post-mine scheme proposed by the operator is subject to review and approval by the state agency, thereby limiting certain aspects of a reclamation plan in some cases.

As part of an All Surface Mining law, some rehabilitation restrictions are clearly defined. For example, under Pennsylvania's All Surface Mining Act, reclamation grades cannot exceed a slope of 35° from the horizontal, including consolidated quarry highwalls. Therefore, any quarry reclamation proposal in that state must adhere to the 35° regulations, thereby limiting some future use potentials.

In addition to restrictions imposed by state legislative action, local governing bodies can influence future planning procedures through zoning laws. Although zoning authorities are usually receptive to improved changes in zoning restrictions, it is important to have prior approval of a proposed land use action before actual implementation of any scheme.

Other regulations, although not directly related to mining, can also affect plans for future mined-land usage. Many states have adopted health, welfare, and safety laws as a means to protect the public from potentially hazardous situations. Items such as unguarded or unfenced highwalls, unprotected water impoundments, abandoned machinery and structures, and other possibly dangerous conditions are often termed *nuisances* under such laws, and would not be permitted as a part of a final reclamation scheme.

Although not normally considered a regulatory body, local, county, and regional planning commissions can offer positive reinforcement to reclamation planning. As part of their function, planning agencies endeavor to formulate a practical, well-organized plan for future developments. Consultation with these agencies prior to final reclamation plan decisions could result in a future land use that will be directly compatible with the areas requirements. A well-planned rehabilitation scheme presented to such an agency might even influence the planning commission's overall strategy enough to utilize the rehabilitation scheme as a focal point for new ideas.

C. Time Restraints

Though planning is an important part of any reclamation program, details of future plans should be proportionate to the time lag before implementation. For long-life operations, the "best planned end-use" may change several times during the life of the mine. Alterations in community development patterns (residential, commercial, industrial, recreational), mine planning and mineral economics, and local or regional planning could render a well-planned scheme ineffective. Too much detailed planning, too soon, may result in wasted time and effort, or an ineffective post-mine land use. Reclamation plans should regularly be reviewed and updated to ensure that the proposed scheme is, in fact, always the "best planned end-use".

D. Planning: Unplanned vs. Planned Reclamation

Although planning is not usually considered a "problem" of reclamations, lack of it can certainly create some costly inconveniences. Unplanned or "fix up" reclamation schemes incur total reclamation expenditures at termination of mining activities. For example, the high cost of overburden and topsoil rehandling would be paid when it comes time to "fix up" an operation before abandonment, while proper placement of overburden and topsoil upon removal could eliminate such a reclamation expense. Other "fix up" costs might include chainlink fence or berm construction, revegetation, impoundment outlet construction, highwall regrading, and pond backfilling.

By not directing mining activities toward a specific post-mine objective, the final result of operations could very well be the creation of undesirable or nonusable land. If an operator were to postpone all rehabilitative procedures until mining has been completed, high reclamation costs with no mining income could cause him to go out of business; consequently, not even site "fix up" would be accomplished. Or, even if an operator could afford to pay the reclamation expense, he might be inclined to look for short-cuts to keep his losses at closing minimized. In any event, an unplanned reclamation scheme would certainly not result in the *best* possible end-use.

By planning reclamation activities concurrent with mine progression, there will be no restoration "bill to pay" upon termination of mining, since reclamation costs will be spread out and amortized over the life of the operation. Actual expenditures will also be reduced, since many *mining* procedures could also be classified as reclamation procedures, if properly executed as part of an overall plan. Men, equipment, and materials are used more efficiently with little or no overburden rehandling.

With concurrent planned reclamation, mining procedures can serve as a means to an end, rather than simply producing minerals. That is, mining can not only provide a source of income, but can also be used as an aid to development of a *desired* future land use scheme, such as a recreational/residential lake-oriented community. Whatever the chosen rehabilitative approach, carrying it out in conjunction with mining, and spreading the work over the life of the mine, maximizes the benefit of reclamation. In many instances, concurrent reclamation provides usable rehabilitated areas while mine progression continues, thus indicating future land-use intentions, and possibly enhancing public relations in the community (Ahearn, 1964).

IV. ACTUAL AND POTENTIAL USES OF REHABILITATED AREAS

Land use potentials of quarries, sand and gravel pits, and borrow areas are virtually limitless. Although influenced by certain physical, legal, and other restraints, reuse alternatives can range from golf courses, to reservoirs, to residential communities, to industrial sites, to sanitary landfills. Several categories of common land re-use schemes are presented below, with brief example descriptions of actual reclaimed sites.

1. RECREATIONAL

Recreational land uses are many and varied, and include both public and private schemes. Private country clubs, game preserves, fishing resorts, parks, playgrounds, or swimming could be developed into a post-mine reuse plan. For example, a sand and gravel producer near Kenosha, Wisconsin, plans to establish an 18-hole golf course around one side of its property, while excavating a 70-ha lake as a focal point for future residential development. Another example of the numerous recreational areas created by quarry and sand and gravel operations is Lamar Park, near Grand Rapids, Michigan. Once a typical sand and gravel operation, the area was reclaimed to provide picnicking, swimming, baseball, and other park-related facilities.

2. INDUSTRIAL/COMMERCIAL

"Industrial/Commercial" can also cover a wide variety of uses, anywhere from drive-in theaters, to shopping centers, to warehouses, to manufacturing plants. An impressive commercial rehabilitation program can be viewed along Dublin Road in North Columbus, Ohio, where surface mining created a 2-km lake, which is now bordered by attractive commercial buildings (Natl. Sand and Gravel Assoc., 1961).

3. RESIDENTIAL

Although residential development near mining areas is not always attractive while mining is in progress, post-mine land use for residential communities has proven to be a very successful reclamation approach. A New York developer has undertaken a plan to establish Highland Lakes, a residential development for about 6,000 people near Northville, Michigan. Utilizing a 100-ha mined-out pit, the community will eventually consist of over 1,300 single family condominium townhouses, 125 single family homes, and 400 apartment units.

4. AGRICULTURAL

Not all post-mine reclamation plans can incorporate development of successful residential communities or elaborate parks. In fact, the vast majority of successful reclamation ventures can be attributed to agricultural-type approaches such as pasture, hay, or cultivated crop production. Many old minesites have been returned to agricultural use, and today appear to be part of the original landscape. One California operator, working along the Stanislaus River in San Joaquin and Stanislaus Counties, is remining areas of abandoned dredge tailings, leaving a properly drained flat surface immediately available for agricultural use (Robertson, 1975).

5. PUBLIC

Public uses for mined land often stem from the land owner's goodwill or from community or regional needs. Donating reclaimed areas for educational facilities, memorial plots, or reservoirs, or making areas available or suitable for landfills, lagoons, or sewage treatment works all reflect public use patterns. An excellent example of preplanned reclamation for public use is displayed at the Dallas Sewage Disposal Plant in Dallas, Texas. Aggregate mining in this area eliminated a major flooding problem, and established correct grades for treatment facility construction, all during the course of mining (Natl. Sand and Gravel Assoc., 1961).

V. CONCLUSION

A depleted quarry or gravel pit does not have to be an unusable piece of land. If unusable, it is because of failure to apply reclamation thinking. Current reclamation techniques, when applied, have shown excellent success, particularly in relation to sand and gravel operations. The National Sand and Gravel Association, in conjunction with the University of Illinois, has sponsored several research projects to determine and present the most practical approaches to sand and gravel pit rehabilitation (Johnson, 1966). Several of their publications are referenced in the bibliography. The Ontario Department of Mines has completed similar work in the quarry field, results of which are also referenced in the bibliography.

Techniques and approaches to successful rehabilitation of aggregate pits and quarries are available and proven. Why then are we faced with the problem of reclaiming mined-out areas? With viable procedures available, the answer certainly cannot be technical inability. Solving problems of pit and quarry reclamation can best be achieved through greater awareness of:

1) Current feasible extraction techniques which are compatible with, and perform major portions of, the desired end-use scheme;
2) Specific site area characteristics such as overburden/mineral ratios, ground water hydrology, and land use patterns;
3) Types of successful reclamation programs at rehabilitated mine sites; and
4) Future land-use planning concepts of local, county, and regional planning commissions.

Becoming familiar with present technology, site specifics, successful restoration, and planning schemes is important, of course, but without a commitment to reclamation and a free imagination, *successful* rehabilitation would be less probable. More communication through trade journals on current mining-reclamation practices, publication and easy access of land-use planning schemes, and more recognition of good restoration programs will allow everyone to become more aware of various reclamation aspects, including some *positive* long-range mining impacts.

LITERATURE CITED

Ahearn, V. P. 1964. Land use planning and the sand and gravel producer. Natl. Sand and Gravel Assoc., Natl. Ready Mixed Concrete Assoc., Silver Spring, Md.

Bauer, A. M. (ed.). 1968. Proc. of the Conf.—Mining in an Urban Landscape, 19–20 Nov., Univ. of Guelph, School of Landscape Architecture, Guelph, Ontario.

Bauer, A. M. 1970. A guide to site development and rehabilitation of pits and quarries. Ontario Dep. of Mines, Toronot, Ontario.

Johnson, C. 1966. Practical operating procedures for progressive rehabilitation of sand and gravel sites. Univ. of Illinois, Urbana, Ill.

National Sand and Gravel Association. 1961. Case histories: Rehabilitation of worked-out sand and gravel deposits. Natl. Sand and Gravel Assoc., Washington, D.C.

Robertson, J. L. 1975. Dredging and reclamation plans govern Kenosha materials sand and gravel operations. Rock Prod. 78:42–45.

Schellie, K. L., and A. M. Bauer. 1968. Shaping the land: Planned use of industrial sand deposits. Natl. Ind. Sand Assoc., Silver Spring, Md.

Schellie, K. L., and D. A. Rogier. 1963. Site utilization and rehabilitation practices for sand and gravel operations. Natl. Sand and Gravel Assoc., Silver Spring, Md.

Chapter 35

Disposition of Dredged Material

RAYMOND J. KRIZEK AND DIMITRIOS K. ATMATZIDIS

The Technological Institute, Northwestern University
Evanston, Illinois

I. INTRODUCTION

Large quantities of bottom sediments are dredged periodically to develop and maintain the harbors and channels necessary to accomodate the ever-increasing tonnage of waterborne commerce that is so vital to the economic welfare of most industrialized nations. In the United States approximately 340 million m³ of bottom sediments are dredged annually to maintain almost 40,000 km of waterways and 1,000 harbors, and an additional 60 million m³ are removed to develop new projects. This work is accomplished at an annual cost of approximately 300 million dollars (Saucier, 1976).

Of the total volume dredged, almost two-thirds is returned to the open water. Although past decisions regarding the disposition of dredged materials were based primarily on economic considerations, recent environmental concerns have dictated alternative criteria in many cases. In particular, certain restrictions on the open water disposal of dredgings that are judged to be polluted have given rise to the trend toward their disposal in diked containment areas. However, the implementation of this alternative requires that thousands of acres of new land be made available; for example, about 28 million m² are required each year to handle the dredged material currently (1976) being placed on land, and it is projected that this land requirement will increase in the future (Kirby et al., 1973; Walsh, 1976).

In order to minimize costs, containment areas have been traditionally located close to the source of the dredged material. However, land availability near the highly developed and industrialized areas associated with harbors and waterways is continuously diminishing, and land appropriation costs are becoming excessively high. Furthermore, the confined disposal of dredged material continues to receive increasing opposition from environmental groups who complain about such factors as the unnatural appearance of dredged material, the visual incompatibility of confinement structures with the natural and man-made surroundings, disturbing odors, and the interference of dredged material disposal sites with existing and proposed land-use patterns (Mann et al., 1975). Accordingly, there is a pressing need to minimize the amount of dredged material that is permanently confined in conventional diked containment areas and to develop methodologies for disposal area reuse and for productive uses of dredged material.

Many activities, although necessary or desirable for the advancement of mankind, have an adverse effect on the environment; for example, many mining operations, such as strip-mining for coal or oil shale, mining for iron or copper ore, and excavations for sand and gravel, result in a drastic disturbance of the land by removing the topsoil, destroying all vegetation, displacing wildlife, and creating huge open pits. Since many of the dredged sediments, especially those located within agricultural watersheds, are rich in nutrients, and since the bulk transport of slurries via pipeline over long distances is both technically and economically feasible in many cases, the potential usefulness of dredged material in the reclamation and revegetation of disturbed lands offers interesting possibilities. Accordingly, a unique solution emerges for the dual problems of reclaiming drastically disturbed lands and disposing of dredged materials, and the ensuing discussion will address (i) problems associated with the confinement of dredged material, (ii) the quality of dredged material landfills, (iii) concepts for disposal area reuse and ultimate use, (iv) unconventional landfill operations, such as the reclamation of drastically disturbed lands and the development of offshore islands, and (v) other productive uses, such as artificial habitat creation, agriculture enhancement, and manufacture of construction materials.

II. CONFINEMENT OF DREDGED MATERIAL

In general, the confined disposal of dredged material involves (i) the aquisition of land, (ii) the construction of confinement dikes, (iii) the placement of the dredged material slurry into the disposal area, and (iv) the dewatering of the slurry. The problems most often encountered in this operation are (i) the diminishing availability of land, (ii) increasing costs, (iii) poor foundation conditions for the confining dikes, (iv) quality control of effluents returned to the open waters, (v) poor quality (with respect to engineering characteristics) of the resulting landfills, (vi) undesirable aesthetic factors, (vii) narrowing and/or distortion of natural waterways, and (viii) the public perception of dredged materials as useless wastes. The typical layout of disposal areas shown in Fig. 1 depicts some of those problems; the disposal sites are located near an industrialized urban area with limited land availability, the dikes are founded in part on soft underlying soils, the cross-section of the river is reduced by the encroachment of the containment areas, the island disposal site at the mount of the river may alter natural flow patterns, and the poor quality of the landfills has thus far precluded their usefulness in regional development projects. However, the depletion of disposal sites is perhaps the most pressing of these problems, and the following three alternatives are offered for its solution: (i) aquisition of upland sites, often necessitating the use of long-distance transport systems for the dredged material, (ii)

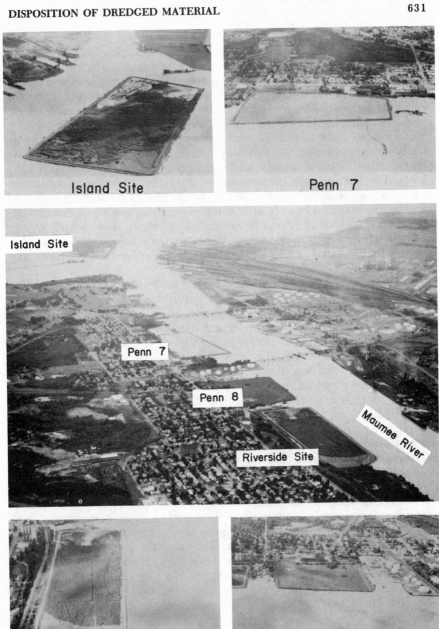

Fig. 1—Aerial views of Toledo disposal areas.

diking in shallow and possibly deep water, and (iii) purchase of large tracts of land for permanent dredged material collection sites (Murphy & Zeigler, 1974). Regardless of the location of a disposal site, certain common problems deal with (i) the transportation of dredged material to the site, (ii) the contamination of the environment and the ground water by effluents and leachates, and (iii) the final productive and/or beneficial use of the resulting landfill.

Dredged material may be conveyed into disposal areas either hydraulically or mechanically, but hydraulic placement is by far the most common method. This is usually accomplished by pumping through a submerged or floating pipeline from either a pipeline or hopper dredge; occasionally a combination of these two methods uses rehandling basins to receive the material from hopper dredges or scows and a pipeline dredge to pump the material into permanent disposal areas. The technology for such short-distance transportation systems is well advanced, and operational, maintenance, and cost details are well understood (Boyd et al., 1972; Murphy & Zeigler, 1974; Mohr, 1974).

Long-distance pumping is often defined as the hydraulic transport of a slurry through pipelines that are sufficiently long to require the placement of one or more booster pumps within the system. The coal and mineral industries have made efficient use of long-distance slurry pipelines to transport materials for hundreds of miles (Thornton, 1970; Murphy & Zeigler, 1974). The U.S. Army Corps of Engineers Philadelphia District (1969) has studied the technical and economic feasibility of long-distance pipelines, and several valuable suggestions have been advanced for the design of such systems to handle dredged material slurries; as two examples, pipelines up to 8 km long have been used to transport slurries along the Gulf Coast (Murphy & Zeigler, 1974), and large quantities of sand dredged from the Hudson River were pumped 11 km across northeastern New Jersey for use as roadbed material in East Rutherford (Walsh, 1976).

Despite its advantages, the concept of long-distance pumping is not without problems. Rehandling stations must be provided to remove objectionable materials, such as scrap iron and large rock fragments, and booster stations, pumps, power requirements, and extra personnel add appreciably to the cost of the system. Easements for long pipelines may be difficult to acquire, and leakage, especially in populated areas, must be avoided. Notwithstanding these problems and considering the successful application of long-distance pipelines in other industries, the concept appears both technically and economically feasible for the dredging industry.

Continuing efforts are being made to study the fate of pollutants from dredged materials placed in disposal areas and to develop methods for preventing pollution of the environment. To date, however, few studies have been completed to aid in determining the environmental impact of dredged material confinement on the surrounding area. Krizek et al. (1976) recently developed a methodology which considers disposal areas as solid-liquid separation systems and provides guidelines for the design of such facilities to control the amount of suspended solids in the effluents being discharged. Based on a water quality study for one typical disposal area in Toledo, Ohio, Krizek et al. (1974a) found that (i) sedimentation in a confined disposal area significantly improves the quality of the effluents that are returned to the receiving water, and (ii) effluents were similar in quality to the ambient river water. In an extensive laboratory study of leachates from actual dredged materials, Krizek et al. (1974b) concluded that the long-term pollution potential of leachates from dredged material landfills may not pose a serious problem in most cases, because the quality of the leachates improves rapidly with time and ground water flow would likely dilute any concentrations of contaminants to acceptable levels. The U.S. Army Corps of Engineers (Boyd et al., 1972; Walsh, 1976) is currently conducting a comprehensive study to characterize the effluents and leachates from confined disposal areas and to determine their effect on the environment.

When the beneficial or productive use of dredged material is considered, attention is often focused on the creation of landfills and the subsequent use of disposal areas for various purposes. Many harbor and port facilities in the coastal areas of the United States have been constructed totally or partly on dredged material landfills. In addition, highways, airports, recreational areas, lakefront residential developments, golf courses, and many similar facilities have been built on dredge spoil in numerous areas. However, a careful review indicates that long-range planning was actually nonexistent in most of these cases, and it was only a fortuitous circumstance that a usable fill area was available in the right place at the right time. Long-range plans are necessary for the proper utilization of dredged material landfills. The final properties of a dredged material landfill depend primarily on the characteristics of the material and the methods used to construct the fill; depending on these factors, fills can be used as construction sites, recreational areas, wildlife refuges, or areas for horticulture or mariculture products.

III. DREDGED MATERIAL LANDFILLS

When dredged material is placed in a diked containment area, it is usually in a slurry form with not more than about 20% solids; natural sedimentation removes most of the suspended solids, and the supernatant waters are returned to the adjoining bodies of open water. Figure 2 shows several views of typical conditions associated with the hydraulic placement of dredged material slurries in diked confinement areas; once the slurry is pumped into the area, the coarse particles and clay lumps are rapidly removed from suspension and the finer solids settle farther from the inflow pipe as they are carried toward a sluicing device from which the excess water is discharged. After the supernatants are removed, the sediments still have an extremely high water content, and this precludes most productive uses of the resulting landfill. Dewatering these materials

Fig. 2—Hydraulic placement of dredged material slurries in diked confinement areas.

serves the dual purpose of reducing their volume and improving their engineering properties, such as strength and compressibility, thereby rendering them more useful as landfill. Based on an evaluation of various dewatering techniques, Krizek et al. (1973) concluded that evaporation is probably the most effective and economical method, especially when thin layers of material are placed sequentially in the disposal area and sufficient time is allowed between lifts for gravity drainage and dessication with or without mechanical agitation. One such dewatering methodology has been developed and pilot tested with excellent results (Garbe & Tsai, 1976); evaporation rates were accelerated by periodic mechanical agitation of the sediments, and the dry density of the materials increased substantially to yield a moderate bearing capacity. Similar conditioning techniques can produce landfills with relatively uniform engineering properties and the ability to support light structures.

IV. REUSE OF DISPOSAL AREAS

Current practice in dredged material confinement is limited to obtaining a disposal area, filling it with dredged material, and then seeking another area; however, this is hardly an acceptable plan for productive land use, and methods are now being developed to promote more effective practices for the confined disposal of dredged material. The objectives of disposal area reuse (Montgomery & Palermo, 1976) are simply to maintain disposal areas convenient to dredging operations for an indefinite period of time while ensuring that disposal operations remain environmentally acceptable. Under such a scheme, the disposal area would serve as a collection and processing site where any valuable portions of the dredged material would be recovered and worthless portions would be treated, if necessary, and discarded under more favorable operating conditions. Disposal area reuse offers the advantages that (i) permanent disposal sites could be established convenient to areas of extensive maintenance dredging, (ii) the expense and objections associated with providing new lands for disposal sites near urban areas are eliminated, and (iii) construction and landfill materials are made available for productive use. The results of preliminary studies by Montgomery and Palermo (1976) are encouraging, but continued effort must be directed toward the development of a workable methodology for disposal area reuse. However, even under such a management concept, it is reasonable to expect that a number of disposal areas will ultimately be filled and rendered inoperational.

V. ULTIMATE USE OF LANDFILLS

As land disposal sites are filled and reuse management schemes are exhausted, the ultimate use of the resulting landfills is of paramount importance to the social and economic well-being of the local community. In previous cases where easements for land disposal have been granted, there has been little control over the subsequent use of the filled areas, except through standard zoning procedures (Walsh, 1976). However, current development pressures in port areas dictate that an overall plan is needed for the phased development and management of all land, including dredged material disposal areas. Accordingly, it is necessary to evolve recreation-oriented and other private and public land use concepts and to assess the technical, economic, institutional, and environmental incentives and constraints that govern the development of dredged material disposal areas as landfill sites. Most urban areas suffer from a severe lack of recreational opportunities, especially for the poor and the aged. The idea of using dredged material landfills as waterfront recreation areas to alleviate this deficiency has been investigated by Skjei (1976) and found to be feasible, despite the constraints associated with the quality of the material, the single-purpose nature of dredging projects, and competing land uses. In a more comprehensive study, deBettencourt et al. (1976) have developed a methodology for quantitatively evaluating the various alternatives in a multi-objective land use planning process.

VI. RECLAMATION OF DRASTICALLY DISTURBED LANDS

Many of the dredged materials obtained from maintenance projects consist of fine-grained silt or clay with various amounts of organics and other nutrients. While the physical and chemical characteristics of untreated fine-grained dredged sediments are not usually conducive to favorable engineering properties, they frequently provide the potential for plant growth. The abundant wild vegetation shown in Fig. 3 developed within 6 to 24 months on several inactive disposal sites; this rapid plant growth gives ample evidence that certain nutrient-rich dredged materials are capable of playing a positive role in land reclamation projects. In cases where the land is drastically disturbed from mining and waste management operations, the placement of dredged material in degraded areas

Fig. 3—Rapid growth of vegetation.

can provide the dual benefit of (i) circumventing the need to acquire new land for a disposal site and (ii) fostering new plant growth on formerly barren areas.

In the one preliminary study to investigate the use of dredged material for reclaiming strip-mined land (Walsh, 1976), both freshwater and brackish samples of fine-grained dredged material were blended with typical strip-mined spoil, a mixture of grasses was sown on the various combinations, and initial plant growth and soil physico-chemical changes were monitored. Although no results are yet available, a field demonstration may be conducted if the results of this preliminary investigation are promising. Without doubt, the potential exists to reclaim large expanses of strip-mined land by dredged material. In abandoned areas in eastern coal regions, dredged material could be incorporated into the strip-mine surface, and in the west where coal is currently being removed from seams up to 30 m thick, considerable quantities of fill material could be used to properly reclaim these large mined-out areas. Although the accessibility of strip-mined lands is unfortunately a major factor affecting the implementation of such ideas, continued improvements in long-distance pipeline technology may provide a technically and economically feasible solution. Another interesting alternative involves the twofold use of trains to transport coal to port areas and dewatered dredged material to mining areas.

Based on the results of a recent poll to investigate the constraints associated with marketing dredged material, Wakeford and McDonald (1974) found that the most popular productive use suggested for dredged material was cover for sanitary landfills. The most desirable physical properties for sanitary landfill cover are that it be dry and relatively impermeable to prevent leachate migration and, after dewatering, fine-grained dredged material can satisfy these requirements; in addition, dredged material may adsorb harmful contaminants in the leachates. However, the high cost of transporting the material may render this course of action economically unfeasible, and the environmental consequences of such a use must be assessed more comprehensively. Other novel ideas in solid waste management include the construction of trash mountains for recreational purposes; despite the proven utility of such projects in many areas the lack of a suitable soil material is frequently a major constraint that impedes their development. Hence, it is possible that major recreational opportunities may evolve from the combination of two very complex disposal problems. However, before such a concept can be implemented, technical design criteria must be documented, and detailed cost-benefit analyses and environmental studies must be undertaken.

VII. CREATION OF OFFSHORE ISLANDS

The desire to utilize dredged materials in a beneficial manner leads to a number of technically feasible, but economically uncertain, possibilities. Perhaps the most obvious alternative is the use of dredged material to form island or waterfront developments. One promising concept, particularly for the Greak Lakes region, is the creation of an "archipelago" near the shoreline. The attractiveness of this scheme lies in its multi-objective nature; in addition to providing space for the disposal of dredged material, the resulting islands can be used for recreational purposes and to enhance beach protection. The significance of this latter advantage is magnified by the present near-record high lake level and the decrease in shore protection by ice due to relatively mild winters. Although the lake level will certainly recede in the coming years (the record low was only 10 years ago), high water and resulting shore erosion will recur from time to time and must either be prevented or endured.

Constructed in stages within the context of a long-term plan, recreational islands could strengthen harbor defenses, provide space for the disposal of dredged materials and solid wastes, and furnish shore protection and shelter for small-boat marinas and anchorages. Such islands could be made topographically interesting as recreational parks with bathing beaches, fishing areas, hiking and cycle trails, tramways, restaurants, facilities for games, etc. However, due to lack of experience, the environmental impact and economic feasibility of such a project is still unclear, and extensive studies are needed before deciding on possible implementation. It is paramount that a long-term plan on the development of an "archipelago" must take into consideration several factors, such as the manner and cost of construction, environmental impact, and legal implications.

This concept can be made more economical if other beneficial uses are included in the actual project. For instance, the idea of simultaneously creating artificial islands and underground pumped storage appears intriguing. The excavated rock from the pumped storage facility could be used to create a dike along the shore of a proposed island, and the enclosed space could be gradually filled with dredged spoil and other waste material. Such an arrangement eliminates many environmental concerns and renders both concepts (that is, underground pumped storage and lake archipelago) much more attractive economically. At the same time, the pumped storage installation would enhance the electric power supply of the adjacent and usually urbanized area by producing valuable peak power and increasing system reliability.

VIII. CREATION OF ARTIFICIAL HABITAT

As mentioned earlier, one of the more feasible alternatives to open water spoil disposal is the construction of artificial habitats, such as spoil islands and new marsh areas. Large volumes of polluted dredge spoil with poor engineering properties could be put to productive use in this way. A comprehensive set of guidelines prepared by Johnson and McGuinness (1975) for material placement in marsh creation enable one to decide (i) if marsh creation warrants significant consideration, (ii) which is the most suitable type of marsh to build, and (iii) what are the most efficient establishment techniques. Adequate steps must be taken to reduce the physical impact of waves and littoral drift on a newly created marsh; this may be accomplished most satisfactorily by careful siting of the marsh and by reinforcing the areas most sensitive to erosion. In addition, when siting and designing the configuration of a marsh, its influence on local circulation patterns and other nearby marshes should be minimized. A cellular layout of the confinement areas and selective placement techniques can be used to alleviate scour and turbidity as the slurry is pumped into the area.

Once the dredged material is in place, suitable marsh vegetation must be established. Based on a survey and evaluation of marsh plant establishment techniques in both fresh and salt water areas, Kadlec and Wentz (1974) and Wentz et al. (1974) determined that the basic problems encountered in establishing marsh plants are (i) physically unsuitable substrates, (ii) nutrient deficiencies in the spoils, (iii) contamination in the sediments, (iv) unfavorable patterns of water fluctuation, (v) excessive wind or current action, (vi) excessive turbidity, and (vii) unfavorable water depths; of these, unsuitable substrate is the major deterrent. In a series of experiments conducted to develop successful techniques for the propagation and establishment of saltmarsh cordgrass (*Spartina alterniflora*) on dredge spoil disposal sites, Woodhouse et al. (1972, 1974) found that, although seeding is more economical and has good results in sheltered areas, transplants can better tolerate the effects of blowing sand and storm waves. The vegetative development of seeded and transplanted areas in the intertidal zone of dredge spoil disposal sites was rapid, and primary production at test sites equaled that of older and more established marshes by the second growing season. However, when marsh plants are established on polluted dredged spoil, there may be a problem with the recycling of heavy metals. Although saltmarsh cordgrass can regulate its uptake of most heavy metals, Windom and Stickney (1972) observed a build-up of methylated mercury in the tissue of this species. Since the detritus of saltmarsh cordgrass is an important food source for estuarine and marine detritivores, the further concentration of methylated mercury in the food chain may present a problem that commands further study before the use of polluted dredge spoil in marsh creation becomes a common practice.

IX. AGRICULTURE ENHANCEMENT

A frequently suggested alternative to the diked containment of dredged material is its use to increase the productivity of marginally suitable agricultural lands. Although some former dredged material disposal areas are now being used as farmland (Walsh, 1976), their capabilities have not yet been documented. The use of dredged material to create or condition agricultural land has been virtually untried in the United States, but several studies involving the use of digested sewage sludge have been made (Boyd et al., 1972). Throughout history, flooding rivers, such as the Mississippi and the Nile, have deposited large amounts of sediments on low-lying lands which are now considered some of the most fertile farmlands in the world, and the basic question is whether man can imitate this natural process. One ongoing effort to partially resolve this problem (Walsh, 1976) involves a greenhouse study on dredged materials selected from various parts of the country; the objectives of this study are to (i) evaluate the resource value of dredged material in agriculture and (ii) develop specific guidelines for deciding whether a specific dredged material can safely and beneficially be applied to agricultural land.

Toth and Gold (1970) applied varying concentrations of dredge spoil from the Delaware River to five different soil types ranging from sandy loam to fine sand, and wheat, corn, peppers, and forage were grown on test plots for 2 years. Although no significant increases in crop production were observed on the better soils, a twofold increase in production was observed on the poorer soils when pH levels were controlled and fertilizers added. Conditioning soils with dredged material changed their percolation rates, aeration, textural characteristics, moisture-holding quality, cation exchange capacity, pH, organic concentration, and clay mineral distribution. The spoils were not sufficiently contaminated to cause reduced plant growth, but measurably higher concentrations of zinc and manganese were found in plant tissue. However, local variations in soil types and spoil characterisics render inadvisable the extrapolation of these results to other areas.

One problem with using dredged material from a saline environment to condition soils is the concentration of salts. Boyd et al. (1972) suggest that saline spoil can be used to create pasture land if certain moderately salt-tolerant forage plants, like African Star (*Cynodon plectostachysis*), are planted until the salts are leached away. Based on a study of the technical and economic feasibility of commercial production of lawn sod and other horticulture products on confined dredged material disposal sites, Arthur D. Little, Inc. (1975) found that weeds, salinity, contaminants, and inundation made horticultural production unfeasible on active dredge spoil disposal sites. In general, the poor accessibility, size, and location of sites rendered them incompatible with production needs but, subject to certain constraints, the commercial production of lawn sod, nursery products, foliage plants, and Christmas trees may be feasible on mature disposal sites.

X. CONSTRUCTION MATERIALS AND PRODUCTS

The possibility of using dredged material or portions thereof for construction purposes has received some attention. Based on an evaluation of methods for separating sand and gravel from dredged material to reduce its volume and create a marketable resource, Mallory and Nawrocki (1974) suggested that the most efficient method of separation depended on the characteristics of the materials to be dredged, the primary dredge site, and the total quantity of material involved. For example, in long-term operations where the dredged materials contain significant fractions of sand and gravel, a semipermanent installation with thickeners and hydraulic scalpers is economically justified, but thickeners and hydrocyclones are more efficient when only small fractions of sand are present in the spoil. The major question, of course, is whether the cost of separating sand and gravel from dredged material is less than its average market value.

Once again, the need for long-range planning and coordination of the dredged material placement program with anticipated regional land developments must be emphasized if there are any intentions of using the treated spoil as landfill. According to Reikenis et al. (1974), regional demands for landfill and construction materials (sand and gravel) vary significantly and are functions of population shifts and the economic growth of specific regions. Because these shifts are relatively rapid and because a long period is required to condition and stockpile large volumes of dredged material, the timing of the placement program is crucial. Finally, the ultimate usage of the spoil should be known before it is placed in the diked area, so that appropriate methods of conditioning can be selected.

The manufacture of construction materials such as bricks from dredge spoil has been studied by Heller and Thelan (1971), and it was determined that the high water-holding capacity of the dredged material and the need to use binders make large scale brick production too expensive to be economically feasible. However, Rhoads et al. (1975) reported that fine-grained muds from northeastern U.S. harbors have been used successfully to produce high quality ceramic materials. For this purpose, muds must contain from 87 to 99% silicate minerals, less than 10% shell carbonates, and less than 3% volatile organics, and 80% (by dry weight) of the particles must be less than 62 μm in diameter (coarse silt). The presence of contaminants seems to create little problem because, as the muds are fired, mercury, cadmium, and lead are released in a gas phase and other contaminants are changed into an inert glass phase. The principal drawback to this approach is that significant volumes of dredge spoil are not likely to be used in the manufacture of ceramic materials.

XI. SUMMARY AND CONCLUSIONS

The disposal of dredged material is becoming more difficult because of diminishing land availability, increasing land acquisition costs, and increasingly stringent environmental constraints. In the future the amount of dredged material to be permanently confined in diked containment areas must be minimized, and a number of solutions are proposed to accomplish this goal; however, most of these solutions are currently under investigation with respect to their technical and economic feasibility and environmental compatibility. Management schemes are being considered for disposal area reuse, but the success of these schemes is dependent in part on the development of methods for using dredged materials productively. In the long-term scheme the ultimate use of dredged material landfills must be planned to avoid the creation of unnatural or disturbed lands. The proliferation of diked disposal areas can be reduced by exploiting the technical and economic feasibility of long-distance pipelines to transfer dredged material to reclamation areas and the high capacity of dredged material to enhance vegetation. In addition to the use of dredge spoil to reclaim drastically disturbed lands, such as those resulting from various mining operations, concepts are also being developed for artificial habitat creation, agriculture enhancement, and other productive uses.

In an effort to attain these objectives, a significant amount of research is currently (1976) being conducted. This research is supported and coordinated in large part through the Dredged Material Research Program at the U.S. Army Engineer Waterways Experiment Station, Vicksburg, Mississippi. This program is scheduled for completion in 1978 and should provide a major contribution toward resolving many of the problems associated with dredging and disposal operations. With due recognition for the fact that considerable research is currently underway, the following conclusions can be advanced:

1) The disposal of dredged material in diked containment areas is very expensive and frequently results in a highly disturbed natural environment; hence, this practice should be minimized in the future. However, with proper planning, existing and future dredged material landfills can be developed and utilized productively as recreational areas, parks, and perhaps sites for light construction.

2) It is technically feasible to utilize dredged material to fill offshore borrow pits, create offshore islands, fill pits and quarries, reclaim strip-mined areas, create artificial habitats, enhance agriculture, and produce construction materials. However, to consider dredged material as such a resource, it must be made readily available at the geographic location where it can be put to productive use and the economic feasibility of the overall plan must be examined.

3) The increased use of dredged material for productive purposes requires that improved information be obtained regarding the (i) conditioning and handling of dredged materials to enhance the engineering properties of resulting landfills, (ii) long-distance transportation of dredged material, (iii) effects of leachates and effluents on the environment, and (iv) selection and use of dredged material for agricultural enhancement and artificial habitat creation.

LITERATURE CITED

Arthur D. Little, Inc. 1975. A feasibility study of lawn sod production and/or related activities on dredged material disposal sites. Contract Rep. D-75-1, U.S. Army Eng. Waterways Exp. Stn., Vicksburg, Miss.

Boyd, M. B., R. T. Saucier, J. W. Keeley, R. L. Montgomery, R. D. Brown, D. B. Mathis, and C. J. Guice. 1972. Disposal of dredge spoil. Problem identification and assessment and research program development. Tech. Rep. H-72-8, U.S. Army Eng. Waterways Exp. Stn., Vicksburg, Miss.

deBettencourt, J. S., R. J. Krizek, and G. L. Peterson. 1976. Site use evaluation for dredged material landfills. J. Urban Planning and Dev. Div., Am. Soc. of Civil Eng. 103(UP1): 39–51.

Garbe, C. W., and K. W. Tsai. 1976. Hydraulic dredge spoil for land reclamation. Natl. Water Resour. and Ocean Eng. Conv., 5–8 Apr. 1976, Preprint 2678. Am. Soc. of Civil Eng., San Diego, Calif.

Heller, H. L., and E. Thelan. 1971. Building materials from dredge spoil. Tech. Rep. F-C3069. Franklin Inst. Res. Lab., Philadelphia, Pa.

Johnson, L. E., and W. V. McGuinness, Jr. 1975. Guidelines for material placement in marsh creation. Contract Rep. D-75-2, U.S. Army Eng. Waterways Exp. Stn., Vicksburg, Miss.

Kadlec, J. A., and W. A. Wentz. 1974. State-of-the-art survey and evaluation of marsh plant establishment techniques: Induced and natural, Vol. I: Report of research. Contract Rep. D-74-9, U.S. Army Eng. Waterways Exp. Stn., Vicksburg, Miss.

Kirby, C. J., J. W. Keeley, and J. Harrison. 1973. An overview of the technical aspects of the Corps of Engineers National Dredge Material Research Program. Misc. Pap. D-73-9, U.S. Army Eng. Waterways Exp. Stn., Vicksburg, Miss.

Krizek, R. J., J. A. FitzPatrick, and D. K. Atmatzidis. 1976. Dredged material confinement facilities as solid-liquid separation systems. p. 609–632. In Proc. of the Specialty Conf. on Dredging and Its Environmental Effects, 26–28 Jan. 1976, Am. Soc. of Civil Eng., Mobile, Ala.

Krizek, R. J., B. J. Gallagher, and G. M. Karadi. 1974a. Water quality study for a dredging disposal area. Tech. Rep. no. 4, by Northwestern Univ. to the Environ. Prot. Agency, EPA Grants 15070-GCK and R-800948, Evanston, Ill.

Krizek, R. J., G. M. Karadi, and P. L. Hummel. 1973. Engineering characteristics of polluted dredgings. Tech. Rep. no. 1, by Northwestern Univ. to the Environ. Prot. Agency, EPA Grants 15070-GCK and R-800948, Evanston, Ill.

Krizek, R. J., G. L. Roderick, and J. S. Jin. 1974b. Stabilization of dredged materials. Tech. Rep. no. 2, by Northwestern Univ. to the Environ. Prot. Agency, EPA Grants 15070-GCK and R-800948, Evanston, Ill.

Mallory, C. W., and M. A. Nawrocki. 1974. Containment area facility concepts for dredged material separation, drying, and rehandling. Contract Rep. D-74-6, U.S. Army Eng. Waterways Exp. Stn., Vicksburg, Miss.

Mann, R., W. A. Niering, R. Sabbatini, and P. Wells. 1975. Landscape concept development for confined dredged material sites. Contract Rep. D-75-5, U.S. Army Eng. Waterways Exp. Stn., Vicksburg, Miss.

Mohr, A. W. 1974. Development and future of dredging. J. of the Waterways Harbors and Coastal Eng. Div., Am. Soc. of Civil Eng. 100(WW2):69–83.

Montgomery, R. L., and M. R. Palermo. 1976. First steps toward achieving disposal area reuse. Misc. Pap. D-76-16, U.S. Army Eng. Waterways Exp. Stn., Vicksburg, Miss.

Murphy, W. L., and T. W. Ziegler. 1974. Practice and problems in the confinement of dredged materials in Corps of Engineers projects. Tech. Rep. D-74-2, U.S. Army Eng. Waterways Exp. Stn., Vicksburg, Miss.

Reikenis, R., V. Elias, and E. F. Drabkowski. 1974. Regional landfill and construction material needs in terms of dredged material characteristics and availability, Vol. 1: Main text. Contract Rep. D-74-2, U.S. Army Eng. Waterways Exp. Stn., Vicksburg, Miss.

Rhoads, D. C., R. B. Gordon, and J. R. Vaisnys. 1975. Conversion of marine muds to lightweight construction aggregate. Environ. Sci. Technol. 9(4):360–362.

Saucier, R. T. 1976. Dredged material as a natural resource—concepts for land improvement and reclamation. Misc. Pap. D-76-13, U.S. Army Eng. Waterways Exp. Stn., Vicksburg, Miss.

Skjei, S. S. 1976. Socioeconomic aspects of dredged material disposal: The creation of recreation land in urban areas. Contract Rep. D-76-6, U.S. Army Eng. Waterways Exp. Stn., Vicksburg, Miss.

Thornton, W. A. 1970. The hydraulic transport of solids in pipes—A bibliography. The British Hydromechanics Res. Assoc., Cranfield, Bedford, England.

Toth, S. J., and B. Gold. 1970. Agricultural value of dredged sediments. Final Rep. Rutgers Univ., New Brunswick, N.J.

U.S. Army Corps of Engineers, Philadelphia District. 1969. Long range spoil disposal study. 6-Vol. Tech. Rep., Philadelphia, Pa.

Wakeford, R. C., and D. McDonald. 1974. Legal, policy and institutional constraints associated with dredged material marketing and land enhancement. Contract Rep. D-74-7, U.S. Army Eng. Waterways Exp. Stn., Vicksburg, Miss.

Walsh, M. R. 1976. Dredged material as a natural resource. Natl. Water Resour. and Ocean Eng. Conf., 5–8 Apr. 1976, Preprint 2714. Am. Soc. of Civil Eng., San Diego, Calif.

Wentz, W. A., R. L. Smith, and J. A. Kadlec. 1974. State-of-the-art survey and evaluation of marsh plant establishment techniques: Induced and natural, Vol. II: A selected annotated bibliography on aquatic and marsh plants and their management. Contract Rep. D-74-9, U.S. Army Eng. Waterways Exp. Stn., Vicksburg, Miss.

Windom, H. L., and R. R. Stickney. 1972. Research to determine the environmental response to the deposition of spoil on salt marshes using diked and undiked techniques. Skidaway Inst. of Oceanography, Savannah, Ga.

Woodhouse, W. W., Jr., E. D. Seneca, and S. W. Broome. 1972. Marsh building with dredge spoil in North Carolina. Bull. 445, Agri. Exp. Stn., North Carolina State Univ., Raleigh, N.C.

Woodhouse, W. W., Jr., E. D. Seneca, and S. W. Broome. 1974. Propagation of *Spartina alterniflora* for substrate stabilization and salt marsh development. Tech. Memo. no. 46, U.S. Army Coastal Eng. Res. Center, Fort Belvoir, Va.

Copyright © 1978 ASA–CSSA–SSSA
677 South Segoe Road, Madison, WI 53711 USA
Reclamation of Drastically Disturbed Lands

Chapter 36

Vegetating Mine Tailings Ponds

REX F. NIELSON AND H. B. PETERSON

Utah State University
Logan, Utah

I. INTRODUCTION

The information presented in this paper is a general overview of the problems associated with establishing vegetation on tailing wastes, based on 10 years of research and experience in the field and laboratory. It is intended as a guide and not a technical report.

Large quantities of low grade ores of copper and uranium are mined and concentrated for smelting. In the process more than 99% of the material is waste solids. The process involves grinding of the rock and ores, tabling or floating out the mineral ores, and transporting the wastes or "tailings" to some retention ponds. These fine wastes range in size from sand to very fine slimes. Tailings are usually transported by water in a pipeline from the mill to a pond. A peripheral discharge allows the tailings to be deposited from the sides of the pond with the water often being decanted for recycle. On very large ponds the material may be discharged from a single point and allowed to run as a meandering stream within the pond. The sides of the pond are known as *berms* and are often built of tailings material; however, they are occasionally constructed with borrow materials from surrounding areas. Solids in the pond are stratified, with the coarse material being dropped near the point of discharge at the berm and the finer materials or slimes moving to the lower areas.

As a result of mining operations, numerous tailings ponds of varying size exist. A currently active unit in Utah is in excess of 20 km² and its depth exceeds 20 m. In contrast, some of the smaller uranium ponds that were built during the 1950's cover only a few hectares. With a few exceptions, most of the sites in the United States are located in an arid climate. It has been estimated that more than a half million metric tons of tailings are being deposited in ponds daily throughout the Intermountain West.

The major environmental problem that develops as a result of tailings ponds is dust. Where a pond is located near a populated area, it is not unusual for dust to be a serious nuisance to the inhabitants, with clouds often traveling many miles, affecting people, vegetation, and the landscape in general. When a pond becomes inactive, the surface drys out and, unless some preventative measures are taken, the fine particules are soon picked up by the winds. As long as a pond is active and kept moist, the dust problem is minimized. On some inactive ponds, when the chemistry of the tailings is favorable, a crust may develop on the surface as a result of acidification. These materials are less likely to be windborne than those where crusts do not form. Ponds with berms constructed exclusively of tailings become vulnerable to high intensity storms and serious wind and water erosion can occur. The aesthetic effects of a tailings pond on a landscape is usually objectionable unless efforts are made to vegetate or improve the site.

II. CHEMISTRY OF TAILINGS

The chemistry of tailings is influenced by the composition of the ore body being processed. Most sites contain small quantities of copper, manganese, iron, and zinc minerals not removed during processing and these move into the ponds as components of the tailings.

A significant effect on the chemistry of tailings is the constituents in the water being used to transport the tailings. The water may be salty and, since it is often decanted and recycled, the salinity tends to increase as a result of evaporation. Salt originating with water used in transport is a major problem affecting plant growth on tailings on the Kennecott site in Utah. In addition, the salinity of the pond is affected by the oxidation of the heavy metals and the salt produced thereby.

With the exception of some uranium ores, most tailings when deposited have a pH ranging from 7 to 10. Chemical changes in the ponds can often be rapid. On sites where pyrites are present, the usual process is for the sulfur to oxidize, lowering the pH to levels as low as 1.7. At pH values below 6, many compounds of the heavy metals are soluble, as indicated by the data in Table 1.

The quantity of heavy metals that eventually solubilize, are controlled by the original amount in the deposit. Measurements have been made on several sites to determine the rate of acidification. On one location in Arizona, copper tailings of known age were sampled. These data indicate that fresh tailings with a pH of 8 reached a value of 4 within 3 years and leveled off at 2 after 10 years. Similar studies with freshly de-

Table 1—The effect of induced pH change on the solubility of several cations in mill tailings

pH	Cu	Fe	Mn	Zn
		ppm		
7.3	0	0	1	0
7.1	0	0	9	0
6.8	0	0	10	0
5.9	6	0	40	2
5.5	45	10	60	10
5.2	140	20	100	14
4.5	400	80	108	33
4.2	625	128	125	37
3.5	1,117	250	166	52
2.3	2,693	508	281	74

posited copper tailings in Utah have shown changes from pH 8.2 to as low as 1.7 within 2.5 years (Nielson & Peterson, 1972). It appears that a threshold exists that may require several years to overcome before a pond starts to become acid. Probably the lime in the waste is neutralized during this period. However, once acidification begins, it proceeds at a rapid rate and, if sufficient sulfide is present, the entire pond will become acidic. It has been noted that the first sites to oxidize are those where heavy concentrations of pyrite exist. Tailings usually acidify first at or very near the surface, with the process continuing to deeper layers.

On experimental sites which were closely observed, it was noted that oxidation first appeared in spots about the size and shape of a tablespoon on the surface of the pond. Within a matter of a few weeks, these areas expanded to about 50 cm. After a year these sites that originally covered an area the size of a spoon spread to cover more than 20 m². At the end of 2 years, the various spots within the test area had coalesced, and the entire site was acidic.

The phenomena of oxidation and acification are restricted to ponds where significant quantities of sulfides are present. The pyrite content of observed ponds has ranged from a low of a few parts per million to a high of nearly 8%. Researchers are not in agreement as to whether the oxidation of pyrites is a biological reaction or a chemical process. Studies conducted by the authors suggest that both processes occur, although one may be dominant at a specific time or site (Utah State University. 1974. Consulting services for research on vegetation to stabilize tailings at Utah concentrators. Final Rep. to Kennecott Copper Corp., Grant no. 29-A-220-280).

III. SELECTING PLANT SPECIES

The problem of selecting plant species for vegetating a tailings pond is complicated by the fact that the composition of all ponds is different, as are the climatic conditions. Plants capable of performing well in the hot desert areas of Arizona are not suited to the mountainous areas of Montana.

Climate is a factor influencing the selection of plant species to be used on an individual site. Temperature extremes throughout the Intermountain West vary from highs in excess 38°C during the summertime to winter extremes of −40°C. In addition to temperature, the amount, frequency, and seasonal distribution of precipitation will also affect plant selection. Some tailings sites are located in summer rainfall zones, while others are restricted to only winter and spring precipitation. The presence of snow cover, its depth and duration, are also important. Winter hardiness in plants is affected by many factors; plants that are able to withstand extremely low temperatures under deep snow may not survive with the same temperatures if snow is not present.

A large number of native and introduced species are available. For example, the lovegrasses (*Erogrostis* sp.) are generally suited to the dry, hot areas of the Southwest. They are drought tolerant and can endure very high temperatures. The wheatgrass (Agropyron sp.) are somewhat drought and salt tolerant but will not endure excessively high temperatures. Their zone of adaptation ranges from the mountainous areas to the cool desert sites. Many of the species in these two genera have been introduced from various parts of the world and have been found to be effective as range or pasture plants.

We have found that species suited to the general environment on a competitive basis are generally good. These are usually vigorous, harsh plants that are not sensitive to nutrient imbalances and are not attractive feed for animals. In most of our arid areas the genotypes should be salt and drought tolerant and be nonsucculent (Nielsen & Peterson, 1973).

The use of native species is highly desirable but generally seeds of native plants are either not available or are difficult to obtain. Native plants adapted to harsh regimes have varying degrees of seed dormancy ranging from months to years and require special treatment before they will germinate. In addition, many of the species are difficult to establish. Once established, however, they are usually long lived.

Numerous efforts have been made throughout the United States and other areas of the world to select plants that are specifically tolerant to soluble salts of heavy metals. Unfortunately, the evolution of most plant species has not allowed this type of selectivity to occur. Researchers in England report some of the bentgrasses (Agrostis L.) grown on old mine heaps for many years have developed measurable tolerances to heavy metals (Gregory & Bradshaw, 1965). It is unfortunate that the bentgrasses are not adapted to the climatic regimes where most of the tailings occur in the western U.S.

The success of a vegetation program on a tailings site requires that stabilization occur and that the plant cover persist on a permanent basis. It has been observed by the authors that native plants invade seeded areas and usually take over. It is likely that the climax vegetation on any site will be made up largely of native species.

A secondary factor that should be considered when selecting plants is whether or not the site is to be used as a sanctuary for birds or animals. If this is one of the goals, then the selection of species may be modified to meet these needs.

IV. ESTABLISHING VEGETATION

Once the selection of plant species has been made, it usually becomes necessary to modify the site so that it will support vegetation. On active ponds where flooding occurs at regular intervals throughout the growing season, it is not practical to make plantings. Where the sites are flooded periodically every several years, it may be desirable to plant on a temporary basis during the period the pond is inactive. Most vegetation programs are carried out on ponds that are no longer active.

A. Toxicities

Prior to planting, an evaluation should be made of the toxicities that exist or may develop (Peterson & Nielson, 1973). a pH measurement will provide some information on the status of heavy metal solubility. If the pH is below 6, it is likely that soluble heavy metals may be present in sufficient quantities to adversely affect plant growth. The addition of lime to bring pH levels up to 7 or higher usually precipitates the heavy metals in forms that are less detrimental to plants. A long-term solution, however, will require an evaluation of the acid-producing potential of the pond, since heavy rates of lime may be required to prevent the pond from reacidifying.

B. Salinity

The salinity or salt content is measured as the electrical conductivity (mmhos/cm^3) of the saturation extract. On agricultural soils with adequate water, salt-sensitive crops are affected when the conductivity ranges from 4 to 8. Only the most salt-tolerant crops will grow within the range of 8 to 16. When readings are in excess of 16, no crops survive. These values are likely too high for use on evaluating tailings material where the soil-water-plant relations are less desirable. Where the conductivity measures in excess of 4, it is desirable to leach the salt from the system with irrigation. Leaching requires a drainage capability which will allow the salt to be moved in the tailings profile to a depth of about 5 feet (1.52 m) or more. On some salty sites that have been studied, rainfall was adequate to move the salt deep enough in the profile to allow plants to grow satisfactorily.

Numerous studies have been conducted on the leaching requirement of tailings, and they have been found to behave somewhat similarly to soils with the same texture. The layering within a tailings pond resulting from alternate deposition of sands and slimes may tend to inhibit the downward free movement of water. Where high levels of salinity exist, the salt profile can vary with the season. Measurements made at the Utah site of Kennecott Copper Corporation show that salt levels in the top 6 inches (15.24 cm) are the highest during mid- and late summer when evaporation has accumulated the salts near the surface. In contrast, the lowest readings are always measured in the spring following the melting of the winter snows and spring rains (Nielson & Peterson, 1972 and 1973).

C. Nutrient Status

All tailings ponds are usually very deficient in plant nutrients (Nielson & Peterson, 1973; Peterson & Nielson, 1973). The only exception is some uranium ponds where ammonia was used in the processing of the ores. On such sites, nitrogen levels are temporarily adequate. The phosphorus and potash status of tailings is dependent on the ore body being processed. Some sites contain sufficient potassium and phosphorus to support adequate plant growth. However, most sites are deficient in phosphorus. It has been observed where large open pit mines are being operated that tailings derived from different sections of the mine contain different levels of phosphorus. For this reason it is possible to have both adequate and deficient levels of phosphorus in the tailings being derived from a single operation. A soil test will provide information on the phosphorus and potassium status of the tailings.

The success of establishing plants on tailings is dependent upon supplying the needed nutrients in quantities necessary to promote good plant growth. The fertilizer rates used are generally similar to those required on agricultural sites of similar character. Since tailings are deficient in nitrogen, usually deficient in phosphorus, and perhaps deficient in potassium, rates to meet these needs should be applied. The long-term nutrient needs for maintaining vegetation on a tailings pond is dependent upon the original nature of the tailings, and the amount and kinds of plant growth that can be developed. Where legumes can be established and maintained, they can supply some needed nitrogen. If plant residues are allowed to recycle, phosphorus and potassium requirements will usually be minimal once the initial threshold levels are established. Most tailings ponds require fertilization for the first 2 or 3 years after establishment. Additional treatments on alternate years will be required until plant residues become adequate to meet the fertilizer needs. In the more humid areas where high rainfall can leach out the plant nutrients, it may be necessary to continue to periodically apply fertilizers.

V. PLANTING PROCEDURES

Site preparation for planting a tailings pond can pose problems not encountered in agriculture. Since tailings ponds are stratified with slimes and sand, physical instability can be a serious problem with equipment where slimes accumulate. These areas have a high retention capability for water and may remain unstable for years after a pond ceases to be active. The history of tailings ponds throughout the west has shown many cases where equipment has been lost in the unstable areas. Sites that have been inactive for some time will usually have developed sand dunes. These require a smoothing operation and incorporating with the finer materials to facilitate planting and moisture control. Wherever possible it is desirable to plow the site to a depth 25 to 30 cm to mix the sand and slime and to break up layers that may inhibit moisture and plant root penetration.

The time of planting is influenced primarily by the climate of the area and the species to be used. In the arid areas of the mountain west where winter snow cover develops, late fall seedings of grass have proven more effective than spring plantings. Where legumes are used, early spring seedings are best. Most native species grown from seed are more likely to succeed if fall planted.

If the site is sufficiently stable to support a tractor and drill, planting can be completed in one operation. When this method cannot be used, a cyclone seeder or aerial application must be used. This type of seeding must be followed with a roughening operation to cover the seed.

VI. IRRIGATION

A critical factor in vegetating a tailings pond is the availability of moisture for plant growth. The distribution of precipitation and the total amount available will determine whether or not irrigation will be required to establish and maintain plantings. Most sites in the west require some irrigation. In the driest areas irrigation is needed to supply the major part of the plant needs. On other sites, supplemental water may be needed only during the periods plants are becoming established. The amount and frequency of irrigation will be governed by the water-holding capacity of the tailings, climate, species being used, and the quantity of plant material being grown (Nielson & Peterson, 1973).

The source of irrigation water should be evaluated, since many of the waters available at the mill site are of poor quality. Water ladened with salts and heavy metals is of little or no value in establishing vegetation (H. B. Peterson and R. F. Nielson. [In press]. Heavy metals in relation to plant growth on mine and mill wastes. Symp. on Waste Disposal and the Renewal and Management of Degraded Environments. July 1973. Advanced Study Inst., NATO).

VII. EROSION CONTROL

The susceptibility of tailings to wind erosion necessitates some type of protection to prevent the young plants from being sand blasted or blown out. A considerable number of chemical binding agents are available that can be sprayed on the tailings following planting. Many of these materials have been proven effective for short-term stabilization while the plants are becoming established. Straw or other plant residues used as a mulch works well unless high velocity winds are encountered for extended periods. In such cases the mulch is either blown away or buried.

Mechanical barriers such as snow fences, when closely spaced, have been effective in preventing blowing on some sites. Fine slag spread uniformly on a pond has also been useful in preventing wind erosion. This material is heavier than sand and is not subject to blowing. Plant growth in areas stabilized with slag may be poor due to high temperatures induced by the dark slag materials.

VIII. CONCLUSIONS

The tailing wastes are highly variable in physical and chemical characteristics. This is related to the kind of operation, the variability of the ore, the pyrite and other sulfides present, the milling process, the quality and quantity of water used to transport the waste, and the age and exposure of the tailings.

An evaluation of site conditions is essential when contemplating establishing vegetation. This is difficult because of the analytical problems and the changes that take place in the waste piles. Sulfides oxidize to increase the acidity, salinity, and solubility of heavy metals. In addition, there may be heavy metals enrichment from outside the pile, such as from smelter stacks or water used for irrigation.

The plants grown most successfully are those suited to the general environment. They are vigorous, nonsucculent species that are not sensitive to nutrient deficiencies or nutrient imbalances. It is best when the plants are not attractive to animals for preferential feeding. In arid climates where some irrigation water is available, such plants as *Agropyron elongatum* and *Festuca arundinacea* are used effectively. Among legumes *Melilotis officinalis* has been the best.

Many of the wastes are low in ion exchange and buffer capacity. All waste pile materials we have studied are deficient in plant nutrients and/ or become acidic. Lime incorporated into the tailings and fertilizers are needed in order to facilitate plant growth. Few, if any, plants will grow in tailings where heavy metals are present at a pH of 5.5 or less. Lime is usually needed to raise the pH and reduce the solubility of the metals. A method is needed to determine the oxidation potential and rate and magnitude of acidification. Methods other than liming are needed to restrict sulfide oxidation. Small uranium tailing ponds can usually be covered with top soil and then plants can easily be established.

In summary, drainage water from the waste pile containing soluble heavy metals constitutes a pollution hazard to receiving waters. Some means for control of wind erosion is usually necessary; cost is a major determining factor as to which material or method is used. In arid climates some irrigation is usually necessary in order to establish an adequate vegetative cover. It is likely some supplemental water would be effective in more humid climates during periods of drought.

LITERATURE CITED

Gregory, R. R. G., and A. D. Bradshaw. 1965. Heavy metal tolerance in populations of *Agrostis tenuis Sibth* and other grasses. Dep. Agric. Bot., Univ. College of North Wales, Bango. New Phytol. 64:131–143.

Nielson, R. F., and H. B. Peterson. 1972. Treatment of mine tailings to promote vegetative stabilization. Utah Agric. Exp. Stn. Bull. 485.

Nielson, R. F., and H. B. Peterson. 1973. Establishing vegetation on mine tailings waste. p. 103–115. *In* Russell J. Hutnik and Grant Davis (ed.) Ecology and reclamation of devastated land. Vol. 2. Gordon and Breach, New York.

Peterson, H. B., and R. F. Nielson. 1973. Toxicities and deficiencies in mine tailings. p. 15–25. *In* Russell J. Hutnick and Grant Davis (ed.) Ecology and reclamation of devastated land. Vol. 1. Gordon and Breach, New York.

Chapter 37

Limitations in the Use of Soil Tests on Drastically Disturbed Lands

W. A. BERG

Colorado State University
Fort Collins, Colorado

I. INTRODUCTION

Surface stabilization, aesthetics, and long-term land use, predominantly for forestry or pasture, are usually the major objectives in reclamation of drastically disturbed lands. Should one then expect soil fertility tests developed largely for soils producing intensively managed annual crops to be a useful tool in management of disturbed lands?

In spite of the different land management objectives, and soil materials that often are not soil in the genesis sense, soil tests have proven useful on disturbed lands. This is apparently because soil tests developed by a combination of empirical and theoretical considerations are reflections of chemical equilibria and biological activity in soils and soil materials (soil materials in this discussion include subsoil, spoils, and tailings used as plant growth media).

However, soil tests have limitations, sometimes rather severe, that some users may be unaware of or give little consideration to. Many of these limitations are discussed in the publication *Soil Testing and Plant Analysis* (Walsh & Beaton, 1973). The objective of this paper is to point out some of the limitations and variations in soil test use on disturbed lands with the hope that it will stimulate discussion and encourage research and publication on the subject.

Soil testing can be divided into fairly distinct phases such as sampling, sample preparation, analytical procedures, correlation, calibration, and recommendations. In the following discussion, sampling and sample preparation will each be covered separately. Then, limiting aspects of individual soil tests will be briefly discussed in relation to analysis, correlation, calibration, and/or recommendations.

Analytical soil test procedures are covered in detail in publications such as Jackson (1958), Black (1965), Hesse (1972), Walsh and Beaton (1973), and in numerous technical journal articles. Thus, only a few items particularly appropriate to soil material samples from disturbed lands will be mentioned here.

654 BERG

The terms *correlation* and *calibration* have been used somewhat interchangeably in soil test discussions (Welch & Wiese, 1973). For this paper, the meaning of *correlation* will be as used by Hanway (1973) in that soil test correlations are usually made in greenhouse or growth chamber studies using a range of soils or soil materials. In such studies it is essential that all nutrients be supplied in adequate amounts except the nutrient under investigation, and that soil materials with factors limiting plant growth and not under study (e.g., toxicities, high soluble salts) should be treated to correct the problem or be eliminated from the study. Many soil test correlations have been made for agronomic crops on soils. Few correlations have been made on soil materials from disturbed lands.

Calibration in this discussion is the relationship found in field studies between soil test values and yield response from incremental rates of the nutrient applied in the field. However, calibration of soil tests such as pH, soluble salts, and potentially toxic trace elements cannot be field tested in relatively simple field studies as can the major nutrients. Thus, calibration may have to be made by many field observations and inferences from greenhouse studies. Field calibration is necessary because plant growth under greenhouse conditions will usually magnify nutrient deficiencies and can underestimate certain toxicities.

Normally, calibrations lead to recommendations for amounts of fertilizer or soil amendments to use. However, recommendations on disturbed lands usually are broader in scope in that recommendations are sometimes made for species that are compatible with the soil material, rather than modifying the soil material to meet the requirements of a species. On overburden core samples the recommendations should include the feasibility of reclamation if disturbed, as well as suggestions on handling and placement of strata.

II. SAMPLING

Guidelines vary widely on the number of samples to take on drastically disturbed lands. Suggestions on the number of samples to take for pH determinations on coal-mine spoils in the eastern U.S. follow. Limstrom (1960) suggests taking individual samples at intervals of 15 to 30 m on transects 120 to 200 m apart on extremely variable spoils—this is a maximum sampling density of 5 samples per ha. The Pennsylvania guide (Davis, 1971) recommends taking 10 to 25 individual samples per ha. Berg (1969) suggests a minimum of 10 individual samples per ha. In contrast, Barnhisel (1975) suggests testing a composite sample made up from a minimum of 10 subsamples on an area of not over 4 ha.

However, sampling of heterogeneous strip-mine spoils in the eastern U.S., particularly those left by outdated mining management techniques, is not suitable criteria for sampling drastically disturbed lands in general. As an example, the work of Yamamoto (1975) shows little variability in the pH of surface and near-surface materials overlying coal in the Fort Union formation in northeastern Wyoming.

The usual recommendation in agronomic soil sampling is to take a composite sample made up of many subsamples (10–30) from within fields or areas of fields that appear uniform. If obvious differences in soils are apparent, such as on ridges or knolls, these are subsampled and composited as a separate sample. This technique is used despite the recognized variability within fields (Peck & Melsted, 1973) apparently because management on a smaller scale is not now realistic.

The heterogeneity of certain drastically disturbed lands leads one to question the use of composite samples. For land management purposes, are not the range and distribution of characteristics of the soil material on a disturbed site more important than averages? Once the range in characteristics is known then a decision can be made on the feasibility of compositing future samplings on the same type of soil material. One should recognize that even what are taken as individual samples are in reality composites of individual particles, which on disturbed lands may be from quite diverse materials.

Statistical methods can be used to calculate the number of samples required to estimate the true mean within set limits for individual plant nutrients in given fields (Peterson & Calvin, 1965). However, such methods require some soil test data before the statistical analyses are made. Thus, this approach is probably not appropriate for those taking samples for on-going reclamation projects.

Sample collection techniques on disturbed lands have been briefly outlined by Berg (1969), Davis (1971), and Barnhisel (1975). They stress that soil materials visibly different in color or composition should be sampled as separate units if extensive enough to be handled separately in the revegetation program. It also has been recognized that considerable vertical as well as horizontal variability may be encountered in soil material on some disturbed lands (Smith et al., 1974).

Deep core sampling for characterization of overburden as plant growth media is a relatively recent development in evaluating rehabilitation potential and predisturbance planning for reclamation. Some problems in sampling, sample preparation by grinding or artificial weathering, analyses, and interpretation of results are similar to the routine soil tests discussed here. The number of cores needed to characterize a given area particularly needs study. The core sampling of Smith et al. (1974) in the Appalachians, Sandoval et al. (1973) and Power and Sandoval (1976) in the northern Great Plains, Miyamoto et al. (1975) in New Mexico, and the USDI EMRIA program (1975) in the western states are noteworthy.

There is and has been considerable interest in changes in spoil chemical characteristics over time. The approach to the question has often been field sampling. Even if staked reference points are established and used, the heterogeneity of certain spoils leads one to question this technique for certain determinations. A confined sample such as used to determine the changes in leachate over time by Ohio researchers (Struthers, 1964) would be preferred; however, the drawback is destructive sampling.

In summary, there are no general guidelines on the number of soil material samples to take in planning for the revegetation of drastically disturbed lands. It is recognized that soil materials on disturbed sites may vary from fairly uniform to quite heterogeneous; the heterogeneity leads one to question the use of composite samples. Meaningful guidelines cannot be established except for specific areas where the variability is known.

III. SAMPLE PREPARATION

Soil material from drastically disturbed lands may contain some to many (80–90%) coarse fragments (>2 mm diameter). Handling and accounting for the coarse fragments when using soil tests poses a problem. One sampling procedure is to sieve out the coarse fragments, determine the mass in relation to the entire sample, and later correct the results to include the coarse fragments as inert material. This correction would appear to be realistic if the soil test concept were always to measure major reservoirs of nutrients, such as exchangeable K. However, when a soil test measures an intensity factor such as in certain tests for plant-available P, the above correction for coarse fragments would tend to dilute the results in terms of P concentrations actually available to the roots.

However, if the coarse fragments are from certain shales, sandstones, or process wastes such as spent oil shales, the coarse fragments may be relatively porous or weather rapidly enough to contribute to the fertility and soluble salt status (Berg, 1973; Chadwick, 1973; U.S. Forest Service, 1974). Extracting large samples including coarse fragments is an approach to this problem (Berg, 1973; U.S. Forest Service, 1974), but the technique is not applicable to efficient routine soil test procedures which commonly extract 1- to 5-g samples. Another approach is to grind the sample as reported on coal-mine spoils by Barnhisel et al. (1975). Drawbacks include exposing more surface area and use of a process that is not readily adaptable to routine processing of soil samples.

Another problem common to soil sample preparation is drying. Nearly all soil tests are correlated for air-dry samples. However, certain soil tests may be correlated with field moist samples. Oven drying of soil materials can change the amount of nutrients extractable by certain soil tests (Hesse, 1972). An example is that the amount of P extractable by the $NaHCO_3$ test increases when samples are oven-dried. Soil material samples usually are not oven-dried prior to soil fertility testing. Sometimes air drying is expedited by forced air and heat not to exceed 50°C.

IV. pH

pH is the most common and often the most important soil test measurement. The low price and increased versatility of modern pH meters make use of the meter the preferred method for pH determinations in both laboratory and field. If other pH indicators are used, information is available on their reliability (Berg, 1969). Several months of weathering after exposure are usually required before soil materials containing acid-producing sulfides develop their lowest pH; thus, a sulfide test (Neckers & Walker, 1952) may be desirable on some materials.

For most soil materials, about the same pH readings are obtained with the electrodes placed in the solution above the settled soil material as in the settled material itself. However, in some materials, particularly on leached acid subsoils, a lower pH (0.3 to 1 pH unit) is recorded when the electrodes are inserted into the settled particles. This is termed *suspension effect* (Thomas, 1967; McLean, 1973). There is no standard way to resolve this suspension effect in making soil pH measurements. One approach is to make soil pH readings in salt solution (e.g. 0.01M CaCl$_2$, 0.1N KCl), however, this modification is not commonly used in the United States. Peech (1965) suggests that "the glass electrode be immersed well into the partially settled suspension." However, electrodes can be broken by sharp contact with coarse particles and, thus, one may wish to insert them only into the liquid. An important point in making pH determinations is the consistency and reporting of the technique used.

The pH of eastern and midwestern coal mine spoils has probably been more extensively correlated (Berg & Vogel, 1968; Vogel & Berg, 1968; Plass & Vogel, 1973) and calibrated (Limstrom, 1960; Ruffner & Steiner, 1973; Miles et al., 1973) with plant growth than any other soil test on disturbed land. A drawback with greenhouse pH correlation tests on acid soil materials is that the major plant growth problem on acid soils is usually aluminum brought into solution by the acid conditions. Stubby roots and the absence of lateral roots are the classical symptoms of Al toxicity; such plants with inadequate root systems may be able to survive and grow under the daily watering regime in greenhouses but they would be subject to extreme water stress in the field.

In field calibrations of pH it is tempting to sample soil material beneath isolated plants in otherwise barren toxic areas. The sample taken may or may not represent the microsite on which the plant germinated and initiated growth. I believe this sampling practice has resulted in reports of species establishing on lower pH materials than is the actual case.

V. LIME REQUIREMENT

The common soil tests for lime requirement (Peech, 1965; Coleman & Thomas, 1967; McLean, 1973) often seriously underestimate the lime requirement for sulfide-containing spoil and tailings. This is because sulfides in soil, spoil, or tailings may continue to oxidize after sampling and liming. The sulfides involved are commonly pyrites. The rate of pyrite oxidation is dependent upon several factors including particle size and type (Caruccio, 1975). Two methods to determine potential acidity from sulfide oxidation have been outlined by Smith et al. (1974); one is by hydrogen peroxide treatment, the other is determination of total sulfur after sulfate sulfur has been removed by leaching. The state of Kentucky has recently initiated a hydrogen peroxide test for potentially acid-producing spoils (personal communication, R. Barnhisel, Agronomy Dep., Univ. of Kentucky). The problem of predicting sulfide oxidation potential when reclaiming poorly drained and submerged soils has been intensively studied. However, Brinkman and Pons (1973) state that the "present methods of identifying and predicting acid sulphate soils take into account quantities only, and not time aspects."

VI. SOLUBLE SALTS

Electrical conductivity (EC) of the water extracted from a distilled water–soil material mixture is the common test for soluble salts. The amount of water added will make a great difference in the concentration of salt in the extract. Thus, the standard procedure (U.S. Salinity Lab., 1954) is to mix water with the soil until a saturated paste is produced. This technique relates the amount of water added to the water-holding capacity of the soil material and, thus, is an indication of the relative soluble salt concentrations encountered by roots in that particular soil material.

However, preparation of saturation extracts requires considerable time and soil material, and on sandy material or those containing considerable coarse fragments the saturation point is difficult to determine. Thus, much wider distilled water–soil material ratios such as 1:1, 2:1, and even 5:1 are sometimes used. These wider water–soil ratios present several major interpretation problems: (i) a sparingly soluble salt like gypsum, if present, will dissolve and give conductivity values which may indicate a salt hazard when none in reality exists; (ii) the soluble salt content is not related to the plant-available water in the soil (e.g., with a given amount of soluble salt a sandy soil will be a much more saline growth medium than a clayey soil containing the same amount of soluble salt); and (iii) soluble salt dilution effects in soils are seldom linear.

At pH's below 4 and above 10, hydrogen and hydroxyl ions, respectively, come into increasing importance as conductors of electricity. Since these ions conduct several times as much electricity as the same concentrations of other common ions, EC values will overestimate the osmotic potential at these pH extremes.

Osmotic pressure (OP) also is overestimated by EC measurements on soil materials dominated by divalent ions because the relationship commonly used assumes equal equivalents of divalent and monovalent ions. This equation is $OP = 0.36 \times EC$ when EC is in mmhos/cm. For divalent systems a factor of 0.28 would be appropriate. Jackson (1958) suggests a factor of 0.30 for soils in humid regions.

Correlations and calibrations of saturation extract EC's and plant growth have been made for some species used in disturbed land situations in the western states (U.S. Salinity Lab., 1954; Dewey, 1960; McKell, 1976; Ries et al., 1976). However, information is limited or unavailable on many species used in more humid areas.

VII. SODIUM ADSORPTION RATIO

High soluble and exchangeable Na poses revegetation problems on certain disturbed soil materials in the western states. The sodium hazard can be predicted by determining the exchangeable sodium percentage

(ESP); however, the procedure is time consuming. A more convenient method to determine the Na hazard is to determine Na, Ca, and Mg in a saturation extract and then calculate the sodium adsorption ratio (SAR) which is empirically related to the ESP (U.S. Salinity Lab., 1954). However, there is recent information that the SAR may overestimate the ESP on core samples from certain western coal overburdens (USDI, 1975) and also that there appears to be little correlation between ESP and SAR on other overburden (Farmer & Richardson, 1976).

VIII. NITROGEN

Plant-available N is usually a major plant growth limiting factor in soils as well as in disturbed soil materials. Predicting the availability of soil N to plants by soil tests has had limited success, although many tests have been evaluated (Dahnke & Vasey, 1973). For convenience in discussion, the soil tests for N will be separated into four categories.

1. TOTAL NITROGEN

Total N analysis on revegetated spoils can be misinterpreted if it is assumed that the N accumulation has all occurred since disturbance and revegetation. This procedure overlooks the N naturally present in geological materials which may range from 10 ppm in some igneous rocks (Stevenson, 1965) to 8,000 ppm in oil shales (Thorne et al., 1951).

Hall and Miller (1908), Power et al. (1974), and J. D. Reeder[1] show that the N mineralization rate in exposed sedimentary rocks is much less than in soils. Thus, determining total N in such materials and comparing and interpreting these measurements by criteria developed for surface soils is not appropriate.

2. ORGANIC MATTER

In soils, the determination of easily oxidized organic matter is sometimes made to estimate N availability. The most common organic matter determination is made by the Walkley-Black method, which supposedly excludes most of the elementary carbon such as charcoal, coal, or graphite (Jackson, 1958). However, Wilson (1965) indicates that the determination may include some carbon from coal. This leads one to question if the determination of organic matter on carbonaceous shales is meaningful if plant growth correlations have not been made.

An interesting question on organic matter is posed by the work of Caspall (1975) who reported increases in organic matter in the surface 15 cm of Illinois spoils from an initial level of 0.4 to 2.5% in 14 years. Did the organic matter buildup come from contemporary vegetation growth and decomposition? If so, this would mean an average of 3,300 kg/ha of organic matter would be added per year. In contrast, Andrew and

---

[1]J. D. Reeder. 1975. N mineralization in Cretaceous shales and coal mine spoils. M.S. Thesis, Colorado State Univ., Fort Collins.

Rhoades (1947) reported an average organic matter increase of 660 kg/ha per year on a railroad cut in glacial till in eastern Nebraska over 75 years. An alternative hypothesis on the buildup of organic matter in the Illinois spoils is that carbon in the spoils that was not initially detectable by the Walkley-Black procedure became more readily oxidizable upon exposure and weathering.

3. INORGANIC NITROGEN

Measurement of inorganic N (nitrate, exchangeable ammonium) in soils is an accepted procedure on certain intensively fertilized crops where substantial carry over of N may occur. In certain shales a reservoir of inorganic N exists that can also be evaluated by this method (Power et al., 1974; Miyamoto et al., 1975; Yamamoto, 1975). However, in most disturbed land soil materials the inorganic N content will be low.

4. INCUBATION METHODS

Incubation methods are probably the most meaningful in determining the plant availability of N in disturbed soil materials (Reeder[1] and Williams, 1975). However, the tests are biological and take considerably more time and expense, and often are not available in laboratories equipped to do routine chemical analyses.

IX. PHOSPHORUS

Phosphorus is often the most limiting fertility factor in plant establishment on drastically disturbed land. Soil tests for P reflect the chemistry of soils and, thus, are more regionalized than tests for the other major nutrients. A number of soil tests have been developed for use on acid soils in the eastern U.S. and others for use on neutral and calcareous soils in the west. However, certain disturbed lands do not reflect the local soils. An example is neutral and calcareous overburden in West Virginia. Here the $NaHCO_3$ soil test for P (commonly used in the western U.S.) was more satisfactory than acid extractants (Smith et al., 1974).

Phosphorus extracted by the Bray no. 1 method was significantly correlated with grass-growth response to added P on N-fertilized Pennsylvanian coal mine spoils. However, P extracted with the two-acid method used in the southeastern U.S. was not correlated (Berg, 1973). Grube et al. (1973) suggest that the reason for the lack of correlation with the latter extractant was that acid-soluble iron in spoils interfered with the analytical color development.

The $NaHCO_3$ extraction (Olsen & Dean, 1965) appears to be satisfactory for estimating plant-available P in neutral and calcareous soil materials for the western U.S. A modification of the procedure uses ascorbic acid as a reducing agent (Watanabe & Olsen, 1965) and eliminates the need for using carbon black as an organic matter decolorizer. However, Power (J. F. Power, ARS, Mandan, N. Dak., personal communication) has found that $NaHCO_3$ extracts of certain coal mine spoils and geological materials require carbon black treatment for correct analytical P determinations.

Considerable P fertilization field work has been done on disturbed land; responses are reported but the reports often do not include soil test P values needed to complete the calibration process. Some soil test P calibration information is available (Bengston et al., 1973; Barnhisel et al., 1975; Bauer et al., Chapter 25 in this book; and U.S. Forest Service, 1974). The calibration data are largely on short-term studies. The importance of long-term studies in calibration of P soil tests for trees has been shown by Ballard and Pritchett (1975).

X. TRACE ELEMENTS

The major current interest in trace elements in disturbed lands, especially mining wastes, is in quantities toxic to plants or animals. Soil tests have been developed for the micronutrients B and Mo (Reisenauer et al., 1973), and Zn, Cu, Mn, and Fe (Viets & Lindsay, 1973). However, most of the soil tests were developed to detect deficiencies rather than toxicity levels. Thus, soil test research is underway to define toxic levels of these micronutrients and other trace elements such as Cd and Se.

Information on potentially toxic elements is required by some mining rehabilitation regulations. This has sometimes resulted in analyses for total amounts of a number of trace elements in overburden. Total analysis has generally proved to be an unfruitful approach to nutrient availability in soils. Viets and Lindsay (1973) suggest that an aqueous extract or saturation extract may be used to show the heavy metal pollution potential of runoff or percolate from mine tailings, land fills, or coal mine spoils. Water extractions were used by Massey and Barnhisel (1972) to characterize Fe, Al, Mn, Zn, Cu, and Ni solubilized in acid coal mine spoils.

Plant species used in revegetation of disturbed soil materials may be less sensitive to trace element deficiencies or toxicities than agronomic crops; thus, calibration under field conditions is needed.

LITERATURE CITED

Andrew, L. E., and H. F. Rhoades. 1947. Soil development from calcareous glacial material in eastern Nebraska during seventy-five years. Soil Sci. Soc. Am. Proc. 12:407–408.

Ballard, R., and W. L. Pritchett. 1975. Evaluation of soil testing methods for predicting growth and response of *Pinus elliotti* to phosphorus fertilization. Soil Sci. Soc. Am. Proc. 39:132–136.

Barnhisel, R. I. 1975. Sampling surface-mined coal spoils. Univ. of Kentucky, Dep. of Agron. AGR-41, Lexington, Ky. 4 p.

Barnhisel, R. I., J. L. Powell, and G. W. Akin. 1975. Keys to successful reclamation in western Kentucky. p. 140–151. *In* 3rd Symp. on Surface Mining and Reclamation, 21–23 Oct. 1975, Louisville, Ky. Vol. II. Natl. Coal Assoc., Washington, D.C.

Bengtson, G. W., S. E. Allen, D. A. Mays, and T. G. Zarger. 1973. Use of fertilizers to speed pine establishment on reclaimed coal mine spoil in Northeastern Alabama: II. Field experiments. p. 227–236. *In* R. J. Hutnik and G. Davis (ed.). Ecology and reclamation of devastated land. Vol. 2. Gordon and Breach, New York.

Berg, W. A. 1969. Determining pH of strip-mine spoils. USDA For. Serv. Res. Note NE-98, Northeast For. Exp. Stn., Upper Darby, Pa. 7 p.

Berg, W. A. 1973. Evaluation of P and K soil fertility tests on coal-mine spoils. p. 93–104. In R. J. Hutnik and G. Davis (ed.) Ecology and reclamation of devastated land. Vol. I. Gordon and Breach, New York.

Berg, W. A., and W. G. Vogel. 1968. Manganese toxicity of legumes seeded in Kentucky strip-mine spoils. USDA For. Serv. Res. Pap. NE-119. Northeast For. Exp. Stn., Upper Darby, Pa. 12 p.

Black, C. A. (ed.). 1965. Methods of soil analysis. 2 Vols. Am. Soc. of Agron., Madison, Wis.

Brinkman, R., and L. J. Pons. 1973. Recognition and prediction of acid sulphate and soil conditions. p. 169–203. In H. Dost (ed.) Acid sulphate soils. Publ. 18, Vol. 1. Int. Inst. Land Reclamation, Wageningen.

Caruccio, F. T. 1975. Estimating the acid potential of coal mine refuse. p. 197–205. In M. J. Chadwick and G. T. Goodman (ed.) The ecology of resource degradation and renewal. Blackwell Sci. Publ., Oxford.

Caspall, F. C. 1975. Soil development on surface mine spoils in western Illinois. p. 221–228. In 3rd Symp. on Surface Mining and Reclamation. 21–23 Oct. 1975, Louisville, Ky. Vol. II. Natl. Coal Assoc., Washington, D.C.

Chadwick, M. J. 1973. Methods of assessment of acid colliery spoil as a medium for plant growth. p. 81–91. In R. J. Hutnik and G. Davis (ed.) Ecology and reclamation of devastated land. Vol. I. Gordon and Breach, New York.

Coleman, N. T., and G. W. Thomas. 1967. The basic chemistry of soil acidity. In R. W. Pearson and F. Adams (ed.) Soil acidity and liming. Agronomy 12:1–41. Am. Soc. of Agron., Madison, Wis.

Dahnke, W. C., and E. H. Vasey. 1973. Testing soil for nitrogen. p. 97–114. In L. M. Walsh and J. D. Beaton (eds.) Soil testing and plant analysis. Soil Sci. Soc. of Am., Madison, Wis.

Davis, G. (chrm.). 1971. A guide for revegetating bituminous stripmine spoils in Pennsylvania. Northeastern For. Exp. Stn., Upper Darby, Pa. 46 p.

Dewey, D. R. 1960. Salt tolerance of twenty-five strains of Agropyron. Agron. J. 52:631–635.

Farmer, E. F., and B. Z. Richardson. 1976. Hydrologic and soil properties of coal mine overburden piles in southeastern Montana. p. 120–130. In 4th Symp. on Surface Mining and Reclamation, 19–21 Oct. 1976, Louisville, Ky. Natl. Coal Assoc., Washington, D.C.

Grube, W. E., Jr., R. M. Smith, R. N. Singh, and A. A. Sobek. 1973. Characterization of coal overburden materials in minesoils in advance of mining. p. 134–152. In 1st Research and Applied Technology Symp. on Mined Land Reclamation, 7–8 Mar. 1973, Pittsburgh, Pa. Natl. Coal Assoc., Washington, D.C.

Hall, A. D., and N. H. J. Miller. 1908. The nitrogen compounds of fundamental rocks. J. Agric. Sci. 2:343–354.

Hanway, J. J. 1973. Experimental methods for correlating and calibrating soil tests. p. 55–66. In L. M. Walsh and J. D. Beaton (ed.) Soil testing and plant analysis. Soil Sci. Soc. of Am., Madison, Wis.

Hesse, P. R. 1972. A textbook of soil chemical analysis. Chemical Publ. Co., New York. 520 p.

Jackson, M. L. 1958. Soil chemical analysis. Prentice Hall, Inc., Englewood Cliffs, N. J. 498 p.

Limstrom, G. A. 1960. Forestation of strip-mined land. USDA Agric. Hbk. 166, Sup. of Documents, Washington, D.C. 74 p.

Massey, H. F., and R. I. Barnhisel. 1972. Copper, nickel, and zinc released from acid coal mine spoil materials of eastern Kentucky. Soil Sci. 113:207–212.

McKell, C. M. 1976. Achieving effective revegetation of disposed processed oil shale. Utah State Univ. Agric. Exp. Stn. Land Rehabilitation Ser. no. 1. 17 p.

McLean, E. D. 1973. Testing soils for pH and lime requirement. p. 77–95. In L. M. Walsh and J. D. Beaton (ed.) Soil testing and plant analysis. Soil Sci. Soc. of Am., Madison, Wis. 491 p.

Miles, V. C., R. W. Ruble, and R. L. Bond. 1973. Performance of plants in relation to spoil classification in Pennsylvania. p. 13–31. In R. J. Hutnik and G. Davis (eds.) Ecology and reclamation of devastated land. Vol. 2. Gordon and Breach, New York.

Miyamoto, S., W. L. Gould, and D. Rai. 1975. Characterizing overburden materials before surface mining in the Fruitland formation of northwestern New Mexico. p. 80–94. In 3rd Symp. on Surface Mining and Reclamation. 21–23 Oct. 1975, Louisville, Ky. Vol. I. Natl. Coal Assoc., Washington, D.C.

Neckers, J. W., and C. R. Walker. 1952. Field test for active sulfides in soil. Soil Sci. 74:467–470.

Olsen, S. R., and L. A. Dean. 1965. Phosphorus. *In* C. A. Black (ed.) Methods of soil analysis. Part 2. Agronomy 9:1035–1049. Am. Soc. of Agron., Madison, Wis.

Peck, T. R., and S. W. Melsted. 1973. Field sampling for soil testing. p. 67–75. *In* L. M. Walsh and J. D. Beaton (ed.) Soil testing and plant analysis. Soil Sci. Soc. of Am., Madison, Wis.

Peech, M. 1965. Hydrogen-ion activity. *In* C. A. Black (ed.) Methods of soil analysis. Part 2. Agronomy 9:914–926. Am. Soc. of Agron., Madison, Wis.

Peterson, R. G., and L. D. Calvin. 1965. Sampling. *In* C. A. Black (ed.) Methods of soil analysis. Part 1. Agronomy 9:54–72. Am. Soc. of Agron., Madison, Wis.

Plass, W. T., and W. G. Vogel. 1973. Chemical properties and particle size distribution in 39 surface-mine spoils in southern West Virginia. USDA For. Serv. Res. Pap. NE-276. Northeast For. Exp. Stn., Upper Darby, Pa. 8 p.

Power, J. F., J. J. Bond, F. M. Sandoval, and W. O. Willis. 1974. Nitrification in Paleocene shale. Science 183:1077–1079.

Power, J. F., and F. M. Sandoval. 1976. Effect of sampling method on results of chemical analysis of overburden samples. Min. Congr. J. 62:(Apr.)37–41.

Ries, R. E., F. M. Sandoval, J. F. Power, and W. O. Willis. 1976. Perennial forage species response to sodium and magnesium sulfate in mine spoil. p. 173–183. *In* 4th Symp. on Surface Mining and Reclamation, 19–21 Oct. 1976, Louisville, Ky. Natl. Coal Assoc., Washington, D.C.

Reisenauer, H. M., L. M. Walsh, and R. G. Hoeft. 1973. Testing soils for sulphur, boron, molybdenum and chlorine. p. 173–200. *In* L. M. Walsh and J. D. Beaton (ed.) Soil testing and plant analysis. Soil Sci. Soc. of Am., Madison, Wis.

Ruffner, J. D., and W. W. Steiner. 1973. Evaluation of plants for use on critical sites. p. 3–12. *In* R. J. Hutnik and G. Davis (ed.) Ecology and reclamation of devastated land. Vol. 2. Gordon and Breach, New York.

Sandoval, F. M., J. J. Bond, J. F. Power, and W. O. Willis. 1973. Lignite mine spoils in the northern Great Plains—characteristics and potential for reclamation. p. 117–133. *In* 1st Symp. on Surface Mining and Reclamation. 7–8 Mar. 1973, Pittsburg, Pa. Natl. Coal Assoc., Washington, D.C.

Smith, R. M., W. E. Grube, Jr., T. Arkle, Jr., and A. Sobek. 1974. Mine spoil potentials for soil and water quality. EPA-670/2-74-070. Sup. of Doc., Washington, D.C. 303 p.

Stevenson, F. J. 1965. Origin and distribution of nitrogen in soil. *In* W. V. Bartholomew and F. E. Clark (ed.) Soil nitrogen. Agronomy 10:1–42. Am. Soc. of Agron., Madison, Wis.

Struthers, P. H. 1964. Chemical weathering of strip-mine spoils. Ohio J. Sci. 64:125–131.

Thomas, G. W. 1967. Problems encountered in soil testing methods. p. 37–54. *In* G. W. Hardy (chm.) Soil testing and plant analysis. Part I. Soil Sci. Soc. of Am., Madison, Wis.

Thorne, H. M., W. I. R. Murphy, K. E. Stanfield, J. S. Ball, and J. W. Horne. 1951. Green River oil shales and products. Oil Shale and Cannel Coal, Proc. Conf. 2nd, 1950, 2:301–341. Inst. of Petroleum, London.

U.S. Department of Interior, Bureau of Land Management. 1975. Energy mineral rehabilitation inventory and analysis (EMRIA). EMRIA Rep. 1-1975 Otter Creek, Mont., 2-1975 Hanna Basin, Wyo., 3-1975 Taylor Creek, Colo., 4-1975 Alton, Utah.

U.S. Forest Service. 1974. Chemical properties of three particle-sized fractions of strip-mine spoils. p. 88–95. *In* Revegetation ARC-71-66-T4. U.S. For. Serv., USDA, Berea, Ky. Natl. Tech. Inf. Serv., Springfield, Va.

U.S. Salinity Laboratory Staff. 1954. Diagnosis and improvement of saline and alkali soils. USDA Agric. Hbk. 60. Sup. of Doc., Washington, D.C. 140 p.

Viets, F. G., Jr., and W. L. Lindsay. 1973. Testing soils for zinc, copper, manganese and iron. p. 153–172. *In* L. M. Walsh and J. D. Beaton (ed.) Soil testing and plant analysis. Soil Sci. Soc. of Am., Madison, Wis.

Vogel, W. G., and W. A. Berg. 1968. Grasses and legumes for cover on acid strip-mine spoils. J. Soil Water Conserv. 23:89–91.

Walsh, L. M., and J. D. Beaton (ed.). 1973. Soil testing and plant analysis. Soil Sci. Soc. of Am., Madison, Wis. 491 p.

Watanabe, F. S., and S. R. Olsen. 1965. Test of an ascorbic acid method for determining phosphorus in water and NaHCO3 extracts from soil. Soil Sci. Soc. Am. Proc. 29:677–678.

Welch, C. D., and R. A. Wiese. 1973. Opportunities to improve soil testing programs. p. 1–11. *In* L. M. Walsh and J. D. Beaton (ed.) Soil testing and plant analysis. Soil Sci. Soc. of Am., Madison, Wis.

Williams, P. J. 1975. Investigations into the nitrogen cycle in colliery spoil. p. 259–274. *In* M. J. Chadwick and G. T. Goodman (ed.) The ecology of resource degradation and renewal. Blackwell Sci. Publ., Oxford.

Wilson, H. A. 1965. The microbiology of strip-mine spoil. Bull. 506T. West Virginia Univ. Agric. Exp. Stn. 44 p.

Yamamoto, Y. 1975. Coal mine spoil as a growing medium: Amax Belle Ayr south mine, Gillette, Wyoming. p. 49–61. *In* 3rd Symp. on Surface Mining and Reclamation. Vol. I. Natl. Coal Assoc., Washington, D.C.

Copyright © 1978 ASA–CSSA–SSSA
677 South Segoe Road, Madison, WI 53711 USA
Reclamation of Drastically Disturbed Lands

Chapter 38

Physical Analyses of Overburden Materials and Mine Land Soils[1]

G. W. GEE,[2] ARMAND BAUER, AND R. S. DECKER

*North Dakota State University, Mandan, North Dakota,
Science and Education Administration (SEA),
USDA, Mandan, North Dakota, and
Hoskins-Western-Sonderegger, Consulting Engineers, Lincoln, Nebraska*

I. INTRODUCTION

Soil water storage, water availability, surface erosion, and land stability are physical processes often altered by mining. Physical characterization is required to evaluate these alterations and assess the reclamation potential of disturbed lands. Physical and chemical characterization of surface-mined soils in the humid, eastern United States is covered in detail elsewhere in this book (see Chapter 9 by Smith and Sobek). The following discussion focuses on physical characterization of western coal mine lands, although the analyses discussed are applicable to other disturbed lands as well.

While overburden characteristics differ widely, coal deposits in the western U.S. generally are overlain by sedimentary deposits composed mainly of shales, sandstones, and siltstones. In some areas, glacial till or windblown sand (eolian) deposits cover the sedimentary materials. It is the mixing of these materials, with their unique physical and chemical characteristics, that largely determines the rehabilitation potential of a mined soil. A *mined soil* is defined here to mean the resultant surface material after mining in which plants are grown. This may either be re-shaped raw spoil or spoil covered with a suitable plant growth media (topsoil).

Rai et al. (1975) determined the suitability of two contrasting overburden materials for reclamation in the Four Corners area of New Mexico. They found cretaceous shale overburden to be high in clay (predominantly montmorillonitic) which exhibited high saturation percentages and high sodium adsorption ratios (SAR), with sodium the dominant cation and sulfate and nitrate the dominant anions. The materials were very slowly permeable. On the other hand, holocene eolian materials tested were lower in clay content, and lower in SAR and satura-

---

[1] This work was supported in part by Old West Regional Commission Grant no. 10470016.
[2] Presently Staff Scientist, Battelle Northwest Laboratories, P.O. Box 999, Richland, WA 99352.

tion percentages, with calcium the dominant cation and sulfate and nitrate and dominant anions. Permeability was very high. Rai et al. (1975)
concluded that the holocene material would be more desirable as surface
material for reclamation than the cretaceous shales.

Extensive sampling in North Dakota (Schroer, 1976) indicates that
palocene shales and sandstone overburden materials from the Fort Union
formation, where the most extensive coal deposits are located, are highly
variable in nature but display the same general traits as the cretaceous
shale overburden of New Mexico. The Fort Union overburden has increasingly higher saturation percentages and higher SAR's with increasing
depth, sodium and sulfate being the dominant cation and anion, respectively. In some localized areas where glacial till is present, the coal is generally deeper and the overburden is low in SAR and saturation percentages. Where a choice is available there are obvious advantages in using
the glacial till as surface material rather than leaving the Fort Union
shales at the surface.

Sandoval et al. (1973) indicate that strip mine spoils in western North
Dakota are often fine-textured (clay % >40), while salinity is seldom
more than moderate with electrical conductivity of the saturated extract
generally below 8 mmhos/cm. Although low in salts, the sodium content
of spoil materials is high, with the SAR often greater than 20. Sandoval et
al. (1973) and Power et al. (1974) indicated that spoil materials with SAR
levels much higher than about 12 produce limited or no vegetative
growth. This is due presumably to the effects of sodium on the physical
properties of the material. Observed high runoff rates, low infiltration,
and surface sealing are factors contributing to low vegetative yields. In
addition, older spoil materials are found to be deficient in both phosphorus and nitrogen.

Sodium-affected (sodic) materials have unusual erosion characteristics. Erosion features such as pipes, tubes, tunnels, and caverns or sink-
holes of rather large extent often develop on nearly level, sodic spoil surfaces and contribute to the instability of the landscape. On steeper slopes,
deep rills develop connecting into larger more developed erosion pipes
and tunnels. Similar natural features have been observed in Colorado
(Brown, 1962), Arizona (Fletcher & Carrol, 1948), and Oklahoma
(Sherard et al., 1976a), and are prominent geologic features of the "badlands" of western North Dakota. Piping erosion is not restricted to the
semiarid and arid western U.S., but has been observed in earth-fill materials throughout the world (Sherard et al., 1976a).

Observation of the physical instability, surface sealing, and low
water infiltration characteristics of sodic mine spoils has led Power et al.
(1974) to recommend topsoiling as a method of overcoming the influence
of the highly sodic material on plant growth. Power, in this book
(Chapter 29), reports on recent research findings regarding topsoil quality
and quantity needed for reclamation of sodic spoils.

There is no way at present to predict the ultimate mix of the overburden after mining. The dragline-dumping method used most extensively in the western U.S. causes overburden inversion and may need to be
modified to produce better defined layering of the mined overburden.

Where certain overburden layers contain chemically or physically unsuitable material, this material must be separated and buried at sufficient depth so that undesirable properties do not affect the rehabilitation potential of the resultant mined soil.

Characterization of soil materials at minesites prior to mining is necessary to determine the suitability of material as a plant root medium. Soil properties, delineated through soil surveys, can be used as an aid in developing criteria for postmine soils. For example, North Dakota law requires detailed soil survey maps for premining plans. These maps, prepared on site by professional soil classifiers, are used to compute extent and thickness of suitable plant growth materials for a given area (Patterson, 1976; Schroer, 1976).

An initial attempt to delineate soil physical and chemical properties important for surface mined soils was made by Omodt et al. (1975) from a study of nonmined soils in western North Dakota. Their study was based on soil surveys taken in the coal impact areas of western North Dakota prior to extensive mining. Soil properties considered important to reclamation include organic matter, soluble salts, exchangeable sodium, free lime, pH, texture, bulk density, structure, and horizon thickness. Productivity indexes developed for nonmined soils suggest that favorable combinations of soil properties optimize productivity.

The significance of any one soil property in influencing productivity depends on the combination of other soil properties that characterize a particular soil. For example, several of the nonmined soils reported by Omodt et al. (1975) were not adversely affected by salts, but were moderately coarse-textured and highly susceptible to wind erosion. Soils developed from glacial till were nonsaline to 150 cm but often had high lime content at the 30-cm depth. High lime content materials have weak structure and for this reason would be undesirable for placement at the surface. Conversely, soils formed from soft shales had high sodium levels (SAR > 10) within 90 cm of the surface, yet had good productivity levels.

Measurement of postmine soil conditions will be necessary to evaluate reclamation. Conventional soil surveys will be useful but additional research and testing will be needed to determine the factors contributing to both sustained productivity and landscape stability. Extensive engineering tests for subsidence and consolidation may be required in addition to the tests listed in the following sections to assess long-term physical stability of reshaped spoil banks.

II. PARTICLE SIZE DISTRIBUTION AND TEXTURE

Particle size in overburden materials varies widely, from large boulders to submicron-size clays. In the following discussion the USDA classification for particle size is used. Individual soil particles ranging in size from 2 to 0.05 mm (50 μm) are classed as sands, those from 50 to 2 μm are silts, and those below 2 μm are clays. Also, the USDA textural classification is followed (Soil Survey Staff, 1951). The work reported here is confined to relatively uniform shale, sandstone, and loessial materials.

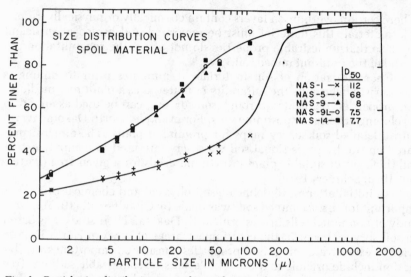

Fig. 1—Particle size distribution curve for spoil materials at a mine site in western North Dakota. D_{50} values are median particle diameters in μm (CO, KR, NA, and NAS refer to mine sites).

A. Methods

The pipette and hydrometer methods are used extensively in soils work to determine particle size distribution of materials < 50 μm in size, while sieving is used for larger materials (Day, 1965). The pipette method is often used as the standard. However, recent work by Kaddah (1974) has indicated that the hydrometer is as reliable as the pipette and allows for a simpler determination of the particle size distribution of a given sample. For both methods, there is some uncertainty regarding sample pretreatment since organic matter and soluble salts are conventionally removed in the pipette method but not in the hydrometer method. For overburden materials high in organic carbon or for samples mixed with coal, the amount of organic matter removed would have an influence on the particle size distribution of the test sample. In this study the hydrometer method (Day, 1965) was used except where noted.

B. Test Results

Examples of summation percentage curves for surface samples from several spoil and nonmined sites are shown in Fig. 1 and 2 and reflect the variable nature of the materials. The D_{50} (median particle diam) for spoil materials NAS9L and NAS1 varies from 7.5 to 112 μm, respectively (Fig. 1). These materials were located on the same shaped slope, separated horizontally by about 150 m. The NAS1 material contains a large percentage of sandstone mixed with some shales, while the NAS9L material is primarily shale sediments. Typical nonmined surface soils shown in Fig. 2

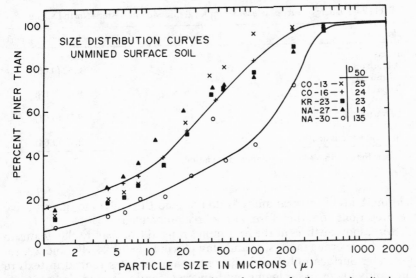

Fig. 2—Paricle size distribution curve for surfaces of nonmined soils near mine sites in western North Dakota. D_{50} values are median particle diameters in μm (*CO*, *KR*, *NA*, and *NAS* refer to mine sites).

tend to be larger in size than the mined materials, with the D_{50} values ranging from 23 to 135 μm. The nonmined surface materials were primarily eolian in nature.

Using the pipette method as a standard, the Day hydrometer method gives reliable results on mine spoil samples (Table 1). The small but consistent difference between clay fraction measurements may be due to differences in sample pretreatment. We conclude that either hydrometer or pipette analysis for particle size will be suitable for mine land studies.

Table 1—Comparisons of two methods for particle size determination on spoil samples

| | Pipette (P) | | | Hydrometer (H) | | | Difference |
Sample	Sand†	Silt‡	Clay	Sand†	Silt‡	Clay	(P-H) clay§
				% by wt			
1	63.9	14.8	21.3	60.4	15.6	24.0	−2.7
2	61.9	16.4	21.7	60.3	16.0	23.7	−2.0
3	57.1	18.8	24.1	55.1	19.6	25.3	−1.2
4	62.3	16.8	20.9	57.6	19.1	23.3	−2.4
5	57.5	20.7	21.8	56.4	20.4	23.2	−1.4
6	56.1	20.6	23.3	54.2	20.4	25.4	−2.1
7	11.3	49.3	39.4	12.0	45.7	42.3	−2.9
8	18.7	51.6	29.7	17.6	49.9	32.5	−2.8
9	17.4	46.1	36.5	16.3	45.9	37.8	−1.3
10	14.4	47.0	38.6	12.3	47.0	40.7	−2.1
Mean	42.0	30.2	27.7	40.2	30.0	29.8	−2.1

† Measured by sieving.
‡ Measured by difference (100 − sand − clay).
§ Clay percentage correlation coefficient, $r = 0.9968$.

Table 2—Particle density of selected samples at minesites in western North Dakota

Sample	Number tested	Particle density, g/cm³
Nonmined		
A Horizon	57	2.56 (0.06)†
Topsoil/mined		
Topsoil	6	2.63 (0.03)
Mined		
Surface spoil	48	2.72 (0.01)
Highwall		
Shale at various depths	48	2.73 (0.04)

† Numbers in parenthesis indicate standard deviation.

Field methods of textural analysis do not lend themselves to quantitative interpretations and, therefore, are not recommended.

Minespoil textures at the four mines ranged from sandy clay loams to clays, with average sand, silt, and clay percentages of 24, 46, and 30, respectively. Surface soils from adjacent nonmined sites ranged in texture from sandy loams to silt loams, with average sand, silt, and clay percentages of 39, 37, and 24, respectively. Although texture was generally finer for mine spoil materials, it will be shown later that factors other than texture per se dominated the physical response of these materials to such processes as water infiltration and water and wind erosion.

III. PARTICLE DENSITY

Particle densities were determined by the pycnometer method (Blake, 1965) for selected surface materials from four mine sites. Samples were taken from nonmined, bare spoil, topsoiled areas, and from overburden samples taken from the face of highwalls at the four mines. Table 2 indicates that the mine spoil and highwall (overburden) samples had considerably higher particle densities than the nonmined sites. This is attributed largely to the lack of organic matter in the mined surface spoil materials.

IV. VOLUME AND DENSITY MEASUREMENTS

A. Overburden Volume

Various methods are presently used to obtain overburden and coal volumes. Among these are use of quandrangular maps, core-boring data, and photogrammetry or detailed topographic surveys. Coe (1976) reviewed these methods and demonstrated that computer-assisted volume analysis using photogrammetry and core borings could provide satisfactory overburden and coal volume estimates as well as depth to seam determinations. For western coal fields, little work has been reported on volume changes in overburden after mining. However, rule of thumb values of 20 to 25% volume increases are often used to estimate the *swell factor* (defined as the percent volume increase) for overburden materials which are common to the Fort Union coal formation in western North Dakota (T. E. Dudley, North American Coal Corp., personal communication). Mining methods (dragline vs. shovel, etc.) and time of year for mining, as well as the overburden physical and chemical characteristics, are all factors which determine the "swell" volume of mined overburden materials.

B. Bulk Density

Bulk density is an important and normally readily measured physical property of soil materials. Total pore volumes, which reflect the percent soil volume for water and air exchange, can be estimated from bulk density measurements. For mined materials, estimates can be made of the degree of volume expansion of the original overburden if bulk densities of overburden and minespoil are known.

Sampling of bulk density in uniform spoil materials composed of sandstone and shales presents no particular problem. Mechanical augers or hydraulic probes can be used for sampling purposes. In glacial tills, however, stone and boulder content may make it difficult to obtain representative samples. Special sampling equipment and procedures must be employed which allow sampling to desired depths and which account for stone volume (Reinhart, 1961; Koshi, 1966).

Samples were taken with a 3.65-cm diam hydraulic probe in 30-cm increments to depths of 2.74 m at 117 sites. These sites consisted of 94 shaped, seeded mine spoil areas, and 23 adjacent nonmined areas. They

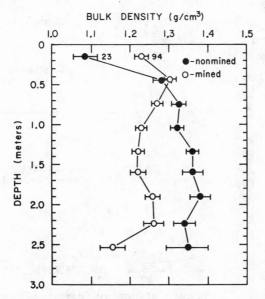

Fig. 3—Bulk density with depth at mine sites in North Dakota. Horizontal bars are standard error of the mean. Numbers by data points indicate number of sites from which samples were taken.

were located near active coal mines at Center, Stanton, Beulah, and Zap, North Dakota.

Figure 3 shows the variation in bulk density with depth at mined and nonmined sites. The average bulk density for all mined sites at all depths was 1.24 ± 0.15 g/cm^3. For the uppermost 30 cm, the average bulk density was 1.23 ± 0.13 g/cm^3 for the mined sites and 1.07 ± 0.15 g/cm^3 for the nonmined sites. Spatial variability in terms of location and depth was less for the mined sites than nonmined sites. This was attributed to overburden mixing from mining. The bulk densities at these mined sites are well within the normal limits of densities observed on most agricultural lands.

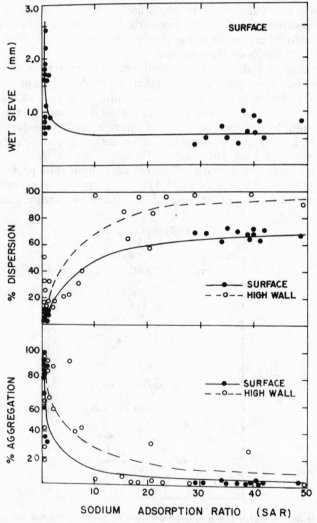

Fig. 4—Structural stability of mine site materials, measured by wet sieve, percent dispersion, and percent aggregation as a function of Na adsorption ratio.

V. SOIL STRUCTURE

Semiarid region soils often contain sufficient amounts of sodium to cause physical degradation (Richards, 1954). Strip mining increases this hazard by exposing sodium-affected materials (Schroer, 1976). A variety of tests are available to measure structural stability and crusting.

Samples tested included A, B, and C horizon materials from soils adjacent to mine sites, surface spoil materials, and overburden materials collected from highwalls at four strip mines in western North Dakota. Water-stable aggregates by wet sieving (Kemper, 1965a), percent dispersion (Sherard et al., 1976a), percent aggregation (Kemper, 1965b), and crust strengths (Richards, 1954) were related to SAR (Fig. 4 and 5).

When SAR levels exceeded 20, >50% dispersion occurred with a reduction in stable aggregates to <20% and a decrease in geometric mean diameter to <1 mm (Fig. 4). For highwall samples, the relationship between percent dispersion and SAR indicated that sodium-affected highwall samples dispersed more readily than spoils (Fig. 4). This is likely because of the mixing and subsequent incorporation of stabilizing agents (organic matter, etc.) into the mine spoil.

Samples with SAR above 10 exhibited high crust strengths (Fig. 5). For agriculturally productive soils, crust strengths are normally <0.5 bars. For both mine spoil and highwall samples, most samples were above 1 bar, with several of the highwall samples exceeding 5 bars. All four tests

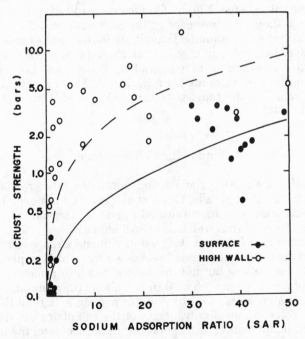

Fig. 5—Crust strength of mine site materials as a function of Na adsorption ratio.

reflect the influence of sodium on soil structure. The dispersion test is rapid and can be run in connection with particle size analysis using the hydrometer (Sherard et al., 1976a). Of the four tests the dispersion test appears to correlate best with visual observations of aggregate breakdown, surface sealing, and crusting of sodium-affected mine spoil materials.

VI. WATER INTAKE

Both physical and chemical properties influence infiltration rates in soils. Physical properties that influence water intake rate are texture, porosity, structure, and initial water content of the surface material. Structural stability is affected by chemical properties which include organic matter, hydrous oxides, and sodium content. Sodium adsorption ratio (SAR) strongly influences structural stability and surface crusting (as shown in the previous section). As a result, SAR should also influence water infiltration rates.

A. Double Ring Infiltrometer

Infiltration rates, using the double ring infiltrometer (Bertrand, 1965), were measured at 15 mined and 7 nonmined sites. A 5-cm head of water was maintained in a 30.5-cm inside diam cylinder and the inflow rate was determined after 1 hour. Duplicated readings were taken at all sites. Figure 6 shows the influence of the SAR on infiltration. The variability in infiltration at nonmined sites is attributed to the surface sealing and dispersive effects of sodium. The data suggest that when SAR is above 20, infiltration rates are severely restricted. Texture was not well correlated with infiltration rates for the mined soils. The site with the lowest infiltration rate had the coarsest texture (63% sand), but also had the highest SAR (>40).

B. Purdue Rainfall Simulator

Infiltration tests using the Purdue rainulator (Meyer, 1960) were conducted on 4 by 22 m plots by Gilley et al. (1977) on mine spoil, topsoil, and rangeland sites. Results confirmed previous observations that little water moves into materials which have SAR above 20.

The Purdue rainulator was designed to simulate a range of rainfall intensities and durations. Aggregate breakdown by rainfall impact is simulated with the rainulator but not the double ring infiltrometer. Also, the larger area of measurement (88 vs. 0.07 m²) allows the rainulator to better estimate the spatial average infiltration for a given area than the double ring infiltrometer. Major disadvantages of the rainulator are the cost of construction, maintenance, and operation. Because of size, the unit lacks portability and must be assembled and dismantled for each test run.

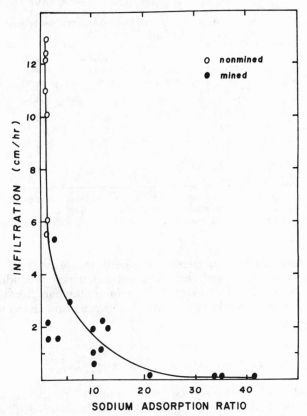

Fig. 6—Infiltration rate after 1 hour as a function of Na adsorption ratio at mine sites in North Dakota.

Smaller, more portable units have been used with some success (Bertrand & Parr, 1961; Meeuwig, 1971; Rauzi & Fly, 1968). For initial characterization of infiltration capacities of mined materials, double ring infiltrometers or small portable rainfall simulators are likely adequate.

VII. WATER RETENTION AND STORAGE

Water retention characteristics of soil materials are determined by measurement of water contents of soil samples equilibrated at specific pressures on a pressure plate or pressure membrane apparatus (Richards, 1954). Water available for plant use is often estimated from the difference in soil water content between 0.1, 0.33, or 0.5 bars (depending on soil texture) and 15 bars. The upper limit of available soil water, or field capacity, is best determined by actual field measurement. Reasonably good correlations have been worked out between laboratory estimates and field values for uniform, deep soils and these values are widely used in engineering and hydrologic studies. However, the correlation between labora-

Table 3—Available water capacity, amount, and percent available water present in
stockpiled topsoil (Gee & Bauer, 1976)

Stock-pile	Age	No. of samples	Depth of sampling	Available water capacity†	Available water present‡	% of available capacity
	years		m	— cm/m —		
SP1	>3	8	2.4	20.0	10.5	52
SP2	<1	29	3.0	24.5	2.7	11
SP3	<1	27	3.0	26.8	-1.0	0
SP4	<1	17	1.8	20.0	6.6	22
SP5	<1	30	3.0	22.2	4.2	19
SP6	<1	30	3.0	20.4	3.9	19

† Mean of all samples at all depths for each stockpile. The available water capacity is estimated by the difference in water retention at 0.33 and 15 bars.
‡ Available water present is the difference in water actually present and water held at 15 bars.

tory estimates and field values depends on the drainage rate and unsaturated conductivity of the soil; hence, unsaturated water conductivity values should be measured. Unsaturated conductivities can be calculated from known saturated conductivities and water retention characteristics (Campbell, 1974).

A. Available Water

Using water retention data, Gee and Bauer (1976) estimated available water in stockpiled topsoil (A and B horizon) materials (Table 3). The data show that except for stockpile SP1, the stored water supply was low, averaging <15% of the estimated available water capacity. The oldest stockpile, SP1, (3 years) averaged 52% of the available water capacity, suggesting that time is a factor in water accumulation in dry stockpiled materials in semiarid regions. The observed values for these stockpiled materials are slightly higher than the estimated available water capacity for 18 soil series common to the coal mine areas of western North Dakota (Schroer, 1976). Where topsoil (A and B horizon) materials are spread over highly sodic spoil (SAR >30) the sodium content of the subsoil hinders water movement sufficiently so that water storage may be limited primarily to the applied topsoil (Gilley et al., 1976). Restricted drainage is a factor in determining the thickness of suitable topsoil needed for reclamation.

B. Unsaturated Conductivity

Measured water transmission properties of topsoil and spoil materials show that for both saturated and unsaturated conductivities the water transmission is less in the spoil material by several orders of magnitude (Table 4). The SAR values of the topsoils tested were all <10, while the spoil SAR values were >25. Topsoil applied on spoil with these character-

Table 4—Saturated and unsaturated conductivities of topsoil and spoil materials from minesites in western North Dakota. Unsaturated conductivities computed by method of Campbell (1974) at −0.1 bar and −0.3 bar water potential

Soil	Texture	Saturated conductivity	Unsaturated conductivity	
			−0.1 bar	−0.3 bar
			cm/day	
Topsoil				
1	Sandy loam	6.0×10^1	2.7×10^0	1.6×10^{-1}
2	Sandy loam	4.4×10^1	2.0×10^0	1.2×10^{-1}
3	Loam	4.7×10^1	4.8×10^0	3.0×10^{-1}
4	Silty clay loam	2.8×10^0	4.2×10^{-1}	3.2×10^{-2}
5	Clay loam	2.2×10^1	4.2×10^0	2.9×10^{-1}
Spoil				
1	Sandy clay loam	8.5×10^{-1}	1.4×10^{-1}	8.5×10^{-3}
2	Sandy clay loam	2.0×10^{-2}	3.4×10^{-3}	2.0×10^{-4}
3	Silty clay	2.4×10^{-2}	4.7×10^{-3}	3.5×10^{-4}

istics drains very little. Observations of restricted drainage in sodic spoils are common at mine sites in North Dakota. Gee et al. (1976) reported that more than 30 days of drainage was required before the soil water potential of applied topsoil dropped below −0.04 bars at one sodic spoil site.

C. Water Storage

Water storage measurements by neutron scatter (Gardner, 1965) provide a nondestructive means to analyze water accumulation from precipitation and water loss by evapotranspiration and drainage. Figures 7 and 8 show overwinter and spring water accumulation in nonmined and mined materials. Materials with SAR >30 showed little water accumulation except in the case where piping erosion holes developed

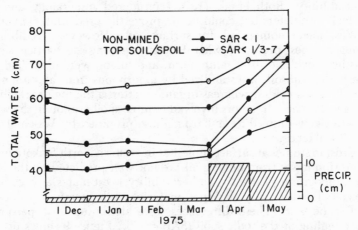

Fig. 7—Total water storage changes to depth of 2.7 m in nonmined and mined overburden at mined sites in western North Dakota.

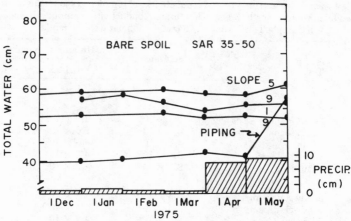

Fig. 8—Total water storage changes to depth of 2.7 m in sodic spoil materials at mine sites in western North Dakota. Numbers by curves are percent slope.

near access tube monitoring sites. Where these erosion features are present they play an important part of surface and subsurface hydrology of reclaimed sodic mine spoils.

VIII. ERODIBILITY

A. Erosion By Water

Predictions of soil loss by water erosion based on soil properties have been made for farmland and construction sites (Wischmeier et al., 1971). The nomograph of Wischmeier et al. (1971) utilizes terms involving particle size, organic matter, structure, and permeability to predict soil erodibility. Roth et al. (1974) considered mineralogy and other chemical parameters but could not improve the prediction capability of the Wischmeier nomograph for surface soils. However, erodibility for subsoils was best predicted when factors involving soil particle size and amorphous oxides of iron, aluminum, and silicon were used. This work suggests that subsoils are stabilized by amorphous iron, aluminum, and silicon hydrous oxides, whereas organic matter is the major stabilizer in surface soils. The soil factors involved in mine spoil erosion in the western U.S. are likely quite different from those proposed by Wischmeier for agricultural lands.

Erosion studies at surface minesites in western North Dakota indicate that erosion losses from mine spoil are not well predicted by the Wischmeier nomograph (Table 5). Soil erodibility K estimates as high as 0.66 were calculated for silty clay spoil material while measured values were found to be 0.08. These differences were attributed to dispersion and surface sealing of the sodic spoil (SAR = 38). Figure 9 shows predicted soil loss by water erosion as a function of slope. Each curve represents erosion loss for specified soil erodibility K values. Soil loss was calculated

Table 5—Predicted and observed soil erodibility K values for water erosion at minesites in western North Dakota

Sample	No. of samples	SAR	K value†	
			Predicted‡	Observed§
Nonmined Topsoil	26	0.6	0.36 (0.08–0.58)¶	--
Stockpiled Topsoil (respread)	15	4	0.26 (0.16–0.49)	--
Sandy loam	6	3	0.22 (0.16–0.26)	0.35
Spoil	31	38	0.48 (0.30–0.66)	--
Spoil (erosion plots)				
Sandy clay loam	3	41	0.41 (0.39–0.44)	0.06
Clay loam	3	37	0.54 (0.53–0.56)	0.10
Silty clay loam	3	33	0.63 (0.59–0.66)	0.08

† F values expressed as soil loss per EI (erosion index of rainfall). Units are in metric ton/ha per metric EI units.
‡ Predicted, using measured soil properties and Wischmeier nomograph (Wischmeier et al., 1971).
§ On-site measurements with simulated rainfall (Gilley et al., 1977).
¶ Mean values. Numbers in parentheses indicate range of individual measurements.

from the universal soil loss equation assuming a uniform slope length of 122 m, a rainfall factor of 87, while the cropping and management factor, C, and the erosion control factor, P were set equal to 1. The K values are expressed in metric units (conversion to English units is obtained by dividing by 1.292). The dashed line for $K = 0.09$ is for an experimentally

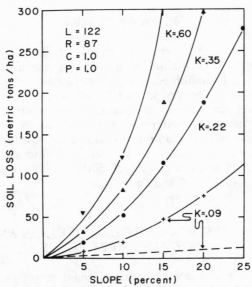

Fig. 9—Soil loss as a function of slope for the specified L, R, C, P, and K parameters as defined in the universal soil loss equation. All parameters are in metric units. Dashed line indicates soil loss from sodic spoil materials with an adjusted slope factor (Gilley et al., 1977). 1977).

Table 6—Wind erodibility data for mined surfaces and fallowed soils in western
North Dakota. Sampled Apr. 1976

Sample	No. of samples	Nonerodible material (%)†	Wind erodibility index (I)‡	Wind erodibility group (WEG)§
Fallowed soil¶	16	40 (20–60)#	119 (0–237)	5 (2–7)
Topsoil-stockpiled	9	50 (33–66)	90 (27–166)	6 (3.5–7)
Topsoil-respread	10	53 (41–72)	76 (22–116)	6 (5–7)
Spoil (with SAR > 30)	5	98 (97–99)	0 (0)	7 (7)

† Aggregates > 0.84 mm equivalent diam.
‡ Refers to wind erodibility relative to a standard plot. Expressed in metric tons/ha per year.
§ Erodibility class: 2—high, 7—low.
¶ Fallowed soils included Arnegard, Belfield, Chama, Flaxton, Rhoades, Temvik, Vebar, and Williams.
# Mean values are reported. Numbers in parentheses reflect the range for the tested materials.

measured slope factor for sodic spoil materials (Gilley et al., 1977). Ranges for calculated and measured values are reported in Table 5. These data suggest that the tested topsoil material is 50% more erosive than predicted.

There are recognized restrictions in applying the universal soil loss equation. Even if the soil erodibility could be predicted or measured with some accuracy, the average K (soil loss per EI unit) used for predicting long-term average soil losses is inadequate for estimating soil losses during specific storms or in specific years (Wischmeier, 1976). Additional work is necessary to evaluate the utility of the universal soil loss equation for minesite erosion in semiarid and arid regions.

B. Erosion By Wind

Wind erosion susceptibility of soils was predicted by measuring air-dry surface aggregates retained on a 0.84-mm screen (Chepil & Woodruff, 1963). Wind erodibility indexes were measured at mined sites in North Dakota using the Chepil and Woodruff procedure (Table 6). In general, wind erosion indexes indicate moderate to minimal wind erosion susceptibility for mined materials. Stockpiled soil materials were more wind erosion-susceptible than mine spoil but less susceptible than fallow soils from adjacent nonmined areas. The low wind erodibility of mine spoil materials is attributed to high SAR which created compacted, crusted surfaces (see Fig. 5 and Table 5).

IX. TESTS FOR DISPERSIVE CLAYS AND PIPING SUSCEPTIBILITY

As previously indicated, sodium-affected materials may offer two major problems to reclamation: (i) Poor plant-water relation characteristics, which could include low infiltration and permeability capacity, and a high degree of crusting causing physical impedence to seedling emergence; and (ii) Instability of surface and subsurface features, which includes piping, jugging, deep rills, and even tunnel-type erosion caused by erosion through cracks and large interstices or uncompacted earth-rock materials. For sodium-affected materials, methods of analysis should be designed to measure the degree to which both problems may likely occur.

A. Methods

Recent work by Sherard et al. (1976a) suggest several tests which may provide satisfactory criteria for piping susceptibility of mine spoils materials. These tests have been used principally for earth-fill dam materials, but should prove suitable for use with mine spoil materials. The three tests are described briefly as follows:

a. **Dispersion or Double Hydrometer Test**—This test is used to determine dispersion percentage (Fig. 4). It is made by using hydrometer techniques for measurement of approximately 5-μm-size particles and running the test sample with and without dispersant and strong mechanical mixing. The ratio of the test without dispersant to the test with dispersant is computed as the dispersion percentage.

b. **Crumb Test**—This test consists of simply placing a crumb of material (about 1 cm in diam), preserved at field water content, into a beaker of distilled water and observing the tendency of the clay to go into colloidal suspension. The results are interpreted on a scale ranging from one to four with one being the least and four being the most dispersive.

c. **Pinhole Test**—A laboratory "pinhole test" designed by Sherard et al. (1976b) simulates the action of a crack or leak in a clay dam. The test was devised specifically for the purpose of identifying dispersive clays. It is intended for qualitative identification only and not for measuring rates of erosion.

In this test, distilled water flows through a 1-mm-diam hole, punched in a 3.8-cm-long sample. The sample is confined in a permeameter (Fig. 10). Initially, water is caused to flow under a head of 5 cm water. The principal differentiation between dispersive clay and erosion-resistant clay is given by the results of the test under 5 cm of head. For dispersive clays, the flow emerging from the specimen is visibly colored with colloids and does not clear with time. Within 10 min, the hole diameter enlarges to about 3 mm or more and the test is complete. For erosion-resistant clay, the flow is completely clear and the hole does not enlarge. At the end of 5 min, the flow rate is unchanged. The hydraulic head is raised in progressive steps each 5 min to 18, 38, and 102 cm. At each higher gradient, the rate of flow is measured and the color of effluent is observed. For highly erosion-resistant clays, the water is always clear and the rate of flow remains constant under each flow condition.

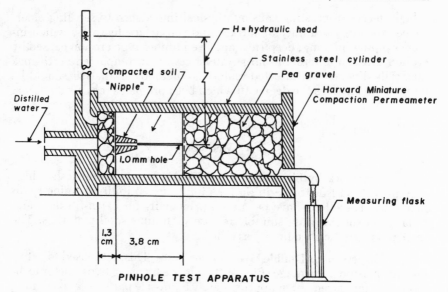

Fig. 10—Pinhole test apparatus used to measure dispersiveness of clays in overburden and spoil materials (after Sherard et al., 1976b).

B. Test Results

Preliminary tests were run by Soil Conservation Service, Soil Mechanics Laboratory personnel on several samples taken from a mine site in western North Dakota. The results suggested that the pinhole test (Sherard et al., 1976b) could accurately describe the piping susceptibility of mine spoil materials. Subsequently, samples from 16 additional sites in western North Dakota were tested. Four samples were taken from the B horizon of typical soils of the area; four from sites where piping erosion was observed; four from topsoil stockpile areas; and four from in-place overburden materials sampled from the face of the highwall. Data in Table 7 indicates the measure particle size, SAR, liquid and plastic limit, percent dispersion, and the results of the crumb and pinhole tests. Figure 11 shows the pinhole test data in relation to the sodium percentage and total dissolved solids in the pore water as determined from a saturation extract. The three zones, A, B, and C corresponding to dispersive, intermediate, and nondispersive, respectively, have been previously defined by Sherard et al. (1976a) by an extensive analysis of dispersive clays using the pinhole test. The data indicate that the North Dakota materials tested fall into the expected categories as determined by their salt concentrations.

From Table 7, it can be seen that high SAR is not always a criterion of dispersive clays. For example, the stockpile sample SP3 has a relatively low SAR of 7.6, but because the total salt concentration of the pore water was relatively low (9.2 meq/liter) and the percent sodium was high (79), the sample dispersed. Similar observations have been reported for sodium-

Table 7—Atterberg limits, plasticity index, and dispersion clay tests for selected samples from mine areas in western North Dakota

Sample	SAR†	Clay, %	Liquid limit	Plasticity index	Crumb test‡	Pinhole test§	Dispersion, %
Nonmined							
BN B	0.2	10	21.5	3.0	1.0	ND2	54
CO B	0.3	18	32.1	10.5	2.0	ND2	26
KR B	0.3	26	36.3	17.3	1.0	ND2	7
NA B	21	33	45.2	24.6	3.5	D2	55
Topsoil							
SP1	1.5	16	21.4	3.0	1.0	ND2	16
SP2	10	43	50.5	28.2	1.5	ND2	6
SP3	7.6	45	47.6	24.6	3.5	D2	11
SP6	0.6	30	30.5	10.2	2.0	ND2	6
Highwall							
BN 4	1.5	22	37.8	14.3	1.5	ND2	16
CO 3	50	60	63.7	40.2	3.5	D2	92
KR 4	21	54	67.7	38.5	3.5	D2	82
NA 4	39	34	87.4	59.4	4.0	D2	98
Mined							
NA P A	24	34	66.1	41.3	4.0	D2	78
NA R 7	56	16	47.6	24.9	3.0	D2	64
NA S 24	28	27	46.1	23.9	2.0	D2	71
NA C	37	16	61.5	40.6	2.5	D2	77

† SAR is the sodium adsorption ratio expressed as $SAR = Na/([Ca + Mg]/2)^{1/2}$.
‡ Crumb test ratings: 1–2 nondispersive, 3–4 dispersive.
§ Pinhole test ratings: ND1–ND2 nondispersive, D1–D2 dispersive.

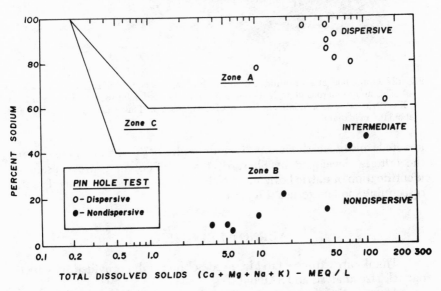

Fig. 11—Relation of pinhole test data to soluble salt status of the soil solution. All data are from saturation extracts. Percent Na is equal to $Na/(Ca + Mg + Na + K) \times 100$.

Fig. 12—Piping hole at a strip-mine site in North Dakota. The SAR of surface material was 40. This and numerous other holes developed on bare, reshaped spoil over the winter of 1974–1975 and were a prominent feature of the landscape. This hole was > 1 m deep and about 0.6 m in diam.

affected soils in North Dakota (Omodt et al., 1975). The pinhole test and the criteria developed by Sherard et al. (1976b) may prove useful in identification of natric horizons in soils, as well as identification of piping susceptible spoil materials (Fig. 12).

ACKNOWLEDGMENT

Thanks are expressed to Mr. Fred Schroer, who provided the pipette particle size analysis and SAR data.

Appreciation is expressed to Baukol-Noonan Coal Company, Center, North Dakota; Consolidation Coal Company, Stanton, North Dakota;

Knife River Coal Company Beulah, North Dakota; and the North American Coal Corporation, Zap, North Dakota for allowing us to conduct experiments at their mine sites.

LITERATURE CITED

Bertrand, A. R. 1965. Rate of water intake in the field. In C. A. Black (ed.) Methods of soil analysis. Part I. Agronomy 9:202-207. Am. Soc. of Agron., Madison, Wis.

Bertrand, A. R., and J. F. Parr. 1961. Design and operations of the Purdue Sprinkling Infiltrometer. Purdue Univ. Res. Bull. no. 723, Lafayette, Ind.

Blake, G. R. 1965. Particle density. In C. A. Black (ed.) Methods of soil analysis. Part I. Agronomy 9:371-373. Am. Soc. of Agron., Madison, Wis.

Brown, G. W. 1962. Piping erosion in Colorado. J. Soil Water Conserv. 17:220-222.

Campbell, G. S. 1974. A simple method for determining unsaturated conductivity from moisture retention data. Soil Sci. 117:311-314.

Chepil, W. S., and N. P. Woodruff. 1963. The physics of wind erosion and its control. Adv. Agron. 15:211-302.

Coe, D. A. 1976. Rigorous volumetric computations using core borings and cross section data. p. 54-63. In 4th Symp. on Surface Mining and Reclamation, 19-21 Oct. 1976, Louisville, Ky. Natl. Coal Assoc., Washington, D.C.

Day, P. R. 1965. Particle fractionation and particle size analysis. In C. A. Black (ed.) Methods of soil analysis. Part I. Agronomy 9:545-567. Am. Soc. of Agron., Madison, Wis.

Fletcher, J. E., and P. H. Carrol. 1948. Some properties of soils associated with piping in southern Arizona. Soil Sci. Soc. Am. Proc. 13:545-547.

Gardner, W. H. 1965. Water content. In C. A. Black (ed.) Methods of soil analysis. Part I. Agronomy 9:84-124. Am. Soc. of Agron., Madison, Wis.

Gee, G. W., and A. Bauer. 1976. Physical and chemical properties of stockpiled materials at a mine site in North Dakota. North Dakota Agr. Exp. Sta. Farm Res. 34(2):44-51.

Gee, G. W., J. E. Gilley, and A. Bauer. 1976. Use of soil properties to estimate soil loss by water erosion on surface-mined lands of western North Dakota. North Dakota Agr. Exp. Sta. Farm Res. 34(2):40-43.

Gilley, J. E., G. W. Gee, A. Bauer, W. O. Willis, and R. A. Young. 1976. Water infiltration at surface-mined sites in western North Dakota. North Dakota Agric. Exp. Stn. Farm Res. 34(2):32-34.

Gilley, J. E., G. W. Gee, A. Bauer, W. O. Willis, and R. A. Young. 1977. Runoff and erosion characteristics of surface-mined sites in western North Dakota. Trans. Am. Soc. Agric. Eng. 20(4):697-704.

Kaddah, M. T. 1974. The hydrometer method for detailed particle size analysis: 1. Graphical interpretation of hydrometer readings and test of method. Soil Sci. 118:102-108.

Kemper, W. D. 1965a. Size distribution of aggregates. In C. A. Black (ed.) Methods of soil analysis: Part I. Agronomy 9:506-508. Am. Soc. of Agron., Madison, Wis.

Kemper, W. D. 1965b. Aggregate stability. In C. A. Black (ed.) Methods of soil analysis: Part I. Agronomy 9:515-518. Am. Soc. of Agron., Madison, Wis.

Koshi, P. T. 1966. Soil-moisture measurements by the neutron method in rocky wildland soils. Soil Sci. Soc. Am. Proc. 30:282-284.

Meeuwig, R. 1971. Infiltration and water repellency in granitic soils. USDA Forest Serv. Res. Pap. INT-111.

Meyer, L. D. 1960. Use of the rainulator for runoff plot research. Soil Sci. Soc. Am. Proc. 24:319-322.

Omodt, H. W., F. W. Schroer, and D. D. Patterson. 1975. The properties of important agricultural soils as criteria for mined land reclamation. North Dakota Agric. Exp. Stn. Bull. 492. p. 52.

Patterson, D. D. 1976. The soil map. A prerequisite to mining and reclamation. North Dakota Agric. Exp. Stn. Farm Res. 34(1):12-13.

Power, J. F., W. O. Willis, F. M. Sandoval, and J. J. Bond. 1974. Can productivity of mined land be restored in North Dakota: North Dakota Agric. Exp. Stn. Farm Res. 31(6):30-32.

Rai, D., P. J. Wierenga, and W. L. Gould. 1975. Chemical and physical properties of soil samples from a coal-bearing formation in San Juan County, New Mexico. New Mexico State Univ. Agric. Exp. Stn. Res. Rep. 294. 24 p.

Rauzi, F., and C. L. Fly. 1968. Water intake on midcontinental rangelands as influenced by soil and plant cover. USDA Tech. Bull. 1390, Washington, D.C. 58 p.

Reinhart, K. G. 1961. The problem of stones in soil-moisture measurement. Soil Sci. Soc. Am. Proc. 25:268-270.

Richards, L. A. 1954. Diagnosis and improvement of saline and alkali soils. Agric. Handb. 60 USDA-ARS, Washington, D.C.

Roth, C. B., D. W. Nelson, and M. J. M. Romkins. 1974. Prediction of subsoil erodibility using chemical, mineralogical and physical parameters. Environ. Prot. Tech. Ser. EPA-660/2-74-043, Washington, D.C. 111 p.

Sandoval, F. M., J. J. Bond, J. F. Power, and W. O. Willis. 1973. Lignite mine spoils in the Northern Great Plains—characteristics and potential for reclamation. In Some environmental aspects of strip-mining in North Dakota. North Dakota Geol. Surv. Educ. Ser. 5:1-24.

Schroer, F. W. 1976. Chemical and physical characterization of coal overburden. North Dakota Agric. Exp. Stn. Farm Res. 34(1):5-11.

Sherard, J. L., L. P. Dunnigan, and R. S. Decker. 1976a. Identification and nature of dispersive soils. Am. Soc. Civil Eng., J. Geotech. Eng. Div. 101(GT4) no. 12052:287-301.

Sherard, J. L., L. P. Dunnigan, R. S. Decker, and E. F. Steele. 1976b. Pinhole test for identifying dispersive soils. Am. Soc. Civil Eng., J. Geo-tech. Eng. Div. 101(GT1) no. 11846: 69-85.

Soil Survey Staff. 1951. Soil survey manual. USDA Handb. no. 18, Washington, D.C. p. 205-223.

Wischmeier, W. H. 1976. Use and misuse of the universal soil loss equation. J. Soil Water Conserv. 31(1):5-9.

Wischmeier, W. H., C. B. Johnson, and B. V. Cross. 1971. A soil nomograph for farmland and construction sites. J. Soil Water Conserv. 26:189-193.

Chapter 39

Methods for Controlling Pollutants

RONALD D. HILL

U.S. Environmental Protection Agency
Industrial Environmental Research Laboratory
Cincinnati, Ohio

I. INTRODUCTION

The extraction of a mineral commodity or fuel by its very nature is a destructive process. Environmental destruction is bound to occur. In Fig. 1, the numerous emissions produced by the extraction process are illustrated. These environmental insults can be divided into several major categories: solid waste handling and disposal, water discharges, air discharges, noise, and aesthetics.

Mining is the largest producer of solid waste in the United States. Not only must large volumes of rock, soil, etc., be removed to extract the ore or fuel, but additional volumes are produced when the material is processed. The handling and disposal of this solid waste is a major problem of drastically disturbed lands. When improperly disposed, ground and surface water pollution, fugitive dust, landslides, and aesthetic problems result.

During mining and beneficiation, environmental problems occur from runoff from the disturbed area, water in the pit area, dust and noise from blasting, extraction, haulage, storage, grinding, etc., and from oil, solvents, and domestic and other waste from the support facilities.

In addition to current mining operations, there exists a legacy of abandoned/inactive mines. A 1969 Congressional study (House document no. 91-180, 1969) reported that inactive coal mines were the source of 78% of acid mine drainage. A recent EPA-supported study (Toups Corporation, 1975) reported that in excess of 1,200 km of streams have been degraded by inactive ore and mineral mines. The major types of pollution were acid, metals, and sediment. Table 1, which presents an estimate of historical production data for these industries, illustrates the magnitude of the past land disturbances.

Pollution control from mining operations is strongly related to whether the mine is active or inactive. Active mining operations are usually under the regulation of some state and/or federal agencies and a responsible party, e.g., the mine owner. In the case of the inactive mine, responsibility and ownership is often unclear, regulations and laws are nonexistent, and funds for pollution control are unavailable or must come from the public sector.

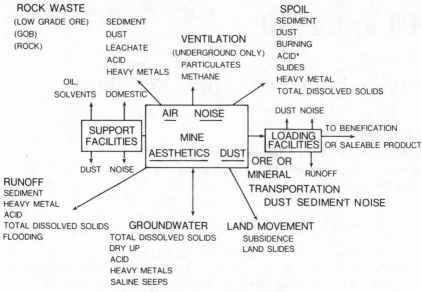

Fig. 1—Emissions from extraction process.

II. MAJOR SOURCES OF POLLUTION

A. Sediment

Sediment in water reduces light penetration and alters the temperature, directly affecting aquatic flora and fauna. Fish production is hindered because food organisms are smothered, spawning grounds destroyed, and pools filled. Sediment places an additional burden on treatment plants and cost as well as on aesthetic and economic values. Sediment deposit in navigable streams must be removed at a high cost. Streams chocked with sediment have reduced carrying capacity and are subject to flooding.

A study by Collier et al. (1964) showed the average annual sediment production from a surface-mined watershed was 42 tons/acre, more than 1,000 times higher than an unmined watershed. Curtis (1974) studied three watersheds in Kentucky and found the sediment yield to range between 0.84 and 1.27 area-inches of area disturbed. He could find little correlation between sediment yield and the amount of land disturbed and concluded that methods of mining and handling the overburden are major factors controlling sediment yield. He also noted that the highest sediment yields were measured during the first 6-month period after mining and that the subsequent sediment yield had a half-life of 6 months, that is, the sediment yield for a second 6-month period would be half that of the preceding 6-month period.

Methods for predicting sediment yield from disturbed land are inadequate. The above example may be representative of the locality of the particular study, but is probably not for others. Sediment yield can best

Table 1—Estimated historical production of major metals and potential waste generated†

Metal	Production	Production base dates	Assumed occurrence in ore‡	Tailings	Tailings and waste
	10³ metric tons		%	— 10⁶ metric tons —	
Base metals					
Copper	57,800	1845	1.0	5,780	14,450
Lead	30,900	1873	2.0	1,550	3,875
Mercury	120	1850	0.5	24	60
Zinc	35,300	1873	4.0	883	2,208
Ferrous metals					
Iron ore	5,420,000	1834	50.0	5,400	5,400
Precious metals					
Gold	10	1792	0.00086	616	1,540
Silver	153	1834	0.014	546	1,365
Rare metals					
Molybdenum	1,294	1914	0.3	430	1,075
Tungsten	140	1900	0.5	28	70
Uranium	253	1957	0.25	101	253
Total				15,358	30,296

† Source: Toups Corp. (1975).
‡ The percentages are a synthesis of published data and the author's experience in mining.

be described by the Universal Soil Loss Equation (USLE), which combines the principal factors that influence surface erosion by water (Roth et al., 1974). The equation takes the form:

$$A = RKLSCP$$

where A is the soil loss in tons/acre; R is the rainfall factor; K is the soil erodibility factor; L is the length of slope factor; S is the steepness of slope factor; C is the cropping and management factor; and P is the erosion control practice factor. Although this equation can serve as a useful guide in planning erosion control practices, its value for determining an accurate sediment yield for a particular disturbed area is questionable because factors K, C, and P have not been determined for land disturbances such as mining. Figures developed from agricultural use are probably grossly inaccurate.

A review of the six factors that influence soil erosion is in order. The rainfall factor, R, reflects the potential of raindrop impact and runoff turbulence to dislodge and transport soil particles. This factor is dependent upon the rainfall pattern and intensity of a specific locality. The mine operator has no control over this factor.

The soil erodibility factor, K, reflects the most significant soil characteristics affecting soil erodibility. For surface soils, the soil texture, organic matter content, soil structure, and permeability are the key parameters. Recently, Roth et al. (1974) have shown for subsoils low in organic matter and high in clay that the chemical properties of the material such as its iron and aluminum content have a major bearing on its erodibility. The K factors for bedrock material fractured during mining and later weathered remains to be defined. The mining company has limited control of their material during the mining operation but they can make every effort during reclamation to place that material with the lowest erodibility factor on the surface. This material should have a high organic matter content, high permeability, and be granular. In many situations, the practice of topsoiling is a step toward obtaining a lower K factor if the soil is properly handled and placed.

The length of slope factor, L, reflects increased sediment detachment and transport as runoff velocities and volume increase with increased slope length. Spoil should be stored and final-graded to prevent long slopes. Where long slopes must be left, control structures should be installed to break up the slope (see P factor).

The degree of slope factor, S, also recognizes that runoff velocity increases as the slope of the land increases. For example, increasing the steepness of a slope from 10 to 40% doubles the flow velocity. Steep slopes should be discouraged in mining operations. Slopes of less than 33% are recommended but are sometimes difficult to obtain in mountain-type surface mining where the original slope equals or exceeds 33%.

The cover management factor, C, reflects the influence of the type of vegetative cover, seeding method, soil tillage, disposition of residues, and general management level. The C value ranges from near zero for excellent sod to 1.0 for bare soil. Mining firms can take advantage of this factor by establishing quick cover of grasses and legumes and using proper tillage techniques. The C values decrease as the percent ground cover and the percent canopy cover increase. The application of mulches such as straw, woodchips, and chemicals also decreases the C factor.

The practice factor, P, accounts for erosion control structures such as terraces and diversions. These practices are used to influence the drainage patterns, runoff concentration, and runoff velocity. Numerous such practices are available and the mining company should take advantage of those applicable to their situation.

For those wanting more information on the USLE, the U.S. Department of Agriculture has prepared a handbook (Wischmeir & Smith, 1965).

B. Acid Mine Drainage and Heavy Metals

One of the most damaging waterborne contaminants from mining operations is the acid generated from the exposure of iron sulfide minerals to the atmosphere. Not only does the acid directly impact stream biota, eat away metal structures, and destroy concrete, but, as a result of the low pH, other ions such as heavy metals become solubilized and carried into water courses. These ions are often toxic to aquatic life and render the water unusable. It has been estimated that in excess of 16,000 km of streams have been degraded by acid mine drainage.

The removal of overburden often exposed rock materials containing pyrite (iron disulfide). As shown in Eq. [1] and [2], the oxidation of pyrite results in the production of ferrous iron and sulfuric acid. The reaction then proceeds to form ferric hydroxide and more acid, as shown in Eq. [3] and [4]:

$$2FeS_2 + 2H_2O + 7O_2 \rightarrow 2FeSO_4 + 2H_2SO_4 \qquad [1]$$

$$(Pyrite) \rightarrow (Ferrous\ Sulfate) + (Sulfuric\ Acid)$$

$$FeS_2 + 14Fe^{3+} + 8H_2O \rightarrow 15Fe^{2+} + 2SO_4^{2-} + 16H^+ \qquad [2]$$

$$(Pyrite) + (Ferric\ Iron) \rightarrow (Ferrous\ Iron) + (Sulfate) + (Acid)$$

$$4FeSO_4 + O_2 + 2H_2SO_4 \rightarrow 2Fe_2(SO_4)_3 + 2H_2O \qquad [3]$$

$$Fe_2(SO_4)_3 + 6H_2O \rightarrow 2Fe(OH)_3 + 3H_2SO_4. \qquad [4]$$

Similar reactions have been proposed to describe the oxidation of other iron sulfide minerals, e.g., chalcopyrite;

$$CuFeS_2 + 4O_2 + 2H_2O \rightarrow CuSO_4 + Fe(OH)_2 + H_2SO_4. \qquad [5]$$

As noted, the products of these various reactions are Fe^{2+}, Fe^{3+}, H_2SO_4, and various heavy metals that may be associated with the host pyrite, such as Cu, Zn, Al, and Mn.

The amount and rate of acid formation, and the quality of water discharged, are a function of the amount and type of pyrite in the overburden rock, ore, and coal, time of exposure, characteristics of the overburden, and amount of available water (Moth et al., 1972). Crystalline forms of pyritic material are less subject to weathering and oxidation than amorphic forms. Since oxidation by oxygen is the primary reaction during early acid formation, the less time pyritic material is exposed to air the less acid is formed. It has also been observed that even under ideal physical and chemical conditions for oxidation the reactions do not proceed at their maximum rate immediately. Thus, a positive preventative method is to cover pyritic materials as soon as possible with earth, which serves as an oxygen barrier. In terms of mining, this step is accomplished by current reclamation techniques and operating with only a small pit.

If the overburden also contains alkaline material such as limestone, acid water may not be discharged even though it is formed, because of in-place neutralization by the alkaline material. Discharges from this situation are usually high in sulfate.

Enough water to satisfy Eq. [1], [2], [4], and [5] is usually available in the overburden and coal material. Water also serves as the transport medium that removes oxidation products from the mining site into streams. Control of this water is a positive pollution preventative method.

Bacteria are almost always present in acid mine drainage. These bacteria obtain their energy for growth from the oxidation of reduced sulfur compounds and ferrous iron. Their role in Eq. [1] through [5] is still under debate. For sure they play a significant role in the oxidation of ferrous iron to the ferric form. From an acid mine drainage control standpoint, the role of the bacteria is unimportant because (i) iron-oxidizing bacteria are common in soils and, thus, the source cannot be controlled, (ii) bactericides have not shown to be effective, and (iii) oxygen control impedes the reaction whether it is chemical or biological.

C. Dissolved Solids

Fracturing the overburden material during extraction exposes many new surfaces to water percolating through it. Numerous ions are subject to removal by solubilization and ion exchange. The type of ions removed are a function of the water quality and the overburden material characteristics. Since many ions are more soluble at lower pH's, acid mine drainage will usually leach more ions than alkaline waters. However, all waters will leach some ions. Increases in concentration of calcium, magnesium, aluminum, sulfate, sodium, chloride, alkalinity, specific conductance, and pH have been reported by Curtis (1972), Plass (1975), and McWhorter et al. (1974). The leaching process can be expected to continue for years because under normal nonacidic conditions the rate is very slow. In most mines the rate of release is low enough that the increase in dissolved solids is not detrimental. However, where extensive areas have been mined, the accumulation of the leachate may create problems. There is little that can be done to control this problem other than keeping the water that would cause leaching to a minimum and, thus, extending the process over a long period.

D. Dust and Other Air Emissions

Dust emission from mining operations result from blasting, excavation, loading and unloading vehicles, vehicle travel, loading and unloading storage areas, backfilling, revegetation, and barren soil and spoil. Dust plumes around mining operations are a common sight during dry weather. Mines in the arid and semiarid western U.S. are acutely sensitive to the problem. Only limited data is available on the magnitude of dust emissions and the significance of these emissions off the mining site.

Many steps within the extraction process cause soil and rock material to be pulverized. These particles are then lifted by rolling wheels, blasts, earth-moving equipment, and strong air currents produced by vehicles and wind. The heavier and coarser material settles back to the ground quickly, whereas the finer material may be carried long distances.

Dust yields from wind erosion can be described by the wind erosion equation (Wilson, 1975):

$$E = IKCLV$$

where E is the gross erosion (tons/acre per year); I is the soil erodibility index; K is the field roughness; C is the climate factor; L is the field length; and V is the vegetative cover.

Soil erodibility index, I, is a function of the ability of the soil to form clods. It is usually determined by sieve analysis. Materials having a larger percentage of coarse material and clays present are less subject to wind erosion.

Surface roughness, K, takes into account that rough surfaces absorb and deflect wind energy and trap some material.

The climatic factor, C, is a function of the windspeed and soil moisture. Areas subject to high windspeeds and dry conditions are subject to greater wind erosion. The USDA has prepared maps with C values (Skidmore & Woodruff, 1968).

The field width index, L, relates to the observation that soil flow is zero at the upwind side of a bare area and increases across the area until it reaches a maximum value. Short areas, or effective short areas because of windbreaks, have less erosion. In regions where the area is dry and regional wind erosion is predominate over site-specific erosion, the upwind side may not have zero soil flow and maximum, L, value is soon reached.

The vegetation factor, V, relates to plant cover. Wind erosion decreases as the protective effects of good ground cover increases.

Some preliminary attempts have been made to develop equations for dust emission factors. Cowherd et al. (1974) developed the following factors for unpaved roads and aggregate storage piles that may have application to mining situations.

$$E \text{ (unpaved roads)} = 0.81 \, S(V)$$

where E is the emission factor (pounds/vehicle-mile); S is the silt content of road surface material (%); and V is the average vehicle speed (mph).

$$E \text{ (storage piles)} = 0.33/(PE/100)2$$

where E is emission factor (pounds/ton placed in storage) and PE is Thornthwaite's precipitation-evaporation index.

The EPA now has a major effort underway to assess the dust emission from coal mining operations in both the eastern and western U.S. A recent study (Blackwood et al., 1976) of the crushed stone industry obtained the emission data presented in Table 2. This data illustrates the major dust sources that might be expected from various mining operations. Another study prepared for EPA (Cavanaugh et al., 1976) has estimated the air emissions from a standard 6,300-tons/day strip mine. These figures are presented in Table 3.

Coal refuse fires are another source of air pollution. Chalebode and Opferbuch (1976) collected data from several burning refuse piles and prepared Table 4.

E. Noise

Many of the operations associated with mining are noisy. Major sources of noise are blasting, heavy equipment operations, loading equipment, and truck haulage. Where mines are remote from urban areas, the

Table 2—Emission factors for crushed stone operations†

Unit operation	Respirable particulates	% of total respirable particulates from all crushed stone operations‡	Total particulates	% of total particulates from all crushed stone operations‡	Respirable particulate, % of total particulates from unit operation
	mg/metric ton		mg/metric ton		
Blasting	8.8	0.27	52.2	0.18	17
Drilling (wet)	16.0	0.49	158	0.56	10
Quarrying	1,050	32.3	10,500	37.02	10
Primary crushing and loading	1,340	41.2	13,400	47.2	10
Secondary crushing and screening	342	10.5	619	2.18	55
Tertiary crushing and screening	66.5	2.05	362	1.28	18
Fines crushing and screening	14.7	0.45	91.8	0.32	16
Conveying	113	3.48	1,730	6.10	7
Loading trucks	45.3	1.39	166	0.58	68
Unloading trucks	53.8	1.65	127	0.45	42
Transport (wet)	202	6.21	1,150	4.05	18
Total	3,250		28,400		11§

† Source: Blackwood et al. (1976).
‡ Rounded off—does not add to 100%.
§ Total respirable particulates as percent of total particulates from all unit operations.

impact of this noise is felt mostly by the mine personnel; however, when the mine is in close relationship to urban areas, noise complaints are common.

Only limited data are available on the severity of this problem. Several operations are inherently noisy and control methods are nonexistent. Proper muffling of vehicles can often lessen the problem from that source. Major steps have been taken to decrease both the noise and vibration from blasting. Adequate stemming, use of millisecond delays, awareness of prevailing wind direction, blasting only during daylight hours, and careful consideration of charge size are all techniques helpful to minimize these problems.

III. AT-SOURCE CONTROL

The prevention and minimization of emissions at their source is the most reasonable approach to controlling pollutants from mine-disturbed lands. Once allowed to form and be discharged from the disturbed area, the control methods become more difficult and costly. For this reason, most efforts are placed at controlling the pollutants at the source. This section describes the various techniques available for at-source control.

Environmental control starts in the mine planning stage. Data

Table 3—Estimated air emissions of strip mining coal module (Basis: 6,300-tons/day run of mine coal)†

Source	Emissions				
	Particulates	SO$_2$	CO	Hydrocarbons	NO$_x$
			lb/day		
Vehicle emissions	20	41	344	66	566
Overburden removal‡	1,160	--	--	--	--
Primary crushing‡	126	--	--	--	--
Loading and unloading at the preparation plant§	39	--	--	--	--
Loading in the pit‡	506	--	--	--	--
Vehicular travel‡	40	--	--	--	--
Thermal drying§	505	1,290	35	17	603
Vehicle emissions from refuse hauling operations	0.9	1.8	15	2.9	25
Total	2,400	1,330	394	86	1,190

† Source: Cavanaugh et al. (1976).
‡ 80% particulate control by water spraying and dust control techniques.
§ 90% particulate control by wet scrubbers.

collected at the proposed mine site on the topography, overburden characteristics, ground and surface water, and climatic conditions are used to plan the mining technique. This insures that proper erosion control is established, and that selected overburden handling is accomplished to prevent acid mine drainage and insure revegetation. Major irreversible problems have resulted when environmental concerns have not been considered along with extraction procedures. Good premining data collection and mine planning are the key to final recovery of the disturbed area.

Table 4—Emission factors for coal refuse fire emissions†

Pollutant	Emission factors			
	kg/hour per m^3 of burning coal refuse	lb/hour per yd^3 of burning coal refuse	kg/hour per metric ton of burning coal refuse	lb/hour per ton of burning coal refuse
Criteria pollutants				
Total particulates	5.1×10^{-7}	8.6×10^{-7}	3.4×10^{-7}	6.8×10^{-7}
Respirable particulates	1.3×10^{-8}	2.2×10^{-8}	8.7×10^{-9}	1.7×10^{-8}
NO$_x$	1.0×10^{-4}	1.7×10^{-4}	6.7×10^{-5}	1.3×10^{-4}
SO$_2$	1.1×10^{-4}	1.9×10^{-4}	7.4×10^{-5}	1.5×10^{-4}
SO$_3$	2.7×10^{-7}	9.6×10^{-7}	3.8×10^{-7}	7.6×10^{-7}
Hydrocarbons	1.0×10^{-4}	1.7×10^{-4}	6.7×10^{-5}	1.3×10^{-4}
CO	1.3×10^{-2}	2.2×10^{-2}	8.7×10^{-3}	1.8×10^{-2}
Noncriteria pollutants				
NH$_3$	6.5×10^{-5}	1.1×10^{-4}	4.3×10^{-5}	8.6×10^{-5}
H$_2$S	4.5×10^{-4}	7.6×10^{-4}	3.0×10^{-4}	6.0×10^{-4}
Hg	6.8×10^{-9}	1.1×10^{-8}	4.6×10^{-9}	9.2×10^{-9}
POM	1.9×10^{-8}	3.2×10^{-8}	1.3×10^{-8}	2.6×10^{-8}

† Source: Chalebode and Opferbuch (1976).

A. Sediment

As described in the preceding section, the Universal Soil Loss Equation describes the factors that influence erosion by water. These factors must be manipulated to obtain the minimum soil loss. The key to most sediment control programs is the establishment of a good vegetative cover. Current technology calls for the rapid development of a grass/legume cover as soon as possible. This development is aided by preparing the area for revegetation as soon as possible and by making grading an integral part of the mining operation. Grading and revegetation should take place as soon as the resource has been extracted or a suitable part of the area is available. The shorter the period an area is bare, the less the erosion. All season planting, nurse crops, and mulching are techniques to accomplish this goal. The utilization of lime, fertilizer, and other soil amendments to assist in germination and survival of the plants is important.

Selection of the best quality of material to place on the surface of the newly regarded area is critical. This material should have desirable physical and chemical characteristics for the establishment of vegetation and the reduction of erosion. In some locations, topsoil removed from the surface as an initial step in mining is the best material because it has good physical characteritics, is high in organic matter and nutrients, has a viable organism community, and contains numerous seeds. In other situations the topsoil is nonexistent or has poor chemical and physical characteristics. Lower horizons may have better soil-forming characteristics and should be utilized. In all cases, if the surface material is not properly "tied" to the base material, erosion will be accelerated.

Length and steepness of slope should be kept to a minimum. Use of control practices such as diversion ditches, terraces, and grading on the contour should be utilized to reduce the impact of slopes. Care must be taken to provide suitable discharge points for water carried away by these structures.

The Environmental Protection Agency (USEPA, 1976) has prepared an erosion control manual for surface mines. It has also produced a comprehensive report on environmental protection in surface mining (Grim & Hill, 1974).

B. Acid Mine Drainage

All techniques for preventing acid formation are based on the control of oxygen. There are two mechanisms by which oxygen can be transported to pyrite—convective transport and molecular diffusion (Ohio State Univ., 1971).

The major convection transport source is wind currents that can easily supply the oxygen requirement for pyrite oxidation at the spoil surface. In addition, wind currents against a steep slope provide sufficient pressure to drive oxygen deeper into the spoil mass. A factor to consider is the degree of slope after regrading. This is especially important on slopes subject to prevailing winds, since the wind pressure on the spoil surface increases as the slope increases. Thus, the depth of oxygen movement into the spoil would increase as the slope increases.

Molecular diffusion occurs whenever there is an oxygen concentration gradient between two points, e.g., the spoil surface and some point within the spoil. Molecular diffusion is applicable to any fluid system, either gaseous or liquid. Thus, oxygen will move from the air near the surface of the spoil, where the concentration is higher, to the gas or liquid-filled pores within the spoil, where it is lower. The rate of oxygen transfer is strongly dependent on the fluid phases and is generally much higher in gases than in liquids. For example, the diffusion of oxygen through air is approximately 10,000 times greater than through water. Therefore, even a thin layer of water (several millimeters) serves as a good oxygen barrier.

The most positive method of preventing acid generation is the installation of an oxygen barrier. Artificial barriers such as plastic films, bituminous, and concrete would be effective, but these have high original and maintenance costs and would be used only in special situations.

Surface sealants such as lime, gypsum, sodium silicate, and latex have been tried, but they too suffer from high cost, require repeated application, and have only marginal effectiveness. The two most effective barrier materials are soil, including nonacid spoil, and water. The minimum thickness of soil or nonacid spoil needed is a function of the soil's physical characteristics (soil compaction and moisture content) and vegetative cover. Deeper layers would be needed for a sandy, dry, granular material with large grain size and porosity than for a tightly packed, saturated clay that is essentially impermeable. Soil thickness should be designed on the basis of the worst situation—such as a dry soil where oxygen can move more readily through cracks and pore spaces devoid of water. A "safety factor" should be included to account for soil losses from such causes as erosion.

Vegetation not only serves to control erosion but, after it dies, it becomes an oxygen user through the decomposing process. This further aids the effectiveness of the barrier. The organic matter that is formed also aids in holding moisture in the soil.

Water is an extremely effective barrier when the pyritic material is permanently covered. Allowing the pyrite to pass through cycles where it is exposed to oxidation and then covered will worsen the AMD problem. Water barriers should be designed to account for water losses such as evaporation and should include at least 30 cm (1 foot) of additional depth as a safety factor.

Additional measures to control AMD are water control and inplace neutralization. Water serves not only as the transport media that carries the acid pollutants from the pyrite reaction sites, it also erodes soil and nonacid spoils to expose pyrite to oxidation. Facilities such as diversion ditches that prevent water from entering the mining area and/or carry the water quickly through the area can significantly reduce the amount of water available to transport the acid products. Sediment and erosion control are needed both during and following mining. Terraces, mulches, vegetation, etc., used to reduce the erosive forces of water are effective measures to prevent further pyrite exposure. These measures usually are performed during reclamation.

Alkaline overburden material and agricultural limestone can be blended with "hot" acidic material to cause inplace neutralization of the acid and assist in establishing vegetation. In some cases, grading directs acid seeps to drain through alkaline overburden. These techniques are more applicable to abandoned surface mines than to current mining, where proper overburden handling should prevent acid formation. The major exception may be those situations where an underground mine was breached and an acid discharge formed.

A problem that has been noted in certain locations is acid seep. These may occur even though the surface mine has been properly graded and is supporting a good vegetative cover. Although the cause of acid seeps is not fully understood, it has been postulated that seeps occur when water percolating through the backfilled spoil reaches the impermeable underclay beneath the coal seam and is forced to move horizontally along the pit bottom and discharge at the toe of the backfill. In many cases the highly pyritic material associated with the coal is buried in the pit bottom where it is subject to leaching by the horizontally flowing water. One solution to this problem is to place the acid-forming material above the pit floor and cover it with an impermeable material. Other solutions would be diversion ditches constructed along the top of the high wall to keep surface runoff from entering the fill area, or thoroughly mixing the acid-forming material with an alkaline overburden material and placing it in the fill above the pit floor.

C. Dust and Other Air Emissions

Fugitive dust controls usually fall into three basic techniques—watering, chemical stabilization, and reduction of surface wind speed across exposed sources.

Water is frequently used to suppress dust on haul roads, material transfer points, and storage piles. Watering has a low first cost, but provides only temporary dust control. Depending on the nature of the dust-producing activity, it is only effective for a few hours. For abandoned/inactive mine sites, it does not offer a solution because equipment and personnel are not available for regular application. Fugitive dust problems are usually more acute in arid/semiarid regions because of low humidity, strong winds, high insolar energy, and low natural surface moisture. At the same time, water is a scarce resource and not readily available for air pollution control. It has been estimated that watering probably is only 50% effective as a control technique (Pedco-Environmental Specialists MC., 1973).

An estimated 100 chemical products are available as dust control agents. These have been shown to be effective under numerous conditions. They are applicable to both active and inactive situations. Because of the larger number available, they can often be "tailor-made" for the particular situation. Limiting factors involved with their use are: (i) cost of material, (ii) life of the chemical and treated surface as impacted by weathering, (iii) inability to withstand travel and handling, (iv) incompatibility with vegetative germination and growth, and (v) possible contamination of material being protected. Chemical stabilizers in general cannot withstand the heavy loads and traffic of a haul road, but can be very effective on storage piles, material being transported, tailing and refuse piles, bare soils, and inactive haul roads.

Wind erosion is a significant contributor to fugitive dust. Reduction of surface wind speed across the source is a positive control action. Control techniques used to control wind speed include windbreaks; enclosures or coverings of the material, for example, mulch or plastic; and establishment of vegetation. Vegetation is one of the best controls. It is discussed further in the sediment control section. The development of good vegetative cover in inadequate moisture areas, where fugitive dust is most prevalent, is a major problem.

Coal refuse pile fires have been controlled by either isolation, blanketing, grouting, or quenching. In the isolation technique, the burning area is segregated from the remainder of the pile by trenches or other means. The burning part is then quenched with water, blanketed with incombustible material, or allowed to burn out. The blanketing technique calls for the sealing of the sides and top of the pile with a heavy dost of incombustible material. Grouting entails the forcing of a slurry of water and finely divided incombustible material into the pile so as to provide some cooling action and also to fill the voids to prevent air from entering the pile. There are several ways to quench a pile. The hot material can be lifted with a dragline and dropped into a pool of water. Another method is to spray water on a burning pile and then mix the refuse with soil and other material and compact. Water cannons can also be used to quench a burning pile.

New construction criteria for refuse piles have been developed by he Mining Enforcement and Safety Administration (E. D'Appolonia Consulting Engineers, Inc., 1975) which should prevent fires in most newly constructed piles. This manual describes methods of construction, operation, maintenance, and closure. The key to fire prevention is to compact the refuse and seal it so that air does not have access to the pile.

IV. TREATMENT

Certain emissions from extraction processes cannot be controlled at the source and, therefore, must pass through some type of treatment process. This is usually the case at an active mine because specific discharge criteria imposed by the state and federal government must be met. Inactive/abandoned mines present another situation because, although treatment may be the only acceptable method to prevent environmentally damaging emission, no party or funds are available to take over the long-term commitment of treatment.

Table 5—Typical effluent guidelines for the mining industry

	Maximum for any 1 day	Average of daily values for 30 consecutive days shall not exceed
pH	6–9	
	mg/liter	
Fe	1–7	0.5–3.5
Cu	0.1	0.05
Zn	0.4–1.0	0.1–0.5
Pb	0.4	0.2
Total suspended solids	30–70	20–35
Hg	0.002	0.001
Cd	0.10	0.05
Cn	0.02	0.01
Al	1.2	0.6
As	1.0	0.5
Mn	4.0	2.0

A. Acid Mine Drainage and Heavy Metals

The EPA has developed effluent guidelines for most of the mining industry. These guidelines in general recommend limits on the concentration of acidity and heavy metals that can be discharged. Typical values are presented in Table 5.

Neutralization is almost the exclusive treatment process used by industry today. The neutralization process provides the following benefits:

1) Removes the acidity and adds alkalinity.
2) Increases pH.
3) Removes heavy metals. The solubility of heavy metals is dependent on pH; that is, up to a point, the higher the pH, the lower the solubility.
4) Ferrous iron, which is often associated with acid mine drainage, oxidizes at a faster rate to ferric iron at higher pH's. Iron is usually removed in the ferric form.
5) Sulfate can be removed if sufficient calcium ion is added to exceed the solubility of calcium sulfate, however, only in highly acidic acid mine drainage does this occur.

Some shortcomings of the neutralization process are:

1) Water hardness is not reduced and may be increased.
2) Sulfate is not reduced to a low level and usually exceeds 2,000 mg/liter.
3) The iron concentration usually is not reduced to less than 3–7 mg/liters.
4) A waste sludge is produced that must be disposed of.

Although several alkaline agents have been demonstrated to be successful in treating acid mine drainage, lime has been almost universally accepted by the industry. A typical lime treatment plant is made up of the following. Acid mine drainage is discharged from the mine to a rapid mix chamber, or to a holding/flow equalizing pond from where it flows to the rapid mix chamber. Hydrated lime is either fed to the rapid mix chamber dry or as a slurry. If the ferrous iron concentration is low (<50 mg/liter), the water is treated to a pH of 6.5 to 8 and flows directly to the settling chamber. If the ferrous iron is high, the pH is usually raised to a higher level (8 to 10) and the water is then passed to an aeration tank where the ferrous sulfate is converted to ferric sulfate. The water then flows to a settling chamber. The settling chamber may be a clarifier, pond, or strip-mine pit. Here the iron, aluminum, calcium sulfate, and other heavy metals precipitate. The supernatant is the treated water. The precipitate or sludge is removed from the settling chamber and disposed of in a second pond, strip-mine pit, underground mine, or landfill. In some cases the pond serves as a settling chamber and permanent storage of the sludge.

Other treatment methods have been developed that produce a very high quality of water. The two methods that have proven most successful are reverse osmosis and ion exchange. The major drawbacks of these methods are their high cost and problems associated with disposal of the waste products. A good discussion of treatment methods is available in Environmental Protection Agency Report 430/9-73-011 (USEPA, 1973).

B. Sediment

Ponds have become the primary sediment treatment method for most surface mines. Several states require their use either by law or regulations. Although frequently used, more often than not they are improperly designed for maximum suspended solids removal, are poorly constructed, receive limited maintenance, and are inadequately "closed down" or abandoned. Most ponds, when designed, are designed not for maximum suspended solids removal, but are based on "rule-of-thumb" suspended solids storage capacity (3.8 to 6.08 ha-cm per ha of disturbed area), proper dam design for safety, and proper location and capacity of over-flow and emergency spillway. All of these factors are important, but may not lead to efficient *sediment removal*. An evaluation by the Environmental Protection Agency (Kathuria et al., 1976) of ponds constructed and in use revealed little correlation between the design submitted with the surface mine permit application and the structure constructed. In many cases the actual pond was a function of the topography of the site, the earth-moving equipment available, and the experience of the operator, rather than of the design. Ponds are often built in locations remote from the operation and in nearly inaccessible locations. Thus, they received little regular attention and maintenance, which leads to reduced efficiency. Often inadequate measures are taken when a pond is abandoned upon completion of mining. Left unattended, dams deteriorate and finally fail, discharging the collected sediment, sometimes as one large mass.

Some factors that need to be considered in the design of ponds for sediment treatment are:

1) *Detention Time:* ponds should be designed on the basis of detention time to remove a specific size particle. Detention times of 2 to

4 hours are used in the water treatment field for properly constructed sedimentation basins. Well-designed settling ponds often provide 8 to 24 hours of detention time.

2) *Number of Ponds:* Some mines, particularly in mountainous areas, use several small ponds. These may be in series or several small ponds may discharge to one large pond. To date the primary reason for using more than one pond is because the topography of the land is unsuited to one single large pond. Several ponds have advantages over one large pond: (i) passing the water from one pond to another may improve retention time and suspended solids removal; (ii) if cleaning is required, smaller ponds can be more easily handled with common equipment; (iii) smaller ponds can be easily removed at the end of mining; and (iv) "turn overs" and wind erosion of banks are less.

One large pond is usually better designed and constructed than smaller ponds which are often dug out with a dozer. They can be designed for the life of the mine and never require cleaning. Cost of several ponds as compared to one pond will depend on the individual situation. Several ponds may require more earth-moving work, whereas one pond may require more expensive dam, outlet, and emergency spillways construction.

3) *Location of Pond:* Some agencies recommend that the pond be built in the main drainway because construction sites are more available and all the surface runoff from the mine area passes through the pond. Others recommend that they be placed out of the main drainway to reduce unnecessary flow from being treated, and to facilitate the removal and abandonment of the pond. Location of the pond will be dictated to a large extent by the topography of the mine area. It is important that access to the pond be available for regular inspection and maintenance.

4) *Size and Depth:* Size and depth of a pond should be based on providing the necessary retention time, with short-circuiting taken into consideration, for maximum suspended solids removal. In addition, sufficient solids storage must be provided for the life of the ponds or for a specified cleaning interval. Retention time should be calculated from the time the pond has reached its full solids storage capacity, not when it is empty, in order to have high performance throughout pond life. Very large and deep ponds are often subject to wave action and turnovers. These factors should be taken into consideration.

5) *Shape of Pond:* The shape of a pond has a major bearing on short-circuiting of flow and, thus, on retention time. Tear drop and toothshaped ponds usually have less short-circuiting than elongated ponds perpendicular to the inlet. The shape of the pond should facilitate suspended solids storage and long retention times, and minimize short-circuiting.

6) *Inlet Design:* Inlet design is very important to minimize short-circuiting. In many ponds the water enters at one point under high velocities. The high velocities are not conducive to good

settling and often stir up solids already settled. The designer should consider multiple inlets, baffles, etc., to spread the flow and reduce inlet velocities.

7) *Outlet Design:* Outlet design is also critical for good pond performance. One discharge point leads to poor performance because of short-circuiting. Trough-type outlets instead of stand pipes and horizontal pipes through the dam should be considered. Using a stand pipe full of holes is a questionable practice, since sediment often is carried away from the pond bottom by scour with the first flow.

8) *Close Down:* During the design phase, the method for removing or stabilizing the pond upon completion of mining should be considered. If the pond is to remain, then the responsibility for its maintenance should be established.

Improved design methods have been proposed recently (USEPA, 1976; Hill, 1976).

LITERATURE CITED

Blackwood, T. R., P. K. Chalebode, and R. A. Wachter. 1976. Source assessment: Crushed stone. EPA Rep. for Contract 68-02-1874, Cincinnati, Ohio.

Cavanaugh, E. C., et al. 1976. Atmospheric pollution potential from fossil fuel resource extraction, on-site processing and transportation. EPA Rep. EPA-600/2-76-064, Research Triangle Park, N.C.

Chalebode, P. K., and T. R. Blackwood. 1976. Source assessment: Coal refuse piles, abandoned mines and outcrops. EPA Rep. for Contract 68-02-1874, Cincinnatio, Ohio.

Collier, C. R., R. J. Pickering, and J. J. Musser. 1964. Influence of strip mining on the hydrologic environment of Beaver Creek Basin, Kentucky, 1955–1959. USGS Prof. Pap. 427-B. Dep. of the Interior, Washington, D.C.

Committee on Public Works. 1969. Acid mine drainage in Appalachia. House Doc. no. 91-180, 91st Congr., 1st Sess., Comm. on Public Works, Washington, D.C.

Cowherd, C., Jr., K. Axetell, Jr., C. M. Guenther, and G. A. Jutze. 1974. Development of emission factors for fugitive dust sources. EPA Rep. EPA-450/3-74-037, Research Triangle Park, N.C.

Curtis, W. R. 1972. Chemical changes in streamflow following surface mining in Eastern Kentucky. p. 19–31. *In* 4th Symp. on Coal Mine Drainage Res., 26–27 Apr. 1972, Pittsburgh, Pa. Bituminous Coal Res., Inc., Monroeville, Pa.

Curtis, W. R. 1974. Sediment yield from strip-mine watersheds in Eastern Kentucky. p. 88–100. *In* 2nd Res. and Applied Technol. Symp. on Mined-Land Reclamation, 22–24 Oct. 1974, Louisville, Ky. Natl. Coal Assoc., Washington, D.C.

E. D'Appolonia Consulting Engineers, Inc. 1975. Engineering and design manual coal refuse disposal facilities. USDI, Mining Enforce. and Safety Admin., Washington, D.C.

Grim, E. C., and R. D. Hill. 1974. Environmental protection in surface mining of coal. Environ. Prot. Technol. Ser. EPA-670/2-74-093. Natl. Environ. Res. Center, Cincinnati, Ohio.

Hill, R. D. 1976. Sedimentation ponds—a critical review. p. 190–199. *In* 6th Symp. on Coal Mine Drainage Research, 19–21 Oct. 1976, Louisville, Ky. Natl. Coal Assoc., Washington, D.C.

Kathuria, D. V., M. A. Nawrocki, and B. C. Becker. 1976. Effectiveness of surface mine sedimentation ponds. Pub. no. EPA-600/2-76-117. Environ. Prot. Technol. Ser., USEPA, Cincinnati, Ohio.

McWhorter, D. B., G. V. Skogerboe, and R. K. Skogerboe. 1974. Water pollution potential of mine spoils in the Rocky Mountain Region. p. 25–38. *In* 5th Symp. on Coal Mine Drainage Res., 22–24 Oct. 1974, Louisville, Ky. Natl. Coal Assoc., Washington, D.C.

Moth, A. H., E. E. Smith, and K. S. Shumate. 1972. Pyritic systems: A mathematical model. Publ. no. EPA-R2-72-002. Environ. Prot. Technol. Ser., USEPA, Washington, D.C.

Ohio State University. 1971. Acid mine drainage formation and abatement. Water Pollut. Control Res. Ser. no. DAST-42, 14010 FPR 04/71. USEPA, Washington, D.C.

Pedco-Environmental Specialists, Inc. 1973. Investigation of fugitive dust—sources, emissions and control. EPA Rep. for Contract 68-02-0044, Research Triangle Park, N.C.

Plass, W. T. 1975. Changes in water chemistry resulting from surface mining coal on four West Virginia watersheds. USFS, Northeastern For. Exp. Stn., Princeton, W. Va.

Roth, C. B., D. W. Nelson, and M. J. M. Romkens. 1974. Prediction of subsoil erodibility using chemical, mineralogical and physical parameters. USEPA Publ. no. EPA-660/2-74-043, Washington, D.C.

Skidmore, E. L., and N. P. Woodruff. 1968. Wind erosion forces in the United States and their use in predicting soil loss. USDA Agric. Hbk. 346, Washington, D.C.

Toups Corporation. 1975. Water pollution caused by inactive ore and mineral mines—A national assessment. Draft Rep. for EPA Contract 68-03-2212, Cincinnati, Ohio.

U.S. Environmental Protection Agency. 1973. Processes, procedures and methods to control pollution from mining activities. EPA Rep. 430/9-73-011, Washington, D.C.

U.S. Environmental Protection Agency. 1976. Erosion and sediment control—surface mining in the Eastern U.S. EPA Technol. Transf. Sem. Pub. EPA-625/3-76-006. Cincinnati, Ohio.

Wilson, L. 1975. Application of the wind erosion equation in air pollution surveys. J. Soil Water Conserv. 30:215-219.

Wischmeir, W. H., and P. D. Smith. 1965. Predicting rainfall-erosion losses from cropland east of the Rocky Mountains. USDA Agric. Hbk. no. 282, Washington, D.C.

Copyright © 1978 ASA–CSSA–SSSA
677 South Segoe Road, Madison, WI 53711 USA
Reclamation of Drastically Disturbed Lands

Chapter 40

Applications of Remote Sensing Technology to Disturbed Lands[1]

T. L. COX AND S. G. WITTER

Remote Sensing Institute
South Dakota State University
Brookings, South Dakota

I. INTRODUCTION

Drastically disturbed lands have become a major concern with recent shortages of petroleum fuel supplies resulting in a shift to other forms of energy, such as coal, which require disturbance of the earth's surface. This, in combination with increasing populations, worldwide demands for agricultural products, and warranted ecological concerns, has forced us to take a closer look at disturbed lands. Reclamation of these lands to restore more natural conditions (vegetation, habitat, animal populations, etc.), to decrease the negative effects on adjacent lands, and to provide food and fiber, has become increasingly important. The rapidly increasing extent and the inaccessibility of these disturbed areas has created a need to develop means by which they can be inventoried and monitored through time with a minimum of costly ground sampling. The application of remote sensing technology to these inventories is increasingly apparent in the literature. Remote sensing involves the acquisition and analysis (photo interpretation, digital analysis, etc.) of spectral data obtained from a remote location. The purpose is to obtain information about an object(s) or large area(s) with a minimum of effort. Recent studies indicate that remote sensing techniques involving the visible, infrared, and microwave regions of the electromagnetic spectrum can be used to measure the reflectance and emittance of plants, soils, water, and other materials which are the major components of disturbed areas.

Many advances have been made in remote sensing technology in the last decade, especially in data acquisition and analysis. It has a potential for providing quantitative inventories and monitoring capabilities applicable to drastically disturbed lands. The purpose of this paper is to acquaint the reader with some technological principles of remote sensing and their applications to analyses of disturbed lands. The present review of remote sensing and the applications to disturbed lands is not ex-

---

[1] Contribution from Remote Sensing Institute, South Dakota State University, Brookings, South Dakota.

haustive; many additional studies have been implemented but have not been published. Remote sensing per se has been covered extensively in the literature. *The Manual of Remote Sensing* (Reeves, 1975) published in 1975 by the American Society of Photogrammetry offers extensive coverage of all facets of remote sensing. Volume I addresses in detail theory, instruments, and techniques, while Volume II covers interpretation and applications. Extensive literature reviews are presented at the end of each chapter. *Remote Sensing in Ecology* (Johnson, 1969) and *Remote Sensing with Special Reference to Agriculture and Forestry* (Natl. Resour. Counc., Comm. on Remote Sensing for Agric. Purposes, 1970) present very readable approaches to the subject.

II. TECHNICAL PRINCIPLES

The acquisition of remote-sensor data is dependent upon the detection and recording of electromagnetic energy reflected or emitted from the surfaces of earth features. The response of the materials (soil, vegetation, water, etc.) vary widely with chemical and physical properties, surface shape and roughness, intensity of illumination, and angle of incidence. These detectable differences in reflectance or emittance, or *signatures* as they are often called, form patterns which provide means for discriminating earth features. However, since earth materials differ widely in their signatures, and since remote sensors record different energy bands, in order to interpret the image patterns an investigator must be aware of the principles and processes involved.

A. Electromagnetic Radiation

Electromagnetic radiation (EMR) refers to energy in the range of wavelengths or frequencies extending from gamma rays to low frequency radiowaves. The electromagnetic spectrum is divided into conventionally known and named segments (Fig. 1), although it is a continuum with no discrete boundaries. This energy is directly or indirectly reflected, absorbed, and reradiated through free space where it can be detected by remote sensors. The EMR most often of interest in remote sensing studies is in the visible and near infrared region. Recently, however, longer wavelengths have been increasingly utilized to monitor changes on the earth's surface as, for example, 3 to 15 μm for temperature variations (thermal infrared scanner) and 0.5 cm to 1 m for microwave and radar studies. Table 1 provides a summary of the conventionally named segments of the electromagnetic spectrum with the remote sensors applied to these segments.

1. SOURCE

The sun is the strongest source of radiant energy for the spectral band of 0.3 to 3.0 μm; other sources are much weaker in this range. A portion of the incident solar radiation (0.4 to 3.0 μm) is immediately reflected away from objects at the earth's surface. Another portion of incident solar radi-

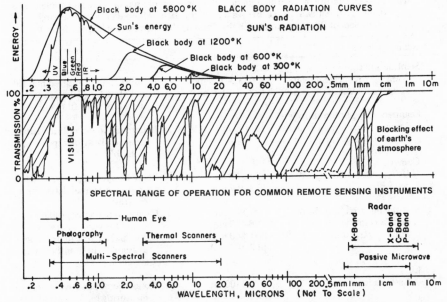

Fig. 1—The electromagnetic energy spectrum (from Sherz & Stevens, 1970).

ation is absorbed and emitted as thermal energy at wavelengths of 3 to 15 μm. Different objects can be identified by the energy they emit as it is a function of the temperature and nature of the surface of the source.

A material which absorbs energy may be heated to a level above its surroundings, causing reemission of energy. Some energy is naturally radiated by objects and sensors which measure this energy are termed *passive remote sensors*. Active remote sensors have their own energy source and transmit energy to an object and measure the portion which is reflected within the view of the sensor. Types of sensors and their capabilities are discussed later.

2. INTERACTION WITH MATTER

The degree electromagnetic energy is reflected, absorbed, or transmitted depends on the properties of the material and the wavelength of the energy. Generally, the fate of the energy can be depicted as in Fig. 2.

Vegetation, soil, and soil moisture are the major components of interest in assessing the conditions of disturbed lands. Therefore, the interactions of these materials with radiation will be discussed in some detail to provide an insight into the technological principles involved in their detection. For a detailed discussion of interaction mechanisms, see Janza (1975).

a. **Plants**—Factors related to the reflectance, absorptance, and transmittance of incident radiation by plants were discussed by Gates (1970). Portions of the following discussion were summarized primarily from his comments.

Table 1—The nature of electromagnetic radiation—remote-sensor types and applications (from G. H. Suits, *In* R. G. Reeves (ed. in ch.) 1975. Manual of remote sensing. Am. Soc. of Photogrammetry, Falls Church, Va. Reproduced by permission)

Remote sensors		Comments
Scintillation counters		
Gamma-ray spectrometer, Geiger counters	<0.003–10 nm (<0.03–100Å)	Measurement of emitted natural radiation by gamma ray detectors; NaI, film, etc.
Scanners with photomultipliers		
Image orthicons and cameras with filtered infrared film >2900Å	10–400 nm	Records incident natural radiation. Imaged ultraviolet spectroscopy available
Cameras		
Using conventional B&W and color film	400–700 nm (0.4–0.7 µm)	B&W film for high spatial detail. Improved spatial detail through contrast.
Using infrared film (B&W and IR color)	600–900 nm (0.6–0.9 µm)	Greater reflectance gradients useful for vegetation surveys.
Multispectral units	300–900 nm (0.3–0.9 µm)	Individual narrow band scenes available with multi-camera systems.
Lidar		
Laser radar	400–1100 nm (0.4–1.1 µm)	Monochromatic active system for measuring backscattered EMR from atmosphere, particularly particulates.
Radiometers (infrared)	Thermal IR band (2.5–14 µm)	Generally measures total radiation in a wide band in the infrared region. Imagery obtained by scanning techniques.
Photometers	400–700 nm (0.4–0.7 µm)	Measures luminous flux in various bands of the optical region for distribution, color, etc.
Spectrometers	In any spectral region	Narrow-band data available sequentially—EMR amplitude vs. frequency.
Solid-state detectors		
Single detectors Linear arrays Matrices	1 µm–1 mm	Single detecting element used in scanners, radiometers. One- and two-dimensional arrays for sequential data gathering.
Radars	1 mm–0.8 m	Narrow-band active systems. Both analog data and imagery available.
Radiometers (microwave)	1 mm–0.8 m	Passive systems. Both analog and imagery available.

The appearance of vegetation, soils, water, rocks, and other materials to remote sensors or the human eye depends on their interaction with radiation. For example, a plant leaf reflects and transmits incident radiation in a manner that is uniquely characteristic of pigmented cells containing water solution. The precise quality and intensity of reflectance or emittance by the plant depends on leaf geometry, morphology, physiology, and chemistry. Of course, these factors are related to and change with soil site and climate. The striking features of leaf spectra summarized by Gates (1970) are the high absorptance in the ultraviolet and blue, the reduced absorptance in the green, the high absorptance in the red, the very

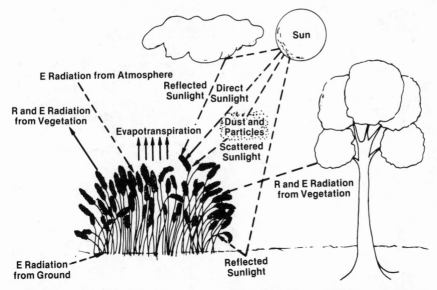

Fig. 2—Energy exchange in the natural environment (from Bauer, 1976. Reproduced with permission).

low absorptance and high reflectance and transmittance in the near infrared (0.7–1.5 μm), and the very high absorptance in the far infrared. Most surfaces which contain chlorophyll exhibit similar spectral reflectances. The spectral reflectances of several plant groups are shown in Fig. 3. Note the high reflectance in the infrared by all groups of plants. Factors influencing the normal reflectance of plants alone include (i) alterations in pigmentation, (ii) variations in water content, and (iii) changes in surface layer of the leaf. Any combination or all three of these factors could be changed by mining or land alterations which affect soil chemistry and soil moisture regimes, and/or physically alter plant structures. Any of these factors or other disturbances (e.g., some stress) which affect a plant canopy may cause the leaves to exhibit a different orientation and perhaps shrink in size, thus not only reducing their reflective surface areas but, by doing so, revealing other reflective surfaces such as stems, branches, other vegetation types, or bare soil; these stress conditions may result in poorer absorption of red by chlorophyll, and subsequent visually distinguishable color differences (Totterdell & Rains, 1973). Therefore, these effects could also be seen as reflectance variations which, in turn, would provide means to monitor vegetation changes to assess revegetation success on, or as a result of, disturbed lands. Totterdell and Rains (1973), Hoffer and Johannsen (1969), and Knipling (1969) discuss important aspects of plant reflectance in relation to color infared (false color) photography.

   b. Soils—Soils are of prime concern on disturbed lands. Recent research in remote sensing has led to the development of various methods of detecting soil conditions. A soil surface exhibits two properties of interest in remote sensing. The first is the reflectance of incident radiation and the

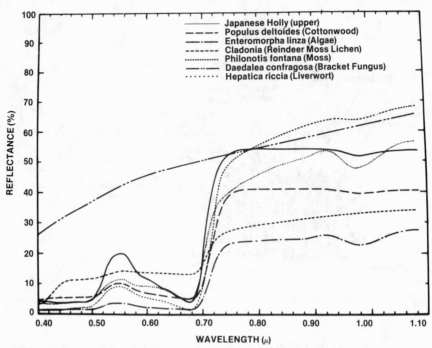

Fig. 3—Spectral reflectance of seven species of plants representing diverse groups (from Gates, 1970. Reproduced with permission of the Natl. Acad. of Sci.).

second is its emittance of long wave radiation and surface temperature. Soil surface reflectance varies with color, texture, surface roughness, moisture content, organic matter, chemical composition, mineral composition, angle of illumination, and the influence of plants, topography, etc. The radiant energy of the sun is partially absorbed by the soil surface and transformed chiefly into heat. A small part of this energy is diffusely reflected. The reflectance patterns of soils at various wavelengths are considerably different than for plants. Relative spectral radiance curves for agricultural scenes including soils are shown in Fig. 4. The influence of soil properties on soil reflectance and/or emission of electromagnetic energy were recently discussed by Myers (1975). Topics such as mineral content, particle size, texture, color, organic matter and iron oxide, and structure and surface roughness were addressed in the context of their affects on reflectance.

In general, soils have a higher reflectance than plants in the visible spectrum. A mix of vegetation and bare soil is less reflective than soil alone. However, in the near infrared band, the opposite is true. In this portion of the spectrum, soils are low in reflectance and plants very high (Fig. 4). A decrease in the size of soil particles usually results in an increase in reflectance because of a smoother boundary (increased light scattering, fewer microshadows, etc). Dry soils often have a higher reflectance than wet soil. Hoffer and Johannsen (1969) demonstrated this

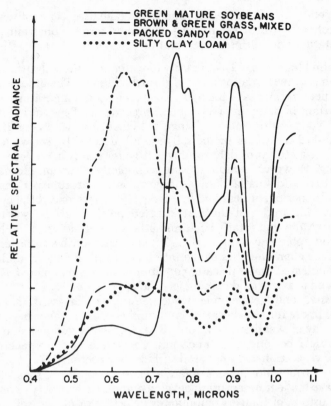

Fig. 4—Relative spectral radiance spectra for agricultural scenes in the range of 0.4–1.05 μm, 30 Aug. 1966, 1150–1156. Curves should be compared in functional form only: gain settings were changed between spectra (from Holmes, 1970. Reproduced with permission of Natl. Acad. of Sci.).

by showing that the reflectances of sandy and clay soils decreased considerably with an increase in moisture.

Temperature and factors influencing interpretation of thermal imagery and time of sensing were discussed by Myers (1975) in relation to energy emitted from soils. Temperature sensing using thermal infrared sensors appears to have considerable promise for identifying some subsurface conditions. The variations in reflectance or emittance with changes in soil characteristics permit a means of assessing soil conditions on disturbed lands using remote sensing technology. Soil temperature is of considerable importance in assessment of disturbed lands as it is related to water losses through evaporation, rate of weathering and chemical dissolution, microbial activity and organic matter decomposition, seed germination, and success and/or rate of plant growth. Soil temperature information obtained using remote sensors has the potential to supply a variety of information related to both disturbance and reclamation. For example, soils could be thermally sensed periodically and the information utilized to determine what time of year each soil would be most amenable to revegetation and the species which should be used. The soil-water conditions of newly disturbed areas could be monitored to determine the soil-water status under different reclamation procedures.

c. **Soil Moisture**—The quantity of water near the soil surface is of extreme importance in assessment of disturbed lands. The amount of moisture indicates changes in the hydrologic cycle, soil temperature, etc., and is important in designing reclamation procedures. Types of vegetation to be planted, amendments to change soil chemistry (acid condition, etc), and physical treatment of the soils are all affected by soil-water conditions. Past methods of determining soil-water status have been by point sampling. However, remote sensing technology offers an alternative approach to provide spatial data for large areas in short time periods.

A number of studies cited by Myers (1975) referenced the use of visible, near infrared and thermal infrared portions of the spectrum for qualitative and quantitative determinations of soil moisture. Reflectances at photographic wavelengths (0.4–0.9 μm) are sensitive to differences in the surface characteristics at the interface of soil, plants, and air. Other studies indicated that soil-water conditions have been depicted using both visible and near infrared in multispectral approaches.

Passive and active microwave sensing (radar) will undoubtedly increase in use for soil subsurface moisture because it is not dependent on time of day or weather conditions. Radar which is responsive to soil surface, subsurface conditions, and moisture content can also penetrate thin layers of vegetation and upper soil surfaces (see Section B2).

The various interactions of land components (plants, soils, etc.) with EMR have made it necessary to develop and utilize a variety of sensors for the acquisition of imagery suitable for detection of plants, soils, and soil moisture regimes in varying circumstances. Some of the more common sensors and platforms will be discussed. For thorough discussions on the influence of these interactions on EMR, see Chapter 4 and 5 in Reeves (1975).

B. Data Acquisition

The acquisition of remote-sensor imagery depends upon the detection and recording of electromagnetic energy reflected or emitted from surface features (natural or man-made) within the field of view of the sensor. Images formed are a function of the interaction between matter and energy within the electromagnetic spectrum. Various sensors are used to detect the record different portions of the electromagnetic spectrum (Table 1). The primary sensors used in remote sensing are aerial cameras, multispectral scanners, thermal-infrared scanners, and passive microwave radiometers.

1. PHOTOGRAPHY

The most common and most developed form of data acquisition is aerial photography. The principle of the aerial camera is the same as the common box camera but its optical-mechanical and electrical features are more complex. Bauer (1976) summarized the advantages of aerial photography as: superior spatial resolution, the relative simplicity of aerial photography and film processing, the relatively low cost of equipment, and the considerable amount of information it provides human interpreters. Disadvantages listed are limited range of sensitivity (0.4 to 1.0 μm) and increased difficulty in return of film to earth for processing as compared to telemetering electronic signals in the case of space photography.

Multiband cameras are used in aerial photography and are especially designed to acquire date from several portions of the spectrum (multispectral data) for a single area. Several approaches are common including use of the multiple-camera system, the multiple-lens camera, and the single lens camera with multiple focal planes. The multiapproach in remote sensing is discussed later (Section C1).

Photographic film may be grouped into three main categories—black and white, color, or false color. There are a number of sources of information on film types, their applications, spectral sensitivity, etc., especially Chapters 2 and 6 in Reeves (1975), and also in Heller (1970).

2. SCANNER SYSTEMS

Multispectral optical-mechanical scanning devices constitute an important component of sensors as they are capable of collecting data in the reflective and thermal portions of the electromagnetic spectrum (0.3–15.0 μm). Basic components are a scanning optics system, a detector or detector array, and a recorder. The energy reflected or emitted from a small area of the earth's surface is detected by the optical scanner (usually a rotating mirror) which reflects it through a system of optics to detectors. The detectors convert the energy to electronic signals which are proportional to the intensity of the radiated energy These signals are recorded on tape (or film in aircraft) or transmitted to ground, and relative values can be used to form analog data on film (shades of gray). An important feature of this type of sensing system is that data are conveniently stored for machine processing.

The optical-mechanical scanners are frequently used as thermal infrared scanners to detect that portion of solar energy reemitted by components of the earth's surface. In studies where temperature variations may be the key to identifying resources or resource conditions, especially where surface water is important, the thermal IR scanner (3 to 14 μm) can be used. The thermal IR scanner employs a photo-conductive transducer to detect temperature variations and then this data is generally displayed in twoforms—cathode ray tube (CRT) display or digital printouts from an analogue tape.

Radar scanners may be used more in disturbed land studies. This sensor can be used day or night in virtually all types of weather and can penetrate thin layers of vegetation to reveal underlying soil patterns. Colwell (1975) reported that the side-looking airborne radar (SLAR) system is capable of providing highly interpretable imagery of the surface of the earth even when the ground is obscured by a dense cover of clouds. At present it appears that the most important application of SLAR is for making rapid inventories of resources in areas where persistent cloud cover is a problem. Consequently, SLAR may have potential for monitoring the reclamation of disturbed areas in zones of persistent cloud cover or haze conditions. Limitations are its single frequency characteristics and course spatial resolution. Scanner systems are discussed in more detail by Orr (1974), Bauer (1976), and in several chapters in Reeves (1975).

3. PLATFORMS

Sensors mounted in either aircraft or satellites are used in remote sensing applications. In early studies, hand-held cameras were used from platforms below the balloons. Later, cameras were attached to cables below the balloons. Until the launching of satellites (1972) most data were acquired from aircraft at altitudes ranging from 500 to 2,000 m (Bauer, 1976). Satellites provide platforms for a variety of sensors and provide data routinely. LANDSAT-1 (1972) and LANDSAT-2 (1975) have demonstrated the feasibility of providing multispectral data from space in practical resource management applications. Each LANDSAT satellite carries a variety of sensor instrumentation (three return beam vidicon cameras, receivers, tape recorders, etc) but the primary sensor is the multispectral scanner system which measures energy in four spectral bands, 0.5–0.6, 0.6–0.7, 0.7–0.8, and 0.8–1.1 μm. The LANDSAT 1 satellite was designed to be operational for approximately 1 year but has been reporting for over 5 years.

On 22 Jan. 1975, LANDSAT-2 was launched into a sun-synchronous orbit corresponding to the middle of the cycle of LANDSAT 1. Thus, satellite coverage may be available every 9 days in certain areas as long as both sensor systems function normally. LANDSAT II is similar in instrumentation and orbit to LANDSAT 1.

Other satellites have been used to investigate a variety of sensors. For example Skylab (altitude 434 km) was launched in May 1973 "to increase man's role as an experimenter in space" (Colvocoresses, 1975). The sensor payload included an infrared spectrometer, a 13-band multispectral scanner, microwave radiometer/scatterometer, multiband camera, and other instrumentation. Unlike the LANDSAT satellites Skylab does not provide continual coverage. The resolution of Skylab imagery is superior to the LANDSAT imagery due to the lower orbiting altitude. The Skylab S190A experiment covered the same area per scene as the LANDSAT Satellites (160 by 160 km). However, the Skylab S190B experiment covered a smaller area (109 by 109 km) and had better resolution than the S190A or LANDSAT.

Favorable characteristics of data collected from satellite platforms are (i) near orthographic view, (ii) large areal coverage and regional perspective, (iii) multispectral capabilities, (iv) temporal coverage, and (v) reduced effects of handling low altitude aerial data (for large areas). The main disadvantage with regularly reporting satellites is lack of resolution.

The history and development of platforms for remote sensors is discussed in detail in Chapter 2 of *The Manual of Remote Sensing* (Fischer et al., 1975).

C. Data Analysis

1. THE MULTIAPPROACH

The use of remote sensors for resource inventories usually consists of a multistage, multispectral, or multitemporal (date) approach. In some cases a combination of two or more of these approaches is warranted. The multiapproach in remote sensing is discussed by Colwell (1975) and Estes (1975).

The multistage approach consists of using progressively more detailed information for progressively smaller subsamples of a study area. For example, satellite imagery might be used to determine general terrain features or general plant associations. Then, a second-stage, large-scale, high-resolution aerial photography would be used to map rock types, plant species, or soil conditions. The utility of different scales (multistage data) of imagery for identification of a variety of mined-land features was discussed by Amato et al. (1975). Figure 5 was formulated as a product of their investigations in three different coal basins. For disturbed areas under study, 1:120,000 scale imagery was sufficient for regional assessment of mining activities, where large scale imagery better provided engineering data and detail of acid mine problems.

The multispectral approach uses different portions of the spectrum to detect different features. For example, Fig. 4 illustrates the different spectral responses of soils and vegetation. Soil reflectance is more pronounced in the visible portion of the spectrum, while plant reflectance is greater in the near infrared. Several portions of the spectrum may be utilized in a variety of combinations.

The benefits of multitemporal or multidate studies should be considered because many types of features exhibit unique changes with the passage of time (Colwell, 1975). This is especially true of vegetated areas where seasonal changes in reflectance occur with plant life cycles. Consequently, with comparative temporal coverage of a disturbed area, changes in reflectances of certain areas on the ground could key the activities taking place. For example, Rehder (1973) mapped changes in stripmining activities in Tennessee using multidate imagery (Fig. 6).

2. IMAGE INTERPRETATION

This is the process of detecting, delineating, and identifying features or conditions on imagery and determining their significance. Tone, texture, pattern, shape, size, color, shadows, location, and association aid the interpreter in identifying, delineating, and evaluating the significance of environmental and cultural objects, patterns, and spatial relationships. In carrying out this task the interpreter may use many more types of data and information than those recorded on the image interpreted. These ancillary data are referred to as *collateral material* and include literature, laboratory measurement and analysis, field work, and ground and/or aerial photography. They vary significantly among remote-sensing pro-

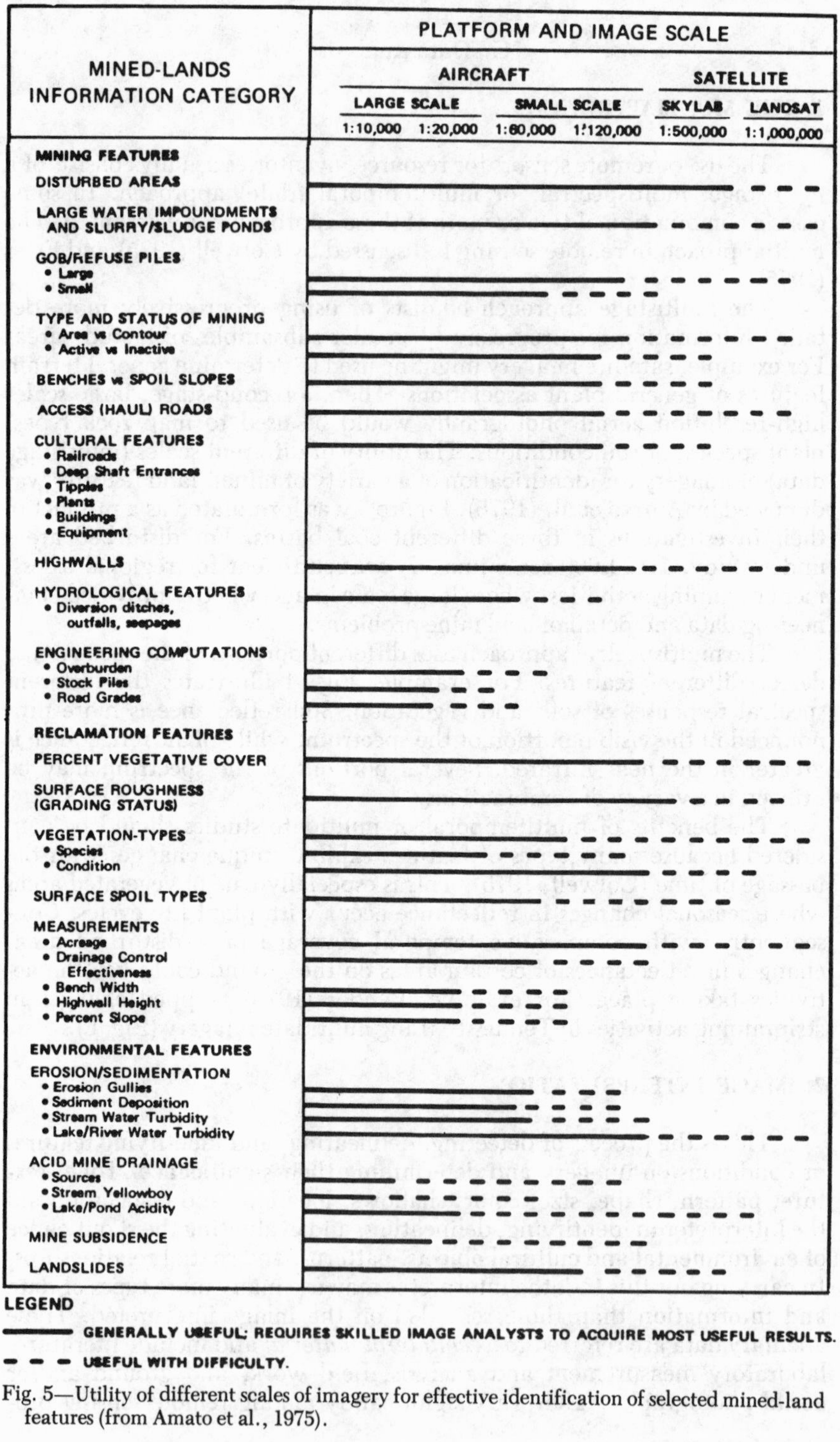

MINED-LANDS INFORMATION CATEGORY	PLATFORM AND IMAGE SCALE					
	AIRCRAFT				SATELLITE	
	LARGE SCALE		SMALL SCALE		SKYLAB	LANDSAT
	1:10,000	1:20,000	1:60,000	1:120,000	1:500,000	1:1,000,000

MINING FEATURES

DISTURBED AREAS

LARGE WATER IMPOUNDMENTS AND SLURRY/SLUDGE PONDS

GOB/REFUSE PILES
- Large
- Small

TYPE AND STATUS OF MINING
- Area vs Contour
- Active vs Inactive

BENCHES vs SPOIL SLOPES

ACCESS (HAUL) ROADS

CULTURAL FEATURES
- Railroads
- Deep Shaft Entrances
- Tipples
- Plants
- Buildings
- Equipment

HIGHWALLS

HYDROLOGICAL FEATURES
- Diversion ditches, outfalls, seepages

ENGINEERING COMPUTATIONS
- Overburden
- Stock Piles
- Road Grades

RECLAMATION FEATURES

PERCENT VEGETATIVE COVER

SURFACE ROUGHNESS (GRADING STATUS)

VEGETATION-TYPES
- Species
- Condition

SURFACE SPOIL TYPES

MEASUREMENTS
- Acreage
- Drainage Control Effectiveness
- Bench Width
- Highwall Height
- Percent Slope

ENVIRONMENTAL FEATURES

EROSION/SEDIMENTATION
- Erosion Gullies
- Sediment Deposition
- Stream Water Turbidity
- Lake/River Water Turbidity

ACID MINE DRAINAGE
- Sources
- Stream Yellowboy
- Lake/Pond Acidity

MINE SUBSIDENCE

LANDSLIDES

LEGEND

───────── GENERALLY USEFUL; REQUIRES SKILLED IMAGE ANALYSTS TO ACQUIRE MOST USEFUL RESULTS.

– – – USEFUL WITH DIFFICULTY.

Fig. 5—Utility of different scales of imagery for effective identification of selected mined-land features (from Amato et al., 1975).

Fig. 6—ERTS-1 Band 5 negative print of strip mines on the Cumberland Plateau in Eastern Tennessee, Oct. 1972. Arrow indicates one of the stripped areas (from Rehder, 1973).

jects in relation to the spatial, temporal, and costs constraints of the projects.

Identification keys, used with great success in field work in the biological and physical sciences, are also useful aids to image interpretation. They are especially necessary when an interpreter must be aware of factors not related to his experience. The key is used to organize the information present in an image form and to guide him to correct identification. The steps and concepts in image interpretation, key formulation and use, modern instrumentation, and many other facets of interpretation are discussed by Estes (1975).

3. ANALYSIS OF DIGITAL DATA

Until recently, imagery was analyzed primarily by manual methods (visual interpretation). This is the more developed and more easily understood approach for most users. However, modern computer technology has led to the development of the numerical approach. This approach uses the spectral variations which are recorded in a digital format to organize and classify remotely sensed data. The numeric analysis techniques are especially applicable where large digital data sets are available (e.g., from scanner systems) or where several bands of multispectral data are analyzed simultaneously. Various systems exist which allow an investigator to interact with digital data to identify spectral signatures and display features of interest. Automatic processing technology can then process large data sets to identify and record these features. Final products include statistics and analog data which can be used to produce photographic products. Steiner and Salerno (1975) discuss the many facets of remote sensor data systems and the processing and management of data. Topics covered include information systems, image data transmission, storage and retrieval, image processing principles, and pattern recognition. Several references to current digital techniques and products are included in the "Applications" section later in this chapter (Section III).

4. IMAGERY ENHANCEMENT

There are a number of techniques which may be applied to imagery to make interpretations easier. For example, optical enhancement can be used. This includes additive color processing of multiband imagery, contrast stretching, density slicing, and enlargement (photographically, or image magnification).

Digital data may be extracted from imagery or magnetic tapes in a variety of formats for enhancement. Most often, digital data is initially displayed as shaded computer printings using conventional printing devices widely available. Data may be also displayed on a cathode ray tube (if available) as shades of gray or color-coded. These data may be printed in black and white or in a color-coded format using one or any combination of electromagnetic bands monitored. Additional information on these procedures can be found in *The Manual of Remote Sensing* (Steiner & Salerno, 1975) and other publications cited in the "Applications" section of this chapter.

The objective of either process is to provide a more easily interpretable product than the original. Enhancement normally increases analysis costs and should be evaluated for cost-effectiveness. In some cases cost may be nominal compared to the overall budget. In general, photolab-type enhancements are less expensive than digital techniques.

III. APPLICATIONS TO DISTURBED LANDS

Remote sensing technology has changed in the past decade from its primarily research and development orientation towards applications and problem-solving. Several studies documenting the use of remote sensing in state resources management were recently summarized by Wobber (1975). Many of the case histories presented involved drastically disturbed lands and are demonstrative of the change toward applications. Wobber (1975) used the results of selected remote sensing case histories to forcast future trends in the utilization of this tool at the state level. He judged that there would be a growth in the number and sophistication of users. This seems to be the trend at a variety of levels from site-specific to national. The following discussion will center on a review of selected applications of remotely sensed data to drastically disturbed lands, as well as on a further look into potential applications and the future.

A. Regional Land Data

In many instances remote sensing technology has been utilized to provide land use data relevant to disturbances at regional levels. In most of these efforts the data are required to form "baseline" information which will be used to measure change in land use through time. A variety of remote sensors have been utilized in relation to the detail required for inventory and analysis.

Johnson et al. (1975) mapped the land use of Mercer County, North Dakota, using black and white and color infrared photographs at a scale of 1:24,000. A map (nine categories) and statistical summation provided a base-line geographical and quantitative land use inventory prior to the major impact associated with the extraction of lignite coal. Conventional photo interpretation techniques were used.

Sweet et al. (1973) reported on the investigation of LANDSAT I in Ohio to provide natural resource and land use data for use in general planning, land use decision-making, and new legislation preparation. Preliminary evaluation of LANDSAT I for all parts of Ohio indicated that the data were more than adequate for periodic mapping and inventorying major surface natural resources at scales of 1:24,000 and smaller. It was also stated that costs were less and accuracies were better with LANDSAT than previous methods using aerial photography. The significance of the land use data from LANDSAT is that for the first time a comprehensive/synoptic overview of the environmental, natural, and cultural surface features and their interrelationships could be viewed. Data are being used for power plant site selection and alternative power transmission corridors, also. Other uses of LANDSAT reported by Sweet et al. (1973) include the detection of abandoned mines and the detection of possible wet areas in which surface water is identified by vegetative patterns and differences in vegetation which may be due to acid mine water pollution.

Remote sensing technology has also been utilized for mapping habitats in relation to site selection for energy facilities and providing land use data for route selection studies. Shanholtzer and Alexander (1975) used digital LANDSAT data and machine processing to provide supportive data for a study along Lake Ontario. They concluded that LANDSAT offers positive economic and practical advantages in the habitat mapping portion of a siting or routing study (i) if good, low altitude coverage is not available; and (ii) when potential sites or corridors have been screened by other disciplines and are not at the final selection stage. Howlett and Lukens (1975) used aerial photography and conventional interpretation methods to provide resource data for siting transmission lines in the United States and Canada. Examples of data interpreted from aerial photos included land use, soils, geology, vegetation types, wetland types, scenic areas, and zones visible from major highway arteries and residential areas.

The potential impact of large-scale energy development in the Canadian Arctic has resulted in considerable remote sensing activity among Canadian governmental agencies responsible for the research, monitoring, and management of the area. Falconer and Lavigne (1975) report that LANDSAT reveals complex hydrology, geology, and vegetation in the region which is not apparent from published maps of the arctic.

Remote sensing technology has also been utilized to provide inventories and insight into understanding the interaction of land use and water quality (Lillesand & Tully, 1975; Rogers et al., 1975). Using this technology, disturbed lands (highly populated, surface mined, etc.) can be inventoried and assessed as to their contributions to water quality.

B. Inventory, Assessment, and Monitoring

One of the primary objectives of any effort to manage drastically disturbed lands is to develop means to provide an accurate inventory of the disturbed areas. Drastically disturbed lands present a variety of land conditions which must be recognized by remote sensing tools. For example, a typical coal mining activity would have the following: (i) areas with freshly disturbed overburden material; (ii) areas where soil has been removed in preparation for mining; (iii) older, ungraded spoil piles which may have been seeded to grasses and trees; (iv) areas which have been graded to a rounded topography and seeded; and (v) natural terrain and a variety of associated vegetation. These different land conditions and associated reflectances require that several types and scales of imagery be used as well as different bands of the spectrum. Most of the studies mentioned initially in this section use a multistage approach. Nearly all the studies use the multiapproach to remote sensing.

In Indiana inventory of coal refuse sites was required to establish a basis for agreement among legislative committees, the coal industry, and state agencies for the acquisition of abandoned and unclaimed mined areas for reclamation purposes (Wobber, 1975). The primary objective was to locate and evaluate coal refuse banks and slurry ponds and estimate reclamation costs for each site. A multistage approach was used. LANDSAT computer-compatible tapes and RB-57 color infrared imagery (1:120,000) were evaluated. The spatial detail provided by high altitude aircraft imagery proved essential to classify coal refuse sites and provide desired environmental parameters for estimating reclamation costs. A comparative analysis indicated that the high-altitude color infrared imagery was more cost-effective in this effort and provided dependable, accurate data.

Borden et al. (1974) successfully mapped coal refuse sites in the anthracite coal region in Pennsylvania using automatic data processing (the ORSER system) and LANDSAT MSS data. However, some problems were encountered in differentiating among some strip mines, towns, and agricultural areas.

The Pennsylvania Environmental Planning Program also demonstrated the use of a multistage remote sensing approach (Wobber, 1975). The project involved the application of satellite and high and low altitude aircraft imagery to (i) identify surface indicators of mine subsidence, (ii) locate areas of potential future subsidence, and (iii) prepare maps of mine subsidence hazards within the Northern Anthracite Basin. Side-looking airborne radar (SLAR) and LANDSAT-I assisted in regional fracture analysis but did not prove useful for "direct" detection of subsidence prone areas.

LANDSAT 1 data (bands 5 and 7) and color infrared imagery (1:120,000 and 1:20,000, respectively) have also been used in a multistage study for fracture mapping and stripmine inventory in Indiana and Illinois (Wier et al., 1973).

Rehder (1973) used a temporal approach and two different types and scales of imagery to monitor landscape changes due to strip mining in the Cumberland Plateau of Eastern Tennessee. In April 1972, RB-57 imagery was used to provide the initial data, while an enhanced Band 5 negative print of LANDSAT I (Fig. 6) was used to detect the newly disturbed (cleared) land. Figure 7 shows the change between April and October of 1972. The black shading (Fig. 7) indicates those mines which were extant in April and the gray shading, the newly stripped areas.

Amato et al. (1975) compared Skylab photography to LANDSAT imagery (Fig. 8) for monitoring surface-mined lands. Due to the higher resolution, Skylab photography, or imagery of similar quality, offers greater potential for acquiring information. Figure 8 shows mine features and mining activities which were delineated using Skylab S-190B. This imagery provided substantial data for updating a 1:24,000-scale mined lands map produced several years earlier from high altitude aerial photography.

In Ohio, remote sensing technology was investigated as a tool to inventory lands for resource management purposes (Sweet et al., 1973). Remote sensor data were applied to (i) detecting, inventorying, and monitoring surface mining activities in relation to recently passed strip mine legislation in Ohio; (ii) updating current land use maps at various scales; and (iii) other real-time problems. The investigators used a variety of modern analysis procedures and equipment to analyze LANDSAT 1, aircraft photos, and on-site radiometric (spectral) signatures of the same strip-mined areas. The investigators concluded that LANDSAT 1 multi-spectral scanner (MSS) data can be utilized to (i) inventory the extent of strip mining, (ii) assess the condition of the stripped terrain, and (iii) monitor actual stripping activity in Ohio. Bands 5 and 7 of LANDSAT were found to actually reveal more information than 1:24,000 aerial photography in cases involving detection of water and residual vegetation. Aircraft data provided greater precision of measurement and interpretation but at a far greater cost in both data collection and analysis. Reflectance curves developed in the Ohio study (Sweet et al., 1973)

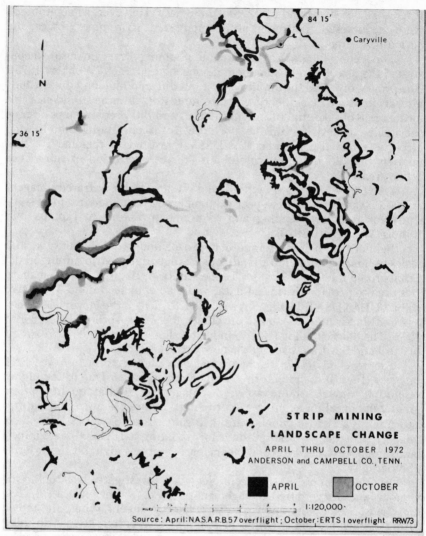

Fig. 7—Landscape change created by strip mining on the Cumberland Plateau Test Site in Eastern Tennessee, Apr.–Oct., 1972 (from Rehder, 1973).

demonstrated the ability to differentiate among different types of surface-mined operations in Ohio using LANDSAT data (Fig. 6). Definite differences were noted among the relative reflectances of limestone quarries, strip mines, and gravel pits (Fig. 9).

Other remote sensing applications to disturbed lands have used automatic data processing and computer-compatible tapes of LANDSAT MSS data. These data have been successfully used to detect acid mine drainage (Alexander et al., 1973). Results indicate that LANDSAT digital data can be used to inventory and monitor stripping, and also to determine the ef-

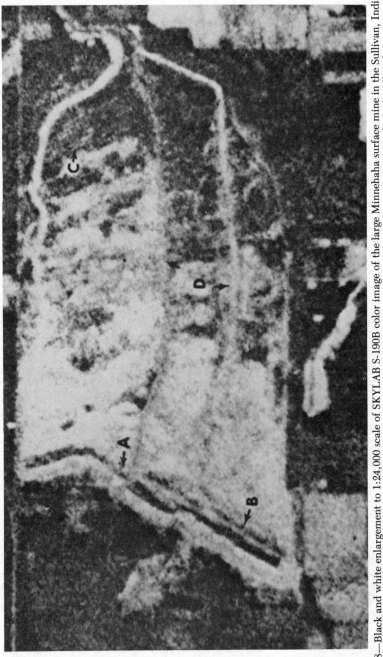

Fig. 8—Black and white enlargement to 1:24,000 scale of SKYLAB S-190B color image of the large Minnehaha surface mine in the Sullivan, Indiana test site. A large dragline used for removing the overburden can be distinguished on the original image at (A) as can be the highwall and the current mining furrow. Two ridges of ungraded mine spoil are evident at (B). Land reclaimed under old mining laws which did not require the ridges to be leveled is identifiable at (C). The older, now unused, road is imaged with less contrast (from Amato et al., 1975).

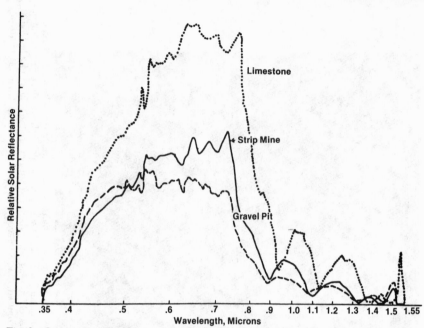

Fig. 9—Comparison of relative reflectance curves of limestone quarry, gravel pit, and strip mine operations in Ohio. These data indicate definite differences in the reflectance characteristics of the visible portion of the electromagnetic spectrum. Such data are necessary for distinguishing types of surface-mine operations in Ohio using ERTS data (from Sweet et al., 1973).

fectiveness of reclamation and pollution abatement procedures. Another study using LANDSAT MSS digital data (Schubert & MacLeod, 1973) measured levels of sedimentation at the confluence of two rivers, as well as inventorying strip mining in adjacent land areas. Rogers et al. (1973) employed automatic data-processing techniques to produce geometrically corrected maps of coal strip mines in east central Ohio. Again, computer-compatible tapes were used.

Anderson et al. (1975) demonstrated the feasibility of monitoring strip mines at a resolution of 2 ha with LANDSAT multispectral data and computer techniques. Accuracy of classification was reported at 93% using band-ratioing techniques and a temporal approach. Anderson and Shubert (1976) indicated that LANDSAT 1 digital data can be used to both monitor and map the extent of strip mining to determine immediately the acreage affected and to indicate where future reclamation and revegetation may be necessary.

One of the main aspects of monitoring reclamation is to be able to assess the establishment of vegetation on disturbed areas. Gilbertson (1973) concluded that LANDSAT may provide suitable data for determining the varying degrees of vegetation on mine dumps in South Africa.

The utility of remote sensing technology to disturbed lands has been well summarized by Amato et al. (1975), who reported that the synoptic and repetitive views of aerial remote sensing records offer valuable environmental and dynamic change data in areas of both surface and underground coal mining. This and other studies cited in this report reveal that remote sensors, if properly selected, can provide timely and accurate information on land use, surface mining status and reclamation progress, coal mine refuse piles and slurry ponds, acid water and siltation problems, and various aspects of environmental impact and reclamation features of disturbed lands.

These studies indicate that LANDSAT, or imagery of a similar resolution, has value for inventorying and monitoring the extent of drastically disturbed lands. Satellite imagery of Skylab 190 B quality has greater potential because of increased resolution. However, it is not routinely collected. High and low altitude aerial photography, particularly color and color infrared types, provide the resolution and spectral qualities for virtually all disturbed land activities. The scale and film type required depend on the particular application. Reliable regional assessments with some detail of the characteristics of the disturbed area (Fig. 5) can be obtained from small-scale imagery (about 1:120,000 to 1:60,00). Detailed data for engineering purposes or detection of acid mine problems requires large-scale photography. Advances in remote sensors, imagery enhancement, and data formats should increase the potential of remote sensing applications to drastically disturbed lands.

IV. FUTURE POTENTIAL APPLICATIONS

The utilization of remote sensing technology to inventory and assess disturbed lands is increasing. Future use is expected to increase rapidly as new remote sensing technology and data analysis methods are developed. Increased usage is forecast because of proposed advances in the resolution capabilities of remote sensors and recorders (film, etc.), imagery enhancement techniques, and the development of more simplified data formats. Also, the experiences gained over the last decade have provided new insights into remote sensing technology as an operational tool.

It appears that remote sensing technology related to satellite sensors has a promising future. There are numerous reasons why investigators have a growing interest in satellite or a similar type of coverage. The most prominent listed by investigators are: (i) the temporal and multispectral aspects of satellite coverage, (ii) the near orthographic format of the data, and (iii) the large regional perspective presented by satellite data (e.g., about 3.2 million ha per scene for LANDSAT). Future satellites are scheduled for an increase in resolution of all sensors over LANDSAT I and II, as well as additional sensors for certain thermal regions and improved instrumentation. Computer-compatible data (digital format) is to be in a geometrically refined and rotated format assigned to a widely used ground coordinate system. These proposed developments, resulting in simplified, and possibly standardized data formats, should greatly increase the utilization of data for monitoring resources (e.g., disturbed lands) and/or combination with other geographic data to characterize land areas in terms of capabilities or suitabilities.

LITERATURE CITED

Alexander, S., J. Dein, and D. P. Gold. 1973. The use of ERTS-1 MSS data for mapping strip mines and acid mine drainage in Pennsylvania. p. 62. *In* Symp. on Significant Results Obtained from ERTS-1, Mar. 1973. (Abstr.). NASA/Goddard Space Flight Center, Greenbelt, Md.

Amato, R. V., O. R. Russell, and K. R. Martin. 1975. Application of EREP, LANDSAT and aircraft image data to environmental problems related to coal mining. p. 309–327. *In* Proc. NASA Earth Resour. Survey Symp., 8–13 June 1975, Houston, Tex. (Also NASA TM X-58168 JSC-09930).

Anderson, A. T., and J. Schubert. 1976. ERTS-1 data applied to strip mining. Photo. Eng. and Remote Sensing 42:211–219.

Anderson, A. T., D. T. Shultz, and N. Buchman. 1975. LANDSAT inventory of surface-mined areas using extendible digital techniques. p. 329–346. *In* Proc. NASA Earth Resour. Survey Symp., 8–13 June 1975, Houston, Tex. (Also NASA TM X-58168 J SC-09930).

Bauer, M. E. 1976. Technological basis and applications of remote sensing of the earth's resources. IEEE Trans. Geosci. Electron. 14(1):3–9.

Borden, F. Y., B. F. Merembeck, D. N. Thompson, B. J. Turner, and D. L. Williams. 1974. Classification and mapping of coal refuse, vegetative cover types, and forest types by digital processing ERTS-1 data. p. 133–152. *In* Proc. of the Int. Symp. on Remote Sensing of Environment. Earth Resour. Inst. of Michigan, Ann Arbor, Mich.

Colvocoresses, A. P. 1975. Platforms for remote sensors. p. 539–588. *In* R. G. Reeves (ed.) Manual of remote sensing. Am. Soc. of Photogramm., Falls Church, Va.

Colwell, R. N. 1975. Introduction. p. 1–25. *In* R. G. Reeves (ed.) Manual of remote sensing. Am. Soc. of Photogramm., Falls Church, Va.

Estes, J. E. 1975. Fundamentals of image interpretation. p. 869–1076. *In* R. G. Reeves (ed.) Manual of remote sensing. Am. Soc. of Photogramm., Falls Church, Va.

Falconer, A., and D. M. Lavigne. 1975. LANDSAT-1 data as an added dimension in the mapping of Arctic ecology. p. 572–581. *In* Proc. Am. Soc. of Photogramm., Phoenix, Ariz.

Fischer, W. A., P. Badgley, D. G. Orr, and G. J. Zissis. 1975. History of remote sensing. p. 27–50. *In* R. G. Reeves (ed.) Manual of remote sensing. Am. Soc. of Photogramm., Falls Church, Va.

Gates, D. M. 1970. Physical and physiological properties of plants. p. 224–252. *In* Remote sensing with special reference to agriculture and forestry. Natl. Acad. of Sci., Washington, D.C.

Gilbertson, B. 1973. Monitoring vegetation cover on mine dumps with ERTS-1 imagery: some initial results. p. 63. *In* Symp. on Significant Results obtained from ERTS-1, Mar. 1973. (Abstr.). NASA/Goddard Space Flight Center, Greenbelt, Md.

Heller, R. C. 1970. Imaging with photographic sensors. p. 35–72. *In* Remote sensing with special reference to agriculture and forestry. Natl. Acad. of Sci., Washington, D.C.

Hoffer, R. M., and C. J. Johannsen. 1969. Ecological potential in spectral signature analysis. p. 1–16. *In* P. L. Johnson (ed.) Remote sensing in ecology. University of Georgia Press, Athens.

Holmes, R. A. 1970. Field spectroscopy. p. 298–323. *In* Remote sensing with special reference to agriculture and forestry. Natl. Acad. of Sci., Washington, D.C.

Howlett, B., and J. Lukens. 1975. Transmission line siting in the United States and Canada using aerial photography. p. 495–507. *In* Proc. Am. Soc. Photogramm., Phoenix, Ariz.

Janza, F. J. 1975. Interaction mechanisms. p. 75–179. *In* R. G. Reeves (ed.) Manual of remote sensing. Am. Soc. of Photogramm., Falls Church, Va.

Johnson, P. L. 1969. Remote sensing in ecology. Univ. of Georgia Press, Athens.

Johnson, G. E., R. D. Mower, and J. R. LaFevers. 1975. Land use mapping of Mercer county, North Dakota. p. 779–787. *In* Proc. Am. Soc. of Photogramm., Phoenix, Ariz.

Knipling, E. B. 1969. Leaf reflectance and image formation on color infrared film. p. 17–29. *In* P. L. Johnson (ed.) Remote sensing in ecology. Univ. of Georgia Press, Athens.

Lillesand, T. M., and W. P. Tully. 1975. Remote sensing, water quality and land use: From the obvious to the insidious. p. 582–618. *In* Proc. Am. Soc. of Photogramm., Phoenix, Ariz.

Myers, V. I. 1975. Crops and soils. p. 1715–1813. *In* R. G. Reeves (ed.) Manual of remote sensing. Am. Soc. of Photogramm., Falls Church, Va.

National Research Council, Committee on Remote Sensing for Agricultural Purposes. 1970. Remote sensing with special reference to agriculture and forestry. Natl. Acad. of Sci., Washington, D.C.

Orr, D. G. 1974. Image forming process. p. II-1 to II-37. *In* ERTS image interpretation workshop. U.S. Dep. of Interior, EROS Data Center, Sioux Falls, S. Dak.

Reeves, R. G. 1975. Manual of remote sensing. Am. Soc. of Photogramm., Falls Church, Va.

Rehder, J. B. 1973. Application of ERTS-1 data to landscape change in Eastern Tennessee. p. 598–609. *In* Proc. Management and Utilization of Remote Sensing Data. Am. Soc. of Photogramm., Falls Church, Va.

Rogers, R. H., L. E. Reed, and W. A. Pettyjohn. 1973. Automated stripmine and reclamation mapping from ERTS. p. 1519–1532. *In* 3rd Earth Resour. Technol. Satellie-1 Symp., Dec. 1973, NASA, Washington, D.C.

Rogers, R. H., L. E. Reed, and N. F. Schmidt. 1975. LANDSAT-1 automated land-use mapping in lake and river watersheds. p. 660–672. *In* Proc. Am. Soc. of Photogramm., Phoenix, Ariz.

Scherz, S. P., and A. R. Stevens. 1970. An introduction to remote sensing for environmental monitoring. Rep. no. 1, Univ. of Wisconsin, Inst. of Environ. Studies, Madison, Wis.

Schubert, J. S., and N. H. MacLeod. 1973. Digital analysis of Potomac river basin imagery: Sedimentation levels at the Potomac-Anacostia confluence and strip mining in Allegheny county, Maryland. p. 72. *In* Symp. on Significant Results Obtained from ERTS-1, Mar. 1973. (Abstr.). NASA/Goddard Space Flight Center, Greenbelt, Md.

Shanholtzer, F. G., and L. D. Alexander. 1975. The application of LANDSAT data to habitat mapping in site and route selection studies. p. 483–494. *In* Proc. Am. Soc. Photogramm., Phoenix, Ariz.

Steiner, D., and A. E. Salerno. 1975. Remote sensor systems, processing, and management. p. 611–803. *In* R. G. Reeves (ed.) Manual of remote sensing. Am. Soc. of Photogramm., Falls Church, Va.

Suits, G. H. 1975. The nature of electromagnetic radiation. p. 51–73. *In* R. G. Reeves (ed.) Manual of remote sensing. Am. Soc. of Photogramm., Falls Church, Va.

Sweet, D. C., P. G. Pincura, C. J. Meier, G. B. Garrett, L. Herd, G. E. Wukelic, J. G. Stephan, and H. E. Smail. 1973. Significant applications of ERTS-1 data to resource management activities at the state level in Ohio. p. 1533–1557. *In* The 3rd Earth Resour. Technol. Satellite-1 Symp., Dec. 1973, NASA, Washington, D.C.

Totterdell, C. J., and A. B. Rains. 1973. Plant reflectance and colour infrared photography. J. Applied Ecol. 10(2):401–407.

Wier, C. E., E. J. Wobber, O. R. Russell, and R. B. Amato. 1973. Fracture mapping and stripmine inventory in the midwest by using ERTS-1 imagery. p. 60. *In* Symp. on significant Results Obtained from ERTS-1, Mar. 1973. (Abstr.). NASA/Goddard Space Flight Center, Greenbelt, Md.

Wobber, F. J. 1975. Remote sensing trends in state resources management. Photo. Eng. and Remote Sensing 41:735–740.

CONVERSION FACTORS FOR U. S. AND METRIC UNITS

To convert column 1 into column 2, multiply by	Column 1	Column 2	To convert column 2 into column 1, multiply by

Length

0.621	kilometer, km	mile, mi	1.609
1.094	meter, m	yard, yd	0.914
0.394	centimeter, cm	inch, in	2.54

Area

0.386	kilometer^2, km^2	mile^2, mi^2	2.590
247.1	kilometer^2, km^2	acre, acre	0.00405
2.471	hectare, ha	acre, acre	0.405

Volume

0.00973	meter^3, m^3	acre-inch	102.8
3.532	hectoliter, hl	cubic foot, ft^3	0.2832
2.838	hectoliter, hl	bushel, bu	0.352
0.0284	liter	bushel, bu	35.24
1.057	liter	quart (liquid), qt	0.946

Mass

1.102	ton (metric)	ton (U.S.)	0.9072
2.205	quintal, q	hundredweight, cwt (short)	0.454
2.205	kilogram, kg	pound, lb	0.454
0.035	gram, g	ounce (avdp), oz	28.35

Pressure

14.50	bar	lb/inch^2, psi	0.06895
0.9869	bar	atmosphere, atm	1.013
0.9678	kg(weight)/cm^2	atmosphere, atm	1.033
14.22	kg(weight)/cm^2	lb/inch^2, psi	0.07031
14.70	atmosphere, atm	lb/inch^2, psi	0.06805

Yield or Rate

0.446	ton (metric)/hectare	ton (U.S.)/acre	2.24
0.892	kg/ha	lb/acre	1.12
0.892	quintal/hectare	hundredweight/acre	1.12

Temperature

$\left(\dfrac{9}{5} \, °C\right) + 32$	Celsius $-17.8C$ 0C 100C	Fahrenheit 0F 32F 212F	$\dfrac{5}{9}\,(°F - 32)$

Water Measurement

8.108	hectare-meters, ha-m	acre-feet	0.1233
97.29	hectare-meters, ha-m	acre-inches	0.01028
0.08108	hectare-centimeters, ha-cm	acre-feet	12.33
0.973	hectare-centimeters, ha-cm	acre-inches	1.028
0.00973	meters^3, m^3	acre-inches	102.8
0.981	hectare-centimeters/hour, ha-cm/hour	feet^3/sec	1.0194
440.3	hectare-centimeters/hour, ha-cm/hour	U.S. gallons/min	0.00227
0.00981	meters^3/hour, m^3/hour	feet^3/sec	101.94
4.403	meters^3/hour, m^3/hour	U.S. gallons/min	0.227

Plant Nutrition Conversion—P and K

P (phosphorus) $\times 2.29 = P_2O_5$
K (potassium) $\times 1.20 = K_2O$

SUBJECT INDEX